GROUP DYNAMICS

Donelson R. Forsyth

University of Richmond

THOMSON
™
WADSWORTH

Australia • Canada • Mexico • Singapore • Spain
United Kingdom • United States

THOMSON
WADSWORTH

Group Dynamics, Fourth Edition
Donelson R. Forsyth

Acquisitions Editor: Michele Sordi
Assistant Editor: Jennifer Wilkinson
Editorial Assistant: Jessica Kim
Technology Project Manager: Erik Fortier
Marketing Manager: Chris Caldeira
Marketing Assistant: Nicole Morinon
Advertising Project Manager: Tami Strang
Project Manager, Editorial Production: Emily Smith
Art Director: Vernon Boes
Print/Media Buyer: Rebecca Cross/Karen Hunt

Permissions Editor: Sarah Harkrader
Production Service: G&S Book Services
Text Designer: John Edeen
Copy Editor: Jan Six
Illustrator: G&S Book Services
Compositor: G&S Book Services
Cover Designer: Denise Davidson
Cover Image: Blue and Yellow Squares ©
    Royalty-Free/CORBIS
Text and Cover Printer: Phoenix Color Corp

Printed in the United States of America
1 2 3 4 5 6 7 09 08 07 06 05

For more information about our products, contact us at:
Thomson Learning Academic Resource Center
1-800-423-0563
For permission to use material from this text or product, submit a request online at **http://www.thomsonrights.com**.
Any additional questions about permissions can be submitted by email to **thomsonrights@thomson.com**.

Library of Congress Control Number: 2004113632

Student Edition: ISBN 0-534-36822-0

Instructor's Edition: ISBN 0-495-00813-3

International Student Edition: ISBN 0-495-00729-3
(Not for sale in the United States)

Thomson Higher Education
10 Davis Drive
Belmont, CA 94002-3098
USA

Asia (including India)
Thomson Learning
5 Shenton Way
#01-01 UIC Building
Singapore 068808

Australia/New Zealand
Thomson Learning Australia
102 Dodds Street
Southbank, Victoria 3006
Australia

Canada
Thomson Nelson
1120 Birchmount Road
Toronto, Ontario M1K 5G4
Canada

UK/Europe/Middle East/Africa
Thomson Learning
High Holborn House
50–51 Bedford Road
London WC1R 4LR
United Kingdom

Latin America
Thomson Learning
Seneca, 53
Colonia Polanco
11560 Mexico
D.F. Mexico

Spain (including Portugal)
Thomson Paraninfo
Calle Magallanes, 25
28015 Madrid, Spain

Brief Contents

CONTENTS

3

THE INDIVIDUAL AND THE GROUP 65

6   STRUCTURE 169

12 CONFLICT   409

15   GROUPS AND CHANGE   523

16 CROWDS AND COLLECTIVE BEHAVIOR 555

PREFACE

Why study groups? Why learn about the processes that unfold in interacting, dynamic groups? Why study theories that explain these processes? Why extend these theories to explain more and more about groups? Because groups are important.

On a *psychological level,* individuals' actions, thoughts, and emotions cannot be understood without taking into consideration the groups they belong to and the groups that surround them. Human behavior is so often group behavior that people cannot be studied in isolation, away from their families, friendship cliques, work groups, and so on. Groups also have a profound impact on individuals; groups shape actions, thoughts, and feelings.

On a *sociological level,* all kinds of societies—hunting/gathering, horticultural, pastoral, industrial, and postindustrial—are defined by the characteristics of the small groups that compose them. Societal forces, such as traditions, values, and norms, do not reach directly to individuals, but instead work through the groups to which each individual belongs.

On a *practical level,* much of the world's work is done by groups, so by understanding groups we move toward making them more efficient. If we want to improve productivity in a factory, problem solving in a boardroom, or learning in the classroom, we must understand groups. Groups, too, hold the key to solving such societal problems as racism, sexism, and international conflict. Any attempt to change society will succeed only if the groups within that society change.

Finally, on a *personal level,* you spend your entire life surrounded by and embedded in groups. Through membership in groups, you define and confirm your values and beliefs and take on or refine a social identity. When you face uncertain situations, in groups, you gain reassuring information about your problems and security in companionship. In groups, you learn about relations with others, the type of impressions you make on others, and the way you can relate with others more effectively. Groups influence us in consequential ways, so we ignore their influence at our own risk.

OVERVIEW

This book serves as an introduction to the theories, studies, and empirical findings pertinent to groups. As a primer rather than an encyclopedia, *Group Dynamics* seeks one basic goal: to inventory the results of scientific explorations of the nature of groups. It achieves this goal by integrating, whenever possible, theory and research, basic science and application, classic and contemporary work, and psychological and sociological analyses of groups.

Theory and Research

The text reviews hundreds of empirical studies of group processes, but most studies extend our *theoretical* understanding of groups. This emphasis on theory-grounded knowledge sometimes means that less central but nonetheless interesting topics are slighted, but whenever possible, the curious reader is referred to other sources for additional information.

Basic and Applied Science

Group dynamics appeals both to theoretically minded, basic research scientists and to applications-oriented individuals who work with groups in industrial, organizational, educational, judiciary, and therapeutic contexts. We take as given, however, Kurt Lewin's dictum, "There is nothing so practical as a good theory." Lewin argued against the traditional distinction between basic and applied science by suggesting that scientific understanding will occur most rapidly if researchers and individuals with applied interests work together to understand groups.

Classic and Contemporary Topics

Our current understanding of groups was shaped by the work of Kurt Lewin and many other scholars of the 19th and 20th centuries. The text concentrates on topics that lie at the heart of contemporary group dynamics, but classic analyses of groups are integrated with current topics to achieve a historically grounded overview.

Psychology, Sociology, and Other Social Sciences

No one discipline holds the exclusive rights to the study of groups. Scientists in such fields as psychology, sociology, social psychology, anthropology, communication, political science, business, education, and psychiatry examine the nature of groups, and whenever possible, the text integrates these perspectives to build an interdisciplinary analysis of group behavior.

FEATURES

Every attempt has been made to create a textbook that teaches group dynamics rather than one that simply exposes the student to basic principles and research findings. The 16 chapters progress from basic issues and processes to the analysis of more specialized topics, but this order is somewhat arbitrary, and many may prefer a different sequence.

Terms, Glossary, and Names

Key terms are presented in boldface type, and they are defined at the bottom of the page where they are first mentioned. Citations are given in the style of the American Psychological Association, and usually include investigators' last names and the date of the publication of the research report or book. When a researcher or theorist is first named in the text, his or her first and last names are included whenever possible.

Outlines, Summaries, and Readings

The first page of each chapter asks several questions examined in that chapter, and also outlines the chapter's contents. Each chapter uses three levels of headings. The primary headings are printed in all capitals, the secondary headings are printed in capital and lowercase letters, and the tertiary headings begin individual paragraphs. Each chapter also ends with a concise summary and a list of sources to consult for more information.

Focuses

Each chapter includes one or more boxed inserts that examine an empirical, theoretical, or practical aspect of groups. These boxes focus on key themes that are woven through the book, such as the impact of computer-mediated communications on group interaction and the differences between men and women when in groups.

Cases

Chapters 3 to 16 use case studies to illustrate and integrate the chapter's contents. The chapter on group formation, for example, focuses on the impressionists, and the chapter dealing with group influence highlights a jury in a murder trial. All the cases are or were real groups rather than hypothetical ones, and the incidents described are documented events that occurred within the group.

CHANGES FROM THE THIRD EDITION

I revised this book because the field of group dynamics has changed dramatically since the third edition was published in 1999. The first three editions of this book were written in a time of steady growth of the field, as investigators and theorists gradually augmented our stock of knowledge pertaining to groups. But in the last

5 years, the amount and quality of research in the field has increased dramatically. Group researchers throughout the social sciences have introduced new topics, new issues, and new methods to the study of groups, and this new edition seeks to integrate this new work with the existing corpus of knowledge pertaining to groups.

This book has matured with each edition, but this edition retains many features of earlier editions, including the heavy emphasis on research findings and the attention to work in a variety of fields. The core topics that I review also remain unchanged from earlier editions, although the order and depth of some treatments have changed. This edition, for example, provides expanded coverage of the impact of technology on groups and social identity processes. It also includes analyses of specific types of groups, such as work groups, teams, and adolescent peer groups. I also shifted the chapters around, primarily based on feedback from people who have strong views on how the material should be sequenced. The two chapters on group conflict (intragroup and intergroup), for example, are now contiguous. Throughout this edition, I sought to improve the consistency in level of analysis by not dipping too deeply into one topic while skimming lightly over another.

Some of these changes were made only reluctantly. The book is heavily referenced, and I have added hundreds of citations to work from the new millennium. But to make space for these new citations, I had to let go of some older references. I also replaced four of the case studies with new ones, but I had a hard time saying goodbye to such groups as the Disney team and Sealab. To balance the loss, boxed inserts, used in the second edition, have returned to this edition. Perhaps boxes will appear only in even-numbered editions. To make room for more content, I also deleted the activities that appeared in the third edition. They are available online, linked to the Group Dynamics Resource Page. I will also post additional resources, including teaching resources, at that site.

To review the chapter-by-chapter changes briefly:

- Chapter 1, Introduction to Group Dynamics, examines the nature of groups and the field's basic paradigm. In earlier editions, I used summaries of the cases examined in the book to introduce readers to the types of groups to be reviewed, but in this edition, I instead review taxonometric analyses of groups.
- Chapter 2, Studying Groups, describes the basic measurement methods and designs that researchers use to test their hypotheses about groups. New to this edition is a more thorough analysis of qualitative methods and the travails associated with studying groups rather than individuals.
- Chapter 3, The Individual and the Group, examines the basic functions of social groups for individual members. I updated this very active area of theory and research by including additional material on ostracism and exclusion, collectivism–individualism, and social identity theory. The chapter's case considers the way C. P. Ellis's life changed as he joined new groups and left others behind.
- Chapter 4, Formation, is bolstered by new material on individual differences in tendencies to join groups, particularly introversion–extraversion

and attachment approaches. The birth of the impressionists is an intriguing case study, at least for those who admire their work.

- Chapter 5, Cohesion and Development, provides a multilevel analysis of group cohesion and applies this concept to explaining team processes. I included more material from groups in organizational settings, and the case study is the 1980 U.S. Olympic Hockey Team. This chapter was Chapter 6 in the previous edition.
- Chapter 6, Structure, describes the tendency of relationships among group members to become organized and predictable. In addition to the analysis of roles, norms, and intermember relations (status, attraction, and communication), group socialization processes are now discussed in this chapter. The case study was not changed, although I omitted some grim details pertaining to the cannibalistic practices of the young men stranded in the Andes.
- Chapter 7, Influence, examines conformity and minority influence, augmented with material pertaining to personality and situational factors that affect rates of conformity, diffusion of responsibility, social pressures in computer-based groups, and jury decision making. The Corona trial is retained as the case study. Newer cases were considered, but none could compete with Victor Villaseñor's (1977) account of this group.
- Chapter 8, Power, still uses Stanley Milgram's studies of obedience to provide the central focus for this chapter, but newer work on reactions to power, changes in powerholders, and power dynamics in bona fide groups (e.g., bullying in children's groups) is also discussed. The chapter's case study, the People's Temple, illuminates stronger forms of social influence.
- Chapter 9, Performance, reviews four basic aspects of group performance—social facilitation, social motivation (social loafing), social combination, and social creativity. Researchers in all these areas continue to pour out new findings, and the chapter integrates them with classic viewpoints such as Robert Zajonc's analyses of social influence and Ivan Steiner's model of group combination. The chapter's case, one of the groups from the seminal Western Electric series, still provides the backdrop for more contemporary studies of loafing, social facilitation of eating behavior, synergistic gains, and so on.
- Chapter 10, Decision Making, uses a collective information-processing model to explain how groups make decisions. Work on group memory, information sharing, and cognitive biases is added to more traditional reviews of group polarization and groupthink. The chapter's case, President Kennedy's Bay of Pigs planners, may be the most studied political advisory group in history.
- Chapter 11, Leadership, uses the first woman to be hired as the CEO of Hewlett-Packard, Carleton ("Carly") Fiorina, as the model of a charismatic, highly capable leader. This chapter follows the chapters on group performance to reflect the greater emphasis on the leader's impact on productivity rather than as a source of social influence.

- Chapter 12, Conflict, has moved to this location in the book to be adjacent to Chapter 13's analysis of intergroup conflict. This chapter was extensively revised in the previous edition and is fine-tuned in this revision. The Steve Jobs vs. John Sculley conflict at Apple Computer is this chapter's case.
- Chapter 13, Intergroup Relations, still uses the classic Robbers Cave Experiment to illustrate factors that influence conflict between groups. New work dealing with the causes of international conflict is added, as are more recent analyses that have reaffirmed the value of contact for reducing intergroup conflict.
- Chapter 14, Groups in Context, is renamed to illustrate the enlarged view adopted in this chapter's review of the relationship between the environment and group behavior. Sealab, used in previous editions as the chapter's case, moved aside to permit the analysis of a more easily visualized group—the crew of Apollo 13. Many of the topics in this chapter are currently not as heavily researched, but this lack of recent work may be due to the fact that previous studies were of such quality that they answered many of the most basic questions about groups and their physical setting.
- Chapter 15, Groups and Change, reviews various means of achieving personal change through membership in groups, with increasing attention to support groups and other nonprofessionally mediated approaches to adjustment. The chapter's case is an interpersonal psychotherapeutic group that illustrates the many curative factors that operate in groups.
- Chapter 16, Crowds and Collective Behavior, considers larger groups and more geographically dispersed aggregates, updated to deal with studies of contagion in groups, imitation, and fast-moving social trends. The large crowd of people that panicked when entering a show by The Who remains a relevant case, for even though the band is old, such disturbances still regularly plague rock concerts. This chapter is moved to the end of the book because it provides a fitting endpoint for the study of groups and their dynamics.

After surveying recent developments in the field of group dynamics, I cannot resist offering an optimistic prediction about its future. This optimism is based, in part, on the field's record of achievement—the outstanding methodological, statistical, and theoretical advances made by those who study groups. Judging from the sheer quantity of new work on groups, groups must be the hot topic in many disciplines, and this revision strives to communicate this excitement to its newest initiates. This optimism is also based on societal developments that have changed the way people live and work in groups. Societies that were once viewed as mere collections of individuals are gradually being transformed into cultures that embrace a more collectivistic orientation. Corporations continue to evolve into multinational organizations, and with that global perspective has come increased interest in harnessing the power of groups for productive purposes. As society adjusts to a more technological and united world, and as the economic success of countries springs from group decisions and work team efforts, understanding groups and their dynamics will become increasingly relevant, practical, and important.

ACKNOWLEDGMENTS

Most things in this world are accomplished by groups rather than by single individuals working alone. This book is no exception. Although I am personally responsible for the ideas presented in this book, many colleagues have also provided me with indispensable comments and suggestions, including Gordon Abra, California State University, Long Beach; Scott Allison, University of Richmond; Russ J. Andaloro, University of Arizona; Thomasina Borkman, George Mason University; Barbara B. Bunker, State University of New York, Buffalo; James Michael Burke, Virginia Commonwealth University; Wynne DuBray, California State University, Sacramento; David Dryden Henningsen, Northern Illinois University; Mark Leary, Wake Forest University; Glenn Littlepage, Middle Tennessee State University; Karen Lohn, University of Minnesota, Duluth; Richard Moreland, University of Pittsburgh; John L. Vohs, University of California, Davis; and Suzan Waller, University of Central Oklahoma.

But groups, as well as individuals, helped with the project. My classes at Virginia Commonwealth University provided me with the opportunity to refine my presentation of the materials, for my students were all too eager to give me feedback about ambiguities and weaknesses. I particularly appreciate the inputs from my undergraduate Group Dynamics class of Spring 2004, who suffered through online drafts of this edition (see Chapter 12's analysis of conflict in groups). The graduate students and faculty of the Social Psychology Division of Virginia Commonwealth University provided me with many opportunities to share my conceptualizations about groups and their processes through classes, colloquia, and informal discussions (see Chapter 5 for an analysis of small, cohesive teams). My colleagues in the department also provided me with many opportunities to experience group dynamics in vivo (for a discussion of intergroup conflict, see Chapter 13). The members of the production teams at Wadsworth, including senior editor Michele Sordi, and at G&S Book Services, including production coordinator Gretchen Otto, also deserve special thanks for their capable efforts, as does Jan Six, copyeditor. They succeeded in transforming my words and sketchy diagrams into a final product, undoubtedly by working together closely in small-group settings (see Chapter 10). Finally, my most important group—my family—deserves my special acknowledgement, for they provided me with substantial social support throughout the process (see Chapter 15's analysis of support groups). They personify the socioemotional, relational perspective that counterbalances my task-oriented, production-focused orientation. So I offer my boundless gratitude to Claire, our son David, our daughter Rachel, and Carmen (the family dog).

Donelson R. Forsyth

1

INTRODUCTION TO GROUP DYNAMICS

CHAPTER OVERVIEW

Group dynamics are the influential interpersonal processes that take place in groups. The tendency to join with others in groups is perhaps the most important single characteristic of humans, and these groups leave an indelible imprint on their members and on society. To understand people, we must understand their groups.

❖ What is a group?

❖ What are some common characteristics of groups?

❖ What assumptions guide researchers in their studies of groups and their processes?

❖ What fields and what topics are included in the scientific study of group dynamics?

CHAPTER OUTLINE

The lone individual—the single man or woman who has no connection to other men and women—is an extraordinarily rare human being. *Homo sapiens* is capable of surviving alone, and the recluse, ascetic, and prisoner in solitary confinement can forge a life on their own. But few humans seek or enjoy the challenges of solitude. Most people prefer to live in groups. Virtually all the activities of our lives—working, learning, worshiping, relaxing, playing, and even sleeping—occur in groups rather than isolated from others. Most people belong to many different groups, so the number of groups in the world probably reaches well beyond six billion. The world is literally teeming with groups.

For centuries, sages and scholars have been fascinated by groups—by the way they form, change over time, dissipate unexpectedly, achieve great goals, and sometimes commit great wrongs. Yet groups remain something of a mystery—unstudied at best, misunderstood at worst. Here we unravel some of their mysteries by examining their basic nature, their processes, and their impact on their members. We begin our task by asking some questions: What is a *group?* What are the characteristics of groups that most interest us? What kinds of group processes do we want to study? What do we mean by *group dynamics?* What assumptions do we embrace as we describe, analyze, and compare the various groups that populate the planet? What approach do we take to the study of groups?

WHAT IS A GROUP?

Hundreds of fish swimming together are called a *school*. A pack of foraging baboons is a *troupe*. A half dozen crows on a telephone wire is a *murder*. A *gam* is a group of whales. But what is a collection of human beings called? A *group*.

Defining Groups

What would you include if you were asked to name all the groups in which you are a member? Would you list your family? Your neighborhood association? People who regularly log into a chat room on the Internet with you? Your political party? The handful of fellow students who often take the same classes you do? Coworkers who go out for drinks after work once in a while? The people standing in line with you at the checkout counter of the supermarket?

Each of these collections of people may seem unique, but each possesses that one critical element that defines a group: connections linking the individual members. We understand intuitively that three persons seated in separate rooms working on unrelated tasks can hardly be considered a group, for they are not connected in any way to each other. If, however, we create a connection among them, then these three individuals can be considered a rudimentary group. The members of a family who live in the same house, for example, are linked to one another by joint tasks, a shared living space, strong emotional bonds, and genetic similarities. People who work together are linked by the collaborative tasks that they must complete together, but in many cases they also become connected through a network of friendships and antagonisms. Even the people who are standing in a queue in a checkout counter are a group, for they are briefly connected in a situation that demands cooperation, communication, and patience. In all these examples, the members are linked together in a web of interpersonal relationships. Thus, a **group** is defined as *two or more individuals who are connected to one another by social relationships*.

TWO OR MORE INDIVIDUALS A group can range in size from two members to thousands of members. Very small collectives, such as dyads (two members) and triads (three members) are groups, but so are very large collections of people, such as mobs, crowds, and congregations (Simmel, 1902). On average, however, most groups tend to be relatively small in size, ranging from two to seven members. One researcher (J. James, 1953), after counting the number of people in 7405 informal, spontaneously formed groups found in public settings, reported an average group size of only 2.4. He also found that deliberately formed groups, such as those created in government or work settings, included an average of 2.3 members (J. James, 1951). In many cases, larger groups are also sets of interlocked smaller groups. Although groups come in all shapes and sizes, they tend to "gravitate to the smallest size, two" (Hare, 1976, p. 215).

The size of a group influences its nature in many ways, for a group with only two or three members possesses many unique characteristics simply because it includes so few members. The dyad is, by definition, the only group that dissolves when one member leaves and the only group that can never be broken down into subgroups (J. M. Levine & Moreland, 1995). Very large collectives, such as mobs, crowds, or congregations, also have unique qualities. In a very large group, for example, the chances for each member to be connected to all other members becomes very small. As groups increase in size, they tend to become more complex and more formally structured (Hare, 1976). By definition, however, all are considered groups.

WHO ARE CONNECTED TO ONE ANOTHER Like a series of interconnected computers, the individuals in any given group are *networked:* They are connected one to another. These connections, or ties, may be strong emotional bonds, like the links between the members of a family or a clique of close friends. The links may also be relatively weak ones that are easily broken with the passage of time or the occurrence of relationship-damaging events. Even weak links, however, can create robust outcomes across an entire group of networked individuals. Nor do these relationships need to link every person directly to every other person in the group. It takes, for example, 6 one-to-one links to connect every member of a 4-person group to every other member of that group (A/B, A/C, A/D, B/C, B/D, and C/D), but a 12-person group would need 66 links to join every member to every other member. Hence, many ties between members in groups are indirect ones. Person A might, for example, talk directly to B, B may talk to C, so A is linked to C through B. But even in large groups, members often feel

---

group Two or more individuals who are connected to one another by social relationships.

TABLE 1-1 Some Definitions of the Word *Group*

Central Feature	Definition
Categorization	A group is "two or more individuals . . . [who] perceive themselves to be members of the same social category" (J. C. Turner, 1982, p. 15).
Communication	"We mean by a group a number of persons who communicate with one another, often over a span of time, and who are few enough so that each person is able to communicate with all the others, not at second hand, through other people, but face-to-face" (Homans, 1950, p. 1).
Influence	"Two or more persons who are interacting with one another in such a manner that each person influences and is influenced by each other person" (M. E. Shaw, 1981, p. 454).
Interaction	"A group is a social system involving regular interaction among members and a common group identity. This means that groups have a sense of 'weness' that enables members to identify themselves as belonging to a distinct entity" (A. G. Johnson, 1995, p. 125).
Interdependence	"A group is a collection of individuals who have relations to one another that make them interdependent to some significant degree" (Cartwright & Zander, 1968, p. 46).
Interrelation	"A group is an aggregation of two or more people who are to some degree in dynamic interrelation with one another" (McGrath, 1984, p. 8).
Psychological significance	"A *psychological group* is any number of people who interact with each other, are psychologically aware of each other, and perceive themselves to be in a group" (D. C. Pennington, 2002, p. 3).
Shared identification	"A group . . . is two or more people possessing a common social identification and whose existence as a group is recognized by a third party" (R. Brown, 2000, p. 19).
Shared tasks and goals	"A group is defined as three or more people who work together interdependently on an agreed-upon activity or goal" (Keyton, 2002, p. 5).
Structure	"A group is a social unit which consists of a number of individuals who stand in (more or less) definite status and role relationships to one another and which possesses a set of values or norms of its own regulating the behavior of individual members, at least in matters of consequence to the group" (Sherif & Sherif, 1956, p. 144).
Systems	"Groups are open and complex systems . . . a complex, adaptive, dynamic, coordinated, and bounded set of patterned relations among members, tasks, and tools" (Arrow, McGrath, & Berdahl, 2000, p. 34).

connected to the majority of the group's members and to the group as a whole (Granovetter, 1973).

BY SOCIAL RELATIONSHIPS Table 1-1 samples theorists' definitions of the word *group*. Some of these definitions do not specify the nature of the connection between group members, but others require members be linked in a particular way before an aggregation of individuals can be considered a group. Some, for example, emphasize the importance of interdependence; they suggest that members depend on one another to achieve their goals and secure positive outcomes. Others insist that the group must be organized in some way; otherwise, it is just a haphazard, accidental gathering of individuals. Still others propose that the connection should be based on mutual influence—the capacity of each group member to influence and be influenced by another. But no matter what the nature of the linkage—whether communication among members, mutual influence, or some type of organization—the group members must be connected at a social level.

The relationship among group members is described as a *social* one to distinguish groups from *categories.* A **category** is an aggregation of individuals who share certain qualities, such as personality traits, physical features, or behavioral regularities. For example, individuals who are quiet and shy are often labeled *introverts,* the residents of New York City are *New Yorkers,* and individuals who routinely wager sums of money on games of chance are *gamblers.* If these categories create an interpersonal connection among the category members, then a category may be transformed into a group. But if the categorization has no social or psychological implications, then the category only describes individuals who are similar in some way, rather than a meaningful social group (Wilder & Simon, 1998).

Classifying Groups

Researchers often begin their analyses of group processes by drawing distinctions between the different types of groups they study. Typologists, no matter what their scientific field, bring order to their individual observations by identifying shared similarities and significant differences among the individual cases they examine. The group typologist asks, "What type of group is this?" and answers by classifying groups into meaningful clusters or categories.

PRIMARY AND SECONDARY GROUPS Sociologist Charles Horton Cooley (1909), in his early studies of groups, distinguished between *primary groups* and *secondary groups.* **Primary groups,** such as family and friends, are small, long-term groups characterized by face-to-face interaction and high levels of cohesiveness, solidarity, and member identification. In many cases, individuals become part of primary groups involuntarily: Most are born into a family, which provides for their well-being until they can join other social groups. Other primary groups form when people interact in significant, meaningful ways for a prolonged period of time. Cooley (1909, p. 23) thought that primary groups protect members from harm, care for them when they are ill, and provide them with

---

category An aggregation of people or things that share some common attribute or are related in some way.

primary group A small, long-term group characterized by face-to-face interaction, solidarity, and high levels of member-to-group interdependence and identification (e.g., families or friendship cliques). Such a group serves as the primary source of socialization for members by shaping their attitudes, values, and social orientation.

shelter and sustenance. But he believed that their most important function was in creating a bridge between the individual and society at large:

> Primary groups are primary in the sense that they give the individual his earliest and completest experience of social unity, and also in the sense that they do not change in the same degree as more elaborate relations, but form a comparatively permanent source out of which the latter are ever springing. (Cooley, 1909, pp. 26–27)

In earlier times, individuals belonged only to primary groups. They could live out their entire lives without leaving their small, close-knit families, tribes, or communities. As societies became more complex, however, so did their groups (Toennies, 1887/1963). Cooley called these more complex social structures **secondary groups.** Such groups are larger and more formally organized than primary groups, and they tend to be shorter in duration and less emotionally involving. However, secondary groups continue to define the individual's place in the social structure of society (T. Parsons, Bales, & Shils, 1953).

PLANNED AND EMERGENT GROUPS Dorwin Cartwright and Alvin Zander (1960) were reluctant to classify groups, because any typology is bound to underestimate the variety and complexity of all groups and may prompt people to feel that they completely understand a group once they have slotted it into a particular category. But they did note that groups tend to fall naturally into two categories: **planned groups,** which are deliberately formed by their members or by an external authority for some purpose, and **emergent groups,** which come into existence spontaneously when individuals join together in the same physical location or form gradually over time as individuals find themselves repeatedly interacting with the same subset of individuals. People *found* planned groups, but they often *find* emergent groups.

Arbitration boards, civil rights groups, commissions, committees, expeditions, juries, legislative bodies, military units, musical groups, research teams, self-help groups, social agencies, sports teams, study groups, task forces, therapy groups, trade associations, veterans organizations, and work groups are all examples of planned groups. Planned groups tend to be organized, task focused, and formal. Such groups generally define their membership criteria clearly and so at all times know who is and who is not in the group. They often operate under a set of bylaws, contracts, or similar regulations that describe the group's acceptable procedures and practices. The group's structure may even be formalized in an organizational chart that defines who has more authority than others, who reports

---

secondary group A relatively large, often formally organized, social group common in more complex societies (e.g., work groups, clubs, congregations). Such a group influences members' attitudes, beliefs, and actions, but as a supplement to the influence of smaller primary groups.

planned group A group deliberately formed by its members or an external authority.

emergent group A group that comes into existence gradually as individuals repeatedly interact with the same subset of individuals.

to whom, and how subgroups within the overall group are connected. Such groups, despite their overall level of organization and definition, may also lack emotional substance. They may be characterized by considerable routines, ceremonies, and procedures, but they may also be devoid of any warmth or emotional depth.

Emergent groups, such as audiences at events, bystanders at a crime scene, crowds, customers at a club, gangs, families, friendship networks in work settings, mobs, people waiting to board an airplane, and all manner of queues and lines, arise over time through repeated association of the eventual members. These groups are not explicitly organized, but they often develop elements of structure as their members determine what kinds of behaviors are expected of members, who is more or less liked, who leads and who follows, and so on. Such groups often have unclear boundaries, for they allow members to come and go rather than requiring them to join in a formal way. They have no written rules, but they likely develop unwritten norms that define what behaviors are appropriate and what behaviors are inappropriate within the group. Unlike planned groups, membership in an emergent group is sought as an end in and of itself: People do not join to gain some goal but because they find satisfaction in associating with the other group members.

Holly Arrow, Joseph E. McGrath, and Jennifer L. Berdahl (2000) extended this distinction between planned and emergent groups by asking another question: Is the group created by forces within the group (*internal origins*) or forces outside of the group (*external origins*)? Arrow and her colleagues combined both the planned–emergent dimension and the internal–external dimension to generate the following fourfold taxonomy of groups:

- *Concocted groups* are planned by individuals or authorities outside the group. A team of laborers digging a trench, the flight crew of an airplane, and a military squad would all be concocted groups, as those who created them are not actually members of the group.
- *Founded groups* are planned by one or more individuals who remain members of the group. A small Internet start-up company, a study group, an expeditionary team, or a grass-roots community action group would all be founded groups.
- *Circumstantial groups* are emergent, unplanned groups that arise when external, situational forces set the stage for people to join together— often temporarily—in a unified group. A group of travelers stranded together when their bus breaks down, a mob breaking shop windows and setting parked cars on fire, and a crowd of patrons at a movie theater would be circumstantial groups.
- *Self-organizing groups* emerge when interacting individuals gradually align their activities in a cooperative system of interdependence. Parties, gatherings of surfers waiting for waves just offshore, drivers leaving a crowded parking lot through a single exit, and a half-dozen adolescents who hang out together are all organized groups, but their organization is generated by implicit adjustments of each member to each other member.

GROUPS, TASK GROUPS, ASSOCIATIONS, AND CATEGORIES Brian Lickel and his colleagues (Lickel et al., 2000), rather than basing their analysis of group types on theoretically prominent dimensions, instead chose to study the way ordinary people intuitively classify the groups they encounter in their daily lives. In a series of studies, they asked college students in the United States and Poland to compare different collectives and rate them in terms of their size, duration, permeability, interaction, importance, and so on. When they examined these data using a statistical procedure called *cluster analysis,* they identified the following basic types of groups:

- *Intimacy groups,* such as families, romantic couples, close friends, and street gangs, were judged to be the most group-like by perceivers. These groups were small in size and moderate in duration and permeability, but characterized by substantial levels of interaction among the members, who considered these groups to be very important to them personally.
- *Task groups* included work groups in employment settings and goal-focused groups in a variety of nonemployment situations. Many of these groups, such as employees at a restaurant, people who worked in a factory, or company committees, were work groups in a business or commercial setting. Task groups outside the employment arena included student service groups, support groups, jury members, and study groups. Members of these groups were thought to be united in pursuing common goals and outcomes.
- *Weak associations* were aggregations of individuals that formed spontaneously, lasted only a brief period of time, and had boundaries that were very permeable. Some of these associations were very transitory, such as people gathered at a bus stop waiting for the next bus, or an audience in a movie theater. Others lasted longer but were marked by very weak relationships or very limited interactions among their members. Examples of these weak social relationship associations were residents of a large neighborhood and students in a college class.
- *Social categories,* as noted earlier, were aggregations of individuals who were similar in terms of gender, ethnicity, religion, and nationality. Such collectives as "women," "Jews," "doctors," and "citizens of Poland" clustered together in this category.

Lickel et al. (2000) also asked the perceivers if they considered all these kinds of aggregations of individuals to be true groups. They did not force people to make an either–or decision about each one, however. Recognizing that the boundary between what is and what is not a group is perceptually fuzzy, they instead asked participants to rate the aggregations on a scale from 1 (*not at all a group*) to 9 (*very much a group*). As they expected, intimacy groups and task groups received high average ratings (6.8 and 6.3), whereas categories and associations were rated lower (4.5 and 4.2, respectively). These findings suggest that people are more likely to consider aggregations marked by strong bonds between members, frequent interactions among members, and clear boundaries to be groups, but that they are less certain that such aggregations as crowds, waiting lines, or categories qualify as groups (see Table 1-2).

TABLE 1-2 Characteristics of Basic Types of Groups

Type of Group	Characteristics	Examples
Primary groups	Small, long-term groups characterized by face-to-face interaction and high levels of cohesiveness, solidarity, and member identification	Families, close friends, tight-knit peer groups, gangs, elite military squads
Secondary groups	Larger, less intimate, more goal-focused groups typical of more complex societies	Congregations, work groups, unions, professional associations
Planned groups	Deliberately formed by the members themselves or by an external authority, usually for some specific purpose or purposes	
Concocted	Planned by individuals or authorities outside the group	Production lines, military units, task forces, crews, professional sports teams
Founded	Planned by one or more individuals who remain within the group	Study groups, small businesses, expeditions, clubs, associations
Emergent groups	Groups that form spontaneously as individuals find themselves repeatedly interacting with the same subset of individuals over time and settings	
Circumstantial	Emergent, unplanned groups that arise when external, situational forces set the stage for people to join together, often only temporarily, in a unified group	Waiting lines (queues), crowds, mobs, audiences, bystanders
Self-organizing	Emerge when interacting individuals gradually align their activities in a cooperative system of interdependence	Study groups, friendship cliques in a workplace, regular patrons at a bar
Intimacy groups	Small groups of moderate duration and permeability characterized by substantial levels of interaction among the members, who value membership in the group	Families, romantic couples, close friends, street gangs
Task groups	Work groups in employment settings and goal-focused groups in a variety of nonemployment situations	Teams, neighborhood associations
Weak associations	Aggregations of individuals that form spontaneously, last only a brief period of time, and have very permeable boundaries	Crowds, audiences, clusters of bystanders
Social categories	Aggregations of individuals who are similar to one another in terms of gender, ethnicity, religion, or nationality	Women, Asian Americans, physicians, U.S. citizens, New Yorkers

Describing Groups

Each one of the billions of groups that exist at this moment is a unique configuration of individuals, processes, and relationships. The family living at 103 Main Street is different in dozens of ways from the family that lives just next door to them. The team of workers building automobiles in Anytown, U.S.A., is unlike any other team of workers in any other factory in the world. The group of five students in a university library reviewing material for an upcoming test displays tendencies and qualities that are unlike any other study group that has ever existed or ever will exist. But all groups, despite their distinctive characteristics, also possess common properties and dynamics. When we study a group, we must go beyond its unique qualities to consider characteristics that appear with consistency in most groups, no matter what their origin, purpose, or membership—qualities such as interaction, interdependence, structure, cohesiveness, and goals.

INTERACTION Groups are systems that create, organize, and sustain **interaction** among the members. Group members get into arguments, talk over issues, and make decisions. They upset each other, give one another help and support, and take advantage of each other's weaknesses. They rally together to accomplish difficult tasks, but they sometimes slack off when they think others will not notice. Group members teach one another new things; they communicate with one another verbally and nonverbally, and they touch each other literally and emotionally. Groups members *do* things to and with each other.

Group interaction is as varied as human behavior itself, for any behavior that an individual can perform alone can also be performed in a group context. Robert Freed Bales (1950, 1999), after observing groups interacting in all types of situations, identified two classes of interaction that are most common in group situations. **Task interaction** includes all group behavior that is focused principally on the group's work, projects, plans, and goals. In most groups, members must coordinate their various skills, resources, and motivations so that the group can make a decision, generate a product, or achieve a victory. When a jury reviews each bit of testimony, a committee argues over the best course of action to take, or a family plans its summer vacation, the group's interaction is task focused.

Relationship interaction (or *socioemotional interaction*), in contrast, is focused on the interpersonal, social side of group life. If group members falter and need support, others will buoy them up with kind words, suggestions, and other forms of help. When group members disagree with the others, they are often

---

interaction The social actions of individuals in a group, particularly those that are influenced either directly or indirectly by the group.

task interaction Actions performed by group members that pertain to the group's projects, tasks, and goals.

relationship interaction Actions performed by group members that relate to or influence the emotional and interpersonal bonds within the group, including both positive actions (social support, consideration) and negative actions (criticism, conflict).

roundly criticized and made to feel foolish. When a coworker wears a new suit or outfit, others in his or her work unit notice it and offer compliments or criticisms. Such actions do not help the group accomplish its designated task, but they do sustain the emotional bonds linking the members to one another and to the group. Bales based his *Interaction Process Analysis (IPA)* on this distinction between task and relationship interaction forms. This model is reviewed in Chapter 2.

INTERDEPENDENCE Most groups create a state of **interdependence,** for members' outcomes, actions, thoughts, feelings, and experiences are determined in part by other members of the group (Wageman, 2001). The acrobat on the trapeze will drop to the net unless her teammate catches her outstretched arms. The assembly line worker is unable to complete his work until he receives the unfinished product from a worker further up the line. The business executive's success (and salary) is determined by how well her staff completes its work. She can fulfill her personal tasks skillfully, but if her staff fails, then she fails as well. In such situations, members are obligated or responsible to other group members, for they provide each other with support and assistance.

Interdependence also results when members are able to influence and be influenced by others in the group. In a business, for example, the boss may determine how employees spend their time, what kind of rewards they experience, and even the duration of their membership in the group. These employees can influence their boss to a degree, but the boss's influence is nearly unilateral: The boss influences them to a greater degree than they influence the boss (see Figure 1-1). In other groups, in contrast, influence is more mutual: One member may influence the next member, who in turn influences the next (*sequential interdependence*) or two or more members may influence each other (*reciprocal* or *mutual interdependence*). Interdependence can also occur because groups are often nested in larger groups, and the outcomes of the larger groups depend on the activities and outcomes of the smaller groups (*multilevel interdependence*).

STRUCTURE Group members are not connected to one another at random, but in organized and predictable patterns. In all but the most ephemeral groups, patterns and regularities emerge that determine the kinds of actions that are permitted or condemned: who talks to whom, who likes whom and who dislikes whom, who can be counted on to perform particular tasks, and whom others look to for guidance and help. These regularities combine to generate **group structure**—the complex of roles, norms, and intermember relations that organizes the group. **Roles,** for example, specify the general behaviors expected of

---

interdependence Mutual dependence or influence, as when one's outcomes, actions, thoughts, feelings, and experiences are determined in whole or in part by others.

group structure Norms, roles, and stable patterns of relations among the members of a group.

role A coherent set of behaviors expected of people who occupy specific positions within a group.

Unilateral interdependence

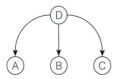

Sequential interdependence

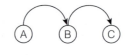

Mutual, reciprocal interdependence

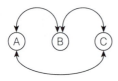

Multilevel interdependence

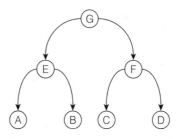

FIGURE 1-1

How do groups create interdependence among members? In some cases, interdependence results from dependence, as when a member's outcomes and experiences are determined by others. In other cases, interdependence is created by patterns of influence in the group and by the group's structure. A leader may, for example, influence others but not be influenced. In other cases, influence is chain-like and hierarchical, as Person A influences B who in turn influences C. Influence is often mutual and reciprocal: All members influence one another.

people who occupy different positions within the group. The roles of *leader* and *follower* are fundamental ones in many groups, but other roles—information seeker, information giver, elaborator, procedural technician, encourager, compromiser, harmonizer—may emerge in any group (Benne & Sheats, 1948). Group members' actions and interactions are also shaped by their group's **norms**—consensual standards that describe what behaviors should and should not be performed in a given context.

Roles, norms, and other structural aspects of groups, although unseen and often unnoticed, lie at the heart of their most dynamic processes. When people join a group, they initially spend much of their time trying to come to terms with the requirements of their role. If they cannot meet the role's demand, they might not remain a member for long. Norms within a group are defined and renegotiated

---

norm A consensual and often implicit standard that describes what behaviors should and should not be performed in a given context.

over time, and conflicts often emerge as members violate norms. In group meetings, the opinions of members with higher status carry more weight than those of the rank-and-file members. When several members form a *subgroup* within the larger group, they exert more influence on the rest of the group than they would individually. When people manage to place themselves at the hub of the group's information exchange patterns, their influence over others also increases. If you had to choose only one aspect of a group to study, you would probably learn the most by studying its structure.

GOALS Groups usually exist for a reason. A team strives to outperform other teams in competitions. A study group wants to raise the grades of all of the students who are members. A jury must make decisions about guilt or innocence. The members of a congregation seek religious and spiritual enlightenment. In each case, the members of the group are united in their pursuit of common **goals.** In groups, people solve problems, create products, create standards, communicate knowledge, have fun, perform arts, create institutions, and even ensure their safety from attacks by other groups. Put simply, groups make it easier to attain our goals. For this reason, much of the world's work is done by groups rather than by individuals.

Groups do so many things that their activities can be classified in a variety of ways. Joseph E. McGrath's **circumplex model of group tasks,** for example, distinguishes among four basic group goals: generating, choosing, negotiating, and executing. As Figure 1-2 indicates, each of these basic categories can be further subdivided, yielding a total of eight basic tasks. When groups work at *generating* tasks, they strive to concoct the strategies they will use to accomplish their goals (*planning tasks*) or to create altogether new ideas and approaches to their problems (*creativity tasks*). When *choosing,* groups make decisions about issues that have correct solutions (*intellective tasks*) or questions that can be answered in many ways (*decision-making tasks*). When groups are *negotiating,* they must resolve differences of opinion among members regarding their goals or decisions (*cognitive conflict tasks*) or resolve competitive disputes among members (*mixed-motive tasks*). The most behaviorally oriented groups actually do things: *Executing* groups compete against other groups (*contests/battles*) or perform (*performances*). Some groups perform tasks from nearly all of McGrath's categories, whereas others concentrate on only one subset of goals (Arrow & McGrath, 1995; McGrath, 1984).

COHESIVENESS Groups are not merely sets of aggregated, independent individuals; instead, they are unified social entities. Groups cannot be reduced down to the level of the individual without losing information about the group as a unit, as a whole. Whenever a group comes into existence, it becomes a system

---

goal The aim or outcome sought by the group and its members.

circumplex model of group tasks A conceptual taxonomy developed by Joseph McGrath that orders group tasks in a circular pattern based on two continua: cooperative–competitive and conceptual–behavioral.

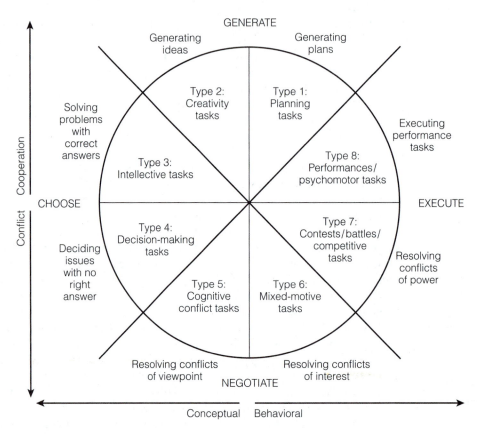

FIGURE 1-2

What do groups *do?* Joseph E. McGrath's task circumplex identifies eight basic activities undertaken by groups: planning, creating, solving problems, making decisions, forming judgments, resolving conflicts, competing, and performing.

with *emergent properties* that cannot be fully understood by piecemeal examination. The Gestalt dictum, "The whole is greater than the sum of the parts," suggests that a group is more than the sum of the individual members.

This quality of "groupness" or unity is determined, in part, by **group cohesion**—the strength of the bonds linking members to one another. A group of executives squabbling among themselves each time the group must reach a decision is clearly less cohesive than a sports team whose members train together

---

group cohesion The strength of the bonds linking individuals to the group, feelings of attraction for specific group members and the group itself, the unity of a group, and the degree to which the group members coordinate their efforts to achieve goals.

FOCUS 1-1   When Does a Group *Look* Like a Group?

I wandered lonely as a cloud . . .
When all at once I saw a crowd
–William Wordsworth

Some collections of people seem to be more like groups than others. Six people playing a game of poker may seem to be a clear case of a group, as would a family of five on a picnic. But what about the audience at a movie? Two lovers walking hand in hand? Thousands of spectators watching a soccer match? Are some groups "groupier" than others?

Donald T. Campbell's (1958a) analysis of *entitativity* suggests that some groups seem more real than other groups. Campbell drew on the work of Gestalt psychologists, who studied how the human mind decides whether something is perceived as a unified entity (a *Gestalt*) or a random collection of unrelated elements. For Campbell, a group's **entitativity** depends on certain perceptual cues that perceivers rely on intuitively to decide if an aggregation of individuals is a true group or just a collection of people. For example, the spectators at a football game may seem to be a disorganized mass of individuals who happen to be in the same place at the same time, but the tendency of the spectators to shout the same cheer, express similar emotions, and move together to create a "wave" gives them entitativity. Entitativity, according to Campbell, is substantially influenced by

- *Common fate:* Do the individuals experience the same or interrelated outcomes?
- *Similarity:* Do the individuals perform similar behaviors or resemble one another?
- *Proximity:* How close together are the individuals in the aggregation?

Consider, for example, four people seated at a table in a library. Is this a group? They could be four friends studying together, or just four independent individuals. To answer the question, you

must consider their common fate, similarity, and proximity. The principle of common fate predicts that the degree of "groupness" you attribute to the cluster would increase if, for example, all the members began laughing together or moved closer to one another. Your confidence that this cluster was a real group would also be bolstered if you noticed that all four were reading from the same textbook or were wearing the same fraternity shirt. Finally, if the members got up and left the room together, you would become even more certain that you were watching a group.

Campbell's analysis of entitativity argues that individuals are intuitively sensitive to information that signals the unity of a group (Hamilton & Sherman, 1996; Hamilton, Sherman, & Lickel, 1998; Lickel et al., 2000). People identify more with their group when all the members share a common fate—for example, if they all fail together or succeed together (Deutsch, 1949a). People recruited for newly formed groups, if told that their group members share many similarities, are more likely to respond as a unified group than people who believe that their group includes dissimilar individuals (Knowles & Brickner, 1981; Schachter, Ellertson, McBride, & Gregory, 1951). When researchers repeatedly told women working in isolation that they were nonetheless members of a group, the women accepted this label and later rated themselves more negatively after their "group" failed (Zander, Stotland, & Wolfe, 1960). Proximity also influences entitativity, for people display more group-level reactions when they meet face to face in a single location than when they meet across long distances in telephone conference calls or through computer-mediated discussions (Kraut, Egido, & Galegher, 1990; Lea & Spears, 1991). Moreover, once a group is judged to be real, this classification leads to a host of perceptual and interpersonal consequences. People who think they are part of a group respond differently than

---

entitativity As described by Donald Campbell, the extent to which an assemblage of individuals is perceived to be a group rather than an aggregation of independent, unrelated individuals; the quality of being an entity.

FOCUS 1-1   (*continued*)

---

people who do not think they are in a group, and observers' impressions of people differ when they think that the people they are watching are members of a unified group. Labeling an aggregation a *group* is not just a matter of semantics. Desig-nating a group as real makes it real in its consequences (W. I. Thomas, 1928). Even if groups are not real, they may nonetheless have important interpersonal consequences if people define them to be real.

---

daily to perfect their coordination and efficiency. However, all groups require a modicum of cohesiveness; else the group would disintegrate and cease to exist as a group (Dion, 2000). A group's unity may also be more perceptual than interpersonal. Even though an aggregation of individuals may not be very cohesive, those who observe the group—and even the members themselves—may believe that the group is a single, unified whole. As Focus 1-1 explains, such groups *look* like groups because they seem to possess the qualities of a real entity.

Groups Are Dynamic

If you were limited to a single word, how would you describe the activities, processes, operations, and changes that transpire in social groups? What word illuminates the interdependence of people in groups? And what word adequately summarizes a group's capacity to promote social interaction, to create patterned interrelationships among its members, to bind members together to form a single unit, and to accomplish its goals?

Kurt Lewin (1943, 1948, 1951), who many have argued is the founder of the movement to study groups scientifically, chose the word *dynamic*. Groups tend to be powerful rather than weak, active rather than passive, fluid rather than static, and catalyzing rather than reifying. Lewin used the term *group dynamics* to stress the powerful impact of these complex social processes on group members. Although Lewin died unexpectedly of a heart attack just as group dynamics was beginning to develop more fully, his students and colleagues have carried on the Lewinian tradition in their theory, research, and applications (Back, 1992; Bargal, Gold, & Lewin, 1992; Marrow, 1969; R. K. White, 1990, 1992).

THE NATURE OF GROUP DYNAMICS

When Kurt Lewin (1951) described the way groups and individuals act and react to changing circumstances, he named these processes **group dynamics.** But Lewin also used the phrase to describe the scientific discipline devoted to the study of these dynamics. Later, Cartwright and Zander, two of the most prolific

---

group dynamics The scientific study of groups; also the actions, processes, and changes that occur in social groups.

researchers in the field, supplied a formal definition, calling group dynamics a "field of inquiry dedicated to advancing knowledge about the nature of groups, the laws of their development, and their interrelations with individuals, other groups, and larger institutions" (1968, p. 7).

Cartwright and Zander also pointed out what group dynamics is *not*. It is not, for example, a therapeutic perspective holding that psychological well-being can be ensured through participation in small groups guided by a skilled therapist. Nor is it the communication of certain rules or guidelines that enable individuals to develop the skills needed for smooth and satisfying social interactions. Finally, group dynamics does not refer to a loose collection of maxims concerning how groups *should* be organized—emphasizing, for example, such niceties as equal participation by all group members, democratic leadership, and high levels of member satisfaction. Rather, group dynamics is an attempt to subject the many aspects of groups to scientific analysis through the construction of theories and the rigorous testing of these theories through empirical research.

Orienting Assumptions

Sociologists and psychologists "discovered" groups almost simultaneously at the beginning of the 20th century (Steiner, 1974). Sociologists, trying to explain how religious, political, economic, and educational systems function to sustain society, highlighted the role played by groups in maintaining social order (Shotola, 1992). Émile Durkheim (1897/1966), for example, argued that individuals who are not members of friendship, family, or religious groups can lose their sense of identity and, as a result, are more likely to commit suicide. Similarly, Cooley suggested that primary groups, such as families, children's play groups, and emotionally close peers, "are fundamental in forming the social nature and ideas of the individual" (1909, p. 23).

At the same time, psychologists were also studying the impact of groups on individuals. In 1895, the French psychologist Gustave Le Bon published his book *Psychologie des Foules* (Psychology of Crowds), which describes how individuals are transformed when they join a group: "Under certain circumstances, and only under those circumstances, an agglomeration of men presents new characteristics very different from those of the individuals composing" the group (1895/1960, p. 23). Although Le Bon's work was speculative, Norman Triplett's (1898) laboratory study of competition confirmed that other people, by their mere presence, can change group members. Triplett arranged for 40 children to play a game that involved turning a small reel as quickly as possible. He found that children who played the game in pairs turned the reel faster than those who were alone, experimentally verifying the shift that occurs when a person moves from a wholly individual circumstance to a social one.

All sciences are based on **paradigms,** which are sets of guiding assumptions or principles shared by researchers in the field (Kuhn, 1970). These early studies

---

paradigm Scientists' shared assumptions about the phenomena they study; also, a set of research procedures.

laid the foundation for the field's paradigm by suggesting that if sociologists and psychologists are to understand society and the individuals in that society, they must understand groups. They also provided examples of the way in which questions about groups could be answered through scientific analysis. Although the group dynamics paradigm continues to evolve and change as theoretical and methodological issues are debated and resolved, several of its core assumptions are considered hereafter (see Gouran, 1999; Harrington & Fine, 2000; J. M. Levine & Moreland, 1990, 1998; McGrath, 1997; Pepitone, 1981; and Steiner, 1986 for more details on the development of group dynamics.)

GROUPS ARE REAL The roots of group dynamics in both sociology and psychology produced a difference in the **levels of analysis** used when studying groups. A *group-level analysis* assumes that each person is "an element in a larger system, a group, organization, or society. And what he does is presumed to reflect the state of the larger system and the events occurring in it" (Steiner, 1974, p. 96). An *individual-level analysis,* in contrast, focuses on the individual in the group. Researchers who took this approach sought to explain the behavior of each group member, and they ultimately wanted to know if such psychological processes as attitudes, motivations, or personality were the true determinants of social behavior. Sociological researchers tended to undertake group-level analyses, and psychological researchers favored the individual-level analysis (Steiner, 1974, 1983, 1986).

Both group-oriented and individualistic researchers asked the question, "Are groups important?" but they often settled on very different answers. Group-level researchers believed that groups and the processes that occurred within them were scientifically authentic. Durkheim (1897/1966) argued that his studies of suicide provided clear evidence of the reality of groups, for it revealed that a very personal act—ending one's life—can be predicted by considering an individual's links to social groups. Durkheim was also impressed by the work of Le Bon and other crowd psychologists and went so far as to suggest that large groups of people sometimes acted with a single mind. He believed that such groups, rather than being mere collections of individuals in a fixed pattern of relationships with one another, were linked by a unifying **groupmind,** or **collective conscious.** Durkheim believed that this force was sometimes so strong that the will of the group could dominate the will of the individual.

Many psychologists who were interested in group phenomena rejected the reality of such concepts as groupmind or collective conscious. Floyd H. Allport,

---

level of analysis The specific focus of study chosen from a graded or nested sequence of possible foci. An individual level analysis examines specific individuals in the group, a group level analysis focuses on the group as a unit, and a multi-level analysis considers both individual- and group-level processes.

groupmind (or **collective conscious**) A hypothetical unifying mental force linking group members together; the fusion of individual consciousness or mind into a transcendent consciousness, suggested by early psychologist Gustave Le Bon.

the foremost representative of this perspective, argued that such terms were unscientific, as they referred to phenomena that simply did not exist. In his 1924 work *Social Psychology,* Allport wrote that "nervous systems are possessed by individuals; but there is no nervous system of the crowd" (p. 5). He added, "Only through social psychology as a science of the individual can we avoid the superficialities of the crowdmind and collective mind theories" (p. 8). Taking the individualistic perspective to its extreme, Allport concluded that groups should never be studied by psychologists, because they did not exist as scientifically valid phenomena. Because Allport believed that "the actions of all are nothing more than the sum of the actions of each taken separately" (p. 5), he thought that a full understanding of the behavior of individuals in groups could be achieved by studying the psychology of the individual group members. Groups, according to Allport, were not real entities.

Allport's reluctance to accept such dubious concepts as groupmind into social psychology helped ensure the field's scientific status. His hard-nosed attitude forced researchers to back up their claims about groups. Many group-level theorists believed in the reality of groups, and they were certain that a group could not be understood by only studying its individual members. Allport's skepticism, however, spurred them to identify the characteristics of groups that set them apart from mere aggregations of individuals.

GROUP PROCESSES ARE REAL Allport was correct in rejecting the concept of groupmind—researchers have never found any evidence that group members are linked by a psychic, telepathic connection that creates a single groupmind. However, the finding that this particular group-level concept has little foundation in fact does not imply that other group-level processes, phenomena, and concepts are equally unreasonable. Consider, for example, the concept of a group norm. As noted earlier, a *norm* is a standard that describes what behaviors should and should not be performed in a group. Norms are not just individual members' personal standards, however, for they are shared among group members. Only when members agree on a particular standard does it function as a norm, so this concept is embedded at the level of the group rather than at the level of the individual.

The idea that a norm is more than just the sum of the individual beliefs of all the members of a group was verified by Muzafer Sherif in 1936. Sherif literally created norms by asking groups of men to state aloud their estimates of the distance that a dot of light had moved. He found that the men gradually accepted a standard estimate in place of their own idiosyncratic judgments. He also found, however, that even when the men were later given the opportunity to make judgments alone, they still based their estimates on the group's norm. Moreover, once the group's norm had developed, the original members of the group could be removed and replaced with fresh members, and the group norm would remain intact. If the individuals in the group are completely replaceable, then where does the group norm "exist"? At the group level rather than the individual level (MacNeil & Sherif, 1976).

The rift between individual-level and group-level researchers closed as the unique contributions of each perspective were integrated in a *multilevel analysis* of

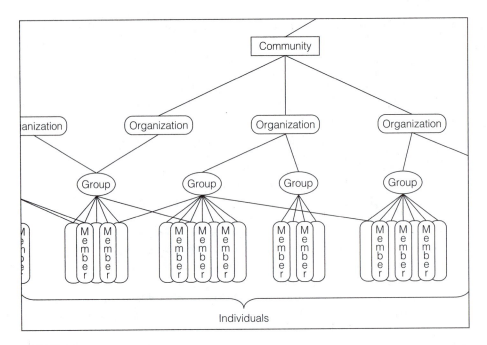

FIGURE 1-3

What is the multilevel view of groups? When researchers study groups, they recognize that individuals are nested in groups, but that these groups are themselves nested in larger social units, such as organizations, communities, tribes, and nations. Thus, the *unit of analysis*—the source of the data the researcher seeks—can be individuals in groups, groups themselves, or groups that are part of organizations, communities, tribes, and societies. Researchers may focus on one level in this multilevel system, such as the group itself, but they must be aware that these groups are embedded in a complex of other relationships.

groups (Hackman, 2003). This perspective, illustrated in Figure 1-3, recognizes that individuals' thoughts, actions, and emotions are shaped by individual-level processes, but that each individual is also shaped by the groups to which he or she belongs. These groups are shaped by their individual members, but they are also nested in larger groups themselves, including communities and organizations. Any analysis that focused only on one level would overlook forces operating at other levels and across levels. Allport, by the way, eventually amended his position and himself conducted extensive studies of such group phenomena as rumors and morale during wartime (F. H. Allport & Lepkin, 1943) and the way norms influence behaviors (the J-curve hypothesis; F. H. Allport, 1934, 1961).

GROUPS ARE MORE THAN THE SUM OF THEIR PARTS   Allport initially believed that group behavior was completely predictable by considering the characteristics and qualities of the individual members. But Kurt Lewin's (1951) *field theory of group dynamics* assumed that groups are more than the sum of their parts. Field theory is premised on the principle of *interactionism,* which assumes that the behavior of people in groups is determined by the interaction of the person and the environment. The formula **B** $=$ $f(P,E)$ summarizes this assumption. In a group context, this formula implies that the behavior (*B*) of group members is a function (*f*) of the interaction of their personal characteristics (*P*) with environmental factors (*E*), which include features of the group, the group members, and the situation. According to Lewin, whenever a group comes into existence, it becomes a unified system with emergent properties that cannot be fully understood by piecemeal examination. Lewin applied the Gestalt dictum, "The whole is greater than the sum of the parts," to groups.

Many group phenomena lend support to Lewin's belief that a group is more than the sum of the individual members. A group's cohesiveness, for example, goes beyond the mere attraction of each individual member to another (Hogg, 1992). Individuals may not like each other a great deal, and yet, when they join together, they experience powerful feelings of unity and esprit de corps. Groups sometimes perform tasks far better—or far worse—than might be expected given the talents of their individual members. When individuals combine synergistically in a group, they sometimes accomplish incredible feats or make horrible decisions that no single individual could ever conceive (Hackman, 1987; Janis, 1983). Such groups seem to possess supervening qualities "that cannot be reduced to or described as qualities of its participants" (Sandelands & St. Clair, 1993, p. 443).

GROUPS ARE LIVING SYSTEMS A holistic perspective on groups prompted researchers to examine how a group, as a unit, changes over time. Some groups are so stable that their basic processes and structures remain unchanged for days, weeks, or even years, but such groups are rare. Bruce W. Tuckman's theory of **group development,** for example, assumes that most groups move through the five stages summarized in Figure 1-4 (Tuckman, 1965; Tuckman & Jensen, 1977). In the *forming* stage, the group members become oriented toward one another. In the *storming* stage, conflicts surface in the group as members vie for status and the group sets its goals. These conflicts subside when the group becomes more structured and standards emerge in the *norming* stage. In the *performing* stage, the group moves beyond disagreement and organizational matters to concentrate on the work to be done. The group continues to function at this level until it reaches the *adjourning* stage, when it disbands. Groups also tend to cycle repeatedly through some of these stages, as group members strive to maintain a balance

---

B $=$ $f(P,E)$ The interactionism formula proposed by Kurt Lewin that assumes each person's behavior (*B*) is a function of his or her personal qualities (*P*), the social environment (*E*), and the interaction of these personal qualities with factors present in the social setting.

group development Patterns of growth and change that emerge across the group's life span.

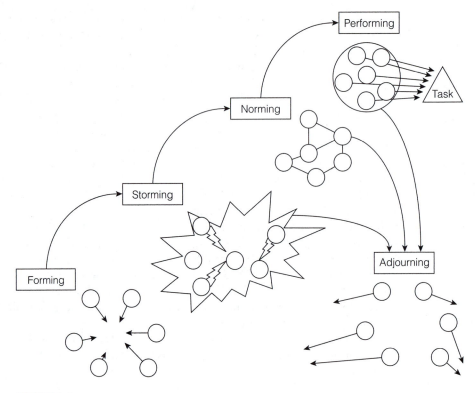

FIGURE 1-4

How do groups change over time? Tuckman's theory of group development argues that nearly all groups pass through the following stages during their development: formation (*forming*), conflict (*storming*), structure development (*norming*), productivity (*performing*), and dissolution (*adjourning*).

between task-oriented actions and emotionally expressive behaviors (Bales, 1965). A group, in a real sense, is alive: It acquires energy and resources from its environment, maintains its structure, and evolves over time.

GROUPS ARE INFLUENTIAL Researchers who study groups are convinced that if one wishes to understand individuals, one must understand groups. Human behavior is, more often than not, group behavior, so people cannot be understood when studied apart from their groups. Groups have a profound impact on individuals; they shape actions, thoughts, and feelings. Some of these changes are subtle ones. Moving from isolation to a group context can reduce our sense of uniqueness, but at the same time it can enhance our ability to perform simple tasks rapidly. Triplett (1898) verified the discontinuity between people's responses when they are isolated rather than integrated, and this shift has been documented time and again in studies of motivation, emotion, and performance. Groups can also change their members by prompting them to change their attitudes and values as they come to agree with the overall consensus of the group (T. M. New-comb, 1943). In primary groups, individuals acquire their attitudes, values, and identities, learn the skills needed to contribute to the group, discover and inter-nalize the rules that govern social behavior, and become practiced at modifying their behavior in response to social norms and others' requirements. Peers are an-other influential group. Children willingly amend their actions and preferences to match the norms of their play groups (Berndt, 1992, 1996). Even very young children imitate the way their playmates dress, talk, and act (Adler, Kless, & Adler, 1992). Children who do not like broccoli will eat it if they are having lunch with a group of broccoli-loving children (Birch, 1987). When anti-achievement norms develop in classrooms, students soon learn to disrupt class and fail tests (Ball, 1981), but teenagers who are part of the "brainy" clique value high academic achievement (B. B. Brown, Mounts, Lamborn, & Steinberg, 1993). As children grow older, the peer group becomes the primary source of social values, replac-ing the influence of the family (Harris, 1995). Twins who have the same friends are more similar to one another in terms of personality and academic achievement than twins who are treated similarly by their parents (Loehlin, 1997).

Groups also change people more dramatically. The earliest group psycholo-gists were struck by the apparent madness of people when immersed in crowds, and many concluded that the behavior of a person in a group may have no connection to that person's behavior when alone. Stanley Milgram's (1963) clas-sic studies of obedience offered further confirmation of the dramatic power of groups over their members, for Milgram found that most people placed in a powerful group would obey the orders of a malevolent authority to harm another person. Individuals who join religious or political groups that stress secrecy, obe-dience to leaders, and dogmatic acceptance of unusual or atypical beliefs (*cults*) of-ten display fundamental and unusual changes in belief and behavior. Groups may just be collections of individuals, but these collections change their members.

GROUPS SHAPE SOCIETY At the same time psychologists began studying how individuals react in group settings, sociologists began studying the role that groups played in maintaining religious, political, economic, and educational systems in society (Shotola, 1992). After the industrial revolution, legal and po-litical systems developed to coordinate actions and make community-level deci-sions. Organized religions provided answers to questions of values, morality, and meaning. Educational systems took over some of the teaching duties previously assigned to the family. Economic systems developed to regulate production and the attainment of financial goals. All these social systems were based, at their core, on small groups and subgroups of connected individuals. Religious groups pro-vide a prime example. Individuals often endorse a specific religion, such as Chris-tianity or Islam, but their connection to their religion occurs in smaller groups known as *congregations*. These groups are formally structured and led by a religious authority, yet they provide members with a sense of belonging, reaffirm the val-ues and norms of the group, and strengthen bonds among members (Finke & Stark, 1992). Groups may just be collections of individuals, but these collections change society (see Focus 1-2).

FOCUS 1-2   Are Groups Good or Bad?

Humans would do better without groups.
–Christian J. Buys (1978a, p. 123)

For centuries, philosophers and scholars have debated the relative value of groups. Some have pointed out that membership in groups is highly rewarding, for it combines the pleasures of interpersonal relations with goal strivings. Groups create relationships between people, and in many cases these connections are more intimate, more enduring, and more sustaining than connections formed between friends or lovers. Groups provide their members with a sense of identity, for the self is not based only on personal traits and qualities (e.g., "I am outgoing") but also on group memberships (e.g., "I am an American"). Groups also provide their members with the means to accomplish goals that they could never achieve alone; they provide their members with support and guidance, and they are often the means of acquiring knowledge, skills, and abilities.

However, the more problematic aspects of groups cannot be ignored. Groups are often the arena for profound interpersonal conflicts that end in violence and aggression. Even though group members may cooperate with one another, they may also engage in competition as they strive to outdo one another. When individuals are members of very large groups, such as crowds, they sometimes engage in behaviors that they would never undertake if they were acting individually. Many of the most misguided decisions have not been made by lone, misguided individuals but by groups of people who, despite working together, still managed to make a disastrous decision. Even though people tend to work together in groups, in many cases, these groups are

far less productive than they should be, given the talents and energies of the individuals in them. Some dysfunctional groups are best avoided—they set the stage for interpersonal conflict while wasting time, turning out poor products, and yielding few benefits. Given these problems, researcher Christian J. Buys whimsically suggested that all groups be eliminated because "humans would do better without groups" (1978a, p.123).

Although Buys's suggestion is a satirical one, it does make the point that groups are neither all good nor all bad. Groups are so "beneficial, if not essential, to humans" that "it seems nonsensical to search for alternatives to human groups" (Buys, 1978b, p. 568), but groups can generate negative outcomes for their members. Researchers, however, are more often drawn to studying negative rather than positive processes, with the result that theory and research in the field tend to stress conflict, rejection, dysfunction, and obedience to malevolent authorities and to neglect cooperation, acceptance, well-being, and collaboration. This negative bias, Buys suggested, has led to an unfair underestimation of the positive impact of groups on people.

Buys's comments, by the way, have prompted a number of rejoinders by other group researchers. One group-authored response (Kravitz et al., 1978) suggested that Buys misassigned responsibility for the problems; its authors argued that humans would do better without other humans rather than without any groups. Another proposed that groups would do better without humans (L. R. Anderson, 1978), whereas a third simply argued that groups would do better without social psychologists (R. B. Green & Mack, 1978).

Contemporary Group Dynamics

The work of early researchers set the foundation for the emerging field of group dynamics. In time, most psychologists abandoned their prejudices against groups as objects of scientific analysis, and Allport himself amended his initial position on the issue by eventually acknowledging the reality of groups (F. H. Allport, 1961, 1962).

By the 1950s, the field was ready to move from its childhood into its adulthood. Armed with new theories of group behavior and a set of increasingly sophisticated research methods, investigators began to examine many more aspects of groups and their dynamics. The field also grew beyond its roots in psychology and sociology to become more interdisciplinary, and many new researchers studied more practical aspects of groups. These developments shaped the content, assumptions, and methods of contemporary group dynamics.

INTERDISCIPLINARY APPROACH Group dynamics was founded by sociologists and psychologists, but it has spread to many other branches of the social sciences. The relevance of groups to topics studied in many academic and applied disciplines gives group dynamics an interdisciplinary character. For example, researchers who prefer to study individuals may find themselves wondering what impact group participation will have on individuals' cognitions, attitudes, and behavior. Those who study organizations may find that these larger social entities actually depend on the dynamics of small subgroups within the organization. Social scientists examining such global issues as the development and maintenance of culture may find themselves turning their attention toward small groups as the unit of cultural transmission.

Table 1-3 summarizes the interdisciplinary breadth of group dynamics. The overall aims of these disciplines may be quite different, but groups are relevant to nearly all the social sciences. Psychologists tend to focus on the behavior of individuals in groups; sociologists, in contrast, focus more on the group and its

TABLE 1-3 Group Dynamics: An Interdisciplinary Field

Discipline	Topics
Anthropology	Groups in cross-cultural contexts; societal change; social and collective identities
Business and Industry	Work motivation; productivity; team building; goal setting; focus groups
Clinical/Counseling Psychology	Therapeutic change through groups; sensitivity training; training groups; self-help groups; group psychotherapy
Communication	Information transmission in groups; discussion; decision making; problems in communication; networks
Criminal Justice	Organization of law enforcement agencies; gangs; jury deliberations
Education	Classroom groups; team teaching; class composition and educational outcomes
Political Science	Leadership; intergroup and international relations; political influence; power
Psychology	Personality and group behavior; problem solving; perceptions of other people; motivation; conflict
Social Work	Team approaches to treatment; family counseling; groups and adjustment
Sociology	Self and society; influence of norms on behavior; role relations; deviance
Sports and Recreation	Team performance; effects of victory and failure; cohesion and performance

relation to society. Anthropologists find that group processes are relevant to understanding many of the common features of various societies; political scientists examine the principles of group relations and leadership; and communication researchers focus more specifically on the communicative relations in groups. Although this listing of disciplines is far from comprehensive, it does convey the idea that the study of groups is not limited to any one field. As A. Paul Hare and his colleagues once noted, "This field of research does not 'belong' to any one of the recognized social sciences alone. It is the common property of all" (Hare, Borgatta, & Bales, 1955, p. vi).

APPLICATIONS Groups are also relevant to many applied areas, as Table 1-3 shows. The study of groups in the work setting has long occupied business-oriented researchers who are concerned with the effective organization of people. Although early discussions of business administration and personnel management tended to overlook the importance of groups, the 1930s witnessed a tremendous growth in management-oriented group research (e.g., Barnard, 1938; Mayo, 1933). People in organizations ranging from businesses to hospitals to the armed forces began to take notice of the critical role that interpersonal relations played in their own organizations, and soon principles of group behavior became an integral part of most philosophies of effective administrative practices. This interest in groups in organizational settings continues to this day, and many group psychologists are also organizational psychologists (N. Anderson, De Dreu, & Nijstad, 2004; Sanna & Parks, 1997).

Social workers frequently found themselves dealing with such groups as social clubs, gangs, neighborhoods, and family clusters, and an awareness of group processes helped crystallize their understanding of group life. Educators were also influenced by group research, as were many of the medical fields that dealt with patients on a group basis. Many methods of helping people to change rely on group principles (A. E. Stewart, Stewart, & Gazda, 1997).

The application of group dynamics to practical problems is consistent with Lewin's call for **action research.** Lewin argued in favor of the intertwining of basic and applied research, for he firmly believed that there "is no hope of creating a better world without a deeper scientific insight into the function of leadership and culture, and of other essentials of group life" (1943, p. 113). To achieve this goal, he assured practitioners that "there is nothing so practical as a good theory" (1951, p. 169) and charged researchers with the task of developing theories that can be applied to important social problems (Cartwright, 1978; Lewin, 1946, 1947).

TOPICS Throughout the history of group dynamics, some approaches that initially seemed promising have been abandoned after they contributed relatively little or failed to stimulate consistent lines of research. The idea of groupmind,

---

action research The term used by Kurt Lewin to describe scientific inquiry that both expands basic theoretical knowledge and identifies solutions to significant social problems.

for example, was discarded when researchers identified more likely causes of crowd behavior. Similarly, such concepts as syntality (Cattell, 1948), groupality (Bogardus, 1954), and lifespace (Lewin, 1951) initially attracted considerable interest but stimulated little research. In contrast, researchers have studied other topics continuously since they were first broached (Forsyth & Burnette, in press; Hare, Blumberg, Davies, & Kent, 1994; J. M. Levine & Moreland, 1990, 1995, 1998; McGrath, 1997).

Table 1-4 samples the topics that currently interest group experts, and it foreshadows the topics considered in the remainder of this book. Chapters 1, 2, and 3 explore the foundations of the field by reviewing the group dynamics perspective (Chapter 1) and the methods and theories of the field (Chapter 2). This introductory section ends with an analysis of what Allport (F. H. Allport, 1961, 1962) called social psychology's "master problem": What is the connection between the individual and the group (Chapter 3)?

Chapters 4, 5, and 6 focus on group development—how groups change and evolve over time. Chapter 4 probes group formation by considering the personal and situational forces that prompt people to join groups or remain apart from them. Chapter 5 focuses more fully on group development by considering the factors that increase the unity of a group and the way those factors wax and wane as the group changes over time. Chapter 6 turns to the topic of group structure—how groups develop systems of roles and intermember relationships—with a particular focus on how structure emerges as groups mature.

A group is a complex social system—a microcosm of powerful interpersonal forces that significantly shape members' actions—and Chapters 7 and 8 examine the flow of influence and interaction in that microcosm. Chapter 7 looks at the way group members sometimes change their opinions, judgments, or actions so that they match the opinions, judgments, or actions of the rest of the group (*conformity*). Chapter 8 extends this topic by considering how group members make use of social power to influence others and how people respond to such influence.

The following chapters turn to questions of group performance. Much of the world's work is done by people working together rather than by individuals working alone. Investigators have identified a host of factors that influence a group's productivity (Chapter 9), and their studies suggest ways to minimize inefficiency and errors when working in groups. We study processes and problems in decision making in Chapter 10 and leadership in Chapter 11.

Chapters 12 and 13 examine conflict and cooperation in groups. Groups are sources of stability and support for members, but in some cases conflicts erupt within groups (Chapter 12) and between groups (Chapter 13).

The final chapters deal with groups in specific settings. All groups are embedded in a social and environmental context, and Chapter 14 considers how the context in which groups exist affects their dynamics. Chapter 15 reviews groups in therapeutic contexts—helping, supportive, and change-promoting groups. Chapter 16 concludes our analysis by considering groups in public, societal contexts, including such relatively large groups as mobs, crowds, and social movements.

TABLE 1-4 Major Topics in the Field of Group Dynamics

Chapter and Topic	Issues
Foundations	
1. Introduction to group dynamics	What are groups and what are their key features? What do we want to know about groups and their dynamics? What assumptions guide researchers in their studies of groups and the processes within groups?
2. Studying groups	How do researchers measure the way groups, and the individuals in those groups, feel, think, and behave? How do researchers search for and test their hypotheses about groups? What are the strengths and weaknesses of the various research strategies used to study groups? What general theoretical perspectives guide researcher's studies of groups and the people in them?
3. The individual and the group	Do humans, as a species, prefer inclusion to exclusion, group membership to isolation? How do groups combine individuals collectively? How do group experiences shape individuals' selves?
Development	
4. Formation	Who joins groups and who remains apart? When and why do people seek out others? Why do people deliberately create groups or join existing groups? What factors influence feelings of liking for others?
5. Cohesion and development	What are the components of group cohesion? How does cohesion develop over time? What are the positive and negative consequences of cohesion and commitment? Does team building enhance group productivity?
6. Structure	What are norms, and how do they structure interactions in groups? What are roles? Which roles occur most frequently in groups? How and why do status networks develop in groups? What factors influence the group's social structure? What are the interpersonal consequences of communication networks in groups?
Influence and Interaction	
7. Influence	When will people conform to a group's standards, and when will they remain independent? How do norms develop, and why do people obey them? Do nonconformists ever succeed in influencing the rest of the group?

Group Dynamics Is Dynamic

The field of group dynamics emerged in the 1940s as theorists and researchers concluded that groups are real and that they should be subjected to scientific analysis. In the 1950s and 1960s, the field grew rapidly as theorists and researchers

TABLE 1-4 (*continued*)

Chapter and Topic	Issues
8. Power	Why are some members of groups more powerful than others? What types of power tactics are most effective in influencing others? Does power corrupt? Why do people obey authorities?

Performance

9. Performance	Do people perform tasks more effectively in groups or when they are alone? Why do people sometimes expend so little effort when they are in groups? When does a group outperform an individual? Are groups creative?
10. Decision making	What steps do groups take when making decisions? Why do some highly cohesive groups make disastrous decisions? Why do groups sometimes make riskier decisions than individuals?
11. Leadership	What is leadership? If a group without a leader forms, which person will eventually step forward to become the leader? Should a leader be task focused or relationship focused? Is democratic leadership superior to autocratic leadership?

Conflict

12. Conflict	What causes disputes between group members? When will a small disagreement escalate into a conflict? Why do groups sometimes splinter into subgroups? How can disputes in groups be resolved?
13. Intergroup relations	What causes disputes between groups? What changes take place as a consequence of intergroup conflict? What factors exacerbate conflict? How can intergroup conflict be resolved?

Contexts and Applications

14. Groups in context	What impact does the social and physical setting have on an interacting group? Are groups territorial? What happens when groups are overcrowded? How do groups cope with severe environments?
15. Groups and change	How can groups be used to improve personal adjustment and health? What is the difference between a therapy group and a self-help group? Are group approaches to treatment effective? Why do they work?
16. Crowds and collective behavior	What types of crowds are common? Why do crowds and collectives form? Do people lose their sense of self when they join crowds? When is a crowd likely to become unruly?

studied more and more topics, the field became more interdisciplinary, and the accumulated knowledge was applied to practical problems.

This rapid expansion slowed once the study of groups gained acceptance in both sociology and psychology, but even today the field remains vibrant. Groups are studied by a range of investigators from a host of different disciplines.

Although these researchers have very different goals, pursuits, and paradigms, they all recognize that groups are essential to human life. Through membership in groups, we define and confirm our values and beliefs and take on or refine our social identity. When we face uncertain situations, we join groups to gain reassurance about our problems and security in companionship. Even though we must sometimes bend to the will of a group and its leaders, through groups we can reach goals that would elude us if we pursued them as individuals. Our groups are sometimes filled with conflict; but by resolving this conflict, we learn how to relate with others more effectively. Groups are fundamental to our social lives, and we must accept the charge of understanding them.

SUMMARY IN OUTLINE

❖ What is a group?

1. No two groups are identical to one another, but a *group,* by definition, is two or more individuals who are connected to one another by social relationships.

2. Groups vary in size from dyads and triads to very large aggregations, such as mobs and audiences.

3. Unlike the members of a *category,* group members are linked together by such interpersonal processes as communication, influence, and identification.

4. Groups come in many varieties.
   - *Primary groups* are smaller and more psychologically influential than are *secondary groups.*
   - *Planned groups* (e.g., concocted groups and founded groups) are deliberately formed, but *emergent groups* (e.g., circumstantial groups and self-organizing groups) come into existence gradually over time.

5. Research suggests that people spontaneously draw distinctions among intimate groups, task-focused groups, loose associations, and more general social categories.

❖ What are some common characteristics of groups?

1. People in groups interact with one another. This *interaction* includes activities that focus on the task at hand (*task interaction*) and activities that concern the interpersonal relations linking group members (*relationship interaction*).

2. Groups create *interdependence* among the group members (unilateral, reciprocal, etc.).

3. Interaction is patterned by *group structure,* including *roles, norms,* and interpersonal relations.

4. Groups seek goals, such as those specified in the *circumplex model of group tasks* (generating, choosing, negotiating, and executing).

5. *Group cohesion,* or cohesiveness, determines the unity of the group. *Entitativity* is the extent to which individuals perceive an aggregation to be a unified group. Entitativity, according to Campbell, is substantially influenced by common fate, similarity, and proximity cues.

❖ What assumptions guide researchers in their studies of groups and the processes within groups?

1. Lewin first used the phrase *group dynamics* to describe the powerful processes that take place in groups, but group dynamics also refers to the scientific study of groups.

2. This relatively young science has roots in both sociology and psychology. Sociolo-

gists have long recognized that groups link individuals to society, and psychologists have studied how people act when they are in groups rather than alone.

3. The field's conceptual *paradigm* includes a number of assumptions:

- *Groups are real.* Early psychologists tended to focus on the psychological processes; they used an *individual level of analysis* in their studies of groups by rejecting such group-level concepts as the *groupmind* and *collective conscious.* In time, researchers recognized that groups are as real as individuals, adopting a multilevel orientation to groups.
- *Group processes are real.* Research studies, such as Sherif's (1936) study of norm formation, suggested that group-level processes were influential determinants of behavior and so supported a multilevel approach to studying individuals and groups.
- *Groups are more than the sum of their parts.* Groups often possess characteristics that cannot be deduced from the individual members' characteristics. This conclusion is consistent with Lewin's (1951) field theory, which maintains that behavior is a function of the person and the environment, or $B = f(P, E)$.
- *Groups are living systems.* Tuckman's (1965) theory of *group development,* for example, assumes that most groups move through the five stages of forming, storming, norming, performing, and adjourning over time.
- *Groups are influential.* Groups alter their members' attitudes, values, and perceptions and in some cases cause radical alterations in personality and actions.
- *Groups shape society.* Groups, although sometimes characterized in negative rather than positive ways, influence many aspects of human society.

❖ **What fields and what topics are included in the scientific study of group dynamics?**

1. The field of group dynamics is an interdisciplinary one, including many researchers outside of sociology and psychology.

2. Many researchers carry out *action research* by using scientific methods to identify solutions to practical problems.

3. Researchers have examined a wide variety of group processes, including group development, structure, influence, power, performance, and conflict.

4. Group dynamics is itself dynamic, for it is the "field of inquiry dedicated to advancing knowledge about the nature of groups" (Cartwright & Zander, 1968, p. 7).

FOR MORE INFORMATION

Introduction to Groups

- *Blackwell Handbook of Social Psychology: Group Processes,* edited by Michael A. Hogg and Scott Tindale (2001), includes 26 chapters dealing with all aspects of small group behavior.
- *Group Dynamics: Research and Theory,* edited by Dorwin Cartwright and Alvin Zander

(1968), is a classic in the scientific field of groups, with chapters dealing with such topics as group membership, conformity, power, leadership, and motivation.

- "Small Groups," by John M. Levine and Richard L. Moreland (1998), provides a serious but compact introduction to the study of groups, with specific sections pertaining to group composition, structure, conflict, and performance.

Group Dynamics: History and Issues

- "Communication in Groups: The Emergence and Evolution of a Field of Study," by Dennis S. Gouran (1999), reviews the recent history of group research in the field of small group communication.
- "The Heritage of Kurt Lewin: Theory, Research, and Practice," edited by David Bargal, Martin Gold, and Miriam Lewin (1992), is an issue of the *Journal of Social Issues* devoted to the contributions of group dynamics' founder, Kurt Lewin.

Groups and the 21st Century

- "Opening the 'Black Box': Small Groups and Twenty-First Century Sociology," by Brooke Harrington and Gary Alan Fine (2000), re-examines the controlling, contesting, organizing, representing, and allocating features of small groups and their relevance to understanding social behavior.
- "The Study of Groups: Past, Present, and Future," by Joseph E. McGrath, Holly Arrow, and Jennifer L. Berdahl (2000) reviews the history of research into groups and predicts future trends.

MEDIA RESOURCES

Visit the Group Dynamics companion website at http://psychology.wadsworth.com/forsyth4e to access online resources for your book, including quizzes, flash cards, web links, and more!

STUDYING GROUPS

CHAPTER OVERVIEW

Just as scientists use exacting procedures to study aspects of the physical and natural environment, so do group researchers use scientific methods to further their understanding of groups. Through research, theorists and researchers separate fact from fiction and truth from myth.

❖ What are the three critical requirements of a scientific approach to the study of groups?

❖ What methods do researchers use to measure individual and group processes?

❖ What are the key characteristics of and differences between case, experimental, and correlational studies of group processes?

❖ What are the strengths and weaknesses of case, experimental, and correlational study designs?

❖ What theoretical perspectives guide researchers' studies of groups?

CHAPTER OUTLINE

MEASUREMENT IN GROUP DYNAMICS
Observational Techniques
Self-Report Measures
FOCUS 2-1: What Dimensions Structure Group Interaction?

TESTING HYPOTHESES: RESEARCH DESIGNS
Case Studies
Experimentation
Nonexperimental Designs
FOCUS 2-2: Are Groups Harder to Study Than Individuals?
Selecting a Research Design

THEORIES IN GROUP DYNAMICS
Motivational Models
Behavioral Approaches
Systems Theories
Cognitive Approaches
Biological Models
Selecting a Theory

Summary in Outline

For More Information

Media Resources

Groups are puzzling, even to those who are thought to be wise. Is a group's potential determined by its weakest link? Yes, said Ralph Waldo Emerson, "There need be but one wise man in a company and all are wise, so a blockhead makes a blockhead of his companions." Do people, when immersed in a crowd, become irrational? Cicero proclaimed that "A mob has no judgment, no discretion, no direction, no discrimination, no consistency." Aristotle believed that leadership is an innate talent: "Men are marked out from the moment of birth to rule or be ruled." Nietzsche questioned the rationality of groups when he wrote, "Madness is the exception in individuals but the rule in groups."

These comments are insightful, but these savants' analyses are limited in one important way: They are all conjectures based on personal opinion rather than scientific research. Can we predict a group's performance by taking into account the skills of its best member and its worst member? How do people behave in crowds? Are leaders born rather than made? Are groups intellectually inferior to individuals? Without scientific analysis, we cannot be certain.

This chapter reviews three basic elements of scientific research: measurement, hypothesis testing, and theory development. As sociologist George Caspar Homans explained, "When the test of the truth of a relationship lies finally in the data themselves, and the data are not wholly manufactured—when nature, however stretched out on the rack, still has a chance to say 'No!'—then the subject is a science"(1967, p. 4). Homans's definition enjoins researchers to "stretch nature out on the rack" by systematically measuring group phenomena and group processes. Researchers must also test "the truth of the relationship" in some way. Emerson's belief that "one bad apple can ruin the barrel" may apply to groups, but we cannot be sure until this hypothesis is put to the test empirically. But scientists do not just test and measure. They also create conceptual frameworks to organize their findings. Homans recognized that "nothing is more lost than a loose fact" (1950, p. 5) and urged the development of theories that provide a "general form in which the results of observations of many particular groups may be expressed"(p. 21).

MEASUREMENT IN GROUP DYNAMICS

Progress in science often depends on the development of tools for conducting research. Biologists made dozens of discoveries when they perfected the compound microscope, as did astronomers when they peered into the night sky with their telescopes. Researchers' success in studying groups was also tied, in large part, to their progress in measuring group members' interpersonal actions and psychological reactions. Here, we trace the growth and impact of two important measurement tools—*observational strategies* and *self-report measures*—that gave group dynamics a foothold in the scientific tradition.

Observational Techniques

Researchers turned to **observational measures** when they first examined groups. Scholars had been watching groups for centuries, but their methods were informal and accidental rather than structured and deliberate. Researchers, in contrast, sought out groups so they could watch and record the verbal and non-verbal actions and interactions of group members. *Verbal actions* include all statements made by the group members, both oral and written, and *nonverbal actions* include gestures, motions, paralinguistic cues such as tone of voice, and even sounds such as grunts and groans.

William Foote Whyte (1943) relied on observational measures in his ethno-graphic study of Italian American gangs in the heart of Boston. He rented a room from an Italian family who lived in the inner city and joined the Nortons, a group of young men who gathered at a particular corner on Norton Street. He also par-ticipated in a club known as the Italian Community Club. Whyte observed and recorded these groups for 3½ years, gradually developing a detailed portrait of this community and its groups. His study underscored the strong link between the in-dividual members and the group, but it also illustrated some key features of ob-servational measures. Whyte focused on observable actions and avoided making inferences about what group members were thinking or feeling if he had no di-rect evidence of their inner states. He also focused his observations, for he realized that he could not record every behavior performed by every corner boy. Instead, he concentrated on communication, leadership, and attempts at gaining status. He also sampled data across time and settings (McGrath & Altermatt, 2001).

Whyte did not, however, use trained, objective observers, as some investiga-tors do. In fact, Whyte actually joined the groups and took part in their activi-ties. He also revealed his identity to the group members, and he did not try to quantify any of his observations; instead, he provided detailed descriptions of what he observed. These decisions, as noted hereafter, all had a great impact on his study and its conclusions.

PARTICIPANT OBSERVATION In many cases, researchers observe groups from a vantage point well outside the group itself. They may arrange for the group to meet in a laboratory equipped with specialized one-way mirrors that permit them to watch the group but prevent the group from watching them. They may also videotape the group members as they interact, so that they can review these records repeatedly to make sure they did not overlook any of the complexities that usually emerge in a full-fledged interacting group. However, some re-searchers, like Whyte, join the groups they study. This **participant observation**

---

observational measure A measurement method that involves watching and recording individual and group actions.

participant observation Watching and recording interpersonal behavior while taking part in the social process.

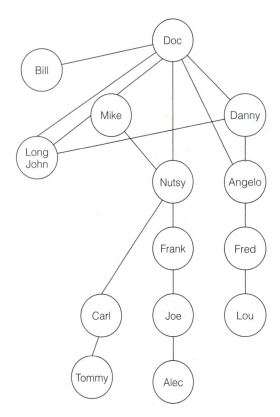

FIGURE 2-1

How were the Nortons organized? Lines between each member indicate interdependence,
and members who are placed above others in
the chart had more influence than those in the
lower positions. Doc was the recognized leader
of the group, and Mike and Danny were second in terms of status. Whyte ("Bill" in the
diagram), the researcher, was connected to
the group through Doc (Whyte, 1955).
Source: From *Street Corner Society* by W. F.
Whyte, p. 13. Copyright © 1943 by University of Chicago Press. Reprinted by permission.

is "a process in which the observer's presence in a social situation is maintained
for the purpose of scientific investigation. The observer is in a face-to-face
relationship with the observed, and, by participating with them in their natural
life setting, he gathers data" (M. S. Schwartz & Schwartz, 1955, p. 344; see also
H. Schwartz & Jacobs, 1979; W. F. Whyte, 1991). Whyte, as a participant observer, gained access to information that would have been hidden from an external observer. His techniques also gave him a very detailed understanding of the
gang. Unfortunately, his presence in the group may have changed the group itself. He went bowling with the Nortons, gambled with them, and even lent
money to some of the members. His presence in the group undoubtedly modified its structure, and, therefore, the group he describes is not a typical corner
gang, but rather a corner gang with a researcher in it (see Figure 2-1).

OVERT AND COVERT OBSERVATION Whyte was an *overt* observer of the
group; the Nortons knew that he was recording their behavior. Such openness
meant that he did not have to mislead the group in any way, but by revealing his
purpose, he may have indirectly influenced the gang's behavior. As one corner
boy remarked, "You've slowed me down plenty since you've been down here.
Now, when I do something, I have to think what Bill Whyte would want to

know about it and how I can explain it. Before, I used to do things by in-stinct"(W. F. Whyte, 1943, p. 301).

This tendency for individuals to act differently when they know they are be-ing observed, is often called the **Hawthorne effect,** after research conducted by Elton Mayo and his associates at the Hawthorne Plant of the Western Electric Company (Landsberger, 1958; Mayo, 1945; Roethlisberger & Dickson, 1939). These researchers studied productivity in the workplace by systematically vary-ing a number of features while measuring the workers' output. They moved one group of women to a separate room and monitored their performance carefully. Next, they manipulated features of the work situation, such as the lighting in the room and the duration of rest periods. They were surprised when *all* the changes led to improved worker output. Dim lights, for example, raised efficiency, but so did bright lights. Mayo and his researchers concluded that the group members were working harder because they were being observed and because they felt that the company was taking a special interest in them.

Subsequent reviews of the Hawthorne studies have suggested that other factors contributed to the increased productivity of the groups, but the term *Hawthorne effect* is still used to describe any change in behavior that occurs when people feel they are being studied (Bramel & Friend, 1981; Franke, 1979; Franke & Kaul, 1978). Because the Hawthorne effect can limit the generaliz-ability of research findings, some researchers prefer to use **covert observation,** whereby the observer records the group's activities without the group's knowl-edge. Such methods are methodologically commendable, but the researchers who use them face ethical issues if their observations invade the privacy of the people they are watching. Nondeceptive methods avoid these moral quagmires, but at the price of less accurate information (Humphreys, 1975; Whitley, 2002).

STRUCTURING OBSERVATIONS Whyte observed the Nortons every day, but he postponed organizing his observations. Like an ethnographer or a field an-thropologist studying a little-known culture, he tried to watch the Nortons with-out any preconceptions about what to look for, so that he would not unwittingly confirm his prior expectations. Nor did he keep track of the frequencies of any of the behaviors he noted or try explicitly to quantify members' reactions to the events that occurred in the group. Instead he watched, took notes, and reflected on what he saw before drawing general conclusions about the group.

Whyte conducted a **qualitative study** of the Nortons. Qualitative methods generate data, but the data describe general qualities and characteristics rather than precise quantities and amounts. Such data are often textual rather than

---

Hawthorne effect A change in behavior that occurs when individuals know they are being studied by researchers.

covert observation A measurement method that records group members' actions with-out the participants' knowledge.

qualitative study A research procedure used to collect and analyze nonnumeric, un-quantified types of data, such as text, images, or objects.

numeric, and may include verbal descriptions of group interactions developed by multiple observers, interview responses collected through open-ended surveys, notes from conversations with group members, or in-depth case descriptions of one or two groups. Such qualitative observational methods require an impartial researcher who is a keen observer of groups. If researchers are not careful to remain objective, they may let initial, implicit expectations shape their records (Dollar & Merrigan, 2002; A. Strauss & Corbin, 1998; Weick, 1985). Albert H. Hastorf and Hadley Cantril (1954) demonstrated just such a perceptual bias by asking college students to watch a film of two teams playing a football game. They selected a game between Dartmouth and Princeton that featured extremely rough play and many penalties against both teams. In fact, both quarterbacks were injured in the game. When Hastorf and Cantril asked Dartmouth and Princeton students to record the number and severity of the infractions that had been committed by the two teams, the Princeton students were not very accurate. Dartmouth students saw the Princeton team commit about the same number of infractions as the Dartmouth players. Princeton students, however, disagreed with the Dartmouth observers; they saw the Dartmouth team commit more than twice as many infractions as the Princeton team. Apparently, the Princeton observers' preference for their own team distorted their perceptions of the group interaction.

Structured observational measures offer one possible solution to the lack of objectivity in observations. Like biologists who classify living organisms under such categories as phylum, subphylum, class, and order, or psychologists who classify people into various personality types, researchers who use a **structured observational method** classify each group behavior into an objectively definable category. They achieve this goal by deciding a priori which behaviors in the group are of interest and which are not. Then they set up the categories to be used in the coding system. The researchers then note the occurrence and frequency of these targeted behaviors. This type of research would be a **quantitative study,** because its results can be described numerically rather than qualitatively (Weingart, 1997).

Researchers can now choose from a wide assortment of structured observational systems; one researcher has actually developed a structured coding system for classifying types of coding systems (Trujillo, 1986). Robert Freed Bales's method, shown in Table 2-1, has proved particularly useful (Bales, 1950, 1970, 1980). Bales called his first coding system **Interaction Process Analysis (IPA).**

---

structured observational method Any research procedure that classifies (codes) the group members' actions into defined categories. For example, the Interaction Process Analysis (IPA) observational system developed by Robert Bales requires observers to classify behaviors into 1 of 12 mutually exclusive categories, such as "asks for information" or "shows tension."

quantitative study A research procedure used to collect and analyze data in a numeric form, such as frequencies, proportions, or amounts.

Interaction Process Analysis (IPA) A structured coding system developed by Robert Bales used to classify group behavior into task-oriented and relationship-oriented categories.

TABLE 2-1 Categories of the Original (1950) and the Revised (1970) Interaction Process Analysis (IPA) System

General Categories	1950 IPA Categories	1970 IPA Categories
A. Positive (and mixed) actions	1. Shows solidarity	1. Seems friendly
	2. Shows tension release	2. Dramatizes
	3. Agrees	3. Agrees
B. Attempted answers	4. Gives suggestion	4. Gives suggestion
	5. Gives opinion	5. Gives opinion
	6. Gives orientation	6. Gives information
C. Questions	7. Asks for orientation	7. Asks for information
	8. Asks for opinion	8. Asks for opinion
	9. Asks for suggestion	9. Asks for suggestion
D. Negative (and mixed) actions	10. Disagrees	10. Disagrees
	11. Shows tension	11. Shows tension
	12. Shows antagonism	12. Seems unfriendly

Source: Personality and Interpersonal Behavior by Robert Freed Bales. Copyright 1970 by Holt, Rinehart, and Winston, Inc.

Researchers who use IPA can classify each bit of behavior performed by a group member into 1 of 12 categories. Six of these categories (1–3 and 10–12) pertain to *relationship activities* (also termed *socioemotional activities*), which sustain or weaken interpersonal ties within the group. Complimenting another person is an example of a positive relationship behavior, whereas insulting a group member reflects a negative relationship behavior. The other six categories (4–9) pertain to *task activity,* or behavior that focuses on the problem the group is trying to solve. Giving and asking for information, opinions, and suggestions related to the problem the group faces are all examples of task-oriented activity.

Observers who use the IPA first learn to identify the 12 types of behavior defined by Bales (see Table 2-1). They must be able to listen to a group discussion, break the verbal content down into "unit acts," and then classify each unit into one of the categories listed in Table 2-1. If Sophia, for example, begins the group discussion by asking "Should we introduce ourselves?" and Barbara answers, "Yes," observers write "Sophia–Group" beside Category 8 (Sophia asks for opinion from whole group) and "Barbara–Sophia" beside Category 5 (Barbara gives opinion to Sophia). If Stephan later angrily tells the entire group, "This group is a boring waste of time," the coders write "Stephan–Group" beside Category 12 (Stephan seems unfriendly to entire group).

If observers are well trained, a structured coding system such as IPA will yield data that are both reliable and valid. **Reliability** is determined by a measure's

---

reliability The degree to which a measurement technique consistently yields the same conclusion at different times. For measurement techniques with two or more components, reliability is also the degree to which these various components all yield similar conclusions.

consistency across time, components, and raters. If a rater, when she hears the statement, "This group is a boring waste of time," always classifies it as a Category 12 behavior, then the rating is reliable. The measure has *interrater reliability* if different raters, working independently, all think that the statement belongs in Category 12. **Validity** describes the extent to which the technique measures what it is supposed to measure. IPA is valid if it actually measures the amount of relationship- and task-oriented activity in the group. If the observers are incorrect in their coding, or if the categories do not accurately reflect the relationship- and task-oriented aspects of a group, the scores are not valid (Bakeman, 2000).

IPA is useful because it records the number of times a particular type of behavior has occurred and, thus, makes possible comparison across categories, group members, and even different groups. Bales has also improved both the reliability and the validity of his coding system over the years. As Table 2-1 indicates, Bales revised the IPA categories in 1970, and more recently he proposed a further elaboration of the entire system. This newest version, which generates more global summaries of group behavior, is called the **Systematic Multiple Level Observation of Groups** (**SYMLOG;** see Focus 2-1).

Given the greater reliability and validity of structured observations, why did Whyte take a qualitative, unstructured approach? Whyte was more interested in gaining an understanding of the entire community and its citizenry, so a structured coding system's narrow focus on specific behaviors would have yielded an unduly narrow analysis. At the time he conducted his study, very few researchers had studied community groups, so Whyte did not know which behaviors he should scrutinize if he wanted to understand the group. Whyte was also unfamiliar with the groups he studied, so he chose to immerse himself in fieldwork. His research was more exploratory, designed to develop theory first and validate hypotheses second, so he used an unstructured observational approach. If he had been testing a hypothesis by measuring specific aspects of a group, then the rigor and objectivity of a structured approach would have been preferable. Qualitative methods, in general, "provide a richer, more varied pool of information" than quantitative ones (L. A. King, 2004, p. 175).

Self-Report Measures

Whyte did not just watch Doc, Mike, Danny, and the others as they interacted with one another and with others in the community. Time and again, Whyte supplemented his observations by questioning the group members. Whenever he

---

validity The degree to which a measurement method assesses what it was designed to measure.

Systematic Multiple Level Observation of Groups (SYMLOG) Robert Bales's theory and observational system which assumes that group activities can be classified along three dimensions (dominance versus submissiveness, friendliness versus unfriendliness, and acceptance versus nonacceptance of authority) and that groups are more effective when these three aspects of the group align.

FOCUS 2-1   What Dimensions Structure Group Interaction?

I have always felt the compulsion to ground my thinking in empirical data.
–Robert Freed Bales (1999, p. xvi).

Robert Freed Bales spent years watching groups interact in all kinds of settings—classrooms, organizations, combat, training, production, and so on—before he developed a general model for summarizing each group member's behavioral tendencies. He called this model *SYMLOG,* which stands for the *Systematic Multiple Level Observation of Groups* (Bales, 1980, 1988, 1999). SYMLOG assumes that three fundamental dimensions structure the interactions of people in groups, and this system seeks to classify each group member at some point along these dimensions:

- *Dominance/submissiveness:* Is this member active, outgoing, and talkative, or passive, quiet, and introverted?
- *Friendliness/unfriendliness:* Is this member warm, open, and positive, or negative and irritable?
- *Acceptance of authority/nonacceptance of authority:* Is this member analytic and task oriented, or emotional, untraditional, and (in some cases) resentful?

Observers, or the group members themselves, can rate each individual in the group using the 26 categories shown in Table 2-2. The group leader's behaviors, for example, might be concentrated in the "active, dominant, talks a lot" category rather than the "passive, introverted, says little" category. A disillusioned group member, in contrast, might get high scores for "irritable, cynical, won't cooperate." These ratings can be used to chart the flow of a group's interaction over time. When a group first begins to discuss a problem, most of the behaviors may be concentrated in the dominant, friendly, and accepting authority categories. But if the group is racked by disagreement, then scores in the unfriendly, nonaccepting authority categories may begin to climb. SYMLOG can also be used to create a graph of the group profile including each member's location on the dominance, friendliness, and authority dimensions (Hare, 1985; Polley, 1989; Polley, Hare, & Stone, 1988).

was curious about their thoughts, perceptions, and emotions, he would ask them, as indirectly as possible, to describe their reactions.

Self-report measures are based on the idea that if you want to know how group members feel about something or why they performed a particular behavior, ask them to tell you. *How* you go about asking can vary; you can administer personality tests, distribute attitude questionnaires, or conduct face-to-face interviews. But these self-report measures are all alike in that they involve asking a question and recording the answer (Judd & McClelland, 1998; N. Schwarz, Groves, & Schuman, 1998).

Jacob L. Moreno used self-report methods to study young women living in 14 adjacent cottages at an institution. The women were neighbors, but they were not very neighborly. Discipline problems were rampant, and disputes continually arose among the groups and among members of the same group who were sharing a cottage. Moreno believed that the tensions would abate if he could regroup the women into more compatible clusters and put the greatest physical distance

---

self-report measure An assessment device, such as a questionnaire, test, or interview, that ask respondents to describe their feelings, attitudes, or beliefs.

TABLE 2-2 Basic Tendencies Identified in the SYMLOG Group Observation System

Label	General Behavior	Description
U	Active, dominant, talks a lot	Material success and power
UP	Extrovert, outgoing, positive	Popularity and social success
UPF	A purposeful, democratic task leader	Social solidarity and progress
UF	An assertive, businesslike manager	Strong effective management
UNF	Authoritarian, controlling, disapproving	A powerful authority, law and order
UN	Domineering, tough-minded, powerful	Tough-minded assertiveness
UNB	Provocative, egocentric, shows off	Rugged individualism, self-gratification
UB	Jokes around, expressive, dramatic	Having a good time, self-expression
UPB	Entertaining, sociable, smiling, warm	Making others feel happy
P	Friendly, egalitarian	Egalitarianism, democratic participation
PF	Works cooperatively with others	Altruism, idealism, cooperation
F	Analytical, task-oriented, problem-solving	Established social beliefs and values
NF	Legalistic, has to be right	Value-determined restraint of desires
N	Unfriendly, negativistic	Individual dissent, self-sufficiency
NB	Irritable, cynical, won't cooperate	Social nonconformity
B	Shows feelings and emotions	Unconventional beliefs and values
PB	Affectionate, likable, fun to be with	Friendship, liberalism, sharing
DP	Looks up to others, appreciative, trustful	Trust in the goodness of others
DPF	Gentle, willing to accept responsibility	Love, faithfulness, loyalty
DF	Obedient, works submissively	Hard work, self-knowledge, subjectivity
DNF	Self-punishing, works too hard	Suffering
DN	Depressed, sad, resentful, rejecting	Rejection of popularity
DNB	Alienated, quits, withdraws	Admission of failure, withdrawal
DB	Afraid to try, doubts own ability	Noncooperation with authority
DPB	Quietly happy just to be with others	Quiet contentment, taking it easy
D	Passive, introverted, says little	Giving up all selfish desires

SYMLOG assumes that behaviors vary in three fundamental dimensions: dominant versus submissive (**U**p versus **D**own), friendly versus unfriendly (**P**ositive versus **N**egative), and acceptance of authority versus nonacceptance of authority (**F**orward versus **B**ackward).

Source: Adapted with permission of The Free Press, a Division of Simon & Schuster Adult Publishing Group, from *SYMLOG: A System for Multiple Level Observation of Groups* by Robert F. Bales and Stephen P. Cohen with Stephen A. Williamson. Copyright © 1979 by The Free Press. All rights reserved.

between hostile groups. So he asked the women to indicate whom they liked the most on a confidential questionnaire. Moreno then used these responses to construct more harmonious groups, and his efforts were rewarded when the overall level of antagonism in the community dwindled (Moreno, 1934).

Moreno called this technique for measuring the relations between group members **sociometry.** A researcher begins a sociometric study by asking group

---

sociometry A research technique developed by Jacob Moreno that graphically and mathematically summarizes patterns of intermember relations.

members one or more questions about the other members. To measure attraction, the researcher might ask, "Whom do you like most in this group?" but such questions as "Whom in the group would you like to work with the most?" or "Whom do you like the least?" can also be used. Researchers often limit the number of choices that participants can make. These choices are then organized in a **sociogram,** which is a diagram of the relationships among group members. As Figure 2-2 illustrates, each group member is represented by a circle, and arrows are used to indicate who likes whom. The researcher can organize the group members' responses into a more meaningful pattern, say, by putting individuals who are frequently chosen by others at the center of the diagram, and the least frequently chosen people could be placed about the periphery. Alternatively, computer programs such as Sociometrics (D. Walsh, 2003) and KrackPlot (Krackhardt, 2003) can generate mathematically accurate sociograms.

A sociogram describes each member's relationship to the other group members and the group's overall structure. Depending on the group, the sociogram may reveal such positions as,

- *populars,* or stars: well-liked, very popular group members picked by many other group members
- *unpopulars,* or rejected members: individuals who are identified as disliked by many group members
- *isolates,* or loners: individuals who are infrequently chosen by any group members
- *positives,* or sociables: individuals who select many others as their friends
- *negatives:* individuals who select few others as their friends
- *pairs:* two people who, by listing each other as their first choice, have reciprocal bonds
- *clusters:* individuals within the group who make up a subgroup, or clique
- *fringers:* pairs that are not selected by anyone else in the group and hence are located at the periphery of the group

The researcher can also use the responses to calculate various *indices of attraction,* including (1) the number of times a person is chosen by the other group members (*choice status*); (2) the number of times a person is rejected by others (*rejection status*); (3) the relative number of mutual pairs in a group (*group cohesion*); and (4) the relative number of isolates (*group integration,* or *inclusiveness*). Sociometric data can also be examined using more elaborate statistical methods, such as path diagrams, factor plots, and cluster analysis (Brandes, Kenis, Raab, Schneider, & Wagner, 1999; Wasserman & Faust, 1994).

Self-report methods, such as sociometry, have both weaknesses and strengths. They depend very much on knowing what questions to ask the group members.

---

sociogram A graphic representation of the patterns of intermember relations created through sociometry. In most cases each member of the group is depicted by a symbol, such as a lettered circle or square, and the types of relations among members (e.g., communication links, friendship pairings) are depicted with capped lines.

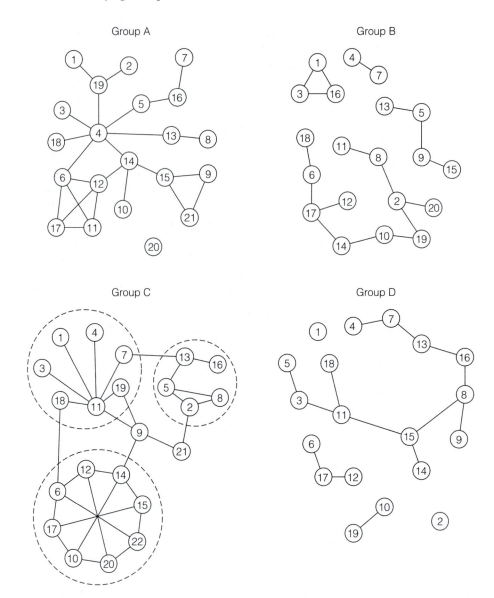

FIGURE 2-2

How can the structure of a group be measured? A *sociogram* charts group structure by identifying relationships among the members. Group A is a centralized group, but B is relatively decentralized. Group C has a number of subgroups that are not well linked, and Group D is relatively disorganized.

A maze of technical questions also confronts researchers designing question-naires. If respondents do not answer the questions consistently—if, for example, Jos indicates that he likes Gerard the most on Monday but on Tuesday changes his choice to Claire—then the responses will be unreliable. Also, if questions are not worded properly, the instrument will lack validity, because the respondents may misinterpret what is being asked. Validity is also a problem if group members are unwilling to disclose their personal attitudes, feelings, and perceptions or are unaware of these internal processes.

Despite these limitations, self-report methods provide much information about group phenomena, but from the perspective of the participant rather than the observer. When researchers are primarily interested in personal processes, such as perceptions, feelings, and beliefs, self-report methods may be the only means of assessing these private processes. But if participants are biased, their self-reports may not be as accurate as we would like. Self-reports may also not be accurate indicators of group-level processes, such as cohesiveness or conflict.

Testing Hypotheses: Research Designs

Good measurement alone does not guarantee good science. Researchers who watch groups and ask group members questions can develop a detailed description of a group, but they must go beyond description if they are to *explain* groups. Measurement "stretches nature out on the rack," but once researchers have collected their data, they must use that information to test hypotheses about group phenomena. Researchers use many techniques to check the adequacy of their suppositions about groups, but the three most common approaches are (1) *case studies* of single groups, (2) *experimental studies* that manipulate aspects of the group situation, and (3) *correlational analyses* of the relationships between various aspects of groups.

Case Studies

One of the best ways to understand groups in general is to understand one group in particular. This approach has a long and venerable tradition in all the sciences, with some of the greatest advances in thinking coming from the **case study**—an in-depth examination of a single group. If the group has not yet disbanded, the researcher may decide to observe it as it carries out its functions. Alternatively, investigators may cull facts about the group from interviews with members, descriptions of the group written by journalists, or members' biographical

---

case study A research technique that involves examining, in as much detail as possible, the dynamics of a single group or individual.

writings. Researchers then use this information to construct an overall picture of the group and estimate the extent to which the examined case supports their hypothesis (Cahill, Fine, & Grant, 1995; Yin, 1993, 1994).

Researchers have conducted case studies of all sorts of groups: search-and-rescue squads (Lois, 1999), cults (Festinger, Riecken, & Schachter, 1956), deep-sea dwelling naval personnel (Radloff & Helmreich, 1968), government leaders at international summits (Hare & Naveh, 1986), religious communes (Stones, 1982), rock-and-roll bands (Bennett, 1980), crisis intervention teams in psychiatric hospitals (Murphy & Keating, 1995), families coping with an alcoholic member (Carvalho & Brito, 1995), focus groups (Seal, Bogart, & Ehrhardt, 1998), and adolescent peer groups (Adler & Adler, 1995). Irving Janis (1972), for example, used this method to study the groups responsible for such fiascoes as the Bay of Pigs invasion, the defense of Pearl Harbor before its attack in World War II, and the escalation of the Vietnam War. Relying on archival methods, Janis sought out available information about several such bumbling groups and then looked for their similarities. He examined historical documents, minutes of meetings, diaries, letters, group members' memoirs, and their public statements before concluding that these groups were victims of **groupthink**—"a deterioration of mental efficiency, reality testing, and moral judgment that results from ingroup pressures" (Janis, 1972, p. 9). Janis specified the major determinants and symptoms of groupthink and suggested steps to avoid it. Chapter 11 examines Janis's theory in more detail.

All research designs offer both advantages and disadvantages, and case studies are no exception. By focusing on a limited number of cases, researchers often provide richly detailed qualitative descriptions of naturally occurring groups. If the groups have disbanded and researchers are relying on archival data, they need not be concerned that their research will substantially disrupt or alter naturally occurring group processes. Janis, for example, studied historical groups, so he did not need to worry about reactivity and the Hawthorne effect. Case studies also tend to focus on **bona fide groups**—that is, groups in everyday, natural contexts. Unlike groups that are concocted by researchers in the laboratory for a brief period of time and then disbanded, bona fide groups are "real" groups, with all the features of full-fledged groups: interaction, interdependence, structure, cohesiveness, and goals. Whyte, for example, studied bona fide groups, for the corner gangs he investigated existed long before he started watching them, and they continued on long after he finished his observations. Families, gangs, work teams, support groups, and cults are just a few of the many naturally occurring groups that researchers have studied by going into the field, locating these groups, and

---

groupthink A strong concurrence-seeking tendency that interferes with effective group decision making, identified by Irving Janis.

bona fide group A naturally occurring group (particularly when compared to an ad hoc group created by a researcher in a laboratory study), such as an audience, board of directors, club, or team.

then collecting information about them by observing their members' activities (Frey, 2002).

Case studies, however, yield only limited information about groups in general. Researchers who use the case study method must bear in mind that the group studied may be so unique that it tells us little about other groups. Also, researchers rarely use objective measures of group processes when conducting case studies, so their interpretations can be influenced by their own assumptions and biases. Even worse, the materials themselves may be inaccurate or unavailable to the researcher. Janis, for example, was forced to "rely mainly on the contemporary and retrospective accounts by the group members themselves . . . many of which are likely to have been written with an eye to the author's own place in history" (1972, p. v). Finally, case studies only imply but rarely establish causal relationships among important variables in the group under study. Janis believed that groupthink was causing the poor decisions in the groups he studied, but some other, unnoticed factor could actually have been the prime causal agent.

Experimentation

Between 1937 and 1940, Kurt Lewin, Ronald Lippitt, and Ralph White studied the way a group's leader can radically change the behaviors of the group members (Lewin, Lippitt, & White, 1939; R. K. White, 1990; R. K. White & Lippitt, 1968). They arranged for 10- and 11-year-old boys to meet after school in five-member groups to work on hobbies such as woodworking and painting. An adult led each group by adopting one of three styles of leadership: autocratic, democratic, or laissez-faire. The *autocratic* leader made all the decisions for the group; the *democratic* leader let the boys themselves make all the group's decisions; and the *laissez-faire* leader gave the group members very little guidance.

The researchers observed the groups as they worked with each type of leader, measuring group productivity and aggressiveness. When they reviewed their findings, they discovered that the autocratic groups spent more time working (74%) than the democratic groups (50%), which in turn spent more time working than the laissez-faire groups (33%). Although these results argued in favor of the efficiency of an autocratic leadership style, the observers also noted that when the leader left the room for any length of time, the democratically led groups kept right on working, whereas the boys in the autocratic groups stopped working. Lewin, Lippitt, and White also discovered a relationship between leadership style and the level of aggression displayed by group members. Observers noted high rates of hostility in the autocratically led groups, as well as more demands for attention, more destructiveness, and a greater tendency to single out one group member to serve as the target of almost continual verbal abuse. The researchers believed that this target for criticism and hostility, or **scapegoat,** provided mem-

---

scapegoat An individual or group who is unfairly held responsible for a negative event and outcome; the innocent target of interpersonal hostility.

bers with an outlet for pent-up hostilities that could not be acted out against the powerful group leader.

THE CHARACTERISTICS OF EXPERIMENTS Lewin, Lippitt, and White's study of leadership styles possesses the three key features of an **experiment.** First, the researchers identified a variable that they believed caused changes in group processes and then systematically manipulated it. They manipulated this **independent variable** by giving groups different types of leaders (autocratic, democratic, or laissez-faire). Second, the researchers assessed the effects of the independent variable by measuring such factors as productivity and aggressiveness. The variables that researchers measure are called **dependent variables,** because their magnitude depends on the strength and nature of the independent variable. Lewin, Lippitt, and White hypothesized that group leadership style would influence productivity and aggressiveness, so they tested this hypothesis by *manipulating* the independent variable (leadership style) and *measuring* the dependent variables (productivity and aggressiveness).

Third, the experimenters tried to maintain control over other variables that might hamper the interpretation of their results. The researchers never assumed that the only determinant of productivity and aggressiveness was leadership style; they knew that other variables, such as the personality characteristics and abilities of the group members, could influence the dependent variables. In the experiment, however, the researchers were not interested in these other variables. Their hypotheses were specifically focused on the relationship between leadership style, productivity, and aggressiveness. Therefore, they made certain that these other variables were controlled in the experimental situation. For example, they took pains to ensure that the groups they created were "roughly equated on patterns of interpersonal relationships, intellectual, physical, and socioeconomic status, and personality characteristics" (R. K. White & Lippitt, 1968, p. 318). The groups were also assigned at random to the experimental conditions. Because no two groups were identical, these variations could have resulted in some groups working harder than others. The researchers used *random assignment* of groups to even out these initial inequalities. Thus, they hoped that any differences found on the dependent measure would be due to the independent variable rather than to uncontrolled differences among the participating groups.

In sum, when researchers conduct experiments they manipulate the independent variable, systematically assess the dependent variable(s), and control other possible contaminating factors. When the experiment is properly designed

---

experiment A research design in which the investigator manipulates at least one variable by randomly assigning participants to two or more different conditions and measuring at least one other variable.

independent variable Those aspects of the situation manipulated by the researcher in an experimental study; the causal variable in a cause–effect relationship.

dependent variable The responses of the participant measured by the researcher; the effect variable in a cause–effect relationship.

and conducted, researchers can assume that any differences among the conditions on the dependent variables are produced by the independent variable that is manipulated, and not by some other variable outside their control.

ADVANTAGES AND DISADVANTAGES Why do researchers so frequently rely on experimentation to test their hypotheses about groups? This preference derives, in part, from the inferential power of experimentation. Researchers who design their experiments carefully can make inferences about the causal relationships linking variables. If the investigators keep all variables constant except for the independent variable, and the dependent variable changes, then they can cautiously conclude that the independent variable caused the dependent variable to change. Experiments, if properly conducted, can be used to detect causal relationships between variables.

Experiments offer an excellent means of testing hypotheses about the causes of group behavior, but they are not without their logistical, methodological, and ethical problems. Researchers cannot always control the situation sufficiently to manipulate the independent variable or to keep other variables constant. Moreover, to maintain control over the conditions of an experiment, researchers may end up studying closely monitored but artificial group situations. Experimenters often work in laboratories with ad hoc groups that are created just for the purpose of research, and these groups may differ in important ways from bona fide groups. Although an experimenter can heighten the impact of the situation by withholding information about the study, such deception can be challenged on ethical grounds. Of course, experiments can be conducted in the field using already existing groups, but they will almost necessarily involve the sacrifice of some degree of control and will reduce the strength of the researchers' conclusions. Hence, the major advantage of experimentation—the ability to draw causal inferences—can be offset by the major disadvantage of experimentation—basing conclusions on contrived situations that say little about the behavior of groups in more naturalistic settings. (These issues are discussed in more detail by C. A. Anderson & Bushman, 1997; and Driskell & Salas, 1992.)

Nonexperimental Designs

When Theodore Newcomb (1943) joined the faculty at Bennington College in the mid-1930s, he could not help but recognize the impressive change in students' opinions during the course of their studies. Most students came from politically conservative New England families who endorsed the Republican candidate in the 1936 presidential election. And most of the first-year students at Bennington shared the attitudes of their families, for 62% preferred the Republican candidate. The juniors and seniors, however, were overwhelmingly pro-Democrat. In fact, only 15% endorsed the Republican candidate.

Why did the relatively conservative first-year students adopt the liberal attitudes of another group of students (the seniors)? Newcomb found evidence that the first-year students tended to accept the seniors as their reference group. A

reference group provides individuals with guidelines or standards for evaluating themselves, their attitudes, and their beliefs (Hyman, 1942). Any group that plays a significant role in one's life, such as a family, a friendship clique, colleagues at work, or even a group one admires but is not a member of, can function as a reference group (E. Singer, 1990). When students first enrolled at Bennington, their families served as their reference group, so their attitudes matched their families' attitudes. The longer students remained at Bennington, however, the more their attitudes changed to match the attitudes of their new reference group—the rest of the college population. Their families had conservative attitudes, but the college community supported mainly liberal attitudes, and Newcomb hypothesized that many Bennington students shifted their attitudes in response to this reference-group pressure.

Newcomb tested this hypothesis by administering questionnaires and interviews to an entire class of Bennington students from their entrance in 1935 to their graduation in 1939. He found a consistent trend toward liberalism in many of the students and reasoned that this change resulted from peer-group pressure because it was more pronounced among the popular students. Those who endorsed liberal attitudes were (1) "both capable and desirous of cordial relations with the fellow community members" (T. M. Newcomb, 1943, p. 149), (2) more frequently chosen by others as friendly, and (3) a more cohesive subgroup than the conservative students. Individuals who did not become more liberal were isolated from the college's social life, or they were very family oriented. These reference groups changed the students permanently, for the students who changed in college were still liberals when Newcomb measured their political beliefs some 25 years later (T. M. Newcomb, Koenig, Flacks, & Warwick, 1967).

CHARACTERISTICS OF NONEXPERIMENTAL STUDIES Newcomb's Bennington study was a **nonexperimental study;** he examined the naturally occurring relationships among several variables without manipulating any of them. Newcomb believed, for example, that as students came to identify more closely with other students, their attitudes and values changed to match those of their peers. Therefore, he assessed students' popularity, their dependence on their families, and changes in their political attitudes. Then he examined the relationships among these variables by carrying out several statistical tests. At no point did he try to manipulate the group situation.

Nonexperimental studies are often called *correlational studies* because researchers usually test the strength and direction of relations among variables by

---

reference group A group or collective that individuals use as a standard or frame of reference when selecting and appraising their abilities, attitudes, or beliefs; includes groups that individuals identify with and admire and categories of noninteracting individuals.

nonexperimental study A research design in which the investigator measures (but does not manipulate) at least two variables and then uses statistical procedures to examine the strength and direction of the relationship between these variables.

calculating a **correlation coefficient,** which in mathematical notation is written as *r*. A correlation can range from +1 to −1, with the distance from zero (0), the neutral point, indicating the strength of the relationship. If Newcomb had found that the correlation between students' popularity and liberal attitudes was close to 0, for example, he would have concluded that the two variables were unrelated to each other. If the correlation was significantly different from 0—in either a positive or a negative direction—his study would have shown that these two variables were related to each other. The sign of the correlation (+ or −) indicates the direction of the relationship. If, for example, the correlation between popularity and attitudes was +.68, this positive correlation would indicate that both variables increased or decreased together: the more popular the student, the more liberal her attitude. A negative correlation, such as −.57, would indicate that the variables were inversely related: More popular students would tend to have less liberal attitudes. Thus, a correlation is a handy way of summarizing a great deal of information about the relationship between two variables.

ADVANTAGES AND DISADVANTAGES Researchers use nonexperimental designs whenever they wish to know more about the relationship between variables. Are group leaders usually older than their followers? Do groups become more centralized as they grow larger? Do people who are more committed to their group tend to express attitudes that match their group's position? These are all questions that researchers might ask concerning the relationship between variables. When coupled with accurate measurement techniques, correlational studies offer a means of clearly describing these relationships without disrupting or manipulating any aspect of the group.

Nonexperimental studies, however, yield only limited information about the *causal* relationship between variables, because no variables are manipulated by the researcher. Newcomb's data, for example, indicated that the attitude changes he measured were related to reference-group pressures, but he could not rule out other possible causes. Perhaps, unknown to Newcomb, the most popular students on campus all read the same books, which contained arguments that persuaded them to give up their conservative attitudes. Newcomb also could not be certain about the *direction* of the relationship he documented. He believed that individuals who joined the liberal reference group became more liberal themselves, but the causal relationship may have been just the opposite: People who expressed more liberal attitudes may have been asked to join more liberal reference groups. Although these alternative explanations seem less plausible, they cannot be eliminated, given the methods used by Newcomb.

----

correlation coefficient A statistic that measures the strength and direction of a relationship between two variables. Often symbolized by *r*, correlations can range from −1 to +1.

FOCUS 2-2   Are Groups Harder to Study Than Individuals?

There is nothing inherently difficult to the analysis of group data, once one appreciates the multiple sources of variation that exist in group data structures and treats groups as the effective unit of analysis.
–Melody Sadler and Charles Judd (2001, p. 523)

Researchers who study groups rather than individual human beings face some unique logistic and statistical problems. Individuals change over time, but their development tends to be gradual and continuous. Groups, in contrast, can change rapidly and dramatically, so that the group that is studied at one point in time may evolve into a very different group when studied again. The group may also change because its composition changes; if a member joins or leaves a group, the group's structures and processes may change. The interactions that take place within groups are also complex and nuanced, so researchers sometimes encounter more data than they can objectively record and process. "Group process carries literally hundreds of messages," so "even after applying one, two, three, or more content analysis schemes to it, more information remains to be gathered and interpreted" (T. M. Mills, 1979, p. 415). Group processes are also *multilevel processes,* for they involve individuals interacting with other individuals in groups that are usually nested in a larger organizational or community context. Tracing causal paths and measuring dynamics is more complex when cause–effect relationships and process systems operate simultaneously at two or more levels (Hackman, 2003).

These complexities do not pose insurmountable barriers to the study of groups, for advances in instrumentation, design, and statistical procedures have combined to ease some of the labor and time costs of conducting group research. Whereas researchers once had to arrange for teams of observers to watch the groups they studied, they can now videotape the groups for later analysis. Sophisticated analysis tools can be used to carry out these process analyses, including computer software that quantifies the content of spoken and written communications in groups (e.g., Nud*ist N6, ethno2). Information technologies provide opportunities to study groups using the Internet, and software can now search out and model the structure of groups. Researchers have even begun developing tools that will allow them to create *virtual reality groups,* where computers are used to immerse individuals in groups that seem to be real but are actually created by virtual environment technologies (Blascovich et al., 2002).

Researchers have also made significant progress in solving the challenges that arise from studying multilevel group processes. If, for example, an investigator wants to know why some people become very loyal to their groups whereas others show little loyalty, she can ask each member to complete a survey that asks such questions as, "Are you loyal to this group?" But a researcher who wants to study characteristics of a group rather than individual-level qualities must use group-level measures. If he wants to know if a climate of loyalty pervades the group—if, like the Nortons, the members share a sense of loyalty and interdependence—he might ask each member, "Are you loyal to this group?" but then average each member's responses to get an index of group loyalty, provided most of the members give similar answers to this question. The researcher may also change the question, so that it asks, "Are most members loyal to the group?" or have the group discuss these types of questions and reach consensus on a single answer that represents the group's score (Chan, 1998; Klein, Conn, Smith, & Sorra, 2001; C. B. Watson, Chemers, & Preiser, 2001).

These advances, taken together, highlight the growing methodological sophistication of group researchers. Although researchers continue to rely on certain basic methods of measurement and design, new techniques have been added to the empiricist's toolbox. Groups are still difficult to study, but these new methods make the researcher's load a little lighter.

Selecting a Research Design

Researchers use a variety of empirical procedures to study groups. Some observe group processes and then perform a qualitative analysis of their observations, whereas others insist on quantitative measurement methods and elaborate controlled experiments. Some researchers conduct their studies in field situations using naturally occurring groups, whereas others bring groups into the laboratory or even create ad hoc groups for the research. Some researchers undertake exploratory studies with no clear idea of what results to expect, whereas other research studies are designed to test hypotheses carefully derived from a specific theory. Some researchers study group phenomena by asking volunteers to role-play group members, and others simulate group interaction with computers.

This diversity of research methods does not reflect researchers' uncertainty about which technique is best. Rather, the diversity stems from the unique advantages and disadvantages offered by each method. Case studies limit the researcher's ability to draw conclusions, to quantify results, and to make objective interpretations. But some topics, such as groupthink, are difficult to study by any other method. As Janis himself pointed out, it would be difficult to examine groups that make decisions about national policies—including war and civil defense—through traditional quantitative methods such as experimentation. But the real forte of the case study approach is its power to provide grist for the theoretician's mill, enabling the investigator to formulate hypotheses that set the stage for other research methods.

Such stimulation of theory is also frequently a consequence of nonexperimental research. Nonexperimental studies are limited in causal power, but they yield precise estimates of the strength of the relationships between variables. Experimentation provides the firmest test of causal hypotheses by showing that variable X will cause such and such a change in variable Y. In a well-designed and -conducted experiment, the researcher can test several hypotheses about groups, making the method both rigorous and efficient (Driskell & Salas, 1992). However, when an artificial setting would yield meaningless results, when the independent variable cannot be manipulated, or when too little is known about the topic even to suggest what variables may be causal, some other approach is preferable. The solution, then, is to study groups using multiple methods (see Focus 2-2). As Joseph E. McGrath explained, "All methods have inherent flaws—though each has certain advantages. These flaws cannot be avoided. But what the researcher can do is to bring more than one approach, more than one method, to bear on each aspect of a problem" (1984, p. 30).

THEORIES IN GROUP DYNAMICS

Successful researchers do not just develop ingenious methods for measuring group processes and testing their hypotheses. They also develop compelling theoretical explanations for group phenomena. Science, more than any other approach to gaining knowledge, advocates the long-term goal of increasing and systematizing our knowledge about the subject matter. Theories provide the means of organizing known facts about groups and so create orderly knowledge out of discrete bits of information. Theories also yield suggestions for future research. When researchers extend existing theories into new areas, they discover new information about groups, while simultaneously testing the strength of their theories.

We will review some of the basic approaches to the study of groups—with the caveat that these approaches are not necessarily mutually exclusive. Most theories embrace assumptions from more than one of the motivational, behavioral, systems, cognitive, and biological perspectives.

Motivational Models

Why do some people vie for leadership in their groups, whereas others remain content with less prominent roles? Why do some groups struggle against adversity, whereas others give up after the first setback? Why do some people shy away from groups, whereas others join dozens of them? Many theorists offer answers that stress the role played by group members' **motivations.** Habits, goals, instincts, expectations, and drives prompt group members to take action (Geen, 1995). The word *motivation* comes from the same root as the verb "to move."

Kurt Lewin's **level-of-aspiration theory** is, at its core, a motivational model, for it explains how people set goals for themselves and their groups (Lewin, Dembo, Festinger, & Sears, 1944). The theory assumes that people enter achievement situations with an ideal outcome in mind—for example, earning an A in the course, winning the game, or making a specific amount of money. Over time, however, people may revise their expectations as they repeatedly fail or succeed in reaching their ideals. Lewin used the term *level of aspiration* (LOA) to describe this compromise between ideal goals and more realistic expectations.

Alvin Zander (1971/1996) applied LOA theory to groups by studying how individual members set goals for their groups and how they revised their goals after each group success or failure. When group members complete a task, they expend considerable mental energy reviewing their efforts and outcomes. They gather and weigh information about their performance and determine if they have met the group's standards. They review the strategies they used to accomplish their task and determine if these strategies require revision. They also plan their future undertakings, ever mindful of the long-term goals they have set for themselves.

---

motivation Wants, needs, and other psychological processes that energize certain responses thereby prompting people to respond in one way rather than another.

level-of-aspiration theory A theoretical perspective developed by Kurt Lewin and his associates that explains how people set goals for themselves and their groups.

Zander found that a group's LOA often slightly exceeds individual members' LOAs. In one study, he arranged for boys to play a simple skill game in groups. After each failure, the boys lowered their own LOA, and after each success, they raised it; but their group LOA was slightly more optimistic than a strict forecast based on past performance would predict. The boys, when discussing their performance, exchanged encouraging suggestions, and this advice may have increased their optimism. Zander also found that groups raised their LOA more after success than they lowered it after failure, and that some groups set themselves up for failure by setting overly optimistic goals. Difficult goals challenge members to work harder to improve performance, but groups that fail consistently have low group morale and high turnover in membership (Zander, 1971/1996).

Behavioral Approaches

Many theories of group behavior are consistent with B. F. Skinner's (1953, 1971) **behaviorism.** Skinner believed that psychological processes, such as motives and drives, may shape people's reactions in groups, but he also believed that such psychological processes are too difficult to index accurately. Instead, Skinner recommended studying the things that people actually do rather than the psychological states that may have instigated their actions. Actions, Skinner believed, tend to be consistent with the *law of effect*—that is, behaviors that are followed by positive consequences, such as rewards, will occur more frequently, whereas behaviors that are followed by negative consequences will become rarer (e.g., Blau, 1964; Foa & Foa, 1971; Homans, 1974; La Gaipa, 1977).

John Thibaut and Harold Kelley's (1959) **social exchange theory** extended Skinner's behaviorism to groups. They agreed that individuals hedonistically strive to maximize their rewards and minimize their costs. However, when individuals join groups, they no longer control their outcomes. Groups create interdependence among members, so that the actions of each group member potentially influence the outcomes and actions of every other group member. Mara, for example, can spend several days working on a project, struggling to complete it successfully. But what if Mara collaborates with Steven on the project? When Mara works alone, she determines her own success. But when she works with Steven, his actions partially shape her outcomes. Mara may enjoy certain aspects of her interaction with Steven, but she may also find some of the

---

behaviorism A theoretical explanation of the way organisms acquire new responses to environmental stimuli through such conditioning processes as stimulus–response associations and reinforcement.

social exchange theory An economic model of interpersonal relationships which argues that individuals seek out relationships that offer them many rewards while exacting few costs.

things he does irritating. Thibaut and Kelley assumed that Mara and Steven would negotiate throughout their interaction to secure greater personal rewards while minimizing costs.

Systems Theories

Researchers in a variety of fields, including engineering, biology, and medicine, have repeatedly found that unique results are obtained when a system is formed by creating dependency among formerly independent components. Systems, whether they are bridges, ecological niches, or organisms, synthesize several parts or subsystems into a unified whole. These systems, because they are based on interrelated parts, can change to an extraordinary degree when one of their constituent components changes.

A **systems theory** approach assumes that groups are systems of interacting individuals. The following definition of a system could easily serve as a definition of a group:

> [A system is] a set of interacting units with relationships among them. The word "set" implies that the units have some common properties. These common properties are essential if the units are to interact or have relationships. The state of each unit is constrained by, conditioned by, or dependent on the state of other units. The units are coupled. Moreover, there is at least one measure of the sum of its units which is larger than the sum of that measure of its units. (James G. Miller, 1978, p. 16)

Just as a system receives inputs from the environment, processes this information internally, and then outputs its products, groups gather information, review that information, and generate products. Groups are also capable of formulating goals and working toward these goals through united action, and group members are responsive to environmental feedback concerning the efficacy of their actions. The communication of information—a key concept in systems theory—similarly plays a central role in groups that must analyze inputs, provide feedback to members, and formulate decisions regarding group action. Indeed, larger groups may be built on a number of smaller groups, all of which are integrated into an overall Gestalt. This organization is, in many cases, initiated by the system itself. Self-organizing systems' structures and processes undergo both regulated, gradual change over time and more chaotic, rapid change.

Systems theory provides a model for understanding a range of group-level processes, including group development, productivity, and interpersonal conflict (McClure, 1998; Tubbs, 2001). A systems approach to group productivity, for example, would highlight the *inputs* that feed into the group setting, the *processes* that take place within the group as it works on the task, and the *outputs*

---

systems theory A general theoretical approach which assumes that groups are *systems*—collections of individual units that combine to form an integrated, complex whole.

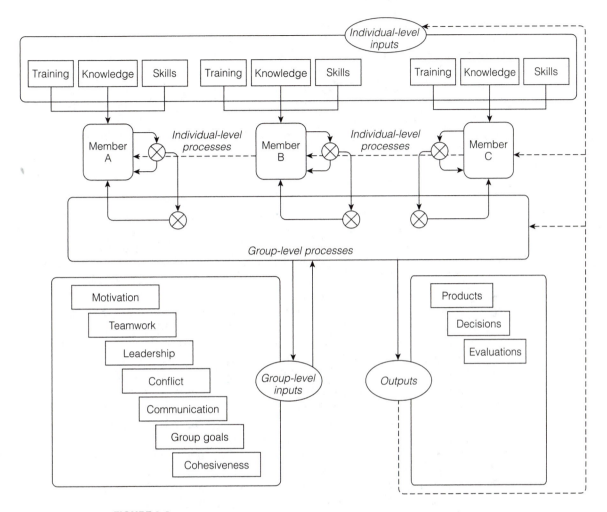

FIGURE 2-3

How is a group like a self-organizing, evolving system? A systems approach to groups assumes that a number of processes, both chaotic and patterned, determine the behavior of groups and individuals within groups. An analysis of some complex aspect of a group, such as its productivity, would need to take into account a number of inter-related components of the system to predict the group's outcomes.

generated by the system (see Figure 2-3). Inputs would include any factors that are present in the situation when the group begins its work on the task, such as the characteristics of the individual members (skill, experience, and training) and group-level factors (group structure and cohesiveness). These input factors all influence, through a variety of paths, the processes that take place within the group as members work together to complete the task, including communication, planning, conflict, and leadership. These processes combine to transform inputs into outputs, which include aspects of the group's performance (e.g., products, decisions, errors) and changes in the factors that serve as inputs to the system. If the group performs poorly, for example, it may become less cohesive, or it may seek out new members. Members of successful groups, in contrast, may become more satisfied with their group and take steps to make sure that the group uses the same procedures to solve the next problem (Hackman, 1987; Hackman & Morris, 1975; Littlepage, Schmidt, Whisler, & Frost, 1995; McGrath, 1964, 1997).

Cognitive Approaches

A group's dynamics, in many cases, become understandable only when we consider the **cognitive processes** that occur within each individual in the group. When people join a group for the first time, they immediately begin to form an impression of the group. This perceptual work prompts them to search for information about the other group members, rapidly identifying those who are outgoing, shy, and intelligent (Albright, Kenny, & Malloy, 1988). Group members also search their memories for stored information about the group and the tasks it must face, and they must retrieve that information before they can use it. A group member must also take note of the actions of others and try to understand what caused the other member to act in this way. Thus, group members are busy perceiving, judging, reasoning, and remembering, and all these mental activities influence their understanding of one another, the group, and themselves (S. T. Fiske & Goodwin, 1994; Nye, 1994).

Joseph Berger and his colleagues offered a cognitive analysis of who will rise to the top and who will fall to the bottom of a group's status hierarchy. Their **expectation–states theory** assumes that group members, while interacting with one another, intuitively take note of two types of cues as they allocate status within the group. *Specific status characteristics* are qualities that attest to each individual's level of ability to perform the specific task at hand. *Diffuse status characteristics* are general qualities that group members think are relevant to ability and evaluation. Any characteristic—sex, age, ethnicity, and so on—can serve as a diffuse status characteristic if people associate that characteristic with certain skills. Those who possess numerous status-earning characteristics are implicitly identified and permitted to perform more numerous and varied group actions, to

---

cognitive process Mental processes that acquire, organize, and integrate information. Cognitive processes include memory systems that store data and the psychological mechanisms that process this information.

expectation–states theory An explanation of status differentiation in groups which assumes that group members allocate status to group members judged to be competent at the task at hand and to group members who have qualities that the members think are indicators of competence and potential.

provide greater input and guidance for the group, to influence others by evaluating their ideas, and to reject the influence attempts of others (J. Berger, Wagner, & Zelditch, 1992; D. G. Wagner & Berger, 1993).

Biological Models

Group members can solve complex problems, communicate with one another using spoken and written language, build and operate massive machines, and plan their group's future. But group members are also living creatures, whose responses are often shaped by biological, biochemical, and genetic characteristics. When conflict arises in the group, heart rates escalate, and other body changes occur to help members cope with the stress (Blascovich, Nash, & Ginsburg, 1978). When groups are trapped in confining, cramped spaces, members often become physiologically aroused, and this arousal can interfere with their work (G. W. Evans & Cohen, 1987). When others encroach on our territories, we instinctively respond to defend our turf.

One biological perspective—**evolutionary psychology** or **sociobiology**—argues that these group behaviors may be genetically determined. This perspective argues that in the last 15 million years, the human species has evolved socially as well as physically. Through the process of natural selection, individuals who were even slightly predisposed to engage in adaptive social behaviors tended to survive longer and to be more successful in passing their genes along to future generations. Over countless generations, this selection process weeded out individuals who lacked these social predispositions, whereas those who possessed them prospered. Even though these tendencies may not enhance our fitness in today's world, the aeons spent in harsher environments have left us genetically predisposed to perform certain social behaviors when situational cues evoke ancient instincts (Buss & Kenrick, 1998; Caporael, 2001; Gaulin & McBurney, 2001).

Evolutionary theory offers insight into a range of group processes, including affiliation, intergroup conflict, and aggression. For example, its explanation of the tendency of many groups to struggle to maintain control over specific geographical areas—**territoriality**—is intriguing. Most modern groups no longer need to defend their turf against outsiders, yet groups and group members retain their territorial ways. Why? Evolutionary psychology suggests that our ancestors lived in tribes that gathered nuts, berries, and other foods from the land as they foraged. These tribes, like the !Kung and the Mescalero Apaches of today, built no

---

evolutionary psychology (or **sociobiology**) A biological approach to understanding behavior which assumes that recurring patterns of behavior in animals ultimately stem from evolutionary pressures that increase the likelihood of adaptive social actions and extinguish nonadaptive practices.

territoriality The tendency for individuals and groups to claim and defend for their exclusive use a specific location or geographic area.

permanent dwellings, but they did establish control over certain geographical areas (Altman & Chemers, 1980). By marking their areas and attacking intruders, they gained an evolutionary edge over others, and their offspring were more likely to survive. Natural selection thus favored individuals who were members of territorial groups, with the result that today's groups are driven by an instinctive need to defend their territories against encroachment by others (R. Kaplan & Kaplan, 1989; Rushton, 1989).

Selecting a Theory

Group dynamics, with its roots in both psychology and sociology, is rich with theory. Some of these theories trace group processes back to psychological processes—the motivations of the individual members, the mental processes that sustain their conception of their social environment, and even their instinctive urges and proclivities. Other theories focus more on the group as a social system that is integrated in the surrounding community and society.

These different theoretical perspectives, however, are not mutually exclusive paradigms, struggling for the distinction as *the* explanation of group behavior. Some researchers test hypotheses derived from only one theory; others draw on several perspectives as they strive to describe, predict, control, and explain groups and their members. Just as the questions, "How should I measure this aspect of the group?" and, "How should I test my hypothesis about groups?" can be answered in more than one way, no one solution can be offered in response to the question, "What theory explains group behavior?" Many of the greatest advances in understanding groups have occurred not when one theory has been pitted against another, but when two or more theories have been synthesized to form a new, more encompassing theoretical perspective. In Homans's (1950) words, "We have a great deal of fact to work with, [and] we also have a great deal of theory. The elements of a synthesis are on hand" (p. 4).

SUMMARY IN OUTLINE

❖ **What are the three critical requirements of a scientific approach to the study of groups?**

1. Researchers must measure group phenomena accurately.

2. Researchers must design research procedures to test their hypotheses about groups.

3. Researchers must develop theories that organize their findings conceptually and comprehensively.

❖ **What methods do researchers use to measure individual and group processes?**

1. *Observational measures* involve observing and recording events transpiring in groups.
   - Whyte used *participant observation* to study a corner gang by joining it.
   - Observational researchers guard against the biasing influences of the *Hawthorne effect* (a change in behavior that occurs when people feel they are

being studied) by keeping their research agenda a secret from the group members they are watching (*covert observation*).

2. *Qualitative studies* require the collection of descriptive data about groups, such as members' verbal statements, detailed narratives, and observers' accounts of the group's activities, but *quantitative* studies require the enumeration and quantification of the phenomena of interest.

   - *Structured observational measures* require observers to assign each coded activity to a specific category.
   - Bales's *Interaction Process Analysis* (*IPA*), a standard group coding system, classifies behaviors into two categories: task and relationship behaviors.

3. *Reliability* and *validity* are essential qualities of all measures, for they must be consistent and they must measure what they are designed to measure.

   - Bales revised his IPA to increase its reliability and validity and, in doing so, created a more advanced structured coding system called *SYMLOG* (*Systematic Multiple Level Observation of Groups*).
   - SYMLOG classifies group behavior along three dimensions: *dominance/ submissiveness, friendliness/unfriendliness,* and *acceptance of authority/nonacceptance of authority.*

4. *Self-report measures* ask group members to describe their own perceptions and experiences. Moreno's *sociometry* method asks members to report whom they like the most. The nominations are used to generate a *sociogram,* or visual image of the interpersonal relations in the group.

❖ **What are the key characteristics of and differences between case,** experimental, and correlational studies of group processes?

1. A *case study* is an in-depth analysis of one or more groups by interviewing members, observation, and so on.

   - Janis's used a case study design in his analysis of *groupthink* in government decision-making groups.
   - By studying naturally occurring, *bona fide groups,* case study researchers can be more certain that the processes they study are not artificial ones influenced by the research process.

2. In an *experiment,* researchers examine cause–effect relationships by manipulating aspects of the group situation (*independent variables*).

   - Lewin, Lippitt, and White studied the impact of autocratic, democratic, and laissez-faire leaders on groups by conducting an experiment. They manipulated the *independent variable* (leadership style), assessed several *dependent variables* (aggressiveness, productivity, etc.), and limited the influence of other possible causal factors by controlling the situation and assigning groups to experimental conditions at random.
   - Lewin, Lippitt, and White's study indicated that productivity was high in both democratic and autocratic groups, but that the participants were more aggressive in the autocratic groups. In some cases, one group member (a *scapegoat*) was bullied by the others.

3. In a *nonexperimental study,* the investigator, rather than manipulating aspects of the situation, gauges the strength of the naturally occurring relationships between such variables.

   - Newcomb studied *reference groups* nonexperimentally by examining the relationship between members' political attitudes and their popularity in the group.

- Nonexperimental studies are sometimes termed *correlational studies* because the magnitude of the relationship between variables is often formalized as a *correlation coefficient.*

❖ **What are the strengths and weaknesses of case, experimental, and correlational designs?**

1. The conclusions drawn from case studies can be highly subjective, but they stimulate theory and provide detailed information about natural, bona fide groups.
2. Groups studied in experimental settings may not display the dynamics of naturally occurring groups, but experimentation provides the clearest test of cause-and-effect hypotheses.
3. Correlational studies provide only limited information about causality, but they yield precise estimates of the strength of the relationship between two variables and raise fewer ethical questions for researchers.
4. All these designs must recognize that group processes are multilevel ones, for individual members are nested in groups, which in turn are nested in

even larger social entities, such as communities and organizations. Researchers who study multilevel processes must be ever wary of interdependence in their data.

❖ **What theoretical perspectives guide researchers' studies of groups?**

1. Motivational models stress members' *motivations,* as illustrated by Lewin's *level-of-aspiration theory.*
2. Theories based on *behaviorism,* such as Thibaut and Kelley's *social exchange theory,* assume that individuals act to maximize their rewards and minimize their costs.
3. A *systems theory* approach assumes that groups are *systems.* An input–process–output model of group performance exemplifies the systems approach.
4. Berger's *expectation-states theory* is a *cognitive process* approach, for it assumes that group members' perceptual, judgmental, and cognitive activities shape their responses.
5. Biological perspectives, such as *evolutionary theory,* or *sociobiology,* argue that some group behaviors, such as *territoriality,* may be rooted in group members' biological heritage.

FOR MORE INFORMATION

Studying Groups

- "Methods of Small Group Research," by Norbert L. Kerr, Joel Aronoff, and Lawrence A. Messé (2000), examines the techniques and measures used by investigators in a wide variety of group research.
- *People Studying People: Artifacts and Ethics in Behavioral Research,* by Ralph L. Rosnow and Robert Rosenthal (1997), is an intriguing

overview of the many technical and ethical problems that researchers encounter when they subject human behavior to scientific scrutiny.

Research Methods

- "Observation and Analysis of Group Interaction Over Time: Some Methodological and Strategic Choices," by Joseph E.

McGrath and T. William Altermatt (2001), is a complete analysis of structured approaches to group observation.

- *Applications of Case Study Research,* by R. K. Yin (1993), updates and reaffirms the advantages of case study methods.
- *Street Corner Society,* by William Foote Whyte (1943), remains one of the best examples of applying the case study method to understanding a group's dynamics.

Advances in Group Research Methods

- "Data Analysis in Social Psychology," by David A. Kenny, Deborah A. Kashy, and Niall Bolger (1998), examines a number of advanced methods for dealing with group-level data.
- "Overcoming Dependent Data: A Guide to the Analysis of Group Data," by Melody S. Sadler and Charles M. Judd (2001), outlines the statistical procedures to use when data are collected from intact groups.
- "Research Methods," a special issue of the journal *Group Dynamics: Theory, Research, and Practice,* edited by Donelson R. Forsyth (1998), includes papers examining a number of emerging new methods for studying groups, including social relations modeling, focus group methods, and multilevel modeling.

MEDIA RESOURCES

 Visit the Group Dynamics companion website at http://psychology.wadsworth.com/forsyth4e to access online resources for your book, including quizzes, flash cards, web links, and more!

The Individual and the Group

CHAPTER OVERVIEW

Humans are a group-seeking species, for most prefer group membership to isolation. When individuals join groups, they retain their personal qualities—their motives, emotions, and outlooks—but add to them a sense of self that incorporates their collective rather than their individual characteristics. Groups blur the boundary between the personal and the interpersonal by transforming the *me* into the *we*.

❖ Do humans prefer solitude or group membership?

❖ What are individualism and collectivism?

❖ Does membership in a group change a person's self-concept and social identity?

CHAPTER OUTLINE

C. P. Ellis:
From Klan Member to Enlightened Humanitarian

Claiborne P. Ellis was a man like any other. He grew up in North Carolina, in the southern United States. He never finished school, but he always found work: pumping gas, cleaning offices, driving a bread truck. He married, raised his children, and worked overtime to get by. He believed in America, he went to church every Sunday, and he obeyed the law. Everyone called him C. P. (Terkel, 1980).

C. P. was an individualist. He worked hard, held firm to his personal beliefs when others disputed them, and looked to no one for favors. But C. P., like most people, did not keep to himself. He supported his family, even quitting school with only an eighth-grade education when his father died and his family needed him to earn money. When he was a young man, he joined a number of groups and associations, including a local chapter of the Ku Klux Klan (KKK), a White supremacy group. In time, he renounced the Klan's racist values and joined a local community group that promoted equal treatment for all. Eventually he served on the local school board and was elected chief steward of his union.

C. P. illustrates the fundamental duality of human nature. He was, like most people, capable of existing both in groups and outside of groups. *C. P. the individualist* was a freethinker, independent, a leader, and so self-reliant that he often took unpopular positions on social issues and spoke his mind freely. But *C. P. the group member* was constantly seeking the company of others rather than remaining alone. He did not live free of the influence of others but, instead, sought out memberships in groups—groups that constrained his individuality in powerful ways. Here, we consider the essential tension between a life alone, as an individual, and a life with others, as a member of groups. We also consider how these two sides of human nature combine to determine individuals' values, identities, and sense of self-worth.

FROM ISOLATION TO BELONGING

Some species of animals are solitary. The cheetah, giant panda, orangutan, and opossum remain apart from other members of their species and congregate in some cases only to mate or rear offspring. Other animals, such as chimps, hyena, deer, and mice, are social creatures, for they usually forage, feed, sleep, and travel in small groups. What about humans? Do we tend to keep to ourselves, guarding our privacy from the incursions of others, or are we group-oriented animals, who prefer the company of other people to a life alone?

Alone or Together

C. P. guarded his privacy and was often very reserved, in that he rarely shared his ideas, attitudes, and values with others. But C. P. also actively sought the company of others—to such a degree that he sometimes found himself joining groups just to be included, rather than because he felt an affinity for the group or its members. As he explained, he never meant to get mixed up with the racist KKK group, but he was drawn to the social rewards that affiliation afforded. When a group of young White men congregated near the gasoline station where he worked, he became curious. "They said they were with the Klan and have meetings close-by. Would I be interested? Boy, that was an opportunity I really looked forward to! To be part of somethin'" (quoted in Terkel, 1980, p. 202). Like most people, he preferred affiliation and togetherness to solitude and separation.

ISOLATION VERSUS INCLUSION Henry David Thoreau spent 2 years secluded at Walden Pond, deliberately keeping his memberships in groups to a minimum. He explained,

> Society is commonly too cheap. We meet at very short intervals, not having had time to acquire any new value for each other. We meet at three meals a day and give each other a taste of that old musty cheese that we are. Certainly less frequency would suffice for all important and hearty communication. (Thoreau, 1962, p. 206)

As Thoreau suggested, spending time alone, away from others, is often a rejuvenating, pleasurable experience. People, when surveyed about their reactions to isolation, report enjoying the self-discovery, contemplation, and increased spirituality that occurs when one is physically isolated from interactions with and observations by others (C. R. Long, Seburn, Averill, & More, 2003). When alone, people say, they can "discover who I am," "determine what I want to be," "meditate and reflect," "try out some new behaviors," "recover my self-esteem," "protect myself from what others say," and "take refuge from the outside world" (Pedersen, 1999, p. 399). Some philosophers, writers, and artists have reached the apex of their creativity during times of isolation, when they were not distracted by other people (Storr, 1988; Suedfeld, 1997).

But even though most people express a desire for privacy, they also seek the company of others. When people were asked to describe their most satisfying experience from the past month, most spoke of events that slaked their need for autonomy; they were able to act in ways that reflected their personal preferences rather than anyone else's. These individuals, however, also prized experiences that satisfied their need for relatedness, connection, and intimacy with others (Sheldon, Elliot, Kim, & Kasser, 2001). Most adults prefer the company of others when threatened or distressed (Rofé, 1984), and they find protracted periods of social isolation disturbing (Zubek, 1973). The diaries of individuals who have been isolated from others for long periods of time—stranded explorers, scientists working in seclusion, and prisoners in solitary confinement—often stress the psychological costs of their ordeal rather than physical deprivations. Like the stranded Robinson Crusoe, they decry their isolation, complaining, "I am singled out and separated, as it were, from all the world, to be miserable. I am divided from mankind, a solitary; one banished from human society. I have no soul to speak to or to relieve me" (Defoe, 1908, p. 51). As their isolation wears on, they report fear, insomnia, memory lapses, depression, fatigue, and general confusion.

Prolonged periods of isolation are also marked by hallucinations and delusions, as when one solo sailor at sea was startled when he thought he saw a pirate steering his life raft (Bone, 1957; Burney, 1961). The psychological effects of forced isolation are so destructive that some cultures consider solitary confinement a form of torture.

Just the prospect of facing life alone, rather than isolation itself, is sufficient to trigger a range of negative psychological and social reactions. Roy Baumeister, Jean Twenge, and their colleagues studied the impact of anticipated aloneness by asking people to fill out an extensive personality test. They then told some people, at random, that their answers indicated their future would be a solitary one: "You're the type who will end up alone later in life. You may have friends and relationships now, but . . . these are likely to be short-lived and not continue . . . the odds are you'll end up being alone more and more" (Baumeister, Twenge, & Nuss, 2002, p. 819). People given this bleak prognostication—in contrast to those who were told that their future would be marked by other sorts of misfortunes—acted more aggressively; they were more critical of others and were more likely to punish others by exposing them to noxious noise levels. They were also more likely to engage in a number of irrational, self-defeating behaviors, such as taking unnecessary risks and procrastinating. And when the researchers asked them to complete a series of general cognitive aptitude measures, they discovered that the forecast of a life alone impaired their capacity for rational, intelligent thought. They concluded that human beings' mental abilities are linked to their capacity to form and sustain relationships (Baumeister et al., 2002; Twenge, Baumeister, Tice, & Stucke, 2001; Twenge, Catanese, & Baumeister, 2002).

INCLUSION VERSUS EXCLUSION Because most people seek inclusion rather than isolation, they are particularly distressed when they are deliberately excluded by a social group. Individuals who seek admission to a group, such as a sorority or fraternity, are disconsolate when they are turned down but elated when they are accepted. Leaders of small cliques of adolescents use the threat of exclusion to control the activities and loyalties of the members (Adler & Adler, 1995). Many religious societies use **shunning** to punish members who have broken rules or traditions. C. P. was thrilled when the KKK accepted him, but disappointed when the group eventually turned against him. This inclusion–exclusion continuum is depicted in Figure 3-1. Although we are maximally satisfied when a group actively seeks us out, any group that takes us in as a member satisfies our need for inclusion. In contrast, we respond negatively when a group ignores or avoids us, but maximal exclusion—the group rejects, ostracizes, abandons, or banishes us—is particularly punishing (Leary, 1990).

Exclusion and ostracism are powerful negative experiences. Targets of exclusion, such as people shunned by their community, children rejected by their

---

shunning Systematic ostracism of an individual by a group, usually taking the form of minimized physical or social contact with the outcast.

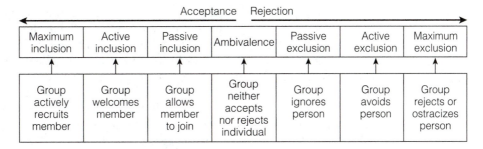

FIGURE 3-1

Is inclusion an all-or-nothing process, or a continuum ranging from maximum inclusion to maximum exclusion? When groups actively seek us out, we experience maximal inclusion, and when they actively ostracize us, we experience maximal exclusion. *Source:* Leary, 1990.

peers, participants ignored by others in an Internet chat room, people at work given the "silent treatment" for whistle-blowing, group members who get the "cold shoulder" from the rest of the group, or children who are not picked for teams during recess, suffer a range of negative cognitive, emotional, and behavioral reactions. When ostracized or ignored by others, people report feeling frustrated, anxious, nervous, and lonely, whereas those who are included in the group feel relaxed, friendly, and comfortable (K. D. Williams, 2001). The ostracized or excluded feel they have been betrayed by the other group members, and they sometimes report frustration, shock, and surprise. Whereas people who are included value their experiences in the group, the excluded sometimes feel as if they are invisible—as if they do not even exist socially (K. D. Williams, 2001; K. D. Williams, Shore, & Grahe, 1998).

Exclusion also influences *self-esteem*—one's feelings of personal worth. Mark R. Leary and his colleagues examined the impact of exclusion on self-esteem by asking sets of five individuals to interact briefly and exchange some sample essays. Participants then rated each other privately on a questionnaire, indicating with whom they would most want to work. The researchers, after examining the questionnaires, told three of the participants that they would be part of a group for the remainder of the research and told the other two that they would be working alone. In half the sessions, the researchers announced that people who were ranked negatively by the other group members would be the isolates, but in the other sessions, they said that the group-versus-individual decision was determined by a random drawing. The individuals who had been excluded from the group reacted the most negatively to their rejection, particularly if they thought the other participants, and not the experimenters' random choice, caused them to be excluded. They reported feeling less competent, adequate, useful, smart, and valuable than did the included group members. The rejected members were also more negative than accepted members when they rated their coparticipants, and they also rationalized their exclusion when asked, "How much did you want to be selected for the three-person 'central' group?" Individuals who were rejected said they did not really want to be in the group after all (Bourgeois & Leary, 2001; Leary, Tambor, Terdal, & Downs, 1995).

These findings support Leary's **sociometer model of self-esteem.** This theory suggests that people intuitively keep track of their inclusion and exclusion in groups, and a drop in self-esteem is an internal signal that warns of possible exclusion. Like a gauge that indicates how much fuel is left in the tank, self-esteem indicates the extent to which a person is included in groups. If the gauge drops, then exclusion is likely. So when we experience a dip in our self-esteem, we search for and correct characteristics and qualities that have put us at risk of social exclusion. The sociometer model concludes that most people have high self-esteem not because they think well of themselves, but because they are careful to maintain inclusion in social groups (Leary & Baumeister, 2000).

The sociometer model explains why people who have been excluded are far more attentive to—and so more likely to accurately recall—the details of a group's interaction: They are searching for the cause of their dismissal from the group (W. L. Gardner, Pickett, & Brewer, 2000). Excluded individuals are also more likely to amend their behaviors—perform extra work, offer apologies, do favors for other group members, and so on—so as to regain acceptance. Kipling D. Williams and his colleagues demonstrated the earnestness of the excluded in three-person groups that included only one real participant and two confederates. When the experimenter left the room, the confederates began to bounce a ball back and forth between them. In some cases, the confederates included the participant in their game, but in other cases, they stopped bouncing the ball to the participant after about a minute. The participants, when later asked how much they liked the other two group members, rated their partners more negatively when they had been ostracized. Women who had been ostracized, however, worked harder on a subsequent collective task, apparently to regain acceptance by the rest of the group. Women were also more likely to blame themselves for their ostracism (e.g., "I have trouble making a good impression with others"). Men, in contrast, did not compensate by working harder, nor did they take the blame for their rejection (K. D. Williams & Sommer, 1997). Williams and his colleagues have also studied how people react when excluded in chat rooms and e-mail conferences—what Williams called **cyberostracism.** As Focus 3-1 notes, people rejected by others via the Internet find that such rejection is upsetting, but they are more likely to reinsert themselves back into the group by increasing their communication with others (K. D. Williams et al., 2002).

---

sociometer model of self-esteem   A conceptual analysis of self-esteem proposed by Mark Leary that argues self-esteem is not an index of perceived self-worth, but instead is a psychological monitor of one's degree of inclusion and exclusion in social groups.

cyberostracism   The exclusion of one or more individuals from a technologically mediated group interaction, such as a computer-based discussion group.

FOCUS 3-1 Does Cyber-Rejection Hurt as Much as Face-to-Face Rejection?

To have one's individuality completely ignored is like being pushed quite out of life—like being blown out as one blows out a light.

–Evelyn Scott

Not all groups meet in face-to-face settings. In some cases, group members communicate with one another over great distances through the use of information technologies, including e-mail, Internet chat rooms, message boards, and mailing lists. Such groups, although unique in many respects, are still groups, and so, in many cases, their dynamics are similar to those of more traditional, face-to-face groups. Such groups develop norms, admit new members, identify goals, and experience conflict. Members of such groups take the lead, offer suggestions, ask questions, and influence one another. And, in some cases, they ostracize one another. New members of Internet chat rooms are sometimes given the derisive label of "newbie," and none of the veteran members will communicate with them. Individuals may refuse to respond to e-mails despite frequent attempts to provoke a response. An entire group of people in a chat room or other type of multi-user computer site may refuse to respond to a person who violates the group's norms about communicating, usually by using profanities or making insulting comments.

Given that the members of computer-based groups communicate at a distance and are, in some cases, completely anonymous, one might think that such cyberostracism is relatively inconsequential. However, the studies of Kipling Williams and his colleagues on online inclusion suggest otherwise. In one study, people from 62 different countries used the World Wide Web to take part in what they thought was a study of creative visualization. They thought they would be linked to two other volunteers and that the three would play a game of virtual catch by passing a flying disk from one player to another. The website allowed players to choose whom they would throw the disk to, and it indicated who possessed the disk, whom it was thrown to, and whether or not the receiver dropped the throw. In actuality, however, the other two players were simulated, and the participants were randomly assigned to one of four conditions: overinclusion (thrown the disk 50% of the time), inclusion (33%), partial ostracism (20%), and complete ostracism (they never received a throw after the initial round of tosses). When the game was over and the participants completed a brief survey over the Web, those who had suffered ostracism displayed the same sorts of negative reactions as evidenced by people in face-to-face groups. Even though the game was meaningless and their partners were total strangers, their social self-esteem dropped, their moods turned negative, and they admitted that they felt rejected (K. D. Williams, Cheung, & Choi, 2000).

Williams reported similar reactions to exclusion in his studies of chat rooms. In this work, he invited participants to join others in online chat rooms—Internet sites where users can type in messages that are read by others who are logged into the site at the same time. Again, some of the participants were excluded by the others in the chat room, who were confederates following a script. Again, the participants reported a variety of negative reactions to the exclusion, but many of them also tried to break into the online conversation by increasing the number of messages they sent. For example, one wrote,

> U 2 can keep talking btw yourselves and ignore me, I don't mind!!! . . . maybe I should start a conversation with myself . . . hi how are yah . . . I'm fine how are you . . . I'm fine too . . . come on talk to me. . .

Williams concluded that these provocative actions provided participants with a way to gain control of the situation and may have partially buffered them from the stressful effects of exclusion (K. D. Williams et al., 2002, p. 73).

ALONE VERSUS LONELY Whereas individuals who are excluded will redouble their efforts to regain acceptance by others, individuals who cannot join together with other people in relationships or groups may experience **loneliness**—an awareness that one's relationships with others are too few or so superficial that one feels a sense of disconnection, sadness, and emptiness. Loneliness, in many cases, occurs when people have trouble establishing a long-term, meaningful, intimate relationship with another person. This distress, termed *emotional loneliness,* might be triggered by divorce, a breakup with a lover, or repeated romantic failures. *Social loneliness,* in contrast, occurs when people feel cut off from their network of friends, acquaintances, and group members. People who have moved to a new city, children who are rejected by their peers, and new employees of large companies often experience social loneliness because they are no longer embedded in a network of friends and acquaintances (L. R. Green, Richardson, Lago, & Schatten-Jones, 2001). Both types of loneliness create feelings of sadness, depression, emptiness, longing, shame, and self-pity.

Groups can provide the antidote to loneliness by (1) organizing and integrating connections with other individuals and (2) promoting the development of warm, supportive, intimate relationships between members (Shaver & Buhrmester, 1983). College students who belonged to a cohesive, satisfying group reported much less loneliness than students who belonged to poorly integrated groups (C. M. Anderson & Martin, 1995; N. Schmidt & Sermat, 1983). Members of groups with extensive interconnections among all the members were less lonely than members of groups with less dense networks (Kraus, Davis, Bazzini, Church, & Kirchman, 1993; Stokes, 1985). Children with friends—even friends who were considered odd or unusual by their peers—were less lonely than friendless children (Asher & Paquette, 2003). People who belonged to groups (e.g., service organizations, religious or church organizations, business or professional organizations, and social clubs) that provided them with social support were healthier and happier than individuals who had few ties to other people (R. E. Harlow & Cantor, 1996). They even lived longer than lonely loners (M. S. Stroebe, 1994; Sugisawa, Liang, & Liu, 1994).

These findings suggest that not all groups are equally effective in buffering their members from both forms of loneliness. As Table 3-1 suggests, transitory, impersonal collectives do little to ease either social or emotional loneliness. Sitting with other people in a theater or striking up a conversation with a stranger on a bus creates a connection momentarily, but only groups that create stable, reliable alliances among members can ward off social loneliness (W. H. Jones & Carver, 1991). Likewise, only groups that connect people together in an intimate, meaningful way reduce feelings of emotional loneliness. Having many superficial relationships with others is far less satisfying than having a few high-quality relationships characterized by high levels of social support, mutual caring, and acceptance (Cacioppo, Hawkley, & Berntson, 2003). In consequence, groups

---

loneliness Feelings of desperation, boredom, self-deprecation, and depression experienced when individuals feel their personal relationships are too few or too unsatisfying.

TABLE 3-1 The Relationships Between Group Structure, Intimacy, and Loneliness

Type of Group	Examples	Impact on Loneliness
Collectives: create only temporary, superficial alliances among members	Ticket buyers standing in a queue, audiences in a theater, passengers in an elevator	No buffering
Structured groups: organize and integrate connections with other individuals	Military squads, work groups, congregations, regulars at a bar, amateur athletic teams, social clubs	Reduce social loneliness
Intimate groups: promote the development of close, intimate relations among members	Small friendship cliques, lovers, roommates	Reduce emotional loneliness
Intimate structured groups: connect members in close, organized relations	Families, communes, family businesses, close-knit teams	Reduce both social and emotional loneliness

that create connections among their members, such as amateur athletic teams, so-cial clubs, or work groups, will reduce members' feelings of social loneliness, but only more intimate, involving types of groups—families, romantic couples, or very close friendship cliques—will meet members' social *and* emotional needs (W. Stroebe, Stroebe, Abakoumkin, & Schut, 1996).

The Need to Belong

Why do people usually choose affiliation over isolation? Why do people respond so negatively when others exclude them? Why do people monitor their accep-tance in groups, and question their self-worth when others shun them? Why is loneliness such a painful experience?

Roy F. Baumeister and Mark R. Leary (1995) suggested that the tendency to prefer membership to isolation, inclusion to exclusion, and sociality to solitude is evidence of our fundamental **need to belong** to social groups. All "human be-ings have a pervasive drive to form and maintain at least a minimum quantity of lasting, positive, and impactful interpersonal relationships" (p. 497). They likened the need to belong to other basic needs, such as hunger or thirst. A person who has not eaten will feel hungry, but a person who has little contact with other people will feel unhappy and lonely. Baumeister and Leary believed that group membership fulfills a generic need to establish positive, enduring relationships with other people (Rook, 1984).

The idea of a "herd instinct" in humans is not a new one (Edman, 1919; McDougall, 1908). Nearly a century ago, William McDougall (1908) argued that

---

need to belong The dispositional tendency to seek out and join with other humans; those who are deprived of human contact will experience discomfort and loneliness.

humans are inexorably drawn to "the vast human herd," which "exerts a baneful attraction on those outside it" (p. 303). Recent advances in evolutionary psychology, however, have sparked new interest in the instinctive basis of human gregariousness. Evolutionary psychology, which was discussed briefly in Chapter 2, draws from Charles Darwin's original theorizing. Darwin maintained that given the natural variation among individual members of a species, some will have more of the qualities needed for survival than others. The individual with more adaptive qualities will tend to survive longer and produce more offspring, who inherit their parents' useful characteristics. Over time, nature will selectively favor individuals with the qualities that match the demands of the environment. Darwin called this process **natural selection.**

Darwin dealt primarily with biological and anatomical adaptations, but evolutionary psychologists assume that recurring patterns of social and psychological tendencies also stem from evolutionary processes that increase adaptive actions and extinguish nonadaptive practices (E. O. Wilson, 1975). Nature did not just encourage the development of webbed feet on ducks or a keen sense of smell in dogs, but also social tendencies, such as banding together to ward off intruders and preferred methods for establishing dominance hierarchies. Contemporary evolutionists have also expanded Darwin's concept of natural selection to include **kin selection**—the selective favoring of qualities that enhance the survival of one's relatives and their offspring. Because copies of our own genes are present in our sisters, brothers, and other relatives, when we help them survive and reproduce, we are indirectly encouraging the survival of our own genes in future generations (W. D. Hamilton, 1964).

Evolutionary psychology draws on these concepts to suggest that humans' propensity to gather in groups is, in part, a genetic adaptation to the environment in which humans lived for thousands and thousands of years. Compared to a single individual, a group of humans roaming the ancient forests and plains probably attracted the attention of more predators. Moreover, when with others, individuals who found a succulent fruit or berry could anticipate losing much of their meal to others in the group. They would also be more likely to suffer from communicable diseases and be harmed by more aggressive humans. But the benefits of sociality are far more substantial than these costs. Those who joined with others in an organized band to hunt large animals or forage for patches of food were likely more successful than individuals who remained alone. Individuals in groups could maintain superior surveillance against predators; they could join forces to ward off predators' attacks, and they could rely on other members of their group to protect them from the aggressive actions of other humans. Rela-

---

natural selection An evolutionary process that results in the survival and proliferation of organisms that have characteristics that enhance their survival and reproductive success in a particular environment.

kin selection A form of natural selection that encourages the survival and proliferation of genes that contribute to the reproductive success of one's relatives rather than one's self.

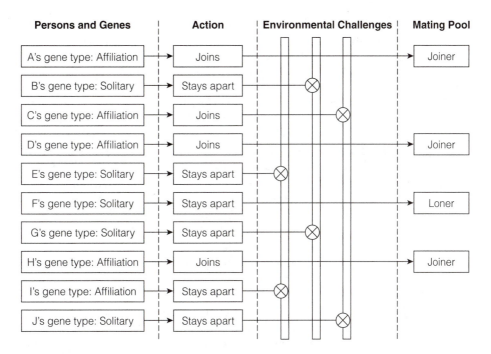

Persons and Genes	Action	Environmental Challenges	Mating Pool
A's gene type: Affiliation	Joins		Joiner
B's gene type: Solitary	Stays apart	⊗	
C's gene type: Affiliation	Joins	⊗	
D's gene type: Affiliation	Joins		Joiner
E's gene type: Solitary	Stays apart	⊗	
F's gene type: Solitary	Stays apart		Loner
G's gene type: Solitary	Stays apart	⊗	
H's gene type: Affiliation	Joins		Joiner
I's gene type: Affiliation	Stays apart	⊗	
J's gene type: Solitary	Stays apart	⊗	

FIGURE 3-2

Do groups give a survival edge to their members? If humanity's ancestors lived in an environment that favored those who lived in groups, then over time those who affiliated would gradually outnumber those who were self-reliant loners. Note that one's genetic endowment interacts with the environment, so not all individuals who are genetically predisposed to affiliate or remain alone will do so (see, e.g., Person I).

tives who lived in close proximity to one another could sustain and nurture children who carried copies of their genes. Because those individuals who were genetically predisposed to join groups ("joiners") were much more likely to survive and breed than people who avoided social contacts ("loners"), with each passing generation, the genes that promoted solitude seeking were weeded out of the gene pool, and the genes that encouraged group joining prospered (P. Marsh & Morris, 1988; see Figure 3-2).

In the modern world, the advantages of group life over solitude are not so clear. People who buy their food in grocery stores and live in houses with dead-bolts on the doors do not need to worry much about effective food-gathering strategies or protection from predation. These modern conditions, however, cannot undo the effects of millions of years of natural selection. Gregariousness remains a part of the biological makeup of humans. Your ancestors were, in all likelihood, joiners rather than loners (Buss, 1996; Gaulin & McBurney, 2001; S. Levine, 1996).

Anthropologists have documented the great diversity of human societies, but across all these variations, they have found one constancy: People live in groups rather than alone (L. Mann, 1988). People seem to be naturally predisposed to identify those who are in their own group. And, with no justification, they treat members of their own group more positively than members of other groups (Rushton, 1989). Studies have indicated that infants seem to be predisposed to form strong attachments to others and that babies who are deprived of close human contact have higher mortality rates (Ainsworth, 1979; Bowlby, 1980). Evidence suggests that cooperative group life is a more stable strategy in evolutionary terms than competition and individualism (Axelrod & Hamilton, 1981).

Evolutionary explanations of social behavior remain controversial, however. Researchers are only now subjecting the theory to close scrutiny, so its assumptions should be considered skeptically. The theory is difficult to test experimentally, and its basic premise—that characteristics that enhance our fitness have a genetic basis—is arguable. Just because groups are useful does not mean that we are instinctively drawn to them (R. C. Francis, 2004). The theory also assumes that humanity's evolutionary past was, for aeons, similar to the living conditions anthropologists have documented in their studies of many nonindustrial societies, and this assumption has been questioned (e.g., Festinger, 1983). Moreover, even if we are gregarious by instinct, other factors also play a role in determining our decision to join or leave a group. Early childhood experiences, for example, may determine the extent to which we prefer solitude or the company of others (H. F. Harlow & Harlow, 1966). Nonetheless, the evolutionary approach offers a compelling answer to the question, "Why do people seek out other people?" We instinctively value the contribution that a group can make to our genetic destiny (Caporael, 2000, 2001).

FROM INDIVIDUALISM TO COLLECTIVISM

Across individuals, societies, and eras, humans consistently prefer to live in groups rather than alone. But once we join with others, we must balance our personal needs against the needs of the group. When C. P. was alone, he could do as he pleased without irritating or offending others. He could spend the day reading, working, or relaxing if he chose to do so. But once C. P. joined a group, his self-centered world was replaced by a group-centered one. He could no longer do anything he pleased, for he had to coordinate his activities with others. How did C. P. manage to be both a unique, autonomous individual and a contributing member of the groups he joined?

Characteristics of Collectivism

Living in groups requires concession and compromise, for the needs and interests of a group do not always completely match the needs and interests of each one of its members. A mother asks her children to stop playing a game and spend an hour doing household chores. A group member thinks he deserves to be the leader, but the other group members will not let him say much during meetings.

An employer asks a worker to take a pay cut so the company can avoid bankruptcy. One dinner guest takes more than her fair share of dessert, so others must have much smaller portions. A social clique may pressure its members into expressing opinions that some members do not personally endorse.

When the group's and its members' needs, interests, and outlooks diverge, whose path should be followed? Should the individuals' needs come first, or does the group take precedence over the individual? Most answers to this question inevitably make their way to the distinction between individualism and collectivism. **Individualism** is a tradition or worldview based on the independence and uniqueness of each individual. This doctrine assumes that people are autonomous and must be free to act and think in ways that they prefer, rather than submit to the demands of the group. Each person is also unique—a true individual—and all people are encouraged to strive to achieve outcomes and goals that will personally benefit them (Kampmeier & Simon, 2001; Simmel, 1902). **Collectivism,** in contrast, puts the group and its goals before those of the individual members. Each person, if even recognized as an independent entity, is inseparably connected to the group or community. Social existence is centered on group relations, for it is the group that creates social obligations based on respect, trust, and a sense of community (Bellah, Madsen, Sullivan, Swidler, & Tipton, 1985).

At their core, these two perspectives differ in their relative emphasis on individuals and groups. In individualism, the person supersedes the group: Each person is unique, autonomous, and free to act in ways he or she considers best. In collectivism, the group supersedes the person: People are group members first, individuals second, and their actions must reflect their position within the confines of the group. Because of these varying priorities, individualistic people, groups, and cultures differ in many ways from ones that are based on collectivism. Table 3-2 and the following sections explore some of these differences, including variations in the nature of interpersonal relationships, norms and roles, motivations, and self-conceptions (Kagitcibasi, 1997; Oyserman, Coon, & Kemmelmeier, 2002; Triandis & Suh, 2002).

"ME" OR "US": RELATIONS, MEMBERSHIPS, AND ASSOCIATIONS Both individualism and collectivism recognize the human need for belonging and connection, but a collectivistic orientation puts more value on these relationships. Collectivists feel close affinity with one another and, so, are more likely to adopt a communal orientation to their groups (Moemeka, 1998). They focus their time and energy on people who belong to their group—the **ingroup**—and are less

---

individualism A tradition, ideology, or personal outlook that emphasizes the primacy of the individual and his or her rights, independence, and relationships with other individuals.

collectivism A tradition, ideology, or personal orientation that emphasizes the primacy of the group or community rather than each individual person.

ingroup Any group one belongs to or identifies with, but particularly one that is judged to be different from, and often superior to, other groups.

TABLE 3-2 Common Attributes of Individualism and Collectivism

Attribute	Individualism	Collectivism
Relationships, memberships, and associations	Concern for maintaining relations that yield personal benefits and few costs (*exchange orientation*); memberships are limited to family and close personal friendships	Concern for nurturing and maintaining harmonious relations with others (*communal orientation*); memberships including family, tribes, villages, organizations, social clubs
Norms, roles, and actions	Behavior is guided by personal attitudes and preferences; context is not as important as personal attitudes	Behavior is guided by group norms and roles; decisions are made by leaders and the group
Motives and goals	Striving for personal success; satisfaction comes from personal triumphs in competition with others	Concern for group success; cooperation among group members; group is protected at all costs; strong sense of duty and pride in group's successes
Self-conceptions	The independent self is based on one's personal, idiosyncratic characteristics; each self is autonomous and unique	The interdependent self is based on group-level relationships, roles, and social identities rather than on individual personal qualities

concerned with people who belong to some other group—the **outgroup.** They value their memberships in their groups more, consider these relationships to be stable and long-lasting, and tend to view boundaries between one group and another to be relatively impermeable. They are less willing to sever their memberships. Individualists, in contrast, do not restrict their relationships to the ingroup, for they tend to interact with more outgroup members. But their social interactions drift toward dyadic encounters, for their daily interactions are often one-on-one encounters rather than group interactions. Although some theorists feel that individualists are as likely as collectivists to interact with family and close friends, all agree that individualists are less likely to spend time in civic, community, or political activities (Cross, Bacon, & Morris, 2000; Oyserman et al., 2002).

Individualists and collectivists also tend to differ in their overall conceptualization of relationships themselves, with individualism associated with an *exchange orientation* and collectivism with a *communal orientation*. Individuals in **exchange relationships** monitor their inputs into the group, strive to maximize the rewards they personally receive through membership, and will become dissatisfied if their group becomes too costly for them. They expect to receive rewards in exchange for their investment of time, energy, and other personal resources. If

---

outgroup Any group one does not belong to or identify with, but particularly one that is judged to be different from, and inferior to, one's own group.

exchange relationship An interpersonal association between individuals based on each person's desire to increase the rewards they receive from others in the relationship.

individuals cannot identify any personal benefit from helping others in the group or community, then they will not offer any help (Ratner & Miller, 2001). In contrast, people in **communal relationships** are more concerned with what their group receives than with their own personal outcomes. When individuals work in communal groups, they help fellow members more, prefer to think of their work as a joint effort, and feel disappointed if other members insist on reciprocating any help given (M. S. Clark, Oullette, Powell, & Milberg, 1987). They are also more likely to consider the consequences of their actions for others and are more diligent in making sure that others' needs are met (J. Mills, Clark, Ford, & Johnson, 2004).

"RIGHTS" OR "DUTIES": NORMS AND ROLES Collectivism, because of its emphasis on the group rather than on the individual, stresses respect for those who hold positions of authority and avoids disagreement or dissent (S. H. Schwartz, 1994). A group, to a collectivist, "binds and mutually obligates" each member (Oyserman et al., 2002, p. 5), and so the individual has no right to create disagreement or to disrupt group proceedings. Collectivists prefer, in fact, acquiescence to disagreement and compromise to conflict. They carry out their duties within their groups, and the successful fulfillment of their roles and responsibilities is the primary source of self-satisfaction (S. H. Schwartz, 1994). Individualists, in contrast, are expected to act on the basis of their attitudes, beliefs, and preferences. Whereas collectivists are enjoined to follow the dictates of social norms when making choices and selecting a course of action, individualists are guided by their personal attitudes and preferences. They have the right to speak their minds and to disagree with others (Triandis, 1996). Researchers illustrated this contrast by asking people to complete a short survey. Collectivists were more likely to comply with the survey takers' request when they were told that many other members of their group had agreed to fill out the form, whereas individualists were more compliant when they were reminded that they had complied with a similar request before (Cialdini, Wosinska, Barrett, Butner, & Gornik-Durose, 1999).

Because of these differences in emphasis on duties versus personal rights, collectivistic groups respond more negatively to group members who violate group norms, procedures, and authority. Their operating principle is, "The tall nail gets pounded down." Individualistic groups are more reserved in their reactions to nonconformity per se, for they assume that "the squeaky wheel gets the grease." Thus, collectivists hold rulebreakers in contempt, whereas individualists tend to display anger toward those who disregard the group's emphasis on autonomy by seeking to impose their will on others (Rozin, Lowery, Imada, & Haidt, 1999).

"MINE" AND "OURS": MOTIVES AND GOALS If the goals of the group perfectly matched the individual members' goals, then individualists and collectivists would be indistinguishable. By helping the group prosper, the members help

---

communal relationship An interpersonal association between individuals who are more concerned with what their partner gets rather than what they themselves receive.

themselves prosper. However, if members must choose between maximizing their own personal goals or helping their group reach its goals, then the self-interest of the individualists will prompt them to further their own ends. Individualists tend to be **self-serving,** or *egocentric*—they strive to extract all the resources they can, while minimizing their contribution of personal resources. Collectivists, in contrast, are **group serving,** or *sociocentric*—they strive to increase the well-being of the community as a whole.

These differences can be clearly seen when members must make decisions about the allocation of resources among group members (Leung, 1997). Whenever groups earn rewards or cover costs, a fair means must be developed to determine how these rewards and costs are distributed across members. Imagine, for example, that your group has earned a reward by winning a lottery or must pay a fine because one of the group members accidentally broke something. The **equity norm** recommends that group members should receive outcomes in proportion to their inputs. If an individual has invested a good deal of time, energy, money, or other types of inputs in the group, then he or she could expect to receive a good deal of the group payoff. Similarly, individuals who contribute little should not be surprised when they receive little. The **equality norm,** on the other hand, recommends that all group members, irrespective of their inputs, should be given an equal share of the payoff. If your group includes all best friends, and collectivism is high, members would likely favor allocating the winnings on an equal-share basis: All should benefit, even if just one of the group members was the one who picked the winning lottery numbers. However, collectivists may also require that the costs be borne more heavily by the individual member who caused the problem, because the group as a whole must be protected against injury (Utz & Sassenberg, 2002). Individualism, in contrast, would favor an equity norm, because the contributions of each member are recognized and rewarded (or punished).

"ME" AND "WE": SELF-CONCEPTIONS Each one of us is, in a sense, a historian who is writing and rewriting his or her own autobiography (Greenwald & Pratkanis, 1984). Each time we acquire new information that we feel defines who we are, we use this information to revise and redefine our sense of self. Most people's selves include both a personal, private side and an interpersonal, public side. Unique, individualistic qualities—traits, beliefs, skills, and so on—

---

self-serving Emphasizing the primacy of one's own needs, perspective, and importance, particularly in contrast to those of other individuals or the group.

group serving Emphasizing the primacy of the group's needs, perspectives, and importance, particularly in contrast to those of individual members or oneself.

equity norm A social standard that encourages distributing rewards and resources to members in proportion to their inputs.

equality norm A social standard that encourages distributing rewards and resources equally among all members.

constitute the **personal identity.** The **collective self,** or **social identity,** includes all those qualities that spring from membership in a vast array of social groups, including families, cliques, work groups, neighborhoods, tribes, cities, regions, and countries (Caporael & Brewer, 1995; J. C. Turner, Hogg, Oakes, Reicher, & Wetherell, 1987). The personal identity is the *me* of the self, and the social identity is the *we.*

Collectivism is more concerned with the *we,* and individualism focuses on the *me.* If asked to describe the self's contents, individualists' list of self-qualities would likely include physical qualities such as height, weight, and physical appearance; enduring personality traits and beliefs; attitudes and interests; and personal goals and experiences (Kanagawa, Cross, & Markus, 2001). They would be less likely to mention other people or their relations with them, because the self is considered to be independent of others: Each person is inherently separate from others. The self of the collectivist, in contrast, includes all those qualities that spring from his or her relationships with other people and group membership (see Table 3-3). *Social roles,* such as spouse, lover, parent, stepparent, caregiver, and worker, define one's position in groups and social networks. C. P. was a father, a husband, a union organizer, and the co-chair of a community action group called the Humans Relations Council. The collective self may also include memberships in social *groups,* such as car pools, clubs, or church groups, and memberships in larger social *categories,* based on ethnicity, age, religion, or some other widely shared characteristic. C. P. was a member of a church, a union, and the Ellis family. Collective identities may also include information based on *relations,* or interpersonal bonds, with other people (Brewer & Gardner, 1996). C. P.'s interdependent, relational self included his close friendship with fellow group member Ann Atwater and his feelings for his son Tim (Brewer & Gardner, 1996; Gecas & Burke, 1995; Rhee, Uleman, Lee, & Roman, 1995; Thoits, 1992).

The self of the collectivist, then, is a more *interdependent* self, for it is based on connections with others. The self of the individualist is a more *independent* self, for it is based on one's unique qualities. This difference has implications for how group members think about themselves and others, and we will consider these self-processes in more detail in the final section of this chapter.

Collectivism Across Cultures

When the French sociologist Alexis de Tocqueville visited the United States in the 1830s, he was struck by Americans' self-reliance and independence. They were, he noted, frequently joining together to achieve some collective goal, but even when they were working in groups, they still took inordinate pride in their

---

personal identity The "me" component of the self-concept that derives from individualistic qualities such as traits, beliefs, and skills.

social identity (or **collective self**) That "we" component of the self-concept that includes all those qualities based on relationships with other people, groups, and society.

TABLE 3-3 Categories of Information in the Interdependent (Collective) Self

Component	Examples
Roles	athlete, caregiver, churchgoer, community volunteer, daughter, friend, group member, neighbor, parent, relative, secretary, son, spouse, stepparent, student, worker
Groups	book club, class, clique, club, committee, department, executive board, fraternity, gang, neighborhood association, research group, rock band, sorority, sports team, squad, work team
Categories	alcoholic, athlete, Christian, deaf person, Democrat, earthling, feminist, gardener, gay, Hispanic, retired person, Republican, salesperson, scientist, smoker, Southerner, welfare recipient
Relations	friend to others, in love, close to other people, helpful to others in need, involved in social causes

personal autonomy and self-reliance. It seemed that all Americans act as if they "owe no man anything and hardly expect anything from anybody. They form the habit of thinking of themselves in isolation and imagine that their whole destiny is in their own hands" (de Tocqueville, 1831/1969, p. 508). He coined a new word, *individualism,* to capture this uniquely American spirit of self-reliance (Bellah, 1986).

The view of people as independent, autonomous creatures may be peculiar to Western society's individualistic leanings. When researchers measured the relative emphasis on the individual and the group in countries all around the world, they found that the United States, other English-speaking countries (e.g., England, Australia), and Western European countries (e.g., Finland, Germany) tended to be more individualistic than Asian, Eastern European, African, and Middle Eastern countries (Hofstede, 1980; Oyserman et al., 2002). Latin and South American countries were more varied, with such countries as Puerto Rico and Chile exhibiting greater individualism than others (e.g., Mexico, Costa Rico). Many Asian, African, and South American societies, in contrast, stress collectivism. The Gahuku-Gama of Highland New Guinea, for example, do not recognize individuals apart from their roles as father, mother, chief, and so on. They do not even grasp the concept of friendship, for such a concept requires liking between two individuals (K. E. Read, 1986). The Akaramas of Peru paint their bodies so elaborately that individuals are unrecognizable. Tribes sleep in same-sex groups of 10 or 12, and when individuals die, their passing goes unnoticed (Schneebaum, 1969). In Japan, the word for self, *jibun,* means "one's portion of the shared space" (Hamaguchi, 1985). To the Japanese, "the concept of a self completely independent from the environment is very foreign," as people are not perceived apart from the existing social context (Azuma, 1984, p. 973).

People who live in collectivistic cultures think of themselves as group members first and individuals second, whereas people who live in individualistic cultures are self-centered rather than group centered (see Focus 3-2). Harry C.

FOCUS 3-2   Do Only Individualists Strive for High Self-Esteem?

If I cannot brag of knowing something, then I can brag of not knowing it. At any rate, brag.
—Ralph Waldo Emerson

Most people prefer to think well of themselves rather than admit their faults, limitations, and foibles. People readily embrace positive feedback, but they question comments that are critical. When they make mistakes, they blame external factors, but when they succeed, they quickly claim credit. People tend to avoid comparing themselves to people who are outperforming them and, instead, prefer to contrast themselves with those who are struggling. The idea that people will go to great lengths to protect and enhance their sense of self-worth is "an old, respected, and when all is said and done, probably one of the great psychological truths" (Markus, 1980, p. 127).

Studies of cultural differences in the nature of the self, however, have challenged this idea, suggesting that only Westerners, with their individualistic selves, strive to enhance their self-worth. Compared to individualists, collectivists do not aspire to a positive self-esteem, do not think they are better than others, and do not blame their failures on other people. They are, in fact, self-critical and unassuming rather than self-enhancing (e.g., Chang & Asakawa, 2003; Heine, Kitayama, & Lehman, 2001; Kanagawa et al., 2001).

A team of international researchers representing England, the United States, and Japan

(Sedikides, Gaertner, & Toguchi, 2003), after considering prior studies of this question, concluded that both collectivists and individualists self-enhance, but they do it in different ways. Individualists stress their superiority over others on attributes that pertain to autonomy and independence, but collectivists think of themselves as more relational and self-sacrificing than others. They tested this hypothesis by asking U.S. and Japanese students to imagine they were part of a large group of their compatriots making a decision. Then they presented these students with a list of traits and asked them to indicate if they considered themselves to be better than, equal to, or worse than the typical member of this group. As they expected (see Figure 3-3), the American students described themselves as superior to others on the individualistic traits (independent, self-reliant, unique, leader), whereas the Japanese students described themselves as superior on the collectivistic traits (agreeable, compromising, cooperative, loyal, respectful). A similar pattern emerged when the participants indicated how likely it would be that they would engage in collectivistic behaviors (e.g., avoid conflict, defend the group, avoid open confrontation) versus individualistic behaviors (e.g., argue for your position, put yourself before your group). On the basis of these and other aspects of their data the researchers concluded that "self-enhancement is a universal human motive" (Sedikides et al., 2003, p. 60).

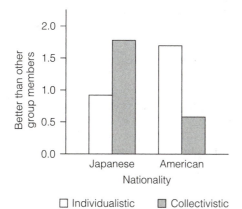

FIGURE 3-3

Is the need for high self-esteem a human universal? When researchers asked Japanese and Americans to rate themselves, both nationalities claimed they were superior to others, but they were culturally selective in their claims. The Japanese noted their superiority when rating their collectivism, and the Americans noted their superiority on traits pertaining to individuality. *Source:* Sedikides, Gaertner, & Toguchi, 2003.

Triandis and his colleagues illustrated this difference by asking people from various countries to describe themselves. As they expected, these self-descriptions contained more references to roles and relationships when people were from collectivistic countries (e.g., Japan, China). Some individuals from the People's Republic of China described themselves exclusively in interpersonal terms. And some U.S. residents used only personal descriptors—they had no elements of a collective self (Triandis, McCusker, & Hui, 1990; cf. Oyserman et al., 2002). Other research has suggested that people from collectivistic countries resist describing their qualities if the social context is not specified. Japanese, for example, described themselves differently when they were with different people and in different social situations. Americans, in contrast, described themselves similarly across different situations (Cousins, 1989). Students in the United States, more than students in China, assume that people's behaviors are caused by personality traits rather than by factors in the situation (Chiu, Hong, & Dweck, 1997). People from individualistic and collectivistic cultures even insult one another differently. Personal insults, such as "You are stupid," characterize conflicts in individualistic cultures, whereas remarks about one's family and group typify disputes between two collectivists (Semin & Rubini, 1990).

These observations are only generalities, for each culture expresses its collectivism and individualism differently. Some collectivistic cultures, for example, are much more hierarchically structured (*vertical*) than others, like the culture of India with its caste system, which stresses tradition, duty, and compliance with authority. Other collectivistic cultures, however, stress equality, and so their society's status and authority structures are relatively flat (*horizontal*). Some collectivistic societies also tolerate considerable conflict within their groups. Members of Israeli kibbutzes, for example, often engage in heated debates, whereas Koreans strive for harmony and avoid discord. Both cultures are relatively collectivistic, yet their approaches to resolving disputes differ substantially (Triandis, 1995, 1996). In contrast, Scandinavians are extremely individualistic, but they are also noncompetitive (A. P. Fiske, 2002). Moreover, as the next section notes, the tendency to classify people into distinct groups on the basis of their nationality overlooks the many subcultures that exist within countries (Joan G. Miller, 2002). It may be that the dichotomy between individualism and collectivism reflects, in part, the cognitive biases of the Western theorists who first proposed this distinction (A. P. Fiske, 2002; Gaines et al., 1997).

Collectivism Across Groups

People's readiness to connect to groups and to put the group's interests above their own varies across racial, ethnic, gender, and other social categories (J. A. Howard, 2000). In the United States, for example, certain areas are more individualistic, whereas others are more collectivistic (Vandello & Cohen, 2004). Communalism is particularly prominent in the southern portions of the United States, where C. P. Ellis lived. This area of the country is more rural, agricultural, and hierarchically structured. When polled, its residents were more likely to agree to such statements as, "It is better to fit in with people around you," and "It is more important to be a cooperative person who works well with others." Individuals living in the western portions of the United States, where the frontier, pioneer tradition stresses self-reliance, are more individualistic. Residents of this part of the country felt that "it is better to conduct yourself according to your own standards, even if that makes you stand out," and "it is more important to be a self-reliant person able to take care of oneself" (Vandello & Cohen, 1999, p. 285).

Ethnic groups in the United States also exhibit remarkable variations in individualism and collectivism. When Oyserman and her colleagues (2002) combined the findings obtained across a number of studies in a meta-analysis, they found that Asian Americans tended to be more collectivistic than European Americans, but that Japanese and Koreans are more similar to European Americans than were the more collectivistic Chinese Americans. Hispanic Americans did not differ from European Americans in their level of individualism, but they were more collectivistic. Even though Afrocentric cultural traditions, like those emphasized in the African American celebration of Kwanzaa, stress strong family ties and mutual help, the researchers discovered that African Americans tended to score higher than European Americans on measures of individualism and lower than European Americans on measures of collectivism.

Collectivism Across People

Just as cultures differ in how much they stress the individual versus the group, individuals within any given culture differ in the emphasis they put on their individuality versus their group memberships. Some people, termed **independents** (or **idiocentrics**) are emotionally detached from their groups; they put their own personal goals above the goals of the group (Markus, Kitayama, & Heiman, 1996; Triandis, 1995). They value equality, social justice, and self-reliance, and they would likely agree with statements such as, "One should live one's life independently of others as much as possible" (Triandis et al., 1990, p. 1013), "I often do what I feel like doing without paying attention to others' feelings" (Kashima et al., 1995, p. 928), and the other statements shown in the top portion of Table 3-4. **Interdependents** (or **allocentrics**), in contrast, put their groups' goals and needs above their own (Markus et al., 1996; Triandis, 1995). They are respectful of other members of their groups, and they value their memberships in groups, their friendships, and tradition. They would likely agree with such statements as, "The well-being of my co-workers is important to me" (Triandis, 1995, p. 207), "I think it is more important to give priority to group

---

independent (or **idiocentric**) An individual who is dispositionally predisposed to put his or her own personal interests and motivations above the group's interests and goals.

interdependent (or **allocentric**) An individual who is dispositionally predisposed to put the group's goals and needs above his or her own.

TABLE 3-4 The Multiple Domains of Individualism and Collectivism

Domain name	Description	Sample item
Individualism		
Independence	Freedom, self-sufficiency, and control over one's life	I tend to do my own thing, and others in my family do the same.
Goals	Striving for one's own goals, desires, and achievements	I take great pride in accomplishing what no one else can accomplish.
Competition	Personal competition and winning	It is important to me that I perform better than others on a task.
Uniqueness	Focus on one's unique, idiosyncratic qualities	I am unique—different from others in many respects.
Privacy	Thoughts and actions private from others	I like my privacy.
Self-knowledge	Knowing oneself; having a strong identity	I know my weaknesses and strengths.
Direct communication	Clearly articulating one's wants and needs	I always state my opinions very clearly.
Collectivism		
Relating	Considering close others an integral part of the self	To understand who I am, you must see me with members of my group.
Belonging	Wanting to belong to and enjoying being part of groups	To me, pleasure is spending time with others.
Duty	The duties and sacrifices that being a group member entails	I would help, within my means, if a relative were in financial difficulty.
Harmony	Concern for group harmony; desire that members get along	I make an effort to avoid disagreements with my group members.
Advice	Turning to close others for help with decisions	Before making a decision, I always consult with others.
Context	Self changes according to context or situation	How I behave depends on who I am with, where I am, or both.
Hierarchy	Focus on hierarchy and status issues	I have respect for the authority figures with whom I interact.
Group	Preference for group work	I would rather do a group paper or lab than do one alone.

Source: Adapted from Oyserman, Coon, & Kemmelmeier, 2002.

interests rather than to personal ones" (Kashima et al., 1995, p. 928), and others shown in the bottom portion of Table 3-4.

One's personal level of interdependence need not correspond to one's culture or ethnic group's collectivism. Triandis and his colleagues (2001) found that about 60% of the people in collectivistic cultures are interdependent types, just as about 60% of the people in individualistic cultures are independent types. They also reported that interdependent individuals in individualistic countries tend to join more groups, but that independent individuals in collectivistic cultures "feel oppressed by their culture and seek to leave it" (Triandis & Suh, 2002, p. 141).

Interdependents seek out groups and become more interconnected with their groups than independents (Cheek, 1989). People who stress their personal, independent identity tend to play sports that require little interaction with other people. They tend to exercise by jogging or swimming, and they say that they exercise because it gives them a feeling of self-satisfaction. People who stress their interdependence, in contrast, more frequently play team sports such as volleyball or soccer, and they do so because they "enjoy competing or exercising with other people" (Leary, Wheeler, & Jenkins, 1986, p. 16). Interdependents seek jobs that will enhance the quality of their relationships with other people, and their satisfaction with their work depends on the quality of their relationships with their coworkers. Independents choose jobs that are personally fulfilling and that offer them opportunities for advancement (Leary, Wheeler, & Jenkins, 1986). Interdependents may also be more loyal to their groups. A high degree of interdependence is associated with patriotism and pride in one's country (Kowalski & Wolfe, 1994). The two types also respond differently to conflicts. Independent individuals respond with greater intensity to interpersonal conflicts—disagreements between two individuals—whereas interdependents respond more intensely to intergroup conflicts—those that involve disagreements with members of the outgroup (Derlega, Cukur, Kuang, & Forsyth, 2002). Men and women tend to differ in collectivism and individualism. In Western cultures, at least, women more often stress connections with other people, whereas men tend to stress independence and autonomy (Cross & Madson, 1997; Josephs, Markus, & Tafarodi, 1992).

Individuals who are more independent than interdependent also tend to stress their unique, unusual qualities. One measure of the tendency to set oneself apart from other people—the *Individuation Scale*—asks people to indicate their willingness to engage in attention-getting behaviors, such as self-disclosure and nonconformity (Maslach, Stapp, & Santee, 1985). People who score high on the Individuation Scale report a greater frequency of owning distinctive possessions (such as a special kind of car), having a unique self-expressive symbol (such as a nickname), expressing unique opinions, criticizing someone in front of others, making controversial statements, and looking directly into someone's eyes while talking to him or her. People scoring low on the scale report a greater frequency of wearing the kind of clothes that others wear, owning standard possessions, avoiding distinctive nicknames, avoiding accessories or colors that get attention, controlling distracting gestures, expressing popular opinions, agreeing with other people, not criticizing others, remaining quiet in a group, and avoiding eye contact. They are more likely to engage in conventional behaviors and seek social acceptance. When these scales are used in collectivistic societies, the respondents distinguish between two forms of individuating behaviors: taking the lead and drawing attention to oneself. Taking the lead was considered to be slightly more acceptable than drawing attention to oneself in one study of Japanese students (Kwan, Bond, Boucher, Maslach, & Gan, 2002).

Although interdependent types of people are often contrasted with independent types, in all likelihood these two orientations are continuous dimensions of personality that vary in their influence across time and situations. As Marilyn Brewer's **optimal distinctiveness theory** suggested, most people probably have at least three fundamental needs: the need to be assimilated by the group, the need to be connected to friends and loved ones, and the need for autonomy and differentiation. She hypothesized that individuals are most satisfied if they achieve optimal distinctiveness: Their unique personal qualities are noted and appreciated, they feel emotionally bonded with intimates, and they feel similar to other group members in many respects (Brewer, Manzi, & Shaw, 1993; Brewer & Pickett, 2002). Achieving a feeling of uniqueness is as important as satisfying the need to belong (Snyder & Fromkin, 1980).

FROM PERSONAL IDENTITY TO SOCIAL IDENTITY

Before C. P. joined groups, he was concerned only with himself and his needs. When he pondered the question, "Who am I?" he answered, "I am C. P." But when he joined with others, he started acting differently—in ways that the group favored rather than in ways he thought were best. When he joined the KKK, he became a racist who despised all non-Whites. But when he quit the KKK and joined a multicultural community group (the Human Relations Council), he adopted an egalitarian outlook. Even his answer to the question, "Who am I?" changed to include elements that were based on his group memberships: He was still C. P., but he thought of himself as a union leader and a reformer. How did these groups manage to embed themselves into C. P.'s sense of self?

Social Identity Theory

As noted earlier, the self includes both personal and interpersonal elements. Whereas one's individualistic qualities make up the personal identity, one's social or collective identity includes all self-conceptions that arise from membership in social groups, including teams, cliques, communities, and so on. The collective self may also reference larger, more categorical aggregates, such as "I am a man" or "I am an American," if individuals consider these qualities important and relevant to their self-concept.

But how does a group become a part of one's social identity? What impact does this acceptance of the group in one's identity have on one's self-concept and

---

optimal distinctiveness theory A conceptual analysis proposed by Marilyn Brewer that assumes individuals strive to maintain a balance between three basic needs: the need to be assimilated by the group, the need to be connected to friends and loved ones, and the need for autonomy and differentiation.

self-esteem? **Social identity theory** suggests that two cognitive processes—*categorization* and *identification*—combine to transform a group membership into an identity (Abrams & Hogg, 2001; Hogg, 2001; Tajfel, 1981; Turner & Onorato, 1999).

CATEGORIZATION IN GROUPS When C. P. first met Howard Clements, he assigned him to the categories *man* and *African American.* When he met Terry Sanford, he thought of him as *European American, man,* and *leader.* Such categories ignore each individual's unique qualities, but they are useful summaries of vast amounts of information about people in general. As Gordon W. Allport (1954) explained, "The human mind must think with the aid of categories. Once formed, categories are the basis for normal prejudgment. We cannot possibly avoid this process. Orderly living depends upon it" (p. 19).

We do not just categorize other people; we also classify ourselves into various groups and categories. Although people vary in the extent to which their self is independent of others or interdependent with others, at any given moment, the self can shift from *me* to *we* if something in the situation makes that group membership salient to us (J. C. Turner & Onorato, 1999). Individuals who find that they are the only representative of a particular group—for example, the only man in a group of five, or the only left-hander in a class of otherwise all right-handers—may suddenly become very aware of that aspect of themselves (W. J. McGuire & McGuire, 1988). People who feel that they are being uniquely scrutinized by other people are more likely to think of themselves as individuals than as group members (Mullen, Rozell, & Johnson, 1996). If people are asked to spend a few minutes thinking about the ways they were similar to their family and friends, their subsequent self-descriptions will be peppered with group-level descriptors (Trafimow, Triandis, & Goto, 1991).

This process of **social categorization** is an automatic cognitive process rather than a controlled one. Controlled cognitive processes are initiated, monitored, and terminated at will. Automatic processes, in contrast, are rapid, autonomous, effortless, and involuntary, and they take place outside of awareness (Bargh, 1990). Hence, even though people may not notice the activation of their social identities, these identities may influence them nonetheless. This automaticity was illustrated by researchers who used a very subtle procedure to activate individuals' group-level identities (Brewer & Gardner, 1996; Experiment 3). They asked participants to circle all the pronouns in a story, and they primed the collective self by manipulating the kinds of pronouns that people read. In some cases, most of the pronouns focused on "we" or "us"; for others, the pronouns

---

social identity theory A theoretical analysis of group processes and intergroup relations that assumes groups influence their members' self-concepts and self-esteem, particularly when individuals categorize themselves as group members and identify with the group.

social categorization The perceptual classification of people, including the self, into categories.

referred to "them" and "they"; and for participants in the control condition, the pronouns referred to "it." When the participants finished their task, they described themselves in their own words. As predicted, people who had searched for "we" pronouns included more collectivistic components in their self-descriptions than did individuals who had searched for "they" or "it." This effect was particularly pronounced when the story containing the pronouns described a large group activity (a football game) rather than a small group activity (an automobile trip).

Researchers are continuing to investigate precisely how individualistic and collectivistic information is stored in memory. Some investigators have stressed the qualitatively distinct nature of these two types of information, but others have argued that social and personal identities are intermingled in our memories (Abrams, 1992; Coats, Smith, Claypool, & Banner, 2000; Reid & Deaux, 1996).

IDENTIFICATION WITH GROUPS Most people belong to many groups and categories, but many of these memberships have no influence on their social identities. C. P. may have been a right-hander, a resident of North Carolina, a Democrat, and brown-eyed, but he never gave much thought to these categories. Only some of his memberships, such as his involvement with a social action group named the Human Relations Council, were core elements of his sense of self. He *identified* with these social categories.

Just as Freud (1922) believed that identification causes children to love and imitate their parents, **social identification** causes individuals to bond with and take on the characteristics of a group. As identification increases, group members become more likely to think that their membership in the group is personally significant. They feel connected and interdependent with other members, are glad they belong to the group, feel good about the group, and experience strong attachment to the group. They are also more involved in the group's activities, as indicated by their participation in meetings, their acceptance of group norms, and their willingness to help the group meet its goals. Figure 3-4 describes social identification with a group graphically (J. E. Cameron, 1999; J. W. Jackson & Smith, 1999; Tropp & Wright, 2001).

In some cases, identification with a group develops over time. C. P., for example, did not immediately identify with the Human Relations Council when he first joined it, for it stood for many ideas that he rejected. Only over time did he abandon his older allegiances and fully embrace his membership in the Human Relations Council. Similarly, people's identification with their ethnic and national groups often develops over time and with experience (Phinney, 1996). One three-stage model of African American ethnic identity, for example, argued that individuals in the first stage of identity development either do not characterize people, including themselves, on the basis of ethnicity (*diffusion*) or they

---

social identification Accepting the group as an extension of the self, and therefore basing one's self-definition on the group's qualities and characteristics.

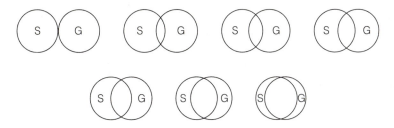

FIGURE 3-4

How much do people identify with their group? When identification is high, the group is included in the individual's sense of self. If asked to select the set of circles that best indicates the extent to which the group (G) overlaps with the self (S), low identifiers should select circles that do not overlap. Increasing identification is indicated by selecting circles where the self and the group overlap to an increasing degree. *Source:* "Ingroup Identification as the Inclusion of Ingroup in the Self," by Linda R. Tropp & Stephen C. Wright, 2001, *Personality and Social Psychology Bulletin,* 27, pp. 585–600. Reprinted by permission of Sage Publications.

accept other people's definition of their ethnicity without question (*foreclosure*). This *unexamined identity stage* ends when individuals begin exploring the meaning of their ethnicity. The *exploration stage* is characterized by immersion in one's ethnic culture and, in some cases, adamant rejection of the values of the majority. The final stage, *identity achievement,* occurs when individuals internalize their ethnicity in their sense of self (Phinney, 1989, 1996; Sellers, Rowley, Chavous, Shelton, & Smith, 1997).

Social identification also becomes more likely when another group is introduced or made salient in some way. If everyone is a member of the same group, this similarity may be unnoticed. But if some people are members of group X and others are in group Y, suddenly people begin to categorize one another, identify with their group (the *ingroup*), and distance themselves from the other group (the *outgroup*).

Self and Social Identity

Once C. P. identified with the Human Relations Council—once he incorporated the group into his social identity "together with the value and emotional significance attached to that membership" (Tajfel, 1981, p. 255)—C. P. changed in fundamental ways. First, the contents of his self were modified as he came to think of himself as more and more similar to the "typical" member of the Council. Second, his evaluation of himself changed as he began to think of himself as a worthy member of this valuable group. As noted hereafter, social identity influences the contents of the self and how those contents are evaluated.

DEFINING THE SELF When people identify strongly with a group, their self-descriptions become increasingly *depersonalized* as they include fewer idiosyncratic elements and more characteristics that are common to the group. Once C. P. identified with the Human Relations Council, he noticed that all the members were concerned with improving social conditions. They were also targets of discrimination and were economically exploited. C. P. soon realized that he, too, was concerned with improving social conditions, and that he was discriminated against and economically exploited.

This process is known as **self-stereotyping** (or **autostereotyping**) because it involves both (1) accepting generalizations about the qualities and characteristics of the members of one's group or social category as accurate and (2) applying those stereotypes to oneself (Abrams & Hogg, 2001). Medical students, for example, did not define themselves as physicians until their training was nearly complete. By graduation, however, their selves included the component of *physician,* and they described themselves in ways that were consistent with stereotypes about physicians (Preiss, 1968). Gay men agreed that gay-stereotypic words (e.g., creative, complicated) described them better than straight-stereotypic words (e.g., able to lead, insensitive), and this tendency to accept the stereotype's content as self-descriptive was particularly pronounced for negative rather than positive characteristics (B. Simon, Glässner-Bayerl, & Stratenwerth, 1991). When women in sororities rated themselves and other women in their sorority on traits often ascribed to sorority women (e.g., popular, well dressed, conceited, shallow, spoiled), they gave themselves and their group nearly identical ratings—the correlation between self-rating and group rating was .98 (Biernat, Vescio, & Green, 1996). When older people's negative stereotypes about old age were primed by displaying words such as *dementia, decrepit,* and *senile* so briefly that they never reported seeing the words themselves, they nonetheless subsequently performed more poorly on memory tasks. Older people exposed to positive words showed improved memories, and younger people exposed to these types of words were unaffected, apparently because they did not identify with this group and its age-based stereotype (B. Levy, 1996).

Any factor that increases members' identification with the group can increase self-stereotyping. In one study, the men in ad hoc groups disagreed with the women in the groups. Because this schism along gender lines made members more aware of their membership in the social categories of *man* and *woman,* when they later rated themselves, the men described themselves as more masculine and the women described themselves as more feminine (Hogg & Turner, 1987).

---

self-stereotyping (or **autostereotyping**) Accepting socially shared generalizations about the prototypical characteristics attributed to members of one's group as accurate descriptions of oneself.

Studies have also suggested that people are more likely to self-stereotype when they are members of a minority group rather than of a larger, dominant, majority group. The experience of being in the minority apparently increases the salience of the social identity based on that membership, and so people are more likely to apply the stereotypical features of the minority group to themselves. Researchers informed some participants that a survey they had just completed suggested that they were extraverted and that only 20% of the population is extraverted. These individuals then gave themselves higher ratings on such traits as *sociable* and *lively* than did people who were told that 80% of the population is extraverted (B. Simon & Hamilton, 1994).

Because individuals who identify with a group take on more and more of the prototypical features of members of that group, they may also adopt the attitudes, preferences, and behaviors that they think typify the group. These attitudes are then likely to influence their behavior, particularly when their membership in the group is salient to them. For example, do all people who realize that exercising regularly is good for them exercise? No, because attitudes are not perfect predictors of behavior. But when researchers distinguished between people who did or did not identify with their group, they discovered that members who identified with a group that valued exercise were far more likely to exercise regularly (Terry & Hogg, 1996). Other researchers confirmed this effect experimentally by directly manipulating the group's norms and the members' degree of identification with the group. Again, identification was associated with greater conformity to the group's norms (Jetten, Spears, & Manstead, 1997).

EVALUATING THE SELF C. P. Ellis felt shame when he was a child, particularly when he compared his tattered shirts and pants with the new clothes his classmates wore to school. But when he joined the KKK, his shame melted away, replaced by self-confidence: "I was led into a large meeting room, and this was the time of my life! It was thrilling. Here's a guy who's worked all his life and struggled all his life to be something, and here's the moment to be something" (Terkel, 1980, p. 203). When C. P. joined this group, he did not just acquire a new identity; he also acquired self-worth.

When individuals join groups, their self-concept becomes connected to that group, and the value of that group comes to influence their feelings of personal worth. People who belong to prestigious groups tend to have higher self-esteem than those who belong to stigmatized groups (so long as they are not reminded that their group's revered social position is undeserved; Branscombe, 1998). High school students, for example, often seek out membership in one of the school's "in crowds." Those who are members of the most prestigious groups generally report feeling very satisfied with themselves and their group. Those students who want to be a part of an "in crowd" but are not accepted by this clique are the most dissatisfied (B. B. Brown & Lohr, 1987). People who were members of prestigious or satisfying groups in high school have higher levels of self-esteem later in life (S. S. Wright & Forsyth, 1997). Sports fans' moods swing up and down as their favorite team wins and looses. After a loss, they feel depressed and

FOCUS 3-3   Can Social Identity Theory Explain Sports Fans?

You may glory in a team triumphant, but you fall in love with a team in defeat. Losing after great striving is the story of man, who was born to sorrow, whose sweetest songs tell of the saddest thought.
–Roger Kahn (1973), *The Boys of Summer*

Fan derives from a slightly longer word: fanatic. A *fanatic* is one who engages in extreme, unreasonable devotion to an idea, philosophy, or practice. Similarly, the die-hard sports fan displays great devotion to a team, with emotions rising and falling with the team's accomplishments. Fans are not actually members of the teams they support. They are only watching the games from the sidelines, and they are not directly involved in the outcome. Yet they often seem to be very closely connected psychologically to their teams. They are elated when their team wins, but after a loss, fans experience a range of negative emotions: anger, depression, sadness, hopelessness, and confusion (Platow et al., 1999; Wann, Dolan, McGeorge, & Allison, 1994). In some cases, fans will even attack the supporters of other teams, with fatal outcomes (Doosje, Ellemers, & Spears, 1999).

Social identity theory offers insight into this odd but exceedingly common group behavior. Die-hard sports fans *identify* with their team and so experience the team's outcomes as their own. When the team wins, they can share in that success. By **basking in reflected glory,** or **BIRGing,** they can stress their association with the successful group, even though they have contributed little to that success (Cialdini et al., 1976; End, Dietz-Uhler, Harrick, & Jacquemotte, 2002). But what happens should their group fail? The casual fan can just downplay the loss by switching his or her allegiance or attention to some other team: **cutting off re-flected failure,** or **CORFing.** But dedicated fans, whose homes are decorated with team insignia, who wear the team's colors, and who have based much of their sense of self on their loyalty to the team, cannot CORF. Their team's loss will be *their* loss (Snyder, Higgins, & Stucky, 1983).

A team of investigators studied these processes by inviting fans of the men's Indiana University (IU) basketball team to watch a live broadcast of a game. In some cases, the IU team won, but in others, the team lost. After the contest, participants rated the IU team, but they also rated their own mood and their own capabilities. As expected, the fans judged the IU team more positively after a win than after a loss. But they also displayed a number of negative reactions when their team lost. Relative to students who watched the team win, the fans were more depressed after a loss; they were more pessimistic when rating their mental ability; and they predicted that an attractive person would be more likely to reject them. These negative reactions were all exacerbated by the strength of the fan's social identity as a fan of the IU team: Those who strongly identified with the team suffered the most after a loss.

The investigators concluded that being a sports fan may yield many social benefits for individuals, but their data indicated that devotion to a group whose performance is beyond one's control is risky. Fans did not feel any better when their teams won, but when the team lost, their moods soured and their outlook for the future became more bleak. The researchers cautiously concluded that "fans are setting themselves up for a great deal of misery by committing themselves to a team" (Hirt, Zillmann, Erickson, & Kennedy, 1992, p. 724).

----

basking in reflected glory (BIRGing) Seeking direct or indirect association with prestigious or successful groups or individuals.

cutting off reflected failure (CORFing) Distancing oneself from a group that performs poorly.

TABLE 3-5 Items from the Collective Self-Esteem Inventory

Subscale	Issue	Example Item
Membership Esteem	Am I a valuable or an ineffective member of the groups to which I belong?	I am a worthy member of the social groups I belong to.
Private Collective Self-Esteem	Do I evaluate the groups I belong to positively or negatively?	I feel good about the social groups I belong to.
Public Collective Self-Esteem	Do other people evaluate the groups I belong to positively or negatively?	In general, others respect the social groups that I am a member of.
Identity	Are the groups I belong to an important or unimportant part of my identity?	In general, belonging to social groups is an important part of my self-image.

Source: "A Collective Self-Esteem Scale: Self-Evaluation of One's Social Identity" by R. Luhtanen and J. Crocker, *Personality and Social Psychology Bulletin,* 18, 1992.

rate themselves more negatively; but after a win, they feel elated and rate themselves more positively (see Focus 3-3).

Jennifer Crocker, Riia Luhtanen, and their colleagues examined the relationship between people's self-esteem and their feelings about the groups to which they belonged by developing a measure of **collective self-esteem** (J. Crocker & Luhtanen, 1990; J. Crocker, Luhtanen, Blaine, & Broadnax, 1994; Luhtanen & Crocker, 1992). Instead of asking people if they felt good or bad about themselves, Crocker and Luhtanen asked individuals to evaluate the groups to which they belonged. Drawing on prior work on social identity and self-esteem, they developed items that tapped four basic issues: membership esteem, private collective self-esteem, public collective self-esteem, and importance to identity (see Table 3-5). When they compared scores on the collective self-esteem scale to scores on more traditional measures of self-esteem, they found that people with high membership, public, and private collective self-esteem scores had higher personal self-esteem, suggesting that group membership contributes to feelings of self-worth.

Even membership in a group that others may not admire is generally associated with higher levels of self-esteem (J. Crocker & Major, 1989). Adolescents with mental retardation do not necessarily have lower self-esteem, even though they know they belong to the negatively stereotyped social category "special education students" (Stager, Chassin, & Young, 1983). African Americans, despite living in a culture where stereotypes about their group are negative, have higher self-esteem than European Americans (Twenge & Crocker, 2002). Members of

------

collective self-esteem A person's overall assessment of that portion of their self-concept that is based on their relationships with others and membership in social groups.

groups that are criticized often respond by defending their group and reaffirming their commitment to it (Dietz-Uhler & Murrell, 1998). When C. P. joined the Human Relations Council, his friends condemned the group as too liberal, but C. P.'s self-esteem rose. So long as individuals believe that the groups they belong to are valuable, they will experience a heightened sense of personal self-esteem (J. Crocker et al., 1994).

PROTECTING THE COLLECTIVE SELF When individuals identify with their group, they also tend to exaggerate the differences between their group and other groups. Once people begin to think in terms of *we* and *us,* they also begin to recognize *them* and *they*. When C. P.'s identification with the Human Relations Council was complete, he came to value the group's work, while at the same time distrusting the motives and goals of people who were not members of the Human Relations Council. The tendency to look more favorably on the ingroup is called the **ingroup–outgroup bias.** Gang members view their group more positively than rival gangs. Teammates praise their own players and derogate the other team. If Group A and Group B work side by side, members of A will rate Group A as better than B, but members of B will rate Group B more favorably than A.

The ingroup–outgroup bias often contributes to conflict between groups (see Chapter 13), but it also contributes to the self-esteem and emotional well-being of group members. Social identity theory posits that people are motivated to maintain or enhance their feelings of self-worth, and because our self-esteem is linked to the groups we belong to, our feelings of self-worth can be enhanced by stressing the relative superiority of our groups to other groups.

Even if our group falters, we can nonetheless find ways to protect the group and, in so doing, protect our self. A setback, particularly at the hands of another group, calls for **social creativity:** Group members compare the ingroup to the outgroup on some new dimension. One researcher illustrated such social creativity by asking members of a last-placed ice hockey team (1 win and 21 losses) to rate their team and their opponents on four key attributes: *aggressive, dirty, skilled,* and *motivated* (Lalonde, 1992). The players admitted that their opponents were more skilled, but they also argued that their opponents were more aggressive and that they played dirty.

PROTECTING THE PERSONAL SELF People protect their collective self-esteem as actively as they protect their personal self-esteem. They deny that their group possesses negative qualities. They consider their group to be superior to

---

ingroup–outgroup bias The tendency to view the ingroup, its members, and its products more positively than other groups, their members, and their products. Ingroup favoritism is more common than outgroup rejection.

social creativity Restricting comparisons between the ingroup and other groups to tasks and outcomes where the ingroup is more successful than other groups and avoiding areas in which other groups surpass the ingroup.

alternative groups. They give their group credit for its successes, but blame outside influences when their group fails. Should other, more rewarding groups stand willing and ready to take them in, individuals remain loyal to their original group. Identity is the glue that binds individuals to their groups (Van Vugt & Hart, 2004).

However, there are limits to what individuals will tolerate. In most cases, people are more disturbed by threats to their personal self-esteem than to their collective self-esteem. They are also more likely to deny the accuracy of negative individualized information relative to negative group information, and they more readily claim positive feedback when it focuses on them rather than on their group (L. Gaertner, Sedikides, Vevea, & Iuzzini, 2002). They will, if the group continues to threaten their personal self-esteem, eventually turn away from the group. When people can choose the groups they belong to or identify with, they often shift their allegiances, leaving groups that are lower in status or prone to failure and seeking membership in prestigious or successful groups (J. Crocker, Blaine, & Luhtanen, 1993; Ellemers, Wilke, & van Knippenberg, 1993). When C. P. could no longer deny the growing rift between his values and the KKK, he resigned from the Klan and joined a more liberal, more egalitarian organization. Such a change in allegiance is termed *individual mobility* (Ellemers, Spears, & Doosje, 1997).

When C. P. left the KKK, he put his individual needs above his group's needs. He sympathized with the Klan members, but he eventually quit that group and joined the Human Relations Council. Once he was accepted into this group, his social identity underwent a substantial change, and his attitudes, values, and beliefs were reshaped once again. In time, he abandoned his prejudiced ways of thinking, earned a high school education, and became a leader in his community. It was

> like bein' born again. It was a new life. I didn't have these sleepless nights I used to have when I was active in the Klan and slippin' around at night. I could sleep at night and feel good about it. . . . My whole life had changed. (quoted in Terkel, 1980, p. 209)

Summary in Outline

❖ **Do humans prefer solitude or group membership?**

1. Solitude is sometimes rewarding, but most adults prefer the company of others, particularly when threatened or distressed. Most people find the prospect of facing life alone to be disturbing.

2. People prefer inclusion to exclusion, and as a result, some religious groups practice

shunning as a means of punishing rule-breakers. Ostracism causes a number of negative psychological and behavioral reactions, including a loss of self-esteem.

- The *sociometer model of self-esteem* explains the relationship between exclusion and self-esteem by hypothesizing that self-esteem evolved to provide individuals with feedback about their degree of inclusion in groups.

- Individuals also react negatively to exclusion from computer-mediated interaction, or *cyberostracism,* but they tend to respond to such exclusion by increasing communication with others.

3. Individuals who feel that their relationships with others are too few or superficial experience *loneliness.*
   - Groups that create reliable alliances among members, such as work groups or clubs, may reduce feelings of *social loneliness.*
   - Emotionally intimate groups, such as romantic dyads or families, are an antidote to *emotional loneliness.*

4. Baumeister and Leary suggested that much of human behavior is motivated by a basic *need to belong.* Evolutionary psychology suggests that this instinct resulted from *natural selection* and *kin selection,* as individuals who affiliated in groups were more likely to survive and to contribute to the survival of close relatives.

❖ **What are individualism and collectivism?**

1. *Individualism* and *collectivism* differ in their relative emphasis on individuals and groups, with individualism stressing the person and collectivism the group. These two orientations differ in a number of ways, including the nature of interpersonal relationships, norms and roles, motivations, and self-conceptions.
   - Collectivism is associated with greater loyalty to the *ingroup* and less concern for the *outgroup,* whereas individualism tends to foster *exchange relationships* rather than *communal relationships.*
   - A collectivistic orientation stresses hierarchy and reacts more negatively to nonconformity.
   - *Self-serving* tendencies are more likely in individualistic settings, in contrast

to the *group-serving* tendencies seen in collectivistic settings. As a result, the *equity norm* often guides the distribution of resources when individualism predominates, whereas *equality norms* hold under collectivism.
   - Self-concepts differ in individualistic and collectivistic contexts, with greater emphasis on *personal identity* in the former and greater emphasis on *social identity* (e.g., roles, memberships, relations) in the latter.

2. Cultures, groups, and individuals vary in their relative emphasis on individualism and collectivism.
   - People who live in collectivistic cultures (e.g., Asian, Eastern European, African, and Middle Eastern countries) think of themselves as group members first and individuals second, whereas people who live in individualistic cultures (Western countries) are self-centered rather than group centered.
   - Some ethnic groups, such as Asian Americans and Hispanic Americans, are more collectivistic than individualistic.
   - Individuals in any given culture differ in the emphasis they put on their individuality versus their group membership, with *independents* stressing individualism and *interdependents* putting their groups' goals and needs above their own. In Western cultures, women tend to be more interdependent, men more independent. Individualists stress their superiority over others on attributes that pertain to autonomy and independence, but collectivists think of themselves as more relational and self-sacrificing than others.
   - Brewer's *optimal distinctiveness theory* suggests that individuals strive to maintain an optimal balance between their personal and collective identities.

❖ **Does membership in a group change a person's self-concept and social identity?**

1. *Social identity theory* traces the development of a collective identity back to two key processes: categorization and identification.
   - Through *social categorization,* individuals automatically classify people, including themselves, into groups.
   - Through *social identification,* individuals come to bond with and take on the characteristics of their groups *(self-stereotyping).* When people identify strongly with a group, their self-descriptions become increasingly depersonalized as they include fewer idiosyncratic elements and more characteristics that are common to the group.
2. Self-esteem is shaped both by individuals' personal qualities and by the value of the groups to which they belong.
   - Those who join prestigious groups often have higher *collective self-esteem* than those who belong to less positively valued groups. However, individuals who are members of stigmatized groups, failing groups, or groups that are derogated by nonmembers often protect their collective self-esteem by rejecting negative information about their groups, stressing the relative superiority of their own groups to other groups (the *ingroup–outgroup bias*), and *social creativity.*
   - Individuals who identify strongly with a group, such as sports fans, experience the group's outcomes as their own.
   - By *basking in reflected glory (BIRGing),* individuals can stress their association with successful groups. By *cutting off reflected failure (CORFing),* they minimize their connection to stigmatized or unsuccessful group identities.
   - In some cases, individuals will choose to promote their own personal interests over their group's, minimizing their association with groups that are performing poorly and resigning from the group *(individual mobility).*

FOR MORE INFORMATION

Chapter Case: C.P. Ellis

- "C. P. Ellis," a chapter in Studs Terkel's book *American Dreams: Lost and Found,* (1980), describes Ellis's transformation from a prejudiced member of a hate group to an advocate of civil rights.

Inclusion, Exclusion, and Belonging

- "The Need to Belong: Desire for Interpersonal Attachments as a Fundamental Human Motivation," by Roy F. Baumeister and Mark R. Leary (1995), marshals evidence in support of their belonging hypothesis.

- *Ostracism: The Power of Silence* (2001), by Kipling D. Williams, examines the nature and consequences of exclusion for both those who are excluded and those who do the excluding.

Individualism and Collectivism

- *Habits of the Heart: Individualism and Commitment in American Life,* by Robert N. Bellah, Richard Madsen, William M. Sullivan, Ann Swidler, and Steven M. Tipton (1985), is a fascinating analysis of the connection between individuals and their groups.

- *Individualism and Collectivism,* by Harry C. Triandis (1995), examines recent theory and research dealing with the two sides of the self: the collective and the personal.
- "Rethinking Individualism and Collectivism: Evaluation of Theoretical Assumptions and Meta-Analyses," by Daphna Oyserman, Heather M. Coon, and Markus Kemmelmeier (2002), thoroughly explores the psychological implications of individual and cultural differences in individualism and collectivism, and is followed by a number of fascinating commentaries by experts in this area (M. H. Bond, 2002; A. P. Fiske, 2002; Kitayama, 2002; Joan G. Miller, 2002).

Social Identity

- "From I to We: Social Identity and the Collective Self," by Michael A. Hogg and Kipling D. Williams (2000), provides a general overview of the basic assumptions of social identity theory.
- "Social Identification," by Kay Deaux (1996), examines the psychological mechanisms involved in identification and the consequences of such identification for various aspects of the self.
- *Social Identity: Context, Commitment, Content,* edited by Naomi Ellemers, Russell Spears, and Bertjan Doosje (1999), examines many aspects of the way the self is transformed by group memberships.

MEDIA RESOURCES

 Visit the Group Dynamics companion website at http://psychology.wadsworth .com/forsyth4e to access online resources for your book, including quizzes, flash cards, web links, and more!

FORMATION

CHAPTER OVERVIEW

Many groups come into existence when individuals, prompted by their personal needs or by the press of environmental circumstances, seek a connection to others. Groups also spring up, sometimes unexpectedly, when people discover that they like one another, and this attraction provides the foundation for the development of interpersonal bonds. Other groups are founded rather than just found—they are deliberately created so that people can, through collaboration, achieve some specific purpose.

❖ Who joins groups?

❖ When do people seek out others?

❖ What processes generate bonds of interpersonal attraction between members of groups?

CHAPTER OUTLINE

The Impressionists: The Group that Redefined Beauty

The classicists dominated the world of art in 19th-century France. They favored religious and historical images, and they belittled any painter who offered a contrasting perspective on artistic form and content. But a dedicated band of radical painters and artists eventually overwhelmed the classicists. Two founding members of the movement, Claude Monet and Camille Pissarro, met in 1860 and immediately became friends. Two years later, Edouard Manet and Edgar Degas joined them in their search for alternative forms of artistic expression. Later that year, Monet met Pierre-Auguste Renoir, Alfred Sisley, and Frédéric Bazille and persuaded them to join the clique.

The young artists developed a new approach to painting, often journeying into the countryside to paint landscapes. They sometimes painted side by side and patiently critiqued one another's work. They also met in cafés in Paris to discuss technique, subject matter, and artistic philosophies. Art critics rejected their approach for years, and the artists scarcely earned enough money to survive. But, in time, they were recognized by the art community as a new school of painting—the *impressionists*—and their paintings are now revered and worth millions of dollars.

We can ask many questions about the artists who founded impressionism. How did they settle the many conflicts that threatened their group? Why did Manet become the group's leader and Degas the malcontent? How did the group counter the constraints imposed by the status quo? But one question—perhaps the most basic of all—concerns the group's origin. Why did it come into existence in the first place? In 1858, Manet, Monet, and the others were busy pursuing their careers independently. But by the mid-1860s, they had joined to form the most influential artists' circle of all time. What were the circumstances that drove these individuals to combine their resources in a group that endured for more than 30 years (Farrell, 1982; Kapos, 1995)?

This chapter answers this question in three parts. It begins with the artists themselves, for people's personalities, preferences, and prior experiences influence the extent to which they seek out membership in groups. Some of us are *joiners;* some of us are *loners.* Next, it considers the *situation,* for even a collection of highly sociable joiners must affiliate on at least one occasion before a group will form. Some situations push people together; others keep them apart. Affiliation, however, only sets the stage for group formation, for if the individuals who find themselves together are not *attracted* to each other, then a long-lasting group like the impressionists will likely not form. Some people like each other; some do not.

JOINING GROUPS

Claude Monet and Vincent van Gogh were both passionate about their art, and they experimented with creative, unconventional techniques. But whereas Monet joined with others whenever possible, van Gogh kept to himself, mostly interacting with his brother and with a few close friends. Why do some seek membership in groups, but others avoid them?

Personality

Not everyone who joins a group is a "joiner," and people who prefer independence over association are not necessarily "loners." But certainly people differ in their overall orientation toward groups. Due to differences in personality, preferences, and past experiences, some people are more like Monet—they seek out membership in groups. Others are like van Gogh—they avoid groups when they can.

INTROVERSION AND EXTRAVERSION The tendency to move toward people or away from people is a basic component of personality (C. G. Jung, 1924). Researchers attempting to distill personality down to a small number of key elements generally agree on five basic dimensions (often referred to as the "Big Five"). The first dimension in most of these models is **introversion–extraversion** (Goldberg, 1993). *Introverts* are withdrawn, quiet, reclusive, and shy; they remain detached, and even move away from others. *Extraverts,* in contrast, seek out contact with other people. They are sociable, outgoing, gregarious, and talkative. Extraverts, more than introverts, are likely to prefer the company of others, particularly in pleasant and enjoyable situations (Lucas & Diener, 2001). Different cultures imbue introversion and extraversion with unique, culture-specific meaning, but people all over the world spontaneously appraise their own and others' social tendencies (Digman, 1990; K. Yang & Bond, 1990).

Extraverts may seek out groups because such interactions are stimulating, and extraverts appreciate stimulating experiences more than introverts do (Eysenck, 1990). Extraverts' affinity for being part of a group may also be based on their relative sensitivity to rewards, and their expectation that social activities are more rewarding than nonsocial activities (Lucas, Diener, Grob, Suh, & Shao, 2000). Groups may also seek out extraverts rather than introverts. Some qualities, like intelligence, morality, and friendliness, are difficult to judge during initial encounters, but observers are particularly good at detecting extraversion in others (Albright, Kenny, & Malloy, 1988; Kenny, Horner, Kashy, & Chu, 1992). If a group is looking for people who will be sociable and connect easily with others, it might recruit extraverts more actively than introverts. As Focus 4-1 suggests, groups may also prefer extraverts as members because they tend to be more positive, enthusiastic, energetic, and happier.

RELATIONALITY Some people are more relationship centered than others. As Chapter 3 suggested, interdependent individuals value their connections with others more than individualists do, and they tend to define themselves in terms

---

introversion–extraversion The degree to which an individual tends to withdraw from or seeks out social contacts. Introverts are oriented primarily toward inner perceptions and judgments of concepts and ideas whereas extraverts are oriented primarily toward the social experiences.

FOCUS 4-1   Are Extraverts Happier than Introverts?

People who need people are the luckiest people in the world.

–Jule Styne and Bob Merrill, *Funny Girl*

Extraverts and introverts diverge in their overall level of gregariousness, but they also differ in their level of happiness, pleasant feelings, and well-being. Do you enjoy talking to strangers? Enjoy working with others? Like making decisions in groups? Do you like to go to parties? If yes, then you are in all likelihood a happier person than someone who prefers to avoid groups and enjoys solitary activities (Lucas et al., 2000, p. 468). This relationship was documented in a meta-analysis of 35 studies of personality and emotions, and it appears to know no cultural or national boundaries (Lucas & Fujita, 2000). When researchers measured the extraversion and emotions of students in 39 countries, extraversion predicted a higher degree of pleasant affect. Extraverts around the world are happier than introverts (Lucas et al., 2000).

Why are extraverts so happy? They may, by basic temperament, just be in good moods, for even when they are alone, extraverts report that they are happier than do introverts. Alternatively, introverts may be more negative in their mood because social demands cause them to associate so frequently with other people, even though they would prefer to be alone. Extraverts may also be more sensitive to rewarding experiences than are

introverts, for they often respond more positively to pleasant events than do introverts.

Research also suggests that the types of behaviors performed by extraverts—connecting with others, behaving in a friendly way, joining groups—are stronger triggers for happiness than the quiet and subdued behaviors performed by introverts. Researchers tested this behavioral hypothesis by giving participants small personal computers and asking them to record, five times a day for 2 weeks, what they did and how happy they felt. Investigators discovered that both introverts and extraverts who reported acting in extraverted ways reported experiencing more positive emotions. Even the introvert, who seeks to be alone, is happier when acting in extraverted ways. Concerned that people's overall level of happiness was influencing their tendency to seek out others, these researchers conducted a study in which they directly manipulated introversion and extraversion. They asked volunteers taking part in a group discussion to act as if they were extraverted (talkative, energetic, active, etc.) or introverted (reserved, quiet, passive, etc.). Those who acted in extraverted ways ended the study in better moods than did people who were told to act as if they were introverted (Fleeson, Malanos, & Achille, 2002). These findings suggest that groups hold the key to happiness, for people are happier when they are seeking out others than when they are limiting their connections to other people.

---

of their relationships with others (Cross & Morris, 2003). Hence, people who are higher in **relationality**—that is, their values, attitudes, and outlooks emphasize and facilitate establishing and maintaining connections to others—are more likely to value group memberships more. In one study, women's relationality did not predict how many relationships and memberships they had, but it did predict their commitment to those relationships. Women interacting briefly in dyads who were high in relationality enjoyed the group interaction more, as did those women who were partnered with someone who was high in relationality (Cross, Bacon, & Morris, 2000).

---

relationality   The degree to which one adopts a set of values, attitudes, and outlooks that emphasize and facilitate establishing and maintaining connections to others.

Social Motivation

Why did Monet rely on other people rather than pursue his goals alone? Motivational theorists argue that **social motives**—such as the need for affiliation, intimacy, and power—guide the choices we make and the goals we seek (Geen, 1995; Murray, 1938).

NEED FOR AFFILIATION People who seek out contact with other people often have a high **need for affiliation.** People with a high need for affiliation tend to join groups more frequently, spend more of their time in groups, communicate more with other group members, and accept other group members more readily (McAdams & Constantian, 1983; McClelland, 1985; Smart, 1965). However, they are also more anxious in social situations, perhaps because they are more fearful of rejection by others (Byrne, 1961; McAdams, 1982, 1995). When others treat them badly or reject them, they avoid people rather than seek them out (C. A. Hill, 1991).

NEED FOR INTIMACY Individuals who have a high **need for intimacy,** like those who have a high need for affiliation, prefer to join with others. Such individuals, however, seek close, warm relations and are more likely to express caring and concern for other people (McAdams, 1982, 1995). They do not fear rejection but, instead, are more focused on friendship, camaraderie, reciprocity, and mutual help. In one study, researchers gave people electronic pagers for one week and asked them to write down what they were doing and how they felt each time they were beeped. People who had a high need for intimacy were more frequently interacting with other people when beeped. They were also happier than people with a low need for intimacy if they were with other people when they were beeped (McAdams & Constantian, 1983).

NEED FOR POWER Because group interactions provide many opportunities to influence others, those with a high **need for power** also tend to seek out groups (McAdams, 1982; Winter, 1973). Researchers studied college students' power needs by asking them to recall 10 recent group interactions that lasted for at least 15 minutes. The students described what had happened in each episode, what had been discussed, and their role in the group. Those with a high power motive took part in relatively fewer dyadic interactions but in more large-group interactions (groups with more than four members). They also reported exercising more control in these groups by organizing and initiating activities, assuming

---

social motive A want or need that is satisfied through social interactions with other people, including the need for affiliation, intimacy, and power.

need for affiliation The dispositional tendency to seek out others

need for intimacy The dispositional tendency to seek warm, positive relationships with others.

need for power The dispositional tendency to seek control over others.

TABLE 4-1 The Fundamental Interpersonal Relations Orientations– Behavior Scale (FIRO-B)

Dimension	Need to Express the Behavior	Need to Receive the Behavior from Others
Inclusion	I try to be with other people.	I like people to invite me to things.
	I join social groups.	I like people to include me in their activities.
Control	I try to take charge of things when I am with people.	I let other people decide what to do.
	I try to have other people do things I want done.	I let other people take charge of things.
Affection	I try to be friendly to people.	I like people to act friendly toward me.
	I try to have close relationships with people.	I like people to act close toward me.

Source: FIRO: A Three-Dimensional Theory of Interpersonal Behavior by W. C. Schutz. Copyright 1958 by Holt, Rinehart, & Winston, Inc.

responsibility, and attempting to persuade others. This relationship between the need for power and participation in groups was strongest for men (McAdams, Healy, & Krause, 1984).

FIRO William C. Schutz (1958, 1992) integrated the need for affiliation, intimacy, and power in his **Fundamental Interpersonal Relations Orientation** theory, or **FIRO** (rhymes with "*I* row"). Schutz identified three basic needs that can be satisfied when we are in groups. *Inclusion*—the desire to be part of a group and to be accepted by a group—is similar to the need for affiliation. The second motive, *control,* corresponds to the need for power; it is the need to guide the group by organizing and maintaining the group's processes. *Affection,* or openness, is the desire to experience warm, positive relations with others, which is similar to the need for intimacy.

Schutz believed that these needs influence group behavior in two ways: They determine how we treat other people and how we want others to treat us. Inclusion involves our desire to join with other people and our need to be accepted by them. Control refers to our need to dominate others but also to our willingness to let others dominate us. Affection includes a desire to like others as well as a desire to be liked by them. The FIRO-B scale, which Schutz developed, measures both the need to express and the need to receive inclusion, control, and affection (see Table 4-1).

Fundamental Interpersonal Relations Orientation (FIRO) A theory of group formation and development proposed by William Schutz that emphasizes compatibility among three basic social motives: inclusion, control, and affection.

Groups offer members a way to satisfy these basic needs. If, for example, Angela has a strong need to receive and express inclusion, she will probably prefer to do things in a group rather than to perform tasks individually. If she needs to express control, she may seek membership in a group that she can control. Or if she wishes to receive affection from others, she may seek out other people who seem warm and friendly. In general, then, the greater the intensity of these needs in any given individual, the more likely that person is to take steps to create or seek out membership in a group (Schutz, 1958, 1992).

Experience and Preference

Not everyone is thrilled at the prospect of joining groups. New residents in a neighborhood, students entering a high school or college, and new employees may find that they are offered many opportunities to take part in such formal and informal groups as neighborhood associations, student government, sororities, unions, and water cooler brigades. The decision to join such groups depends on one's previous experiences with such groups. Those with little prior experience or with negative experiences in groups avoid membership in groups, whereas group veterans or those with many positive prior experiences seek them out (Bohrnstedt & Fisher, 1986; Corning & Myers, 2002; Ickes & Turner, 1983).

Richard Moreland, John Levine, and their colleagues' studies of college students' decision to join one of the many groups that abound on university campuses underscore the impact of one's past history with groups on one's future in groups. In one study, they surveyed more than a thousand first-year students at the University of Pittsburgh, asking them if they took part in groups in high school and if they expected to join groups in college. They discovered that students came to college with widely differing opinions about the value of groups. Some felt that their high school groups were enjoyable and important, but others saw little of value in these past affiliations. Significantly, as Figure 4-1 indicates, those with positive prior experiences were more positive about the value of groups in college, and they were more likely to seek out groups when they reached college (Brinthaupt, Moreland, & Levine, 1991; Moreland, 1987; Pavelchak, Moreland, & Levine, 1986).

Social Anxiety and Shyness

Just as one's personality and social motives may push people toward groups, other personal qualities may push them away. Shyness reduces the frequency and quality of one's group experiences. As early as age 2, some children begin to display fear or shyness when they encounter a person they do not recognize (Kagan, Snidman, & Arcus, 1992). Some grade school children consistently seek out other people, whereas others show signs of shyness and withdrawal when they are in groups (Asendorpf & Meier, 1993). Shy adults report feeling awkward, uncomfortable, and tense when interacting with people they do not know very well

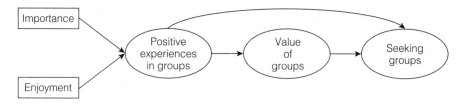

FIGURE 4-1

Does a person's past experience with groups influence their future with groups? Students who had positive experiences in groups in high school were more likely to seek out groups to join in college (the direct relationship between "positive experiences in groups" and "seeking groups"). Also, prior experiences influenced their evaluation of groups as a means to reach their goals, and this attitude influenced their tendency to seek out groups to join (the indirect relationship from "positive experiences" to "value of groups" to "seeking groups"). *Source:* Pavelchak et al., 1986, p. 59.

(Cheek & Buss, 1981). Shy people join groups less frequently than nonshy individuals (Zimbardo, 1977b).

Most people manage to cope with their shyness. In some cases, however, shyness escalates into **social anxiety** (Vertue, 2003). Historical accounts of the troubled life of van Gogh, for example, comment on his anxiety over his failed relationships. He had some friends, and he tried to join his fellow artists, but he could not sustain these relationships.

Social anxiety sets in when people want to make a good impression, but they do not think that their attempts to establish relationships will succeed (Leary, 2001; Leary & Kowalski, 1995). Because of these pessimistic expectations, when these individuals interact with other people, they suffer troubling emotional, physiological, and behavioral side effects. They feel tense, awkward, uncomfortable, and scrutinized. They become physiologically aroused to the point that their pulse races, they blush and perspire, and they feel "butterflies" in their stomach. This anxiety can cause them to *disaffiliate*—to reduce the amount of social contact they have with others (Leary & Kowalski, 1995, p. 157). Socially anxious people, even when they join groups, do not actively participate; they can be identified by their silence, downcast eyes, and low speaking voice. They may also engage in *innocuous sociability* (Leary, 1983): They merge into the group's background by indicating general interest in the group and agreement with the other group members while consistently minimizing their personal involvement in the group interaction.

---

social anxiety A feeling of apprehension and embarrassment experienced when anticipating or actually interacting with other people.

Attachment Style

Developmental psychologists recognize that infants and young children differ in the way they respond to their parents. Some seem very secure and comfortable in their relationship to their caregivers, and so, when placed in a strange environment, they feel free to explore it so long as their parent is nearby. Other children, in contrast, seem to be more uncertain of their parents' supportiveness, and some even seem to ignore their parents altogether.

These observations formed the basis of *attachment theory,* which explains the way people differ in their relationships, or attachments, to others. The theory suggests that these childhood differences emerge in adulthood in variations in **attachment style**—one's basic cognitive, emotional, and behavioral orientation when in a relationship with others. Studies of children's attachments to their parents and adults' relationships with romantic partners have identified at least three basic attachment styles (Hazan & Shaver, 1987):

- *Secure* individuals are comfortable with intimacy. They enjoy forming close relationships with other people, and they do not worry about being abandoned by their loved ones.
- *Avoidant* types evade intimacy with others. They are uncomfortable relying on other people, and they complain that their partners ask for more intimacy than they can easily provide.
- *Anxious* people desire intimacy, but they are nonetheless worried that their loved ones will reject them.

These types appear to be based on two underlying dimensions: anxiety about relationships and avoidance of closeness and dependency on others (Brennan, Clark, & Shaver, 1998).

People's attachment style influences their romantic and family relationships, but it also influences their group relationships. The *Group Attachment Scale,* for example, asks group members to indicate their agreement with such statements as "I find it difficult to allow myself to depend on my group," "I sometimes worry that I will be hurt if I allow myself to become too close to my group," and "I am somewhat uncomfortable being close to my group." People with anxious group attachment styles questioned their acceptance by their group and reported feeling as if they were unworthy of membership. They spent less time in their groups, engaged in fewer collective activities, and were less satisfied with the level of support they received from the group. Those with avoidant group attachment styles felt that the group was less important to them, and they were more likely to claim that they were planning to leave the group (E. R. Smith, Murphy, & Coats, 1999). When researchers observed people with varying attachment styles interacting in small groups, they discovered that people with secure attachment styles contributed to both the instrumental and the relationship activities of the

---

attachment style One's characteristic approach to relationships with other people; the basic styles include secure, avoidant, and anxious.

group. Those with more anxious attachment styles, in contrast, contributed less to the group's instrumental work, and those with avoidant attachment styles contributed less to both instrumental and relationship activities (Rom & Mikulincer, 2003).

Men, Women, and Groups

Nearly all the impressionists were men; Morisot and Cassatt were exceptions. Why? Are men more likely to join together with other men, or are women the more social sex?

Studies of men and women have found some differences in their tendency to join groups, but the differences are far from clear. Women tend to be somewhat more extraverted than men, particularly on aspects of this trait concerned with interpersonal warmth and gregariousness (Costa, Terracciano, & McCrae, 2001). Women remember more details about their relationships than do men, and they more accurately recount events that occurred in their social networks (M. Ross & Holmberg, 1992; S. E. Taylor et al., 2000). Women, if asked "Are close relationships an important reflection of who you are?" or "Do you usually feel a strong sense of pride when someone close to you has an important accomplishment?" are more likely to reply "yes" than are men (Cross et al., 2000). When asked to take photographs that describe how they see themselves, women are more likely to include pictures of themselves with other people rather than alone (Dollinger, Preston, O'Brien, & DiLalla, 1996). Overall, women tend to adopt more collectivistic, interdependent orientations than do men (see Chapter 3).

Other studies, however, have questioned the magnitude and meaning of these differences between the sexes. Even though women may put more value on their relationships, they may not be any more social than men. When investigators sampled 800 adults in the United States, they found that men belonged to more professional groups, governing boards, political parties, and military organizations than women. Men had more friends than women, but women reported closer ties with members of their family, and they spent more time in their groups than did men (Booth, 1972). Another survey found that women belonged to more religious and informal recreational groups than men and that women's associations were more intimate and caring (Umberson, Chen, House, Hopkins, & Slaten, 1996). Survey researchers also found that younger men (18- to 26-year-olds) visited with friends and attended parties more frequently than younger women, and that women spent more time with their families. Boys are also more oriented toward the group than are girls, who tend to be more oriented toward specific individuals, with whom they build close relationships (Benenson, Apostoleris, & Parnass, 1997). The sexes do not differ in the time spent in solitary activities (Osgood, Wilson, O'Malley, Bachman, & Johnston, 1996). Studies of community action groups also find no consistent sex differences (Parkum & Parkum, 1980), and women are just as likely as men to join atypical groups, such as cults, satanic covens, and communes (Pittard-Payne, 1980). Women-only groups can be, but are not necessarily, more cohesive than groups with only male members (Rogelberg & Rumery, 1996).

The differences that emerge, although subtle, indicate that women seek membership in smaller, informal, intimate groups, whereas men seek membership in larger, more formal, task-focused groups. These tendencies may reflect women's and men's differing interpersonal orientations. Men tend to define themselves as individuals separate and distinct from others, whereas women's self-definitions may be more interpersonal, defining themselves in terms of their memberships in groups and their relationships with other people (S. E. Taylor et al., 2000). The differences may also reflect the emphasis that the two sexes put on achieving power and establishing connections with others (Baumeister & Sommer, 1997). Both these goals can best be achieved in groups, but they require membership in different types of groups. Men, seeking power and influence, join competitive, goal-oriented groups, where they can vie for status. Women, seeking intimate relationships, would be more likely to join small, supportive groups. Indeed, women's groups tend to be more unified than men's groups (Booth, 1972; C. T. Hill & Stull, 1981; Winstead, 1986).

These sex differences are also entangled with role differences and cultural stereotypes. In cultures where men and women tend to enact different roles, the roles may shape opportunities for involvement in groups. If women are primarily responsible for domestic duties and childbearing, their opportunities for membership in groups may be limited (J. M. Nielsen, 1990). Hence, as attitudes toward the role of women have changed in contemporary society, differences in social participation have also begun to diminish (Lal Goel, 1980; D. H. Smith, 1980). Sexist attitudes may also work to exclude women and men from certain types of groups. Women, for example, were until recently deliberately excluded from juries in the United States. (The United States' Supreme Court ruled that women could not be excused from jury duty because of their sex in 1975.) As sexist attitudes decline, differences in membership in various types of groups may also abate.

GROUP AFFILIATION

Why do people join together with others in groups? In part, the motivation comes from *within* the members themselves, for people's personalities, preferences, and other personal qualities predispose them to affiliate with others. But the tendency to affiliate with others also comes from *without*—from the situation itself. People often seek the company of others when they find themselves in ambiguous, frightening, and difficult circumstances.

Social Comparison

The young impressionists faced uncertainty each time they stood before a blank canvas. They were convinced that the methods taught by the traditional Parisian art schools were severely limited, but they were not sure how to put their

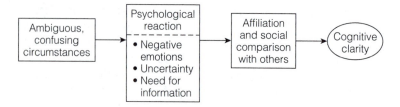

FIGURE 4-2

How do people respond when they are uncertain and confused?
Festinger's (1954) theory of *social comparison* assumes that people rely
on others for information.

alternative approach into practice. So they often painted together, exchanging
ideas about colors and techniques, as they refined their approach to art.

Many years ago, Leon Festinger (1950, 1954) suggested that in many cases,
people seek out others because they require information about themselves and
the environment. Although, in some instances, physical reality provides an objective standard for the validation of personal opinions, beliefs, or attitudes, in
other cases, individuals must turn to social reality to test their validity. People engage in **social comparison** to determine if their beliefs, opinions, or attitudes
are consistent with the interpretations of appropriate others (see Figure 4-2). Although Festinger believed that social comparison is usually guided by the need
for accurate information, researchers now believe that people engage in social
comparison for a variety of different reasons—to evaluate their own qualities, to
set personal goals, to help other people, or to (they hope) discover that they are
superior to the people around them (Suls & Wheeler, 2000; J. V. Wood, 1996).

MISERY LOVES COMPANY Social comparison theory suggests that people join
with others to acquire information, by comparing their personal viewpoints to
the views expressed by others to determine if those views are "correct," "valid,"
or "proper" (Goethals & Darley, 1987). Stanley Schachter (1959) tested this hypothesis by convincing participants that they faced an ambiguous and possibly
dangerous situation. When the women he recruited for his study arrived, the researcher introduced himself as Dr. Gregor Zilstein from the Medical School's
Departments of Neurology and Psychiatry. In serious tones, he explained that he
was studying the effects of electric shock on human beings. In one condition (*low
anxiety*), the room contained no electrical devices; the experimenter explained
that the shocks would be so mild that they would "resemble more a tickle or a
tingle than anything unpleasant" (p. 14). Participants assigned to the *high-anxiety*

---

social comparison Evaluating the accuracy of personal beliefs and attitudes by comparing oneself to others.

condition, however, faced a vast collection of electrical equipment and were informed, "These shocks will hurt, they will be painful . . . but, of course, they will do no permanent damage" (p. 13). The researcher then asked the participant if she wanted to wait for her turn alone or with others. Many more of the women in the high-anxiety condition (63%) than in the low-anxiety condition (33%) chose to wait with others. Schachter concluded that "misery loves company" (1959, p. 24).

MISERY LOVES MISERABLE COMPANY Schachter, by placing people in a threatening situation, discovered that people preferred to await their fate with others rather than alone. But what was their primary motivation for joining with others? Did they wish to acquire information through social comparison, or were they just so frightened that they did not want to be alone? Schachter examined this question by replicating the high-anxiety condition of his original experiment, complete with the shock equipment and Dr. Zilstein. He held anxiety at a high level, but manipulated the amount of information that could be gained by affiliating with others. He told half of the women that they could wait with other women who were about to receive shocks—who were *similar* to the participants. He told the others that they could join women "waiting to talk to their professors and advisors" (1959, p. 22)—the *dissimilar* condition. Schachter hypothesized that if the women believed that the others could not provide them with any social comparison information, there would be no reason to join them. The findings confirmed his analysis: 60% of the women asked to wait with others if they all faced a similar situation, but no one in the dissimilar condition expressed affiliative desires. Schachter, recognizing that people prefer to compare themselves to similar rather than dissimilar others, concluded "Misery doesn't love just any kind of company, it loves only miserable company" (Schachter, 1959, p. 24).

Subsequent studies confirmed Schachter's conclusion but added several important qualifications. Schachter assumed that people preferred to join with someone who was facing the same threat because they would provide more useful information. But how would participants have reacted if they had been offered the chance to wait with someone who had participated in the study the previous day? Such individuals would be ideal sources of clarifying information, for they did not just face the same situation; they had already gone through the same situation. In a replication of Schachter's work, participants preferred to join someone who had already gone through the procedure (L. A. Kirkpatrick & Shaver, 1988). Similarly, 60% of the patients about to undergo surgery chose a roommate who was recovering from the same type of operation, whereas only 17% wanted "miserable company"—a roommate who was also about to undergo the operation (Kulik & Mahler, 1989). They also reported talking with their roommate about the operation more if their roommate had already had the operation and was recovering (Kulik, Mahler, & Moore, 1996). These studies suggest that people are more interested in gaining clarifying information than in sharing the experience with someone, particularly when the situation is a dangerous one and they can converse openly with other group members (Kulik & Mahler, 2000).

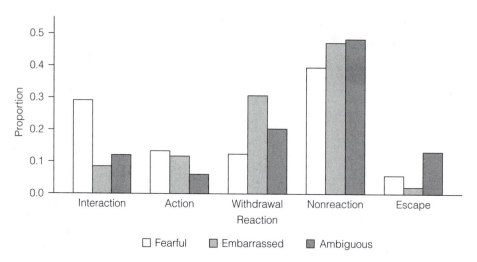

FIGURE 4-3

When do people seek social comparison information? People who faced an ambiguous situation did not talk among themselves (*interaction*) as much as people who were fearful. People who were anxious and embarrassed, in contrast, interacted the least, and they often withdrew from the group. *Source:* Morris et al., 1976.

EMBARRASSED MISERY AVOIDS COMPANY People who find themselves in ambiguous, threatening circumstances seek out the company of others, but what if the situation is more embarrassing than dangerous? Researchers examined this question by watching the way group members reacted in frightening, ambiguous, and embarrassing situations. The investigators asked four to six strangers to meet in a room labeled with the sign "Sexual Attitudes—Please Wait Inside." In the *fear-provoking* condition, the room contained several electrical devices and information sheets that suggested that the study involved electric shock and sexual stimulation. In the *ambiguous* condition, the participants found only two cardboard boxes filled with computer forms. In the *anxiety-provoking* (embarrassing) condition, the equipment and boxes were replaced by contraceptive devices, books on venereal disease, and color pictures of nude men and women. Observers behind a one-way mirror watched the group for 20 minutes, recording the five types of behavior shown in Figure 4-3: *interaction* (talking about the situation), *action* (e.g., examining the equipment), *withdrawal* (e.g., reading a book), *controlled nonreaction* (e.g., talking about something other than the experiment), and *escape* (Morris et al., 1976).

The observers discovered that the group members engaged in social comparison the most when they were fearful. As Figure 4-3 indicates, groups who faced the ambiguous situation spent about 12% of the time talking among themselves, but groups sitting in a room with the fear-inducing electrical equipment spent nearly 30% of the time gathering information through communication. Groups who thought that the study involved sexual behavior interacted the least, and they also showed more withdrawal. When people worry that they will be embarrassed when they join a group, they *usually* do not affiliate with others. However, when their need for information or support becomes overwhelming, their embarrassment-related anxieties may not keep them away from the group (Buunk & Hoorens, 1992; Davison, Pennebaker, & Dickerson, 2000).

MISERY LOVES MORE MISERABLE COMPANY (SOMETIMES) Monet, by joining with the other artists, gained information about art, technique, and ways of dealing with the officials who judged art exhibitions in Paris. This information undoubtedly reduced his confusion, but this cognitive clarity may have come at an emotional cost. Renoir, like Monet, was experimenting with many new methods, but Renoir was prospering; his art sold well in the Parisian market. Compared to Renoir, Monet was a failure. And how did Monet feel when he spoke to his friend Sisley? Sisley's work was never considered to be collectible, and he lived on the brink of poverty for much of his life. When Monet compared himself to Sisley, he must have felt a sense of relief that his own situation was not so bleak, but at the same time, he must have worried that his own career could take a turn for the worst at any moment.

Monet engaged in **downward social comparison** when he chose Sisley as a target for his comparison and in **upward social comparison** when he compared himself with Renoir. In many cases, people prefer downward social comparison to upward comparison. Downward social comparisons remind us that we are doing better than others. Our own plight often seems less bleak and our coping more effective in comparison to people who are doing worse than we are (J. V. Wood, 1989). Upward social comparison, in contrast, can leave us feeling like failures. When students were asked to keep track of the people they compared themselves to over a two-week period, they reported feeling depressed and discouraged when they associated with superior people (L. Wheeler & Miyake, 1992). Because these negative consequences of upward social comparison appear to be greatest when the comparisons involve attributes or skills that are central to individuals' self-definitions, individuals may deliberately avoid joining groups that include people who outperform them in spheres they consider to be personally important (Lockwood & Kunda, 1997; see Focus 4-2). However, these negative consequences of upward social comparison diminish when the person who outperforms us is a source of inspiration and hope (R. L. Collins, 2000). We also react more positively when the person who outperforms us is a member of our ingroup. In such cases, their success reflects on the accomplishments and status of our group, our identity, and ourselves (Blanton, Crocker, & Miller, 2000; M. T. Schmitt, Silvia, & Branscombe, 2000).

---

downward social comparison Comparing oneself to others who are performing less effectively relative to oneself.

upward social comparison Comparing oneself to others who are performing more effectively relative to oneself.

FOCUS 4-2   How Do People React to Others' Triumphs and Tragedies?

schadenfreude \SHAHD-n-froy-duh\, *noun:*
"A malicious satisfaction in the misfortunes of
others."
–Word of the Day (2000)

A single player out of 42 is chosen for the all-star team. One of the members of your study group gets the lowest grade on the exam. A member of the work squad is singled out by management for a raise. How do we react when a member of our group succeeds or fails? Abraham Tesser's **self-evaluation maintenance (SEM) model** suggests that we often graciously celebrate others' accomplishments. When our comembers shine, we can brag about our close connection to them, bask in the reflected glory (BIRG) of their accomplishments, and even hint that we helped them along the way to their goals. But what if they surpass us in areas that we ourselves value greatly? What if *we* wanted to make the all-star team, wanted the best grade for ourselves, or were seeking the promotion they received? The SEM model suggests that when someone bests us in a domain that we value greatly, their success will more likely trigger resentment, envy, and shame rather than pride and admiration (R. H. Smith, 2000). The SEM model predicts a preference for friends and coworkers who (1) perform worse than we do on tasks that we think are important but (2) perform very well on tasks that we

do not think are important (Beach & Tesser, 2000; Tesser, 1988, 1991).

Tesser and his colleagues examined this tension between sharing others' successes and highlighting their failures by asking elementary school students to identify the types of activities (sports, art, music, math) that were personally important to them. The students also identified their most and least preferred classmate. One week later, the students rated their ability, their close classmate's ability, and their distant classmate's ability in one area they felt was important and one area they felt was unimportant. As Figure 4-4 indicates, if the students thought that the task was important, they judged their performance to be superior to that of their close friend. If the task was not important to them personally, they felt that they had performed relatively worse (Tesser, Campbell, & Smith, 1984). Similarly, in a study of married couples, Tesser and his colleagues discovered that happy couples felt that it was more pleasant to be outdone by one's partner in an area that their partner valued but to outperform the partner in an area that he or she did not value. Unhappy couples did not recognize this secret to a successful relationship (Beach et al., 1998).

Other investigators have even discovered that the desire to outperform others—especially those that are close to us and are seeking goals that we value—may cause people to withhold

Social Support

Monet initially sought to change the art world single-handedly, but he soon found that he needed help from others. When his work was condemned by the critics, he shared his feelings of rejection with the other artists, who offered him encouragement and advice. Frequently penniless, he sold his work to other artists so he could buy food and pay for his lodging. He could not afford his own

---

self-evaluation maintenance (SEM) model A theory proposed by Abraham Tesser that assumes individuals maintain and enhance self-esteem by associating with high-achieving individuals who excel in areas that are not relevant to one's own sense of self-esteem and avoiding association with high-achieving individuals who excel in areas that are important to one's sense of self-esteem.

FOCUS 4-2   (*continued*)

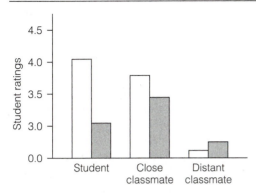

FIGURE 4-4

Do we like people who outperform us on tasks that we think are important? When students rated their own performance on a task they felt was important to them, they rated themselves as somewhat better than their close friend and much better than their distant classmate. However, students rated their friend more positively than themselves when the task had no implications for their self-worth. *Source:* "Friendship Choice and Performance: Self-Evaluation Maintenance in Children" by A. Tesser, J. Campbell, and M. Smith. In J. Suls and A. G. Greenwald (Eds.), *Psychological Perspectives on the Self* (vol. 2). Copyright 1983 by Lawrence Erlbaum Associates, Inc. Reprinted by permission.

help from others. Investigators asked students to keep track of every single one of their interactions with other people for 6 days. After each interaction, they were to note if the interaction involved academic matters or social matters, what their relationship to the person was (e.g., acquaintance, stranger, close friend), and if they shared information with that person that they thought would help the other to improve. As the SEM model suggests, these students gave helpful information to their friends when the interactions pertained to social matters, but when it came to academics, they helped their friends less than they helped strangers. This tendency was even more pronounced when the students thought that their friend was already performing better than they were (Pemberton & Sedikides, 2001).

studio, so Bazille and Renoir invited him to share one with them. When Monet injured his leg, Bazille cared for him. It seemed that whenever Monet encountered a problem, a disaster, or a difficulty, his group helped him cope with each adversity.

COPING WITH STRESS IN GROUPS Schachter (1959) did not just place people in a confusing, ambiguous situation. He put people into a frightening, stressful situation. The women he studied affiliated with others to acquire clarifying information through social comparison, but they were probably also seeking reassurance. Two people, facing the prospect of receiving electric shocks, could examine the situation, but they could also talk about their misgivings, calm each other down, and help one another should problems arise. Given a choice between people who are equal in their knowledge of the situation but vary in their emotional reaction to the threat—some are very fearful, but others are calm—people choose to wait with those who are calm (Rabbie, 1963).

Chapter 3 noted that humans are group-seeking animals, but our gregariousness becomes particularly robust under conditions of stress. In times of trouble, such as illness, divorce, catastrophe, natural disaster, or personal loss, people seek out friends and relatives (Dooley & Catalano, 1984). When people experience strong emotions, they share those emotions by talking to friends and loved ones in about 90% of the cases (Rimé, Philippot, Boca, & Mesquita, 1992). College students who are experiencing problems, academically or socially, spend between 28% and 35% of their time interacting with people they feel are supportive (R. E. Harlow & Cantor, 1995). Individuals experiencing work-related stress, such as layoffs, time pressures, or inadequate supervision, cope by joining with coworkers (R. D. Caplan, Vinokur, Price, & Van Ryn, 1989; C. L. Cooper, 1981). Individuals who have been reminded of their own mortality are more likely to sit closer to other people, even if these other individuals do not share their opinions on important social issues (Wisman & Koole, 2003). People also react to large-scale traumatic events by seeking out others. When U.S. President John F. Kennedy was assassinated, 60% of adult Americans reported seeking solace by talking to others (Sheatsley & Feldman, 1964). In the days following the terrorist attack on September 11, 2001, 98% of all adult Americans reported talking to others about the attack, 60% reported taking part in a group activity, and 77% sought to strengthen their connection to their loved ones (M. A. Schuster et al., 2001). Many individuals joined virtual groups via the Internet. Internet usage declined overall, but discussion areas, forums, and chat room use surged, as did e-mail rates. Nearly three quarters of all Internet users (72%) used e-mail to contact family and friends or to share news about the attack (Ranie & Kalsnes, 2001).

Affiliation with others plays a key role in both "*fight-or-flight*" responses and "*tend-and-befriend*" responses to stress. In the **fight-or-flight response** to stress, an animal reacts to imminent danger by fleeing from it or striking back against the threat. When in groups, individuals can work together to fight against a common threat—they can rally against attackers, organize a concerted response to a disaster, and so on. Groups also enhance escape behaviors, in some cases. If escape routes are not restricted, the dispersion of a group can confuse attackers and increase the chances that all members of the group will escape unharmed. A group can also organize its escape from danger, with stronger members of the group helping less able members to reach safety. Groups also play a central role in the **tend-and-befriend response** to stress recently proposed by Shelley E. Taylor and her colleagues (2000). Taylor suggested that some people, but women in particular, respond to chronic stress by increasing their nurturing, protective,

---

fight-or-flight response A physiological response to stressful events characterized by the activation of the sympathetic nervous system (increased heart rate, pupil dilation) that readies the individual to counter the threat (fight) or to escape the threat (flight).

tend-and-befriend response An interpersonal response to stressful events characterized by increased nurturing, protective, and supportive behaviors (tending) and by seeking out connections to other people (befriending).

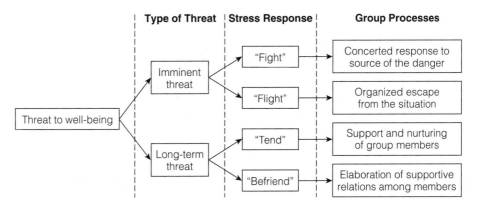

FIGURE 4-5

How do groups help members cope with stressful events? The two basic responses to stress—*fight-or-flight* and *tend-and-befriend*—are both enhanced when members rely on resources made available by their groups.

and supportive behaviors (*tending*) and by seeking out connections to other people (*befriending*). Women not only tend to respond to stress by affiliating with others, but others also show a disproportionate preference to join with women rather than men when they themselves are stressed (see Figure 4-5).

SOURCES OF SUPPORT IN GROUPS How do groups help their members to cope with stressful experiences? Groups offer members **social support**—personal actions and resources that help members cope with minor aspects of everyday living, daily hassles, and more significant life crises (Finch et al., 1997; E. A. Skinner, Edge, Altman, & Sherwood, 2003). As Table 4-2 indicates, group members provide *emotional support* when they compliment and encourage one another, express their friendship for others, and listen to others' problems without offering criticism or suggestions. They offer *informational support* when they give directions, offer advice, and make suggestions about how to solve a particular problem. Groups also provide *instrumental support* when members help each other with their work, do favors for each other, or lend each other money. A group may also be a source of *spiritual support* when it helps members to resolve existential dilemmas or resolve threats to one's worldview. Finally, groups may comfort members just by including them. A group offers members a safe haven—a shelter from the storm of stress.

Admittedly, some groups fail to deliver on their promise of support. They add stressors by stirring up conflicts, increasing responsibilities, and exposing members to criticism (Hays & Oxley, 1986; M. Seeman, Seeman, & Sayles, 1985). Overall,

---

social support Emotional support, advice, guidance, tangible assistance, and spiritual perspective given to others when they experience stress, daily hassles, and more significant life crises.

TABLE 4-2 Some Forms of Social Support Provided by Groups

Type of Support	Example
Approval	Expressing acceptance of person Expressing approval for entire group Demonstrating friendship
Emotional	Complimenting and encouraging others Showing respect for abilities or skills Listening to others' problems Sharing feelings Responding nonverbally to others' disclosures (e.g., hugging, nodding)
Informational	Providing information Giving directions, advice, and suggestions Demonstrating a way to perform a task Explaining problems, approaches
Instrumental	Helping one another with work Doing favors Lending money
Spiritual	Providing explanations for challenging events Allaying existential anxiety, fear of death

however, groups are more frequently supportive than burdensome. People who receive support from others tend to experience less stress in their lives, are less likely to suffer from depression and other psychological problems, and are physically healthier (Barrera, 1986; Herbert & Cohen, 1993; Uchino, Cacioppo, & Kiecolt-Glaser, 1996). Social support is particularly valuable when people find themselves in threatening circumstances—a divorce, a job change, a move, or the like. Stressful life circumstances leave us at risk for psychological and physical illness, but groups can serve as protective buffers against these negative consequences (S. Cohen & Wills, 1985; Wills & Cleary, 1996). Researchers verified this *buffering effect* in one study of individuals trying to recover from a devastating crisis (e.g., the death of a spouse or child). People who were more firmly embedded in a social network of friends, relatives, and neighbors were less depressed than people who were not integrated into groups (Norris & Murrell, 1990).

Collaboration

The impressionist artists' circle was both a found group and a founded group. It emerged, for the most part, as personal and situational forces combined to create relationships among individuals who found themselves repeatedly interacting with one another in the streets, cafés, and studios of Paris. But the impressionists' group was also the result of deliberate planning. Monet and his small circle of close confidants founded it in an attempt to influence the opinions of the Academy of Fine Arts.

TABLE 4-3 Some of the Many Goals Accomplished by Groups

Purpose of the Group	Typical Groups
Accomplish heavy, arduous tasks	Construction crew, assembly line, expeditionary team
Administer a company or organization	Executive committee, trustees, regents, administrators
Advise others	Consulting group, quality circles
Build and repair	Roofers, team of carpenters, an auto shop
Discover new information	Research team, professional society
Effect social change	Citizens action group, political party
Entertainment—fine arts	Orchestra, dance company, drama troupe
Entertainment—informal	Parties, dinners, cook-outs
Entertainment—leisure	Hobby club, discussion group, book club
Entertainment—sports	Baseball team, soccer club, intramural team
Heal members and nonmembers	Surgery team, emergency room staff
Home life and care of relatives	Families, communes, kibbutzes
Maintain and enforce the law	Police, citizen security groups, judicial groups
Make resources available	Bank, rental agency
Observe and celebrate	Patriotic society, veterans' groups
Plan strategy, direct others, lead	Executives, board of directors
Production	Factory, production line
Protect members from harm	Neighborhood watch association, gangs, army platoons, police units
Reduce costs for members	Buyers' cooperative, trade association
Reduce monotony	Quilting groups, cohesive work teams
Render decisions on guilt	Jury, hearing panel
Respond to problems	Firefighters, paramedic squad
Set standards for others to follow	Legislative body, ethics review board
Solve problems	Committee, commission, task force, research staff
Teach and learn	School, class, study group
Transport	Airplane crew, ship captain and crew
Worship	Religious body, congregation, cult

Sources: Adapted from Arrow, McGrath, & Berdahl, 2000; D. J. Devine, 2002; Zander, 1985.

GROUPS WITH A PURPOSE Groups are often spawned when one or more individuals confront an obstacle, a problem, or a task they wish to overcome, solve, or complete; but they recognize that the solution is beyond the reach of a single individual. Such situations require collaboration among individuals, who combine their personal energies and resources in joint activities aimed at reaching both individual and group goals (Zander, 1985).

Table 4-3 samples only a portion of the astonishing variety of groups that people have founded in their efforts to reach their goals. Some of these groups, such as families, social movements, communes, and parties, are typically begun by one or more individuals who then remain in the group as it works to reach its designated goals. A small Internet start-up company, a study group, an expeditionary team, or a grassroots community action group would all be *member-founded groups*. Other groups, in contrast, are begun by individuals or authorities outside the group. A team of laborers digging a trench, the flight crew of an airplane, and a military squad would all be *mandated groups* (or *concocted* groups), because those who created them are not actually members of the group (Arrow, McGrath, & Berdahl, 2000). Complex organizations, such as large corporations, usually include both types of groups. A manufacturing company, for example, may include a group of executives and their subordinates who make decisions about procedures and policies (a *command group*) and a number of interdependent task groups that complete the work necessary to generate the company's products (*work groups*).

COLLABORATIVE GROUP TASKS Collaborative groups differ in size, duration, and complexity, but they are all alike in that their raison d'être is a task that can be best accomplished through the interdependent action of multiple individuals. In general, as tasks become more difficult, complex, and consequential, the more likely people will prefer to complete them through coordinated activity rather than individual action (Karau & Williams, 1993; Zander, 1985).

- *How difficult is the task?* In some circumstances, people are faced with tasks that are well beyond the skills and resources of a single individual. No one person, no matter how talented, can compile a dictionary of all the words in the English language, construct a nuclear power plant, or overthrow a political dictator. Other tasks are difficult ones because they require enormous amounts of time or strength. One talented individual could build a car or dig a 100-yard-long trench, but a crew of workers will accomplish these tasks more quickly and with better results. The duration of the task also influences its difficulty. Projects that take months or years to complete are best attempted by multiple individuals, so that the work continues even when specific individuals leave the team.
- *How complex is the task?* A single person cannot perform Beethoven's Fifth Symphony or compete against the New York Yankees. Individuals may be able to carry out specific assignments with great skill, but some tasks involve multiple interdependent subtasks that must each be completed in a specific sequence before the goal is reached.
- *How important is the task?* Problems are not equal in their overall significance. A flat tire or a bad head cold pale in importance when compared to inequalities in the criminal justice system, uncontrolled pollution, and global warming. When the effects of succeeding or failing at a task are consequential for many people for a long period of time, individuals are more likely to collaborate with others.

Other, more psychological and interpersonal factors also influence people's interest in collaborating with others. When individuals fear that they will be blamed for a bad decision or outcome, they might form a group to make the decision to avoid full responsibility for the negative outcome (Leary & Forsyth, 1987). People also form groups when they are dissatisfied with the status quo and feel that the system can be changed only through collective action. A community group seeking lower taxes, the civil rights movement, Mothers Against Drunk Driving (MADD), or street gangs exemplify such groups (see Focus 4–3). People may even found a group or join an existing group so that they can enjoy the fruits of the group's labors without having to invest very much of their own personal time. As shown in Chapter 9, when people's individual contributions to a group's goal are not easily identified, they often do less than their fair share.

Group Attraction

Monet met Pissarro, quite by happenstance, when they were both attending art classes in Paris. Their desire to learn more about their craft and their enrollment in the same school combined to bring them together. But this chance meeting by itself was not sufficient to spark the formation of the group that would, in time, become the impressionists. Monet and Pissarro would not have chosen to spend more and more time together discussing art, politics, and Parisian society if they had disliked each other. Affiliation may set the stage for a group to form, but *attraction* among the members transforms acquaintances into friends.

Interpersonal Attraction and Group Formation

Theodore Newcomb was intrigued by the way networks of likes and dislikes generate groups. He decided to bring together a small number of people who were strangers to one another for a prolonged period of time, and then observe how the naturally occurring attraction between individuals would create groups within the overall set of participants. He offered 17 young men starting their studies at the University of Michigan free rent if they answered a detailed survey of their attitudes, likes, and dislikes each week. Then he watched as the 17 students sorted themselves out into friendship pairs and distinct groups. Even though the participants were assigned to their rooms at random, most of them ended up liking their roommate the most of all the other group members. Newcomb also found, however, that the 17-man group split into two subgroups containing 9 and 7 members (one person was an outcast from both subgroups). The 7-man group was particularly unified, for when asked to indicate who they liked in the total group, they gave relatively high rankings to one another. The remaining members of the total group did not show the same level of mutual attraction as the smaller clique (T. M. Newcomb, 1960, 1961, 1979, 1981).

Newcomb confirmed his basic hypothesis. Groups are, in many cases, "mutual admiration societies," for they form when two or more individuals find that they like each other. But his study also offered insights into the reasons why certain members liked each other and why others disliked one another. As the

FOCUS 4-3   Why Join a Gang?

It's like a comfortable feeling, you got someone to back you up and protect you.

—"Billy," 21-year-old North Side Crip (Decker & Van Winkle, 1996, p. 74)

Gangs are often characterized as disruptive, violent groups of delinquents who commit robberies, hijack cars, distribute drugs, murder, and generally live outside the boundaries of "normal" society. But objective analyses of the characteristics of these "neighborhood associations" suggest that violence is rarely the defining feature of such groups. Gangs do tend to contend against legal authorities, but in many cases, the members are connected to their community through their membership in more traditional social groups (church congregations, families, schools). Some gangs are also just loose associations of smaller cliques of three or four members, and these subgroups are "much more important to the individual boy than his relationship to the gang" (Thrasher, 1927, p. 322; see also Coughlin & Venkatesh, 2003).

Gangs also emerge for many of the same reasons that any group is formed. One study of gangs in East Los Angeles, for example, traced many of these groups back to a much smaller cluster of friends who lived near one another (J. Moore, 1991). The founders of the group were very similar to one another in terms of ethnicity and age, and they were committed to increasing the level of safety in their neighborhoods. Over time, more people joined the groups, which gradually became more formally organized, more territorial, and more likely to engage in criminal behavior. Gangs also tend to be relatively task focused. When members were asked why they joined the gang, most stressed the usefulness of the gang as a means of achieving valued goals. As Figure 4-6 indicates, nearly all the gang members interviewed in one study said that safety was a major reason for joining a gang. They also agreed that gangs provided members with a means of earning money—usually by selling drugs. As one member remarked, "There's money in a gang. I want to be in it, you see a lot of money in it man. That's why I really got in the gang, money and all" (quoted in Decker & Van Winkle, 1996, p. 74). Many gang members also agreed that gang membership increased their status in the community and helped them socially. "One thing I like about gangs it's more people to be around, more partners to go places with . . . social stuff" (quoted in Decker & van Winkle, 1996, p. 75).

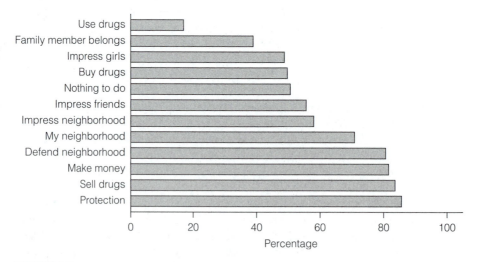

FIGURE 4-6

How do members of gangs explain their decision to join? They are more likely to mention instrumental concerns—such as protection and the need to make money selling drugs—than a concern for gaining status and impressing other people. Other factors, such as having a family member in the gang or the gang's access to drugs, were also mentioned as reasons for joining.

sections that follow indicate, people are more likely to associate with certain people—those who are nearby, those who express similar attitudes and values, and those who respond positively to them—and such associations often culminate in the creation of a group.

THE PROXIMITY PRINCIPLE Group members often assume that their groups result from rational planning or common interests. But the **proximity principle** suggests that in some cases, people join groups that just happen to be close by. When teachers assign students seats in classrooms, cliques of pupils in adjacent seats develop (M. W. Segal, 1974). Newcomb (1960) discovered that young men assigned to rooms at random were more likely to form friendships with their roommates or with students assigned to nearby rooms. Commuters who regularly use the same subway stops in New York City eventually gel into identifiable groups, as do students who patronize the same bars near college campuses (Milgram, 1992; Willsie & Riemer, 1980). Monet, Manet, Degas, and many other impressionists lived in the same neighborhood in Paris. Their paths crossed and crossed again, until eventually a group was formed.

We do not form groups with people who happen to be nearby because we are shallow or indiscriminating. Rather, proximity increases interaction between people, and interaction cultivates attraction. As Richard L. Moreland (1987) noted in his *social integration theory* of group formation, groups emerge gradually over time as individuals find themselves interacting with the same subset of individuals with greater and greater frequency. Repeated interactions may foster a sense of "groupness," as the interactants come to think of themselves as a group, and people outside the group begin to treat them as a group (Arkin & Burger, 1980). Close proximity also sets the stage for mere exposure. We are likely to more frequently see people whose offices, homes, and desks are located near ours, and this frequent exposure may increase our liking for them (R. F. Bornstein, Leone, & Galley, 1987). Close proximity may also, as the following section notes, promote the growth of social networks.

THE ELABORATION PRINCIPLE Groups, as self-organizing, dynamic systems, tend to increase in complexity over time. A group that begins with only two members tends to grow in size as these individuals become linked to other nearby individuals. According to systems theory, "the basic dynamic of elaboration is the proliferation of elements and ties," which "are linked together to form a functional unit called a group" (Arrow et al., 2000, pp. 91–92).

Newcomb's groups, for example, conformed to this **elaboration principle,** for cliques usually evolved from smaller, dyadic pairings. The first friendships

---

proximity principle The tendency for individuals to form interpersonal relations with those who are close by.

elaboration principle The tendency for groups to expand as members form dyadic associations with someone who is not in the group and thereby draw the nonmember into the group.

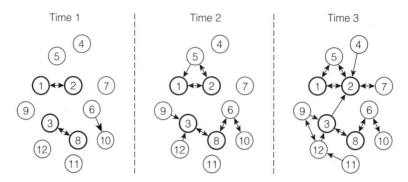

FIGURE 4-7

Do groups form through elaboration? A systems theory approach to groups suggests that groups form as simple groups (such as dyads) become more complex and unpatterned relationships become self-organized. Through dyadic elaboration, individuals who are initially linked together only in one-to-one, dyadic relationships (e.g., Person 1 and 2, Person 3 and 8) expand their networks to include additional elements (members). When centralized elaboration occurs, single individuals (Persons 2 and 3) become the hub for the formation of groups.

were two-person pairs—usually roommates or people living in adjoining rooms who became friends. Over time, these dyads expanded to include other individuals who were attracted to one or both of the original members. This same kind of self-organizing process has been documented in other emerging groups, such as adolescents' peer group associations, leisure groups, and social movements (Benford, 1992). A gang is formed when three friends refer to themselves with a shared name and recruit other friends to join the group (J. Moore, 1991). Friendships were very likely to form between students who were linked to the same individuals (Gibbons & Olk, 2003). Groups form when otherwise unrelated individuals are drawn to a single individual, who becomes the hub for gradually developing bonds among the various members (Redl, 1942). The impressionists developed into a group through such a self-organizing process. Monet and Pissarro became friends first; then other artists bonded with either Monet or Pissarro (see Figure 4-7).

THE SIMILARITY PRINCIPLE When Newcomb examined the subgroups that emerged spontaneously in his dormitory study, he noticed that subgroup members' values, beliefs, and interests were similar. One clique, for example, contained men who endorsed liberal political and religious attitudes, were all registered in the arts college, came from the same part of the country, and shared similar aesthetic, social, theoretical, economic, political, and religious values. The members of the second subgroup were all veterans, were majors in engineering, and shared similar religious, economic, and political values. (T. M. Newcomb,

1960, 1961, 1963). Newcomb had found strong evidence for the **similarity principle:** We like people who are similar to us in some way.

Similarity is a social magnet that creates all kinds of relationships. People tend to marry people who are similar to them; they join groups composed of others who are like them; and they live in communities where people are more alike than different. Although these similarities often reflect agreements in attitudes, values, and beliefs, they are also based on irrelevant demographic characteristics, such as race, ethnicity, sex, and age (Lazarsfeld & Merton, 1954). As a result, most groups are characterized by **homophily.** The cliques that form in large volunteer organizations tie together people who are similar in some way rather than dissimilar (Feld, 1982). If a group decreases in size, the first individual who is dropped from membership will likely be the one who is the least similar to the other members; ties between similar people are maintained, but ties with dissimilar people dissolve. "Birds of a feather flock together" describes most groups.

Why are people drawn to others who are similar to them in some way? Homophily appears to be sustained by a number of psychological, sociological, and relational factors that combine to promote contacts between people who share similarities rather than differences (McPherson, Smith-Lovin, & Cook, 2001). Because people who adopt the same values and attitudes that we do reassure us that our beliefs are accurate, we find association with such people very rewarding (Byrne, 1971). People may also assume, with some justification, that future group interactions will be more cooperative and conflict free when members are all similar to one another (Insko & Schopler, 1972). Similarity may also increase a sense of connectedness to the other person (Arkin & Burger, 1980). Two strangers chatting casually on an airplane, for example, feel united if they find that they share even the smallest similarity, such as the same middle name or favorite television program. Disliking a person who seems similar may also be psychologically distressing. After all, if a person is similar to us, it follows logically that he or she must be attractive (Festinger, 1957; Heider, 1958). Homophily also tends to beget homophily. Because communities, schools, and most workplaces bring people together who are similar in terms of race, attitudes, religion, and ethnicity, people's options for relationships are limited to those who are already similar to them in these ways (McPherson et al., 2001).

THE COMPLEMENTARITY PRINCIPLE The similarity principle exerts a powerful influence on groups, but sometimes we prefer the company of people who are dissimilar to us. If, for example, Claude enjoys leading groups, he will not be attracted to other individuals who also strive to take control of the group.

---

similarity principle The tendency to affiliate with or be attracted to similar others; this tendency causes groups and other interpersonal aggregates to be composed of individuals who are similar to one another rather than dissimilar.

homophily The tendency for group members to display certain affinities, such as similarities in demographic background, attitudes, values, or so on; the overall degree of similarity of individuals within the same group.

Instead, he will respond more positively to those who accept his guidance. According to the **complementarity principle,** we are attracted to people who possess characteristics that complement our own personal characteristics (Kerckhoff & Davis, 1962; Levinger, Senn, & Jorgensen, 1970; Meyer & Pepper, 1977).

Which tendency is stronger, similarity or complementarity? Some investigators, working primarily with dyads, have found that similarity is much more common than complementarity (Levinger et al., 1970; Magaro & Ashbrook, 1985; Meyer & Pepper, 1977). Other researchers, however, have found that the members of close-knit groups tend to possess compatible but somewhat dissimilar needs (Kerckhoff & Davis, 1962; O'Connor & Dyce, 1997). In all likelihood, group members respond positively to both similarity and complementarity. We may, for example, be attracted to people whose qualities complement our own, yet we may also feel that we are very similar to such people (Dryer & Horowitz, 1997). We may also prefer people who are similar to us in some ways, but who complement us in other ways. Studies of interpersonal complementarity indicate that people prefer to interact with others who match their general level of friendliness, warmth, and positivity. Positive behaviors, such as seeming sociable, reassuring, and considerate, tend to elicit similar levels of friendliness in response. However, people generally respond to dominant behaviors by acting submissively, and vice versa, so leaders seek out followers, and the strong seek out the weak (e.g., Tracey, Ryan, & Jaschik-Herman, 2001).

Similarly, William Schutz (1958) distinguished between *interchange compatibility* and *originator compatibility*. **Interchange compatibility** exists when group members have similar expectations about the group's intimacy, control, and inclusiveness. Interchange compatibility would be high if all the members expect that their group will be formally organized with minimal expressions of intimacy, but low if some think that they can share their innermost feelings whereas others want a more reserved exchange. **Originator compatibility** exists when people who wish to act on their needs for control, inclusion, and affection join with people who wish to accept these expressions of control, inclusion, and affection. For example, originator compatibility would be high if a person with a high need to control the group joined a group whose members wanted a strong leader.

Schutz tested his theory by constructing groups of varying compatibility. He created originator compatibility by placing in each group one member with a high need for control, one member with a high need for inclusion, and three

---

complementarity principle The tendency for group members to like people who are dissimilar to them in ways that complement their personal qualities.

interchange compatibility As described by William Schutz, compatibility between group members based on their similar needs for inclusion, control, and affection.

originator compatibility As described by William Schutz, compatibility between group members that occurs when individuals who wish to express inclusion, control, or affection within the group are matched with individuals who wish to receive inclusion, control, or affection from others.

members with lower needs for control and inclusion. Moreover, interchange compatibility was established by grouping people with similar needs for affection. All the groups in this set were compatible, but levels of affection were high in half of the groups and low in the other half. A set of incompatible groups was also created by including group members who varied significantly in their need for affection, ranging from high to low. As Schutz predicted, (1) cohesiveness was higher in the compatible groups than in the incompatible groups, and (2) the compatible groups worked on problems far more efficiently than the incompatible groups. He found similar results in studies of groups that formed spontaneously, such as street gangs and friendship circles in fraternities (Schutz, 1958).

THE RECIPROCITY PRINCIPLE When Groucho Marx joked, "I don't want to belong to any club that will accept me as a member," he was denying the power of the **reciprocity principle**—that liking tends to be met with liking in return. When we discover that someone else accepts and approves of us—they give friendly advice, compliment us, or declare their admiration for us—we usually respond by liking them in return (S. C. Jones, 1973; Shrauger, 1975). Newcomb (1979) found strong evidence of the reciprocity principle, as did other investigators (Kandel, 1978; M. W. Segal, 1979; T. L. Wright, Ingraham, & Blackmer, 1984). Some group members, like Groucho Marx, may not like to be liked, but these exceptions to the reciprocity principle are relatively rare.

Negative reciprocity also occurs in groups: We dislike those who seem to reject us. In one study, college students discussed controversial issues in groups. Unknown to the true participants in the experiment, two of the three group members were confederates of the experimenter, who either accepted or rejected the comments of the participant. During a break between the discussion and the completion of a measure of attraction to the group, the rejecting confederates excluded the participant from their discussion by talking among themselves and giving the participant an occasional "dirty" look. Naturally, participants were less attracted to their comembers if they had been rejected by them. The rejection also served to lower participants' opinions of themselves (Pepitone & Wilpinski, 1960).

THE MINIMAX PRINCIPLE What draws people toward some groups, and what pushes them away from others? As noted in Chapter 2, social exchange theory is based on the **minimax principle:** People will join groups and remain in groups that provide them with the maximum number of valued rewards while incurring the minimum number of possible costs (Kelley & Thibaut, 1978; Moreland & Levine, 1982; Thibaut & Kelley, 1959). Rewards include acceptance by others,

---

reciprocity principle The tendency for liking to be met with liking in return; if A likes B then B will tend to like A.

minimax principle The tendency to prefer relationships and group memberships that provide the maximum number of valued rewards and incur the fewest number of possible costs.

camaraderie, assistance in reaching personal goals, social support and comparison information, exposure to new ideas, and opportunities to interact with people who are interesting and attractive. But groups have costs as well—time, money, energy, and the like. When researchers asked prospective group members to identify the rewards and costs they felt the group might create for them, 40% mentioned such social and personal rewards as meeting people, making new friends, developing new interests, or enhancing their self-esteem. They also mentioned such rewards as learning new skills, increased opportunities for networking, and fun. The prospective members also anticipated costs, however. More than 30% expected to lose time and money by joining a group. Other frequently mentioned costs were social pressures, possible injury or illness, and excessive demands made by the group for their time. The prospective members in this study, by the way, optimistically felt that the groups they were considering joining would offer them far more rewards than costs (Brinthaupt, Moreland, & Levine, 1991; Moreland, Levine, & Cini, 1993).

The group members themselves are also an important source of rewards and costs. People are usually attracted to groups whose members possess positively valued qualities and avoid groups of people with objectionable characteristics. We prefer to associate with people who are generous, enthusiastic, punctual, dependable, helpful, strong, truthful, and intelligent (Bonney, 1947; Thibaut & Kelley, 1959). We tend to dislike and reject as potential group members those individuals who possess socially unattractive personal qualities—people who seem pushy, rude, self-centered, or boring (Gilchrist, 1952; Iverson, 1964). People who complain too frequently are also viewed negatively (Kowalski, 1996), as are bores who sidetrack the group unnecessarily, show little enthusiasm, and seem too serious and preoccupied with themselves (Leary, Rogers, Canfield, & Coe, 1986). Many of the impressionists, for example, considered having to interact with Degas a major cost of membership. In a letter to Pissarro, Gustave Caillebotte wrote, "Degas introduced disunity into our midst. It is unfortunate for him that he has such an unsatisfactory character. He spends his time haranguing at the Nouvelle-Athènes or in society. He would do much better to paint a little more" (quoted in Denvir, 1993, p. 181).

The Economics of Membership

Why did such artists as Manet, Pissarro, and Bazille join with Monet to create an artists' circle? As we have seen, the group offered its members a number of advantages over remaining alone. By joining Monet, the impressionists gained a sounding board for ideas, social support, help with tasks they could not accomplish alone, and friends. But the group also created costs for members, who had to spend time and personal resources before they could enjoy the benefits the group offered. The minimax principle argues that those who joined the group must have felt that the benefits outweighed the costs.

Do we, then, join *any* group that promises us a favorable reward/cost ratio? Howard Kelley and John Thibaut argued that although we may be attracted to such groups, our decision to actually join is based on two factors: our *comparison level* and our *comparison level for alternatives*. **Comparison level (CL)** is the standard by which individuals evaluate the desirability of group membership. The CL derives from the average of all outcomes known to the individual and is usually strongly influenced by previous relationships. If, for example, Degas's prior group memberships yielded very positive rewards with very few costs, his CL should be higher than that of someone who has experienced fewer rewards and more costs through group membership. According to Thibaut and Kelley, groups that "fall above CL would be relatively 'satisfying' and attractive to the member; those entailing outcomes that fall below CL would be relatively 'unsatisfying' and unattractive" (Thibaut & Kelley, 1959, p. 21; see also Kelley & Thibaut, 1978).

Comparison level, however, only predicts when people will be *satisfied* with membership in a group. If we want to predict whether people will join groups or leave them, we must also take into account the value of other, alternative groups. What if Degas could have joined several artists' circles, all of which surpassed his CL? Which one would he then select? According to Thibaut and Kelley (1959), the group with the best reward/cost balance will determine Degas's **comparison level for alternatives (CL_{alt}).** Thibaut and Kelley argued that "CL_{alt} can be defined informally as the lowest level of outcomes a member will accept in the light of available alternative opportunities" (1959, p. 21).

Entering and exiting groups is largely determined by CL_{alt}, whereas satisfaction with membership is determined by CL (see Table 4-4). For example, why did Degas initially join the impressionists, but eventually leave the group? According to Thibaut and Kelley, Degas intuitively calculated the positive and negative outcomes that resulted from membership in the group. This index, at least at first, favored the impressionists. If Degas believed that joining the group would surpass his comparison level (CL), then he would likely be satisfied with membership. But over time, the demands of the group became too great and the rewards too small, the group's value dropped below his CL, and he became dissatisfied. If the group's value dropped below Degas's intuitive estimations of the value of other groups (his CL_{alt}), then he would likely leave the impressionists and join another, more promising group. In Degas's case, the alternative of remaining alone established the lower level of his CL_{alt}.

The rest of the impressionists, however, remained friends. They often exhibited their works individually and spent months in isolation, but they still

----

comparison level (CL) In John Thibaut and Harold Kelley's social-exchange theory, the standard by which the individual evaluates the quality of any social relationship. In most cases individuals whose prior relationships yielded positive rewards with few costs will have higher CLs than those who experienced fewer rewards and more costs in prior relationships.

comparison level for alternative (CL_{alt}) In John Thibaut and Harold Kelley's social-exchange theory, the standard by which individuals evaluate the quality of other groups that they may join.

TABLE 4-4 The Impact of Comparison Level (CL) and Comparison Level for Alternatives (CL$_{alt}$) on satisfaction with group membership and the decision to join a group

Membership in the Group is	Membership in the Group is	
	Above CL	Below CL
Above CL$_{alt}$	Membership is satisfying, will join group	Membership is dissatifying, but will join group
Below CL$_{alt}$	Membership is satisfying, but will not join group	Membership is dissatisfying and will not join group

Source: Adapted from Thibaut & Kelley, 1959.

provided each other with help as necessary. Indeed, for many years, they met regularly at the Café Riche, where they would discuss art, politics, and literature. In time, they reached their goal of fame and fortune. By the turn of the century, most were invited, at last, to present in traditional shows, and collectors payed handsome prices for their work. They came to Paris to learn to paint as individuals, but they changed the world's definition of fine art as a group.

SUMMARY IN OUTLINE

❖ Who joins groups?

1. The tendency to join groups is partly determined by individuals' personal qualities, including traits, social motives, and gender.

2. The personality trait *introversion–extraversion* predicts the extent to which individuals are drawn to other people and groups (*extravert*) or tend to avoid groups (*introvert*), as does their level of *relationality*. Perhaps for that reason, extraverts tend to be happier than introverts.

3. The strength of *social motives*, such as the *need for affiliation*, the *need for intimacy*, and the *need for power* also predict one's group-joining proclivities. Schutz's *Fundamental Interpersonal Relations Orientation* (*FIRO*) theory explains how people use groups to satisfy their need to receive and express inclusion, control, and affection.

4. Individuals who have had prior positive experiences in groups tend to seek out memberships, whereas those individuals who experience shyness and *social anxiety* are less likely to join groups.

5. Differences in *attachment style* also predict one's willingness to join groups, and in some cases, men and women exhibit differences in their orientation toward groups.

❖ When do people seek out others?

1. People often seek the company of others when they find themselves in ambiguous, frightening, and difficult circumstances.

2. Schachter found that people who face an ambiguous situation affiliate to acquire information through *social comparison.* However,

- When people worry that they will be embarrassed when they join a group, they usually do not affiliate with others.
- By choosing comparison targets who are performing poorly compared to themselves (*downward social comparison*), individuals bolster their own sense of competence, and by choosing superior targets (*upward social comparison*), individuals refine their expectations.
- The *self-evaluation maintenance (SEM) model* argues that people prefer to associate with individuals who do not outperform them in areas that are very relevant to their self-esteem.

3. Individuals often seek out group members when facing stressful situations.

- Group behaviors facilitate both the "*fight-or-flight*" and the "*tend-and-befriend*" responses to stress.
- Groups can be sources of *social support* and so provide a protective buffer during times of stress.

4. Groups are useful on a practical level. People often found groups when they face goals that they cannot attain working alone. Even gang members often note pragmatic reasons for joining these groups.

❖ **What processes generate bonds of interpersonal attraction between members of groups?**

1. Newcomb, in his studies of the acquaintance process, found that people who like one another often bond together to form a group. Attraction patterns are generally consistent with the following principles:

- *Proximity principle:* People tend to like those who are situated nearby.
- *Elaboration principle:* Groups often emerge as complex systems when additional elements (people) become linked to the original members.
- *Similarity principle:* People like others who are similar to them in some way. In consequence, most groups tend toward increasing levels of *homophily.*
- *Complementarity principle:* People like others whose qualities complement their own qualities.
- *Reciprocity principle:* Liking tends to be mutual.
- *Minimax principle:* Individuals are attracted to groups that offer them maximum rewards and minimal costs.

2. *Social exchange theory* maintains that satisfaction with group membership is primarily determined by *comparison level* (CL), whereas the *comparison level for alternatives* (CL$_{alt}$) determines whether members will join, stay in, or leave a group.

FOR MORE INFORMATION

Chapter Case: The Impressionists

- *Canvases and Careers: Institutional Change in the French Painting World,* by Harrison C. White and Cynthia A. White (1993), com-

prehensively examines the sociological mechanisms that set the stage for the impressionists' success.

- *The Chronicle of Impressionism,* by B. Denvir (1993), provides the timeline for the development of the impressionists and includes reproductions of both their art and their personal correspondence.

Affiliation

- *Social Anxiety,* by Mark R. Leary and Robin M. Kowalski (1995), is a highly informative discussion of the causes and consequences of social anxiety.
- *The Psychology of Affiliation,* by Stanley Schachter (1959), describes the exacting scientific methods he used to document when and why we seek out others.

- *Handbook of Social Comparison: Theory and Research,* edited by Jerry Suls and Ladd Wheeler (2000), includes chapters on virtually all aspects of social comparison processes.

Attraction

- "The Formation of Small Groups," by Richard L. Moreland (1987), provides an overall framework for understanding group formation by describing four ways individuals become integrated into a group: environmental integration, behavioral integration, affective integration, and cognitive integration.

MEDIA RESOURCES

 Visit the Group Dynamics companion website at http://psychology.wadsworth.com/forsyth4e to access online resources for your book, including quizzes, flash cards, web links, and more!

5

Cohesion and Development

CHAPTER OVERVIEW

In physics, cohesion is the molecular integrity of matter. In group dynamics, cohesion is the solidarity and integrity of a group. All groups must be at least minimally cohesive—otherwise the members would drift apart—but some groups are more cohesive than others. As cohesion and commitment ebb and flow with time, the group's influence over its members rises and falls.

❖ What is group cohesion?

❖ Does cohesion develop over time?

❖ What are the positive and negative consequences of cohesion?

❖ Should organizations rely on teams to enhance productivity?

CHAPTER OUTLINE

CASE STUDY
The U.S. Olympic Hockey Team: Miracle Makers

THE NATURE OF GROUP COHESION
Cohesion Is Attraction
Cohesion Is Unity
FOCUS 5-1 Hazing: Do Initiations Create Cohesion?
Cohesion Is Teamwork
What Is Group Cohesion?

COHESION AND COMMITMENT OVER TIME
Stages of Group Development
Cycles of Group Development

CONSEQUENCES OF COHESION
Member Satisfaction and Adjustment
Group Dynamics and Influence
Group Productivity
FOCUS 5-2 Does Stress Lead to a Loss of Team Perspective?

COHESION AT WORK: TEAMS
Teams in Organizations
Building Teams in Organizations
Are Teams Effective?

Summary in Outline

For More Information

Media Resources

The U.S. Olympic Hockey Team: Miracle Makers

They were underdogs, and they knew it. Their mission: To represent their country, the United States, in the 1980 Winter Olympics. Their goal: To win a bronze, silver, or gold medal in hockey. Their task: To defeat teams from such hockey-rich countries as Sweden and Germany. Their major obstacle: The world-famous U.S.S.R. National Championship Team. The Russian players were practically professionals—as members of the Russian army, they were paid to practice and play their sport. They had beaten all their previous opponents in the Olympics easily, and were poised to take their 5th consecutive gold medal in the sport. In fact, in an exhibition game held just a few days before the start of the Olympic Games, Russia beat the U.S. team 10 to 3.

But strange things happen when groups compete against groups. The U.S. team made its way through the preliminary rounds and faced the awesome Russian team in the medal round. The U.S. team fell behind by two goals, and it looked as though the Russians would take victory with ease. But the plucky U.S. team kept struggling, finally taking the lead with 8 minutes left to play. During the game's last minutes, the Russians launched shot after shot, but all the while the U.S. coach, Herb Brooks, calmed his players by telling them "Play your game!" As the game's end neared, the announcer counted down the seconds over his microphone before asking his listeners, "Do you believe in miracles?" What else could explain the game's outcome? The U.S. Olympic Hockey Team, expected to win a game or two at most in the entire series, had just beaten an unbeatable team.

The U.S. team was inferior to the Russian team in nearly all respects. The U.S. players were mostly college students or recent graduates. They were smaller, slower, and inexperienced. The team was relatively unpracticed, for only 6 months before, Herb Brooks had recruited each player from schools and jobs across the country. But for all their weaknesses, they had one quality that the Russian team lacked: They were cohesive. They were filled with a sense of purpose, of duty, and esprit de corps. No one player took credit for the victory, but instead spoke only of "we," repeating "we beat those guys" over and over as the bewildered Russian team looked on.

Many believed that their cohesiveness was the deciding factor in their victory. But what is group cohesion, after all? Why did the U.S. team have this unique quality, and why did the Russian team lack it? Is cohesiveness such a valuable commodity that it can offset inadequate training and skills and thereby turn a mediocre group into a great group? Is cohesiveness so wondrous that we should strive to transform all our groups into cohesive teams? This chapter considers the mysteries of cohesiveness by specifying its nature, causes, and consequences.

THE NATURE OF GROUP COHESION

Cohesive groups come in many shapes and sizes. Consider the executive board of a company that meets weekly for many years. It is an efficient, productive group, yet the members never associate with one another after work. In fact, most dislike one another. The fictional coterie of six men and women living in New

York as *Friends* is also cohesive. The members accomplish very little in their time together, but they are so closely interconnected that they move through one problematic experience after another without a loss of synchrony. The U.S. Hockey Team, too, was cohesive. Each member feared he would be cut from the team before the Olympics, so competition among players ran high, but in the end they bonded together and managed to win a gold medal against all odds.

All of these groups are cohesive, but they are cohesive in different ways. In some cases, their cohesion springs from the bonds between group members: The members are close friends who are networked together in a group. Other groups, in contrast, are cohesive because their members share a deep sense of belonging to the group itself; they use words such as *family, community,* or just *we* to describe their group. Some groups, too, are cohesive because the members are all striving together to accomplish some goal. As the following sections note, these three interrelated social processes—attraction, unity, and shared commitment to tasks—are the glues that hold groups together.

Cohesion Is Attraction

Kurt Lewin, Leon Festinger, and their colleagues conducted some of the first studies of group cohesion at the Research Center for Group Dynamics. As early as 1943, Lewin used the term *cohesion* to describe the forces that keep groups intact by pushing members together and countering forces that push them apart (Zander, 1979). Festinger and his colleagues, in their studies of groups that spring up spontaneously in housing complexes, defined *group cohesion* as "the total field of forces which act on members to remain in the group" (Festinger, Schachter, & Back, 1950, p. 164). But when they measured cohesion, they focused on one "force" more than all others: attraction. They asked the group members (residents) to identify all their good friends and calculated the ratio of ingroup choices to outgroup choices. The greater the ratio, the greater was the cohesiveness of the residential group (Dion, 2000).

Cohesion, then, can be considered a form of *attraction*—"that group property which is inferred from the number and strength of mutual positive attitudes among the members of a group" (A. J. Lott & Lott, 1965, p. 259). As Figure 5-1 indicates, this attraction creates connections at two levels: the individual level and the group level. At the individual level, specific group members may be attracted to other group members. The players on the hockey team, for example, roomed with each other, ate their meals together, and practiced for hours together, and, in time, friendships developed. At the group level, the members of a cohesive group develop a positive attitude toward the group itself. Most of the players on the hockey team, for example, became very positive toward the team as a whole, and considered it to be the best hockey team in the world. They were proud to be members. These two forms of attraction—individual and group—usually covary, for friendship among the members of a group tends to generate liking for and pride in the group as a whole (Mullen & Copper, 1994). But friendship need not always go hand-in-hand with group pride, particularly if groups focus on work or performance rather than leisure or socializing. When cohesion is based

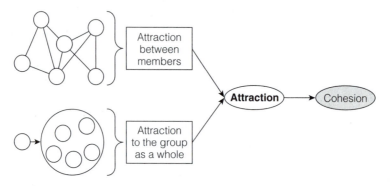

FIGURE 5-1

Is cohesion attraction? Some theorists feel that the members of cohesive groups both like each other individually and like the group as a whole.

on friendships and the friends leave the group, the remaining members are more likely to quit. When cohesion is based on pride in the group, people remain members even when specific members leave the group (Carron, Widmeyer, & Brawley, 1988; Mobley, Griffeth, Hand, & Meglino, 1979).

Some researchers prefer to reserve the term *cohesion* for group-level attraction only. Michael Hogg and his colleagues, for example, argued that although members of cohesive groups usually like one another, this personal attraction is not group cohesion. Rather, group cohesion corresponds to a form of group-level attraction that Hogg labeled *social attraction*—a liking for other group members that is based on their status as typical group members. Unlike personal attraction, which is grounded on relationships between specific members, social attraction is depersonalized, for it is based on admiration for individuals who possess the kinds of qualities that typify the group. Hogg found that any factor that increases members' tendency to categorize themselves as group members (e.g., conflict with other groups, the presence of an outgroup, activities that focus members' attention on their group identity) will reduce personal attraction but increase depersonalized, social attraction (see Hogg, 1992, 2001, for a review).

Cohesion Is Unity

In physics, the molecular integrity of matter is known as *cohesiveness*. When matter is cohesive, the particles that constitute it bond together so tightly that they resist any competing attractions. But when matter is not cohesive, it tends to disintegrate over time as the particles drift away or adhere to some other nearby object. Similarly, in human groups, cohesion is the integrity, solidarity, and sense of community of aggregated individuals. A cohesive group is a unified one, so members literally "stick together"—they stand closer together and they position themselves to prevent nonmembers from intruding on the group's space (Knowles & Brickner, 1981). When members talk about themselves and their

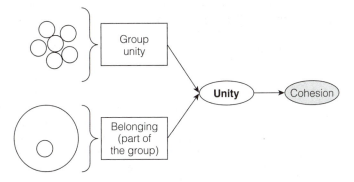

FIGURE 5-2
Is cohesion unity? Some theorists feel that a cohesive group is a unified group and that members feel closely connected to such groups.

group, they use more plural pronouns than personal pronouns: "We won that game" or "We got the job done" rather than "I got the job done" (Cialdini et al., 1976). Cohesive therapy groups end their sessions with longer "group hugs" than noncohesive ones (Kirshner, Dies, & Brown, 1978). Members of a cohesion-as-unity group are more likely to agree with such statements as,

- "There is a feeling of unity and cohesion in this group" (Moos, Insel, & Humphrey, 1974)
- "I spend time when not on duty with people in this company" (P. D. Bliese & Halverson, 1996)
- "The group members stick together outside of the team project" (A. Chang & Bordia, 2001, p. 392).

This group-level sense of unity and solidarity is usually accompanied by individual-level perceptions of belonging to the group (see Figure 5-2). Members not only feel that "we are one" and "we are family," but also "I am one with the group." When asked to comment directly on their sense of belonging to the group, members of cohesive groups are more likely to agree that

- "I feel a sense of belonging to my group" (Bollen & Hoyle, 1990)
- "I think of this group as a part of who I am" (Henry, Arrow, & Carini, 1999)
- "I feel included in the group" (N. J. Evans & Jarvis, 1986, p. 207)

Individuals who are members of cohesive groups—with *cohesion* defined as a strong sense of belonging to an integrated community—are more actively involved in their groups, are more enthusiastic about their groups, and even suffer from fewer social and interpersonal problems (Hoyle & Crawford, 1994). Members are also more committed to their groups, where commitment is indicated by the degree of attachment to the group, a long-term orientation to the group, and intentions to remain within the group (Arriaga & Agnew, 2001; Wech,

---

FOCUS 5-1   Hazing: Do Initiations Create Cohesion?

A participant who is asked to give up something of value for their group becomes, because of this sacrifice, more attracted to that body
—Alvin Zander (1982, p. 7)

Many groups require prospective members to pass an initiation test before they join the group. Initiates in biker gangs, for example, must earn the right to wear the letters and emblems of their gang—their "colors"—by performing a variety of distasteful behaviors (J. R. Davis, 1982). Pledges to fraternities at some universities are ritually beaten, subjected to ridicule and embarrassment, and required to drink unhealthy amounts of alcohol (Goldstein, 2002).

What is the purpose of **hazing**? Leon Festinger's (1957) *cognitive dissonance theory* suggests that initiations force the prospective members to invest in the group, and that these investments will increase their commitment. Because the two cognitions, "I have invested in the group" and "The group is loathsome" are dissonant, these beliefs cause the members psychological discomfort. Although people can reduce cognitive dissonance in many ways, one frequent method is to emphasize the rewarding features of the group while minimizing the costly characteristics.

Festinger and his colleagues investigated this process in their classic study of an atypical group

that formed around a psychic, Marion Keech. Keech convinced her followers that the world was coming to an end, but that the inhabitants of a planet named Clarion would rescue the group before the apocalypse. Many members of the group committed all their personal resources to the group or gave away their personal possessions in the weeks before the scheduled departure from the planet. Yet the group did not disband even when the rescuers never arrived. Keech claimed that the dedication of the group had so impressed God that the Earth had been spared, and many of the members responded by becoming even more committed to their group. Membership was costly, but each investment tied them more strongly to the group. (See also Atlas, 1990; Batson, 1975; J. R. Bliese, 1990; Hardyck & Braden, 1962.)

Other researchers have tested the impact of costs and commitment using more traditional research procedures (Aronson & Mills, 1959; Axsom, 1989; Gerard & Mathewson, 1966). Elliot Aronson and Judson Mills, for example, manipulated the investments that individuals made before joining a group discussing topics related to sexual behavior. They randomly assigned female college students to one of three experimental conditions: a severe initiation condition, a mild initiation condition, and a control

---

Mossholder, Steel, & Bennet, 1998). They will even sacrifice their own individual desires for the good of the group (Prapavessis & Carron, 1997).

Was the U.S. Hockey Team cohesive in this sense? Not at first, for many of the players had competed against each other in college, and they remembered their bitter rivalries. But the team coach, Herb Brooks, required each player to pass a series of difficult psychological and physical challenges before earning a spot on the team, and these qualifying trials created a sense of shared adversity (see Focus 5-1). Brooks also stressed the importance of team unity. His goal was to "build a 'we' and 'us' in ourselves as opposed to an 'I,' 'me,' 'myself'" (Warner HBO, 2001). This unity reached its peak in the medal ceremonies after the U.S.

---

hazing An initiation into a group that subjects the new member to mental or physical discomfort, harassment, embarrassment, ridicule, or humiliation.

FOCUS 5-1 *(continued)*

condition. Participants assigned to the *severe initiation* condition had to read aloud to the male experimenter a series of obscene words and two "vivid descriptions of sexual activity from contemporary novels." In the *mild initiation* condition, participants read five sex-related but nonobscene words. In the *control* condition, participants were not put through any kind of initiation whatsoever.

After the initiation, they listened in, through the use of an intercom system, to the group they were about to join. To their chagrin, the group's discussion (which was actually a tape recording of a group following a script) was exceedingly boring and uninteresting. After listening for a while, the researchers asked the participants to rate the group they listened to on a number of dimensions. When they totaled up these ratings, they found that the people who had worked hardest to join the boring group were more positive than those who had experienced a mild initiation or no initiation at all.

Aronson and Mills concluded that the initiation increased cohesion by creating cognitive dissonance; but other factors may also account for the initiation–attraction relationship. Individuals may find strict, demanding groups attractive because their stringent standards ensure that other group members will be highly involved in the group, too, so one's investments in the group will be matched by everyone else's (Iannaccone, 1994). Their public expressions of liking for such groups may also stem more from a desire to save face after making a faulty decision than from the psychic discomfort of cognitive dissonance (Schlenker, 1975). Initiations also fail to heighten attraction if they frustrate new members or make them angry (Lodewijkx & Syroit, 1997).

Severe initiations are also dangerous. Although some hazings are relatively mild—as when new members must take a public oath of loyalty or endure mild pranks—in other cases, new members must endure physical and psychological abuse before they are accepted into the group. Many university fraternities, for example, continue to haze new members because they believe that hazing has many positive benefits, including building group unity, instilling humility in new members, and perpetuating group traditions (Baier & Williams, 1983). Each year, however, many students are killed or seriously injured in hazing incidents (Goldstein, 2002). Hazing is illegal in a number of states because of its aggressive character and its unhealthy consequences, so groups turn to other methods to increase new members' commitment to the group and the group's overall cohesiveness.

---

team had won its gold medal. Team captain Eruzione waved to the team to join him on the small stage, and somehow the entire team crowded onto the small platform. The captain did not represent the group. The entire group, as a whole, received the medal.

Cohesion Is Teamwork

Each year since 1954, the magazine *Sports Illustrated* has identified one individual from the world of sports for the honor of "Athlete of the Year"—but not in 1980. That year, the Athlete of the Year was a group: the U.S. Hockey Team. The U.S. Women's World Cup Soccer Team was similarly honored in 1999.

Many theorists believe that cohesion has more to do with members' willingness to work together to accomplish their objectives than it does with positive interpersonal relations or feelings of unity. Studies of sports teams, for example, find

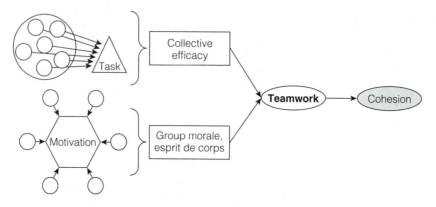

FIGURE 5-3

Is cohesion teamwork? Some theorists feel that a cohesive group is a character-ized by coordinated task performance and team spirit.

that most players, when asked to describe their team's cohesiveness, stress the quality of their **teamwork** (Carron, 1982; Yukelson, Weinberg, & Jackson, 1984). Task-oriented groups, such as military squads or flight crews, are unified by members' shared drive to accomplish their goals (Guzzo, 1995). Much of the unity of the U.S. Hockey Team was based on the members' commitment to their sport and their quest for a gold medal. Groups that are cohesive, in the sense that they work as a team to achieve chosen goals, are characterized by positive ex-pectations about the group's capabilities and enthusiasm for the group and its work (see Figure 5-3).

A group whose cohesiveness is generated by a shared task focus tends to be high in **collective efficacy.** Unlike general optimism or overall confidence in the group, collective efficacy is based on group members' shared beliefs that they can accomplish all the components of their group's task competently and efficiently. Group members may think, "We are a powerful, successful hockey team," but this overall conception of the group is not collective efficacy. Mem-bers of a group with collective efficacy think, "We are fast on the ice," "We can block effectively," and "We have an excellent transition game." These be-liefs must also be widely shared by group members. One or two members may doubt the group's potential for success, but overall, the consensus is positive rather than negative. This confidence is also based on the members' belief that

---

teamwork The combined activities of two or more individuals who coordinate their efforts to make or do something; in many cases, each individual performs a clearly defined portion of the task which, when combined, yield a total group product.

collective efficacy The belief, shared among a substantial portion of the group mem-bers, that the group is capable of organizing and executing the actions required to attain the group's goals and successfully complete its tasks.

the group members will competently coordinate their individual actions in skilled, collective performance, so there is a sense of interdependence and shared resources (Zaccaro, Blair, Peterson, & Sazanis, 1995). Hence, collective efficacy is "a group's shared belief in its conjoint capabilities to organize and execute the courses of action required to produce given levels of attainment" (Bandura, 1997, p. 476).

Task cohesiveness is also associated, in some cases, with **esprit de corps.** The Russian and U.S. hockey teams were equal in confidence and collective efficacy, for both groups had the talent needed to win at hockey. But they differed dramatically in esprit de corps. The Russian team was confident but unenthusiastic. The U.S. team was not so confident, but the team was brimming with energy, enthusiasm, and team spirit. A group with high levels of collective efficacy may expect to succeed, but a group with esprit de corps has emotional vitality, passion, vim, and vigor. Esprit de corps, or *positive affective tone,* predicts a number of positive behaviors in the group, including helping teammates, protecting the organization, making constructive suggestions, improving one's personal performance, and spreading goodwill (George, 1990; George & Brief, 1992; Zhou & George, 2001). It was this emotional intensity that Coach Brooks whipped up to its peak intensity before the U.S. team's game with the Russians. He told them that the Russians were taking their victory for granted, but "we can beat them." He told his team, "you were born to be a player," you were "destined to be here today," and this is "our time." When he told them to "spit in the eye of the tiger," they did.

What Is Group Cohesion?

Table 5-1 suggests that group cohesion is a combination of (1) the unity or solidarity of a group, as indicated by the strength of the bonds linking group members to each other and to the group as a whole; (2) the sense of belonging and community within the group; and (3) the degree to which the group members coordinate their efforts to achieve goals. But there is no one best way to define cohesion. Indeed, "the ease with which cohesiveness can be described has been accompanied by an astonishing difficulty in defining it in an agreed-on manner" (Mullen, Driskell, & Salas, 2000, p. 225). Some, dismayed by this diversity, have suggested that the concept should be discarded as too ambiguous to be useful (Mudrack, 1989; Wekselberg, Goggin, & Collings, 1997). Others, however, have noted that this diversity reflects the complexity inherent in the concept itself. Even though attraction to individual members and to the group itself, unity, and teamwork are all components of cohesiveness, a cohesive group may not exhibit all of these qualities. Cohesiveness may also be based on very different criteria in different kinds of groups: What unifies the members of a work group may not

---

esprit de corps A feeling of unity, commitment, confidence, and enthusiasm for the group shared by most or all of the members.

TABLE 5-1 Various types of cohesion

Component	Description	Examples
Cohesion as Attraction		
Member-to-member attraction	Number of friends in the group; strength of friendship bonds between members	I have many friends in this group. We are close friends.
Attraction to the group	Liking for the group as a whole; group pride (in some models)	I am proud to be in this group. I like my group.
Cohesion as Unity		
Unity	The coherence of the group; the extent to which it is, or is seen to be, a single entity; entitavitity	This group is unified. We are one. United we stand.
Belonging	A sense of community with the group	I belong to this group. I am one with this group.
Cohesion as Teamwork		
Task cohesion	Capacity to perform successfully as a coordinated unit	This group is effective. I do my best for this group
Esprit de corps	Emotional intensity of the group; team spirit	This group has tremendous energy. The group has team spirit.

unify the members of a religious congregation, a classroom, or a military squad (Ridgeway, 1983). As a result, there is no such thing as a typical cohesive group (Cota, Evans, Dion, Kilik, & Longman, 1995; Dion, 1990).

Neither is there one best way to measure a group's cohesion. Some researchers use sociometric methods to measure attraction within the group. Others rely on observational strategies, monitoring interpersonal relations among members, noting instances of conflict or tension, and judging how smoothly the group works together as a unit (e.g., Adler & Adler, 1995; Fine & Holyfield, 1996). In many cases, too, investigators hope that group members are accurate observers of their group's cohesiveness and, if asked, will share these perceptions. Investigators have used a variety of questions to tap into cohesion, including, "Do you want to remain a member of this group?" and "How strong a sense of belonging do you feel you have to the people you work with?" (Schachter, 1951; Indik, 1965, respectively). Researchers also use multi-item scales that include many questions that can be combined to yield a single index of cohesiveness, such as the *Group Environment Scale* (Moos & Humphrey, 1974), *Group Attitude Scale* (N. J. Evans & Jarvis, 1986), *Group Environment Questionnaire* (Widmeyer, Brawley, & Carron, 1992), *Perceived Cohesion Scale* (Bollen & Hoyle, 1990), *Group Identification Scale* (Henry et al., 1999), *Sports Cohesiveness Questionnaire* (Martens, Landers, & Loy, 1972), and *Gross Cohesion Questionnaire* (Stokes, 1983).

Cohesion, as a multilevel concept, can also be measured at multiple levels (see Chapter 2). Those who consider cohesion to be a psychological quality that is rooted in members' feelings of attraction for others, the group, and a sense of unity measure cohesion at the individual level. They might ask members of a group to only describe their own attraction to and commitment to the group through such questions as, "Are you attracted to the group?" or "Do you feel a strong sense of belonging to the group?" Other researchers, in contrast, may feel that only a group can be cohesive, and so cohesion should be located at the group level (Mason & Griffin, 2002). These investigators may ask group members to estimate the group's cohesion directly through such questions as, "Are members attracted to this group?" and "Is this group a cohesive one?" They might also decide to have the group answer these types of questions as a group (see Paskevich, Brawley, Dorsch, & Widmeyer, 1999).

This plethora of operational definitions can create challenges for researchers. When they measure cohesiveness in different ways, they often report different conclusions. A study using a self-report measure of cohesion might find that cohesive groups outproduce groups that are not cohesive, but other investigators may not replicate this finding when they use observational measurement methods (Mullen, Anthony, Salas, & Driskell, 1994). Moreover, some operational definitions of cohesion may correspond more closely to the theoretical definition than others. A measure that focuses only on group members' perceptions of their group's cohesiveness, for example, may be assessing something very different than a measure that focuses on the actual strength of the relationships linking individuals to their group. In any case, these varied methods of measurement will likely yield very different conclusions about the group's cohesion.

COHESION AND COMMITMENT OVER TIME

The U.S. Olympic Hockey Team that faced the Russian team in February of 1980 was, without question, cohesive. The team was extraordinarily unified—most of the members liked one another, and they worked diligently to achieve their goals. But the group did not become cohesive all at once. When Coach Brooks first invited the best amateur hockey players to a training camp in Colorado Springs in July 1979, the players showed few signs of camaraderie, fellowship, or cohesion. Coach Brooks was tough on them; many had played against one another in college and still held grudges, and some were so temperamental that no one would befriend them. But the hockey team changed over time. Initial uncertainties gave way to stable patterns of interaction; tensions between members waned; many players were cut from the team and replaced by new ones; and members abandoned old roles to take on new ones. Over time, the team grew from a collection of talented individuals into a cohesive team.

The U.S. Hockey Team's evolution over time followed a predictable course. Few groups become cohesive, efficient teams from the moment their members first meet. Instead, they experience *group development*—a pattern of growth and change beginning with initial formation and ending, in most cases, with dissolution.

Stages of Group Development

The group dynamicist William Fawcett Hill was at one time so intrigued by developmental processes in groups that he diligently filed away each theory that he found on that subject. Over the years, his collection grew and grew, until finally the number of theories reached 100. At that moment, Hill noted, the "collecting bug was exterminated, as the object of the quest had lost its rarity" (W. F. Hill & Gruner, 1973, p. 355; see also Hare, 1982; Lacoursiere, 1980).

The morass of theoretical models dealing with group development, though daunting, is not altogether irremediable. Theoreticians are at variance on many points, but most agree that groups pass through several phases, or *stages,* as they develop. Just as humans mature from infancy to childhood, adolescence, adulthood, and old age, stage models of group development theorize that groups move from one stage to the next in a predictable, sequential fashion. The U.S. Hockey Team, for example, became unified, but only after earlier stages marked by confusion, conflict, and growing group structure.

What stages typify the developmental progression of groups? The number and names of the stages vary among theorists. Many models, however, highlight certain interpersonal outcomes that must be achieved in any group that exists for a prolonged period. Members of most groups must, for example, discover who the other members are, achieve a degree of interdependence, and deal with conflict (Hare, 1982; Lacoursiere, 1980; Wheelan, 1994). Therefore, most models include the basic stages shown in Table 5-2 and illustrated earlier in Figure 1-4. First, the group members must become oriented toward one another. Second, they often find themselves in conflict, and some solution is sought to improve the group environment. In the third phase, norms and roles develop that regulate behavior, and the group achieves greater unity. In the fourth phase, the group can perform as a unit to achieve desired goals. The final stage ends the sequence of development with the group's adjournment. Bruce W. Tuckman (Tuckman, 1965; Tuckman & Jensen, 1977) labeled these five stages *forming* (orientation), *storming* (conflict), *norming* (structure development), *performing* (work), and *adjourning* (dissolution).

FORMING: THE ORIENTATION STAGE The first few minutes, hours, days, or even weeks of a newly formed group's life are often marked by tension, guarded interchanges, and relatively low levels of interaction. During this initial *orientation stage,* members monitor their behavior to avoid any embarrassing lapses of social poise and are tentative when expressing their personal opinions. Because the group's structure has not had time to develop, the members are often uncertain

TABLE 5-2 Stages of group development

Stage	Major Processes	Characteristics
Orientation: *Forming*	Members become familiar with each other and the group; dependency and inclusion issues; acceptance of leader and group consensus	Communications are tentative, polite; concern for ambiguity, group's goals; leader is active; members are compliant
Conflict: *Storming*	Disagreement over procedures; expression of dissatisfaction; tension among members; antagonism toward leader	Criticism of ideas; poor attendance; hostility; polarization and coalition formation
Structure: *Norming*	Growth of cohesiveness and unity; establishment of roles, standards, and relationships; increased trust, communication	Agreement on procedures; reduction in role ambiguity; increased "we-feeling"
Work: *Performing*	Goal achievement; high task orientation; emphasis on performance and production	Decision making; problem solving; mutual cooperation
Dissolution: *Adjourning*	Termination of roles; completion of tasks; reduction of dependency	Disintegration and withdrawal; increased independence and emotionality; regret

Source: Data from Tuckman, 1965.

about their role in the group, what they should be doing to help the group reach its goals, or even who is leading the group.

With time, tension is dispelled as the ice is broken and group members become better acquainted (Thibaut & Kelley, 1959). After the initial inhibitions subside, group members typically begin exchanging information about themselves and their goals. To better understand and relate to the group, individual members gather information about their leaders and comembers by formulating attributions concerning their personality characteristics, interests, and attitudes (Heider, 1958). Also, through self-disclosure of their own characteristics, group members reveal enough information about themselves to enable others to get to know them better (Jourard, 1971). Eventually, the group members feel familiar enough with one another that their interactions become more open and spontaneous.

STORMING: THE CONFLICT STAGE As the relatively mild tension caused by the newness of a group wanes, tension over goals, procedures, and authority often waxes. On the U.S. Hockey Team, for example, the players from the schools in the eastern part of the United States often excluded the players from the Midwest. Several players were considered hotshots, who were more interested in their personal performance than in team success. And nearly all the players rebelled against the hard-driving coaching style of Herb Brooks. He would yell, insult, swear, and curse the players whenever they failed to perform up to his standards, and he often threatened to cut players from the team.

The *conflict stage* is marked by personal conflicts between individual members who discover that they just do not get along, procedural conflict over the group's goals and procedures, and competition between individual members for authority, leadership, and more prestigious roles. In groups that have an official leader, like the U.S. Hockey Team, the conflict often centers on relationships between the leader and the rest of the group. In the orientation stage, members accept the leader's guidance with few questions, but as the group matures, leader–member conflicts disrupt the group's functioning. Members may oscillate between fight and flight. Some may openly challenge the leader's policies and decisions (*fight*), whereas others may respond by minimizing contact with the leader (*flight*). In groups that have no formally appointed leader, conflicts erupt as members vie for status and roles within the group. Once stable patterns of authority, attraction, and communication have developed, conflicts subside, but until then, group members jockey for authority and power (Bennis & Shepard, 1956; Wheelan & McKeage, 1993).

Many group members are discouraged by this outbreak of conflict in their young groups, but conflict is as common as harmony in groups. As Chapter 12's analysis of the roots of conflict suggests, the dynamic nature of the group ensures continual change, but along with this change come stresses and strains that surface in the form of conflict. In rare instances, group members may avoid all conflict because their actions are perfectly coordinated; but in most groups, the push and pull of interpersonal forces inevitably exerts its influence. Low levels of conflict in a group can be an indication of remarkably positive interpersonal relations, but it is more likely that the group members are simply uninvolved, unmotivated, and bored (B. A. Fisher, 1980).

Conflict is not just unavoidable, however; it may actually be a required ingredient for creating group cohesion. If conflict escalates out of control, it can destroy a group. But more often, conflict has positive consequences. Members of cohesive groups must understand one another's perspectives, and such understanding cannot deepen until hostility has surfaced, been confronted, and been resolved (Bennis & Shepard, 1956; Deutsch, 1969). Conflicts "serve to 'sew the social system together' by canceling each other out, thus preventing disintegration along one primary line of cleavage" (Coser, 1956, p. 801). Conflict provides a means of venting personal hostilities that, if never faced, may build up to a point where the group can no longer continue as a unit. Some evidence also suggests that conflict helps groups to clarify their goals and thereby improves performance, but the evidence of this benefit of conflict is mixed (De Dreu & Weingart, 2003).

NORMING: THE STRUCTURE DEVELOPMENT STAGE With each crisis overcome, the U.S. Hockey Team became more stable, more organized, and more cohesive. Erusione emerged as the group's leader and was selected to be captain. The players revised their initial impressions of each other and reached more benevolent conclusions about their teammates. The players still complained about the team rules, the practice schedules, and the coach's constant criticisms, but they became fiercely loyal to the team, their teammates, and their coach.

Groups in the third stage of group development, the *structure development stage,* become both unified and organized. Whereas groups in the orientation and conflict stages are characterized by low levels of intimacy, friendship, and unity, the group becomes a unified whole when it reaches the structure development stage. Mutual trust and support increase, members cooperate more with each other, and members try to reach decisions through consensus. The group becomes cohesive (Hare, 1976; Tuckman, 1965; Wheelan, 1994).

The group also becomes more organized. It resolves the problems that caused earlier conflicts—uncertainty about goals, roles, and authority—and prepares to get down to the work at hand. Norms, those taken-for-granted rules that dictate how members should behave, emerge more clearly and guide the group members as they interact with one another. Differences of opinion still arise, but now they are dealt with through constructive discussion and negotiation. Members communicate openly with one another about personal and group concerns, in part because members know one another better. On the U.S. Hockey Team, the players did not always agree with the coach, but they changed the way they dealt with disagreement. Instead of grumbling about their treatment, several players started compiling a book of *Brooksisms*—the odd expressions Coach Brooks used during practice to motivate his players. Nearly every player, interviewed 20 years after they played for Brooks, remembered such Brooksisms as "You are playing worse every day and now you are playing like the middle of next week" and "Gentlemen, you don't have enough talent to win on talent alone."

PERFORMING: THE WORK STAGE Few groups are productive immediately; instead, productivity must usually wait until the group matures. Various types of groups, such as conferences, factory workers assembling relay units, workshop participants, and the members of expeditions, become more efficient and productive later in their group's life cycle (Hare, 1967, 1982; Hare & Naveh, 1984). The more "mature" a group, the more likely the group will spend the bulk of its time working rather than socializing, seeking direction, or arguing. When the content of group members' remarks is systematically coded, task-focused remarks are found to occur later rather than sooner in the group's life (Bales & Strodtbeck, 1951; Borgatta & Bales, 1953; Heinicke & Bales, 1953). Conflict and uncertainty also decrease over time as work-focused comments increase. When researchers studied the verbal remarks of 26 teams that varied in "age" from 1 month to 18 months, they found that the groups that had been together longer talked more about work-related matters, whereas the younger groups were more likely to express conflict or uncertainty and make requests for guidance (Wheelan, Davidson, & Tilin, 2003).

The U.S. Hockey Team's effectiveness increased when it reached the *work stage* in its development. They played 41 games against other teams in preparation for the Olympics and won 30 of those matches. They reached their peak of performance when they beat the Russian team to qualify for the final, gold-medal game against Finland. Before that game, Coach Brooks did not give them a pep talk, as he had before the Russian game. Instead, he only said, "You lose this game and you will take it to your . . . graves" (Warner HBO, 2001). They won.

However, not all groups reach this productive work stage. If you have never been a member of a group that failed to produce, you are a rare individual indeed. In a study of neighborhood action committees, only 1 of 12 groups reached the productivity stage; all the others were bogged down at the conflict or cohesion stages (Zurcher, 1969). An early investigation of combat units found that out of 63 squads, only 13 could be clearly classified as effective performance units (Goodacre, 1953). An analysis of 18 personal growth groups concluded that only 5 managed to reach the task performance stage (Kuypers, Davies, & Hazewinkel, 1986; see also Kuypers, Davies, & Glaser, 1986). These studies and others suggest that time is needed to develop a working relationship, but time alone is no guarantee that the group will be productive (Gabarro, 1987).

ADJOURNING: THE DISSOLUTION STAGE Susan Wheelan's (1994) *Group Development Questionnaire,* summarized in Table 5-3, measures the group's stage of development by asking members to describe their group's success in dealing with issues of orientation, conflict, structure, and productivity. Some groups, however, move through these four basic stages to a fifth one: the dissolution stage. The U.S. Olympic Hockey Team, for example, was invited to the White House to meet the President of the United States after their victory. That ceremony marked the end of the group's existence, for the team never reconvened or played again. After meeting the president, the members of the U.S. Hockey Team clapped one another on the back one last time, and then the group disbanded.

A group's entry into the *dissolution stage* can be either planned or spontaneous. *Planned dissolution* takes place when the group accomplishes its goals or exhausts its time and resources. The U.S. Hockey Team meeting the President, a wilderness expedition at the end of its journey, a jury delivering its verdict, and an ad hoc committee filing its final report are all ending as scheduled. *Spontaneous dissolution,* in contrast, occurs when the group's end is not scheduled In some cases, an unanticipated problem may arise that makes continued group interaction impossible. When groups fail repeatedly to achieve their goals, their members or some outside power may decide that maintaining the group is a waste of time and resources. In other cases, the group members may no longer find the group and its goals sufficiently satisfying to warrant their continued membership. As social exchange theory maintains, when the number of rewards provided by group membership decreases and the costly aspects of membership escalate, group members become dissatisfied. If the members feel that they have no alternatives or that they have put too much into the group to abandon it, they may remain in the group even though they are dissatisfied. If, however, group members feel that other groups are available or that nonparticipation is preferable to participation in such a costly group, they will be more likely to let their current group die (Rusbult, 1983, 1987; Rusbult & Martz, 1995; Rusbult, Zembrodt, & Gunn, 1982).

The dissolution stage can be stressful for members (C. Johnson, 1974; Mayadas & Glasser, 1985; Sarri & Galinsky, 1985). When dissolution is unplanned, the final group sessions may be filled with conflict-laden exchanges

TABLE 5-3 A sampling of items from the *Group Development Questionnaire* (GDQ)

Stage	Sample Items
Orientation	Members tend to go along with whatever the leader suggests. There is very little conflict expressed in the group.
Conflict	People seem to have very different views about how things should be done in this group. Members challenge the leader's ideas
Structure	The group is spending its time planning how it will get its work done. Members can rely on each other. They work as a team.
Work	The group gets, gives, and uses feedback about its effectiveness and productivity. The group encourages high performance and quality work

Source: "Validation Studies of the Group Development Questionnaire" by S. A. Wheelan and J. M. Hochberger, *Small Group Research, 27,* February 1996. Copyright © 1996 by Sage Publications, Inc. Reprinted by permission of Sage Publications, Inc.

among members, growing apathy and animosity, or repeated failures at the group's task. Even when dissolution is planned, the members may feel distressed. Their work in the group may be over, but they still mourn for the group and suffer from a lack of personal support. Members of disbanding partnerships sometimes blame one another for the end of the group (Kushnir, 1984).

Cycles of Group Development

Tuckman's model, which can be operationalized using measures like the one in Table 5-3, is a *successive-stage theory:* It specifies the usual order of the phases of group development. Sometimes, however, group development takes a different course. Although interpersonal exploration is often a prerequisite for other interpersonal outcomes, and cohesion and conflict often precede effective performance, this pattern is not universal. Some groups manage to avoid particular stages; others move through the stages in a unique order; still others seem to develop in ways that cannot be described by Tuckman's five stages (Seeger, 1983). Also, the demarcation between stages is not clear-cut. When group conflict is waning, for example, feelings of cohesion may be increasing, but these time-dependent changes do not occur in a discontinuous, stepwise sequence (Arrow, 1997).

Many theorists believe that groups repeatedly cycle through stages during their lifetime, rather than just moving through each stage once (Arrow, 1997; W. F. Hill & Gruner, 1973; Mennecke, Hoffer, & Wynne, 1992; Shambaugh, 1978). These *cyclical models* agree that certain issues tend to dominate group interaction during the various phases of a group's development, but they add that these issues can recur later in the life of the group. Very long-term groups, such as teams of software engineers who work on products for many years, show signs of shifting from task-focused stages back to conflict (*re-storming*) and norming (*re-norming*) stages (McGrew, Bilotta, & Deeney, 1999). Similarly, the discussion groups that Bales (1965) studied tended to oscillate between periods of group effort and periods of cohesion-creating, interpersonal activity. Bales's **equilibrium model** of group development therefore assumes that group members strive to maintain a balance between accomplishing the task and enhancing the quality of the interpersonal relationships within the group. In consequence, groups cycle back and forth between what Tuckman called the norming and performing stages: A period of prolonged group effort must be followed by a period of cohesion-creating, interpersonal activity (Bales & Cohen, 1979).

Punctuated equilibrium models agree with Bales's view, but they add that groups often go through periods of relatively rapid change. These changes may be precipitated by some internal crisis, such as the loss of a leader, or by changes in the type of task the group is attempting (Eldredge & Gould, 1972). The halfway point in the group's life, too, can trigger dramatic changes in the group, as members realize that the time they have available to them is dwindling (Arrow, 1997; Gersick 1989). The U.S. Hockey Team's development, although stage-like in many respects, also changed more rapidly following specific, critical events. Perhaps the most dramatic turning point in the group's life occurred when the team lost an exhibition game to a relatively weak team. Coach Brooks believed the team played without any heart or energy, and after the game he kept them on the ice rather than letting them shower and change. He made the players skate back and forth between the goals (the players called these drills "Herbies") for what seemed like hours. Even when the arena manager turned off the lights and went home, Brooks kept the team skating back and forth in the dark. The experience created a feeling of unity in the group, and this cohesiveness carried them through the remainder of their games and on to victory. Such turning points may, however, be relatively rare in groups. More typically, the shift from an initial orientation focus to a task focus occurs gradually as groups and their members pace their progress toward the completion of their final goal (Seers & Woodruff, 1997).

CONSEQUENCES OF COHESION

Cohesion is something of a "purr word." Most of us, if asked to choose between two groups—one that is cohesive and another that is not—would likely pick the cohesive group. But cohesiveness has its drawbacks. A cohesive group is an *intense* group, and this intensity affects the members, the group's dynamics, and the group's performance in both positive and negative ways. Cohesion leads to a range of consequences—not all of them desirable.

---

equilibrium model A conceptual analysis of group development, proposed by Robert Bales, that assumes the focus of a group shifts back and forth between the group's tasks and the interpersonal relationships among group members.

punctuated equilibrium model A group development theory that assumes groups change gradually over time but that the periods of slow growth are punctuated by brief periods of relatively rapid change.

Member Satisfaction and Adjustment

Many of the men of the U.S. Hockey Team, years later, said that their 6 months together in 1980 were a special time in their lives. People are usually much more satisfied with their groups when the group is cohesive rather than noncohesive. Across a range of groups in industrial, athletic, and educational settings, people who are members of highly compatible, cohesive groups report more satisfaction and enjoyment than members of noncohesive groups (Hackman, 1992; Hare, 1976; Hogg, 1992; D. F. Roy, 1973). One investigator studied teams of masons and carpenters working on a housing development. For the first 5 months of the project, the men worked at various assignments in groups formed by the supervisor. This period gave the men a chance to get to know virtually everyone working on the project, and natural likes and dislikes soon surfaced. The researcher then established cohesive groups by making certain that the teams only contained people who liked each other. As anticipated, the masons and carpenters were much more satisfied when they worked in cohesive groups. As one of them explained, "Seems as though everything flows a lot smoother. . . . The work is more interesting when you've got a buddy working with you. You certainly like it a lot better anyway" (Van Zelst, 1952, p. 183).

A cohesive group creates a healthier workplace, at least at the psychological level. Because people in cohesive groups respond to one another in a more positive fashion than the members of noncohesive groups, people experience less anxiety and tension in such groups (A. E. Myers, 1962; M. E. Shaw & Shaw, 1962). In studies conducted in industrial work groups, for example, employees reported less anxiety and nervousness when they worked in cohesive groups (Seashore, 1954). Investigations of therapeutic groups routinely find that the members improve their overall level of adjustment when their group is cohesive (I. D. Yalom, 1995). People also cope more effectively with stress when they are in cohesive groups (C. A. Bowers, Weaver, & Morgan, 1996; Zaccaro, Gualtieri, & Minionis, 1995).

Cohesive groups can, however, be emotionally demanding (Forsyth & Elliott, 1999). The **old sergeant syndrome,** for example, is more common in cohesive military squads. Although the cohesiveness of the unit initially provides psychological support for the individual, the loss of comrades during battle causes severe distress. When the unit is reinforced with replacements, the original group members are reluctant to establish emotional ties with the newcomers, partly in fear of the pain produced by separation. Hence, they begin restricting their interactions, and these "old sergeants" can eventually become completely isolated within the group. Some highly cohesive groups may also purposefully sequester members from other groups in an attempt to seal members off from competing interests. Individuals who leave high-demand religious groups due to changes in

---

old sergeant syndrome Symptoms of psychological disturbance, including depression, anxiety, and guilt, exhibited by noncommissioned officers in cohesive units that suffer heavy casualities. Strongly loyal to their unit and its members, these leaders feel so responsible for their unit's losses that they withdraw psychologically from the group.

beliefs or social mobility may experience loneliness, chronic guilt and isolation, a lingering distrust of other people and groups, and anxiety about intimate relationships (Yao, 1987).

Group Dynamics and Influence

As cohesion increases, the internal dynamics of the group intensify. In consequence, the pressure to conform is greater in cohesive groups, and individuals' resistance to these pressures is weaker. When members of cohesive groups discovered that some others in their group disagreed with their interpretations of three ambiguous stimuli, they tried to exert greater influence over their partners than did members of noncohesive groups. Partners also conformed more in cohesive dyads, perhaps because they wanted to avoid confrontation (Back, 1951). When the group norms emphasize the value of cooperation and agreement among members, members of highly cohesive groups avoid disagreement more than members of noncohesive groups. Irving Janis's (1982) theory of *groupthink* suggests that these pressures undermine a group's willingness to critically analyze its decisions. As Chapter 11 explains, in some cases, this breakdown in decision-making effectiveness can be disastrous.

Anecdotal accounts of highly cohesive groups—military squads, adolescent peer groups, sports teams, fraternities and sororities, and cults—often describe the strong pressures that these groups put on their members (Goldhammer, 1996). Drug use and illegal activities are often traced back to conformity pressures of adolescents' peer groups (Giordano, 2003). Cohesive gangs exert strong pressure on members (Coughlin & Venkatesh, 2003). Cults may demand extreme sacrifices from members, including suicide. Even sports teams, if highly cohesive, may extract both compliance and sacrifice from members (Prapavessis & Carron, 1997). Cohesion can also increase negative group processes, including hostility and scapegoating (French, 1941; Pepitone & Reichling, 1955). In one study, cohesive and noncohesive groups worked on a series of unsolvable problems. Although all the groups seemed frustrated, coalitions tended to form in noncohesive groups, whereas cohesive groups vented their frustrations through interpersonal aggression: overt hostility, joking hostility, scapegoating, and domination of subordinate members. The level of hostility became so intense in one group that observers lost track of how many offensive remarks were made; they estimated that the number surpassed 600 comments during the 45-minute work period (French, 1941).

Group Productivity

Most people consider cohesion to be a key ingredient for group success. The cohesive, unified group has, throughout history, been lauded as the most productive, the most likely to win in battle, and the most creative. The Spartans who held the pass at Thermopylae were a model of unity, courage, and strength. The explorers on the ship *Endurance,* which was crushed by ice floes during a voyage to the Antarctic, survived by working together under the able leadership of Ernest Shackleton. The engineers at the Palo Alto Research Center (PARC) worked as a team, and together they managed to create the personal computer and other assorted technologies, including the mouse, a graphical interface (clickable icons), e-mail, and laser printers. When the U.S. Hockey Team won, most sports commentators explained the victory by pointing to the U.S. team's cohesiveness, even suggesting that a unified team could work "miracles." But is this folk wisdom consistent with the scientific evidence? Are cohesive groups really more productive?

DO COHESIVE GROUPS OUTPERFORM LESS UNIFIED GROUPS? Studies of all kinds of groups—sports teams, work groups in business settings, expeditions, military squads, and laboratory groups—generally confirm the cohesion–performance relationship: Cohesive groups tend to outperform less unified groups. But a study by Brian Mullen and Carolyn Copper (1994) suggested that the relationship does not emerge in all studies and in all groups. Mullen and Copper combed the research literature looking for studies of cohesion and performance. They found 49 studies of 8702 members of a variety of groups, and when they combined these studies statistically, they discovered that 92% of them supported cohesive groups over noncohesive ones. However, they also found that this cohesion–performance relationship was stronger (1) in bona fide groups than in ad hoc laboratory groups, (2) in correlational studies than in experimental studies, and (3) in smaller groups than in larger groups. The relationship between cohesion and performance was strongest in studies of sports teams, somewhat weaker in military squads, weaker still in nonmilitary bona fide groups, and weakest overall in ad hoc, artificial groups (Carron, Colman, Wheeler, & Stevens, 2002).

ARE COHESION AND PERFORMANCE CAUSALLY CONNECTED? Prior studies of groups that work on tasks have found that "nothing succeeds like success" when it comes to cohesion. When a group performs well at its identified task, the level of cohesion in the group increases, but should it fail, disharmony, disappointment, and a loss of esprit de corps are typically observed. These effects of performance on cohesion occur even when groups are identical in all respects except one—when some are arbitrarily told they performed well, but others are told they did not do well. Even under these highly controlled circumstances, groups given positive feedback became more cohesive than groups that are told they performed poorly (e.g., Forsyth, Zyzniewski, & Giammanco, 2001). These studies suggest that cohesion is related to performance, not because cohesion causes groups to perform better, but because groups that perform better become more cohesive.

Mullen and Copper (1994) examined the flow of causality in the cohesion–performance relationship by comparing experimental studies that manipulated cohesion with studies that used correlational designs. Because the cohesion–performance relationship emerged in both types of studies, they concluded that cohesion causes improved performance. However, the relationship between cohesion and performance is stronger in correlational studies. This disparity suggests that cohesion aids performance, but that performance also causes changes in cohesiveness. Mullen and Copper closely examined seven correlational studies that measured cohesion and performance twice rather than once. These studies suggested that a group's cohesiveness at Time 1 predicted its performance at

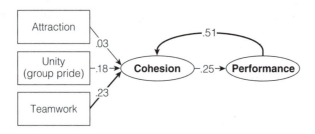

FIGURE 5-4

Does cohesion cause improved task performance, or do groups that succeed become more cohesive? Mullen and Copper's (1994) meta-analysis suggested that cohesion does influence performance (and that teamwork is the strongest predictor of cohesion), but the impact of performance on cohesion is stronger than the impact of cohesion on performance.

Time 1 and at Time 2. But in these studies, group performance at Time 1 was a particularly powerful predictor of *cohesiveness* at Time 2! These findings prompted Mullen and Copper to conclude that the cohesion−performance relationship is bidirectional: Cohesion makes groups more successful, but groups that succeed also become more cohesive (see Figure 5-4).

WHAT IS IT ABOUT COHESIVE GROUPS THAT MAKES THEM MORE EF-FECTIVE? Cohesive groups do outperform less cohesive groups. But what is it about a cohesive group that makes it more successful? Does the high level of attraction among members reduce conflict, making it easier for the group to concentrate on its work? Or perhaps group members are more dedicated to their group if it is cohesive, and this sense of dedication and group pride prompts them to expend more effort on behalf of their group.

The success of cohesive groups lies, in part, in the enhanced coordination of their members. In noncohesive groups, members' activities are uncoordinated and disjointed, but in cohesive groups, each member's contributions mesh with those of the other group members. Cohesion thus acts as a "lubricant" that "minimizes the friction due to the human 'grit' in the system" (Mullen & Copper, 1994, p. 213). Members of cohesive groups all share the same "mental model" of the group's task and its demands, and this shared prescription for how the task is to be accomplished facilitates their performance (in most cases; see Focus 5-2 for an exception). Hence, cohesive groups are particularly likely to outperform noncohesive groups when the group's task requires high levels of interaction and interdependence (Gully, Devine, & Whitney, 1995).

The tendency for members of cohesive groups to be unified in their drive to accomplish their goals also gives such groups an edge over noncohesive groups. Cohesion based on attraction or pride in one's group may not improve performance nearly as much as cohesion based on commitment to the task. Mullen and

FOCUS 5.2   Does Stress Lead to a Loss of Team Perspective?

Every man for himself, his own ends, the Devil for all.
–Robert Burton

In December of 1978, United Airlines Flight 173 crashed near Portland, Oregon. When the National Transportation Safety Board (NTSB) investigated the crash, they concluded that the flight crew, faced with the emergency situation of a malfunctioning landing gear, experienced a breakdown in teamwork. The captain of the plane was distracted by the mechanical problem, and the rest of the crew failed to communicate critical information to him as he worked to solve the problem. The plane eventually ran out of fuel.

James E. Driskell, Eduardo Salas, and Joan Johnston (1999) suggested that this tragic failure by a cohesive but malfunctioning group may have been caused by a loss of team perspective. They suggested that the members of cohesive groups, in most cases, share a collective perception of the "interrelations of actors and actions in the group system" (p. 293). This perspective is strongest when (1) members are focused on the group rather than on themselves (i.e., they have a "sense of being part of a team versus a more individualistic self-focus"; p. 293) and (2) they share a collective representation of the tasks that the group must perform (i.e., a "team mental model" that describes "how team members must interact with one another to perform the task"; p. 293).

Driskell et al. tested this hypothesis with naval personnel working in teams linked by a computer network. The task simulated a critically important naval decision—deciding on the basis of radar and database information whether an unidentified contact was a threat to the ship or nonhostile. All the participants worked in teams of three, but in the *coaction* condition, members made their decisions independently of one another. In the *interdependent* condition, the members had to work together to gather information about the possible target. The researchers also manipulated stress by exposing some of the groups to distracting sound and noise while they worked and by increasing the number of contacts presented on the radar screens. They also pressured these groups by telling members to "work harder" and to "hurry up."

The study's results confirmed their initial suspicions: Interdependent groups working in a stressful situation lost their group perspective. They were more likely to report feeling like three individuals rather than like a team, and they were not focused on the task. They were also less likely to use plural pronouns such as *we, us, our, ours,* and *ourselves* when describing their response to the simulation. Moreover, groups that lost their team perspective tended to perform more poorly—they were more likely to identify a harmless contact on their radar screens as hostile, and less likely to correctly identify contacts that were dangerous. These findings suggest that cohesive groups cope well with routine problems, but that the advantages of cohesion may be lost when groups face extraordinary difficulties (Milanovich et al., 1998; Weick, 1990).

Copper (1994) confirmed this possibility in their meta-analysis by reviewing each study's approach to measuring or manipulating cohesion. They found that in the experimental studies, attraction, group pride, and commitment to the task were all related to improved performance, but in studies of bona fide groups, only task commitment reliably predicted improved performance.

These findings explain why some groups, even though they are cohesive, are not productive—because the members are not committed to the group's performance goals. A survey of 5871 factory workers in 228 groups found that the more cohesive the group, the less the productivity levels *varied* among members;

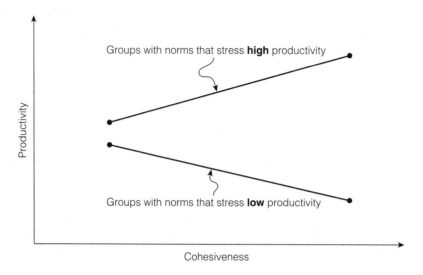

FIGURE 5-5

Do cohesive groups always outperform less cohesive groups? If the group's norms encourage productivity, cohesiveness and productivity will be positively correlated. If the group's standards for performance are low, however, cohesiveness will actually undermine productivity.

members of cohesive groups produced nearly equivalent amounts, but individuals in noncohesive groups varied considerably more in their productivity. Furthermore, fairly low standards of performance had developed in some of the highly cohesive groups; thus, productivity was uniformly low in these groups. In contrast, in cohesive groups with relatively high performance goals, members were extremely productive (Seashore, 1954; Langfred, 1998). This tendency for the group's norms about productivity to moderate the strength of the cohesion–performance relationship was also confirmed experimentally by manipulating both cohesion and production norms (Berkowitz, 1954; Gammage, Carron, & Estabrooks, 2001). In one illustrative study, cohesive and noncohesive groups worked on a simple assembly-line type task. Then, during the task, messages were ostensibly sent from one worker to another to establish performance norms. In some instances, the messages called for increased production (*positive messages*), but in other instances, the messages requested a slowdown (*negative messages*). As expected, the impact of the messages was significantly greater in the cohesive groups than in the noncohesive groups. Furthermore, the decreases in productivity brought about by the negative messages were greater than the increases brought about by the positive messages (Schachter et al., 1951). In sum, so long as group norms encourage high productivity, cohesiveness and productivity are positively related: The more cohesive the group, the greater its productivity. If group norms encourage low productivity, however, the relationship is negative (see Figure 5-5).

Cohesion at Work: Teams

How should businesses, governments, hospitals, and military units be designed to maximize productivity? For many years, experts assumed that people do not like to work and must be prodded into action by the promise of financial incentives, close supervision, and clear goals that they can attain with little effort. The experts considered workers to be mere "adjuncts to machines," and they designed workplaces in which employees did not waste time talking to one another (F. W. Taylor, 1923). But as corporations became larger and pressures to compete against other companies became more intense, many organizations began relying on **teams** for production, management, distribution, and general decision making. Half the workers in the United States now belong to at least one team at work. Teams are used by at least 50% of all larger organizations in the United States, and in countries like Sweden and Japan, the use of teams approaches 100% (Applebaum & Blatt, 1994; D. J. Devine, Clayton, Philips, Dunford, & Melner, 1999). Nonprofit organizations, such as health care organizations and public service corporations, are particularly heavy adopters of team approaches to work (81%), followed by such blue collar industries as construction, manufacturing, and retail sales (50%), and white collar industries like banking, real estate, and insurance (34%). The modern organization is no longer a network of individuals, but rather a network of interconnected teams (see Kozlowski & Bell, 2003, for a review).

Teams in Organizations

Teams perform a wide range of tasks in organizations (see Table 5-4). *Management groups,* such as administrative units, review panels, boards of directors, and corporate executive teams, identify and solve problems, make decisions about day-to-day operations and production, and set the goals for the organization's future. *Project teams,* or *cross-functional teams,* include individuals with different backgrounds and areas of expertise who join together to develop innovative products and identify new solutions to existing problems. *Advisory groups,* such as review panels, quality circles, and steering committees are sometimes called *parallel groups* because they work outside the usual supervisory structures of the company. **Quality circles,** for example, are self-managed groups of employees who monitor productivity and operations during meetings held independently of the usual working hours and using their own methods of review. *Work groups,* such as assembly lines, manufacturing teams, and maintenance crews, are responsible for the company's tangible output; they create the organization's products (*production teams*) or deliver its services (*service teams*). Some of these groups can also be

---

team An organized, task-focused group.

quality circle A small, self-regulated group of employees charged with identifying ways to improve product quality.

TABLE 5-4 Types of teams common in organizational settings

Type and Subtypes	Function	Examples
Management		
Executive	Plan, direct	Board of directors, city council
Command	Integrate, coordinate	Control tower, combat center
Project		
Negotiation	Deal, persuade	Labor management, international treaty
Commission	Choose, investigate	Search committee, jury
Design	Create, develop	Research and development team, marketing group
Advisory	Diagnose, suggest	Quality circle, steering committee
Service	Provide, repair	Fast food, auto service team
Production	Build, assemble	Home construction, automotive assembly
Action		
Medical	Treat, heal	Surgery, ER
Response	Protect, rescue	Fire station, paramedics
Military	Neutralize, protect	Infantry squad, tank crew
Transportation	Convey, haul	Airline cockpit, train crew
Sports	Compete, win	Baseball, soccer

Source: Adapted from D. J. Devine, 2002.

considered *action groups*. Sports teams, surgery teams, police squads, military units, and orchestras are specialized groups that generate a product or a service through highly coordinated actions (Sundstrom, McIntyre, Halfhill, & Richards, 2000; see also D. J. Devine, 2002, for a comprehensive review of various taxonomies of work groups).

Despite this diversity in terms of focus, composition, and design, teams in organizations are fundamentally groups, and they possess the basic characteristics of any group:

- *Interaction.* Teams create, organize, and sustain group behavior. Teams focus primarily on task-oriented activity, because they are based in workplaces, and their members are paid to address work-related concerns. Teams also promote relationship-sustaining interactions (e.g., social support, self-disclosure, mutual aid).
- *Interdependence.* Team members' interactions are cooperative and coordinated. Specific team members usually have specialized knowledge, skills, and abilities that they contribute to the team, and the team's success depends on combining these individual inputs effectively.
- *Structure.* Teams are structured groups. Group norms, members' specific roles in the group, and communication patterns are often explicitly stated. The membership of teams tends to be clearly defined, as does their duration.
- *Goals.* Teams are goal oriented. Teammates' interdependence is based on the coordination of actions in pursuit of a common goal.

■ *Cohesiveness*. Teams are typically cohesive, particularly in the sense that their members are united in their efforts to pursue a common goal.

Teams vary widely in their autonomy. Some teams are semi-autonomous or supervisor led, for they have a formally recognized leader who is responsible for organizing the members and reviewing their performance. Other teams, in contrast, are autonomous, self-regulating, self-managing, or self-directed. These groups can manage their own work-related activities, including their own operating procedures and structures (Sundstrom et al., 2000). Because teams are part of a larger organization, the tasks that they work on and the decisions they make have an impact on larger projects. Teams also often work under some kind of pressure, such as a heavy workload, limited time, or competition with other groups.

Building Teams in Organizations

Organizational experts often draw on principles of group dynamics to identify ways to design, develop, and improve organizational teams. **Team building** begins with the assumption that success in teams results from a collaborative interdependence that develops through practice. In many ways, team training in the workplace parallels team building in sports. Coach Brooks began with very talented players, but these players had to learn how to pool their individual abilities and energies to maximize the team's performance. They had to learn who was particularly skilled in offense and defense, who was faster and slower, and who could be trusted to pass off the puck to another player who had a better shot. Similarly, organizational teams must learn to coordinate their efforts with those of the other group members. Group goals must be set, work patterns structured, and a sense of group identity developed. Individual members must learn how to coordinate their actions, and any strains and stresses in interpersonal relations need to be identified and resolved (S. G. Cohen & Bailey, 1997; Guzzo & Dickson, 1996; Ilgen, 1999; LaFasto & Larson, 2001).

SETTING GOALS   The U.S. Hockey Team's goal was clear to every member—to win the gold medal by defeating all other competing teams. But in many organizations, groups meet routinely with no clear purpose. If the members do not understand the point of the group, then they do not know what they are supposed to do to help the group reach its goals. An effective team should therefore know what goals it is seeking and what tasks must be accomplished in order to reach these goals. In some cases, a team will spend time developing a mission or vision statement that articulates the group's more important goals (E. H. Schein, 1990). Once the overall purpose of the team is clarified—ideally through a consensus-building

---

team building Interventions, such as trust-building exercises and goal-setting workshops, that are used to increase the extent to which a group functions as a team.

process—the group can identify the tasks that must be completed to achieve the group's overarching goals. In general, groups function more effectively when goals are explicit and members regularly receive feedback about their progress toward those goals (LeFasto & Larson, 2001; Locke & Latham, 1990).

DESIGNING THE TEAM Sports teams have one major advantage over teams in organizations: The size, structure, and responsibilities of each member do not need to be strategically planned, because the team's design is defined by the rules of the sport. Many people may be on a hockey team's roster, but only nine play at any one time. The responsibilities of each player are defined by his or her position, as are the types of skills needed for each player in each role. Organizational teams, in contrast, must be designed, for "there is no single recipe for optimal team design—it depends on the type of work the team is doing, the structure of the organization, and so on" (Thompson, 2004, p. 73). However, some consideration must be given to the group's size, its focus, its longevity, its membership composition, the skills and abilities of its members, and the overall autonomy of the group.

- *How many people will be on the team?* More members provide more resources, but as groups increase in size, fewer members have an opportunity to express themselves. Large groups require more management and tend to be less productive.
- *How will members interact with each other?* In many cases, members communicate in meetings that provide the opportunity for information gathering and decision making. Many teams also communicate by using various information technologies, such as e-mail conferencing.
- *How much authority will the group have?* Many teams in organizations are created by management, and a member of the management remains on the team to act as the group's leader. Other groups, in contrast, may have the authority to manage their own processes and make decisions without getting those decisions approved by others.
- *How will the group be organized?* Decisions must be made about which various roles the members will occupy, who will lead and who will follow, and what norms will govern the group interactions.
- *How long with the team last?* Teams in organizations are, in some cases, limited in duration. A problem-solving team, for example, may be required to develop a report that outlines its solution by a particular date, and once the report is completed, the group disbands.
- *Who will be on the team?* The composition of the team is critical to the group's success. If a team does not include individuals with the knowledge, skills, and attributes demanded by the task, then the group will likely not succeed.

PRACTICING AND PERFORMING Just as athletes must learn how to pool their individual abilities and energies to maximize the team's performance, employees must learn to work together. This learning requires members not only to learn the job itself, but also to develop the social skills they need to get along with others productively (Cannon-Bowers, Tannenbaum, Salas, & Volpe, 1995). One model of team functions identifies no fewer than seven components of teamwork (Fleishman & Zaccaro, 1992): *orienting* (e.g., exchange of information among members, setting priorities), *distributing resources* (e.g., apportioning work to each member), *pacing* (e.g., identifying when work will be completed), *coordinating responses, motivating members* (e.g., developing standards, acknowledging and rewarding performance), *monitoring systems* (e.g., gathering feedback about work quality), and *monitoring procedures* (e.g., gathering feedback about methods used by the team).

Members of teams must also learn to coordinate their efforts; they must learn to back up their teammates, share responsibilities, support one another, complete tasks in a timely and efficient fashion, and accept feedback from one another. New teams often cannot perform as well as more mature ones simply because their members have not learned to coordinate their efforts, and groups with many new members also suffer coordination losses, as coordination takes practice (Argote, Insko, Yovetich, & Romero, 1995; Arrow & McGrath, 1995; Littlepage, Robison, & Reddington, 1997; Wittenbaum & Stasser, 1996). Those members who are new to the group must also be taught how they should work with the groups and its individual members. Individuals who are experienced in working in teams may adapt quickly, but those who are new to teams may need to learn, through training, the task and interpersonal skills they need.

Ideally, this training should focus on the entire group rather than on individual members (Salas & Cannon-Bowers, 2001). Many organizations continue to train employees by sending them to off-site seminars, by providing them with a structured sequence of informational instruction, or by allowing them to observe existing teams. Ironically, by training their employees individually, the organization is failing to train their teams. When groups first form, members are unable to determine which member can be counted on for what type of information. Over time, however, members become more proficient at recognizing and taking advantage of the strengths of each group member (Littlepage, Robison, & Reddington, 1997; Littlepage & Silbiger, 1992). Work groups typically improve their performance over time, as members learn to coordinate both their efforts and their informational resources (P. S. Goodman & Leyden, 1991). Evidence indicates that groups that are trained together are far more effective than groups whose members have received training as individuals but not as members of the group that will actually be doing the work (Moreland, Argote, & Krishnan, 1999; Paris, Salas, & Cannon-Bowers, 1999). For example, surgical teams whose members are more experienced outperform those who have performed an operation less frequently. However, different teams learn new procedures at drastically different rates, and much of that difference in learning is related to the time spent practicing the procedures with intact groups (Pisano, Bohmer, & Edmondson, 2001).

In some cases, the team members may need special training in interpersonal skills and group process management. An external consultant who is an expert on interpersonal relations may work with the group members as they learn to communicate better, use better decision methods, avoid conflict, and trust each other. Team builders also make use of **process consultation** to help group members develop insight into the nature of their group's work culture (E. H. Schein, 1971). A process consultation begins when an expert observes the unit at work and takes note of patterns of communication and attraction, decision-making procedures, sources of power, informal social norms, the potency of within-group pressures, and varieties of intermember conflict. Once the consultant understands how the group is working, he or she discusses these observations with the unit. Through didactic instruction, role playing, and training in observational methods, the consultant and the group members develop ways to improve the group's dynamics.

BUILDING COHESION AND EFFICACY Coach Brooks developed a cohesive team by creating an environment that pitted the individual members against him. He placed them repeatedly in challenging, difficult circumstances, and the players eventually bonded together in opposition to him. This method is often used to create a sense of unity in work groups. In many teams, the manager is very demanding, and the group members ally with one another in their shared contempt for the manager. This approach has its risks, however. The Russian team coach was despised by his players, but this shared enmity did not create a sense of cohesion among them.

A more reliable method of building cohesion requires augmenting its components—attraction, unity, and task-focus. Any factor that promotes *attraction,* such as proximity, similarity in attitudes, and the absence of negative personal qualities (see Chapter 4) will prompt team members to become friends, and thereby the team to become more cohesive. Organizations can also communicate a *communal perspective* to the group through rhetoric that stresses unity, by not singling out individual members, and by providing financial incentives for good group work rather than for individual work. Organizations may also place their groups in challenging environments, so that the members will learn teamwork skills but also develop a sense of unity as a result of surviving the ordeal. Team-building adventures, such as backpacking together in the wilderness, spending the day in a ropes course, or playing a paintball game against a rival team, continue to be popular methods of increasing cohesion.

Particular attention should be paid to building *collective efficacy.* Just as studies of self-efficacy indicate that people learn more, work harder, and achieve better outcomes when they believe that they have the skills required by the tasks they face, so groups with collective efficacy outperform groups that doubt their competence (Guzzo, Yost, Campbell, & Shea, 1993; Little & Madigan, 1997; Silver & Bufanio, 1996, 1997). In general, leaders who believe that the group is compe-

---

process consultation Training group members to identify and better deal with group processes (leadership, conflict) through didactic instruction, role playing, structured process analysis, and training in observational methods.

tent and effective create teams that have higher collective efficacy (Pescosolido, 2001, 2003). Certain types of leaders—those who act as role models for members, who talk optimistically about the group's future, and who help group members develop their strengths—are also more likely to increase the cohesiveness of a group than are more traditional, task-focused leaders (D. I. Jung & Sosik, 2002).

Are Teams Effective?

Organizational experts recommend using teams to achieve organizational excellence. No matter what system the experts propose—quality circles, total quality management (TQM), job enrichment, self-managing teams, or management by objectives (MBO)—most will tout the benefits of using teams to get work done.

But is a team approach always the best approach? Anecdotal evidence and research findings converge on a verdict that favors teams. Even though groups in organizations are sometimes spectacularly ineffective, absenteeism, turnover, and employee complaints can decrease when organizations shift to more group-centered methods (Rayner, 1996; Sundstrom et al., 1990, 2000; Woodman & Sherwood, 1980). Case studies of organizations also confirm the effectiveness of teams (Applebaum & Blatt, 1994). Texas Instruments, for example, increased productivity when it organized its employees into small groups whenever possible, took steps to build up team cohesiveness, and went to great lengths to establish clear goals based on realistic levels of aspiration (Bass & Ryterband, 1979). When a manufacturer in the United States shifted to teams, supportive supervision, participant leadership, organizational overlap among groups, and intensity of group interaction, employee satisfaction increased and turnover decreased (Seashore & Bowers, 1970). Field studies of the use of groups and team development also support the wisdom of relying on teams (Sundstrom et al., 2000). The Harley-Davidson Motor Company, for example, dramatically transformed their production methods by shifting from a traditional command-and-control culture to one based on self-managing work teams, and the positive results of this conversion appear to depend in large part on the high level of cohesiveness maintained by these groups (Chansler, Swamidass, & Cammann, 2003). When researchers, through meta-analysis, examined the link between organizational change and performance, they found that companies that made multiple changes usually improved their performance and that group-level interventions were more closely linked to productivity than individual-level interventions (Macy & Izumi, 1993).

A team approach does not, however, ensure success. Cohesive groups, as noted earlier, can be strikingly unproductive if the group's norms do not call for high productivity. Also, some kinds of team-building interventions appear to be more useful than others. Interventions that increase group members' control over and involvement in work, for example, are more powerful than interventions that focus on morale boosting or envisioning goals (Cotton, 1993; D. I. Levine & D'Andrea Tyson, 1990). When teams cannot move past personality conflicts and tensions, they perform poorly (D. J. Devine et al., 1999). In many cases, too, organizations create groups but then do little to help group members develop the skills they need to work in teams. Only 29% of the organizations in one survey gave their teams any kind of training in teamwork or interpersonal skills, and only 26% based compensation (salary, bonuses) on team performance (D. J. Devine et al., 1999). If untrained teams fail, should the concept of teamwork be blamed, or the failure to implement the concept properly?

Work teams are only one of the interfaces between group dynamics and the field of organizational behavior. Because most work is carried out in groups, groups substantially influence a range of business and organizational outcomes. When managers intervene to help their group become more productive, they are raising questions of leadership (Hollander & Offermann, 1990; Ilgen, 1999). Management teams that routinely make faulty decisions after spending months reviewing the issues may be suffering from groupthink. If productivity drops when members who once worked individually now pool their efforts in a communal project, the problem may be traced to social motivation problems. The study of organizations raises questions that are eminently practical, yet they are also ones that can be answered by drawing on theory and research in group dynamics.

Summary in Outline

❖ What is group cohesion?

1. Group cohesion springs from a number of interrelated sources, including interpersonal attraction, a sense of unity, and the collaborative pursuit of shared goals.

2. Members of cohesive groups tend to like their fellow members (personal attraction) and the group itself (social attraction).

3. Cohesive groups tend to be unified, with group members expressing a sense of "we-ness" and belonging to the group. *Hazing* can generate increased commitment to a group, but severe initiations can harm members and have been banned in many jurisdictions.

4. Cohesive groups coordinate their efforts to achieve goals (*teamwork*). Cohesiveness is often associated with increases in *collective efficacy* and *esprit de corps*.

5. Researchers have developed a number of operational definitions of cohesion, using observation, structured observation, and self-report methods. Cohesion, as a multilevel concept, can also be measured at multiple levels.

❖ Does cohesion develop over time?

1. Cohesion is, in most cases, the consequence of a period of group development—a pattern of growth and change beginning with initial formation and ending, in most cases, with dissolution.

2. Many theorists agree with Tuckman's five-stage model:
   • Orientation (forming) stage: Members experience tentative interactions, tension, concern over ambiguity, growing interdependence, and attempts to identify the nature of the situation.
   • Conflict (storming) stage: Members express dissatisfaction with the group, respond emotionally, criticize one another, and form coalitions.

- Structure development (norming) stage: Unity increases, membership stabilizes, members report increased satisfaction, and the group's internal dynamics intensify.
- Work (performing) stage: The group's focus shifts to the performance of tasks and goal attainment. Not all groups reach this stage, for even highly cohesive groups are not necessarily productive.
- Dissolution (adjourning) stage: The group disbands. A group's entry into the dissolution stage can be either planned or spontaneous, but even planned dissolution can create problems for members as they work to reduce their dependence on the group.

3. Tuckman's model is a successive-stage theory —it specifies the usual order of the phases of group development. *Cyclical* models, such as Bales's *equilibrium model,* maintain that groups cycle through various stages repeatedly. *Punctuated equilibrium models* suggest that groups sometimes move through periods of accelerated change.

❖ **What are the positive and negative consequences of cohesion?**

1. In most instances, cohesion is associated with increases in member satisfaction and decreases in turnover and stress.

2. Cohesion intensifies group processes. Dependence, pressure to conform, and acceptance of influence are greater in cohesive groups. Cohesive groups can be so psychologically demanding that they cause emotional problems for members (e.g., the *old sergeant's syndrome*).

3. Cohesion and performance are linked, both because success increases a group's cohesion and because cohesive groups tend to outperform less cohesive groups.

- Even though cohesive groups tend to outperform less cohesive groups, this relationship between cohesion and performance is strongest when members are committed to the group's tasks.
- If group norms do not encourage high productivity, or if the group members are working in a stressful situation, cohesiveness and productivity are not positively related.

❖ **Should organizations rely on teams to enhance productivity?**

1. *Teams* are specialized types of performance groups. They stress cooperation among members, higher levels of structure and coordination, cohesion and identity, and goal attainment.

2. Examples of teams in business and industry include management and advisory groups (e.g., *quality circles*), production groups, project groups, and action groups.

3. *Team building* uses a variety of methods to increase the effectiveness of work teams, including
- clarifying goals and roles;
- designing teams by intentionally controlling their size, composition, organizational structure, and so on;
- training members to identify and control group processes, such as orienting, distributing resources, pacing, coordinating responses, motivating members, and so on;
- carrying out a *process consultation* that involves observing, documenting, and analyzing the group's processes;
- building cohesion.

4. Team approaches do not ensure success, but they are reliably associated with increases in effectiveness and member satisfaction.

FOR MORE INFORMATION

Chapter Case: U.S. Olympic Hockey Team

- *Do You Believe in Miracles? The Story of the 1980 U.S. Hockey Team,* a videotape produced by Warner HBO (2001), provides excellent details about the team and the coach.

Defining and Measuring Cohesion

- "Group Cohesion: From 'Field of Forces' to Multidimensional Construct," by Kenneth L. Dion (2000), reviews key issues in the study of cohesion, with a focus on definitional debates and problems in measurement.
- *The Social Psychology of Group Cohesiveness: From Attraction to Social Identity,* by Michael A. Hogg (1992), thoroughly reviews conceptual analyses of the concept of cohesion and bases its integrative theoretical reinterpretation on social identity theory.

Group Development

- *Group Process: A Developmental Perspective,* by Susan A. Wheelan (1994), provides an extensive analysis of each stage that marks the maturation of most groups.

Consequences of Cohesion

- "Relationship Between Collective Efficacy and Team Cohesion: Conceptual and Measurement Issues," by David M. Paskevich, Lawrence R. Brawley, Kim D. Dorsch, and W. Neil Widmeyer (1999), is a lucid, informative analysis of the problems encountered when studying such multilevel concepts as cohesion and collective efficacy. See also James E. Maddux's (1999) comments on issues of nomenclature and measurement.
- "The Relation Between Group Cohesion and Performance: An Integration," by Brian Mullen and Carolyn Copper (1994), presents the results of their comprehensive and sophisticated meta-analysis of 47 studies of the link between cohesion and performance.

Teams

- "Teams Embedded in Organizations: Some Implications," by Daniel R. Ilgen (1999), briefly examines the conceptual issues involved in generalizing from traditional studies of groups to teams in organizations.
- "Work Groups and Teams in Organizations," by Steve W. J. Kozlowksi and Bradford Bell (2003), provides a succinct, up-to-date analysis of the use of teams in organizational settings.
- *Making the Team,* by Leigh L. Thompson (2004), is a fine-grained, well-researched analysis of team processes that offers useful insights for managers, leaders, and executives who want to use teams but want these teams to be successful.

MEDIA RESOURCES

 Visit the Group Dynamics companion website at http://psychology.wadsworth.com/forsyth4e to access online resources for your book, including quizzes, flash cards, web links, and more!

6

STRUCTURE

CHAPTER OVERVIEW

Each group is unique in many ways, but beneath the surface lie certain structures that are common to virtually all groups. All but the most ephemeral groups develop written and unwritten norms that dictate conduct in the group, expectations about members' roles, and networks of connections among the members.

❖ What are norms?

❖ What are roles?

❖ What are status networks?

❖ What are attraction networks?

❖ What are communication networks?

CHAPTER OUTLINE

Andes Survivors: One Group's Triumph over Extraordinary Adversity

The chartered Fairchild F-227 was en route from Uruguay to Chile. Most of the passengers were players on the "Old Christians" amateur rugby team, family members, or friends of the players. But the plane never reached Chile. The pilot and copilot misjudged their location and began their descent from cruising altitude too soon. Their plane crashed deep in the snow-covered Andes of South America.

Rescue teams searched through the mountains, but the plane had been so far off course when it crashed that the search was fruitless. Thus, those passengers who survived the crash faced another challenge—surviving in the harsh, subzero temperatures of the Andes. Despite incredible hardships, the survivors managed to band together and overcome every adversity they faced. They organized their work, with some cleaning their sleeping quarters, some tending the injured, and others melting snow into drinking water. When their food ran out, they made the difficult decision to eat the frozen bodies of those who had died in the crash. And when starvation seemed imminent, they sent two men down the mountain to seek help. The two walked for 14 days before they reached a small farm on the edge of the great mountain range. Their sudden appearance after 70 days was followed by a rescue operation that lifted the remaining 14 survivors from the crash site.

The group lived and worked together at the crash site for nearly 3 months. But the group that came down from the Andes was not the same group that began the chartered flight; the pattern of relationships among the group members—that is, the group's *structure*—had been altered. The survivors developed new standards and values that were unlike any of the rugby team's norms. The group began with a captain but ended up with "commanders," "lieutenants," and "explorers." Men who were at first afforded little respect or courtesy eventually earned considerable status within the group. Some who were well liked before the crash became outcasts. Some who had hardly spoken to the others before became active communicators within the group.

Any group, whether stranded in the Andes, sitting around a conference table, or working to manufacture some product, can be better understood by studying its *group structure*—the underlying pattern of stable relations that organizes groups. Just as physicists, when studying an unknown element, analyze its basic atomic structure rather than its superficial features, those who study groups look beyond the unique features of groups for evidence of these underlying basic structures—norms, roles, and intermember relations (see Hechter & Op, 2001; L. H. Lofland, 1995; D. T. Miller & Prentice, 1996; Scott & Scott, 1981; for reviews).

NORMS

The survivors of the crash needed to coordinate their actions if they were to survive. With food, water, and shelter severely limited, the group members were forced to interact with and rely on each other continually, and any errant action on the part of one person would disturb and even endanger several other people. So members soon began to follow a shared set of rules that defined how the group would sleep at night, what types of duties each healthy individual was expected to perform, and how food and water were to be apportioned.

Norms are the emergent, consensual standards that regulate group members' behaviors. **Prescriptive norms** define the socially appropriate way to respond in a social situation—the *normal* course of action—and **proscriptive norms** identify the types of actions that should be avoided if at all possible (Sorrels & Kelley, 1984). For example, some of the prescriptive norms of the Andes group were "Food should be shared equally," "Those who can should work to help those who are injured," and "Follow the orders of the leader," whereas some proscriptive norms were "Do not urinate inside the airplane" and "Do not take more than your share of food and water." *Social norms* structure actions in a wide variety of contexts and cultures, whereas *group norms* are specific to a particular group. In some groups, it may be appropriate to interrupt others when they are talking, to arrive late and to leave early, and to dress informally. In other groups, such behaviors would be considered inappropriate because they violate the group norms of dress and decorum.

Some norms describe the kinds of behavior that people *usually* perform. These **descriptive norms** define what most people would do, feel, or think in a particular situation. Most people arrive for the meeting on time. Very few people fall asleep during the meeting. Most people clap when the speaker finishes. **Injunctive norms** are more evaluative—they describe the sorts of behaviors that people *ought* to perform. People who do not comply with descriptive norms may be viewed as unusual, but people who violate injunctive norms are considered "bad" and are open to sanction by the other group members. Not only do very few people lie, cheat, and steal, but lying, cheating, and stealing are all considered immoral, and people who break these social rules are usually punished in some way. In the Andes group, for example, those who failed to do their fair share of work were criticized by the others, given distasteful chores, and sometimes even denied food and water (Cialdini, Reno, & Kallgren, 1990; D. T. Miller & Prentice, 1996).

Norms are a fundamental element of a group's structure, for they provide direction and motivation, organize social interactions, and make other people's

---

prescriptive norm A consensual standard that identifies preferable, positively sanctioned behaviors.

proscriptive norm A consensual standard that identifies prohibited, negatively sanctioned behaviors.

descriptive norm A consensual standard that describes how people typically act, feel, and think in a given situation.

injunctive norm An evaluative consensual standard that describes how people *should* act, feel, and think in a given situation rather than how people *do* act, feel, and think in that situation.

responses predictable and meaningful. Simple behaviors such as choice of clothing ("Wear shoes in public"), manners ("Do not interrupt others"), and conventions of address ("Call the professor 'Dr.'") reflect norms, but so do general societal principles of fairness ("Help others when they are in need"), morality ("Do not lie to members of the group"), and value ("Work hard for the group"). Each group member is restrained to a degree by norms, but each member also benefits from the order that norms provide.

The Development of Norms

Groups sometimes write down and formally adopt norms as their group's rules, but more frequently, a group's norms are implicit standards rather than explicit ones. Because members gradually align their behaviors until they match certain standards, they are often not even aware that their behavior is dictated by the norms of the situation. People do not spend a great deal of time wondering, "Should I be quiet in the library?" "Should I nap during the group meeting?" or "Should I eat another human being?" They take these norms for granted so fully that they comply with them automatically (Aarts, Dijksterhuis, & Custers, 2003).

The Andes survivors, for example, had been raised in a culture that condemned cannibalism, but this taboo was largely unstated. By the fourth day, the group was growing weak from starvation, and one group member remarked that the only source of nourishment was the frozen bodies of the crash victims. The others took the remark to be a joke until the tenth day, when "the discussion spread as these boys cautiously mentioned it to their friends or those they thought would be sympathetic" (P. P. Read, 1974, p. 76). When the topic was discussed by the entire group, a small subgroup of boys argued in favor of eating the corpses, and a second group claimed that they could not bring themselves to think of their dead friends as food. The next day, however, their hopes of rescue were crushed when they learned by radio that the air force had given up the search. The realization that help was not forthcoming forced most of the group members to consume a few pieces of meat, and, in the end, cannibalism became the norm.

A group of people in an ambiguous situation may start off with little internal consensus and great variability in behavior, but in time, its members reach a consensus through reciprocal influence. Group members do not actively conform to the judgments of others, but they use the information contained in others' responses to revise their own opinions and beliefs. Norms, then, emerge when "the external surroundings lack stable, orderly reference points," and "the individuals caught in the ensuing experience of uncertainty mutually contribute to each other a mode of orderliness to establish their own orderly pattern" (Sherif, 1936, 1966, pp. xxi–xiii). Norms are, in many cases, self-generating.

Muzafer Sherif, as noted briefly in Chapter 1, studied this norm emergence process by taking advantage of the *autokinetic effect*. This illusion of vision occurs when a person stares at a pinpoint of light in an otherwise dark room. Even though the light is stationary, the dot will appear to move. Sherif found that when

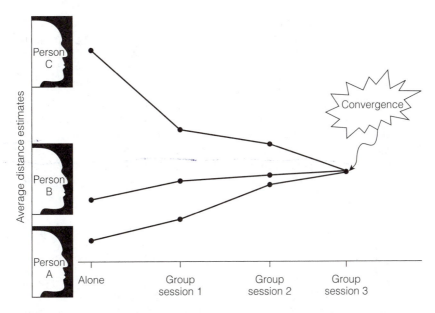

FIGURE 6-1

How do norms develop in groups? Participants' judgments in Sherif's study converged over time. Their private, pregroup judgments differed markedly, but when they joined with others, their judgments converged. *Source:* Data from M. Sherif *The Psychology of Social Norms,* 1936, Harper & Row.

individuals judged the dot's movement repeatedly, they usually established their own idiosyncratic average estimates, which varied from 1 to 10 inches. But when people made their judgments in groups, their personal estimates blended with those of other group members. One group, for example, included three people who had already been tested individually. During these initial tests, Person A thought the light moved very little—about 1 inch. Person B estimated the movement at 2 inches, but C's estimates were higher, averaging about 7 inches. When these three people made their estimates of the movement aloud when seated together, their judgments converged. It took three meetings, but by the third session, a norm had emerged: All the members felt the light was moving about 3 inches. Figure 6-1 graphs this convergence process: Over time, individuals with the highest and lowest estimates revise their judgments to match the group average.

The Transmission of Norms

Norms, by definition, are shared, consensual standards. Sherif, for example, did not just find that each individual adopted some idiosyncratic standard, but that the entire group came to adopt the same standard. But Sherif also discovered that norms are often personally accepted by group members. Sherif did not think that the group members whose initial judgments differed substantially from the group's estimates were just agreeing with the others publicly, whereas privately, they still felt that their own idiosyncratic estimates were more accurate. He instead believed that the group members fully endorsed the group's standard of movement estimation, and that even if removed from the group, they would continue to adhere to the group's norm. So he arranged for people to make their judgments alone again after taking part in the group sessions. He discovered that they continued to base their estimates on the standard that emerged in the group that they belonged to previously (Sherif, 1966). They obeyed their group's norm even when there was no external pressure to do so, suggesting that they had *internalized* the norm—that they personally accepted the standard as their own (Kelman, 1961).

Norms, because they are both consensual (accepted by many group members) and internalized (personally accepted by each individual member), are social facts—taken-for-granted elements of the group's stable structure. Even if the individuals who originally fostered the norms are no longer present, their normative innovations remain a part of the organization's traditions, and newcomers must change to adopt that tradition. Researchers have studied this norm transmission experimentally using a *generational* paradigm: They create a group, and then add newcomers to it and retire old-timers until the entire membership of the group has turned over. Do these succeeding generations of members remain true to the group's original norms, even if these norms are arbitrary or cause the group to make errors and mistakes (see Focus 6-1)? In one autokinetic effect study, researchers established an extreme norm by putting a confederate in each three-member group. The confederate steadfastly maintained that the dot of light was moving about 15 inches—clearly an excessive estimate, given that most estimates averaged about 3 to 4 inches. Once the confederate deflected the group's distance norm upward, he was removed from the group and replaced by a naive participant. The remaining group members, however, still retained the large distance norm, and the newest addition to the group gradually adapted to the higher standard. The researchers continued to replace group members with new participants, but new members continued to shift their estimates in the direction of the group norm. This arbitrary group norm gradually disappeared as judgments of distance came back down to an average of 3.5 inches, but in most cases, the more reasonable norm did not develop until group membership had changed five or six times (R. C. Jacobs & Campbell, 1961; MacNeil & Sherif, 1976; Pollis, Montgomery, & Smith, 1975). In another generational study, researchers gave groups feedback that suggested that their norm about how decisions should be made was causing them to make errors, but this negative feedback did not reduce the norm's longevity across generations (M. E. Nielsen & Miller, 1997).

Because norms tend to resist revision, some group's norms may seem pointless and arbitrary rather than reasonable and functional. They are, however,

FOCUS 6-1   Do Eating Disorders Run in Groups?

*Everyone on the [cheerleading] squad binges and
vomits. That's how I learned.*
—Laura (quoted in Squire, 1983, p. 48)

Theodore Newcomb, in his 1943 study of political attitudes discussed in Chapter 2, discovered
that students changed their attitudes until their
political preferences matched the attitudes of
their classmates and professors. Some 40 years
later, Christian Crandall (1988) documented
similar shifts in a study of *bulimia*—a pernicious
cycle of binge eating followed by self-induced
vomiting or other forms of purging. Certain social groups, such as cheerleading squads, dance
troupes, sports teams, and sororities, tend to have
strikingly high rates of eating disorders (Crago,
Yates, Beutler, & Arizmendi, 1985; D. M. Garner & Garfinkel, 1980; Squire, 1983). In explanation, Crandall noted that such groups adopt
norms that encourage binging and purging.
Rather than viewing these actions as abnormal
and a threat to health, the sororities that Crandall
studied accepted purging as a normal means of
controlling one's weight. The women who were
popular in such groups were the ones who
binged at the rate established by the group's

norms. Even worse, women who did not binge
when they first joined the group were more
likely to take up the practice the longer they remained in the group.

Similar results have been obtained in studies of
other sorts of socially undesirable or unhealthy
behaviors (W. A. Fisher & Fisher, 1993). In many
cases, group members believe they are conforming to the group's norm, but in fact they have
misperceived the norm itself. College students,
for example, often misperceive the extent to
which other students drink excessive amounts of
alcohol. Most of the students who participated in
one study were personally opposed to overindul-
gence, but they believed that their campus's
norms encouraged heavy alcohol consumption.
The men responded to this norm by gradually
internalizing the misperceived norm. They began
to drink more the longer they stayed at the
school. The women, in contrast, responded by
distancing themselves from their university and
its norms about drinking (Prentice & Miller,
1993). These studies explain how norms that run
counter to society's general traditions can establish a life of their own in small subgroups within
that society.

aspects of the group's structure, and even odd or unusual norms organize interactions, increase predictability, and enhance solidarity. The newcomer to a work
crew that always refers to its afternoon break as "banana time" may be baffled by
this odd label initially, but in short order, the newcomer will himself be announcing, "It's banana time" as break time draws near (D. F. Roy, 1973). Adults
who want to take part in an ongoing game of "pickup" basketball learn to ask the
question "Who has next?" to inform the other players that they wish to play and
that they will complain if they are passed over for a player who arrived after they
did (Jimerson, 1999). When a Little League baseball team takes to calling an opposing team "the string beans" because of the greenish color of their uniform,
the players share a sense of collusion and secrecy when their shortstop calls out
"bean the bean" to the pitcher (Fine, 1979). Norms do not just maintain order
in the group; they also maintain the group itself (see Table 6-1).

TABLE 6-1 Various types of norms—the standards that structure behavior in groups and other social situations

Common Features	Description
Descriptive	Describe how most members act, feel, and think
Consensual	Shared among group members, rather than personal, idiosyncratic beliefs
Injunctive	Define which behaviors are "bad" or "wrong" and which are "good" or "acceptable"
Prescriptive	Set the standards for expected behavior
Proscriptive	Identify behaviors that should not be performed
Informal	Describe the unwritten rules of conduct in the group
Implicit	Often so taken for granted that members follow them automatically
Self-generating	Emerge as members reach a consensus through reciprocal influence
Stable	Once they develop, resistant to change and passed from current members to new members

ROLES

On the day after the Andes crash, Marcelo, the captain of the rugby team, organized the efforts of those who could work. Two young men and one of the women administered first aid to the injured. One subgroup of boys melted snow for drinking water, and another team cleaned the cabin of the airplane. These various positions in the group—leader, doctor, snow melter, cabin cleaner—are all examples of *roles*—coherent sets of behaviors expected of people in specific positions within a group or social setting.

Roles in a group are similar in some respects to roles in a play. A play's roles describe the characters that the actors portray before the audience. To become Juliet in Shakespeare's *Romeo and Juliet,* for example, an actor must perform certain actions and recite her dialogue accordingly. Similarly, roles in groups structure behavior by dictating the "part" that members take as they interact. Once cast in a role such as leader, outcast, or questioner, group members perform certain actions and interact with other group members in a particular way. Their actions and activities reflect the demands of their role rather than their personal predilections or inclinations. But members can, in many cases, negotiate within the group as they move in and out of different roles. Group members who want to influence others may seek the role of leader, and those who wish to maintain a low profile may seek out the role of follower (Biddle, 1979; Callero, 1994).

Just as some variability is permitted in theatrical roles, group roles do not structure group members' actions completely. An actor playing the role of Juliet must perform certain behaviors as part of her role—she would not be Shakespeare's Juliet if she did not fall in love with Romeo. She can, however, recite her lines in an original way, change her stage behaviors, and even ad-lib. In social groups, too, people can fulfill the same role in somewhat different ways, and so long as they do not stray too far from the role's basic requirements, the group tolerates this variation. However, like the stage director who replaces an actor who presents an unsatisfactory Juliet, the group can replace members who repeatedly fail to play their part within the group. The role often supersedes any particular group member. When the role occupant departs, the role itself remains and is filled by a new member (Hare, 1994; Stryker & Burke, 2000; Stryker & Statham, 1985).

Role Differentiation

Sometimes, groups deliberately create roles to organize the group and thereby facilitate the attainment of the group's goals (Stempfle, Hübner, & Badke-Schaub, 2001). A group may decide that its efficiency would be augmented if someone takes charge of the meetings and different tasks are assigned to subcommittees. In some cases, too, someone outside the group, such as the group's supervisor, may create roles within the group by mandate. But even without a deliberate attempt at creating a formal group structure, the group will probably develop an informal role structure. Members may initially consider themselves to be just members, basically similar to each other. But in time, some group members will begin to perform specific types of actions and interact with other group members in a particular way. As this **role differentiation** process unfolds, the number of roles in the group increases, whereas the roles themselves gradually become more narrowly defined and specialized. In the Andes survivors, for example, the roles of *leader, doctor,* and *cleaner* emerged first, soon followed by the *inventor,* who created makeshift snowshoes, hammocks, and water-melting devices; *explorer,* who was determined to hike down from the mountain; and *complainer, pessimist, optimist,* and *encourager.* This rapid proliferation of roles is typical of groups facing difficult problems or emergencies (Bales, 1958).

TYPES OF ROLES What roles tend to emerge as a group becomes organized? Certainly, the role of *leader* is a fundamental one in many groups, but other roles should not be overlooked. Many of these roles, such as *expert, secretary,* and *organizer,* are similar in that they revolve around the task the group is tackling. People who fulfill a **task role** focus on the group's goals and on the members' attempts to support one another as they work. Marcelo, in the Andes group, was a task-oriented leader, for he organized work squads and controlled the rationing of the group's meager food supplies, and the rest of the members obeyed his

---

role differentiation An increase in the number of roles in a group, accompanied by the gradual decrease in the scope of these roles as each one becomes more narrowly defined and specialized.

task role Any position in a group occupied by a member who performs behaviors that promote completion of tasks and activities, such as initiating structure, providing task-related feedback, and setting goals.

orders. He did not, however, satisfy the group members' interpersonal and emotional needs. As if to offset Marcelo's inability to cheer up the survivors, several group members became more positive and friendly, actively trying to reduce conflicts and to keep morale high. Liliana Methol, in particular, provided a "unique source of solace" (P. P. Read, 1974, p. 74) to the young men. She came to fill a **relationship role** (also frequently termed *socioemotional role*) in the Andes group. A group may need to accomplish its tasks, but it must also ensure that the interpersonal and emotional needs of the members are met. Whereas the *coordinator* and *energizer* structure the group's work, such roles as *supporter, clown,* and even *critic* help satisfy the emotional needs of the group members.

The tendency for groups to develop both task roles and relationship roles is consistent with Kenneth D. Benne and Paul Sheats's (1948) studies conducted at the National Training Laboratories (NTL), an organization devoted to the improvement of groups. Benne and Sheats concluded that a group, to survive, must meet two basic demands: The group must accomplish its tasks, and the relationships among members must be maintained. Table 6-2 lists the typical task roles that Benne and Sheats identified, including *coordinator, elaborator, energizer, evaluator/critic, information giver, information seeker,* and *opinion giver.* Table 6-2 also lists the relationship roles that most frequently emerge in groups, including *compromiser, encourager, follower,* and *harmonizer.* The task roles facilitate the group's attainment of its goals, and the relationship roles reduce interpersonal strains and stresses within the group. Benne and Sheats also identified a third set of roles— *individualistic roles.* Like the malingerers in the Andes group—several young men who did little work and demanded that others care for them—those who adopt individualistic roles emphasize their own needs over the group's needs.

WHY DIFFERENTIATION? Why do task roles and relationship roles emerge in so many different groups? One answer, proposed by Bales and his colleagues, suggests that very few individuals can simultaneously fulfill both the task and the relationship needs of the group (Bales, 1955, 1958; T. Parsons et al., 1953). When task specialists try to move groups toward their goals, they must necessarily issue orders, restrict the behavioral options of others, criticize other members, and prompt them into action. These actions may be necessary to reach the goal, but the group members may react negatively to the task specialists' prodding. Because most of the members believe the task specialist to be the source of the tension, "someone other than the task leader must assume a role aimed at the reduction of interpersonal hostilities and frustrations" (P. J. Burke, 1967, p. 380). The peacekeeper who intercedes and tries to maintain harmony is the relationship specialist. Task and relationship roles, then, are a natural consequence of these two partly conflicting demands.

---

relationship role Any position in a group occupied by a member who performs behaviors that improve the nature and quality of interpersonal relations among members, such as showing concern for the feelings of others, reducing conflict, and enhancing feelings of satisfaction and trust in the group.

TABLE 6-2 Types of roles in groups

Role	Function
Task Roles	
Initiator/contributor	Recommends novel ideas about the problem at hand, new ways to approach the problem, or possible solutions not yet considered
Information seeker	Emphasizes getting the facts by calling for background information from others
Opinion seeker	Asks for more qualitative types of data, such as attitudes, values, and feelings
Information giver	Provides data for forming decisions, including facts that derive from expertise
Opinion giver	Provides opinions, values, and feelings
Elaborator	Gives additional information—examples, rephrasings, implications—about points made by others
Coordinator	Shows the relevance of each idea and its relationship to the overall problem
Orienter	Refocuses discussion on the topic whenever necessary
Evaluator/critic	Appraises the quality of the group's methods, logic, and results
Energizer	Stimulates the group to continue working when discussion flags
Procedural technician	Cares for operational details, such as materials, machinery, and so on
Recorder	Takes notes and maintains records
Relationship Roles	
Encourager	Rewards others through agreement, warmth, and praise
Harmonizer	Mediates conflicts among group members
Compromiser	Shifts his or her own position on an issue in order to reduce conflict in the group
Gatekeeper/expediter	Smooths communication by setting up procedures and ensuring equal participation from members
Standard setter	Expresses or calls for discussion of standards for evaluating the quality of the group process
Group observer/ commentator	Points out the positive and negative aspects of the group's dynamics and calls for change if necessary
Follower	Accepts the ideas offered by others and serves as an audience for the group
Individual Roles	
Aggressor	Expresses disapproval of acts, ideas, and feelings of others; attacks the group
Blocker	Negativistic; resists the group's influence; opposes the group unnecessarily
Dominator	Asserts authority or superiority; manipulative
Evader/self-confessor	Expresses personal interests, feelings, and opinions unrelated to group goals
Help seeker	Expresses insecurity, confusion, and self-deprecation
Recognition seeker	Calls attention to him- or herself; self-aggrandizing
Playboy/girl	Uninvolved in the group; cynical, nonchalant
Special-interest pleader	Remains apart from the group by acting as representative of another social group or category

Source: Adapted from "Functional Roles of Group Members" by K. D. Benne and P. Sheats, Journal of Social Issues, 1948, 4(2), 41–49. Copyright 1948 by the Society for the Psychology of Social Issues. Reprinted by permission.

Bales's research team identified these tendencies by tracking the emergence of task and relationship experts in decision-making groups across four sessions. Bales used his *Interaction Process Analysis* (IPA) system to identify certain specific types of behavior within the groups. As noted in Chapter 2 (see Table 2-1), half of the categories in IPA focus on task-oriented behaviors—either attempts to solve specific problems in the group or attempts to exchange information via questioning. The remaining six categories are reserved for positive relationship behaviors (*shows solidarity, tension release, agreement*) or negative relationship behaviors (*disagrees, shows tension, shows antagonism*). Bales found that individuals rarely performed both task and relationship behaviors: Most people gravitated toward either a task role or a relationship role. The task specialist (labeled the "idea man") offered mostly suggestions and expressed his or her opinions. The relationship specialist (labeled the "best-liked man") showed solidarity, more tension release, and greater agreement with other group members. The task specialist tended to elicit more questions, displays of tension, antagonism, and disagreement, whereas the relationship specialist received more demonstrations of solidarity, tension reduction, and solutions to problems. Moreover, this differentiation became more pronounced over time. During the first session, the same person was both the task specialist and the relationship specialist in 56.5% of the groups. By the fourth session, only 8.5% of the leaders occupied both roles. In most cases, individuals dropped their role as task leader in favor of the relationship role (Bales, 1953, 1958; Bales & Slater, 1955; Slater, 1955).

The task and relationship roles are most likely to emerge as separate roles when the group is experiencing conflict about its goals. In one study of such groups, task and relationship behaviors were very negatively correlated ($-.73$; see P. J. Burke, 1967). But role differentiation is not an inevitable occurrence in all groups (R. H. Turner & Colomy, 1988). Some individuals are the small-group equivalent of great heroes and leaders, for they are both well liked and they focus on the work to be done (Borgatta, Couch, & Bales, 1954). When players on football teams were asked to identify the best players on the team (task experts) and those who contributed most to the group's harmony (relationship experts), many of the seniors and first-string players were identified as fulfilling both roles (Rees & Segal, 1984). When students in classroom groups rated their fellow group members on Benne and Sheats's (1948) roles listed in Table 6-2, they often attributed task and relationship roles to the same individual. The correlation between the two roles was .25. Groups with members who filled both roles were also more cohesive and performed more effectively (Mudrack & Farrell, 1995). Differentiation of these two types of roles is more common than their combination, however, perhaps because few people have the interpersonal and cognitive skills needed to enact both roles successfully.

Group Socialization

An actor answering a casting call may hope to land the lead role of Juliet, but the director may instead offer her only a smaller part, such as the role of the nurse or Lady Capulet. She may decide that the role is too unsubstantial for her talents and not accept it, or she may decide that any role in the production is better than no

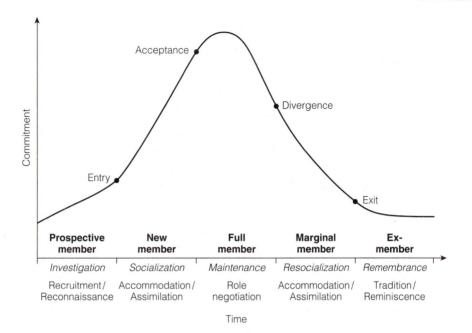

FIGURE 6-2

What stages mark members' transition from one role to the next in a group? Moreland and Levine's (1982) model of group socialization identifies five types of roles (e.g., prospective member, new member), five role stages (e.g., investigation, socialization), five role socialization processes (e.g., recruitment/reconnaissance, accommodation/assimilation), and four role transition points (e.g., entry, acceptance). The curved line represents the gradual increase—and eventual decrease—of a hypothetical member's commitment to the group. Commitment increases as the member moves from prospective member to new member to full member, then declines as the member moves to the role of marginal member and ex-member.

role at all. Similarly, individuals often seek particular roles in groups, but the group may not permit them to occupy these roles. In the Andes group, for example, many sought to be one of the "expeditionaries"—explorers who were selected to hike away from the crash site and seek help. But only three were chosen. The group also selected some group members to perform certain tasks, and although some members openly complained about their roles, the group insisted that they take on the role despite their protestations.

Richard Moreland and John Levine (1982) described this negotiation of roles between the individual and the group in their theory of **group socialization.** This theory, which is summarized in Figure 6-2, recognizes that individuals are

group socialization A pattern of change in the relationship between an individual and a group that begins when an individual first considers joining the group and ends when he or she leaves it.

often asked to take on roles that they would prefer to avoid. Newcomers must "learn their place" in the group and acquire the behaviors required by the roles to which they have been assigned. Veteran group members must, in some cases, be ready to take on new roles within the group that force them to learn new skills and seek new challenges. But group members also feel that their groups should be flexible enough to change to meet their particular needs. So individuals attempt to influence the group. Hence, group socialization is a mutual process; through assimilation, the individual accepts the group's norms, values, and perspectives, and through accommodation, the group adapts to fit the newcomer's needs.

Moreland and Levine's theory distinguishes between five classes of roles— *prospective member, new member, full member, marginal member,* and *ex-member.* Prior to actually joining a group, individuals may study the group and the resources it offers, and part of this reconnaissance involves identifying the type of role they will be given should they join. The group, in contrast, seeks to recruit new members, often by promising them roles and responsibilities that—once they are in the group—they will not actually be given (R. M. Kramer, 1998). Should the individuals choose to enter the group (*entry*), their commitment to the group increases, and their socialization by the full members begins in earnest (Moreland & Levine, 2002). To the full members, the newcomers are inexperienced and cannot be completely trusted until they accept the group's norms and role allocations. Newcomers can prolong their assimilation into the group by remaining cautiously aloof or by misinterpreting other members' reactions. Moreland (1985) studied how people react when they think they are newcomers by arranging for groups of five unacquainted individuals to meet for several weeks to discuss various topics. He told two of the five that the group had been meeting for some time and that they were the only newcomers. Although the role of newcomer existed only in the minds of these two participants, the people who thought themselves newcomers behaved differently from the others. They interacted more frequently and more positively with each other, they were less satisfied with the group discussion, and their descriptions of the group made reference to members' seniority. Thus, the belief that one is a newcomer who will be treated differently by the old-timers can act as a self-fulfilling prophecy: The newcomers may act in ways that slow their acceptance by the rest of the group (Major, Kozlowski, Chao, & Gardner, 1995). They may also have second thoughts about the group once they learn more about it. Peripheral members, if they feel that the group will accept them fully in the future, come to identify strongly with the group. But if they worry that their future is uncertain, these members' loyalty to the group will wane, and they will begin looking for an alternative (J. M. Levine, Moreland, & Choi, 2001).

The socialization process does not end when individuals become full-fledged group members. Even seasoned group members must adjust as the group adds new members, adopts new goals in place of its old objectives, or modifies status and role relationships. Much of this maintenance phase is devoted to role negotiation. The group may, for example, require the services of a leader who can organize the group's activities and motivate members. The individual, in contrast, may wish instead to remain a follower who is responsible for relatively routine matters. During this phase, the group and the individual negotiate the nature and quantity of the member's expected contribution to the group.

Many group members remain in the maintenance period until their membership in the group reaches a scheduled conclusion. An employee who retires, a student who graduates from college, or an elected official whose term in office expires all leave the group after months or years of successful maintenance. In some cases, however, the maintenance process builds to a transition point that Moreland and Levine labeled *divergence*. The group may, for example, force individuals to take on roles that they do not find personally rewarding. Individuals, too, may fail to meet the group's expectations concerning appropriate behavior, and role negotiation may reach an impasse.

When the divergence point is reached, the socialization process enters a new phase—*resocialization*. During resocialization, the former full member takes on the role of a marginal member, whose future in the group is uncertain. The individual sometimes precipitates this crisis—often in response to increased costs and dwindling rewards, waning commitment to the group, and dissatisfaction with responsibilities and duties. The group, too, can be the instigator, reacting to a group member who is not contributing or is working against the group's explicit and implicit purposes. Moreland and Levine identified two possible outcomes of resocialization. The group and the individual, through accommodation and assimilation, can resolve their differences. In this instance, *convergence* occurs, and the individual once more becomes a full member of the group. Alternatively, resocialization efforts can fail (see Figure 6-2). The group may conclude that the individual is no longer acceptable as a member and move to expel him or her. Similarly, the individual may reevaluate his or her commitment to the group and decide to leave. As a result, the divergence between the group and the individual becomes so great that a final role transition is reached—*exit*.

Roles, Stress, and Well-Being

Roles influence group members' happiness and well-being in significant ways. By taking on a role in a group, individuals secure their connection to their fellow members, building the interdependence that is essential for group cohesion and productivity. But roles also permit group members to express themselves, for even though roles constrain individuals, they are not so rigid that they undermine the role occupants' sense of control and autonomy (Bettencourt & Sheldon, 2001).

But some roles are more satisfying than others. People prefer to occupy roles that are prestigious and significant rather than roles that are menial and unimportant, but they also like roles that require specialized skills and talents more than unchallenging, uninvolving roles (Rail, 1987; Rentach & Steel, 1998). The demands of a role can also be stressful for the occupants of that role. One of the young men in the Andes group, for example, was told to act as a doctor and tend the sick, but he did not have any medical training and was worried that he was doing more harm than good. When a role is ambiguously defined, internally inconsistent, or fits the occupant poorly, roles can be great challenges for group members (R. L. Kahn, Wolfe, Quinn, Snoek, & Rosenthal, 1964).

ROLE AMBIGUITY The responsibilities and activities that are required of a person who occupies a role are not always clear either to the occupant of the role (the *role taker*) or to the rest of the group (the *role senders*). Even when a role has a long history in the group (e.g., many groups have always had a leader, a secretary, and a treasurer) or the group deliberately creates the role for some specific purpose (e.g., a note taker is appointed) the responsibilities of the role may be ill-defined. In such cases, role takers will likely experience **role ambiguity**—they wonder if they are acting appropriately, they perform behaviors that others in the group should be carrying out, and they question their ability to fulfill their responsibilities (House, Schuler, & Levanoni, 1983).

ROLE CONFLICT In some instances, group members may find themselves occupying several roles at the same time, with the requirements of each role making demands on their time and abilities. If the multiple activities required by one role mesh with those required by the other, role takers experience few problems. If, however, the expectations that define the appropriate activities associated with these roles are incompatible, **role conflict** may occur (Brief, Schuler, & Van Sell, 1981; Graen, 1976; Van Sell, Brief, & Schuler, 1981).

Interrole conflict develops when role takers discover that the behaviors associated with one of their roles are incompatible with those associated with another one of their roles. When assembly line workers are promoted to managerial positions, for example, they often feel torn between the demands of their new supervisory role and their former roles as friend and workmate. Similarly, college students often find that their student role conflicts with other roles they occupy, such as spouse, parent, or employee. If the student role requires spending every free moment in the library studying for exams, other roles will be neglected.

Intrarole conflict results from contradictory demands within a single role. A supervisor in a factory, for example, may be held responsible for overseeing the quality of production, training new personnel, and providing feedback or goal-orienting information. At another level, however, supervisors become the super-

---

role ambiguity Unclear expectations about the behaviors to be performed by an individual occupying a particular position within the group, caused by a lack of clarity in the role itself, a lack of consensus within the group regarding the behaviors associated with the role, or the individual role taker's uncertainty with regard to the types of behaviors expected of them.

role conflict A state of tension, distress, or uncertainty caused by inconsistent or discordant expectations associated with one's role in the group.

interrole conflict A form of role conflict that occurs when individuals occupy multiple roles within a group and the expectations and behaviors associated with one of their roles are not consistent with the expectations and behaviors associated with another of their roles.

intrarole conflict A form of role conflict that occurs when the behaviors that make up a single role are incongruous, often resulting in inconsistent expectations on the part of the person who occupies the role and other members of the group.

vised, because they take directions from a higher level of management. Thus, the members of the team expect the manager to keep their secrets and support them in any disputes with the management, but the upper echelon expects obedience and loyalty (D. Katz & Kahn, 1978; Miles, 1976).

Role conflict also arises when role takers and role senders have different expectations. The newly appointed supervisor may assume that leadership means giving orders, maintaining strict supervision, and criticizing incompetence. The work group, however, may feel that leadership entails eliciting cooperation in the group, providing support and guidance, and delivering rewards.

PERSON–ROLE CONFLICT Sometimes, the behaviors associated with a particular role are completely congruent with the basic values, attitudes, personality, needs, or preferences of the person who must enact the role: A stickler for organization is asked to be in charge of organizing the group's records; a relationship expert must take on a role that requires sensitivity and warmth. In other cases, though, **role fit** is poor. An easygoing, warm person must give performance appraisals to the unit's employees. An individual with high ethical standards is asked to look the other way when the company uses illegal accounting practices.

When role fit is low, people do not feel that they can "be themselves" in their roles. College students who held roles in campus groups were asked if they felt that their role "reflected their authentic self and how much they felt free and choiceful as they fulfilled their role" (Bettencourt & Sheldon, 2001, p. 1136). Those who felt more authentic when enacting their role reported more positive mood, less negative mood, and a higher level of satisfaction with life overall. Feeling competent when enacting one's role was also a powerful predictor of well-being. In another study, students first rated themselves on 20 different traits (e.g., cooperative, outgoing, imaginative). Later in the semester, they were given a list of five discussion roles (idea person, devil's advocate, moderator, secretary, and announcer) and then asked to indicate how valuable these 20 traits were for enacting each role. For example, how important is it for the idea person to be cooperative? Outgoing? Imaginative? Then they were assigned to one of these roles in a class discussion. As the concept of role fit suggests, individuals assigned to roles that required the kinds of characteristics that they believed they possessed felt more authentic, and their moods were more positive (Bettencourt & Sheldon, 2001).

ROLE CONFLICT AND GROUP PERFORMANCE Role ambiguity, conflict, and poor role fit all predict decreased satisfaction, reduced productivity, and increased stress. In one study, accountants and hospital employees who reported experiencing role stress also displayed high levels of tension, decreased job

---

role fit The degree of congruence between the demands of a specific role and the attitudes, values, skills, and other characteristics of the individual who occupies the role.

satisfaction, and increased employee turnover (Kemery, Bedeian, Mossholder, & Touliatos, 1985). In another study, athletes who complained of role ambiguity also felt less confident in their ability to fill their roles adequately, and they also played more poorly (Beauchamp, Bray, Eys, & Carron, 2002). When the results of dozens of studies of role ambiguity and conflict are synthesized, they suggest that role stress is detrimental to group and organizational success. The size of the relationship between role conflict and group performance varied considerably across studies, but increases in role ambiguity and conflict were usually associated with an increased desire to leave the organization and with decreases in commitment to the organization, involvement, satisfaction, and participation in decision making (S. P. Brown, 1996; C. D. Fisher & Gitelson, 1983; S. E. Jackson & Schuler, 1995; L. A. King & King, 1990; M. F. Peterson, Smith, Akande, & Ayestaran, 1995; Tubre & Collins, 2000).

What can organizations do to help their employees cope with role stress? One solution involves making role requirements explicit: Managers should write job descriptions for each role within the organization and provide employees with feedback about the behaviors expected of them. The workplace can also be designed so that potentially incompatible roles are performed in different locations and at different times. In such cases, however, the individual must be careful to engage in behaviors appropriate to the specific role, because slipping into the wrong role at the wrong time can lead to considerable embarrassment (E. Gross & Stone, 1964). Some companies, too, develop explicit guidelines regarding when one role should be sacrificed so that another can be enacted, or they may prevent employees from occupying positions that can create role conflict (Sarbin & Allen, 1968). Managers and the leaders of groups should also be mindful of the characteristics of the members of their groups and be careful to maximize role fit when selecting members for particular tasks.

INTERMEMBER RELATIONS

On the 17th day of their ordeal, an avalanche swept down on the Andes survivors as they slept, filling their makeshift shelter with snow. Many were killed, and soon a new order emerged in the group. Three young men stepped forward to take over control of the group. They were cousins, and their kinship bonds connected them to one another securely, but they also were friends with many of the remaining group members.

Connections among the members of a group provide the basis for the third component of group structure—the network of intermember relations. The Andes survivors were a group, but they were also many individuals who were connected to one another in different ways. Norms and roles describe the kinds of behaviors that group members perform when they occupy particular positions within the group, but they do not specify the linkages among the individual members. Which one of the three cousins had the most authority? Who in a group is most liked by others, and who is an isolate? How does information flow

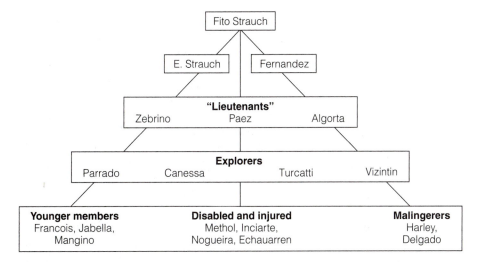

FIGURE 6-3

Did a chain of command exist in the Andes group? Before the avalanche killed the team captain, the survivors' authority structure was based on the rugby team's structure and seniority. After the avalanche, however, the group became organized in a hierarchical, centralized authority structure based on kinship.

through a group from one person to the next? The answers depend on the group's status, attraction, and communication networks.

Status Relations

The roles that emerged in the Andes group following the crash defined who would lead, who would explore, and who would care for the injured. The individuals who took on these roles, however, were not equal in terms of authority in the group. After the avalanche, Fito Strauch was more influential than the other group members; when he gave orders, most of the others obeyed. Also, the group's explorers were afforded more authority than the rank-and-file members. These stable variations in members' relative dominance and authority have many different names: *authority, power,* or *status networks; pecking orders; chains of command;* and *prestige rankings.*

Status networks are often hierarchical and centralized. In the Andes group, as Figure 6-3 illustrates, Fito Strauch, E. Strauch, and Fernandez formed a coalition that controlled most of the group's activities. Their "lieutenants" supported them by enforcing their orders and carrying out certain minor duties. The lieutenants' requests carried less force than those of Fito Strauch, but they still commanded a fair amount of respect. The explorers ("expeditionaries") occupied a niche just below the lieutenants. These individuals had been chosen to hike down the mountain in search of help. In preparing for their journey, they were given special privileges, including better sleeping arrangements and more clothing, food, and water. They were not leaders per se, but they could require lower echelon members to obey their orders. The rank-and-file members included the youngest men in the group, four men who had received disabling injuries, and two group members who were considered malingerers.

Figure 6-3 depicts the levels of authority that existed in the group. The power holders at the top of the hierarchy made more decisions, took more responsibility, and served as the foci for communication within the group. Below this top level was a second stratum of members who had less power than the leaders but more prestige than the occupants of lower echelons. Further down the chain of command, authority diminished and the number of occupants at each subordinate level increased. Hence, the lines of group authority formed a pyramid pattern, rather like that of formally organized groups such as businesses and military organizations (Dale, 1952). Status rankings violate our expectations of "equal treatment for all," but in the microsociety of the group, equality is the exception and inequality the rule. Initially, group members may start off on an equal footing, but over time, **status differentiation** takes place: Certain individuals acquire authority by laying claim to a position of greater status and by having their claim accepted by the other members of the group.

CLAIMING STATUS All social animals know how to communicate the message, "I am in charge." Dominant chimpanzees chatter loudly at potential rivals, the leader of the wolf pack growls and bares his teeth at low-ranking wolves, and the ranking lioness in the pride swats another with her paw. Members of these social groups compete for status, for the individual at the top of the hierarchy—the so-called *alpha* male or female—enjoys greater access to the group's resources. These high-ranking members maintain their position by threatening or attacking low-ranking members, who in turn manage to avoid these attacks by performing behaviors that signal deference and submissiveness. This system of dominance and submission is often called a **pecking order** because (at least in chickens) it determines who will do the pecking and who will be pecked. Biologists argue that pecking orders limit conflict in groups and increase individual and group survival (Bergman, Beehner, Cheney, & Sayfarth, 2003; Mazur, 1973).

Humans, too, compete for status in their groups. Humans rarely snarl at one another to signal their status, but they do use such nonverbal cues as a firm handshake, an unwavering gaze, a relaxed but poised posture, or an unsmiling countenance to let others know that they should be respected (Leffler, Gillespie, & Conaty, 1982). In the boardroom, for example, a dark suit, an expensive watch, and a conservative hairstyle connote power, but in a small group of friends, a

---

status differentiation The gradual rise of some group members to positions of greater authority, accompanied by decreases in the authority exercised by other members.

pecking order A stable, ordered pattern of individual variations in prestige, status, and authority among group members.

more casual look may be more appropriate. Large, sweeping gestures using the hands and head, a relaxed but poised posture, an attentive (but unsmiling) expression, a direct gaze, and a firm handshake or touch are all actions that lay claim to status. People also seek status by speaking clearly and loudly, whereas those who speak softly and pepper their comments with nervous giggles are afforded less authority (Damhorst, 1990; M. T. Lee & Ofshe, 1981; Mazur et al., 1980; Patterson, 1991). Displays of emotion also signal differences in status. Group members who seem angry are thought to be more influential and accorded higher status, whereas those who seem sad are thought to be lower in status (Tiedens, 2001; Tiedens, Ellsworth, & Mesquita, 2000).

People also signal their authority through their verbal communications. Those seeking status often initiate conversations and shift the discussion to their own areas of competence (Godfrey, Jones, & Lord, 1986). A person seeking high status would be more likely to (1) tell other people what they should do, (2) interpret other people's statements, (3) confirm or dispute other people's viewpoints, and (4) summarize or reflect on the discussion (Stiles et al., 1997). In a study group, for example, a high-status member may say, "I've studied this theory before," "I know this stuff backward and forward," or "I think it's more important to study the lecture notes than the text." A low-status individual, in contrast, may lament that "I always have trouble with this subject" or "I'm not sure I understand the material." Status seekers use strong rather than weak influence tactics, and they talk the most when they are in groups (Bonito & Hollingshead, 1997; Cappella, 1985; Dovidio et al., 1988). Group members also assert their authority over the group by interrupting other speakers frequently (Schmid Mast, 2002).

PERCEIVING STATUS People's status-seeking efforts will be for naught if the group rejects them. In the Andes group, one young man, to attain the high-status role of explorer, tried to impress others by undertaking risky physical adventures. The other group members, however, wanted explorers to be cautious rather than risk takers, and so they selected someone else for the role. The young man displayed characteristics and actions that he felt would earn him status, but because these claims did not match the group members' intuitive beliefs about who deserved status, his bid for authority failed.

Expectation-states theory, developed by Joseph Berger and his colleagues, provides a detailed analysis of the impact of group members' expectations on the status-organizing process. As noted briefly in Chapter 2, expectation-states theory assumes that status differences are most likely to develop when members are working collectively on a task that they feel is important. Because the group hopes that it can successfully complete the project, group members intuitively take note of one another's *status characteristics*—personal qualities that they think are indicative of ability or prestige. Those who possess numerous status characteristics are implicitly identified and permitted to perform more numerous and varied group actions, to provide greater input and guidance for the group, to influence others by evaluating their ideas, and to reject the influence attempts of others. (The basic propositions of this theory are discussed by J. Berger &

Zelditch, 1998; Fisek, Berger, & Norman, 1995; Ridgeway, 2001; Ridgeway & Walker, 1995; and M. Webster & Hysom, 1998.)

Expectation-states theorists believe that we generally take two types of cues into consideration when formulating expectations about ourselves and other group members. **Specific status characteristics** are qualities that attest to each individual's level of ability at the task to be performed in the given situation. On a basketball team, for example, height may be a specific status characteristic, whereas prior jury duty may determine status in a jury (Strodtbeck & Lipinski, 1985). In the Andes group, the higher status explorers were chosen on the basis of several specific status qualities: strength, determination, health, and maturity.

We also notice **diffuse status characteristics**—general qualities of the person that the members think are relevant to ability and evaluation. Sex, age, wealth, ethnicity, status in other groups, or cultural background can serve as diffuse status characteristics if people associate these qualities with certain skills, as did the members of the Andes group. Among the survivors, age was considered an important diffuse status characteristic, with youth being negatively valued.

Researchers have largely confirmed expectation-states theory's prediction that individuals with positively evaluated specific status and diffuse status characteristics usually command more authority than those who lack status-linked qualities (Wilke, 1996). In police teams, officers with more work experience exercised more authority than their less experienced partners (Gerber, 1996). Members of dyads working on a perceptual task deferred to their partner if he or she seemed more skilled at the task (Foddy & Smithson, 1996). People who are paid more are permitted to exert more influence over people who are paid less (Harrod, 1980; P. A. Stewart & Moore, 1992). When air force bomber crews work on nonmilitary tasks, rank predicts influence (Torrance, 1954). Juries allocate more status to jurors who have previously served on juries or who have more prestigious occupations (Strodtbeck, James, & Hawkins, 1957). The bulk of the research also confirms the following causal sequence in status allocation: (1) group member X displays specific and diffuse status characteristics, (2) group members form higher expectations about X's capabilities, and (3) group members allow X to influence them (Driskell & Mullen, 1990).

INCONGRUENCIES IN STATUS ALLOCATIONS Groups do not always allocate status fairly (J. Schneider & Cook, 1995). Imagine, for example, a jury that includes these three individuals:

- Dr. Prof, a 40-year-old European American woman who teaches in the School of Business and who has written several books on management.

---

specific status characteristic In status characteristics theory, task-specific behavioral and personal characteristics that people consider when estimating the relative competency, ability, and social value of themselves and others.

diffuse status characteristic In status characteristics theory, general personal qualities such as age, race, and ethnicity that people consider when estimating the relative competency, ability, and social value of themselves and others.

- Mr. Black, a 35-year-old African American executive with outstanding credentials and long experience in a leadership position.
- Dr. White, a 58-year-old European American male physician who has an active practice.

Considerable evidence suggests that a jury of middle-class European Americans, when selecting a foreman, would be biased against Dr. Prof and Mr. Black and in favor of Dr. White. Dr. Prof and Mr. Black, despite their specific status credentials, may be disqualified from positions of status in the group by their (completely irrelevant) diffuse status characteristics. In contrast, Dr. White poses little incongruency for the group if the group members unfairly consider advanced age, pale skin, and an M.D. degree to be positive features. This phenomenon is known as **status generalization:** Group members let general status (i.e., diffuse status) characteristics influence their expectations, even though these characteristics are irrelevant in the given situation (Molm, 1986; Ridgeway & Balkwell, 1997).

Status generalization explains why women and African Americans are given less status and authority in groups than European Americans and men. Despite changes in sexist and racist attitudes in society, stereotypical biases still make gaining status in small groups a difficult task for women, African Americans, and other minorities (J. M. Nielsen, 1990). Women and African Americans report more dissatisfaction about how status is allocated in groups (Hembroff, 1982). Women are less likely to be selected as leaders of their groups, and they are more likely to be assigned to lower status roles (Eagly & Karau, 2002). Women and minorities must put extra effort into their groups and reach higher performance standards just to reach the same level of respect and authority granted to less productive European American men (Biernat & Kobrynowicz, 1997; Foschi, 1996).

These unfair status allocation processes are magnified when individuals who are members of stereotyped minority societal groups are also underrepresented in the group itself. Women, for example, react more negatively than do men to **solo status**—being the only representative of their social category (in this case, the only woman) in the group. Solo status causes minority members to feel that the other group members are categorizing them in terms of their social group rather than as a comember. In consequence, they are less likely to identify with the group, will not be as loyal to the group, and will not contribute as much to the group's activities—especially when they do not feel they will be able to influence prestige allocations (Branscombe, Spears, Ellemers, & Doosje, 2002; Jetten, Branscombe, Spears, & McKimmie, 2003). They may experience a decline in

---

status generalization The tendency for individuals known to have achieved or been ascribed authority, respect, and prestige in one context to enjoy relatively higher status in other, unrelated, contexts (e.g., a celebrity who exercises influence in a group even though this diffuse status characteristic is not relevant in the current group context).

solo status The state of being the only group member who is a representative of a specific social category in an otherwise homogenous group (e.g., a man in an otherwise all female group).

FOCUS 6-2 Do Online Groups Allocate Status More Fairly than Face-to-Face Groups?

Somewhere in desolate wind-swept space
In Twilight land, in No-man's land
Two hurrying Shapes met face to face
–Thomas Bailey Aldrich

When people meet in face-to-face groups to make decisions or solve problems, their impact on the final outcome is often a function of their status in the group. Those who have risen to the top of the group's hierarchy have more of an impact on others. In the typical face-to-face group, the leader will speak as much as 40 to 50% of the time (F. F. Stephan & Mischler, 1952). Two or three other group members will also contribute a great deal, but as one's rank in the "speaking hierarchy" drops, so does his or her contribution to the group's discussion (Gibson, 2003). Those at the bottom of the hierarchy may say nothing at all during the course of a meeting. Contributions to the discussion also tend to be clustered. Once individuals enter the discussion stream, they tend to concentrate their comments during periods of high vocality, or *megaturns* (Dabbs & Ruback, 1987; Parker, 1988). This pattern oc-

curs, in part, because some individuals are too slow to speak when the previous speaker concludes, so they never manage to capture the "floor." Moreover, as expectation-states theory suggests, individuals who are more influential are given more latitude in speaking than are those who are low in status (Bonito & Hollingshead, 1997).

What happens when groups meet via the Internet rather than face to face? In many online groups, the effects of status on participation are muted, resulting in a *participation equalization effect* (Hollingshead, 2001). One early investigation of participants who varied in status tracked their involvement in discussions conducted via e-mail or in face-to-face meetings. E-mail reduced the participation differences between group members, with the result that low-status members participated more and high-status members participated relatively less (Dubrovsky, Kiesler, & Sethna, 1991). Studies of online discussions in college classes also indicated that students participate more equally than they do in face-to-face discussions and that differences in participation due to

self-confidence when they work in the group, and their performance may also suffer (Biernat et al., 1998; Sekaquaptewa & Thompson, 2002, 2003). In one study, women preferred reassignment to a different group if they were going to be a solo member, whereas men showed no aversion to being the only man in the group (L. L. Cohen & Swim, 1995). Solo members are also rarely allocated status in groups (Carli, 2001).

These negative status effects often fade over time as group members gain experience in working together. Groups that initially allocate status unfairly revise their hierarchies as they recognize the skills and abilities of previously slighted members (W. E. Watson, Kumar, & Michaelsen, 1993). Given enough time, women and minorities find that they no longer need to continually prove themselves to the others (Hembroff & Myers, 1984; Markovsky, Smith, & Berger, 1984). Women and minorities who communicate their involvement in the group to the other members also tend to gain status more rapidly, as do those who act in a group-oriented rather than a self-oriented way (Carli et al., 1995; Ridgeway, 1982). If a solo woman in an otherwise all-male group remains actively involved in the group by asking questions, the negative effects of her solo status are elim-

FOCUS 6-2 *(continued)*

the cultural background (K. Kim & Bonk, 2002) or the sex of the student (Davidson-Shivers, Morris, & Sriwongko, 2003) are reduced. Students who eventually earn better grades are more active in such online discussions, but these differences in contribution likely reflect motivational differences rather than status differences (Wang, Newlin, & Tucker, 2001).

Other studies, however, have suggested that people in online groups behave, in most respects, like those in face-to-face groups. Many of the cues that people implicitly use to allocate status to others are minimized when people interact via computers—a group member's height, age, sex, and race can be kept private in online groups, and the computer-mediated format prevents the exchange of nonverbal signs of dominance and authority. There can be no raised voice, no long stare, and no rolling of the eyes when members are connected only by a computer. Online groups, however, still exhibit signs of structural differentiation. Participants, through the content of their messages, level of involvement, style of communication (e.g., punctuation; capitalization such as I AGREE TOTALLY!!!!; slang; humor;

and "emoticons"—those little text-based faces created with periods, commas, parentheses, semicolons, and so on) lay claim to characteristics that define their place within the group. In some cases, group members may even be *more* influenced by irrelevant diffuse status characteristics in online groups, because they have no other information to use to guide their perceptions of the other members. If all Ed knows about his partner in a discussion is that his or her name is Jolina, then he may inevitably draw conclusions about her personality and interests from her name alone (Postmes & Spears, 2002).

In consequence, in most studies, the format of the group has little impact on status and attraction differentiation. Those who possess qualities that would likely earn them high status in face-to-face groups tend to participate more in computer-based groups as well (Driskell, Radtke, Salas, 2003). The goal of creating online groups that escape the implicit biases introduced by a group's tendency to favor the powerful—the utopian vision of a group where all members are created equally—remains elusive (McKenna & Green, 2002).

---

inated (Fuegen & Biernat, 2002). Similarly, when men who deliberately adopted either a cooperative, friendly interaction style or an emotionally distant, self-absorbed style joined otherwise all-female groups, they achieved high status no matter what style they exhibited. Women solo members in male groups, in contrast, achieved high status only if they displayed a group-oriented motivation. External authorities can also undo unfair status generalizations by explicitly stressing the qualifications of women and minorities or by training group members to recognize their biases (Ridgeway, 1989). Moreover, groups may reduce biases in the allocation of status to their members by making use of computer-based technology to make decisions and exchange information (see Focus 6-2).

Attraction Relations

Some of the 19 Andes survivors rose to positions of authority, whereas others remained relatively powerless. Yet to describe the group in just these terms would miss a vital part of the group's structure. The individuals were not just leaders and followers, powerful and powerless; they were also friends and enemies. This

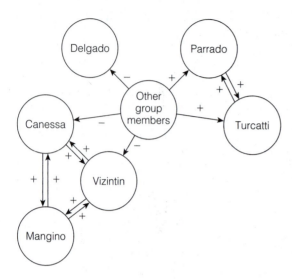

FIGURE 6-4

Who liked whom in the Andes group? This sociogram of the Andes survivors suggests that two subgroups of well-liked and less well-liked members emerged within the group. The lines marked with a plus sign indicate attraction, those marked with a minus sign indicate dislike, and arrows indicate the direction of the affect.

network of likes and dislikes among group members is called by many names, including **attraction network,** *social status,* or *sociometric structure.*

SOCIOMETRIC DIFFERENTIATION Jacob Moreno, the developer of sociometry, maintained that the tendency to react to one another on a spontaneous, affective level imparts a unique quality to human groups. Our relationships with other group members take on many different shades—hate, condemnation, liking, friendship, love, and so on—but only rarely do we react neutrally to one another (Moreno, 1960). Consider, for example, the relationships among the rank-and-file group members and the four explorers, Turcatti, Parrado, Vizintin, and Canessa (see Figure 6-4). Nearly everyone admired Turcatti and Parrado; their warmth, optimism, and physical strength buoyed the sagging spirits of the others. Vizintin and Canessa, in contrast, "did not inspire the same affection" (P. P. Read, 1974, p. 141). They liked each other but had few other friends within the group. Mangino, one of the younger men, was an exception; he liked them both. Most of the others, however, quarreled with them constantly.

Attraction patterns like those in the Andes group are not a disorganized jumble of likes and dislikes but a network of stable social relationships (Doreian, 1986). Just as status differentiation results in variations in status, so, too, **sociometric differentiation** results in a stable ordering of members from least liked

---

attraction network Patterns of liking–disliking, acceptance–rejection, and inclusion–exclusion among members of a group.

sociometric differentiation The development of stronger and more positive interpersonal ties between some members of the group, accompanied by decreases in the quality of relations between other members of the group.

to most liked (Maassen, Akkermans, & van der Linden, 1996). *Popular* individuals (*stars*) receive the most positive sociometric nominations within the group; *rejected* group members (*outcasts*) get picked on the most when group members identify whom they dislike; *neglected* group members (*isolates* or "fringers") receive few nominations of any kind; and the *average* members are liked by several others in the group (Coie, Dodge, & Kupersmidt, 1990; A. F. Newcomb, Bukowski, & Pattee, 1993). In the Andes group, for example, Parrado was admired by all; he was, sociometrically, the star of the group. Delgado, in contrast, was the group's outcast; he had no friends in the group, and the young men ridiculed him constantly for not doing his share of the work.

Like sociometric relations in most groups, the Andes survivors' showed signs of *reciprocity, transitivity,* and *homophily.* Vizintin liked Canessa, and Canessa liked Vizintin in return. Such reciprocity, as noted in Chapter 4, is a powerful tendency in most settings; it has been documented repeatedly in a variety of groups, including football teams, police squads, psychotherapy groups, and classroom groups (Kandel, 1978; T. M. Newcomb, 1979; M. W. Segal, 1979; T. L. Wright, Ingraham, & Blackmer, 1984). Exceptions to reciprocity sometimes occur, and some forms of attraction tend to be less reciprocal than other forms of attraction, but these exceptions to the reciprocity principle are relatively rare (M. W. Segal, 1979). The Andes group also showed signs of network transitivity: Canessa liked Mangino, Mangino liked Vizintin, and, in confirmation of transitivity, Canessa liked Vizintin (A likes B, B likes C, so A likes C).

Clusters, or *cliques,* also existed in the Andes group, for Vizintin, Canessa, and Mangino formed a unified coalition within the larger group. Others rarely hesitated to show their disdain for the members of this subgroup, but these three were joined by strong bonds of attraction. In many cases, subgroups display *homophily*—members of cliques tend to be more similar to one another than they are to the members of the total group. Members of the same racial category, for example, may join to form a coalition, or the group may separate naturally into all-male and all-female cliques (Hallinan, 1981; Schofield & Whitley, 1983; Thorne, 1993). Group members also often deliberately form and manipulate cliques within larger groups by systematically including some individuals and excluding others (Adler & Adler, 1995).

Membership in a clique or small subgroup within the larger group does not, in all cases, undermine one's level of social participation in the group as a whole. Researchers examined the balance between subgroup membership and attachment to the larger group in a study of women who were members of a sorority. Through sociometry, they identified 3 large subgroups of members, one small 3-woman clique, and 10 isolates. Those women who occupied more central positions in the group were more emotionally attached to the group than those who were isolated or occupied more peripheral positions in the attraction network. Membership in the subgroups did not interfere with emotional attachment to the group, so long as the subgroups were densely connected to the group as a whole. Those who were members of subgroups that lacked cross-cutting ties throughout the sorority were not as attached to the group (Paxton & Moody, 2003).

MAINTAINING STRUCTURAL BALANCE Why do most groups tend toward reciprocity, transitivity, and homophily? According to Fritz Heider's **balance theory,** attraction relations in groups are balanced when they fit together to form a coherent, unified whole. A dyad, for example, is balanced only if liking (or disliking) is mutual. If Vizintin liked Canessa but Canessa disliked Vizintin, the dyad would be unbalanced, and the result would be structural strain (Cartwright & Harary, 1956, 1970; Heider, 1958; T. M. Newcomb, 1963).

The sociometric structures of larger groups also tend to be balanced. The triad containing Vizintin, Canessa, and Mangino, for example, was balanced because everyone in it liked one another; all bonds were positive. What would happen, however, if Mangino came to dislike Canessa? According to Heider, this group would be *unbalanced,* because the product of the three relationships (Vizintin likes Canessa, Mangino likes Vizintin, and Mangino dislikes Canessa) is negative. In general, a group is balanced if (1) all the relationships are positive, or (2) an even number of negative relationships occur in the group. Conversely, groups are unbalanced if they contain an odd number of negative relations.

Because unbalanced sociometric structures generate tension among group members, people are motivated to correct the imbalance and restore the group's equilibrium. Heider noted, however, that this restoration of balance can be achieved either through psychological changes in the individual members or through interpersonal changes in the group. If Mangino initially likes only Vizintin and not Canessa, he may change his attitude toward Canessa when he recognizes the strong bond between Vizintin and Canessa. Alternatively, group members who are disliked by the other group members may be ostracized, as in the case of Delgado (H. F. Taylor, 1970). Finally, because the occurrence of a single negative relationship within a group can cause the entire group to become unbalanced, large groups tend to include a number of smaller, better balanced cliques (T. M. Newcomb, 1981). The Andes group, for example, was somewhat unbalanced overall, but its subgroups tended to be very harmonious (Cartwright & Harary, 1956, 1970; T. Mayer, 1975). As a result, the group was high in cohesiveness.

DETERMINANTS OF ATTRACTION STRUCTURE Why did Parrado gain social standing in the group, and why was Delgado held in disregard? One's popularity, in large part, is determined by the interpersonal factors reviewed in Chapter 4—similarity, complementarity, reciprocity, personal qualities, and even physical attractiveness can influence one's sociometric ranking in a group. Parrado was similar to the others in age and background, and he possessed qualities

---

balance theory A conceptualization advanced by Fritz Heider that assumes interpersonal relationships can be either balanced (integrated units with elements that fit together without stress) or unbalanced (inconsistent units with elements that conflict with one another). Heider believed that unbalanced relationships create an unpleasant tension that must be relieved by changing some element of the system.

that the others admired: He was optimistic, handsome, dependable, helpful, and strong. Delgado, unfortunately, did not possess such attributes. Interaction with Delgado incurred considerable costs and yielded very few interpersonal rewards (Thibaut & Kelley, 1959).

Popularity cannot be predicted solely on the basis of the group members' personal qualities, for different groups value different attributes. The qualities that earn a person popularity in a boardroom differ from those that predict sociometric standing on a baseball team or in a biker gang. Thus, predictions of social standing must take into account the person–group fit—the degree to which individuals' attributes match the qualities valued by the group to which they belong. In another group, Delgado might have been well liked, for he was quite articulate and socially skilled. In the Andes group, however, the fit between his personal qualities and the group was poor (C. Anderson, John, Keltner, & Kring, 2001).

The impact of person–group fit on social standing has been studied extensively in children's groups (Bukowski, Newcomb, & Hartup, 1996). Researchers in one study used sociometric methods to identify popular, rejected, neglected, and average boys in elementary school classes. Trained observers also rated each boy's behavior during several free-play periods, looking for evidence of aggressiveness, cooperation, and withdrawal. Supporting a "social misfit" hypothesis, the investigators found that in nonaggressive groups and socially active groups, the rejected boys engaged in the most aggressive behaviors or too frequently played by themselves. Aggressive boys who were members of groups characterized by relatively high levels of hostility, fighting, and verbal abuse were more popular than less aggressive ones, but only if their aggression was reactive (a defense against others' aggression) rather than proactive (unprovoked aggression aimed at influencing others). These results suggest that popularity in one group does not guarantee popularity in another group; a sociometric star in one group can become an outcast or misfit in another (J. C. Wright, Giammarino, & Parad, 1986; see also Boivin, Dodge, & Coie, 1995; Hubbard et al., 2001).

Communication Relations

In the Andes group, the three leaders stayed in close communication, discussing any problems among themselves before relaying their interpretations to the other group members. The other members usually routed all information to the threesome, who then informed the rest of the group. In contrast, the injured members were virtually cut off from communication with the others during the day, and they occasionally complained that they were the last to know of any significant developments. These regular patterns of information exchange among members of a group are called **communication networks.**

---

communication network Patterns of information transmission and exchange that describe who communicates most frequently and to what extent with whom.

CENTRALIZATION EFFECTS Patterns of communication among group members, like other structural features of groups, are sometimes deliberately set in place when the group is organized. Many companies, for example, adopt a centralized, hierarchical communication network that prescribes how information is passed up to superiors, down to subordinates, and horizontally to one's equals. Even when no formal attempt is made to organize communication, an informal communication network will usually take shape over time. Moreover, this network tends to parallel status and attraction patterns. Take the Andes group as a case in point: Individuals who occupied high-status roles—the explorers, the food preparers, and the lieutenants—communicated at much higher rates and with more individuals than individuals who occupied the malingerer and injured roles (Shelly, Troyer, Munroe, & Burger, 1999).

Communication networks become more complex and varied as groups increase in size, but some of their basic forms are graphed in Figure 6-5. In a *wheel* network, for example, all group members communicate with just one person. In a *comcon,* all members can and do communicate with all other members. In a *chain,* communication flows from one person to the next in a line. A *circle* is a closed chain, and a *pinwheel* is a circle where information flows in only one direction (M. E. Shaw, 1964).

One of the most important features of these networks is their degree of *centralization* (M. E. Shaw, 1964, 1978). With centralized networks, one of the positions is located at the crossroads (the *hub*) of communications, as in the wheel and Y of Figure 6-5. Groups with this type of structure tend to use the hub position as the data-processing center, and its occupant typically collects information, synthesizes it, and then sends it back to others. In decentralized structures, like the circle or comcon, the number of channels at each position is roughly equal, so no one position is more "central" than another. These groups tend to use a variety of organizational structures when solving their problems, including the so-called *each to all* pattern, in which everyone sends messages in all directions until someone gets the correct answer. Centralization can also be more precisely indexed by considering the relative number of links joining the positions in the network (Bavelas, 1948, 1950; L. C. Freeman, 1977; Grofman & Owen, 1982; Moxley & Moxley, 1974).

Early studies of communication networks suggested that groups with centralized networks outperformed decentralized networks (Bavelas, 1948, 1950; Bavelas & Barrett, 1951; Leavitt, 1951). A group with a wheel structure, for example, took less time to solve problems, sent fewer messages, detected and corrected more errors, and improved more with practice than a group with a decentralized structure, such as a circle or comcon (M. E. Shaw, 1964, 1978). The only exceptions occurred when the groups were working on complicated tasks such as arithmetic, sentence construction, problem solving, and discussions. When the task was more complex, the decentralized networks outperformed the centralized ones.

These results led Marvin E. Shaw to propose that network efficiency is related to *information saturation.* When a group is working on a problem, ex-

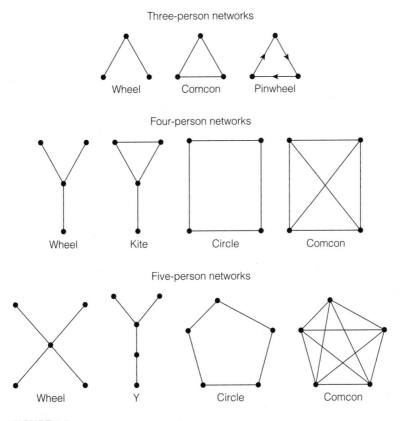

FIGURE 6-5

What kinds of communication networks are common in small groups? These networks are a sample of the various kinds of communication networks that can be created by opening and closing lines of communication among members. Studies of communication networks distinguish between *centralized* networks (such as the *wheel,* the *kite,* and the *Y*) and *decentralized* networks, such as the *circle* and the *comcon.* Most of the networks are bidirectional, with information flowing back and forth between members. Only the *pinwheel* has one-way communication links. Adapted from "Communication Networks," by M. E. Shaw. In L. Berkowitz (ed.), *Advances in Experimental Social Psychology* (Vol. 1). Copyright © 1964 by Academic Press. Reprinted by permission.

changing information, and making a decision, the central position in the network can best manage the inputs and interactions of the group. As work progresses and the number of communications being routed through the central member increases, however, a saturation point can be reached at which the individual can no longer efficiently monitor, collate, or route incoming and outgoing messages.

Shaw noted that saturation can occur in a decentralized network, but it becomes more likely when a group with a centralized structure is working on complex problems. Because the "greater the saturation the less efficient the group's performance" (M. E. Shaw, 1964, p. 126), when the task is simple, centralized networks are more efficient than decentralized networks; when the task is complex, decentralized networks are superior. In consequence, groups tend to gravitate naturally to more decentralized network structures when the tasks they must accomplish become more complex and multifaceted (T. M. Brown & Miller, 2000).

POSITIONAL EFFECTS Parrado occupied a position near the center of the Andes group. Although he was not one of the leaders, he was well liked by nearly everyone, so people often sought out his company. He was an explorer, so he communicated frequently with the group's leadership and with the other explorers. In contrast to Parrado, the injured members rarely communicated with the other group members, and when they did, it was to complain about the food, their living conditions, and their leadership. Their morale was low, but the rest of the group hardly noticed because they so rarely communicated with them directly.

The centrality of a particular position in a communication network depends on three factors—degree, betweenness, and closeness (L. C. Freeman, 1979). A position with a high *degree of centrality* is one that connects the occupant to many other occupants. If Parrado communicates with 15 of the 19 people in a group, and Harley communicates with only 5 of the 19, then Parrado has a higher degree of centrality. A position with a high degree of *betweenness,* in contrast, is one that is located between many of the other individuals in the network. An individual in such a position often acts as the "go-between," linking people in the network who could otherwise not contact one another. If most of the other members of the group ignore the injured members, but Parrado regularly checks on them and gives them news about their situation, then Parrado would have high betweenness. Finally, a position with a high degree of *closeness* is one that is located near the heart of the network. If Parrado can communicate with most members of the group directly without having his message relayed by someone else, then he has high closeness.

These different types of centrality have different effects on group processes and members' satisfaction. Degree of centrality, for example, tends to be associated with one's sociometric status in the group, because interaction tends to increase attraction between group members. Betweenness, in contrast, is associated with increased status and information control, for individuals who can control the flow of information in the group can act as gatekeepers. Individuals who are high in closeness, because they are directly connected to so many other individuals, tend to be influential in their groups, but indirectly rather than directly (Granovetter, 1973). In general, however, these three indicators of centrality are correlated, for people who have more connections tend to be closer to others, and they can usually control the flow of information through the network

(Krackhardt & Kilduff, 1999). All three of these indicators also predict role allocations, overall commitment, and satisfaction with membership in the group (Krackhardt & Porter, 1986; Lovaglia & Houser, 1996). Individuals who occupy positions of high betweenness in centralized communication networks, such as a wheel or a Y (see Figure 6-5), are nearly always thought to be the leader of their group, even when they are randomly assigned to this position (Leavitt, 1951). In studies of employees in work groups, those who are more central in their network, both in terms of degree and closeness, are less likely to quit than are employees at the periphery of the company's communication network (Feely, 2000). Peripheral members are also more likely to quit in clumps. Because individuals in decentralized positions are connected to very few of the other members, when one peripheral member leaves the group, the individuals located near that person in the network also tend to leave the group (Krackhardt & Porter, 1986). Finally, centralized networks, by definition, have fewer centralized positions than decentralized positions. In consequence, the overall level of satisfaction in a centralized group is almost always lower than the level of satisfaction in a decentralized group (M. E. Shaw, 1964).

DIRECTIONAL (UP–DOWN) EFFECTS Only small groups with decentralized communication networks outperform groups with centralized networks. Once the group becomes too large, members can no longer keep up with the high rate and quantity of information they are receiving. Therefore, most larger groups and organizations manage information flow by adopting *hierarchical* communication networks (Goetsch & McFarland, 1980). In such networks, information can pass either horizontally—between members on the same rung of the communication ladder—or vertically—up and down from followers to leaders and back (Jablin, 1979).

Upward communications tend to be very different from downward communications (Browning, 1978; Sias & Jablin, 1995). What type of information passes downward from superior to subordinate? Explanations of actions to be taken, the reasons for actions, suggestions to act in a certain manner, and feedback concerning performance are examples. Upward communications from subordinates to superiors, in contrast, include information on performance, insinuations about a peer's performance, requests for information, expressions of distrust, factual information, or grievances concerning the group's policies. These upward communications, moreover, tend to be fewer in number, briefer, and more guarded than downward communications. In larger organizations, the upward flow of information may be much impeded by the mechanics of the transferral process and by the low-status members' reluctance to send information that might reflect unfavorably on their performance, abilities, and skills (Bradley, 1978; Browning, 1978; Manis, Cornell, & Moore, 1974). This reticence of low-status members means that good news travels quickly up the hierarchy, whereas the top of the ladder will be the last to learn bad news (see Jablin, 1979, 1982, for a detailed review of communication in hierarchical organizations).

The Ties That Bind

On December 21, 1972, the radio announcer told Uruguay and the world the news: Two of the passengers from the missing airplane, Fernando Parrado and Roberto Canessa, had been found in a place called Los Maitenes on the River Azufre. The two explorers, running low on food and supplies, had stumbled into a farmer tending his cattle. Parrado himself guided the rescue helicopters back to the crash site, and by Christmas Day, the men were back in civilization. All of them, when asked how they survived, credited the "unity" of the group (P. P. Read, 1974, p. 310). And when they read the book that described their ordeal on the mountainside, they complained of only one inaccuracy: They felt that author Piers Paul Read failed to capture the "faith and friendship which inspired them" for 70 days.

SUMMARY IN OUTLINE

❖ What is group structure?

1. Groups are not unorganized, haphazard collections of individuals, but organized systems of interactions and relationships regulated by group structure.
2. Three important elements of group structure are norms, roles, and networks of connections among the members.

❖ What are norms?

1. Norms are implicit, self-generating, and stable standards for group behavior.
   - *Prescriptive norms* set the standards for expected group behavior.
   - *Proscriptive norms* identify behaviors that should not be performed.
   - *Descriptive norms* define what most people do, feel, or think in the group.
   - *Injunctive norms* differentiate between desirable and undesirable actions.
2. Norms develop gradually over time as members align their actions with those displayed by others, but Sherif's work indicates that group members do not merely imitate others—rather, they often internalize these consensual standards.
3. Because norms are transmitted to other group members, they tend to be con-

sensual, implicit, self-generating, and stable.

❖ What are roles?

1. Roles specify the types of behaviors expected of individuals who occupy particular positions within the group.
2. As members interact with one another, their role-related activities become patterned (*role differentiation*) with
   - *Task roles* pertaining to the work of the group, and
   - *Relationship roles* pertaining to maintaining relations among members.
3. The same person rarely holds both the task role and the relationship role in the group.
4. Moreland and Levine's theory of *group socialization* describes the way roles are allocated to individuals and the way in which members transition through the roles of prospective member, new member, full member, marginal member, and former member.
5. The role differentiation and socialization processes often create stress and tension for groups and group members.

- *Role ambiguity* occurs when the behaviors associated with a role are poorly defined.
- *Role conflict* occurs when group members occupy two or more roles that call for incompatible behaviors (*interrole conflict*) or when the demands of a single role are contradictory (*intrarole conflict*).
- When *role fit* is low, members do not feel that they match the demands of their roles.

❖ **What are status networks?**

1. Most groups develop a stable pattern of variations in authority and power (e.g., status networks, chains of command) through a *status differentiation* process.

2. In some instances, people compete with one another for status in groups; the resulting *pecking order* determines who is dominant and who is submissive.

3. Group members' perceptions of one another also determine status. *Expectation-states theory* argues that group members allocate status by considering *specific status characteristics* and *diffuse status characteristics*.

4. When *status generalization* occurs, group members unfairly allow irrelevant characteristics such as race, age, or ethnic background to influence the allocation of prestige.
   - Status allocations are particularly unfair when individuals who are members of stereotyped minority societal groups are also underrepresented in the group itself, with the most extreme case being *solo status* (being the only individual of that category in the group).
   - In many online groups, the effects of status on participation are muted, resulting in a *participation equalization* effect.

❖ **What are attraction networks?**

1. A group's *attraction network,* or *sociometric structure,* develops through a *sociometric*

differentiation process that orders group members from least liked to most liked.

2. Attraction relations tend to be reciprocal and transitive, and clusters or coalitions often exist within the group that are higher in homophily than the group as a whole.

3. As Heider's *balance theory* suggests, sociometric structures also tend to reach a state of equilibrium in which likes and dislikes are balanced within the group.

4. Sociometric differentiation generally favors individuals who possess socially attractive qualities, such as cooperativeness or physical appeal, but social standing also depends on the degree to which the individual's attributes match the qualities valued by the group (person–group fit).

❖ **What are communication networks?**

1. A group's *communication network* may parallel formally established paths, but most groups also have an informal network that defines who speaks to whom most frequently.

2. *Centralized* networks are most efficient for simple tasks.

3. A group's network, in addition to structuring communication, influences a variety of group and individual outcomes, including performance, effectiveness, and members' level of satisfaction. Individuals who occupy more central positions in communication networks (as defined by the number of connections, betweenness, and closeness) are often more influential than those located at the periphery.

4. More information generally flows downward in hierarchical networks than flows upward, and the information that is sent upward is often unrealistically positive.

FOR MORE INFORMATION

Chapter Case: The Andes Survivors

- *Alive,* by Piers Paul Read (1974), is the best-selling account of the young men who crashed in the Andes and survived by creating a potent group.

Norms and Roles

- "The Construction of Social Norms and Standards," by Dale T. Miller and Deborah A. Prentice (1996), examines the nature of social norms, with particular emphasis on their impact on perceptions and social judgments.
- "Norms," by Donelson R. Forsyth (1994), is a concise summary of the concept of norms and its application in social psychology.
- *Social Norms,* edited by Michael Hechter and Karl-Dieter Op (2001), is a collection of outstanding theoretical and empirical reviews of the nature of norms and their influence in groups.
- "Role Conflict and Role Ambiguity: A Critical Assessment of Construct Validity," by Lynda A. King and Daniel W. King (1990), summarizes past research dealing with role stress and offers a compelling assessment of the validity of such concepts as role conflict and role ambiguity.

Intermember Relations

- "Birds of a Feather: Homophily in Social Networks," by M. McPherson, L. Smith-Lovin, and J. M. Cook (2001), exhaustively reviews and synthesizes prior studies of homophily in groups.
- "Organizational Culture," by Edgar H. Schein (1990), applies the concept of structure and networking to the functioning of large organizations in his conception of organizational culture.
- *Social Network Analysis: Methods and Applications,* by Stanley Wasserman and Katherine Faust (1994), is a relatively technical analysis of methods that can be used to measure connections among members of a group or aggregate.
- "Social Status and Group Structure," by Cecilia L. Ridgeway (2001), offers a brief overview of the voluminous research and theory dealing with expectation states and status allocations in groups.

MEDIA RESOURCES

 Visit the Group Dynamics companion website at http://psychology.wadsworth.com/forsyth4e to access online resources for your book, including quizzes, flash cards, web links, and more!

7

INFLUENCE

CHAPTER OVERVIEW

Group members must sometimes change their opinions, judgments, or actions to match those favored by their group. But groups are not inflexible, for any individual can influence the group in return. Groups require both conformity and rebellion if they are to endure.

❖ When do people conform to the demands of the group?

❖ When do people resist the group's influence and, instead, change the group?

❖ Why do people conform?

❖ Do social influence processes shape juries' verdicts?

CHAPTER OUTLINE

The Corona Trial Jury:
The Group as Arbiter of Justice

The crime shook the community to its moral core. The police in Yuba City, California, discovered the shallow graves of 25 men in a lonely orchard outside of town. After analysis of evidence uncovered at the scene, investigators arrested and charged Juan Corona, a labor contractor who worked in the area. Corona was put on trial for the crime, and the prosecution built its case on hundreds of bits of evidence that implicated Corona and no one else. The trial lasted for 5 long months and ended when the question of Corona's guilt was put to a jury of his peers—a group of men and women, strangers to one another, chosen at random from the community, unschooled in legal principles, and unpracticed in group decision making (see Table 7-1). The jurors deliberated for eight days, reviewing the evidence, sharing their own interpretations of that evidence, pointing out inconsistencies in one another's reasoning, and voting again and again by secret ballot. At last, they reached a final decision: Corona was guilty (Villaseñor, 1977).

How did the jury reach its verdict? The answer lies in **social influence**—interpersonal processes that change group members' thoughts, feelings, and behaviors. The jury member changing her vote, clique members mimicking the mannerisms of the group's leader, children endorsing the political views of their parents, and the uncertain restaurant patron putting house dressing on his salad because everyone else at the table used that dressing are all changed by other people's influence rather than by their own private ideation. Much of this influence flows from the group to the individual, as Figure 7-1 suggests. When the majority of the group's members champion a particular view, they may pressure the few dissenting group members to change for the sake of the group's unity. However, social influence also flows from the individual to the group. If the group is to meet new challenges and improve over time, it must recognize and accept ideas that conflict with the status quo. In the Corona jury, the majority prevailed, but the minority influenced the outcome, too. No one wanted to make a mistake, so the jury carefully considered the misgivings of the undecided jurors. Whereas **majority influence** increases the consensus within the group, **minority influence** sustains individuality and innovation (see Figure 7-1). Here we consider the nature of this give-and-take between majorities and minorities and the implications of this influence process for understanding how juries make their decisions.

---

social influence Interpersonal processes that change the thoughts, feelings, or behaviors of another person.

majority influence Social pressure exerted by the larger portion of a group on individual members and smaller factions within the group.

minority influence Social pressure exerted by a lone individual or smaller faction of a group on members of the majority faction.

The Corona Trial Jury (*continued*)

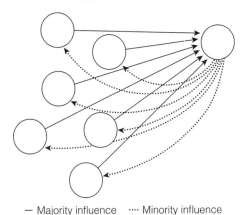

— Majority influence   ···· Minority influence

FIGURE 7-1
Who influences whom? In many cases, group members change as a result of direct group pressure by the majority (*majority influence*), but in other cases, one or more group members succeed in changing the entire group. This *minority influence* is indicated by the curved lines of influence from the lone minority back to the majority group members.

TABLE 7-1 The Corona trial jurors

Juror	Age	Occupation	Characteristics
Faye Blazek	66	Retired teacher	Well educated; spoke with precision; backed up points with compelling arguments
Rick Bremen	26	Welder	Defended his points vehemently, often to the irritation of the other jurors
Frank Broksell	58	Retired toolmaker	Skeptical of the legal process; made very few comments during the deliberation
Larry Gallipeo	41	Ship construction	Quiet; seemed casual and relaxed during the deliberations
Matt Johnson	54	Retired sergeant	Easygoing, active contributor who diffused tension through humor
Victor Lorenzo	45	Grocer	Reserved; contributed only when knowledgeable on the subject
George Muller	43	Employee at air base	Enthusiastic and outgoing; moderately involved in the discussion
Jim Owen	39	Shipyard inspector	Thoughtful contributor; offered appropriate and provocative insights
Ernie Phillips	53	Retired sergeant	Foreman of the jury; talkative and task oriented; accepted by jurors
Donald Rogers	60	Retired machinist	Cigar smoker; irritated others by speaking loudly, brusquely
Naomi Underwood	61	Retired clerk	Prior experience in jury duty; high-strung; raised issues that others felt were irrelevant
Calvin Williams	51	School custodian	Frequent participant; guided the group and maintained discussion norms; only African American on the jury

Source: Adapted from *Jury: The People vs. Juan Corona* by V. Villasenor. Copyright 1977 by Little, Brown, Inc.

MAJORITY INFLUENCE: THE POWER OF THE MANY

The lone individual is free to think and act as he or she chooses, but group members must abandon some of their independence. Once they walked into the jury room, the 12 jurors had to coordinate their actions with the activities of the other group members. Each one strove to change the group to suit his or her personal inclinations, but at the same time, the group influenced its members: It swayed their judgments, favored one interpretation of reality over another, and encouraged certain behaviors while discouraging others. Four jurors initially believed that Corona was innocent, but one by one, they changed their vote to guilty. They displayed **conformity**—a change in opinion, judgment, and action to match (1) the opinions, judgments, or actions of other people or (2) the normative standards of a social group or situation.

How strong is the urge to conform? Muzafer Sherif (1936; see Chapter 5) verified that group members modify their judgments so that they match those of others in their groups. Theodore Newcomb, in his 1943 study of Bennington students (see Chapter 2), showed that members of a group will gradually take as their own the group's position on political and social issues. But it was Solomon Asch who provided definitive evidence of the power of the many to influence the few (Asch, 1952, 1955, 1957).

Majority Influence

How would you have reacted if you were a participant in Asch's study of conformity in groups? You would have entered the study thinking you were taking part in a simple study of visual acuity. After you and the rest of the participants sat down around the table, the experimenter would explain that he wanted the group to make a series of judgments about the length of some test lines. On each trial, he would show you two cards. One card had a single line that was to serve as the standard. Three lines, numbered 1, 2, and 3, were displayed on the second card (see Figure 7-2). Your job? Just pick the line that matched the standard line in length. As one test line was always the same length as the standard line, the correct answer was fairly obvious. Few people made mistakes when making such judgments alone.

On each trial, the experimenter displayed two cards and asked the participants to state their answers aloud, starting at the left side of the table. The first few trials passed uneventfully, with everyone in the group picking the correct answer. But on the third trial, the first participant picked Line 2, even though Line 1 was a closer match to the standard stimulus. To your surprise, each of the other group members followed the first participant's lead by selecting Line 2 as the correct answer. When your turn came to answer, would you go along with the group and select Line 2, or would you stand your ground and select Line 1?

---

conformity A change in opinion, judgment, or action to match the opinions, judgments, or actions of other group members or the group's normative standards.

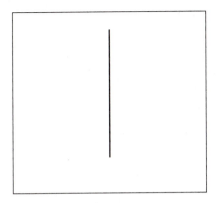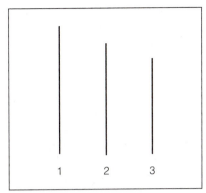

FIGURE 7-2

Would you have conformed if you were a participant in the Asch study? Participants were told to look at the standard line (the card on the left) and then match it to one of the three lines on the card at the right. The task was an easy one, but all group members save the one true participant were Asch's confederates, who deliberately made many mistakes. For example, on the cards shown here, the standard line was 8 inches long, and comparison Line 1 was the correct answer. However, the confederates chose Line 2, which was actually 7 inches long. *Source:* Adapted from "An Experimental Investigation of Group Influence" by S. E. Asch. In Symposium on Preventive and Social Psychiatry, April 15–17, Walter Reed Army Institute of Research. Washington, DC: Government Printing Office.

The majority's mistaken choice was no accident, for only one group member was an actual participant; all other "participants" were trained confederates who deliberately made errors on 12 of the 18 trials to see if the real participant would conform to a unanimous majority's judgments. When the participant arrived, he was seated so that he would answer only after most of the other participants did. He would study the lines, identify the correct answer, but hear everyone else make a different selection. When his turn came, he could disagree with the other participants' judgments, or he could conform to the group's wrong answer.

How did the people whom Asch studied react? When they heard the first person name the incorrect line as the best match, they probably thought little of it. But when the second person agreed with the first, they must have started to wonder. Then a third, a fourth, and a fifth person—all agreeing with one another, all selecting the wrong answer. What should they do? Many conformed, changing their answer to match the answer given by the other group members. In fact, across several studies, Asch discovered that people conformed on about one third of the trials. Some participants, as Table 7-2 indicates, never conformed, but most did so at least once, and a few did so on every single trial of the experiment! Between 75% and 80% of the participants agreed with the erroneous group at least once.

TABLE 7-2 Results of Asch's study of conformity

Measure	Result
How many members made at least one error?	76.4%
How many times did the average member conform?	36.8%
How many group members never conformed?	24.0%
How many group members conformed 10 times or more?	11.0%
How many individuals made at least one error when tested alone?	5.0%

Source: Data from Asch, 1952, 1957.

Asch himself was surprised by his findings (Gleitman, Rozin, & Sabini, 1997). He had expected that his participants would resist the pressure to conform and speak out against the incorrect majority's view (Leyens & Corneille, 1999). Yet they did not. Had the group been making important decisions—deliberating over a verdict in a murder trial, forging a plan to deal with an emergency, or crafting a solution to a difficult problem—then the participants would have let the group make a mistake at least one out of every three times. In search of an explanation, Asch and other researchers asked a series of probing questions about the innocuous **Asch paradigm.** First, did it matter that the participants faced the others alone—just one voice disagreeing with an entire group? Second, what about group size? Did people conform so much because the group was so big that it overwhelmed them? Finally, did the people in Asch's study really accept the others' estimates as more accurate than their own, or were they just acquiescing? In other words, did they publicly agree, but privately disagree?

UNANIMITY INCREASES INFLUENCE On the sixth day of deliberations, the Corona trial jury was split 9 to 3 favoring guilt. Naomi Underwood looked around the table, wondering who else had voted not guilty and hoping that others would swing that way too. But when the jury voted again later that day, the tally was 11 to 1. Naomi realized that she was the only person who thought that Corona was innocent of the murders, and on the next ballot, she changed her vote to guilty.

Like Naomi, Asch's participants had no partner—all the other members of the group agreed among themselves, so each participant faced a unanimous majority. Whereas the lone person stands little chance of resisting the majority, a minority *coalition,* even if it contains only two individuals, is more likely to withstand the majority's influence. Asch demonstrated this effect by telling one of the confederates to agree with the participant on some trials. As predicted, when par-

---

Asch paradigm An experimental procedure developed by Solomon Asch in his studies of conformity to group opinion. Participants believed they were making perceptual judgments as part of a group, but the other members were confederates who made errors on certain trials.

ticipants had an ally, their conformity rates were cut to one fourth their previous levels. In yet another variation, Asch arranged for some confederates to disagree with the majority but still give an incorrect answer. Participants did not agree with the erroneous nonconformist, but his dissent made it easier for them to express their own viewpoint (Asch, 1955).

Why is a unanimous majority uniquely influential? First, individuals who face the majority alone, without a single ally, bear the brunt of all the group's pressure. When three jurors voted not guilty, all three became targets for the majority's influence, but they also provided each other with support for their own position (V. L. Allen, 1975). But when only Naomi disagreed with the others, she became the sole recipient of all the group's influence, and these pressures were too great to resist (Asch, 1955). Second, individuals who discover that they are unlike all other members of their group may be too embarrassed to admit their uniqueness. The kinds of judgments that Asch studied were very simple ones, so most participants probably realized that if they dissented, they would make an odd impression on others. After all, "the correct judgment appeared so obvious that only perceptual incompetents, fools, or madmen could err" (L. Ross, Bierbrauer, & Hoffman, 1976, p. 149). But if a single other member of the group disagreed, then their answer—and they themselves—seemed more reasonable (Morris & Miller, 1975). Third, the larger the size of the minority coalition, the smaller the majority's coalition. A minority of two against four is far stronger than a minority of one against five (R. D. Clark, 1990).

LARGER GROUPS ARE MORE INFLUENTIAL (UP TO A POINT) How many people does it take to create maximum conformity? Is two against one enough? Are smaller groups less influential, because a small group has fewer sources of influence relative to larger ones? But is 11 to 1 too many? Do lone individuals feel relatively anonymous in large groups, so they can resist group forces? Asch explored these questions by studying groups with 2 to 16 members. His findings, summarized in Figure 7-3, confirm that larger majorities are more influential— but only up to a point. People in two-person groups conformed very little; most were unsettled by the erroneous choices of their partner, but they did not go along with him or her (3.6% error rate). But the error rate climbed to 13.6% when participants faced two opponents, and when a single individual was pitted against three others, conformity jumped to 31.8%. Asch studied even larger groups, but he found that with more than three opponents, conformity increased only slightly (reaching its peak of 37.1% in the seven-person groups); even 16 against 1 did not raise conformity appreciably above the level achieved with three against one (Asch, 1952, 1955).

Asch's conclusion—that larger groups are more influential up to a point—is consistent with Bibb Latané's **social impact theory.** This theory suggests that

---

social impact theory An analysis of social influence developed by Bibb Latané that proposes the impact of any source of influence depends upon the strength, the immediacy, and number of people (sources) present.

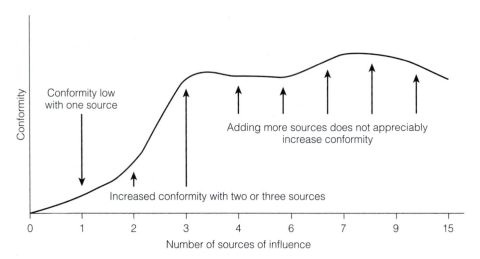

FIGURE 7-3

When do conformity pressures reach their peak in groups? Studies conducted in a number of settings suggest that few people conform when they face just one other person who disagrees with them, but that conformity rises rapidly when a lone individual faces a group of two or three. Adding more than three people to the majority does not appreciably increase conformity.

social influence is related to how many sources of influence are present, as well as to the strength and psychological immediacy of these sources. Latané noted that in general, stronger stimuli generate more intense psychological reactions. Imagine, for example, that you turn on a single lamp in an otherwise dark room. The room becomes lighter, although not too bright if the bulb is weak and the room is large. But what if you turn on more lights? The room will get brighter with each light, but eventually, the room will become so bright that adding another light will make no difference. In an analogous fashion, the more sources of social influence, the greater their impact—up to a point. Just as the first few lights have a greater effect than the hundredth, so the first few persons or sources of influence have more impact than the hundredth person added to the majority. Thus, conformity pressures increase, but at a gradually decreasing rate (Latané, 1981, 1996, 1997; Latané & Bourgeois, 2001; Latané & Wolf, 1981).

The precise shape of the relationship between size and influence, however, depends on a number of situational factors. A single individual, for example, can influence another individual if he or she appears to be very knowledgeable on the issue, is an expert, or is designated the group's leader (Hare, 1976). In contrast, a large group can lose some of its influence when its members do not reach their decisions independently of one another. If individuals learn that a six-person group disagrees with them, but they believe that the group members worked together as a group to make their decision, then the size of the dissenting group matters little. But when individuals believe that the other group members reached their conclusions independently of one another, then their influence increases as the number of sources increases. In fact, two 2-person groups (two separate entities) are more influential than one 4-person group who worked together (Wilder, 1977, Experiment 2; see also J. M. Jackson, 1987; Latané, 1981; Mullen, 1987; Wolf, 1987).

CONFORMITY DOES NOT ALWAYS EQUAL CONVERSION All four jurors who initially thought that Corona was innocent eventually conformed to the group's verdict, but they conformed for very different reasons. Naomi, for example, became exhausted during the deliberations, and she decided to go along with the majority even though she had doubts. Calvin, in contrast, initially voted not guilty because he did not know if general circumstantial evidence, such as bloodstains in Corona's truck, should be considered as evidence of particular murders. He changed his vote when this point was clarified during the deliberations.

When people respond by changing their stated position, one of at least two different processes may be occurring. **Compliance** (or *acquiescence*) occurs when group members privately disagree with the group, but publicly express an opinion that matches the opinion expressed by the majority of the group. **Conversion** (or *private acceptance*), in contrast, represents a true change of opinion that occurs when the target of social influence personally accepts the influencer's position. Nonconformity, too, can involve one of two different processes. People who refuse to bend to the will of the majority may be displaying **independence**—the public expression of ideas, beliefs, and judgments that are consistent with their personal standards. On ballot after ballot, Jim refused to vote guilty. Only at the very end, when he reconsidered his own moral values, did he change his opinion. Up to the end, however, he remained independent. Second, nonconformity can reflect **anticonformity** (or **counterconformity**)—the expression of ideas or the taking of actions that are the opposite of whatever the group recommends.

---

compliance Change that occurs when the targets of social influence publicly accept the influencer's position but privately maintain their original beliefs.

conversion Change that occurs when group members personally accept the influencer's position; also, the movement of all members of a group to a single, mutually shared position, as when individuals who initially offer diverse opinions on a subject eventually come to share the same position.

independence Expressing opinions, making judgments, or acting in ways that are consistent with one's personal beliefs but inconsistent with the opinions, judgments, or actions of other group members or the group's norms.

anticonformity (or **counterconformity**) Deliberately expressing opinions, making judgments, or acting in ways that are different from those of the other group members or the group's norms in order to challenge the group and its standards rather than express one's personal preferences.

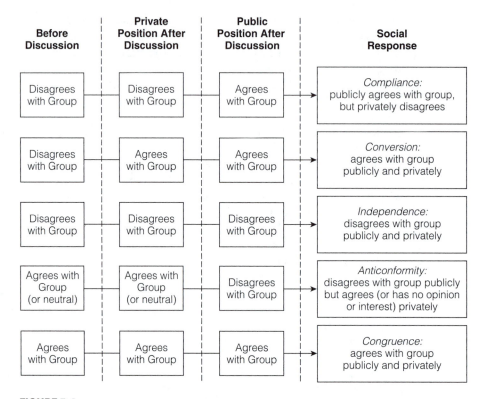

Before Discussion	Private Position After Discussion	Public Position After Discussion	Social Response
Disagrees with Group	Disagrees with Group	Agrees with Group	*Compliance:* publicly agrees with group, but privately disagrees
Disagrees with Group	Agrees with Group	Agrees with Group	*Conversion:* agrees with group publicly and privately
Disagrees with Group	Disagrees with Group	Disagrees with Group	*Independence:* disagrees with group publicly and privately
Agrees with Group (or neutral)	Agrees with Group (or neutral)	Disagrees with Group	*Anticonformity:* disagrees with group publicly but agrees (or has no opinion or interest) privately
Agrees with Group	Agrees with Group	Agrees with Group	*Congruence:* agrees with group publicly and privately

FIGURE 7-4

What is the difference between compliance, conversion, independence, counter-conformity, and congruence? When people react to group pressures, conformity can be labeled *compliance,* and nonconformity can be thought of as *counterconformity.* In the opposite situation, when the response is prompted by one's personal standards, conformity becomes private acceptance or *conversion,* and nonconformity entails *independence.* Technically, people who agree with the group from the outset are not conformists, because they do not shift their opinion in the direction advocated by the group; they already hold that position. They display *congruence* with their groups.

In some cases, anticonformity is motivated by rebelliousness or obstinacy rather than by the need to accurately express oneself. In other cases, however, members will play the "devil's advocate" to make sure that the group considers alternatives carefully. Donald, on the Corona jury, initially voted "not guilty," even though he was certain of Corona's guilt. He later explained that he had voted "not guilty" only because he wanted to ensure that the jury would review all the evidence thoroughly. Figure 7-4 summarizes these four types of social responses. (Nail, MacDonald, & Levy, 2000, provided a detailed analysis of these and other forms of social response.)

The Asch paradigm generated mostly compliance rather than conversion. A few participants assumed they were mistaken in their personal judgment, but most went along with the majority even though they thought the majority was dead wrong. As Asch explained,

> Among the extremely yielding persons we found a group who quickly reached the conclusion: "I am wrong, they are right." Others yielded in order "not to spoil your results." Many of the individuals who went along suspected that the majority were "sheep" following the first responder, or that the majority were victims of an optical illusion; nevertheless, these suspicions failed to free them at the moment of decision. (1955, p. 33)

Limits to Majority Influence

Asch studied young men (mostly) making public judgments about relatively inconsequential matters. All lived in the United States at a time when their culture was politically conservative. Would his findings hold at other times, with other kinds of people, from other cultures, and in other groups facing different issues? (see V. L. Allen, 1975; R. Bond & Smith, 1996; Hare, 1976; C. A. Kiesler & Kiesler, 1976.)

CONFORMITY ACROSS CULTURES AND ERAS In the years since Asch first published his findings, other researchers have replicated his basic procedure in more than a dozen countries, including the United States, Britain, Belgium, Fiji, Holland, Kuwait, Portugal, and Zimbabwe. When Rod Bond and Peter B. Smith (1996) surveyed these studies, they concluded that Asch may actually have underestimated conformity by studying people living in a relatively individualistic culture. As noted in Chapter 3, the individualistic cultures typical of Western societies tend to place the individual above the collective. Collectivistic societies, which are more prevalent in Asia, Africa, and South America, stress shared goals and interdependence. As a result, people tend to conform more in collectivistic cultures, especially when the source of influence is family members or friends (Frager, 1970).

Bond and Smith also checked for changes in conformity during the period from 1952 to 1994 to determine if conformity rates fluctuated as society's tolerance of dissent waxed and waned. When Asch carried out his work in the 1950s, social norms stressed respect for authority and traditional values, whereas the late 1960s were marked by student activism and social disobedience. This period of rebelliousness was followed by a prolonged period of social stability. Do entire generations of people become more or less conforming, depending on the sociopolitical climate of the times in which they live? Bond and Smith discovered that conformity rates have dropped since the 1950s, but they found no support for the idea that conformity is a "child of its time." Conformity is decreasing, but this decline was not sharper in the 1960s or more gradual in the relatively placid 1970s and 1980s (Larsen, 1982; Perrin & Spencer, 1980, 1981).

CONFORMITY ACROSS THE SEXES Did Asch underestimate the urge to conform by studying mostly men? Is it not true, "at least in our culture, that females supply greater amounts of conformity under almost all conditions than males" (Nord, 1969, p. 198)? That "women have been found to yield more to a bogus group norm than men" (Hare, 1976, p. 27)? Alice H. Eagly and her colleagues reviewed dozens of studies before concluding that women conform more than men—but only when group members are sitting face to face and when they must state their opinions aloud. In more anonymous, low surveillance situations, differences between men and women are almost nonexistent (H. M. Cooper, 1979; Eagly & Carli, 1981; cf. R. Bond & Smith, 1996). Women conform less when interacting via computer than they do in face-to-face discussions (Guadagno & Cialdini, 2002).

Why do women only conform more than men in face-to-face groups? The difference may reflect women's relatively greater concern for maintaining positive relationships with others (Eagly et al., 1981). Whereas men tend to use disagreement to dominate others or even separate themselves from the group, women may use agreement to create consensus and cohesion (Maslach, Santee, & Wade, 1987; Santee & Jackson, 1982; Santee & Maslach, 1982). These differences may also reflect continuing biases in the allocation of status to women. Eagly suggested that despite changes in stereotypes about women and men, groups traditionally reward men for acting in dominant, nonconforming ways and women for acting in cooperative, communal ways. If women feel that they should behave in a traditional way, they may conform more than men (Eagly, Wood, & Fishbaugh, 1981). Women who do not accept the traditional role of women, however, do not conform more than men (S. L. Bem, 1975, 1985). Sexism in groups and in society at large may also prevent women from expressing their dissent in groups. The studies of status allocation reviewed in Chapter 6, for example, have indicated that groups only grudgingly allocate status to qualified women. This sexist bias against women undermines their resistance to influence and weakens their power to influence others (Eagly, 1987). As women have become more successful in work and educational settings, their social status has risen, along with their independence and assertiveness (Twenge, 2001).

CONFORMITY ACROSS PEOPLE People differ at the individual level in their response to social influence. Asch found, for example, that some group members conformed on every trial—not once giving the correct answer when the group had erred. Others, though, never gave in to group pressure and held strong to their own beliefs. As one participant remarked, "The answers of the others didn't change my mind—an honest answer was expected. I did not change my answer once." When asked about the others in the group, he simply said "They were wrong" (Asch, 1952, p. 467).

Group members' reactions to influence depends, in part, on their age, personality, and expertise (see Table 7-3). Conformists are often authoritarians: Their

TABLE 7-3 A sampling of personality characteristics that are reliably associated with conformity and nonconformity

Characteristic	Reaction to Influence
Age	Conformity increases with age (M. B. Walker & Andrade, 1996).
Authoritarianism	Authoritarians respect and obey authorities and social conventions (Altemeyer, 1988; Feldman, 2003).
Birth order	First born children tend to conform more than later-born children, who tend to be more rebellious and creative (Sulloway, 1996).
Dependency	People who are high in dependency display heightened compliance, conformity, and suggestibility as well as sensitivity to interpersonal cues (R. F. Bornstein, 1992).
Gender identity	Masculine individuals and androgynous individuals conform less on gender-neutral tasks than feminine individuals (S. L. Bem, 1982).
Individualism–collectivism	People from collectivistic cultures (e.g., Asians) value conformity as a means of achieving harmony with others, whereas those from individualistic cultures (e.g., European Americans) value uniqueness (H. Kim & Markus, 1999).
Individuation	People with a high desire to publicly differentiate themselves from others (*high individuators*) are more willing to express dissenting opinions and contribute more to group discussions (K. Whitney, Sagrestano, & Maslach, 1994).
Intelligence	Less intelligent people and individuals who are uncertain of their abilities conform more (Crutchfield, 1955).
Need for closure	Conformity pressures are stronger in groups with a preponderance of members with a high need for closure (De Grada, Kruglanski, Mannetti, & Pierro, 1999).
Need for uniqueness	Individuals with a high need for uniqueness (NFU) are more likely to make unusual choices and prefer the unconventional to the conventional (Simonson & Nowlis, 2000).
Self-blame	Adolescents who tend to blame themselves for negative outcomes conform more than individuals with low self-blame (Costanzo, 1970).
Self-esteem	Individuals with low self-esteem conform more than individuals with moderate and high-self esteem (Berkowitz & Lundy, 1957); however, adolescents with high self-esteem conform more than those with low self-esteem (L. J. Francis, 1998).
Self-monitoring	High self-monitors, because of their higher self-presentational tendencies, conform more when striving to make a positive impression (S. Chen, Shechter, & Chaiken, 1996).
Stability	Stability, conscientiousness, and agreeability are associated with greater conformity (DeYoung, Peterson, & Higgins, 2002).
Yea-saying	Yea-sayers, particularly when working under a cognitive load, say "yes" faster and more frequently than individuals who thoughtfully consider their position (Knowles & Condon, 1999).

conventionality, conservative values, and unwillingness to confront authority increase their willingness to accept the majority's opinion. Conformists also tend to let the situation and other people influence their perceptions, opinions, and outlooks. People who rely on situational cues when making perceptual judgments, self-conscious individuals, and high self-monitors are more likely to make certain that their actions match the group's standards. People who conform show a greater interest, overall, in other people. They have a higher need for social approval, are more interpersonally oriented, and are more fearful of social rejection. Factors that undermine self-confidence—low self-esteem, incompetence, low intelligence—also increase conformity.

CONFORMITY ACROSS GROUP SETTINGS Asch studied conformity in newly formed groups working on a very simple task that was not particularly consequential. The members did not know each other; they sat together in a well-lit room, and they made their decisions by announcing their choice aloud. The Corona jury members, in contrast, had spent months together; their group had a leader charged with keeping order, and the members voted by secret ballot as they made a decision that would forever alter another human being's life.

Just as some individuals lean toward conformity rather than independence, so some group situations create more pressure to conform than do others (see Table 7-4). As Asch (1952) himself discovered, groups with four or more members are more influential than smaller groups, as are groups that are united against a single dissenter. Participants in Asch's studies also stated their choices aloud under the watchful eyes of all the other members, and this procedure likely increased their feelings of evaluation and embarrassment. This conclusion is supported by studies of conformity using the so-called **Crutchfield apparatus.** Asch ingeniously captured the essentials of many group decision settings in his studies, but his procedure was inefficient. Many confederates were required to study just one participant. Richard S. Crutchfield (1955) solved this problem by leaving out the confederates. In Crutchfield's laboratory, the participants made their judgments while seated in individual cubicles (see Figure 7-5). They flipped a small switch on a response panel to report their judgments to the researcher, and their answers would supposedly light up on the other group members' panels as well. Crutchfield told each person in the group that he or she was to answer last, and he himself simulated the majority's judgments from a master control box.

Crutchfield apparatus An experimental procedure developed by Richard Crutchfield to study conformity. Participants who signaled their responses using an electronic response console believed that they were making judgments as part of a group, but the responses of the other members that appeared on their console's display were simulated.

TABLE 7-4 A sampling of group and situational characteristics that reliably increase and decrease conformity

Factor	Conformity Increases If	Conformity Decreases If
Accountability (A. Quinn & Schlenker, 2002)	Individuals are striving for acceptance by others whose preferences are known	Individuals are accountable for their actions and are striving for accuracy
Accuracy (Mausner, 1954)	Majority's position is reasonable or accurate	Majority position is unreasonable or mistaken
Ambiguity (R. W. Spencer & Huston, 1993)	Issues are simple and unambiguous	Issues are complex and difficult to evaluate
Anonymity (Deutsch & Gerard, 1955)	Responses are made publicly in face-to-face groups	Responses are anonymous and members cannot see each other
Attraction (C. A. Kiesler & Corbin, 1965)	Members are attracted to the group or its members	Members dislike each other
Awareness (Krueger & Clement, 1997)	Individuals are aware they disagree with the majority	Individuals do not realize their position is unusual
Cohesion (Lott & Lott, 1961)	Group is close-knit and cohesive	Group lacks cohesion
Commitment to position (Gerard, 1964)	Individuals are publicly committed to their position from the outset	Uncommitted individuals are confronted by the group
Commitment to group membership (C. A. Kiesler, Zanna, & DeSalvo, 1966)	Individuals are committed to remaining in the group	Groups or membership are temporary
Priming (Epley & Gilovich, 1999)	Unnoticed cues in the setting prime conformity	Situational cues prime independence
Size (Asch, 1955)	Majority is large	Majority is small
Task (Baron, Vandello, & Brunsman, 1996)	Task is important but very difficult	Task is important and easy, or task is trivial
Unanimity (Asch, 1955)	Majority is unanimous	Several members disagree with the majority

Thus, during the critical trials, Crutchfield could lead participants to think that all the other participants were giving erroneous answers.

Crutchfield's method sacrificed face-to-face interaction between the participant and confederates, but it was efficient: He could study five or more people in a single session, and he did not need to recruit confederates. Because group members' responses were private, however, fewer people agreed with the majority in the Crutchfield situation relative to the Asch situation (R. Bond & Smith, 1996). Indeed, the change that takes place in such groups may reflect conversion rather than a temporary compliance that disappears when the individual is away from the group and its influence (see Focus 7-1).

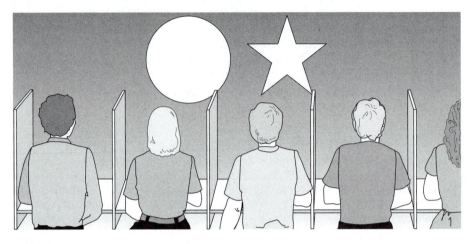

FIGURE 7-5

What is the *Crutchfield apparatus?* Richard Crutchfield studied conformity by seating participants in individual booths and gathering their responses electronically. When asked a question such as, "Which one of the figures has a greater area, the star or the circle?" participants answered by flipping the appropriate switch in their booth. They thought that their answers were being transmitted to the experimenter and to the other participants, but in actuality, the experimenter was simulating the majority's judgment from a master control panel. *Source: Social Psychology* by L. S. Wrightsman, Brooks/Cole Publishing Company, 1977.

MINORITY INFLUENCE: THE POWER OF THE FEW

Despite pressure from religious authorities, Galileo insisted that the planets revolve around the Sun rather than the Earth. Two members of the jury in the trial of Oklahoma City bomber Terry Nichols convinced the other 10 jury members to change their votes from innocent to guilty. Martin Luther King Jr. promoted equality in America until he was assassinated by a White supremacist. The composer Igor Stravinsky was denounced as a musical heretic when *The Rite of Spring* was first performed, but he refused to change a note. These dissenters stood firm against the majority's pressure. They became the sources of influence in their groups rather than the targets of influence, and eventually they changed the majority (Cialdini & Goldstein, 2004; Crano, 2000).

Minority Influence

In most of his studies, Asch (1952) recorded the reactions of a single person to the pressure of a larger majority. But in a few of his experiments, he reversed this procedure by planting one confederate in each group and watching the group's

FOCUS 7-1   Are Pressures to Conform Minimized in Groups that Interact via Computers?

No one today disputes that the Internet is likely to have a significant impact on social life; but there remains substantial disagreement as to the nature and value of this impact.
–John A. Bargh and Katelyn Y. A. McKenna (2004, p. 575)

Many groups meet at a distance, with members seated at computers rather than face to face in conference rooms. Computers provide a way to exchange ideas, opinions, and information, but they strip away some of the features of communication that are common in face-to-face settings. When group members interact via computers, their nonverbal reactions, their personal characteristics, and even their identities may be unknown to others. Freed from the constraints of public evaluation and the immediate scrutiny of others, individuals might be expected to conform less and dissent more when their interactions take place via e-mail, in chat rooms, or through instant messaging.

Studies of groups engaged in computer-mediated interactions, however, have suggested that online groups are no more likely to violate norms, disregard pressures to conform, or dissent than are face-to-face groups (Bargh & McKenna, 2004). Although early studies of computer-mediated interactions suggested that *flaming*—the expression of hostility, name-calling, and insults in e-mail exchanges—is a common occurrence in computer-based communication, more recent work has suggested that personal attacks are relatively rare occurrences (Straus,

1997). Social identity theorists Russell Spears, Tom Postmes, and their colleagues suggested that, in many cases, people conform *more* when they interact via computers rather than face to face. They argued that individuals experience increased depersonalization when they are interacting via computers, and that this depersonalization increases the salience of their group-level social identities. In consequence, they are more likely to conform to the group's norms (Spears, Postmes, Lea, & Wolbert, 2002).

The prediction that people will conform more when interacting via computers, although counterintuitive, has been confirmed empirically. When group identity is made salient, individuals on computers conform more than when their individual identities are emphasized (Spears, Lea, & Lee, 1990). When individuals making decisions via computer receive electronic messages from other individuals whom they do not know and will not communicate with in the future, they are more likely to change their decision to match the recommendations of these anonymous strangers (E. Lee & Nass, 2002). When small groups of students use e-mail in classes, each group develops idiosyncratic norms that regulate the group's interactions, and conformity to these norms increases through the semester (Postmes, Spears, & Lea, 2000). Apparently the urge to conform, which Asch found so powerful in face-to-face settings, is no less powerful when people who are separated by space and time are united by an Internet connection.

reaction when the confederate disagreed with the group on many of the trials. Asch found that the groups held firm—they did not waver from their choice when confronted by the lone, erroneous minority. In many cases, they ridiculed the confederate, laughing openly at his mistaken choices.

But the majority does not always ignore the voices of dissenters in the group. Groups tend to favor the status quo and choose the path favored by the majority, but they do not entirely ignore novel ideas, new directions, or untried opportunities. If groups were entirely immune to influence, then they would remain static and unchanging, but in fact, groups are dynamic; they change over time as members shed outmoded beliefs and practices and adopt new ways, practices, and positions. But when will the majority listen to the minority?

CONSISTENT MINORITIES ARE INFLUENTIAL The drama *Twelve Angry Men* captures the frustrations of a jury trying to reach a verdict in a murder trial. Eleven jurors agree in the first straw poll that the defendant is guilty. The majority attacks the lone holdout's position. But the holdout stands firm, and one by one, the rest of the group members change their minds. The jury eventually returns a verdict of not guilty (Rose, 1954).

The juror in *Twelve Angry Men* was influential because he was *consistent*—he always rejected the majority's guilty verdict during the long hours of the deliberation. Similarly, Serge Moscovici and his colleagues have demonstrated that minorities are most influential when they adopt a consistent behavioral style—when they unwaveringly argue their position. In one early study, these researchers asked six-person groups to judge the color and brightness of a series of color slides. All the slides were blue, but Moscovici planted confederates in each group, and the confederates consistently argued that the slides were green. Overall, 8.4% of the participants shifted their judgments from blue to green—not as much influence as that found by Asch in his studies of majority influence, but a significant amount of influence nonetheless. If the confederates labeled the slides as green on only two thirds of the trials, their influence on the majority was nil (Moscovici, Lage, & Naffrechoux, 1969; Moscovici & Personnaz, 1980).

Consistent minorities are particularly influential when the majority interprets the consistency positively (W. Wood, Lundgren, Ouellette, Busceme, & Blackstone, 1994). In the Corona jury, for example, Naomi's dissent was viewed negatively by the majority of the group, who felt she was stubborn and confused rather than confident and insightful. Naomi would have been more influential if she had offered coherent, compelling arguments that contradicted the majority's position (R. D. Clark, 1990). She also would have been more influential if she had signaled her confidence in her opinion—say, by sitting at the head of the table (Nemeth & Wachtler, 1974) or by reminding the jury of her prior service on other juries (Shackelford, Wood, & Worchel, 1996). Consistent minorities who signal their reasonableness by granting minor concessions to the majority are also more influential than rigid, uncompromising minorities (Pérez & Mungy, 1996), as are individuals who engage in "small talk" about unrelated matters prior to revealing their position (Dolinski, Nawrat, & Rudak, 2001). In general, minorities are more influential when they are perceived to be "team players" who are committed, competent, and group centered (J. M. Levine & Russo, 1987).

MINORITIES WITH "CREDITS" ARE INFLUENTIAL Minorities who consistently disagree influence the majority, but so do minority members who preface their dissent with conformity. Edwin P. Hollander (1971) studied the impact of early conformity in five-man groups working on a complex decision task. Hollander's confederate systematically violated certain rules of procedure either during the early phases of problem solving or later in the session. Hollander found that the confederate's influence over the others tended to increase over time but that a confederate who prefaced his nonconformity with conformity exerted somewhat more influence than an early nonconformist. Similar findings were reported when children with well-developed leadership skills were placed in new groups (Merei, 1958). Those who tried to change the group immediately were rejected, whereas those who worked within the group for a time before attempting innovations became successful influencers.

Hollander (1971) developed the concept of **idiosyncrasy credits** to explain the group's positive reaction to the minority who prefaced dissent with conformity. According to Hollander, idiosyncrasy credits are "the positive impressions of a person held by others, whether defined in the narrower terms of a small face-to-face group or a larger social entity such as an organization or even a total society" (1971, p. 573). These credits accumulate as members interact—typically as the member contributes to the progress of the group toward desired goals. Because high-status members have usually contributed more in the past and possess more valued personal characteristics, they have more idiosyncrasy credits. Therefore, if they do not conform, their actions are more tolerable to the other members. The low-status members' balance of credits is, in comparison, very low; hence, they are permitted a smaller latitude for nonconformity. The idiosyncrasy model suggests that influence levels in a group are increased by careful conformity to group norms during the early phases of group formation, followed by dissent when a sufficient balance of idiosyncrasy credit has been established (Hollander, 1958, 1960, 1961, 1971, 1981).

Hollander's advice about early conformity contrasts to some extent with Moscovici's recommendations concerning consistent nonconformity. Hollander warned that dissenters who challenge the majority without first earning high status in the group will probably be overruled by the majority, but Moscovici argued that consistent nonconformity will lead to innovation and change. Both tactics, however, may prove effective. Researchers compared the two in group discussions of three issues. One minority built up idiosyncrasy credits by agreeing on the first two issues that the group discussed, but then disagreeing on the third. The second minority built up consistency by disagreeing with the group on all three issues. Both minorities were influential, but the minority who built up idiosyncrasy credits was more influential in all-male groups (Bray, Johnson, & Chilstrom, 1982).

LARGER (AND GROWING) MINORITIES ARE INFLUENTIAL Naomi Underwood was a consistent minority, but eventually she stood alone against the others. Had more of the members taken up her minority view, then the odds of a

---

idiosyncrasy credit In Edwin Hollander's explanation for the leniency groups sometimes display toward high status members who violate group norms, the hypothetical interpersonal credit or bonus that is earned each time the individual makes a contribution to the group but erased each time the individual influences others, makes errors, or deviates from the group's norms.

shift in the verdict would have increased. Lone dissenters usually change their vote, but larger minorities are more influential. In fact, a computer model that simulates jury deliberations (DICE) assumes that a 3-person coalition in a standard 12-person jury will be relatively weak, but a 4- or 5-person coalition will be fairly influential (Hastie et al., 1983; Penrod & Hastie, 1980; Tanford & Penrod, 1983).

Naomi also failed to grow her minority group. She never succeeded in garnering any support for her views; no one publicly renounced their prior view and enthusiastically embraced her position. Yet minority influence, by its very nature, requires more change than majority influence. At some point along this conversion process, the position once favored by the minority must be accepted by so many in the group that it becomes the majority position (N. L. Kerr, 2001; Prislin & Christensen, 2002).

Russell D. Clark (1999, 2001) examined this process by measuring observers' verdicts after each round of balloting in a jury trial. He first provided observers with a detailed description of a hypothetical trial and jury deliberation patterned after the one described in *Twelve Angry Men*. He then asked the observers to rate the guilt of the defendant after learning that on the first ballot, the vote was 11 against 1, with the majority favoring guilty. Nearly all the observers agreed with the majority, but as the deliberations progressed, the observers learned that the minority position was growing from 9 to 3, to 6 to 6, to 3 to 9, and eventually 0 to 12. With each progressive vote, the observers shifted their own ratings from guilty to not guilty. Other research has suggested that individuals are particularly likely to join an expanding minority when the minority offers cogent arguments supporting its position and when other defectors are thought to have been swayed by the logic of the minority's arguments rather than by self-interest (Gordijn, De Vries, & De Dreu, 2002). Perhaps for this reason, individuals who know they will be arguing against the views of the majority prepare more diligently for their meetings (Van Hiel & Franssen, 2003).

An influential minority must not, however, threaten the integrity of the group itself. Many groups will tolerate debate and disagreement, but if the dissent creates deep divisions in the group, the majority may take steps to quash the minority or exclude its members from the group. If a group is just a loose conglomeration of individuals with no clear sense of identity, then the members of this "group" do not feel threatened by disagreement. But if the group members identify strongly with their group, and they feel that the dissenter is undermining its collective identity, they are more likely to feel a sense of loss when members begin to take a minority's arguments seriously (Prislin, Brewer, & Wilson, 2002). In such cases, an individual who is not even a member of the group may be more influential than an ingroup member (K. W. Phillips, 2003).

MINORITIES INFLUENCE INDIRECTLY Majorities influence members *directly;* they create compliance as individuals compare their own judgments with other group members' judgments. Minorities, in contrast, influence members *indirectly;* they create conversion to the minority's position as individuals struggle to validate their judgments. Because minority influence tends to be less blatant than majority influence, it often leads to true convergence rather than mere compliance. Many of the Corona jurors, for example, expressed misgivings after they filed their final decision. Naomi Underwood, in particular, regretted her decision to side with those who favored guilt; she had complied, but she had not converted (Moscovici, 1994; see also Maass, West, & Cialdini, 1987; Nemeth, 1986).

Moscovici theorized that this indirect influence of minorities occurs at a latent level, becoming evident only when the group has completed its initial deliberations and moved on to another task. Researchers demonstrated this tendency in one study by asking five-person groups to make an award in a simulated personal-injury case. One of the five group members was a confederate who consistently argued for an award of $3000, which was substantially below the $15,000 award favored by the majority. On the final vote, the majority's position was unchanged, but when the participants turned to a second case, they gave significantly smaller awards than participants who had never been exposed to the minority (Nemeth & Wachtler, 1974).

This delayed, indirect impact of minorities on the majority has been documented in a wide variety of laboratory and field studies, which indicate that "minorities tend to produce profound and lasting changes in attitudes and perceptions that generalize to new settings and over time . . . whereas majorities are more likely to elicit compliance that is confined to the original influence setting" (Maass et al., 1987, pp. 56–57). Minorities, then, are a source of innovation in groups, for they shake the confidence of the majority and force the group to seek out new information about the situation. In one series of studies, when people worked on problems in groups, they often accepted the majority's solutions, even if those solutions were flawed. If, however, a minority argued for a nonobvious solution, the group members abandoned the flawed solutions and sought solutions that were both novel and correct. They did not accept the minority's proposal as they had the majority's, but they did reevaluate their original answer (Nemeth, 1994; Nemeth & Wachtler, 1983).

Influence as Social Impact

Influence in groups is two-sided. From the majority's perspective, change takes place when the minority abandons its radical ideas and conforms. From the minority's perspective, change takes place when the majority reexamines and possibly revises its position. But change in groups is actually a mutual process—the majority influences the minority, and the minority influences the majority (Crano, 2000; R. Martin & Hewstone, 2001; Tanford & Penrod, 1984).

Latané's extension of his social impact theory, or **dynamic social impact theory,** uses systems theory to explain this tension between majorities and mi-

---

dynamic social impact theory Bibb Latané's extension of his social impact theory which assumes that influence is a function of the strength, the immediacy, and the number of sources present, but that this influence results in consolidation, clustering, correlation, and continuing diversity in groups that are spatially distributed and interacting repeatedly over time.

norities in groups. Like social impact theory, dynamic social impact theory assumes that minorities and majorities influence each other. But unlike the original model, dynamic social impact theory assumes that groups are complex systems rather than static, simple systems. Simple systems can usually be understood once the laws underlying the behavior of the system are identified. Complex systems, in contrast, follow an intricate, unstable pattern that is governed by many interlinked components that act, in some cases, as random influences on the system. Complex systems appear to be ever changing, aperiodic, and utterly unpredictable, but closer examination reveals an order to this apparent chaos. When Latané studied groups discussing issues repeatedly, he identified four tendencies—consolidation, clustering, correlation, and continuing diversity (Latané, 1996, 1997; Latané & Bourgeois, 1996, 2001; Nowak, Szamrej, & Latané, 1990).

1. *Consolidation.* Over time, the majority grows in size, and the minority dwindles in size. Just as the Corona jury converged on the guilty verdict, groups become more unified in their opinions over time.
2. *Clustering.* As the law of social impact suggests, people are more influenced by their closest neighbors, so clusters of group members with similar opinions emerge in groups. Clustering is more likely when group members communicate more frequently with members who are close by and less frequently with more distant group members. Clustering can also occur, however, if group members can move around within the group. In the Corona trial, the jurors who voted not guilty moved so that they could sit together.
3. *Correlation.* Over time, the group members' opinions on other issues—even ones that are not discussed in the group—converge, so that their opinions on a variety of matters are correlated. In the Corona jury, for example, members of the majority might find that they also agreed on when to break for lunch or what program to watch on television. Members of the minority also agreed with one another, but they disagreed with the majority's choices on these unrelated matters.
4. *Continuing diversity.* Because of clustering, members of minorities are often shielded from the influence attempts of the majority, and their beliefs continue within the group. Diversity drops if the majority is very large and if the members of the minority are physically isolated from one another, but diversity continues when the minority members who communicate with the majority resist the majority's influence attempts.

Latané and his colleagues identified all four patterns in a study of classroom groups (Harton, Green, Jackson, & Latané, 1998). They asked students to answer several multiple-choice questions twice—once on their own, and once after talking about the questions with the two people sitting on either side of them. *Consolidation* occurred on several of the questions. On one question, 17 of the 30 students favored an incorrect alternative before discussion. After discussion, 5 more students changed their answers and sided with the incorrect majority—

including 3 students who had initially answered the question correctly! The majority increased from 57% to 73%. *Clustering* was also apparent; 11 students disagreed with both of their neighbors initially, but after discussion, only 5 students disagreed with both neighbors—indeed, two large clusters of 6 and 13 students who all agreed with one another emerged. Students within clusters also tended to give the same answers on other items (*correlation*), and some individuals refused to change their answers, even though no one else agreed with them (*continuing diversity*).

These four patterns vary depending on the number of times the group holds its discussion, the dispersion of the group members, the group's communication network, the status of particular individuals, the group members' desire to reach agreement, and other aspects of the situation (Kameda, 1996; Kameda & Sugimori, 1995; Latané, 1997). The four tendencies are robust, however, and answer some key questions about influence in groups. Do most groups eventually converge on a single opinion that represents the average across all members? Dynamic social impact theory says no—groups tend to become polarized on issues as clusters form within the group. Does social pressure eventually force all those who disagree with the minority to conform? Again, dynamic social impact theory suggests that minorities, particularly in spatially distributed groups, are protected from influence. So long as minorities can cluster together, diversity in groups is ensured (Nowak, Vallacher, & Miller, 2003).

SOURCES OF GROUP INFLUENCE

At the beginning of the trial, the 12 members of the Corona jury differed in their opinions about politics, the law, and the defendant's guilt. But when their deliberations ended, the group had reached consensus on a single verdict. Why did the group members who initially believed that Corona was innocent change their vote to guilty?

Many people think of conformity in a negative way. They assume that the jurors who changed their vote yielded to the group's pressure and so failed to stand up for their personal beliefs. This pejorative view underestimates the complexity of social influence. Individuals in any group, including the Corona jury, change their behavior for a variety of reasons (see Figure 7-6). **Informational influence** occurs when group members use the responses of others in the group as reference points and informational resources. If everyone in the group favors Plan A over Plan B, and you have no opinion on the issue, it is wise to let the

---

informational influence Interpersonal processes that promote change by challenging the correctness of group members' beliefs or the appropriateness of their behavior directly (e.g., though communication and persuasion) or indirectly (e.g., through social comparison processes).

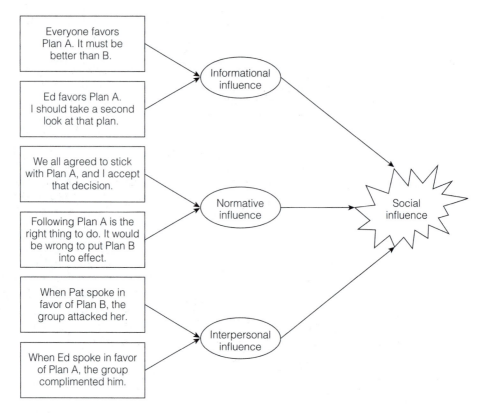

FIGURE 7-6

What are the psychological and interpersonal processes that mediate social influence in groups? *Informational influence* takes place whenever group members look to others for information. *Normative influence* prompts group members to feel, think, and act in ways that are consistent with their group's social standards. *Interpersonal influence* occurs when other people selectively encourage conformity while discouraging or even punishing nonconformity. In this example, all three sources influence a group member's decision to select Plan A rather than Plan B.

group guide your choice. **Normative influence** occurs when group members tailor their actions to match the group's standards. Individuals adhere to their group's norms because, as responsible group members, they accept the legitimacy of the established norms and recognize the importance of supporting these

---

normative influence Personal and interpersonal processes that cause individuals to feel, think, and act in ways that are consistent with social norms, standards, and convention. Because individuals internalize their group's norms they strive to act in ways that are consistent with those norms.

norms. **Interpersonal influence,** in contrast, occurs when the group uses verbal and nonverbal influence tactics to induce change. Those who violate their group's norms, even to a small degree, are often reminded of their duty and told to change their ways (Deutsch & Gerard, 1955; Forsyth, 1990; Kelley, 1952).

Informational Influence

Calvin Williams changed his verdict from not guilty to guilty, but he did not mindlessly go along with the majority's verdict. Rather, when Calvin learned that most of the jury believed that Corona was guilty, he wondered, "Why did so many of the jurors draw different conclusions about the case than I did?" and "Am I correct in my interpretation of the evidence?" Calvin reconsidered his position because the other group members provided him with clarifying information.

SOCIAL COMPARISON Social comparison theory assumes that group members, as active information processors, evaluate the accuracy of their beliefs and gauge the quality of their personal attributes by comparing themselves to other individuals. Individuals facing questions with no clear solution—"Is Corona guilty?" "Is Plan A better than Plan B?" "Are the New York Yankees the best team in baseball?" "Is majority influence stronger than minority influence?"— cannot reduce this uncertainty by consulting objective sources of information so they reach conclusions by comparing their views to the views endorsed by others in the group (Darley, 2001; Festinger, 1954). Festinger and his colleagues put it this way:

> The "social reality" upon which an opinion or attitude rests for its justification is the degree to which the individual perceives that this opinion or attitude is shared by others. An opinion or attitude that is not reinforced by others of the same opinion will become unstable generally. There are not usually compelling facts which can unequivocally settle the question of which attitude is wrong and which is right in connection with social opinions and attitudes as there are in the case of what might be called "facts." (Festinger et al., 1950, pp. 168–169)

In some cases, groups deliberately gather information about their members' opinions. The Corona trial jurors, for example, took a vote before they had done very much deliberating, because they were "anxious to know where everyone else stood before expressing their own views" (Villaseñor, 1977, p. 63). In most cases, however, information about others' views is gathered during routine discussion (Gerard & Orive, 1987). Festinger and his colleagues (1950), for example, discovered that the students who lived in a campus housing unit discussed attitudinal issues during their daily interaction and thereby gained information about the consensus of opinion within their groups and the relative uniqueness

---

interpersonal influence Social influence that results from other group members selectively encouraging conformity and discouraging or even punishing nonconformity.

of their attitudes. Those who expressed deviant attitudes tended to be individuals who, due to isolation from others, could not engage in this comparative process. But those closely connected by friendship or membership in a clique shared "a common fund of information about a variety of matters. . . . they will know and they will not know many of the same things" (p. 167). Interestingly, Festinger also found that this intuitive surveying of others' opinions is often biased. Members of the majority often underestimate the size of their own group, but minority members overestimate the degree to which others agree with them. This tendency, called the **false consensus effect,** leaves them thinking that there is more support for their position than there actually is (S. R. Gross & Miller, 1997; Krueger, 2000; Krueger & Clement, 1997; Mullen & Hu, 1988).

DUAL PROCESS APPROACHES Judging from the number of models proposed by theorists, those who study majority and minority influence must be nonconformists themselves. Robin Martin and Miles Hewstone (2001) counted no fewer than nine distinct theories that seek to explain when group members change their opinions and judgments and when they hold fast to their original position. Most of these theories, however, agree that change often results from two processes. In many cases, group members, when confronted with an opinion that is different from their own, undertake a relatively systematic review of their position. They review the arguments, look for weaknesses, reexamine their own ideas on the topic, and revise their position if revision is warranted. Yet at other times, group members are less thoughtful. They do not pay much attention to what they are told, they do not really understand the arguments completely, they forget what other people have suggested, yet they still change their minds.

Dual process theories of influence recognize that both direct (*systematic*) and indirect (*peripheral,* or *heuristic*) processes can lead to social influence (De Vries & De Dreu, 2001). Diane Mackie (1987), for example, traced much of the impact of a majority on a minority back to direct informational influence. She led her participants to believe that they were part of a small minority that disagreed with a majority on such matters as foreign policy and juvenile justice. After they listened to members of both the minority and the majority argue their positions, Mackie asked them to record their thoughts and reactions. When Mackie examined these cognitive reactions, she found that participants recalled more of the arguments offered by the majority, and they had more positive reactions to the majority's view after the discussion. Mackie also found that people who more extensively processed the majority's message changed their opinions more than those who did not process the message (see also De Dreu & De Vries, 1996; Trost, Maass, & Kenrick, 1992). Exposure to others' positions—in addi-

---

false consensus effect Perceivers' tendency to assume that their personal qualities and characteristics are common in the general population.

dual process theories of influence In general, a conceptual analysis arguing that individuals change in response to direct forms of influence (such as persuasion) and indirect forms of influence (such as mimicking another's response).

tion to providing further information and prompting a more thorough analysis of that information—can also cause group members to reinterpret or cognitively restructure key aspects of the issue (V. L. Allen & Wilder, 1980; Buehler & Griffin, 1994; Tindale et al., 1996; W. Wood, Pool, Leck, & Purvis, 1996).

Minorities, too, can stimulate cognitive elaboration of decision-relevant information. As Moscovici argued, minorities influence majorities by creating "cognitive conflicts" that challenge the status quo of the group by calling for a reevaluation of issues at hand. Such a minority undermines the majority's certainty and forces the group to seek out new information about the situation. When a minority is present, groups take longer to reach their conclusions and are more likely to consider multiple perspectives when drawing conclusions (R. S. Peterson & Nemeth, 1996). If the majority considers the minority members to be part of the ingroup, it will think positively rather than negatively about the minority position (Alvaro & Crano, 1997). Minorities also prompt group members to use more varied strategies in solving problems and to devise more creative solutions (Nemeth, 1986; Nemeth & Kwan, 1985, 1987; Nemeth, Mosier, & Chiles, 1992). In some cases, group members remember information presented by the minority better than information presented by the majority (Nemeth, Mayseless, Sherman, & Brown, 1990; cf. Walther et al., 2002).

These direct informational influence processes are complemented by more indirect, less rational processes (Moskowitz & Chaiken, 2001). Particularly when group members' cognitive resources are limited, or when they are not motivated to do the cognitive work necessary to weigh the information available to them, group members will use simplifying inferential principles or rules of thumb to reach decisions quickly (Baker & Petty, 1994; R. S. Peterson & Nemeth, 1996; W. Wood et al., 1996). One such rule, or **heuristic,** is the principle of *social proof*—we "view behavior as correct in a given situation to the degree that we see others performing it" (Cialdini, 2001, p. 100). If a group member learns that 99 other people favor Plan A over Plan B, that individual will likely adopt Plan A simply because "everyone else does." If one group member rubs her nose, soon after, another group member will begin rubbing his nose (Chartrand & Bargh, 1999). If a sufficiently large number of people begin to adopt a new fashion, hairstyle, or attitude, the rest of the group and community may adopt the craze as well (Gladwell, 2000). As Focus 7-2 suggests, in some cases, this tendency to respond as others are responding can cause people to act inappropriately in response to emergencies.

Normative Influence

The Corona jurors did not change their vote simply because they acquired relevant information from the other jurors. Rather, they changed because the group's norms changed. Just as Sherif's (1936) participants eventually agreed on how

---

heuristic An inferential principle or rule of thumb that people use to reach conclusions when the amount of available information is limited, ambiguous, or contradictory.

FOCUS 7-2   Why Are Groups Less Helpful than Individuals?

We are discreet sheep; we wait to see how the drove is going, and then go with the drove.

–Mark Twain

In the early morning of March 13, 1964, a young woman named Catherine Genovese ("Kitty" to her friends) was attacked and killed in Queens, New York. Thirty-eight people witnessed the murder, but none of them helped. Only one person even called the police (A. A. Seeman & Hellman, 1975).

Many blamed this failure on the bystanders, suggesting that the urbanites were cruel, apathetic, or lacking the moral compunction needed to compel them to act. But when Bibb Latané and John Darley read about the murder of Kitty Genovese, they were struck by the large number of witnesses. Could it be, they wondered, that people are less likely to help when they are in groups rather than alone? Latané and Darley created a false emergency in their laboratory (1970). While male college students completed some bogus questionnaires, Latané and Darley pumped white smoke through an air vent into the test room. Some participants were alone in the room, but others were part of three-person groups con-

sisting of one participant and two confederates. The confederates pretended to be participants, but they were trained to ignore the emergency. As the room filled with smoke, they nonchalantly glanced at the vent, shrugged, and went back to their questionnaires. If the participant mentioned the smoke to them, they said merely "I dunno." In a third condition, all three members of the group were actual participants.

When tested alone, participants usually left the room to report the smoke within 2 minutes; 75% reported the emergency within the 6-minute time limit. Puzzled, most stared at the vent, went over to get a closer look at the smoke, and finally left the room to get help. Participants tested in groups, however, behaved very differently. Only 10% of the participants tested with the passive confederates ever reported the smoke, and the percentage reached no higher than 15% even when all three group members were actual participants. By the time the 6-minute period was up, the room was so smoky that participants could not see the far wall. They coughed and rubbed their eyes, but they stayed at their tables, fanning the fumes away from their papers so they could finish their questionnaires. Latané and

much a pinpoint of light in an otherwise dark room moved, the jury eventually settled on a verdict. The group waffled from guilt to innocence for a week, but on the eighth day, a new norm emerged: Corona is guilty. When the judge later asked each one of the group to give his or her personal decision on each count, every single juror said "guilty."

Normative influence causes us to feel, think, and act in ways that are consistent with our group's norms. At an interpersonal level, people feel compelled to act in accordance with norms because a variety of negative consequences could result from nonconformity. People who consistently violate their group's norms are often reminded of their duty and told to mend their ways. They are often disliked, assigned lower status jobs, and in some cases dismissed from the group (Schachter, 1951). Normative influence, however, also has a personal component, for people obey norms to fulfill their own expectations about proper behavior. Norms are not simply external constraints but internalized standards; people feel duty bound to adhere to norms because, as responsible members of their groups, they accept the legitimacy of the established norms, and they recognize the importance of supporting these norms. Thus, people obey norms not only because they fear the negative interpersonal consequences—ostracism, rid-

FOCUS 7-2   *(continued)*

Darley had succeeded in documenting the **by-stander effect**—people are less likely to help in groups than when they are alone.

These findings may seem surprising, but they have been replicated in approximately four dozen studies of nearly 6000 people who faced various apparent emergencies alone or in a group. Across these various studies, about 75% of the participants tested alone intervened, but only 53% of the participants in groups helped (Latané & Nida, 1981).

But why do people in groups not help as much as single individuals? Latané and Darley believed that the presence of other bystanders inhibits helping for three basic reasons. The first factor, **diffusion of responsibility,** leaves bystanders feeling that it is not their responsibility to help. "The pressures to intervene do not focus on any one of the observers; instead, the responsibility for intervention is shared among all the onlookers and is not unique to any one" (Darley & Latané, 1968, p. 378). Simply imagining that one will be with others in a group is sufficient to reduce feelings of accountability and helpfulness (Garcia, Weaver, Moskowitz, & Darley, 2002).

Second, *informational influence* prompts individuals to rely on the actions of the other bystanders to guide their interpretation of the situation. Unfortunately, because emergencies are sometimes ambiguous, each nonresponding bystander sends the same inaccurate message to every other nonresponding bystander: "It's OK; no help is needed."

Third, the bystander effect is also caused by **evaluation apprehension**—onlookers' fear that they will embarrass themselves by doing something inappropriate. Most people prefer to appear poised and "normal" in social settings, and actively avoid doing anything that may lead to embarrassment. In an ambiguous emergency, we look and feel foolish if we offer assistance to someone who does not need it (S. H. Schwartz & Gottlieb, 1976).

These factors dispel some of the mystery surrounding helping and failure to help, for they explain the nature of the forces that immobilized the bystanders. They also suggest practical advice should you ever witness someone in need of help: Intervene, instead of looking first to see how others are reacting.

---

icule, punishment—that their nonconformity may produce, but also because they feel personally compelled to live up to their own expectations.

Stanley Milgram (1992) documented the personal consequences of violating norms. His student researchers broke the "first-come, first-served" norm of subway seating by asking subway riders in New York City to give up their seats. Many people turned over their seats to the students, but Milgram was more interested in how the students felt. The students were volunteers who were

---

bystander effect The tendency for people to help less when they know others are present and capable of helping. The effect was initially thought to be the result of apathy and a selfish unwillingness to get involved, but research suggests a number of cognitive and social processes, including diffusion of responsibility and misinterpretation that help is not needed, contribute to the effect.

diffusion of responsibility A reduction of personal responsibility experienced by individuals in groups and social collectives identified by John Darley and Bibb Latané in their studies of bystanders' failures to help someone in need.

evaluation apprehension An anxiety-creating concern to appear normal or competent.

deliberately breaking the situational norms in the name of research, but all "felt anxious, tense, and embarrassed. Frequently, they were unable to vocalize the request for a seat and had to withdraw" (Milgram, 1992, p. 42). Milgram, who also performed the norm violation task himself, described the experience as wrenching and concluded that there is an "enormous inhibitory anxiety that ordinarily prevents us from breaching social norms" (p. xxiv).

These powerful reactions make normative influence a more potent and longer lasting form of influence than informational influence. Robert Cialdini and his colleagues contrasted these two forms of influence in their studies of pro-environment actions (Cialdini, Kallgren, & Reno, 1991; Cialdini, Reno, & Kallgren, 1990). Cialdini's research team put handbills under the windshield wipers of cars in a parking lot, and then watched to see if people threw these scraps of paper on the ground when they returned to their cars. They then manipulated the salience of norms about littering across three conditions. To create information influence, some participants, while walking toward their car, passed by a confederate who carefully dropped a bag of trash into a garbage can. This condition suggested, "most people do not litter." In a second condition, participants saw a confederate actually pick up a piece of litter (the same bag of trash) and dispose of it in the garbage can. Cialdini and his colleagues believed that this confederate made salient the injunctive norm, "It is wrong to litter!" In the control condition, the confederate merely walked by the participant. Participants encountered the confederate either in the lot where the participant's car was parked or on the path leading to the parking lot.

These researchers discovered that the informational influence worked only for a short period of time. Participants who saw the confederate throw away his trash just before they got to their car were less likely to litter than those who saw him on the path leading to their car. In contrast, the injunctive norm became more powerful over time. No one who saw the confederate pick up litter on the path leading to the parking lot littered (Reno, Cialdini, & Kallgren, 1993, Study 3).

Interpersonal Influence

Just before a key vote by the jurors, Naomi interrupted the proceedings (Villaseñor, 1977, p. 149):

> "Wait. I got one thing to say. If Corona is so guilty, then why didn't the sheriff come and tell us that he knows Corona is guilty?"
>
> Everyone looked at Naomi. Victor and Matt, almost in unison, pushed back their chairs and lowered their heads, trying not to laugh. Frank and Larry looked at each other. Rogers yelled:
>
> "Because that's not evidence! That would be hearsay! Dammit, why don't you ask why God doesn't come down here and tell us everything about everybody, then we don't even need the jury system and we can all go home!"

More is going on here than informational or normative influence. The jurors have detected a nonconformist in their midst, and they are deliberately trying to change her behavior through interpersonal influence. Instead of providing

Naomi with information or reiterating the group's norms, the jurors are using verbal and nonverbal tactics—complaining, demanding, threatening, pleading, negotiating, pressuring, manipulating, rejecting, and so on—to induce change.

Stanley Schachter (1951) documented interpersonal influence by planting three kinds of confederates in a number of all-male discussion "clubs." The *deviant* always disagreed with the majority. The *slider* disagreed initially, but conformed over the course of the discussion. The *mode* served as a control; he consistently agreed with the majority. Schachter also manipulated the groups' cohesiveness by putting some of the participants in clubs that interested them and others in clubs that did not interest them. He assumed that people with common interests would be more cohesive than those with disparate interests. Moreover, the groups discussed a topic that was either relevant or irrelevant to the group's stated purpose.

Schachter was interested in how group members would pressure the deviant during the course of the discussion, so he kept track of each comment directed to the deviant, slider, and mode by the other group members. He predicted that the group would initially communicate with the mode, deviant, and slider at equal rates. But once the group became aware of the deviant's and slider's disagreement, group members would concentrate on these two participants. Schachter believed that communication would continue at a high rate until the dissenter capitulated to the majority opinion (as in the case of the slider) or until the majority concluded that the deviant would not budge from his position (as in the case of the persistent deviant), but that this reaction would be exacerbated by the group's cohesiveness, the relevance of the task, and the group members' dislike for the deviant.

INFLUENCE AND OSTRACISM Figure 7-7 summarizes Schachter's findings. In most cases, the group communicated with the slider and the mode at a relatively low rate throughout the session, whereas communications with the deviant increased during the first 35 minutes of discussion. At the 35-minute mark, however, some groups seemed to have rejected the deviant. These groups were cohesive ones working on a task that was relevant to the group's goals and whose members developed a negative attitude toward the deviant. If the group liked the deviant, communication increased all the way up to the final minute. If the group disliked the deviant, however, communication dropped precipitously.

Schachter's findings highlight the difference between inclusive and exclusive reactions to minorities (Berkowitz, 1971; Emerson, 1954; T. M. Mills, 1962; Mucchi-Faina, 1994; Orcutt, 1973). Most of the groups displayed an *inclusive* reaction to the deviant: Communication between the majority and the minority was intensive and hostile, but the minority was still perceived to be a member of the ingroup. If an *exclusive* reaction occurred, however, communication with the deviant dwindled along with overt hostility, and the deviant was perceptually removed from the group by the majority members. An exclusive reaction becomes more likely when group members think that their group is very heterogeneous (Festinger, Pepitone, & Newcomb, 1952; Festinger & Thibaut, 1951). Highly cohesive groups, too, will sometimes "redefine the group's boundary" if the dissenter

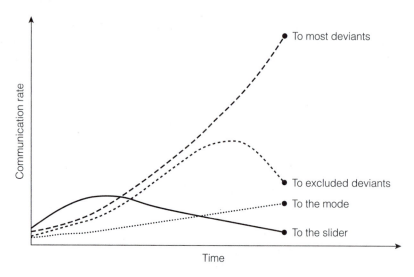

FIGURE 7-7

How does a group react to a lone dissenter who refuses to conform? Schachter (1951) found that the person who disagreed with the others (the *deviant*) usually received the most communication throughout the discussion period. The only exception occurred in cohesive groups working on a relevant task who disliked the deviant; in this case, communications tapered off. The average number of communications addressed to the *mode* increased slightly over the session, whereas communication with the *slider* (who initially dissented but later conformed) decreased over time. Adapted from "Deviance, Rejection, and Communication" by S. Schachter, *Journal of Abnormal and Social Psychology,* 1951, 46, 190–207.

is inflexible and the issue is important (Gerard, 1953). So-called *double minorities*—individuals who disagree with the group and also possess one or more other unique qualities that distinguish them from the rest of the group—are also more likely to face exclusion (E. E. Sampson, 1971; E. E. Sampson & Brandon, 1964).

INTERPERSONAL REJECTION The group members did not just argue with the deviant—they also rejected the deviant. When Schachter's participants rated each other on likability, the deviant was the sociometric outcast, whereas the mode was liked the most. The deviant was also saddled with the secretarial chores of the group; the mode and slider were assigned more desirable positions. This rejection was more pronounced in the more cohesive groups. Schachter also found that the slider, who disagreed with the majority only briefly, was not as well liked as the mode; apparently, even a little dissent can lead to a little rejection. John Levine and his associates have confirmed this tendency in their studies of individuals who shift their position during a group discussion (see J. M. Levine, 1980, for a comprehensive review). They, like Schachter, found that nonconformists and those who were initially neutral but eventually disagreed were liked the least. Moreover, even the individual who abandons his or her initial position to agree with the group is liked less than a conformist. These reactions to the dissenter likely reflect group members' sensitivity to the size of shifting majorities and minorities. Majority members are gratified when a member of the minority converts, but they are particularly troubled when a member of the majority "goes over to the other side" (Prislin, Limbert, & Bauer, 2000).

Subsequent studies have replicated this relationship between rejection and nonconformity, although these studies have frequently noted that certain situational factors increase the magnitude of this relationship (Tata et al., 1996). Task relevance, cohesiveness, interdependence, behavior extremity, and the degree of threat posed by the dissenter all work to increase rejection. The deviant's contribution to the task, apologies for deviation, group norms that encourage deviation and innovation, and a history of previous conformity reduce the likelihood of rejection. In many cases, too, social identity processes play a key role in determining members' reactions to deviants and conformists. Jose Marques, Dominic Abrams, and their colleagues, in a series of studies of what they termed "subjective group dynamics," suggested that group members find deviants within their midst to be distressing because they call into question the group's positive identity and make hazy the distinctiveness of the ingroup relative to outgroups. In consequence, group members react more positively to an ingroup member who acts in ways that are consistent with the group's norms than they do to an outgroup member who performs the exact same behavior. However, when ingroup members engage in negative behavior, they are evaluated more unfavorably than outgroup members who engage in similar behavior. This effect has been termed the **black-sheep effect** (Marques, 1990; see also Abrams, Marques, Bown, & Henson, 2000; Marques, Abrams, & Serôdio, 2001).

APPLICATION: UNDERSTANDING JURIES

Groups have served as the final arbiter of guilt and innocence for centuries. As far back as the 11th century, the neighbors of those accused of wrongdoing were asked both to provide information about the actions of the accused and to weigh the evidence. Witnesses and experts now provide the evidence, but the jury remains responsible for weighing the testimony of each person before rendering a verdict. More than 300,000 juries convene each year in American courtrooms (see Hyman & Tarrant, 1975; and L. E. Moore, 1973; for discussions of the history of juries).

---

black-sheep effect The tendency for group members to evaluate a disliked ingroup member who performs an offensive behavior more harshly than an outgroup member who performs the same offense.

Jury Dynamics

The jury situation is designed to foster careful decision making and tolerance for all viewpoints, but at their core, juries are groups. The jury's final decision depends not only on the evidence presented at the trial, the attorneys' arguments, and the judge's instructions, but also on social influence.

VERDICT-DRIVEN AND EVIDENCE-DRIVEN JURIES Reid Hastie, Steven Penrod, and Nancy Pennington (1983), in their book *Inside the Jury*, described the processes that typically unfold once the jury is sequestered in the jury room. Most juries begin by electing a leader and deciding if balloting will be secret or public. Some juries immediately take a straw poll of their initial preferences, and more than 30% reach complete consensus on that first ballot (Penrod & Hastie, 1980). But when members disagree, they initiate a consensus-seeking process. During this phase of the deliberation, the group may ask the judge for instructions and request additional information concerning the evidence. The group spends most of its time, however, discussing points favoring the two possible verdicts.

The jury's approach to the deliberations depends, in part, on how it structures the task. Hastie, Penrod, and Pennington noted that jurors generally approach the decision in one of two ways. Some jurors appear to be *verdict driven*. They reach a decision about the verdict before deliberation and cognitively organize the evidence into two categories: evidence that favors a verdict of guilty and evidence that favors a verdict of not guilty. *Evidence-driven* jurors, in contrast, resist making a final decision on the verdict until they have reviewed all the available evidence; then they generate a "story" that organizes the evidence (Hastie, Penrod, & Pennington, 1983; N. Pennington & Hastie, 1986, 1992). When juries contain both verdict-driven and evidence-driven jurors, the approach preferred by the majority of the jurors is generally used to structure the deliberations. When researchers created mock three-person juries containing two members who shared the same type of cognitive orientation, this cognitive majority dominated the deliberations, and in most cases, the individual with the alternative viewpoint restructured his or her approach so that it matched the majority's approach (Kameda, 1994).

MINORITY INFLUENCE AND VERDICTS In the play *Twelve Angry Men*, a single insistent juror convinces the other eleven jurors to change their guilty verdicts to not guilty. This plot is dramatic, but statistically a rarity in real juries. The verdict favored by 7 to 11 jurors (a majority) on the first ballot becomes the jury's final decision in 90% of all jury trials (D. J. Devine, Clayton, Dunford, Seying, & Pryce, 2001; Hans, Hannaford-Agor, Mott, & Munsterman, 2003; Kalven & Zeisel, 1966). Most jurors implicitly adopt a "majority rules" decision norm: If a significant majority of the members (say, two thirds) favor a verdict, then everyone in the group should agree with that verdict (J. H. Davis, Bray, & Holt, 1977; J. H. Davis, Kameda, Parks, Stasson, & Zimmerman, 1989; J. H. Davis, Stasson, Ono, & Zimmerman, 1988).

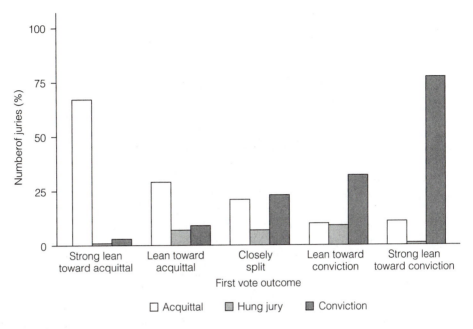

FIGURE 7-8

How strong is majority and minority influence in juries? In most cases, the decision favored by the majority of the jurors when deliberations begin is the verdict eventually returned by that jury. Minority influence, although rare, occurred in about 10% of the cases when the majority favored acquittal, and in 15% of the cases when the majority favored conviction.

Even though the majority tends to prevail in juries, the statistics displayed in Figure 7-8 suggest that the *Twelve Angry Men* scenario—a staunch minority persuading the majority to adopt its view—occurs in 10% to 15% of deliberations. For example, in the trial of the second defendant in the Oklahoma City Bombing, Terry Nichols, the first vote was 10 to 2 for acquittal (Bartels, 2001). But the two lone jurors who favored guilt dug in to their position and carefully reviewed the evidence for 6 long days. One of the jurors, Todd Fockler, was a geophysicist who used his skill, logic, and persuasive talents to craft a compromise verdict of guilty on conspiracy but not guilty of first-degree murder. He was successful, in part, because of his recognized expertise and the rapid change in votes by four of the other jurors. These findings confirm the importance of allowing juries to deliberate before rendering a final decision (Hans et al., 2003).

Minorities can also deadlock the jury by refusing to conform to the majority's verdict, resulting in a *hung jury* if a unanimous verdict is required. The origin of the term "hung jury" is not certain, but it was apparently first used to describe American juries that could not reach a verdict. It matches "most closely to the meaning of the word hung as caught, stuck, or delayed" (Hans et al., 2003, p. 33). Hung juries generally occur when the evidence does not clearly favor one verdict, and even then they only occur in approximately 10% of such cases. When a hung jury does occur, it is often just one or two jurors holding out against the majority (Hans et al., 2003).

STATUS AND INFLUENCE Some members of the Corona jury had higher status within the group than the other rank-and-file members: Ernie, the foreman, Faye, the retired teacher, and Jim, the shipyard inspector. Is it a coincidence that the verdict they favored was the final verdict of the jury?

Fairly or unfairly, people who have high prestige or status are more influential than low-status members. Fred L. Strodtbeck and his colleagues, in their studies of mock juries, carefully replicated all aspects of an actual trial. They selected sets of 12 individuals from a pool of eligible jurors, simulated the pretrial interview process designed to eliminate biased jurors (*voir dire*), and assembled the group in the courtroom. A bailiff then played a recording of a trial and asked the group to retire to a jury room to decide on a verdict. Except for the use of a recording, the groups were treated just like actual juries (Strodtbeck & Hook, 1961; Strodtbeck et al., 1957; Strodtbeck & Mann, 1956).

Consistent with expectation-states theory (see Chapters 2 and 6), juries favored people of higher socioeconomic status (proprietors and clerical workers) over those of lower socioeconomic status (blue-collar workers) when choosing a foreman, even though no mention of occupation was made (Strodtbeck & Lipinski, 1985). High-status members also participated more frequently in the jury's discussions, often by offering more suggestions and providing more orientation to the task. High-status members were also more successful in convincing the others that their judgments on the case were the most accurate. The correlation between private predeliberation opinion and the jury's final decision was .50 for proprietors, but it dropped all the way down to .02 for laborers (Strodtbeck et al., 1957). Sex differences were also apparent, for women joined in the discussion less frequently than men (R. James, 1959; Strodtbeck et al., 1957). Furthermore, women's comments were more often relational in nature, showing solidarity and agreement, whereas men's comments were more task focused (Strodtbeck & Mann, 1956; see also Nemeth, Endicott, & Wachtler, 1976).

How Effective Are Juries?

Given what we know about conformity and nonconformity in groups, should the jury system be modified? Asch's studies tell us that people often conform and that even a correct minority often loses to an incorrect majority. As we have seen, normative, informational, and interpersonal influence are powerful forces in groups, and they can quash individuals' freedom to speak their minds. Juries are a time-honored tradition, but are they effective?

Determining the effectiveness of juries as deciders of guilt or innocence is a complicated task, for we can never know when the jury has been correct or incorrect in condemning or freeing a defendant. If a clear criterion for determining guilt existed, juries would not be necessary in the first place. Several bits of evidence, however, provide partial support for the effectiveness of juries as decision makers. First, jurors seem to take their role very seriously. As Villaseñor's account of the Corona jury vividly illustrates, jurors strive to reach the fairest decision possible (Hastie et al., 1983). One jury expert, after studying the responses of more than 2000 jurors participating in a Chicago law project, concluded,

> The most consistent theme that emerged from listening to the deliberations was the seriousness with which the jurors approached their job and the extent to which they were concerned that the verdict they reached was consistent with the spirit of the law and with the facts of the case. (R. J. Simon, 1980, p. 521)

Second, juries do well when compared with judges' preferences. In a survey of nearly 8000 actual criminal and civil trials, judges and juries disagreed on only 20% of the cases; for criminal trials, the jury was somewhat more lenient than the judge, but for civil trials, the disagreements were evenly split for and against the defendant. Furthermore, 80% of these disagreements occurred when the weight of the evidence was so close that the judge admitted that the verdict could have gone either way. This concord between verdicts may explain why 77% of the judges surveyed felt that the jury system was satisfactory, 20% felt that it had disadvantages that should be corrected, but only 3% felt that the system was so unsatisfactory that its use should be curtailed (Kalven & Zeisel, 1966).

Third, jurors are hardly unbiased, rational weighers of evidence; the defendant's physical appearance, the lawyer's style of questioning, and the sequencing of evidence are just a few of the factors that bias jurors' decisions (Dane & Wrightsman, 1982; Hastie et al., 1983; M. F. Kaplan, 1982; Wrightsman, Nietzel, & Fortune, 1998). These biases are largely controlled, however, by relying on group decisions rather than individual decisions. Simulations of juries suggest that the lone juror's initial biases and preferences have very little impact on the group's final decision, no matter what the size of the jury (N. L. Kerr & Huang, 1986).

Each of these pro-jury arguments, however, can also be countered by other, more disquieting data about juries and their capabilities. In recent years, a number of very high-profile juries have made decisions that in retrospect appear to have been based on emotion and prejudice rather than on the thoughtful analysis of the evidence. Studies of their deliberation processes indicate that a handful of group members dominated the group discussion, and these individuals succeeded, in most cases, in determining the final verdict. When investigators have asked jurors about their understanding of the legalities of the case, they discovered that many understood less than half of the judges' instructions to the jury (Ellsworth & Reifman, 2000). Jury members also have a particularly difficult time following the arguments and evidence introduced in complex, time-consuming trials (Cecil, Hans, & Wiggins, 1991). These findings have prompted some to suggest that the jury system should be abolished, but others favor a more moderate solution—improving juries by modifying their structure and dynamics.

Improving Juries

The judicial system is long on tradition, but in recent years, several innovations have been suggested and even implemented (Penrod & Heuer, 1998; Saks, 1977). Some of these reforms, such as reducing the size and the decision rules of juries, are designed to improve the general efficiency of juries and the fairness of their procedures. Others, such as note taking, help jurors to process the evidence and testimony that they must consider when reaching their decision.

JURY SIZE In 1970, the U.S. Supreme Court returned a landmark ruling in the case of *Williams v. Florida* (National Center for State Courts, 1976). Williams sought to have his conviction overturned on the grounds that the deciding jury had included only six persons. The Supreme Court, however, found in favor of the state, ruling that a six-person jury is large enough to promote group deliberation, protect members from intimidation, fairly represent the community, and weigh the facts in the case (*Williams v. Florida,* 1970). Psychology and law expert Michael J. Saks, however, has suggested that the Supreme Court should have taken group dynamics research into consideration before making its decision. As he noted, modifying jury size could influence

- *Group structure.* Members of smaller juries participate at more equal rates; smaller juries are more cohesive; and members of larger juries exchange more information.
- *Representativeness.* Smaller groups are not as representative of the community as larger ones. For example, if a community was 10% Latino and 90% Anglo, in all probability, about 80% of the 12-person juries selected from that community would include at least one Latino, but only 40% of the 6-person juries would contain Latinos.
- *Majority influence.* The majority's influence may be greater in smaller juries, because the likelihood of finding a partner for one's minority coalition becomes smaller.

The Supreme Court erred in assuming that a 5 to 1 vote in a 6-person jury was the same as a 10 to 2 split in a 12-person group. With the 10 to 2 vote, one is joined by a dissenting partner, whereas in the 5 to 1 vote, one must face the majority alone. As a result, the likelihood of a hung jury is greater in larger juries (N. L. Kerr & MacCoun, 1985). Saks also noted, however, that despite size-related changes in group dynamics, small juries and large juries do not appear to differ significantly in the types of verdicts reached—except in certain civil cases, where smaller juries tend to return larger damages (Saks, 1977; Saks & Hastie, 1978; Saks & Marti, 1997).

UNANIMITY In 1972, three men were convicted, in separate trials, of assault, grand larceny, and burglary by the court system of Oregon. They appealed to the U.S. Supreme Court on the grounds that their right to a fair trial had been violated because the votes of the juries had not been unanimous. To the defendants' dismay, the Supreme Court ruled in favor of Oregon (*Apodoca v. Oregon,* 1972), concluding that the Sixth Amendment to the U.S. Constitution guarantees only that a "substantial majority of the jury" must be convinced of the defendant's guilt. Later in the ruling, the Supreme Court suggested that 75% agreement constitutes an acceptable minimum for most juries.

The court's conclusion is, for the most part, justified by the empirical evidence. The verdict preferred by the majority of the jurors on their first vote usually becomes the final verdict in a large percentage of the cases, with or without a unanimity rule. The minority's opinion sometimes prevails, but in such cases, the minority is usually so substantial that a 9 out of 12 majority would not have been reached anyway. Most juries implicitly operate according to either a basic two-thirds or a 10 out of 12 rule (J. H. Davis, Kerr, Atkin, Holt, & Meek, 1975; J. H. Davis, Kerr, Stasser, Meek, & Holt, 1977; Stasser, Kerr, & Bray, 1982).

Relaxing the requirement for unanimity, however, changes the decision-making process in juries. Juries that do not have to reach a unanimous decision render their judgments twice as quickly and are far less likely to come to a stalemate (Foss, 1981; N. L. Kerr et al., 1976). Saks and Hastie (1978) feared that juries that do not deliberate to unanimity do not deliberate sufficiently and make more mistakes—"convictions when the correct decision is acquittal; acquittals when the correct decision is conviction" (pp. 84–85).

PROCEDURAL INNOVATIONS Whereas jurors were once forbidden from taking notes or discussing the case prior to deliberations, in a series of modifications, the courts have experimented with various types of procedural changes to determine if they help jurors to remember and process the volumes of information they receive during the trial. For example, the courts have worked to try to clarify information about the legal terms used in the case under consideration. The revised wording of such concepts as "reasonable doubt" and "preponderance of evidence," for example, has triggered changes in how long juries deliberate and in their eventual verdicts (Horowitz & Kirkpatrick, 1996). The courts have studied ways to make the instructions given to the jurors prior to deliberation clearer and more understandable (Ellsworth & Reifman, 2000). Some courts also permit jurors to (1) take notes during the presentation of evidence and use these notes during deliberation; (2) submit questions to the courts that, after review by judge and legal counsel, can be considered in summary statements during the trial or in the presentation of additional evidence; and (3) discuss the trial with the other jurors while the trial is ongoing. These innovations are generally associated with increased involvement of jurors in the deliberation process, but their impact on decision outcomes appears to be modest (D. J. Devine et al., 2001).

VOIR DIRE The courts select jury members from a pool of potential participants through a process known as **voir dire.** Voir dire—an alteration of the French

---

voir dire The oral or written questioning of prospective jurors by counsel.

phrase *vrai dire,* which means "to speak truly"—calls for verbal or written questioning of prospective jurors to uncover any biases or prejudices that may stand in the way of fairness and impartiality (Hans & Vidmar, 1982).

Until the 1970s, voir dire was primarily left up to the judge's discretion; defense lawyers could submit questions, but judges were free to omit them if they desired. However, when convictions were overturned because trial judges had disallowed defense participation in voir dire (e.g., *Ham v. S. Carolina,* 1973), the courts began opening up the procedure to attorneys. Systematic jury selection, whereby lawyers carefully study the prospective jurors in the pool and use voir dire to identify sympathetic and antagonistic jurors, is now a common practice in major trials. Voir dire is regularly used, for example, in cases in which the defendant, if convicted, faces the death penalty. By rejecting from the jury anyone who objects to the death penalty, the prosecution can assemble what is termed a *death-qualified jury.*

Systematic jury selection is controversial. Proponents argue that in many political and criminal trials, biases produced by unfair publicity, regional prejudices, and unrepresentative jury rosters must be controlled if the defendant is to receive just treatment. Critics feel that systematic jury selection is tantamount to jury rigging, as it produces biased rather than fair juries and works to exclude certain types of people from juries. Death-qualified juries, for example, are not just willing to impose a death sentence, but they are also more conviction prone than non−death-qualified juries (Filkins, Smith, & Tindale, 1998).

Lawrence Wrightsman, an expert on psychology and the law, has argued that judges should limit the number of jurors that lawyers can challenge during voir dire. He also recommended stricter guidelines for lawyers, who sometimes use the voir dire process to influence the jurors in their favor. Wrightsman suggested that voir dire questioning be carried out carefully, so that jurors will respond honestly, and that judges supervise the process more closely. Voir dire is a useful way of identifying highly biased individuals, but it should not be a means of manipulating the composition of the jury (Wrightsman et al., 1998).

SUMMARY IN OUTLINE

❖ When do people conform to the demands of the group?

1. *Social influence* in groups occurs when the majority of the members influence smaller subgroups within the group (the minority) to change (*majority influence*) and when the minority members succeed in converting the majority of the group members to their position (*minority influence*).

2. Asch studied *conformity* by measuring people's decisions when the majority of their group's members made blatant errors in judgment (the *Asch paradigm*).

   • Approximately one third of the people that Asch studied conformed to erroneous judgments.

   • Conformity increased when the majority was large and unanimous, but increasing the majority beyond four did not significantly increase conformity. This decreasing impact of increased numbers of sources of influence is consistent with Latané's *social impact theory.*

- When group members change their position, their conformity may result from temporary *compliance* to the group's pressure rather than true *conversion* (private acceptance). Those who do not comply may be displaying *independence* or deliberate defiance of the group (*anticonformity*).
- Fewer group members conform when they can respond anonymously via secret ballot or by the so-called *Crutchfield apparatus.*

3. Conformity rates vary across time, cultures, sexes, and group settings.
   - Group members in collectivistic societies yield to majority influence more often than those in individualistic societies.
   - Conformity rates have dropped slightly in the last half of the 20th century.
   - Women conform more than men, albeit only in face-to-face groups. Women may use conformity to increase group harmony, whereas men use nonconformity to create the impression of independence.
   - Certain personality traits are related to conformity. People who conform consistently in groups tend to be more authoritarian but seek social approval. Nonconformists are more self-confident.
   - Majority influence varies in strength depending on the size, structure, cohesiveness, and goals of the group and the nature of its tasks.
   - Individuals in groups engaged in computer-mediated interactions conform at rates equal to face-to-face groups.

❖ When do people resist the group's influence and instead change the group?

1. Moscovici studied minority influence by measuring people's reactions to one or more consistent dissenters.
   - Moscovici found that a minority, particularly if behaviorally *consistent,* can change the majority.
   - Minorities that are accorded high status in the group can also influence the majority, for their *idiosyncrasy credits* protect them from sanctions when they display nonconformity.
   - Minorities that can convince members of the majority to join them are more influential.

2. The minority's influence is more indirect than the majority's, sometimes becoming evident only when the group has completed its initial deliberations and moved on to another task. Minorities therefore create more conversion and innovation, whereas majorities tend to create compliance.

3. Latané's *dynamic social impact theory* uses the processes of consolidation, clustering, correlation, and continuing diversity to explain majority and minority influence in spatially distributed groups that interact repeatedly over time.

❖ Why do people conform?

1. *Informational influence* takes place whenever group members look to others for information.
   - As social comparison theory notes, people are a valuable source of information, although individuals often misjudge the extent to which others agree with their viewpoint (the *false consensus effect*).

- *Dual process theories* of influence recognize that social influence occurs when group members systematically process available information (*direct process*) or base their choices on nonrational processes, such as *heuristics* and emotional responses (*indirect process*).
- Individuals sometimes take others' inaction in emergencies (the *bystander effect*) to be a sign that no help is needed. *Diffusion of responsibility,* informational influence, and *evaluation apprehension* all contribute to the bystander effect.

2. *Normative influence* prompts group members to feel, think, and act in ways that are consistent with their group's social standards.
   - Milgram documented the negative emotions associated with violating norms in his study of norm violations on the subway.
   - In some cases, normative influence is a more potent and longer lasting form of influence than informational influence.

3. *Interpersonal influence* includes verbal and nonverbal tactics—complaining, demanding, threatening, pleading, negotiating, pressuring, manipulating, rejecting, and so on—designed to induce change.
   - Schachter's analysis of group rejection indicates that a nonconformist is generally less liked by others in the group.
   - Communication with a disliked deviant eventually diminishes, at least when cohesive groups are working on relevant tasks.
   - Group members who violate norms can trigger the *black-sheep effect*—they will be evaluated more negatively than an individual who is not a group member who performs the same type of action.

❖ **Do social influence processes shape juries' verdicts?**

1. The magnitude of social influence suggests that the decisions reached by groups, including juries, are shaped by social processes rather than by an unbiased weighing of evidence.
   - Juries tend to use either *verdict-driven* or *evidence-driven* deliberation strategies. In most cases, they choose the method of deliberation favored by the majority of the members.
   - The verdict favored by the majority of the members prior to deliberation (or on the first straw poll) is usually the jury's final verdict.
   - Jurors who have higher status occupations tend to dominate the group's discussion.

2. Available evidence suggests that juries are satisfactory vehicles for making legal decisions.
   - Despite size-related changes in group dynamics, small and large juries do not appear to differ significantly in the types of verdicts reached.
   - Juries that do not have to reach a unanimous decision render their judgments twice as quickly and are far less likely to be hung juries.
   - Several alterations of procedure have been developed to help jurors remember and process trial information, but their impact is not yet known.
   - *Voir dire* procedures are often used to select jury members, but the effectiveness of this systematic selection process continues to be debated.

FOR MORE INFORMATION

Chapter Case: The Corona Jury

- *Jury: The People vs. Juan Corona,* by Victor Villaseñor (1977), offers a vivid case study of how juries make decisions, as carefully constructed by a journalist who interviewed all the jurors after the trial.

Majority and Minority Influence

- "Culture and Conformity: A Meta-Analysis of Studies Using Asch's (1952b, 1956) Line Judgment Task," by Rod Bond and Peter B. Smith (1996), is a scholarly analysis of nearly 50 years of research into conformity.
- *Group Consensus and Minority Influence: Implications for Innovation,* edited by Carsten K. W. De Dreu and Nanne K. De Vries (2001), includes state-of-the-art literature reviews by leading experts on social minority influence.
- "Conformity and Independence in Groups: Majorities and Minorities," by Robin Martin and Miles Hewstone (2001) is a succinct but comprehensive review of current theoretical models pertaining to social influence.

Social Influence

- *Social Influence: Direct and Indirect Processes,* edited by Joseph P. Forgas and Kipling D. Williams (2001), includes empirically focused and theoretically based chapters on virtually all aspects of social influence.
- "Social Influence: Compliance and Conformity," by Robert B. Cialdini and Noah J. Goldstein (2004) reviews the literature on social influence published between 1997 and 2002.

Juries

- *Inside the Jury,* by Reid Hastie, Steven D. Penrod, and Nancy Pennington (1983), presents a masterful analysis of communication, influence, and decision making in juries.
- "Jury Decision Making: 45 Years of Empirical Research on Deliberating Groups," by Dennis J. Devine, Laura D. Clayton, Benjamin B. Dunford, Rasmy Seying, and Jennifer Pryce (2001), provides a clear review of social science analyses of key aspects of juries as decision makers.

MEDIA RESOURCES

Visit the Group Dynamics companion website at http://psychology.wadsworth .com/forsyth4e to access online resources for your book, including quizzes, flash cards, web links, and more!

8

POWER

CHAPTER OVERVIEW

Power is essential to group life. Authorities, by exerting control over others, coordinate members' activities and guide them toward their goals. Power, however, can be used against the group, for authorities sometimes demand actions that members would otherwise never consider. We would not be social beings if we were immune to the impact of power, but power can corrupt.

❖ What are the limits of an authority's power over group members?

❖ What are the sources of power in groups?

❖ How do those without power react when power is used to influence them?

❖ How do people react when they use their power to influence others?

The People's Temple:
The Metamorphic Effects of Power

Jim Jones was the People's Temple Full Gospel Church's founder and minister. Under his able leadership, the congregation grew to 8000 members. Many of the People's Temple members thought that Jones was a visionary, inspiring leader, but some had their doubts. Former members reported that at some services, people were beaten before the whole congregation, with microphones used to amplify their screams. Jones, some said, insisted on being called Father, and he demanded absolute dedication and obedience from his followers. He asked members to donate their property to the church, and he even forced one family give him their 6-year-old son.

Jones, for reasons that remain unclear, decided to move his entire church to Guyana, in South America, and he called the settlement Jonestown. Jones claimed that Jonestown was an ideal community where everyone found love, happiness, and well-being. But the men, women, and children of Jonestown did not find contentment. They found, instead, a group that exercised incredible power over their destiny. Jones asked members to make great personal sacrifices for the group, and time and again they obeyed. They worked long hours in the fields. They were given too little to eat. They could not communicate with their loved ones back in the United States. Then disaster struck when church members attacked and killed members of a congressional delegation from the United States. Jones, fearing the dismantling of his empire, ordered his followers to take their own lives. Authorities who first reached the settlement were met by a scene of unbelievable ghastliness. On Jones's orders, more than 900 men, women, and children had killed themselves. Jones's body lay near his chair, where he sat beneath the motto "Those who do not remember the past are condemned to repeat it" (Krause, 1978).

Why did the group members obey his order? What force is great enough to make parents give poison to their children? Many blamed Jim Jones—his persuasiveness, his charisma, his depravity. Others emphasized the kind of people who join such groups—their psychological instability, their willingness to identify with causes, and their religious fervor. Still others suggested more fantastic explanations—mass hypnosis, government plots, and even divine intervention.

Such explanations underestimate the power of groups and their leaders—their capacity to influence members, even when the members try to resist this influence (Cartwright, 1959). As Chapter 7 noted, groups influence the way their members feel, think, and act. But groups do more than create uniformity through subtle social influence; they also compel obedience among members who would otherwise resist the group's wishes. Here we consider the sources of that power and the consequences of power for those who wield it and those who are subjected to it.

OBEDIENCE TO AUTHORITY

Bertrand Russell concluded many years ago that "the fundamental concept in social science is Power, in the same sense in which Energy is the fundamental concept in physics" (1938, p. 10). Few interactions advance very far before elements of power and influence come into play. The coach demanding obedience from a player, the police officer asking the driver for the car's registration, the teacher scowling at the errant student, and the boss telling an employee to get back to work are all using social power to influence others (Cartwright, 1959). A powerful person can use and control others for his or her own ends, "without their consent, against their will, or without their knowledge or understanding" (Buckley, 1967, p. 186). Powerholders can "produce intended and foreseen effects on others" (Wrong, 1979, p. 21), even when the others try to resist.

But can **social power**—a commonplace process that shapes nearly all group interactions—generate such a dramatic and disastrous outcome as the Jonestown mass suicide? Can group members be so bent to the will of an authority that they would follow any order, no matter how nocuous? Stanley Milgram's (1974) laboratory studies of obedience to authority suggest that the answer to these questions is *yes*.

The Milgram Experiments

Milgram analyzed power by creating small groups in his laboratory at Yale University. In most cases, he studied three-man groups: One member was a volunteer who had answered an advertisement; one member was the experimenter who was in charge of the session; and one member appeared to be another participant recruited from the community but was in actuality a confederate, who was part of the research team. The confederate looked to be in his late 40s, and he seemed friendly and a little nervous. The experimenter, in contrast, acted self-assured as he set the group's agenda, assigned tasks to the group members, and issued orders. He assigned the participants to one of two roles—teacher or learner. Those given the "teacher" role read a series of paired words (*blue box, nice day, wild day,* etc.) to the "learner," who was supposed to memorize the pairings. The teacher would later check the learner's ability to recall the pairs by reading the first word in the pair and several possible answers (e.g., *blue: sky, ink, box, lamp*). Failures would be punished by an electric shock. What the teacher did not know, however, was that the confederate was always assigned to the learner role and that he did not actually receive shocks.

After assigning the participants to their roles, the experimenter took both group members into the next room. The teacher then watched as the experimenter strapped the learner into a chair that was designed "to prevent excessive

---

social power The capacity to influence others, even when these others try to resist influence.

movement during the shock." The learner sat quietly while an electrode was attached to his wrist. When he asked if the shocks were dangerous, the experimenter replied, "Oh, no. Although the shocks can be extremely painful, they cause no permanent tissue damage" (Milgram, 1974, p. 19).

The experimenter then led the participant back to the other room and seated him at the shock generator. This bogus machine, which Milgram himself fabricated, featured a row of 30 electrical switches. Each switch, when depressed, would supposedly send a shock to the learner. The shock level of the first switch on the left was 15 volts, the next switch was 30, the next was 45, and so on, all the way up to 450 volts. Milgram also labeled the voltage levels, from left to right, *Slight Shock, Moderate Shock, Strong Shock, Very Strong Shock, Intense Shock, Extreme Intensity Shock,* and *Danger: Severe Shock.* The final two switches were marked *XXX.* The rest of the face of the shock generator was taken up by dials, lights, and meters that flickered whenever a switch was pressed.

The experimenter administered a sample shock of 45 volts to each participant, supposedly to give him an idea of the punishment magnitude. The study then began in earnest. Using a microphone to communicate with the learner, the teacher read the list of word pairs and then began "testing" the learner's memory. Each time the teacher read a word and the response alternatives, the learner indicated his response by pushing one of four numbered switches that were just within reach of his bound hand. His response lit up on the participant's control panel. Participants were to deliver one shock for each mistake and increase the voltage one step for each mistake.

Milgram set the stage for the order-giving phase by having the learner make mistakes deliberately. Although participants punished that first mistake with just a 15-volt jolt, each subsequent failure was followed by a stronger shock. At the 300-volt level, the learner also began to protest the shocks by pounding on the wall, and after the next shock of 315 volts, he stopped responding altogether. Most participants assumed that the session was over at this point, but the experimenter told them to treat a failure to respond as a wrong answer and to continue delivering the shocks. When the participants balked, the experimenter, who was seated at a separate desk near the teacher's, would use a sequence of prods to goad them into action (Milgram, 1974, p. 21):

- ❏ Prod 1: "Please continue," or "Please go on."
- ❏ Prod 2: "The experiment requires that you continue."
- ❏ Prod 3: "It is absolutely essential that you continue."
- ❏ Prod 4: "You have no other choice; you must go on."

The situation was extremely realistic and served as a laboratory analog to real-world groups where authorities give orders to subordinates. The experimenter acted with self-assurance and poise. He gave orders crisply, as if he never questioned the correctness of his own actions, and he seemed surprised that the teacher would try to terminate the shock sequence. Yet from the participants' point of view, this authority was requiring them to act in a way that might be harmful to another person. When they accepted the $4.50 payment, they implicitly agreed to carry out the experimenter's instructions, but they were torn between this duty and their desire to protect the learner from possible harm. Milgram designed his experiment to determine which side would win in this conflict.

Did They Obey? Milgram's Findings

Milgram was certain that very few of his participants would carry out the experimenter's orders. He went so far as to purchase special equipment that would let him record precisely the duration of each shock administered, expecting that few participants would give more than four or five shocks (Elms, 1995). He also polled a number of psychological researchers and psychiatrists on the subject, asking them to predict how people would react in his study. None believed that participants would shock to the 450-volt level; they predicted that most would quit at the 150-volt level.

Milgram and the other experts, however, underestimated the power of the situation. Of the 40 individuals who served as teachers in the initial experiment, 26 (65%) administered the full 450 volts to the helpless learner (see Figure 8-1). None broke off before the 300-volt level, and several of the eventually disobedient participants gave one or two additional shocks before finally refusing to yield to the experimenter's prods. The comments made by the participants during the shock procedure and their obvious psychological distress revealed that they were unwilling to go on but felt unable to resist the experimenter's demands for obedience.

Milgram studied nearly 1000 people in a series of replications and extensions of his original study. In these later studies, some of which are discussed here,

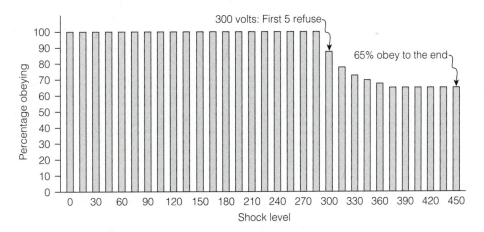

FIGURE 8-1

Would group members, if ordered to give another person painful electric shocks, obey? Milgram (1974) found that all participants obeyed the authority's orders up to the 300-volt level. More people resisted the authority's order as the shocks became more powerful, but 26 of the 40 participants (65%) were completely obedient up to the maximum voltage level.

different aspects of the setting were systematically manipulated, allowing Milgram to assess their influence on obedience rates. Although he continued to search for the limits of obedience, again and again his participants buckled under the pressure of the experimenter's power.

HARM AND PROXIMITY Surprised that so few people disobeyed the authority, Milgram wondered if the participants realized they were hurting the learner. All they heard was an ambiguous pounding on the wall, which the experimenter told them to ignore. So Milgram made the harm more obvious by adding additional cues that clearly signaled the learner's suffering.

- *Voice-feedback condition.* The learner's shouts and pleas (carefully rehearsed and tape-recorded) could be heard through the wall. The learner grunted when shocked at levels below 120 volts and complained about the pain. At 150 volts, he cried out, "Experimenter, get me out of here! I won't be in the experiment any more! I refuse to go on!" (Milgram, 1974, p. 23). He continued screaming and demanding release until the 300-volt level, when he refused to answer any more questions. Still, 62.5% of the participants obeyed to the 450-volt level.
- *Proximity condition.* The learner sat in the same room as the teacher, voicing the same complaints used in the voice-feedback condition and writhing with pain at each shock. Obedience dropped to 40%.
- *Touch-proximity condition.* The learner sat next to the teacher and received his shock when he put his hand on a shock plate. At the 150-volt level, he refused to put his hand down on the plate, so the experimenter gave the participant an insulated glove and told him to press the learner's hand down onto the plate as he depressed the shock switch. Still, 30% obeyed.
- *Heart condition.* The learner was once more seated in the adjoining room, but as the experimenter connected the wires to his arm, the learner mentioned that he had a heart condition and asked about complications. The experimenter said that the shocks would cause no permanent damage. During the shock phase, the learner's groans and shouts of protest could be heard through the wall, and he also repeatedly complained that his heart was bothering him. Even though he stopped responding after 330 volts, 65% of the participants continued to administer shocks to the 450-volt level.

PRESTIGE AND OBEDIENCE Milgram conducted his initial studies on the campus of Yale University, which most people recognize as a prestigious center of learning and science. Milgram was concerned that people obeyed the experimenter because he was perceived to be a "Yale scientist" and could therefore be trusted to act appropriately. So Milgram moved the study away from prestigious Yale University. He set up the study in an office building located in a shopping area. "The laboratory was sparsely furnished, though clean, and marginally respectable in appearance. When subjects inquired about professional affiliations, they were informed only that we were a private firm conducting research for industry" (Milgram, 1974, pp. 68–69). Obedience dropped to 48%—still a surprisingly large figure given the unknown credentials of the staff.

SURVEILLANCE How would people react if the authority could not see them carry out his orders? Would they still obey? Milgram manipulated surveillance by having the experimenter leave the room after he reviewed the procedures with the participant. He continued giving orders to the participant by telephone; 25% of the participants stopped as soon as the learner insisted on release (the 150-volt level). Only 20% of the participants were obedient to the 450-volt level, and many participants disobeyed by deceiving the authority—they assured the experimenter that they were administering increasingly large shocks with each mistake, when they were actually only delivering 15 volts.

EXPERTISE Milgram's experimenter was a trained actor who exuded confidence and scientific expertise; he seemed to know clearly what he was doing throughout the shock process. Milgram therefore arranged, in some conditions, for the orders to come from someone other than the expert experimenter. In one variation, he added a fourth member to the group. The experimenter explained the study, as in other conditions, but gave no instructions about shock levels before he was called away. The new participant, who was actually a confederate, filled the role of the authority; he suggested that shocks be given in increasingly strong doses and ordered the participant to continue giving shocks when the learner started to complain. Obedience dropped to 20%. Once the participants refused to continue, the confederate left the experimenter's desk and began administering the shocks. Most of the participants (68.75%) failed to intervene by stopping the confederate.

In a particularly creative episode, the experimenter agreed to take the role of the learner, supposedly to convince a reluctant learner that the shocks were not harmful. The experimenter tolerated the shocks up to 150 volts, but then he shouted, "That's enough, gentlemen!" The confederate, who had been watching the procedure, then insisted, "Oh, no, let's go on. Oh, no, come on, I'm going to have to go through the whole thing. Let's go. Come on, let's keep going" (Milgram, 1974, p. 102). In all cases, the participant released the experimenter; obedience to the ordinary person's command to harm the authority was nil.

GROUP EFFECTS Milgram also demonstrated some interesting effects of other group members' behaviors on the participant's obedience. Milgram arranged for two more confederates to pose as volunteers, and in these sessions, the three men worked together to deliver the shocks to the learner. One read the list of words, one gave the verbal feedback to the learner, and the participant pushed the shock button (see Figure 8-2). The confederates, however, defied the authority when the learner began to cry out in pain. In this variation, only 10% of the participants were fully obedient—although these individuals had to administer the shocks as the disobedient confederates looked on. Obedience jumped considerably, however, when the participant merely recorded information and performed other ancillary tasks while an accomplice flipped the shock switches. In this

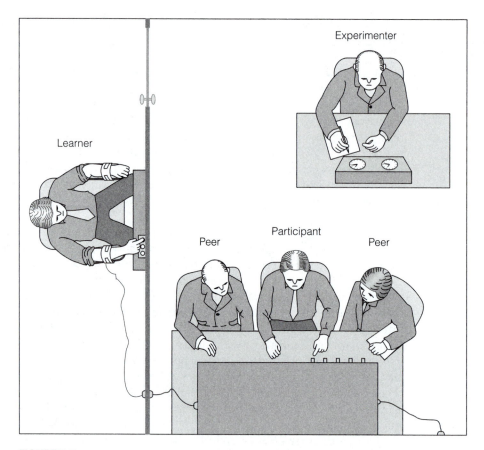

FIGURE 8-2

Are groups more obedient than individuals? When the participants worked with two other "teachers" who obeyed the experimenter's orders, very few disobeyed. But if their comembers refused to continue to shock the learner, most of the participants also refused to obey the experimenter.

variation, 92.5% obediently fulfilled their tasks without intervening. Also, if two experimenters ran the research but one demanded continued shocking, whereas the other argued for stopping the shocks, all the participants obeyed the commands of the benevolent authority.

The Power of the Milgram Situation

Milgram's results sparked controversies that are unresolved even today (Blass, 2000; A. G. Miller, Collins, & Brief, 1995a). Some researchers believe that the participants were not taken in by Milgram's subterfuge; they knew that no shocks were being administered, but they played along so as not to ruin the study (Mixon, 1977; Orne & Holland, 1968). Milgram's research team, however, carefully interviewed all the participants, and fewer than 20% challenged the reality of the situation (Elms, 1995). Moreover, if participants saw through the elaborate duplicity, then why did they become so upset? According to Milgram,

> Many subjects showed signs of nervousness in the experimental situation, and especially upon administering the more powerful shocks. In a large number of cases the degree of tension reached extremes that are rarely seen in sociopsychological laboratory studies. Subjects were observed to sweat, tremble, stutter, bite their lips, groan, and dig their fingernails into their flesh. (1963, p. 375)

The distress of the participants was so great that the publication of the study sparked a controversy over the ethics of social–psychological research (A. G. Miller, 1995). Even a museum exhibit that featured the Milgram experiment sparked public debate over its ethics when it toured the U.S. science museums (C. Marsh, 2000).

Other experts, when trying to explain why so many people obeyed in the study, have pointed to the participants themselves—their personalities, their temperaments, their society's views of obedience. Just as many people, when first hearing of the Guyana tragedy, wondered, "What strange people they must have been to be willing to kill themselves," when people are told about Milgram's findings, they react with the question, "What kind of evil, sadistic men did he recruit for his study?" Yet by all accounts, Milgram's participants were normal and well adjusted, and subsequent attempts to link obedience to personality traits have been relatively fruitless (see Blass, 1991, for an analysis). Also, even though Milgram's participants were mostly men, they were paid for their time, and they lived at a time when people trusted authorities more than they do now, his findings appear to be highly reliable over time and across situations. Replications of the study using different procedures and participants have generally confirmed Milgram's initial findings (see Blass, 2000a). Many believe that the level of obedience that Milgram documented in his laboratory matches levels found in military, educational, and organizational settings (Brief et al., 1995a; A. G. Miller et al., 1995a; see Focus 8-1).

POWER IN GROUPS

More than 4000 members of the Unification Church married each other in a mass ceremony because their leader, Reverend Sun Myung Moon, told them to do so. The Branch Davidians remained barricaded in their compound until their leader, David Koresh, ordered them to set it on fire. Thirty-seven members of the religious group Heaven's Gate took their own lives because their leader convinced them that they were leaving their bodies to join extraterrestrials in a nearby spaceship. Members of the People's Temple drank cyanide-laced punch

FOCUS 8-1 How Strong Are Pressures to Obey in the Cockpit?

The pilot in command of an aircraft is directly responsible for, and is the final authority as to, the operation of that aircraft.

−Federal Aviation Agency, Code of Federal Regulation, Paragraph 91.3

Commercial jetliners are not piloted by individuals, but by groups. No one individual could carry out the many and varied actions needed when taxiing, at takeoff, when aloft, in final approach, and when landing, so the captain and crew work together to pilot the plane safely to its destination. In some cases, however, the smooth teamwork of the crew is disrupted by power and its dynamics. Most larger aircraft require the services of a pilot, a copilot, and a flight engineer but, as a signal of the relative authority of each position, these roles are also labeled captain, first officer, and second officer. Captains are, by law, the final authority on board, and in many cases, they exert their power over the rest of the crew in both subtle and unsubtle ways. The flight deck of the craft is often called the *cockpit,* which is also the name of the pen where contests between fighting roosters (cocks) are held (Foushee, 1984).

Investigations conducted by the National Transportation Safety Board (NTSB) traced several fatal crashes back to two group-level sources: (1) a captain's refusal to comply with the suggestions of other crew members, and (2) the crew's excessive obedience to the captain's authority (NTSB, 1994). When a DC-8 ran out of fuel and crashed in Portland, analysis of the flight recorder indicated that the flight engineer repeatedly reminded the pilot of their dwindling fuel, but the pilot ignored him (Milanovich, Driskell, Stout, & Salas, 1998). The pilot of Northwest Express Flight 5719 spent much of the flight issuing orders to the first officer, many of which were considered unnecessary. The copilot eventually failed to correct the pilot's error on the approach, and the plane crashed (Tarnow, 2000). A copilot on a flight involved in a *near miss*—two aircraft almost colliding in midair—claimed that he warned the captain to reduce airspeed, but that the captain ignored him (Foushee, 1984, p. 888):

> After several attempts to convey the information, the captain responded by saying, "I'll do what I want." Air traffic control inquired as to why the aircraft had not been slowed, advised the crew that they had almost collided with another aircraft, and issued a new clearance that was also disregarded by the captain despite repeated clarification by the copilot. Following the last advisory from the copilot, the captain responded by telling the copilot to "just look out the damn window."

Aviation and group experts, recognizing the destructive impact of excessive obedience by flight crews and the abuse of power by pilots, have instituted changes in personnel training. Rather than attempt to change the long-standing norms of hierarchy, control, and deference in the cockpit, these programs instead seek to improve communications between all members of the flight crew. Through workshops, structured group activities, and simulations, copilots learn how to challenge errors made by the pilot, and pilots are encouraged to accept warnings from crew members rather than ignore them. Many airlines carry out team-based training using advanced flight simulators (Line-Oriented Flight Training, or LOFT) and deliberately simulate emergencies that can only be solved if the crew members communicate clearly and decisively with the captain (Ginnett, 1993; Helmreich & Foushee, 1993; Merritt & Helmreich, 1996.

and died. Sixty-five percent of Milgram's participants administered painful electric shocks to an innocent person as he begged them to stop.

Reverend Moon, Jim Jones, Milgram's experimenter, coaches, police officers, and teachers exact obedience from others. But where does this remarkable power come from?

TABLE 8-1 French and Raven's six bases of power

Power Base	Definition
Reward	The capability of controlling the distribution of rewards given or offered to the target.
Coercive	The capacity to threaten and punish those who do not comply with requests or demands.
Legitimate	Authority that derives from the powerholder's legitimate right to require and demand obedience.
Referent	Influence based on the target's identification with, attraction to, or respect for the powerholder.
Expert	Influence based on the target's belief that the powerholder possesses superior skills and abilities.
Informational	Influence based on the potential use of informational resources, including rational argument, persuasion, or factual data.

Source: Data from French & Raven, 1959.

Bases of Power

John R. P. French and Bertram Raven (1959) summarized many of the sources of power in interpersonal settings in their **power bases** model of influence. They traced power in groups back to the six key sources, or *bases,* summarized in Table 8-1. Group members who can reward or punish other group members, who are liked and respected, who are accepted by the members as legitimate authorities, and who have some special skill or information are more influential than group members who fail to secure a base of power.

REWARD POWER In many cases, power is closely tied to the control of valued resources. The members of the People's Temple, for example, thought that Jim Jones possessed the things that they needed—security, economic support, companionship, political reform, and spirituality. His ability to control, exclusively and completely, the distribution of material and symbolic rewards, secured his **reward power** within the group.

Rewards can take many forms—gold stars for students, salaries for workers, social approval for participants in experiments, positive feedback for employees, food for the starving poor, freedom for prisoners, and even suicide for those who are leading tortured lives. In general, rewards that have a high social value are

---

power base Sources of social power in a group, including one's degree of control over rewards and punishment, authority in the group, attractiveness, expertise, and access to and control over information needed by group members.

reward power Influentiality (the capacity to influence others) based on one's control over the distribution of rewards given or offered to group members.

more potent sources of power, particularly during times of scarcity. Money and food, for example, are valued resources, but they become a source of power when the rest of the group is penniless and starving. Rewards that one controls exclusively are also more likely to augment one's power, for group members who depend on someone for a reward will likely comply with that individual's requests (Pfeiffer & Salancik, 1978). Jones, for example, offered members rewards and outcomes that they valued when the group was located in the United States, but once it moved to Jonestown, he became the sole source of these rewards (Emerson, 1962, 1981).

Ironically, the tendency for the "rich to get richer" also applies to reward power, because group members often implicitly assume that the rewards given them by powerful people are more valuable than the rewards given them by those without power. When members of groups were given the opportunity to trade goods of equal monetary value with other group members, most were willing to pay more for goods they received from a high-status group member, and they considered those resources to be more valuable, important, and worth having. Because powerful individuals' rewards were overvalued by others, they did not need to expend as many of their resources to achieve the same level of success in the exchange as did those members with low power, so their resources tended to grow rather than diminish (Thye, 2000).

COERCIVE POWER Accounts of the People's Temple describe Jones's reliance on physical and psychological punishment as a means of exacting obedience from his followers. When members broke the rules or disobeyed his orders, he was quick to punish them with beatings, solitary confinement, denials of food and water, and long hours of labor in the fields.

Coercive power derives from one's capacity to dispense punishments to others. Examples of coercive influence abound: Terrorists attack the citizens of other countries, or threaten them with attack. Employers threaten employees with the loss of pay, a transfer to an undesirable job, or even dismissal. Teachers punish mischievous students with extra assignments, detention, or a scowl. Disagreeing friends insult and humiliate one another; gang members coerce other members through acts of physical violence, and religious leaders threaten members with loss of grace or ostracism. People also use coercion to influence other group members. When asked to describe the way they influence others, they report using a variety of coercive techniques, including bullying members, name-calling, criticizing, finding fault, making demands, nagging, insulting, and threatening (see Focus 8-2).

Certain kinds of people appear to prefer influencing others through coercion rather than through reward. Most people, though, turn to coercive power when they feel it is the only means they have to influence others. In consequence, and

---

coercive power Influentiality based on one's ability to punish or threaten others who do not comply with requests or demands.

FOCUS 8-2 Bullying: A Harmless Phase or Coercive Abuse?

Courage is fire, and bullying is smoke.

—Benjamin Disraeli

Each day, as Erick boards the bus, Jonathan berates him, making fun of his hair and clothes. No one will sit with Erick for fear of being drawn into the abuse. Donzella and her friends deliberately circulate nasty rumors about Carol, who was once part of the Donzella clique but who is now considered an outcast. Each day at recess, Greg finds Albert on the playground and, after teasing him, pushes him up against the school wall and punches him. At Columbine High School, a clique of athletes made loud, negative remarks about a group of outcasts who did not fit into any of the school's other cliques.

Bullying is a form of coercive interpersonal influence. It involves deliberately inflicting injury or discomfort on another person repeatedly through physical contact, verbal abuse, exclusion, or other negative actions. Bullying, as Dan Olweus (1997) noted, signals a marked imbalance in the power relationship between the bully and his or her victim. The victim of abuse "has difficulty in defending himself or herself and is somewhat helpless against" the bully (p. 216). Bullying, then, is not retaliation between parties in a dispute or conflict, but the mistreatment of a powerless person by someone with power. Bullying was once considered a phase that children pass through on their way to adulthood, but instances of bullying escalating into violence and catastrophic reactions of victims to bullying have caused a shift in this view. Bullying is not "child's play" but aggression—a form of peer abuse. Bullying is common in school settings, but it also occurs in military, business, and professional organizations (Hogh & Dofradottir, 2001; Liefooghe & Davey, 2001).

Bullying is also a group behavior. Victims are sometimes isolated and friendless children abandoned to their fate by the rest of the school, but in many cases, groups of children are abused by groups of bullies. Bullying also takes place in a larger social context, as other children are drawn into the harmful bully–victim exchange. Some children take the role of henchmen or facilitators; they do not initiate the abuse, but they take an active part once the bullying event has begun. Others shout encouragement to the bullies or signal support by smiling and laughing. Others impassively watch the interaction without speaking, and a few members of the bystander group may intercede on behalf of the victim, either directly or by seeking help from officials or authorities (O'Connell, Pepler, & Craig, 1999; Olweus, 2000).

Because bullying is rooted in both power dynamics and group dynamics, experts recommend school- and group-level interventions for preventing peer abuse. Olweus's (1997) pioneering program stresses restructuring the role of teachers in schools to increase their control over social behavior as well as instruction. Olweus recommended creating a school atmosphere that is warm and supportive, but also closely monitored by authorities who consistently enforce anti-bullying norms. These norms must be supported through the dissemination of information about bully–victim problems and by discussing expectations with students in classes and schoolwide assemblies. Victims of bullying can also be supported through the development of buddy systems, cooperative learning activities, and the use of peer-conflict mediation programs. Families, too, should be involved in reducing bullying by monitoring children's behavior closely and by setting standards for appropriate conduct (Giannetti & Sagarese, 2001; Goldstein, 2002).

----

bullying Repetitively teasing, ridiculing, provoking, or tormenting others through various types of irritating, harassing, or aggressive actions, such as name-calling, threats, insults, and physical injury.

ironically, individuals in positions of authority who feel relatively powerless are more likely to use coercion than more powerful individuals. Some parents and teachers, for example, feel that their children and students are controlling them even though they occupy a position of greater authority in the home or school. These individuals feel relatively powerless, and so, in contentious situations, they tend to use coercive threats, punishments, and abuse more than do empowered authorities (Bugental & Lewis, 1999). In contrast, when individuals who are equal in coercive power interact, they often learn over time to avoid the use of their power (Lawler, Ford, & Blegen, 1988; Lawler & Yoon, 1996). Group members also prefer to use reward power rather than coercive power if both are available—particularly if they fear reprisals from others in the group should they act in a coercive way (Molm, 1997).

LEGITIMATE POWER Individuals who have **legitimate power** have the recognized right to ask others to obey their orders. The security personnel at the airport telling a passenger to remove her shoes, the drill sergeant ordering the squad to attention, the professor waiting for the class to become quiet before a lecture, and the minister interpreting the Gospel for the congregation are powerful because they have the right to command the target person, and the target is obligated to obey. Jones, for example, was the legitimate head of the People's Temple. He was also an ordained minister; his work was commended by many political and religious leaders, and he received such honors as the Martin Luther King, Jr., Humanitarian Award. When individuals joined the People's Temple, they tacitly agreed to follow Jones's orders. In fact, "consent is the necessary condition of a stable system of power. Legitimacy is important because it gives rise to consent" (Zelditch & Walker, 1984, p. 1).

When individuals obey the commands of another because they hope to earn a reward or avoid a punishment, their obedience dwindles when the power-holder's control over the resources diminishes. Members obey legitimate authorities, however, because they personally accept the norms of the group; they voluntarily obey from an internalized sense of duty, loyalty, or moral obligation. Legitimate power also "minimizes the need for maintaining means of coercion in constant readiness, continual surveillance of the power subjects, and regular supplies of economic or non-economic rewards. For these reasons, naked (that is, coercive) power always seeks to clothe itself in the garments of legitimacy" (Wrong, 1979, p. 52). As noted later in this chapter, these "garments of legitimacy" spring from the structure of the group itself and its dynamics. Leaders who achieve their position of authority through methods that the group does not consider to be fair or proper will likely be less influential than those who follow the rules for advancement in the group.

---

legitimate power Influentiality that is based on an individual's valid claim to a position or role that gives the occupant the right to require and demand compliance with his or her directives.

REFERENT POWER Who is the best-liked member of the group? Who is the most respected? Is there someone in the group whom everyone wants to please? The individual with referent power lies at the interpersonal center of the group. Just as group members seek out membership in selective, desirable groups, so they identify with and seek close association with respected, attractive group members. The members of the People's Temple were devoted to Jones—to the point where they loved, admired, and identified with him. Many made financial and emotional sacrifices in the hope of pleasing him. As one observer commented, "To his followers, Jones was a god whose power they could take into themselves merely by obeying him" (H. Allen, 1978, p. 121).

The concept of **referent power** explains how charismatic leaders manage to exert so much control over their groups. It was sociologist Max Weber who first used the term *charisma* to account for the almost irrational devotion that followers exhibit for their leaders. **Charisma** originally described a special power given by God to certain individuals. These individuals were capable of performing extraordinary, miraculous feats, and they were regarded as God's representatives on Earth (Weber, 1921/1946). Weber argued that **charismatic leaders** do not have unique, wondrous powers, but they succeed because their followers *think* they have unique, wondrous powers. Weber himself was struck by the charismatic leader's power to demand actions that contradict established social norms: "Every charismatic authority . . . preaches, creates, or demands new obligations" (1921/ 1946, p. 243; see also Cavalli, 1986; Lepsius, 1986; Lindholm, 1990).

People sometimes refer to a charming, dynamic leader's charisma, as in "Kennedy's good looks and warm smile made him a charismatic leader" (Bradley, 1978; Conger & Kanungo, 1987). Weber, however, reserved the term to describe the tremendous referent and legitimate power of the "savior–leader." Charismatic leaders such as Jones usually appear on the scene when a large group of people is dissatisfied or faces a distressful situation. The leader offers these people a way to escape their problems, and the masses react with intense loyalty. In the vivid words of social critic Eric Hoffer (1951), the charismatic leader

> personifies the certitude of the creed and justifies the resentment dammed up in the souls of the frustrated. He kindles the vision of a breathtaking future so as to justify the sacrifice of a transitory present. He stages the world of make-believe so indispensable for the realization of self-sacrifice and united action. He evokes the enthusiasm of communion—the sense of liberation from a petty and meaningless individual existence. (p. 105)

---

referent power Influentiality that is based on group members' identification with, attraction to, or respect for the powerholder.

charisma Derived by Max Weber from the Greek *xarisma* (a devine gift of grace), the ascription of extraordinary or supernatural acumen, ability, and value to a leader by his or her followers.

charismatic leader An inspirational leader who is widely admired, respected, or loved by his or her followers.

EXPERT POWER Group members often defer to and take the advice of those who seem to possess superior skills and abilities. A physician interpreting a patient's symptoms, a local resident giving directions to an out-of-towner, a teacher spelling a word for a student, and a computer technician giving advice to a PC user can all transform their special knowledge into **expert power.**

As with most of the power bases identified by French and Raven, a person does not actually need to be an expert to acquire expert power; the person must only be *perceived* by others to be an expert (Kaplowitz, 1978; Littlepage & Mueller, 1997). Researchers demonstrated the impact of perceived expertise on influence by arranging for dyads to work on a series of problems. Half of the participants were led to believe that their partner's ability on the task was superior to their own, and the rest were told that their partner possessed inferior ability. As the concept of expert power suggests, individuals who thought that their partners were experts accepted their recommendations an average of 68% of the time, whereas participants paired with partners perceived as inferior accepted their recommendations only 42% of the time (Foschi, Warriner, & Hart, 1985; see also Schopler & Layton, 1972a, 1972b).

INFORMATIONAL POWER In 1965, Raven added **informational power** to his list of power bases. Group members can turn information into power by providing it to others who need it, by keeping it from others, by organizing it, increasing it, or even falsifying it. Group leaders, because their role requires substantial communication and coordination, often know more about the group, its tasks, and its members than anyone else. They are the group's interpersonal database, as are the long-term members whose memories provide a record of the group's traditions. Some individuals achieve informational power by deliberately manipulating or obscuring information, or at least making certain that the information remains a secret shared by only a few group members (Messick, 1999). Other individuals are recognized as the keepers of the group's truths or secrets, and these individuals must be consulted before the group makes a decision (Fine & Holyfield, 1996). Even gossips can achieve informational power, by passing unverified and, in some cases, private information through the group's "grapevine" (Kurland & Pelled, 2000).

POWER BASES AND OBEDIENCE French and Raven's power base theory explains why so many people obeyed Jim Jones, but it also offers insights into participants' reactions in the Milgram experiments. Even though the experimenter was not an authority in a traditional sense—he was not formally identified as the group's leader and given an impressive title such as *captain, president, director,* or *doctor*—he did draw power from all six of the bases identified by French and

---

expert power Influentiality that derives from subordinates' assumption that the power-holder possesses superior skills and abilities.

informational power Influentiality based on the potential use of informational resources, including rational argument, persuasion, or factual data.

Raven (1959; Raven, 1965, 1992, 1999). His power to reward was high, because he gave out the payment, and also because he was an important source of positive evaluations; participants wanted to win a favorable appraisal from this figure of authority. He also used coercive prods: "The experiment requires that you continue," and, "You have no other choice, you must go on" warn of possible negative consequences of disobedience. Many participants also assumed that the experimenter had a legitimate right to control their actions and that the learner had no right to quit the study. The participants also respected Yale and recognized the importance of scientific research, so the experimenter had referent power. Very few participants knew much about electricity, either, so they considered the experimenter an expert. He also persuaded them to continue by telling them that the study was important and that its findings would answer questions about how people learn.

Thomas Blass (2000a) confirmed the power of the experimenter in the Milgram study by asking a group of unbiased observers to review a 12-minute videotape of Milgram's procedures. The observers then reviewed six possible reasons why the participant obeyed the experimenter's orders. The reasons were derived from French and Raven's power base model. The coercive power explanation, for example, asked if people obeyed because the experimenter insisted they continue and seemed to "warn of negative consequences" (Blass, 2000a, p. 42) The expert power explanation, in contrast, suggested that the participants assumed that the experimenter was an expert and that his explanation of the procedure reassured them. These observers ranked the experimenter as higher on expert, legitimate, coercive, and informational power, but lower on reward power, and lower still on referent power. The experimenter adopted a very brusque manner during the study, so he did not seem particularly likable; hence his low referent power. His stern, no-nonsense manner, however, apparently made him seem like a duly appointed expert whose orders could not be disobeyed.

Power Processes

The microsociety of the group is not, in most cases, egalitarian. The members of a newly formed group begin as equals, but before long, the interpersonal processes discussed in Chapter 6 create differences in roles, status, attractiveness, and communication. These group structures and processes do not just determine who is best liked or who talks the most, but also who is in charge and who is not. Jones and the Milgram experimenter were powerful because they controlled the bases of power in their groups, and their followers were weak because they lacked a power base. But they were also powerful because groups—with their status hierarchies, their systems of roles and duties, and their reciprocal networks of influence among members—tend to create and sustain differences in power (Stolte, Fine, & Cook, 2001).

SUPERIOR–SUBORDINATE RELATIONS Jack Washington, a participant in Milgram's experiment, administered all the shocks up to 450 volts with barely a hesitation. The experimenter never prodded Jack to continue, but throughout he seemed subdued—almost sad. When later asked why he followed orders, he said "I merely went on. Because I was following orders. I was told to go on. And I did not get a cue to stop" (Milgram, 1974, p. 50).

Washington believed he had been hired by the researchers at Yale University to do a job as part of a study on learning. He was part of a small group, but he knew he was by no means the group's leader. That position was occupied by the experimenter who, as Washington's superior in the hierarchy of authority, gave the orders, directions, guidance, and instruction. Washington, as his subordinate, was duty bound to follow those orders, directions, and so on. The experimenter was in charge—the top dog, the boss, the chief, the head honcho, "the man." Washington was just a worker bee, a minion, an underling, a "tool."

As Milgram (1974) noted, "each member's acknowledgement of his place in the hierarchy stabilizes the pack" (p. 124). Individuals who occupy positions that are located at the bottom of the status hierarchy—the low men or women on the totem pole—tend to do as they are told by those with higher status. Researchers confirmed this prediction by replicating Milgram's findings with a chain of command (Kilham & Mann, 1974). Because orders are often passed down from superiors to subordinates through a chain of command, the basic Milgram experiment was modified to include a *transmitter,* who relayed orders, and an *executant,* who actually delivered the shocks. As predicted, transmitters were more obedient than executants (54% versus 28%). In this study, men were more obedient than women, but other studies found either no difference between men and women (Milgram, 1974) or heightened obedience among women (Sheridan & King, 1972).

Interpersonal theories of social behavior also suggest that group members are more ready to obey authorities than they are to rebel against them (e.g., Carson, 1969). Interpersonal theory assumes that each group member's action tends to evoke, or "pull," a predictable set of actions from the other group members. If, for example, an individual seems agreeable, pleasant, and cooperative, the other group members would tend to react in kind: they would behave in positive, friendly ways. Friendly behaviors are complimented by more friendly behaviors. But what if group members act in dominant, firm, directive ways—issuing orders, taking charge, giving advice? According to interpersonal theory, such behaviors would tend to evoke submissive responses from the other group members. The **interpersonal complementarity hypothesis** predicts that (1) positive behaviors evoke positive behaviors and negative behaviors evoke negative behaviors, and (2) dominant behaviors evoke submissive behaviors and submissive behaviors evoke dominant behaviors (P. Sadler & Woody, 2003).

Stanley Strong and his colleagues tested the interpersonal complementarity hypothesis by videotaping women as they interacted with a confederate who had

---

interpersonal complementarity hypothesis The predicted tendency for certain behaviors to evoke behaviors from others that are congruous with the initial behavior, with positive behaviors evoking positive behaviors, negative behaviors evoking negative behaviors, dominant behaviors evoking submissive behaviors, and submissive behaviors evoking dominant behaviors.

been trained to adopt one of several styles of interaction. When in a dominant role, the confederate exuded confidence and authority. In one variation of the role, the confederate also mixed dominance with friendliness, frequently intervening to keep the group working. In another variation, the confederate was dominant, but less friendly. In this case, she stressed her superiority and autonomy, and her self-confidence bordered on self-absorption and conceit. The confederate also enacted more submissive, self-effacing roles with some participants. Rather than take charge, she would seem timid, uncertain, passive, and inhibited.

When the investigators studied the transcripts of the sessions, they detected clear evidence of complementarity. As interpersonal theory predicts, participants who were paired with a dominant confederate acted submissively; they acquiesced, behaved passively, and showed respect for their partner. Only rarely did a participant respond in a dominant manner when faced with a dominant interaction partner. Conversely, if the confederate behaved in a docile manner, then the participants tended to take charge by acting in a dominant fashion. Other studies suggest that group members feel more comfortable when interacting with someone who displays complementary rather than similar reactions. Group members who display signs of submissiveness when talking to someone who seems powerful are better liked, as are those who take charge when interacting with docile, submissive individuals (Tiedens & Fragale, 2003).

POWER AND RESPONSIBILITY One's power in a group and one's responsibility for what happens in the group tend to covary. Those who occupy positions of authority within the group—leaders, executives, managers, and bosses—are generally viewed as more accountable than those who occupy such low-status positions as subordinate or employee (Blass, 1995, 1996; V. L. Hamilton & Sanders, 1995). Because responsibility is thought to be concentrated in the role of the superior, however, subordinates in hierarchically organized groups sometimes no longer feel personally responsible for their own actions. They enter what Milgram called the **agentic state**—they become agents of a higher authority (Milgram, 1974). They feel "responsibility to the authority" but "no responsibility for the content of the actions that the authority prescribes" (Milgram 1974, pp. 145–146). Like Jack Washington, who was just "following orders" when he shocked the screaming learner, many individuals who have little power in the group assume that they are supposed to carry out the orders of the authority without questioning those orders. They no longer feel that they are in control of their own actions, and so they become willing cogs in the group machine, carrying out authorities' orders without considering their implications or questioning their effects (V. L. Hamilton & Sanders, 1999; Kelman & Hamilton, 1989).

Milgram documented this tendency by asking his participants to allocate responsibility for the situation among the three participants—the experimenter,

---

agentic state A psychological state described by Stanley Milgram that occurs when subordinates in an organized status hierarchy experience such a marked reduction in autonomy that they are unable to resist authorities' orders.

the teacher, and the learner. Obedient participants gave more responsibility to the experimenter than they gave to themselves. They also gave twice as much responsibility to the victim as did disobedient participants. These disobedient participants, in contrast, took more responsibility than they attributed to the experimenter (Mantell & Panzarella, 1976; Meeus & Raaijmakers, 1995; West, Gunn, & Chernicky, 1975). Milgram's analysis of responsibility is also consistent with studies of diffusion of responsibility: People feel less personally responsible when they are in groups than when they are alone. Other negative group behaviors, such as reductions in collective effort, conflict, mob behaviors, and vandalism have all been attributed to the diffusion of responsibility that occurs in groups (see Focus 7-2).

THE POWER OF ROLES When participants arrived for the Milgram experiment, they were carefully cast into the role of teacher. The duties of that role were made clear to them, and it was not until the shock sequence progressed that they realized the demands that their role would put on them. Their role required their actions.

Phillip Zimbardo and his colleagues examined the power of roles in their Stanford Prison Study. Zimbardo selected two dozen healthy, intelligent, and psychologically normal men from a large group of student volunteers to serve as either guards or prisoners in a simulated prison. The students randomly assigned to the role of prison guard were issued khaki uniforms, billy clubs, whistles, and reflective sunglasses. They were then put in charge of a mock prison that Zimbardo and his colleagues had constructed in the basement of the psychology building at Stanford University. The students assigned to the role of prisoner were "arrested" by uniformed police, booked, and transported to the prison. There they were sprayed with a deodorant, searched, issued an identification number, and outfitted in a dresslike shirt, heavy ankle chain, and stocking cap.

The study was scheduled to run for 2 weeks, but was terminated after only 6 days. Why? According to Zimbardo, the participants became too immersed in their roles. The prisoners seemed literally to become prisoners; although some rebelled, the majority became withdrawn and depressed. The guards also changed as the study progressed; many became increasingly tyrannical and arbitrary in their control of the prisoners. They woke the prisoners in the middle of the night and forced them to stand at attention for hours, locked them in a closet, required them to clean toilets with their bare hands, strictly enforced pointless rules, and censored prisoners' mail. Zimbardo confessed that even he found himself sinking too deeply into the role of warden, worrying over possible "prison breaks" and autocratically controlling visiting procedures (Haney, Banks, & Zimbardo, 1973; Zimbardo, Maslach, & Haney, 2000).

Why did the prisoners respond so obediently and the guards so autocratically? Zimbardo believed that the participants felt compelled to act consistently with their roles. All of the participants had a general idea of what it meant to act like a prisoner or like a guard. As the study progressed, they became more and more comfortable in their roles. Eventually, to be a guard meant controlling all aspects of the prison and protecting this control with force if necessary. Prisoners, on the other hand, were supposed to accept this control and try to get through the experience as easily as possible by obeying all the prison's rules. Participants who refused to obey these norms were pressured by the other participants to bring their behavior back in line; nonconformity was not tolerated.

THE POWER OF COMMITMENT Jim Jones's order to commit suicide did not surprise his followers. Jones had talked about mass suicide even before the People's Temple moved to Guyana. On more than one occasion, Jones had told the congregation that he had poisoned the sacramental wine and that all would be dead within the hour. He went so far as to plant confederates in the audience who feigned convulsions and death. He repeated this ceremony in Jonestown, calling it the White Night. After enough repetitions, the thought of suicide, so alien to most people, became commonplace in the group.

Jones's White Night tactic illustrates the power of *behavioral commitment*. Jones did not suddenly order his followers to commit suicide. Instead, he prefaced his request with months of demands that increased in their intensity. Similarly, Milgram did not ask participants to push a lever that would deliver 450 volts to the learner at the outset of the study. Instead, he asked them only to give the learner a mild shock if he answered incorrectly. No one refused. Over time, however, the demands escalated, and participants were unable to extricate themselves from the situation. Once they began, they could not stop (Gilbert, 1981; Modigliani & Rochat, 1995).

Studies of the influence tactics used by panhandlers, salespeople, fundraisers, and authorities confirm the power of gradually escalating demands (Cialdini, 2001). The **foot-in-the-door technique,** for example, works by prefacing a major request with a minor one that is so inconsequential that few people would refuse to comply. Investigators demonstrated the strength of this technique by asking home owners to post a large, unattractive sign in their yards. Nearly all refused—unless this major request had been preceded by a smaller request (Freedman & Fraser, 1966). Similar studies have also found that the two requests called for by the foot-in-the-door technique are superior to a single request for many types of behaviors, although such factors as the sex of the influencer and the amount of time that elapses between the two requests moderate the power of the foot-in-the-door method (Beaman et al., 1983; Dillard, 1991).

The Chinese incorporated the foot-in-the-door tactic in the so-called "brainwashing" indoctrination methods that they used with U.S. prisoners captured during the Korean War. They began by subjecting the POWs to physical hardships and stressful psychological pressures. The men were often fatigued from forced marches, and their sleep was disrupted. Their captors broke down the chain of command in these units by promoting nonranking soldiers to positions of authority, and friendships among the men were systematically discouraged.

---

foot-in-the-door technique A method of influence in which the influencer first makes a very small request that the target will probably agree to; once the target agrees to the minor request, he or she is more likely to agree to the influencer's more important request.

Although the Chinese relied heavily on traditional methods of influence, such as persuasion, indirect techniques proved more effective. The prisoners were initially asked to perform inconsequential actions, such as copying an essay out of a notebook or answering some questions about life in the United States. Once the men agreed to a minor request, a more significant request followed. They might be asked to write their own essays about communism or discuss the problems of capitalism. Each small concession led to a slightly larger one, until the men found themselves collaborating with the Chinese. The Chinese rarely succeeded in permanently changing the men's attitudes and values, but they did extract obedience to their authority: Morale within the prison was poor, and the men rarely tried to escape (E. H. Schein, 1961; H. A. Segal, 1954).

THE DYNAMICS OF AUTHORITY A church member obediently swallowing poison. A soldier executing innocent civilians. A worker installing substandard building materials. A participant in an experiment giving an innocent victim painful shocks. On first hearing about such events, people often fall prey to the **fundamental attribution error** (FAE): They blame the personalities of the individuals rather than the powerful group processes at work that forced them to obey (Vorauer & Miller, 1997; West et al., 1975). In extreme instances, when a powerholder inflicts tremendous suffering and misfortune on people, the group members blame themselves for their misery. The members of the People's Temple may have felt so deserving of their fate that they chose to suffer rather than escape suffering. These feelings of self-condemnation may account for their willingness to take their own lives (K. B. Clark, 1971; Fanon, 1963; Gamson, 1968).

Yet obedience is not a reflection of the nature of the individuals in the group, but an indication of the power of the group itself. By controlling key bases of power, using power tactics, exploiting the nature of the subordinate–authority relationship, and prefacing large demands with minor ones, authorities exert great influence on group members. As John Darley explained, "Many evil actions are not the volitional products of individual evil-doers. Instead, they are in some sense societal products, in which a complex series of social forces interact to cause individuals to commit multiple acts of stunning evil" (Darley, 1992, p. 204).

THE METAMORPHIC EFFECTS OF POWER

Once power is used, its effects reverberate through the group, creating changes in both those it influences and those who exercise the influence (Kipnis, 1974, 1984). Some of the members of the People's Temple, when first subjected to Jones's coercive influence, became so angry that they left the group. Others

---

fundamental attribution error (**FAE**): The tendency to overestimate the causal influence of dispositional factors and underemphasize the causal influence of situational factors.

accepted their punishment passively or even joined with Jones to inflict harm on others. Furthermore, Jones himself changed as his influence in the group grew, morphing from an inspirational religious leader into a tyrant.

Reactions to the Use of Power

Power, by its very nature, suggests tension, conflict, and turmoil. In many cases, power does not just include power *over* people, but also power *against* people. Powerholders can influence, sometimes dramatically, the outcomes of those who have little power, for power is "the interaction between two parties, the powerholder and the target person, in which the target person's behavior is given new direction by the powerholder" (Kipnis, 1974, p. 9). How do people respond—behaviorally, cognitively, and emotionally—when the "new direction" they are given by those with power conflicts with the goals they have set for themselves?

COMPLIANCE AND CONVERSION Both Milgram's participants and the People's Temple members did as they were told, but the two groups differed in one crucial respect: Most of Milgram's participants struggled to withstand the authority's pressure, for they believed that the learner should not be harmed. Many of Jones's followers, in contrast, zealously followed his orders. They did not strain against his authority; they had converted to his way of thinking (Darley, 1995; Lutsky, 1995; Staub, 1989, 1996).

Herbert Kelman (1958, 1961) identified three basic reactions that people display in response to coercive influence (see Table 8-2). In some cases, the powerholder only produces *compliance*—the group members do what they are told to do, but only because the powerholder demands it. Privately, they do not agree with the powerholder, but publicly they yield to the pressure. Like Milgram's participants, they obey only when the powerholder maintains surveillance. *Identification* occurs when the target of the influence admires and therefore imitates the powerholder. When group members identify with the powerholder, their self-image changes as they take on the behaviors, characteristics, and roles of the person with power. Many members of the People's Temple admired Jones and wanted to achieve his level of spirituality. They obeyed his orders because they identified with him.

Identification, if prolonged and unrelenting, can lead to the final stage—internalization. When *internalization* occurs, the individual "adopts the induced behavior because it is congruent with his value system" (Kelman, 1958, p. 53). The group members are no longer merely carrying out the powerholder's orders; instead, their actions reflect their own personal beliefs, opinions, and goals. Even if the powerholder is not present, the group members will still undertake the required actions. Extreme obedience—such as occurred with Jonestown, the murder of millions of Jews by the Nazis during World War II, the My Lai massacre, and the Heaven's Gate group—often requires internalization. The group members' actions reflect their private acceptance of the authority's value system (V. L. Hamilton & Sanders, 1995, 1999; Kelman & Hamilton, 1989).

TABLE 8-2 Kelman's three-stage theory of conversion

Stage	Description
Compliance	Group members comply with the powerholder's demands, but they do not personally agree with them. If the powerholder does not monitor the members, they will likely not obey.
Identification	Group members' compliance with the actual or anticipated demands of the powerholder are motivated by a desire to imitate and please the authority. The members mimic the powerholder's actions, values, characteristics, and so on.
Internalization	Group members follow the orders and advice of the powerholder because those demands are congruent with their own personal beliefs, goals, and values. They will perform the required actions even if not monitored by the powerholder.

Source: Kelman, 1958.

Kelman's three-step model of conversion explains how groups convert recruits into fervent members over time. Cults, for example, insist that the members adopt the group's ideology, but in the early stages of membership, they only require compliance. New recruits are invited to pleasant group functions, where they are treated in a warm, positive way. Once they agree to join the group for a longer visit, the veteran members disorient them by depriving them of sleep, altering their diet, and persuading them to join in physically exhilarating activities. The recruits are usually isolated from friends and family to prevent any lapses in influence, subjected to lectures, and asked to take part in group discussions. Compliance with these small requests is followed by greater demands, as with the Korean POWs. Eventually, the recruits freely agree to make personal sacrifices for the group, and these sacrifices prompt a further consolidation of their attitudes (R. S. Baron, 2000; R. S. Baron, Kerr, & Miller, 1992). Once recruits reach the consolidation stage, they have fully internalized the group's ideology and goals.

RESISTANCE TO COERCIVE INFLUENCE Authorities do not always succeed. Sometimes, the targets of influence do not obey but, instead, escape the powerholder's region of control or apply influence in return. In many cases, members contend against those in power individually—particularly when they feel that others in the group have more power than they do. But when members feel a sense of shared identity with the other low-power members of the group, they are more likely to join with them in a **revolutionary coalition** that opposes the powerholder (Dijke & Poppe, 2004; Lawler, 1975). In one study of group rebellion, group members worked under the direction of a leader who was appointed

---

revolutionary coalition A subgroup formed within the larger group that seeks to disrupt or change the group's authority structure.

to that post because he or she had outscored them on a bogus test of ability. The leader then proceeded to keep more than half of the money earned by the work, giving each participant less than one fourth. If the leader had personally decided how to apportion payment, 58% of the participants rebelled by forming a coalition with the other low-status participants. If the leader was not responsible for the payment scheme, only 25% revolted (Lawler & Thompson, 1978, 1979).

Group members are also more likely to resist an authority who lacks referent power, uses coercive influence methods, and asks the group members to carry out unpleasant assignments (Yukl, Kim, & Falbe, 1996). Such conditions can generate *reactance* in group members. When **reactance** occurs, individuals strive to reassert their sense of freedom by affirming their autonomy (J. W. Brehm, 1976; S. S. Brehm & Brehm, 1981). In one study, in which teammates had to make a choice between two alternatives marked 1-A and 1-B, 73% chose 1-A if their partner said, "I prefer 1-A," but only 40% chose 1-A if the partner demanded, "I think we should both do 1-A" (J. W. Brehm & Sensenig, 1966). In another study, 83% of the group members refused to go along with a group participant who said, "I think it's pretty obvious all of us are going to work on Task A" (Worchel & Brehm, 1971, p. 299).

Coercive tactics also tend to generate a range of negative emotions, including hostility, depression, fear, and anger (Keltner et al., 1998). Studies of reciprocity in groups indicate that when people are rewarded by a powerholder, they tend to reciprocate with cooperation; if, in contrast, powerholders employ coercion, they provoke animosity (Schlenker, Nacci, Helm, & Tedeschi, 1976). Moreover, even when mildly coercive methods, such as threats, are used, people often overreact and respond with even stronger threats. This escalating pattern sets in motion an upward spiral of conflict (Youngs, 1986). Hence, although coercive powerholders may be successful in initial encounters, influence becomes more difficult in successive meetings as the target's anger and resistance to pressure grow. Coercive and reward power can also cause group members to lose interest in their work. Supervisors who create feelings of autonomy sustain their subordinates' intrinsic interest in their work, whereas those who use coercive or rewarding methods find that productivity dwindles when they are not monitoring the group (Deci, Nezlek, & Sheinman, 1981; Pelletier & Vallerand, 1996). Organizational experts advocate sharing power with subordinates by delegating responsibilities, empowering workers, and making use of self-directed work teams (Hollander & Offermann, 1990).

The conflict created by coercive influence can disrupt the entire group's functioning. Studies of classrooms, for example, indicate that many teachers rely heavily on coercion, but that these methods cause rather than solve disciplinary problems (Kounin, 1970). Coercive tactics, such as physical punishment, displays of anger, and shouting, not only fail to change the target student's behavior but also lead to negative changes in the classroom's atmosphere (Kounin & Gump,

---

reactance A complex emotional and cognitive reaction that occurs when individuals feel that their freedom to make choices has been threatened or eliminated.

1958). When misbehaving students are severely reprimanded, other students often become more disruptive and uninterested in their schoolwork, and negative, inappropriate social activity spreads from the trouble spot throughout the classroom. This *disruptive contagion,* or *ripple effect,* is especially strong when the reprimanded students are powerful members of the classroom authority structure or when commands by teachers are vague and ambiguous. On the basis of these findings, researchers have suggested that teachers avoid the ripple effect by relying on other influence bases, including reward power, referent power, and expert power.

Group members, however, do not always rebel against a "benevolent despot." A powerholder who uses coercive influence tactics, such as threats and punishments, is often tolerated by group members when the group is successful (Michener & Lawler, 1975), the leader is trusted (Friedland, 1976), and the use of such tactics is justified by the group's norms (Michener & Burt, 1975b). Coercive methods are also more effective when they are applied frequently and consistently to punish prohibited actions (Molm, 1994).

REACTIONS TO POWER TACTICS Individuals' reactions to power also vary depending on how powerholders exert their authority. Powerholders who shout at subordinates, impose fines, or make threats will generate a very different reaction than those who use more egalitarian methods of influence. Studies of the types of methods that people use to influence others—**power tactics**—suggest that people's reactions depend on the directness, rationality, and fairness of the powerholder's method of influence (Falbo, 1977; Falbo & Peplau, 1980; Kipnis, 1984).

- *Directness.* Direct tactics are explicit, overt methods of influence—threats, demands, and *faits accomplis* (i.e., simply going ahead and doing what you want despite objections). *Indirect* tactics, in contrast, involve covert manipulation and indirect influence. When we drop hints, use ingratiation, or evade the issue, we are using indirect methods. David Kipnis (1984) used the terms *strong* and *weak* tactics, rather than direct and indirect.
- *Rationality.* Tactics that emphasize reasoning, logic, and good judgment are *rational* tactics; bargaining and persuasion are examples. Tactics such as ingratiation and evasion are nonrational tactics of influence, because they rely on emotionality and misinformation.
- *Bilaterality.* Some tactics are interactive, involving give-and-take on the part of both the influencer and the target of the influence. Such *bilateral* tactics include persuasion, discussion, and negotiation. *Unilateral* tactics, in contrast, can be enacted without the cooperation of the target of influence. Such tactics include demands, faits accompli, evasion, and disengagement.

---

power tactic Any one of many specific methods people use to attain the goal of influencing others, such as persuasion, fait accompli, bargaining, and evasion.

Reliance on direct, irrational influence methods tends to undermine the quality of the relationship between the powerholder and the target. When people met in same-sex groups of three to five persons, those who relied on discussion, persuasion, and expertise were most favorably evaluated, whereas those who emphasized manipulation, evasion, and threat received the most negative evaluations (Falbo, 1977). Moreover, people who used (or at least reported using) indirect or rational strategies, such as persuasion or ingratiation, were rated as more considerate and friendlier than people who used direct or irrational strategies, such as threats and faits accomplis. Other researchers have confirmed these findings, using a variety of research methods (Caldwell & Burger, 1997; French, Morrison, & Levinger, 1960; Litman-Adizes, Fontaine, & Raven, 1978; Pandey & Singh, 1987; J. I. Shaw & Condelli, 1986).

POWER, ACTIVATION, AND INHIBITION When individuals must live and work for prolonged periods of time under the influence of powerful others, they tend to become inhibited. The outspoken member, after months of ridicule and teasing, eventually falls silent in the group. The nonconforming worker eventually changes his ways and no longer spreads gossip about the company executives.

These changes in actions, perceptions, and emotions are consistent with an *approach–inhibition model of power* (Keltner, Gruenfeld, & Anderson, 2003). This model notes that most organisms display one of two basic types of reactions to environmental events. One reaction, *approach,* is associated with action, self-promotion, seeking rewards and opportunities, increased energy, and movement. The second reaction, *inhibition,* is associated with reaction, self-protection, avoiding threats and danger, vigilance, loss of motivation, and an overall reduction in activity. Significantly, the approach–inhibition power model suggests that power increases approach tendencies, whereas reductions in power trigger inhibition. In consequence, those with high and those with low power display contrasting emotions and actions across situations. As Table 8-3 indicates, high-power individuals usually feel good about things—their moods are elevated, they report higher levels of such positive emotions as happiness and satisfaction, and they even smile more than low-power group members (D. Watson & Clark, 1997). Those without power, in contrast, report more negative moods and emotions (C. Anderson & Berdahl, 2002).

Power prompts people to take action rather than remain passive. In one investigation, researchers primed people to feel they had power and then watched how they responded to minor problems and dilemmas. In all cases, those primed did not adopt a "wait-and-see" approach—they took steps to deal with the problems (Galinsky, Gruenfeld, & Magee, 2003). Those without power, in contrast, were inhibited. They were less likely to express their attitudes, and they kept their disagreements to themselves (C. Anderson & Berdahl, 2002).

One's level of power also influences what one notices in others and in the situation. Individuals with power seek out rewards and are more likely to realize when desirable resources can be acquired. Those without power, in contrast, are more likely to be watching out for threats and punishments and, therefore, are more likely to interpret ambiguous situations as threatening ones (Keltner et al.,

TABLE 8-3 The approach–inhibition power model

Type of Reaction	Approach Reaction (High Power)	Inhibitory Reaction (Low Power)
Experience and expression of affect	Positive affect	Negative affect
Social attention	Sensitive to rewards	Sensitive to threat and punishment
Perceptions of others	Views others as a means to one's own ends	Views the self as a means to others' ends
Social cognition	Automatic processing	Controlled processing
Social behavior	Approach-related behaviors	Behavioral inhibition
Behavioral consistency	Self-determined and personally consistent	Situationally contingent
Behavioral regulation	Socially inappropriate behavior	Socially appropriate behavior

Source: Data from Keltner, Gruenfeld, & Anderson, 2003.

2003). When success depends on recognizing the strengths and weaknesses of subordinates, powerholders are discerning judges of those who work for them (Overbeck and Park, 2001). But when the number of subordinates grows and their relationship to the powerholder becomes more formal, powerholders are more likely to let their perceptions be guided by stereotypes rather than by a thorough review of each subordinates' qualities (Goodwin, Gubin, Fiske, & Yzerbyt, 2000). As the final section of this chapter notes, when individuals acquire power, they sometimes undergo a metamorphosis in action, thought, and emotion.

Changes in the Powerholder

The metamorphic effects of power have long fascinated observers of the human condition (Kipnis, 1974). In their tragedies, the Greeks dramatized the fall of heroes who, swollen by past accomplishments, conceitedly compared themselves to the gods. Myth and folklore are replete with tales of temptation to seek too much power, as in the case of Icarus, whose elation at the power of flight caused his death. In our own century, we find examples of political thinkers who, like Jim Jones, began their careers envisioning utopian societies but became cruel and inhuman dictators when they achieved positions of power. As Lord Acton warned, "Power tends to corrupt, and absolute power corrupts absolutely."

WHO SEEKS POWER? Not everyone seeks power in a group. Some members are content to be ordinary members, equal in responsibilities and influence to most of the others in the group, and they do not need or desire to rise upward in the group's hierarchy. Other individuals, in contrast, actively seek out power.

Motivation theorists (as noted briefly in Chapter 4) suggest that people vary in their basic need to control other people and situations. People who are high in their *need for power* tend to pursue status and prestige more vigorously than others, and they are more likely to hold offices in groups and organizations (Winter, 1973). Individuals' need for power measured when they were first hired for a large company predicted their position in the corporation's management hierarchy some 8 to 16 years later (McClelland & Boyatzis, 1982). Individuals with a high need for power also report *feeling* more powerful when they interact with others (Fodor & Riordan, 1995), but if they are not able to act on this need, they tend to have high blood pressure and other health problems (McClelland, 1975).

Individuals who seek and use power also tend to view the world—and the individuals and groups within it—as ordered in terms of relative dominance. This **social dominance orientation** (**SDO**) is, at its core, a general predisposition toward anti-egalitarianism within and between groups, manifested by a preference for "group-based hierarchy and the domination of 'inferior' groups by 'superior' groups" (Sidanius & Pratto, 1999, p. 48). Individuals who are high in SDO strive to protect and even increase the differences between group members, and they prefer membership in hierarchical groups. Interpersonally, individuals who are high in SDO are dominant and assertive rather than submissive and passive. Men are more likely higher in SDO than women (M. S. Wilson & Liu, 2003), and they tend to be less idealistic (M. S. Wilson, 2003).

SDO also predicts reactions to outgroups. Just as individuals who are high in SDO believe that a pecking order of individuals structures groups, so they feel that a group-level pecking order ranks all societies. They would tend to agree with such statements as, "Some groups of people are simply inferior to other groups" and "It's probably a good thing that certain groups are at the top and other groups are at the bottom" (Sidanius & Pratto, 1999, p. 67). In consequence, SDO is a powerful predictor of stereotyping and prejudice (Whitley, 1999).

DOES POWER CORRUPT? Lord Acton's warning that power corrupts, and that absolute power corrupts absolutely, applies to those who are given authority over others in small-group settings. Under such conditions, powerful people's self-evaluations grow more favorable, whereas their evaluations of others grow more negative (Georgesen & Harris, 1998). Some individuals (primarily men) associate power with sexuality, and so when they are empowered, they engage in inappropriate sexual behaviors, including sexual harassment (MacKinnon, 2003). Individuals with a high need for power generate negative emotional reactions in their subordinates, particularly when there is disagreement and conflict in the group (Fodor & Riordan, 1995). Some individuals, driven by their need for power, overstep the boundaries of their authority (Emler & Cook, 2001; see Lee-Chai & Bargh, 2001). In 1937, for example, Franklin D. Roosevelt was elected president of the United States by an overwhelming majority and subsequently

---

social dominance orientation (SDO) A dispositional tendency to accept and even prefer circumstances that sustain social inequalities combined with a general preference for hierarchical social structures.

went about increasing the powers of the presidency beyond those specified in the U.S. Constitution. This reaction to increased power brought on by overwhelming support from the group has been labeled the **mandate phenomenon** (R. D. Clark & Sechrest, 1976).

Powerful people use their position to exert influence, yet at the same time, they often derogate their subordinates. Kipnis (1972) arranged for advanced business students to participate as managers in a simulated manufacturing company after telling them that their performance would be a good indicator of their leadership potential in other executive situations. In one condition, the participants were given a good deal of reward power and coercive power over their subordinates: They could award bonuses, cut pay, threaten and actually carry out transfers to other jobs, give additional instructions, and even fire a worker. The participants in the second condition could use only persuasion or extra instructions to influence their subordinates.

The procedure was designed so that the managers could not actually see their workers but were kept informed of their production levels by an assistant, who brought in the finished products from the four workers. This arrangement was chosen so that Kipnis could control the level of productivity of the fictitious workers (all performed adequately) and provide a reason for the use of an intercom system in giving orders to subordinates. These communications were surreptitiously recorded. Subsequent analyses revealed that the powerful managers initiated roughly twice as many attempts at influence as the nonpowerful managers, and the difference between the two types of managers became more apparent as the sessions progressed. Moreover, the powerful and nonpowerful managers used different power tactics—the powerless ones relied on persuasion, whereas the powerful ones coerced or rewarded their workers. Other studies have yielded similar support for the idea that people with power tend to make use of it (Deutsch, 1973; Kipnis & Consentino, 1969), but they also suggest that the magnitude of this effect depends on many other factors (Bedell & Sistrunk, 1973; Black & Higbee, 1973; Goodstadt & Hjelle, 1973; Michener & Burt, 1975a).

Once power has been used to influence others, changes in powerholders' perceptions of themselves and of the target of influence may take place. In many instances, the successful use of power as a means of controlling others leads to self-satisfaction, unrealistically positive self-evaluations, and overestimations of interpersonal power (Erez, Rim, & Keider, 1986; Kipnis, 1974; Raven & Kruglanski, 1970; Sorokin & Lundin, 1959). In the Kipnis simulation described here, for example, participants were asked if their subordinates were performing well because of (1) the workers' high self-motivation levels, (2) their manager's comments and suggestions, or (3) their desire for money. Analyses showed that the high-power managers believed that their workers were only in it for the money (which the manager could control), whereas the low-power managers believed that the workers were "highly motivated." In fact, in the powerful manager condition,

---

mandate phenomenon A tendency for leaders to overstep the bounds of their authority when they feel they have the overwhelming support of the group.

the correlation between the number of messages sent to the workers and the manager's agreement with the statement, "My orders and influence caused the workers to perform effectively" was quite strong ($r = .65$; Kipnis, 1974). Other studies have also revealed this tendency for powerful individuals to assume that they themselves are the prime cause of other people's behavior (Kipnis, Castell, Gergen, & Mauch, 1976).

Devaluation of the target of the influence also tends to covary with increased feelings of control over people. In a classic study of power dynamics in a mental hospital, Alvin Zander and his colleagues found that psychiatrists tended to underestimate the abilities of the psychologists they supervised (Zander, Cohen, & Stotland, 1959). Although the psychologists believed themselves to be capable of developing diagnoses and conducting therapy, the psychiatrists considered them qualified only to conduct psychological testing. Evidence also suggests that powerholders tend to (1) increase the social distance between themselves and nonpowerful individuals, (2) believe that nonpowerful individuals are untrustworthy and in need of close supervision, and (3) devalue the work and ability of less powerful individuals (Kipnis, 1972; R. V. Sampson, 1965; Strickland, 1958; Strickland, Barefoot, & Hockenstein, 1976). Powerful individuals also spend less time gathering and processing information about their subordinates and, as a result, may perceive them in a stereotypical fashion (S. T. Fiske, 1993a)—particularly if their primary loyalty is to the organization rather than to the individuals who are subordinate to them (Overbeck & Park, 2001). This tendency to derogate the target person while simultaneously evaluating oneself more positively widens the gap between group members who have varying degrees of power (see Focus 8-3).

THE IRON LAW OF OLIGARCHY Some people are power hungry. They seek power, not because they can use it to achieve their goals, but because they value power per se (Cartwright & Zander, 1968). Hence, once such people attain power, they take steps to protect their sources of influence. This protective aspect of power translates into a small-group version of Robert Michels's (1915/1959) **iron law of oligarchy**—individuals in power tend to remain in power. Eventually, too, powerholders may become preoccupied with seeking power, driven by a strong motivation to acquire greater and greater levels of interpersonal influence (McClelland, 1975, 1985; Winter, 1973). This need for power, as noted earlier in the chapter, is a prominent personality characteristic in individuals who rise to positions of authority in organizations and politics. Evidence also indicates, however, that when those with a high power motivation cannot exercise that power, they experience increased tension and stress (McClelland, 1985). Under such conditions, they also exaggerate the amount of conflict that exists in the group and overlook group members' efforts at cooperation (Fodor, 1984, 1985).

---

iron law of oligarchy Robert Michel's principle of political and social control which predicts that in any group where power is concentrated in the hands of a few individuals (an oligarchy), these individuals will tend to act in ways that protect and enhance their power.

FOCUS 8-3 Does Power Corrupt?

Any man can withstand adversity; if you want to test his character, give him power.

−Abraham Lincoln

David Kipnis (1974), in his book *The Powerholders,* warned of the corruptive impact of power on people. Power, he suggested, can become a reward in itself, with the result that people seek to expand their dominion, even though this expansion serves no useful purpose. Once empowered, people tend to make use of their power, so they tend to influence people more directly than is necessary. Kipnis also felt that power can change the way people perceive themselves and others and can undermine the quality of people's relationships.

Not all leaders, however, are seduced by power's rewards. Some individuals, when they have the capacity to influence others through various means, choose to promote the interests and outcomes of others rather than themselves. Individuals who are more *group focused*—more concerned with communal needs and outcomes than with their own needs—may use their power to help others. Those who are more *self-focused*—who view interpersonal relationships as an exchange where one must monitor their rewards as well as their costs—may use power to further their own ends (J. Mills, Clark, Ford, & Johnson, 2004; see Chapter 3).

Serena Chen, Annette Y. Lee-Chai, and John A. Bargh (2001) examined these two different reactions to the experience of power by subtly priming individuals' sense of power and then measuring their reaction, using an equally subtle measure of responsiveness to others' needs. They first used a personality measure to identify *communals* (individuals who are concerned with others' needs and outcomes) and *exchangers* (individuals who are mindful of the exchange of rewards among group members). Participants then completed a word search task that involved looking for words embedded in a table of letters. Power was primed by including such power-related words as *authority, boss, control, executive,* and *influence* on some participants' word search lists. After finishing this task, the experimenter told the participant that he or she would be working with another student in completing a series of 10 exercises, but that the other student was delayed. While waiting, the participant was given the opportunity to pick which tasks he or she would complete and which ones the tardy second participant would complete. The list of tasks included information about the time that each task took to complete, so participants could minimize their time commitment by selecting the shortest tasks. Such a strategy was selfish, however, because it would increase the time the second participant would need to devote to the study.

Did people exploit their tardy partner by saving the shorter tasks for themselves? When power was not primed, communal and exchange-oriented participants did not differ in their choice of assignments for themselves. When power was primed, however, exchangers chose substantially shorter exercises for themselves, whereas communal individuals selected some of the longer ones—thereby helping to reduce their nonexistent partner's burden. Chen's group replicated these findings in a second study, which they conducted in a professor's office. In this study, they manipulated power by arranging for some participants to sit in the professor's desk chair or in a chair where a visitor would typically sit, and they again found that exchangers made choices that favored them personally, whereas communal individuals made choices that enhanced their partner's outcomes. Taken together, these studies suggest that power does corrupt selfish and self-centered people, but not people who are driven more by prosocial, communal goals (Bargh & Alvarez, 2001).

Questioning Authority

In 1976, Jim Jones fought for the improvement of housing and for progressive political change in the San Francisco area, and his followers worked diligently toward the goals outlined by their leader. In 1978, he was accused of human rights violations, physical assault, and illicit sexual practices. Power changed all the members of the People's Temple, including Jones himself.

Authority is essential to group life. Without its organizing guidance, group members could not coordinate their efforts and achieve their goals. Yet authorities that overstep their boundaries can undermine members' motivations, create conflict, and break the bonds between members. Authorities, too, must be wary of their own power, for power is easily misused. Who should question authority? Those who have it and those who are controlled by it.

SUMMARY IN OUTLINE

❖ **What are the limits of an authority's power over group members?**

1. *Social power* is the capacity to influence others, even when these others try to resist this influence.

2. Milgram tested people's ability to resist a powerful authority who ordered them to give painful and potentially harmful electric shocks to a confederate.
   - A majority (65%) of Milgram's participants obeyed, apparently because they felt powerless to refuse the orders of the authority.
   - Obedience rose and fell systematically as Milgram manipulated various aspects of the setting, including the proximity of the victim to the group member, the prestige of the research location, surveillance by the experimenter, and the presence of groups.
   - Critics noted methodological flaws of the procedures and suggested that the personal characteristics of Milgram's participants prompted them to obey, but Milgram argued that his studies underscored the power of authorities.

3. Milgram's studies suggest that obedience is common in hierarchically organized groups, such as those found in military, educational, and organizational settings. Studies of flight crews, for example, suggest that aircraft accidents are in some cases due to excessive obedience to the pilot's authority.

❖ **What are the sources of power in groups?**

1. French and Raven's theory of *power bases* emphasizes six sources of power— *reward power, coercive power, legitimate power, referent power, expert power,* and *informational power.*

2. *Bullying* is the use of coercive influence against another, less powerful person. It can involve physical contact, verbal abuse, exclusion, or other negative actions. Bullying can and should be prevented by restructuring the group situation.

3. Group members' influence over others depends on their control of these six power bases. Weber's concept of *charisma*

suggests that certain *charismatic leaders,* for example, exert their influence by relying on legitimate power and referent power.

4. A number of group and structural processes sustain variations in power in groups.

   • Individuals tend to obey orders in groups with clear superior–subordinate hierarchies.

   • As interpersonal theory notes, individuals tend to respond submissively when they confront authority, and they tend to behave assertively when they encounter someone who is submissive (the *interpersonal complementarity hypothesis*).

   • Milgram's theory of the *agentic state* traces obedience back to the nature of the authority–subordinate relationship. When individuals become part of an organized hierarchy, they tacitly agree to follow the leader's orders. They also experience a reduction of responsibility.

   • Individuals feel compelled to comply with the requirements of the role they occupy within the group, as Zimbardo's simulated prison study confirms.

   • Powerholders extract obedience from group members by taking advantage of *the foot-in-the-door technique,* prefacing major demands with minor, inconsequential ones.

   • People who blame obedience on the individuals in the situation may be displaying the *fundamental attribution error (FAE),* which underestimates the power of group-level processes.

❖ **How do those without power react when power is used to influence them?**

1. Targets of influence may begin by merely complying with the authority's request, but over time, they may experience *identification* and *internalization.* When group members identify with the authority or internalize the authority's demands, their obedience reflects their personal beliefs rather than the constraints of the situation.

2. Coercive methods have been linked to a number of dysfunctional group processes, including,

   • *revolutionary coalitions;*

   • *reactance;*

   • increases in conflict as more group members rebel against authority (the ripple effect);

   • disrupted interpersonal relations.

3. People also react more negatively to direct, irrational *power tactics* than to power tactics that are more indirect, rational, and bilateral.

4. The approach–inhibition model of power posits that power increases approach tendencies, whereas reductions in power trigger inhibition. This approach–inhibition mechanism leads to negative processes for those without power and to more positive processes for those with power.

❖ **How do people react when they use their power to influence others?**

1. Individuals vary in their desire for power in the group, depending on their need for power and their *social dominance orientation* (SDO).

2. Kipnis's studies of the metamorphic effects of power found that people who are given coercive power will use this power, and that once it is used, the powerholders tend to overestimate their control over others and devalue their targets.

3. Powerholders who are very secure in their position may overstep the bounds of their authority in a process termed the

mandate phenomenon, or they may become so enamored of power that they
are preoccupied with gaining it and using it to the exclusion of all other goals
(*the iron law of oligarchy*).

4. Some group members—those who are
   more communal than exchange oriented—use power to improve others'
   outcomes rather than their own.

FOR MORE INFORMATION

Chapter Case: The People's Temple

■ *Guyana Massacre: The Eyewitness Account,* by
Charles A. Krause (1978), provides a factual analysis of the demise of the People's
Temple, as well as commentaries on cults in
general.

Obedience to Authority: The Milgram Studies

■ *Obedience to Authority: Current Perspectives on
the Milgram Paradigm,* edited by Thomas Blass
(2000b), provides both a personal and an objective analysis of the study that some feel is
"one of the best carried out in this generation" (Etzioni, 1968, pp. 278–280).
■ *Obedience to Authority,* by Stanley Milgram
(1974), describes his classic obedience studies
in graphic detail.
■ "Perspectives on Obedience to Authority:
The Legacy of the Milgram Experiments,"
edited by Arthur G. Miller, Barry E. Collins,
and Diana E. Brief (1995b), is an issue of the
Journal of Social Issues devoted to Milgram's
research specifically, and to obedience in
general.

Source of Power in Groups

■ *Crimes of Obedience: Toward a Social Psychology
of Authority and Responsibility,* by Herbert C.
Kelman and V. Lee Hamilton (1989), analyzes
the factors that sustain obedience in contemporary society.
■ *Influence: Science and Practice,* by Robert B.
Cialdini (2001), is an exceptionally well-
written excursus on the techniques that
"compliance professionals"—salespeople, advertisers, charity workers, and panhandlers—
use to influence us in our daily lives.

Metamorphic Effects of Power

■ "Power, Approach, and Inhibition," by
Dacher Keltner, Deborah H. Gruenfeld, and
Cameron Anderson (2003), describes an intriguing new theory of power that synthesizes
prior approaches to power and offers new insights into power dynamics in small groups.
■ "Social Influence and Social Power: Using
Theory for Understanding Social Issues," edited by Irene Hanson Frieze (1999), is an issue
of the *Journal of Social Issues* devoted to theory
and research examining power.

MEDIA RESOURCES

Visit the Group Dynamics companion
website at http://psychology.wadsworth
.com/forsyth4e to access online resources for your book, including quizzes,
flash cards, web links, and more!

9

PERFORMANCE

CHAPTER OVERVIEW

We turn to groups to get things done. Groups are the world's workers, protectors, builders, decision makers, and problem solvers. When individuals combine their talents and energies in groups, they accomplish goals that would overwhelm individuals. Even though groups often prevail, however, they do not always reach the goals they set for themselves.

❖ Do people work better alone or with others?

❖ Do people work as hard when in groups as they do when working by themselves?

❖ When are groups more productive than individuals?

❖ What steps can be taken to encourage creativity in groups?

The Relay Test Room:
Enhancing Productivity Through Teamwork

Nora, Helen, Dorothy, Olivia, and Flora worked at the Hawthorne Plant of the Western Electric Company. Each day, they sat at their workbenches, building telecommunications relays out of an assortment of clamps, pins, coils, and electronic parts. In May, their boss asked them if they would take part in an experiment. Management, he said, wanted to learn more about Western's employees, and so they had set up an observation room where a small group could be studied for an extended period. The Relay Test Room group would consist of the five workers, one person to restock parts, an inspector, and at least one observer.

The Relay Test Room group spent the next 5 years turning out a total of 3.3 million electronic components. During that period, researchers monitored the women's rates of production and observed their interactions. They expected that changes in the work setting—better lighting, fewer breaks, more vacations—would improve productivity. Their observations, however, prompted them to reach a different conclusion: Group processes, not aspects of the physical work setting, were the principal determinants of productivity (Hare, 1967; Mayo, 1933; Roethlisberger & Dickson, 1939; Whitehead, 1938).

Many people believe that the best way to get a job done is to form a group. Many of the billions of groups in the world exist to get a particular job done. People use groups to discuss problems, concoct plans, forge products, and make decisions. When a task would overwhelm a single person's time, energy, and resources, individuals turn to groups. Even when tasks can be accomplished by people working alone (such as assembling hardware for telecommunications systems), people often prefer to work in the company of others. Table 4-3 offers a sampling of various tasks accomplished by groups.

The world relies on groups to achieve its goals, but people sometimes challenge the wisdom of this custom. Although groups sometimes turn out excellent products, they often fall short of expectations. One task force may formulate an effective plan for dealing with a problem, whereas another may create a plan that ends in disaster. A team may practice diligently, yet still play miserably during the big game. A group of women working together in a factory may assemble relays with incredible efficiency, but they may also spend so much time in conversation that their work suffers. Why do some groups perform impressively whereas others disappoint? Chapter 5 examined this question with an emphasis on the productivity of *teams.* This chapter extends this analysis by considering the processes that facilitate and inhibit productivity and performance in all types of groups. Chapter 10 examines groups making decisions.

Social Facilitation

Nora could build a relay by herself. She sat at a workbench stocked with all the materials and tools needed to complete the task. The work was repetitive but called for a high degree of skill. Nora had to remember where each part went and cull faulty parts from her supplies when she ran across them. The task also demanded manual dexterity, for assembling a single relay required more than 30 different movements of each hand. Nora did not need to talk to the others, but she often did (Whitehead, 1938).

Such situations lie at the boundary between nonsocial, purely individualistic settings and social, interpersonal settings. Each woman in the Relay Test Room could complete her task by herself. No teamwork was required; but neither did they work in isolation. They worked in each others' presence, as most people do when they work in a group. They did not influence each other directly, but working with others nearby was enough to change them from independent individuals into interdependent group members.

Working with Others: Social Facilitation

Do people in groups outperform people who are working by themselves? Norman Triplett (1898) asked this question after he noticed that bicyclists performed better in races against other cyclists than they did when they were timed riding the course alone. Triplett concocted a host of possible explanations for the improvement, which he tested by arranging for 40 children to perform a simple reel-turning task in pairs or alone. The children turned the reels faster in pairs than when they were alone. This enhancement of performance when another person is present has come to be known as **social facilitation.**

COACTION, AUDIENCES, AND INCONSISTENCIES The children in Triplett's study and the women in the relay wiring room worked on the same task in the same room, but they did not interact with one another. This type of situation is a **coaction** task. Eating in a restaurant, taking a test in a classroom, and riding a bicycle with a friend are everyday instances of coaction that may trigger social facilitation. But researchers soon discovered that social facilitation also occurs when individuals perform a task in front of an audience. One of the first scientific demonstrations of social facilitation in the presence of a passive spectator occurred in an exercise laboratory. People who worked out lifting weights reached a fairly uniform level of performance, but when a researcher unexpectedly returned to the weight room one night, a person whose performance had been constant for several days improved. Audiences, as well as coactors, can stimulate social facilitation (Meumann, 1904).

But coactors and audiences do not always stimulate improved performance. Floyd H. Allport (1920), for example, discovered that people who are "coworking" do not always outperform people working in isolation. He arranged for his participants to complete tasks twice—once while alone in a small testing

---

social facilitation Improvement in task performance that occurs when people work in the presence of other people.

coaction Performing a task or other type of goal-oriented activity in the presence of one or more other individuals who are performing a similar type of activity.

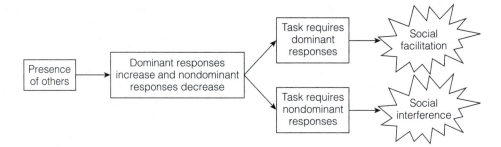

FIGURE 9-1

Do people work better when alone or in groups? Zajonc (1965) integrated previous research by noting that people display more dominant responses—and perform dominant behaviors more rapidly—when others are present. If the dominant response is appropriate in the situation, the presence of others is facilitating. If, however, the situation calls for a nondominant response, the presence of others will interfere with performance.

cubicle, and once with others at a table. To reduce competition, he cautioned his participants not to compare their scores with one another, and he also told them that he himself would not be making comparisons. He found that people in groups produced more than people working in isolation, but that their products were often lower in quality. Likewise, other researchers sometimes reported gains in performance through coaction or when an audience was watching, but they also documented performance decrements (Aiello & Douthitt, 2001).

ZAJONC'S RESOLUTION Researchers were puzzled by the elusiveness of social facilitation until Robert B. Zajonc (1965) integrated the divergent results by drawing a distinction between *dominant responses* and *nondominant responses.* Zajonc noted that some behaviors are easier to learn and perform than others. These *dominant responses* are located at the top of the organism's response hierarchy, so they dominate all other potential responses. Behaviors that are part of the organism's behavioral repertoire but are less likely to be performed are *nondominant responses.* Zajonc pointed out that extensive studies of many organisms had repeatedly demonstrated that increases in arousal, activation, motivation, or drive level enhance the emission of dominant responses and impede the performance of nondominant responses. His review of prior studies of audience and coaction indicated that nearly all the studies that documented social facilitation studied well-learned or instinctual responses, such as lifting weights, bicycling, or eating rapidly. Studies involving novel, complicated, or unpracticed actions, such as solving difficult math problems or writing poetry, usually found little evidence of social facilitation.

Zajonc's insight was that the presence of others increases the tendency to perform dominant responses and decreases the tendency to perform nondominant responses. If the dominant response is the correct or most appropriate response in a particular situation, then social facilitation occurs; people will perform better when others are present than when they are alone. If the task calls for non-dominant responses, however, then the presence of other people interferes with performance (see Figure 9-1). Consider these examples:

- *Making speeches*. Allport found that people could generate words more rapidly when others were present, but when a second researcher replicated Allport's study, he discovered that people were less fluent when others watched. The studies used nearly identical procedures, but the participants in the second study stuttered when they spoke. For these people, verbal production was not a dominant response, so the presence of an audience impeded their performance (Travis, 1928).

- *Running mazes*. Zajonc and his colleagues taught 32 female cockroaches (*Blatta orientalis*) to complete a complex maze or a simple maze by putting a bright light at one end of the maze and a dark hole at the other. Some roaches worked alone, others were part of a coacting pair, and still others were watched by other cockroaches (the cockroach spectators watched from their side of a plastic barrier; we can only assume that they were actually watching). Both facilitating and inhibiting effects were obtained, just as Zajonc expected. When the maze was a simple runway with no turns, single roaches reached home base in an average of 40.6 seconds. Coacting roaches managed to trim 7.6 seconds off this time, returning in just 33 seconds flat. This tendency reversed, however, when the maze was complex: Single roaches crawled to the finish line 19.6 seconds faster than did coacting roaches. Roaches watched by an audience were the slowest contestants of all, but they were particularly slow when the maze was complex—taking nearly 2 minutes longer than single roaches (Zajonc, Heingartner, & Herman, 1969).

- *Getting dressed*. Hazel Markus (1978) compared how quickly people performed a familiar task (taking off their own shoes and socks) and a more unfamiliar task (putting on a robe that tied in the back) when alone and when with another person. As Figure 9-2 indicates, people removed their shoes and socks 3 seconds faster if another person was in the room. They were even faster—by 2 seconds on average—when the observer watched as they removed their footware. In contrast, they donned the unfamiliar clothes more slowly when the observer was present and watchful.

- *Playing games*. Researchers first surreptitiously watched people playing a game of pool to identify skilled and unskilled players. Skilled players made at least two thirds of their shots, and unskilled players missed at least two thirds. Researchers then moved near the pool table and observed their play. Skilled players' performance improved 14% when they were observed, but unskilled players' performance dropped by more than 30% (Michaels, Blommel, Brocato, Linkous, & Rowe, 1982).

Charles F. Bond and Linda J. Titus (1983) confirmed Zajonc's analysis in their meta-analysis of nearly 24,000 human participants performing tasks alone and with others. When Bond and Titus combined the results of 241 studies

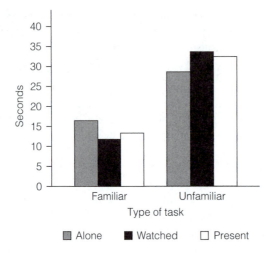

FIGURE 9-2
Does the presence of others facilitate the performance of familiar tasks (such as taking off one's shoes and socks) and interfere with the performance on a more unfamiliar task (putting on a robe that tied in the back)? Markus (1978) found that when they were observed, people performed the familiar task faster but the more unfamiliar task more slowly.

statistically, they concluded that people work faster and produce more when others are present, but only when they work at simple tasks. The presence of others rarely enhances the quality of performance, and it decreases both the quantity and quality of work on complex tasks. Bond and Titus also noted that the gains that occurred when people worked together on simple tasks were not as great as the losses that occurred when people worked on complex tasks.

Why Does Social Facilitation Occur?

Zajonc's analysis explains *when* social facilitation occurs. But *why* does the presence of others enhance dominant responses? Triplett (1898) offered several explanations for his observations of cyclists: Perhaps the lead rider creates a partial vacuum, and followers are pulled along with less effort. Maybe the lead rider breaks the wind resistance and makes the followers' job easier. Also, the presence of other riders may buoy up the spirits of the competitors, encouraging them to expend greater effort. His laboratory study, however, eliminated most of these explanations and suggested, instead, that the presence of others is psychologically stimulating. But what is the source and nature of this mysterious "psychological stimulation"? (For other reviews, see Aiello & Douthitt, 2001; Geen, 1991; Geen & Bushman, 1987; Guerin, 1993, 1999; B. Strauss, 2002.)

DRIVE PROCESSES Zajonc coined the word *compresence* to describe the state of responding in the presence of others. Compresence, he hypothesized, touches off a basic arousal response in most social species "simply because one never knows, so to speak, what sorts of responses—perhaps even novel and unique—may be required in the next few seconds" when others are nearby (Zajonc, 1980, p. 50). Zajonc believed that compresence in and of itself is sufficient to elevate drive levels, and this drive triggers social facilitation when tasks are so easy that only dominant responses are needed to perform them.

Zajonc's **drive theory** uniquely predicts that social facilitation will occur even when all forms of social interaction, communication, and evaluation between the individual and the observer are blocked. Investigators tested this hypothesis by asking people to work on simple or complex tasks in the presence of an "observer" who was blindfolded and wore earplugs. Even though the observer could not interact with participants in any way, his mere presence still enhanced their performance when they worked on simple tasks and slowed their performance on complex ones (B. H. Schmitt, Gilovich, Goore, & Joseph, 1986).

But do people actually show signs of physiological arousal whenever they are joined by other humans? Some studies have found evidence of increased heart rate and blood pressure, but the physiological effects of compresence depend on the type of situation and on who is watching (Mullen, Bryant, & Driskell, 1997). James Blascovich and his colleagues (Blascovich, Mendes, Hunter, & Salomon, 1999), for example, verified that an audience triggers increases in cardiac and vascular reactivity. Blascovich's team also discovered, however, that this arousal was physiologically very different when people worked on an easy task rather than on a hard one. When the task was easy, physiological measures indicated that people were challenged by the task, and their bodies responded in ways that facilitated their performance. But when the task was difficult, people responded physiologically as if they were threatened by the situation, and their performance deteriorated. Other studies found that the presence of certain people—such as close friends—can have a calming rather than an arousing influence. When women performed a difficult math test with a friend who was merely present—the friend could touch the participant's wrist but was preoccupied with another task and was wearing a headset that blocked all sound—the participant's cardiovascular responses were lowered (Kamarck, Manuck, & Jennings, 1990).

MOTIVATIONAL PROCESSES When Dora worked in isolation, she alone judged her productivity. But once she was joined by Dorothy, Olivia, and the others, the group provided a standard for evaluating productivity. The group could commend Dora for her efficiency, but it could also decide that her rate was substandard.

In many cases, evaluative pressures motivate people to work harder. Nickolas B. Cottrell's (1972) **evaluation apprehension theory,** for example, proposed that people learn through experience that other people are the source of

---

drive theory In general, an analysis of human motivation that stresses the impact of psychological or physiological needs or desires on individuals' thoughts, feelings, and actions; also an explanation of social facilitation proposed by Robert Zajonc, which maintains that the presence of others evokes a generalized drive state characterized by increased readiness and arousal.

evaluation apprehension theory An analysis of performance gains in groups arguing that individuals working in the presence of others experience a general concern for how these others are evaluating them, and that this apprehension facilitates their performance on simple, well-learned tasks.

most of the rewards and punishments they receive. Thus, individuals learn to associate social situations with evaluation, so they feel apprehensive whenever other people are nearby. This *evaluation apprehension* enhances performance on simple tasks, but it becomes debilitating when people attempt more difficult projects. Cottrell thus believed that apprehension, and not the arousal response identified by Zajonc, is the source of social facilitation effects (Henchy & Glass, 1968; Weiss & Miller, 1971).

Self-presentation theory also underscores the motivational impact of evaluation apprehension (Goffman, 1959). Self-presentation theory assumes that group members actively control others' impressions of themselves by displaying social behaviors that establish and maintain a particular social image, or *face*. Group members do not want the others to think that they possess negative, shameful qualities and characteristics, so they strive to make a good impression. Performance situations create self-presentational challenges for members, particularly when they feel they might fail. To avoid that embarrassment, group members redouble their efforts, particularly when self-presentational pressures are strong (C. F. Bond, 1982; C. F. Bond, Atoum, & VanLeeuwen, 1996).

The primary hypothesis that derives uniquely from motivational models—that any stimulus increasing the organism's apprehension over future rewards or punishments should increase drive levels—has received some support. When people find themselves in evaluative situations, they tend to perform dominant rather than nondominant responses (J. L. Cohen, 1979; Guerin, 1986; J. J. Seta, Crisson, Seta, & Wang, 1989). When, for example, individuals who were watched by an observer were told that the observer was evaluating them, their performance improved, but only when they were working on a simple task (Bartis, Szymanski, & Harkins, 1988; Geen, 1983). When people who had already failed once tried the task a second time, they performed worse when others were present (Sanna & Shotland, 1990; C. E. Seta & Seta, 1995). Also, situational factors that decrease evaluation apprehension, such as allowing for private responses, unevaluative audiences, and the absence of a definable task that can be evaluated, often eliminate social facilitation effects (Griffin, 2001; Henchy & Glass, 1968; Martens & Landers, 1972; Sasfy & Okun, 1974). Finally, individuals who are highly confident perform better when evaluated by others, whereas those who doubt their ability to succeed perform better when alone (Sanna, 1992).

The presence of other people—even friends—also increases physiological reactivity if these friends are evaluative. As noted earlier, people were more relaxed when working on a task with a friend nearby. Their friend, however, was wearing earphones and could not evaluate the participant's performance (Kamarck et al., 1990). What would happen if the friend was a potential source of evaluation? When people are watched closely by a friend, they tend to show signs of physiological arousal rather than relaxation (K. M. Allen, Blascovich, Tomaka, & Kelsey, 1991; Hilmert, Kulik, & Christenfeld, 2002). In fact, people

---

self-presentation theory An analysis of performance gains in groups that assumes that social facilitation is caused by individuals striving to make a good impression when they work in the presence of others.

are more relaxed when they are with their pets rather than with other people. Pets are an ideal source of social support, for they provide reassurance through their presence but they do not (we assume) evaluate their owner's performance (K. Allen, Blascovich, & Mendes, 2002; K. M. Allen et al., 1991).

Other findings, though, do not support this emphasis on evaluation. Even when the companion refrains from attending to the individual in any way, social facilitation still occurs (R. E. Berger, 1981; Platania & Moran, 2001; Worringham & Messick, 1983). Animals that likely lack the capacity to feel nervous or embarrassed—puppies, chickens, mice, rats, monkeys, armadillos, ants, opossums, and even cockroaches—perform simple tasks better when other members of their species are present (Cottrell, 1972). Moreover, activities that involve little threat of evaluation, such as eating, drinking, or getting dressed, still show social facilitation effects (see Focus 9-1).

COGNITIVE PROCESSES Zajonc stressed drive levels, Cottrell underscored the importance of evaluation, but several cognitive theories have suggested that the presence of others changes our capacity to process information adequately. When people work in the presence of other people, they must split their attention between the task they are completing and the other person (Guerin, 1983; Guerin & Innes, 1982). The presence of an audience may also increase individuals' self-awareness, and as a result, they may focus their attention on themselves and fail to pay sufficient attention to the task (Carver & Scheier, 1981; Duval & Wicklund, 1972; Mullen & Baumeister, 1987).

Distractions, however, do not inevitably undermine performance. **Distraction-conflict theory,** for example, suggests that distraction interferes with the attention given to the task, but that these distractions can be overcome with effort. Therefore, on simple tasks, the interference effects are inconsequential compared with the improvement that results from concentrating on the task, so performance is facilitated. On more complex tasks, the increase in drive is insufficient to offset the effects of distraction, and performance is therefore impaired (R. S. Baron, 1986; G. S. Sanders, Baron, & Moore, 1978). As this model predicts, working with others is often distracting; people forget key aspects of the task when they complete it in the presence of others rather than alone (Gastorf, Suls, & Sanders, 1980; G. S. Sanders et al., 1978). Social facilitation is more pronounced when participants' attention is divided between the task and the other people who are present. If people are present but do not draw the participants' attention, facilitation does not occur (C. F. Bond et al., 1996; Groff et al., 1983; G. S. Sanders et al., 1978).

Studies of people's performance when completing the *Stroop Task* with others or alone also support the distraction-conflict model. In the *Stroop Task,* participants are shown a color name (e.g., *Red, Blue*) printed in a primary color (such

---

distraction-conflict theory An analysis of performance gains in groups assuming that when others are present, attention is divided between the other people and the task; this attentional conflict increases motivation and so it facilitates performance on simple, well-learned tasks.

FOCUS 9-1   Are Groups Good for the Appetite?

A good meal tastes better if we eat it in the company of friends.
–Harry F. Harlow (1932, p. 211)

One of the most ubiquitous of all groups is the one that eats. At breakfast, lunch, dinner, feasts, fêtes, and snack time, people gather to consume nutrition as a group. Most people report that they prefer to eat with others rather than dine alone (Clendenen et al., 1994). A shared meal, however, is a complex interpersonal event that sets the stage for social facilitation. When researchers ask people to keep track of how much they eat and whom they eat with, they usually find that people eat more—sometimes 40% to 50% more—when they dine in groups (e.g., de Castro et al., 1997; Patel & Schlundt, 2001). As meals eaten by groups are longer in duration than the ones eaten by solo individuals, people have more opportunity to keep eating when in groups than alone. Watching someone else eat also increases social imitation of the eating response. When the participants in one study witnessed another person eating 20 soda crackers, they ate far more crackers themselves than did participants who saw someone eat only one (Nisbett & Storms, 1974). People even seem to prepare relatively larger portions for meals to be eaten in groups than individually, as if they anticipate that the group members will be able to consume more than they

would if alone. So long as the group does not include a substantial portion of dieters, the group may continue to eat until all the available food is consumed. Solitary eaters are more likely to eat only until they are sated (Herman, Roth, & Polivy, 2003). In general, larger groups trigger greater increases in eating, although at a decreasing rate, similar to that suggested by social impact theory (Latané, 1981).

The social facilitation of eating is strongest when co-eaters are known and liked. In some studies, the correlation between group size and amount of eating was only significant when people dined with families and friends. Social facilitation of eating is also limited to coaction rather than audience situations. People eat more when others with them are eating, but they tend to eat less when the other people who are present are observing them. One explanation for the inhibiting impact of others on eating suggests that the observers may trigger excessive evaluation apprehension, so individuals may reduce their consumption because they expect that observers will not think well of them if they eat too much. Diners may also engage in social comparison as they eat, for only by comparing their own consumption amounts to those of others at the table can they determine if they are eating too much or too little (Herman et al., 2003).

---

as red or blue) and asked to name the color of the *ink*. For example, if the word *Red* is printed in blue ink, the participant should answer *blue*. When the ink and the color word match, people have no problems. But when the ink and the color word are incongruent, reaction time and errors increase. These errors, however, decrease when individuals complete the task with others—apparently because the presence of others reduces the impact of the distracting color name cue (Huguet, Galvaing, Monteil, & Dumas, 1999).

Conclusions and Applications

Social facilitation occurs because human beings, as social beings, respond in predictable ways when joined by other members of their species (see Table 9-1). Some of these reactions, as Zajonc suggested, are very basic ones, for the mere presence of other people elevates drive levels. But arousal becomes more sub-

TABLE 9-1 Three general explanations of social facilitation

Theory	Mediating Process	Evidence
Drive theory (Zajonc, 1965)	*Unlearned drive:* The mere presence of others elevates drive levels; this drive triggers social facilitation when tasks are so easy that only dominant responses are needed to perform them.	People show signs of physiological arousal when others are present Many species perform basic tasks more efficiently in the presence of other species members Facilitative arousal occurs primarily for simple tasks
Evaluation apprehension theory (Cottrell, 1972)	*Motivational process:* Through experience, people learn to associate the presence of others with evaluation; this concern for evaluation facilitates performance on well-learned tasks.	The presence of others is facilitative only when the observers can evaluate the quality of the performance Facilitative effects are strongest when individuals are striving to make a good impression
Distraction-conflict theory (R.S. Baron, 1986; G. S. Sanders, 1981)	*Cognitive process:* When others are present, attention is divided between the other people and the task; attentional conflict increases motivation, which facilitates performance so long as the task is a simple one.	Recall is poorer when original stimulus was presented in presence of others (suggesting that people are distractions) Facilitation is reduced if the others in the situation are not noticed Presence of others improves performance on interference tasks (e.g., the *Stroop Task*)

stantial when group members realize that the people around them are evaluating them and might form negative impression of them if they perform badly. Cognitive mechanisms that govern how individuals process information and monitor the environment also come into play when people work in the presence of others. As the following examples illustrate, these physiological, motivational, and cognitive processes influence group members' reactions across a wide range of performance settings.

PREJUDICE AND SOCIAL FACILITATION *Prejudices* are deeply ingrained negative attitudes about the members of other groups. Such prejudices as racism and sexism are increasingly recognized as unfair and socially inappropriate, so individuals who are prejudiced often try to keep their prejudices to themselves. Prejudiced people do not express negative attitudes toward the members of other groups to avoid being labeled a racist or sexist (Kleinpenning & Hagendoorn, 1993).

Prejudice, however, is a well-learned, *dominant* response; so, ironically, the presence of other people may lead individuals to express even more biased opinions when they are in public rather than in private. Even though individuals may wish to keep their prejudices hidden, when they are with others—or just anticipate being with others—their attitudes may surface in their public statements. Researchers demonstrated the facilitating impact of anticipated interaction by first measuring White students' anti-Black attitudes before asking them to evaluate a fictitious Black student named "Donald." If the participants anticipated meeting with others to discuss their evaluation of Donald, their attitudes predicted their evaluations, especially for socially anxious individuals: Prejudiced individuals rated Donald more negatively, whereas unprejudiced individuals ratings were more positive. A second study, which used a priming procedure to determine if prejudiced people would unconsciously associate Blacks with violent images and Whites with nonviolent images, yielded similar results. Anxious individuals made more mistakes processing information when they anticipated meeting with others in a group. These studies suggest that even individuals who are striving to control their prejudices may nonetheless more readily express their biases when they are part of a group rather than alone (Lambert, Cronen, Chasteen, & Lickel, 1996; Lambert et al., 2003).

ELECTRONIC PERFORMANCE MONITORING (EPM) Social facilitation is not limited to face-to-face group settings. The *electronic presence* of others—made possible by computers, telephones, or other surveillance systems—can also enhance performance on simple tasks but undermine performance on complicated ones. John Aiello, for example, drew on studies of social facilitation in his analyses of **electronic performance monitoring** (EPM). Many businesses can now track the performance of their employees throughout the workday with computer information networks. When workers use their computer to enter data, communicate with one another, or search databases for stored information, their activity can be monitored automatically. Does EPM enhance performance, or does it create so much evaluation anxiety that performance suffers? Aiello found that EPM may enhance employees' productivity, but in ways that are consistent with social facilitation effects. He studied people working on a data entry task. Some were alone, some were working with others, and some were members of a cohesive group. Aiello discovered that EPM enhanced the performance of highly skilled workers, but interfered with the performance of less skilled participants. Monitoring also increased workers' feeling of stress, except among those who were part of a cohesive work group (Aiello & Kolb, 1995). Individuals who believed they could turn off the monitoring also showed no negative effects of EPM, as did individuals who had been given the opportunity to express their opinions on the use of the monitoring system (Douthitt & Aiello, 2001).

SOCIAL FACILITATION IN EDUCATIONAL SETTINGS Groups are used in a variety of ways in educational settings (small seminars, group discussions, problem-based learning teams, etc.), but perhaps the most common of all educational

---

electronic performance monitoring (EPM) The use of information technologies, such as computer networks, to track, analyze, and report information about workers' performance.

collectives is the **study group.** Unlike groups created and monitored by the instructor, study groups are self-organized and self-directive, for they are formed by students themselves for the purpose of studying course material.

"Join a study group" is the advice often given to college students who are struggling in their classes, but do study groups fulfill their promise? Study groups offer members some advantages over studying alone. Some groups enhance members' motivation and help students stay focused on their academic goals (Dudley, Johnson, & Johnson, 1997; Finn & Rock, 1997). Moreover, if students receive useful instruction from other group members, then students who are members of study groups outperform students who do not study in groups (Webb, Troper, & Fall, 1995). Students who are committed to their groups and value the learning experiences they provide generally outperform students who react negatively to such groups (K. A. Freeman, 1996).

Study groups may, however, inhibit the acquisition of new concepts and skills. The presence of others can be distracting, and during the early phases of learning, this distraction can interfere with learning. The presence of other people also interferes with overt and covert practicing. When the participants in one project needed to learn a list of words, they were too embarrassed to rehearse the material by saying it aloud, and their performance suffered (S. M. Berger et al., 1981). Studies of athletes acquiring new skills, of students learning a second language, and of clinicians developing their therapeutic skills have indicated that learning proceeds more rapidly, at least initially, when students work alone rather than in groups (S. M. Berger, Carli, Garcia, & Brady, 1982; Ferris & Rowland, 1983; MacCracken & Stadulis, 1985; Schauer, Seymour, & Geen, 1985).

Once they have learned their skills, however, people should perform with others present if possible (Utman, 1997). Zajonc recommends that the student

> study all alone, preferably in an isolated cubicle, and arrange to take his examinations in the company of many other students, on stage, and in the presence of a large audience. The results of his examination would be beyond his wildest expectations, provided, of course, he had learned his material quite thoroughly. (Zajonc, 1965, p. 274)

SOCIAL LOAFING

The Relay Test Room group was a success. The women were experts, so the presence of others enhanced their performance. Their output jumped by as much as 25% when they worked in the Relay Test Room. But this high level of productivity did not mean that they were maximally productive. During any given week, some members of the group would reach their usual levels of productivity, whereas others—especially Nora and Helen—would work below their maximum efficiency. As a result, the group produced more than individuals working in isolation, but the difference was not astonishing.

---

study group A self-organized, self-directive group formed by students for the purpose of studying course material.

Why did the Relay Test Room women not reach their full potential as a working group? Ivan Steiner (1972) drew on the concept of **process losses** to provide an answer. Steiner recognized that groups have great potential, for their resources, expertise, and abilities outstrip those of any single individual. But Steiner also realized that groups rarely reach their full potential because a variety of interpersonal processes detracts from their overall proficiency. His "law" of group productivity predicts that

Actual productivity = Potential productivity − Losses owing to faulty processes

Thus, even when a group includes skilled members who possess all the resources they need to accomplish their tasks, faulty group processes may prevent them from succeeding. When process losses proliferate, the group's chance to become greater than the sum of its parts dwindles.

Productivity Losses in Groups

Max Ringelmann (1913) was a French agricultural engineer who, in the late 19th century, studied the productivity of horses, oxen, men, and machines in various agricultural applications. Should you plow a field with two horses or three? Can five men turn a mill crank faster than four? Ringelmann did not just speculate about the answers to these questions. Instead, he set up teams of varying sizes and measured their collective power. (Kravitz & Martin, 1986, present an excellent summary and interpretation of Ringelmann's work.)

Ringelmann's most startling discovery was that workers—and that includes horses, oxen, and men—all become less productive in groups. A group of five persons making relays can easily outperform a single person, just as a team pulling a rope is stronger than a single opponent or an audience applauding makes more noise than an individual. But even though a group outperforms an individual, the group does not usually work at maximum efficiency. When Ringelmann had individuals and groups pull on a rope attached to a pressure gauge, groups performed below their theoretical capabilities (Moede, 1927). If Dorothy and Olivia could each pull 100 units when they worked alone, could they pull 200 units when they pooled their efforts? No, their output reached only 186. A three-person group did not produce 300 units, but only 255. An eight-person group managed only 392, not 800. Groups certainly outperformed individuals—but as more and more people were added, the group became increasingly inefficient (see Figure 9-3). To honor its discoverer, this tendency for groups to become less productive as group size increases is now known as the **Ringelmann effect** (Ingham, Levinger, Graves, & Peckham, 1974; Steiner, 1972).

---

process loss Reduction in performance effectiveness or efficiency caused by actions, operations, or dynamics that prevent the group from reaching its full potential, including reduced effort, faulty group processes, coordination problems, and ineffective leadership.

Ringelmann effect The tendency, first documented by Max Ringelmann, for people to become less productive when they work with others; this loss of efficiency increases as group size increases, but at a gradually decreasing rate.

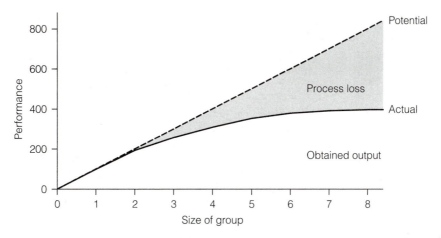

FIGURE 9-3

Do many hands make light the work? Ringelmann (1913) recorded the work output of single individuals as well as groups ranging in size from two to eight members. If a group's performance were based strictly on addition of members' individual efforts, then a two-person group could produce 200 units, a three-person group 300 units, and so on. Ringelmann found much lower productivity. The means for his groups were 186, 255, 308, 350, 378, 392, and 392, for two- to eight-person groups, respectively.

Why might people working on such simple tasks fail to be as productive as they could be? Ringelmann identified two key sources of process losses when people worked together. First, *coordination losses,* caused by "the lack of simultaneity of their efforts" (Ringelmann, 1913, p. 9) interfere with performance. On a task such as rope pulling, for example, people tend to pull and pause at different times, resulting in a failure to reach their full productive potential. Second, Ringelmann speculated that people may not work so hard when they are in groups. After watching a group of prisoners turning the crank of a flour mill, he noted that their performance was "mediocre because after only a little while, each man, trusting in his neighbor to furnish the desired effort, contented himself by merely following the movement of the crank, and sometimes even let himself be carried along by it" (p. 10; translation from Kravitz & Martin, 1986, p. 938). This reduction of effort by individuals working in groups is called **social loafing** (K. D. Williams, Harkins, & Latané, 1981).

Bibb Latané, Kipling Williams, and Stephen Harkins studied both coordination losses and social loafing by measuring how loudly people cheered when alone and when in groups. They asked the participants to wear blindfolds and headsets, so their performance would not be influenced by "the effects of sensory feedback" (1979, p. 824). They then asked participants to shout as loudly as they could while the headsets played a stream of loud noise. Consistent with the

---

social loafing The reduction of individual effort exerted when people work in groups compared to when they work alone.

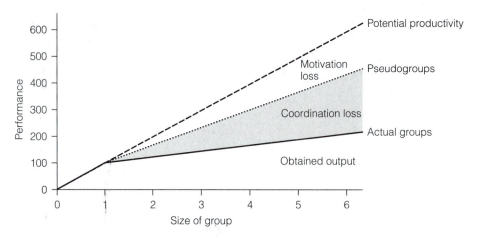

FIGURE 9-4

What causes the Ringelmann effect? Latané and his colleagues disentangled the two major causes of productivity losses in groups working on additive tasks by leading people to think they were working in groups when they actually were not. The people in these "groups" (labeled "pseudogroups") suffered from motivation loss, but not from coordination loss, as they were actually working alone. The unshaded portion between the dashed line and the dotted line represents motivation loss (social loafing), and the shaded portion between the dotted line and the solid line represents coordination loss. They combine to create the Ringelmann effect.

Ringelmann effect, groups of participants made more noise than individuals, but groups failed to reach their potential. When the participants were tested alone, they averaged a rousing 9.22 dynes/cm² (about as loud as a pneumatic drill). In dyads, each participant shouted at only 66% of capacity, and in six-person groups, at 36%. This drop in productivity is charted in Figure 9-4 (Latané, Williams, & Harkins, 1979, Experiment 2, p. 826; see also Harkins, Latané, & Williams, 1980; K. D. Williams et al., 1981).

But how much was this drop in productivity due to coordination problems and how much due to social loafing? Latané and his colleagues separated out these sources of process loss by testing noise production in "pseudogroups." In these conditions, participants were led to believe that either one other participant or five other participants were shouting with them, but in actuality, they were working alone. (The blindfolds and headsets made this deception possible.) Thus, any loss of production obtained in these pseudogroup conditions could not be due to coordination problems, because there were no other group members shouting. Instead, any decline in production could only be blamed on the reduced effort brought about by social loafing. Figure 9-4 summarizes these findings. When participants thought that one other person was working with them, they shouted only 82% as intensely, and if they thought that five other persons were shouting, they reached only 74% of their capacity. These findings suggest that even if work groups are so well organized that virtually all losses due to faulty coordination are eliminated, individual productivity might still be below par because of social loafing.

Causes of and Cures for Social Loafing

Social loafing is not limited to groups that must exert physical effort. Groups working at such diverse tasks as maze performance, vigilance exercises, creativity problems, job selection decisions, typing, and swimming tend to perform below their capability. Men and women, people of all ages, and groups in many different cultures exert less effort when they are working together (Karau & Williams, 1993). But social loafing is not inevitable. For every slack group—workers leaning on their shovels instead of digging with them, meetings that degenerate into gabfests, task forces that perform no tasks—there is a group whose members strive to reach new levels of efficiency and productivity. When is loafing the exception rather than the rule in groups?

INCREASE IDENTIFIABILITY Studies of social loafing suggest that people are *less* productive when they work with others. But studies of social facilitation, discussed earlier in this chapter, find that people are *more* productive when others are present (at least when the task is easy). Which is it?

Both. When people feel as though their level of effort cannot be ascertained because the task is a collective one, then social loafing becomes likely. But when people feel that they are being evaluated, they tend to exert more effort, and their productivity increases. If the task is an individualistic one, and is easy, the presence of other people increases evaluation apprehension, so social facilitation occurs. But when group members are anonymous, and their contributions are unidentifiable, the presence of others reduces evaluation apprehension, and social loafing becomes more likely (Harkins & Szymanski, 1987, 1988; J. M. Jackson & Latané, 1981).

Researchers illustrated the importance of evaluation by asking the members of a four-person group to generate as many ideas as possible for a common object. The participants did not discuss their ideas out loud but simply wrote them on slips of paper. Some of the participants thought that their ideas were individually identifiable, whereas others thought that their ideas were being collected in a common pool. Moreover, some participants believed that everyone was devising uses for the same object, but others thought that each group member was working with a different object. In this study, loafing occurred not only when ideas were pooled, but also when the participants believed that their individual outputs were not comparable or could not be evaluated (Harkins & Jackson, 1985). When each individual member's output was identifiable, on the other hand, loafing was virtually eliminated (Hardy & Latané, 1986; N. L. Kerr & Bruun, 1981; Sanna, 1992; K. D. Williams et al., 1981).

Consider the problem of the pickle packer, whose job involves selecting the right size pickle to pack into the pickle jar. As Kipling Williams and his colleagues noted, only "dill halves of a certain length can be used. Those that are too long will not fit and those that are too short will float and dance inside and look cheap and crummy" (K. D. Williams et al., 1981, p. 310). They suggested that the tendency to loaf could be reduced if each pickle packer's productivity could be measured and reviewed, and that workers be paid only for those jars that meet quality standards, for "How many pickles could a pickle packer pack if pickle packers were only paid for properly packed pickles?"

MINIMIZE FREE RIDING Thousands of people listen to public radio without making a contribution when the radio asks for donations. Some audience members do not clap during the call for an encore because they know their applause will not be missed. Many students avoid group projects where the entire group receives the same grade, because inevitably one or more members of the group will not do their share of the work (Hoffman & Rogelberg, 2001).

All these situations invite **free riding**—members doing less than their share of the work because others will make up for their slack. Although norms of fairness warn members to do their part, if they feel that the group does not need them or their contribution, they will be tempted to free-ride. When group members think that they are an indispensable part of the group—perhaps because their contribution is unique or essential for the group's success—they work harder (N. L. Kerr & Bruun, 1983). They also free-ride less in smaller groups, because each person plays a larger role in determining the group's outcomes (Kameda, Stasson, Davis, Parks, & Zimmerman, 1992). But free riding increases when members become suspicious of the level of effort being invested by the other group members. Rather than looking like a "sucker" by working harder than the others, group members reduce their efforts to match the level that they think other group members are expending. This **sucker effect** is strongest when they feel that their fellow group members are competent but lazy (Hart, Bridgett, & Karau, 2001).

SET GOALS Groups that set clear, challenging goals outperform groups whose members have lost sight of their objectives. When truck drivers who hauled logs from the woods to the mill were initially told to do their best when loading the logs, the men only carried about 60% of what they could legally haul (Latham & Baldes, 1975). When the drivers were later encouraged to reach a goal of 94% of the legal limit, they increased their efficiency and met this specific goal. In a study of groups generating ideas, members were more productive when they had a clear standard by which to evaluate the quality of their own work and the group's work (Harkins & Szymanski, 1989). Other research has suggested that clear goals stimulate a number of production-enhancing processes, including increases in effort, better planning, more accurate monitoring of the quality of the group's work, and increased commitment to the group (E. Weldon, Jehn, & Pradhan,

---

free riding Contributing less to a collective task when one believes that other group members will compensate for this lack of effort.

sucker effect The tendency for individuals to contribute less to a group endeavor when they expect that others will think negatively of someone who works too hard or contributes too much (considering them to be a "sucker").

1991). The group's goals should also be challenging rather than too easily attained. The advantages of working in a group are lost if the task is so easy that it can be accomplished even if the group loafs, so care should be taken to set the standards high—but not so high that they are unattainable (Hinsz, 1995; Locke & Latham, 2002; E. Weldon & Weingart, 1993).

INCREASE INVOLVEMENT   Loafing is less likely when people work at exciting, challenging, and personally involving tasks (Wageman, 1999; Zacarro, 1984). When individuals feel that a poor group performance will affect them personally, they do not loaf (Brickner, Harkins, & Ostrom, 1986). They also do not loaf if a high-quality performance will be rewarded (Shepperd, 1993, 1995; Shepperd & Wright, 1989). Social loafing is also reduced when rewards for successful performance are group based rather than individually based—so long as the group is not too large in size (DeMatteo, Eby, & Sundstrom, 1998) and the reward is divided nearly equally among all the group members (Honeywell-Johnson & Dickinson, 1999).

Involvement may even prompt group members to compensate for the expected failures or incompetencies of their fellow group members by expending extra effort. Kipling Williams and Steven Karau (1991) documented **social compensation** by convincing individuals that their group's task was a meaningful one, but that the motivation of other group members was in doubt (apparently because one of the other experimenters considered the research topic to be boring). Participants were also led to expect that their partners were either skilled or unskilled at the task. Williams and Karau discovered that group members worked hardest when the task was meaningful and the members believed that their coworkers' ability was minimal.

These findings are consistent with Karau and Williams's (1993) **collective effort model** (CEM). Drawing on classic expectancy-value theories of motivation, they suggested that two factors determine group members' level of motivation: their expectations about reaching a goal, and the value of that goal. Motivation is greatest when people think that the goal is within their reach (expectations are high) and they consider the goal to be valuable. Motivation diminishes if expectations are low or individuals do not value the goal. Working in a group, unfortunately, can diminish both expectations about reaching a goal and the value that is placed on that goal. In groups, the link between our effort and the chance of success is ambiguous. Even if we work hard, others may not, and the group may fail. Moreover, even if the group does succeed, we personally may not benefit much from the group's good performance. Earning a good grade on a

---

social compensation The tendency for group members to expend greater effort on important collective tasks to offset the anticipated insufficiencies in the efforts and abilities of their co-members.

collective effort model (CEM) A theoretical explanation of group productivity developed by Steven Karau and Kipling Williams that traces losses of productivity in groups to diminished expectations about successful goal attainment and the diminished value of group goals.

project completed by a group may not be as satisfying as earning a good grade on a project that we completed working on our own. Karau and Williams tested the CEM's basic predictions in a meta-analysis. Their review of 78 studies indicated that loafing is reduced if individuals' expectations for success are high and they feel that the goal they are seeking is a valuable one.

INCREASE IDENTIFICATION WITH THE GROUP The Relay Test Room did more than just bring together individuals to work in the same room. The women changed from a collection of independent individuals into a work group. They developed a shared sense of identity and began to take pride in their group's productivity rates. Friendships formed within the group, and the observers decided that "social sentiment and activity, so far from being one of the constants, was necessarily showing itself to be the dominating variable in the experiment" (Whitehead, 1938, p. 117).

Social identity theory suggests that the difference between a hard-working group and a loafing group is the match between the group's tasks and its members' self-definitions. If people are working together, but the group and its tasks have no meaning to them, they care very little if their group succeeds or fails. But when individuals derive their sense of self and identify from their membership in a group, then *social loafing* is replaced by *social laboring* as members expend extra effort for their groups (Haslam, 2001; Worchel, Rothgerber, Day, Hart, & Butemeyer, 1998). Individuals sometimes work hard when they think, "This task is important to me," but they are likely to work even harder when they think, "This task is important to *us*."

SOCIAL COMBINATION

By the winter of 1927, the Relay Test Room team had far surpassed the standards set by operators working in the main department. Despite problems with coordination loss and social loafing, the Relay Test Room group surpassed all expectations. But the observers could not help noticing that two of the group members were not very involved in the experiment or in the group. When they were transferred out of the group, and two new women took their place, the group's chemistry changed. Conflicts smoothed out. Absenteeism declined. Satisfaction increased. Productivity skyrocketed. In the main shop, workers averaged 50 relays per hour, but in the Relay Test Room, the rate reached more than 70 units per hour (Whitehead, 1938).

Group productivity expert Ivan Steiner (1972, 1976) likened a group performing a task to a cook baking a cake. Just as a cook needs the ingredients that the recipe requires, so a group can only accomplish its goals if its members have the resources—talents, energies, and skills—needed to complete the task. Good ingredients, however, do not guarantee that the cake will be a tasty one, just as recruiting talented group members does not guarantee that the group will be a productive one. These raw materials must be combined correctly if the group will be a success. In many cases, the task itself dictates how members' resources should be combined, just as different recipes call for different combinations of ingredients. In other cases, however, the group itself decides how to combine its resources, and mistakes during this combination process ultimately undermine the quality of the final product. Two heads may be better than one, but sometimes too many cooks spoil the broth (or the cake).

Group Composition: Building the Effective Group

Management did not pick the women of the Relay Test Room for their dedication to the company or their special expertise as operators. Nora was productive, but she did not take any special interest in the experiment. Olivia came from a very cohesive family, and during the first years of the study, she kept to herself. In contrast, Dorothy was "naturally gregarious, lively, and fond of a joke" (Whitehead, 1938, p. 155). Flora was not as productive as some workers, but she "worked faithfully for her pay, she never showed petulance, and she thoroughly appreciated the real advantages of the Relay Test Room" (Whitehead, 1938, p. 156).

Group performance depends, in part, on **group composition.** All groups are composites formed by the joining together of multiple, relatively independent individuals. Each member of the group brings with him or her a set of unique personal experiences, interests, skills, abilities, and motivations, which merge together with the personal qualities of all the other individual members to form the group as a whole. The Relay Test Room, for example, included five women who differed from one another in terms of age, personality, motivations, and attitudes, and these differences fundamentally influenced their personal performance and the group's performance (Moreland, Levine, & Wingert, 1996).

KNOWLEDGE, SKILL, AND ABILITY (KSA) Some groups fail because they simply do not include people with the qualities and characteristics needed to get the job done. A group struggling to generate solutions to math puzzles may not have any mathematicians at the table. A soccer team made up of slow-moving defensive fullbacks but no offensive goal scorers will likely lose. A group's performance depends, in part, on its members' knowledge, skills, and abilities, or **KSAs.**

What KSAs are important to groups? On the task side, groups whose members are more skilled at the work to be done outperform groups composed of less skilled members. A group of mediocre individuals can, with enough practice, good leadership, and determination, reach lofty goals, but it is difficult to make a silk purse out of a bunch of sow's ears. The Relay Test Room was productive

---

group composition The individuals who compose the group and their unique and common qualities (e.g., knowledge, skills, abilities) that combine to create the group as a whole.

KSAs Acronym for knowledge, skills, abilities, and other characteristics that are needed to complete a job or task successfully.

FOCUS 9-2   What Makes a Group Great?

Great Groups are inevitably forged by people unafraid of hiring people better than themselves.
–Warren Bennis and Particia Ward Biederman (1997, p. 12)

There are good groups, but there are also great groups. Many work crews can build houses and put out fires, but only a handful are capable of building a 40-story skyscraper or capping a burning wellhead on an oil derrick. Many sports teams play excellent soccer and baseball, but there is only one Manchester United; only one Boston Red Sox. There are excellent performing orchestras, but only one Berlin Philharmonic. Many space crews have flown into orbit around the Earth, but only a few have traveled to the Moon and back.

What are the ingredients for a group that makes remarkable advances in science, technology, art, and education? Warren Bennis and Patricia Ward Biederman (1997) studied seven such groups, including the Walt Disney Studios of the 1930s, which created the first full-length animated film; the members of Lockheed's Skunk Works, who designed the first supersonic jets and stealth fighters; and the Palo Alto Research Center (PARC), which invented, among other things, the laser printer, ethernet and e-mail, the mouse, and a graphical user interface for personal computers. Although each group was unique in many ways, Bennis and Biederman traced much of their success back to their composition. Walt Disney, the founder and leader of the Disney Studios, recruited the finest animators in the world to work together to create his films. The members of PARC were creative engineers who knew more about computing than anyone else on the planet. Those at Skunk Works were recruited from every unit in Lockheed and charged to work in secret to build planes that could fly faster than sound. Many of the members of these groups were relatively young men and women who lacked experience, but they had no fear of failure. Many were "fueled by an invigorating, completely unrealistic view of what they can accomplish" (Bennis & Biederman, 1997, p. 15).

Bennis and Biederman admitted that all these great groups had great leaders, but the primary task for the leaders was the recruitment and retention of gifted individual members. Leaders must not be afraid to hire people who are far more talented than they are, for "recruiting the right genius for the job is the first step in building many great collaborations. Great groups are inevitably forged by people unafraid of hiring people better than themselves" (p. 12).

---

because only highly skilled women were recruited for the group. Groups that succeed in creating new products and solutions to long-standing problems are staffed by individuals of high intelligence, motivation, and energy (see Focus 9-2). Studies of sport teams indicate that the "the best individuals make the best team" (Gill, 1984, p. 325). In many sports, the players' offensive and defensive performance can be tracked so that their skill level can be identified accurately. These qualities can then be used to calculate the statistical aggregation of the talent level of the team, which can be compared to the team's outcomes. These analyses indicate that the correlation between the aggregation of individual members' ability and group performance is very strong: .91 in football, .94 in baseball, and .60 in basketball (M. B. Jones, 1974; Widmeyer, 1990). The relationship is somewhat reduced in basketball because this sport requires more coordination among members and the teams are smaller in size. Hence, the team members' ability to play together may have a larger impact on the outcome of a basketball game, whereas the sheer level of ability of players has a greater impact on a football or baseball game's outcome.

On the interpersonal side, members must be able to work well with others on joint tasks. Communication skills, leadership ability, and a talent for managing conflicts are some of the qualities possessed by members of successful work teams (C. A. Bowers, Braun, & Morgan, 1997; Cannon-Bowers, Tannenbaum, Salas, & Volpe, 1995; Stout, Salas, & Fowlkes, 1997). The two women who were transferred out of the Relay Test Room, for example, caused a variety of interpersonal problems for the group, and productivity increased when they were replaced with two women who were more interpersonally skilled (Whitehead, 1938).

DIVERSITY The Relay Test Room was a relatively homogeneous group. Members were similar in terms of ethnicity, socioeconomic background, sex, and expertise. Would their performance have differed if some group members had unique personal qualities that distinguished them from the others? Do diverse, heterogeneous groups outperform homogeneous ones?

Diversity, at least in terms of skills and abilities, tends to increase productivity (C. A. Bowers, Pharmer, & Salas, 2000). When members vary in ability, then by definition the group will include at least one individual with high ability. Some homogeneous groups will be uniformly unskilled, so these groups will perform particularly badly at their task. Heterogeneous groups may also become more productive because the low-performing members are motivated by the high standards set by the others in the group, and the others in the group may also be a source of help and assistance as the low performers work to increase their performance. In heterogeneous groups, individuals who are of moderate or high ability show relatively little improvement in performance, whereas those who initially have low performance show the greatest gains. This *spillover effect* is due both to motivation gains and to learning gains (F. W. Goldman & Goldman, 1981; M. Goldman, 1965, 1966).

Other types of diversity, such as variations in ethnicity, race, age, and sex, influence performance less reliably (K. Y. Williams & O'Reilly, 1998). Teams of researchers were more productive when they joined with researchers from other disciplines (Pelz, 1956, 1967), but top management teams and work groups were less productive and experienced more turnover when their members varied noticeably in age and tenure (Pelled, Eisenhardt, & Xin, 1999). Management teams in banks that were diverse in terms of their educational histories and backgrounds were more innovative than teams that were homogeneous (S. E. Jackson, 1992), but in some cases, members of minority groups were given unfairly negative evaluations by supervisors (Greenhaus, Parasuraman, & Wormley, 1990). Groups that included Asian, African, Hispanic, and European Americans outperformed groups that only included European Americans (McLeod, Lobel, & Cox, 1996), but classroom groups performed best when they were composed of individuals whose personality characteristics were similar and focused on goal attainment (M. H. Bond & Shiu, 1997).

These conflicting findings attest to the mixed benefits and limitations offered by diversity in groups. Diverse groups may be better at coping with changing work conditions, because their wider range of talents and traits enhances their flexibility. Diversity should also help groups seek alternative solutions to problems and increase creativity and innovation. Diverse groups, however, may lack cohesion, because members may perceive one another as dissimilar. Heterogeneity may increase conflict within the group (S. E. Jackson, May, & Whitney, 1995; K. Y. Williams & O'Reilly, 1998).

MEN AND WOMEN IN GROUPS Would the Relay Test Room group have performed any differently if its members had been men, or if the group had consisted of both men and women? Wendy Wood (1987), after reviewing 52 studies of sex differences in group performance, noted that some studies suggested that women outperform men, but other studies suggested that all-male groups are superior to all-female groups. She noted, however, that two factors covaried with sex differences in group performance—task content and interaction style. First, in the studies that favored men, the content of the task was more consistent with the typical skills, interests, and abilities of men than of women. Groups of men were better at tasks that required math or physical strength, whereas groups of women excelled on verbal tasks. Second, Wood suggested that sex differences in performance are influenced by the different interaction styles that men and women often adopt in groups. Men more frequently enact a task-oriented interaction style, whereas women tend to enact an interpersonally oriented interaction style. Thus, men outperform women (to a small extent) when success is predicated on a high rate of task activity, and women outperform men when success depends on a high level of social activity (W. Wood, Polek, & Aiken, 1985).

These findings suggest that men would not have outperformed the women in the Relay Test Room. Although the task required manual dexterity, the women were all experts. Also, although men show a slight tendency to excel at tasks that require maximal productivity, positive social activities within the group were responsible for the high level of motivation maintained by the workers. If the group had become too task oriented, this source of motivational encouragement might have been lost (Eagly & Wood, 1991).

But what of mixed-gender groups—groups that include both men and women? As noted earlier, studies of diversity suggest that groups that are more heterogeneous—whether based on abilities, skills, or sex—sometimes often outperform more homogeneous groups (S. E. Jackson, 1992; K. Y. Williams & O'Reilly, 1998). However, groups that achieve diversity by adding only one or two members of a social category, such as a group with one woman and many men, or a group with several European Americans and a single Hispanic American, may encounter more problems than homogeneous groups. When work groups include a single "token, solo" woman, for example, coworkers are more likely to categorize each other in terms of their sex (Wilder, 1986b). As noted in Chapter 6, solo members are also scrutinized more than other group members, and this unwanted attention may make them so apprehensive that their performance suffers (Kanter, 1977). Token members are more often targets of sexism and prejudice (S. T. Fiske, 1993b). Token members must, in many cases, work harder and express higher levels of commitment to the group to overcome other members' biases (Eagly & Johnson, 1990; Ridgeway, 1982).

In some cases, groups with token members will outperform homogeneous groups, even when the groups attempt tasks that are traditionally reserved for homogeneous groups. For example, one team of researchers watched groups working on a wilderness survival exercise—an activity that favors people who have a knowledge of the outdoors. Groups of men generally outperformed women, but groups of men that included one woman performed best of all. The researchers speculated that the addition of a woman in the otherwise all-male groups may have tempered the men's tendency to compete with one another and, thus, helped them to function as a team (Rogelberg & Rumery, 1996).

The studies of Richard Hackman and his colleagues on orchestras have suggested that gender diversity depends, in part, on the group's history and the larger social context in which the group is embedded (Allmendinger, Hackman, & Lehman, 1996; Hackman, 2003). Many of the orchestras they studied were in the midst of a transition from all-male groups to groups that included both men and women. Some orchestras were only beginning this transition, for they included very few women (2% was the lowest), whereas others were more heterogeneous (up to 59% women). When Hackman et al. measured members' work motivation and overall satisfaction with their orchestras, they discovered that orchestras with a larger proportion of female members were viewed more negatively. This tendency was more pronounced among the men in the group, and also in countries with traditional conceptions of the role of men and women in society. Hackman wrote,

> Life in a homogeneously male orchestra surely is not much affected by the presence of one or two women, especially if they play a gendered instrument such as a harp. Larger numbers of women, however, can become a worrisome presence on high-status turf that previously had been an exclusively male province, engendering intergroup conflicts that stress all players and disrupt the social dynamics of the orchestra. (2003, p. 908)

Steiner's Taxonomy of Tasks

The performance of a group cannot be predicted by considering only the characteristics of the individuals in the group. Had Nora, Helen, and the others worked alone at assembling relays, their productivity would have been determined strictly by each one's personal resources—their individual talents, skills, effort, temperaments, and so forth. But because they worked together as a unit, their performance was determined by each individuals' resources *plus* the interpersonal processes that determined how these resources were combined. Even the best cooks working with excellent ingredients need a good recipe.

Steiner (1972), in his taxonomy of group tasks, suggested that in many cases, the recipe for how group members' inputs will be combined is determined by the task itself. A group that is assembling relays, for example, must combine members' products in ways that differ from the combination process used by a team playing baseball or by workers on an assembly line. Steiner called the combination processes dictated by the problem or group activity the **task demands.**

---

task demand The effect that a problem or task's features, including its divisibility and difficulty, have on the procedures the group can use to complete the task

TABLE 9-2 A summary of Steiner's taxonomy of tasks

Question	Task Type	Qualities	Examples
Divisibility: Can the task be broken down into subtasks?	Divisible	Subcomponents can be identified and assigned to specific members	Playing a football game Building a house Preparing a six-course meal
	Unitary	The task does not have subcomponents	Pulling on a rope Reading a book Solving a math problem
Quantity versus quality: Is the quantity produced more important than the quality of performance?	Maximizing	*Quantity:* The more produced, the better the performance	Generating many ideas Lifting a great weight Scoring the most goals
	Optimizing	*Quality:* A correct or optimal solution is needed	Developing the best answer Solving a math problem
Interdependence: How are individual inputs combined to yield a group product?	Additive	Individual inputs are added together	Pulling a rope Shoveling snow
	Compensatory	Decision is made by averaging together individual decisions	Estimating a pig's weight by asking 3 people to guess and averaging their guesses Averaging ratings of job applicants
	Disjunctive	Group selects one solution or product from a pool of members' solutions or products	Picking one person's answer to a math problem to be the group's answer Letting one art project represent the entire school
	Conjunctive	All group members must contribute to the product for it to be completed	Climbing a mountain Eating a meal as a group
	Discretionary	Group decides how individual inputs relate to group product	Deciding to shovel snow together Choosing to vote on the best answer to a problem

Source: Adapted from *Group Processes and Productivity* by I. D. Steiner. Copyright © 1972 by Academic Press.

These demands vary depending on the divisibility of the task, the type of output desired, and the combination rules required to complete the task (see Table 9-2).

First, some tasks are *divisible*—they can be broken down into subtasks that can be assigned to different members—whereas other tasks are *unitary*. Building a house, planting a garden, or working a series of math problems by assigning one to each group member are all **divisible tasks,** because the entire task can be split into parts. **Unitary tasks,** however, cannot be divided: Only one painter is needed for a small closet in a house, only one gardener can plant a single seed, and only one person is needed to solve a simple math problem.

Second, some tasks call for a high rate of production (*maximization*), whereas others require a high-quality, correct outcome (*optimization*). With **maximizing tasks,** quantity is what counts. In a relay race, tug-of-war, or block-stacking problem, performance depends on sheer quantity; the emphasis is on maximal production. For **optimizing tasks,** a good performance is the one that most closely matches a predetermined criterion. Examples of optimizing tasks include estimating the number of beans in a jar or coming up with the best solution to a problem.

Third, members' contributions to the group task can be *combined* in different ways. On an assembly line, for example, the members perform a specific task repeatedly, and the product is finished when each member has made his or her contribution. The members of a rock band, in contrast, all play and sing together, so each member's contribution must mesh with the other members' contributions. The five basic combinatorial strategies described by Steiner (1972)—*additive, compensatory, disjunctive, conjunctive,* and *discretionary*—are described hereafter.

ADDITIVE TASKS **Additive tasks** are divisible and maximizing, for they require the summing together of individual group members' inputs to maximize the group product. In consequence, so long as each group member can perform the simple, individualistic task required—such as pulling on a rope, cheering at a football game, clapping after a concert, or raking leaves in a yard—the productivity of the group will probably exceed the productivity of the single individual. However, as studies of social loafing have suggested, people in groups do not always work hard at additive tasks; as the saying goes, "many hands make light work."

COMPENSATORY TASKS When groups attempt **compensatory tasks,** the members must average their individual judgments or solutions together to yield the group's outcome (see Table 9-2). A group may not want to meet in a

---

divisible task A task that can be broken down into subcomponents which can then be assigned to individuals or to subgroups within the group.

unitary task A task that cannot be performed piecemeal because it does not break down into any subcomponents.

maximizing tasks A task or project that calls for a high rate of production.

optimizing task A task or project that has a best solution and outcome, thus the quality of the group's performance can be judged by comparing the product to a quality-defining standard.

additive task A task or project that a group can complete by cumulatively combining individual members' inputs.

compensatory task A task or project that a group can complete by literally averaging together (mathematically combining) individual members' solutions or recommendations.

face-to-face meeting, for example, so members submit their votes to the chair, who tallies them up to reach a conclusion (Lorge, Fox, Davitz, & Brenner, 1958).

Marvin E. Shaw (1981), after thoroughly reviewing studies of a wide variety of groups, concluded that groups outperform individuals on compensatory tasks. Consider, for example, a group of people who were asked to estimate the temperature of their classroom (H. C. Knight, 1921). Naturally, some people overestimated the temperature, and others underestimated, so the "group" judgment, which was an average of all the estimates offered, was more accurate than the judgments made by 80% of the individuals. Shaw noted, however, that the increased accuracy of compensatory methods springs more from the use of multiple judgments than from the greater accuracy of groups per se. When single individuals make multiple estimates, and their estimates are averaged, their judgments are also more accurate (Stoop, 1932).

DISJUNCTIVE TASKS When groups work at **disjunctive tasks,** they must generate a single solution that will stand as the group's outcome. Juries making decisions about guilt or innocence, computer technicians deciding which program bug to fix first, or the coaching staff setting the lineup for the day's game are all performing disjunctive tasks. These types of tasks tend to be both unitary and optimizing, for they cannot be broken down into subtasks, and they require a high-quality or correct solution rather than a large quantity of product.

Disjunctive tasks often require discussion and decision, and Chapter 10 provides a more detailed analysis of how groups tackle such tasks. In general, however, groups perform disjunctive tasks better than most of the individual members. For example, if four students complete a quiz as a group, the group will likely outscore most of the individual students, because more heads means more information and better detection of errors. If the students would have gotten 70%, 80%, 80%, and 90% when tested as individuals, the group will likely score at least 80%.

The group may even score 90% if it accepts the recommendations of its highest scoring member. In some cases, once someone in the group mentions the correct answer, the group adopts it as the group solution—a *truth-wins rule.* Sometimes, however, the group rejects the correct answer. Rosa may be certain that the answer to the question, "Who first documented the reduction of individual productivity when in groups?" is "Ringelmann," but her group may not accept her solution, because they doubt her skills or because someone of higher status may propose a different solution. Ringelmann is the correct answer, but this truth will not win out over error unless someone in the group supports Rosa and her answer—a *truth-supported-wins rule.*

The truth-wins rule usually holds for groups working on *Eureka problems,* whereas the truth-supported-wins rule holds for groups working on *non-Eureka problems.* When we are told the answer to a *Eureka problem,* we are very certain

---

disjunctive task A task or project that is completed when a single solution, decision, or recommendation is adopted by the group.

that the answer offered is correct. It fits so well, we react with an "Aha!" or "Eureka!" The answers to *non-Eureka problems,* in contrast, are not so satisfying. Even after arguing about them, we often wonder if the recommended answer is the correct answer. Consider, for example, the famous horse-trading problem:

> A man bought a horse for $60 and sold it for $70. Then he bought it back for $80 and again sold it for $90. How much money did he make in the horse-trading business? (Maier & Solem, 1952, p. 281)

When 67 groups discussed this problem, many included a member who knew the correct answer, but many of these groups nonetheless adopted the wrong solution. In this case, truth lost because knowledgeable members had a difficult time persuading the other members to adopt their solutions. In fact, some people later changed their answers to match the incorrect solution advocated by their groups (Maier & Solem, 1952; the answer, by the way, is $20). Thus, groups perform at the level of the best member of the group only if (1) the member who knows the answer shares his or her answer with the others and (2) the group adopts this answer as the group's solution (J. H. Davis, 1973; Littlepage, 1991; Lorge & Solomon, 1955; Smoke & Zajonc, 1962; E. J. Thomas & Fink, 1961).

Groups can, in even rarer instances, outperform the best member of the group. If students score 70%, 80%, 80%, and 90% individually, they may, through discussion, manage to score a perfect 100% when tested as a group. As Focus 9-3 notes, however, such *synergistic* effects are very rare in groups.

CONJUNCTIVE TASKS The Relay Test Room did not use an assembly-line procedure to build its products. With an *assembly line,* workers repeatedly perform the same task, such as adding a particular part to a product as it passes by on the conveyor belt. Because such **conjunctive tasks** are not finished until all members of the group complete their portion of the job, the speed and quality of the work depends on the group's least skilled member. The speed of a group of mountain climbers moving up the slope is determined by its slowest member. The trucks in a convoy can move no faster than the slowest vehicle (Frank & Anderson, 1971; Steiner, 1972).

Groups often take steps to improve their proficiency on conjunctive tasks. In some cases, groups may urge their weakest members to work harder, and the members with less ability may respond with increased effort—the so-called **Köhler effect** (Köhler, 1926; Messe et al., 2002; W. Stroebe, Diehl, & Abakoumkin, 1996). If the conjunctive tasks are divisible, then the group can assign

---

conjunctive task A task that can be completed successfully only if all group members contribute.

Köhler effect An increase in performance by groups working on conjunctive tasks that require persistence but little coordination of effort and is likely due to the increased effort expended by the less capable members.

FOCUS 9-3   Does Synergy Occur in Groups?

Let's form proactive synergy restructuring teams.
–Dogbert, organizational consultant in Scott Adams' cartoon *Dilbert*

Synergy is a critical concept in a number of theoretical analyses of biological, physiological, chemical, and physical systems. **Synergy** occurs whenever the combined effect of two or more discrete systems is greater than the effect of these systems when they operate independently. Two drugs, for example, combine synergistically if their effects are greater when they are taken together rather than separately. In groups, if synergy occurs, the group as a whole is greater than the sum of its parts. For example, four students taking a test may score 70%, 80%, 80%, and 90%, but when they work together—if synergy occurs—they should be able to score better than 90%. Synergy is sometimes called an **assembly bonus effect** because "the group is able to achieve collectively something which could not have been achieved by any member working alone or by a combination of individual efforts" (B. E. Collins & Guetzkow, 1964, p. 58).

Synergy in groups is relatively rare, however. When individuals work on a collective task, the whole is often much less than the sum of the parts, as members exert less effort (*social loafing*) or let others do their share of the work (*free riding*). Groups often outperform the most incompetent group member (the "better than the worst" effect), and they may perform as well as the most competent member (the "equal to the best" ef-

fect), but the "better than the best" effect occurs only rarely. Patrick Laughlin and his colleagues, for example, found evidence of synergy when groups worked on extremely complex logic problems, but only when group members who did not know the right answer could recognize the correct solution when it was proposed, and group members who knew the right answer could convince the others they were correct (Laughlin, Bonner, & Miner, 2002; Laughlin, Zander, Knievel, & Tan, 2003).

Synergy also becomes more likely when the group members are highly motivated to find the correct solution—when grades, jobs, or lives depend on finding the best solution, synergy becomes more likely. In one study, 222 classroom groups took multiple-choice tests that were counted toward their course grades. These groups often outperformed their best members, suggesting that the groups could identify new and better solutions when they worked together in collaborative groups (Michaelsen, Watson, & Black, 1989). Other investigators replicated these findings, although they concluded that the synergistic effects occurred primarily because someone in the group other than the best member knew the right answer and could correct the best member. Thus, synergistic gains in groups are not due to mystical processes whereby groups generate new knowledge, ideas, and energies; instead, they result when the group abandons incorrect answers when better ideas are proposed by someone in the group.

group members to the subcomponents that best match their skill levels. If the least competent member is matched with the easiest task, a more satisfying level of performance may be obtainable. If the least competent member is matched with a difficult subtask, group performance will, of course, decline still further (see

---

synergy The combining of two or more independent systems that yields an effect that is greater than the sum of the individual effects.

assembly bonus effect Producing an outcome as a group that is superior to the results that could have been achieved by a simple aggregation or accumulation of group members' individual efforts; a gain in performance that is caused by the way the members fit together to form the work group.

TABLE 9-3 A summary of the potential productivity of groups working on various tasks

Type of Task	Productivity Effect
Additive	*Better than the best:* The group exceeds the performance of even the best individual member.
Compensatory	*Better than most:* The group exceeds the performance of a substantial number of the individual members.
Disjunctive	*Better than average* on most tasks and *equal to the best* if the group accepts the most capable member's input as the group solution; groups rarely perform *better than the best* member (synergy, or assembly bonus effect).
Conjunctive: Unitary	*Equal to the worst:* The group equals the performance of its least capable member.
Conjunctive: Divisible	*Better than the worst:* Performance will be superior if subtasks are matched to members' capabilities.
Discretionary	*Variable:* Performance depends on the combination rules adopted by the group.

Steiner, 1972, Chapter 3, for a detailed review of group performance on divisible tasks).

DISCRETIONARY TASKS Steiner noted that a group can complete some of the tasks it faces by using a variety of combination procedures. How, for example, would a group estimate the temperature of the room in which it is working? One simple method would involve averaging individual judgments. Alternatively, members could determine whether anyone in the group was particularly good at such judgments and then use this person's answer as the group solution. Judging the temperature of the room is a **discretionary task,** because the members themselves can choose the method for combining individual inputs.

Two Heads Are Better—Sometimes

Is a group more or less capable than a single individual? Steiner's theory argued that a group's success depends, ultimately, on the resources that the group members contribute and the processes that determine how their inputs are combined and coordinated. In general, as indicated in Table 9-3, groups outperform the most skilled individual when the task is an additive one, and they generally perform better than the average group member on many other kinds of tasks (compensatory, disjunctive, divisible conjunctive with matching, and discretionary).

---

discretionary task A relatively unstructured task that can be completed by using a variety of social-combination procedures, thus leaving the methods used in its completion to the discretion of the group or group leader.

Note, however, that these predictions describe the group's *potential* level of productivity. Groups working on additive tasks, in principle, will outperform an individual. Groups that include at least one person who knows the correct answer have the potential to solve a disjunctive problem. Groups do not always reach their full potential, however, because processes unfolding within them detract from their proficiency (N. L. Kerr, MacCoun, & Kramer, 1996b; Laughlin, 1996; Shiflett, 1979). Steiner's law assumes that productivity in groups is equal to potential productivity minus losses owing to such negative processes as coordination problems and social loafing.

But cannot groups actually exceed their potential? Social loafing and coordination problems may reduce productivity, but when people work in groups, they may gain new solutions, energy, and insights into old problems that they would never have achieved if they worked as individuals. If good group processes can yield benefits for groups, then the revised law of productivity states,

$$\begin{aligned} \text{Actual productivity} = &\text{ Potential productivity} \\ &- \text{ Losses owing to faulty processes} \\ &+ \text{ Gains owing to good processes} \end{aligned}$$

The final section of this chapter examines several ways to push groups to the limits of their creative potential.

GROUP CREATIVITY

Groups seeking novel, creative solutions to problems often meet in **brainstorming** sessions (Osborn, 1957). Brainstorming groups are urged adopt a set of norms that encourage the flow of ideas among members, including,

1. *Be expressive.* Express any idea that comes to mind, no matter how strange, wild, or fanciful. Do not be constrained or timid; freewheel whenever possible.
2. *Postpone evaluation.* Do not evaluate any of the ideas in any way during the idea generation phase. All ideas are valuable.
3. *Seek quantity.* The more ideas, the better. Quantity is desired, for it increases the possibility of finding an excellent solution.
4. *Piggyback ideas.* Because all ideas belong to the group, members should try to modify and extend others' ideas whenever possible. Brainstorming is conducted in a group, so that participants can draw from one another.

Do groups that follow these rules produce more and better ideas than groups that use more traditional methods of group discussion?

---

brainstorming A method for enhancing creativity in groups that calls for heightened expressiveness, inhibited evaluation, quantity rather than quality, and deliberate attempts to build on earlier ideas.

Does Brainstorming Work?

Studies conducted in the late 1950s found that brainstorming groups out-performed individuals. Brainstorming groups also generated more ideas than **nominal groups**—groups created by having individuals work alone and then pooling their ideas. A four-person brainstorming group, for example, would not only outperform any single individual, but also four individuals whose ideas were combined to create a nominal group (a group "in name" only). However, these investigations stacked the deck against the nominal groups; brainstorming groups were told to follow the four basic brainstorming rules, whereas the individuals composing the nominal group were not given any special rules concerning creativity (D. J. Cohen, Whitmyre, & Funk, 1960; Meadow, Parnes, & Reese, 1959). When individuals working alone were better informed about the purposes of the study and the need for highly creative responses, they often offered more solutions than individuals working in groups. In one study, for example, four-person groups came up with an average of 28 ideas in their session, whereas four individuals working alone suggested an average of 74.5 ideas when their ideas were pooled. The quality of ideas was also lower in groups—when the researchers rated each idea on creativity, they found that individuals had 79.2% of the good ideas. Groups also performed more poorly even when given more time to complete the task (Diehl & Stroebe, 1987; Mullen, Johnson, & Salas, 1991).

Brainstorming groups produce fewer ideas because their members tend to loaf. Individuals do not work as hard to generate ideas as they would if they worked alone. But brainstorming groups also suffer both process losses and cognitive losses. The originators of brainstorming thought that hearing others' ideas would stimulate the flow of ideas, but the clamor of creative voices instead resulted in **production blocking.** In brainstorming groups, members must wait their turn to get the floor and express their ideas, and during that wait, they forget their ideas or decide not to express them. Hearing others is also distracting and can interfere with one's ability to do the cognitive work needed to generate ideas. Even when researchers tried to undo this blocking effect by giving brainstormers notepads and organizing their speaking turns, the groups still did not perform as well as individuals who were generating ideas alone (Diehl & Stroebe, 1987, 1991).

Evaluation apprehension can also limit the effectiveness of brainstorming groups, even though the "no evaluation" rule was designed to free members from such concerns (Diehl & Stroebe, 1987). Groups become even less effective when

---

nominal group A collection of individuals that meets only the most minimal of requirements to be considered a group, and so is a group in name only; in studies of performance, a control or baseline group created by having individuals work alone and then pooling their products.

production blocking A loss of productivity that occurs when group and procedural factors obstruct the group's progress toward its goals, particularly when individuals in a brainstorming session are delayed in stating their ideas until they can gain the floor and when group members are distracted by others' ideas and so generate fewer of their own.

an authority watches them work. Apparently, members worry that the authority may view their ideas negatively (Mullen et al., 1991). Individuals with high social anxiety are particularly unproductive brainstormers and report feeling more nervous, anxious, and worried than group members who are less anxiety prone (Camacho & Paulus, 1995).

Social comparison processes also conspire to lower standards of performance in brainstorming groups. Although undercontributors are challenged to reach the pace established by others, overcontributors tend to reduce their contributions to match the group's mediocre standards. This *social matching effect* tends to lower performance levels overall, but it can be minimized by increasing feelings of competition among members (V. Brown & Paulus, 1996; Paulus & Dzindolet, 1993; J. J. Seta, Seta, & Donaldson, 1991).

Brainstorming groups are also unproductive because they often overestimate their productivity. In many cases, groups have no standard to determine how well their group is performing, so individual members can only guess at the quantity and quality of their group's product and their personal contributions to the endeavor. These estimates, however, are often unrealistically positive, resulting in an **illusion of group productivity** (Homma, Tajima, & Hayashi, 1995; W. Stroebe, Diehl, & Abakoumkin, 1992). Members of groups working on collective tasks generally think that their group is more productive than most (Polzer, Kramer, & Neale, 1997). Nor do group members feel that they are doing less than their fair share. When members of a group trying to generate solutions to a problem were asked to estimate how many ideas they provided, each group member claimed an average of 36% of the ideas, when in reality they generated about 25% of the ideas (Paulus, Dzindolet, Poletes, & Camacho, 1993). Evidently, people are not aware that they are loafing, or they are simply unwilling to admit it (Karau & Williams, 1993).

Improving Brainstorming Sessions

Studies of brainstorming offer a clear recommendation: Do not use face-to-face deliberative groups to generate ideas unless special precautions are taken to avoid production blocking, evaluation apprehension, social matching, and social loafing. Any group can be a creative one, provided its members take certain precautions, such as,

- Members should be trained to follow brainstorming rules and be given feedback if they violate any of the basic principles. Groups that have not practiced brainstorming methods usually generate only mediocre ideas (Bouchard, 1972b; cf. M. W. Kramer, Kuo, & Dailey, 1997).
- Members should be given the opportunity to record their ideas individually during and after the session. Paul Paulus and his colleagues recom-

---

illusion of group productivity The tendency for members to believe that their groups are performing effectively.

mended a variation of brainstorming called **brainwriting**—members write down ideas on paper, and then pass the paper along to others, who add their ideas to the list (V. R. Brown & Paulus, 2002; Paulus, 2000). A postgroup session during which members generate ideas by themselves enhances idea generation (Dugosh, Paulus, Roland, & Yang, 2000).

- Members should deliberately stop talking periodically to think in silence. Pauses and silences help members collect their thoughts and improve the results (Ruback, Dabbs, & Hopper, 1984).
- Members should have plenty of time to complete the task. Groups that work under time pressure often produce more solutions initially, but the quality of those solutions is lower than if they had spent more time on the task (Kelly, Futoran, & McGrath, 1990; Kelly & Karau, 1993).
- Members should remind each other to stay focused on the task and to avoid telling stories, talking in pairs, or monopolizing the session (Paulus & Putman, 1996).
- Members' efforts should be coordinated by a skilled discussion leader (Offner, Kramer, & Winter, 1996). A skilled leader can motivate members by urging them on ("We can do this!"), correcting mistakes in the process ("Remember, the rules of brainstorming forbid criticism"), and providing them with a clear standard ("Let's reach 100 solutions!"). A facilitator can also record all ideas in full view of the participants, as exposure to others' ideas is critical for successful brainstorming (Dugosh et al., 2000).

ALTERNATIVES TO BRAINSTORMING Many individuals often feel that creativity is a rare quality, and that only some people—and some groups—are capable of generating fresh ideas and new insights into old problems. Yet nearly all groups can expand their creativity by using creativity-building techniques (Sunwolf, 2002). When stumped for new ideas, members can break up into *buzz groups,* which are small subgroups that generate ideas that can later be discussed by the entire group. Members can jot down a *bug list* of small irritations pertaining to the problem under discussion, and the group can then discuss solutions for each bug. Groups can use the *stepladder technique,* which requires asking each new member of the group to state his or her ideas before listening to the group's position (Rogelberg & O'Connor, 1998). Groups can even use an elaborate system of idea generation called **synectics,** in which a designated leader guides the group through a discussion of members' goals, wishes, and frustrations using analogies, metaphors, and fantasy. Groups that use synectics are more effective than traditional brainstorming groups (Bouchard, 1972a; Bouchard, Barsaloux, & Drauden, 1974; Bouchard, Drauden, & Barsaloux, 1974).

---

brainwriting Brainstorming sessions that involve generating new ideas in writing rather than orally, usually by asking members to add their own ideas to a circulating list.

synectics A technique for improving problem solving in groups that uses creativity-building exercises to enhance members' involvement and inventiveness.

Another approach, the **nominal group technique** (NGT), minimizes blocking and loafing by reducing interdependence among members. André L. Delbecq and Andrew H. Van de Ven developed this method by integrating face-to-face groups and nominal groups whose members do not interact (Delbecq & Van de Ven, 1971; Delbecq, Van de Ven, & Gustafson, 1975; Van de Ven & Delbecq, 1971). NGT involves four basic phases:

- *Step 1.* The group discussion leader introduces the problem or issue in a short statement that is written on a blackboard or flip chart. Once members understand the statement, they silently write ideas concerning the issue, usually working for 10 to 15 minutes.
- *Step 2.* The members share their ideas with one another in a round-robin; each person states an idea, which is given an identification letter and written beneath the issue statement, and the next individual then adds his or her contribution.
- *Step 3.* The group discusses each item, focusing primarily on clarification.
- *Step 4.* The members rank the five solutions they most prefer, writing their choices on an index card.

The leader then collects the cards, averages the rankings to yield a group decision, and informs the group of the outcome. Delbecq and Van de Ven suggested that at this point, the group leader may wish to add two steps to further improve the procedure: a short discussion of the vote (optional Step 5) and a re-voting (optional Step 6; Delbecq et al., 1975).

NGT is an effective alternative to traditional brainstorming (Gustafson, Shukla, Delbecq, & Walster, 1973; Van de Ven, 1974). Van de Ven (1974), for example, found that when groups discuss issues that tend to elicit highly emotional arguments, NGT groups produce more ideas and also report feeling more satisfied with the process than unstructured groups. The ranking and voting procedures also provide for an explicit mathematical solution that fairly weights all members' inputs and provides a balance between task concerns and socioemotional forces.

ELECTRONIC BRAINSTORMING (EBS) Group members can also avoid some of the disadvantages of traditional brainstorming sessions by using electronic mail, computer-based bulletin boards, and electronic conferencing (online discussions with shared information screens) to pool ideas over wide distances and at different times (Hollingshead & McGrath, 1995). **Electronic brainstorming** (EBS), offers group members a way to generate ideas even when spatially separated. Using software designed specifically for use by groups (called *group decision*

---

nominal group technique (NGT) A group performance method wherein a face-to-face group session is prefaced by a nominal-group phase during which individuals work alone to generate ideas.

electronic brainstorming (EBS) Generating ideas and solving problems using computer-based communication methods such as online discussions and real-time e-mail rather than face-to-face sessions.

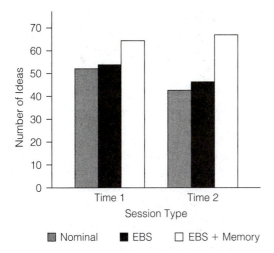

FIGURE 9-5

Are computer-based groups better at brainstorming than individuals? In most prior studies of brainstorming, face-to-face groups did not generate as many ideas as individuals working together whose ideas were then combined in a "nominal group." But when groups brainstormed via computer (*electronic brainstorming; EBS*), they produced as many ideas as nominal groups. Their creativity was further enhanced if members were told to pay attention to the ideas that other group members contributed to the discussion (the "memory" condition). The effect held at Time 2, when participants completed the task again as individuals.

support systems or *groupware*), group members seated at individual computers can share information rapidly and more completely. One program, *GroupSystems,* opens up several windows on each group member's computer—one window is for entering ideas, another displays all the ideas, and another shows a counter that tracks how many ideas the group has generated.

EBS eliminates some of the problems that rob face-to-face groups of their productive potential. Because members can type in ideas simultaneously, EBS reduces production blocking. EBS minimizes interpersonal pressures, particularly if brainstormers are not identified (Gallupe & Cooper, 1993; M. C. Roy, Gauvin, & Limayem, 1996). EBS also enhances one of the key features of brainstorming—idea building—for online exposure to others' ideas tends to stimulate the production of additional novel ideas (Paulus & Yang, 2000).

Groups using EBS, although they are freed from some of the constraints created by face-to-face meetings, still display problems of social coordination and motivation. Computer-mediated discussions can overwhelm group members with a flood of information to process (Nagasundaram & Dennis, 1993). Social matching can also occur in groups if members know how many ideas each group member has contributed (M. C. Roy et al., 1996). EBS sessions are also not particularly productive if the group members become so focused on generating ideas that they ignore the ideas generated by other members. When researchers arranged for groups and individuals to use *GroupSystems* to generate solutions to a problem, they discovered that EBS groups generated, on average, only two more ideas than nominal groups (see Figure 9-5). However, when the EBS group members were told to pay close attention to the other group members' ideas—because their memory of the ideas expressed by others would be tested later—then EBS groups generated, on average, 13 more ideas than nominal groups. This substantial gain also increased the number of ideas that the group members could generate when they worked alone in a second, individualized brainstorming session (Dugosh, Paulus, Roland, & Yang, 2000). These findings suggest that technology can improve many aspects of group functioning but is no panacea for basic problems of social coordination and motivation that occur whenever people use groups to achieve goals (Dennis & Valacich, 1999; Pinsonneault, Barki, Gallupe, & Hoppen, 1999).

SUMMARY IN OUTLINE

❖ **Do people work better alone or with others?**

1. Triplett's 1898 study of *social facilitation* confirmed that people work more efficiently when other people are present. Social facilitation occurs for both *coaction* tasks and audience tasks.

2. As Zajonc noted, social facilitation usually occurs only for simple tasks that require dominant responses, whereas social interference or impairment occurs for complex tasks that require nondominant responses. Studies of a variety of species have supported Zajonc's conclusion.

3. Researchers have linked social facilitation to several personal and interpersonal processes, including arousal, evaluation apprehension, and distraction (see Table 9-1).
   - Zajonc's *drive theory* argues that the mere presence of a member of the same species raises the performer's arousal level by touching off a basic alertness response.
   - Cottrell's *evaluation apprehension theory* proposes that the presence of others increases arousal only when individuals feel that they are being evaluated. *Self-presentation theory* suggests that this apprehension is greatest when performance may threaten the group member's public image.
   - The *distraction-conflict theory* emphasizes the mediational role played by distraction, attentional conflict, and increased motivation.

4. Eating in groups, some forms of prejudice, reactions to *electronic performance monitoring,* and the performance of *study groups* can all be explained as forms of social facilitation.

❖ **Do people work as hard when in groups as they do when working by themselves?**

1. Few groups reach their potential, because negative group processes (*process losses*) place limits on their performance.

2. Groups become less productive as they increase in size. This *Ringelmann effect* is caused by coordination losses and by *social loafing*—the reduction of individual effort when people work in a group.

3. Latané and his colleagues identified the relative contributions of coordination losses and social loafing to the Ringelmann effect by studying groups and pseudogroups producing noise.

4. Social loafing depends on a number of group-level factors, including,
   - Identifiability: When people feel as though their level of effort cannot be ascertained because the task is a collective one, then social loafing becomes likely. But when people feel that they are being evaluated, they tend to exert more effort, and their productivity increases (leading to social facilitation if the task is easy).
   - *Free riding:* Individuals in collective work sometimes work less, knowing that others will compensate for their

lack of productivity. They also work less to avoid being the "sucker" who works too hard (the *sucker effect*).

- Goals: Groups that set clear, challenging goals outperform groups whose members have no clear standard to evaluate their performance.
- Involvement: Loafing is less likely when people work at exciting, challenging, and involving tasks. According to Karau and Williams's *collective effort model* (CEM), such tasks reduce loafing and even trigger *social compensation* (highly involved group members work harder to compensate for the poor performance of others in the group).
- Identity: According to social identity theory, when individuals derive their identity from their membership in a group, social loafing is replaced by social laboring as members expend extra effort for their groups.

❖ **When are groups more productive than individuals?**

1. Steiner's taxonomy of group tasks argued that group effectiveness depends in large part on the *group composition* and the type of task the group is attempting.
   - Performance depends on members' knowledge, skills, and abilities (*KSAs*).
   - Highly effective groups tend to be staffed by highly effective individuals, both in terms of specific task skills and general social skills.
   - Group diversity is positively associated with performance. However, diverse groups may lack cohesion, because their members may perceive each other as dissimilar. If cohesion is essential for the group to succeed, a diverse group will be disadvantaged.
   - Sex differences in group performance are minimal.

- Groups that include a lone representative of a particular social category (tokens, or solos) may encounter problems of fairness, influence, and so on. Studies of performing groups indicate that the group's history and the larger social context in which the group is embedded influence the impact of a group's gender heterogeneity on performance.

2. *Task demands* depend on the task's divisibility (*divisible tasks* versus *unitary tasks*), the type of output desired (*maximizing tasks* versus *optimizing tasks*), and the social combination rule used to combine individual members' inputs.
   - Groups outperform individuals on *additive tasks* and *compensatory tasks*.
   - Groups perform well on *disjunctive tasks* if the group includes at least one individual who knows the correct solution. The truth-wins rule usually holds for groups working on Eureka problems, whereas the truth-supported-wins rule holds for groups working on non-Eureka problems.
   - Groups rarely perform better than the best member (*synergy*, or *assembly bonus effect*).
   - Groups perform poorly on *conjunctive tasks*, unless less skilled members increase their efforts (the *Köhler effect*) or the task can be subdivided, with subtasks matched to members' abilities.
   - The effectiveness of groups working on *discretionary tasks* covaries with the method chosen to combine individuals' inputs (see Table 9-3).

❖ **What steps can be taken to encourage creativity in groups?**

1. *Brainstorming* groups strive to find creative solutions to problems by following four basic rules that encourage the

flow of ideas among members: "Be expressive," "Postpone evaluation," "Seek quantity," and "Piggyback ideas."

2. **Brainstorming groups rarely generate as many ideas as individuals in *nominal groups*.** Their less than expected performance has been linked to social loafing, *production blocking,* social matching, and the *illusion of productivity.*

3. Other methods, including *brainwriting, synectics,* the *nominal group technique (NGT),* and *electronic brainstorming (EBS),* offer advantages over traditional brainstorming.

For More Information

Chapter Case: The Relay Test Room

■ *The Industrial Worker,* by Thomas North Whitehead (1938), provides a thorough analysis of early studies of industrial productivity, including the women of the Relay Test Room.

Social Facilitation and Loafing

■ "Social Facilitation from Triplett to Electronic Performance Monitoring," by John R. Aiello and Elizabeth A. Douthitt (2001), reviews the literature on social facilitation before offering an integrative model of performance processes in groups.

■ "Group Performance and Decision Making," a chapter in the *Annual Review of Psychology,* by Norbert L. Kerr and R. Scott Tindale (2004), reviews much of the recent work on performance in both simple and complex groups.

Coordination, Independence, and Performance

■ *Group Process and Productivity,* by Ivan D. Steiner (1972), is a timeless analysis of groups that includes entire chapters examining the relationship between group composition, motivation, size, and performance.

■ *Groups That Work (and Those That Don't),* edited by J. Richard Hackman (1990), offers endless insights into group performance by documenting the causes and consequences of success and failure in over two dozen management groups, task forces, performing groups, and other assorted work groups.

■ *Motives and Goals in Groups,* by Alvin Zander (1971; with a new introduction, 1996), systematically examines the intricate relationship between individual goals, group goals, and performance.

■ *Organizing Genius: The Secrets of Creative Collaboration,* by Warren Bennis and Patricia Ward Biederman (1997), offers a close look at seven of the most productive groups of the 20th century, including Disney Studios, Xerox's Palo Alto Research Center (PARC), and Lockheed's Skunk Works.

■ *Team Performance Assessment and Measurement: Theory, Methods, and Applications,* edited by Michael T. Brannick, Eduardo Salas, and Carolyn Prince (1997), is a compendium of cutting-edge instruments and techniques that can be used to measure a group's effectiveness.

Media Resources

 Visit the Group Dynamics companion website at http://psychology.wadsworth .com/forsyth4e to access online resources for your book, including quizzes, flash cards, web links, and more!

DECISION MAKING

CHAPTER OVERVIEW

People turn to groups when they must solve problems and make decisions. Groups often make better decisions than individuals, for groups can process more information more thoroughly. But groups, like individuals, sometimes make mistakes. When a group sacrifices rationality in its pursuit of unity, the decisions it makes can yield calamitous consequences.

❖ Why make decisions in groups?

❖ What problems undermine the effectiveness of decision making in groups?

❖ Why do groups make riskier decisions than individuals?

❖ What is groupthink, and how can it be prevented?

CHAPTER OUTLINE

The Bay of Pigs Planners: Disastrous Decisions and Groupthink

In October 1962, the world stood on the brink of nuclear war. The Union of Soviet Socialist Republics was installing weapons of mass destruction on the island of Cuba, located just off the coast of Florida. U.S. military and political experts, led by President John F. Kennedy, crafted a series of responses to this threat and, during 13 tense days, negotiated with the Russians to dismantle the bases. These experts considered the issues, debated possible solutions, and disagreed over strategies. They finally recommended a plan that included a naval blockade of all Cuban ports. The strategy worked, and the Russians agreed to dismantle the weapon systems.

This same group, less than one year earlier, had made one of the greatest group blunders of all time. Kennedy and his advisors (see Figure 10-1), guided by the Central Intelligence Agency (CIA), developed a detailed plan to invade Cuba in hopes of overthrowing that country's government. The plan assumed that a squad of well-trained troops could capture and defend a strip of land in the Bahía de Cochinos (Bay of Pigs) on the southern coast of Cuba. The men would then launch raids and encourage civilian revolt in Havana. But nothing went according to plan. The entire attacking force was killed or captured within days, and the U.S. government had to send food and supplies to Cuba to ransom them back. Group expert Irving Janis described the decision as one of the "worst fiascoes ever perpetrated by a responsible government" (1972, p. 14), and President Kennedy lamented, "How could I have been so stupid?" (quoted in Wyden, 1979, p. 8).

The Bay of Pigs planners were not unique. Like many other groups, they faced a problem needing a solution. Through discussion, the members pooled their

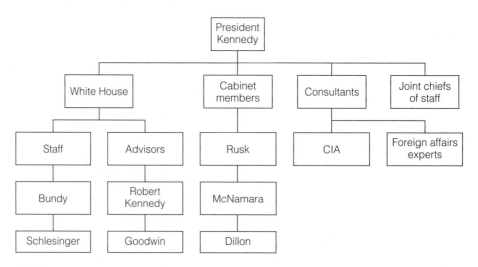

FIGURE 10-1

Who made the decision? The members of the committee who planned the Bay of Pigs invasion included many excellent decision makers, but when they combined in the group, they failed to use their skills to critically examine the plan.

expertise and information. They sought out information from available sources, and they thoroughly weighed alternatives and considered the ramifications of their actions. When their alternatives were narrowed down to two—to invade or not to invade—they made a decision as a group. But the committee was typical in another way. Like so many other groups, it made the wrong decision.

We owe much to groups. Groups put the first humans on the moon, built the Empire State Building, performed the first symphony, and invented the personal computer. But groups also killed innocent civilians at My Lai, marketed thalidomide, doomed the space shuttles *Challenger* and *Columbia,* and piloted Air Florida's Flight 90 into Washington's 14th Street Bridge. Groups have great strengths, but their limitations can only be ignored at great risk.

GROUPS AND DECISIONS

On February 3, 1961, President Kennedy was given the secret document JCSM-57-61, "Military Evaluation of the CIA Paramilitary Plan—Cuba" (Wyden, 1979, p. 90). It suggested that the United States should arm and train a group of Cuban exiles, who would then return to their homeland and lead a revolt against that country's current leader, Fidel Castro. Kennedy could have studied the report and made a decision at that moment. Instead, he turned the decision over to a group rather than make the choice alone.

Individual and Group Decision Making

In office buildings, executives hold conferences to solve problems of management and production; at the dinner table, families talk over moving to a new neighborhood; in courthouses, juries weigh evidence to determine guilt and innocence; in schools, parents meet with teachers to discuss their son's or daughter's progress; on the battlefield, a combat squad identifies a target and plans an attack. In these and thousands of other similar settings, interdependent individuals make decisions in groups.

Why this reliance on groups? People turn to groups because, in most cases, groups are better at choosing, judging, estimating, and problem solving than are individuals (Stasser & Dietz-Uhler, 2001). Investment groups outperform single investors in the stock market. Groups form more accurate perceptions of people than do individuals (Ruscher & Duval, 1998). Teams of physicians making a diagnosis are more accurate than single physicians. Students taking a test in groups get better grades than individual students (Zimbardo, Butler, & Wolfe, 2003). Burglars who work in groups are less likely to be caught than are thieves who work alone (Warr, 2002). Even very powerful leaders—presidents of the United States, for example—rarely make decisions without consulting others. Instead, people rely on groups, for they assume that the weighty problems that they must handle on a daily basis would overwhelm a lone individual. Apparently "none of us alone is as smart as all of us together" (D. G. Myers, 2002, p. 317).

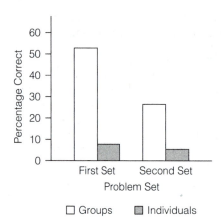

FIGURE 10-2

Do groups make better decisions than individuals? When Marjorie E. Shaw (1932) arranged for people to work either alone or in groups on a series of difficult problems, she found that individuals solved fewer of the problems correctly than did groups. When she reversed her procedure for a second set of problems by having those who worked alone join groups and those who had been in groups work alone, she once more found that groups outperformed individuals.

Researcher Marjorie E. Shaw (1932) demonstrated the superiority of groups by asking 21 individuals and five 4-person groups to work on several problems, including the famous missionary–cannibal dilemma:

> Three missionaries and three cannibals are on one side of the river and want to cross to the other side by means of a boat that can only hold two persons at a time. All the missionaries can row, but only one cannibal can row. For obvious reasons, the missionaries must never be outnumbered by the cannibals, under any circumstances or at any time, except where no missionaries are present at all. How many crossings will be necessary to transport the six people across the river?

When the groups and individuals finished the first set of problems, Shaw switched them—those who worked alone initially solved the problems in groups and those who initially worked in groups solved the problems individually.

Shaw's findings, summarized in part in Figure 10-2, indicated that groups outperformed individuals on both sets of problems. Groups not only generated more correct solutions, but they were also better at detecting errors in calculations and faulty inferences about the problems. If a group member recommended a solution that was inaccurate, groups were more likely to reject that solution. Groups, when they did make mistakes, also erred later in the decision process than did individuals, in part because groups were more proficient at noticing and correcting errors than were individuals. Groups, however, took longer to complete the task than did individuals.

(The answer to the missionary–cannibal problem, by the way, is 13 crossings! If we assume that M1, M2, and M3 are the three missionaries, C1 and C2 are the two non-rowing cannibals, and CR is the cannibal who can row, then the crossings are as follows: M1 and C1 cross, M1 returns, CR and C2 cross, CR returns, M1 and M2 cross, M1 and C1 return, CR and M1 cross, M1 and C2 return, M1 and M3 cross, CR returns, CR and C1 cross, CR returns, CR and C2 cross. Note, too, that this study was conducted by Marjorie E. Shaw—no relation to Marvin E. Shaw, who also studied groups and whose classic 1981 text, *Group Dynamics,* is this book's intellectual progenitor.)

The relative superiority of groups to individuals depends on a variety of situational and task factors. Groups, not unexpectedly, do not perform well when tasks are very difficult, complex, unfamiliar, or uninteresting to members (M. E. Shaw, 1981). When time is limited, groups sometimes perform poorly, although they are often remarkably resilient to such pressures (Karau & Kelly, 1992, Kelly & Karau, 1999). Group effectiveness also depends, as Patrick Laughlin and his colleagues convincingly argued, on the extent to which the task has a *demonstrably correct solution.* **Intellective tasks,** to use Laughlin's (1980) terms, yield solutions that can be objectively reviewed and judged as right or wrong, but **judgmental tasks** require evaluative judgments for which no correct answer can be authoritatively determined. Logic and math problems are intellective tasks, whereas a jury's decision in a trial or the issues decided the Bay of Pigs planners would be judgmental tasks. Groups are more clearly superior when performing intellective tasks than when performing judgmental tasks (Laughlin, 1996, 1999; Laughlin, Bonner, & Miner, 2002; Laughlin, Zander, Knievel, & Tan, 2003).

The Anatomy of Group Decision Making

What is the secret to groups' superiority in making decisions? A **functional theory of group decision making** suggests that skilled decision-making groups are more likely to make use of group procedures that enhance the way they gather, analyze, and weigh information. Although no two groups reach their decisions in precisely the same way (and no two theorists agree on *the* definitive list of decision functions), the stages shown in Figure 10-3 often appear when groups make decisions. The group defines the problem, sets goals, and develops a strategy in the *orientation phase.* Next, during the *discussion phase,* the group gathers information about the situation and, if a decision must be made, identifies and considers options. In the *decision phase,* the group chooses its solution by reaching consensus, voting, or using some other social decision process. In the final, *implementation phase,* the decision must be put into action and the impact of the decision assessed. Groups that follow these four stages, as noted hereafter, are more likely to make better decisions than those who sidestep or mishandle information at any particular stage (Hirokawa & Salazar, 1999; Wittenbaum et al., 2004).

---

intellective task A project, problem, or other type of task with results that can be evaluated objectively using some normative criterion, such as a mathematics problem with a known solution or the spelling of a word.

judgmental task A project, problem, or other type of task with results that cannot be evaluated objectively because there are no clear criteria to judge them against.

functional theory of group decision making A conceptual analysis of the steps or processes that groups generally follow when making a decision, with a focus on the intended purpose of each step or process in the overall decision-making sequence.

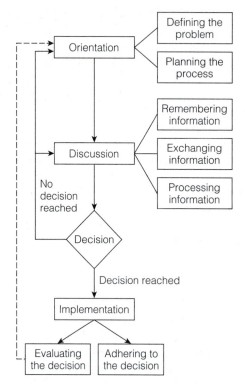

FIGURE 10-3

How does a group make a decision? Although no two groups reach their decisions in precisely the same way, many groups, after a brief orientation period, discuss the matter, make a decision, and then implement it.

ORIENTATION During the orientation phase, groups create the organization for their actions. They identify objectives, set goals, develop strategies, make plans, and select tactics. All this planning provides the blueprint for "the order in which a sequence of operations is to be performed" (G. A. Miller, Galanter, & Pribram, 1960, p.16) and so structures actions effectively. Key components of this orientation phase include,

- Clarifying the group's desire to identify the best solution possible
- Identifying the resources needed to make the decision
- Enumerating any obstacles that must be overcome or avoided
- Specifying the procedures to be followed in gathering information and making the decision
- Establishing ground rules for meetings (paraphrased from Gouran & Hirokawa, 1996, p. 76–77)

One particularly valuable outcome of this period of orientation is the development of a **shared mental model**—a mental representation of the problem

---

shared mental model Knowledge, expectations, conceptualizations, and other cognitive representations that members of a group have in common pertaining to the group's members, tasks, procedures, and resources.

that is held by all the members of the group (Klimoski & Mohammed, 1994). Armed with a shared plan, groups no longer react to situations; rather, they proactively control situations so that their expectations are affirmed.

A group may still function without a shared mental model, but when group members adopt the same general conceptualization of their tasks, goals, and procedures, their final choices reflect these criteria rather than the group members' personal biases (Tindale, Meisenhelder, Dykema-Engblade, & Hogg, 2001). When groups worked on a role-playing problem involving survival on the Moon, the only factor that distinguished successful groups from failing groups was the number of strategy-planning remarks made during the group discussion (Hirokawa, 1980). In a study of six conferences in which panels of experts evaluated new medical technologies, participants were more satisfied when the decisional procedures had been discussed in advance (Vinokur, Burnstein, Sechrest, & Wortman, 1985). Similarly, in a project that experimentally manipulated the use of process planning, groups were more productive when they were encouraged to discuss their performance strategies before working on a task requiring intermember coordination (Hackman, Brousseau, & Weiss, 1976). Process planning also leads to more positive ratings of group atmosphere, more verbal interaction, greater satisfaction with leadership, and more flexibility in performing tasks (Hackman & Morris, 1975).

The more time a group spends on orientation, the better its overall performance, but group members rarely show much interest in process planning (Tindale et al., 2001). When a group member raises questions about planning, very rarely do any of the other group members respond (Hackman & Morris, 1975). When groups are given a task, their first tendency is to begin their task rather than consider process-related issues (Varela, 1971). Group members also believe that planning activities are less important than actual task activities, even when they are cautioned that proper planning is critical (Shure, Rogers, Larsen, & Tassone, 1962). This belief stems, in part, from the group members' willingness to apply whatever method they used in the past to current and future projects (Hackman & Morris, 1975). Even Kennedy's group moved through the orientation stage too hastily. Kennedy had just taken over the office of president, and his advisors had not worked together before, so the members should have spent several meetings talking about the problem and the strategy they would take in solving it. Instead, the planners immediately began to discuss logistics and operations (Stern 1997).

DISCUSSION If information is the lifeblood of decision making, then the discussion phase must be the heart of that process (Kowert, 2002). During the discussion stage, group members gather and process the information needed to make a decision. As Robert Freed Bales (1955) and his colleagues discovered when they watched and recorded groups at work, more than 30% of all comments made by members are expressions of opinion, evaluations, and analysis of issues. Group members also share information about the problem during a discussion (18% of all comments) and express agreement (16.5%). Members also express disagreement with others, release tension in various ways (e.g., by making humorous remarks), and ask for more information and clarification. Communication within the group peaks during this phase.

What is the value of all this discussion and debate? An *information processing approach* to decisions assumes that people strive, in most cases, to make good decisions by (1) acquiring the information that is relevant to the issue at hand and (2) processing that information thoroughly, so that its implications are clearly understood. A **collective information processing approach** to decision making also assumes that people seek out and process relevant information, but that they do this cognitive work during the group discussion. Three information processing gains that result from discussion are noted in Figure 10-3—improved memory for information, increased information exchanged, and more thorough processing of information (Hinsz, Tindale, & Vollrath, 1997; J. R. Larson & Christensen, 1993; Propp, 1999).

First, two heads are better than one because groups have superior memories for information relative to individuals (see Focus 10-1). Schlesinger knew a great deal about international relations, but he could not compete with the **collective memory** of the Bay of Pigs planners (N. K. Clark, Stephenson, & Kniveton, 1990). The president's planners required a vast array of information about Cuba, Castro, the invasion force, weaponry, and even the terrain of the beach where the troops would land. These informational demands would have overwhelmed a lone individual, but the group's greater memory resources were sufficient for the task at hand. *Cross-cueing* and *transactive memory systems* may also enhance members' ability to retrieve important information. When group members discuss information, they may give each other cues that help them remember things that they would not recall if working alone. This process is known as **cross-cueing.** For example, President Kennedy may not remember where the force will land, but perhaps he will say, "I think it's a bay." This cue may trigger someone else's memories, so that the name "Bay of Pigs" is retrieved by the group, even though none of the members could generate this name individually (Meudell, Hitch, & Boyle, 1995; Meudell, Hitch, & Kirby, 1992; Stasson & Bradshaw, 1995). **Transactive memory systems** also enhance group memory by dividing up information among the members. In the committee, for example,

---

collective information processing model A general theoretical explanation of group decision making assuming that groups use communication and discussion among members to gather and process the information needed to formulate decisions, choices, and judgments.

collective memory A group's combined memories, including each member's memories, the group's shared mental models, and transactive memory systems.

cross-cueing The enhancement of recall that occurs during group discussion when the statements made by group members serve as cues for the retrieval of information from the memories of other group members.

transactive memory system A process by which information to be remembered is distributed to various members of the group who can then be relied on to provide that information when it is needed.

FOCUS 10-1   Why Do Groups Keep Minutes?

The palest ink is better than the best memory.
–Japanese Proverb

Groups' collective memories are shared reservoirs of information held in common by two or more members of a group. Groups remember more than individuals, because groups draw on more memories. When individuals and groups take a standard memory test—for example, a brief story or a list of 100 words is read aloud to test participants who are later asked to remember the information—groups remember more of the information than the individuals.

But groups are not mnemonic marvels. When researchers compared the memories of collaborative groups, nominal groups (groups of noninteracting individuals), and individuals, collaborative groups outperformed both the average single individual and the best single individual. Collaborative groups did not, however, perform as well as nominal groups, and the groups displayed many of the characteristics typically seen in individual memory. Individuals, for example, generally have better memory for information that they process more deeply, and better memory for pictures than for words. Groups displayed these same tendencies when their memories were tested (M. S. Weldon & Bellinger, 1997). Groups also reported words that were not on the original list, and their memories were also less well structured (Finlay, Hitch, & Meudel, 2000).

Groups do not remember as much as they could because members free-ride and loaf. As noted in Chapter 9, when members know that others will be on hand should they forget any details, they put less effort into processing and storing the information. But even when factors that produce loafing are eliminated—members are made identifiable, each individual is promised a substantial reward for performing well, and group cohesion is high—three-person groups who worked together at a memory task still remembered less information than three individuals whose memories were tested when alone (M. S. Weldon, Blair, & Huebsch, 2000). Apparently, the complexity of the group setting disrupts group members' ability to organize information in memory and subsequently retrieve that information. In consequence, collaborating groups perform particularly poorly when trying to remember badly organized information, but perform equally to noninteracting (nominal) groups when trying to remember organized information (Basden, Basden, Bryner, & Thomas, 1997).

Groups' memories are improved if members can talk to each other about the information in a joint recall session. When researchers tested group members' memories for a list of words, groups outperformed individuals if the members were given a chance to talk over their decision and make a single choice that would represent the group answer (S. E. Clark, Hori, Putnam, & Martin, 2000). Groups also enhance their collective memories by redistributing information among members through discussion, particularly during the early stages of the discussion process (Bangerter, 2002). They achieve this redistribution of information procedurally by selecting one individual in the group to act as the *recorder* or *secretary*. This individual is charged with keeping the group's *minutes,* which are a written record of the group's deliberations and decisions. Although few group members relish the role of recorder, without minutes, details of the group's actions may be forgotten.

the CIA was recognized as the source of all information about the invasion force, so other group members spent little effort deliberately storing information on that topic. When anyone needed to check a fact pertaining to the commandos, they turned to the CIA and their memory stores (Hollingshead, 2001a; Wegner, Giuliano, & Hertel, 1985).

Second, groups have more information than do individuals, and this information is exchanged through discussion. The CIA operatives who met with the Bay of Pigs planners knew all about the weapons, tactics, and the morale of Castro's troops, but Dean Rusk was an expert on the relationship between Cuba and the Soviet Union. When they joined together, they could pool their individual expertise to form the group's decisions. (Unfortunately, no one in the group knew that the Bay of Pigs was Castro's favorite fishing spot, so he was thoroughly familiar with ever path, road, and hill in the area.) In a team-based trivia contest, one player may know a great deal about sports, and another may know about literature, so when they join forces, they can correctly answer questions about both sports and literature. Similarly, when students are permitted to take examinations as a group, they usually outperform individuals, for the student who is stumped by the question, "Name four common phases of group decision making," may be saved by a group member who remembers the mnemonic acronym ODD-I: Orientation, Discussion, Decision, and Implementation (Michaelsen, Watson, & Black, 1989; Stasson & Bradshaw, 1995). Groups can also *get* more information than individuals can, if more information is needed. In many cases, decision-making groups are staffed by individuals who have widely differing experiences, backgrounds, and positions, so each one can acquire a unique set of information that they can contribute to the discussion (Cummings, 2004).

Third, groups also process the information they have more thoroughly through discussion. Members ask questions, and others offer answers. Alternative options are discussed, and the strengths and weaknesses of each option are considered. Group members critique each others' ideas and offer corrections when they note errors. Members dialogue with one another, sharing viewpoints and seeking a shared meaning. Ideas are debated, with some group members seeking to convince others that their position is better. The group members also monitor their work and intervene as necessary to bring the group back on task. Most group discussions also include an interpersonal element that complements the focus on the work to be done (Barge, 2002). Decision-making groups do not only share and evaluate information, but they also encourage each other, express commitment to the group, and help each other (Jehn & Shah, 1997; Weingart & Weldon, 1991; E. Weldon, Jehn, & Pradhan, 1991).

Just as the orientation period is essential to effective decision making, so the time spent in active discussion increases the quality of the group's decision (R. Katz & Tushman, 1979). When researchers monitored group members' communications while working on a problem that could be solved only by properly sequencing individuals' responses, they found that the group's use of essential information through discussion proved to be the best predictor of success (Lanzetta & Roby, 1960). Moreover, project groups in a college class were more successful when members actively discussed their task (Harper & Askling, 1980). Groups working on *collective induction problems*—tasks that require a cycle of hypothesis generation and testing—performed best when members discussed the problems actively and focused their analysis on evidence rather than on hypotheses (Laughlin & Hollingshead, 1995). Flight crews that confront sudden emergencies often overcome the problem if they share information with one another; but those crews that do not take advantage of group discussion often make errors in judgment that are not corrected by the group (Paris, Salas, & Cannon-Bowers, 1999; see Focus 8-1). Studies of online groups have found that the online format substantially hampers the group's ability to make an informed decision if the rate of information exchange is too low and too slow (Baltes, Dickson, Sherman, Bauer, & LaGanke, 2002). When researchers watched groups make decisions, they found that information sharing (talking a great deal, free expression of ideas, thoughts, and feelings) and critical evaluation of ideas (critically evaluating each other's ideas or works, differences of opinion, disagreement among group members, disagreements on who should do what or how something should be done) were correlated with judgmental accuracy (Jehn & Shah, 1997).

DECIDING By early April, the Bay of Pigs committee was ready to make its decision. The members had spent months examining the CIA's plan, and even though many questions remained unanswered, the group could delay no longer. Word of the plan had leaked to the press, and the group was worried that Castro might begin to shore up his defenses. They needed to make up their minds.

A **social decision scheme** is a group's method for combining individual members' inputs in a single group decision. In many cases, the social decision scheme is an implicit one. The *truth-wins rule,* noted in Chapter 9, is one such decision rule, as is the more frequently observed *majority-rules model.* This social decision scheme predicts that any decision favored by more than 50% of the group members will be selected by the group as its final decision, even in the absence of any explicit, formalized rule about how the final decision is to be made (J. H. Davis, 1996; Laughlin, 1999).

In other cases, however, the group may adopt an explicit social decision scheme that describes the procedures that the group must follow when making its decisions. Some common social decision schemes are *delegation, statistical aggregation, voting, consensus* (discussion to unanimity), and *random choice.*

- *Delegating decisions:* An individual or subgroup within the group makes the decision for the entire group. Under a *dictatorship* scheme, the chairperson or some other authority makes the final decision with or without input from the group members. When an *oligarchy* operates in the group, a coalition speaks for the entire group. Other forms of delegation include asking an expert to answer or forming a subcommittee made up of a few members to study the issue and reach a conclusion (Smoke & Zajonc, 1962).
- *Statisticized decisions:* Each group member makes his or her decision individually (either before or after a group discussion) and these private recommendations are averaged together to yield a nominal group decision.

---

social decision scheme A strategy or rule used in a group to select a single alternative from among various alternatives proposed and discussed during the group's deliberations, including explicitly acknowledged decision rules (e.g., the group accepts the alternative favored by the majority) and implicit decisional procedures (e.g., the group accepts the alternative favored by the most powerful members).

For example, to choose among five possible candidates for a job opening, each member of the hiring committee could rank the candidates from 1 (the best) to 5, and the group could then average these rankings.

- *Plurality decisions:* Members express their individual preferences by voting, either publicly or by secret ballot. In most cases, the group selects the alternative favored by the majority of the members (50% or more), but in some cases, a more substantial plurality (such as a two-thirds majority) is needed before a decision becomes final. Some groups also use ranking methods, with more points awarded to alternatives that are ranked higher than others (the *Borda count method*).

- *Unanimous decisions (consensus):* The group discusses the issue until it reaches unanimous agreement without voting (although the group may take a series of straw polls to gauge the group's general sentiments on the issue).

- *Random decisions:* The group abandons reason altogether and leaves the final decision to chance. If the group cannot reach consensus or is bewildered by the problems it faces, members may decide by flipping a coin.

How the group makes its decision influences the group members' satisfaction and willingness to act on the decision. *Autocratic* procedures, such as mandates from the group's leadership, may leave members feeling disenfranchised and ignored. When groups average individual members' inputs, all the group members' opinions are considered, and this procedure often cancels out errors or extreme opinions. But a group that just averages without discussion may make an arbitrary decision that fails to satisfy any of the group members, all of whom may end up feeling little responsibility for implementing the decision. Still, autocratic and averaging methods save time, as the group need not hold a face-to-face meeting.

Voting, at least in Western groups, is by far the most frequently chosen method for reaching a decision. Voting is a way of making a clear-cut decision, even on issues that deeply divide the group. This strength, however, is also a drawback, for when the vote is close, some members of the group may feel alienated and defeated. In consequence, they become dissatisfied with membership and are less likely to follow through on the decision (Castore & Murnighan, 1978). Voting can also lead to internal politics, as members get together before meetings to apply pressure, form coalitions, and trade favors to ensure the passage of proposals that they favor. Also, if the vote is taken publicly, individuals may conform to previously stated opinions rather than expressing their personal views (J. H. Davis, Stasson, Ono, & Zimmerman, 1988).

Some groups avoid these drawbacks by relying on *consensus* to make decisions. Consensus decision schemes are involving and often lead to high levels of commitment to the decision and to the group. Unfortunately, groups may not be able to reach consensus on all issues. Consensus building takes a good deal of time, and if rushed, the strategy can misfire. In many cases, too, groups explicitly claim to be using the unanimity scheme, but the implicit goal may be something less than unanimity. When nine people on a jury all favor a verdict of guilty, for example, the three remaining jurors may hold back information that they believe would cause dissent within the group. Thus, a consensus decision scheme is not necessarily superior to the other schemes (Kameda & Sugimori, 1993; Kameda, Takezawa, Tindale, & Smith, 2002).

Groups often prefer to reach consensus on questions that require sensitive judgments, such as issues of morality—but they favor a majority-rules voting scheme on problem-solving tasks (M. F. Kaplan & Miller, 1987). Members also prefer procedures that increase their sense of control over the discussion and outcome (Folger, 1993; Gilliland, 1994; J. Greenberg, 1994). People are more likely to regard a decision as a fair one if the decisional procedures are implemented "(a) consistently, (b) without self-interest, (c) on the basis of accurate information, (d) with opportunities to correct the decision, (e) with the interests of all concerned parties represented, and (f) following moral and ethical standards" (Brockner & Wiesenfeld, 1996, p. 189; Leventhal, Karuza, & Fry, 1980). Self-interest also plays a large role in shaping members' reactions to their group's decisions. When our group's decisions benefit us, we are quick to say that the decision is a just and wise one, even when unfair procedures were used. But if the decision harms us, we are far more likely to cry "foul" when the group used questionable methods to reach its decision (Brockner & Wiesenfeld, 1996). Even a dictator's judgment satisfies group members when it coincides with their own (C. E. Miller, Jackson, Mueller, & Schersching, 1987).

IMPLEMENTATION   When the die is cast and the decision made, two significant pieces of work remain to be done. First, the decision must be *implemented*. If a union decides to strike, it must put its strike plan into effect. If a city planning commission decides that a new highway bypass is needed, it must take the steps necessary to begin construction. If an advisory committee approves an invasion, its members must mobilize the necessary military forces. Second, the quality of the decision must be *evaluated*. Was the strike necessary? Did we put the highway where it was needed the most? Was it really such a good idea to invade Cuba?

If the group's decision pertains to the group itself—its rules, its procedures, or its mission—implementation proceeds more smoothly when members have had an active role or voice in the decision-making process (Lind, Kanfer, & Earley, 1990; cf. Locke, Alavi, & Wagner, 1997). Lester Coch and John R. P. French, Jr. (1948) documented this tendency in their classic analysis of procedural changes in a clothing mill. Management modified production methods frequently as a result of engineering advances and product alterations, and line workers reacted to each modification with protests. Turnover was high, productivity was down, and the amount of time needed for retraining after each production change was excessive.

Coch and French suspected that employees would be more compliant if they were involved more in planning changes, so they devised three different training programs. Employees in the *no-participation* program were not involved in the planning and implementation of the changes, but they were given an explanation for the innovations. Those in the *participation-through-representation* program attended group meetings where the need for change was discussed openly and an informal decision was reached. A subgroup was then chosen to become the "special" operators, who would serve as the first training group. Employees in the third program—*total participation*—followed much the same procedures as those in the second program, but here *all* the employees, not a select group, were transferred to the training system.

Just as Coch and French predicted, the no-participation group improved very little—hostility, turnover, and inefficiency remained high. In fact, 17% of these workers quit rather than learn the new procedure, and those who remained never reached the goals set by management. The two participation conditions, in contrast, responded well. These workers learned their new tasks quickly, and their productivity soon surpassed prechange levels and management goals. Morale was high, only one hostile action was recorded, and none of the employees quit in the 40 days following the change. Furthermore, when the members of a control condition were run through a participation program several months later, they, too, reached appropriate production levels.

Quality circles, autonomous work groups, and *self-directed teams* are the modern-day counterparts to Coch and French's total-participation groups (Cascio, 1995). These groups vary considerably in composition and goals, but in most cases, they are charged with identifying problems that are undermining productivity, efficiency, quality, or job satisfaction. These groups spend considerable time discussing the causes of the problems and suggesting possible solutions, either with or without a formal leader or supervisor. Once decisions are made about changes (usually by consensus), these changes are implemented and evaluated. If the changes do not have the desired effect, the process is repeated. Quality circles, in particular, base their analyses on statistical data pertaining to productivity (O. L. Crocker, Chiu, & Charney, 1984; Deming, 1975). These approaches increase workers' levels of satisfaction, and they may even increase productivity (Chansler, Swamidass, & Cammann, 2003; J. A. Wagner, 1994). They can, however, be short-lived if they are not integrated into the organization's overall structure (Guzzo & Shea, 1992).

Who Decides—Individuals or Groups?

Making a decision in a group offers a number of advantages over making a decision alone. Groups, with their greater informational resources and capacity to process that information, may be able to identify better solutions and to detect errors in reasoning. Members may also find a group's decision more satisfying than that of a single individual, particularly if the group uses a consensus-building decision process. Group decisions, however, can take more time than people wish to give to them, and so groups too often sacrifice quality for timeliness. Some issues, too, are so trivial, so convoluted, or so contentious that a group approach may end in failure.

Given this mixture of benefits and liabilities, Victor Vroom's **normative model of decision making** suggests that different types of situations call for different types of decision-making methods (Vroom, 1973, 1974, 1976; Vroom &

---

normative model of decision making A theory of decision making and leadership developed by Victor Vroom that predicts the effectiveness of group-centered, consultative, and autocratic decisional procedures across a number of group settings.

Jago, 1988; Vroom & Yetton, 1973). In some cases, the decision maker should not even consult with others before he or she makes a choice. In other cases, however, the leader should seek input from the group or even turn the decision over to the group entirely. Although procedures can fall anywhere along the continuum from leader-centered, authoritarian to group-centered, democratic decision making, Vroom stressed these five basic types:

- *Autocratic I (AI):* The leader solves the problem or makes the decision, using the information available to him or her at that time.
- *Autocratic II (AII):* The leader obtains the necessary information from group members and then decides on the solution to the problem. In getting the information, the leader may choose not to tell the group members what the problem is. The role played by the group members is one of providing information rather than suggesting or evaluating alternative solutions.
- *Consultative I (CI):* The leader shares the problem with the relevant group members individually, getting their ideas and suggestions without bringing them together as a group. Then the leader makes the decision, which may not reflect the group members' influence.
- *Consultative II (CII):* The leader discusses the problem with the members as a group, collectively obtaining their ideas and suggestions. Then the leader makes the decision, which may not reflect the group members' influences.
- *Group II (GII):* The leader discusses the problem with the members as a group. Together, the leader and members devise and evaluate alternatives and attempt to reach agreement (consensus) on a solution. The leader's role is much like that of the chairperson of a committee. The leader does not try to influence the group to adopt a particular solution and is willing to accept and carry out any solution that is supported by the entire group. (paraphrased from Vroom & Yetton, 1973, p. 13)

Vroom's normative model argues that no single method will be best in all situations. In general, leaders should probably meet with the group whenever a major decision is to be made, but in some situations, a group approach may prove ineffective, time consuming, and dissatisfying to members. In these instances, a more centralized decision method may be the most successful approach. Choosing between an individual and a group approach is complex, however, so Vroom and his colleagues listed a number of rules of thumb to serve as guidelines (Vroom, 1976; Vroom & Jago; 1978, 1988; Vroom & Yetton, 1973). Some of these rules are designed to protect the quality of the decision the group is making. For example, the *unstructured problem rule* warns against using AI, AII, or CI if a high-quality decision is needed and the leader lacks sufficient information to solve an unstructured problem alone. Other rules are designed to ensure the acceptance of the decision by the group. For example, the *acceptance rule* recommends using either consultative (CI and CII) or group (GII) methods if acceptance of the decision by subordinates is critical to effective implementation and if it is not certain that an autocratic decision will be accepted (paraphrased from Vroom & Jago, 1978, pp. 151–162).

Does the normative model work? The available evidence, although scant, is supportive. For example, Vroom and his colleagues reported that when expert managers read a case study of a leadership decision and then made a recommendation about an appropriate leadership method, their suggestions coincided with the predictions of the normative model (T. E. Hill & Schmitt, 1977; Jago, 1978; Vroom & Yetton, 1973). More research, however, is needed to examine the impact of each of the five key methods in each situation specified by Vroom (Field, 1979; Field & House, 1990; T. E. Hill & Schmitt, 1977; Vroom & Jago, 1978).

Groups as Imperfect Decision Makers

People often have harsh words to say about the decisions made by groups. Members complain about time wasted in groups and swap jokes such as "An elephant is a mouse designed by a committee," "Trying to solve a problem through group discussion is like trying to clear up a traffic jam by honking your horn," and "Committees consist of the unfit appointed by the unwilling to do the unnecessary." Although groups, with their vastly greater informational and motivational resources, have the *potential* to outperform individuals, they do not always reach that potential. When and why do groups make poor decisions?

Group Discussion Pitfalls

Most experts on group communication agree that misunderstanding seems to be the rule in groups, with accurate understanding being the exception. Too many group members simply lack the skills needed to express themselves clearly. They fail to make certain that their verbal and nonverbal messages are accurate and easily decipherable and so unintentionally mislead, confuse, or even insult other members (Gulley & Leathers, 1977). Inaccuracies also arise from the information processing limitations and faulty listening habits of human beings. Listeners can *level* (simplify and shorten), *sharpen* (embellish distinctions made by the speaker), and *assimilate* (interpret messages so that they match personal expectations and beliefs) information offered by others during a discussion (D. T. Campbell, 1958b; B. E. Collins & Guetzkow, 1964).

Nor do all group members have the interpersonal skills that a discussion demands. When researchers asked 569 full-time employees who worked at jobs ranging from clerical positions to upper-level management to describe "in their own words what happens during a meeting that limits its effectiveness," they received nearly 2500 answers. The problems they reported, which are summarized in Table 10-1, fell into seven basic categories—bad communication, egocentric behavior, nonparticipation, failure to stay focused (tendency to become sidetracked), interruptions, negative leadership behaviors, and negative attitudes and emotions. The participants in this research suggested that their groups failed more frequently than they succeeded at solving problems (Di Salvo, Nikkel, & Monroe, 1989).

Groups also sometimes use discussion to *avoid* making a decision rather than *facilitate* making a decision. As Irving Janis and Leon Mann (1977) suggested, most

TABLE 10-1   Group members' descriptions of problems experienced when trying to make a group decision

Problem	Frequency	Description
Communication skills	10%	Poor listening skills, ineffective voice, poor nonverbal communication, lack of effective visual aids, misunderstands or does not clearly identify topic, is repetitive, uses jargon
Egocentric behavior	8%	Dominates conversation and group. Behaviors are loud, overbearing. One-upmanship, show of power, manipulation, intimidation, filibustering. Talks to hear self talk. Followers or brown-nosers; clowns and goof-offs.
Nonparticipation	7%	Not all participate, do not speak up, do not volunteer, are passive, lack discussion, silent starts
Sidetracking	6.5%	Leaves main topic
Interruptions	6%	Members interrupt speaker; talk over others; socialize; allow phone calls, messages from customers/clients
Negative leader behavior	6%	Unorganized and unfocused, not prepared, late, has no control, gets sidetracked, makes no decisions
Attitudes and emotions	5%	Poor attitude, defensive or evasive, argumentative, personal accusations, no courtesy or respect, complain or gripe, lack of control of emotions

Source: Adapted from Di Salvo, Nikkel, & Monroe, 1989.

people are reluctant decision makers, so they use a variety of tactics during discussion to avoid having to face the decision. These tactics include the following:

- *Procrastination.* Rather than spending its time studying alternatives and arguing their relative merits, the group postpones the decision.
- *Bolstering.* The group quickly but arbitrarily formulates a decision without thinking things through completely, and then bolsters the preferred solution by exaggerating the favorable consequences and minimizing the importance and likelihood of unfavorable consequences.
- *Avoiding responsibility.* The group denies responsibility by delegating the decision to a subcommittee or by diffusing accountability throughout the entire assembly.
- *Ignoring alternatives.* The group engages in the fine art of muddling through (Lindblom, 1965) by considering "only a very narrow range of policy alternatives that differ to only a small degree from the existing policy" (Janis & Mann, 1977, p. 33).
- *"Satisficing."* Members accept as satisfactory any solution that meets only a minimal set of criteria, instead of working to find the best solution. Although superior solutions to the problem may exist, the "satisficer" is content with any alternative that surpasses the minimal cutoff point.

FOCUS 10-2   Do Groups Waste Time?

Groups take minutes but waste hours.
–Unknown

Making decisions in groups requires, in many cases, a trade-off between efficiency and accuracy. Groups' decisions are often superior to those of individuals, but groups require more time to draw conclusions and to reach agreement. The humorist C. Northcote Parkinson (1957) has identified two fundamental "laws" that groups all too frequently obey. Parkinson's first law, which he modestly named *Parkinson's law,* states that a task will expand so as to fill the time available for its completion. Hence, if a group gathers at 1 PM for a one-hour meeting to discuss five items of business, the group will likely adjourn at 2 PM no matter how simple or routine the issues.

Parkinson's second law, the *law of triviality,* states that the time a group spends on discussing

any issue will be in inverse proportion to the consequentiality of the issue (Parkinson, 1957, paraphrased from p. 24). Parkinson described a hypothetical finance committee dealing with Item 9 on a long agenda, a $10-million allocation to build a nuclear reactor. Discussion is terse, lasting about 2½ minutes, and the committee unanimously approves the item. However, when the group turns to Item 10, the allocation of $2350 to build a bicycle shed to be used by the office staff, everyone on the committee has something to say. As Parkinson explained,

> A sum of $2350 is well within everybody's comprehension. Everybody can visualize a bicycle shed. Discussion goes on, therefore, for forty-five minutes, with the possible result of saving some $300. Members at length sit back with a feeling of achievement. (1957, p. 301)

- *Trivializing the discussion.* The group avoids dealing with larger issues by focusing on minor issues. In many cases, the *law of triviality* holds: The time a group spends discussing any issue will be in inverse proportion to the consequentiality of the issue (see Focus 10-2).

The Shared Information Bias

The Bay of Pigs planners spent much time talking about how U.S. citizens would react to the invasion and the incompetence of Castro's forces. They did not spend as much time talking about the weapons that the troops would carry, the political climate in Cuba, the terrain of the area where the invasion would take place, or the type of communication system used by Cuban military forces. Only the CIA representatives knew that the morale of the invasion force was very low, but they never mentioned that information during the discussion. Joseph Newman, a journalist just back from visiting Cuba, met with President Kennedy privately and told him that the Cuban people would not rebel against Castro. Kennedy kept this information to himself during the group discussions.

The good news is that groups can pool their individual resources to make a decision that takes into account far more information than any one individual's decision might take into account. The bad news is that groups spend too much of their discussion time examining *shared information*—details that two or more group members know in common—rather than unshared information (Stasser, 1992a, 1992b; Stasser, Taylor, & Hanna, 1989; Wittenbaum & Stasser, 1996). If all the members of a group discussing an invasion plan know that the majority of U.S. citizens oppose communism, then this topic will be discussed at length. But if only the CIA representative knows that the invading troops are poorly trained or only Kennedy knows that Cuban citizens support Castro, these important— but unshared—pieces of information might never be discussed.

The harmful consequences of this **shared information bias** are substantial when the group must have access to the unshared information if it is going to make a good decision. If a group is working on a problem where the shared information suggests that Alternative A is correct, but the unshared information favors Alternative B, then the group will only discover this so-called *hidden profile* if it discusses the unshared information. To examine this type of problem, Garold Stasser and William Titus (1985) gave the members of four-person groups 16 pieces of information about three candidates for student body president. Candidate A was the best choice for the post, for he possessed eight positive qualities, four neutral qualities, and four negative qualities. The other two candidates had four positive qualities, eight neutral qualities, and four negative qualities. When the group members were given all the available information about the candidates, 83% of the groups favored Candidate A—a slight improvement over the 67% rate reported by the participants before they joined their group. But groups did not fare so well when Stasser and Titus manipulated the distribution of the positive and negative information among the members to create a hidden profile. Candidate A still had eight positive qualities, but Stasser and Titus made certain that each group member received information about only two of these qualities. Person 1, for example, knew that Candidate A had positive qualities P1 and P2; Person 2 knew that he had positive qualities P3 and P4; Person 3 knew that he had positive qualities P5 and P6; and Person 4 knew that he had positive qualities P7 and P8. But they all knew that Candidate A had negative qualities N1, N2, N3, and N4. Had they pooled their information carefully, they would have discovered that Candidate A had positive qualities P1 to P8, and only four negative qualities. But they oversampled the shared negative qualities and chose the less qualified candidate 76% of the time (Stasser & Titus, 1985, 1987).

WHAT CAUSES THE SHARED INFORMATION BIAS? The shared information bias reflects, in part, the dual purpose of discussion. As a form of *informational influence,* discussions help individuals marshal the evidence and information they need to make good decisions. But as a form of *normative influence,* discussions give members the chance to influence each other's opinions on the issue. Discussing unshared information may be enlightening, but discussing shared information helps the group reach consensus on the matter. Hence, when groups are motivated more by a desire to make a decision and get closure than by a drive to make the best possible decision, the shared information bias becomes more pronounced (Kelly & Karau, 1999; Postmes, Spears, & Cihangir, 2001). The bias is strongest

---

shared information bias The tendency for groups to spend more time discussing information that all members know (shared information) and less time examining information that only a few members know (unshared).

when groups work on judgmental tasks that do not have a demonstrably correct solution, as the goal of the group is to reach agreement rather than to find the right answer (D. D. Stewart & Stasser, 1998). Groups are also more biased when their members think that they do not have enough information to make a fully informed decision (Stasser & Stewart, 1992).

The shared information bias also reflects the psychological and interpersonal needs of group members. If group members enter into the group discussion with a clear preference, they will argue in favor of their preference and resist changing their minds. If the shared information all points in one direction—as it did in Stasser and Titus's (1985) study of hidden profiles—then all the group members begin the discussion with a negative opinion of Candidate A. The group's final choice reflects these initial preferences (Brodbeck, Kerschreiter, Mojzisch, Frey, & Schulz-Hardt, 2002; Gigone & Hastie, 1997; Greitemeyer & Schulz-Hardt, 2003). Group members also consider shared information to be highly diagnostic, so in their quest to make a good impression with the group, people dwell on what everyone knows rather than on the points that only they understand. For example, they feel that people who discuss shared information are more knowledgeable, competent, and credible than are group members who contribute unshared information to the discussion (Wittenbaum, Hubbell, & Zuckerman, 1999). In consequence, group members who anticipate a group discussion implicitly focus on information that they know others also possess, instead of concentrating on information that only they possess (Wittenbaum, Stasser, & Merry, 1996).

CAN THE SHARED INFORMATION BIAS BE AVOIDED? Even though groups prefer to spend their time discussing shared information, experienced members avoid this tendency, and they often intervene to focus the group's attention on unshared data (Wittenbaum, 1998). When researchers studied medical teams making decisions, they noted that the more senior group members repeated more shared information, but they also repeated more unshared information than the other group members. Moreover, as the discussion progressed, they were more likely to repeat unshared information that was mentioned during the session— evidence of their attempt to bring unshared information out through the discussion (J. R. Larson, Christensen, Abbott, & Franz, 1996). Groups can also avoid the shared information bias if they spend more time actively discussing their decisions. Because group members tend to discuss shared information first, groups are more likely to review unshared information in longer meetings (J. R. Larson, Foster-Fishman, & Keys, 1994; Winquist & Larson, 1998).

Group decision support systems (GDSS) may also offer a means of reducing this bias. If a group uses a group decision support system (GDSS), its

---

group decision support systems A set of integrated tools groups use to structure and facilitate their decision making, including computer programs that expedite data acquisition, communication among group members, document sharing, and the systematic review of alternative actions and outcomes.

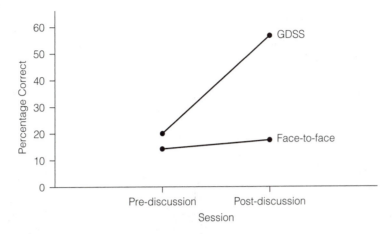

FIGURE 10-4

Does the use of information technology to structure group decisions—
by means of *group decision support systems* (GDSS)—help groups to avoid
the shared information bias? Groups that met in a traditional face-to-
face group session fell prey to the shared information bias, for very few
of them solved a hidden-profile problem correctly. But groups that met
via computer and could access a shared list of discussion items were
more likely to select the best solution to the problem. *Source:* Lam &
Schaubroeck, 2000.

members can work from individual computers that might be located anywhere
in the world. Depending on the GDSS, the group would have access to an array
of decision-making tools, such as databases, search engines for locating information, communication tools for sending messages to specific individuals and to
the entire group, shared writing and drawing areas where members can collaborate on projects, and computational tools that will poll members automatically
and help them to estimate costs, risks, probabilities, and so on (Hollingshead,
2001b). In one recent study of a relatively simple GDSS—it automated communication among members but did not structure voting or information
search—group members were asked to select between three applicants for a
job. As in previous hidden-profile studies, in some cases the information about
the candidate was distributed to group members so that the shared information
favored Candidate B, but if all the information was considered, Candidate A
would be selected. Participants worked either in face-to-face groups or used
the GDSS, and they also made their choices before any discussion and after
the discussion. As Figure 10-4 indicates, groups that used the GDSS were
much more likely to select the best candidate after their discussion (Lam &
Schaubroeck, 2000).

Cognitive Limitations

Groups generate decisions through processes that are both active and complex. Members formulate initial preferences, gather and share information about those preferences, and then combine their views in a single group choice. Although these tasks are relatively ordinary ones, they sometimes demand too much cognitive work from members. The president's committee, for example, wanted to weigh all the relevant factors carefully before making its choice, but the complexity of the problem outstripped the members' relatively meager cognitive capacity. People's judgments in such demanding situations are often systematically distorted by cognitive and motivational biases. People use the information they have available to them inappropriately, putting too much emphasis on interesting information and ignoring statistical information. People sometimes form conclusions very quickly and then do not sufficiently revise those conclusions once they acquire additional information. When people cannot easily imagine an outcome, they assume that such an outcome is less likely to occur than one that springs easily to mind. People overestimate their judgmental accuracy because they remember all the times their decisions were confirmed and forget the times when their predictions were disconfirmed. People make mistakes (Arkes, 1993; Brownstein, 2003; Plous, 1993).

Groups, unfortunately, are not immune from these judgmental biases. When Norbert Kerr and his colleagues (N. L. Kerr, MacCoun, & Kramer, 1996a, 1996b) reviewed the research literature looking for studies of these mental glitches in decision making, they identified three general categories of potential bias: (1) errors in how information is used (*sins of commission*), such as reliance on information that has already been reviewed and found to be inaccurate (*belief perseverance*), reluctance to abandon a course of action once an investment has been made in that action (*sunk cost bias*), the use of information that one has been told explicitly to ignore (*extraevidentiary bias*), and the tendency to overestimate the accuracy of one's prior knowledge of an outcome (*hindsight bias*); (2) errors caused by overlooking useful information (*sins of omission*), such as failure to pay attention to information about general tendencies (*base rate bias*) and stressing dispositional causes when making attributions about the cause of people's behaviors (*fundamental attribution error*); and (3) errors caused by reliance on mental rules of thumb (*heuristics*) that oversimplify the decision (*sins of imprecision*), such as basing decisions on information that is readily available (*availability heuristic*), failing to recognize that the probability of two events occurring together will always be less than the probability of just one of the events occurring (*conjunctive bias*), and excessive reliance on salient but misleading aspects of a problem (*representativeness heuristic*). After reviewing studies that compared individuals' and groups' resistance to these biases, Kerr and his colleagues cautiously ruled against groups: Groups amplify rather than suppress these biases (see Arkes, 1993; Sniezek & Buckley, 1993; Tindale, 1993).

Groups can hold these biased tendencies in check if they are careful to use more thorough decision-making procedures (Härtel & Härtel, 1997; Littlepage & Karau, 1997). Consider, for example, individuals' and groups' resistance

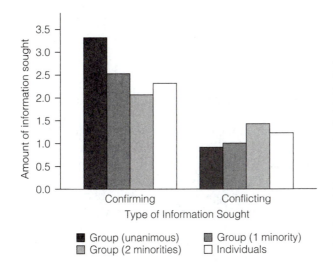

FIGURE 10-5
Is the confirmation bias stronger in groups? Individuals, when they must make a decision, tend to seek out information that supports their initial preferences. This tendency is even stronger in groups, for groups showed a stronger preference for confirming information (and a somewhat weaker tendency to avoid conflicting information). Groups that include 2 members who initially disagree with the position taken by the majority of the members, however, are somewhat less biased than individuals.

to the **confirmation bias.** In decision-making situations, people often start off with an initial preference and then seek out additional information to test the accuracy of their initial inclinations. Unfortunately, this review is biased in many cases, for people usually seek out information that confirms their preferences, and they avoid disconfirming evidence. Groups, too, seek out information that supports the prediscussion preferences of most members, but they can minimize this bias if they deliberately ban any public statements of initial preferences (Dawes, 1988). Groups also avoid the confirmation bias when they include individuals who adopt divergent minority positions on the issue. Researchers studied this possibility by giving individuals some background information about a company that was considering relocating its production facilities. Participants indicated their initial preference on the matter, and the experimenters then used those choices to create three kinds of groups: (1) unanimous groups, composed of individuals who shared the same initial preference; (2) groups with one member who took a minority position on the issue; and (3) groups with two minority members. Participants in these three conditions were given the opportunity to select and review 10 additional background readings, which were summarized by short thesis statements that indicated they either supported or opposed relocation. A fourth set of participants made these choices as individuals. As predicted, unanimous, highly homogeneous groups showed a strong preference for confirming information and a tendency to avoid disconfirming information. Groups that included individuals who initially disagreed actually showed a tendency to avoid the bias relative to individuals (see Figure 10-5). These results confirm the value of including people with a range of experiences and opinions as members of

---

confirmation bias The tendency to seek out information that confirms one's inferences rather than disconfirms them.

groups that must make critical decisions (Schulz-Hardt, Frey, Luethgens, & Moscovici, 2000; see also Schulz-Hardt, Jochims, & Frey, 2002).

Group Polarization

Historians cannot say why President Kennedy decided to create a committee to help him review the invasion plan, but he may have acted on the intuitively appealing notion that groups have a moderating impact on individuals. He may have assumed that a group, if faced with a choice between a risky alternative (invade Cuba) and a more moderate alternative (use diplomatic means to influence Cuba), would prefer the moderate route. Unfortunately for Kennedy, for his advisers, and for the members of the attack force, groups' decisions are more extreme than individuals' decisions. Groups do not urge restraint; instead, they *polarize*.

THE RISKY SHIFT PHENOMENON At about the time that Kennedy's committee was grappling with the problems inherent in the invasion plan, group experts were initiating studies of the effects of group discussion on decision making. Although some researchers discovered that groups preferred more conservative solutions than individuals, others found a surprising shift in the direction of greater risk (Stoner, 1961, 1968). One research team, for example, studied people's willingness to take risks by asking individuals and groups to read 12 hypothetical situations involving a choice between one of two possible courses of action (Wallach, Kogan, & Bem, 1962). In all the situations, the more rewarding outcome was also the riskier one, and the participants were asked, "What would the probability of success have to be before you would advise the character in the story to choose the riskier course of action?" The first item from this **Choice-Dilemmas Questionnaire,** along with the format used to measure the participants' responses, follows:

> Mr. A, an electrical engineer, who is married and has one child, has been working for a large electronics corporation since graduating from college five years ago. He is assured of a lifetime job with a modest, though adequate, salary and liberal pension benefits upon retirement. On the other hand, it is very unlikely that his salary will increase much before he retires. While attending a convention, Mr. A is offered a job with a small, newly founded company which has a highly uncertain future. The new job would pay more to start and would offer the possibility of a share in the ownership if the company survived the competition of the larger firms.
>
> Imagine that you are advising Mr. A. Listed below are several probabilities or odds of the new company proving financially sound. Please check the lowest probability that you would consider acceptable to make it worthwhile for Mr. A to take the new job.

Choice-Dilemmas Questionnaire A self-report measure of willingness to make risky decisions that asks respondents to read a series of scenarios involving a course of action that may or may not yield financial, interpersonal, or educational benefits, then indicate what the odds of success would have to be before they would recommend the course of action.

_____ The chances are 1 in 10 that the company will prove financially sound.
_____ The chances are 3 in 10 that the company will prove financially sound.
_____ The chances are 5 in 10 that the company will prove financially sound.
_____ The chances are 7 in 10 that the company will prove financially sound.
_____ The chances are 9 in 10 that the company will prove financially sound.
_____ Place a check here if you think Mr. A should not take the new job no matter what the probabilities. (Pruitt, 1971, p. 359)

These researchers documented an increase in risk taking when people made their choices in groups. When they added together choices for all 12 items, the investigators found that the mean of prediscussion individual decisions was 66.9 for men and 65.6 for women. The mean of the group's consensual decision, however, was 57.5 for men and 56.2 for women—a shift of 9.4 points in the direction of greater risk. This shift also occurred when individual judgments were collected after the group discussion and when the individual postdiscussion measures were delayed 2 to 6 weeks (the delayed posttests were collected from male participants only). Participants in a control condition shifted very little.

The finding that groups seem to make riskier decisions than individuals was dubbed the **risky-shift phenomenon.** Shifts were reliably demonstrated in countries around the world, including Canada, the United States, England, France, Germany, and New Zealand, and with many kinds of group participants (Pruitt, 1971). Although commentators sometimes wondered about the generality and significance of the phenomenon (M. B. Smith, 1972), laboratory findings were eventually bolstered by field studies (Lamm & Myers, 1978).

GROUP POLARIZATION During this research period, some investigators hinted at the possibility of the opposite process—a _cautious shift._ For example, when the early risky shift researchers examined the amount of postdiscussion change revealed on each item of the _Choice-Dilemmas Questionnaire,_ they frequently found that group members consistently advocated a less risky course of action than did individuals on one particular item (Wallach et al., 1962). Intrigued by this anomalous finding, subsequent researchers wrote additional choice dilemmas, and they, too, occasionally found evidence of a cautious shift. Then, in 1969, researchers reported evidence of individuals moving in both directions after a group discussion, suggesting that both cautious and risky shifts were possible (Doise, 1969).

Researchers also discovered that group discussions not only amplify choices between risky and cautious alternatives, but also group members' attitudes, beliefs, values, judgments, and perceptions (D. G. Myers, 1982). In France, for example, where people generally like their government but dislike Americans, group discussion improved their attitude toward their government but exacerbated their negative opinions of Americans (Moscovici & Zavalloni, 1969). Similarly, strongly prejudiced people who discussed racial issues with other prejudiced individuals became even more prejudiced. But when only mildly

---

risky-shift phenomenon The tendency for groups to make riskier decisions than individuals.

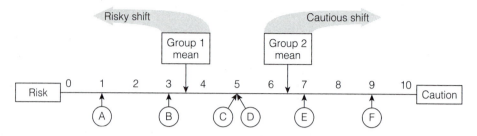

FIGURE 10-6

Why does group discussion polarize opinions? Imagine that Group 1 includes Person A (who chose 1), Person B (who chose 3), and Persons C and D (who both chose 5); the average of pregroup choices would be $(1 + 3 + 5 + 5)/4$, or 3.5. Because this mean is less than 5, a risky shift would probably occur in Group 1. If, in contrast, Group 2 contained Persons C, D, E, and F, their pregroup average would be $(5 + 5 + 7 + 9)/4$ or 6.5. Because this mean is closer to the caution pole, a cautious shift would probably occur in the group.

prejudiced persons discussed racial issues with other mildly prejudiced individuals, they became less prejudiced (D. G. Myers & Bishop, 1970).

Somewhat belatedly, researchers realized that risky shifts after group discussions were a part of a more general process. When people discuss issues in groups, they sometimes settle on a more extreme course of action than would be suggested by the average of their individual judgments, but the direction of this shift depends on their average initial preferences. David G. Myers and Helmut Lamm called this process **group polarization** because the "average postgroup response will tend to be more extreme in the same direction as the average of the pregroup responses" (D. G. Myers & Lamm, 1976, p. 603; see also Lamm & Myers, 1978).

Imagine two groups of four individuals whose opinions vary in terms of preference for risk. As Figure 10-6 indicates, when the average choice of the group members before discussion is closer to the risky pole of the continuum than to the cautious pole (as would be the case in a group composed of Persons A, B, C, and D), a risky shift will occur. If, in contrast, the group is composed of Persons C, D, E, and F, a cautious shift will take place, because the pregroup mean of 6.5 falls closer to the cautious pole. This example is, of course, something of an oversimplification, because the shift depends on the distance from the psychological rather than the mathematical midpoint of the scale. As D. G. Myers and Lamm (1976) noted, on choice dilemmas, an initial pregroup mean of 6 or smaller is usually sufficient to produce a risky shift, whereas a mean of 7 or greater is necessary to produce a cautious shift. If the pregroup mean falls between 6 and 7, shifting is unlikely.

---

group polarization The tendency to respond in a more extreme way when making a choice or expressing an opinion as part of a group, as opposed to when responding individually.

WHAT CAUSES GROUP POLARIZATION? How do groups intensify individuals' reactions? Early explanations suggested that groups feel less responsible for their decisions and are overly influenced by risk-prone leaders, but in time, investigators recognized that polarization results from such common social influence processes as *social comparison, normative influence,* and *social decision schemes.*

When people make decisions individually, they have no way to determine whether they are risk-averse or risk-takers; whether they are responding as most people do or are overreacting; whether the position they are defending is reasonable or whether they are arguing for an idea that most people think is bizarre. But when group members make choices together, they use others as reference points to evaluate their own preferences and positions (Goethals & Zanna, 1979; D. G. Myers, 1978). As social comparison theory suggests, individuals spontaneously compare themselves to others, and if they find a difference between their view and the group's, they may move toward the group's view (G. S. Sanders & Baron, 1977). Polarization occurs because group members, through discussion, discover the group's norm on the issue, and then they stake a claim to a position that exceeds that norm in whatever direction the majority of the members endorse. As Roger Brown (1974) explained, "To be virtuous . . . is to be different from the mean—in the right direction and to the right degree" (p. 469). If, for example, the group discussion indicates that the majority of the group likes Plan A, then a desire to create a positive impression in the group may prompt members to claim that they *really* like Plan A (Weigold & Schlenker, 1991). Discussion may also reveal that a more extreme position on the issue is prototypical for the group, so self-categorization processes prompt members to shift their attitude in that direction (Abrams, Wetherell, Cochrane, Hogg, & Turner, 1990).

Group members also change their opinions in response to others' arguments and ideas. If, for example, the discussion reveals several strong arguments that favor Plan A rather than Plan B, members will shift in that direction. But as **persuasive-arguments theory** notes, groups usually generate more arguments that support the position endorsed by the majority of the group, or the position that is most consistent with dominant social values—in part because members may be more willing to express arguments that are consistent with social norms. As a result, the group persuades itself, as more arguments favoring the dominant viewpoint are brought up during the discussion (Burnstein & Vinokur, 1973, 1977; Vinokur & Burnstein, 1974, 1978). The group's social decision scheme may also favor extreme rather than moderate positions. If, for example, a group adopts a "risk-supported-wins" rule, and two members of the group express a willingness to tolerate extreme risk, then the group may shift in that direction (J. H. Davis, 1982; J. H. Davis, Kameda, & Stasson, 1992; Ohtsubo, Masuchi, Nakanishi, 2002; Zuber, Crott, & Werner, 1992).

---

persuasive-arguments theory An explanation of polarization in groups assuming that group members change their opinions during group discussion, generally adopting the position favored by the majority of the members, because the group can generate more arguments favoring that position.

Group polarization, then, is not caused by any one mechanism, but by several processes that combine to amplify attitudes and choices (Isenberg, 1986; M. F. Kaplan & Miller, 1983). Studies have indicated, for example, that the direction of polarization in a group depends on the preponderance of arguments for risk and caution—as persuasive-arguments theory suggests. Also, when discussants are asked to repeat the arguments raised in the discussion, they are more likely to be persuaded, and in such cases polarization increases (Brauer, Judd, & Gliner, 1995). But group members also shift their opinions when they discover others' positions but not their arguments, suggesting that knowledge of group norms is sufficient to generate a shift (Blascovich, Ginsburg, & Howe, 1975, 1976). Polarization also depends on the network of communication in the group and the relative status of members, suggesting that polarization is, at its core, the result of social influence processes that operate routinely in groups (Friedkin, 1999; Liu & Latané, 1998).

WHAT ARE THE CONSEQUENCES OF POLARIZATION? Would people who believe that environmental pollution is a serious problem be more likely, after discussion, to insist on severe measures to prevent pollution? Do individuals who enjoy a challenge, when they join a group, seek even greater challenges than they would if they were alone? Would a group of government experts who slightly favored an invasion plan enthusiastically endorse the plan after they discuss it? Do groups amplify group members' shared tendencies? Studies of polarization say *yes*.

Sometimes, polarization can cause a group to misstep. Polarization processes likely contributed to the escalation of the Vietnam War by President Johnson's administration (McCauley, 1989), the Japanese high command's decision to attack Pearl Harbor (G. Whyte, 1998), and the Bay of Pigs fiasco. Polarization may also play a role in groups' tendency to become so committed to a plan or choice that members refuse to reconsider the decision, even when its costs mount (G. Whyte, 1993). But polarization may also yield positive effects. A group's collective efficacy may rise as individually optimistic members join together and discuss their chances for success. The members of a support group may become far more hopeful of their chances for recovery when they gather together with others who are moderately optimistic. Innovations and new ideas may be adopted by large numbers of people as polarization amplifies enthusiasm for the new products, methods, or outlooks. Thus, polarization, though sometimes a source of error and bias, can in some cases have a beneficial impact on the group and its members.

GROUPTHINK: A WORST-CASE SCENARIO

Irving Janis was intrigued by President Kennedy's Bay of Pigs committee. This group, like so many others, failed to make the best decision it could. The committee's failure, though, was so spectacular that Janis wondered if something more

TABLE 10-2 Five fiascoes in U.S. history: Was groupthink to blame?

Group	Fiasco
Admiral H. E. Kimmel and his senior naval advisors, including 20 captains, vice-admirals, and other executive naval officers	In 1941, this group concentrated on Pearl Harbor's importance as a training base to such an extent that the U.S. Pacific fleet was left vulnerable to attack by the Japanese.
President H. S. Truman's policy-making staff, including the Joint Chiefs of Staff and members of the National Security Council	This group authorized the movement of U.S. troops across the 38th parallel during the Korean War, prompting China to join North Korea in its war against the United States.
President J. F. Kennedy's ad hoc advisory committee, including top CIA officers, the Joint Chiefs of Staff, and the secretaries of state and defense	In 1961, this group planned and approved the invasion of Cuba at the Bay of Pigs.
President L. B. Johnson's "Tuesday Lunch Group," consisting of White House staff, the chair of the Joint Chiefs of Staff, the CIA director, and cabinet members	From 1965 to 1968, this group met over lunch to discuss military operations in Vietnam, including the selection of nonmilitary bombing targets.
President R. M. Nixon's White House staff, including John Dean, John Ehrlichman, Charles E. Colson, and H. R. Haldeman	In 1971 and 1972, this group tried to cover up the activities surrounding the Watergate break-in by destroying evidence and lying to investigators.

than such common group difficulties as faulty communication and judgmental biases was to blame.

Janis pursued this insight in a series of extensive case studies of groups like those described in Table 10-2. After studying these groups and their gross errors of judgment, he concluded that they suffered from *groupthink*—a distorted style of thinking that renders group members incapable of making a rational decision. According to Janis (1982), groupthink is "a mode of thinking that people engage in when they are deeply involved in a cohesive ingroup, when the members' strivings for unanimity override their motivation to realistically appraise alternative courses of actions" (p. 9). During groupthink, members try so hard to agree with one another that they make mistakes and commit errors that could easily be avoided.

Symptoms of Groupthink

To Janis, groupthink is like a disease that infects healthy groups, rendering them inefficient and unproductive. Like the physician who searches for symptoms that signal the onset of the illness, Janis has identified a number of symptoms that occur in groupthink situations (Janis, 1972, 1982, 1983, 1985, 1989; Janis & Mann, 1977; Longley & Pruitt, 1980; D. D. Wheeler & Janis, 1980). He organized the eight most important symptoms into three categories: *overestimation of the group, closed-mindedness,* and *pressures toward uniformity* (Janis, 1982).

OVERESTIMATION OF THE GROUP Groups that have fallen into the trap of groupthink are actually planning fiascoes and making all the wrong choices. Yet the members usually assume that everything is working perfectly. They even express enthusiasm in their public statements about their wrong-headed decisions (Tetlock, 1979). Janis traced this unwarranted optimism to illusions of invulnerability and illusions of morality.

The Bay of Pigs planners, like many groups, overestimated their group's decisional savvy. Members felt that they were performing well, even though they were not. This illusory thinking, though commonplace, becomes so extreme during groupthink that Janis has called it an *illusion of invulnerability.* Feelings of assurance and confidence engulfed the group. The members felt that their plan was virtually infallible and that their committee could not make major errors in judgment. Such feelings of confidence and power may help athletic teams or combat units reach their objectives, but the feeling that all obstacles can be easily overcome through power and good luck can cut short clear, analytic thinking in decision-making groups (Silver & Bufanio, 1996).

The planners also believed in the inherent morality of their group and its decisions. Yet the plan to invade Cuba could unsympathetically be described as an unprovoked sneak attack by a major world power on a virtually defenseless country. But the decision makers, suffering from *illusions of morality,* seemed to lose their principles in the group's desire to bravely end Castro's regime. Although groups are capable of reaching admirable levels of moral thought, this capability is unrealized during groupthink (McGraw & Bloomfield, 1987).

CLOSED-MINDEDNESS Groups that are overtaken by groupthink are not open-minded groups, searching for new ideas and perspectives. Rather, they are *closed-minded*—rigidly shut off from alternatives and seeking to bolster their initial decision through *rationalization.* One key element of this closure is the tendency to view other groups in biased, simplistic ways. For example, the members of the planning group shared an inaccurate and negative opinion of Castro and his political ideology, and they often expressed these *stereotypes about the outgroup* during group discussions. Castro was depicted as a weak leader, an evil communist, and a man too stupid to realize that his country was about to be attacked. His ability to maintain an air force was discredited, as was his control over his troops and the citizenry. The group participants' underestimation of their enemy was so pronounced that they sent a force of 1400 men to fight a force of 200,000 and expected an easy success. The group wanted to believe that Castro was an ineffectual leader and incompetent military officer, but this oversimplified picture of the dictator turned out to be merely wishful thinking.

PRESSURES TOWARD UNIFORMITY The struggle for consensus is an essential and unavoidable aspect of life in groups, but in groupthink situations, interpersonal pressures make agreeing too easy and disagreeing too difficult. Tolerance for any sort of dissent seems virtually nil, and groups may use harsh measures to bring those who disagree into line. In the president's committee, criticism was taboo, and members who broke this norm were pressured to conform. Janis highlighted four indicators of this pressure: self-censorship, the illusion of unanimity, direct pressure on dissenters, and self-appointed mindguards.

Self-censorship is Janis's term for a personal ban on expressing disagreements about the group's decisions. In the planning group, many of the members of the group privately felt uncertain about the plan, but they kept their doubts to themselves. Some even sent private memorandums to the president before or after a meeting; but when the group convened, the doubting Thomases sat in silence. As Schlesinger (1965) later wrote,

> In the months after the Bay of Pigs I bitterly reproached myself for having kept so silent during those crucial discussions in the Cabinet Room, though my feelings of guilt were tempered by the knowledge that a course of objection would have accomplished little save to gain me a name as a nuisance. I can only explain my failure to do more than raise a few timid questions by reporting that one's impulse to blow the whistle on this nonsense was simply undone by the circumstances of the discussion. (p. 225)

This self-imposed gag order created an *illusion of unanimity* in the group. The members seemed to agree that the basic plan presented by the CIA was the only solution to the problem and, in later discussions, appeared to just be "going through the motions" of debate. Retrospective accounts reveal that many of the group's members objected to the plan, but these objections never surfaced during the meetings. Instead, a "curious atmosphere of assumed consensus" (Schlesinger, 1965, p. 250) characterized the discussion, as each person wrongly concluded that everyone else liked the plan. As Janis (1972) explained, the group members played up "areas of convergence in their thinking, at the expense of fully exploring divergences that might disrupt the apparent unity of the group" (p. 39). The Bay of Pigs planners, like the group discussed in Focus 10-3, apparently felt that it would be "better to share a pleasant, balmy group atmosphere than be battered in a storm" (p. 39).

This easygoing, supportive atmosphere did not extend to those who disagreed with the group, however. *Direct pressure* was applied to dissenters, often by self-appointed vigilantes, or **mindguards,** who shielded the group from information that would shake the members' confidence in themselves or their leader. The mindguard diverts controversial information away from the group by losing it, forgetting to mention it, or deeming it irrelevant and thus unworthy of the group's attention. Alternatively, the mindguard may take dissenting members

---

mindguard A group member who shields the group from negative or controversial information by gatekeeping and suppressing dissent.

FOCUS 10-3   How Do Groups Get Trapped by Decisions?

We'd just done the opposite of what we wanted to do.
–Jerry Harvey (1988, p. 14)

The day was hot and dusty, as was often the case in July in the small town of Coleman, Texas. Jerry Harvey, his wife, and his wife's parents were fanning themselves on the back porch, playing dominoes and drinking lemonade. Suddenly, Jerry's father-in-law suggested, "Let's get in the car and go to Abilene and have dinner at the cafeteria" (Harvey, 1988, p. 13). Abilene was 53 miles away, it was 104 degrees in the shade, and the only available means of transportation was an unairconditioned 1958 Buick. But the rest of the family chimed in with "Sounds great," and "Sure, I haven't been to Abilene in a while." They traveled all the way to Abilene, had a miserable time, and only when they were back on the porch did they realize that none of them had wanted to go in the first place. After blaming each other for the bad decision,

we all sat back in silence. Here we were, four reasonably sensible people who—of our own volition—had just taken a 106-mile trip across a godforsaken desert in furnace-like heat and dust storm to eat unpalatable food in a hole-in-the-wall cafeteria in Abilene, when none of us had really wanted to go. To be concise, we'd just done the opposite of what we wanted to do. (Harvey, 1988, p. 14)

Groups sometimes make decisions that veer far from the plans, desires, and preferences of their individual members. Organizational expert Jerry Harvey's *Abilene paradox* aptly illustrates this tendency, highlighting two factors that can combine to lead groups astray.

First, the Abilene group suffered from a severe case of **pluralistic ignorance.** The group members mistakenly believed that their private opinion about the Abilene outing was discrepant from the other group members' opinions. Therefore, each group member, wishing to be seen as

---

aside and pressure them to keep silent. The mindguard may use a variety of strategies to achieve this pressure: requesting the change as a personal favor, pointing out the damage that might be done to the group, or informing the dissenter that in the long run, disagreement would damage his or her position in the group (Uris, 1978). But whatever the method, the overall goal is the same—to contain dissent before it reaches the level of group awareness.

President Kennedy, Rusk, and the president's brother, Robert Kennedy, all acted as mindguards. Kennedy, for example, withheld memorandums condemning the plan from both Schlesinger and Fulbright. Rusk suppressed information that his own staff had given him. One extreme example of this mindguarding occurred when Rusk, unable to attend a meeting, sent Undersecretary of State Chester Bowles. Although Bowles was said to be horrified by the plan under discussion, President Kennedy never gave him the opportunity to speak during the meeting. Bowles followed bureaucratic channels to voice his critical misgivings, but his superior, Rusk, did not transmit those concerns to the committee, and he told Bowles that the plan had been revised. Ironically, Bowles was fired several weeks after the Bay of Pigs defeat.

---

pluralistic ignorance   When members of a group hold a wide range of opinions, beliefs, or judgments but express similar opinions, beliefs, or judgments publicly because each member believes that his or her personal view is different from that of the others in the group.

FOCUS 10-3 *(continued)*

a cooperative member of the family, publicly conformed to what they thought was the group's norm, each one erroneously assuming that he or she was the only one with misgivings. Jerry went to Abilene because that is what everyone else wanted to do—or so he thought. Unfortunately, everyone else was thinking the same thing (D. T. Miller & McFarland, 1991). Pluralistic ignorance prompts people to conform to norms that do not actually exist—except in their minds.

Second, the group committed to its decision quickly, and did not reconsider its choice when negative consequences—the heat, the cost, the discomfort—mounted. This process is sometimes termed **entrapment**—a special form of escalation that occurs when the group expends "more of its time, energy, money, or other resources than seems justifiable by external standards" (J. Z. Rubin, Pruitt, & Kim, 1994, p. 112). Entrapment occurs when groups become so invested in a course of action that they

refuse to reverse their decisions (Brockner, 1995; Brockner & Rubin, 1985). Such situations often lure in groups by raising concerns over *sunk costs* (Arkes & Blumer, 1985). If a group discovers that the costs for a project are escalating, then the members will rarely consider canceling the project altogether. Instead, they will continue to fund the project, because the initial investment, or **sunk cost,** must be honored. Unfortunately, the money and time invested in a plan of action is already spent and should no longer be considered in weighing the ultimate value of the project. Sunk costs, however, can cause groups to continue to expend resources on projects that will ultimately fail. Analyses of truly massive, much-criticized projects that cost millions of dollars—such as the Millennium Dome in London, EuroDisneyland, and the Denver International Airport—can often be traced to entrapment (Nutt, 2002).

Symptoms of Defective Decision Making

If luck had been on the side of the Bay of Pigs planners—if, for example, one of Castro's generals had decided to take over the military on the same day as the invasion—then the attack might have succeeded. But the Bay of Pigs planners would still have been a groupthink group. Janis did not consider the group to be one overtaken by groupthink only because it made a bad decision, but because it displayed symptoms of groupthink *and* symptoms of defective decision making. The committee, for example, discussed two extreme alternatives—either endorse the Bay of Pigs invasion or abandon Cuba to communism—while ignoring all other potential alternatives. Moreover, the group lost sight of its overall objectives as it became caught up in the minor details of the invasion plan, and it failed to develop contingency plans. The group actively avoided any information that pointed to limitations in its plans, while seeking out facts and opinions that buttressed its initial preferences. The group members did not just make a few small errors. They committed dozens of blunders. The invasion was a fiasco, but

---

entrapment A form of escalating investment in which individuals expend more of their resources in pursuing a chosen course of action than seems appropriate or justifiable by external standards.

sunk cost An investment or loss of resources that cannot be recouped by current or future actions.

it was the faulty decisional strategies of the group that indicated that the group suffered from groupthink.

Causes of Groupthink

Did these conformity pressures, illusions, misperceptions, and faulty decision-making strategies cause the group's error? Janis suggested that these processes undoubtedly contributed to the poor judgments (Janis, 1989), but he labeled them *symptoms* of the problem rather than actual *causes* (see Figure 10-7). The causes of groupthink include *cohesiveness, structural faults* of the group or organization, and *provocative situational factors* (Janis, 1989).

COHESIVENESS The members of the president's committee felt fortunate to belong to a group that boasted such high morale and esprit de corps. Problems could be handled without too much internal bickering, personality clashes were rare, the atmosphere of each meeting was congenial, and replacements were never needed, because no one ever left the group. However, these benefits of cohesiveness did not offset one fatal consequence of a close-knit group—group pressures so strong that critical thinking degenerated into groupthink.

Of the many factors that contribute to the rise of groupthink, Janis emphasized cohesiveness above all others. He agreed that groups that lack cohesion can also make terrible decisions—"especially if the members are engaging in internal warfare"—but they cannot experience groupthink (Janis, 1982, p. 176). In a cohesive group, members refrain from speaking out against decisions, avoid arguing with others, and strive to maintain friendly, cordial relations at all costs. If cohesiveness reaches such a level that internal disagreements disappear, then the group is ripe for groupthink.

Measures of cohesiveness were, of course, never collected for the president's committee. But many signs point to the group's unity. The committee members were all men, and they were in many cases close personal friends. These men, when describing the group in their memoirs, lauded the group, suggesting that their attitudes toward the group were exceptionally positive. The members also identified with the group and its goals; all proudly proclaimed their membership in such an elite body. Robert Kennedy's remarks, peppered with frequent use of the words *we* and *us,* betrayed the magnitude of this identification:

> It seemed that with John Kennedy leading *us* and with all the talent he had assembled, nothing could stop *us. We* believed that if *we* faced up to the nation's problems and applied bold, new ideas with common sense and hard work, *we* would overcome whatever challenged *us.* (quoted in Guthman, 1971, p. 88; italics added)

STRUCTURAL FAULTS OF THE GROUP OR ORGANIZATION Cohesion is a necessary condition for groupthink, but the syndrome becomes more likely when the group is organized in ways that inhibit the flow of information and promote carelessness in the application of decision-making procedures. *Insulation* of the group from other groups, for example, can promote the development of unique, potentially inaccurate perspectives on issues and their solution. The Bay of Pigs planners worked in secret, so very few outsiders ever came into the group to participate in the discussion. The committee was virtually insulated from criticisms. Many experts on military questions and Cuban affairs were available and, if contacted, could have warned the group about the limitations of the plan, but the committee closed itself off from these valuable resources.

President Kennedy's *leadership style* also shaped the way the Bay of Pigs planners worked and may have contributed to groupthink. By tradition, the committee meetings, like cabinet meetings, were very formal affairs that followed a rigid protocol. The president could completely control the group discussion by setting the agenda, permitting only certain questions to be asked, and asking for input only from particular conferees (Stasson, Kameda, & Davis, 1997). He often stated his opinion at the outset of each meeting; his procedures for requiring a voice vote by individuals without prior group discussion paralleled quite closely the methods used by Asch (1952) to heighten conformity pressures in discussion groups. Ironically, Kennedy did not give his advisors opportunities to advise him (Kowert, 2002).

PROVOCATIVE SITUATIONAL CONTEXT A number of provocative situational factors may push the group in the direction of error rather than accuracy. As humans tend to be reluctant decision makers in the best of circumstances, they can unravel when they must make important, high-stakes decisions. Such decisions trigger greater tension and anxiety, so group members cope with this provocative *decisional stress* in less than logical ways. Through collective discussion, the group members may rationalize their choice by exaggerating the positive consequences, minimizing the possibility of negative outcomes, concentrating on minor details, and overlooking larger issues. Because the insecurity of each individual can be minimized if the group quickly chooses a plan of action with little argument or dissension, the group may rush to reach closure by making a decision as quickly as possible (Callaway, Marriott, & Esser, 1985). Janis also suggested that any factors that work to lower members' *self-esteem,* such as a history of mistakes or prior lapses of morality, may further increase the possibility of groupthink.

The Emergence of Groupthink

Figure 10-7 summarizes Janis's revised model of groupthink. The model specifies three key sets of causal factors (cohesion, structural faults, and provocative situational contexts) that can combine to cause a strong *concurrence-seeking tendency* (groupthink), which in turn leads to two classes of observable consequences: symptoms of groupthink (e.g., overestimation of the group, closed-mindedness) and symptoms of defective decision making.

Because of the complexity of the groupthink model, few tests of the entire model have been conducted. Researchers have, however, attempted to replicate Janis's findings through archival case studies of other historical and political groups. They have also examined specific aspects of the theory—such as the impact of cohesion and stress on decision-making groups—to determine if its key

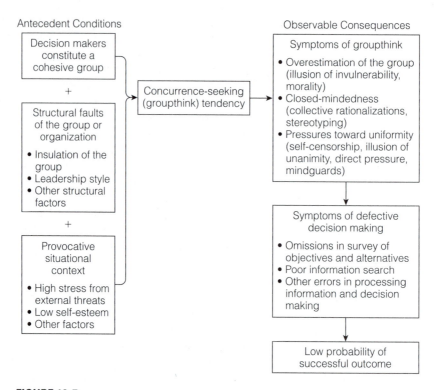

Antecedent Conditions

Observable Consequences

FIGURE 10-7

Why do groups sometimes make disastrous decisions? Irving Janis's (1982) theory of *groupthink* specifies three key sets of antecedent conditions that set the
stage for groupthink, including *cohesion, structural faults* of the group or organization, and *provocative situational contexts.* These conditions cause members to
seek out agreement with others (*concurrence-seeking tendency*), which in turn
leads to two classes of observable consequences: symptoms of groupthink and
symptoms of defective decision making.

assumptions hold up under empirical scrutiny. These studies, which are reviewed
briefly hereafter, sometimes support, sometime challenge, and sometimes clarify
Janis's theory.

ARCHIVAL CASE STUDIES Janis, using an archival method, compared groups
that made very poor decisions to groups that made excellent choices to determine
if the error-prone groups exhibited more of the symptoms of groupthink. In later
work, he enlarged his pool of cases to a total of 19 decision-making groups and
had external raters who worked from the same historical texts rate the groups'
symptoms. As predicted, the higher the number of groupthink symptoms, the
more unfavorable the outcome of the group's deliberations ($r = .62$; Herek,
Janis, & Huth, 1987, 1989; Welch, 1989).

Other archival studies have yielded checkered support for the groupthink model (J. K. Esser, 1998; M. E. Turner & Pratkanis, 1998). Philip E. Tetlock (1979), for example, analyzed the content of leaders' public speeches when in groupthink and vigilant decision-making situations. He discovered that those in the groupthink situations showed signs of reduced complexity and that they were more likely to make positive statements about the ingroup. Tetlock and his colleagues extended these findings in several studies by applying a sophisticated rating system (a *Q-sort*) to several successful and unsuccessful groups in political and organizational contexts. They found that structural faults were related to groupthink, but cohesiveness and provocative situational context factors were not (R. S. Peterson, Owens, Tetlock, Fan, & Martorana, 1998; Tetlock, Peterson, McGuire, Chang, & Feld, 1992). Studies of other disasters and mistake-prone groups, such as the launch the of the *Challenger* and the Iran-Contra affair, also provided partial support for Janis's model (e.g., J. K. Esser & Lindoerfer, 1989; Hensley & Griffin, 1986; Manz & Sims, 1982; Moorhead, Ference, & Neck, 1991; Schafer & Crichlow, 1996; 't Hart, 1991).

COHESION AND GROUPTHINK Janis maintained that groupthink was a characteristic of cohesive groups only. If a group lacked cohesion, it might make poor decisions, but those decisions would be due to processes other than groupthink. His basic prediction was that cohesion, combined with one or more of the other potential causes of groupthink (e.g., structural faults, provocative situational context), would trigger groupthink. He admitted that cohesive groups are not necessarily doomed to be victims of groupthink, but "a high degree of group cohesiveness is conducive to a high frequency of symptoms of groupthink, which, in turn, are conducive to a high frequency of defects in decision-making" (Janis, 1972, p. 199).

Researchers have reported that cohesive groups do sometimes display groupthink tendencies, provided one or more of the other triggering conditions for groupthink are present (Callaway & Esser, 1984; Flowers, 1977; Moorhead & Montanari, 1986; Moorhead, Neck, & West, 1998; Neck & Moorhead, 1995; Street, 1997). For example, John A. Courtright (1978) checked to see if high cohesion, when combined with a high level of "discussion constraint," would undermine performance. After increasing the cohesiveness of some groups, he told constrained groups that they had little time left for discussion and that "the best solutions usually come when one good idea cooperatively evolves from a small number of initial ideas" (p. 233). Groups in the unconstrained condition were told that sufficient time was available to fully discuss the issue and that "the best solutions usually come from vigorous competition among a large number of incompatible ideas" (p. 233). A control condition received no special instructions. Unconstrained groups made better decisions when they were cohesive, and the constrained but cohesive groups disagreed less with one another (Courtright, 1978). The cohesion hypothesis also received limited support in a meta-analysis that combined the results of seven different studies involving more than 1300 participants (Mullen, Anthony, Salas, & Driskell, 1994).

The cohesion−groupthink relationship may depend on the source of the group's cohesion. Groups that derived their cohesiveness from their members' commitment to the task, for example, displayed significantly fewer symptoms of groupthink, whereas groups that were interpersonally cohesive displayed more symptoms of groupthink (Bernthal & Insko, 1993). Social identity theory also offers a more theoretically precise analysis of the roots of the cohesion–groupthink connection. This theory suggests that it is not group unity per se that increases groupthink symptoms, but rather the threat to a shared social identity that may result should the group fail. Marlene E. Turner and her colleagues examined this idea by increasing the salience of group identity by giving some groups names, group name tags, and the opportunity to discuss similarities and commonalities. They discovered that group performance declined when group identity was salient and the situation threatened that identity (Turner, Pratkanis, Probasco, & Leve, 1992; Turner & Pratkanis, 1998).

STRUCTURAL FAULTS AND GROUPTHINK Janis identified several structural features of groups that can contribute to groupthink, but researchers have concentrated most of their attention on the group leader (Z. Chen, Lawson, Gordon, & McIntosh, 1996; Flowers, 1977; Hodson & Sorrentino, 1997). In one project, group members discussed evidence pertaining to a civil trial. Researchers told some of the groups' assigned leaders to adopt a *closed style* of leadership: They were to announce their opinions on the case prior to discussion. *Open-style* leaders were told to withhold their own opinions until later in the discussion. Groups with a leader who adopted a closed style were more biased in their judgments, particularly when many of the group members had a high need for certainty (Hodson & Sorrentino, 1997). Groups with leaders with a strong need for power also performed less effectively, irrespective of the group's level of cohesion (Fodor & Smith, 1982). Other evidence, however, suggests that leaders who are highly directive improve their group's decisions, provided that they limit their control to the group's decisional processes rather than the group's decisional outcomes (R. S. Peterson, 1997).

PROVOCATIVE SITUATIONAL CONTEXT Do situational factors, such as time pressure and the importance of the decision, contribute to faulty decision processes? Although not designed to test Janis's theory, studies by Arie Kruglanski and his colleagues have verified that high stress can lead to a need for closure that can undermine the quality of group decisions. Drawing on his lay epistemic theory, Kruglanski noted that individuals vary in their **need for cognitive closure**—"a desire for a definite answer to a question, any firm answer, rather than uncertainty, confusion, or ambiguity" (Kruglanski, Shah, Pierro, & Mannetti, 2002, p. 649). Individuals who seek closure are cognitively rushed, seeking to make a judgment on the basis of insufficient information. Those with a low need for cognitive closure work more slowly, searching extensively for informa-

---

need for cognitive closure The psychological desire to reach a final decision swiftly and completely; also, the relative strength of this tendency, as indicated by a preference for order, predictability, decisiveness, and closed-mindedness.

tion and generating varied interpretations and solutions. When individuals face situations that interfere with their capacity to process information—time pressures, severe ambiguity, noise, or fatigue—this need for cognitive closure increases. The result is that groups rush to reach consensus. They are more likely to reject a member who disagrees with the group, and they express a stronger desire for agreement with other members. Stereotyped thought and tendencies to favor the ingroup over the outgroup increase, and willingness to compromise to reach integrative solutions during bargaining decreases. Increased need for closure—whether due to aspects of personality or triggered by a stressful situation—also increases the emergence of particular kinds of group structures. When groups are working under situations that induce a need for cognitive closure, they develop hierarchical authority structures with autocratic leaders. These groups' discussions are dominated by high-status group members who have a much greater impact on the group's communications and decisions than the rank-and-file members (De Dreu, 2003; Kruglanski et al., 2002; Kruglanski & Webster, 1991; Pierro, Mannetti, De Grada, Livi, & Kruglanski, 2003; Shah, Kruglanski, & Thompson, 1998; D. M. Webster & Kruglanski, 1998). These consequences of the need for closure are consistent with the symptoms of groupthink identified by Janis.

THE GROUPTHINK MODEL: CONCLUSIONS How well does Janis's groupthink model explain mistaken choices made by high-level decision-making groups? Theorists and researchers are divided on this issue. Some, noting the theory's limited support, suggest that it should be drastically revised. Others feel that the jury is still out, and encourage more research (Aldag & Fuller, 1993; Fuller & Aldag, 1998; Longley & Pruitt, 1980; McCauley, 1998; Raven, 1998; M. E. Turner & Pratkanis, 1998). Nearly all researchers agree, however, that the model has great heuristic value. A mere 3 years after the publication of Janis's 1972 analysis, the term *groupthink* appeared in *Webster's New Collegiate Dictionary* (M. E. Turner & Pratkanis, 1998). The theory offers insight into very puzzling groups—those that make wrong-headed decisions—and has been applied to political decision makers, cults, businesses, and communities. In 2004, for example, the U.S. Senate Select Committee on Intelligence concluded that the intelligence community of the U.S. government had displayed a number of the symptoms of groupthink when it erroneously concluded that the country of Iraq was assembling weapons of mass destruction. The theory serves as a reminder that if we are to understand political events that change the lives of tens of thousands of people the world over, we must understand groups.

Preventing Groupthink

Kennedy did not take his Bay of Pigs failure lightly. In the months following the defeat, he explored the causes of his group's poor decision making. He fired those he felt had misled him, put in place improved procedures for handling information, and learned how to decipher messages from his military staff. These changes prepared him for the next great issue to face his administration—the Cuban

Missile Crisis of 1962. When Kennedy learned that the Soviet Union was constructing a missile base in Cuba, he called together his top advisers to form the Executive Committee of the National Security Council. This time, Kennedy and his advisors made the right decision. Essentially the same people meeting in the same room and guided by the same leader worked equally hard under similar pressures. Both crises occurred in the same area of the world, involved the same foreign powers, and could have led to equally serious consequences. Why did the Missile Crisis advisors succeed where the Bay of Pigs committee had failed?

LIMITING PREMATURE SEEKING OF CONCURRENCE If conformity was the norm in the Bay of Pigs group, dissent was championed by the group during the Missile Crisis. Kennedy deliberately suspended the rules of discussion that guided such meetings; agendas were avoided, and new ideas were welcomed. Although pressures to conform surfaced from time to time during the discussion, the members felt so comfortable in their role as skeptical, critical thinkers that they were able to resist the temptation to go along with the consensus. In fact, the group never did reach 100% agreement on the decision to turn back Soviet ships.

The atmosphere of open inquiry can be credited to changes designed and implemented by Kennedy. He dropped his closed style of leadership to become an open leader as he (1) carefully refused to state his personal beliefs at the beginning of the session, waiting instead until others had let their views be known; (2) required a full, unbiased discussion of the pros and cons of each possible course of action; (3) convinced his subordinates that he would welcome healthy criticism and condemn "yea-saying"; (4) arranged for the group to meet without him on several occasions; and (5) encouraged specific members of the group to take the role of dissenter, or *devil's advocate,* during the group discussions.

Kennedy also arranged for this committee to meet separately in two subgroups. The committee members had practiced this approach on other policy issue decisions, and they were satisfied that it yielded many benefits: Arbitrary agreement with the views of the other subgroup was impossible; the lower level staff members felt more at ease expressing their viewpoints in the smaller meetings, and the presence of two coalitions in the subsequent combined meetings virtually guaranteed a spirited debate (D. D. Wheeler & Janis, 1980).

CORRECTING MISPERCEPTIONS AND BIASES Janis's image of people as reluctant decision makers does not quite match the executive committee members. The participants fully realized that some course of action had to be taken, and they resigned themselves to their difficult task. Their decisional conflict was fanned by doubts and worries over questions that they could not answer, and at times, they must have been tempted to ease their discomfort by overestimating American superiority, belittling the Russians, and denying the magnitude of the dangers. Yet through vigilant information processing, they succeeded in avoiding these misperceptions, illusions, and errors.

No trace of the illusion of superiority that had permeated the planning sessions of the Bay of Pigs invasion was in evidence during the executive committee meetings. The men knew that they and their decision were imperfect and that wishful thinking would not improve the situation. President Kennedy repeatedly told the group that there was no room for error, miscalculation, or oversight in their plans, and at every meeting, the members openly admitted the tremendous risks and dangers involved in taking coercive steps against the Russians. Each solution was assumed to be flawed, and even when the blockade had been painstakingly arranged, the members developed contingency plans in case it failed.

As members admitted their personal inadequacies and ignorance, they willingly consulted experts who were not members of the group. No group member's statements were taken as fact until independently verified, and the ideas of younger, low-level staff members were solicited at each discussion. Participants also discussed the group's activities with their own staffs and entered each meeting armed with the misgivings and criticisms of these unbiased outsiders.

The committee discussed the ethics of the situation and the proposed solutions. For example, although some members felt that the Russians had left themselves open to any violent response the Americans deemed appropriate, the majority argued that a final course of action had to be consistent with "America's humanitarian heritage and ideals" (Janis, 1972, p. 157). Illusions of morality and invulnerability were minimized along with biased perceptions of the outgroup.

USING EFFECTIVE DECISION-MAKING TECHNIQUES The executive committee is not an example of an effective decision-making body simply because its solution to the missile crisis worked. Rather, just as the decision-making methods used by the Bay of Pigs committee ensured its failure, the executive committee's use of effective decision-making techniques increased its chances of success ('t Hart, 1998). Members analyzed a wide range of alternative courses of action, deliberately considered and then reconsidered the potential effects of their actions, consulted experts, and made detailed contingency plans in case the blockade failed to stop the Russians. Many initially favored military intervention, but the majority of the group's members insisted that other alternatives be explored. This demand led to an expanded search for alternatives, and soon the following list emerged:

1. Do nothing.
2. Exert pressure on the Soviet Union through the United Nations.
3. Arrange a summit meeting between the two nations' leaders.
4. Secretly negotiate with Castro.
5. Initiate a low-level naval action involving a blockade of Cuban ports.
6. Bombard the sites with small pellets, rendering the missiles inoperable.
7. Launch an air strike against the sites with advance warning to reduce loss of life.
8. Launch an air strike without advance warning.
9. Carry out a series of air attacks against all Cuban military installations.
10. Invade Cuba.

Once this list was complete, the men focused on each course of action before moving on to the next option. They considered the pros and cons, fleshed out unanticipated drawbacks, and estimated the likelihood of success. During this process, outside experts were consulted to give the members a better handle on the problem, and contingency plans were briefly explored. Even those alternatives that had initially been rejected were resurrected and discussed, and the group invested considerable effort in trying to find any overlooked detail. When a consensus on the blockade plan finally developed, the group went back over this alternative, reconsidered its problematic aspects, and meticulously reviewed the steps required to implement it. Messages were sent to the Russians, military strategies were worked out to prevent any slipups that would escalate the conflict, and a graded series of actions was developed to be undertaken should the blockade fail. Allies were contacted and told of the U.S. intentions, the legal basis of the intervention was established by arranging for a hemisphere blockade sanctioned by the Organization of American States, and African countries with airports that could have been used by Russia to circumvent the naval blockade were warned not to cooperate. To quote Robert Kennedy, "Nothing, whether a weighty matter or a small detail, was overlooked" (1969, p. 60).

Summary in Outline

❖ Why make decisions in groups?

1. Groups are more effective decision makers than individuals, particularly when dealing with problems that have a known solution (*intellective tasks*) rather than problems that have no clear right or wrong answer (*judgmental tasks*).

2. A *functional theory of group decision making* identifies four stages that appear consistently in many groups: orientation, discussion, decision, and implementation (see Figure 10-3).

   • *Orientation stage:* The group identifies the problem to be solved and plans the process to be used in reaching the decision. Although many groups bypass this stage, one useful result of this period of orientation is the development of a mental representation of the problem that is shared by all the members of the group (a *shared mental model*).

   • *Discussion stage:* The group gathers information about the situation, identifies and weighs options, and tests its assumptions. A *collective information*

processing model assumes that groups gather information and process that information to generate decisions and judgments. Three information processing gains that result from discussion are improved memory for information, increased exchange of information, and more thorough processing of information. A group's *collective memory* includes the combined memories of all individual members, and *cross-cueing* and *transactive memory systems* work to enhance group memory. Group memory is weakened by social loafing, free riding, and by the complexity of the group setting, which disrupts group members' ability to organize information in memory and subsequently retrieve that information.

   • *Decision stage:* The group relies on an implicit or explicit *social decision scheme* to combine individual preferences into a collective decision. Common schemes include delegating decisions, statisticized decisions, plurality decisions, unanimous decisions (consensus), and random decisions. Groups generally use consensus when dealing with sensitive issues, but they tend to use a plurality voting scheme when making choices.

- *Implementation stage:* The group carries out the decision and assesses its impact. As Coch and French's classic study of motivation in the workplace suggests, members are more satisfied and more likely to implement decisions when they were actively involved in the decision-making process. Contemporary management methods, such as quality circles and self-directed teams, are based on this insight.

3. Vroom's *normative model of decision making* suggests that different types of situations call for different types of autocratic, consultative, or group decision-making methods.

❖ **What problems undermine the effectiveness of decision-making groups?**

1. The usefulness of group discussion is limited, in part, by members' inability to express themselves clearly and by their limited listening skills. Groups sometimes use discussion to avoid making decisions, and they often spend more time discussing minor matters instead of important ones.

2. Groups are prone to the *shared information bias*—they spend more of their discussion time examining details that two or more of the group members know in common than discussing unshared information. This oversampling of shared information leads to poorer decisions when a hidden profile would be revealed by considering the unshared information more closely.

- The shared information bias increases when tasks have no demonstrably correct solution and when group leaders do not actively draw out unshared information.

- Groups can avoid the shared information bias if they spend more time actively discussing their decisions or if they make use of *group decision support systems* (GDSS).

3. Judgment errors that cause people to overlook important information and overuse unimportant information are often exacerbated in groups, including errors in how information is used (*sins of commission*), errors caused by overlooking useful information (*sins of omission*), and errors caused by reliance on mental rules of thumb (*heuristics*) that oversimplify the decision (*sins of imprecision*). For example, groups, more so than individuals, fall prey to the *confirmation bias*—they start off with an initial preference and then seek out additional information to confirm the accuracy of their initial inclinations.

❖ **Why do groups make riskier decisions than individuals?**

1. Common sense suggests that groups would be more cautious than individuals, but early studies carried out using the *Choice-Dilemmas Questionnaire* found that group discussion generates a shift in the direction of a more risky alternative (the *risky shift phenomenon*).

2. When researchers later found evidence of cautious shifts as well as risky shifts, and a tendency for various types of attitudes to become more extreme in groups, they realized that the risky shift was a specific case of *group polarization:* a shift in the direction of greater extremity in individuals' responses (e.g., choices, judgments, expressions of opinions) when in groups.

3. Group polarization is sustained by the desire to evaluate one's own opinions by comparing them to those of others (social comparison theory), by exposure to other

members' pro-risk or pro-caution arguments (*persuasive-arguments theory*), and by groups' implicit reliance on a "risk-supported-wins" social decision scheme.

❖ What is groupthink, and how can it be prevented?

1. Janis argued that fiascoes and blunders such as the decision to invade Cuba at the Bay of Pigs occur when group members strive for solidarity and cohesiveness to such an extent that any questions or topics that could lead to disputes are avoided. Janis called this process *groupthink*.

2. Groupthink has multiple symptoms, which Janis organized into three categories:
   - overestimation of the group (illusion of invulnerability and illusion of morality);
   - closed-mindedness (rationalizations, stereotypes about the outgroup); and
   - pressures toward uniformity (self-censorship, the illusion of unanimity, direct pressure on dissenters, and self-appointed *mindguards*).

3. Studies of *pluralistic ignorance* have verified the tendency for group members to erroneously assume that their private opinion is discrepant from the other group members' opinions. Groups also experience *entrapment* when they become committed too quickly to a decision and continue to invest in it despite high *sunk costs*.

4. Groupthink groups also display defective decision-making processes.

5. Janis identified three sets of causes of groupthink: cohesiveness, structural faults of the group or organization (such as isolation and a closed leadership style), and provocative situational factors (including decisional stress).

6. Research has yielded partial—but not robust—support for many of Janis's hypotheses regarding decision making in groups:
   - Archival studies have found mixed support for the theory's most basic prediction—that groups that display more of the symptoms of groupthink tend to make poorer decisions.
   - Studies have suggested that cohesive groups sometimes display groupthink tendencies, provided that one or more of the other triggering conditions for groupthink are present.
   - Social identity theory suggests that a threat to a shared social identity will trigger groupthink-like decisions.
   - Groups whose members have a high *need for cognitive closure* are more likely to make poorer decisions.

7. Janis noted that groups need not sacrifice cohesiveness to avoid the pitfall of groupthink. Rather, he recommended limiting premature seeking of concurrence, correcting misperceptions and errors, and improving the group's decisional methods.

FOR MORE INFORMATION

Chapter Case:
The Bay of Pigs Planners

- *Bay of Pigs: The Untold Story*, by Peter Wyden (1979), offers a wealth of detail about the group that planned the invasion, and draws on

personal interviews with many of the original group members.

Making Decisions in Groups

- "The Emerging Conceptualization of Groups as Information Processors," by Verlin B.

Hinsz, R. Scott Tindale, and David A. Vollrath (1997), is a wide-ranging synthesis of
how such cognitive mechanisms as attention,
encoding, storage, retrieval, processing, and
learning shape group decisions.

- *Group Performance,* by James H. Davis (1969),
is a brief but seminal analysis of decision making in groups, with chapters examining social
facilitation, group tasks, social transition
schemes, composition, and communication
networks.

- "Group Performance and Decision Making,"
by Norbert L. Kerr and R. Scott Tindale
(2004), reviews studies of group decision
making published between 1990 and 2003.

- *The Handbook of Group Communication Theory
and Research,* edited by Lawrence R. Frey
(with associate editors Dennis S. Gouran and
Marshall Scott Poole; 1999), is a collection of
20 chapters dealing with virtually all aspects of
group communication and decision making.

Faulty Decision Making in Groups

- *Groupthink: Psychological Studies of Policy Decisions and Fiascos,* by Irving Janis (1982), takes
a sobering look at the pitfalls of group decision making and recommends many ways to
avoid groupthink. Excellent reading for anyone who regularly takes part in groups that
make important decisions.

- "Theoretical Perspectives on Groupthink:
A Twenty-Fifth Anniversary Appraisal," edited by Marlene E. Turner and Anthony R.
Pratkanis (1998), is a special issue of *Organizational Behavior and Human Decision Processes*
that focuses on Janis's theory of groupthink.

- *Why Decisions Fail: Avoiding the Blunders and
Traps that Lead to Debacles,* by Paul C. Nutt
(2002), reviews a series of terrible mistakes
made by corporate leaders in the United
States, including the construction of Euro-
Disneyland and the failure to recall dangerous
automobiles with known risks.

MEDIA RESOURCES

 Visit the Group Dynamics companion
website at http://psychology.wadsworth
.com/forsyth4e to access online resources for your book, including
quizzes, flash cards, web links, and more!

LEADERSHIP

CHAPTER OVERVIEW

Leaders are as universal as the groups they lead, but their ubiquity has not robbed them of their mystery. Leadership binds together the leader and the follower, the coach and the team, the manager and the staff, and the president and the citizenry in an interface that can fundamentally shape the group's future. If asked, "What one thing would you change to turn an inept group into a productive one?" most people would answer, "The leader."

❖ What is leadership?

❖ Who will lead?

❖ Why do some leaders succeed and others fail?

CHAPTER OUTLINE

Carly Fiorina: Transforming Groups Through Leadership

When Stanford University classmates Bill Hewlett and Dave Packard agreed to form a company to manufacture electronics, they flipped a coin to decide whose name to list first. Hewlett-Packard (HP) began building a variety of small products in Packard's garage and, over time, added more products, employees, offices, and factories. The company that began by making a foul-line indicator for bowling alleys now builds and markets such high-tech products as personal computers, calculators, software, printers, and medical technology. They started their company with $538. HP's annual revenue is now over $76 billion.

HP traces its success back to its excellent leaders. From the beginning, Hewlett and Packard avoided hierarchy and titles, insisting that all employees be called by their first names only; Hewlett and Packard were just "Bill" and "Dave." Their style of leadership, the "HP Way," was based on a can-do attitude, minimal corporate bureaucracy, reliance on small teams, and strong employee–management relations (Packard, 1995). When Bill and Dave retired, new leaders took over their work guiding the company, and in 1999, Carleton ("Carly") Fiorina was hired as HP's CEO. Fiorina began her career in business as a receptionist, but moved quickly into positions requiring management and leadership. Fiorina developed skills in all aspects of leadership, including planning, delegating, decision making, coordinating, and communicating with others. She transformed the "HP Way" into the "Carly Way" (until she resigned in 2005).

Fiorina's successes, and the successes of others like her, raise many questions about the complicated and intricate interpersonal process called *leadership*. First, what did Fiorina do to motivate her employees, ensure the smooth functioning of her teams, and solve problems in the company? What do leaders do? Second, why did executives at HP choose Fiorina to be a leader? Why are some people recognized as leaders, but others are not? And third, in her first few years as CEO of HP, Fiorina dramatically changed the nature of the company, vastly increasing its size and profits. Why did she succeed where others might have failed?

QUESTIONS ABOUT LEADERSHIP

People have probably been puzzling over leadership since the first cave dweller told the rest of the group, "We're doing this all wrong. Let's get organized." Leadership is an inevitable element of life in groups—a necessary prerequisite for coordinating the behavior of group members in pursuit of common goals. Leadership may be one of the few universals of human behavior (L. Mann, 1980). The great epics, such as *Beowulf*, the *Song of Roland*, and the *Odyssey*, are filled with the exploits of leaders of small bands of adventurers. Egyptian hieroglyphics written 5000 years ago include the terms *leader* and *leadership* (Bass, 1990). Anthropological evidence indicates that "there are no known societies without leadership in at least some aspects of their social life" (Lewis, 1974, p. 4). But what is leadership?

TABLE 11-1 Political leaders' comments on the nature of leadership

Source	Conception of Leadership
George W. Bush	"Leadership to me means duty, honor, country. It means character, and it means listening from time to time."
Benjamin Disraeli	"I must follow the people. Am I not their leader?"
Dwight D. Eisenhower	"Leadership is the ability to decide what is to be done, and then to get others to want to do it."
Adolf Hitler	"To be a leader means to be able to move masses."
Jesse Jackson	"Time is neutral and does not change things. With courage and initiative, leaders change things."
Ho Chi Minh	"To use people is like using wood. A skilled worker can make use of all kinds of wood, whether it is big or small, straight or curved."
Theodore Roosevelt	"The best executive is the one who has the sense enough to pick good men to do what he wants done, and self-restraint enough to keep from meddling with them while they do it."
Margaret Chase Smith	"Leadership is not manifested by coercion, even against the resented."
Margaret Thatcher	"If you want something said, ask a man; if you want something done, ask a woman."
Harry S. Truman	"A leader is a man who has the ability to get other people to do what they don't want to do, and like it."
Lao Tzu	"A leader is best when people barely know that he exists, not so good when people acclaim him, worst when they despise him."

Leadership Myths

The political scientist James McGregor Burns (1978) has asserted that leadership is "one of the most observed and least understood phenomena on earth" (p. 2). Other experts have expressed dismay at the prevalence of misunderstanding about leadership, complaining, for example, that most people "don't have the faintest concept of what leadership is all about" (Bennis, 1975, p. 1), that "the nature of leadership in our society is very imperfectly understood" (J. W. Gardner, 1965, p. 3) and that "many public statements about it are utter nonsense" (J. W. Gardner, 1965, p. 12). Scholars and laypeople are constantly offering prescriptive suggestions to leaders, but they often base their recommendations on some questionable assumptions about leadership (Bass, 1990; Yukl, 2002).

IS LEADERSHIP POWER? Many people, including some prominent political leaders, assume that good leaders are those capable of manipulating, controlling, and forcing their followers into obedience. Adolf Hitler, for example, defined leadership as the ability to move the masses, whether through persuasion or violence, and Ho Chi Minh once said that a good leader must learn to mold, shape, and change people just as a woodworker must learn to use wood (see Table 11-1). But people who use domination and coercion to influence others—whether they are kings, presidents, bosses, or managers—are not leaders. Constructive leaders act in the best interests of a group with the consent of that group. Leadership is a form of power, but power *with* people rather than *over* people—a reciprocal relationship between the leader and the led. Nor do leaders hoard their power. A leader may control the sources of power within the group, but he or she shares this power with other members (Hollander & Offermann, 1990; Sankowsky, 1995). As Fiorina (2004) explained, "leadership isn't about title, or hierarchy, or how many people report to you, or the size of your budget . . . leadership is about helping people see a different set of possibilities for themselves."

ARE LEADERS BORN OR MADE? Aristotle believed that leadership was an innate talent: "Men are marked out from the moment of birth to rule or be ruled." Some people, he believed, are "born leaders," for their unique dispositional qualities predestine them for the role of leader, just as others are born to be followers. But studies of leadership development and effectiveness, which we will examine later in this chapter, suggest that a person—through diligent effort and careful mentoring—can acquire the skills needed to become an effective leader. Certain personality variables are associated with effective leadership, but "nurture is far more important than nature in determining who becomes a successful leader" (Bennis & Nanus, 1997, p. 207).

DO ALL GROUPS HAVE LEADERS? The role of leader is not an absolute necessity for a group to function, but one of the first roles to emerge in a newly formed group is that of the leader (see Chapter 6). In small groups, and in groups that exist only briefly, all members may share leadership responsibilities, so no one individual emerges as the leader (Pearce & Conger, 2003). But as John K. Hemphill (1950) explained, larger groups encounter problems of coordination, administration, and communication that can be ameliorated by a leader. Therefore, members of large groups are more open to attempts by possible candidates to gain leadership. When Hemphill (1950) tested this hypothesis by comparing the behaviors of large-group leaders with those of small-group leaders, he found evidence of a greater reliance in the larger groups on the leader to make rules clear, keep members informed, and make group decisions. Hemphill (1961) also suggested that leaders appear in groups when (1) members feel that success on the group task is within their reach, (2) the rewards of success are valued, (3) the task requires group effort rather than individual effort, and (4) an individual with previous experience in the leadership role is present in the group. A group that is facing a stressful situation—such as a potential failure or danger—is also likely to embrace a leader's guidance (Hamblin, 1958; Helmreich & Collins, 1967; Moreland, 1997; Mulder & Stemerding, 1963; Pillai, 1996).

DO FOLLOWERS RESIST LEADERS? Some laypersons and experts have suggested that groups function best without leaders—that reliance on a central authority figure weakens the group and robs members of their self-reliance. Some, too, have noted that groups chafe under the control of a leader, for they begrudge the authority and power of the leader (Gemmill, 1986; Heifetz, 1994). Yet most people prefer to be led rather than be leaderless. Group members are usually more satisfied and productive when their groups have leaders (Berkowitz, 1953). Group members often complain about the quality of their leaders, but they seek out better leaders rather than avoiding them altogether (Hogan, Curphy, & Hogan, 1994). Most people do not just accept the need for a leader, but appreciate the contribution that the leader makes to the group and its outcomes (Friedman & Saul, 1991; G. L. Stewart & Manz, 1995). This "need for a leader" becomes particularly strong in groups that are experiencing interpersonal turmoil and can sometimes cause members to see leadership potential in people where none exists. Members of troubled groups, compared to more tranquil groups, exaggerate the potential of possible leaders. They even misremember crucial details, tending to recall their prospective leader as having performed any number of leader-consistent behaviors and forgetting any past behaviors that conflict with their image of the person as a suitable leader. Thus, members do not resist having a leader; instead, they conspire to create leaders both interpersonally and psychologically (Emrich, 1999).

DO LEADERS MAKE A DIFFERENCE? What would have happened if Fiorina had taken a job with IBM or Microsoft instead of HP? Would the company be as successful today? Leaders do influence their groups. Studies of leaders in all kinds of group situations—flight crews, politics, schools, military units, and religious groups—all suggest that some groups prosper when guided by good leaders (Bass, 1990; Cannella & Rowe, 1995). When a company gets a new CEO, its performance often climbs (Weiner & Mahoney, 1981). Professional baseball teams who begin their season with a new manager improve their performance over their play in the previous season (Fabianic, 1994). Newly appointed leaders who inspire and excite members with fresh ideas and strategies can spur the group on to great achievements and successes (Zaccaro & Banks, 2001). But even though a leader can inspire and transform, people sometimes attribute too much influence to leaders. In Western cultures, in particular, people assume that leaders are so influential that they, and they alone, determine their group's outcomes. This **romance of leadership** ignores both the limited influence wielded by most leaders (Finkelstein & Hambrick, 1996) and the many other factors that influence a group and its dynamics (Meindl, 1995; Shamir, 1992). When a team fails, those in charge often replace the group's leaders, for they assume that a different leader could have rescued the failing team (Gamson & Scotch, 1964). When people give all the credit for a group's success to the leader, or blame him or her for a failure, they overlook the contributions of the other group members (Meindl, Ehrlich, & Dukerich, 1985). Leaders are influential, but few leaders deserve all the blame for their group's failures, and fewer still are heroes who can fairly claim the lion's share of credit for their group's achievements.

---

romance of leadership The tendency to overestimate the amount of influence and control leaders exert on their groups and their groups' outcomes.

What Is Leadership?

Leadership is not the power to coerce others, an inborn trait, a necessity of group life, or a mysterious capacity to heal sick groups. Instead, **leadership** is the process by which an individual guides others in their pursuits, often by organizing, directing, coordinating, supporting, and motivating their efforts. Dave Packard and Carly Fiorina, despite their widely differing methods, were both leaders, for they organized and guided networks of individuals and groups. They directed the efforts of their subordinates, but they were also responsive to their employees' needs and interests. They also provided help and support to others in exchange for their time and energy. As Fiorina (2004) explained, "one of the most important qualities a leader can bring is the ability, the energy, the desire to unlock potential in others. I think leadership is ultimately about helping other people achieve more than they think is possible."

Leadership, then, is not a static characteristic of an individual or a group, but a complex of interpersonal processes whereby cooperating individuals are permitted to influence and motivate others to promote the attainment of group and individual goals. These processes are reciprocal, transactional, transformational, cooperative, and adaptive.

- Leadership is a *reciprocal* process, involving the leader, the followers, and the group situation. The leader does not just influence the group members; rather, the leader–follower relationship is mutual. An interactional view assumes that leadership cannot be understood independently of *followership*—the skills and qualities displayed by nonleaders (Barrow, 1977; Hollander, 1985, 1993; Hollander & Offermann, 1990).

- Leadership is a *transactional* process, in which leaders and followers work together, exchanging their time, energies, and skills to increase their joint rewards (Graen & Uhl-Bien, 1991; Hollander & Julian, 1969; Pigors, 1935).

- Leadership is a *transformational* process, for leaders heighten group members' motivation, confidence, and satisfaction by uniting members and changing their beliefs, values, and needs (Bass, 1985a, 1985b, 1997; Bass, Avolio, & Goldheim, 1987).

- Leadership is a *cooperative* process of legitimate influence rather than sheer power (Grimes, 1978). In a small group, for example, the individual who influences others the most is often designated the leader (Hollander, 1985). The right to lead is, in most instances, voluntarily conferred on the leader by some or all members of the group (Kochan, Schmidt, & DeCotiis, 1975).

- Leadership is an *adaptive, goal-seeking* process, for it organizes and motivates group members' attempts to attain personal and group goals (D. Katz & Kahn, 1978).

---

leadership   Guidance of others in their pursuits, often by organizing, directing, coordinating, supporting, and motivating their efforts; also, the ability to lead others.

What Do Leaders Do?

Fiorina was hired to lead HP, and her official title was Chairman of the Board and Chief Executive Officer. But what does Fiorina do as a leader? What behaviors define the role of leader?

A work group demands different things of a leader than does a discussion group or a huge corporation, but some similarities in leadership behavior emerge in a wide variety of groups. In the Ohio State University Leadership Studies, for example, investigators first developed a list of hundreds of types of behaviors observed in military and organizational leaders—behaviors that included initiating new practices, providing praise, interacting informally with subordinates, delegating responsibilities, representing the group, and integrating group action. They then refined the list by asking members of various groups to indicate how many of these behaviors their leaders displayed. Using a statistical technique called *factor analysis,* they identified clusters of related behaviors and identified relatively peripheral qualities that were rarely used to describe leaders. These analyses suggested that 80% of the variability in followers' ratings could be explained by two basic factors, as summarized in Table 11-2: *task leadership* (initiation of structure) and *relationship leadership* (consideration for group members; Fleishman, 1953; Halpin & Winer, 1952).

- *Task leadership* focuses on the group's work and its goals. To facilitate the achievement of group goals, the leader initiates structure, sets standards and objectives, identifies roles and positions members in those roles, develops standard operating procedures, defines responsibilities, establishes communication networks, gives evaluative feedback, plans activities, coordinates activities, proposes solutions, monitors compliance with procedures, and stresses the need for efficiency and productivity (Lord, 1977; Yukl, 2002).
- *Relationship leadership* focuses on the interpersonal relations within the group. To increase socioemotional satisfaction and teamwork in the group, the leader boosts morale, gives support and encouragement, reduces interpersonal conflict, helps members to release negative tensions, establishes rapport, and shows concern and consideration for the group and its members (Lord, 1977; Yukl, 2002).

The Ohio State researchers built these two dimensions into their *Leader Behavior Description Questionnaire* (LBDQ; S. Kerr, Schriesheim, Murphy, & Stogdill, 1974; Schriesheim & Eisenbach, 1995). Group members complete the LBDQ by rating their leader on items like those presented in the right-hand column of Table 11-2. The totals from the two separate sets of behaviors index the two dimensions of leadership.

Researchers in many countries who have studied many different types of groups have repeatedly confirmed this two-dimensional model of leadership behaviors. Although the labels vary—*work-facilitative* versus *supportive* (D. G. Bowers & Seashore, 1966), *production-centered* versus *employee-centered* (Likert, 1967), *administratively skilled* versus *relations-skilled* (F. C. Mann, 1965), *goal achievement*

TABLE 11-2 Task and relationship leadership: Definitions, related terms, and sample behaviors

Factor	Term	Sample Behavior
Task leadership: actions that promote task completion; regulating behavior, monitoring communication, and reducing goal ambiguity	Task oriented, goal oriented, work facilitative, production centered, administratively skilled, goal achievement	Assigns tasks to members, makes attitudes clear to the group, is critical of poor work, sees to it that the group is working to capacity, coordinates activity
Relationship leadership: actions that maintain and enhance positive interpersonal relations in the group; friendliness, mutual trust, openness, recognizing performance	Relationship oriented, socioemotional, supportive, employee centered, relations skilled, group maintenance	Listens to group members, is easy to understand, is friendly and approachable, treats group members as equals, is willint to make changes

versus *group maintenance* (Cartwright & Zander, 1968), and *performance* versus *maintenance* (Misumi, 1995)—the two basic clusters emerge with great regularity. These two elements of leadership also emerge when leaders talk about their work. Bill Hewlett, for example, emphasized the importance of creating strong, trusting relationships with his employees. He was more of a relationship leader. Dave Packard was also concerned about his employees' levels of satisfaction, but he was quicker to criticize faulty work. Packard's task leadership orientation earned him the nickname "The Mean One" (Anders, 2003).

The two-dimensional model of leadership behavior predicts that leaders, despite their widely varying methods and styles, tend to do two basic things when they lead others—they coordinate the work that the group must accomplish, and they attend to the group's interpersonal needs (see Focus 11-1). But these two forms of leadership, though commonplace, are not necessary conditions for leaders. As **leadership substitutes theory** posits, substitutes for leadership sometimes "negate the leader's ability to either improve or impair subordinate satisfaction and performance" (S. Kerr & Jermier, 1978, p. 377). As Table 11-3 indicates, aspects of the group (e.g., members' indifference to rewards), the task (e.g., the level of intrinsic reward), and the group or organization (e.g., the cohesiveness of the group) can make leadership unnecessary and unlikely (Dionne, Yammarino, Atwater, & James, 2002; Podsakoff & MacKenzie, 1997; Podsakoff, MacKenzie, & Bommer, 1996).

---

leadership substitutes theory A conceptual analysis of the factors that combine to reduce or eliminate the need for a leader.

FOCUS 11-1   Do Men and Women Lead Differently?

In contrast to popular writers, leadership researchers generally seem to agree that there are few and negligible gender differences in actual leader behavior.
–Karin Klenke (1996, pp. 159–160)

Leadership has two sides—the task side and the relationship side—and humans come in two varieties—man and woman. Do these variations in leadership correspond to sex differences in leadership? Do men tend to be task oriented, whereas women are more relationship oriented?

Despite changes in the role of men and women in contemporary society, when men and women gather in groups, the men tend to be *agentic*—task oriented, active, decision focused, independent, goal oriented—whereas women are more *communal*—helpful to others, warm in relation to others, understanding, aware of others' feelings (Abele, 2003). Women, when asked to describe themselves to others in just-formed groups, stress their communal qualities with such adjectives as open, fair, responsible, and pleasant. Men describe themselves as influential, powerful, and skilled at the task to be done (Forsyth, Schlenker, Leary, & McCown, 1985). Women, more so than men, engage in relationship maintenance, including giving advice, offering assurances, and managing conflict (Stafford, Dainton, & Haas, 2000). In day-to-day activities with same-sex friends, women tend to be more agreeable than men (Suh, Moskowitz, Fournier, & Zuroff, 2004). Women connect more positively to other group members by smiling more (LaFrance, 1985), maintaining eye contact (Exline, 1963), and responding more tactfully to others' comments (Ickes & Barnes, 1977). When same-sex groups work at tasks that require good interpersonal relations, groups of women outperform groups of men (W. Wood, 1987). These differences can even be seen in groups of children, with boys undertaking physical activities, competing with one another, and playing in rough ways, and girls carrying out coordinated activities with a minimum of conflict (Maccoby, 2002). These differences may even reflect evolutionary pressures that encouraged the development of communal tendencies in women and task-focused activity in men (Eagly & Wood, 1999; W. Wood & Eagly, 2002).

This sex difference is only a tendency, and it does not manifest itself across all groups and situations. Nor does it determine how men and women respond when they become a group's leader. When Alice Eagly and Blair Johnson (1990) reviewed more than 150 studies that compared the leadership styles adopted by men and women, they discovered that as the agentic–communal tendency suggests, women performed more relationship-oriented actions in laboratory groups and also described themselves as more relationship oriented on questionnaires. The sexes did not differ, however, in studies conducted in organizational settings (Dobbins & Platz, 1986). Indeed, as managers, women tended to be both task and relationship oriented, whereas men were primarily task oriented (Stratham, 1987). Women and men often adopted different styles of leadership, but they did not differ in their agentic and communal tendencies.

LEADERSHIP EMERGENCE

Manet was the leader of the impressionist painters. Fito Strauch took control of the day-to-day activities of the Andes survivors. Jim Jones was the charismatic leader of the People's Temple. John F. Kennedy was elected president of the United States. Carly Fiorina was chosen to be the president and CEO of HP. But why Manet and not Degas? Why Strauch and not Canessa? Why Kennedy and not Nixon? Why did the board of directors of HP ask former CEO Lew Platt to

TABLE 11-3 Characteristics that can substitute for and neutralize relationship and task leadership

Characteristic	Relationship Leadership	Task Leadership
Of the group member		
1. Has ability, experience, training, knowledge		Substitute
2. Has a need for independence		Substitute
3. Has a "professional" orientation	Substitute	Substitute
4. Is indifferent to group rewards	Neutralize	Neutralize
Of the task		
5. Is unambiguous and routine		Substitute
6. Is methodologically invariant		Substitute
7. Provides its own feedback concerning accomplishment		Substitute
8. Is intrinsically satisfying	Substitute	
Of the organization		
9. Is formalized (has explicit plans, etc.)		Substitute
10. Is inflexible (rigid, unbending rules, etc.)		Neutralize
11. Has specified staff functions		Substitute
12. Has cohesive work groups	Substitute	Substitute
13. Has organized rewards not controlled by leader	Neutralize	Neutralize
14. Has physical distance between leader and members	Neutralize	Neutralize

Source: S. Kerr & Jermier, 1978.

step down so they could hire Carly Fiorina to replace him? What determines which individuals emerge as the leaders of their groups, organizations, and countries? What determines **leadership emergence**?

Scholars have debated this question for centuries. In the 19th century, for example, the historian Thomas Carlyle offered up his **great leader theory** of history (Carlyle called it the "great man" theory). He asserted that leaders do not achieve their positions by accident or twist of fate. Rather, these individuals possess certain characteristics that mark them for greatness. Carlyle (1841) believed that leaders are different from followers, so history could be best studied by considering the contributions of the few great men and women. The Russian novelist Leo Tolstoy disagreed. To Tolstoy, such leaders as Alexander the Great

---

leadership emergence The process by which an individual becomes formally or informally, perceptually or behaviorally, and implicitly or explicitly recognized as the leader of a formerly leaderless group.

great leader theory A view of leadership, attributed to historian Thomas Carlyle, that successful leaders possess certain characteristics that mark them for greatness, and that such great leaders shape the course of history.

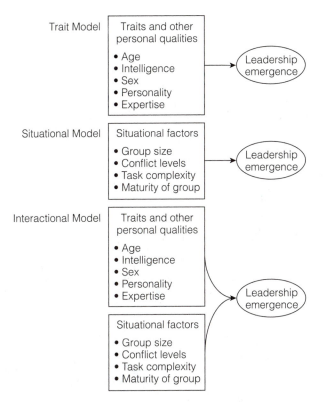

FIGURE 11-1

Who will emerge as leader? An interactional model suggests that characteristics of the individual (traits) interact with situational factors to determine who will emerge as the leader of a group.

and Napoleon came to prominence because the spirit of the times—the *zeitgeist*—was propitious for the dominance of a single individual, and the qualities of the person were largely irrelevant to this rise to power. Tolstoy's **zeitgeist theory** posited that the conquests and losses of military leaders such as Napoleon were caused not by their decisions and skills but by uncontrollable aspects of the historical situation (Tolstoy, 1869/1952).

These two perspectives—Carlyle's great leader theory and Tolstoy's zeitgeist approach—continue to shape theoretical analyses of leadership emergence. As Figure 11-1 indicates, the great leader theory is consistent with *trait models,* which

---

zeitgeist theory A view of leadership, attributed to Leo Tolstoy, that history is determined primarily by the "spirit of the times" rather than by the actions and choices of great leaders.

assume that leaders possess certain personality traits and characteristics and that these characteristics are responsible for their rise in the leadership ranks. Tolstoy's zeitgeist view, in contrast, is consistent with *situational models,* which suggest that leadership is determined by a host of variables operating in the leadership situation, including the needs of the group members, the availability of resources, and, most importantly, the type of task to be performed (Immelman, 2003; Simonton, 1980, 1987).

An *interactional* approach to leadership, however, reconciles these two models by asserting that traits and situations interact to determine who will lead and who will not. If a group is about to disintegrate because of heated conflicts among the members, for example, the effective leader will be someone who can improve the group's interpersonal relations (R. Katz, 1977). Similarly, if individuals possess skills that facilitate performance on intellectual tasks but undermine performance on artistic tasks, then they are likely to emerge as effective leaders only if the group is working on intellectual tasks (Stogdill, 1974). Lewin's $B = f(P, E)$ formula for interactionism, applied to leadership, suggests that a leader's behavior is a function both of the characteristics of the person (traits) and the characteristics of the group environment (situations; House & Aditya, 1997).

Personal Qualities of Leaders

Carly Fiorina possesses qualities that set her apart from others. She has extensive experience in business leadership, for before joining HP, she spent nearly 20 years at AT&T and Lucent Technologies. She is extremely intelligent, articulate, self-assured, energetic, and achievement oriented. Are these the personal qualities we expect to find in a leader?

PERSONALITY Early leadership researchers believed that leaders possessed certain personality traits that set them apart from others. This *trait view,* which in its strongest form assumed that some people were natural-born leaders, faded in popularity as researchers reported a series of failures to find any consistent impact of personality on leadership behavior across a wide variety of situations. After conducting hundreds of studies, several reviewers concluded that the correlation between personality traits and leadership was too small to serve much predictive purpose (J. H. Mann, 1959; Stogdill, 1948).

In retrospect, this rejection of the trait model was premature (House & Aditya, 1997). When Ralph Stogdill re-reviewed more than 160 studies of personality and leadership in 1970, he concluded that leaders, relative to followers, were higher in ascendancy and energy level, sociability, achievement orientation, responsibility taking, adaptability, and self-confidence. Bernard Bass's (1990) list of key predictors of leadership emergence added several other personality traits, including adjustment, aggressiveness, alertness, emotional control, independence, creativity, and integrity. Robert Lord and his colleagues, after a meta-analytic review, recommended that dominance, masculinity–femininity, and intelligence be added to the list of key personality traits that predict leadership (Lord, De Vader, & Alliger, 1986).

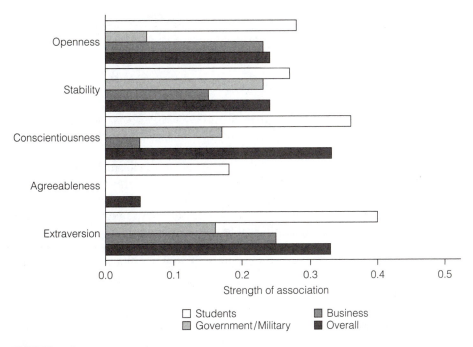

FIGURE 11-2

What is the relationship between personality traits and leadership emergence? When researchers used meta-analysis to combine the results of 222 correlational findings generated in 73 samples of the personality–leadership relationship, they found that extraversion was the strongest predictor of leadership emergence and agreeableness the weakest. *Source:* Judge, Bono, Ilies, & Gerhardt, 2002.

In general, the pattern of relationships is consistent with the so-called "big five" dimensions of personality identified by dozens of different researchers (Hogan et al., 1994):

- *extraversion:* outgoing, sociable, interpersonal, expressive, gregarious
- *agreeableness:* friendly, warm, likable, generous, kind
- *conscientiousness:* responsible, achievement oriented, dependable, self-controlled
- *stability:* emotionally controlled, assured, not anxious, balanced
- *openness to experience:* intellectually able, open to new ideas and experiences, cultured

As Figure 11-2 indicates, leaders tend to have elevated personality scores on four of these dimensions, with extraversion, conscientiousness, and openness emerging as particularly consistent indicators in a number of studies conducted in organizational and small-group settings (Barrick & Mount, 1991; S. A. Kirkpatrick & Locke, 1991; Ones, Mount, Barrick, & Hunter, 1994). Studies involving students, including laboratory studies of leaderless groups, generally found stronger relationships between personality and leadership emergence than studies of leaders in military, government, and business settings (Judge, Bono, Ilies, & Gerhardt, 2002).

INTELLIGENCE Stogdill (1948, 1974) cited 48 studies of the link between intellectual ability and leadership. Although the average correlation is small—on the order of .25 to .30—small-group and managerial leaders tend to score higher than average on standard intelligence tests, make superior judgments with greater decisiveness, be more knowledgeable, and speak more fluently. Leaders typically do not, however, exceed their followers in intellectual prowess by a wide margin (Simonton, 1985). Groups appear to prefer leaders who are more intelligent than the average group member, but too great a discrepancy introduces problems in communication, trust, and social sensitivity. Although highly intelligent individuals may be extremely capable and efficient leaders, their groups may feel that large differences in intellectual abilities translate into large differences in interests, attitudes, and values. Hence, although high intelligence may mean skilled leadership, a group prefers to be "ill-governed by people it can understand" (C. A. Gibb, 1969, p. 218).

In addition to basic intelligence, leaders also require a modicum of social and emotional intelligence. When people think of intelligence, they often stress cognitive abilities such as mathematics, verbal skill, and intellectual problem solving. But some people are also interpersonally intelligent: They have the ability to understand and relate to people, for they deal with others wisely and effectively (Thorndike, 1920). Social intelligence is indicated by higher than average empathy for others, initiative in social interactions, emotional expressivity, and self-control in interpersonal contexts, and these qualities are all associated with leadership tendencies. **Emotional intelligence,** which is a key component of interpersonal intelligence, "is a type of social intelligence that involves the ability to monitor one's own and others' emotions, to discriminate among them, and to use the information to guide one's thinking and actions" (J. D. Mayer & Salovey, 1993, p. 433). This form of intelligence is linked to behaviors associated with leadership, including willingness to cooperate with others, empathy for others, the tendency to take others' perspectives, and the emotional intensity of one's interpersonal relations (Goleman, 1995; Schutte et al., 2001; Wolff, Pescosolido, & Druskat, 2002).

Stephen Zaccaro and his colleagues have confirmed the importance of social intelligence by studying how people react when they move from one group to another and from one task assignment to another. Using a rotational design, Zaccaro repeatedly changed the membership composition of several groups as they worked on different tasks. Some of the tasks, such as group discussions of controversial topics, called for a leader who was good with people. Other tasks, in

---

emotional intelligence The component of social intelligence that relates to one's capacity to accurately perceive emotions, to use information about emotions when making decisions, and to monitor and control one's own and others' emotional reactions.

contrast, called for a leader who was task oriented. Even though the researchers dissolved the groups and re-formed them before assigning new tasks to each group, the same individuals tended to emerge as leaders in each newly reformulated group. Later analysis indicated that these individuals were able to alter their behaviors to fit the demands of the situation. If their group was working on a task that required good "people skills," they became more interpersonally oriented. But when the group needed a directive, task-oriented leader, these individuals stressed the task. These findings suggest that *flexibility* may be one of the most important qualities to look for in an effective leader (Kenny & Zaccaro, 1983; Zaccaro, 1995; Zaccaro, Foti, & Kenny, 1991; Zaccaro, Gilbert, Thor, & Mumford, 1991; see also Borgatta, Couch, & Bales, 1954).

EXPERTISE AND EXPERIENCE When groups work collectively on tasks, individuals with more expertise usually rise higher in the group's leadership hierarchy. In a review of 52 studies of characteristics typically ascribed to the leader, Stogdill (1974) found that technical, task-relevant skills were mentioned in 35% of the studies. Groups are more accepting of leaders who have previously demonstrated task ability (M. Goldman & Fraas, 1965) and are more willing to follow the directions of a task-competent person than those of an incompetent person (Hollander, 1965). Furthermore, although high task ability facilitates leadership, low task ability seems to be an even more powerful factor in disqualifying individuals from consideration as leaders (Palmer, 1962). Given enough experience in working together, most group members can distinguish between the skilled and the unskilled (Littlepage, Robison, & Reddington, 1997; Littlepage & Silbiger, 1992).

Field studies of leadership in organizational and military settings suggest that individuals who possess valued skills are more often recognized as leaders. The successful head of the accounting department, for example, is usually recognized as a better accountant than his or her subordinates or other, less highly regarded managers (Tsui, 1984). Studies of ratings of military leadership ability have also found that physical ability and task performance skills are highly correlated with leadership emergence (R. W. Rice, Instone, & Adams, 1984). Fiorina's emergence as a leader was probably due to her general leadership skills, however, rather than to her skills in technology. She was the first CEO of Hewlett-Packard who did not have a degree in engineering. In fact, she was a history major in college.

PARTICIPATION The relationship between expertise and leadership is heartening, for it suggests that groups tend to favor leaders who are qualified for that role. Studies of participation rates and leadership, however, offer an important qualification, for they suggest that the person who talks the most in the group is the most likely to emerge as leader (P. J. Burke, 1974; Stein & Heller, 1979, 1983). These data are surprising. The correlation between leadership emergence and most personal characteristics usually averages in the low .20s, but the correlation between participation rate and leadership ranges from .61 to .72 (Littlepage & Mueller, 1997; Malloy & Janowski, 1992; Stein & Heller, 1979).

Nor does it matter what the leader says. Supporting the so-called *babble effect,* researchers found that people who make many useless remarks are more likely to emerge as leaders than individuals who make relatively few useful remarks. When researchers manipulated both the quantity and quality of the statements of a trained confederate in a problem-solving group, quantity overpowered quality (Sorrentino & Boutillier, 1975). The researchers created four-person groups and set them to work, but one of the group members was a confederate who systematically offered either many comments or few comments that were either high in quality (they promoted success on the tasks) or low in quality (they promoted failure on the tasks). When the participants later rated on 5-point scales the confederate's confidence, interest in the problem, competence, influence over others, and contributions to solving the task, only the quantity of his comments significantly influenced his ratings of confidence and interest. Furthermore, although the participants viewed the confederate as more competent and more influential when he interjected high-quality comments rather than when he made low-quality comments, the effects due to quantity were still stronger.

Why pick leaders based on the sheer quantity of their remarks? This tendency may stem from our assumption that the individual who is actively involved in the group discussion is interested in the group and is willing to take responsibility for its performance. Low participation rates, in contrast, are taken to imply that the individual has little interest in the group or its problems: "Quality is not positively related to leadership unless the competent person demonstrates his willingness to share his resources with the group members and is perceived as seriously trying to contribute to the group's goals" (Sorrentino & Boutillier, 1975, p. 411). These perceptions can apparently be best fostered by participating at high levels (Mullen, Salas, & Driskell, 1989; Sorrentino & Field, 1986).

Demographics of Leadership Emergence

When Fiorina (2003) was selected to be the CEO of HP, she expected to be asked, "What is it like to be the first non-technologist to run HP?" But this question was never voiced. Instead, interviewers and colleagues repeatedly queried, "What is it like to be the first woman to run HP?" Leadership emergence depends not only on personal qualifications and achievements, but also on general demographic characteristics, such as age, race, and sex.

HEIGHT, WEIGHT, AND AGE Leaders tend to differ physically from their subordinates. They are often older, taller, and heavier than the average group member. Ralph Stogdill (1948, 1974), after thoroughly reviewing the relationship between height and leadership, noted that correlations varied from −.13 to +.71, but the average was about .30. Group members seem to associate height with power, but the relationship is not so strong that height is a prerequisite for leadership. Dave Packard, for example, was 6 foot 5, but Bill Hewlett was 5 foot 8. Leaders also tend to be more physically fit. The smaller a man's waist-to-hip ratio (an indicator of fitness, because those with larger ratios tend to be out of shape), the more others rated him as leader-like when working in leaderless groups that were observed by others (L. Campbell, Simpson, Stewart, & Manning, 2002).

Stogdill found that the link between age and leadership emergence is more complicated. Leaders in informal discussion groups vary in age, whereas political and business leaders are often older than their subordinates. Stogdill suggested that in organizations and political settings, the climb up the ladder of leadership takes time. Fewer than 1% of the corporate executives for the top Fortune 700 companies are under 40 years of age, and 81% are 50 or older (Spencer Stuart, 2004). As Stogdill noted, "Organizations tend to rely upon administrative knowledge and demonstration of success that comes with experience and age" (1974, p. 76). Furthermore, if group members assume that age is an indicator of wisdom, experience, and sagacity, they are likely to prefer a leader who is older rather than younger (B. S. Lawrence, 1996; Zajac & Westphal, 1996).

ETHNICITY Leaders emerge all over the world, no matter what the culture, ethnicity, or race of the group members (Hunt & Peterson, 1997). Leadership may even be more common in cultures and subcultures that stress collectivistic, group-centered values. African American groups, for example, are often centered on strong leaders, even though Afrocentric groups stress unity more than European American groups (Warfield-Coppock, 1995). The role of leader is also firmly embedded in the traditions of Latin American, Asian American, and Native American groups (P. B. Smith & Bond, 1993; Zamarripa & Krueger, 1983).

But how do the members of a subculture fare in groups where they are outnumbered by members of another ethnic group? First, minorities tend to be less influential in heterogeneous small groups and, as a result, are less likely to emerge as leaders (Bass, 1990; Mai-Dalton, 1993). For example, when Mexican American and European American women interacted in groups, the Mexican American women exerted less influence than the European American women (Roll, McClelland, & Abel, 1996). In a study conducted in Australia that paired Chinese students with Australian students, the Chinese students were less influential than the Australian students (E. S. Jones, Gallois, Callan, & Barker, 1995). Second, minorities tend to be underrepresented in leadership roles in business and organizational settings (Bass, 1990). African Americans in U.S. organizations and military groups, for example, are typically denied leadership positions in racially diverse groups, even if their qualities and experiences qualify them for these roles (Molm, 1986; M. Webster & Driskell, 1983). When senior managers review the leadership potential of lower level managers, they give higher marks to European Americans than to African Americans and Asian Americans (Landau, 1995). Asian Americans, despite their success in scientific and technical fields, are less likely than European Americans and African Americans to achieve positions of leadership in those fields (Tang, 1997). Ethnic and racial minorities are underrepresented in the leadership world (Hooijberg & DiTomaso, 1996; Scandura & Lankau, 1996).

SEX Fiorina, as both a woman and a leader, is something of an exception. Although the gender gap in leadership has narrowed in recent years, it has not closed. Social roles are still apportioned by sex, with men more likely to work outside the home (Eagly, Wood, & Diekman, 2000). Men's overrepresentation in organizations and business settings provides them with far more leadership opportunities than are available to women. The number of women working in first-line managerial roles in sales and office settings has risen steadily over the years—reaching nearly 52% of the total positions—but men hold a near monopoly on high-level leadership positions (D. Jones, 2003). In 2004, Fiorina was one of only six female CEOs of Fortune 500 companies. Female managers are more likely to feel excluded from career-related and informal interactions with senior managers than are male managers (Cianni & Romberger, 1995), and some have also expressed less confidence in their leadership abilities (C. Watson & Hoffman, 1996). A "glass ceiling" has been said to block women's rise into top management positions.

This gender difference also shapes men's and women's actions in small-group settings (Eagly & Karau, 2002). Men are five times more likely to enact leadership behaviors than women in small, mixed-sex, leaderless groups (H. A. Walker, Ilardi, McMahon, & Fennell, 1996) and so are more likely to emerge as leaders (Eagly, 1987). Both leaders and subordinates perceive female leaders to be less dominant than male leaders (Carli, 2001). The lone man in an otherwise all-female group often becomes the leader, whereas the lone woman in an otherwise all-male group has little influence (J. Crocker & McGraw, 1984). The tendency for men to dominate women in informal discussion groups was observed even when the men and women were all deemed to be androgynous (Porter, Geis, Cooper, & Newman, 1985), when group members were personally committed to equality for men and women (Sapp, Harrod, & Zhao, 1996), when the women in the group were dispositionally more dominant than the men (Megargee, 1969; Nyquist & Spence, 1986), and when the men and women were equally extraverted (L. Campbell et al., 2002). When researchers paired together a person who tended to be interpersonally powerful with one who was more submissive, the dispositionally dominant person emerged as the leader in 73% of same-sex dyads. But in mixed-sex dyads, the dominant man became the leader 90% of the time, and the dominant woman became the leader only 35% of the time (Nyquist & Spence, 1986).

This tendency for men to emerge as leaders more frequently than women is particularly ironic because studies of sex differences in the qualities that have been shown to predict leadership effectiveness—skill in working with others, acknowledging the good work of subordinates, communicating clearly, and facilitating others' development—all suggest that women are superior on these qualities to men. Hence, although women are more qualified to be leaders, they are less likely to become leaders (Eagly, Johannesen-Schmidt, & Engen, 2003).

Who Will Lead? A Cognitive Explanation

Does this maze of relationships between leadership emergence and such qualities as personality, age, and sex follow any discernible pattern? Research suggests that leadership emergence is, in part, an orderly process that reflects the rationality of groups. The individual who is most likely to take charge of the group is the one who is most skilled, most experienced, most socially intelligent, and most capable. But groups are not always so rational, for in many cases, they select people to be leaders simply because they talk a great deal, are older, or are men.

Implicit leadership theories (ILTs) offer a cognitive explanation for these partially conflicting tendencies (Lord & Maher, 1991). Each group member comes to the group equipped with a set of expectations, beliefs, and assumptions about leaders and leadership. These cognitive structures are termed *implicit leadership theories* (Lord et al., 1986) or *leader prototypes* (Foti, Fraser, & Lord, 1982). Although each group member may have a unique conception of leadership, most people's ILTs include task skills—the leader should be active, determined, influential, and in command—and relationship skills—the leader should be caring, interested, truthful, and open to others' ideas (Kenney, Schwartz-Kenney, & Blascovich, 1996). Group members also expect their leaders to be prototypical of their group. Groups that prize intellectual prowess and analytic ability should have different ILTs than groups that stress action and adventure (Fielding & Hogg, 1997; Hogg, 1996).

Members rely on their ILTs to sort group members into one of two categories—leader or follower. They intuitively note the actions and characteristics of the individuals in their group, compare them to their ILTs, and favor as leader the individual who matches that prototype of a leader (Lord, Foti, & De Vader, 1984; Lord & Maher, 1991). ILTs also guide subordinates' evaluations of their leaders (Ilgen & Fujii, 1976; Lord, Binning, Rush, & Thomas, 1978; Rush, Thomas, & Lord, 1977). If members believe that leaders should be dominant, for example, they may only remember their leader acting dominantly and forget the times when their leader engaged in submissive behavior (Cronshaw & Lord, 1987; Lord, 1985; Lord & Alliger, 1985; Lord et al., 1984). Lord and his colleagues illustrated the biasing effects of ILTs in one study by arranging for raters to watch a videotape of a group interaction. After the tape, they asked the observers to identify behaviors that the leader had or had not performed. Lord found that the raters were less accurate, less confident, and slower to respond when trying to judge behaviors that were part of their ILTs but had not been performed by the leader they had watched. He also found that the raters were less accurate but more confident when rating the leader on traits that were not part of their ILTs (Foti & Lord, 1987). Lord concluded that when subordinates describe their leaders, these ratings reflect the subordinates' ILTs more than their leaders' actions (Lord, 1985; J. S. Phillips & Lord, 1986).

If ILTs were like actual scientific theories, then group members would discard them when they fail to explain who is and who is not an effective leader. But ILTs, because they are *implicit* theories, are rarely recognized or revised. In consequence, if individuals' ILTs are biased in favor of individuals who are White, masculine, tall, or just highly vocal, then members with these qualities will rise to positions of authority in the group, even if they are not qualified for these positions. As Focus 11-2 indicates, ILTs explain why leaders in groups in many societies tend to be men rather than women (Nye, 2002).

---

implicit leadership theories (ILTs) Group members' taken-for-granted assumptions about the traits, characteristics, and qualities that distinguish leaders from the people they lead.

FOCUS 11-2   Are Groups Biased Against Female Leaders?

True capabilities, true leadership, I think cannot be defined by gender or limited by gender.

–Carly Fiorina, HP Chief Executive Officer (2004)

Despite widespread changes in the roles of women and men in contemporary society, most leaders are men rather than women. A group without a leader, when asked to select one, generally opts for a man rather than for a woman (Eagly & Karau, 1991, 2002). Both men and women, when surveyed, express a preference for a male rather than a female boss (e.g., Simmons, 2001). Women receive lower evaluations and fewer promotions than men, even when actual performance data or behaviors are held constant (Geis, Boston, & Hoffman, 1985; Heilman, Block, & Martell, 1995). When a woman exerts influence in a group, members tend to frown and tighten their facial muscles; but when a man takes charge, members are more likely to nod in agreement (D. Butler & Geis, 1990). When people think "leader," they think "male" (V. E. Schein, 2001).

Alice Eagly's (1987) **social role theory** traces this bias to two intertwined misunderstandings— one pertaining to men and women, and one pertaining to leadership. Although gender stereotypes vary across time and place, people in virtually all cultures, when asked to describe women, speak of their expressive qualities, including nurturance, emotionality, and warmth. They expect a "she" to be sentimental, affectionate, sympathetic, soft hearted, talkative, gentle, and feminine. When describing men, they stress their instrumental qualities, including productivity, energy, and strength (J. E. Williams & Best, 1990). But when group members are asked to describe the qualities needed in a leader, their implicit leadership theories prompt them to emphasize the instrumental side of leadership (Dodge, Gilroy, & Fenzel, 1995; Nye & Forsyth, 1991); a leader must, they suggest, command and control. In consequence, the expectations associated with leadership mesh with the male gender role stereotype, but the leadership role is inconsistent with widely held stereotypes about women (Forsyth, Heiney, & Wright, 1997).

This *role incongruity* not only disqualifies women from taking the lead in groups, but it also creates a double standard for women once they achieve a position of leadership. Women, to be evaluated as positively as men, must outperform men. When Eagly and her colleagues reviewed 61 different studies that asked people to evaluate the performance of male and female leaders, they found that the behaviors and outcomes achieved by men were viewed more positively than the exact same outcomes achieved by women (Eagly, Makhijani, & Klonsky, 1992). Ironically, this bias reaches its peak when a female leader adopts a more task-oriented approach to leadership. In a classic example of a "catch-22," women are urged to act more like male leaders, but when they do, they are denigrated for not being "ladylike" (Heilman, 2001; Rudman & Glick, 2001). As Fiorina (2004) noted, "when it's clear that a woman is perhaps equally ambitious as her male counterparts, then she is too driven, too hard-bitten. In short, we may not like her." In situations where group members would "call a man aggressive and commanding," group members "call a woman domineering and demanding" (Fiorina, 2004). Perhaps these biases explain why men, in general, are more interested in becoming leaders than are women (Eagly, Karau, Miner, & Johnson, 1994).

Fiorina (2003) urged women to ignore the pressures of these biases and strive to overcome them. Eagly, in contrast, urged groups and group members to discard the prejudicial tendencies that drive these biases. If group members' implicit assumptions about leadership did not prize task-oriented actions over relational ones, and if they did not expect men to be more task oriented than women, then the tendency to "think leader, think male" would fade away (Eagly & Karau, 2002; V. E. Schein, 2001).

---

social role theory A conceptual analysis of sex differences developed by Alice Eagly recognizing that men and women take on different types of roles in many societies, and that these role expectations generate gender stereotypes and differences in the behavior of women and men.

LEADER EFFECTIVENESS

Alexander the Great controlled a huge empire without any modern means of transportation or communication. General George S. Patton inspired those under his command by displaying high levels of personal confidence, sureness, and an immense strength of character. Carly Fiorina, after taking charge of HP, steered the company through a period of economic downturn by cutting costs, streamlining procedures, laying off unproductive workers, and merging HP with a competitor (Compaq Computers). Alexander, Patton, and Fiorina are not simply leaders. They are *effective* leaders. But what is the key to their effectiveness?

Fiedler's Contingency Model

Fred Fiedler spent years studying groups that worked to achieve collective goals under the direction of an appointed, elected, or emergent leader. He focused his attention on groups that generated products and performances that could be evaluated, and he measured aspects of the groups' settings and their leaders to see what combinations consistently led to good results. His basic conclusion was that a leader's effectiveness cannot be predicted just by considering the leader's qualities. Nor can it be predicted on the basis of the situation the leader faces. Rather, Fiedler's **contingency theory** assumes that leadership effectiveness is contingent on both the leaders' motivational style and the leader's capacity to control the group situation (Fiedler, 1978, 1981, 1996).

MOTIVATIONAL STYLE Fiedler, like many other researchers, drew a distinction between relationship-motivated leaders, who try to find acceptance within their groups, and task-motivated leaders, who concentrate on completing the group's task. Fiedler measured these leadership styles with the *Least Preferred Co-Worker Scale* (LPC). Respondents first think of the one individual with whom they have had the most difficulty working at some time. They then rate this person, dubbed the *least preferred coworker,* on bipolar adjective scales such as "pleasant–unpleasant," "friendly–unfriendly," and "tense–relaxed." People who make high scores on the LPC are assumed to be relationship oriented; after all, they even rate the person they do not like to work with positively. Low LPC scorers are assumed to be task oriented.

SITUATIONAL CONTROL Just as leadership style is the key *personal* variable in contingency theory, control is the key *situational* factor in the model. If leaders can control the situation, they can be certain that decisions, actions, and

---

contingency theory Fred Fiedler's conceptual analysis of leadership assuming that a leader's success is determined by his or her leadership style and the favorability of the group situation; more generally, any analysis of leadership that suggests that the effectiveness of leaders depends on the interaction of their personal characteristics and the group situation.

suggestions will be carried out by the group members. Leaders who have trouble gaining control, in contrast, cannot be certain that the group members will carry out their assigned duties. What factors determine control? Fiedler highlighted leader–member relations, task structure, and position power.

■ *Leader–member relations.* What is the quality of the relationship between the leader and the group? If the group is highly cohesive and relatively conflict free, the leader will be less concerned with peacekeeping and monitoring behavior.

■ *Task structure.* Do group members clearly understand what is expected of them? When task structure is high, the group's tasks are straightforward and have only one right solution, whose correctness is easily checked. Tasks that are unstructured, in contrast, are ambiguous, admit many correct solutions, and offer no one right way of reaching the goal.

■ *Position power.* How much authority does the leader possess? Leaders with high position power can control rewards, punishments, salaries, hiring, evaluation, and task assignment. In some groups, on the other hand, the leader may have relatively little power.

Figure 11-3 summarizes the relationship between these three variables and the favorability of the leadership situations. Octant I in the chart is the most favorable setting—leader–member relations are good, the task is structured, and the leader's power is strong. Octant VIII is the least favorable situation, for all three variables combine in a group that is difficult for the leader to control.

PREDICTING LEADERSHIP EFFECTIVENESS Fiedler did not believe that either type of leader—task motivated or relationship motivated—is better overall. Instead, he predicted that task-oriented leaders (low LPC score) would be most effective in situations that are either highly favorable or highly unfavorable, whereas relationship-oriented leaders (high LPC score) would be most effective in middle-range situations. Assume, for example, that Fiorina is a low-LPC leader—task rather than relationship motivated. When will the groups she leads perform the best? According to Figure 11-3, Fiorina will get the most out of groups in Octants I, II, and III, where situational favorability is high, and groups in Octant VIII, the least favorable situation. If she is a high-LPC leader, her groups will perform best in the middle-range situations—Octants IV to VI. This relationship between motivational style and situational favorability is thought to be caused by the way relationship- and task-oriented leaders respond to difficult leadership situations. In difficult groups (Octant VIII), task-oriented leaders drive the group toward its goals, but the relationship-oriented leader spends too much time repairing relations. In highly favorable (Octants I through III) situations, in contrast, task-oriented leaders become more considerate and enjoy more positive leader–member relations than relationship-oriented leaders (Bons & Fiedler, 1976; Fiedler, 1986; Fiedler & Chemers, 1974; Fiedler & Garcia, 1987).

Studies of a variety of working groups support the complex predictions charted in Figure 11-3 (Fiedler, 1967, 1971a, 1971b, 1978, 1993). For example, when Fiedler (1964) studied anti-aircraft artillery crews, he measured both the

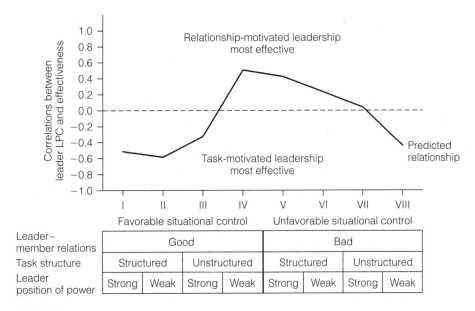

FIGURE 11-3

When is a task-motivated leader more effective than a relationship-motivated leader? Fiedler's (1964) contingency model argues that effectiveness depends on three aspects of the group situation: leader–member relations, task structure, and the leader's position of power. Octant I (left) corresponds to the most controllable and favorable situation, and Octant VIII (right) corresponds to the least controllable and least favorable setting. The vertical axis indicates the predicted relationship between *Least Preferred Co-Worker Scale* (LPC) scores and task performance. If the correlation is higher than 0 (positive), effectiveness is positively related to LPC score; that is, relationship-motivated leaders are more effective. If the correlation is lower than 0 (negative), effectiveness is negatively related to LPC score; task-motivated leaders are more effective. The graph suggests that a task-oriented leader is more effective when the situation is either favorable (Octants I, II, and II) or highly unfavorable (Octant VIII) for the leader.

commander's leadership style (high or low LPC) and the favorability of the situation. In most crews, the leaders enjoyed a strong position power because their authority was determined by rank. Moreover, task structure was high in most crews because the same sequence of decisions had to be made for each target. In some crews, however, the commander was well liked, whereas in other crews, the commander was disliked. As Figure 11-3 indicates, some crews were located in Octant I, because leader–member relations were good, the task was structured, and position power was strong. Others, though, fell into Octant V because the leader–member relations were bad. Thus, a low-LPC leader should be more effective for Octant I crews, but groups in Octant V should perform better with a high-LPC leader. Supporting this prediction, Fiedler (1955) found that LPC scores were negatively correlated with effectiveness for artillery squads in Octant I ($r = -.34$), but positively correlated with effectiveness in Octant V ($r = .49$).

The effectiveness of a unique leadership training program, called *Leader Match,* also supports the validity of contingency theory. Although many different programs and techniques have been developed to train leaders, the results of these procedures are typically disappointing (Stogdill, 1974). Fiedler, however, suggested that these programs fail because they place too much emphasis on changing the leaders—making them more supportive, more decisive, more democratic, and so on. He suggested instead that the situation should be engineered to fit the leader's particular motivational style. He called his training program *Leader Match* because he taught trainees to modify their group situation until it matched their personal motivational style (Fiedler, Chemers, & Mahar, 1976). Studies of the effectiveness of this innovative training program suggest that trained leaders outperform untrained leaders (M. J. Burke & Day, 1986; Csoka & Bons, 1978; Fiedler, 1978).

QUESTIONS AND CONCLUSIONS   Contingency theory, like all theories, has both weaknesses and strengths. Despite years of research, experts are divided on the model's validity, with some arguing that evidence supports the model and others arguing against it (see Chemers, 1997, for a review). Investigators have challenged not only the strength of the relationships that provide the basis of the predictions in the eight octants in Figure 11-3, but they have also questioned the methods that Fiedler used to measure leaders' motivational style (Hare, Hare, & Blumberg, 1998). In defense of contingency theory, however, the contingency model was one of the first theories of leadership effectiveness that fully considered both personal factors (LPC score) and situational factors (situational control). Few would dispute its key take-home message—that the effectiveness of a leader cannot be predicted without taking into account both the leader's perceptions of his or her followers and the leader's degree of control in the situation (Avolio et al., 2003; Chemers, 2000; Nahavandi, 2003; R. W. Rice, 1979).

"Style" Theories

Fiedler's contingency model assumes that leaders have a preferred "style" of leading: Some tend to be relationship-oriented leaders, and others are task-oriented leaders. Many other leadership theories accept this basic premise, but add that some leaders integrate both task and relationship elements in their approach to leadership. These style theories argue that effective leaders balance these two basic ingredients in the groups they lead (e.g., D. G. Bowers & Seashore, 1966; Hersey & Blanchard, 1977; House, 1971; S. Kerr et al., 1974; Likert, 1967; Misumi, 1985; Reddin, 1970).

THE LEADERSHIP GRID   Robert Blake and Jane Mouton hypothesized that leadership style depends on how one answers two basic questions: (1) How important is the production of results by the group? (2) How important are the feelings of group members? To some leaders, the key goal is achieving results. For others, positive feelings in the group are so important that they emphasize team-

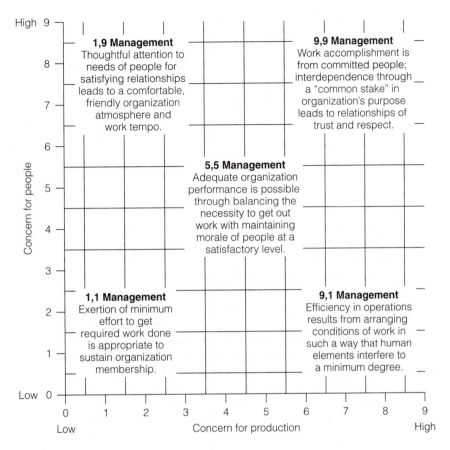

FIGURE 11-4

What is the one best style to use when leading people? The *Leadership Grid* (formerly the *Managerial Grid*) distinguishes between five basic leadership styles and recommends the 9,9 style above all others. *Source:* Adapted from *Leadership Dilemmas— Grid Solutions,* p. 29, by Robert R. Blake and Anne Adams McCanse. Copyright 1991 © by Robert R. Blake and the Estate of Jane S. Mouton. Used with permission. All rights reserved.

work and personal satisfaction. Others may feel that both these goals are important (Blake & McCanse, 1991; Blake & Mouton, 1964, 1978, 1980).

Blake and Mouton summarized these differences in their **Leadership Grid** (formerly called the *Managerial Grid*), which is presented in Figure 11-4. Both

---

Leadership Grid A theory of management and leadership, proposed by Robert Blake and Jane Mouton, assuming that people vary in their concern for people and their concern for results, and that individuals who are high on both dimensions (9,9) are the best leaders.

dimensions—concern for people and concern for results—are represented as 9-point scales ranging from *low concern* to *high concern*. Although a person's orientation could fall at any of 81 possible positions on the grid, Blake and Mouton emphasized five orientations: those located at the four corner positions and the one in the very center. An apathetic, impoverished 1,1 leader is hardly a leader, for he or she is not interested in either subordinates' feelings or the production of results. The 9,1 individual (high on concern for production, but low on concern for people, located in the lower right corner of the grid) is a taskmaster, who seeks productivity at any cost. The 1,9 leader, in contrast, adopts a "country club" approach that makes subordinates feel comfortable and relaxed in the group. The "middle-of-the-roader," located at 5,5, tries to balance both performance and morale but sometimes sacrifices both when results and individuals' feelings come into conflict. Finally, the 9,9 leader values both people and products highly and therefore tackles organizational goals through teamwork—"a high degree of shared responsibility, coupled with high participation, involvement, and commitment" (Blake & Mouton, 1982, p. 41).

Blake and Mouton (1982) were not contingency theorists; they felt that the 9,9 leadership style was the "one best style" to use when leading people. In their initial studies (Blake & Mouton, 1964), they found that managers who adopted the 9,9 style were far more successful in their careers than managers who adopted other methods. They also noted that studies conducted in educational, industrial, and medical organizations supported the utility of the 9,9 leadership style, as did the favorable results of their management training system (Blake & Mouton, 1980, 1982, 1985, 1986). These results are impressive, but many experts still question their strong claim that the 9,9 style works in *all* situations (S. Kerr et al., 1974; L. L. Larson, Hunt, & Osborn, 1976; Nystrom, 1978; R. E. Quinn & McGrath, 1982).

SITUATIONAL LEADERSHIP THEORY Paul Hersey and Kenneth Blanchard also described leadership in terms of the relationship and task dimensions. Unlike Blake and Mouton's grid, however, their **situational leadership theory** suggests that effective leaders combine supportive behaviors with directive behaviors depending on the developmental level, or *maturity,* of the group or subordinate. Mature individuals or groups are ones who are committed to the group and its task, and they are usually confident, self-assured, and highly motivated. Maturity is also related to competence, for mature members possess the skills and knowledge needed to perform their assigned tasks, perhaps because they have been trained, or because they have experience (Hersey & Blanchard, 1976, 1977, 1982; Hersey, Blanchard, & Johnson, 2001).

Figure 11-5 describes the theory's predictions. When group members are low in both commitment and competence, they work most effectively with a

situational leadership theory A theory of leadership, proposed by Paul Hersey and Kenneth Blanchard, suggesting that groups benefit from leadership that meshes with a group's stage of development.

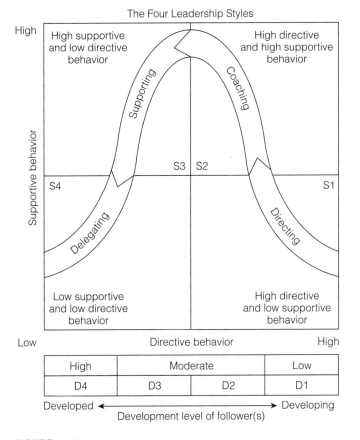

The Four Leadership Styles

FIGURE 11-5

Which style of leadership works best across the life cycle of the group? Hersey and Blanchard's (1982) *situational leadership theory* assumes that leaders must be flexible. When the group forms, they must use a directing leadership style (S1), but over time they should shift to other styles as the group develops.

directing leader who is not supportive (S1). As the group develops and gains experience on the task and commitment to the group's goals, the leader can increase relationship behavior and adopt a *coaching* style (S2; high direction and support). Still later in the group's development, the leader can ease off on both types of leadership, starting first with direction. In moderately mature groups, the *supporting* leader is most effective (S3), and in fully mature groups, a *delegating* leadership style is best (S4). Thus, an effective leader must display four different leadership styles as the group moves through its life cycle—directing, coaching, supporting, and delegating (Hersey et al., 2001).

Some critics have argued that situational leadership theory puts too much emphasis on matching the maturity of the members; these experts call for a careful balancing of task and relationship orientation at all developmental levels (Nicholls, 1985). But the basic premise on which the model rests—that different groups need varying amounts of task and relationship leadership—has been confirmed in a number of investigations. For example, newly hired employees needed and appreciated greater task structuring from their manager than did veteran employees (Vecchio, 1987). Conversely, members with higher levels of education and greater levels of job tenure preferred a leader who provided less task structure (Vecchio & Boatwright, 2002). Moreover, measures of leadership flexibility based on the theory, such as the *Leader Behavior Analysis II,* are useful tools for assessing rigidity in leadership style (Hersey, 1985; Lueder, 1985a, 1985b; cf. Graeff, 1983, 1997). The theory's training methods are also very popular among business professionals. Situational leadership theory forms the basis for the "one-minute management" approach to leadership in organizational settings (K. Blanchard & Johnson, 1981; K. Blanchard, Zigarmi, & Nelson, 1993; Carew, Parisi-Carew, & Blanchard, 1986).

Leader–Member Exchange Theory

Most theories of leadership, such as Fiedler's (1978) contingency theory and Blake and Mouton's (1980) *Leadership Grid,* focus on the leader's style or strategy and how the group responds as a whole to various interventions. But such a "one size fits all" approach does not always match the needs of specific group members. Whereas one group member may work well with a task-oriented leader, others may prefer a leader who provides them with support.

One approach to leadership, **leader–member exchange theory** (LMX), uniquely stresses the quality of the one-to-one relationship between a leader and a subordinate. LMX theory (and its predecessor, *vertical dyad linkage theory*) notes that leaders have dyadic relationships with each group member and that these dyadic relationships may be substantially different within the total group. In some cases, the member and leader may work well together. The leader may be satisfied with the member's work and provide him or her with extra responsibilities and rewards. The follower, in turn, may extend his or her role and express higher levels of satisfaction with the group. Other group members, however, may not respond as positively to the leader, so their responses are defined by their role and their fixed responsibilities (Dansereau, Graen, & Haga, 1975; Graen & Cashman, 1975; Graen & Uhl-Bien, 1995).

LMX theory suggests that group members tend to cleave into subgroups within the overall group. One group, the *ingroup* or *inner group,* includes those individuals with positive linkages to the leader. Leaders spend more time working with these members, value their inputs more, and also provide them with more

---

leader–member exchange theory (LMX) A dyadic, relational approach to leadership assuming that leaders develop exchange relationships with each of their subordinates, and that the quality of these leader–member exchange (LMX) relationships influences subordinates' responsibility, decision influence, access to resources, and performance.

resources. These group members respond by working harder for the group, taking on additional role responsibilities, and declaring their loyalty to the leader and the group. The second group, the *outgroup* or *outer group,* includes individuals with less satisfying linkages to the leader. These individuals do their work, but do not contribute as much to the group. They also express less loyalty and support for the leader (Dienesch & Liden, 1986).

LMX theory's basic assumptions have been verified empirically (Gerstner & Day, 1997). Individuals who feel that they have a good working relationship with their leader are less likely to leave the group and more likely to earn higher performance evaluations, get promoted more rapidly, express more commitment to the organization, voice more positive attitudes about their work and the group, and garner more attention and support from their leader. They often view their relationship with their boss as a *partnership.* Individuals who are not satisfied with their relationship think of their leader as someone who monitors their work but is otherwise uninterested in them as individuals (Duchon, Green, & Taber, 1986; Dunegan, Uhl-Bien, & Duchon, 2002; Graen & Uhl-Bien, 1995; Hofmann, Morgeson, & Gerras, 2003; Kacmar, Witt, Zivnuska, & Gully, 2003; Sherman, 2002; Varma & Stroh, 2001; Yrle, Hartman, & Galle, 2002). Researchers have also documented the natural tendency for subgroups to develop within groups, and for disparities in performance to exist between these two cliques (Bass, 1990). Leaders who recognize this tendency can improve their overall relations with their group by minimizing the number of people in the outer group (Graen & Uhl-Bien, 1991).

LMX theory's dyadic approach—stressing the relationship between each member and the leader—also provides an additional way of looking at leadership in general. Researchers have returned to other leadership theories, such as Fiedler's contingency model, and have begun to explore the type of leadership style that leaders use with each group member. These dyadic-level approaches add a second layer of information about leadership to the more common group-level analysis (Ayman, Chemers, & Fiedler, 1995; Dansereau, Yammarino, & Markham, 1995; R. J. Hall & Lord, 1995; Schriesheim, Cogliser, & Neider, 1995; Somech, 2003; Yammarino & Bass, 1991).

Participation Theories

Some leaders do all the leading—they, and they alone, make decisions, dole out assignments, supervise work quality, communicate with other groups, set goals, and so on. Such leaders adopt a command-and-control approach to leadership, which is common in military organizations. They give the orders, and their subordinates carry them out. Other leaders, however, share their leadership with others in the group. Dave Packard did not make decisions without consulting the members of his team. Similarly, Carly Fiorina (2004) set the general goals for HP, but she expected the other executives, managers, and workers to make choices, create structures, and recommend changes in procedures. Should leadership, as Fiorina and Packard suggested, be distributed across the group, or should it be concentrated in the hands of a single individual?

THE LEWIN–LIPPITT–WHITE STUDY As noted in Chapter 2, Kurt Lewin, Ronald Lippitt, and Ralph White conducted one of the earliest laboratory studies of interacting groups to determine the relative effectiveness of shared and unshared approaches to leadership. They arranged for groups of 10- and 11-year-old boys to meet after school to work on various hobbies. In addition to the boys, each group included a man who adopted one of three leadership styles (Lewin, Lippitt, & White, 1939; White & Lippitt, 1960, 1968):

- The *authoritarian,* or *autocratic,* leader took no input from the members in making decisions about group activities, did not discuss the long-range goals of the group, emphasized his authority, dictated who would work on specific projects, and arbitrarily paired the boys with their work partners.
- The *democratic* leader made certain that all activities were first discussed by the entire group. He allowed the group members to make their own decisions about work projects or partners and encouraged the development of an egalitarian atmosphere.
- The *laissez-faire* leader rarely intervened in the group activities. Groups with this type of atmosphere made all decisions on their own without any supervision, and their so-called leader functioned primarily as a source of technical information.

In some cases, the boys were rotated to a different experimental condition, so that they could experience all three types of participation.

The three types of leadership resulted in differences in efficiency, satisfaction, and aggressiveness. The autocratic groups spent as much time working on their hobbies as the democratic groups, but the laissez-faire groups worked considerably less (see Figure 11-6). When the leader left the room, however, work dropped off dramatically in the autocratically led groups, remained unchanged in the democratic groups, and actually increased in the laissez-faire groups. Furthermore, members of groups with an autocratic leader displayed greater reliance on the leader, expressed more critical discontent, and made more aggressive demands for attention. Democratic groups tended to be friendlier and more group oriented. Overall, the boys preferred democratic leaders to the other two varieties.

Although these findings seem to recommend democratic leadership over the two alternatives, the findings of Lewin, Lippitt, and White were not as clear-cut as Figure 11-6 implies. Several of the groups reacted to the autocratic leader with hostility, negativity, and scapegoating, but others responded very passively to their authoritarian leaders. In these latter groups, productivity was quite high (74%) when the leader was present, but it dropped to 29% when he left the room. Aggression—very apparent in some of the autocratically led groups—was replaced in these passive groups by apathy and acceptance of the situation. Although the group became aggressive if the autocratic leader was replaced with a more permissive one, when he was present, the group members worked hard, demanded little attention, only rarely engaged in horseplay, and closely followed his recommendations. As a methodological aside, the findings should also be interpreted with caution because the laissez-faire condition was not originally included when Lewin and his team designed the study. But when one of the

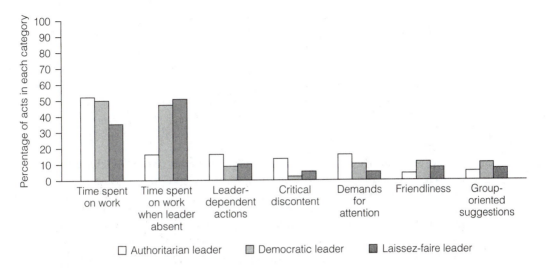

FIGURE 11-6

How do group members react to authoritarian, democratic, and laissez-faire leaders? Lewin, Lippitt, and White (1939) answered this question by recording a variety of behaviors of group members working under the direction of one of three types of leaders. Groups with either authoritarian or democratic leaders were more productive than the laissez-faire groups, but the autocratic groups were less productive when the leader left the room. Other findings suggest that the democratic groups were more cohesive. *Source:* Adapted from *Autocracy and Democracy* by R. K. White and R. Lippitt. Copyright © 1960 by the authors. Reprinted by permission of Harper-Collins Publishers, Inc.

experimenters was unable to enact an autocratic style correctly and instead just distanced himself from the groups, the investigators relabeled the leadership style he used as laissez-faire leadership (R. K. White, 1990).

SHARED LEADERSHIP Lewin, Lippitt, and White's (1939) findings, although far from definitive evidence of the superiority of democratic leadership, offer some support for sharing leadership responsibility across the entire group. Such decentered leadership models go by many names—co-leadership, collective leadership, democratic leadership, delegated leadership, empowerment, peer leadership, self-leadership, shared leadership, and participatory leadership—but underlying these various models is a common emphasis on breaking the leader's monopoly on power, influence, and authority in the group and shifting responsibility for core leadership functions to the rest of the group members (Seers, Keller, & Wilkerson, 2003).

Craig L. Pearce and Henry Sims, Jr. (2002) examined the relative effectiveness of a group-centered approach in a study of a manufacturing plant shifting away from a traditional organizational matrix to a flatter, group-based structure. This shift was precipitated by a series of severe labor–management disputes that culminated in bomb threats, conflict, and a drop in productivity. The leadership of the organization worked closely with the union in an attempt to develop a team-based approach. Over the course of several years, production was shifted to *change-management teams* (CMTs) that were designed to enhance productivity, product quality, and satisfaction with the work process itself. These groups were responsible for identifying areas of positive change in the organization, but they could also implement changes. Each CMT had a leader, but this individual was charged with adopting a shared rather than centralized approach to leadership (see Manz & Sims, 2001).

Pearce and Sims measured group members' perceptions at two levels—the leader level and the group level. To measure how much each leader adopted a positive, participatory style, members responded to items pertaining to self-reward, teamwork, goal setting, independent actions, opportunity thinking, and self-development (e.g., "My team leader urges me to reward myself with something I like when I have successfully completed a major task."). The members also completed these same items, but rating the group rather than the leader (e.g., "My team urges me to reward myself with something I like when I have successfully completed a task."). Significantly, Pearce and Sims found that groups that had high levels of group-level participatory leadership outperformed groups that had lower levels of participatory leadership.

Other studies, taken together, have suggested that if the members' reactions to their work are a key factor in maintaining and evaluating success, a participatory approach will be superior to a more leader-centered method (K. I. Miller & Monge, 1986). As Stogdill (1974) noted after reviewing more than 40 studies of various leadership methods that ranged along the participation continuum, satisfaction with the group seems to be highest in democratic groups, as opposed to autocratic and laissez-faire groups. Shared methods of leadership are also more effective in smaller rather than in larger groups (Vroom & Mann, 1960), and so are well suited to organizations that rely on small, self-directed teams or networks of distributed, relatively independent employees. A group-centered approach is also recommended when the leader does not have the information, time, or skill needed to adequately structure and regulate the group's work. As Victor Vroom's normative model (discussed in Chapter 10) posits, the choice between autocratic, consultative, or participative leadership depends on such factors as the importance of the decision to made, the availability of information to the leader, and so on (Vroom & Jago, 1988).

Transformational, Charismatic, and Visionary Leadership

Carly Fiorina is no ordinary CEO. She does not just set goals and plan future initiatives, but she inspires, excites, and captures the imaginations of those who work for her. When she spoke to HP employees and executives, she reiterated her vision of HP, her respect and admiration for people who work for HP, and her hope that the company will become the greatest company that has ever existed (Fiorina, 2002). People have described her as "courageous," a "warrior," "inspirational," "mesmerizing," and an Armani-wearing "rock star" (Hatcher & McCarthy, 2003).

Fiorina is a transformational, charismatic, visionary leader. Through the force of her personality, her spoken word, and her dynamic presentational style, she has a profound effect on her subordinates' dedication to her and to their work. Max Weber (1921/1946), as noted in Chapter 8, used the Greek word *charisma* to describe such leaders, for they seem possess a "divinely inspired gift" that sets them apart from other, more commonplace leaders. Such leaders, Weber believed, derived their power from their followers' devotion to them. Charismatic leaders are often inspirational speakers, expressing ideas that are both appealing and easily understood. Group members often express great affection for such leaders and accept their pronouncements on faith. Members also tend to become emotionally involved with the group and willingly sacrifice their own interests for the good of the group (Burns, 1978; House & Baetz, 1979).

Bernard Bass's (1997) theory of **transformational leadership** identifies the processes that charismatic leaders use to influence their followers. Bass (1997) believed that most leaders are *transactional* rather than *transformational*. They treat their relationship with their followers as a transaction: They define expectations, offer rewards, "formulate mutually satisfactory agreements, negotiate for resources, exchange assistance for effort, and provide commendations for successful follower performance" (Bass, 1997, p. 134). They also, in too many cases, lead by pointing out members' failings or by just ignoring problems until they become dire. Transformational leaders, however, go beyond rewards and punishments. These leaders tend to be self-confident and determined, and their communications with their followers are usually eloquent and enthusiastic (Waldman, Bass, & Yammarino, 1990; Yammarino & Bass, 1990).

Bass, in seeking the source of such leaders' social power, identified four components of transformational leadership: idealized influence (or charisma), inspirational motivation, intellectual stimulation, and individualized consideration:

- *Idealized influence.* Leaders express their conviction clearly and emphasize the importance of trust; they take stands on difficult issues and urge members to adopt their values; they emphasize the importance of purpose, commitment, and the ethical consequences of decisions.
- *Inspirational motivation.* Leaders articulate an appealing vision of the future; they challenge followers with high standards, talk optimistically with enthusiasm, and provide encouragement and meaning for what needs to be done.
- *Intellectual stimulation.* Leaders question old assumptions, traditions, and beliefs; they stimulate in others new perspectives and ways of doing things, and they encourage the expression of ideas and reasons.
- *Individualized consideration.* Leaders deal with others as individuals; they consider individual needs, abilities, and aspirations; they listen attentively

---

transformational leadership As described by Bernard Bass, a charismatic, inspiring method of leading others that often includes heightening followers' motivation, confidence, and satisfaction, uniting them in the pursuit of shared, challenging goals, and changing their beliefs, values, and needs.

and further individual members' development; they advise, teach, and coach. (paraphrased from Bass, 1997, p. 133)

Leaders who combine all four of these components of transformational leadership will, according to Bass, be effective in any group situation, at any level of an organization, and in any culture. Supporting this view, in a number of studies, leaders who display the qualities stressed in the model are viewed more positively by their subordinates, and their subordinates tend to be more productive as well (Hoyt & Blascovich, 2003; Lowe, Kroeck, & Sivasubramaniam, 1996). Charismatic leaders also change their followers for the better by raising their self-confidence, providing them with a shared set of goals for future activities, and increasing the group's sense of common identity (Conger, 1999).

Cross-cultural studies of leadership also support, at least in part, the idea that people all over the world consider charismatic leaders to be preferable to transactional ones. Researchers in the Global Leadership and Organizational Behavior Effectiveness (GLOBE) Program, for example, asked 15,022 managers in 62 different countries around the world to describe desirable and undesirable characteristics in a leader. The investigators then identified those qualities that nearly all of the individuals agreed were critical by calculating indexes of agreement for each country. As Table 11-4 suggests, many of the qualities identified as desirable in an outstanding leader were charismatic, transformational ones. Those qualities that were considered to be most undesirable in a leader were those associated with a lack of integrity, self-centeredness, and asocial tendencies (Den Hartog, House, Hanges, Ruiz-Quintanilla, Dorfman, et al., 1999). Bass and his colleagues also offered leaders clear suggestions for improving their motivational impact on members, and studies of the impact of training designed to increase tranformational leadership skills have yielded positive results (e.g., Dvir, Eden, Avolio, & Shamir, 2002).

Women, Men, and Leadership

The future promises many changes in the nature and application of leadership principles. As organizations continue to become more decentralized—flatter rather than hierarchically organized—leadership methods will likely shift from leader-centered approaches to group-centered ones. The increase in the use of information technologies will also likely change the way leaders interact with their followers, as traditional forms of leadership give way to new forms of *e-leadership* (Avolio, Kahai, & Dodge, 2000). Increases in diversity across groups will also create challenges for leaders, particularly if they must adapt their methods and style to match the varied needs of heterogeneous work groups (Hooijberg & DiTomaso, 1996). The future will also likely see increased numbers of women rising to positions of leadership in groups and organizations. As noted earlier, male and female leaders do not differ significantly in their basic approaches to leadership; the sexes are equivalent when it comes to providing members with task-orientation and relational support (Eagly, Karau, & Makhijani, 1995). However, the sexes do differ consistently in their styles of leadership, for women tend to adopt participative and transformational styles of leadership,

TABLE 11-4 Cross-cultural, universal qualities that are considered desirable and undesirable in a leader

Type	General Dimension	Specific Examples
Desirable qualities	Visionary, inspiritional, integrity, group focused, diplomatic, administratively competent, decisive, performance oriented	Has foresight, plans ahead, dynamic, positive, encouraging, confidence builder, motivational, trustworthy, just, honest, informed, communicative, coordinator, team builder, win–win problem solver, effective bargainer
Undesirable qualities	Self-centered, malevolent, ruthless, egocentric, face saver	Asocial, loner, irritable, noncooperative, nonexplicit

Source: Data from Den Hartog, House, Hanges, Ruiz-Quintanilla, Dorfman, et. al., 1999.

whereas men are more likely to enact autocratic, laissez-faire, and transactional styles (Eagly, Johannesen-Schmidt, & van Engen, 2003; Eagly & Johnson, 1990; van Engen, 2001). Because the styles favored by women are more closely associated with increased group performance and improved subordinate satisfaction, as prejudicial biases give way to fairer promotional practices, the Carly Fiorinas of the world should begin to outnumber the Bill Hewletts and Dave Packards.

SUMMARY IN OUTLINE

❖ What is leadership?

1. Myths and misunderstandings pertaining to leadership are common among lay-persons and professionals.
   - Leadership is a form of power, but power *with* people rather than *over* people.
   - Certain personality variables are associated with effective leadership, but leadership is not an inborn trait.
   - All groups do not have leaders, but as groups increase in size and complexity, most select someone to lead.
   - Most people prefer to be led rather than be leaderless.

- Leaders make a difference, for groups prosper when guided by good leaders. However, people sometimes assume that leaders are so influential that they, and they alone, determine their group's outcomes (the *romance of leadership*).

2. *Leadership* is the process by which an individual guides others in their pursuits, often by organizing, directing, coordinating, supporting, and motivating their efforts. This process can be characterized as reciprocal, transactional, transformational, cooperative, and adaptive.

3. Studies of leaders' actual behaviors, such as the Ohio State University Leadership Studies, identify two clusters of leadership activities:
   - Task leadership focuses on the group's work and its goals.
   - Relationship leadership focuses on the interpersonal relations within the group.
   - The *Leader Behavior Description Questionnaire* (LBDQ) assesses both task and relationship leadership.

4. *Leadership substitutes theory* suggests that certain features of the situation can fulfill critical interpersonal and task functions and so reduce the need for a leader.

5. Men tend to be more agentic and task oriented in groups, whereas women are more communal and relationship oriented. The sexes differ only negligibly, however, in their emphasis on task versus relationship leadership when they occupy positions of leadership.

❖ **Who will lead?**

1. Early theories of *leadership emergence* adopted either a trait model (*great leader theory*) or a situational model (*zeitgeist theory*), but most modern theories are *interactional* models that base predictions on the reciprocal relationships among the leader, the followers, and the nature of the group situation.

2. Certain personal qualities (traits) are associated with the rise to a position of leadership, including,
   - personality traits, such as extraversion, conscientiousness, and openness.
   - intelligence (with groups preferring leaders who are somewhat more intelligent than the average group member) and *emotional intelligence* (degree of social skill).
   - expertise, skill, and experience.

- level of participation in discussion, for people who speak more in groups are likely to emerge as leaders, irrespective of the quality of their contributions.

3. Leadership is also associated with demographic variables:
   - Leaders tend to be older, taller, and heavier than the average group member.
   - Ethnic minorities and women are less likely to be selected as leaders in groups.
   - The bias against women is ironic because, in general, women possess more of the skills needed to be a successful leader.

4. *Implicit leadership theory* suggests that individuals who act in ways that match the group members' leader prototypes are likely to emerge as leaders. *Social role theory* maintains that sex roles and leadership roles can create negative expectations for women leaders.

❖ **Why do some leaders succeed and others fail?**

1. Fiedler's *contingency model* suggests that leadership effectiveness is determined by the leader's motivational style and the favorability of the situation.
   - The leader's motivational style can be either task motivated or relationship motivated, as measured by the *Least Preferred Co-Worker Scale* (LPC).
   - Situational favorability is determined by leader–member relations, the task structure, and the leader's power.
   - Fiedler's theory predicts that task-motivated (low-LPC) leaders will be most effective in situations that are either extremely unfavorable or extremely favorable, whereas relationship-motivated leaders are most effective in intermediate situations.

2. Leadership style theorists assume that effectiveness depends on the leader's task and relationship behaviors.
   - The *Leadership Grid,* proposed by Blake and Mouton, assumes that people vary in their concern for others and in their concern for results, and that individuals who are high on both dimensions (9,9) are the best leaders.
   - The *situational leadership theory,* proposed by Hersey and Blanchard, suggests that groups benefit from leadership that meshes with the developmental stage of the group.

3. *Leader–member exchange theory* (LMX) focuses on the dyadic relationship linking the leader to each member of the group and notes that in many cases, two subgroups of linkages exist (the inner group and the outer group). Groups with more inner-group members are more productive.

4. Participation theories of leadership extend the early findings of Lewin, Lippitt, and White regarding the effects of autocratic, democratic, and laissez-faire leaders. This approach provides the theoretical and empirical basis for shared leadership models, such as co-leadership, collective leadership, and peer leadership.

5. Transformational, charismatic, and visionary leadership models, such as Bass's *transformational model,* identify the processes that charismatic leaders use to influence their followers. Bass emphasizes four components of transformational (rather than transactional) leadership: idealized influence (or charisma), inspirational motivation, intellectual stimulation, and individualized consideration.

6. Women tend to adopt participative and transformational styles of leadership, whereas men are more likely to enact autocratic, laissez-faire, and transactional styles. Women's skills are particularly well suited for organizations of the future, which will be less hierarchical and require a collaborative, shared approach to leadership.

FOR MORE INFORMATION

Chapter Case: Carly Fiorina

- *Perfect Enough: Carly Fiorina and the Reinvention of Hewlett-Packard,* by George Anders (2003), describes the leadership methods used by Fiorina, with a particular focus on the difficult controversy that arose when she proposed merging Hewlett-Packard with another company.

The Nature of Leadership

- *Bass and Stogdill's Handbook of Leadership: Theory, Research, and Managerial Applications,* by Bernard M. Bass (1990, 3rd ed.), is the definitive reference for research into leadership. Its 1000 pages and 7500 references provide insight into virtually all aspects of the leadership process.

- *Leadership in Organizations,* by Gary Yukl (2002), is a masterful integration of theory, research, and application of leadership studies in business and organizations.

- "Leadership Models, Methods, and Applications," by Bruce J. Avolio, John J. Sosik, Dong I. Jung, and Yair Berson (2003), is a concise but comprehensive analysis of recent advances in the analysis of leadership.

- *Shared Leadership: Reframing the Hows and Whys of Leadership,* edited by Craig L. Pearce and Jay A. Conger (2003), draws together 14 papers that carefully analyze emerging issues pertaining to the distribution of leadership within groups.

Women and Leadership

- "Gender, Hierarchy, and Leadership," edited by Linda L. Carli and Alice H. Eagly (2001), is an issue of the *Journal of Social Issues* that focuses on social and group processes pertaining to sex differences and sexism in leadership.

- *Women and Leadership: A Contextual Perspective,* by Karin Klenke (1996), is a multidisciplinary analysis of women as leaders, with chapters on female leaders in history, the media, popular literature, politics, and the workplace.

MEDIA RESOURCES

 Visit the Group Dynamics companion website at http://psychology.wadsworth.com/forsyth4e to access online resources for your book, including quizzes, flash cards, web links, and more!

12

CONFLICT

CHAPTER OVERVIEW

The word *conflict* comes from the Latin *confligere,* "striking together with force." During group conflict, words, emotions, and actions "strike together" to produce disruptive effects. Yet conflict is an unavoidable outgrowth of group life, for by entering into relations with others, we must negotiate and renegotiate our undertakings and our outcomes.

❖ What is conflict?

❖ What are the sources of conflict in groups?

❖ Why does conflict escalate?

❖ How can group members manage their conflict?

❖ Does conflict, when resolved, lead to improved group functioning?

CHAPTER OUTLINE

Jobs Versus Sculley:
When Group Members Turn Against Each Other

They were business partners and good friends. Steve Jobs, the chief executive officer (CEO) of Apple Computer, handpicked John Sculley to be his successor. He convinced Sculley to leave his job as CEO of Pepsico, and the two joined forces to build Apple into the premier computer company in the world. They admired each other's strengths as leaders and visionaries, and they conferred constantly on all matters of production and policy. Sculley and Jobs were often seen taking long walks around the grounds of their corporate headquarters, deep in discussion of strategy, design, and direction.

But then the trouble started. They wrangled over how much to charge for their new product, the Macintosh. Sculley did not agree with Jobs's plan for organizing the various units of the company. Jobs wondered if Sculley knew enough about the computer industry. Their working relationship dissolved into a series of disagreements that reached a climax in May of 1985. Sculley, just before a scheduled trip to China, heard a rumor that Jobs was planning a corporate coup once Sculley was out of the country. Sculley canceled his trip and called a board meeting. He opened the meeting by confronting Jobs:

> "It's come to my attention that you'd like to throw me out of the company, and I'd like to ask if that's true."
>
> Jobs's answer: "I think you're bad for Apple and I think you're the wrong person to run this company. . . . You really should leave this company. . . . You don't know how manufacturing works. You're not close to the company. The middle managers don't respect you."
>
> Sculley, voice rising in anger, replied, "I made a mistake in treating you with high esteem. . . . I don't trust you, and I won't tolerate a lack of trust."
>
> Sculley then polled the board members. Did they support Sculley or Jobs? All of them declared great admiration for Jobs, but they felt that the company needed Sculley's experience and leadership. Jobs then rose from the table and said, "I guess I know where things stand," before bolting from the room. Sculley transferred Jobs to a development position. Jobs later resigned from the company he had founded. (Sculley, 1987, pp. 251–252)

Jobs versus Sculley was one of corporate America's most spectacular conflicts, but it was no anomaly. Groups of all kinds experience periods of disagreement, discord, and friction. Good friends disagree about their weekend plans and end up exchanging harsh words. Families argue over finances, rules, and responsibilities. Work teams struggling to improve their productivity search for a person who can be blamed for their inefficiency. College classes, angered by their professors' methods of teaching, lodge formal complaints with the Dean. Rock bands split up when artistic tensions between members become unacceptable. Teammates blame one another for a loss and never regain their sense of unity and cohesion.

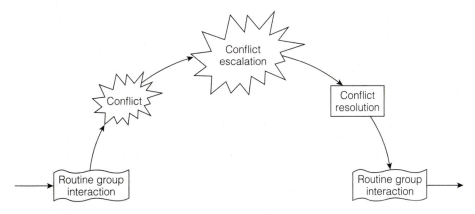

FIGURE 12-1

What is the course of conflict in groups? The typical conflict cycle begins when routine group interaction is disrupted by disagreement, discord, and friction among the members. This conflict often *escalates* as the group members become more involved in the dispute, but in time, it abates as problems are resolved.

When **conflict** occurs in a group, the actions or beliefs of one or more members of the group are unacceptable to and resisted by one or more of the other group members. Members stand against each other rather than in support of each other (Boardman & Horowitz, 1994; J. M. Levine & Thompson, 1996; Pruitt, 1998; Tjosvold, 1986).

Why do allies in a group sometimes turn into adversaries? This chapter answers that question by tracing the course of conflict in groups. As Figure 12-1 suggests, the process begins when the routine course of events in a group is disrupted by an *initial conflict*—differences of opinion, disagreements over who should lead the group, individuals competing with each other for scarce resources, and the like. Whatever the cause of the initial disunity, the conflict grows as persuasion gives way to arguing, emotions take the place of logic, and the once unified group splits into factions and coalitions. This period of *conflict escalation* is, in most cases, followed by a reduction in conflict and, ideally, by *conflict resolution*. The board of directors at Apple, for example, settled their conflict by backing Sculley and demoting Jobs—a rather severe means of resolving the dispute (J. A. Wall & Callister, 1995). This chapter, then, focuses on conflict inside a group, or

---

conflict Disagreement, discord, and friction that occur when the actions or beliefs of one or more members of the group are unacceptable to and resisted by one or more of the other group members.

intragroup conflict. A second form of conflict—conflict between groups, or **intergroup conflict**—is examined in the next chapter.

THE ROOTS OF CONFLICT

Conflict is everywhere. When the members of 71 groups were asked, "Did your group experience any conflict?" they identified 424 instances of interpersonal irritation (V. D. Wall & Nolan, 1987). When Robert Bales and his colleagues used *Interaction Process Analysis* (IPA) to record group interactions, some of the groups they observed spent as much as 20% of their time making hostile or negative comments (Bales & Hare, 1965). When researchers asked group members to work together on a frustrating, impossible-to-solve task, the researchers were startled by the intensity of the conflict that overtook the groups. In one particularly hostile group, members averaged 13.5 antagonistic comments *per minute* (French, 1941).

Most people, if given the choice, avoid situations that are rife with conflict (Witteman, 1991). Yet conflict seems to be an unavoidable consequence of life in groups. When individuals are sequestered away from other people, their ambitions, goals, and perspectives are their own concern. But a group, by its very nature, brings individuals into contact with other people—people who have their own idiosyncratic interests, motivations, outlooks, and preferences. As these individuals interact with one another, their diverse interests and preferences can pull them in different directions. Instead of working together, they compete against one another. Instead of sharing resources and power, members selfishly claim more than their fair share. Instead of accepting each other for who they are, members treat those they like better than those they dislike.

Winning: Conflict and Competition

When Sculley first joined Apple, he worked with Jobs in a cooperative, friendly way. But then Sculley and Jobs ran headlong into a dispute over the Macintosh computer. Sculley thought the Mac should be engineered for business applications, but Jobs envisioned a simple, elegant computer that nearly anyone could use. The two men refused to change their minds, and so their once *cooperative* relationship turned into a *competitive* one. For Sculley to succeed, Jobs would have to fail. For Jobs to succeed, Sculley would have to fail.

---

intragroup conflict Disagreement or confrontation between members of the same group.

intergroup conflict A disagreement or confrontation between two or more groups and their members that can include physical violence, interpersonal discord, and psychological tension.

Many social situations promote competition between people. When two people play backgammon, one must win and the other must lose. When two rivals in a business go after the same account, one will succeed and the other will fail. In a footrace, only one runner will end up in first place. As Morton Deutsch explained, such situations involve **competition:** The success of any one person means that someone else must fail. Deutsch (1949b) called this form of interaction *contrient interdependence*. Other situations, in contrast, are based on **cooperation:** The success of any one member of the group will improve the chances of success for the other members. Deutsch called this form of interaction *promotive interdependence* (Deutsch, 1949b).

Competition is a powerful motivator of behavior. When individuals compete against one another, they sometimes expend greater effort, express more interest and satisfaction in their work, and set their personal goals higher (Tauer & Harackiewicz, 2004). But competition promotes conflict between individuals. When people compete, they must look out for their own interests, instead of the group's interests or their comembers' interests. They cannot take pride in other group members' accomplishments, for each time someone else in the group excels, their own outcomes shrink. In cooperative groups, members enhance their outcomes by helping other members achieve success, but in competitive groups, members profit from others' errors. Because competing group members can only succeed if others fail, they may even sabotage others' work, criticize it, and withhold information or materials that others might need (Franken & Prpich, 1996; Steers & Porter, 1991).

Deutsch studied the dark side of competition by creating two different grading systems in his college classes. In competitive classes, students' grades were relative: The individual who did the best in the group would get the highest grade, whereas the individual who did the worst would get the lowest grade. Deutsch created cooperative groups as well. These students worked together to learn the material, and everyone in the group received the same grade. As Deutsch predicted, conflict was much more pronounced in the competitive groups. Members reported less dependency on others, less desire to win the respect of others, and greater interpersonal animosity. Members of cooperative groups, in contrast, acted friendlier during the meetings, were more encouraging and supportive, and communicated more frequently (Deutsch, 1949a, 1949b, 1973, 1980, 1985, 1994, 2000).

Other researchers, too, have found that cooperative situations tend to be friendly, intimate, and involving, whereas competitive situations are viewed as unfriendly, nonintimate, and uninvolving (Graziano, Hair, & Finch, 1997; G. A. King & Sorrentino, 1983). Work units with high levels of cooperation have fewer

---

competition A performance situation that is structured in such a way that success depends on performing better than others.

cooperation A performance situation that is structured in such a way that the success of any one member of the group improves the chances of other members' succeeding.

latent tensions, personality conflicts, and verbal confrontations (Tjosvold, 1995). Students in classrooms that stress cooperation rather than individualism or competition work harder, show greater academic gains, and display better psychological adjustment (D. W. Johnson & Johnson, 1989; D. W. Johnson, Maruyama, Johnson, Nelson, & Skon, 1981; cf. Cotton & Cook, 1982). Sports teams, too, tend to be more cohesive and—depending on the demands of the particular sport—more successful when coaches instill a desire for team success rather than individual success (Zander, 1977; see D. W. Johnson & Johnson, 2003, and D. R. Schmitt, 1981, for detailed reviews).

MIXED-MOTIVE CONFLICT Few situations involve pure cooperation or pure competition; the motive to compete is often mixed with the motive to cooperate. Sculley wanted to gain control over the Mac division, but he needed Jobs's help with product development. Jobs valued Sculley's organizational expertise, but he felt that Sculley misunderstood the company's goals. The men found themselves in a **mixed-motive situation**—they were tempted to compete and cooperate at the same time.

Social psychologists use a specialized technique, known as the **prisoner's dilemma game** (PDG), to study conflict in mixed-motive situations (Poundstone, 1992). This procedure takes its name from an anecdote about two prisoners. The criminals, when interrogated by police detectives in separate rooms, are offered an intriguing deal. They are told they can retain their right to remain silent, or they can confess and implicate their accomplice. If both remain silent, then they will be set free. If both confess, both will receive a moderate sentence. But if one confesses and the other does not, then the one who confesses will receive a minimal sentence, and his partner will receive the maximum sentence. The prisoners, as partners in crime, want to cooperate with each other and resist the demands of the police. However, by competing with each other (i.e., by confessing in the hope that the other does not), they may end up with a lighter sentence (Luce & Raiffa, 1957).

When researchers use the prisoner's dilemma to study conflict, the participants play for points or money (see Figure 12-2). The two participants must individually pick one of two options, labeled A and B. Option A is the *cooperative choice*. If both players pick A, then both will earn money. Option B is the *competitive choice*. If only one of the two players picks B, that player will make money, and the other will lose money. But if both pick B, both will lose money. Figure 12-2 shows the payoff matrix that summarizes how much money the two will win or lose in each of the four possible situations:

---

mixed-motive situation A performance setting in which the interdependence among interactants involves both competitive and cooperative goal structures.

prisoner's dilemma game (PDG) A simulation of social interaction in which players must make either cooperative or competitive choices in order to win; used in the study of cooperation, competition, and the development of mutual trust.

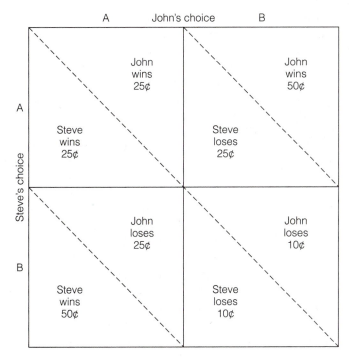

FIGURE 12-2

What is the prisoner's dilemma game? This conflict problem is based on the story of two prisoners who are tempted to implicate each other in a crime. In studies of conflict, participants are not threatened with jail time but instead earn points or money by playing the game. Our two hypothetical participants, John and Steve (who usually cannot communicate with each other), would be told that they must select either Option A (*cooperate*) or Option B (*compete*). These choices are shown along the sides of the matrix. The payoffs for these joint choices are shown within each cell of the matrix. In each cell, John's outcomes are shown above the diagonal line, and Steve's outcomes are shown below the diagonal. For example, if John picks A and Steve picks A, they each earn 25¢. But if John picks A and Steve picks B, then John loses 25¢ and Steve wins 50¢.

1. If John chooses A and Steve chooses A, both earn 25¢.
2. If John chooses A and Steve chooses B, John loses 25¢ and Steve wins 50¢.
3. If John chooses B and Steve chooses A, John wins 50¢ and Steve loses 25¢.
4. If John chooses B and Steve chooses B, both lose 10¢.

The PDG captures the essence of a mixed-motive situation (Rapoport, 1985; Schlenker & Bonoma, 1978; Wrightsman, O'Connor, & Baker, 1972). Players want to maximize their own earnings, so they are tempted to pick Option B. But most people realize that their partner also wants to maximize his or her profit—and if both select B, then they will both lose money. So they are drawn to Option A, but are wary that their partner may pick B. Players usually cannot communicate with each other, and they cannot wait to pick until after they learn their partner's choice. In most cases, players also make their choices several times. Each pair of choices between alternatives A and B is termed a *trial.*

Many people choose to compete rather than cooperate, although the proportion varies depending on the value of the rewards offered, the players' personality traits, the relative advantages of each strategy, and a variety of other factors (Mori, 1996; Parks, Henager, & Scamahorn, 1996; Rapoport, 1988; Vinacke, 1971). When female college students seated in individual cubicles played the game using the payoff matrix shown in Figure 12-2, 56% competed on the first trial (Messé & Sivacek, 1979). But in another study, where men and women sat face to face before making their choices, only 20% competed. Competitiveness, however, jumped to 68% when they were partnered with a computer with human-like features (S. Kiesler, Sproull, & Waters, 1996).

When people play the PDG for several trials, their choices are substantially influenced by their partner's choices. When playing with someone who consistently makes cooperative choices, people tend to cooperate themselves. Those who encounter competitors, however, soon adopt this strategy, and they, too, begin to compete. As the **norm of reciprocity** suggests, cooperation begets cooperation, and competition begets competition. *Negative reciprocity,* however, is stronger than *positive reciprocity.* A cooperative person who runs into a competitive partner is likely to begin to compete *before* the competitive person begins to cooperate (Kelley & Stahelski, 1970a, 1970b, 1970c). Negative reciprocity is kept in check if cooperatively oriented individuals have the opportunity to withdraw from the interaction or can communicate their "good" intentions to their partners (K. Garner & Deutsch, 1974; D. T. Miller & Holmes, 1975), but in most situations, a partner turns into an opponent faster than an opponent turns into an ally (Carroll, 1987; Schlenker & Goldman, 1978).

WHO COMPETES? Both Jobs and Sculley were tough-minded entrepreneurs who sought to maximize their gains whenever possible. Did their personalities contribute to the conflict? Studies of group members' **social values orientation** have suggested that some people are natural competitors, whereas others are more cooperative or individualistic (Beggan & Allison, 1994; Van Lange, 1999, 2000).

---

norm of reciprocity A societal standard that enjoins individuals to pay back in kind what they receive from others.

social values orientation The dispositional tendency to respond to conflict settings in a particular way; cooperators, for example, tend to make choices that benefit both parties in a conflict, whereas competitors act to maximize their own outcomes.

TABLE 12-1 Three basic social value orientations

Social Motive	Motivation
Competitor	Strives to maximize own outcomes and minimize others' out comes; views disagreements as win–lose situations
Cooperator	Strives to maximize joint outcomes (seeks to maximize own outcomes *and* others' outcomes); seeks win–win solutions to disagreements
Individualist	Strives to maximize own outcomes only; either helps or harms others if these actions increase own outcomes; seeks own goals

As Table 12-1 indicates, competitors view group disagreements as *win–lose situations* and find satisfaction in forcing their ideas on the others. Concessions and compromise, they believe, are only for losers. A *competitor* believes that "each person should get the most he can" and plays to win even when playing a game with a child (Brenner & Vinacke, 1979, p. 291). Cooperators, in contrast, are prosocial people who value accommodative interpersonal strategies that generate *win–win situations* (De Dreu & Van Lange, 1995). A *cooperator* would argue that "when people deal with each other, it's better when everyone comes out even," and if playing a game with a child would "try to arrange it so that no one really wins or loses" (Brenner & Vinacke, 1979, p. 291). *Individualists* are concerned only with their own outcomes. They make decisions based on what they think they personally will achieve, with no concern for others' outcomes. They neither interfere with nor assist others' attempts to reach their goals.

Individuals with competitive value orientations are more likely to find themselves in conflicts. The competitor's style is abrasive, spurring cooperative members to react with criticism and requests for fairer treatment. Competitors, however, rarely modify their behavior in response to these complaints, because they are relatively unconcerned with maintaining smooth interpersonal relations (De Dreu, Weingart, & Kwon, 2000). Hence, competitors try to overwhelm cooperators, who sometimes respond by becoming competitive themselves. For cooperators, the perception of others' cooperativeness is *positively* correlated with their own cooperativeness. If they think that others will cooperate, they cooperate. For competitors, perceptions of others' cooperativeness is *negatively* correlated with their own cooperativeness. If they think that others will cooperate, they compete (Smeesters, Warlop, Van Avermaet, Corneille, & Yzerbyt, 2003). When two competitors meet, the result is an intense conflict like that seen at Apple, and when competitors lose, they often withdraw from the group altogether (Shure & Meeker, 1967). Competitors tend to think "it could have been worse," whereas cooperative individuals think of ways the interaction "could have been better" (Parks, Sanna, & Posey, 2003).

These differences in social values orientations have been linked to other personal qualities, including agreeableness, achievement orientation, interpersonal orientation, and trust in others (Graziano et al., 1997; Swap & Rubin, 1983; Yamagishi, 1986). Social values also vary systematically across cultures. Many Western societies, for example, openly value competition. Their economic systems are based on competition, their schools teach children the importance of surpassing others' achievements, and popular games and sports have winners and losers. More cooperative—and more peaceful—societies, in contrast, condemn competition, devalue individual achievement, and avoid any kind of competitive games (Bonta, 1997; Fry & Björkqvist, 1997; Van Lange, De Bruin, Otten, & Joireman, 1997).

MEN, WOMEN, AND COMPETITION What if John Sculley were Joanna Sculley—a woman rather than a man? Would she and Jobs have battled as fiercely? Or would Joanna have used other, less competitive methods for settling the dispute?

Common gender role stereotypes generally assume that men are more competitive than women. Stories of executives conjure up images of individuals who are driven, ruthless, self-seeking, and male. Yet experimental studies of cooperation and competition suggest that women are just as competitive as men (Sell, 1997; Sell, Griffith, & Wilson, 1993). One review of previous work found that in 21 experiments, women were more competitive, but 27 other studies suggested that women were less competitive (J. Z. Rubin & Brown, 1975). Both men and women use more contentious influence methods when they are paired with a man than with a woman, perhaps because they anticipate more conflict (Carli, 1989, 1999). When it comes to social values orientations, however, more women are cooperators and more men are competitors (G. P. Knight & Dubro, 1984). Women also tend to base their choices in conflict situations on factors other than the rewards they stand to gain. If, for example, their partner is attractive, women make more cooperative choices. If they do not like their partner, they are more likely to compete (A. Kahn, Hottes, & Davis, 1971).

Sharing: Conflict over Resources

Steve Jobs faced a dilemma. The board of directors of Apple had hired John Sculley to be CEO, and they expected all the company's employees to follow the lead and direction of Sculley as the company moved to increase its profits. But Sculley's plan called for sacrifices, for he wanted to shift personnel and financial resources away from Jobs's division. Jobs could have accepted this decision and gone along with the group's decision, but instead he chose his own path.

Group life, by its very nature, creates **social dilemmas** for group members. The members, as individuals, are motivated to maximize their own rewards and minimize their costs. They strive to extract all they can from the group, while minimizing the amount of time and energy the group takes from them. Yet, as

---

social dilemma An interpersonal situation where individuals must choose between maximizing their personal outcomes or maximizing their group's outcomes.

group members, they also wish to contribute to the group, for they realize that their selfishness can destroy the group. Conflicts arise when individualistic motives trump group-oriented motives, and the collective intervenes to redress the imbalance.

COMMONS DILEMMAS   Consider the "tragedy of the commons." A group of shepherds all use a common grazing land. The land can support many sheep, so the system works smoothly. However, some selfish members of the community want to maximize their personal profit, so they add animals to their own flocks. Others notice the extra sheep, so they, too, add to their flocks. Soon, the commons is overgrazed, and all the sheep die of starvation (Hardin, 1968).

This **social trap,** or **commons dilemma** (Pruitt, 1998), occurs when members share a common resource that they want to maintain for their group, but individual members are tempted to take more than their fair share. But if everyone acts selfishly, the common resource will be destroyed. Members are tempted by the short-term gains that will bring about long-term losses to the collective (Allison, Beggan, & Midgley, 1996; Komorita & Parks, 1994; Shepperd, 1993).

Researchers have studied when people choose self-interest over group interest by giving groups of four or five people the chance to draw as many tokens as they want from a pool of available tokens. The pool is a *renewable resource,* for after each round of harvesting, it regenerates in direct proportion to the number of tokens remaining in the pool. If members quickly draw out all the tokens, the pool is permanently exhausted; cautious removal of only a small number of tokens ensures replenishment of the resource. Nonetheless, group members tend to act in their own self-interest by drawing out all the tokens, even when they realize that the pool is quite small (Brewer & Kramer, 1986; Yamagishi, 1994).

How can groups escape this dilemma? Both experience with the situation and communication among members appear to be critical factors (Allison & Messick, 1985a; Edney & Bell, 1984). In one study, triads harvested from either a large or a small token pool. The members of half of the groups could communicate with one another, but the rest could not. The differences between these groups were striking. More than 80% of the groups that could not communicate bankrupted their pool within a minute. Even when the pool was large, the noncommunicating groups still had problems with overharvesting. Many of these groups realized the long-term negative consequences of overharvesting, but they did not manage their resources as well as the communicating groups. These results suggest that groups can avoid traps if their members can plan a strategy for dealing with the situation through face-to-face communication (Brechner, 1977).

---

social trap (or **commons dilemma**) A social dilemma where individuals can maximize their outcome by seeking personal goals rather than the collective goals, but if too many individuals act selfishly then all members of the collective will experience substantial long-term losses.

PUBLIC GOODS DILEMMAS In a commons dilemma, group members take more than their fair share. In a **public goods dilemma,** they fail to give as much as they should (Komorita & Parks, 1994; Orbell, Dawes, & van de Kragt, 1995. At the community level, individuals may be able to use public parks, enjoy the protection of the police, and send their children to public school, even though they do not contribute to the community by paying taxes. At the group level, when people work on a task together, not everyone does the share of the work they are assigned. *Free riding,* discussed in Chapter 9, is a kind of public goods dilemma. Because the task is a collective one and individual inputs cannot be identified, group members do not exert maximum effort on the task—they socially loaf. In such cases, group members coast along, letting others do their share of the work. They also contribute less because they do not want to be exploited by the other loafers in the group (the *sucker effect;* N. L. Kerr, 1983).

Free riding can cause conflict in a group. When group members in a college class described the sources of conflicts in their project groups, more than 35% of their comments targeted disputes over work load. People had much to say about the dedication of their comembers to the group's goals, for some did not put in as much time, effort, and resources as the others expected (V. D. Wall & Nolan, 1987). When too many individuals reduce their input to the group, the quality of the group's product declines along with the group's cohesiveness (K. D. Williams, Jackson, & Karau, 1995). Free riding transfers too much of the responsibility for the group's output to some group members, who may object to the added burden. Some groups respond to free riding by implementing negative sanctions to minimize inequities in contributions, by extracting promises of satisfactory contributions from members, and by subjecting free riders to verbal abuse. Some individual group members, to counter the inequity of working in a group with free riders, may reduce their own contributions or withdraw from the group (see Komorita & Parks, 1994, for a review).

FAIRNESS DILEMMAS Groups must often make decisions about how their resources will be apportioned to members. A company issues wages to workers. More personnel must be assigned to more important work units. Office space must be allocated to executives, along with company cars, staff support, and budgets. Because resources are limited, groups must develop a fair means of doling them out to members. But what is fair or unfair is often open to debate.

Distributive justice pertains to judgments of the fairness of the amount of a resource allocated by the group to a member. When one's piece of cake seems smaller than it should be, when others get the best seats right up near the front of the bus, when workers who do the same job are paid different salaries, or when group leaders give all their attention to one or two favorite members and ignore

---

public goods dilemma A social dilemma where one cannot contribute any resources in support of a public good (such as a park or a highway system) but not be excluded from the benefits for failing to contribute.

distributive justice Perceived fairness of the distribution of rights and resources.

the others, group members feel that distributive justice has not been done. **Procedural justice,** in contrast, is concerned with the methods used to make decisions about the allocation of resources. Rather than focusing on the outcome per se—"How much did I get?"—questions of procedural justice arise when groups do not use consistent, open, and agreed-upon methods for allocating their resources. Procedural justice asks, "Did they make the decision in a fair way?" (van den Bos, Wilke, & Lind, 1998).

Judgments of fairness are also shaped by the allocation norms adopted by the group. As noted in Chapter 3, the *equity norm* prescribes basing members' outcomes on their inputs: An individual who has invested a good deal of time, energy, money, or other type of input in the group should receive more from the group than individuals who have contributed little. The *equality norm,* in contrast, recommends that all group members, irrespective of their inputs, be given an equal share of the payoff: Even though a person contributes only 20% of the group's resources, he or she should receive as much as the person who contributes 80%. Other norms, such as the *power norm* ("to the victor go the spoils") and the *need norm* ("the greatest good to those with the greatest needs"), can also be used to determine how the group allocates its resources (Deutsch, 1975; N. L. Kerr, 1995).

Money (and other resources) may not be the root of all evil, but its distribution often causes conflicts within groups (Allison & Messick, 1990; Samuelson & Allison, 1994; Samuelson & Messick, 1995). Members who contribute less to the group often argue in favor of the equality norm, whereas those who contribute more tend to favor the equity norm. Women prefer equality over equity even when they outperform their coworkers (Leventhal & Lane, 1970). Members of larger groups prefer to base allocations on equity, whereas members of smaller groups stress equality (Allison, McQueen, & Schaerfl, 1992). Members of groups working on tasks where one individual's contributions are critically important for success prefer equitable distributions over egalitarian ones (Elliott & Meeker, 1984; C. E. Miller & Komorita, 1995). Group members who feel that they are receiving too little for what they are giving (*negative inequity*) sometimes withdraw from the group, reduce their effort, and turn in work of lower quality. Group members who feel that they are receiving too much for what they are giving (*positive inequity*) sometimes increase their efforts (Adams & Rosenbaum, 1962; Dittrich & Carrell, 1979). Negative inequity, however, is a much more likely cause of conflict than the more personally favorable experience of positive inequity (Rivera & Tedeschi, 1976).

These reactions are driven, in part, by self-interest. Group members strive to maximize their personal rewards, so they react negatively when they are denied what they feel they deserve. But group members are also concerned with the issues of fairness and justice, because these are indications of their status and inclusion in groups. When group members feel that their group has acted with

---

procedural justice Perceived fairness of the processes used to make decisions about rights and resources.

integrity while allocating rewards, they feel a sense of pride in their group. They also feel that the rewards they receive from the group are an indication of their prestige and respect within the group. These reactions are shaped more by the group's procedural justice than by its distributive justice (Blader & Tyler, 2003; Tyler & Blader, 2003).

RESPONSIBILITY DILEMMAS When a group completes its work, members often dispute who deserves credit and who deserves blame. The board of directors at Apple blamed Jobs's devotion to the Mac for the company's economic misfortunes. Sculley credited his skilled marketing interventions for Apple's prosperity in the years following Jobs's dismissal. Jobs blamed Sculley for ruining the company.

Just as individuals carry out extensive appraisals of their own successes and failures, so do group members devote significant cognitive resources to the analysis and comprehension of their collective endeavors. This appraisal, however, is complicated by the collaborative nature of group activities. Group members must identify the factors that contributed to each member's performance, assign credit and blame, and make decisions regarding rewards, power, and status (Forsyth & Kelley, 1996). Group members' postperformance reactions are often *group serving* (or *sociocentric*). After success, members may praise the entire group for its good work with such comments as "We all did well," or "Our hard work really paid off." Likewise, after failure, members may join together in blaming outside forces and absolving one another of blame. Too frequently, however, members are *self-serving* (or *egocentric*); they take undue personal credit for success and blame one another for the group's misfortunes (Forsyth, 1980; Forsyth, Zyzniewski, & Giammanco, 2002). As Focus 12-1 indicates, group-serving tactics unite the group, whereas self-serving tactics contribute to conflict (Leary & Forsyth, 1987).

Controlling: Conflict over Power

The conflict between Sculley and Jobs was rooted in each man's desire to control the company. Jobs thought that he would be content to allow another person to make key decisions about Apple's future, but when those decisions did not mesh with his own vision, he sought to regain control. Sculley believed that Jobs was undermining his authority. Both Jobs and Sculley sought the power they needed to control the company, and their "power games" caused turmoil within the group.

As noted in earlier chapters, the differentiation of members in terms of status, prestige, and power is a ubiquitous feature of groups. Some group members with a high need for power make use of strong methods to increase their influence over others. As the group strives to coordinate its members' task-directed activities, some individuals will begin to assert more authority over the others. Those who occupy positions of authority have the right to issue orders to others, who are expected to follow those directives. Once individuals gain power over

FOCUS 12-1   Should You Take the Blame for Your Group's Failure?

Success has many parents, but failure is a bastard.
–Anonymous

When a group runs into problems, members often search for a cause. The officers at the Enron Corporation, when explaining their company's abuses, blamed their accountants for using the wrong "auditing" methods. The accountants refused the responsibility and said that blame rested with Enron's executives (Taub, 2001). Tom and Susan Klebold, the parents of Dylan Klebold, the student who shot and killed 13 fellow students at Columbine High School, said that their family was not responsible for Dylan's actions: "Dylan did not do this because of the way he was raised. He did it in contradiction to the way he was raised" (quoted in D. Brooks, 2004). When the *Challenger* space shuttle exploded, NASA scientists blamed the engineers who designed the O-rings, but the engineers blamed NASA for launching the shuttle in cold weather. When members of the anti-logging groups ACT UP and Earth First! destroyed expensive equipment used by loggers, the movement's leaders disavowed any responsibility, pointing out that the vandals were acting as individuals without the approval of the group (Elsbach & Sutton, 1992).

Groups, like individuals, must often track down who is responsible for their successes and failures. Did we fail because of bad luck? Did we not work hard enough? Was the task too difficult? But this search for the cause of outcomes is more complicated in groups. Group members must identify the factors that contributed to each member's performance, assign credit and blame, and make decisions regarding rewards, power, and status. The members must also calibrate their chances of succeeding in the future, given the resources of the members, and set in motion any needed changes in the group's composition, structures, and strategies if the analysis indicates that their future outcomes are in jeopardy (Forsyth & Kelly, 1994; Rantilla, 2000).

In most cases, group members settle on group-serving attributions of responsibility—they blame failures and mistakes on factors outside of the group, but they credit the group for its successful accomplishments. During conflict, however, this sociocentric pattern is replaced by more egocentric, self-serving attributions of responsibility, as members deny responsibility for failure but claim all the credit for successes. Members of failing groups may, for example, deny personal responsibility ("It's not my fault we failed"), blame another group member ("Ed really ruined it for us"), remind the group that they personally performed well ("I had a good game; I was 3 for 4 and made some great catches"), or even disavow membership in the group ("I'm not really part of that group").

Naturally, group-serving attributions tend to unite the group, whereas self-serving attributions result in conflict and a loss of cohesion (Leary & Forsyth, 1987). In one study, two teams competed in a game situation. Certain members of each team were confederates of the researcher, and they systematically blamed one of the actual participants for the team's losses. Relative to others who had escaped blame, the unfairly accused group members were less satisfied with their teams, belittled their teammates' abilities, and preferred to work with other groups on future tasks (M. E. Shaw & Breed, 1970).

Similar consequences of self-serving reactions in the face of failure occurred in small groups working on decision-making tasks. After the groups learned that they had succeeded or failed, they were asked to complete a confidential report of their responsibility and others' responsibilities for the outcome. Then, to their surprise, this report was shared with other group members. Unbeknownst to the group members, the actual reports were switched with standard ones indicating that another group member either took high, moderate, or low responsibility for the outcome. As shown in Figure 12-3, group members who blamed others for failure or tried to claim the lion's share of responsibility after success were not well liked (Forsyth, Berger, & Mitchell, 1981). Other studies confirmed that those who engage in self-serving attributions in groups are often viewed as braggarts, narcissists, or even untrustworthy liars, but that those who share responsibility appropriately are considered trustworthy teammates (J. Greenberg, 1996; Schlenker, Pontari, & Christopher, 2001).

FIGURE 12-3

How do group members respond to someone who claims the credit for a group's success? When the group failed, the self-serving members who claimed low responsibility were liked significantly less than the more group-serving members who claimed moderate or high responsibility. Conversely, when the group did well, individuals who claimed all the credit were liked the least, and those who claimed moderate responsibility were liked the most. *Source:* Forsyth, Berger, & Mitchell, 1981.

others, they tend to defend their sources of power through manipulation, the formation of coalitions, information control, and favoritism. These power processes occur with great regularity in groups, but they nonetheless cause waves of tension, conflict, and anger to ripple through the group (Coleman, 2000; Sell et al., 2004).

Infighting, power struggles, and disputes are particularly common in business and corporate settings. Calvin Morrill (1995) spent several years collecting ethnographic data on the sources and consequences of conflict between executives in corporations. His analysis confirmed the image of companies as arenas for power struggles, where group members compete with each other for power, promotions, and prominence, often by using manipulative, illicit tactics. Contests of authority and power were so commonplace in one company that the executives developed an elaborate set of terms and expressions pertaining to company politics, which Morrill recorded much like an anthropologist would record the rituals and incantations of the members of an isolated tribe. An *ambush* was a "covert action to inconvenience an adversary" (synonyms: *bushwhack* and *cheap shot*); *blindsiding* was "an intentional and surprising public embarrassment by one executive at another's expense"; an *outlaw* was "an executive who handles conflict in unpredictable ways but who is regarded as especially task competent." In some cases, this maneuvering would result in a *meltdown*—a "physical fight between executives" (1995, pp. 263–265).

Deciding: Conflict over Choices

When people discuss their problems and plans, they sometimes disagree with one another's analyses. These **substantive conflicts** do not stem from personal disagreements between individuals, but from disagreements about issues that are relevant to the group's real goals and outcomes. Groups and organizations use such conflicts to make plans, increase creativity, solve problems, decide issues, and resolve conflicts of viewpoint (McGrath, 1984). Sculley and Jobs, as the leaders of Apple, were supposed to argue and debate.

Although substantive conflicts help groups reach their goals, these disagreements can turn into personal, unpleasant conflicts. People who disagree with the group, even when their position is a reasonable one, often provoke considerable animosity within the group. The dissenter who refuses to accept others' views is liked less, assigned low-status tasks, and sometimes ostracized. As the group struggles to reach consensus on the substantive issues at hand, it responds negatively to those group members who slow down this process (Kruglanski & Webster, 1991). In one study, groups of men who were supposed to reach a unanimous decision were hindered by one of the group members. This individual, who was a member of the research team, deliberately interrupted and questioned the group. In some groups, he explained that he had a hearing problem, but other groups were given no explanation for the member's frustrating behavior. At the end of the study, when given the opportunity to eliminate one person from the group, 100% of the group members chose the individual who interrupted the group without any excuse (Burnstein & Worchel, 1962).

Substantive conflicts occur when ideas, opinions, and interpretations clash. **Procedural conflicts** occur when strategies, policies, and methods clash. Group members may find themselves uncertain about how to resolve a problem, with some championing continued discussion and others favoring a vote. The leader of the group may make decisions and initiate actions without consulting the group; but the group may become irritated if denied an opportunity to participate in decision making (Smoke & Zajonc, 1962). During procedural conflicts, groups do not just disagree—they disagree on *how* to disagree.

Many groups minimize procedural ambiguities by adopting formal rules— bylaws, constitutions, statements of policies, or mission and procedure statements—that specify goals, decisional processes, and responsibilities (Houle, 1989). Many decision-making groups also rely on specific rules to regulate their

---

substantive conflict Disagreements over issues that are relevant to the group's recognized goals and procedures.

procedural conflict Disagreement over the methods the group should use to complete its basic tasks.

discussions. The best-known set of rules was developed by Henry M. Robert, an engineer who was irritated by the conflict that characterized many of the meetings he attended. Robert's *Rules of Order,* which he first published in 1876, explicated not only "methods of organizing and conducting the business of societies, conventions, and other deliberative assemblies," but also such technicalities as how motions should be stated, amended, debated, postponed, voted on, and passed (Robert, 1915/1971, p. i). No less than 7 pages were used to describe how the group member "obtains the floor," including suggestions for proper phrasings of the request, appropriate posture, and timing. More complex issues, such as the intricacies of voting, required as many as 20 pages of discussion. Robert purposely designed his rules to "restrain the individual somewhat," for he assumed that "the right of any individual, in any community, to do what he pleases, is incompatible with the interests of the whole" (1915/1971, p. 13). In consequence, his rules promote a formal, technically precise form of interaction, sometimes at the expense of openness, vivacity, and directness. Furthermore, the rules emphasize the use of voting procedures, rather than discussion to consensus, to resolve differences.

Liking and Disliking: Personal Conflicts

Beth Doll and her colleagues (2003) studied conflict at recess—the period of relatively unsupervised interaction that many schoolchildren consider to be an oasis of play in the otherwise work-filled school day. They discovered that many conflicts stemmed from disagreements and power struggles, as children argued about the rules of games, what is fair and what is not, and who gets to make decisions. But the most intense conflicts were personal. Children who disliked each other got into fights. Children who had irritating personal habits were routinely excluded by others. Children in one clique were mean to the children in other cliques and to those who were excluded from all cliques. When children who said they had a rotten time at recess were asked why, in most cases they explained, "I had to play alone" and, "Other kids would not let me join in" (Doll, Murphy, & Song, 2003).

Adults do not always play well together, either. **Personal conflicts,** also called *affective conflicts* (Guetzkow & Gyr, 1954), *personality conflicts* (V. D. Wall & Nolan, 1987), or *emotional conflicts* (Jehn, 1995), are rooted in individuals' antipathies for other group members. Personal likes and dislikes do not always translate into group conflict, but people often mention their disaffection for another group member when they air their complaints about their groups (Alicke et al., 1992; Kelley, 1979; V. D. Wall & Nolan, 1987). Morrill's (1995) study of high-level corporate executives, for example, revealed that these professionals argued with each other over company matters and struggled for power, but in more than 40% of the cases, their disputes were rooted in "individual enmity between the

---

personal conflict Interpersonal discord that occurs when group members dislike one another.

principals without specific reference to other issues." Disputants questioned each others' moral values, the way they treated their spouses, and their politics. They complained about the way their adversaries acted at meetings, the way they dressed at work and at social gatherings, their hobbies and recreational pursuits, and their personality traits. They just did not like each other very much (Morrill, 1995, p. 69).

Just as any factor that creates a positive bond between people can increase a group's cohesion, so any factor that creates disaffection can increase conflict. In many cases, people explain their conflicts by blaming the other person's negative personal qualities, such as moodiness, compulsivity, incompetence, communication difficulties, and sloppiness (Kelley, 1979). People usually dislike others who evaluate them negatively, so criticism—even when deserved—can generate conflict (Ilgen, Mitchell, & Fredrickson, 1981). Group members who treat others unfairly or impolitely engender more conflict than those who behave politely (Ohbuchi, Chiba, & Fukushima, 1996). People who have agreeable personalities are usually better liked by others, and they also exert a calming influence on their groups. In a study of dyads that included people who were either high or low in agreeableness, dyads with two highly agreeable individuals displayed the least conflict, whereas dyads that contained two individuals with low agreeableness displayed the most conflict (Graziano, Jensen-Campbell, & Hair, 1996). Agreeable people also responded more negatively to conflict overall. When people described their day-to-day activities and their daily moods, they reported feeling unhappy, tense, irritated, and anxious on days when they experienced conflicts—especially if they were by nature agreeable people (Suls, Martin, & David, 1998).

The relationship between disaffection and conflict explains why groups with greater diversity sometimes display more conflict than homogeneous groups. Just as similarity among members increases interpersonal attraction, dissimilarity tends to increase disaffection and conflict (Rosenbaum, 1986). Groups whose members had dissimilar personalities (e.g., differences in authoritarianism, cognitive complexity, and temperament) did not get along as well as groups composed of people whose personalities were more similar (Haythorn, Couch, Haefner, Langham, & Carter, 1956; M. E. Shaw, 1981). Heterogeneous teams developing new information technologies were better than homogeneous teams when identifying their goals and gathering information from other groups, but their overall level of performance was inferior because they could not work well together (Ancona & Caldwell, 1992). When group members were led to believe that they were similar to one another, cohesiveness increased and conflict decreased (Back, 1951). Groups whose members vary in terms of ability, experience, opinions, values, race, personality, ethnicity, and so on can capitalize on their members' wider range of resources and viewpoints, but these groups often suffer high levels of conflict (Moreland, Levine, & Wingert, 1996).

Heider's balance theory goes so far as to suggest that arguing and fighting with someone we dislike is cognitively "harmonious"; the elements of the situation all "fit together without stress" (Heider, 1958, p. 180). If Steve likes John but the two do not agree on important issues facing the group, John will experience psychological stress, which he will reduce by changing his opinion of Steve,

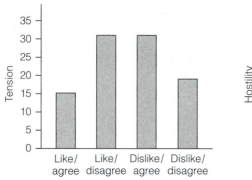
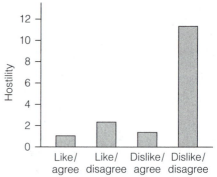

FIGURE 12-4

What happens when we argue with someone we like? When people who disagreed or agreed on an issue and either liked or disliked each other talked for 30 minutes, *tension* was greatest in groups of disagreeing people who liked each other and agreeing people who disliked each other. The greatest amount of *antagonism,* however, occurred in groups where discussants both disagreed and disliked each other. *Source:* H. F. Taylor, 1970.

changing his opinion on the issues so that he agrees with Steve, or avoiding situations where the disagreement will surface.

Howard F. Taylor (1970) tested these predictions by arranging for male college students to discuss an issue with a confederate of the researcher whom they either disliked or liked. This confederate either agreed with the participant or argued against him. Taylor coded the 30-minute discussion, searching for evidence of conflict, including *tension* (nervousness, stammering, blushing, expressions of frustration, and withdrawal), *tension release* (giggling, joking, cheerfulness, silliness), and *antagonism* (anger, hostility, taunting, and defensiveness).

Figure 12-4 partly summarizes Taylor's findings. As balance theory suggests, tension was highest in the unbalanced pairs—when disagreeing people liked each other or when people who disliked each other agreed. The greatest amount of antagonism, however, occurred in pairs where discussants both disagreed and disliked each other. Taylor concluded that the most harmonious groups are ones whose members like each other and find themselves in agreement. The least harmonious groups are balanced, but by negative rather than positive forces: Members dislike each other and they disagree. Taylor suspected that such groups would not endure for long outside the confines of the laboratory.

CONFRONTATION AND ESCALATION

Early in 1985, Sculley and Jobs began moving toward a showdown, pushed into conflict by their incompatibilities, their marked differences of opinion about the company, the competitive nature of their interdependence, and their refusal to take less than they felt was their due. They tried to quell the tension, but by spring, the men were trapped in an escalating conflict.

Conflicts *escalate*. Although the parties to the conflict may hope to reach a solution to their dispute quickly, a host of psychological and interpersonal factors can frustrate their attempts to control the conflict. As Sculley continued to argue with Jobs, he became more committed to his own position, and his view of Jobs and his position became biased. Sculley used stronger influence tactics, and soon other members of Apple were drawn into the fray. All these factors fed the conflict, changing it from a disagreement to a full-fledged corporate war (see J. Z. Rubin, Pruitt, & Kim, 1994).

Uncertainty → Commitment

As conflicts escalate, group members' doubts and uncertainties are replaced by a firm commitment to their position. Sculley, for example, became more certain that his insights were correct, and his disagreement with Jobs only increased his commitment to them (Staw & Ross, 1987). When people try to persuade others, they search out supporting arguments. If this elaboration process yields further consistent information, they become even more committed to their initial position (Petty & Cacioppo, 1986). People rationalize their choices once they have made them: They seek out information that supports their views, they reject information that conflicts with their stance, and they become entrenched in their original position (L. Ross & Ward, 1995). Moreover, people feel that once they commit to a position publicly, they must stick with it. They may realize that they are wrong, but to save face, they continue to argue against their opponents (S. R. Wilson, 1992). Finally, if other group members argue too strongly, *reactance* may set in. As noted in Chapter 8, when reactance occurs, group members become even more committed to their position (S. S. Brehm & Brehm, 1981; Curhan, Neale, & Ross, 2004).

The *dollar auction* illustrates the impact of commitment on conflict. Members bid for $1, but one special rule is added. The highest bidder gets to keep the dollar bill, but the second highest bidder gets no money *and* must pay the amount he or she bid. Bids flow slowly at first, but soon the offers climb over 50 cents toward the $1 mark. As the stakes increase, however, quitting becomes costly. If a bidder who offers 50 cents for the $1 is bested by someone offering 60 cents, the 50-cent bidder will lose 50 cents. So he or she is tempted to beat the 60-cent bid. This cycle continues upward—well beyond the value of the dollar bill in some cases. On occasion, players have spent as much as $20 for the $1 (Teger, 1980).

Perception → Misperception

Individuals' reactions during conflict are shaped in fundamental ways by their perception of the situation and the people in that situation. When group members argue, they must determine why they disagree. If they conclude that their disagreement stems merely from the group's attempts to make the right decision, the disagreement will probably not turn into true conflict. If, however, participants attribute the disagreement to another's incompetence, belligerence, or argumentativeness, a simple disagreement can escalate into conflict (Messé, Stollak, Larson, & Michaels, 1979; L. Ross & Ward, 1995).

If perceptions were always accurate, people would understand one another better. Unfortunately, perceptual biases regularly distort individuals' inferences. They tend to oversimplify conflicts to the point that they misunderstand their own position. They exaggerate the scope of the conflict, turning molehill-sized disputes into mountains of discord (Thompson & Nadler, 2000). They fall prey to the *fundamental attribution error* (FAE) and assume that other people's behavior is caused by personal (dispositional) rather than situational (environmental) factors (L. Ross, 1977). If Jobs was affected by the FAE, he may have blamed Sculley's personality, beliefs, attitudes, and values for the conflict, rather than pressure from the board of directors, the shareholders, or Jobs's own actions.

Because of the FAE, group members assume that people who give them critical feedback, argue with them, or mistreat them in some way do so deliberately, and that their actions reflect basic flaws in their personalities (Baumeister, Stillwell, & Wotman, 1990; Cunningham, Starr, & Kanouse, 1979; Messé et al., 1979; Murata, 1982). One team of researchers verified this tendency by pairing people playing a PDG-like game with partners who used one of four possible strategies: *competition* (they maximized personal gains while minimizing their partners' gains), *cooperation* (they maximized joint gains, striving to increase their own and their partners' outcomes), *individualism* (they ignored their partners' gains but maximized personal gains), and *altruism* (they ignored their own personal gains but maximized their partners' gains). When describing their partners' motives, the players were most accurate when playing an individualistic or competitive person, and least accurate in interpreting cooperation and altruism (Maki, Thorngate, & McClintock, 1979).

People with competitive social values orientations are the most inaccurate in their perceptions of cooperation. When cooperators play the PDG with other cooperators, their perceptions of their partner's strategy are inaccurate only 6% of the time. When competitors play the PDG with cooperators, however, they misinterpret their partner's strategy 47% of the time, mistakenly believing that the cooperators are competing (Kelley & Stahelski, 1970a, 1970b, 1970c; Sattler & Kerr, 1991). Competitors are also biased in their search for information, for they are more likely to seek out information that confirms their suspicions—"I am dealing with a competitive person"—rather than information that might indicate the others are attempting to cooperate (Van Kleef & De Dreu, 2002). Competitors also tend to deliberately misrepresent their intentions, sometimes claiming to be more cooperatively intentioned than they actually are (Steinel & De Dreu, 2004).

Weak Tactics → Stronger Tactics

We can influence people in dozens of different ways. As noted in Chapter 8, we can promise, reward, threaten, punish, bully, discuss, instruct, negotiate, manipulate, supplicate, ingratiate, and so on. Some of these tactics are stronger than

TABLE 12-2 Influence methods used in groups sharing scarce resources

Behavior	Example	Percentage Using
Requests	May I use the glue?	100.0
Statements	We need the glue.	100.0
Demands	Give me the glue, now!	88.9
Complaints	What's wrong with you? Why don't you share?	79.2
Problem solving	You can use our stapler if you share the glue.	73.6
Third party	Make them share!	45.8
Angry	I'm mad now.	41.7
Threat	Give me the glue or else.	22.2
Harassment	I'm not giving you any more ribbon until you return the glue.	16.7
Abuse	You are a selfish swine.	0.7

Source: Mikolic, Parker, & Pruitt, 1997.

others. Threats, punishment, and bullying are all strong, contentious tactics because they are direct, nonrational, and unilateral. People use weaker tactics at the outset of a conflict, but as the conflict escalates, they shift to stronger and stronger tactics. Sculley gradually shifted from relatively mild methods of influence (discussion, negotiation) to stronger tactics (threats). Eventually, he demoted Jobs (Carnevale & Pruitt, 1992).

Researchers have studied this escalation process by paying participants to construct birthday cards using paper, colored markers, and ribbons. Participants' efforts were frustrated by a confederate of the researchers who deliberately hoarded materials that the participants needed. As the hour wore on, it became clear that the confederate was going to make far more money than the participants, and the participants became more and more frustrated. They responded by using stronger and more contentious influence tactics. As Table 12-2 indicates, all the participants tried to solve their problem initially with statements and requests. When those methods failed, they shifted to demands and complaints. When those methods failed, they tried problem solving and appeals to a third party (the experimenter). In the most extreme cases, they used threats, abuse, and anger to try to influence the irritating confederate (Mikolic, Parker, & Pruitt, 1997).

People who use stronger tactics often overwhelm their antagonists, but such methods intensify conflicts. Morton Deutsch and Robert Krauss (1960) examined this intensification process in their classic **trucking game experiment.**

---

trucking game experiment A research procedure developed by Morton Deutsch and Robert Krauss in their studies of conflict between individuals who differ in their capacity to threaten and punish others.

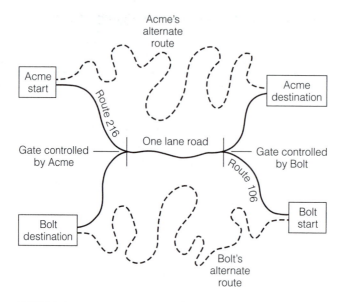

FIGURE 12-5

How did Deutsch and Krauss create conflict using their trucking game simulation? Players took the role of either Acme or Bolt, and maneuvered their trucks along Route 216, Route 106, or the longer, alternate routes. In some cases, one or both of the players were given gates that they could close to bar access by their opponent. *Source: The Resolution of Conflict: Constructive and Destructive Processes,* by M. Deutsch. Copyright 1973 by Yale University Press. Reprinted by permission.

They asked pairs of women to role-play the owners of a trucking company. The two companies, Acme and Bolt, carried merchandise over the roads mapped in Figure 12-5. Acme and Bolt each earned 60 cents after each complete run, minus 1 cent for each second taken up by the trip.

The truck route set the stage for competition and conflict between Acme and Bolt. The shortest path from start to finish for Acme was Route 216 and for Bolt was Route 106, but these routes merged into a one-lane highway. When trucks encountered each other along this route, one player had to back up to her starting position to let the other through. Acme and Bolt could avoid this confrontation by taking the winding alternate route, but this path took longer.

All the pairs played the same basic game, but some were provided with the power to threaten their opponents, and others were not. In the *unilateral threat* condition, Acme was told that a gate, which only she could open and close, was located at the fork in Route 216. When the gate was closed, neither truck could pass this point in the road, making control of the gate a considerable benefit to

Acme. If Bolt attempted to use the main route, all Acme had to do was close the gate, forcing Bolt to back up and enabling Acme to reopen the gate and proceed quickly to her destination. Thus, when only Acme possessed the gate, Bolt's profits were greatly threatened. In the *bilateral threat* condition, both sides had the use of gates located at the ends of the one-lane section of Route 216, and in the *control* condition, no gates were given to the players.

Deutsch and Krauss's control participants soon learned to resolve the conflict over the one-lane road. Most of these pairs took turns using the main route, and on the average, each participant made a $1 profit. Winnings dwindled, however, when one of the players was given a gate. Participants in the unilateral threat condition lost an average of $2.03. Bolt's losses were twice as great as Acme's, but even Acme lost more than $1 at the game. Conflict was even worse when both Acme and Bolt had gates. In the bilateral threat condition, both players usually took the longer route because the gates on the main route were kept closed, and their losses in this condition averaged $4.38.

These findings convinced Deutsch and Krauss that the capacity to threaten others intensifies conflict. They also noted that establishing a communication link between adversaries does not necessarily help them to solve their dispute (Krauss & Morsella, 2000). If one party can or does threaten the other party, the threatened party will fare best if he or she cannot respond with a counterthreat (Borah, 1963; Deutsch & Lewicki, 1970; Froman & Cohen, 1969; Gallo, 1966). Equally powerful opponents, however, learn to avoid the use of their power if the fear of retaliation is high (Lawler, Ford, & Blegen, 1988).

Reciprocity → Upward Conflict Spiral

Conflict-ridden groups may seem normless, with hostility and dissatisfaction spinning out of control. Yet upward conflict spirals are in many cases sustained by the norm of *reciprocity,* for that norm suggests that people who harm you are also deserving of harm themselves. The converse of "You scratch my back and I'll scratch yours" is "An eye for an eye, a tooth for a tooth" (e.g., Tedeschi, Gaes, & Rivera, 1977; Tedeschi, Smith, & Brown, 1974). If one group member criticizes the ideas, opinions, or characteristics of another, the victim of the attack will feel justified in counterattacking unless some situational factor legitimizes the hostility of the former.

If interactants followed the norm of reciprocity exactly, a mild threat would elicit a mild threat in return, and an attack would lead to a counterattack. But interactants tend to follow the norm of *rough* reciprocity—they give too much (*overmatching*) or too little (*undermatching*) in return. In one study, women playing a PDG-like game against a confederate could send notes to their opponent and penalize her by taking points from her winnings. Reciprocity guided the player's actions, for the more often the confederate sent threats, the more often the participant sent threats; when the confederate's threats were large, the participant's threats were large; and confederates who exacted large fines triggered large fines from the participant. This reciprocity, however, was rough rather than exact. At low levels of conflict, the participants overmatched threats and punishments, and at high levels of conflict, they undermatched their threats. The overmatching that occurs initially may serve as a strong warning, whereas the undermatching at high levels of conflict may be used to send a conciliatory message (Youngs, 1986).

Few → Many

During the Jobs–Sculley conflict, Jobs tried to persuade each member of the board to side with him in the dispute. His goal was to form a powerful coalition that would block Sculley's plans and swing the vote of the board in his favor.

Coalitions exist in most groups, but when conflict erupts, group members use coalitions to shift the balance of power in their favor. The initial disagreement may involve only two group members, but as conflicts intensify, previously neutral members often join with one faction. Similarly, even when members initially express many different views, with time, these multiparty conflicts are reduced to two-party blocs through coalition formation. Coalitions can even link rivals who decide to join forces temporarily to achieve a specific outcome (a mixed-motive situation). Although allies may wish to compete with one another, no single individual has enough power to succeed alone. Hence, while the coalition exists, the competitive motive must be stifled (Komorita & Parks, 1994).

Coalitions contribute to conflicts because they draw more members of the group into the fray. Coalitions are often viewed as contentious, heavy-handed influence tactics because individuals in the coalition work not only to ensure their own outcomes but also to worsen the outcomes of non–coalition members. Coalitions form *with* people and *against* other people. In business settings, for example, the dominant coalition can control the organization, yet it works outside the bounds of the formal group structure. Those who are excluded from a coalition react with hostility to the coalition members and seek to regain power by forming their own coalitions. Thus, coalitions must be constantly maintained through strategic bargaining and negotiation (Mannix, 1993; Murnighan, 1986; W. B. Stevenson, Pearce, & Porter, 1985).

Irritation → Anger

Few people can remain calm and collected in a conflict. When disputes arise, tempers flare, and this increase in negative emotions exacerbates the initial conflict. Most people, when asked to talk about a time when they became angry, said that they usually lost their temper when arguing with people they knew rather than with strangers. Many admitted that their anger increased the negativity of the conflict; 49% became verbally abusive when they were angry, and 10% said they became physically aggressive (Averill, 1983). Participants in another study reported physically attacking someone or something, losing emotional control, or imagining violence against someone else when they were angry (Shaver, Schwartz, Kirson, & O'Connor, 1987). Even when group members begin by discussing their points calmly and dispassionately, as they become locked into their positions, emotional expression begins to replace logical discussion (Allred, 2000; Blascovich et al., 1978). Unfortunately, all manner of negative behaviors, including the rejection of concessions, the tendering of unworkable initial offers, and the use of contentious influence strategies, increase as members' affect becomes more negative (Pillutla & Murnighan, 1996; Van Kleef, De Dreu, & Manstead, 2004). Anger is also a contagious emotion in groups (Kelly, 2001). Group members, when negotiating with someone who has become angry, tend to become angry themselves (Van Kleef et al., 2004).

CONFLICT RESOLUTION

In one way or another, conflicts subside. Even when members are committed to their own viewpoints, high levels of tension cannot be maintained indefinitely. In time, disputants regain control of their tempers and break the upward conflict spiral. When group members confront their problems and work toward a solution, conflict becomes a valued resource rather than a problem that must be eliminated. In time, group hostility devolves into harmony.

Commitment ➜ Negotiation

Just as conflicts escalate when group members become firmly committed to a position and will not budge, conflicts de-escalate when group members are willing to negotiate with others to reach a solution that benefits all parties. **Negotiation** is a reciprocal communication process whereby two or more parties to a dispute examine specific issues, explain their positions, and exchange offers and counteroffers. Negotiation sometimes amounts to little more than simple bargaining or mutual compromise. In such *distributive negotiations,* both parties retain their competitive orientation and take turns making small concessions until some equally dissatisfying middle ground is reached. Haggling and bartering ("I'll give you $20 for it, and not a penny more!") illustrate this form of negotiation (Druckman, 1994; McKersie & Walton, 1992; Pruitt & Carnevale, 1993; Raiffa, Richardson, and Metcalfe, 2003; Thompson, 1990; Zartman & Rubin, 2000).

Integrative negotiation, in contrast, is not a competitive conflict management method (J. Z. Rubin, 1994). As Roger Fisher and William Ury noted, integrative negotiators work with other group members to achieve cooperative, integrative outcomes that benefit both sides. Fisher and Ury, drawing on studies and conferences conducted as part of the Harvard Negotiation Project, distinguished between three types of negotiators—soft negotiators, hard negotiators, and principled negotiators (see Table 12-3). *Soft bargainers* see negotiation as too close to competition, so they choose a gentle style of negotiation. They make offers that are not in their best interests, they yield to others' demands, they avoid any

---

negotiation A reciprocal communication process whereby two or more parties to a dispute examine specific issues, explain their positions, and exchange offers and counteroffers to reach agreement or achieve mutually beneficial outcomes.

TABLE 12-3 Comparisons between the three approaches to negotiation

Element	Soft Negotiation	Hard Negotiation	Principled Negotiation
Perception of others	Friends	Adversaries	Problem solvers
Goals	Agreement	Victory	A wise outcome reached efficiently and amicably
Concessions	Make concessions to cultivate the relationship	Demand concessions as a condition of the relationship	Separate the people from the problem
People vs. problems	Be soft on the people and the problem	Be hard on the problem and the people	Be soft on the people, hard on the problem
Trust	Trust others	Distrust others	Proceed independently of trust
Positions	Change your position easily	Dig into your position	Focus on interests, not positions
Negotiation	Make offers	Make threats	Explore interests
Bottom line	Disclose your bottom line	Mislead as to your bottom line	Avoid having a bottom line
Losses and gains	Accept one-sided losses to reach agreement	Demand one-sided gains as a price of agreement	Invent options for mutual gains
Search	Search for a single answer—the one they will accept	Search for a single answer—the one you will accept	Develop multiple options to choose from; decide later
Criteria	Insist on agreement	Insist on your position	Insist on using objective criteria
Contest of will	Avoid a contest of wills	Win the contest of wills	Reach a result based on standards, independent of will
Pressure	Yield to pressure	Apply pressure	Reason and be open to reason; yield to principle, not pressure

Source: Adapted from R. Fisher & Ury, 1981.

confrontation, and they maintain their friendship. *Hard bargainers,* in contrast, use tough, competitive tactics during negotiations. They begin by taking an extreme position on the issue, and then they make small concessions only grudgingly. The hard bargainer uses contentious strategies of influence and says such things as "Take it or leave it," "This is my final offer," "This point is not open to negotiation," "My hands are tied," and "I'll see you in court" (R. Fisher, 1983).

Principled negotiators, meanwhile, seek integrative solutions by sidestepping commitment to specific positions. Instead of risking entrapment, principled negotiators focus on the problem rather than the intentions, motives, and needs of the people involved. Positional bargaining, Roger Fisher and William Ury (1981) argued, is too dangerous:

When negotiators bargain over positions, they tend to lock themselves into those positions. The more you clarify your position and defend it against attack, the more committed you become to it. The more you try to convince the other side of the impossibility of changing your opening position, the more difficult it becomes to do so. Your ego becomes identified with your position. (p. 5)

Fisher and Ury recommended that negotiators explore a number of alternatives to the problems they face. During this phase, the negotiation is transformed into a group problem-solving session, with the different parties working together in search of creative solutions and new information that the group can use to evaluate these alternatives. Fisher and Ury's principled negotiators base their choice on objective criteria rather than on power, pressure, self-interest, or an arbitrary decisional procedure. Such criteria can be drawn from moral standards, principles of fairness, objective indexes of market value, professional standards, tradition, and so on, but they should be recognized as fair by all parties (Kolb & Williams, 2003).

Misperception → Understanding

Many conflicts are based on misperceptions. People often assume that others are competing with them, when in fact those other people only wish to cooperate. They think that people who criticize their ideas are criticizing them personally. They do not trust other people because they are convinced that their motives are selfish ones. They assume that their goals are incompatible when they are not (Thompson & Hrebec, 1996).

Group members must undo these perceptual misunderstandings by actively communicating information about their motives and goals through discussion. In one study, group members were given the opportunity to exchange information about their interests and goals, yet only about 20% did (Thompson, 1991). Those who did, however, were more likely to discover shared goals and were able to reach solutions that benefited both parties to the conflict (Thompson, 1991; Weingart, Thompson, Bazerman, & Carroll, 1990). Other studies have suggested that conflict declines when group members communicate their intentions in specific terms, make explicit references to trust, cooperation, and fairness, and build a shared ingroup identity (Harinck, 2004; N. L. Kerr & Kaufman-Gilliland, 1994; Sell et al., 2004).

Communication is no cure-all for conflict, however. Group members can exchange information by communicating, but they can also create gross misunderstandings and deceptions. Communication offers group members the means to establish trust and commitment, but it can also exacerbate conflict if members verbalize feelings of hatred, disgust, or annoyance. For example, when Deutsch and Krauss (1960) let participants in their trucking game experiment communicate with each other, messages typically emphasized threats and did little to reduce conflict (Deutsch, 1973). Communication is detrimental if these initial messages are inconsistent, hostile, and contentious (McClintock, Stech, & Keil, 1983; Pilisuk, Brandes, & van den Hove, 1976; R. K. Wilson & Sell, 1997). Communication can be beneficial, however, if interactants use it to create cooperative norms, if it increases trust among participants, and if it generates increased cohesion and unity in the group (Messick & Brewer, 1983).

Strong Tactics → Cooperative Tactics

Group members cope with conflict in different ways. Some ignore the problem. Others discuss the problem, sometimes dispassionately and rationally, sometimes angrily and loudly. Still others seek a neutral party to serve as a mediator. Some actually resort to physical violence (Sternberg & Dobson, 1987). Most of the tactics that people use to deal with conflict can be classified into one of four basic categories, as shown in Table 12-4.

- *Avoiding.* Inaction is a favorite means of dealing with disputes. Students in small groups often said that they dealt with conflicts by adopting a "wait and see" attitude, hoping that they would eventually go away (V. D. Wall & Nolan, 1987). Many executives say that they "tolerate" conflicts, allowing them to simmer without doing anything to minimize them (Morrill, 1995). Rather than openly discussing disagreements, people who rely on avoidance change the subject, skip meetings, or even leave the group altogether (Bayazit & Mannix, 2003).
- *Yielding.* People solve both large and small conflicts by giving in to the demands of others. Sometimes, they yield because they realize that their position is in error, so they agree with the viewpoint adopted by others. In other cases, however, they may withdraw their demands without really being convinced that the other side is correct, but—for the sake of group unity or in the interest of time—they withdraw all complaints. Thus, yielding can reflect either genuine conversion or superficial compliance.
- *Fighting.* Some people manage their disputes by forcing others to accept their view. They see the conflict as a win–lose situation and use competitive, powerful tactics to intimidate others. Fighting (*forcing, dominating,* or *contending*) can take many forms, including authoritative mandate, challenges, arguing, insults, accusations, complaining, vengeance, and even physical violence (Morrill, 1995). These conflict resolution methods are all contentious ones because they involve imposing one's solution on the other party.
- *Cooperating.* People who rely on cooperation to resolve disputes search for solutions that are acceptable to both sides in the conflict. Cooperating people identify the issues underlying the dispute and then work together to identify a solution that is satisfying to both sides. This orientation, which is also described as collaboration, problem solving, or a win–win orientation, entreats both sides in the dispute to consider their opponent's outcomes as well as their own.

Some theorists consider *conciliation* to be a fifth distinct way to resolve conflicts, but trying to win over others by accepting some of their demands can also be thought of as either yielding or cooperating (van de Vliert & Euwema, 1994).

TABLE 12-4 The four basic methods of dealing with conflict

Dimension	Negative	Positive
Active	*Fighting:* competing, forcing, dominating, contending; win–lose; maximize own outcome and minimize others' outcomes; high concern for self and low concern for others	*Cooperating:* sharing, collaborating, problem solving; win–win; synthesis, negotiation; maximize joint outcomes; high concern both for self and for others
Passive	*Avoiding:* Inaction, withdrawal; lose–lose; "wait and see" attitude; denial, evasion; exit the group, minimize own losses; low concern both for self and for others	*Yielding:* Acceptance, smoothing, accommodating, giving in, yielding, losing; maximize others' outcomes; low concern for self and high concern for others

These conflict management methods differ from one another in at least two important ways. First, some of the dispute resolution modes are negative rather than positive. The *negative* methods (avoidance and fighting) do not take into account others' outcomes (Pruitt, 1983), they intensify conflicts (Sternberg & Dobson, 1987), and they are viewed as more disagreeable (Jarboe & Witteman, 1996; van de Vliert & Euwema, 1994). The *positive* methods (yielding and cooperation) recognize and try to accommodate others' needs, mitigate conflict, and are viewed as more agreeable. Second, some of the methods are active, whereas others are more passive. Fighting and cooperating are both *active* approaches to coping with conflict, whereas yielding and avoidance are *passive* methods (Sternberg & Dodson, 1987; Sheppard, 1983; K. W. Thomas, 1992; van de Vliert & Janssen, 2001).

When conflict erupts, group members can use any or all of the basic modes of conflict resolution shown in Table 12-4, but only one of them—*cooperation*—offers an integrative solution to the group's problem. Avoidance, fighting, and yielding are often only temporary solutions, for they quell conflicts at the surface without considering the source. Cooperation, in most cases, yields both immediate and long-term benefits for the group (Deutsch, 1973; K. W. Thomas, 1992; see Focus 12-2).

Upward → Downward Conflict Spirals

Consistent cooperation among people over a long period generally increases mutual trust. But when group members continually compete with each other, mutual trust becomes much more elusive (Haas & Deseran, 1981). When people cannot trust one another, they compete simply to defend their own best interests (Lindskold, 1978).

How can the upward spiral of competition and distrust, once initiated, be reversed? Robert Axelrod (1984; Axelrod & Hamilton, 1981) explored this question by comparing a number of strategies in simulated competitions. After

FOCUS 12-2   What Is the Best Way to Manage Conflict?

*He who turns and runs away, lives to fight
another day.*
–English proverb

What should you do when a conflict takes over
your group? Should you encourage members to
deal, up front and directly, with their dispute? Or
is it sometimes best to just look the other way,
and let the hard feelings fade with the passage
of time?

Many corporate consultants, confident that
reason, cooperation, and fair play will heal all
group wounds, recommend dealing with conflicts directly by "working things out," "putting
your cards on the table," and "airing out differences." Such advice is predicated on the assumption that if groups root out the cause of their
conflicts, they will become more cohesive and
productive. But what if the group's conflict
springs from interpersonal sources—differences
in personality, values, lifestyles, likes, and dislikes—rather than from the group's task? Are
collaborative, integrative methods of dealing
with conflict always best, or do problems sometimes go away (to a degree) if groups ignore them
(Torrance, 1957)?

Carsten De Dreu and his colleagues cautiously argued against a one-size-fits-all approach
to dealing with conflict, for their studies suggested that collaborative approaches sometimes
aggravate the group conflict more than they mol-
lify it (e.g., De Dreu, 1997; De Dreu & Van
Vianne, 2001; De Dreu & Weingart, 2003). In
one field study, members of semi-autonomous
teams working on complex, nonroutine tasks

were asked about the ways they handled conflicts
in their teams. All these teams included both men
and women, and they ranged in size from 4 to
13 members. Members of these teams typically
interacted with each other in face-to-face settings at least once a week in planning sessions,
and they reported interacting with each other informally nearly every day. As expected, negative
methods of dealing with conflicts, such as arguing and forcing one's views onto others, were associated with negative team functioning. In these
groups, however, collaborative methods of conflict resolution (e.g., "discussing the issues," "cooperating to better understand others' views,"
"settling problems through give and take") were
also negatively correlated with team functioning.
Only avoiding responses, such as "avoiding the
issues," "acting as if nothing has happened," and
"hushing up the quarrel" were associated with
increases in group adjustment to the conflict.
Apparently, the consistent use of collaboration
to deal with intractable differences or petty
disagreements distracted the groups from the
achievement of their task-related goals (De
Dreu & Van Vianne, 2001).

These findings suggest that groups may wish
to heed the advice of one member of a successful
musical quartet who, when asked how his group
managed conflicts, explained, "We have a little
saying in quartets—either we play or we fight"
(Murnighan & Conlon, 1991, pp. 177–178).
Sometimes, the best way to deal with someone
who is disagreeable, irritating, or aggravating is
to ignore the conflict and focus, instead, on the
work to be done.

---

studying dozens of different strategies, ranging from always competing with a
competitor to always cooperating with one, the most effective competition re-
verser to emerge was a strategy called **tit for tat** (TFT). When using TFT, you
begin bargaining by cooperating. If the other party cooperates, too, then you

---

tit for tat (TFT) A bargaining strategy that begins with cooperation, but then imitates
the other person's choice so that cooperation is met with cooperation and competition
with competition.

continue to cooperate. But if the other party competes, then you compete as well. Each action by the other person is countered with the matching response—cooperation for cooperation, competition for competition. Axelrod felt that TFT works because it is both a provocable strategy and a forgiving strategy. It is *provocable* in the sense that it immediately retaliates against individuals who compete. It is *forgiving,* however, in that it immediately reciprocates cooperation should the competitor respond cooperatively.

TFT is a *reciprocal* strategy, for it fights fire with fire and rewards kindness in kind. Individuals who follow a tit-for-tat strategy are viewed as "tough but fair"; those who cooperate with a competitor are viewed as weak, and those who consistently compete are considered unfair (McGillicuddy, Pruitt, & Syna, 1984). Because the effectiveness of TFT as a conflict reduction method is based on its provocability, any delay in responding to cooperation reduces the effectiveness of TFT. If a group member competes, and this defection is not countered quickly with competition, TFT is less effective (Komorita, Hilty, & Parks, 1991). TFT also loses some of its strength in "noisy" interactions, when behaviors cannot be clearly classified as either competitive or cooperative (Van Lange, Ouwerkerk, & Tazelaar, 2002; Wu & Axelrod, 1995). It is also less effective in larger groups, although this decline is minimized if individual members believe that a substantial subgroup within the total group is basing its choices on the TFT strategy (Komorita, Parks, & Hulbert, 1992; Parks & Komorita, 1997).

Many → Few

Conflicts grow larger when others take sides, but they shrink when third-party **mediators** help group members reach a mutually agreeable solution to their dispute (Kressel, 2000). Although uninvolved group members may wish to stand back and let the disputants "battle it out," impasses, unflagging conflict escalation, or the combatants' entreaties may cause other group members or outside parties to help by

- creating opportunities for both sides to express themselves while controlling contentiousness.
- improving communication between the disputants by summarizing points, asking for clarification, and so on.
- helping disputants save face by framing the acceptance of concessions in positive ways and by taking the blame for these concessions.
- formulating and offering proposals for alternative solutions that both parties find acceptable.
- manipulating aspects of the meeting, including its location, seating, formality of communication, time constraints, attendees, and agenda.
- guiding the disputants through a process of integrative problem solving.

---

mediator One who intervenes between two persons who are experiencing conflict, with a view to reconcile them.

However, if the disputants want to resolve the conflict on their own terms, third-party interventions are considered an unwanted intrusion (Carnevale, 1986a, 1986b; Pruitt & Rubin, 1986; Raiffa, 1983; J. Z. Rubin, 1980, 1986).

Go-betweens, facilitators, diplomats, advisers, judges, and other kinds of mediators vary considerably in terms of their power to control others' outcomes (LaTour, 1978; LaTour, Houlden, Walker, & Thibaut, 1976). In an *inquisitorial procedure,* the mediator questions the two parties and then hands down a verdict that the two parties must accept. In *arbitration,* the disputants present their arguments to the mediator, who then bases his or her decision on the information they provide. In a *moot,* the disputants and the mediator openly and informally discuss problems and solutions, but the mediator can make no binding decisions. Satisfaction with a mediator depends on how well the intermediary fulfills these functions and also on the intensity of the conflict. Mediational techniques such as arbitration are effective when the conflict is subdued, but they may not work when conflict intensity is high. Overall, most people prefer arbitration, followed by a moot, mediation, and inquisitorial procedures (LaTour et al., 1976; W. H. Ross, Brantmeier, & Ciriacks, 2002; W. H. Ross & Conlon, 2000).

Anger → Composure

Just as negative emotions encourage conflicts, positive affective responses increase concession making, creative problem solving, cooperation, and the use of non-contentious bargaining strategies (Forgas, 1998; Van Kleef et al., 2004). Hence, when tempers flare, the group should encourage members to regain control over their emotions. "Count to ten," calling a "time-out," or expressing concerns in a written (and carefully edited) letter or e-mail are simple but effective recommendations for controlling conflict, as is the introduction of humor into the group discussion (Mischel & DeSmet, 2000). Apologies, too, are effective means of reducing anger. When people are informed about mitigating causes—background factors that indicate that the insult is unintentional or unimportant—conflict is reduced (Betancourt & Blair, 1992; Ferguson & Rule, 1983). Groups can also control anger by developing norms that explicitly or implicitly prohibit shows of strong, negative emotion or by holding meetings on controversial topics online (J. Yang & Mossholder, 2004).

The Value of Conflict

Conflict is a natural consequence of joining a group. Groups bind their members and their members' outcomes together, and this interdependence can lead to conflict when members' qualities, ideas, goals, motivations, and outlooks clash. Conflict is also an undeniably powerful process in groups. In the case of Apple, the conflict between Jobs and Sculley permanently changed the entire company. Before the conflict, Apple was an unconventional, risk-taking trendsetter. After the conflict, the company focused on costs, increasing sales, and turning a profit. This change helped the company compete successfully against competitors, even though some of the original employees regretted the change. Sculley remained with Apple for nearly 10 years before he moved on. Ironically, Steven Jobs rejoined Apple in 1997 as chief executive officer, and has reinstated some of his original policies to improve Apple.

But is conflict always harmful—a pernicious process that should be avoided? This question remains open to debate. Insofar as conflict is resolved successfully, it could stabilize the group and serve as a unifying force. As noted in Chapter 5's analysis of group development, many groups pass through a period of conflict as they mature. This conflict phase expands the range of options, generates new alternatives, and enhances the group's unity by making explicit any latent hostilities and tensions. Conflict can make a group's goals more explicit and help members understand their role in the group (Bormann, 1975; Jehn, 1994; Thibaut & Coules, 1952).

In general, however, conflict causes more harm than good. It undermines satisfactions, engenders negative emotions, disrupts performance, and can even trigger violence. When Carsten W. De Dreu and Laurie R. Weingart (2003) conducted a meta-analysis of dozens of studies of conflict in groups, they discovered that, in study after study, conflict undermined satisfaction and lowered performance. They even distinguished between types of conflict: *relationship conflict* (which should cause interpersonal disruptions) and *task conflict* (which should stimulate members to improve the way they work together). The negative relationship still held—conflict of any kind undermined outcomes. De Dreu and Weingart (2003) concluded that

> Conflict may have positive consequences under very specific circumstances, and we need to detect those circumstances in new research. While waiting for these studies, however, it seems safe to stop assuming that, whereas relationship conflict is detrimental to team performance, task conflict improves team performance. Clearly, it does not. (p. 748)

SUMMARY IN OUTLINE

❖ What is conflict?

1. When *conflict* occurs in a group, the actions or beliefs of one or more members of the group are unacceptable to and resisted by one or more of the other members.

2. *Intergroup conflict* involves two or more groups, and *intragroup conflict* occurs within a group.

3. Conflict follows a cycle from conflict escalation to resolution.

❖ What are the sources of conflict in groups?

1. Many group and individual factors conspire to create conflict in a group, but the most common sources are competition, conflicts over the distribution of resources, power struggles, decisional conflicts, and personal conflicts.

2. *Competition* creates conflict by pitting members against one another, whereas *cooperation* leads to mutual gain.

- *Mixed-motive situations,* like the *prisoner's dilemma game* (PDG), stimulate conflict because they tempt individuals to compete rather than cooperate.
- The *norm of reciprocity* encourages responding to competition by competing.
- Individuals differ in their basic orientation toward conflict. Those with a competitive *social values orientation* are more likely to compete than are those with cooperative or individualistic orientations, even if they think that others will be acting in a cooperative fashion.
- Men and women are equally competitive, although both sexes use more contentious influence methods when they are paired with a man rather than with a woman, perhaps because they anticipate more conflict.

3. *Social dilemmas* stimulate conflict by tempting members to act in their own self-interest to the detriment of the group and its goals. Disputes arise when one or more members
   - exploit a shared resource (a *commons dilemma* or *social trap*).
   - do not contribute their share in a *public goods dilemma* (free riding).
   - disagree on how to divide up resources (*distributive justice*) or on the procedures to following in dividing the resources (*procedural justice*).
   - do not agree on the norms to follow when apportioning resources (the *equality norm* versus the *equity norm*).
   - avoid blame for group failure or take too much personal responsibility for group successes (self-serving attributions of responsibility).

4. These reactions are driven, in part, by self-interest, but group members respond negatively to perceived mistreatment because it calls into question their status and inclusion.

5. Power struggles are common in groups as members vie for control over leadership, status, and position.

6. *Substantive conflict* stems from disagreements about issues that are relevant to the group's goals and outcomes. Even though substantive conflicts help groups reach their goals, these disagreements can turn into personal, unpleasant conflicts.

7. *Procedural conflicts* occur when members do not agree on group strategies, policies, and methods. Groups avoid such conflicts by clarifying procedures.

8. *Personal conflict* occurs when individual members do not like one another.
   - Any factor that causes disaffection between group members (e.g., differences in attitudes, objectionable personal qualities) can increase personal conflict.
   - Personal conflict is more prevalent in groups that are diverse.
   - Balance theory predicts that group members will respond negatively when they disagree with those they like or agree with those they dislike, but in most cases, conflict is greatest when group members both disagree with and dislike each other.

❖ Why does conflict escalate?

1. Once conflict begins, it often intensifies before it begins to abate.

2. When individuals defend their viewpoints in groups, they become more committed to their positions; doubts and uncertainties are replaced by firm commitment.

3. Conflict is exacerbated by members' tendency to misperceive others and to assume that the other party's behavior is caused by personal (dispositional) rather than situational (environmental) factors (*fundamental attribution error*).

4. As conflicts worsen, members shift from weak to strong tactics. Deutsch and Krauss studied this process in their *trucking game experiment*. Conflict between individuals escalated when each side could threaten the other.

5. Other factors that contribute to the escalation of conflict in groups include
   - negative reciprocity, as when negative actions provoke negative reactions in others.
   - the formation of coalitions that embroil formerly neutral members in the conflict.
   - angry emotions that trigger expressions of anger by others.

❖ **How can group members manage their conflict?**

1. In many cases, members use *negotiation* (including integrative negotiation) to identify the issues underlying the dispute and then work together to identify a solution that is satisfying to both sides.

2. Because many conflicts are rooted in misunderstandings and misperceptions, group members can reduce conflict by actively communicating information about their motives and goals through discussion.

3. Four frequently identified and used means of dealing with conflicts—avoiding, yielding, fighting, and cooperating—differ along two dimensions: negative–positive and active–passive.

- In many cases, cooperation is more likely to promote group unity than all other tactics.
- Personal conflicts—ones that are rooted in basic differences in attitude, outlook, and so on—may not yield to cooperative negotiations, and in such cases, an avoiding method may be the best way to cope with the conflict.

4. If a group member continues to compete, the *tit-for-tat* (TFT) strategy has proved useful as a conflict management strategy.

5. Third-party interventions—*mediators*—can reduce conflict by imposing solutions (inquisitorial procedures and arbitration) or guiding disputants to a compromise (moot and mediation procedures).

6. Just as negative emotions encourage conflict, positive affective responses reduce conflict.

❖ **Does conflict, when resolved, lead to improved group functioning?**

1. Conflict is a natural consequence of joining a group and cannot be avoided completely.

2. Some evidence suggests that conflicts, when resolved successfully, promote positive group functioning, but in general, conflict causes more harm than good.

FOR MORE INFORMATION

Chapter Case: The Jobs–Sculley Conflict

■ *Odyssey: Pepsi to Apple . . . A Journal of Adventure, Ideas, and the Future,* by John Sculley (with J. A. Byme; 1987), describes one side in the great Jobs versus Sculley confrontation.

Causes of Conflict

■ "Conflict in Groups," a chapter by John M. Levine and Leigh Thompson (1996), is a relatively high-level analysis of the causes, benefits, and liabilities of conflict in small groups.

- *Social Conflict: Escalation, Stalemate, and Settlement* (2nd ed.), by Jeffry Z. Rubin, Dean G. Pruitt, and Sung Hee Kim (1994), provides a thorough analysis of the causes and consequences of interpersonal conflict.
- *The Executive Way,* by Calvin Morrill (1995), is a compelling analysis of the causes and consequences of conflict in the upper echelons of large corporations.
- *Resolving Social Dilemmas: Dynamic, Structural, and Intergroup Aspects,* edited by Margaret Foddy, Michael Smithson, Sherry Schneider, and Michael Hogg (1999), is a compilation of 23 chapters by leading experts on a wide array of problematic collaborative activities, including social and environmental traps.

Conflict Resolution

- *Getting to YES: Negotiating Agreement Without Giving In* (2nd ed.), by Roger Fisher, William Ury, and Bruce Patton (1991), describes a step-by-step strategy for resolving conflicts to the mutual benefit of both parties.
- *The Handbook of Conflict Resolution,* edited by Morton Deutsch and Peter T. Coleman (2000), is the definitive sourcebook for general analyses of conflict resolution but also provides practical recommendations for resolving conflicts.
- *The Resolution of Conflict: Constructive and Destructive Processes,* is Morton Deutsch's (1973) foundational, "must-read" analysis of conflict.

Media Resources

Visit the Group Dynamics companion website at http://psychology.wadsworth .com/forsyth4e to access online resources for your book, including quizzes, flash cards, web links, and more!

13

INTERGROUP RELATIONS

CHAPTER OVERVIEW

As a social species, humans strive to establish close ties with one another. Yet the same species that seeks out connections with others also metes out enmity and rejection when it confronts members of another group. Intergroup relations are more often contentious than harmonious.

❖ What interpersonal factors disrupt relations between groups?

❖ What are the cognitive foundations of conflict between groups?

❖ How can intergroup relations be improved?

CHAPTER OUTLINE

The Rattlers and the Eagles: Group Against Group

On two midsummer days in 1954, twenty-two 11-year-old boys from Oklahoma City boarded buses for their trip to summer camp. They were "normal, well-adjusted boys of the same age, educational level, from similar sociocultural backgrounds and with no unusual features in their personal backgrounds" (Sherif, Harvey, White, Hood, & Sherif, 1961, p. 59). Their parents had paid a $25 fee, signed some consent forms, and packed them off to a camp situated in Robbers Cave State Park, which legend claimed was once a hideout for desperadoes.

Robbers Cave was not your everyday summer camp. All the boys had been handpicked by a research team that included Muzafer Sherif, O. J. Harvey, Jack White, William Hood, and Carolyn Sherif. The Sherifs and their colleagues had spent more than 300 hours interviewing the boys' teachers, studying their academic records, reviewing their family backgrounds, and unobtrusively recording their behavior in school and on the playground. The parents knew that the camp was actually part of a group dynamics research project, but the boys themselves had no idea that they were participants in the **Robbers Cave Experiment**. The staff randomly assigned the boys to one of two groups and brought them to camp in two separate trips. Each group spent a week hiking, swimming, and playing sports in their area of the camp, and both groups developed norms, roles, and structure. Some boys emerged as leaders, others became followers, and both groups established territories within the park (see Figure 13-1). The boys named their groups the Rattlers and the Eagles and stenciled these names on their shirts and painted them onto flags. The staff members, who were also collecting data, noted clear increases in group-oriented behaviors, cohesiveness, and positive group attitudes. For example,

> At the hideout, Everett (a non-swimmer when camp started) began to swim a little. He was praised by all and for the first time the others called him by his preferred nickname. Simpson yelled, "Come on, dive off the board!" All members in the water formed a large protective circle into which Everett dived after a full 2 minutes of hesitation and reassurance from the others. (Sherif et al., p. 79)

When each group realized that another group was camping nearby, references to "those guys," "they," and "outsiders" became increasingly frequent. Both teams wanted to compete with the other group and asked the staff to set up a tournament. Of course, a series of competitions between the two groups was exactly what the staff had in mind, so they held a series of baseball games, tugs-of-war, tent-pitching competitions, cabin inspections, and a (rigged) treasure hunt.

As the competition wore on, tempers flared. When the Eagles lost a game, they retaliated by stealing the Rattlers' flag and burning it. The Rattlers raided the Eagles' cabin during the night, tearing out mosquito netting, overturning beds, and carrying off personal belongings. When the Eagles won the overall tournament, the Rattlers absconded with the prizes. When fistfights broke out between the groups,

---

Robbers Cave Experiment A field study performed by Muzafer and Carolyn Sherif and their colleagues that examined the causes and consequences of conflict between two groups of boys at Robbers Cave State Park.

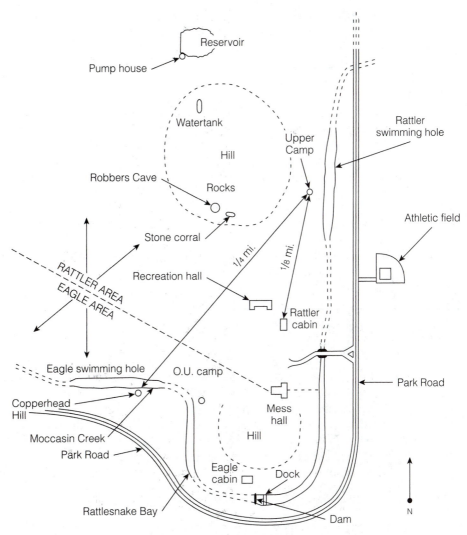

Robbers Cave State Park Area

FIGURE 13-1

How did the Sherifs and their colleagues create intergroup conflict? Instead of observing conflict between naturally occurring groups, the Sherifs created groups at a
summer camp in the Robbers Cave State Park in Oklahoma, and then recorded the
conflict that unfolded over time. This diagram shows the general layout of the campsite and the respective areas used by the two groups. *Source:* Sherif, Harvey, White,
Hood, & Sherif, 1961.

the staff had to intervene to prevent the boys from seriously injuring one another. They moved the two groups to different parts of the camp, amid shouts of "poor losers," "bums," "sissies," "cowards," and "little babies."

Groups are everywhere, and so are conflicts between them. *Intergroup conflict* occurs at all levels of social organization—fights between gangs, organized disputes in industrial settings, race riots, and even conflicts between nations. Groups provide us with the means to achieve our most lofty goals, but when groups oppose each other, they are sources of hostility, abuse, and aggression. Although conflict between groups is one of the most complicated phenomena studied by social scientists, the goal of greater understanding and the promise of reduced tension remain enticing. Here, we consider the nature of intergroup relations, with a focus on the sources of intergroup conflict and the ways such conflicts can be resolved (for reviews, see G. Bornstein, 2003; Dovidio, Gaertner, Esses, & Brewer, 2003; W. G. Stephan & Stephan, 2000).

COMPETITION AND CONFLICT: US VERSUS THEM

On the ninth day of the Robbers Cave Experiment, the Rattlers and the Eagles saw the tournament prizes for the first time: the shining trophy, medals for each boy, and—best of all—four-blade camping knives. The boys wanted these prizes, and nothing was going to stand in their way. From then on, all group activities revolved around the ultimate goal of winning the tournament. Unfortunately, although both groups aspired to win the prizes, success for one group meant failure for the other. When groups are pitted against each other in a contest for resources, intergroup relations that were once amicable often become antagonistic.

Realistic Group Conflict Theory

Many of the things that people want and need are available in limited supply. Should one group acquire and control a scarce commodity—whether it be food, territory, wealth, power, natural resources, energy, or the prizes so desperately desired by the Rattlers and the Eagles—other groups must do without that resource. According to **realistic group conflict theory,** this struggle between groups to acquire resources inevitably leads to conflict (D. T. Campbell, 1965; R. A. LeVine & Campbell, 1972). All groups would prefer to be "haves" rather than "have-nots," so they take steps to achieve two interrelated outcomes—

---

realistic group conflict theory A conceptual framework arguing that conflict between groups stems from competition for scarce resources, including food, territory, wealth, power, natural resources, and energy.

attaining the desired resources and preventing the other group from reaching its goals. Theorists have traced many negative intergroup dynamics—including struggles between the classes of a society (Marx & Engels, 1947), rebellions (Gurr, 1970), international warfare (Streufert & Streufert, 1986), racism (Gaines & Reed, 1995), religious persecutions (S. Clark, 1998), tribal rivalries in East Africa (Brewer & Campbell, 1976), police use of lethal force against citizens (D. Jacobs & O'Brien, 1998), interorganizational conflicts (Jehn & Mannix, 2001), and even the development of culture and social structure (Simmel, 1955)—to competition over scarce resources.

Robert Blake and Jane Mouton documented the close connection between competition and conflict in their work with business executives. They assigned participants in a 2-week management training program to small groups that worked on a series of problem-solving tasks. Blake and Mouton never explicitly mentioned competition, but the participants knew that a group of experts would decide which group had produced the most adequate solution. Many viewed the project as a contest to see who was best, and they wholeheartedly accepted the importance of winning. Leaders who helped the group beat the opponent became influential, whereas leaders of losing groups were replaced. The groups bonded tightly during work and coffee breaks, and only rarely did any participant show liking for a member of another group. In some cases, hostility between the two groups became so intense that the "experiment had to be discontinued" and special steps taken to restore order, tempers, and "some basis of mutual respect" (Blake & Mouton, 1984, 1986, p. 72). These findings and others suggest that *competition*—even competition that is only anticipated—can spark intergroup hostility (G. Bornstein, Budescu, & Zamir, 1997; Horwitz & Rabbie, 1982; Polzer, 1996; van Oostrum & Rabbie, 1995).

The Discontinuity Effect

Just as Chapter 12 concluded that many conflicts in groups occur when group members compete with each other, realistic group conflict theory argues that relations between groups deteriorate when groups compete against each other. The competition–conflict relationship is particularly robust, however, at the group level. Chet Insko, John Schopler, and their colleagues called the tendency for groups to respond more competitively than individuals the **discontinuity effect,** because the competitiveness of groups is out of proportion to the competitiveness displayed by individuals when interacting with other individuals. Even though individuals in the group may prefer to cooperate, when they join groups, this cooperative orientation tends to be replaced by a competitive one (L. Gaertner & Insko, 2001; Hoyle, Pinkley, & Insko, 1989; Insko et al., 1987, 1988, 1992, 1993, 1994, 2001; Insko, Schopler, Hoyle, Dardis, & Graetz, 1990; Insko,

---

discontinuity effect The markedly greater competitiveness of groups when interacting with other groups, relative to the competitiveness of individuals interacting with other individuals.

Schopler, & Sedikides, 1998; D. M. McCallum et al., 1985; Schopler & Insko, 1992; Schopler et al., 1993, 1994, 1995; Schopler, Insko, Graetz, Drigotas, & Smith, 1991; Wildschut, Lodewijkx, Hein, & Insko, 2001).

STUDIES OF DISCONTINUITY Insko, Schopler, and their colleagues documented this discontinuity effect by asking individuals and groups to play the *prisoner's dilemma game* (PDG). As noted in Chapter 12, this mixed-motive game offers the two participating parties a choice between *cooperative* responding and *competitive* responding, and competition yields the highest rewards only if one of the two parties cooperates. The sample PDG matrix in Figure 13-2 illustrates the

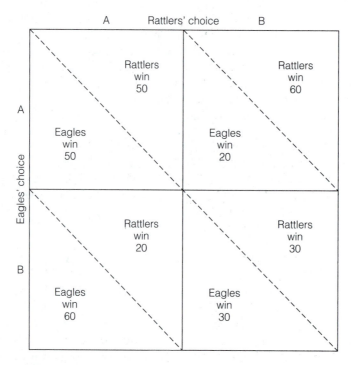

FIGURE 13-2

Are people in groups greedy or fearful? Chet Insko and his colleagues studied the discontinuity effect by asking two groups (in this example, the Rattlers and the Eagles) to play the *prisoner's dilemma game*. Group members earn points by selecting either Option A or B. In each cell, the Rattlers' outcomes are shown above the diagonal line, and the Eagles' outcomes are shown below. In this example matrix, both groups would be tempted to select Option B to maximize their payoff, but if they both select B, their rewards will be halved. Groups tend to select Option B much more frequently than Option A, because they are seeking to maximize their profits (*greed*) and do not trust the other group to cooperate (*fear*), group's dilemma. Members will earn 60 points if they pick Option B, but only if the other group picks Option A. If both groups seek Option B, then their rewards will be cut in half. Option A will yield the best outcomes for both groups if they both select A, but if one picks A (the *cooperative choice*) and the other picks B (the *competitive choice*), then the cooperative group's payoff will be small compared to the competitive group's payoff.

When the Insko-Schopler research teams had two individuals play the game, they averaged only 6.6% competitive responses over the course of the game. Competition was also rare when three independent, noninteracting individuals played three other independent individuals (7.5%). But when an interacting triad played another interacting triad, 36.2% of their choices were competitive ones, and when triads played triads but communicated their choices through representatives selected from within the group, competition rose to 53.5% (Insko et al., 1987). These findings are remarkably consistent—a meta-analysis of 48 separate studies conducted in 11 different group dynamics laboratories confirmed that groups are disproportionately more competitive than individuals (Wildschut, Pinter, Vevea, Insko, & Schopler, 2003).

This discontinuity between individuals and groups is not confined to laboratory groups playing a structured conflict game. When researchers examined everyday social interactions, they found that group activities were marked by more competition than one-on-one activities. Participants diligently recorded their interpersonal activities for an entire week, classifying them into one of five categories:

- *One-on-one interactions:* playing chess, walking to class with another person, and so on.
- *Within-group interactions:* interactions with members of the same group, such as a club meeting or a classroom discussion.
- *One-on-group interactions:* the individual participant interacting with a group, such as a student meeting with a panel of faculty for career information.
- *Group-on-one interactions:* the individual is part of a group that interacts with a single individual.
- *Group-on-group interactions:* a soccer game, a joint session of two classes, and the like.

As Figure 13-3 indicates, the proportion of competitive interactions within each type of interaction climbed steadily as people moved from one-on-one interactions to group interactions. These effects also emerged when sports activities, which could have exacerbated the competitiveness of groups, were eliminated from the analysis (Pemberton, Insko, & Schopler, 1996).

CAUSES OF DISCONTINUITY Insko, Schopler, and their colleagues have identified three key factors that combine to create the discontinuity effect. Their *greed hypothesis* suggests that the members of interacting groups support each other's selfishness, and as a result, competition increases and cooperation decreases. Their *identifiability hypothesis* argues that the anonymity of the group situation frees members to make more competitive choices. Their *fear hypothesis* suggests that

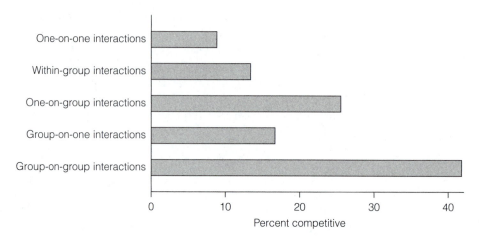

FIGURE 13-3

Are groups more competitive than individuals? Pemberton, Insko, and Schopler (1996) asked people to identify which of their week's interactions were competitive or cooperative. More of the interactions that involved groups rather than one-on-one dyadic interactions were considered competitive rather than cooperative.

groups may be more competitive than individuals because people expect intergroup relations to be more unfriendly, threatening, and aggressive. People are more wary of groups. They describe them as more abrasive (competitive, aggressive, proud) and less agreeable (cooperative, trustworthy, helpful) than individuals. This pessimistic outlook also colors their expectations about specific group interactions, for people who were about to play the PDG against a group felt that the experience would be more abrasive than did individuals about to play the game as individuals (Hoyle, Pinkley, & Insko, 1989).

This lack of trust between groups also surfaces when members talk about their choices and plan their strategies. Members of groups expecting to play the PDG against another group question the motives of their opponents and refer to the likelihood that the other group will try to exploit them (Insko et al., 1994; Schopler et al., 1995). If people are given a third option in the PDG—*withdrawing* instead of either competing or cooperating—they choose this safe, defensive option more frequently when playing in groups rather than as individuals (Insko et al., 1990, 1993; Schopler et al., 1993, 1995). Moreover, when individuals playing the PDG can communicate with one another, they often become more cooperative, but giving groups the chance to communicate with each other does not increase their cooperativeness (Insko et al., 1993). Groups were more likely to say such things as "We don't trust you" and "You better not cheat us" to their opponents (Insko et al., 1994).

Insko's studies have also identified ways to reduce the discontinuity effect. One common but ineffective way of dealing with the conflict is *appeasement*—responding cooperatively even when the other party competes. When groups play the PDG against groups whose members cooperate even when they encounter competition, groups exploit these cooperators by continuing to make competitive choices. A reciprocal strategy, such as *tit for tat* (TFT), is a more effective strategy to counter discontinuity. As noted in Chapter 12, TFT matches competition with competition and cooperation with cooperation. This strategy, Insko suggests, allays groups' fears that they will be exploited, for it reassures them that they can trust the other group. Other methods for reducing the discontinuity effect include decreasing the rewards of competition (by changing the values in the PDG matrix) and leading group members to believe that their individual choices will be known (Wildschut et al., 2003).

Norms of Engagement

Conflicts between groups—protests between rioters and police, gang fights, or even the conflict between the Rattlers and the Eagles—are not out-of-control, atypical interpersonal actions that occur when the social order breaks down. Normatively, competition and hostility between groups are often completely consistent with the standards of conduct in that situation.

RECIPROCITY Groups, like individuals, tend to obey the *norm of reciprocity.* They answer threats with threats, insults with insults, and aggression with aggression. The infamous Hatfield–McCoy feud, for example, began after the Civil War with the theft of some hogs by Floyd Hatfield (O. K. Rice, 1978). The McCoys countered by stealing hogs from another member of the Hatfield clan, and soon members of the two families began taking potshots at one another. Between 1878 and 1890, more than 10 men and women lost their lives as a direct result of interfamily violence. Likewise, studies of gangs indicate that many street fights stem from some initial negative action that in reality may pose little threat to the offended group. The target of the negative action, however, responds to the threat with a counterthreat, and the conflict spirals. Battles resulting in the death of gang members have begun over an ethnic insult, the intrusion of one group into an area controlled by another group, or the theft of one gang's property by another gang (Gannon, 1966; Yablonsky, 1959). Large-scale intergroup conflicts, such as race riots and warfare between countries, have also been caused by gradually escalating hostile exchanges (Goldberg, 1968; Holsti & North, 1965; D. J. Myers, 1997; Reicher, 2001).

A *spiral model of conflict intensification* accurately describes the unfolding of violence at Robbers Cave. The conflict began with minor irritations and annoyances but built in intensity. *Exclusion,* a mild form of rejection, occurred as soon as the boys realized that another group was sharing the camp. This antipathy escalated into *verbal abuse* when the groups met for the tournament. Insults were exchanged, members of the opposing team were given demeaning names, and verbal abuse ran high. Next, *intergroup discrimination* developed. The groups isolated themselves from each other at meals, and the boys expressed the belief that it was wrong for the other team to use the camp facilities or to be given an equal amount of food. Last came the acts of *physical violence*—the raids, thefts, and

FOCUS 13-1 Are Collectivists Peacemakers?

Ye have heard that it hath been said, Thou shalt love thy neighbour, and hate thine enemy. But I say unto you, Love your enemies, bless them that curse you, do good to them that hate you.

—Matthew 5:43–44

Individuals and societies vary in their degree of individualism and collectivism. *Individualism* stresses the rights of the individual; *collectivism* exults the rights of the group. Individualists tend to make choices that maximize their own outcomes, so in general they respond more competitively in conflict situations. Collectivists are more likely to adopt harmony-enhancing strategies that minimize conflict, including following rules that will yield a fair resolution to the disagreement (Gire, 1997; P. B. Smith, Dugan, Peterson, & Leung, 1998; see Chapter 3).

Collectivists' pacifism may not, however, extend to individuals who are not part of their ingroup. Even though collectivists express less anger, hostility, and aggression when dealing with members of their own group, when interacting with a member of the outgroup, they display more hostility than individualists (Leung, 1988). In one investigation, students from countries with collectivistic and individualistic cultures were asked to identify how they would respond to a conflict with another individual (*in-*

terpersonal or *intragroup conflict*), to a conflict between their group and another group (*intergroup conflict*), and to a conflict between their country and another country (*international conflict*). Students from collectivistic countries responded more negatively to intergroup and international conflicts than to interpersonal conflicts. Those from more individualistic countries differed less in their endorsement of conflict resolution strategies in an international versus an interpersonal conflict (Derlega, Cukur, Kuang, & Forsyth, 2002).

Collectivists and individualists also responded differently when they played a conflict game that simulated a social dilemma. All participants were members of three-person groups, but some played the game against an ingroup member and others played against a member of another three-person group. The results, shown in Figure 13-4, suggest that collectivism tempered competition only when people were interacting with a member of their own group. Within their own group, collectivism was inversely related to competition. But when the opponent was a member of the outgroup, collectivism was positively associated with competition—the more collectivist the individual, the more he or she competed against an outgroup member (Probst, Carnevale, & Triandis, 1999).

---

fistfights. Thus, the conflict at Robbers Cave built in a series of progressively more dangerous stages from exclusion to verbal abuse to discrimination and, finally, to physical assault (Streufert & Streufert, 1986).

CULTURAL NORMS The extent to which groups respond in hostile ways to other groups varies from culture to culture. The Mbuti Pygmies of Africa, !Kung, and many native American tribes (e.g., the Blackfoot and Zuñi) traditionally avoid conflict by making concessions. The members of these societies live in small groups and, rather than defend their territories when others intrude, they withdraw to more isolated areas. Men are not regarded as brave or strong if they are aggressive, and war with other groups is nonexistent (Gorer, 1986). In contrast, the Yanomanö of South America and the Mundugumor of New Guinea seem to thrive on violence (Chagnon, 1997; Mead, 1935). The anthropologist Napoleon Chagnon called the Yanomanö the "fierce people," for they choose

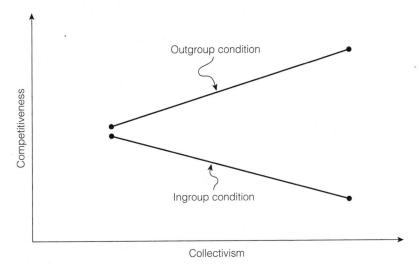

FIGURE 13-4.

Do the harmony-promoting tendencies of collectivists extend to members of the outgroup? When participants played a competition simulation game against a member of the ingroup (*ingroup condition*), as collectivism increased, competition decreased. But when participants played against a member of the outgroup (*outgroup condition*) increases in collectivism were associated with increases in competitiveness.

violence over peace at every opportunity. Among the Yanomanö, prestige is accorded to those who are most aggressive, and bravery is the most revered personal quality one can have. Villages routinely attack other villages, and personal conflicts are usually settled through violence. Chagnon reported that more than one third of the men in this society are murdered or killed during wars and battles. Variations in collectivism and individualism are also related to intergroup conflict, as noted in Focus 13-1.

SUBCULTURAL NORMS Some groups within the larger society adopt unique norms and values pertaining to intergroup conflict. In the United States, the Mennonites and the Amish avoid interpersonal conflict and strive instead for cooperative, peaceful living. Urban youth gangs, in contrast, accept norms that emphasize dominance over other groups. When one gang or gang member offends another gang, violence is the normal method of settling the dispute. Violence is sometimes so strongly ingrained in the normative structure of the group that individuals behave aggressively simply to establish a reputation among their peers. In one study of 69 men who were convicted of violent crimes, approximately 76% claimed to use violence to create a image of dominance and authority (Toch, 1969).

Richard Nisbett (1993) presented a normative analysis of regional differences in various types of violent crime committed by male European Americans in the

United States. Nisbett noted that nearly three times as many men are murdered each year in the southern U.S. states as in other parts of the country. In explanation, Nisbett suggested that the "culture of honor" in the South encourages men to respond violently to defend their families and their property. Southerners are not more positive about aggression in general, but they are more likely to prefer aggressive responses if their family group is threatened or if they are insulted (D. Cohen & Nisbett, 1993; Vandello & Cohen, 2003).

Power and Domination

Intergroup conflicts, though initially rooted in competition for scarce resources, can escalate into *intergroup exploitation* as one group tries to dominate the other. Not only do groups wish to monopolize and control scarce resources, but they also wish to gain control over the other group's land, resources, peoples, and identity (Rouhana & Bar-Tal, 1998). As Herbert Spencer wrote in 1897, the first priority of most governments is the identification of "enemies and prey" (p. 547).

Just as groups seek to subdue and exploit other groups, the targets of these attacks struggle to resist this exploitation. In some cases, this competition is purely economic. By manufacturing desirable goods or performing valuable services, one group can come to dominate others in the intergroup trade system (Service, 1975). But domination can also occur through force and coercion (Carneiro, 1970). The Greeks and Romans dominated Europe not only by trading effectively, but also by conquest. European countries, during their period of colonialism, established colonies throughout the world and exploited the original inhabitants of these areas both economically and through military force. Europeans seized the lands of native Americans and used captured Africans as slaves in their workforce. Both Napoleon and Hitler sought to expand their empires through the conquest of other nations. In Russia, the ruling class exploited workers until the workers rose up in revolution and established a communist nation.

This cycle of domination and resistance occurs between nations, classes, ethnic groups, the sexes, and even small groups in controlled experimental situations. Chet Insko and his colleagues examined exploitation and conflict by creating a simulated social system in the laboratory. Insko's *microsocieties* included three interdependent groups, multiple generations of members, a communication network, products, and a trading system (Insko et al., 1980, 1983). Insko assigned the microsocieties to one of two experimental conditions. In the *economic power condition,* one group could produce more varied products, so it quickly became the center of all bargaining and trading. In the *coercive power condition,* the group whose members were supposedly better problem solvers was given the right to confiscate any products it desired from the other groups. (Insko referred to these conditions as the *Service condition* and the *Carneiro condition,* respectively.)

These differences in power had a dramatic effect on productivity and intergroup relations. In the economic power condition, all three groups reached very high levels of productivity, with the advantaged group slightly outperforming the others. In contrast, none of the groups in the coercive power condition were very productive. As the "idle rich" hypothesis suggests, the members of the powerful group spent less time working when they could confiscate others' work. But the other groups reacted very negatively to this exploitation, and as the powerful group continued to steal their work, the members of the other groups held strikes and work slowdowns and sabotaged their products. (Men, in particular, were more likely to strike back against the oppressive group.) Eventually, the groups worked so little that the dominant group could not confiscate enough products to make much profit. These results suggest that as with intragroup conflict, one sure way to create conflict is to give one party more coercive power than the other (Deutsch & Krauss, 1960). Apparently, when it comes to power, more is not always better.

Anger and Frustration

When intergroup competitions end, one side is often branded the *winner* and one the *loser*. Like the victorious Eagles, winners experience a range of positive emotions, including pride, pleasure, happiness, and satisfaction. Losers, in contrast, experience the "agony of defeat"—humiliation, anger, embarrassment, and frustration (J. D. Brown & Dutton, 1995). These emotions can contribute to continuing conflict between groups, for negative emotional experiences such as frustration and anger can provoke aggression and retaliation (Berkowitz, 1962). The Rattlers, for example, were very angry when they lost, and they responded by vandalizing the Eagles' cabin and stealing the prizes.

In most cases, if a group interferes with another group, the injured party retaliates against the perpetrator. If, however, the aggressor is extremely powerful, too distant, or difficult to locate, then the injured party may respond by turning its aggression onto another group. This third group, although not involved in the conflict in any way, would nonetheless be blamed and thereby become the target of aggressive actions. The third group, in this case, would be the *scapegoat*—a label derived from the biblical guilt transference ritual. Anger originally aroused by one group becomes displaced on another, more defenseless group. Attacking the guiltless group provides an outlet for pent-up anger and frustration, and the aggressive group may then feel satisfied that justice has been done. At the Robbers Cave, for example, the cause of the Rattlers' failure was not the Eagles—who beat them in a fair contest. Rather, it was the experimenters, who rigged the contest so that the Rattlers would fail.

The **scapegoat theory** of intergroup conflict explains why frustrating economic conditions often stimulate increases in prejudice and violence (Poppe, 2001). Studies of anti-Black violence in southern areas of the United States between 1882 and 1930 have indicated that outbreaks of violence tended to occur whenever the economy of that region worsened (Hovland & Sears, 1940). The correlation between the price of cotton (the main product of that area at the time) and the number of lynchings of Black men by Whites ranged from $-.63$ to $-.72$, suggesting that when Whites were frustrated by the economy, they took

---

scapegoat theory An explanation of intergroup conflict arguing that hostility caused by frustrating environmental circumstances is released by taking hostile actions against members of other social groups.

out these frustrations by attacking Blacks (see also Hepworth & West, 1988, for a more sophisticated analysis of the Hovland-Sears data). Scapegoating can even prompt oppressed groups to lash out at other oppressed groups. Even though the minority group is victimized by the majority group, the group responds by turning against another minority group rather than against the more powerful majority (Harding, Proshansky, Kutner, & Chein, 1969; D. J. Myers, 1997; Rothgerber & Worchel, 1997).

SOCIAL CATEGORIZATION: PERCEIVING US AND THEM

The boys at Robbers Cave displayed antipathy toward the other group even before the idea of a competitive tournament was mentioned. The Rattlers and Eagles had not even seen each other when they began to refer to "those guys" in a derogatory way:

> When the ingroup began to be clearly delineated, there was a tendency to consider all others as outgroup. . . . The Rattlers didn't know another group existed in the camp until they heard the Eagles on the ball diamond; but from that time on the outgroup figured prominently in their lives. Hill (Rattler) said "They better not be in our swimming hole." The next day Simpson heard tourists on the trail just outside of camp and was convinced that "those guys" were down at "our diamond" again. (Sherif et al., 1961, p. 94)

The Sherifs suggested that the conflict between the two groups resulted from their competition, but this explanation cannot fully account for the almost automatic rejection of members of the other group. Group members reject members of other groups not because they fear them or because they must compete with them, but simply because they belong to a different group.

The Ingroup–Outgroup Bias

When Mills, a Rattler, met an Eagle on the path to the dining hall, he spontaneously classified him as an Eagle rather than a Rattler. This *social categorization* process, although undeniably adaptive in the long run, nonetheless provides a cognitive foundation for intergroup conflict (Wilder, 1986a, 1986b). People do not simply segment people into the categories "member of my group" and "member of another group" and then stop. Once people are categorized, members of the ingroup are evaluated more favorably than people in the outgroup. At the group level, this tendency is called the *ingroup–outgroup bias;* among larger social groups, such as tribes, ethnic groups, or nations, this bias is termed **ethnocentrism** (Sumner, 1906).

---

ethnocentrism The belief that one's own tribe, region, or country is superior to other tribes, regions, or countries.

The magnitude of the bias depends on a host of situational factors, including the group's outcomes, the way perceptions are measured, ambiguity about each group's characteristics, and members' identification with the group. Overall, however, the ingroup–outgroup bias is robust. A rock band not only thinks that its music is very good, but also considers a rival band's music inferior. One ethnic group prides itself on its traditions and also views other groups' traditions with disdain. One team of researchers thinks that its theory explains intergroup conflict and criticizes other researchers' theories as inadequate. After a bean-collecting game, the Rattlers overestimated the number of beans collected by Rattlers and slightly underestimated the number of beans supposedly collected by Eagles. Across a range of group and organizational settings, members rate their own group as superior to other groups (Hewstone, Rubin, & Willis, 2002; Hinkle & Schopler, 1986).

INGROUP FAVORITISM VERSUS OUTGROUP REJECTION The ingroup–outgroup bias is really two biases combined: (1) the selective favoring of our own group, its members, and its products, and (2) the derogation of another group, its members, and its products. But at Robbers Cave, the pro-ingroup tendency went hand in hand with the anti-outgroup tendency. When they were asked to name their friends, 92.5% of the Eagles' choices were Eagles, and 93.6% of the Rattlers' choices were fellow Rattlers. When asked to pick the one person they disliked the most, 95% of the Eagles selected a Rattler, and 75% of the Rattlers identified an Eagle. In many intergroup conflicts, however, ingroup favoritism tends to be stronger than outgroup rejection. For example, during a conflict between the United States and Iraq, U.S. citizens may feel very positive about the United States and its people, but they may not condemn Iraqis. Marilyn Brewer, after surveying a number of studies of intergroup conflict, concluded that the expression of hostility against the outgroup depends on the similarity of ingroup and outgroup members, anticipated future interactions, the type of evaluation being made, and the competitive or cooperative nature of the intergroup situation (see Brewer, 1979; Brewer & Brown, 1998; Hewstone et al., 2002).

CATEGORIZATION AND COHESION Lewis Coser (1956) agreed that the pro-ingroup bias is stronger than the anti-outgroup bias, and suggested that this asymmetry may explain the impact of intergroup conflict on cohesion (1956, p. 87). At Robbers Cave, for example, as the competitions progressed, the two groups became more tightly organized. The attitudes of each group toward the other became more and more negative, but the cohesiveness of each group became increasingly stronger. Although every defeat was associated with initial dejection and internal bickering, the groups channeled this animosity in the direction of the opponent. As time passed, the groups became better organized, and the group structure solidified.

Intergroup conflict does not invariably lead to increased cohesion (Tyerman & Spencer, 1983), nor is intergroup conflict a prerequisite for intragroup cohesion (M. Goldman, Stockbauer, & McAuliffe, 1977). In general, however, Coser's speculations concerning the solidifying effects of cohesion have been confirmed empirically. Rises in intergroup conflict tend to go hand in hand with increases in intragroup cohesion (Dion, 1973, 1979; Worchel, Lind, & Kaufman, 1975).

DIFFERENTIATION As groups become more distinct from one another, members tend to differentiate between people who belong to the ingroup and those who are members of the outgroup (Jetten & Spears, 2004; Jetten, Spears, & Postmes, 2004). As Coser stated, "conflict serves to establish and maintain the identity and boundary lines of groups" (1956, p. 38). As the conflict between the Eagles and the Rattlers escalated, each group tended to emphasize the major distinctions between the two groups of combatants. The groups began to isolate themselves from each other and asked that they be allowed to eat separately. Unique group norms also began to develop, and if one group adopted a style of action, this behavior was soundly rejected by the other group. For example, the Rattlers cursed frequently; to distinguish themselves from those "bad cussers," the Eagles adopted the norm of no profanity. Later, their leader decided that the Rattlers were such poor sports that "the Eagles should not even talk to them anymore" (Sherif et al., 1961, p. 106). Proprietary orientations toward certain portions of the camp also developed, along with mottoes, uniforms, and secret passwords.

Such *differentiation* is typical of intergroup conflict. Rather than noting shared similarities, the groups tend to emphasize their differences (Sherif, 1966). Competing groups also distance themselves from one another, whereas cooperating groups minimize distances (Ryen & Kahn, 1975). Members of competing groups even take pains to display nonverbal postures that are different from those displayed by members of the other group (LaFrance, 1985) or try to speak differently from the outgroup members. When people from different cultures find themselves in conflict, they often adopt a dialect, accent, or language form that is unique to their ingroup and foreign to the outgroup (Giles, 1977; Giles & Johnson, 1981; Krauss & Chiu, 1998).

DOUBLE-STANDARD THINKING The ingroup–outgroup bias often fuels **double-standard thinking.** Members rationalize their own group's actions as fair and just and condemn the actions of the outgroup as unfair and unjust. Our warnings are *requests,* but the other side calls them *threats.* We are *courageous,* though they consider us *stubborn.* Pride in our own group is *nationalism,* but the other group takes it as evidence of *ethnocentrism.* We offer them *concessions,* but they interpret them as *ploys* (De Dreu, Nauta, & Van de Vliert, 1995). Ralph K. White found that both sides in the major Middle East wars of 1948, 1956, 1967, and 1973 believed the other side to have been the aggressor in all four wars. In two of these wars (1956, 1967), the Palestinians believed that Israel had simply

---

double-standard thinking The tendency to consider the actions and attributes of one's own group as positive, fair, and appropriate, but to consider these very same behaviors or displays to be negative, unfair, and inappropriate when the outgroup performs them.

attacked without provocation. In the remaining two (1948, 1973), the Palestinians admitted that they had initiated hostilities, but believed that they had been forced to do so by the expansionistic policies of Israel. Conversely, the Israelis felt that the 1948 and 1973 wars were examples blatant, unmitigated Palestinian aggression and that the 1956 and 1967 wars had been indirectly caused by the threats and malevolent intentions of the Palestinians (R. K. White, 1965, 1966, 1969, 1977, 1998). Similar biases have been found when students in the United States are asked to evaluate actions performed by their country and by the Soviet Union (Oskamp & Hartry, 1968) and when Whites' and Blacks' judgments of ambiguously aggressive actions committed by either a Black or a White person are compared (Sagar & Schofield, 1980). People judge actions that their own group performs positively, but they negatively evaluate these same actions when they are performed by the outgroup. People also attribute another nations' harmful actions more to internal factors—things about that country—but their nation's actions to external factors (Doosje & Branscombe, 2003).

OUTGROUP MORAL EXCLUSION   Throughout history, the members of one group have done great harm to the members of other groups. When the intergroup conflict reaches extreme levels, with members of one group attacking, harming, and killing members of other groups, the ingroup–outgroup bias becomes equally extreme. During extreme intergroup conflicts, group members view their own group as morally supreme and members of the outgroup as less than human (Leyens et al., 2003).

Ervin Staub's (1989, 1990) concept of **moral exclusion** explains cases of extreme violence perpetrated by one group against another—European Americans enslaving Africans; Nazi Germany's attempted genocide of Jews; "ethnic cleansing" in Croatia and Serbia; and the continuing warfare between Israelis and Palestinians. Staub has suggested that those who subjugate others tend to rationalize their violence by attributing it to the actions, intentions, or character of their victims. As their aggression intensifies, however, their rationalizations prompt them to increasingly devalue their victims. Eventually, the aggressors denigrate the outgroup so completely that the outsiders are excluded from moral concern, for it is difficult to intensely harm people whom one evaluates positively or strongly identifies with (Staub, 1990, p. 53). Groups that have a history of devaluing segments of their society are more likely to engage in moral exclusion, as are groups whose norms stress respect for authority and obedience. These groups, when they anticipate conflict with other groups, rapidly revise their opinions of their opponents so that they can take hostile actions against them (Bandura, 1999; Bar-Tal, 2000; B. Lott, 2002; Opotow, 2000).

---

moral exclusion   A psychological process whereby opponents in a conflict come to view each other as less than human, so that issues or principles of morality no longer apply to them; such dehumanization serves to rationalize the extremely negative treatment often afforded to members of other groups.

Robert J. Sternberg (2003) similarly suggested that outgroup rejection, when extreme, can become **group hate.** This hatred, when it reaches its apex, includes a sense of repulsion (negation of intimacy), passion, and commitment.

- *Negation of intimacy:* Groups avoid any type of intimate contact with the rejected group, as the outgroup is thought to be repulsive and disgusting. The only contact that is tolerated is that required to inflict harm on the rejected group.
- *Passion:* Groups display one of two types of negative emotions (*fear* and *anger*) in response to the rejected group.
- *Commitment:* Groups are committed to their negative characterization of the outgroup, which is often viewed as barely human, or even subhuman.

Sternberg, after studying a series of extreme intergroup conflicts, found that in most cases, cultural myths about the target group supported one or more of the elements of group hate. The victimized group is not just inferior, but "impure," "evil," "godless," "morally bankrupt," "barbaric," "greedy," "murderous," and "subhuman." In such conflicts, leaders may further encourage the development of group hate through propaganda. Hitler's incendiary speeches to the German people used imagery, propaganda, and threats to bolster all three components of group hate toward Jews.

Cognitive Consequences of Categorization

Categorization is, in all likelihood, an automatic cognitive process; without much thought, people rapidly pigeonhole other people into categories (Ashburn-Nardo, Voils, & Monteith, 2001; Greenwald et al., 2002; Mackie, Devos, & Smith, 2000). But once an individual is recognized as a member of our group or of some other group, we rush to make generalizations about their qualities, their interests, and their unseen attributes. These generalizations, however, are often overgeneralizations that are driven more by the categorization process than by the evidence of our senses.

OUTGROUP HOMOGENEITY BIAS Most group members are quick to point out the many characteristics that distinguish them from the other members of their own group ("Why, I'm not like them at all!"), but when they evaluate members of outgroups, they underestimate their variability ("They all look the same to me"). If you were an Eagle, for example, you would describe the Rattlers as poor sports who cheated whenever possible. When describing the Eagles, in contrast, you might admit that a few of the members were sissies and that maybe one Eagle liked to bend the rules, but you would probably argue that the Eagles were so heterogeneous that sweeping statements about their typical qualities could not be formulated. Studies of a variety of ingroups and outgroups—

---

group hate Intense feelings of repulsion, anger, fear, and contempt for another group.

women versus men, physics majors versus dance majors, Sorority A versus Sorority B, Princeton students versus Rutgers students, Canadians versus Native Americans, and Blacks versus Whites—have documented this **outgroup homogeneity bias**—the tendency for people to assume that the outgroup is much more homogeneous than the ingroup. Group members' conceptualizations of other groups are simplistic and undifferentiated, but when they turn their eye to their own group, they note its diversity and complexity (Linville & Fischer, 1998; Linville, Fischer, & Salovey, 1989; Ostrom & Sedikides, 1992; Park & Rothbart, 1982; Quattrone, 1986).

The outgroup homogeneity bias does not emerge across all intergroup settings. The group that is disadvantaged in some way is usually viewed as more homogeneous, whereas the more powerful group is viewed as more variable (Guinote, Judd, & Brauer, 2002). The bias can also reverse entirely, with group members describing all the members of the ingroup as very similar and the outgroup as highly differentiated (Haslam & Oakes, 1995; B. Simon, Pantaleo, & Mummendey, 1995). Such an *ingroup homogeneity bias* usually occurs when the ingroup is threatened in some way. When psychology majors, for example, were told that an outgroup (business majors) was more intelligent, the psychology students who strongly identified with their major viewed all psychology majors as relatively similar (Doosje, Ellemers, & Spears, 1995). Under conditions of extreme conflict, both tendencies may emerge, prompting group members to assume that "none of us deserve this treatment," and "they have harmed us; they must all be punished" (Rothgerber, 1997).

GROUP ATTRIBUTION ERROR Group members tend to make sweeping statements about the entire outgroup after observing one or two of the outgroup's members. If an African American employee is victimized by a European American boss, the victim may tend to assume that all European Americans are racists. Similarly, a visitor to another country who is treated rudely by a passerby may leap to the conclusion that everyone who lives in that country is discourteous. Individuals in intergroup situations tend to fall prey to the **law of small numbers:** They assume that the behavior of a large number of people can be accurately inferred from the behavior of a few people (Quattrone & Jones, 1980).

The opposite process—assuming that the characteristics of a single individual in a group can be inferred from the general characteristics of the whole group—can also lead us astray. If we know our group's position on an issue, we are reluctant to assume that any one of us agrees with that position. When we know another group's position, however, we are much more willing to assume that each and every person in that group agrees with that position. Scott Allison

---

outgroup homogeneity bias The perceptual tendency to assume that the members of other groups are very similar to each other, whereas the membership of one's own group is more heterogeneous.

law of small numbers The tendency for people to base sweeping generalizations about an entire group on observations of a small number of individuals from that group.

and his colleagues studied this **group attribution error** by telling students that an election had recently been held either at their college or at another college to determine how much funding should be given to the college's athletics programs. They then told the students the results of the vote and asked them to estimate the opinion of the "typical student" at the college where the vote was taken. When the students thought that the vote had been taken at their own college, they did not want to assume that the individual's opinion would match the group's opinion. But when they thought that the vote was taken at another college, they were much more confident that the individual's opinions would match the group's opinions (Allison & Messick, 1985b; Allison, Worth, & King, 1990).

ULTIMATE ATTRIBUTION ERROR When individuals form impressions of other individuals, the *fundamental attribution error* (FAE) prompts them to attribute the actions of others to their personal qualities rather than to the constraints of the situation. But when group members form impressions of outgroup members, the **ultimate attribution error** (UAE) prompts them to attribute only negative actions to outgroup members' dispositional qualities (Hewstone, 1990; Pettigrew, 2001). If outgroup members rob a bank or cheat on a test, then their actions are explained by reference to their personality, genetics, or fundamental lack of morality. But should an outgroup member perform a positive behavior, that action is attributed to a situational factor—perhaps good luck or a special advantage afforded the outgroup member. In any case, the perceiver will conclude that the good act, and the outgroup member who performed it, is just a special case. Because of the UAE, the perceiver concludes that there is no need to reappraise the group because the outgroup member is not responsible for the positive act.

The **linguistic intergroup bias** is a more subtle form of the UAE. Instead of attributing the behavior to dispositional factors or to the situation, group members describe the action differently depending on who performs it. If an ingroup member engages in a negative behavior, such as crying during a game, then members would describe that behavior very concretely—Elliott "shed some tears." If an outgroup member performed the same behavior, they would describe the action more abstractly—Elliott "acted like a baby." Positive behaviors, in contrast, are described in abstract terms when attributed to an ingroup member but in very concrete terms when performed by an outgroup member (Maass,

---

group attribution error The tendency for perceivers to assume that specific group members' personal characteristics and preferences, including their beliefs, attitudes, and decisions, are similar to the preferences of the group to which they belong; for example, observers may assume that each member of a group that votes to reelect the president supports the president, even though the group's decision was not a unanimous one.

ultimate attribution error The tendency for perceivers to attribute negative actions performed by members of the outgroup to dispositional qualities and positive actions to situational, fluctuating circumstances.

linguistic intergroup bias The tendency to describe positive ingroup and negative outgroup behaviors more abstractly and negative ingroup and positive outgroup behaviors more concretely.

Ceccarelli, & Rudin, 1996; Maass, Milesi, Zabbini, & Stahlberg, 1995; Semin, Gil de Montes, & Vlencia, 2003; Zyzniewski, 2002).

STEREOTYPES Social categorization makes it possible for us to distinguish between the members of our group and the members of other groups. When an Eagle met another Eagle on the trail, he probably expected the boy to be friendly, helpful, and brave. But if he encountered a Rattler, he expected the boy to be unfriendly, aggressive, and deceitful.

These expectations are based on **stereotypes**—cognitive generalizations about the qualities and characteristics of the members of a particular group or social category. In many ways, stereotypes function as cognitive labor-saving devices by helping us make rapid judgments about people based on their category memberships (D. J. Schneider, 2004). Because they are widely adopted by most of the ingroup, stereotypes are shared social beliefs rather than individualistic expectations (Bar-Tal, 2000). But stereotypes tend to be exaggerated rather than accurate, negative rather than positive, and resistant to revision even when we encounter individuals who directly disconfirm them. People also tend to cling to stereotypes so resolutely that they become unreasonable beliefs rather than honest misconceptions. As Gordon W. Allport (1954) wrote, "Prejudgments become prejudices only if they are not reversible when exposed to new knowledge" (p. 8).

If stereotypes have all these perceptual and cognitive limitations, why do they persist? Walter Lippmann (1922), who first used the word *stereotype* to describe our intuitive assumptions about people, argued that the stereotype resists disconfirmation because "it stamps itself upon the evidence in the very act of securing the evidence." When group members see people through eyes clouded by stereotypes, they misperceive and misremember people and events. Because individuals tend to interpret ambiguous information so that it confirms their expectations, stereotypes can act as self-fulfilling prophecies (G. W. Allport & Postman, 1947). Stereotypes also influence memory, so that recall of information that is consistent with stereotypes is superior to recall of stereotype-inconsistent information (Howard & Rothbart, 1980; Rothbart, Sriram, & Davis-Stitt, 1996). Because members expect outgroup members to engage in negative behavior and can more easily remember the times that they acted negatively rather than positively, they feel vindicated in thinking that membership in the outgroup and negative behaviors are correlated (D. L. Hamilton & Sherman, 1989).

Does Categorization Cause Conflict?

Categorization, though an essential cognitive tool for understanding ourselves and others, limits the veridicality of our perceptions. When we formulate impressions of others by relying on stereotypes and expectations, we underestimate the complexity of the outgroup, overlook information that is inconsistent with

---

stereotype A socially shared set of cognitive generalizations (e.g., beliefs, expectations) about the qualities and characteristics of the members of a particular group or social category.

our expectations, and formulate judgments that are more extreme than they should be. But does social categorization, in and of itself, cause conflict? Does the mere existence of identifiable groups within society, and the cognitive biases generated by these perceived groups, inevitably push groups into conflict?

Henri Tajfel, John Turner, and their colleagues have examined this question in their studies of the **minimal intergroup situation.** They began by randomly assigning participants to one of two groups, but they told the participants that the division was based on some irrelevant characteristic, such as art preference. Next, the participants read a series of booklets asking them to decide how a certain amount of money should be allocated to other participants in the experiment. The names of the individuals were not given in the booklets, but the participant could tell which group a person belonged to by looking at his or her code number. The groups were *minimal* ones, for (1) members of the same group never interacted in a face-to-face situation, (2) the identities of ingroup and outgroup members were unknown, and (3) no one gained personally by granting more or less money to any particular person. The groups were "purely cognitive"; they existed only in the minds of the participants themselves (Tajfel & Turner, 1979, 1986).

Tajfel and Turner's research revealed a systematic ingroup bias even in this minimal intergroup situation. Participants did not know one another; they would not be working together in the future, and their membership in the so-called group had absolutely no personal or interpersonal implications. Yet the participants not only awarded more money to members of their own group, but they seemed to keep money from members of the other group. The ingroup bias even persisted when the researcher went to great lengths to make it clear that assignment to a group was being done on a random basis and that giving money to the outgroup would not cause any monetary loss for any ingroup member. Tajfel and Turner concluded that the "mere perception of belonging to two distinct groups—that is, social categorization per se—is sufficient to trigger intergroup discrimination favoring the ingroup" (Tajfel & Turner, 1986, p. 13; see also Hogg & Abrams, 1999).

SOCIAL IDENTITY AND CATEGORIZATION Tajfel and his colleagues turned to social identity theory to explain the biases they documented in the minimal intergroup situation. This theory, as noted in Chapter 3, assumes that membership in groups can substantially influence members' sense of self. When the boys joined the Robbers Cave Experiment and became firmly embedded in their groups, their identities changed. They came to think of themselves as Rattlers or Eagles, and they accepted the group's characteristics as their own. The theory also suggests that as the boys came to identify with their group, their own self-worth became more closely tied to the worth of the group. If a Rattler dedicated himself to the group and the Rattlers failed, the boy would likely experience a distressing reduction in his own self-esteem. Group members, therefore, stress the

---

minimal intergroup situation A research procedure developed by Henri Tajfel and John Turner in their studies of intergroup conflict that involved creating temporary groupings of anonymous, unrelated people.

value of their own groups relative to other groups as a means of indirectly enhancing their own personal worth (Tajfel & Turner, 1986).

Researchers have confirmed some but not all of social identity theory's assumptions about the source of the ingroup–outgroup bias (Aberson, Healy, Romero, 2000; Mummendey, 1995; M. Rubin & Hewstone, 1998). Ingroup biases become more robust the greater the extent to which group members identify with their group (Branscombe & Wann, 1994). When individuals feel that the value of their group is being questioned, they respond by underscoring the distinctiveness of their own group and by derogating others (Dietz-Uhler & Murrell, 1998; Grant, 1993; Spears, Doosje, & Ellemers, 1997). Individuals who experience a threat to their self-esteem do indeed tend to discriminate more against outgroups, and low-status, peripheral members of the group are often the most zealous in their defense of their group and in the rejection of the outgroup (Noel, Wann, & Branscombe, 1995). Individuals are also more likely to draw comparisons between their group and other groups in areas where the comparison favors the ingroup. The Rattlers, for example, lost the tournament, so they admitted that the Eagles were better than the Rattlers at sports. But the Rattlers could stress their superiority in other spheres unrelated to the games, such as toughness or endurance (Mullen, Brown, & Smith, 1992; Reichl, 1997). Group members also display group-level *schadenfreude*. They take malicious pleasure when other groups fail, particularly when the failure is in a domain that is self-relevant and when the ingroup's superiority in this domain is uncertain (Leach, Spears, Branscombe, & Doosje, 2003).

But does condemning other groups raise one's self-esteem? The effectiveness of this technique for sustaining self-esteem has not been confirmed consistently by researchers. In some cases, derogating outgroup members raises certain forms of self-esteem, but praising the ingroup tends to bolster self-esteem more than condemning the outgroup (Abrams & Hogg, 2001; Branscombe & Wann, 1994; Hunter, Platow, Bell, Kypri, & Lewis, 1997; Jetten, Spears, & Manstead, 1996). Also, though people are quick to praise their ingroup, they still think that they are superior to most people—including all the members of their own group (Lindeman, 1997).

The Evolution of Intergroup Conflict

Evolutionary psychology offers yet another explanation for the built-in biases that accompany social categorization. The tendency to categorize people into groups is so pervasive that some experts believe that it may have a genetic basis. Evolutionary psychologists believe that human beings are "herd animals" because groups provided individuals with survival advantages. In harsher environments, lone individuals survived only rarely, whereas those who banded together with others in groups were more likely to survive and procreate. However, this natural selection for sociality may apply only to members of one's own small group or tribe (Insko, Schopler, & Sedikides, 1998). In all likelihood, early humans lived in small tribes composed of people who were genetically similar. Therefore, by helping members of one's own group, one was also helping to protect copies of one's genes that were present in these other people. Because members of other groups were less genetically similar and less likely to be available to reciprocate any help if help was given them, human beings favored their own group over the outgroup. The outgroup, too, likely competed with the ingroup for land, food, water, and shelter and may have attempted to mate with the women of the ingroup through coercion. Because outsiders were a danger, people with the ability to recognize and avoid them tended to survive, whereas the less cautious tended to die off. After aeons of this natural selection process, the Earth was populated primarily by human beings with a built-in readiness to respond positively to the ingroup and negatively to the outgroup (Caporael, 2000; Gould, 1991; Rushton, 1989).

RESOLVING INTERGROUP CONFLICT: UNITING US AND THEM

The Robbers Cave researchers were left with a problem. The manipulations of the first two phases of the experiment had worked very well, for the Rattlers–Eagles war yielded a gold mine of data about intergroup conflict. Unfortunately, the situation had degenerated into a summer camp version of William Golding's (1954) *Lord of the Flies*. The two groups now despised each other. As conscientious social scientists, the Sherifs and their colleagues felt compelled to try to undo some of the negative effects of the study—to seek a method through which harmony and friendship could be restored at the Robbers Cave campsite.

Intergroup Contact

The Robbers Cave researchers first tried to reduce the conflict by uniting the groups in shared activities. They based their intervention on the **contact hypothesis,** which assumes that ingroup–outgroup biases will fade if people interact regularly with members of the outgroup. So the Sherifs arranged for the Rattlers and the Eagles to join in seven pleasant activities, such as eating, playing games, viewing films, and shooting off firecrackers. Unfortunately, this contact had little impact on the hostilities. During all these events, the lines between the two groups never broke, and antilocution, discrimination, and physical assault continued unabated. When contact occurred during meals, "food fights" were particularly prevalent:

> After eating for a while, someone threw something, and the fight was on. The fight consisted of throwing rolls, napkins rolled in a ball, mashed potatoes, etc. accompanied by yelling the standardized, unflattering words at each other. The throwing continued for about 8–10 minutes, then the cook announced that cake and ice cream were ready for them. Some members of each group went after their dessert,

---

contact hypothesis The prediction that equal-status contact between the members of different groups will reduce intergroup conflict.

but most of them continued throwing things a while longer. As soon as each gobbled his dessert, he resumed throwing. (Sherif et al., 1961, p. 158)

THE CONTACT HYPOTHESIS REVISITED *Contact* lies at the heart of such social policies as school integration, foreign student exchange programs, and the Olympics, but simply throwing two groups together in the same setting is a risky way to reduce intergroup tensions. Contact between racial groups at desegregated schools, for example, rarely reduces prejudice (Gerard, 1983; Schofield, 1979). When units of an organization that clash on a regular basis are relocated in neighboring offices, the conflicts remain (R. Brown, Condor, Matthews, Wade, & Williams, 1986). College students studying in foreign countries become increasingly negative toward their host countries the longer they remain in them (Stangor, Jonas, Stroebe, & Hewstone, 1996). Competing groups in laboratory studies remain adversaries if the only step taken to unite them is mere contact (W. G. Stephan, 1987; Worchel, 1986). Even before they initiated the contact, the Sherifs predicted that a "contact phase in itself will not produce marked decreases in the existing state of tension between groups" (Sherif et al., 1961, p. 51).

Why does contact sometimes fail to cure conflict? Few people would argue that *any* kind of contact is sufficient to reduce animosity, antipathy, and prejudice between groups. If members of the two groups use the contact situation as one more opportunity to insult, argue with, physically attack, or discriminate against one another, then certainly such contact should not be expected to yield beneficial effects (Riordan & Riggiero, 1980). The setting must, instead, create *positive contact* between groups by including such ingredients as

- *Equal status.* The members of the groups should have the same background, qualities, and characteristics that define status levels in the situation. Differences in academic backgrounds, wealth, skill, or experiences should be minimized if these qualities will influence perceptions of prestige and rank in the group (Mullen et al., 1992; Schwarzwald, Amir, & Crain, 1992).
- *Personal interaction.* The contact should involve informal, personal interaction with outgroup members rather than superficial, role-based contacts. If the members of the groups do not mingle with one another, they learn very little about the other group, and cross-group friendships do not develop (Cook, 1985; Pettigrew, 1997; Schofield, 1979).
- *Supportive norms.* The contact should encourage friendly, helpful, egalitarian attitudes and condemn ingroup–outgroup comparisons. These norms must be endorsed explicitly by authorities and by the groups themselves (W. G. Stephan & Rosenfield, 1982).
- *Cooperation.* Groups should work together in the pursuit of common goals (S. L. Gaertner, Dovidio, Rust, et al., 1999).

These ingredients were identified by a team of researchers led by Kenneth Clark and including Isidor Chein, Gerhart Saenger, and Stuart Cook. This group developed the social science statement filed in the U.S. Supreme Court case of *Brown vs. Board of Education,* which ruled that segregation of schools was unconstitutional (Benjamin & Crouse, 2002).

Do these factors stimulate conflict reduction? Thomas Pettigrew and Linda R. Tropp (2000) examined this question by surveying the results of 203 separate studies of contact and conflict. This large pool of studies examined the responses of more than 90,000 participants who resided in 25 different nations. They found that face-to-face contact between group members reduced prejudice in 94% of these studies, and that the basic correlation between contact and conflict was −.20; the more contact, the less prejudice between groups. They also noted, however, that contact had a stronger impact on conflict when researchers studied high-quality contact situations that included equal status, cooperation between groups, and so on. In such studies, the correlation between contact and conflict climbed to −.27.

The effects of contact also varied across situations. Contact in work settings had the strongest impact on conflict, whereas contact that occurred when group members visited another group's country (i.e., as tourists) had the least impact on conflict (see Figure 13-5). The impact of contact on conflict also varied across countries. For example, the impact of contact was greatest in the United States and South Africa; followed by Australia, Canada, and New Zealand; then Europe; and then Bangladesh, India, Zambia, and Zimbabwe. Some types of intergroup conflicts were also more resistant to the curative power of contact than others. Heterosexuals' attitudes toward gay men and lesbians improved the most

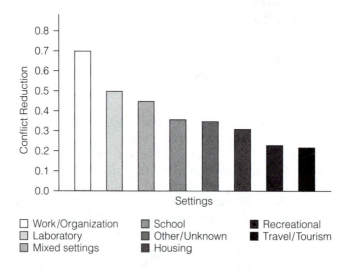

FIGURE 13-5

What kind of intergroup contact is most effective for reducing prejudice? When the results of contact studies conducted in many different settings were compared statistically, those that involved contact between individuals in work or organizational settings generated the greatest reduction in conflict, whereas those studies of contact in recreational or tourist encounters showed the least impact on conflict.

after contact, followed by attitudes related to race and ethnicity. Contact lost some of its strength in studies of contact between people of different nationalities and ages. Also, contact had less effect on the attitudes of members of minority groups relative to members of majority groups.

CONTACT AND SUPERORDINATE GOALS   Contact also reduced the conflict at the Robbers Cave site once the Sherifs improved the quality of the contact between the Rattlers and Eagles. Following the failure of simple contact, they arranged for the groups to work together in the pursuit of **superordinate goals**— that is, goals that can be achieved only if two groups work together. The staff created these superordinate goals by staging a series of crises. They secretly sabotaged the water supply and then asked the boys to find the source of the problem by tracing the water pipe from the camp back to the main water tank, located about ¾ mile away. The boys became quite thirsty during their search and worked together to try to correct the problem. Eventually, they discovered that the main water valve had been turned off by "vandals," and they cheered when the problem was repaired. Later in this stage, the boys pooled their monetary resources to rent a movie that they all wanted to see, worked together to pull a broken-down truck, prepared meals together, exchanged tent materials, and took a rather hot and dusty truck ride together. Like feuding neighbors who unite when a severe thunderstorm threatens to flood their homes, or like warring nations that pool their technological skills (in a recurring science fiction theme) to prevent the collision of the Earth with an asteroid, the Rattlers and the Eagles were reunited when they sought goals that could not be achieved by a single group working alone.

Other factors that enhance the impact of contact are friendship, success, and time. Stephen C. Wright and his colleagues, for example, have tested what they called the *extended contact hypothesis:* When group members learn that one or more members of their group have a friend in the outgroup, they express more positive intergroup attitudes (S. C. Wright, Aron, McLaughlin-Volpe, & Ropp, 1997; see Focus 13-2). Intergroup experiences that lead to successes, too, are more effective than intergroup experiences that lead to negative outcomes (Worchel, 1986). A disastrous performance during cooperation will only serve to further alienate groups (F. A. Blanchard, Adelman, & Cook, 1975; F. A. Blanchard & Cook, 1976; Cook 1978, 1984). Contact is also more effective when groups share a common fate and when cues that signal status differences between the groups are minimized (S. L. Gaertner, Dovidio, Rust, et al., 1999; Gardham & Brown, 2000).

Contact also takes *time* to work its cure. In the Robbers Cave research, a whole series of superordinate goals was required to reduce animosity. Similarly, when students from two different colleges worked together on problems, students who worked with the outgroup just once or not at all rated the members of the outgroup more negatively than students who worked with the outgroup

---

superordinate goal A goal that can only be attained if the members of two or more groups work together by pooling their efforts and resources.

FOCUS 13-2   Is Friendship Stronger Than Hate?

Tis but thy name that is my enemy:
Thou art thyself, though not a Montague.
What's Montague? It is nor hand nor foot
Nor arm nor face nor any other part
Belonging to a man. O be some other name.
What's in a name? That which we call a rose
By any other word would smell as sweet.

–Shakespeare, *Romeo and Juliet,* Act 2, Scene 2

The Robbers Cave Experiment was Sherif's third field study of intergroup conflict. One of the earlier studies, in which the Panthers battled the Pythons, had to be aborted when the two groups realized that the camp administration was creating the intergroup friction (Sherif, White, & Harvey, 1955). The other, conducted in 1949 in a camp in northern Connecticut, pitted friendship against the ingroup bias (Sherif & Sherif, 1953). Unlike the campers at Robbers Cave, the boys were not separated into groups until a full week of campwide activities had been held. During that time, strong patterns of friendship developed between the boys, but the researchers deliberately separated friends when they segregated the two groups during the second week. Many of the Red Devils had friends on the Bull Dogs team and many Bull Dogs had Red Devil friends.

Categorization, however, virtually obliterated these original friendships. Boys who continued to interact with members of the outgroup were branded traitors and threatened with bodily harm unless they broke off their friendships. One member of the Bull Dogs who did not completely identify with the group was partially ostracized, and eventually his parents had to remove him from the camp. A Red Devil who suggested that the two groups get together for a party was punished by the Red Devil's leader. This observational evidence was buttressed by the sociometric choice data collected before and after the groups were formed. Before the intergroup conflict, more than 60% of the boys reported that their best friends were members of what would eventually become the outgroup.

Later, after the groups were separated, cross-group friendships dwindled down to 10%.

Other studies, however, have suggested that friendship can sometimes cure intergroup conflict. Thomas Pettigrew, in a study of 3,806 people living in four countries in Europe, discovered that people who reported having friends who were members of an outgroup (another race, nationality, culture, religion, or social class) were less prejudiced than those who had no outgroup friends. Other investigations have confirmed this tendency (Pettigrew & Tropp, 2000). For example, Stephen Wright and his colleagues conceptually replicated the Robbers Cave Experiment with college students who spent an entire day working in one of two groups on a variety of tasks. Groups first developed a sense of cohesiveness by designing a logo for their team and sharing personal information. The groups then competed against each other, and during lunch, they watched as each group was given prizes and awards for defeating the other group. Later in the day, the groups worked on solitary tasks, except for two individuals who met together—supposedly to take part in an unrelated study. This meeting, however, was designed to create a friendly relationship between these two individuals, who then returned to their groups just before a final competition.

Wright discovered that the two group members who were turned into friends were more positive toward the outgroup. More importantly, however, this positivity generalized throughout the rest of the group. Even though the other group members had not themselves developed friendships with members of the outgroup, the knowledge that someone in their group considered an outgroup member to be likable moderated the ingroup–outgroup bias. Wright concluded that intergroup conflict sometimes prevents friendships from forming, but that friendships that cut across groups can undo some of the pernicious effects of the ingroup–outgroup bias (S. C. Wright et al., 1997).

twice (Wilder & Thompson, 1980). Similar findings have been obtained in studies of desegregated schools. A long period of favorable intergroup contact may reduce prejudice, but if this favorable contact is followed by an equally long period in which contact is not encouraged, the groups inevitably drift apart once again (Schofield & Sagar, 1977).

Cognitive Cures for Conflict

Intergroup contact does more than just promote positive interactions between people who were once antagonists. When individuals cooperate with the outgroup, their "us versus them" thinking fades, along with ingroup favoritism, outgroup rejection, and stereotyping (Brewer & Brown, 1998; Brewer & Miller, 1984; N. Miller & Brewer, 1986a, 1986b).

DECATEGORIZATION During the waning days at the Robbers Cave, the boys began to abandon their collective identities. Some boys became less likely to think of themselves as Rattlers, but instead viewed themselves as individuals with specific interests, skills, and abilities. This **decategorization,** or *individuation,* of group members reduces intergroup conflict by reminding group members to think of outgroup members as individuals rather than as typical group members (Brewer & Brown, 1998). In one study, researchers personalized the outgroup by merging two distinct groups and giving them problems to solve. Some of the groups were urged to focus on the task, but others were encouraged to get to know one another. This manipulation decreased the magnitude of the ingroup–outgroup bias, although it did not eliminate it completely (Bettencourt, Brewer, Croak, & Miller, 1992). Individuation can also be increased by changing the perceived homogeneity of the outgroup. When group members were told that one member of the outgroup strongly disagreed with his or her group during an episode of intergroup conflict, ingroup–outgroup biases were muted (Wilder, 1986b). The participants looked at the outgroup and saw a collection of individuals rather than a unified group (Wilder, Simon, & Faith, 1996).

RECATEGORIZATION The **common ingroup identity model,** developed by Samuel L. Gaertner, John F. Dovidio, and their colleagues, recommends reducing bias by shifting group members' representations of themselves away from two separate groups into one common ingroup category. This **recategorization**

---

decategorization Reducing social categorization tendencies by minimizing the salience of group memberships and stressing the individuality of each person in the group.

common ingroup identity model An analysis of recategorization processes and conflict, developed by Samuel L. Gaertner, John F. Dovidio, and their colleagues, predicting that intergroup conflict can be reduced by emphasizing membership in inclusive social categories and the interdependence of the individuals in the groups.

recategorization A reduction of social categorization tendencies by collapsing groups in conflict into a single group or category.

will undo the conflict-exacerbating cognitive factors that that are rooted in the ingroup−outgroup bias, but will also permit members to retain their original identities (so long as they do not conflict with the recategorized groups). Because people belong to multiple groups, they may be able to conceive of themselves as members of different groups who are currently members of one, more superordinate group. Recategorization can also be achieved by systematically manipulating the perceptual cues that people use to define "groupness." When the members of competing groups were urged to adopt a single name, space was minimized between the members, and their outcomes were linked, these cues increased the perceived unity, or *entitativity,* of the group members, and ingroup−outgroup biases diminished (Dovidio, Gaertner, Isen, Rust, & Guerra, 1998; S. L. Gaertner & Dovidio, 2000; S. L. Gaertner, Dovidio, Nier, Ward, & Banker, 1999; S. L. Gaertner, Dovidio, Rust, et al., 1999; S. L. Gaertner et al., 2000).

Jason Nier and his colleagues (2001) confirmed this shifting of identities at a football game between the University of Delaware and Westchester State University. They arranged for European and African American interviewers to approach European American fans and ask them if they would answer a few questions about their food preferences. The interviewers manipulated shared social identity by wearing different hats. For example, when interviewers approached a Delaware fan, they wore a Delaware hat to signal their shared identity, but a Westchester hat to indicate they were members of the outgroup. Ingroup−outgroup identity did not influence European Americans' compliance with a European American interviewer's request. However, the participants were more likely to agree to be interviewed by an African American if the interviewer and interviewee apparently shared a common university affiliation.

The Sherifs made use of recategorization in their 1949 study by pitting a softball team made up of members from both groups against an outside camp (Sherif & Sherif, 1953). This *common-enemy approach* was partially successful in that during the game, the boys cheered one another on and, when the home team won, congratulated themselves without paying heed to group loyalties. By introducing the third party, the common-enemy approach forced the boys to redefine themselves in terms of a single shared group identity. The Sherifs pointed out, however, that combining groups in opposition to a common enemy "enlarges" the conflict as new factions are drawn into the fray (Kessler & Mummendey, 2001). The old conflicts can also return once the common enemy is dispatched.

CROSS-CATEGORIZATION Ingroup−outgroup biases are also minimized when group members' other classifications—in addition to their group identity that is the focus of the conflict—are made salient to them. **Cross-categorization,**

---

cross-categorization A reduction of the impact of social categorization on individuals' perceptions by making salient their memberships in two or more social groups or categories that are not related to the categories that are generating ingroup−outgroup tensions.

instead of uniting all individuals in a single group or breaking down groups altogether, decreases the power of the problematic group identity by shifting attention to alternative memberships that are less likely to provide ingroup–outgroup tensions. The Sherifs, if they had implemented this strategy at the Robbers Cave, would have introduced at least one other category and split the Rattlers and the Eagles into two new groups. The boys, for example, were drawn from both the north and the south side of Oklahoma City, so the Sherifs could have separated them into these two groups and introduced activities that would have made these identities salient. The Sherifs could have also reduced the boys' "cognitive load" in the situation so that they would not fall back on the older, better known Eagles–Rattlers distinction, and introduced the cross-categorizations at times when the boys were in positive rather than negative moods (Brewer, 2000; Marcus-Newhall, Miller, Holtz, & Brewer, 1993; N. Miller, Urban, & Vanman, 1998).

CONTROLLING STEREOTYPED THINKING Rather than attacking the categorization process, Patricia G. Devine (1989) recommended controlling the impact of stereotypes on perceptions. Stereotypes are automatically activated whenever one encounters a member of another group or even is merely reminded of that other group by some symbol or other meaningful stimulus. A person's skin color, hair length, accent, or style of shoes may be enough to trigger a stereotype, which, once activated, may then influence responses. Even cues that are so subtle that we do not consciously recognize them may prime our stereotypes.

Although we may not be able to avoid the activation of stereotypes, we can control our subsequent thoughts to inhibit ingroup–outgroup biases. Devine found that the European Americans she studied could easily list the contents of their culture's stereotype about African Americans. She also found that European Americans who were low in prejudice could describe the stereotype as accurately as those who were high in prejudice. The unprejudiced European Americans, however, could control their thoughts after the stereotypes were activated. When asked to list their thoughts about African Americans, the unprejudiced participants listed such things a "Blacks and Whites are equal" and "It's unfair to judge people by their color—they are individuals." Prejudiced people, in contrast, listed negative, stereotypical thoughts. Devine and her colleagues have also found that unprejudiced European Americans feel guilty when they find themselves responding to African Americans in stereotypical ways, whereas prejudiced European Americans do not (P. G. Devine, 1995; P. G. Devine, Monteith, Zuwerink, & Elliot, 1991; P. G. Devine, Plant, Amodio, Harmon-Jones, & Vance, 2002; P. G. Devine, Plant, & Buswell, 2000).

Conflict Management

People often try to resolve intergroup conflicts through bargaining and negotiation. Such methods, as noted in Chapter 12, involve meetings where all parties to the dispute can discuss their grievances and recommend solutions. Both sides draw up a list of problems that are sources of dissatisfaction. Next, the two groups together consider each issue and seek a solution that is satisfying to both sides. When one issue is solved, the negotiations proceed to the next item on the agenda.

Unfortunately, few people have the necessary skills to manage intergroup conflict effectively. Negotiation, for most people, is only competition disguised as cooperation. The two parties refuse to accept each other's arguments, insist on maximizing their own interests, and use contentious bargaining tactics. These tactics, instead of quelling the conflict, intensify it (R. J. Fisher, 1994; J. Z. Rubin, 1994). In the Sherifs' 1949 study, an informal attempt by one of the Bull Dogs' leaders to negotiate with the Red Devils ended in increased antagonism:

> Hall . . . was chosen to make a peace mission. He joined into the spirit, shouting to the Bull Dogs, "Keep your big mouths shut. I'm going to see if we can make peace. We want peace." Hall went to the Red Devil cabin. The door was shut in his face. He called up that the Bull Dogs had only taken their own [belongings] . . . and they wanted peace. His explanation was rejected, and his peaceful intentions were derided. He ran from the bunkhouse in a hail of green apples. (Sherif & Sherif, 1953, p. 283)

Conflict experts, such as Herbert Kelman (1992), recommend training people to be more effective managers of intergroup conflict. Kelman and his colleagues have met repeatedly with high-ranking representatives from countries in the Middle East to solve problems in that region of the world. Kelman has carefully structured the workshops so that participants can speak freely, and he intervenes only as necessary to facilitate the communication process. The workshops are completely confidential, discussion is open but focused on the conflict, and expectations are realistic. The workshops are not designed to resolve the conflict, but to give participants the behavioral skills needed to solve conflicts themselves (Rouhana & Kelman, 1994). Examples of such programs include jigsaw learning groups, constructive controversy groups, and GRIT training.

JIGSAW LEARNING GROUPS Studies of U.S. public schools suggest that desegregation often fails to eliminate racial and ethnic prejudices. Although integrated schools bring students from various groups into contact, they rarely promote cooperation between these groups (Amir, 1969, 1976; Cook, 1985; Schofield, 1979; Worchel, 1986). Instead of including the necessary ingredients for positive intergroup interaction, many school systems fail to encourage interaction among the members of various subgroups, and staff openly express hostile attitudes toward outgroup members (Brewer & Miller, 1984). Some schools, too, group students on the basis of prior academic experiences; as a result, educationally deprived students are segregated from students with stronger academic backgrounds (Schofield, 1979).

Desegregation will reduce prejudice only when supplemented by educational programs that encourage cooperation among members of different racial and ethnic groups. One technique that has yielded promising results involves forming racially mixed teams within the classroom. In the **jigsaw method,** for example, students from different racial or ethnic groups are assigned to a single learning group. These groups are then given an assignment that can be completed only if each individual member contributes his or her share. Study units are broken down into various subareas, and each member of a group must become an expert on one subject and teach that subject to other members of the group. In a class studying government, for example, the teacher might separate the pupils into three-person groups, with each member of the group being assigned one of the following topics: the judiciary system (the Supreme Court of the United States), the duties and powers of the executive branch (the president's office), and the functions of the legislative branch (Congress). Students can, however, leave their three-person groups and meet with their counterparts from other groups. Thus, everyone assigned to study one particular topic, such as the Supreme Court, would meet to discuss it, answer questions, and decide how to teach the material to others. Once they have learned their material, these students rejoin their original groups and teach the other members of their group what they had learned. Thus, the jigsaw class uses both group learning and student teaching techniques (Aronson & Patnoe, 1997; Aronson, Stephan, Sikes, Blaney, & Snapp, 1978).

Studies of classrooms that use cooperative learning groups have shown some promising results. When reviewers statistically combined the results of 31 separate studies, they found that ingroup–outgroup hostility was reduced in cooperative classrooms (D. W. Johnson, Johnson, & Maruyama, 1984). These programs can be made even more effective by structuring the task so that each group member makes a contribution, randomly assigning students to roles within the group, and making certain that all groups contain an equal number of representatives from the group being merged. The procedure used to assign grades—either giving the entire group the same grade or giving grades to individuals in the group—had little impact on the success of the intervention, nor did the degree to which each individual's contribution was made public affect the outcome (N. Miller & Davidson-Podgorny, 1987).

CONSTRUCTIVE CONTROVERSY David W. Johnson and Roger T. Johnson have also created school-based conflict management programs. They designed their program to achieve three major goals—to decrease the amount of tension between groups in schools and colleges; to increase students' ability to solve problems without turning to authorities; and to give students skills they can use when they become adults. The program itself teaches students a five-step approach to resolving conflicts: (1) define the conflict; (2) exchange information about the nature of the conflict; (3) view the situation from multiple perspectives; (4) generate solutions to the conflict; (5) select a solution that benefits all parties. Johnson

---

jigsaw method A team-learning technique developed by Elliot Aronson and his colleagues that involves assigning topics to each student, allowing students with the same topics to study together, and then requiring these students to teach their topics to the other members of their groups.

and Johnson, in evaluations of the program, reported substantial reductions in discipline problems after training, as well as increases in academic achievement (D. W. Johnson & Johnson, 1999; D. W. Johnson, Johnson, & Tjosvold, 2000).

GRADUATED AND RECIPROCAL INITIATIVE IN TENSION REDUCTION (GRIT) Svenn Lindskold's (1978, 1979, 1986) **Graduated and Reciprocal Initiative in Tension Reduction** (GRIT) program pertains to extremely hostile intergroup conflict situations. When disputants have a prolonged history of conflict, misunderstandings, misperceptions, and hostility, attempts at cooperation are often misinterpreted by the opponent as attacks. Lindskold therefore focused on developing mutual trust by teaching group members to communicate their desire to cooperate, engage in behaviors that are consistent with cooperative intentions, and initiate cooperative responses even in the face of competition.

The first three stages of GRIT call for adequate communication between the groups in the hope of establishing the "rules of the game." The next three stages are designed to increase trust between the two groups as the consistency in each group's responses demonstrates credibility and honesty. Lindskold suggested that these phases are crucial to overwhelm the skepticism of the opponents as well as the tendency for other parties to assume that the concessions are merely "smokescreens" or propaganda tactics. The final four steps are necessary only in extremely intense conflict situations, in which the breakdown of intergroup relations implies a danger for the group members. In the case of military conflict, for example, the failure to stem the conflict could have disastrous consequences. Hence, each side must make concessions at a fixed rate while at the same time maintaining retaliatory capability.

The GRIT model clarifies the difficulties inherent in establishing mutual trust between parties that have been involved in a prolonged conflict. Although some of the stages are not applicable to all conflicts, the importance of clearly announcing intentions, making promised concessions, and matching reciprocation are relevant to all but the most transitory conflicts. Furthermore, case studies (Etzioni, 1967), simulations (Crow, 1963), and experiments (Lindskold, 1986; Lindskold & Aronoff, 1980) have lent considerable support to the recommendations of the GRIT model for inducing cooperation. At minimum, the model offers a good deal of promise as a guide for better relationships between groups.

Resolving Conflict: Conclusions

In his classic treatise *The Nature of Prejudice,* Gordon W. Allport (1954) wrote that "conflict is like a note on an organ. It sets all prejudices that are attuned to it into simultaneous vibration. The listener can scarcely distinguish the pure note from the surrounding jangle" (p. 996).

————

Graduated and Reciprocal Initiative in Tension Reduction (GRIT) A 10-step system for reducing intergroup conflict by increasing trust and cooperation.

The Sherifs and their colleagues created just such a "jangle" at the Robbers Cave. The Rattlers and the Eagles were only young boys camping, but their conflict followed patterns seen in disputes between races, between regions, and between countries. But just as the Robbers Cave Experiment is a sobering commentary on the pervasiveness of conflict, so the resolution of that conflict is cause for optimism. The Sherifs created conflict, but they also resolved it. When it came time to return to Oklahoma City, several of the group members asked if everyone could go in the same bus:

> When they asked if this might be done and received an affirmative answer from the staff, some of them actually cheered. When the bus pulled out, the seating arrangement did not follow group lines. Many boys looked back at the camp, and Wilson (E) cried because camp was over. (Sherif et al., 1961, p. 182)

If the Robbers Cave conflict can end peacefully, others can as well.

SUMMARY IN OUTLINE

❖ What interpersonal factors disrupt relations between groups?

1. Muzafer and Carolyn Sherif and their colleagues' carried out the *Robbers Cave Experiment* to identify the causes of intergroup conflict.

2. As *realistic group conflict theory* maintains, competition contributes significantly to conflict. When groups and individuals play the *prisoner's dilemma game,* groups respond much more competitively than individuals. This *discontinuity effect* is likely caused by individuals' distrust of groups (fear), desire to maximize profit (greed), and the lack of identifiability.

3. Normative processes also instigate and sustain conflict.
   - Intergroup conflict, like intragroup conflict, tends to escalate over time. Both the norm of reciprocity and the use of contentious influence tactics stimulate conflict spirals.
   - The extent to which groups respond in hostile ways to other groups varies from culture to culture, with some cultures eschewing intergroup conflict and others accepting it routinely.
   - Collectivism encourages the resolution of conflict through harmony-enhancing strategies within the ingroup, but not when interacting with a member of the outgroup.
   - Subgroups within the large cultural context may adopt unique norms pertaining to violence. For example, in the South of the United States men tend to respond more aggressively to threat.

4. Conflict increases when one group attempts to dominate and exploit another group, and the target group resists exploitation. Groups exploit other groups both economically and coercively, but coercive influence is associated with greater increases in conflict.

5. Negative emotional reactions can trigger anti-outgroup reactions. *Scapegoat theory* explains why groups that experience setbacks sometimes fight other, more defenseless groups.

❖ **What are the cognitive foundations of conflict between groups?**

1. Social categorization leads perceivers to classify people into two mutually exclusive groups—the ingroup and the outgroup.

2. Groups tend to favor the ingroup over the outgroup (the ingroup–outgroup bias). This bias, when applied to larger groups such as tribes or nations, is called *ethnocentrism*.

3. Ingroup favoritism tends to be stronger than outgroup rejection, but both forms of ingroup–outgroup bias emerged at Robbers Cave. Over time, the groups became more cohesive, more clearly differentiated, and more favorable toward the ingroup.

4. When conflicts become more intense, members may display more extreme misperceptions of the outgroup, including
   - *Double-standard thinking:* Group members frame the behaviors and characteristics of the ingroup in more positive terms than these same behaviors and characteristics displayed by the outgroup.
   - *Moral exclusion:* Group members feel that the outgroup is not due any kind of fair treatment or justice.
   - *Group hate:* Feelings of repulsion toward the outgroup, intensely negative feelings, and commitment to a negative characterization of the outgroup.

5. During intergroup conflict, group members' judgments are often distorted by the following biases:
   - *Outgroup homogeneity bias:* The outgroup is assumed to be much more homogeneous than the ingroup. Members assume that their own group is diverse and heterogeneous, although when the group is threatened, members may exaggerate the similarity of everyone in their group.
   - *Law of small numbers:* The behaviors and characteristics exhibited by a small number of outgroup members are generalized to all members of the outgroup.
   - *Group attribution error:* Group decisions are assumed to reflect individual group members' attitudes, irrespective of the particular procedures used in making the decisions.
   - *Ultimate attribution error:* Group members attribute the negative behaviors performed by outgroup members to internal dispositions, but their positive behaviors are explained away as situationally caused aberrations.
   - *Linguistic intergroup bias:* Actions performed by the ingroup are described differently than actions performed by the outgroup.
   - *Stereotypes:* Cognitive generalizations are made about the qualities and characteristics of the members of a particular group or social category.

6. People in Tajfel and Turner's *minimal intergroup situation* displayed the ingroup–outgroup bias, leading researchers to conclude that social categorization may be sufficient to create conflict. Social identity theory suggests that individuals, by championing the ingroup, maintain and even raise their self-esteem.

7. Intergroup conflict may be instinctive—the result of evolutionary pressures that favored individuals who preferred ingroup members over outgroup members.

❖ **How can intergroup relations be improved?**

1. The Sherifs' first, relatively unsuccessful attempt to reduce conflict was based on the *contact hypothesis*.

2. The key to contact's effectiveness as a means of reducing intergroup conflict is the nature of the contact. Contact is more effective when it creates cooperation between the groups, when participants are equal in status, when interaction is intimate enough to sustain the development of friendships across the groups, and when norms encourage cooperation.

- Pettigrew and Tropp's review of the contact hypothesis indicated that contact is more effective in work and organizational settings than in recreational and tourist settings.
- The Sherifs successfully reduced conflict in the Robbers Cave camp by prompting the boys to work toward *superordinate goals.*
- Encouraging the development of friendship relations has reduced prejudice in a number of studies.

3. Cognitive approaches to conflict reduction seek to reverse the negative biases that follow from parsing individuals into ingroups and outgroups.

- *Decategorization* encourages members to recognize the individuality of the outgroup members.
- The *common ingroup identity model* suggests that *recategorization*—collapsing the boundaries between groups— reduces conflict yet can promote the retention of identities. The common-enemy approach is an example of recategorization.
- *Cross-categorization* involves making salient multiple group memberships.

4. Conflict management methods promote adaptive ways to deal with conflict situations by teaching group members the skills they need to resolve interpersonal disputes through negotiation and mediation.

- The *jigsaw method* is an educational intervention that reduces prejudice by assigning students from different racial or ethnic groups to a single learning group.
- Conflict management programs in schools and colleges are designed to reduce conflict between groups by teaching students to recognize conflict, communicate about the source of the conflict, and identify mutually acceptable solutions.
- The *Graduated and Reciprocal Initiative in Tension Reduction (GRIT)* is a formal method for dealing with conflict in extreme situations where the threat of retaliation is great.

FOR MORE INFORMATION

Chapter Case:
The Robbers Cave Experiment

- *Intergroup Conflict and Cooperation: The Robbers Cave Experiment,* by Muzafer Sherif, O. J. Harvey, B. Jack White, William R. Hood, and Carolyn W. Sherif (1961), describes in detail the well-known study of conflict between two groups of boys at a summer camp.

Intergroup Processes

- "Intergroup Relations," by Marilyn B. Brewer and Rupert J. Brown (1998), is a theoretically sophisticated review of the theory and research pertaining to intergroup processes.
- *Theories of Intergroup Relations,* by Donald M. Taylor and Fathali M. Moghaddam (1994;

2nd ed.), systematically reviews all major theoretical perspectives on intergroup processes, including realistic conflict theory and social identity theory.

Cognitive Approaches to Intergroup Relations

- "Intergroup Bias," by Miles Hewstone, Mark Rubin, and Hazel Willis (2002), provides a comprehensive but efficient review of research dealing with the causes and consequences of the intergroup bias.
- *Intergroup Cognition and Intergroup Behavior,* edited by Constantine Sedikides, John Schopler, and Chester A. Insko (1998), draws together the theoretical and empirical work dealing with the cognitive foundations of intergroup conflict.
- *The Psychology of Stereotyping,* by David J. Schneider (2004), not only examines issues of stereotype and bias, but also reviews a wide variety of cognitive processes that pertain to groups, including perceptions of entitativity, categorization, and ingroup–outgroup bias.

Resolving Intergroup Conflict

- *Reducing Intergroup Bias: The Common Ingroup Identity Model,* by Samuel L. Gaertner and John F. Dovidio (2000), uses the common group identity model to offer suggestions for reducing intergroup conflict.

MEDIA RESOURCES

 Visit the Group Dynamics companion website at http://psychology.wadsworth.com/forsyth4e to access online resources for your book, including quizzes, flash cards, web links, and more!

14

GROUPS IN CONTEXT

CHAPTER OVERVIEW

Just as individuals are embedded in groups, so groups are embedded in physical and social environments. Groups alter their environments so substantially—erecting cities, creating organizations and communities, building comfortable homes and efficient workplaces—that we assume that groups shape their spaces and places. But in many cases, it's the place that shapes the group. As Kurt Lewin's (1951) formula, $B = f(P, E)$, reminds us, group behavior (B) is a function of the persons (P) who are in the group and the environment (E) in which the group is embedded.

❖ How does the social and physical environment influence groups and their dynamics?

❖ What is the ecology of a group?

❖ What are the causes and consequences of a group's tendency to establish territories?

CHAPTER OUTLINE

Apollo 13: The Group that Lost the Moon

James A. Lovell, Jr., John L. Swigert, Jr., and Fred Wallace Haise, Jr., piloted the National Aeronautics and Space Administration (NASA) Apollo 13 into space on April 11, 1970. Lovell and his crew were to spend 4 days crowded together in their command module, named the *Odyssey,* before reaching the moon (see Figure 14-1). The team members had trained for years for the mission, and throughout the trip

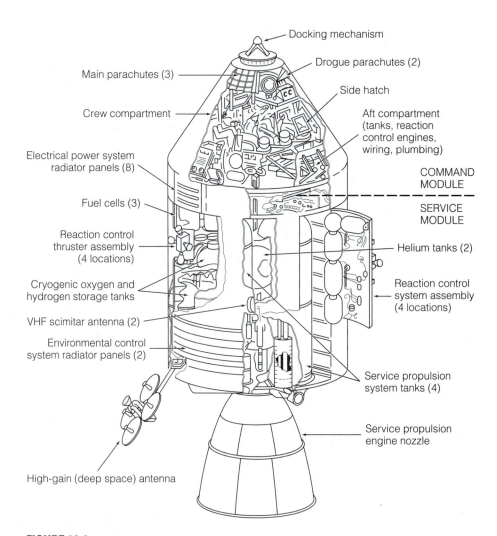

Docking mechanism

Drogue parachutes (2)

Main parachutes (3)

Side hatch

Crew compartment

Aft compartment (tanks, reaction control engines, wiring, plumbing)

Electrical power system radiator panels (8)

COMMAND MODULE

SERVICE MODULE

Fuel cells (3)

Reaction control thruster assembly (4 locations)

Helium tanks (2)

Cryogenic oxygen and hydrogen storage tanks

Reaction control system assembly (4 locations)

VHF scimitar antenna (2)

Environmental control system radiator panels (2)

Service propulsion system tanks (4)

Service propulsion engine nozzle

High-gain (deep space) antenna

FIGURE 14-1

What was the physical layout of the space where the Apollo 13 crew lived? For the first part of the mission, the crew lived in the command and service module. When the oxygen tank (labeled *cryogenic oxygen and hydrogen storage tanks* in the diagram) exploded, the crew powered down the command module and survived in the lunar module (not shown in this diagram).

they would remain in constant communication with ground control teams in Houston, Texas. Once in orbit around the moon, Lovell and Haise would descend to the surface of the moon in the Lunar Excursion Module (LEM), the *Aquarius.*

But 56 hours into the mission, Swigert initiated a procedure designed to stir the cryogenic oxygen tanks. One of the tanks exploded. With oxygen escaping from their ship and battery power dwindling, Lovell coolly radioed NASA his famous understatement, "Houston, we have a problem." (Actually, he said "Houston, we've had a problem.") During the next 3 days, the crew and the teams on the ground identified and responded to one life-threatening challenge after another, including near-freezing temperatures and a buildup of carbon dioxide in the cabin. The group managed to return to Earth, and landed safely in the Pacific Ocean on April 17, 1970.

The extraordinary actions and experiences of the Apollo 13 crew raise many questions. How did the group respond when Ken Mattingly, who was originally assigned to the flight, was removed from the team days before the mission and replaced by backup crewman Jack Swigert? Was the team's success determined by its high level of interpersonal cohesiveness or by the group's commitment to the task they had set for themselves? How did Jim Lovell, the commander of the mission, facilitate the group's performance of its tasks and assuage members' anxieties during the crisis? How did the crew coordinate the exchange of information about the ship and its problems with the members of various control teams located in Houston? But beneath all these questions lies a more fundamental one: How did the group's *environment*—the place where the group existed in time and space—shape its dynamics and outcomes?

GROUP SETTINGS

Few groups travel into space to visit other worlds, but all groups are embedded in a particular social and physical environment. The impressionists thrived in Paris in the 1860s in the midst of its countless galleries, art schools, restaurants, bistros, and parks. The 1980 U.S. Olympic hockey team trained and played for hours and hours on hockey rinks across the world. The Bay of Pigs planners met in an elegantly appointed conference room, speaking to each other in subdued voices across an imposing mahogany table. The Rattlers and the Eagles met, fought, and befriended each other at the cabins, in the rivers, and on the fields of the Robbers Cave State Park. Each one of these groups slept, worked, played, interacted, argued, fought—in short, lived—in a specific environmental context, which they actively shaped as it was shaping them.

Many disciplines, including environmental psychology, ethology, human ecology, demography, and ecological psychology, affirm the important impact of environmental variables on human behavior (Bell, Fisher, Baum, & Green, 2001; C. M. Werner, Brown, & Altman, 2002; Wicker, 2002). All share a concern for the *setting* or *context* in which behavior occurs. Just as a group-level orientation assumes that individuals' actions are shaped by the groups to which they belong, an environmental orientation assumes that groups are shaped by their

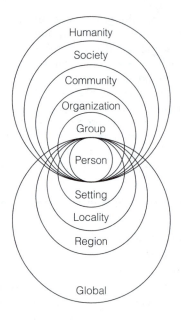

FIGURE 14-2

What is the group's environment? A context-sensitive approach to groups suggests that each individual is nested in a hierarchy of increasingly inclusive social aggregates (e.g., groups, organizations, communities), but at the same time physically occupies a place that is located within larger and larger geographic domains (e.g., settings, localities, regions).

environments. As Figure 14-2 suggests, a multilevel analysis of human behavior recognizes that individuals are nested in a hierarchy of increasingly inclusive social aggregates, such as groups, organizations, and communities. But individuals and their groups also exist in a physical setting located in a particular geographic locality in a specific region of the world.

Environmental Settings

Groups can be found in both natural and built environments. At a post office, workers sort mail in noisy rooms bathed in fluorescent light. Hikers trek through the woods, taking care to leave no evidence of their passing. Rows of college students sit in a classroom listening to a lecturer drone. Members of a gang stand on and around a picnic bench in a park, harassing passersby. In a corporate conference room, executives sit in leather chairs and stare impassively at reports projected on a computer screen. The crew of Apollo 13 lived in a high-tech environment filled with multiple controls and few comforts.

In some cases, people report feeling rejuvenated and energized by the places that their groups occupy (Hartig, Mang, & Evans, 1991; Staats & Hartig, 2004). People also report benefits from spending time in places they feel attached to, including their homes, their rooms, or even cubicles in an office (Altman & Churchman, 1994; Carlopio, 1996). Environments, however, are often a source of **stress**—strain caused by environmental circumstances that threaten one's

---

stress Negative physiological, emotional, cognitive, and behavioral responses to circumstances that threaten—or are thought to threaten—one's sense of well-being and safety.

sense of well-being and safety. Groups do not exist in neutral, passive voids, but in fluctuating environments that are sometimes too hot, too cold, too impersonal, too intimate, too big, too little, too noisy, too quiet, too restrictive, or too open—but rarely just right (G. W. Evans & Stecker, 2004; Halpern, 1995).

TEMPERATURE   One of the minor miseries of life occurs when people must work in a room that is either too hot or too cold. Although people generally rate temperatures from the mid-60s to the mid-80s Fahrenheit as "comfortable," temperatures that fall outside this range cause discomfort, irritability, and reduced productivity (Bell, 1981, 1992). When groups were assigned to work either in a room at normal temperature (72.4 F) or in a hot room (93.5 F), the overheated group members reported feelings of fatigue, sadness, and discomfort, whereas participants in the normal-temperature room reported feeling more elated, vigorous, and comfortable (Griffitt & Veitch, 1971). Studies have also suggested that extremes in temperature can reduce interpersonal attraction (Griffitt, 1970) and interfere with successful task performance (H. M. Parsons, 1976). Also, one of the concomitants of high temperatures in groups is exposure to others' body odors— a sensation that most people find objectionable (McBurney, Levine, & Cavanaugh, 1977). The odor of men's sweat is perceived as particularly repugnant (R. J. Stevenson & Repacholi, 2003).

Groups tend to be more aggressive when they are hot, as colloquialisms like "hot under the collar" and "flaring tempers" suggest. Mob violence is seasonal, with more riots occurring in the summer than the winter (C. A. Anderson & Bushman, 1997; Rotton & Cohn, 2002). Groups may also disband when the environment they occupy becomes unpleasantly hot. In one study, researchers measured people's aggressiveness in a comfortable room versus a hot room. Instead of acting more aggressively in the hot room, the participants responded as rapidly as possible, so that they could escape the noxious environmental setting. Thus, the heat-stressed participants were angry, but they were so uncomfortable that their primary concern was to finish the experiment as quickly as possible (R. A. Baron & Bell, 1975, 1976; Bell, 1992).

Extreme temperatures are also physically harmful (Folk, 1974). When temperatures are high, people are more likely to suffer from exhaustion, stroke, and heart attacks. Extreme cold can lead to hypothermia and death. The Apollo 13 astronauts, for example, struggled to maintain their body heat at healthy levels when the loss of power forced them to turn off the cabin heaters. It was, as Lovell characteristically understated, "very uncomfortable. Basically, the cold made it uncomfortable" (quoted in Godwin, 2000, p. 109). Accounts of groups struggling in extremely cold natural environments, such as teams wintering over in Antarctica or mountain climbers, document the lethal effects of exposure to extremely cold temperatures.

NOISE   The crew of the Apollo 13 lived with noise constantly during their 5 days in space. The Saturn V rockets were deafening, burning 3400 gallons of fuel per second. Once in orbit, the cabin was filled with the humming of computers, the whirring of fans and pumps circulating air and liquids, and the crackling of transmissions between the crew and COMCON, the flight controller back in

Houston. There was also the one sound that signaled to the crew that something was wrong; Lovell described it as a "bang-whump-shudder" that was felt more than heard (Lovell & Kluger, 1994, p. 94).

Noise is any sound that is unwanted. Sounds in the range of 0 to 50 decibels (dB) are very soft and generally produce little irritation for the listener. Sounds of more than 80 dB, in contrast, may be bothersome enough to be called noise. In general, the louder the noise, the more likely it will produce distraction, irritation, and psychological stress (S. Cohen & Weinstein, 1981). Group communication becomes impossible in such environments, so members have problems coordinating their efforts. Coping with chronic noise also exacts a psychological toll. Groups in noisy places—people who work in noisy offices, families living in homes near airports, and children on playgrounds located near major highways—generally find that the noise has a disruptive impact on their social behaviors. People are less likely to interact with other people in noisy places, and they also tend to be less helpful (Edelstein, 2002; Mathews, Canon, & Alexander, 1974; Veitch, 1990).

Groups can cope with noise for short periods of time. When researchers bombarded people working on both simple and complex tasks with tape-recorded noise, the participants quickly became so inured to the stimulus that they no longer noticed it (Glass & Singer, 1972; Glass, Singer, & Pennebaker, 1977). Groups cannot, however, cope for long periods of time with noise. As "individuals expend 'psychic energy' in the course of the adaptive process," they become "less able to cope with subsequent environmental demands and frustrations" (Glass et al., 1977, p. 134). These aversive aftereffects of *chronic* exposure to noise include increased physical illness (headaches, heart disease, allergies, and digestive disorders), infant and adult mortality rates, mental illness, interpersonal conflict, and even impotence (Bronzaft, 2002). Noise may even be partly responsible for the differences in school performance displayed by children attending schools in urban rather than rural settings. Children attending a school located near an airport had higher blood pressure and were more likely to give up when working on a difficult task than children who attended a school in a quieter neighborhood. Even when the noise was reduced, children who were exposed for prolonged periods to the noise exhibited performance deficits (S. Cohen, Evans, Stokols, & Krantz, 1986; S. Cohen, Glass, & Singer, 1973; G. W. Evans, Hygge, & Bullinger, 1995).

AMBIANCE AND LOAD Physical settings are often said to have **ambiance,** or *atmosphere,* for they can create a distinctive cognitive and emotional reaction in people who occupy these spaces.

> We have strong feelings in and about places. Some places make us feel good: glad to be there, relaxed, excited, warm all over. We are drawn to these places and return to them as often as we can. Other places make us feel bad: uncomfortable, insignificant,

---

ambiance The psychological reaction (mood, feelings, emotions) evoked by a setting.

unhappy, out of place. We avoid these places and suffer if we have to be in them (Farbstein & Kantrowitz, 1978, p. 14)

Although people's evaluations of places vary depending on their culture, experiences, and personal preferences, most are based on two dimensions: How *pleasant* is the place (positive versus negative), and how *intense* is the place (exciting versus relaxing)? A group environment that is orderly, tastefully decorated, clean, and spacious usually prompts a more favorable reaction than one that is poorly designed, shabby, unkempt, and odorous. Groups also respond to their environment by implicitly considering its intensity. Whereas some places are restful, others are so stimulating that they arouse their occupants rather than relax them. The astronauts and engineers working in the control room at Houston all responded positively to their highly arousing habitat, and so they considered it an exhilarating place. Visitors to the control room, in contrast, often reacted negatively to its harsh lights, countless monitors, displays, and cacophony of voices issuing orders, relaying information, and asking questions. Few considered it boring or tranquil (Mehrabian & Russell, 1974, 1975; J. A. Russell & Lanius, 1984; J. A. Russell & Mehrabian, 1975).

Groups generally respond best, in terms of performance and satisfaction, in positive, stimulating environments. Studies of manufacturing teams in factories, students in classrooms, and workers in offices, for example, have found that they respond better when working in attractive spaces that are visually interesting rather than drab (Sundstrom, Bell, Busby, & Asmus, 1996). Physical features that stimulate or provoke positive emotions—including music, furnishings, art, decor, decorations, color, and lighting—tend to be associated with a range of positive group dynamics, including increased cohesion, improved communication, productivity, and reduced absenteeism (Brief & Weiss, 2002). An attractive environment is not, however, a requirement for group effectiveness. Many successful groups, including the impressionists, the technicians at Lockheed's Skunk Works, and the Palo Alto Research Center (PARC) discussed in Chapter 9, worked in relatively shabby settings (Bennis & Biederman, 1997).

Groups also thrive in stimulating, but not in excessively stimulating, spaces. Studies of groups living in harsh circumstances, such as teams stationed in Antarctica and explorers living for months on end in a confined space, complain more about the *monotony* of the environment than about the danger, discomfort, or isolation (Stuster, 1996). As one officer aboard a research ship wintering in the Arctic wrote, "Monotony was our enemy, and to kill time our endeavor; hardship there was none. . . . Monotony, as I again repeat, was the only disagreeable part of our wintering" (quoted in Mowat, 1977, p. 272). Such groups strive to make their environments more interesting, often by decorating common areas extensively. But too much stimulation can contribute to **overload** when complex, stimulating environments overwhelm group members. In everyday situations,

---

overload A psychological reaction to situations and experiences that are so cognitively, perceptually, or emotionally stimulating that they tax or even exceed the individual's capacity to process incoming information.

people cope with overload by reducing their contact with others, limiting the amount of information they notice and process, or ignoring aspects of the situation. In Apollo 13, the only way astronauts could control the overload was to sleep—which they rarely did (C. I. Greenberg & Firestone, 1977; Saegert, 1978).

These coping strategies are often effective. Students living in high-density dormitories who used screening strategies to limit their contact with other people, for example, were better adjusted than those who did not (Baum, Calesnick, Davis, & Gatchel, 1982). In other cases, though, these strategies may not reduce members' stress. Men who coped with environmental stress by withdrawing from the very people who could have helped them cope with the situation (friends and loved ones), for example, were more maladjusted than men who did not withdraw (G. W. Evans, Palsane, Lepore, & Martin, 1989; Lepore, Evans, & Schneider, 1991). Similarly, when researchers masked the sounds of a busy office, performance improved, but the workers experienced heightened arousal (Loewen & Suedfeld, 1992).

DANGEROUS PLACES The astronauts sat atop millions of pounds of rocket fuel at launch, traveled though space in a thin-shelled spacecraft at speeds of nearly 25,000 miles an hour, and during reentry relied on a heat shield to deflect the heat away from the command module and parachutes that would slow the craft's descent. All the dangers were minimized through planning, design, and training, but one danger that all crews faced but could not protect themselves against was always present—a collision with a meteor.

> Of all the possible disaster scenarios that astronauts and controllers consider in planning a mission, few are more ghastly—or more capricious, or more sudden, or more total, or more feared—than a surprise hit by a rogue meteor. At speeds encountered in Earth orbit, a cosmic sand grain no more than a tenth of an inch across would strike a spacecraft with an energetic wallop equivalent to a bowling ball traveling at 60 miles per hour. (Lovell & Kluger, 1994, p. 94)

Groups sometimes live and work in places filled with dangers, both recognized and unknown. Some hazards are unavoidable and unpredictable. Some natural calamity, such as a flood, earthquake, or blizzard, may overtake a group. Some groups, too, work at jobs that are riskier than most: Miners, ship crews, police officers, and military units often live and work in circumstances that can be life threatening. The group, too, may occupy an inhospitable environment. Some people live in neighborhoods where violence and aggression are so commonplace that their lives are often at risk.

Groups generally cope with danger by taking precautions designed to make the situation safer. Astronauts, military combat squads, and explorers all minimize the possibility of error or exposure to danger by training, stressing cooperation among members, and monitoring each individual's connection to the group (Harrison & Connors, 1984; Suedfeld, 1987). In consequence, dangerous circumstances often promote an increased level of teamwork. During routine flights, astronauts and the mission specialists on the ground tend to adopt an "us versus them" orientation (Bechtel, 2002). Disagreements and disputes are com-

FOCUS 14-1   Why Is Mount Everest So Deadly to Groups?

I felt disconnected from the climbers around me—emotionally, spiritually, physically—to a degree I hadn't experienced on any previous expedition. We were a team in name only.

–Jon Krakauer (1997, p. 163)

On May 10, 1996, two groups led by experts set off to scale Mount Everest, the highest peak in the world. One group, Adventure Consultants Guided Expedition, was led by Rob Hall, who had reached the summit of Mount Everest four times between 1990 and 1995. Scott Fischer was the leader of Mountain Madness Guided Expedition. Fisher was also an expert guide and climber.

Both teams met with disaster, caused in part by the dangerous environment of Mount Everest. Everest is subject to high winds, bitter temperatures, and icy conditions. Climbers prepare for the summit attempt at a camp high on the mountain, but they must reach the peak and return to that camp in a single day, because the chances of surviving a night on the summit of Everest are slim. But the teams were overtaken by an unexpectedly powerful storm as they descended and they could not reach the shelter of their camp. Several members of the team also suffered from a lack of oxygen, for the air is thin at that altitude. Everest climbers usually carry tanks of oxygen, but even these supplements cannot counteract the negative effects of climbing treacherous terrain 29,000 feet above sea level.

These negative environmental events interacted with negative group dynamics in both teams. Jon Krakauer (1997), a member of Hall's group, suggested that an inattention to teamwork may have contributed to the failure. Even though the climb is extremely dangerous and many who attempt it are killed, the groups did not practice together, did not establish routines for dealing

with supplies (including oxygen), and did not set up contingency plans. A hierarchy of authority was not established, despite the possibility that one of the leaders could be injured. Hall and Fisher did not share their plans for the summit with the group, and they did not remain in contact with the other guides during the climb. The leaders of both teams also made errors in judgment, possibly due to inexperience, the ill effects of too little oxygen (hypoxia), and the desire to outdo the other team. Even though the climbers, before attempting the summit, agreed on a turn-around time—the time during the day when they must turn back from the summit it they were to reach their base safely before nightfall—Hall and Fisher ignored that deadline and continued on. The other guides recognized the danger in not returning at the turnaround time, but they did not feel that they had the authority to intervene. As a result, several climbers managed to reach the summit, but they were overtaken by the snowstorm during the descent and perished.

As Krakauer later described, a sense of isolation pervaded the camp on the night before the summit attempt:

> The roar of the wind made it impossible to communicate from one tent to the next. In this godforsaken place, I felt disconnected from the climbers around me—emotionally, spiritually, physically—to a degree I hadn't experienced on any previous expedition. We were a team in name only, I'd sadly come to realize. Although in a few hours we would leave camp as a group, we would ascend as individuals, linked to one another by neither rope nor any deep sense of loyalty. (Krakauer, 1997, p. 163)

Krakauer's misgivings proved prophetic. Everest claimed the lives of eight members of the two teams, including Rob Hall and Scott Fisher.

mon, with both sides viewing the other side as stubborn and misinformed. These tensions dissolve, however, during the crucial moments of each mission, and they were nearly nonexistent during the flight of the Apollo 13—the crew and mission control worked together seamlessly to solve each problem as it arose. Groups that face dangerous circumstances but do not manage to work as a team to overcome their problems place themselves at risk (see Focus 14-1).

Behavior Settings

The Apollo 13 was more than a metal spacecraft filled with expensive instrumentation and equipment. It was also a **behavior setting**—a physical location where people's actions are prescribed by the features and functions of the situation. The counter at a fast food restaurant, the waiting area in a doctor's office, a computer lab on a college campus, a conference room in a business office, and a bench in a park are all behavior settings, for once people enter these spaces, their behavior is shaped more by the space than by their personal characteristics. For example, when people enter a fast food restaurant, they join a line, place their order, pay for their food, and then find a table where they eat their meal. A group in a conference room sits in chairs, exchanges information, and eventually decides to adjourn. The astronauts, once they entered the Apollo 13, acted in ways that the situation required.

The concept of a behavior setting was developed by ecological psychologist Roger Barker and his colleagues in their studies of common interpersonal situations. Barker, after studying offices, homes, schools, neighborhoods, communities, and entire towns, concluded that most behavior—at least, most routine, ordinary behavior—is determined by the environmental settings in which it occurs. These behavior settings tend to be specific spatial areas—actual places where group members interact with one another. These places often have *boundaries*—such as walls, doors, or fences—that identify the edge of one behavior setting and possibly the beginning of the next. Some boundaries can also be temporal, as when a group is present only during a certain time (e.g., a group may occupy a classroom only on Mondays and Wednesdays from 9 to 10:30). Most settings also include both people (group members) and things (equipment, chairs, etc.); Barker called them both *components* of the setting. Barker noted that individuals and settings are often inseparable, for the meaning of actions often depends on the physical features of the situation, just as a situation takes it meaning from the individuals in the setting. Barker believed that people routinely follow a *program* that sequences their actions and reactions in behavior settings. They may, for example, make use of the settings' objects in very predictable, routine ways, as when people who enter a room with chairs in it tend to sit on them (Barker, 1968, 1987, 1990; Barker et al., 1978).

Not every physical setting is a behavior setting. Some situations are novel ones, which group members have never before encountered, so they have no expectations about how they should act. Some individuals, too, may enter a behavior setting, but they are not aware of the norms of the situation, or they simply do not accept them as guides for their own action. But in most cases, group members act in predictable, routine ways in such situations. Libraries, for example, are behavior settings because they create a readiness for certain types of action: One should be subdued, quiet, and calm when in a library. These normative expecta-

---

behavior setting As defined by Roger Barker in his theory of ecological psychology, a physically and temporally bounded social situation that determines the actions of the individuals in the setting.

tions guide behavior directly, and in many cases, group members are not even aware of how the situation automatically channels their actions. To demonstrate this automatic, unconscious impact of place on people, researchers first showed people a picture of either a library or a railroad station. Later, their reaction times to various words, including words relevant to libraries (e.g., *quiet, still, whisper*), were measured. As expected, people recognized library-related words more quickly after seeing the picture of a library, suggesting that the picture activated norms pertaining to the situation (Aarts & Dijksterhuis, 2003).

SYNOMORPHY AND STAFFING Barker and his colleagues noted that in some behavior settings, the people are seamlessly embedded in the place itself. The cockpit of the Apollo 13, for example, was designed so that the astronauts could monitor all their instruments and reach all their controls. A fast food restaurant may use a system of guide chains and multiple cash registers to handle large numbers of customers efficiently. A classroom may contain areas where students can work on individual projects, a reading circle where the teacher can lead small groups, and an art area where students can easily access the supplies they need. In other behavior settings, however, the people do not fit the place. A classroom may have chairs bolted to the floors in rows, so the teacher can never have students work in small groups. An office may have windows that provide workers with a view of the city, but the light from the windows prevents them from reading their computer screens. A concert hall may have so few doors that concert-goers clog the exits. Barker used the word **synomorphy** to describe the degree of fit between the setting and its human occupants. When settings are high in synomorphy, the people fit into the physical setting and use its objects appropriately. The people and the place are unified. Settings that are low in synomorphy lack this unity, for the people do not mesh well with the physical features and objects in the place.

Allan Wicker's **staffing theory** draws on the concept of synomorphy to explain group performance (Wicker, 1979, 1987, 2002). Consider office workers in a small business, university, or government agency who are responsible for typing papers and reports, answering the telephone, duplicating materials, and preparing paperwork on budgets, schedules, appointments, and so on. If the number of people working in the office is sufficient to handle all these activities, then the setting is *optimally staffed*. But if telephones are ringing unanswered, reports are days late, and the photocopier is broken and no one knows how to fix it, then the office lacks "enough people to carry out smoothly the essential program and maintenance tasks" and is *understaffed* (Wicker, 1979, p. 71). On the other hand, if the number of group members exceeds that needed in the situation, the group is *overstaffed* (Sundstrom, 1987).

---

synomorphy In ecological psychology, the quality of the fit between the human occupants and the physical situation.

staffing theory An ecological analysis of behavior settings arguing that both understaffing (not enough people) and overstaffing (too many people) can be detrimental.

TABLE 14-1 Group members' reactions to understaffed and overstaffed work settings

Reaction	Understaffed groups	Overstaffed groups
Task performance	Members engage in diligent, consistent, goal-related actions	Members are perfunctory, inconsistent, and sloppy
Performance monitoring	Members provide one another with corrective, critical feedback as needed	Members exhibit little concern for the quality of the group's performance
Perceptions	Members are viewed in terms of the jobs they do rather than their individual qualities	Members focus on the personalities and uniqueness of members rather than on the group
Self-perceptions	Members feel important, responsible, and capable	Members feel lowered self-esteem, with little sense of competence
Attitude toward the group	Members express concern over the continuation of the group	Members are cynical about the group and its functions
Supportiveness	Members are reluctant to reject those who are performing poorly	Members are less willing to help other members of the group

Source: Adapted from Barker, 1968; Wicker, 1979.

Table 14-1 summarizes staffing theory's predictions about the relationship between staffing and performance. Overstaffed groups may perform adequately—after all, so many extra people are available to carry out the basic functions—but overstaffing can lead to dissatisfaction with task-related activities and heightened rejection of other group members. Understaffed groups, in contrast, often respond positively to the challenging workload. Instead of complaining about the situation, understaffed groups sometimes display heightened involvement in their work and contribute more to the group's goals (Arnold & Greenberg, 1980; Wicker & August, 1995). Four-man groups, for example, when placed in an overstaffed situation (too few tasks to keep all members active), reported feeling less important, less involved in their work, less concerned with performance, and less needed. These effects were reversed in understaffed groups (Wicker, Kirmeyer, Hanson, & Alexander, 1976). In another study, the increased workload brought on by understaffing increased professionals' and long-term employees' involvement in their work, but understaffing also led to decreased commitment among new employees and blue-collar workers. Understaffing was also associated with more negative attitudes toward the group (Wicker & August, 1995). Staffing theory also explains why individuals who are part of smaller groups and organizations get more involved in their groups; for example, even though a large school offers more opportunities for involvement in small-group

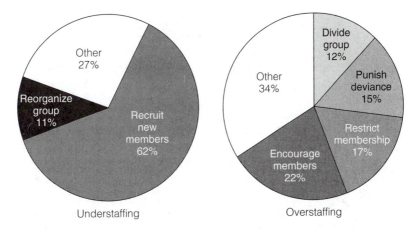

FIGURE 14-3

How do groups cope with staffing problems? Leaders of student groups recommended dealing with understaffing by recruiting more members or by
reorganizing the group so that it worked more efficiently. They frequently
mentioned encouraging members and dividing the group as methods for
dealing with overstaffing. *Source:* "Group Staffing Levels and Responses to
Prospective and New Group Members" by M. A. Cini, R. L. Moreland,
and J. M. Levine, *Journal of Personality and Social Psychology,* 65. Copyright
© 1993 American Psychological Association. Reprinted by permission.

activities, the proportion of students who join school-based groups is higher in
smaller schools (Gump, 1990).

How do groups cope with staffing problems? When researchers asked leaders of student groups this question, nearly 75% recommended recruiting more
members or reorganizing the group as the best ways to deal with understaffing.
Other solutions included working with other groups and adopting more modest
group goals (see Figure 14-3). These leaders offered a wider range of solutions
for overstaffing, including encouraging members to remain active in the group
(often by assigning them specific duties), enforcing rules about participation, dividing the group, taking in fewer members, changing the group's structure to include more positions, and adopting more ambitious goals (Cini, Moreland, &
Levine, 1993).

DESIGNING GROUP SPACES In many cases, people fail to recognize the close
connection between individuals, groups, and their environment. They may realize that they are part of nature, but they do not as easily recognize their connection to an artificial, built environment (Mowday & Sutton, 1993; Schultz,
Shriver, Tabanico, & Khazian, 2004). Unfortunately, not all physical settings are
designed so carefully as the Apollo 13, and as a result, many groups may not even
realize that they are working and playing in areas that lack synomorphy.

Studies of all types of behavioral settings—classrooms, factories, offices, playgrounds, highways, theaters, and so on—frequently find that these areas need to be redesigned to maximize the fit between the people and the place. Groups in workplace settings, for example, will increase their productivity if their work areas are redesigned to promote interaction, communication, task completion, and adaptation. The group members should have access to shared spaces, where members can interact on a regular basis without interruption and interference. This *shared group space* should encourage the development of a group identity through decorative styles, boundaries, the use of signs and labels, and so on. The setting should also encourage communication among members. In many cases, buildings are designed around formally recognized locations for communication—such as conference rooms—but groups also meet informally and spontaneously, and these locations should be incorporated into the building's design. Many high-performance organizations go so far as to integrate work areas with other areas to promote additional interaction among group members, as when shared eating facilities and fitness facilities are included in the building's design. The setting should, however, promote rather than inhibit task performance. The materials and equipment needed for the group members to do their work should be readily available and in good working order (Becker, 2004; McCoy, 2002).

The kind of space needed by a group will also depend on the type of tasks the group must accomplish. A group that is working on tasks that require high levels of collaboration and creativity will need a very different space than a group working on divisible tasks that are highly structured. Francis Duffy (1997), by examining a number of groups working in large corporations, identified four types of groups that needed four types of spaces—hives, cells, dens, and clubs.

- *Hives.* Members who function as "worker bees" by performing divisible, highly structured tasks require little interaction with other group members. Such groups function well in open, cubicle-type offices where each individual has a defined, relatively small workspace.
- *Cells.* Members working on complex, long-term, relatively individualized projects need private spaces to carry out their work. They may also be able to work by telecommuting from a home office.
- *Dens.* When members who are similar in terms of skills and responsibilities work together on collective tasks and projects, they need an open space that all members share. So long as the task is highly structured and is facilitated by a high rate of collaboration and interaction, such groups do not need individualized areas.
- *Clubs.* Members who are talented, well trained, or possess very specialized skills often work on diverse tasks and projects that vary greatly in their collaborative demands. Their work space must be flexible, permitting them to collaborate as needed but also to secure privacy.

Duffy found that club offices tend to be the most productive, but he added that nearly all group spaces must be changed to increase the fit between the group and its tasks. Even the most carefully designed and implemented setting may, when filled with the group, fail to meet members' needs and so require revision.

SMALL-GROUP ECOLOGY

Ecology is the science of the interrelationship of organisms and their habitats (R. J. Lawrence, 2002). Ecologists examine how organisms—whether they are plant, animal, or microbe—interact with and adapt to other organisms in their environment and to the environment itself. Similarly, those who study the ecology of small groups explore how individuals interact with and adapt to the group habitat. Just as frogs issue their croaks from their favorite places in the stream, and birds neatly space themselves along a telephone wire, so humans display consistent patterns of spacing and seating when immersed in a group habitat.

Personal Space

Anthropologist Edward T. Hall (1966) argued that much of our behavior is shaped by a "hidden dimension." In Apollo 13, this dimension determined where each astronaut sat as he carried out scheduled tasks; how crew members moved through the tunnel between the command module and the service module; where they positioned themselves when they looked out the windows of their ship as it passed over the surface of the moon. What is this hidden dimension? *Space*.

People prefer to keep some space between themselves and others. This **personal space** provides a boundary that limits the amount of physical contact between people. This boundary extends farther in the front of the person than behind, but the individual is always near the center of this invisible buffer zone. Personal space is portable, but it is actively maintained and defended. When someone violates our personal space, we tend to take steps to correct this problem (Aiello, 1987). The term *personal space* is something of a misnomer, as the process actually refers to distances that people maintain between one another. Hence, it is an *interpersonal space* (Patterson, 1975). Some people seem to require more space than others, but as we will see, our spatial processes operate across a broad range of people and situations (Aiello, 1987; Altman & Chemers, 1980; Hayduk, 1978, 1983; Knowles, 1980).

INTERPERSONAL ZONES Different group activities require different amounts of personal space. Hall, in describing these variations, proposed four types of interpersonal zones (see Table 14-2). The *intimate zone* is appropriate only for the most involving and personal behaviors, such as arm wrestling and whispering. The *personal zone,* in contrast, is reserved for a wide range of small-group experiences, such as discussions with friends, interaction with acquaintances, and conversation. More routine transactions are conducted in the *social zone*. Meetings held over large desks, formal dining, and professional presentations to small

---

personal space The area that individuals maintain around themselves into which others cannot intrude without arousing discomfort.

TABLE 14-2 Types of social activities that occur in each interpersonal zone

Zone	Distance	Characteristics	Typical Activities
Intimate	Touching to 18 inches	Sensory information concerning the other is detailed and diverse; stimulus person dominates perceptual field	Sex, hugging, massage, comforting, jostling, handshakes, slow dancing
Personal	18 inches to 4 feet	Other person can be touched if desired; gaze can be directed away from the other person with ease	Conversations, discussion, car travel, viewing performances, watching television
Social	4 feet to 12 feet	Visual inputs begin to dominate other senses; voice levels are normal; appropriate distance for many informal social gatherings	Dining, meeting with business colleagues, interacting with a receptionist
Public	12 feet or more	All sensory inputs are beginning to become less effective; voices may require amplification; facial expressions unclear	Lectures, addresses, plays, dance recitals
Remote	Different locations	Primarily verbal inputs; facial and other behavioral and nonverbal cues unavailable	Electronic discussions, conference calls, telephone voice mail, e-mail

Source: Adapted from E. T. Hall, 1966.

groups generally take place in this zone. The *public zone* is reserved for even more formal meetings, such as stage presentations, lectures, or addresses. Table 14-2 also adds a fifth zone to those described by Hall. In the years since Hall proposed his taxonomy of interpersonal zones, groups have begun to meet more frequently in the *remote zone*. In this zone, group members are physically separated but communicate with each other through such technologies as radio, telephone, and computers (Sommer, 2002). The Apollo 13 astronauts and the flight control engineers back in Houston interacted in this remote zone.

Closer, smaller spaces are generally reserved for friendlier, more intimate interpersonal activities. As a result, cohesive groups tend to occupy smaller spaces than noncohesive gatherings (G. W. Evans & Howard, 1973); extraverted people maintain smaller distances from others than do introverted ones (Patterson & Sechrest, 1970); people who wish to create a friendly, positive impression usually choose smaller distances than less friendly people (G. W. Evans & Howard, 1973); and groups of friends tend to stand closer to one another than groups of strangers (Edney & Grundmann, 1979). Physical distance has little impact on remote groups, although individuals communicating via computer respond differently when their interface includes facial information as well as verbal information (S. Kiesler, Sproull, & Waters, 1996).

Why does distance influence so many group processes? One explanation, based on an **equilibrium model of communication,** suggests that personal space, body orientation, and eye contact define the level of intimacy of any interaction. If group members feel that a low level of intimacy is appropriate, they may sit far apart, make little eye contact, and assume a relatively formal posture. If, in contrast, the members are relaxing and discussing personal topics, they may move close together, make more eye contact, and adopt more relaxed postures (Argyle & Dean, 1965; Patterson, 1996). By continually adjusting their nonverbal and verbal behavior, group members can keep the intimacy of their interactions at the level they desire (Burgoon, 1983; K. J. Kaplan, Firestone, Klein, & Sodikoff, 1983).

MEN, WOMEN, AND SPACE Would the amount of personal space maintained by the astronauts in Apollo 13 have differed if they had been women? Probably, for studies suggest that women's personal spaces tend to be smaller than men's (Hayduk, 1983). Relative to men, women allow others to get closer to them, and they approach other people more closely. Women also take up less space by sitting with their arms close to their sides and by crossing their legs, whereas men enlarge their personal space by assuming expansive, open positions (Edwards, 1972; Heshka & Nelson, 1972; Mehrabian, 1972). The interactions between the men of Apollo 13 occurred almost exclusively in the personal zone, except when Lovell hugged the shivering Haise, who had become increasingly ill during the mission.

STATUS The type of relationship linking interactants plays a particularly significant role in determining personal space. A study of 562 U.S. Navy personnel, for example, found that subordinates conversing with superiors required more space than when conversing with peers (Dean, Willis, & Hewitt, 1975). Furthermore, many studies suggest that when we are with friends rather than with strangers or mere acquaintances, our personal space needs become relatively small. This effect occurs in both same-sex and mixed-sex dyads, although the effect is sometimes seen only in women (Hayduk, 1983).

CULTURE Edward T. Hall (1966) argued that cultures differ in their use of space. People socialized in the *contact cultures* of the Mediterranean, the Middle East, and Latin America prefer strong sensory involvement with others, and so they seek direct social contact whenever possible. In contrast, residents in such *noncontact cultures* as the United States, England, and Germany try to limit their spatial openness with others. Given that the crew of Apollo 13 included only Americans, they shared similar norms about how much distance should be

---

equilibrium model of communication An explanation of distancing behavior in interpersonal settings arguing that the amount of eye contact, the intimacy of the topic, and the frequency of smiling influence the amount of personal space required by interactants.

maintained. Crews on space stations, such as Mir or Salyut, involve astronauts from different cultural backgrounds, so misunderstandings caused by spatial confusions may be more common (Remland, Jones, & Brinkman, 1995). Culture also influences how people interact in the remote zone, for people with different cultural backgrounds vary in how much emotion, personal information, and responsiveness to others they express when communicating via the Internet (Reeder, MacFadyen, Roche, & Chase, 2004).

Reactions to Spatial Invasion

Individuals cannot always protect their personal space from intrusion by others. In some cases, group members may find themselves in places where the available space is so limited that people cannot maintain appropriate distances between one another. In other instances, the group may have sufficient space, but for some reason, a member approaches so closely that he or she seems "too close for comfort."

How do group members react to such intrusions? High density does not always lead to feelings of crowding and other negative interpersonal outcomes. As Daniel Stokols (1972, 1978) noted, **density** refers to a characteristic of the environment—literally, the number of people per unit of space. **Crowding,** in contrast, refers to a psychological, experiential state that occurs when people *feel* that they do not have enough space. Although the density of a given situation, such as a party, a rock concert, or Apollo 13, may be very high, the interactants may not feel crowded at all. Yet two people sitting in a large room may still report that they feel crowded if they expected to be alone, are engaged in some private activity, or dislike each other intensely.

AROUSAL AND ATTRIBUTIONS Physiologically speaking, what happens to people when they find themselves in high-density situations? In many cases, they become *aroused*—their heart rate and blood pressure increase, they breathe faster, and they sometimes perspire more (G. W. Evans, 1979). This link between personal space violations and arousal was confirmed in a study of men micturating in a public restroom (Middlemist, Knowles, & Matter, 1976). Reasoning that arousal would lead to a general muscular contraction that would delay micturation and reduce its duration, the researchers set up a situation in which men using wall-mounted urinals were joined by a confederate who used either the next receptacle (*near condition*) or one located farther down the wall (*far condition*). When onset times and duration for men in the near and far condition were compared with those same times for men in a no-confederate control condition, the researchers found that personal space invasion significantly increased general arousal.

---

density The number of individuals per unit of space.

crowding A psychological reaction that occurs when individuals feel that the amount of space available to them is insufficient for their needs.

This arousal is not always stressful, however. If the intruder is a close friend, a relative, or an extremely attractive stranger, closeness can be a plus (Willis, 1966). Similarly, if we believe that the other person needs help or is attempting to initiate a friendly relationship, we tend to react positively rather than negatively (Murphy-Berman & Berman, 1978). These findings suggest that the *label* that individuals use to interpret their arousal determines the consequences of crowding. If people attribute the arousal to others' standing too close, then they will conclude, "I feel crowded." If, in contrast, they explain the arousal in some other way—"I drank too much coffee," "I'm in love," "I'm afraid our ship will burn up in the atmosphere," and so on—they will not feel crowded.

Steven Worchel and his colleagues tested this attributional model of crowding by seating five-person groups in chairs placed either 20 inches apart or touching at the legs. These researchers told the groups that an inaudible noise would be played in the room as they worked on several tasks. They told some groups that the noise was detectable subconsciously and would lead to stressful, discomforting effects. They told other groups that the noise would have relaxing and calming effects, or they gave no explanation for the noise at all. The groups were not actually exposed to any noise, but as Worchel predicted, crowded groups who thought that the noise would arouse them felt less crowded. Why? Because they attributed the arousal caused by crowding to the supposed noise rather than to the proximity of other people (Worchel & Yohai, 1979; see also Worchel & Teddlie, 1976).

INTENSITY Jonathan Freedman also argued that high-density situations are not always aversive situations. His **density–intensity hypothesis** suggests that high density merely intensifies whatever is already occurring in the group situation (Freedman, 1975, 1979). If something in the situation makes the group interaction unpleasant, high density will make the situation seem even more unpleasant. If the situation is a very pleasant one, however, high density will make the good situation even better. Freedman tested this notion by placing groups of people in large or small rooms and then manipulating some aspect of the group interaction to create either unpleasantness or pleasantness. In one investigation, groups of 6 to 10 high school students sat on the floor of either a large room or a small room. Each delivered a speech and then received feedback from the other group members. Freedman made certain that in some groups, the feedback was always positive, whereas in other groups, the feedback was always negative. When the participants later rated the room and their group, Freedman discovered that crowding *intensified* the effects of the feedback: People liked their group the most when they received positive feedback under high-density conditions, and they liked their group the least when they got negative feedback when crowded.

---

density–intensity hypothesis An explanation of crowding proposed by Jonathan Freedman, predicting that high density makes unpleasant situations more unpleasant but pleasant situations more pleasant.

Furthermore, Freedman found that these effects were clearest for all-female groups as opposed to all-male or mixed-sex groups (see also Storms & Thomas, 1977).

CONTROLLABILITY Crowded situations are unsettling because they undermine group members' control over their experiences. Crowded situations bring people into contact with others they would prefer to avoid, and if working groups cannot cope with the constraints of their environment, they may fail at their tasks. Group members can therefore cope with crowding by increasing their sense of control over the situation. Just as a sense of high personal control helps people cope with a range of negative life events, including failure, divorce, illness, and accidents, people are less stressed by environmental threats when they feel they can control their circumstances (G. W. Evans & Lepore, 1992; Rodin, 1976; Rodin & Baum, 1978; D. E. Schmidt & Keating, 1979; Sherrod & Cohen, 1979).

Researchers tested the benefits of controllability by asking groups of six men to work on tasks in either a small laboratory room or a large one. One problem was a 15-minute discussion of censorship, and the second involved blindfolding members one at a time and letting them wander about within a circle formed by the rest of the group. To manipulate control, one of the participants was designated the *coordinator;* he was responsible for organizing the group, dealing with questions concerning procedures, and blindfolding members for the second task. A second participant, the *terminator,* was given control over ending the discussion and regulating each member's turn in the center of the circle. Significantly, the two group members who could control the group tasks through coordination or termination were not as bothered by the high-density situation as the four group members who were given no control (Rodin, Solomon, & Metcalf, 1978).

INTERFERENCE Crowding is particularly troublesome when it interferes with the group's work. The Apollo 13 crew, for example, did not react negatively to their high-density living conditions so long as the crowding did not undermine their group's effectiveness. Difficulties only occurred when they needed to fix a problem—such as a hatch that would not secure properly, but there was only enough room for one person to reach it. Similarly, studies that find no ill effects of crowding generally study groups working on coaction problems that require little interaction. Studies that require the participants to complete interactive tasks, in contrast, tend to find negative effects of crowding (e.g., Heller, Groff, & Solomon, 1977; Paulus, Annis, Seta, Schkade, & Matthews, 1976).

Researchers demonstrated the importance of interference by deliberately manipulating both density and interaction. All-male groups worked in either a small laboratory room or in a large one collating eight-page booklets. The order of the pages was not constant, however, but was determined by first selecting a card that had the order of pages listed in a random sequence. In the *low-interaction condition,* each person had all eight stacks of pages and a set of sequence cards. In the *high-interaction condition,* the stacks were located at points around the room, so participants had to walk around the room in unpredictable patterns. In fact, the participants often bumped into one another while trying to move from one stack to another. The interference created in the high-interaction condition led to decrements in task performance—provided that density was high (Heller et al., 1977; see also R. McCallum, Rusbult, Hong, Walden, & Schopler, 1979; Morasch, Groner, & Keating, 1979; Paulus et al., 1976; Sundstrom, 1975).

Seating Arrangements

At launch and during most key maneuvers, the three Apollo 13 astronauts were seated side by side in front of the control panel, but the seat on the left was reserved for the mission commander, or the officer who was piloting the ship. As Robert Sommer (1967) noted, seating arrangements play a large role in creating a group's ecology. Although often unrecognized, or simply taken for granted, seating patterns influence interaction, communication, and leadership in groups.

SEATING PATTERNS AND SOCIAL INTERACTION Groups behave very differently if their seating pattern is sociopetal rather than sociofugal. **Sociopetal spaces** promote interaction among group members by heightening eye contact, encouraging verbal communication, and facilitating the development of intimacy. **Sociofugal spaces,** in contrast, discourage interaction among group members and can even drive participants out of the situation altogether. A secluded booth in a quiet restaurant, a park bench, or five chairs placed in a tight circle are sociopetal environments, whereas classrooms organized in rows, movie theaters, waiting rooms, and airport waiting areas are sociofugal. Sommer felt that airport seating was deliberately designed to disrupt interaction. He noted that even people seated side by side on airport chairs cannot converse comfortably:

> The chairs are either bolted together and arranged in rows theater-style facing the ticket counters, or arranged back-to-back, and even if they face one another they are at such distances that comfortable conversation is impossible. The motive for the sociofugal arrangement appears the same as that in hotels and other commercial places—to drive people out of the waiting areas into cafés, bars, and shops where they will spend money. (Sommer, 1969, pp. 121–122)

Group members generally prefer sociopetal arrangements (Batchelor & Goethals, 1972; Giesen & McClaren, 1976). This preference, however, depends in part on the type of task undertaken in the situation (Ryen & Kahn, 1975; Sommer, 1969). Sommer found, for example, that college students' preferences varied depending on whether they were conversing, cooperating on some task, competing, or coacting on individual tasks. As Figure 14-4 shows, corner-to-corner and face-to-face arrangements were preferred for conversation, and

---

sociopetal spaces Environmental settings that promote interaction among group members, including seating arrangements that facilitate conversation.

sociofugal spaces Environmental settings that discourage or prevent interaction among group members.

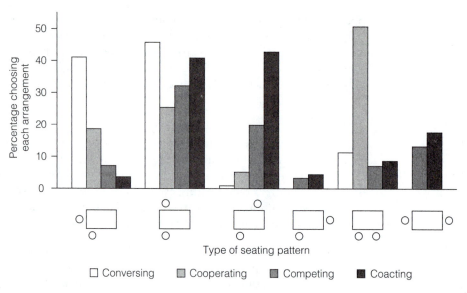

FIGURE 14-4

How do different chair arrangements influence group interaction? When Sommer (1969) compared six different kinds of seating arrangements, he discovered that corner-to-corner and face-to-face arrangements were preferred for conversation, and side-by-side seating was selected for cooperation. No one chose the arrangement where both interactants sit at the ends of the table when cooperating or conversing. *Source: Personal Space* by Robert Sommer, © 1969 by Prentice-Hall, Inc. Reprinted by permission of the author.

side-by-side seating was selected for cooperation. Competing pairs either took a direct, face-to-face orientation (apparently to stimulate competition) or tried to increase interpersonal distance, whereas coacting pairs preferred arrangements that involved a visual separation. As one student stated, such an arrangement "allows staring into space and not into my neighbor's face" (Sommer, 1969, p. 63). Similar choices were found with round tables.

Groups in sociopetal environments act differently than groups in sociofugal spaces. In one study, dyads whose members sat facing each other seemed more relaxed, but dyads whose members sat at a 90-degree angle to each other were more affiliative (Mehrabian & Diamond, 1971). When researchers compared circle seating with L-shaped seating, the circle was associated with feelings of confinement but fostered greater interpersonal attraction (Patterson, Kelley, Kondracki, & Wulf, 1979; Patterson, Roth, & Schenk, 1979). People seated in the L-shaped groups, on the other hand, engaged in more self-manipulative behaviors and fidgeting, and they paused more during group discussions. Overall, the positive effects of the circle arrangement relative to the L-shaped arrangement were stronger in female groups than in male groups.

MEN, WOMEN, AND SEATING PREFERENCES Women and men diverge, to a degree, in their preferences for seating arrangements. Men prefer to position themselves across from those they like, and women prefer adjacent seating positions (Sommer, 1959). Conversely, men prefer that strangers sit by their side, whereas women feel that strangers should sit across from them. Researchers studied the confusion that this difference can cause by sending confederates to sit at the same table as solitary women and men working in a library. After a brief and uneventful period, the confederate left. When a second researcher then asked the participant some questions about the confederate and the library, the researchers discovered that men were the least favorably disposed toward the stranger who sat across from them but that women reacted more negatively to the stranger who sat next to them (J. D. Fisher & Byrne, 1975). Clearly, group members should be sensitive to the possibility that their spatial behaviors will be misinterpreted by others and should be willing to make certain that any possible misunderstandings will be short-lived.

COMMUNICATION PATTERNS Bernard Steinzor's early studies of face-to-face discussion groups indicated that spatial patterns also influence communication rates in groups. Although at first he could find few significant relationships between seat location and participation in the discussion, one day, while watching a group, he noticed a participant change his seat to sit opposite someone he had argued with during the previous meeting. Inspired by this chance observation, Steinzor (1950) reanalyzed his findings and discovered that individuals tended to speak after the person seated opposite them spoke. He reasoned that we have an easier time observing and listening to the statements of people who are seated in a position central to our visual field, so that their remarks serve as stronger stimuli for our own ideas and statements. The tendency for members of a group to comment immediately after the person sitting opposite them is now termed the **Steinzor effect.** The phenomenon appears to occur primarily in leaderless discussion groups, for later research has suggested that when a strong leader is present, group members direct more comments to their closest neighbor (Hearne, 1957).

HEAD-OF-THE-TABLE EFFECT Where should the leader sit—at the head of the table or in one of the side chairs? With great consistency, leaders seek out the head of the table. Sommer (1969), for example, found that people appointed to lead small discussion groups tended to select seats at the head of the table. Those who move to this position of authority also tend to possess more dominant personalities (Hare & Bales, 1963), talk more frequently, and often exercise greater amounts of interpersonal influence (Strodtbeck & Hook, 1961).

Steinzor effect The tendency for members of a group to comment immediately after the person sitting opposite them.

Sommer suggested two basic explanations for this intriguing **head-of-the-table effect**—*perceptual prominence* and the *social meaning* associated with sitting at the head of the table. Looking first at prominence, Sommer suggested that in many groups, the chair at the end of the table is the most salient position in the group and that the occupant of this space can therefore easily maintain greater amounts of eye contact with more of the group members, can move to the center of the communication network, and (as the Steinzor effect suggests) can comment more frequently. Moreover, in Western cultures, where most studies of leadership have been conducted, the chair at the head of the table has been virtually defined as the most appropriate place for the leader to sit. Sommer was careful to note that this norm may not hold in other societies, but in most Western cultures, leadership and the head of the table go hand in hand.

Both factors play a role in the head-of-the-table effect. Investigators manipulated salience by having two persons sit on one side of the table and three on the other side. Although no one sat in the end seat, those seated on the two-person side of the table could maintain eye contact with three of the group members, but those on the three-person side could focus their attention on only two members. Therefore, group members on the two-person side should be able to influence others more and hence be the more likely leaders. As predicted, 70% of the leaders came from the two-person side, and only 30% came from the three-person side (Howells & Becker, 1962).

In another study, the tendency for people to automatically associate the head of the table with leadership was examined by arranging for confederates to voluntarily choose or be assigned to the end position or to some other position around a table (Nemeth & Wachtler, 1974). These confederates then went about systematically disagreeing with the majority of the group members on the topic under discussion, and the extent to which the participants altered their opinions to agree with the deviant was assessed. Interestingly, the deviants succeeded in influencing the others only when they had freely chosen to sit in the head chair. Apparently, disagreeing group members sitting at the "normal" locations around the table were viewed as "deviants," whereas those who had the confidence to select the end chair were viewed more as "leaders" (Riess, 1982; Riess & Rosenfeld, 1980).

TERRITORIALITY

When Lovell, Swigert, and Haise entered the Apollo 13 spaceship for their mission, they entered a cylinder filled with computers, controls, equipment, and supplies. But within days, this physical space was transformed into the group's territory. The men stowed personal gear in their lockers. The controls over

---

head-of-the-table effect The tendency for group members to associate the leadership role and its responsibilities with the seat located at the head of the table; as a result, individuals who occupy such positions tend to emerge as leaders in groups without designated leaders.

TABLE 14-3 Three types of territories established and protected by individuals and groups

Type	Degree of Control	Duration of Claim	Examples
Primary	*High:* Occupants control access and are very likely to actively defend this space.	*Long-term:* Individuals maintain control over the space on a relatively permanent basis; ownership is often involved.	A family's house, a bedroom, a clubhouse, a dorm room, a study
Secondary	*Moderate:* Individuals who habitually use a space come to consider it to be "theirs." Reaction to intrusions is milder.	*Temporary but recurrent:* Others may use the space, but must vacate the area if the usual occupant requests.	A table in a bar, a seat in a classroom, a regularly used parking space, the sidewalk in front of your home
Public	*Low:* Although the occupant may prevent intrusion while present, no expectation of future use exists.	*None:* The individual or group uses the space only on the most temporary basis and leaves behind no markers.	Elevator, beach, public telephone, playground, park, bathroom stall, restaurant counter

Source: The Environment and Social Behavior by Irving Altman, Brooks/Cole Publishing Company, 1976.

which they had primary responsibility became "their controls," and they were wary when any of the other crew members would carry out procedures in their area. Haise, more so than either Lovell and Swigert, became attached to *Aquarius,* the lunar excursion module. When the time came to jettison the module prior to their descent, Haise collected small objects as momentos, and mission control remarked, "Farewell, *Aquarius,* and we thank you" (Lovell & Kluger, 1994, p. 329).

Like so many animals—birds, wolves, lions, seals, geese, and even seahorses—human beings develop proprietary orientations toward certain geographical locations and defend these areas against intrusion by others. A person's home, a preferred seat in a classroom, a clubhouse, a football field, and *Aquarius* are all **territories**—specific areas that an individual or group claims, marks, and defends against intrusion by others.

When people establish a territory, they generally try to control who is permitted access. As Irwin Altman noted, however, the degree of control depends on the type of territory (see Table 14-3). Control is highest for *primary territories*—areas that are maintained and "used exclusively by individuals or groups . . . on a relatively permanent basis" (Altman, 1975, p. 112). Individuals maintain only a moderate amount of control over their *secondary territories*. These

territory A specific geographic area that individuals or groups of individuals claim, mark, and defend against intrusion by others.

areas are not owned by the group members, but because the members use such an area regularly, they come to consider it "theirs." College students, for example, often become very territorial about their seats in a class (Haber, 1980, 1982). Control over *public territories* is even more limited. Occupants can prevent intrusion while they are physically present, but they relinquish all claims when they leave. A bathroom stall or a spot on the beach can be claimed when occupied, but when the occupant leaves, another person can step in and claim the space. (B. B. Brown, 1987, thoroughly reviewed much of the work on human territoriality.)

Group Territories

Territoriality is, in many cases, a group-level process. Instead of an individual claiming an area and defending it against other individuals, a group will lay claim to its turf and prevent other groups from using it. South American howler monkeys, for example, live together in bands of up to 20 individuals, and these groups forage within a fairly well-defined region. The bands themselves are cohesive and free of internal strife, but when another group of howlers is encountered during the day's wandering, a fight begins. Among howlers, this territorial defense takes the form of a "shouting match," in which the members of the two bands simply howl at the opposing group until one band—usually the invading band—retreats. Boundaries are rarely violated, because each morning and night, the monkeys raise their voices in a communal and far-carrying howling session (Carpenter, 1958).

Human groups have also been known to territorialize areas. Classic sociological analyses of gangs, for example, have often highlighted the tendency for young men to join forces in defense of a few city blocks that they considered to be their turf (Thrasher, 1927; W. F. Whyte, 1943; Yablonsky, 1962). Many gangs took their names from a street or park located at the very core of their claimed sphere of influence and sought to control areas around this base. Contemporary gangs, despite changes in size, violence, and involvement in crime, continue to be rooted to specific locations. Gangs in San Diego, California, for example, can be traced to specific geographical origins: the Red Steps and the Crips to Logan Heights, and the Sidros to San Ysidro (W. B. Sanders, 1994).

Gangs mark their territories through the placement of graffiti, or "tags," and also attack intruders. Philadelphia researchers found that the number of graffiti mentioning the local gang's name increased as one moved closer and closer to the gang's home base, suggesting that the graffiti served as *territorial markers,* warning intruders of the dangers of encroachment. This marking, however, was not entirely successful, for neighboring gangs would occasionally invade a rival's territory to spray-paint their own names over the territorial markers of the home gang or, at least, to append a choice obscenity. In fact, the frequency of graffiti attributable to outside groups provided an index of group power and prestige, for the more graffiti written by opposing gangs in one's territory, the weaker was the home gang (Ley & Cybriwsky, 1974b).

Human groups also maintain secondary and public territories. People at the beach, for example, generally stake out their claim by using beach towels, coolers, chairs, and other personal objects (Edney & Jordan-Edney, 1974). These temporary territories tend to be circular, and larger groups command bigger territories than smaller groups. Groups also create territories when they interact in public places, for in most cases, nonmembers are reluctant to break through group boundaries. Just as individuals are protected from unwanted social contact by their invisible bubble of personal space, so groups seem to be surrounded by a sort of "shell" or "membrane" that forms an invisible boundary for group interaction. Various labels have been used to describe this public territory, including **group space** (Edney & Grundmann, 1979; Minami & Tanaka, 1995), *interactional territory* (Lyman & Scott, 1967), *temporary group territory* (Edney & Jordan-Edney, 1974), *jurisdiction* (Roos, 1968), and *group personal space* (Altman, 1975). No matter what this boundary is called, the evidence indicates that it often effectively serves to repel intruders.

Eric Knowles examined the impermeability of groups by placing two or four confederates in a hallway (Knowles, 1973). Participants who wished to move through this space were forced either to walk between the interactants or to squeeze through the approximately 2-foot space between the group and the hallway wall. Knowles found that 75% of the passersby chose to avoid walking through the group, but this figure dropped to about 25% in a control condition in which the interacting individuals were replaced by waste barrels. Knowles and his colleagues (Knowles, Kreuser, Haas, Hyde, & Schuchart, 1976) also discovered that when passing by an alcove that was occupied by a group, people would shift their path to increase the distance between themselves and the group. People begin invading a group's public territory only if the distance between interactants becomes large (Cheyne & Efran, 1972) or if the group is perceived as a crowd rather than as a single entity (Knowles & Bassett, 1976). Furthermore, mixed-sex groups whose members are conversing with one another seem to have stronger boundaries (Cheyne & Efran, 1972), as do groups whose members are exhibiting strong emotions (Lindskold, Albert, Baer, & Moore, 1976).

BENEFITS OF TERRITORIES   Studies of territoriality in prisons (Glaser, 1964), naval ships (Heffron, 1972; Roos, 1968), neighborhoods (Newman, 1972), and dormitories (Baum & Valins, 1977) have suggested that people feel far more comfortable when their groups can territorialize their living areas. For example, Andrew Baum, Stuart Valins, and their associates confirmed the benefits of territories in their studies of college students who were randomly assigned to one of two types of dormitories. Many lived in the more traditionally designed, corridor-style dorm, which featured 17 double-occupancy rooms per floor. These residents could only claim the bedrooms they shared with their roommates as their territories. In contrast, students who lived in the suite-style dorms controlled a fairly well-defined territory that included a private space shared with a roommate as well as a bathroom and lounge shared with several suitemates (Baum & Davis, 1980; Baum, Davis, & Valins, 1979; Baum, Harpin, & Valins, 1975).

---

group space A temporary spatial boundary that forms around interacting groups and serves as a barrier to unwanted intrusion by nonmembers.

Even though nearly equal numbers of individuals lived on any floor in the two types of designs, students in the corridor-style dormitories reported feeling more crowded, complained of their inability to control their social interactions with others, and emphasized their unfulfilled needs for privacy. Suite-style dorm residents, on the other hand, developed deeper friendships with their suitemates, worked with one another more effectively, and even seemed more sociable when interacting with people outside the dormitory. Baum and Valins concluded that these differences stemmed from the corridor-style dorm residents' inability to territorialize areas that they had to use repeatedly.

TERRITORIES AND INTERGROUP CONFLICT Group members often feel more comfortable when they can establish a territory for their group, but territoriality can be a source of conflict between groups. All kinds of intergroup conflicts—from disputes between neighbors, to drive-by gang shootings, to civil wars, to wars between nations—are rooted in disputes over territories (Ardry, 1970). Such conflicts may be based on ancient group traditions. Because most human cultures harvest the animals and plants from the land around them, they establish control over certain geographical areas (Altman & Chemers, 1980). Territories are also defended for symbolic reasons. A group's power is often defined by the quality and size of the space it controls, so groups protect their turf as a means of protecting their reputations. An urban gang, for example, must be ready to attack intruding gangs because "a gang cannot lay any legitimate claim to public areas otherwise" (W. B. Sanders, 1994, p. 18). Most drive-by shootings are territorial disputes, occurring when the members of one gang deliberately enter an area controlled by a rival gang and shoot a member of that gang. Disputes over territories are often one-sided, however, for groups that are defending their territory usually triumph over groups that are invading territories (see Focus 14-2).

Territoriality Within Groups

Territoriality also operates at the level of each individual in the group. Although members develop attachment to the group's space, they also develop spatial attachments to specific areas within the group space (Moser & Uzzell, 2003). Such *individual territories* help group members maintain their privacy by providing them with a means of reducing contact with others. As Altman (1975) noted, depending on the situation, people prefer a certain amount of contact with others, and interaction in excess of this level produces feelings of crowding and invasion of privacy. The student in the classroom who is distracted by a jabbering neighbor, employees who are unable to concentrate on their jobs because of their noisy officemates' antics, and the wife who cannot enjoy reading a novel because her husband is playing the stereo too loud are all receiving excessive inputs from another group member. If they moderated their accessibility by successfully establishing and regulating a territorial boundary, they could achieve a more satisfying balance between contact with others and solitude.

Territories also work as organizers of group members' relationships (Edney, 1976). Once we know the location of others' territories, we can find or avoid

FOCUS 14-2   The Home Advantage: Real or Myth?

We didn't rally them there. We never went looking for trouble. We only rallied on our own street, but we always won there.
–Doc, leader of the Nortons (W. F. Whyte, 1943, p. 51)

When individuals and groups establish a proprietary claim to a place, they usually strive to control who is allowed to enter. Nations patrol their borders to make certain that people from neighboring countries cannot enter the country easily. Neighborhood associations erect fences and gates to keep others out. When families move into a new home or apartment, they often install locks and elaborate burglar alarms to prevent intrusions by nonmembers. Students who find someone sitting in their usual chair will ask the intruder to leave (Haber, 1980).

These territorial disputes, curiously enough, most often end with the defender of the territory vanquishing the intruder—the **home advantage.** Case studies of street gangs, for example, find that defending groups usually succeed in repelling invading groups, apparently because they are more familiar with the physical layout of the area and have access to necessary resources (W. F. Whyte, 1943). One member of a gang in New York explained that his group never lost a fight ("rally") so long as it took place on his group's turf:

> Once a couple of fellows in our gang tried to make a couple of girls on Main Street. The boy friends of these girls chased our fellows back to Norton Street. Then we got together and chased the boy friends back to where they came from. They turned around and got all Garden Street, Swift Street, and Main Street to go after us. . . . It usually started this way. Some kid would get beaten up by one of our boys. Then he would go back to his street and get his gang. They would come over to our street, and we would rally them. . . . I don't remember that we ever really lost a rally. Don't get the idea that we never ran away. We ran sometimes. We ran like hell. They would come over to our street and charge us. We might scatter, up roofs, down cellars, anywhere. We'd get ammunition there. . . . Then we would charge them—we had a good charge. They might break up, and then we would go back to our end of the street and wait for

them to get together again. . . . It always ended up by us chasing them back to their street. We didn't rally them there. We never went looking for trouble. We only rallied on our own street, but we always won there. (W. F. Whyte, 1943, p. 51)

Individuals, too, are often more assertive when they are within their own territorial confines rather than encroaching on others' turf. College students working with another student on a cooperative task spent more time talking, felt more "resistant to control," and were more likely to express their own opinions when they were in their own room rather than in their partner's room (Conroy & Sundstrom, 1977; Edney, 1975; R. B. Taylor & Lanni, 1981). Individuals and groups seem to gain strength and resolve when the dispute takes place on their home territory, even if they are encountering an opponent who is physically stronger or more socially dominant.

This home advantage also influences the outcome of sporting events, for the home team is more frequently the victor than the loser (Schlenker, Phillips, Boniecki, & Schlenker, 1995a). When a basketball team must travel to the rival team's home court to play, they often make more errors, score fewer points, and end up the losers rather than the winners of the contest (B. Schwartz & Barsky, 1977). This advantage becomes even greater when the visiting team must travel longer distances and when the fans watching the game support the home team and boo the opponent (Courneya & Carron, 1991; Greer, 1983). Playing at home, however, can become something of a disadvantage in rare circumstances. When athletes play must-win games on their home field and they fear that they will fail, the pressure to win may become too great. And when a team is playing a series of games and it loses an early game at home, it may lose its home advantage to the emboldened adversary. Overall, however, groups tend to win at home (for more details, see Baumeister, 1984, 1985, 1995; Baumeister & Showers, 1986; Schlenker et al., 1995a, 1995b).

---

home advantage The tendency for individuals and groups to gain an advantage over others when interacting in their home territory.

them with greater success. Furthermore, because we often grow to like people we interact with on a regular basis, people with contiguous territories tend to like one another (Moreland, 1987). Territories also work to regularize certain group activities—such as preparing and eating food, sleeping, or studying—by providing a place for these activities. Finally, territories define what belongs to whom; without a sense of territory, the concept of stealing would be difficult to define, because one could not be certain that the objects carried off actually belonged to someone else.

Territories also help individual group members define and express a sense of personal identity. Office walls often display posters, diplomas, crude drawings produced by small children, pictures of loved ones, or little signs with trite slogans, even when company regulations specifically forbid such personalizing markings. Although such decorations may seem insignificant to the chance visitor, to the occupant of the space, they have personal meaning and help turn a drab, barren environment into home.

Researchers studied personal territories by photographing the walls over the beds of students living in campus dormitories. As an incidental finding, they discovered that most of the decorations on these walls fit into one of the categories listed in Table 14-4. They also found that students who eventually dropped out of school seemed to mark their walls more extensively—particularly in the categories of personal relations and music and theater—than students who stayed in school. Although "stay-ins" used fewer markers, their decorations revealed greater diversity, cutting across several categories. Whereas a dropout's wall would feature dozens of skiing posters or high school memorabilia, the stay-in's decorations might include syllabi, posters, wall hangings, plants, and family pho-

TABLE 14-4 Displays and decorations used by students to mark personal territories in dorm rooms

Category	Examples of Markers and Identifiers
Entertainment or equipment	Bicycles, skis, radios, stereos, climbing gear, tennis rackets, computers, phones
Personal relations	Pictures of friends and family, flowers, photographs of vacations, letters, drawings by siblings
Values	Religious or political posters, bumper stickers, ecology signs, flags, sorority signs
Abstract	Prints or posters of flowers, landscapes, art reproductions, cartoons
Reference items	Schedules, syllabi, calendars, maps
Music or theater	Posters of ballet, pictures of rock groups, theater posters
Sports	Ski posters, pictures of athletes, motorcycle races, magazine covers, hiking posters
Idiosyncratic	Handmade items (wall hangings, paintings), plants, unique items (e.g., stolen road signs), animal skins, stuffed animals

Source: "Privacy Regulation, Territorial Displays, and Effectiveness of Individual Functioning" by A. Vinsel, B. B. Brown, I. Altman, and C. Foss, *Journal of Personality and Social Psychology,* 1980, 1104–1115. Copyright 1980 by the American Psychological Association.

tos. The researchers concluded that the wall decorations of dropouts "reflected less imagination or diversity of interests and an absence of commitment to the new university environment" (Hansen & Altman, 1976; Vinsel, Brown, Altman, & Foss, 1980, p. 1114).

TERRITORY AND STATUS The size and quality of individuals' territories within a group often indicates their social status within the group. In undifferentiated societies, people rarely divide up space into "yours," "mine," and "ours." The Basarawa of Africa, for example, do not make distinctions between people on the basis of age, sex, or prestige. Nor do they establish primary territories or build permanent structures (Kent, 1991). But stratified societies with leaders, status hierarchies, and classes are territorial. Moreover, the size and quality of the territories held by individuals tend to correspond to their status within society. The political and social elite in the community live in large, fine homes rather than small, run-down shacks (Cherulnik & Wilderman, 1986). Executives with large offices hold a higher, more prestigious position with the company than executives with small offices (Durand, 1977). Prison inmates who control the most desirable portions of the exercise yard enjoy higher status than individuals who cannot establish a territory (A. H. Esser, 1973). As one informal observer has noted, in many large corporations, the entire top floor of a company's headquarters is reserved for the offices of the upper echelon executives and can only be reached by a private elevator (Korda, 1975). Furthermore, within this executive area, offices swell in size and become more lavishly decorated as the occupant's position in the company increases. Substantiating these informal observations, a study of a large chemical company headquarters, a university, and a government agency found a clear link between office size and status (Durand, 1977). The correlation between size of territory and position in each group's organization chart was .81 for the company, .79 for the government agency, and .29 for the university.

The link between territory and dominance in small groups tends to be more variable. Several studies have suggested that territory size increases as status increases (A. H. Esser, 1973; Sundstrom & Altman, 1974). Other studies, however, indicated that territory size seems to decrease as status in the group increases (A. H. Esser, 1968; A. H. Esser, Chamberlain, Chapple, & Kline, 1965). Eric Sundstrom and Irwin Altman (1974) suggested that these contradictory results occur because territorial boundaries are more fluid in small groups. In one study that they conducted at a boys' rehabilitation center, they asked each participant to rank the other boys in terms of ability to influence others. Also, an observer regularly passed through the residence bedrooms, lounge, TV area, and bathrooms and recorded territorial behaviors. The boys evaluated each area to determine which territories were more desirable than others.

Sundstrom and Altman found evidence of the territory–dominance relation, but the strength of this relation varied over time. During the first phase of the project, the high-status boys maintained clear control over more desirable areas, but when two of the most dominant boys were removed from the group, the remaining boys competed with one another for both status and space. By the end of the tenth week, however, the group had quieted back down, although certain highly dominant members continued to be disruptive. When formal observations were finally terminated, the available evidence suggested that the group's territorial structures were once more beginning to stabilize.

These findings suggest that dominance–territory relations, like most group processes, are dynamic. In many small groups, the higher status members possess larger and more aesthetically pleasing territories, but chaotic intermember relations or abrupt changes in membership can create discontinuities in territorial behavior. Moreover, the hostility that surfaced in the group when spatial claims were disputed suggests that territories can work as tension reducers by clarifying the nature of the social situation and increasing opportunities for maintaining privacy.

TERRITORY AND STRESS IN EXTREME AND UNUSUAL ENVIRONMENTS
Groups often find themselves in an *EUE*—an *Extreme and Unusual Environment* (Suedfeld & Steel, 2000). During the International Geophysical Year (1957–1958), for example, several countries sent small groups of military and civilian personnel to outposts in Antarctica. These groups were responsible for collecting various data concerning that largely unknown continent, but the violent weather forced the staff to remain indoors most of the time. Equipment malfunctioned regularly, radio contact was limited, and water rationing restricted bathing and laundering. As months went by and these conditions remained, interpersonal friction often surfaced, and the group members found themselves arguing over trivial issues. The members summarized their group malaise with the term *antarcticitis*—lethargy, low morale, grouchiness, and boredom brought on by their unique living conditions (Gunderson, 1973; see also Carrere & Evans, 1994; Stuster, 1996).

These Antarctic groups are by no means unique, for accounts of sailors confined in submarines (Weybrew, 1963), divers living in Sealab (Helmreich, 1974; Radloff & Helmreich, 1968), astronauts in a spacecraft (Sandal, Vaernes, Bergan, Warncke, & Ursin, 1996), work teams on large naval ships (Luria, 1990), and crews on space stations (Stuster, 1996) have reported evidence of stress produced by EUEs. Although technological innovations make survival in even the most hostile environments possible, groups living in these space-age settings must learn to cope with age-old problems of interpersonal adjustment. Leaders must make certain that group members remain active and busy, and conflicts must be handled quickly and decisively. Groups that achieve high levels of teamwork tend to be more successful than ones with rigid, traditional hierarchies. Attention to spatial concerns, however, is also critical, for groups that develop individual and group territories tend to prosper, whereas those that fail to territorialize their spaces founder (Harrison, Clearwater, & McKay, 1991; Harrison & Connors, 1984; Leon, 1991; Palinkas, 1991).

Irwin Altman, William Haythorn, and their colleagues at the Naval Medical Research Institute in Bethesda, Maryland, studied territoriality in EUEs by confining pairs of volunteers to a 12-by-12-foot room equipped with beds, a toilet cabinet, and a table and chairs (see Altman, 1973, 1977; Haythorn, 1973). The groups worked for several hours each day at various tasks, but were left to amuse themselves with card games and reading the rest of the time. The men in the isolation condition never left their room during the 10 days of the experiment;

matched pairs in a control condition were permitted to eat their meals at the base mess and sleep in their regular barracks.

The members of isolated groups quickly claimed particular bunks as theirs. Furthermore, this territorial behavior increased as the experiment progressed, with the isolated pairs extending their territories to include specific chairs and certain positions around the table. Not all of the groups, however, benefited by establishing territories. In some of the groups, territories structured the group dynamics and eased the stress of the situation, but in other dyads, these territories worked as barricades to social interaction and exacerbated the strain of isolation. Overall, withdrawal and time spent sleeping increased across the 10 days of the study, whereas time spent in social interaction decreased. Other measures revealed worsened task performance and heightened interpersonal conflicts, anxiety, and emotionality for isolates who drew a "psychological and spatial 'cocoon' around themselves, gradually doing more things alone and in their own part of the room" (Altman & Haythorn, 1967, p. 174).

Altman and his colleagues followed up these provocative findings in a second experiment by manipulating three aspects of the group environment: (1) availability of privacy (half of the groups lived and worked in a single room; the remaining groups had small adjoining rooms for sleeping, napping, reading, etc.); (2) expected duration of the isolation (pairs expected the study to last either 4 days or 20 days); and (3) amount of communication with the outside world. Although the study was to last for 8 days for all the pairs, more than half terminated their participation early. Altman explained this high attrition rate by suggesting that the aborting groups tended to "misread the demands of the situation and did not undertake effective group formation processes necessary to cope with the situation" (1973, p. 249). On the first day of the study, these men tended to keep to themselves, never bothering to work out any plans for coping with what would become a stressful situation. Then, as the study wore on, they reacted to increased stress by significantly strengthening their territorial behavior, laying increased claim to particular areas of the room. They also began spending more time in their beds, but they seemed simultaneously to be increasingly restless. Access to a private room and an expectation of prolonged isolation only added to the stress of the situation and created additional withdrawal, maladaptation, and eventual termination (Altman, Taylor, & Wheeler, 1971).

Groups that lasted the entire 8 days seemed to use territoriality to their advantage in structuring their isolation. On the first day, they defined their territories, set up schedules of activities, and agreed on their plan of action for getting through the study. Furthermore, the successful groups tended to relax territorial restraints in the later stages of the project, thereby displaying a greater degree of positive interaction. As Altman (1977) described,

> The epitome of a successful group was one in which the members, on the first or second day, laid out an eating, exercise, and recreation schedule; constructed a deck of playing cards, a chess set, and a Monopoly game out of paper. (p. 310)

The men who adapted "decided how they would structure their lives over the expected lengthy period of isolation" (Altman, 1977, p. 310). Although territorial behavior worked to the benefit of some of the groups, the last-minute attempts of some of the faltering groups to organize their spatial relations failed to improve their inadequate adaptation to the isolation.

Groups in Context: Beyond Apollo 13

The Apollo 13 astronauts were not the first group to face difficult environmental circumstances. For centuries, explorers have hiked, sailed, flown, and rocketed from their homes to distant lands and planets, and many of these groups have endured very long periods of isolation in harsh climates. Sir Ernest Shackleton and the crew of *Endurance* survived the destruction of their ship on an ice floe in the Antarctic. Fridtjof Nansen and Hjalmar Johansen spent 9 months in a hut in the Arctic. Teams of divers have lived for weeks on end in Sealab, 200 feet beneath the ocean's surface. NASA's crews have endured for months in space, and plans are being laid for a 3-year voyage to Mars that will begin as soon as 2020 (Bechtel, 2002; Stuster, 1996).

These groups survived and achieved their goals because they did not overlook the impact of the environment on their groups. Whereas harsh environments and circumstances overwhelm lone individuals, groups are capable of overcoming the limiting conditions created by these environmental stressors. Some groups may not survive in a hostile environment, but others respond to stress by becoming better groups—more organized, more cohesive, and more efficient. Certainly these groups experience conflicts, and some degenerate as members continually squabble over insignificant matters. But many groups not only persevere in these adverse circumstances; they find the experience to be exhilarating. Groups like Apollo 13 and the Shackleton explorers have faced disaster, death, and ruin at each turn, yet their autobiographical accounts of their experience speak eloquently about their adventure—which they do not regret, but instead describe as "a cherished and important part of their life, perceived as an impetus to growing, strengthening, and deepening, to be remembered with pride and enjoyment" (Suedfeld & Steel, 2000, p. 229).

SUMMARY IN OUTLINE

❖ **How does the social and physical environment influence groups and their dynamics?**

1. An environmental approach recognizes that individuals and their groups are embedded in a physical and social setting, and that the characteristics of that setting can substantially influence group dynamics.

2. Features of the natural environment and artificial, built environments, such as extremes in temperature and noise, information overload, and dangerousness, can engender *stress* in groups and undermine performance.

   • High temperatures are linked to loss of attention as well as a number of other unpleasant consequences, including discomfort, aggression, and reduced productivity. Extremes in heat and cold are also physically hazardous.

- Group members can cope with exposure to noise for a short duration, but prolonged exposure is associated with psychological and physical difficulties.

- Physical settings are often said to create a distinctive cognitive and emotional reaction in people (*ambiance*). People generally prefer positive, stimulating environments, but excessive stimulation can lead to *overload*.

- Groups that must live or work in dangerous settings adapt by improving communication and teamwork. Groups that do not emphasize a team approach in such environments, such as the 1996 expeditions to Mount Everest, are less likely to escape such situations unharmed.

3. Barker, after studying many groups in their natural locations, concluded that most behavior is determined by the *behavior setting* in which it occurs.

- The boundaries, components, and programs of such settings define the functions of the situation and the type of behaviors performed in it.

- Behavior settings that lack *synomorphy* are inefficient and distressing.

- *Staffing theory* describes the causes and consequences of understaffing and overstaffing.

4. Some groups work and interact in spaces that need to be redesigned to maximize the fit between the people and the place. The kind of space needed by a group will depend on the type of task the groups must accomplish.

❖ What is the ecology of a group?

1. Researchers who study the ecology of small groups explore how individuals interact with and adapt to the group habitat.

2. Studies of *personal space* suggest that group members prefer to keep a certain distance between themselves and others.

- Closer distances are associated with greater intimacy, so space requirements tend to increase as the situation becomes less intimate. The five interpersonal zones are the intimate, personal, social, public, and remote zones.

- The *equilibrium model of communication* predicts that individuals will moderate their distances to achieve the desired level of intimacy, but researchers have also found that variations in space are linked to the gender, status, and cultural background of the interactants.

3. *Density* describes the number of people per unit of space, whereas *crowding* is a psychological reaction to high physical density.

4. Crowding is exacerbated by a number of factors, including cognitive processes that prompt individuals to make attributions about the causes of their arousal, group members' overall evaluation of the high-density setting (the *density–intensity hypothesis*), perceptions of control, and the degree to which others interfere with task performance.

5. Seating arrangements make up an important part of the ecology of small groups. *Sociopetal* spaces tend to encourage interaction, whereas *sociofugal* patterns discourage interaction. People generally prefer interaction-promoting, sociopetal patterns, but these preferences vary with the type of task being attempted and the gender of the interactants.

6. Seating arrangements significantly influence patterns of attraction, communication, and leadership. For example, in

many groups, individuals tend to speak immediately after the person seated opposite them (the *Steinzor effect*), and leadership is closely associated with sitting at the end of the table (the *head-of-the-table effect*).

❖ **What are the causes and consequences of groups' tendency to establish territories?**

1. Like many other animals, humans establish *territories*—geographical locations that an individual or group defends against intrusion by others.

2. Altman distinguished between primary territories, secondary territories, and public territories.
   • Various groups, including gangs, territorialize areas; they prevent nongroup members from entering them and they mark them in various ways.
   • Studies of *group space* suggest that groups, like individuals and their personal space, are surrounded by an interaction boundary that prevents nongroup members from approaching too closely.

   • Individuals feel more comfortable when their groups can territorialize their living areas. Territories promote adjustment and reduce stress, but they also promote intergroup conflict, as in the case of gang-related territoriality.
   • Groups with a *home advantage* tend to outperform groups that are outside their territories.

3. Individual members of the group establish their own personal territories within the group's territory.
   • Personal territories fulfill privacy, organizing, and identity functions for individual members. Territorial markings, for example, are associated with membership stability.
   • Higher status individuals generally control larger and more desirable territories; changes in status hierarchies can disrupt the allocation of territory.

4. A group's capacity to adapt and even thrive in extreme and unusual environments (EUEs) depends on its members' judicious management of the environment, including territories.

FOR MORE INFORMATION

Chapter Case: Apollo 13

■ *Apollo 13: The NASA Mission Reports,* edited by Robert Godwin (2000), provides complete documentation of the mission, including press releases, transcripts of the crew debriefing, the text of the committee investigations of the cause of the accident, and recordings of the crew transmissions during the flight.

■ *Lost Moon: The Perilous Journey of Apollo 13,* by Jim Lovell and Jeffrey Kluger (1994), is a forthright summary of the Apollo 13 mission, with details about the group's dynamics and

relations with ground control teams and family members.

Groups in Context

■ *Handbook of Environmental Psychology,* edited by Daniel Stokols and Irwin Altman (1987), contains chapters written by leading researchers and theorists in the field of person–environment relations. The 22 chapters in Volume One focus on basic processes, and the 21 chapters in Volume Two consider applications and cross-cultural implications. The

2002 edition of the *Handbook of Environmental Psychology,* edited by Robert B. Bechtel and Arzah Churchman, provides a comprehensive update of the field that supplements the 1987 handbook.

■ *Personal Space,* by Robert Sommer (1969), takes an entertaining look at interpersonal distancing processes.

Small-Group Ecology and Territoriality

■ *The Environment and Social Behavior,* by Irwin Altman (1975), remains the definitive analysis of privacy, personal space, territoriality, and crowding in groups.

Groups in Extreme and Unusual Environments

■ *Bold Endeavors: Lessons from Polar and Space Exploration,* by Jack Stuster (1996), draws on interviews, historical documentation, and empirical research to develop a comprehensive, detailed analysis of the dynamics of groups that live and work in atypical environments, such as bases in Antarctica and space stations.

■ "The Environmental Psychology of Capsule Habitats," by Peter Suedfeld and G. Daniel Steel (2000), examines the social and psychological consequences of prolonged stays in secluded and dangerous environments.

MEDIA RESOURCES

 Visit the Group Dynamics companion website at http://psychology.wadsworth .com/forsyth4e to access online resources for your book, including quizzes, flash cards, web links, and more!

15

GROUPS AND CHANGE

CHAPTER OVERVIEW

People often rely on groups to improve their psychological adjustment and social relations. Groups, by their very nature, provide their members with information, support, and guidance, and so many personal and interpersonal problems can be resolved more readily when confronted in a group rather than alone.

❖ What are some of the ways that groups are used to help members change?

❖ How do groups promote change?

❖ How effective are groups in bringing about change?

The Therapy Group: Groups as Interpersonal Resources

The psychotherapy group included Ann, John, Gene, Bob, Linda, Carl, Jerome, Barry, Ida, Dan, Ted, and two facilitators, Dr. C. and Dr. F. The members were all united by their desire to change themselves for the better. John, for example, was trying to recover from a string of failed relationships. He had spent some time in the military, was in college, but felt lonely. Gene had a very close, protective relationship with his mother. He believed that she and other women were superior to men, but had trouble achieving a sense of independence. Linda did not get along with her mother, whose constant criticisms made Linda question her own value. Carl was gay and still exploring his sexuality. In addition to several developmental issues, he was also helping many of his friends cope with the health problems caused by AIDS. Ted's problems stemmed from his depression, which was related to a spinal cord injury that prevented him from walking. Others had joined and dropped out of the group over the past 3 years, but the core of the group had remained stable. They met in a comfortable room each week for about an hour to explore their psychological, emotional, and social problems (Forsyth & Corazzini, 2000).

The idea that a group can be used as a change-promoting agent is not a new one. Throughout history, personal change has often been achieved through social mechanisms rather than by individualistic, asocial processes. As early as 1905, a Boston physician arranged for patients who were suffering from tuberculosis to meet in groups to ward off feelings of depression and to discuss ways to overcome their disease (Pratt, 1922). Jacob L. Moreno (1934), who developed sociometry, advocated acting out troubling relationships and feelings in groups. Sigmund Freud (1922) presented a cogent analysis of group processes that provided the foundation for conducting psychoanalysis in groups, and Kurt Lewin (1936) was a champion of group approaches to achieving social and personal change. It was Lewin who stated the basic "law" of change in groups: "It is usually easier to change individuals formed into a group than to change any one of them separately" (1951, p. 228).

This chapter asks three questions about groups and change. First, what are some of the ways that groups are used to achieve change in their members? Second, how do groups and group processes promote change? Third, are groups effective means of bringing about change? The group led by Dr. C. and Dr. F. helped its members, but do groups sometimes do more harm than good?

GROUP APPROACHES TO CHANGE

People join groups to solve many different kinds of problems. Some want to get rid of something—weight, sadness, irrational thoughts, or overwhelming feelings of worthlessness and despair. Others are seeking something—new skills and outlooks, insight into their own characteristics, or a new repertoire of behaviors they can use to improve their relationships with others. Still others seek the strength

TABLE 15-1 Ways groups are used as agents of personal and interpersonal change

Type	Basic Goal	Leader	Examples
Therapy group	Improve psychological functioning and adjustment of individual members	Mental health professional: psychologist, psychiatrist, clinical social worker	Psychoanalytic and Gestalt groups, psychodrama, interpersonal, cognitive–behavioral group therapy
Interpersonal learning group	Help members gain self-understanding and improve their interpersonal skills	Varies from trained and licensed professionals to untrained amateurs	T-groups, encounter groups, seminars and workshops
Self-help group	Help members cope with or overcome specific problems or life crises	Usually a volunteer layperson; many groups do not include a leadership position	Alcoholics Anonymous, Grow (a group for ex-mental patients), support groups for caregivers

they need to resist an addiction or obsession—the temptation to drink alcohol, use drugs, or batter their spouse.

The variety of change-promoting groups reflects the variety of individuals' goals. The early group formats devised by Moreno, Freud, and Lewin have evolved into today's jogging and fitness clubs; consciousness-raising groups; support groups for parents, children, grandparents, and ex-spouses; workshops and leadership seminars; marriage and family counseling groups; religious retreats; self-help groups; psychotherapy groups; and so on. These groups, despite their many varieties, all help individuals to achieve goals that they cannot reach on their own. Moreover, most fit one of the three categories shown in Table 15-1. **Psychotherapy groups** help people overcome troublesome psychological problems. **Interpersonal learning groups** help individuals gain self-understanding and improve their relationships with others. **Self-help groups,** or *mutual support groups,* are voluntarily formed groups of people who help one another cope with or overcome a common problem. But not all change-promoting groups fall neatly into one and only one of these three categories. Many support groups, for example, are formed and organized by health care professionals, but they nonetheless have many of the other properties of member-led self-help groups (Schubert & Borkman, 1991).

---

psychotherapy group (or **group psychotherapy**) Individuals seeking treatment for a psychological problem who meet as a group with a trained mental health professional.

interpersonal learning group A group formed to help individuals extend their self-understanding and improve their relationships with others (e.g., experiential group, growth group).

self-help group (or **mutual support group**) A group of people who meet regularly to help one another cope with or overcome a problem they hold in common.

Group Therapy

Dr. C. and Dr. F. were both trained to help people overcome troublesome psychological and personal problems. Both of them frequently worked with clients in one-on-one psychotherapy sessions, but they also treated some of their clients in group sessions. These sessions involved treating individuals "in groups, with the group itself constituting an important element in the therapeutic process" (Slavson, 1950, p. 42). When such groups were initially proposed, skeptics questioned the wisdom of putting people who were suffering from psychological problems together in one group. How, they asked, could troubled individuals be expected to cope in a group when they had failed individually? How could the therapist guide the therapeutic process in a group? History, however, has proved the skeptics wrong. Group psychotherapy is currently used to treat all types of psychiatric problems, including addictions, thought disorders, depression, eating disorders, post-traumatic stress disorder, and personality disorders (Barlow, Burlingame, & Fuhriman, 2000; Kanas, 1999; S. Long, 1988; Spira, 1997).

Group therapists vary widely in theoretical orientation. Some, for example, are primarily psychoanalytic in orientation, for their basic approach is based on Sigmund Freud's therapeutic principles. Others, in contrast, adopt a more interpersonal perspective that stresses the exploration of the social processes that unfold in the group. But most group therapists are eclectic—they draw on any number of perspectives as they work with the group. Dr. C., for example, encouraged members to explore their emotions, but he would also frequently ask members to consider the parallels between their actions in the group and their reactions to their parents or their children (Forsyth & Corazzini, 2000).

GROUP PSYCHOANALYSIS The first psychotherapy, Sigmund Freud's psychoanalysis, also generated the first group therapy. Psychoanalysis, by tradition, was used with one patient and one therapist who, through directives, free association, interpretation, and transference, helped the patient gain insight into unresolved unconscious conflicts. But in *Group Psychology and the Analysis of Ego,* Freud (1922) recognized that groups, in many cases, become an unconscious means of regaining the security of the family. Some have suggested that Freud himself practiced **group psychoanalysis** when he and his students met to discuss his theories and cases (Kanzer, 1983; Roth, 1993). In such groups, the therapist is very much the leader, for he or she directs the group's discussion during the session, offers interpretations, and summarizes the group's efforts. Just as the goal of individual therapy is the gradual unfolding of repressed conflicts, in group therapy, as members talk about their memories, fantasies, dreams, and fears, they will gain insight into their unconscious motivations.

---

group psychoanalysis An approach to group therapy that is grounded in Sigmund Freud's method of treatment, and so includes a directive therapist who makes use of free association, interpretation, and transference processes.

Freud believed that therapy stimulates **transference**—patients transfer wishes, fantasies, and feelings associated with the significant people in their lives to the therapist. Group psychoanalysis also stimulates transference, but in a group, the therapist and the other group members are included in the process. Members may find themselves reacting to one another inappropriately, but their actions, when examined more closely, may parallel the way they respond to a family member. In the therapy group, for example, Gene explicitly demonstrated transference when he looked at Dr. C. during an emotionally upsetting point in the session and said "I want to hear more from my dad." In psychoanalytic terms,

> Unlike two-person therapy, in which the introjects are slowly brought into consciousness, in the group each member or parts of each member become the projected introjects, and the ensuing communications may be symbolically to a patient's father, mother, sister, brother, or lover. The intensive verbal and nonverbal interchange quickly unmasks the repetitive maladaptive personality traits. Frequently the peers, not the therapist, confront and retaliate against the narcissistic exhibitionist, the dramatic histrionic patient, the overclinging complainer, or the manipulator. (Azima, 1993, p. 394)

Some therapists are more fully Freudian in their orientation than others, but rare is the therapist who does not deal with transference processes, the interpretation of fantasies or dreams, familial tensions, and other latent conflicts during a group session (Forsyth, 2001).

GESTALT GROUPS AND PSYCHODRAMA Frederick ("Fritz") S. Perls, the founder of Gestalt therapy, frequently conducted his therapeutic sessions in groups rather than with single individuals. Perls drew his theoretical principles from Gestalt psychologists, who argued that perception requires the active integration of perceptual information. The word *Gestalt,* which means both "whole" and "shape," suggests that we perceive the world as unified, continuous, and organized. Like Freud, Perls assumed that people often repress their emotions to the point that unresolved interpersonal conflicts turn into "unfinished business." Perls, however, believed that people are capable of self-regulation and great emotional awareness, and he used therapy to help patients reach their potential (Perls, 1969; Perls, Hefferline, & Goodman, 1951).

In some cases, **Gestalt group therapy** is one-to-one Gestalt therapy conducted in a group setting: Group members observe one another's "work," but

---

transference The displacement of emotions from one person to another during the treatment, as when feelings for a parent are transferred to the analyst or feelings about siblings are transferred to fellow group members.

Gestalt group therapy An approach to group therapy in which clients are taught to understand the unity of their emotions and cognitions through a leader-guided analysis of their behavior in the group situation.

they do not interact with each other. More frequently, however, interaction takes place among group members, with the therapist actively orchestrating the events. Many group therapists make use of unstructured interpersonal activities, such as the "hot seat" or the "empty chair," to stimulate members' emotional understanding. When using the *hot seat,* one person in the group sits in the center of the room and publicly works through his or her emotional experiences. The *empty chair* method involves imagining that another person or a part of oneself is sitting in an empty chair and then carrying on a dialogue with that person. These techniques, when properly applied, can trigger strong emotional reactions among members, but Gestalt therapists resist offering interpretations to their patients (Goulding & Goulding, 1979; Greve, 1993).

Psychodrama, developed by Jacob Moreno (1953), also makes use of exercises to stimulate emotional experiences in group members. Moreno conducted therapeutic groups perhaps as early as 1910, and he used the term *group therapy* in print in 1932. Moreno believed that the interpersonal relations that developed in groups provided the therapist with unique insights into members' personalities and proclivities, and that by taking on roles, the members become more flexible in their behavioral orientations. He made his sessions more experientially powerful by developing psychodrama techniques. When *role playing,* for example, members take on the identity of someone else and then act as he or she would in a simulated social situation. *Role reversal* involves playing a role for a period of time before changing roles with another group member. *Doubling* is the assignment of two group members to a single role, often with one member of the pair playing him- or herself. Moreno believed that psychodrama's emphasis on physical action was more involving than passive discussion, and that the drama itself helped members overcome their reluctance to discuss critical issues (Kipper & Ritchie, 2003; Rawlinson, 2000).

INTERPERSONAL GROUP PSYCHOTHERAPY An interpersonal approach to psychological disturbances assumes that many psychological problems, such as depression, anxiety, and personality disorders, can be traced back to *social* sources—particularly, interactions with friends, relatives, and acquaintances. Rather than searching for psychodynamic causes, interpersonal theorists assume that maladaptive behavior results from "an individual's failure to attend to and correct the self-defeating, interpersonally unsuccessful aspects of his or her interpersonal acts" (D. J. Kiesler, 1991, pp. 442–443).

Many group therapists, recognizing the interpersonal basis of psychological problems, use the group setting to help members examine their interpersonal behavior. Irvin D. Yalom's (1995) **interpersonal group psychotherapy** (also

---

psychodrama A therapeutic tool developed by Jacob Moreno that stimulates active involvement in the group session through role playing.

interpersonal group psychotherapy An approach to the treatment of psychological, behavioral, and emotional problems that emphasizes the curative influence of interpersonal learning.

called *interactive group psychotherapy*), for example, uses the group as a "social microcosm," where members respond to one another in ways that are characteristic of their interpersonal tendencies outside of the group. Therapy groups, as groups, display a full array of group dynamics, including social influence, structure, conflict, and development. The therapist takes advantage of the group's dynamics to help members learn about how they influence others and how others influence them. Members do not discuss problems they are facing at home or at work, but instead focus on interpersonal experiences within the group—the *here and now* rather than the *then and there*. When, for example, two members begin criticizing each other, someone uses powerful or bizarre influence tactics, or another refuses to get involved in the group's meetings, therapists prompt group members to examine and explain the members' interactions (Flores, 2002; I. D. Yalom, 1995).

COGNITIVE–BEHAVIORAL THERAPY GROUPS Some therapists, rather than searching for the cause of the problematic behavior in unseen, unconscious conflicts or interpersonal transactions, take a behavioral approach to mental health. This approach assumes that problematic thoughts and behaviors are acquired through experience. Thus, interventions are based on principles derived from learning theories (B. F. Skinner, 1953, 1971). The goals of behavior therapy are defined in terms of desirable cognitions and behaviors that will be encouraged (e.g., expressing positive emotions) versus undesirable cognitions and behaviors that will be extinguished (e.g., drinking alcohol).

Cognitive–behavioral therapy groups use these principles with two or more individuals (Beck, 2002; Liese, Beck, & Seaton, 2002). If Drs.C. and F. were cognitive–behavioral therapists, they would follow a series of standard procedures before, during, and after the group intervention. Prior to treatment, they would measure the members' degree of functioning, using behavioral rating methods, if possible. They would also review with each patient the purpose of the therapy and, in some cases, ask the patient to watch videotaped examples of group therapy sessions. Such *pretherapy reviews* not only create change-enhancing expectancies, but they also help members identify the specific goals of the therapeutic intervention (Higginbotham, West, & Forsyth, 1988). At this point, the therapists might also ask the patients to sign a *behavioral contract* that describes in objective terms the goals the group members are trying to achieve.

During the therapy itself, Drs. F. and C. would rely on a number of behavioral methods, including modeling, rehearsal, and feedback. *Modeling* involves demonstrating particular behaviors while the group members observe. The group leaders may engage in a brief interaction, videotape the interaction, and then play it back to the group and identify the key nonverbal and verbal behaviors. During *rehearsal,* group members practice particular skills themselves, either with one another or through role-playing exercises. These practice sessions can be

------

cognitive–behavioral therapy group The treatment of interpersonal and psychological problems through the application of behavioral principles in a group setting.

videotaped and played back to the group so that the participants can see precisely what they are doing correctly and what aspects of their behavior need improvement. This *feedback* phase involves not only reassurance and praise from the leaders but also support from the other group members (e.g., Franklin, Jaycox, & Foa, 1999; Whittal & McLean, 2002).

Interpersonal Learning Groups

Many psychologists are united in their belief that the human race too frequently fails to reach its full potential. Although our relationships with others should be rich and satisfying, they are more often than not superficial and limiting. Also, although we are capable of profound self-understanding and acceptance, most of us do not understand ourselves very well. These limitations are not so severe that we seek treatment from a psychotherapist, but our lives would be richer if we could overcome them.

Lewin was one of the first to suggest using small groups to teach people interpersonal skills and self-insight. Lewin believed that groups and organizations often fail because their members are not trained in human relations. He therefore recommended close examination of group experiences to give people a deeper understanding of themselves and their groups' dynamics. Other theorists expanded on this basic idea, and by 1965, the human potential movement was in high gear (Back, 1973; Gazda & Brooks, 1985; Lakin, 1972).

TRAINING GROUPS (T-GROUPS) How can people learn about group dynamics? Members could learn the facts about effective interpersonal relations by attending lectures or by reading books about group dynamics (as you are doing now), but Lewin argued that good group skills are most easily acquired by directly experiencing human relations. Hence, he developed specialized **training groups,** or **T-groups.** Lewin discovered the utility of such groups when running educational classes dealing with leadership and group dynamics. At the end of each day, he arranged for observers to discuss the dynamics of the groups with the group leaders who conducted the training sessions. These discussions were usually held in private, until one evening, a few of the group members asked if they could listen to the observers' and leaders' interpretations. Lewin agreed to their request, and sure enough, the participants confirmed Lewin's expectations by sometimes vehemently disagreeing with the observations and interpretations offered by Lewin's observers. However, the animated discussion that followed proved to be highly educational, and Lewin realized that everyone in the group was benefiting enormously from the analysis of the group's processes and dynamics (Highhouse, 2002).

One of the most noteworthy aspects of T-groups is their lack of structure. Although, from time to time, the trainees might meet in large groups to hear lec-

---

training group or **T-group** A skill development training intervention in which individuals interact in unstructured group settings and then analyze the dynamics of that interaction.

tures or presentations, most of the learning takes place in small groups. Even though the group includes a designated leader, often called a *facilitator* or *trainer,* this individual acts primarily as a catalyst for discussion rather than as a director of the group. Indeed, during the first few days of a T-group's existence, group members usually complain about the lack of structure and the ambiguity, blaming the trainer for their discomfort. This ambiguity is intentional, however, for it shifts responsibility for structuring, understanding, and controlling the group's activities to the participants themselves. As the group grapples with problems of organization, agenda, goals, and structure, the members reveal their preferred interaction styles to others. They also learn to disclose their feelings honestly, gain conflict reduction skills, and find enjoyment from working in collaborative relationships.

After Lewin's death in 1947, his colleagues organized the National Training Laboratory (NTL). The laboratory was jointly sponsored by the National Education Association, the Research Center for Group Dynamics, and the Office of Naval Research (ONR). Researchers and teachers at the center refined their training methods in special workshops, or *laboratories*. Although the long-term effectiveness of T-groups is still being debated, training groups continue to play a key role in many organization development interventions (Bednar & Kaul, 1979; M. J. Burke & Day, 1986; R. E. Kaplan, 1979).

GROWTH GROUPS The T-group was a precursor of group techniques designed to enhance spontaneity, increase personal growth, and maximize members' sensitivity to others. As the purpose of the group experience shifted from training in group dynamics to increasing sensitivity, the name changed from T-group to **sensitivity training group,** or **encounter group** (F. Johnson, 1988; Lieberman, 1994).

The humanistic therapist Carl Rogers (1970) was a leader in the development of encounter groups. Rogers believed that most of us lose sight of our basic goodness because our needs for approval and love are rarely satisfied. We reject many aspects of ourselves, deny our failings, and hold our feelings in when interacting with other people. Rogers believed that the encounter group helps us restore our trust in our own feelings, our acceptance of our most personal qualities, and our openness when interacting with others. If Drs. C. and F. were "Rogerians," they would have encouraged the members to "open up" to one another by displaying their inner emotions, thoughts, and worries. Recognizing that the group members probably felt insecure about their social competencies, Drs. C. and F. would have given each one unconditional positive regard and helped them express their feelings by mirroring any statements they made. They would also have used role playing and other exercises to encourage them to experience and express intense feelings of anger, caring, loneliness, and helplessness.

---

sensitivity training group An unstructured group designed to enhance spontaneity, increase personal awareness, and maximize members' sensitivity to others.

encounter group A form of sensitivity training that provides individuals with the opportunity to gain deep interpersonal intimacy with other group members.

Stripped of defensiveness and facades, Rogers believed, group members would encounter each other "authentically" (R. C. Page, Weiss, & Lietaer, 2002).

STRUCTURED LEARNING GROUPS Both T-groups and encounter groups are open-ended, unstructured approaches to interpersonal learning. Members of such groups follow no agenda; they examine events that unfold spontaneously within the confines of the group itself, and give one another feedback about their interpersonal effectiveness when appropriate. **Structured learning groups,** in contrast, are planned interventions that focus on a specific interpersonal problem or skill. Integrating behavioral therapies with experiential learning, the group leaders identify specific learning outcomes before the sessions. They then develop behaviorally focused exercises that will help members practice these targeted skills. In a session on nonverbal communication, for instance, group members may be assigned a partner and then be asked to communicate a series of feelings without using spoken language. During assertiveness training, group members might practice saying no to one another's requests. In a leadership training seminar, group members may be asked to role-play various leadership styles in a small group. These exercises are similar in that they actively involve the group members in the learning process.

Thousands of local and national institutes use structured learning groups in their seminars and workshops. Although the formats of these structured experiences differ substantially, most include the components summarized in Figure 15-1. The leader begins with a brief *orientation* session, in which he or she reviews the critical issues and focuses members on the exercise's goals. Next, the group members *experience* the event or situation by carrying out a structured group exercise. When they have completed the exercise, the members engage in a general *discussion* of their experiences within the group. This phase can be open-ended, focusing on feelings and subjective interpretations, or it, too, can be structured through the use of questioning, information exchange procedures, or videotape recording. This discussion phase should blend into a period of *analysis,* during which the consultant helps group members to identify consistencies in their behavior and the behaviors of others. In many cases, the consultant guides the group's analysis of underlying group dynamics and offers a conceptual analysis that gives meaning to the event. The interpersonal learning cycle ends with *application,* as the group members use their new-found knowledge to enhance their relationships at work and at home.

Self-Help Groups

Instead of seeking help from a mental health professional, the men and women in the therapy group could also have joined a *self-help group*—a voluntary group whose members share a common problem and meet for the purpose of exchang-

---

structured learning group A planned intervention, such as a workshop, seminar, or retreat, focusing on a specific interpersonal problem or skill.

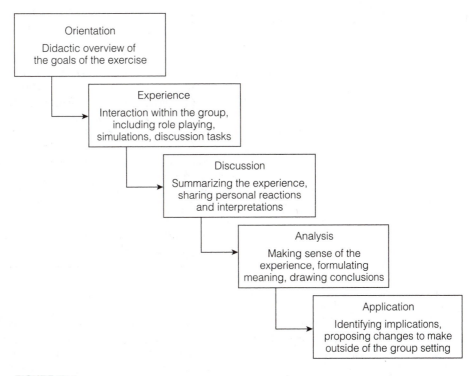

FIGURE 15-1

What are the essential steps in an experiential learning cycle? In most structured learning groups, individuals not only complete some type of active learning exercise, but they also examine their experience carefully, both in an open discussion session and in a guided analysis with the group trainer.

ing social support. Self-help groups, also known as *mutual support groups,* exist for nearly every major medical, psychological, or stress-related problem. There are groups for sufferers of heart disease, cancer, liver disease, and AIDS; groups for people who provide care for those suffering from chronic disease, illness, and disability; groups to help people overcome addictions to alcohol and other substances; groups for children of parents overcome by addictions to alcohol and other substances; and groups for a wide variety of life problems, including groups to help people manage money or time (see Table 15-2). Self-help groups are growing in terms of both numbers and members, with perhaps as many as 10 million people in the United States alone belonging to such groups (G. Goodman & Jacobs, 1994; A. H. Katz, 1993; L. H. Levy, 2000).

These groups differ from each other in many ways, but most are self-governing, with members rather than experts or mental health professionals determining the group's activities. They also tend to stress the importance of treating all members fairly and giving everyone an opportunity to express their

TABLE 15-2 Varieties of self-help groups

Type of Group	Examples
Anti-addiction	Alcoholics Anonymous, Gamblers Anonymous, TOPS (Take Off Pounds Sensibly), Weight Watchers
Family support	In Touch (for parents of children with mental handicaps), Adult Children of Alcoholics, Al-Anon
Medical and rehabilitation	The Bell's Palsy Network, CARE (Cancer Aftercare and Rehabilitation Society), Recovery, Inc. (for recovering psychotherapy patients), Reach to Recovery (for breast cancer patients)
Social rights	Campaign for Homosexual Equality, local chapters of the National Organization for Women, the Gay Activists' Alliance
General social support	Association of the Childless and Childfree, Parents without Partners, Singles Anonymous

viewpoints. The members face a common predicament, problem, or concern, so they are "psychologically bonded by the compelling similarity of member concerns" (M. K. Jacobs & Goodman, 1989, p. 537). These groups value reciprocal helping, for members are supposed to give help to others as well as receive it from others. Self-help groups usually charge little in the way of fees, for in most cases they are not operated by health care professionals. In fact, they often stand in contrast to more traditional forms of treatment, for they arise spontaneously because their members' needs are not being satisfied by existing educational, social, or health agencies. The groups meet at a wide variety of locations in the community, including churches, schools, universities, and private homes. They also meet, in some cases, via computer connections to the Internet. As Focus 15-1 notes, *Internet support groups* provide individuals with advice, support, and information 24 hours a day, 7 days a week (Alexander, Peterson, & Hollingshead, 2003).

Alcoholics Anonymous (AA) is an example of a self-help group. AA was founded by Bill Wilson in 1935. Wilson had tried to quit drinking for years, but no matter what he tried, he always returned to his addiction. After a fourth hospital stay for acute alcoholism, Wilson experienced a profound, almost mystical experience that convinced him that he could overcome his drinking problem. To explain the experience, he examined the writings of psychologists William James and Carl Jung and eventually concluded that such experiences could be triggered by periods of negativity, depression, and helplessness. Wilson then connected with a small spiritual group, the Oxford Group Movement, and with his physician friend William D. Silkworth developed a support system that included self-examination, admitting past wrongs, rebuilding relationships and making amends, and reliance on and helping others.

Wilson's program formed the basis of Alcoholics Anonymous, which grew to be an international organization with millions of members. Despite AA's size,

FOCUS 15-1   Can Groups Give Support Online?

No one should have to face cancer alone.
–Online Cancer Care Support Group
(http://supportgroups.cancercare.org)

Just as information technology has changed the way groups solve problems, collaborate on projects, and make decisions, so too has it altered many self-help groups. Such groups, by tradition, meet regularly at designated locations where members share information and support. Information technology, however, has made it possible for these groups to "meet" across great distances and at any time. Members, instead of leaving their homes and traveling to a meeting, can now take part in a range of group activities using a computer and a connection to the Internet (Tate & Zabinski, 2004). No matter what problem an individual faces—a serious physical illness, stress caused by providing care for an ill family member, a negative life event such as divorce or the death of a loved one, addiction and drug dependency, social rejection, prejudice, or problems of adjustment and mental health—an online group likely exists somewhere on the Internet that can provide self-care information, support, and referral services. Some of these sites are primarily repositories of information about the problem or issue, and may be sponsored by professionals who treat these problems. Others, however, are true self-help groups, for they were created by individuals who all face the same difficulty and are designed to help fellow sufferers connect to and support each other.

Some support groups create *synchronous* communication among members using *Internet relay chat* (IRC) software. Members log into a chat room at a preset time, and then all in attendance can send and receive messages during the session. In many cases, the software identifies all those who are logged into the group by their user name, and members are asked to announce their presence and departure from the group. Other support groups are *asynchronous,* with members using e-mail and electronic bulletin boards to read messages from others and to post messages

and responses to others' postings. Both synchronous and asynchronous groups can be moderated by a group leader who facilitates the discussion (and intervenes to remove content as necessary).

How helpful can these online support groups be, given that they meet in a relatively sterile online world? Studies of online groups for problems ranging from cancer to sexual abuse to psychological disorders suggest that these groups are surprisingly effective, and may even rival face-to-face groups in terms of functionality (Tate & Zabinski, 2004). Participants report that they feel supported and valued by their group and, after taking part in an online session, feel more hopeful about their situation. Members stress the quality and quantity of the information they receive from others in the online community, and instances of inappropriate commentary or hostile postings ("flaming") are rare and inconsequential (J. K. Miller & Gergen, 1998).

Some aspects of the online format may even enhance aspects of a self-help approach to coping with negative events. Because members are not identifiable, they report being able to reveal more intimate information about their experiences and to respond more emotionally to others than they would if interacting face to face. Members of online sessions also tend to exchange more practical advice and factual information than they do in face-to-face sessions, and members value this aspect of online groups as well. They report that the information is useful to them in understanding their condition and in dealing more effectively with their health care providers (Houston, Cooper, & Ford, 2002). Internet support groups are also particularly valuable for individuals whose illness restricts their mobility and for those who are suffering from a stigmatized illness, such as prostate cancer or AIDS. Individuals may feel self-conscious about their condition, but the comfort they experience by joining with others who are "in the same boat" overwhelms this concern about embarrassment (Davison, Pennebaker, & Dickerson, 2000).

change is still achieved through local chapters of alcoholics who meet regularly to review their success in maintaining their sobriety. AA meetings emphasize testimonials, mutual self-help, and adherence to the 12-stage program (the "12 steps") described by the AA doctrine. These steps recommend admitting one's powerlessness over alcohol; surrendering one's fate to a greater power; taking an inventory of personal strengths, weaknesses, and moral failings; and helping others fight their addiction (Flores, 1997).

SOURCES OF CHANGE IN GROUPS

The members of the therapy group led by Dr. C. and Dr. F. changed over the course of their treatment. Ann gained control over her anger and her relationship with her husband. Gene was dating, and no longer expressed inappropriate comments about the female interns who sometimes met with the group. Ted, who used a wheelchair, left the group to begin an internship. He had stopped his self-destructive activities and reported feeling happier and better adjusted. Dan, an athlete who had a severe problem with alcohol addiction, stopped drinking and became one of the more active members of the group. He eventually completed his treatment and enrolled in a PhD program in another state.

The group was a successful one, for the members changed in ways they desired. After many weekly sessions, most of the group members felt that their problems had been corrected. But what was the source of the group's therapeutic power?

Group approaches to change, despite their wide variations in method, structure, and procedure, have certain key elements in common (Ingram, Hayes, & Scott, 2000). Some of these common therapeutic, **curative factors** are equivalent to the change-promoting forces that operate in individualistic, one-on-one therapies, but others are unique to group approaches to change. All therapies, for example, help clients gain self-insight, but only group approaches stimulate interpersonal comparisons and provide members with a forum for practicing their interpersonal skills. All therapies provide clients with support and help, but in groups, members are also sources of help rather than only recipients.

Although no one list of curative factors has been verified by researchers and accepted by practitioners, Table 15-3 summarizes some of the most frequently identified change-promoting factors. Some of these factors, such as giving hope to group members, are more influential during the early stages of the group's history, whereas others become more potent with time (e.g., self-insight). Some focus on cognitive processes, whereas others promote changes in behavior directly. But all these processes, as noted hereafter, combine to generate changes in group mem-

---

curative factor An aspect of group settings that aids and promotes personal growth and adjustment; includes such factors as the installation of hope, universality, imparting of information, altruism, and interpersonal learning.

TABLE 15-3 Factors that promote change in groups

Factor	Definition	Meaning to Member
Universality	Recognition of shared problems, reduced sense of uniqueness	We all have problems.
Hope	Increased sense of optimism from seeing others improve	If other members can change, so can I.
Vicarious learning	Developing social skills by watching others	Seeing others talk about their problems inspired me to talk, too.
Interpersonal learning	Developing social skills by interacting with others	I'm learning to get along better with other people.
Guidance	Offering and accepting advice and suggestions to and from the group	People in the group give me good suggestions.
Cohesion and support	Comfort, confirmation of feelings; acceptance	The group accepts, understands, and comforts me.
Self-disclosure	Revealing personal information to others	I feel better for sharing things I've kept secret for too long.
Catharsis	Releasing pent-up emotions	It feels good to get things off my chest.
Altruism	Increased sense of efficacy from helping others	Helping other people has given me more self-respect.
Insight	Gaining a deeper understanding of oneself	I've learned a lot about myself.

bers' adjustment and well-being (Bloch & Crouch, 1985; T. Butler & Fuhriman, 1983a; Crouch, Bloch, & Wanlass, 1994; Kivlighan & Goldfine, 1991; MacNair-Semands & Lese, 2000; I. D. Yalom, 1995; V. J. Yalom & Vinogradov, 1993.)

Universality and Hope

When individuals face their problems alone, they often blame themselves, or they spend so much time wondering "Why me?" that they fail to identify ways to overcome their problems. Some sink into a depression that saps their motivation, and they end up convinced that their situation is hopeless (Bulman & Wortman, 1977). Groups, however, set the stage for health-promoting social comparison processes. When suffering alone, individuals may not realize that many of their feelings and experiences are relatively common ones. But when surrounded by other people who are similarly suffering, members recognize the *universality* of the problems they face. Self-help groups, in particular, create a sense of shared suffering among members (Lieberman, 1993). Everyone at an AA meeting, for example, publicly states, "I am an alcoholic," and this ritual reassures all the other participants that their problem is shared by others. When people are with others who face similar problems or troubling events, they feel better, in terms of self-esteem and mood, than when they are with dissimilar people (Frable, Platt, & Hoey, 1998).

Social comparison, when directional, can also be a source of reassurance and *hope*. When the group includes individuals who are experiencing particularly negative outcomes, these individuals can serve as targets for *downward social comparison*. Such comparisons reduce group members' own sense of victimization and can raise their overall sense of self-esteem (Wills & Filer, 2000). The group may also include individuals who are coping well with many difficulties, and these *upward social comparison* targets can encourage members by symbolizing the possibility of progress (Buunk, Oldersma, & de Dreu, 2001; S. E. Taylor & Lobel, 1989). Although successful group members—the fellow cancer survivor who is in complete remission, the AA member who has stayed sober for 3 years, or the caregiver who is managing to care for her elderly mother and still attend college—may make some group members feel like failures, they also provide a standard for future gains (Tennen, McKee, & Affleck, 2000). Group members who are successfully dealing with their problems increase all other group members' optimism by elevating two key components of hope identified by C. R. Snyder and his colleagues—a *sense of efficacy* about reaching their goals, and the identification of *multiple pathways* to reach those goals (Snyder, Ilardi, Michael, & Cheavens, 2000). Groups that are structured to elevate members' sense of hope tend to be more powerful agents of change than groups that use other procedures (e.g., Klausner, Snyder, & Cheavens, 2000; Worthington et al., 1997).

Social Learning

When an individual who is striving to change meets with one other person—whether a trained therapist, counselor, friend, or relative—he or she can discuss problems, identify solutions, and receive support and encouragement. But even in the most therapeutic dyads, the individual shares perspectives, feedback, guidance, acceptance, and comfort with only one other person. A larger group, with its multiple members, is richer in terms of its interpersonal and curative resources. Within the social microcosm of the small group, individuals experience a fuller range of interpersonal processes, including feedback about their strengths and weaknesses, pressure to change behaviors that other members find objectionable, role models whose actions they can emulate, and opportunities to practice the very behaviors they are seeking to refine. Of the 10 curative factors in Table 15-3, vicarious learning, interpersonal learning, and guidance are most closely related to social learning processes that help members explore themselves, their problems, and their social relationships with others.

VICARIOUS LEARNING **Social learning theory,** developed by Albert Bandura (1977, 1986), maintains that people can acquire new attitudes and behaviors *vicariously*—by observing and imitating others' actions. This theory, which explains how infants learn their native language, why adolescents adopt the un-

---

social learning theory A conceptualization of learning developed by Albert Bandura that describes the processes by which new behaviors are acquired by observing and imitating the actions displayed by models, such as parents and peers.

healthy habits of their peers, and how viewers of televised violence mimic the aggressive actions they watch, suggests that group members can learn by observing other group members, provided they (1) are motivated to learn from their peers; (2) attend closely to the behavior being modeled by the other group member; (3) are able to remember and reenact the behavior they observed; and (4) are aware that the consequences of the model's behavior are positive rather than negative (Shebilske, Jordon, Goettl, & Paulus, 1998).

Groups provide members with multiple models to emulate, including the leader or leaders. When, for example, group members who are skilled in expressing their feelings deftly describe their emotional reactions, the less verbally skilled members may learn how they, too, can put their feelings into words. When two members who regularly disagree with each other reach an accord, other group members who watch this reconciliation unfold learn how they can resolve interpersonal conflicts. Group leaders can also model desirable behaviors by treating the group members in positive ways and avoiding behaviors that are undesirable (Dies, 1994). In one study, the coleaders of therapy groups modeled social interactions that the group members considered difficult or anxiety provoking. The leaders then helped the group members perform these same behaviors through role playing. Groups that used explicit modeling methods showed greater improvement than groups that only discussed the problematic behaviors (Falloon, Lindley, McDonald, & Marks, 1977).

INTERPERSONAL LEARNING In the therapy group, Gene practiced, in every session, speaking to the women in the group. He improved, with feedback from the group, and eventually developed the skills he needed to maintain a relationship. Linda also learned how to express her feelings of frustration and anger in constructive ways, primarily by watching the way the group's leaders discussed their emotions clearly and carefully.

How did Gene, Linda, and the other members of the therapy group acquire new ways of relating effectively to others? To a large extent, this learning occurs gradually as group members implicitly monitor their impact on the other people in their group and draw conclusions about their own qualities from others' reactions to them. The other group members become, metaphorically, a "mirror" that members use to understand themselves (Cooley, 1902). A group member may begin to think that she has good social skills if the group always responds positively each time she contributes to the group discussion. Another member may decide that he is irritating if his comments are always met with anger and hostility. This indirect feedback helps members perceive themselves more accurately. Individuals who are socially withdrawn, for example, tend to evaluate their social skills negatively even though the other group members view them positively (P. N. Christensen & Kashy, 1998). Individuals also tend to rate themselves as more anxious than others tend to perceive them as being (Marcus, 1988; Marcus & Wilson, 1996). Extended contact with others in a group setting should repair these negative, inaccurate perceptions.

Groups are also very willing to give direct, unambiguous feedback to members when they engage in objectionable or praiseworthy actions (Kivlighan,

1985). Kurt Lewin was one of the first theorists to borrow the term *feedback* from engineering and use it to describe how others' responses to group members served as corrective guides for subsequent actions (Claiborn, Goodyear, & Horner, 2001). The individual who is lonely because he alienates everyone by acting rudely may be told, "You should try to be more sensitive," or "You are always so judgmental, it makes me sick." Some groups exchange so much evaluative information that members withdraw from the group rather than face the barrage of negative feedback (Scheuble, Dixon, Levy, & Kagan-Moore, 1987). Most group leaders, however, are careful to monitor the exchange of information between members so that individuals receive the information they need in positive ways (Morran, Stockton, Cline, & Teed, 1998).

GUIDANCE When group members discuss issues, concerns, problems, and crises, other group members frequently help by providing advice, guidance, and direction. Members of support groups, for example, exchange considerable factual and personal information about their disorder or concern, as well as suggestions for problem management (e.g., LaBarge, Von Dras, & Wingbermuehle, 1998). Group leaders, in addition to guiding the flow of the session through questioning, summarizing, and rephrasing members' statements, also provide information, suggest solutions, confront the members' interpretations of problems, and offer their own interpretation of the causes of the members' problems (C. E. Hill et al., 1988). This guidance ranges from explicit suggestions and directions to suggestions of minor adjustments to deepen an emotional process or cognitive interpretation (Heppner et al., 1994).

Group facilitators, like all group leaders (see Chapter 11), vary considerably along the directive–nondirective dimension. Those who adopt a leader-centered approach—typical of psychoanalytic, Gestalt, and behavioral groups—are more directive. They guide the course of the interaction, assign various tasks to the group members, and occupy the center of the centralized communication network. In some instances, the group members may not even communicate with one another, but only with the group leader. Other facilitators, however, advocate a nondirective style of leadership, in which all group members communicate with one another. These group-oriented approaches, which are typified by interpersonal approaches, encourage the analysis of the group's processes, with the therapist/leader sometimes facilitating the process but at other times providing no direction whatsoever.

Both directive and nondirective approaches are effective, so long as the leaders are perceived to be caring, help members interpret the cause of their problems, keep the group on course, and meet the members' relationship needs (Lieberman & Golant, 2002; Lieberman, Yalom, & Miles, 1973). Moreover, just as effective leaders in organizational settings sometimes vary their interventions to fit the situation, so effective leaders in therapeutic settings shift their methods as the group matures. During the early stages of treatment, members may respond better to a task-oriented leader, whereas in the later stages, a relationship-oriented leader may be more helpful (Kivlighan, 1997).

Several studies have suggested that groups with two leaders are more effective than groups with only one leader. **Coleadership** eases the burdens put on the group's leader (Dugo & Beck, 1997). The two leaders can lend support to each other, and they can also offer the group members their combined knowledge, insight, and experience. Also, male–female teams may be particularly beneficial, as they offer a fuller perspective on gender issues and serve as models of positive but nonromantic heterosexual relationships. The advantages of coleadership, however, are lost if the leaders are unequal in status or engage in power struggles during group sessions (Arnardottir, 2002).

Group Cohesion

Just as cohesion is a key ingredient for effective sports, production, and management teams, so cohesion is a critical ingredient for effective change-promoting groups. Without cohesion, feedback would not be accepted, norms would never develop, and groups could not retain their members. Dorwin Cartwright (1951) suggested that if groups are to be used as change agents, the members should have a strong sense of group identity and belonging; otherwise, the group would not exert sufficient influence over its members. Others, too, have noted that the "cotherapeutic influence of peers" (Bach, 1954, p. 348) in the therapy group requires group cohesion (see also J. D. Frank, 1957).

ACCEPTANCE AND SUPPORT Cohesive groups are superior sources of emotional and social support for their members (Burlingame, Fuhriman, & Johnson, 2001). A cohesive group accepts its members, and this feeling of *acceptance* is considered by many group members to be the most central benefit of group membership (Kivlighan & Mullison, 1988). When a group is cohesive, the members are more engaged in the group and its change-promoting processes. Members rarely miss meetings; they take part in the planning of the group's topics and activities, and they express a sense of closeness with the other members. Avoidance and conflict, in contrast, are clear indicators of a lack of cohesiveness (Kivlighan & Tarrant, 2001; Ogrodniczuk & Piper, 2003). In many cases, members who are hostile and socially inhibited attend sessions infrequently, and as a result, are not sufficiently engaged in the group change process (MacNair-Semands, 2002).

Cohesive groups also provide members with a source of support that they can draw upon outside of the therapy session in times of stress and adversity. Dr. C., for example, would sometimes remind members to rely on the group even when the group was not in session by "putting the group in your pocket: Carry us with you. Rely on us when you need support, guidance, and feel alone" (Marmarosh & Corazzini, 1997, p. 65). When members of a therapeutic group were

---

coleadership Two or more individuals sharing the organizational, directive, and motivational duties of the leadership role.

encouraged to increase their degree of identification with the group and its goals through a series of interventions (including carrying a card that identified them as a member of the group), their collective self-esteem increased relative to individuals in a control condition (Marmarosh & Corazzini, 1997).

COHESION OVER TIME   A group's cohesiveness fluctuates over time, depending on its longevity and stage of development. Even when the group's task is a therapeutic one, time is needed to achieve cohesiveness. In one study, investigators observed and coded the behaviors displayed by adolescents in a program of behavioral change. These groups did not immediately start to work on self-development issues, nor did the group members try to help one another. Rather, the groups first moved through orientation, conflict, and cohesion-building stages before they began to make therapeutic progress (W. F. Hill & Gruner, 1973).

Other studies have also suggested that the success of the group depends to a large extent on its movement through several stages of development. Although these stages receive various labels from various theorists, many accept the five emphasized by Bruce Tuckman (1965)—forming, storming, norming, performing, and adjourning (see Chapter 1, Figure 1-4). During the *forming* stage, individual members are seeking to understand their relationship to the newly formed group and strive to establish clear intermember relations. During the *storming* stage, group members often find themselves in conflict over status and group goals; consequently, hostility, disruption, and uncertainty dominate group discussions. During the next phase (*norming*), the group strives to develop a group structure that increases cohesiveness and harmony. The *performing* stage is typified by a focus on group productivity and decision making. Finally, when the group fulfills its goals, it reaches its last stage of development—*adjourning*. If a group does not move through these stages, its members will not be able to benefit from the experience (MacKenzie, 1994, 1997; I. D. Yalom, 1995).

Dennis Kivlighan and his colleagues illustrated the important impact of group development on therapeutic outcomes by matching interventions to the developmental "maturity" of the group. Group members were given structured help in expressing either anger or intimacy before either the fourth or the ninth group session of their therapy. The information dealing with anger clarified the value of anger as a natural part of group participation and provided suggestions for communicating it. The information dealing with intimacy clarified the value of intimacy in groups and provided suggestions for its appropriate expression toward others. As anticipated, when the interventions were matched to the most appropriate developmental stage—for example, when group members received the information on anger during the storming phase (Session 4) and the information on intimacy during the norming phase (Session 9)—the participants displayed more comfort in dealing with intimacy, more appropriate expressions of intimacy and anger, fewer inappropriate expressions of intimacy, and more congruence between self-ratings and other ratings of interpersonal style (Kivlighan, McGovern, & Corazzini, 1984).

Disclosure and Catharsis

Groups become more unified the more the members engage in **self-disclosure**—the sharing of personal, intimate information with others (Corey & Corey, 1992; Leichtentritt & Shechtman, 1998). When groups first convene, members usually focus on superficial topics and avoid saying anything too personal or provocative. In this *orientation stage,* members try to form a general impression of each other and also make a good impression themselves. In the *exploratory affective stage,* members discuss their personal attitudes and opinions, but they avoid intimate topics. This stage is often followed by the *affective stage,* when a few topics still remain taboo. When the group reaches the final stage, *stable exchange,* all personal feelings are shared (Altman & Taylor, 1973).

Self-disclosure can be something of a challenge for some individuals. Individuals experiencing personality or psychological disturbances, for example, often disclose the wrong sorts of information at the wrong time (J. P. McGuire & Leak, 1980). Men and boys, too, are generally more reserved in their self-disclosure (G. R. Brooks, 1996; Kilmartin, 1994; Shechtman, 1994). Thus, therapists must sometimes take special steps to induce the male members of therapy groups to share personal information about themselves, including modeling disclosure and incorporating disclosure rituals in the group (Horne, Jolliff, & Roth, 1996). Men's reluctance to disclose can even undermine the quality of the group experience for all participants: The more men in the therapeutic group, the fewer benefits are reported by participants (Hurley, 1997).

Self-disclosure and cohesion are reciprocally related. Each new self-disclosure deepens the group's intimacy, and this increased closeness then makes further self-disclosures possible (Agazarian, 2001). By sharing information about themselves, members are expressing their trust in the group and signaling their commitment to the therapeutic process (Rempel, Holmes, & Zanna, 1985). Disclosing troubling, worrisome thoughts also reduces the discloser's level of tension and stress. Individuals who keep their problems secret but continually ruminate about them display signs of physiological and psychological distress, whereas individuals who have the opportunity to disclose these troubling thoughts are healthier and happier (Pennebaker, 1997).

Members can also vent strong emotions in groups, although the value of such emotional venting continues to be debated by researchers. Some side with Freud's initial analysis of emotions and tension. Freud believed that strong emotions can build up, like steam in a boiler. If this psychological steam is not vented from time to time, the strain on the system can cause psychological disorders. Therefore, healthy people discharge these emotions in a process Freud called **catharsis.** Others, however, have suggested that "blowing off steam" is rarely

---

self-disclosure The process of revealing personal, intimate information about oneself to others.

catharsis The release of emotional tensions.

FOCUS 15-2   How Can We Cope with Disasters and Trauma?

Each time I tell my story, I remove one small bit of hurt from inside me. I ease my wound.
–Carol Staudacher, *Time to Grieve* (1994, p. 61).

In rural India, a bus carrying 25 college students and their guides crashes, killing 7 and injuring all the other passengers. A series of tornadoes crisscrosses North Carolina, leaving a path of devastation and death. In Columbine High School, Eric Harris and Dylan Klebold kill 13 people and wound dozens of others before killing themselves. When a cloud of gas from a leak at a petrochemical plant in Texas ignites, 23 workers are killed and hundreds injured. In September 2001, millions of Americans grieve the loss of thousands of fellow citizens killed by terrorist attacks.

People the world over experience catastrophes, crises, and disasters. Some of these stressful events—such as volcanoes, floods, hurricanes, blizzards, and tornadoes—can be blamed on naturally occurring disruptions in the planet's meteorological and geological systems. Others, however, are man-made—wars, terrorist attacks, violence, nuclear accidents, transportation accidents, building fires, industrial accidents, and so on.

These events take their toll on human adjustment and well-being. One comprehensive review of dozens of published studies of psychological reactions to disasters concluded that people who survive a stressful event are more likely to suffer from anxiety, sleeplessness, and fearfulness. Such stressors also lead to small increases in drug use and depression among people exposed to a hazard. Between 7% and 40% of the survivors of disasters will exhibit some sign of psychopathology (Rubonis & Bickman, 1991). Many victims of disasters, such as Americans who lived and worked near the sites of the 2001 terrorist attacks, civilians in Bosnia, and victims of Sarin attack in Japan, show evidence of *post-traumatic stress disorder,* even if not directly harmed.

These negative mental health consequences (anxiety, depression, sleeplessness, compulsions, intrusive thoughts) can be reduced through stress management crisis interventions. These interventions—usually designed and implemented by community health professionals—often make use of group-level therapeutic coping processes, including social comparison, social support, and social learning (R. D. Allen, 1993; Layne et al.,

helpful, for in the extreme, venting heightens members' psychological distress and upset (Ormont, 1984).

Altruism

The group's leader is not the only source of help available to group members. Other group members can sometimes draw on their own experiences to offer insights and advice to one another. This mutual assistance provides benefits for both parties. Even though the group's leader is the official expert in the group, people are often more willing to accept help from people who are similar to themselves (Wills & DePaulo, 1991). The helper, too, "feels a sense of being needed and helpful; can forget self in favor of another group member; and recognizes the desire to do something for another group member" (Crouch et al., 1994, p. 285). Mutual assistance teaches group members the social skills that are essential to psychological well-being (Ferencik, 1992).

FOCUS 15-2 (*continued*)

2001). The students who survived the bus crash in India met with counselors for 6 weeks to deal with issues of trauma, coping, and grief (A. L. Turner, 2000). In the aftermath of the devastating tornadoes, North Carolina residents met at the local community college to share worries and anxieties, recount their stories of surviving the storm, and exchange information about resources, insurance claim procedures, and cleanup efforts (McCammon & Long, 1993). Following the explosion at the petrochemical plant, a response team provided a constant flow of information to the community, conducted group sessions for individuals who lost family members in the accident, and organized *critical incident stress debriefing* (CISD) sessions for workers who were part of the emergency team that sought, in vain, to fight the blaze (Lloyd, Creson, & D'Antoni, 1993).

The effectiveness of such interventions depends, in part, on timing, procedures, and the characteristics of the individuals involved. Ideally, the intervention occurs immediately following the event, and provides continuing treatment as group members progress through the cumulative stages of the coping process. Interventions

should also be planned carefully in advance, and in some cases, methods used in traditional therapeutic circumstances must be replaced by methods that will work in the chaos and confusion of a disaster or community trauma (Butcher & Hatcher, 1988; G. A. Jacobs, Quevillon, & Stricherz, 1990). Interventions must also take into account the characteristics of the individuals involved. Children and elderly people, for example, require a different set of group experiences than do adults, family members, and emergency personnel. Interventions must also be sensitive to each individual's reaction to the event. Some may appreciate the opportunity to interact with others who are coping with a disaster, but others may not respond well to the evocative demands of the group (E. D. Schwarz & Kowalski, 1992). Not everyone can share their grief with others, and the continued discussion of the event may only exacerbate their anxieties and emotional reprocessing (Melamed & Wills, 2000). A group approach to treatment works for many people, but some will require individual assistance rather than group help.

Mutual assistance is particularly important in self-help groups. Mended Hearts—a support group that deals with the psychological consequences of open-heart surgery—tells its members that "you are not completely mended until you help mend others" (Lieberman, 1993, p. 297). AA groups formalize and structure helping in their 12-step procedures. Newcomers to the group are paired with sponsors, who meet regularly with the new member outside of the regular group meetings. As Focus 15-2 notes, collective helping is also an essential component of group-level approaches to dealing with traumatic events.

Insight

Individuals' perceptions of their own personal qualities are generally accurate. Individuals who think of themselves as assertive tend to be viewed that way by others, just as warm, outgoing individuals tend to be viewed as friendly and approachable (Kenny, Kieffer, Smith, Ceplenski, & Kulo, 1996; Levesque, 1997). In some cases, however, individuals' self-perceptions are inaccurate (Andersen, 1984). An individual may believe that he is attractive, socially skilled, and friendly, when in fact he is unattractive, interpersonally incompetent, and hostile.

Groups promote self-understanding by exposing us to the unknown areas of our selves. Although we are not particularly open to feedback about our own attributes, when several individuals provide us with the same feedback, we are more likely to internalize this information (A. Jacobs, 1974; Kivlighan, 1985). Also, when the feedback is given in the context of a long-term, reciprocal relationship, it cannot be so easily dismissed as biased or subjective. Group leaders, too, often reward members for accepting rather than rejecting feedback, and the setting itself works to intensify self-awareness. In a supportive, accepting group, we can reveal hidden aspects of ourselves, and we therefore feel more open and honest in our relationships.

Even qualities that are unknown to others and to ourselves can emerge and be recognized during group interactions (Luft, 1984). As self-perception theory suggests, people often "come to 'know' their own attitudes, emotions, and other internal states partially by inferring them from observations of their own behavior and/or the circumstances in which this behavior occurs" (D. J. Bem, 1972, p. 2). If individuals observe themselves acting in ways that suggest that they are socially skilled—for example, disclosing information about themselves appropriately and maintaining a conversation—then they may infer that they are socially skilled (Robak, 2001).

Studies of group members' evaluations of the therapeutic experience attest to the importance of insight. When participants in therapeutic groups were asked to identify the events that took place in their groups that helped them the most, they stressed universality, interpersonal learning, cohesion (belonging), and insight (see Figure 15-2). During later sessions, they stressed interpersonal learning even more, but universality became less important (Kivlighan & Mullison, 1988; Kivlighan, Multon, & Brossart, 1996). In other studies that asked group members to rank or rate the importance of these curative factors, the group members emphasized self-understanding, interpersonal learning, and catharsis (T. Butler & Fuhriman, 1983a; Markovitz & Smith, 1983; Maxmen, 1973, 1978; Rohrbaugh & Bartels, 1975; Rugel & Meyer, 1984). In general, individuals who stress the value of self-understanding tend to benefit the most from participation in a therapeutic group (T. Butler & Fuhriman, 1983b).

THE EFFECTIVENESS OF GROUPS

What would you do if you were bothered by some personal problem? Perhaps you have trouble making friends. Maybe you are having problems adjusting to a new job or wish that you could be more productive when you are at work. Perhaps you have finally resolved to stop smoking or drinking, or you just cannot seem to get over the depression that has enveloped you since your mother passed

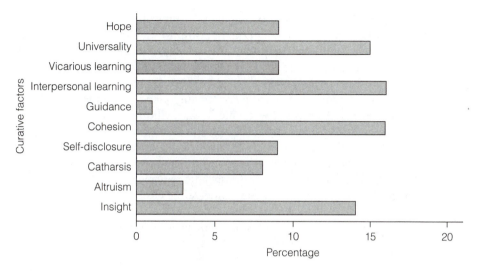

FIGURE 15-2

Which group experiences do members of therapeutic groups value the most? Participants in therapeutic groups stressed universality, interpersonal learning, cohesion (belonging), and insight when identifying the events that were most important to them personally. During later sessions, they stressed interpersonal learning even more, but universality became less important. *Source:* Kivlighan & Mullison, 1988.

away last year. Whatever the problem, you have not succeeded in changing on your own. So you decide to join a change-promoting group.

Would this group really help you achieve the changes you desire? Researchers and therapists have been debating this question for many years. Reviewers, after sifting through hundreds of studies evaluating the effectiveness of group interventions, rejected many studies as so methodologically flawed that they yielded no information whatsoever (Bednar & Kaul, 1978, 1979, 1994; Burlingame, Kircher, & Taylor, 1994; Fuhriman & Burlingame, 1994a; Kaul & Bednar, 1986). Those studies that did use valid methods, however, generally weighed in favor of group-level interventions. Gary M. Burlingame, Addie Fuhriman, and their colleagues, in a series of meta-analytic reviews of hundreds of experimental, quasi-experimental, and correlational studies, concluded that group methods are effective treatments for a wide variety of psychological problems (Burlingame, Fuhriman, & Mosier, 2003; Fuhriman & Burlingame, 1994a; McRoberts, Burlingame, & Hoag, 1998). Group methods have also been found to be effective (1) when used to treat children and adolescents (Hoag & Burlingame, 1997), (2) when used for the primary prevention of health problems in children (Kulic, Horne, & Dagley, 2004), and (3) with incarcerated individuals, particularly when cognitive–behavioral methods are paired with homework assignments to be completed after the sessions (Morgan & Flora, 2002). A comprehensive review of self-help groups also suggested that individuals gain positive outcomes through membership in such groups, relative to individuals in control conditions (Barlow, Burlingame, Nebeker, & Anderson, 2000).

Individuals who have participated in group therapy—the consumers of group-based treatments—also give group approaches relatively high marks. One study, conducted by *Consumer Reports,* asked respondents to rate a variety of treatments. All psychological methods, including group interventions, were rated positively. AA received particularly positive evaluations in this study (Seligman, 1995, 1996; see also A. Christensen & Jacobson, 1994). In sum, the "accumulated evidence indicates that group treatments have been more effective than no treatment, than placebo or nonspecific treatments, or than other recognized psychological treatments, at least under some circumstances" (Bednar & Kaul, 1994, p. 632).

These positive conclusions, however, require some qualification. First, the changes brought about by group experiences are often more perceptual than behavioral. Second, in some cases, groups can do more harm than good for participants. Third, all groups are not created equal; some may be more effective in promoting change than others. These issues are examined next.

Perceptions Versus Behaviors

Richard Bednar and Theodore J. Kaul (1979), after culling the studies of change that were methodologically flawed, concluded that most studies had reported changes only on self-report data, but not on behavioral data. Reviews of experiential groups, for example, generally found stronger evidence of perceptual changes than of behavioral changes (Bates & Goodman, 1986; Berman & Zimpfer, 1980; Budman, Demby, Feldstein, & Gold, 1984; Ware, Barr, & Boone, 1982). One review, for instance, identified 26 controlled studies of personal growth groups that (1) used both pretest and posttest measures, (2) met for at least 10 hours, and (3) had a long-term follow-up (at least 1 month after termination). Summarizing these methodologically superior studies, the reviewers concluded that group treatments did result in enduring positive changes, particularly at the self-report level (Berman & Zimpfer, 1980). These and other findings suggest that groups are most useful in promoting changes in the "ability to manage feelings, directionality of motivation, attitudes towards the self, attitudes towards others, and interdependence," but that behavior changes are slight (J. R. Gibb, 1970, p. 2114; M. E. Shaw, 1981).

Evidence of Negative Effects

Not everyone who joined the therapy group conducted by Dr. C. and Dr. F. remained in the group. Some attended only one or two sessions, never to return. Two members who attended regularly for several months, Bob and Linda, dropped out of the group unexpectedly, and could not be contacted by the staff.

Before they left the group, they became more withdrawn from the discussion and unresponsive to the facilitator's interventions.

Bednar and Kaul noted that groups can fail in two distinct ways. First, a participant may decide to leave the group before he or she has benefited in any way; such an individual is usually labeled a **premature termination,** or *dropout* (Holmes, 1983). A **casualty,** in contrast, is significantly harmed by the group experience. A casualty might, for example, commit suicide as a result of the group experience, require individual therapy to correct harm caused by the group, or report continued deteriorations in adjustment over the course of the group experience. The number of casualties reported in studies has ranged from a low of none among 94 participants in a human relations training lab followed up after 5 months (P. B. Smith, 1975, 1980) to a high of 8% of the participants in a study of 17 encounter groups (Lieberman et al., 1973). A relatively high casualty rate (18%) was obtained in one study of 50 married couples who participated in marathon encounter groups, but this rate was inflated by the problems the couples were experiencing before entering the group (Doherty, Lester, & Leigh, 1986). No evidence is available concerning the rate of casualties in self-help groups, but statistics maintained by the NTL indicate that 25 individuals who participated in the program prior to 1974 experienced a severe psychological reaction (Back, 1974). This number represented less than 0.2% of the participants.

Bednar and Kaul (1978) noted that most premature terminations result from failed expectations about the purposes of the group or from an inadequate match between the group member's goals and the leader's methods. Casualties, in contrast, can most often be traced to a particularly negative event in the group. In one study, for example, an individual sought psychiatric treatment immediately after the group attacked her for being overweight:

> She stated that the group was an extremely destructive one for her. The group operated by everybody "ganging up on one another, thirteen to one, and bulldozing them until they were left on the ground panting." She was bitterly attacked by the group and finally dropped out after an attack on her in which she was labeled "a fat Italian mama with a big shiny nose." She was also told that she probably had "a hell of a time getting any man to look at her." (Lieberman et al., 1973, p. 189)

Given these potential problems, group therapists, trainers, facilitators, and members themselves are urged to use care when interacting in their groups. Casualties can be minimized by limiting conflict during sessions and by making certain that the group atmosphere is supportive, nonevaluative, and nonthreatening (Mitchell & Mitchell, 1984; Scheuble et al., 1987).

---

premature termination The withdrawal of a participant from a change-promoting group that occurs before the individual has reached his or her therapeutic goals.

casualty An individual whose psychological well-being declines rather than improves as a result of his or her experiences in a change-promoting group.

Types of Groups and Effectiveness

Change-promoting groups conform to no single set of procedures: Some groups are leader centered (psychoanalytic or Gestalt groups), whereas others are group focused (encounter groups and T-groups); and the group's activities can range from the highly structured (interpersonal learning groups) to the wholly unstructured (encounter groups). In some groups, the members themselves are responsible for running the meeting (self-help groups), whereas in other situations, the facilitator runs the session (structured groups). Group practitioners also vary greatly in their orientations and techniques: Some focus on emotions with Gestalt exercises, others concentrate on the here and now of the group's interpersonal processes, and still others train members to perform certain behaviors through videotaped feedback, behavioral rehearsal, and systematic reinforcement.

Given this diversity of purposes and procedures, one might expect some types of groups to emerge as more effective than others. Yet differences in treatment effectiveness are relatively rare. Morton Lieberman, Irvin Yalom, and Matthew Miles (1973), for example, investigated the overall impact of a 12-week experiential group on members' adjustment. They began by assigning 206 Stanford University students to 1 of 18 therapy groups representing 10 different theoretical orientations. Trained observers coded the groups' interactions, with particular attention to leadership style. Before, during, immediately after, and 6 months following the participation, they administered a battery of items assessing group members' self-esteem, attitudes, self-satisfaction, values, satisfaction with friendships, and so on. Measures were also completed by the comembers, the leaders, and by group members' acquaintances.

Somewhat unexpectedly, the project discovered that no one theoretical approach had a monopoly on effectiveness. For example, two separate Gestalt groups with different leaders were included in the design, but the members of these two groups evidenced widely discrepant gains. One of the Gestalt groups ranked among the most successful in stimulating participant growth, but the other Gestalt group yielded fewer benefits than all of the other groups.

A number of factors could account for this apparent equivalence of therapies (Stiles, Shapiro, & Elliott, 1986). First, the various group therapies may be differentially effective, but researchers' measures may not be sensitive enough to detect these variations. Second, a group's effectiveness may depend as much on who is in the group and who leads the group as on the methods used. The question is not "Is Therapy X more effective than Therapy Y?" but, "What type of group run by which therapist is effective for this individual with this type of problem?" (Paul, 1967). Third, although group interventions are based on widely divergent theoretical assumptions, these assumptions may not lead to differences in practice. The leader of a Gestalt group and the leader of a psychodynamic group, for example, may explain their goals and methods in very different theoretical terms, but they may nonetheless rely on identical methods in their groups. Fourth, as the concept of curative factors suggests, despite their heterogeneity in purposes and procedures, therapeutic groups have certain characteristics in common, and these common aspects of groups and their dynamics may account for their therapeutic effects.

The Value of Groups

Groups are not all benefit with no cost. Groups can demand great investments of time and energy from their members. Although groups provide social support, they are also a source of considerable stress for their members. Groups, too, can socialize members in ways that are not healthy and set social identity processes in motion that increase conflict between groups (Forsyth & Elliott, 2000).

The checkered impact of groups, however, in no way detracts from their significance in shaping mental health. Groups help their members define and confirm their values, beliefs, and identities. When individuals are beset by problems and uncertainties, groups offer reassurance, security, support, and assistance. Groups are places where people can learn new social skills and discover things about themselves and others. Groups, too, can produce changes in members when other approaches have failed. Both researchers and mental health professionals who understand groups agree with Lewin's law: "It is usually easier to change individuals formed into a group than to change any one of them separately" (1951, p. 228).

SUMMARY IN OUTLINE

❖ **What are some of the ways that groups are used to help their members change?**

1. Individuals often turn to groups for help in achieving personal and therapeutic change. As Lewin stated, "It is usually easier to change individuals formed into a group than to change any one of them separately."

2. Most change-oriented groups focus either on therapeutic adjustment (*psychotherapy groups*), interpersonal and emotional growth (*interpersonal learning groups*), or overcoming addictions or other life stresses (*self-help groups*).

3. Group psychotherapy sessions, conducted by a mental health professional, focus on psychological problems.
   - In *group psychoanalysis,* the therapist helps members to gain insight into

their problems by offering interpretations and working through sibling and parental *transference* effects.
   - In *Gestalt group therapy,* the therapist promotes emotional growth by using experiments, avoiding interpretations, and, in some cases, by extensive role-playing methods.
   - *Psychodrama,* developed by Moreno, also uses role play and physical activities.
   - In *interpersonal group psychotherapy,* the leader takes advantage of the group's dynamics to help members learn about how they influence others and how others influence them.
   - In *cognitive–behavioral therapy groups,* the therapist uses principles derived from learning theory to encourage specific behaviors while extinguishing others. This approach makes use

of behavioral methods, including behavioral contracts, modeling, behavior rehearsal, and feedback.

4. Interpersonal learning groups involve attempts to help relatively well-adjusted individuals improve their self-understanding and relationships with others.

- In *training groups,* or *T-groups,* members are encouraged to actively confront and resolve interpersonal issues through unstructured discussions.

- In growth groups, such as *sensitivity training groups* or *encounter groups,* individuals are urged to disclose personal aspects of themselves to others and to provide other members with positive feedback.

- In *structured learning groups,* members take part in planned exercises that focus on a specific interpersonal problem or skill. Most of these interventions involve a learning cycle that begins with an orienting overview and then moves from experience to discussion to analysis to application.

5. *Self-help groups* often form spontaneously when people combine their energies and efforts in an attempt to cope with or overcome a common problem.

- Many support groups, such as Alcoholics Anonymous (AA), emphasize inspirational testimonials, mutual help, shared similarities, and collective encouragement.

- Studies of online support groups for problems ranging from cancer to sexual abuse to psychological disorders have suggested that these groups provide many of the same resources to members as do face-to-face support groups.

❖ **How do groups promote change?**

1. A number of *curative factors* (or *therapeutic factors*) operate in groups to promote change.

2. Groups, by providing opportunities to engage in social comparison and mutual support, convince members of the universality of their problems and give them hope.

3. Because groups include multiple individuals, rather than just a single therapist/helper and a single client, they can make use of the sources of interpersonal learning described in Bandura's *social learning theory.*

- Groups facilitate vicarious learning (modeling of behaviors), interpersonal feedback, and guidance (direct instruction).

- *Coleadership* (two leaders are present at all sessions) provides more opportunities for social learning and feedback. Group facilitators, like all group leaders, vary considerably along the directive–nondirective dimension.

4. Cohesive groups offer individuals the opportunity to help others and to be helped by them, and they serve as buffers against stress. Therapeutic groups, like all groups, generally become more cohesive over time.

5. Groups become more intimate as members reveal private information about themselves (*self-disclosure*). When group members vent strong emotions, the resulting *catharsis* may reduce their stress.

6. Group members also benefit from the increased self-confidence produced by helping others and by gaining insight about their personal qualities from other group members.

7. Many stress management crisis interventions implemented following community disasters and crises make use of group-level therapeutic coping processes, including social comparison, social support, social learning, and mutual help.

❖ **How effective are groups in bringing about change?**

1. Most group approaches are effective methods for helping individuals change their thoughts, emotions, and actions. However,
   - Changes fostered by group experiences are often more perceptual than behavioral.

- Participation in groups can also lead to a number of negative consequences, although not every *premature termination* from a group is necessarily a psychological *casualty.*

2. Group methods, despite their diversity, tend to be equally effective. This general but nonspecific effectiveness may reflect the operation of common curative factors across most therapeutic groups.

FOR MORE INFORMATION

Chapter Case: The Therapy Group

- "Groups as Change Agents" by Donelson R. Forsyth and the late John G. Corazzini (2000), provides the transcripts and analysis of the growth-oriented treatment group examined in this chapter, as well as a general overview of group approaches to treatment.

Group Approaches to Change

- "Group-Based Interventions for Trauma Survivors," a special issue of the journal *Group Dynamics: Theory, Research, and Practice,* edited by Gary M. Burlingame and Christopher M. Layne (2001), examines theory and research pertaining to group methods for helping people cope with disasters and catastrophes.
- *Group Psychotherapy with Addicted Populations: An Integration of Twelve Step and Psychodynamic Theory,* by Philip J. Flores (1997), examines the interpersonal and intrapersonal processes that operate in "12-step programs" (such as Alcoholics Anonymous) and therapeutic groups.
- "Self-Help Groups," by Leon H. Levy (2000), reviews a number of forms of self-help groups, and thoroughly reviews the empirical literature pertaining to their effectiveness.
- *The Theory and Practice of Group Psychotherapy* (4th ed.), by Irvin D. Yalom (1995), sets forth Yalom's basic principles of interpersonal group therapy, which stresses the basic curative factors common to all group approaches to change.

Group Effectiveness

- *Handbook of Group Psychotherapy: An Empirical and Clinical Synthesis,* edited by Addie Fuhriman and Gary M. Burlingame (1994b), is a comprehensive synthesis of research studies that have investigated the nature and efficacy of group psychotherapy.

MEDIA RESOURCES

 Visit the Group Dynamics companion website at http://psychology.wadsworth .com/forsyth4e to access online resources for your book, including quizzes, flash cards, web links, and more!

16

CROWDS AND COLLECTIVE BEHAVIOR

CHAPTER OVERVIEW

Groups are not always small, intimate, and stable. Large groups, such as crowds of people that exist only temporarily, and even larger groups, such as social movements, are similar to smaller groups in many respects. Yet these collectives possess unique features as well. We expect individuals and small groups to act rationally, but who is surprised when a crowd, mob, or movement acts in odd and unusual ways?

❖ What is collective behavior?

❖ What theories explain collective behavior?

❖ How different are collectives from other types of groups?

CHAPTER OUTLINE

The Who Concert Stampede: A Crowd Gone Mad?

The crowd, nearly 8000 strong, was waiting to get into Cincinnati's Riverfront Coliseum to hear a concert by the rock band The Who. Many fans had festival seating, no-reserved-seats tickets, so they came early to claim a spot closer to the stage. But they had been joined now by thousands of others, and the throng was packed so tightly that whenever someone near the fringe pushed forward, ripples spread through the rest of the group. When pranksters pushed against people standing at the periphery of the crowd, the shove passed like a wave through the group (see Figure 16-1).

The doors opened at 7:30, and the crowd surged forward. A crowd of 8000 people is loud, but above the din, the concertgoers could hear the band warming up. As those on the periphery pushed forward, people near the doors were packed together tighter and tighter. The ticket takers worked as fast as they could,

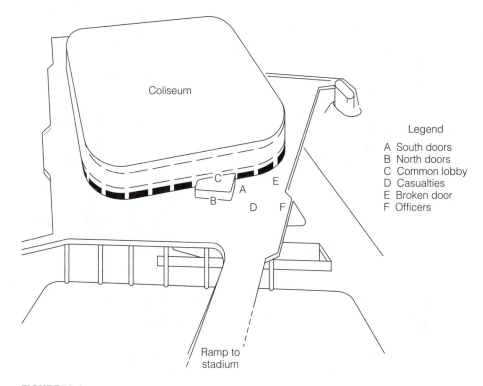

Coliseum

Legend

A South doors
B North doors
C Common lobby
D Casualties
E Broken door
F Officers

Ramp to
stadium

FIGURE 16-1

What happened at The Who concert at Cincinnati's Riverfront Coliseum? When the Coliseum staff opened the doors for the show an estimated 8000 people were in the area leading from the ramp to the doors. Density was very high outside the south doors, and the flow of people jammed. When concertgoers behind the jam pushed forward, many were caught in the crowd and crushed. *Source:* "Panic at 'The Who Concert Stampede': An Empirical Assessment," by N. R. Johnson. Reprinted from *Social Problems*, Vol. 34, No. 4, p. 366 by permission. Copyright © 1987 by The Society for the Study of Social Problems.

but too few doors were opened to handle the large collective. The back of the group moved faster than the front, and the flow jammed near the clogged doors. People were literally swept off their feet by the surge and slipped to the concrete floor. Those around them tried to pull them back to their feet, but the rest of the crowd saw the open doors and heard only the music. They pushed forward relentlessly, and the helpers fell themselves or were pushed past those who had fallen.

Eleven people died in the crowd, and many others were injured. Most suffocated, caught so long in the press of the crowd that they could not breathe. Some were physically injured by the crowd, for their "bodies were marked with multiple contusions, bruises and the victims had suffered hemorrhages" ("The Who," 1979, p. A-19). Survivors' descriptions reported by the news media revealed the gruesome details:

- "People were hitting other people, and a girl fell down in front of me. I helped her up finally."
- "All of a sudden, I went down. . . . I couldn't see anything."
- "My face was being pressed to the floor. I felt I was smothering."
- "I saw people's heads being stepped on. I fell and couldn't get up. People kept pushing me down."
- "People just didn't seem to care. I couldn't believe it. They could see all the people piled up and they still tried to climb over them just to get in."

This tragedy is a grim example of **collective behavior**—the actions of a large group of people who are responding in a similar way to an event or situation (McPhail, 1991). In earlier chapters, we focused on smaller groups—cliques, work squads, juries, sports teams, corporate boards, crews, and bands of explorers. But individuals can also—sometimes unwittingly and sometimes purposely— become members of much larger aggregates (Blumer, 1964). Some collectives, like the concertgoers at the Who concert, form when people are concentrated in a specific location. Others, however, occur when widely dispersed individuals engage in markedly similar actions, as when all the individuals in a community, city, or country begin to adopt a fad or fashion style. In most cases, collectives do not behave in odd, atypical ways. Each day, thousands upon thousands of collectives form and disband around the world, and in nearly all cases, these collectives help rather than hurt their members. But collectives are, at their core, groups, and like any other group, they can go wrong.

In this chapter, we turn our attention to such groups by first examining their forms and variations, for they range from the accidental convergences of unrelated individuals to groups with faithful followers who remain members for many years. We will also review both classic and contemporary theoretical analyses of collective behavior, beginning with the provocative arguments presented by Gustave Le

---

collective behavior The actions of a group of people who are responding in a similar way to an event or situation, including people who all occupy the same location (a *crowd*) as well as mass phenomena in which individuals are dispersed across a wide area (*collective movements*).

Bon (1895/1960) in his book *The Crowd* and ending with new theories that offer fresh insights into the limits and potentials of human action in groups.

THE NATURE OF COLLECTIVES

In 10th-century Italy (and again in Germany and the Low Countries in the 13th and 14th centuries), an epidemic of "dancing mania" caused thousands of people to writhe compulsively for days at a time. In 1943, Mrs. Mullane, a contestant on a radio program, was told to collect pennies as a service to the nation's war effort. The announcer then suggested that listeners should send Mrs. Mullane a penny, and gave her address on the air. Within weeks, she received more than 200,000 letters and well over 300,000 pennies. In 1978, only 8% of households in the United States had microwave ovens. This percentage increased slowly until 1985, when the percentage jumped from 34% to 61%. In 1999, in Minsk, Belarus, an audience at a Mango Mango concert sought shelter from a storm in a nearby subway station—53 people were crushed to death by the crowd. On a recent Thursday evening, 200 strangers massed at a ledge in New York City's Central Park, made bird calls for a few minutes, repeated the chant "Na-ture" 30 times, and then dissolved into the night. It was a "flash crowd" or "smart mob," organized by the use of cell phone technology and instant messaging (Rheingold, 2002). On the ninth day of the month of Hijjah, at noon, more than two million people gather on the Plain of Arafat, the site of the prophet Mohammed's farewell sermon—arguably the largest gathering of people in one place at any time in history (McPhail, 1991).

The science of group dynamics is based on one core assumption—that people act collectively. Much of this collective action occurs in relatively small groups, and the field of group dynamics (and this book) has concentrated on such groups. But as these historical examples reveal, people also join very large groups, and the impact of these groups on their members can be large as well.

What Is a Collective?

The term *collective,* if taken literally, would describe any aggregate of two or more individuals and, hence, would be synonymous with the term *group* (Blumer, 1951). Most theorists, however, reserve the term for larger, more spontaneous social groups. A baseball team, a company's board of directors, and a family at a meal are all groups, but they are small, organized, and stable. **Collectives,** in contrast, are large groups whose members act in similar and sometimes unusual ways. A list of collectives (see Table 16-1) would include a street crowd watching a building burn, an audience at a movie, a line (*queue*) of people waiting to purchase tickets, a mob of college students protesting a government policy, and a

---

collective A relatively large aggregation or group of individuals who display similarities in actions and outlook.

TABLE 16-1 Various types of collectives

Type	Defining Characteristics
Crowd	A temporary gathering of individuals who share a common focus of interest
Audience	Spectators at an exhibition, performance, or event
Queue	A waiting line or file of individuals
Mob	An acting crowd, often aggressive in character
Riot	A large, less localized and less organized mob
Panic	A threatened crowd, either seeking escape from danger or competing for a scarce commodity
Mass hysteria and rumor	The spontaneous outbreak of atypical thoughts, feelings, or actions in a group or aggregate, including psychogenic illness, common hallucinations, and bizarre actions
Trends (fads, crazes, fashions)	An abrupt but short-lived change in the opinions, behaviors, lifestyle, or dress of a large number of widely dispersed individuals
Social movement	A deliberate, organized attempt to achieve a change or resist a change in a social system

Sources: R. W. Brown, 1954; McPhail, 1991; Milgram & Toch, 1969.

panicked group fleeing from danger. But the list would also include mass movements of individuals who, though dispersed over a wide area, display common shifts in opinion or actions.

The diversity of collectives is staggering, so no single classification scheme is sufficient to categorize their many forms. They tend to be large, but some collectives are huge—as when millions of individuals respond similarly to some fashion craze. In some cases, all the members of a collective are together in one place, and so they "can monitor each other by being visible to or within earshot of one another" (Snow & Oliver, 1995, p. 572). Some collectives, in contrast, involve individuals who are dispersed across great distances. All collectives, however, are distinguished from categories of individuals by their members' "common or concerted" form of behavior or reaction (McPhail, 1991, p. 159). Members of a crowd, for example, may move in the same direction or perform the same general types of behaviors. Members of social movements, although not interacting in face-to-face settings, as are individuals in crowds and mobs, act in similar ways to achieve a common purpose.

Collectives also vary in their duration and cohesion. Although some collectives are concocted, planned groups that are created for a specific purpose, in most cases they are emergent groups that result from the press of circumstances or through self-organizing dynamics (Arrow et al., 2000). They tend to be open groups, for they have no standards for defining membership and do not adopt operational strategies. In consequence, the relationships between members are more superficial and impersonal than those that link members of smaller groups. If a typical group is two or more individuals who are connected to one another by interpersonal relationships, a typical collective is a large number of individuals who are connected to one another by some similarity in action and outlook rather than by close, intimate relationships. Collectives are often weak associations of individuals rather than cohesive groups (Lickel et al., 2000). Collectives, too, are by reputation more unconventional than other groups. They tend to exist outside of traditional forms of social structures and institutions, and as a result, their members also sometimes engage in atypical, unruly, unconventional, or even aberrant behaviors.

Crowds

The throng of concertgoers massed outside the Who show was a **crowd**—a group of individuals sharing a common focus and concentrated in a single location. Individuals who are sitting on benches in a park or walking along a city block occupy a common location, but they do not become a crowd unless something happens—a fire, a car collision, or a mugging, for example—to create a common focus of attention (Milgram & Toch, 1969). Shoppers in a mall are just individuals, until a woman spanks her small child when he cries too loudly. Suddenly, the hundred pairs of eyes of an instantly formed crowd focus on the woman, who hurries out the door.

The most common crowd is a *street crowd*—a group of otherwise unrelated individuals who, while going about their own personal business, end up in the same general vicinity and share a common experience (R. W. Brown, 1954; McPhail, 1991). Although such crowds are often short-lived, even these fleeting collectives possess boundaries that limit their size and extent. These boundaries are relatively permeable at the edges of the crowd, where individuals are allowed to enter and exit freely, but permeability diminishes as one moves nearer the center of the crowd. Also, roles, status hierarchies, and other group structures may not be very evident in such crowds, but close probing usually reveals some underlying structure. For example, they usually take on one of two distinctive shapes—*arcs* (half-circles with all members facing some focal point) and *rings* (full circles). The focal point is known as a *crowd crystal*—one or more individuals who, by drawing attention to themselves or some event, prompt others to join them (Canetti, 1962). Subgroups also exist in these crowds, for in many cases, the people who populate public places are part of small groups rather than lone individuals. At the Who concert, for example, groups of friends waited together for the concert to begin, and these subgroups remained intact even during the fatal crush at the entrance doors. Evidence also indicates that those who occupy central positions in crowds are likely to be more actively involved in the experience than those who are content to remain on the fringes (Milgram & Toch, 1969).

Stanley Milgram and his colleagues examined the formation of street crowds by watching 1424 pedestrians walking along a busy New York City sidewalk. As the pedestrians passed by one section of the sidewalk, they encountered one or

---

crowd A gathering of individuals, usually in a public place, who are present in the same general vicinity and share a common focus.

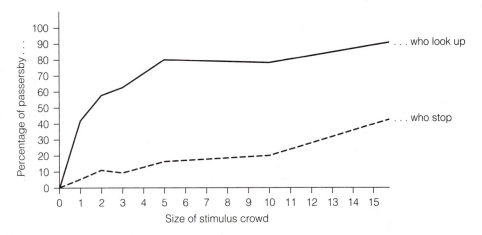

FIGURE 16-2

How many people, when they passed by one or more people who were looking up at a building, (1) looked in the same direction as the starers or (2) actually stopped walking and stood with the starers? *Source:* "Note on the Drawing Power of Crowds of Different Size," by S. Milgram, L. Bickman, and L. Berkowitz, *Journal of Personality and Social Psychology*, 1969, 13, 79–82. Copyright 1969 by the American Psychological Association.

more confederates who were gazing at the sixth floor of a nearby building. These confederates acted as crowd crystals by watching the building for 1 minute before gradually dispersing. Meanwhile, a camera filmed the passersby to determine how many looked up at the building or stopped and joined this crowd. If we define crowd membership as (1) occupying the same vicinity and (2) sharing the same focus of attention, the results in Figure 16-2 indicate that even a small group of three persons was sufficient to trigger the formation of a crowd. If, in contrast, we require that passersby stop walking and stand with the confederates before we consider them part of the crowd (see Focus 16-1), then the larger the crowd, the greater the likelihood that others will join it (Milgram, Bickman, & Berkowitz, 1969).

AUDIENCES A crowd that deliberately gathers in a particular area to observe some event or activity is called an **audience** (or *conventional crowd*). Unlike a crowd that forms spontaneously when some event creates a shared focus, individuals join audiences deliberately, and they are also bound more by social conventions that dictate their location and movements (Blumer, 1946). They enter the focal area via aisles or pathways and occupy locations that are determined by

audience A gathering of onlookers who observe some performance, event, or activity; audiences tend to be conventional in behavior, and they disperse when the event they are watching concludes.

FOCUS 16-1   People Watching: What Do Crowds Do?

The realm of activity that is generated by face-to-face interaction and organized by norms of co-mingling. . . has never been sufficiently treated as a subject matter in its own right.

–Erving Goffman (1971, p. ix)

The crowds that form in public and semi-public places come in many shapes and sizes, and their members undertake a variety of actions (Blumer, 1946; R. W. Brown, 1954; Milgram & Toch, 1969). Whereas some crowds are hostile, others are fearful, greedy, or even joyful; some remain stationary, whereas others move about collectively; some watch events passively, whereas others take part actively. But beneath this variability, one can discern patterns and regularities in the behavior of people in public places. People in collectives, like the people in most groups, often communicate with one another verbally and nonverbally. Collectives are often mobile groups, and so their members are not stationary but moving— either within the context of the group itself or from one place to another. Some collectives also interact directly with objects in the environment, as when bystanders at an accident scene help the injured or when a mob turns over parked cars.

Clark McPhail and his colleagues, after observing all kinds of public gatherings, identified a number of elementary behaviors common to such groups (McPhail, 1991; Tucker, Schweingruber & McPhail, 1999). Their listing includes,

- *Movement:* Actions taken in common by group members, such as clustering, queueing, surging, marching, jogging, and running.
- *Positioning:* The stance assumed by members in the space, including sitting, standing, jumping, bowing, and kneeling.
- *Manipulation:* Alternation of objects in the setting, such as throwing or moving objects.

- *Gesticulation:* Gesturing, such as saluting and signaling (e.g., the raised middle finger, power fist).
- *Verbalization:* Communicating through language forms, such as chanting, singing, praying, reciting, or pledging.
- *Vocalization:* Communicating with paralinguistic sounds, such as ooh-ing and ahh-ing, cheering, booing, whistling, laughing, or wailing.
- *Orientation:* Moving into a particular formation within the space, such as clustering, arcing, ringing, gazing, facing, or vigiling.

These categories provide observers of crowds and collectives with a means of structuring their observations. Traditional group behavior coding systems, such as Interaction Process Analysis (IPA; Bales, 1970), were designed for analysis of small, face-to-face groups. Such systems tend to focus on the individuals within the group rather than on the group itself. McPhail's categories, in contrast, offer a means of objectively recording the behavior of the group as a whole and are not constrained by the number of participants present in the situation.

McPhail agreed that collective behavior can be far more complex than these simple forms suggest, but his coding scheme is an effective way of recording the most common behaviors performed by people in collectives. These categories, he noted, provide "a way of specifying our ignorance about the composition of and variation across gatherings" (McPhail, 1991, p. 186). Even though any particular group may act in odd or unusual ways, "it is difficult to deny that people collectively engage in these behaviors in a great variety of gatherings around the world" (p. 163).

seating arrangements or by custom. While observing, they may perform a variety of behaviors, including clapping, cheering, shouting, or questioning, but these actions are usually in accord with the norms of the particular setting. Moreover, when the event or performance has ended, the audience disperses in an orderly fashion (Hollingworth, 1935).

QUEUES A **queue**—a group of persons awaiting their turn—is a unique type of crowd. *Queue* comes from the French word for a braid of hair and so pays etymological homage to the queue's most common shape—a relatively straight line. But some settings, such as theme parks, lobbies, and registration offices, shape the queue into a zigzag pattern through the use of stanchions and ropes. Other establishments create dispersed queues by assigning queuers a number and then summoning them through a beeper or announcement when it is their turn. Queues can also be segmented into subgroups that are permitted to enter together, as when passengers board a plane in groups based on seat assignment. Some queues, too, are not at all linear, as when those waiting to board a bus (or to enter a crowded concert venue) move in a relatively unregulated way toward the entryway.

Like the common crowd, the queue includes strangers who will probably never meet again. But like the members of an audience, those in a queue have joined deliberately to achieve a particular goal, and thus, as members of the collective, they are bound by certain norms of behavior (L. Mann, 1969, 1970). Queues are an interference, for they prevent us from immediately achieving our goal of purchasing tickets, services, or other commodities, but they also protect us from late-arriving competitors for these commodities. As Milgram and his colleagues noted,

> As in the case of most social arrangements, people defer to the restraints of the form, but they are also its beneficiary. The queue thus constitutes a classic illustration of how individuals create social order, on the basis of a rudimentary principle of equity, in a situation that could otherwise degenerate into chaos. (Milgram, Liberty, Toledo, & Wackenhut, 1986, p. 683)

But what prevents the queue from breaking down into a disorderly crowd? Milgram noted that in addition to environmental supports, such as ushers and ropes, queues are also protected by norms of civility and justice. People in many cultures implicitly recognize the basic fairness of the principle "first come, first served," which the queue protects (Brady, 2002). When members join the queue, they accept its rules, and even though the group will disband as soon as the event begins, members conform to its norms and enforce them as needed (D. T. Miller, 2001).

Milgram studied queues by having both male and female accomplices break into 129 lines waiting outside ticket offices and the like in New York City. Working either alone or in pairs, the accomplices would simply say, "Excuse me, I'd like to get in here," and then insert themselves in the line. In an attempt to determine who would be most likely to enforce the norm, Milgram also included either one or two passive confederates in some of the queues he studied. These individuals, who were planted in the line in advance, stood directly behind the point of intrusion (Milgram et al., 1986).

---

queue A line, file, or set of people who are waiting for some service, commodity, or opportunity.

Objections occurred in nearly half of the lines studied. In a few cases (10.1%), queuers used physical action, such as a tap on the shoulder or a push. In 21.7% of the lines, the reaction was verbal, such as "No way! The line's back there. We've all been waiting and have trains to catch," or "Excuse me, it's a line." In another 14.7% of the lines, queuers used dirty looks, staring, and hostile gestures to object to the intrusion nonverbally. Objections were also more prevalent when two persons broke into the line rather than one, and they were least prevalent when two confederates separated the intruders from the other queuers. Overall, 73.3% of the complaints came from people standing behind the point of intrusion rather than from people standing in front of the intrusion. Other investigators found that queue-breakers encountered less hostility when they appeared to be joining someone they knew and when they only broke in near the very end of the line (B. H. Schmitt, Dubé, & Leclerc, 1992). These findings suggest that self-interest, as well as the normative force of the queue's rules, mediated reactions to the queue-breakers' actions.

MOBS When a gathering of people—a crowd, an audience, or even a queue—becomes emotionally charged, the collective can become a **mob.** Mobs tend to form when some event, such as a crime, a catastrophe, or a controversial action, evokes the same kind of affect and action in a substantial number of people. The hallmark of the mob is its emotion (J. Lofland, 1981). Early accounts of mobs argued that individuals in mobs were so overwhelmed by their emotions that they could no longer control their actions. Unless the situation is diffused, the mob becomes volatile, unpredictable, and capable of violent action. Mobs, as their name implies, are often highly *mobile,* with members moving together from one location to another, massing in a single location, or just milling about in unpatterned ways (Hughes, 2003).

Mobs, even though they stimulate their members' emotions, are not necessarily irrational, nor are they necessarily violent. When sports fans celebrate a victory, when partiers parade New Orleans streets during Mardi Gras, or when patriots celebrate the end of a conflict, the members of a mob share positive emotions—joy, jubilation, and exhilaration (Vider, 2004). Their aggressive counterparts, however, tend to be more common—or at least they receive more attention in the media (Milgram & Toch, 1969). *Lynch mobs* terrorized Black men in the southern United States until recently. The first documented lynch mob occurred in the United States in 1882, but by 1950, lynch mobs had killed thousands. Virtually all the victims were Black, and many of the killings were savagely brutal (Mullen, 1986a; Tolnay & Beck, 1996). *Hooliganism* is common in Europe. Large numbers of football (soccer) fans, often intoxicated, spill into the streets around the stadiums, fighting among themselves and with fans who support the opposing team (E. G. Dunning, Murphy, & Williams, 1986; Oyserman & Saltz, 1993). The abuse of low-status group members by groups of bullies, which is

---

mob A disorderly, emotionally charged crowd; mobs tend to form when some event, such as a crime, a catastrophe, or a controversial action, evokes the same kind of affect and action in a substantial number of people.

sometimes termed *mobbing,* is a regular occurrence in both school and work settings (B. Schuster, 1996; I. Whitney & Smith, 1993).

Riots can be construed as mobs on a grander scale. They often begin when a relatively peaceful crowd is transformed by a negative experience into a violent mob. For example, on the final night of the 1999 Woodstock music festival, an anti-violence group named PAX asked the audience to light candles as an expression of unity. A small group of concertgoers instead used the candles to burn down the outdoor venue. MTV news correspondent Kurt Loder described the incident as "the history of human terrestrial evolution recounted in reverse" (quoted in Vider, 2004, p. 114). In other cases, riots are an expression of unrest and protest in the general population. In 1921, for example, Whites in Tulsa, Oklahoma, attacked the highly successful Black business community of Greenwood. Hundreds died, and 35 city blocks of Black-owned businesses were destroyed. In the 1960s, riots diffused throughout many large American cites due, in part, to intergroup competition and racial tensions (D. J. Myers, 1997). In 1980 and 1992, residents of Liberty City, Florida, and Los Angeles, California, rioted when police officers charged with brutality were found not guilty. Riots are also sometimes motivated by the desire to loot and steal rather than by group-level processes. For example, in 1969, when the police force of Montreal went on strike for 17 hours, riots broke out all over the city. As expected, professional crimes skyrocketed, but the noncriminal population also ran amok. A heterogeneous crowd of impoverished, rich, and middle class people rampaged along the central business corridor, looting and vandalizing (G. Clark, 1969).

PANICS Some mobs are charged with a different set of emotions than anger; they are fearful, anxious, and frightened. These mobs have *panicked,* for they are either fleeing from an aversive situation (*escape panics*) or seeking out a limited resource that they fear will run out (*acquisitive panics*). Escaping mobs occur when crowds of people are overtaken by some catastrophe, such as a fire, flood, or earthquake, and they must escape en masse from the dangerous situation. Many groups exit such situations calmly, but if the situation is seen as very dangerous, and the escape routes are limited, a crowd can become a panicked mob (A. L. Strauss, 1944). Members, fearing personal harm or injury, struggle to escape both from the situation and from the crowd itself:

> The individual breaks away and wants to escape from it because the crowd, as a whole, is endangered. But because he is still stuck in it, he must attack it. . . . The more fiercely each man "fights for his life," the clearer it becomes he is fighting against all the others who hem him in. They stand there like chairs, balustrades, closed doors, but different from these in that they are alive and hostile. (Canetti, 1962, pp. 26–27)

Panics often result in a staggering loss of life. In 1903, for example, a panic at Chicago's Iroquois Theater killed nearly 600 people. When a small fire broke

---

riot A large and often widely dispersed crowd whose wanton and unrestrained behavior violates rules of civil and legal authority (e.g., harassment, looting, destruction of property, assault, violence).

out backstage, the management tried to calm the audience. But when the lights shorted out and the fire was visible behind the stage, the crowd stampeded for the exits. Some were burned, and others died by jumping from the fire escapes to the pavement, but many more were killed as fleeing patrons trampled them. One observer described the panic this way:

> In places on the stairways, particularly where a turn caused a jam, bodies were piled seven or eight feet deep. Firemen and police confronted a sickening task in disentangling them. An occasional living person was found in the heaps, but most of these were terribly injured. The heel prints on the dead faces mutely testified to the cruel fact that human animals stricken in terror are as mad and ruthless as stampeding cattle. Many bodies had the clothes torn from them, and some had the flesh trodden from their bones. (Foy & Harlow, 1928/1956)

Experimental simulations of panicked crowds suggest that individuals who must take turns exiting from a dangerous situation are most likely to panic when they believe that the time available to escape is very limited and when they are very fearful of the consequences of a failure to escape (Kelley, Contry, Dahlke, & Hill, 1965; Mintz, 1951). Larger groups, even if given more time to effect their escape, are also more likely to panic than smaller ones (Chertkoff, Kushigian, & McCool, 1996).

The group waiting for the Who concert was initially a queue—a disorganized queue, but a queue nonetheless. But when the doors opened, the queue became a surging crowd, and then a panic. Although the news media described the crowd as a drug-crazed stampede bent on storming into the concert, police interviews with survivors indicated that the crowd members in the center of the crush were trying to flee from the dangerous overcrowding rather than to get into the concert. Also, some individuals in the crowd were clearly fighting to get out of the danger, but some were Good Samaritans who helped others to safety (N. R. Johnson, 1987).

Collective Movements

Not all collective phenomena transpire at close distances. In some cases, individuals who are physically dispersed may act and react in similar and often atypical ways. Such curious phenomena are variously termed **collective movements,** *mass movements,* or *dispersed collective behavior,* although this terminology is by no means formalized or universally recognized (Genevie, 1978; Smelser, 1962). But like crowds, collective phenomena come in many varieties, including rumors, trends, and social movements (see Figure 16-3).

RUMORS AND MASS HYSTERIA In 1954, rumors that windshields were being damaged by nuclear fallout began circulating in the Seattle area. The rumors escalated into a mild form of mass hysteria as reporters devoted much attention

---

collective movement A large aggregation of individuals who strive to attain common goals, interests, or aspirations that is widely dispersed across space and time.

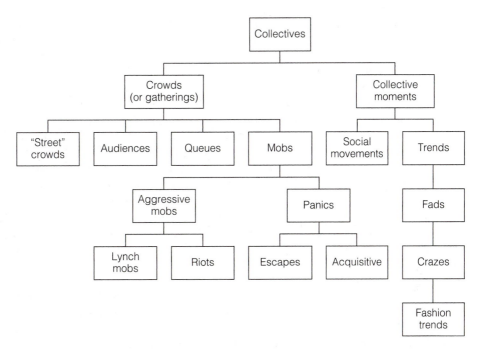

FIGURE 16-3

What are collectives? Gatherings of people are so diverse that they defy categorization, but most forms of collective action fit into two basic clusters—crowds (or gatherings) and social movements. *Sources:* R. W. Brown, 1954; Goffman, 1983; J. Lofland, 1981; McPhail, 1991.

to the issue, residents jammed police telephone lines reporting damage, and civic groups demanded government intervention. Subsequent investigation revealed that no damage at all had occurred (Medalia & Larsen, 1958).

Rumors provide people with a means of exchanging information about threatening situations and, in many cases, have a calming effect on groups and communities. In some cases, however, rumors can instigate more negative reactions to uncertainty, and play a part in triggering riots and panics. Future rioters, for example, often mill about for hours swapping stories about injustices before taking any aggressive action. Panics and crazes, too, are often sustained by rumors, particularly when the mass media perpetuate hearsay in news reports and announcements (G. W. Allport & Postman, 1947; Milgram & Toch, 1969). A recent epidemic of *koro* (a rare delusion characterized by the fear that one's sex organs will disappear) that swept through the Han region of China, for example, was traced to exposure to rumors about the fictitious malady (Cheng, 1997). Similarly, the riot that occurred at the 1999 Woodstock music festival was preceded by a day of rumors circulating through the crowd about what the final night of the concert would bring (Vider, 2004).

Ralph L. Rosnow (1980) argued that two conditions tend to influence the spread of rumor—the degree of *anxiety* that individuals are experiencing and their *uncertainty* about the true nature of the situation. He argued that just as individuals often affiliate with others in threatening situations, "ambiguous or chaotic" situations tend to generate rumors. By passing rumors, individuals convey information (albeit false) about the situation. Rumors also reduce anxiety by providing, in most cases, reassuring reinterpretations of the ambiguous event (C. J. Walker & Berkerle, 1987). After the Three Mile Island nuclear power plant accident, for example, rumors circulated so rampantly that a rumor control center had to be opened to supply more accurate information. Rosnow, after studying this incident, maintained that even though many of the rumors were preposterous, they gave people a sense of security in a time of great anxiety (Rosnow & Kimmel, 1979; Rosnow, Yost, & Esposito, 1986).

Rumors also provide the basis for **mass hysteria**—the spontaneous outbreak of atypical thoughts, feelings, or actions in a group or aggregation, including psychogenic illness, common hallucinations, and bizarre actions (Pennebaker, 1982; Phoon, 1982). Such episodes are uncommon, but they have occurred regularly throughout the modern era. For example, the *Werther syndrome* is named for Johann Wolfgang von Goethe's (1749–1832) novel *Die Leiden des Jungen Werthers* (The Sorrows of Young Werther), which triggered a fashion fad (many young men of the time imitated the eccentric style of dress of the book's hero, Werther) but also led to cluster suicides—many readers also killed themselves in the same way as Werther did. *Choreomania* is the term used to describe the compulsive dancing crazes of the late Middle Ages. *Tulipmania* caused financial ruin for many who speculated in the bulb market in Holland. In the 1600s, the price of tulip bulbs skyrocketed in the Netherlands, and trading for the precious bulbs was frenzied. Many traders lost their life savings when the price of bulbs plummeted in 1637. *Biting mania* was a 15th-century epidemic of mass hysteria, which began when a German nun developed a compulsive urge to bite her associates, who in turn bit others, until the mania spread to convents throughout Germany, Holland, and Italy. In more modern times, a large segment of U.S. residents panicked on Halloween night in 1938 when Orson Welles broadcast the radio play *The War of the Worlds*. When listeners thought they were hearing an actual news broadcast, many reacted by warning relatives, taking defensive precautions, contemplating suicide, and fleeing from the "invaded" areas (Cantril, 1940).

In some cases, unexplained epidemics of illnesses are thought to have been cases of **psychogenic illness** rather than organic illness. For example, in June 1962, workers at a garment factory began complaining of nausea, pain, disorientation, and muscular weakness; some actually collapsed at their jobs or lost consciousness. Rumors spread rapidly that the illness was caused by "some kind of insect" that had infested one of the shipments of cloth from overseas, and the owners began making efforts to eradicate the bug. No bug was ever discovered,

---

mass hysteria The spontaneous outbreak of atypical thoughts, feelings, or actions in a group or aggregation, including psychogenic illness, common hallucinations, and bizarre actions.

psychogenic illness A set of symptoms of illness in a group of persons when there is no evidence of an organic basis for the illness and no identifiable environmental cause.

however, and experts eventually concluded that the "June Bug incident" had been caused by mass hysteria (Kerckhoff & Back, 1968; Kerckhoff, Back, & Miller, 1965).

Researchers can never definitively determine which cases of widespread illness are socially produced rather than biologically produced, but one study of work groups identified 23 separate cases that involved large numbers of individuals afflicted with "physical symptoms . . . in the absence of an identifiable pathogen" (Colligan & Murphy, 1982, p. 35). More than 1200 people were affected by these outbreaks, with most reporting symptoms that included headaches, nausea, dizziness, and weakness. Many were women working in relatively repetitive, routinized jobs, and the illness often spread through friendship networks. Similarly, studies of pupils in school often conclude that many epidemics, such as outbreaks of fainting or nausea, are caused by hysterical contagion (Bartholomew, 1997; Bartholomew & Sirois, 1996; P. W. H. Lee, Leung, Fung, & Low, 1996). Some experts believe that as many as 75% of the epidemics that are blamed on the presence of irritants in buildings—the so-called *sick building syndrome*—are actually psychogenic illnesses (Rothman & Weintraub, 1995).

How can group-level delusions be controlled? Organizational experts suggest that as soon as the possibility of a physical cause is eliminated, workers should be told that their problems are more psychological than physical. A second means of limiting the spread of such delusions involves altering the setting. The outbreaks often occur when employees have been told to increase their productivity, or when they have been working overtime. Poor labor–management relations have also been implicated, as have negative environmental factors, such as noise, poor lighting, and exposure to dust, foul odors, or chemicals (Colligan, Pennebaker, & Murphy, 1982). Larger outbreaks of rumors and hysteria that sweep across whole regions and countries can be countered by providing citizens with clear, accurate information from trusted sources.

TRENDS In 1929, as the United States plunged into the Great Depression, people had little time or money to spend playing golf. But several entrepreneurs set up "miniature golf courses" in cities, and the idea took hold of the nation with a vengeance. Miniature golf spread over the entire country, and some people were predicting that the game would replace all other sports as the country's favorite form of recreation. The craze died out within 6 months (LaPiere, 1938).

Trends are changes in attitudes, actions, and behaviors that influence large segments of a population, such as whole communities or regions. Many of these changes are relatively pedestrian ones; shifts in the use of the Internet, for example, illustrate the diffusion of a technological innovation across the world. Others, in contrast, are more capricious and unpredictable. A *fad,* for example, is an unexpected, short-lived change in the opinions, behaviors, or lifestyles of a large number of widely dispersed individuals. Fads such as the Hula Hoop, the disco, reality television, and low-carbohydrate diets are remarkable both because

---

trend The general direction in which the attitudes, interests, and actions of a large segment of a population change over time, including fashion trends, fads, and crazes.

they influence so many people so rapidly and because they disappear without leaving any lasting impact on society. *Crazes* are similar to fads in most respects, except that they are just a bit more irrational, expensive, or widespread. Streaking (running naked) on college campuses, the rapid proliferation of cellular telephones, and the widespread use of cocaine all qualify as crazes. Finally, fads that pertain to styles of dress or manners are generally termed *fashion trends.* Clamdiggers gave way to hiphuggers, which were supplanted by bellbottoms, which lost out to blue jeans, which gave way to khaki. Ties and lapels expand and contract, women's hemlines move up and down, and last season's color takes a backseat to this season's shade (Ragone, 1981).

SOCIAL MOVEMENTS In 1096, thousands upon thousands of Europeans, urged on by Pope Urban II, marched to Jerusalem to "free the Holy Land from the pagans." In 1789, large bands of French citizens fought government forces and eventually overthrew the government. In December 1955, Dr. Martin Luther King, Jr., and a dozen other ministers founded the Montgomery Improvement Association, which succeeded in dismantling the segregated bus system in Montgomery, Alabama. In 1971, a group of protesters, calling themselves Greenpeace, organized a campaign to prevent environmental degradation. Greenpeace now claims 2.8 million members and is involved in 40 countries across Europe, the Americas, Asia, and the Pacific.

A **social movement** is a deliberate, relatively organized attempt to achieve a change or resist a change in a social system. Social movements, like other forms of collective behavior, often arise spontaneously in response to some problem, such as unfair government policies, societal ills, or threats to personal values. They are, in a sense, very large self-help groups, seeking to improve the lives of both members and nonmembers (de la Roche, 1996). Social movements are not short-lived, however. Over time, social movements tend to gain new members, set goals, and develop leadership structures, until eventually they change from spontaneous gatherings of people into *social movement organizations,* or *SMOs.* SMOs have all the structural characteristics of any organization, including clearly defined goals, rational planning, and bureaucratic leadership structures (Zald & Ash, 1966; see Gamson, 1992; McAdam, McCarthy, & Zald, 1988; and Snow & Oliver, 1995; for detailed reviews of social movements.)

Social movements, like crowds, vary in their longevity and their goals (Appelbaum & Chambliss, 1995; W. B. Cameron, 1966). *Reformist movements* seek to improve existing institutions, often through civil disobedience and demonstrations. The U.S. civil rights movement, for example, sought to change existing laws that gave unfair power to Whites, but the movement did not challenge the basic democratic principles of the country. *Revolutionary movements,* in contrast, seek more sweeping changes in existing social institutions. The revolts in France in the late 1700s, for example, were revolutionary movements, for the protesters

---

social movement A collective movement making a deliberate, organized attempt to achieve a change or resist a change in a social system.

sought to overthrow the monarchy and replace it with a democracy. *Reactionary movements,* instead of trying to achieve change, seek to resist it or even to reinstate extinct social systems. The Ku Klux Klan is one such movement, as are many militia groups and groups that argue against alternative lifestyles. *Communitarian movements* strive to create more ideal living conditions than currently exist in modern society, often by withdrawing from contact with nonmembers. The communes of the 1960s were communitarian movements, as are such radical religious groups as Heaven's Gate, the Branch Davidians, the People's Temple, and the Solar Temple.

COLLECTIVE DYNAMICS

Groups that undertake extreme actions—crowds, mobs, riots, cults—fascinate layperson and researcher alike. Although groups are so commonplace that they usually go unnoticed and unscrutinized, atypical groups and their members invite speculation, raising questions such as, "What unseen forces control people when they are part of an extraordinary group? Why do crowds sometimes turn into violent mobs? Do human beings lose their rationality when they are immersed in mobs?" (D. L. Miller, 1985; McPhail & Wohlstein, 1983; R. H. Turner & Killian, 1987).

Le Bon's Crowd Psychology

Gustave Le Bon published his classic analysis of mobs and movements, *The Crowd,* in 1895. Le Bon was fascinated by large groups, but he also feared their tendency to erupt into violence. Perhaps because of these biases, he concluded that a crowd of people could, in certain instances, become a unified entity that acted as if guided by a single collective mind. Le Bon wrote,

> Whoever be the individuals that compose it, however like or unlike be their mode of life, their occupations, their character, or their intelligence, the fact that they have been transformed into a crowd puts them in possession of a sort of collective mind which makes them feel, think, and act in a manner quite different from that in which each individual of them would feel, think, and act were he in a state of isolation. (1895/1960, p. 27)

Le Bon believed that no matter what the individual qualities of the people in the group, the crowd would transform them, changing them from rational, thoughtful individuals into impulsive, unreasonable, and extreme followers. Once people fall under the "law of the mental unity of crowds" (1895/1960, p. 24), they act as the collective mind dictates.

Le Bon was a physician, so he viewed the collective mind as a kind of disease that infected one part of the group and then spread throughout the rest of the crowd (see Focus 16-2). After observing many crowds firsthand, Le Bon concluded that emotions and behaviors could be transmitted from one person to

FOCUS 16-2 Are Social Trends Infectious?

In a crowd every sentiment and act is contagious.
–Le Bon (1895/1960, p. 50)

Society changes gradually over time as new ideas, behaviors, and innovations pass from one person and group to another in waves, except in the cases of fads, crazes, and other fast-moving trends that diffuse rapidly across large segments of society. In 1978, few people owned microwave ovens. By 1990, nearly everyone did. The compact disc was a novelty for several years, until it suddenly and almost completely replaced vinyl records. Sales of Hush Puppy shoes jumped from 30,000 pairs to 430,000 pairs in one year.

Malcolm Gladwell's (2000) *tipping point theory* suggests that fast-moving trends are flu-like, spreading like contagious diseases through social groups. Gladwell drew the concept of a tipping point from studies of rapid changes in residential composition that occurred in predominantly White neighborhoods in the 1980s. These neighborhoods changed little when a few Black families moved in. But when the number of Black families reached a certain value—the *tipping point*—a large proportion of the prejudiced White residents moved out, and the neighborhood resegregated. Unlike most social changes, which are gradual and ubiquitous, this "White flight" was an abrupt, threshold-crossing process.

An illness, such as the flu, passes from one person to another, and individuals who interact with large numbers of people when their flu is in its communicable stage will infect far more people than will a person who stays at home. Similarly, Gladwell noted that certain types of individuals play prominent roles in the generation of social change. They are the people with large social networks (*connectors*), the individuals who are opinion authorities (*mavens*), and those who are able to persuade others to change their minds (*salespeople*). Relative to most people, these influential individuals can push an idea much more rapidly to many more people. Connectors, for example, have been identified as one source of the rapid shift in popularity of new musical groups. When investigators asked fans of a new musical group how many other people they told about the band, they discovered that most fans told only a few other people. But a small number of the fans—the connectors—told many more of their friends about the group, including one individual who claimed to have spread the message to more than 150 people (Reifman, Lee, & Apparala, 2004). Advertisers now target such influential persons, in the belief that if they win them over as customers, the rest of their network will follow (Keller & Berry, 2003).

another just as germs can be passed along, and he believed that this process of **contagion** accounted for the tendency of group members to behave in very similar ways (L. Wheeler, 1966).

The occurrence of contagion in groups is quite common. People unconsciously mimic each other during everyday social interaction—if one person stands with her arms crossed over her chest, before long several of the others in the group will also cross their arms (Chartrand & Bargh, 1999). One person laughing in an audience will stimulate laughter in others. Question and answer sessions after a lecture usually begin very slowly, but they soon snowball as more and more questioners begin raising their hands. Individuals' emotions tend to converge over time when they interact frequently in groups (C. Anderson, Keltner, & Oliver,

---

contagion The spread of behaviors, attitudes, and affect through crowds and other types of social aggregations from one member to another.

2003). Le Bon believed that such contagion processes reflected the heightened suggestibility of crowd members, but other processes may be at work as well. Because many crowd settings are ambiguous, social comparison processes may prompt members to rely heavily on other members' reactions when they interpret the situation (J. E. Singer, Baum, Baum, & Thew, 1982). Contagion may also arise in crowds through imitation, social facilitation, or conformity (Chapman, 1973; Freedman & Perlick, 1979; Nosanchuk & Lightstone, 1974; Tarde, 1903).

Herbert Blumer combined these various processes when he argued that contagion involves circular reactions rather than interpretive reactions (Blumer, 1946, 1951, 1957). During interpretive interactions, group members carefully reflect on the meaning of others' behavior and try to formulate valid interpretations before making any kind of comment or embarking on a line of action. During circular reactions, however, the group's members fail to examine the meaning of others' actions cautiously and carefully and, therefore, tend to misunderstand the situation. When they act on the basis of such misunderstandings, the others in the group also begin to interpret the situation incorrectly, and a circular process is thus initiated that eventually culminates in full-blown behavioral contagion.

Convergence Theories

Why do people join collectives? **Convergence theory** assumes that individuals who join rallies, riots, movements, crusades, and the like all possess particular personal characteristics that influence their group-seeking tendencies. Although these predisposing features may be latent and unrecognizable, they are hypothesized to be the true causes of the formation of both large and small collectives. Such aggregations are not haphazard gatherings of dissimilar strangers; rather, they represent the convergence of people with compatible needs, desires, motivations, and emotions. By joining in the group, the individual makes possible the satisfaction of these needs, and the crowd situation serves as a trigger for the spontaneous release of previously controlled behaviors. As Eric Hoffer (1951) wrote, "All movements, however different in doctrine and aspiration, draw their early adherents from the same types of humanity; they all appeal to the same types of mind" (p. 9).

But what "types of mind" are likely to join a crowd or movement? Are crowd members "joiners"? Are people who seek out membership in collective movements different, in terms of their personalities and values, than people who do not join such groups? Early conceptions of crowds, which portrayed their members as less intelligent, more easily influenced, more impulsive, and more violent, have not received consistent empirical support (E. D. Martin, 1920; Meerloo, 1950). Participants in mobs—particularly in connection with sports—tend to be younger men who have engaged in aggressive crowd activities in the past (Arms & Russell, 1997; G. W. Russell & Arms, 1998). People who join radical religious groups are usually teenagers or young adults, and although they tend to

---

convergence theory An explanation of collective behavior assuming that individuals with similar needs, values, or goals tend to converge to form a single group.

be more idealistic and open to new experiences, and also higher in psychological dependency, they show no signs of psychological disturbance (Bromley, 1985; S. V. Levine, 1984; Y. Walsh, Russell, & Wells, 1995). People who join social movements do tend to be higher in *personal efficacy*—they believe that through their personal involvement, they can make a difference (Snow & Oliver, 1995). Self-confidence, achievement orientation, need for autonomy, dominance, self-acceptance, and maturity are also positively correlated with social activism (P. Werner, 1978). Individuals who have a history of taking part in collectives tend to jump at the chance to join new ones (Corning & Myers, 2002), but those who have a history of avoiding conflict tend to avoid them (Ulbig & Funk 1999).

People who are particularly frustrated by their economic or social situation are also more likely to take part in social movements. As the concept of **relative deprivation** suggests, people who are suffering the most—those who are the most impoverished, persecuted, or endangered—are not necessarily the most likely to join revolutionary social movements. Rather, those who join social movements tend to be people who have higher expectations but who have not succeeded in realizing these expectations. Consider, for example, the Black Power movement of the 1960s (Milgram & Toch, 1969). African Americans who joined this collective were often individuals who had succeeded in escaping from poverty, crime, and discrimination. These gains, however, served to raise their expectations, which remained largely unfulfilled. These individuals thus experienced greater frustration and anger than African Americans who experienced more intense privations but expected little better. They responded by taking part in change-promoting groups (N. Caplan, 1970; Crosby, 1976).

The tendency to take part in social movements appears to be more closely linked to fraternal deprivation than to egoistic deprivation. *Egoistic deprivation* occurs when individuals are dissatisfied with the gains they have personally achieved. *Fraternal deprivation* occurs when one is a member of a group that does not enjoy the same level of prosperity as other groups (Runcimann, 1966). Individuals who are active in revolutionary social movements, such as the national separatist movement in Quebec and Ireland, are more likely to be dissatisfied with their group's outcomes than with their own personal outcomes (Abrams, 1990; Guimond & Dubé-Simard, 1983).

Emergent Norm Theory

Ralph H. Turner and Lewis M. Killian's **emergent norm theory** questions the idea that unusual social processes operate in crowds and collectives (R. H. Turner, 1964; R. H. Turner & Killian, 1972). Turner and Killian rejected one of the

---

relative deprivation The psychological state that occurs when individuals feel that their personal attainments (*egoistic* deprivation) or their group's attainments (*fraternalistic* deprivation) are below their expectations.

emergent norm theory An explanation of collective behavior suggesting that the uniformity in behavior often observed in collectives is caused by members' conformity to unique normative standards that develop spontaneously in those groups.

fundamental assumptions of most collective behavior theories—that crowds are extremely homogeneous—and concluded that the mental unity of crowds is primarily an illusion. Crowds, mobs, and other collectives only seem to be unanimous in their emotions and actions because the members all adhere to norms that are relevant in the given situation. Granted, these *emergent norms* may be unique and sharply contrary to more general societal standards, but as they emerge in the group situation, they exert a powerful influence on behavior.

Turner and Killian based their analysis on Sherif's (1936) classic analysis of the gradual alignment of action in groups. As noted in Chapter 6, norms emerge gradually in ambiguous situations as members align their actions. Individuals do not actively try to conform to the judgments of others, but instead use the group consensus when making their own behavioral choices. In most cases, the group's norms are consistent with more general social norms pertaining to work, family, relations, and civility. In other cases, however, norms emerge in groups that are odd, atypical, or unexpected.

A normative approach partly explains **baiting crowds**—groups that form below a person who is threatening to commit suicide by jumping from a building, bridge, or tower (L. Mann, 1981). These crowds, rather than merely watching, often begin to bait the jumper who fails to act swiftly. When Leon Mann studied members of such crowds, he was unable to identify any similarities in personality or demographic characteristics (as convergence theory would suggest). He did note, however, that baiting became more likely as crowd size increased. Mann suggested that larger crowds are more likely to include at least one person who introduces the baiting norm into the group. "In a large crowd at least one stupid or sadistic person will be found who is prepared to cry 'Jump!' and thereby provide a model suggestible for others to follow" (L. Mann, 1981, p. 707). Mann reported evidence of conformity to the baiting norm in crowds that not only encouraged the victim to "end it all" but also jeered and booed as rescuers attempted to intervene.

Emergent norm theory, in contrast to other analyses of crowds and collectives, argues that collectives are not out of control or normless. Rather, their behavior is socially structured, but by an unusual, temporary norm rather than by more traditional social standards. For example, cults, such as Heaven's Gate, condone mass suicide. Adolescent peer cliques pressure members to take drugs and commit illegal acts (Corsaro & Eder, 1995; Giordano, 2002). Groups of women, such as sororities, can develop norms that promote unhealthy actions, such as binge eating and purging (Crandall, 1988). Urban gangs accept norms that emphasize toughness, physical strength, and the use of drugs (Coughlin & Venkatesh, 2003; Jankowski, 1991). Groups of hooligans at British soccer matches consider violence a normal part of the event, and the mass media sustain this view (D. Dunning, Murphy, & Williams, 1986; Ward, 2002). Although these actions—when viewed from a more objective perspective—may seem out of control and very strange, for the group members they are literally "normal."

---

baiting crowd A gathering of people in a public location whose members torment, tease, or goad others.

Deindividuation Theory

Philip Zimbardo's (1969) process model of deindividuation offers a counterpoint to emergent norm theory. This model, which is summarized in Figure 16-4, suggests that people *escape* normative regulation in mobs and crowds. If people become so deeply submerged in their group that they feel as though they no longer stand out as individuals, this feeling can create a "reduction of inner restraints" (Festinger, Pepitone, & Newcomb, 1952). Zimbardo's model assumes that anonymity, reduced responsibility, and other situational features can create **deindividuation**—a subjective experience in which the individual group members experience "a lowered threshold of normally restrained behavior" (Zimbardo, 1969, p. 251, 1975, 1977a).

ANONYMITY Zimbardo believed that anonymity was a variable of paramount importance in the deindividuation process. Group members achieve anonymity in many ways—wearing disguises, using an alias, avoiding acquaintances, or joining a group whose members are very similar to one another. If people conform to norms only because they fear legal reprisals, anonymity decreases the likelihood that those in authority will locate and punish them for engaging in strange or illegal activities (Dodd, 1985; Ley & Cybriwsky, 1974a). In such cases, anonymity and atypical action go hand in hand. Leon Mann (1981) found that baiting crowds gather at night, when their members' identities are masked by darkness. Studies of people communicating by computer have found that *flaming*—the use of inappropriately expressed criticism when communicating with others—is more likely when people feel anonymous (S. Kiesler, Siegel, & McGuire, 1984; T. W. McGuire, Kiesler, & Siegel, 1987). According to anthropological evidence, warriors in 92.3% (12 out of 13) of the most highly aggressive cultures—ones known to practice headhunting and to torture captives—disguised themselves prior to battle, whereas only 30% (3 out of 10) of the low-aggression cultures featured similar rituals (R. I. Watson, 1973). Even groups assembled in classroom and laboratory settings behave more inappropriately when their members are anonymous: They use obscene language, break conventional norms governing conversation, express themselves in extreme ways, criticize one another, and perform embarrassing behaviors (Cannavale, Scarr, & Pepitone, 1970; Lindskold & Finch, 1982; Mathes & Guest, 1976; J. E. Singer, Brush, Lublin, 1965).

Research also suggests that anonymity increases aggression (Donnerstein, Donnerstein, Simon, & Ditrichs, 1972; L. Mann, Newton, & Innes, 1982; Mathes & Kahn, 1975; R. A. Page & Moss, 1976). Zimbardo (1969), under an elaborate pretense, asked all-female groups to give 20 electric shocks to two women. *Anonymous* women wore large lab coats (size 44) and hoods over their heads, and they were not permitted to use their names. Women who were *identifiable* were greeted by name and wore large name tags, and the experimenter

---

deindividuation An experiential state caused by a number of input factors, such as group membership and anonymity, that is characterized by the loss of self-awareness, altered experiencing, and atypical behavior.

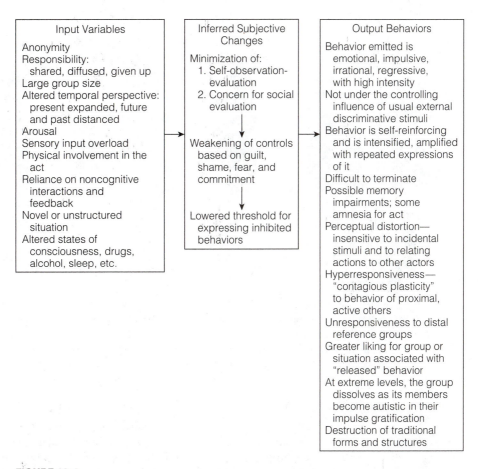

Input Variables	Inferred Subjective Changes	Output Behaviors

Anonymity
Responsibility:
  shared, diffused, given up
Large group size
Altered temporal perspective:
  present expanded, future
  and past distanced
Arousal
Sensory input overload
Physical involvement in the
  act
Reliance on noncognitive
  interactions and
  feedback
Novel or unstructured
  situation
Altered states of
  consciousness, drugs,
  alcohol, sleep, etc.
	Minimization of:
	1. Self-observation-
	  evaluation
	2. Concern for social
	  evaluation
	
	↓
	
	Weakening of controls
	based on guilt,
	shame, fear, and
	commitment
	
	↓
	
	Lowered threshold for
	expressing inhibited
	behaviors
		Behavior emitted is
		  emotional, impulsive,
		  irrational, regressive,
		  with high intensity
		Not under the controlling
		  influence of usual external
		  discriminative stimuli
		Behavior is self-reinforcing
		  and is intensified, amplified
		  with repeated expressions
		  of it
		Difficult to terminate
		Possible memory
		  impairments; some
		  amnesia for act
		Perceptual distortion—
		  insensitive to incidental
		  stimuli and to relating
		  actions to other actors
		Hyperresponsiveness—
		  "contagious plasticity"
		  to behavior of proximal,
		  active others
		Unresponsiveness to distal
		  reference groups
		Greater liking for group or
		  situation associated with
		  "released" behavior
		At extreme levels, the group
		  dissolves as its members
		  become autistic in their
		  impulse gratification
		Destruction of traditional
		  forms and structures

FIGURE 16-4

What is deindividuation? Zimbardo's (1969) model specifies the conditions of deindividuation—features of the group situation, such as anonymity and responsibility, that stimulate or retard the onset of the process. These features lead to the deindividuated state, which in turn generates a series of deindividuated behaviors that represent the outputs of the process.

emphasized their uniqueness and individuality. Although identifiability was unrelated to the number of shocks given (the average was 17 of 20), the unidentifiable participants held their switches down nearly twice as long as the identifiable participants (0.90 second versus 0.47 second).

Zimbardo's decision to dress his participants in hoods—the garb of lynch mobs and other criminals—may have exaggerated the relationship between anonymity and aggression. His participants might have responded to the experimenter's orders to deliver the shock differently if prosocial cues rather than antisocial cues had been present in the setting. Researchers verified this tendency, giving the White women who acted as participants costumes to wear under the guise of masking individual characteristics. In the *prosocial cues condition,* the ex-

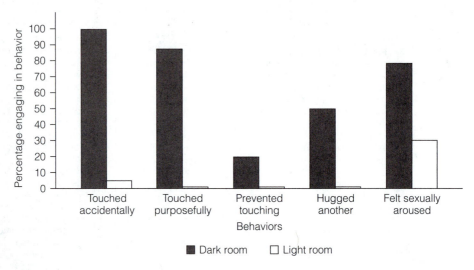

FIGURE 16-5

What would a group of people do if they found themselves in a totally darkened room with strangers? Groups in a darkened room engaged in many behaviors that under more usual circumstances would have been odd. *Source:* "Deviance in the Dark" by K. J. Gergen, M. M. Gergen, and W. H. Barton. Reprinted with permission from *Psychology Today Magazine.* Copyright © 1973 (Sussex Publishers, Inc.).

perimenter explained that "I was fortunate the recovery room let me borrow these nurses' gowns." But in the *antisocial cues condition,* the experimenter mentioned that the costumes resembled Ku Klux Klan outfits: "I'm not much of a seamstress; this thing came out looking kind of Ku Klux Klannish" (R. D. Johnson & Downing, 1979, p. 1534). Anonymity *polarized* the groups, making them more prosocial or more antisocial depending on the valence of the situational cues.

Anonymity also polarized responses of participants who were sitting in a totally darkened room. All the participants in this study were escorted to and from the room and were assured that the other participants would not be told their identities. The individuals in the dark room reported feeling aroused, but in no case did the anonymous (and possibly deindividuated) group members exhibit hostility, aggressiveness, or violence. Rather, nearly all became more intimate and supportive. In the words of one participant, a "group of us sat closely together, touching, feeling a sense of friendship and loss as a group member left. I left with a feeling that it had been fun and nice" (Gergen, Gergen, & Barton, 1973, p. 129). Apparently, the situation helped people express feelings that they would have otherwise kept hidden, but these feelings were those of affection rather than aggression (see Figure 16-5).

RESPONSIBILITY As Le Bon argued many years ago, the crowd is "anonymous, and in consequence irresponsible" (1895/1960, p. 30). When individuals are part of a group, they tend to feel less responsible. This *diffusion of responsibility* has been verified in dozens of studies of people who faced various emergencies alone or in a group (see Chapter 7). Members of groups may also experience a reduction in responsibility if an authority demands compliance (Milgram, 1974) or if they do not recognize the connections between their personal actions and their final consequences. Some groups actually take steps to ensure the diffusion of responsibility, as when murderers pass around their weapons from hand to hand so that responsibility for the crime is distributed through the entire group rather than concentrated in the one person who pulls the trigger or wields the knife (Zimbardo, 1969).

GROUP MEMBERSHIP Deindividuation is a group-level process—individuals may feel anonymous or uncertain as to their identity, but only groups create the sense of anonymity and diffusion of responsibility that generates deindividuation. Edward Diener and his associates tested this assumption in an ingenious study of Halloween trick-or-treating (Diener, Fraser, Beaman, & Kelem, 1976). Their participants were 1352 children from the Seattle area who visited one of the 27 experimental homes scattered throughout the city. An observer hidden behind a decorative panel recorded the number of extra candy bars and money (pennies and nickels) taken by the trick-or-treaters who were told to take one candy bar each. The children came to the house alone or in small groups (exceedingly large groups were not included in the study, nor were groups that included an adult). An experimenter manipulated anonymity by asking some children to give their names and addresses. As expected, the children took more money and candy in groups than alone and when they were anonymous rather than identified. The effects of anonymity on solitary children were not very pronounced, however, whereas in the group conditions, the impact of anonymity was enhanced (see Figure 16-6). These findings, which have been supported by other investigations, suggest that the term *deindividuation* is used most appropriately in reference to people who perform atypical behavior while they are members of a group (Cannavale, Scarr, & Pepitone, 1970; Mathes & Guest, 1976; Mathes & Kahn, 1975).

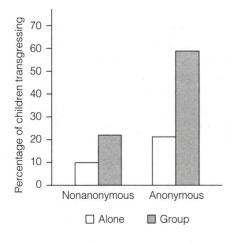

FIGURE 16-6

What are the combined effects of anonymity and group membership on counternormative behavior? Both anonymity and group membership contributed to transgression, but anonymity combined with group membership produced a more substantial increase in transgression. *Source:* "Effects of Deindividuating Variables on Stealing by Halloween Trick-or-Treaters," by E. Diener, S. C. Fraser, A. L. Beaman, and R. T. Kelem, *Journal of Personality and Social Psychology,* 1976, 33, 178–183. Copyright 1976 by the American Psychological Association. Reprinted by permission.

GROUP SIZE Are larger groups more likely to act in unusual ways? Leon Mann's (1981) study of baiting crowds found that large crowds (more than 300 members) baited more than small crowds. Mann also discovered that people are more likely to respond to religious messages when they are part of a larger rather than a smaller group (Newton & Mann, 1980). At the end of many religious meetings, audience members are invited to become "inquirers" by coming forward and declaring their dedication to Christ. In 57 religious meetings, the correlation between crowd size and the proportion of people who moved down to the stage to become inquirers was .43. On Sundays, the correlation rose to .78. Larger lynch mobs are also more violent than smaller ones. When Brian Mullen (1986a) examined the records of 60 lynchings in which the number of victims ranged from one to four and the size of the mob ranged from 4 to 15,000, he found that as the ratio of victims to mob size decreased, atrocities increased.

AROUSAL Zimbardo listed a number of other variables that stimulate deindividuated action, including altered temporal perspective, sensory overload, heightened involvement, lack of situational structure, and use of drugs. Many of these factors, he suggested, function by both arousing and distracting group members. Zimbardo even suggested that certain rituals, such as war dances and group singing, are actually designed to arouse participants and enable them to be deindividuated when the fighting starts: "Among cannibals, like the Cenis or certain Maori and Nigerian tribes, the activity of ritual bonfire dance which precedes eating the flesh of another human being is always more prolonged and intense when the victim is to be eaten alive or uncooked" (1969, p. 257). Aroused individuals, as deindividuation theory suggests, tend to respond more aggressively, particularly when in a group (Goldstein, 2003).

SELF-AWARENESS Zimbardo's deindividuation theory posits that situational variables, such as anonymity and membership in a group, can in some cases combine to induce psychological changes in group members. Deindividuated people, Zimbardo predicted, should feel very little self-awareness, and this minimization of self-scrutiny is the most immediate cause of the atypical behaviors seen in collectives.

Edward Diener (1979, 1980) tested this hypothesis by making use of an Asch-type experimental situation. He created eight-person groups, but he included in each group six accomplices trained to facilitate or inhibit the development of deindividuation. In the *self-aware condition,* the confederates seemed restless and fidgety. Everyone wore name tags as they worked on tasks designed to heighten self-awareness, such as providing personal responses to questions, sharing their opinions on topics, and disclosing personal information about themselves. In the *non-self-aware condition,* Diener shifted the participants' focus of attention outward by having them perform a series of mildly distracting tasks. The problems were not difficult, but they required a good deal of concentration and creativity. In the *deindividuation condition,* Diener tried to foster feelings of group cohesiveness, unanimity, and anonymity by treating the members as interchangeable and by putting the groups through a variety of arousing activities.

TABLE 16-2   Characteristics of factors that combine to create a state of deindividuation

Factor	Typical Characteristics
Loss of self-awareness	Minimal self-consciousness
	Lack of conscious planning as behavior becomes spontaneous
	Lack of concern for what others think of one
	Subjective feeling that time is passing quickly
	Liking for the group and feelings of group unity
	Uninhibited speech
	Performing uninhibited tasks
Altered experiencing	Unusual experiences, such as hallucinations
	Altered states of consciousness
	Subjective loss of individual identity
	Feelings of anonymity
	Liking for the group and feelings of group unity

Source: "Deindividuation, Self-Awareness, and Disinhibition," by E. Diener, *Journal of Personality and Social Psychology,* 1979, 37, 1160–1171. Copyright 1979 by the American Psychological Association. Adapted by permission.

When Diener asked the participants to describe how they felt during the study, he identified the two clusters, or factors, shown in Table 16-2. The first factor, *self-awareness,* encompasses a lack of self-consciousness, little planning of action, high group unity, and uninhibited action. The second dimension, *altered experiencing,* is also consistent with the deindividuation theory in that it ties together a number of related processes, such as "unusual" experiences, altered perceptions, and a loss of individual identity. When Diener compared the responses of participants in the three conditions of his experiment, he discovered that (1) deindividuated participants displayed a greater loss of self-awareness than both the non-self-aware and the self-aware participants and (2) deindividuated participants reported more extreme altered experiencing than the self-aware participants.

Steven Prentice-Dunn and Ronald W. Rogers (1982) extended these findings by leading the members of four-man groups to believe that they were going to deliver electric shocks to another person. Half of the participants were led through a series of experiences that focused their attention on the situation, whereas the others were frequently reminded to pay attention to their personal feelings. Moreover, some participants were told that their actions would be carefully monitored, whereas others were led to believe that their actions were not going to be linked to them personally. The results of the study supported Diener's two-factor model of deindividuation on three counts. First, the participants who were prompted to focus on the situation were lower in private self-awareness, and they tended to behave more aggressively. Second, analysis of the participants' questionnaire responses revealed the two components emphasized by Diener: low self-awareness and altered experiencing. Third, using a statistical procedure known as path analysis, Prentice-Dunn and Rogers found that both of these components mediated the relationship between the variables they manipulated and the participants' aggressive response (Prentice-Dunn & Rogers, 1980, 1982, 1983; Prentice-Dunn & Spivey, 1986; R. W. Rogers & Prentice-Dunn, 1981).

However, other studies of the nature of the deindividuated state—and the impact of this state on group members' behavior—have not consistently supported Zimbardo's model. When Tom Postmes and Russell Spears (1998) conducted a meta-analysis of 60 studies of the theory, they found that such situational factors as anonymity, group size, and group membership were associated, albeit weakly, with antinormative behavior. They found little support, however, for the assumption that these factors trigger psychological changes, and that these changes mediate the relationship between situational factors and aberrant actions. Their analysis also yielded more support for emergent norm theory's prediction that anonymity and group membership increase conformity to norms that emerge spontaneously in the group setting. They concluded that crowd members are not rule breakers but rather conformists who are following the example set by others in the group situation.

Collectives and Identity

Deindividuation theory assumes that when individuals in collectives lose their sense of identity, they are more likely to act in unusual ways. Yet in many cases, collectives sustain rather than undermine individuals' identities. The act of joining a social movement, for instance, can be one of self-definition (Polletta & Jasper, 2001). For example, the alcoholic who joins Alcoholics Anonymous proclaims, "I am an alcoholic," just as the man who joins Promise Keepers lays public claim to his religiosity and masculinity (Melucci, 1989). Collectives are also intergroup settings, so when individuals join them, their personal and social identities change (Reicher & Levine, 1994; Reicher, Spears, & Postmes, 1995).

SOCIAL IDENTITY AND INTERGROUP CONFLICT Mobs, riots, and gangs are often intergroup phenomena. Riots in inner cities, for example, usually occur when inner-city residents contend against another group: the police (Goldberg, 1968). Violence during athletic competitions often occurs when the fans of one team attack, en masse, the fans or players of another team (Leonard, 1980). Protests on college campuses pit students against the university administration (Lipset & Wolin, 1965). Inner-city gangs vie for turf against other gangs (W. B. Sanders, 1994). Militia groups rise up to confront civil and judicial authorities (Flynn & Gerhardt, 1989). Lynch mobs were crowds of Whites with high solidarity who attacked Blacks (de la Roche, 2001). A lone collective is a rarity, for in most cases, collectives emerge in opposition to other collectives.

Collectives, as intergroup phenomena, provide members with an enlarged view of the self, based not just on individual qualities but also on collectivistic qualities. Such collectives do not lead to deindividuation, but to a depersonalized sense of self that reflects group-level qualities rather than individual ones. The presence of an outgroup increases the salience of the collective identity, and members begin to perceive themselves and the situation in ways that reflect the ingroup–outgroup bias: Other members of the ingroup are viewed positively, as are their actions, whereas outgroup members and their actions are denigrated (see Chapter 13).

Stephen D. Reicher's (1984, 1987, 1996, 2001) analyses of rioters' social identities are consistent with social identity theory. One riot occurred when members of the National Union of Students organized a demonstration in London. The leaders of the group planned to march to the Houses of Parliament, but when the police blocked their path, conflict erupted. As the tension between the groups escalated, the students became more unified. When one member of the group was arrested by the police, students attacked the police unit as a group. They also felt that the police were behaving violently and that they themselves only responded in self-defense. As one student put it, "To some extent there was a feeling of there was the students and there was the police and you knew which side you were on so you had to be up in the front with students, you know. And there was a lot of crowd empathy" (quoted in Reicher, 1996, p. 126).

INDIVIDUATION A paradox permeates the analysis of individuality and collectives. On the one hand, many theorists assume that submersion in a group results in the attainment of power and an escape from societal inhibitions; hence, group members seek and try to maintain the experience of deindividuation. In contrast, many psychologists believe that people can enjoy psychological well-being only when they are able to establish and maintain their own unique identities. In the words of R. D. Laing (1960, p. 44), "A firm sense of one's own autonomous identity is required in order that one may be related as one human being to another. Otherwise, any and every relationship threatens the individual with loss of identity" (Dipboye, 1977; Fromm, 1965; Laing, 1960; Maslow, 1968).

An *identity affirmation* approach to collective behavior suggests that group members who feel "lost" in a group will try to reestablish their individual identities. People in large crowds, for example, may act oddly to regain a sense of individuality, not because they feel anonymous. Individuals who take part in riots may do so not to protest their group's unfair treatment, but to reaffirm their individual identities. As one resident of the riot-torn community of Watts (in Los Angeles) explained, "I don't believe in burning, stealing, or killing, but I can see why the boys did what they did. They just wanted to be noticed, to let the world know the seriousness of their state of life" (Milgram & Toch, 1969, p. 576). Similarly, members of large groups, such as industrial workers, students in large classrooms, people working in bureaucratic organizations, and employees in companies with high turnover rates, may perform atypical actions just to stand apart from the crowd.

Christina Maslach (1972) examined this *individuation* process by making two people in a four-person group feel individuated; she referred to them by name, made more personal comments to them, and maintained a significant amount of eye contact. She made the other two feel deindividuated by avoiding close contact with them and addressing them impersonally. When these individuals were later given the opportunity to engage in a free-response group discussion and to complete some questionnaires, the deindividuated participants evidenced various identity-seeking reactions. Some attempted to make themselves seem as different as possible from the other group members by giving more unusual answers to the questions, making longer comments, joining in the discussion more frequently, and attempting to capture the attention of the experimenter. Other participants seemed to redefine their identities by revealing more intimate details of their personalities and beliefs through longer and more unusual self-descriptions.

COLLECTIVES ARE GROUPS

All groups are intriguing, but groups that undertake extreme actions under the exhortation of exotic, charismatic leaders—cults, mobs, crowds, and the like—fascinate both layperson and researcher. Although groups are so commonplace that they often go unnoticed and unscrutinized, atypical groups invite speculation and inquiry. But are such groups mad? Do human beings lose their rationality when they are immersed in mobs?

The Myth of the Madding Crowd

For well over a century, most theorists and researchers have assumed that crowds are unique social aggregations, a "perversion of human potential" (Zimbardo, 1969, p. 237) where impulse and chaos replace reason and order. Le Bon argued that crowds develop a collective mind that leaves individual members unable to think for themselves. Convergence theories assume that atypical groups are staffed by atypical people. Groups often develop odd, unusual norms, and members may forget who they are when they sink too deeply into their groups. This belief in the "madness of crowds" is so deeply ingrained in our conception of collectives that some individuals who commit violent crimes in groups face reduced sentences. Deindividuated and driven to conform to their group's norms, they are not held personally responsible for their actions (Colman, 1991).

Yet collectives are, at their core, groups, and so the processes that shape group behaviors also shape collective behaviors. Many contemporary theorists, rather than assuming that collectives are atypical groups that require special theories that include novel or even mysterious processes, argue that the "madding crowd" is more myth than reality. Collective behavior is not bizarre, but instead a rational attempt by a number of individuals to seek change through united action. These groups form, change, and disband following the same patterns that govern other groups, and the internal structures and processes of a collective and a group are more similar than they are different (J. Lofland, 1981; McPhail, 1991; Snow & Oliver, 1995).

Clark McPhail (1991) elaborated this viewpoint in his book *The Myth of the Madding Crowd*. McPhail maintained that early theorists were too biased by their preconceived belief that crowds are crazed. McPhail himself carried out extensive field studies of actual collective movements over a 10-year period so that he could determine firsthand what such groups do. His conclusions were threefold:

> First, individuals are not driven mad by crowds; they do not lose cognitive control! Second, individuals are not compelled to participate by some madness-in-common, or any other sovereign psychological attribute, cognitive style, or predisposition that distinguishes them from nonparticipants. Third, the majority of behaviors in which members of these crowds engaged are neither mutually inclusive nor extraordinary, let alone mad. (McPhail, 1991, p. xxii)

One hundred years of theory and research is a stalwart legacy that cannot be easily dismissed. Yet the available evidence favors the view that the crowd is a group. Le Bon's (1895/1960) crowd psychology and Zimbardo's (1969) theory of deindividuation make dire predictions about crowds and mobs, but when Postmes and Spears (1998) combined the results of 60 independent experimental studies, they found that dramatic changes in self-control and inappropriate behavior are rare.

Field observations of crowds and collectives also attest to these groups' rationality and normality rather than to their irrationality and impulsivity. McPhail (1991), for example, concluded that violence is very rare in crowds. In most cases, individuals in the crowd are committed to particular goals, and like any performing group, they do their share of the work to increase the group's chances for success. Moreover, when violence does occur, it takes the form of intergroup conflict rather than mindless savagery. Even the group at the Who concert did not behave badly. Many experts condemned the crowd, calling it a stampede, but when Cincinnati sociologist Norris R. Johnson looked more closely at the evidence, he concluded that the crowd did not "stampede" or engage in selfish, destructive behavior. Indeed, the amount of helping shown by the people in the crowd exceeded what we would normally expect to find among a group of bystanders.

The crowd-as-mad and the crowd-as-group views must be reconciled in a more complete understanding of collective behavior. Crowds do, on occasion, perpetrate great wrongs—wrongs that seem more malevolent than any one individual's capacity for evil. Yet people in crowds usually act in ways that are unremarkable. Crowds are groups, and collective dynamics are for the most part group dynamics. Hence, the next time you hear of a crowd behaving oddly, do not dismiss its actions as one more illustration of a group gone wrong.

Studying Groups and Collectives

In this book, we have examined many different groups—a band of outcasts from the art community that generated a cohesive movement that redefined the world of art; a sports team that survived against all odds when their plane crashed in the Andes; a cohesive hockey team that outperformed a superior opponent; a jury reaching a verdict by carefully reviewing its mission and the evidence it was given; a group led by a powerful authority figure who manipulated the members through deceit and subterfuge; teams that worked to make products and decisions, including military and political experts who planned an ill-fated invasion; groups that had to deal with conflict within their ranks and conflict with other groups; a heroic group trying to return to Earth after circling the Moon; and a group of people who made use of the restorative, curative impact of a group to gain self-understanding and improve their well-being. In this final chapter we have turned to examine crowds, mobs, and social movements.

These analyses have illuminated many of a group's most basic processes—how groups take in and reject members; evolve over time; organize their members in hierarchies of authority; perform tasks, both effectively and ineffectively; make plans and decisions; and succor their members and regulate behavior in context. But these analyses have also revealed that groups, like large collectives, are often misunderstood and mismanaged. It is ironic that whereas scientists have studied aspects of the physical world for centuries, only in the last 100 years have they turned their attention to human experiences, and human groups in particular. Yet the theories and studies of group dynamics we have examined here have repeatedly confirmed the important role that groups play in all aspects of social life. Human beings are in many ways individuals who are seeking their personal, private objectives, yet they are also members of larger social units that may be seeking collective outcomes. As social creatures, embedded in a rich network of mutual, collective, and reciprocal relationships, individuals cannot be understood fully without considering the social groups to which they belong.

Fortunately, the field of group dynamics offers the means of reducing our ignorance of this fundamental aspect of the human condition. Stanley Milgram and Hans Toch, writing 35 years ago, asked this question: If we "do not take up the job of understanding riots, panics, and social movements, who will?" (1969, p. 590). Their question applies, with equal force, to the study of groups in general. If we do not take up the job of understanding groups, who will?

SUMMARY IN OUTLINE

❖ **What is collective behavior?**

1. The term *collective behavior* has many interpretations, but in general, it describes instances in which a relatively large group of people respond in a similar way to an event or situation. *Collectives* differ from other types of groups in terms of
   - Size: Collectives tend to be large rather than small.
   - Proximity: In some cases, members of a collective are together in one place (e.g., crowds), but other collectives involve individuals who are dispersed across great distances (e.g., social movements).
   - Duration: Collectives sometimes, but not always, form and disband rapidly.
   - Conventionality: Members sometimes engage in atypical, unconventional, or even aberrant behaviors.
   - Relationships between members: Collectives are often weak associations of individuals rather than cohesive groups.

2. Two basic forms of collective behavior are crowds and collective movements.
   - *Crowds* include common crowds, such as street crowds or public gatherings,

audiences, queues, and *mobs* (aggressive mobs and panics). In general, members of most crowds conform to social norms, whereas members of mobs and crowds in panic display hostile and fearful actions, respectively. *Riots* are more widely dispersed, and usually more aggressive, mobs.

- McPhail's analyses of behavior in public places identified a number of forms of elementary collective behavior, including movement, positioning, manipulation, gesticulation, verbalization, vocalization, and orientation.
- Individuals need not be concentrated in a single location to display convergence in action, for such *collective movements* as rumors, *trends* (fads, crazes, fashion trends), *mass hysteria, psychogenic illness,* and *social movements* can influence widely dispersed individuals.

❖ **What theories explain collective behavior?**

1. Le Bon maintained that crowds are governed by a collective mind and that *contagion* causes crowd members to experience similar thoughts and emotions. Tipping point theory suggests that fast-moving trends can spread like contagious diseases through social groups.

2. *Convergence theories* propose that the individuals who join groups often possess similar needs and personal characteristics. Studies of *relative deprivation,* for example, suggest that people whose attainments fall below their expectations are more likely to join social movements.

3. Turner and Killian's *emergent norm theory* posits that crowds often develop unique standards for behavior and that these atypical norms exert a powerful influence on behavior. The *baiting crowd,* for example, forms when a group of onlookers collectively urges someone to injure him- or herself.

4. Zimbardo's deindividuation theory traces collective phenomena back to *deindividuation,* which can be broken down into three components—inputs, internal changes, and behavioral outcomes. Inputs, or causes, of deindividuation include feelings of anonymity, reduced responsibility (diffusion of responsibility), membership in large groups, and a heightened state of physiological arousal.

5. The deindividuated state itself appears to involve two basic components—reduced self-awareness (minimal self-consciousness, etc.) and altered experiencing (disturbances in concentration and judgment, etc.). The impact of this state on group members' behavior has not been empirically supported, however. Most studies indicate that individuals usually act in ways that are consistent with—rather than in opposition to—situational norms that regulate behavior.

6. Social identity theory notes that collective behavior is often intergroup behavior, and so (1) collectives sustain rather than undermine individuals' identities and (2) collective behavior in some cases represents an attempt to reestablish a sense of individuality.

❖ **How different are collectives from other types of groups?**

1. Recent analyses of crowds and collectives have questioned the "crowd-as-mad" assumption. Collectives differ from more routine groups in degree rather than in kind.

2. Collectives, like groups in general, are often misunderstood and mismanaged, but the field of group dynamics offers a means of reducing this ignorance.

FOR MORE INFORMATION

Chapter Case: The Who Concert

- "Panic at 'The Who Concert Stampede': An Empirical Assessment," by Norris R. Johnson (1987), provides considerable background information and theoretical analysis of the crowd that pushed through the doors at Cincinnati's Riverfront Coliseum in 1979.

Crowds and Collectives

- "Collective Behavior: Crowds and Social Movements," by Stanley Milgram and Hans Toch (1969), though written 35 years ago, still offers fundamental insights into collective behavior.
- *The Crowd: A Study of the Popular Mind* (translation of *Psychologie des foules*), by Gustave Le Bon (1895/1960), has been described as one of the most influential books dealing with social behavior ever written.
- "The Human Choice: Individuation, Reason, and Order Versus Deindividuation, Impulse, and Chaos," by Phillip G. Zimbardo (1969), is a wide-ranging analysis of the causes and consequences of the loss of identity that sometimes occurs in groups.
- "Deindividuation and antinormative behavior: A meta-analysis," by Tom Postmes and Russell Spears (1998), summarizes much of the empirical work on deindividuation processes and offers an alternative to the traditional "groups as mad" interpretation of crowds and mobs.
- "Social Movements and Collective Behavior: Social Psychological Dimensions and Considerations," by David A. Snow and Pamela E. Oliver (1995), reviews theory and research dealing with the factors that prompt people to join social movements.

Collectives as Groups

- *The Myth of the Madding Crowd,* by Clark McPhail (1991), expertly synthesizes prior theoretical work on crowds with McPhail's field studies of actual crowds to dispel many absurd myths about crowds and replace them with data-based propositions.
- "Rethinking Crowd Violence: Self-Categorization Theory and the Woodstock 1999 Riot," by Stephen Vider (2004), is a conceptually rich case study of a riot that occurred, ironically, during a music festival celebrating the peace movement of the 1960s.

MEDIA RESOURCES

 Visit the Group Dynamics companion website at http://psychology.wadsworth .com/forsyth4e to access online resources for your book, including quizzes, flash cards, web links, and more!

REFERENCES

Aarts, H., & Dijksterhuis, A. (2003). The silence of the library: Environment, situational norm, and social behavior. *Journal of Personality and Social Psychology, 84,* 18–28.

Aarts, H., Dijksterhuis, A., & Custers, R. (2003). Automatic normative behavior in environments: The moderating role of conformity in activating situational norms. *Social Cognition, 21,* 447–464.

Abele, A. E. (2003). The dynamics of masculine–agentic and feminine–communal traits: Findings from a prospective study. *Journal of Personality and Social Psychology, 85,* 768–776.

Aberson, C. L., Healy, M., & Romero, V. (2000). Ingroup bias and self-esteem: A meta-analysis. *Personality and Social Psychology Review, 4,* 157–173.

Abrams, D. (1990). *Political identity: Relative deprivation, social identity, and the case of Scottish nationalism.* London: Economic and Social Research Council.

Abrams, D. (1992). Processes of social identification. In G. M. Breakwell (Ed.), *Social psychology of identity and self-concept* (pp. 57–99). New York: Surrey University Press.

Abrams, D., & Hogg, M. A. (2001). Collective identity: Group membership and self-conception. In M. A. Hogg & R. S. Tindale (Eds.), *Blackwell handbook of social psychology: Group processes* (pp. 425–460). Malden, MA: Blackwell.

Abrams, D., Marques, J. M., Bown, N., & Henson, M. (2000). Pro-norm and anti-norm deviance within and between groups. *Journal of Personality and Social Psychology, 78,* 906–912.

Abrams, D., Wetherell, M., Cochrane, S., Hogg, M. A., & Turner, J. C. (1990). Knowing what to think by knowing who you are: Self-categorization and the nature of norm formation, conformity and group polarization. *British Journal of Social Psychology, 29,* 97–119.

Adams, J. S., & Rosenbaum, W. B. (1962). The relationship of worker productivity to cognitive dissonance about wage inequities. *Journal of Applied Psychology, 46,* 161–164.

Adler, P. A., & Adler, P. (1995). Dynamics of inclusion and exclusion in preadolescent cliques. *Social Psychology Quarterly, 58,* 145–162.

Adler, P. A., Kless, S. J., & Adler, P. (1992). Socialization to gender roles: Popularity among elementary school boys and girls. *Sociology of Education, 65,* 169–187.

Agazarian, Y. M. (2001). *A systems-centered approach to inpatient group psychotherapy.* Philadelphia: Jessica Kingsley.

Aiello, J. R. (1987). Human spatial behavior. In D. Stokols & I. Altman (Eds.), *Handbook of environmental psychology* (Vol. 1, pp. 389–504). New York: Wiley.

Aiello, J. R., & Douthitt, E. A. (2001). Social facilitation: From Triplett to electronic performance monitoring. *Group Dynamics, 5,* 163–180.

Aiello, J. R., & Kolb, K. J. (1995). Electronic performance monitoring and social context: Impact on productivity and stress. *Journal of Applied Psychology, 80,* 339–353.

Ainsworth, M. D. S. (1979). Infant–mother attachment. *American Psychologist, 34,* 932–937.

Albright, L., Kenny, D. A., & Malloy, T. E. (1988). Consensus in personality judgments at zero acquaintance. *Journal of Personality and Social Psychology, 55,* 387–395.

Aldag, R. J., & Fuller, S. R. (1993). Beyond fiasco: A reappraisal of the groupthink phenomenon and a new model of group decision processes. *Psychological Bulletin, 113,* 533–552.

Alexander, S. C., Peterson, J. L., & Hollingshead, A. B. (2003). Help is at your keyboard: Support groups on the Internet. In L. R. Frey (Ed.), *Group communication in context: Studies of bona fide groups* (2nd ed., pp. 309–334). Mahwah, NJ: Erlbaum.

Alicke, M. D., Braun, J. C., Glor, J. E., Klotz, M. L., Magee, J., Sederholm, H., & Siegel, R. (1992). Complaining behavior in social interaction. *Personality and Social Psychology Bulletin, 18,* 286–295.

Allen, H. (1978). Cults: The battle for the mind. In C. A. Krause, *Guyana massacre: The eyewitness account* (pp. 111–121). New York: Berkley.

Allen, K., Blascovich, J., & Mendes, W. B. (2002). Cardiovascular reactivity in the presence of pets, friends, and spouses: The truth about cats and dogs. *Psychosomatic Medicine, 64,* 727–739.

Allen, K. M., Blascovich, J., Tomaka, J., & Kelsey, R. M. (1991). Presence of human friends and pet dogs as moderators of autonomic responses to stress in women. *Journal of Personality and Social Psychology, 61,* 582–589.

Allen, R. D. (1993). Organizing mental health services following a disaster: A community systems perspective. *Journal of Social Behavior and Personality, 8,* 179–188.

Allen, V. L. (1975). Social support for nonconformity. *Advances in Experimental Social Psychology, 8,* 2–43.

Allen, V. L., & Wilder, D. A. (1980). Impact of group consensus and social support on stimulus meaning: Mediation of conformity by cognitive restructuring. *Journal of Personality and Social Psychology, 39,* 1116–1124.

Allison, S. T., Beggan, J. K., & Midgley, E. H. (1996). The quest for "similar instances" and "simultaneous possibilities": Metaphors in social dilemma research. *Journal of Personality and Social Psychology, 71,* 479–497.

Allison, S. T., McQueen, L. R., & Schaerfl, L. M. (1992). Social decision making processes and the equal partitioning of shared resources. *Journal of Experimental Social Psychology, 28,* 23–42.

Allison, S. T., & Messick, D. M. (1985a). Effects of experience on performance in a replenishable resource trap. *Journal of Personality and Social Psychology, 49,* 943–948.

Allison, S. T., & Messick, D. M. (1985b). The group attribution error. *Journal of Experimental Social Psychology, 21,* 563–579.

Allison, S. T., & Messick, D. M. (1990). Social decision heuristics in the use of shared resources. *Journal of Behavioral Decision Making, 3,* 195–204.

Allison, S. T., Worth, L. T., & King, M. C. (1990). Group decisions as social inference heuristics. *Journal of Personality and Social Psychology, 58,* 801–811.

Allmendinger, J., Hackman, J. R., & Lehman, E.V. (1996). Life and work in symphony orchestras. *Musical Quarterly, 80,* 194–219.

Allport, F. H. (1920). The influence of the group upon association and thought. *Journal of Experimental Psychology, 3,* 159–182.

Allport, F. H. (1924). *Social psychology.* Boston: Houghton Mifflin.

Allport, F. H. (1934). The J-curve hypothesis of conforming behavior. *Journal of Social Psychology, 5,* 141–183.

Allport, F. H. (1961). The contemporary appraisal of an old problem. *Contemporary Psychology, 6,* 195–197.

Allport, F. H. (1962). A structuronomic conception of behavior: Individual and collective. I. Structural theory and the master problem of social psychology. *Journal of Abnormal and Social Psychology, 64,* 3–30.

Allport, F. H., & Lepkin, M. (1943). Building war morale with news-headlines. *Public Opinion Quarterly, 7,* 211–221.

Allport, G. W. (1954). *The nature of prejudice.* New York: Addison-Wesley.

Allport, G. W., & Postman, L. J. (1947). *The psychology of rumor.* New York: Holt.

Allred, K. G. (2000). Anger and retaliation in conflict: The role of attribution. In M. Deutsch & P. T. Coleman (Eds.), *The handbook of conflict resolution: Theory and practice* (pp. 236–255). San Francisco: Jossey-Bass.

Altemeyer, B. (1988). *Enemies of freedom: Understanding right-wing authoritarianism.* San Francisco: Jossey-Bass.

Altman, I. (1973). An ecological approach to the functioning of socially isolated groups. In J. E. Rasmussen (Ed.), *Man in isolation and confinement* (pp. 241–269). Chicago: Aldine.

Altman, I. (1975). *The environment and social behavior.* Pacific Grove, CA: Brooks/Cole.

Altman, I. (1977). Research on environment and behavior: A personal statement of strategy. In D. Stokols (Ed.), *Perspectives on environment and behavior* (pp. 303–324). New York: Plenum Press.

Altman, I., & Chemers, M. M. (1980). *Culture and environment.* Pacific Grove, CA: Brooks/Cole.

Altman, I., & Churchman, A. S. (Eds.). (1994). *Human behavior and the environment: Advances in theory and research: Place attachment* (Vol. 12). New York: Plenum Press.

Altman, I., & Haythorn, W. W. (1967). The ecology of isolated groups. *Behavioral Science, 12,* 169–182.

Altman, I., & Taylor, D. A. (1973). *Social penetration: The development of interpersonal relationships.* New York: Holt, Rinehart & Winston.

Altman, I., Taylor, D. A., & Wheeler, L. (1971). Ecological aspects of group behavior in social isolation. *Journal of Applied Social Psychology, 1,* 76–100.

Alvaro, E. M., & Crano, W. D. (1997). Indirect minority influence: Evidence for leniency in source evaluation and counter-argumentation. *Journal of Personality and Social Psychology, 72,* 949–964.

Amir, Y. (1969). Contact hypothesis in ethnic relations. *Psychological Bulletin, 71,* 319–342.

Amir, Y. (1976). The role of intergroup contact in change of prejudice and ethnic relations. In P. A. Katz (Ed.), *Towards the elimination of racism.* New York: Pergamon Press.

Ancona, D. G., & Caldwell, D. F. (1992). Demography and design: Predictors of new product team performance. *Organization Science, 3,* 321–341.

Anders, G. (2003). *Perfect enough: Carly Fiorina and the reinvention of Hewlett-Packard.* New York: Portfolio.

Andersen, S. M. (1984). Self-knowledge and social inference: II. The diagnosticity of cognitive/affective and behavioral data. *Journal of Personality and Social Psychology, 46,* 294–307.

Anderson, C., & Berdahl, J. L. (2002). The experience of power: Examining the effects of power on approach and inhibition tendencies. *Journal of Personality and Social Psychology, 83,* 1362–1377.

Anderson, C., John, O. P., Keltner, D., & Kring, A. M. (2001). Who attains social status? Effects of personality and physical attractiveness in social groups. *Journal of Personality and Social Psychology, 81,* 116–132.

Anderson, C., Keltner, D., & Oliver J. (2003). Emotional convergence between people over time. *Journal of Personality and Social Psychology, 84,* 1054–1068.

Anderson, C. A., & Bushman, B. J. (1997). External validity of "trivial" experiments: The case of laboratory aggression. *Review of General Psychology, 1,* 19–41.

Anderson, C. M., & Martin, M. M. (1995). The effects of communication motives, interaction involvement, and loneliness on satisfaction: A model of small groups. *Small Group Research, 26,* 118–137.

Anderson, L. R. (1978). Groups would do better without humans. *Personality and Social Psychology Bulletin, 4,* 557–558.

Anderson, N., De Dreu, C. K. W., & Nijstad, B. A. (2004). The routinization of innovation research: A constructively critical review of the state-of-the-science. *Journal of Organizational Behavior, 25,* 147–173.

Apodoca v. Oregon, 406 U.S. 404 (1972).

Applebaum, E., & Blatt, R. (1994). *The new American workplace.* Ithaca, NY: ILR.

Appelbaum, R. P., & Chambliss, W. J. (1995). *Sociology.* New York: HarperCollins.

Ardry, R. (1970). *The territorial imperative: A personal inquiry into the animal origins of property and nations.* New York: Atheneum.

Argote, L., Insko, C. A., Yovetich, N., & Romero, A. A. (1995). Group learning curves: The effects of turnover and task complexity on group performance. *Journal of Applied Social Psychology, 25,* 512–529.

Argyle, M., & Dean, J. (1965). Eye-contact, distance, and affiliation. *Sociometry, 28,* 289–304.

Arkes, H. R. (1993). Some practical judgment and decision-making research. In N. J. Castellan, Jr. (Ed.), *Individual and group decision making: Current issues* (pp. 3–18). Mahwah, NJ: Erlbaum.

Arkes, H. R., & Blumer, C. (1985). The psychology of sunk cost. *Organizational Behavior and Human Decision Processes, 35,* 124–140.

Arkin, R. M., & Burger, J. M. (1980). Effects of unit relation tendencies on interpersonal attraction. *Social Psychology Quarterly, 43,* 380–391.

Arms, R. L., & Russell, G. W. (1997). Impulsivity, fight history, and camaraderie as predictors of a willingness to escalate a disturbance. *Current Psychology: Developmental, Learning, Personality, Social, 15,* 279–285.

Arnardottir, A. A. (2002). *Leadership style in colead psychotherapy groups, assessed from leaders', co-leaders', and group members' perspective.* Unpublished doctoral dissertation. Richmond: Virginia Commonwealth University.

Arnold, D. W., & Greenberg, C. I. (1980). Deviate rejection within differentially manned groups. *Social Psychology Quarterly, 43,* 419–424.

Aronson, E., & Mills, J. (1959). The effects of severity of initiation on liking for a group. *Journal of Abnormal and Social Psychology, 59,* 177–181.

Aronson, E., & Patnoe, S. (1997). *Cooperation in the classroom: The jigsaw method.* New York: Longman.

Aronson, E., Stephan, C., Sikes, J., Blaney, N., & Snapp, M. (1978). *The jigsaw classroom.* Thousand Oaks, CA: Sage.

Arriaga, X. B., & Agnew, C. R. (2001). Being committed: Affective, cognitive, and conative components of relationship commitment. *Personality and Social Psychology Bulletin, 27,* 1190–1203.

Arrow, H. (1997). Stability, bistability, and instability in small group influence patterns. *Journal of Personality and Social Psychology, 72,* 75–85.

Arrow, H., & McGrath, J. E. (1995). Membership dynamics in groups at work: A theoretical framework. *Research in Organizational Behavior, 17,* 373–411.

Arrow, H., McGrath, J. E., & Berdahl, J. L. (2000). *Small groups as complex systems: Formation, coordination, development, and adaptation.* Thousand Oaks, CA: Sage.

Asch, S. E. (1952). *Social psychology.* Upper Saddle River, NJ: Prentice Hall.

Asch, S. E. (1955). Opinions and social pressures. *Scientific American, 193*(5), 31–35.

Asch, S. E. (1957). An experimental investigation of group influence. In *Symposium on preventive and social psychiatry.* Washington, DC: U.S. Government Printing Office.

Asendorpf, J. B., & Meier, G. H. (1993). Personality effects on children's speech in everyday life: Sociability-mediated exposure and shyness-mediated reactivity in social situations. *Journal of Personality and Social Psychology, 64,* 1072–1083.

Ashburn-Nardo, L., Voils, C. I., & Monteith, M. J. (2001). Implicit associations as the seeds of intergroup bias: How easily do they take root? *Journal of Personality and Social Psychology, 81,* 789–799.

Asher, S. R., & Paquette, J. A. (2003). Loneliness and peer relations in childhood. *Current Directions in Psychological Science, 12,* 75–78.

Atlas, J. (1990). A psychohistorical view of crusade origins. *Journal of Psychohistory, 17,* 412–415.

Averill, J. R. (1983). Studies on anger and aggression: Implications for theories of emotion. *American Psychologist, 38,* 1145–1160.

Avolio, B. J., Kahai, S., & Dodge, G. E. (2000). E-leadership: Implications for theory, research, and practice [Electronic version]. *Leadership Quarterly, 11,* 615–668.

Avolio, B. J., Sosik, J. J., Jung, D. I., & Berson, Y. (2003). Leadership models, methods, and applications. In W. C. Borman, D. R. Ilgen, R. J. Klimoski, & I. B. Weiner (Eds.), *Handbook of psychology: Industrial and organizational psychology* (Vol. 12, pp. 277–307). New York: Wiley. Retrieved May 12, 2004, from http://www.netlibrary.com

Axelrod, R. (1984). *The evolution of cooperation.* New York: Basic Books.

Axelrod, R., & Hamilton, W. D. (1981). The evolution of cooperation. *Science, 211,* 1390–1396.

Axsom, D. (1989). Cognitive dissonance and behavior change in psychotherapy. *Journal of Experimental Social Psychology, 25,* 234–252.

Ayman, R., Chemers, M. M., & Fiedler, F. (1995). The contingency model of leadership effectiveness: Its levels of analysis. *Leadership Quarterly, 6,* 147–167.

Azima, F. J. (1993). Group psychotherapy with personality disorders. In H. I. Kaplan & B. J. Sadock (Eds.), *Comprehensive group psychotherapy* (pp. 393–406). Baltimore: Williams and Wilkins.

Azuma, H. (1984). Secondary control as a heterogeneous category. *American Psychologist, 39,* 970–971.

Bach, G. R. (1954). *Intensive group psychotherapy.* New York: Ronald Press.

Back, K. W. (1951). Influence through social communication. *Journal of Abnormal and Social Psychology, 46,* 9–23.

Back, K. W. (1973). *Beyond words: The story of sensitivity training and the encounter movement.* Baltimore: Penguin.

Back, K. W. (1974). Intervention techniques: Small groups. *Annual Review of Psychology, 25,* 367–387.

Back, K. W. (1992). This business of topology. *Journal of Social Issues, 48*(2), 51–66.

Baier, J. L., & Williams, P. S. (1983). Fraternity hazing revisited: Current alumni and active member attitudes toward hazing. *Journal of College Student Personnel, 24,* 300–305.

Bakeman, R. (2000). Behavioral observation and coding. In H. T. Reis & C. M. Judd (Eds.), *Handbook of research methods in social and personality psychology* (pp. 138–159). New York: Cambridge University Press.

Baker, S. M., & Petty, R. E. (1994). Majority and minority influence: Source–position imbalance as a determinant of message scrutiny. *Journal of Personality and Social Psychology, 67,* 5–19.

Bales, R. F. (1950). *Interaction process analysis: A method for the study of small groups.* Reading, MA: Addison-Wesley.

Bales, R. F. (1953). The equilibrium problem in small groups. In T. Parsons, R. F. Bales, & E. A. Shils (Eds.), *Working papers in the theory of action* (pp. 111–161). New York: Free Press.

Bales, R. F. (1955). How people interact in conferences. *Scientific American, 192*(3), 31–35.

Bales, R. F. (1958). Task roles and social roles in problem-solving groups. In E. E. Maccoby, T. M. Newcomb, & E. L. Hartley (Eds.), *Readings in social psychology* (pp. 437–447). New York: Holt, Rinehart & Winston.

Bales, R. F. (1965). The equilibrium problem in small groups. In A. P. Hare, E. F. Borgatta, & R. F. Bales (Eds.), *Small groups: Studies in social interaction* (2nd ed., pp. 444–476). New York: Knopf.

Bales, R. F. (1970). *Personality and interpersonal behavior.* New York: Holt, Rinehart & Winston.

Bales, R. F. (1980). *SYMLOG case study kit.* New York: Free Press.

Bales, R. F. (1988). A new overview of the SYMLOG system: Measuring and changing behavior in groups. In R. B. Polley, A. P. Hare, & P. J. Stone (Eds.), *The SYMLOG practitioner: Applications of small group research* (pp. 319–344). New York: Praeger.

Bales, R. F. (1999). *Social interaction systems: Theory and measurement.* New Brunswick, NJ: Transaction.

Bales, R. F., & Cohen, S. P. (with Williamson, S. A.). (1979).

SYMLOG: A system for the multiple level observation of groups. New York: Free Press.

Bales, R. F., & Hare, A. P. (1965). Diagnostic use of the interaction profile. *Journal of Social Psychology, 67,* 239–258.

Bales, R. F., & Slater, P. E. (1955). Role differentiation in small decision-making groups. In T. Parsons & R. F. Bales (Eds.), *Family, socialization, and interaction process* (pp. 259–306). New York: Free Press.

Bales, R. F., & Strodtbeck, F. L. (1951). Phases in group problem solving. *Journal of Abnormal and Social Psychology, 46,* 485–495.

Ball, S. J. (1981). *Beachside comprehensive: A case study of secondary schooling.* New York: Cambridge University Press.

Baltes, B. B., Dickson, M. W., Sherman, M. P., Bauer, C. C., & LaGanke, J. (2002). Computer-mediated communication and group decision making: A meta-analysis. *Organizational Behavior and Human Decision Processes, 87,* 156–179.

Bandura, A. (1977). *Social-learning theory.* Upper Saddle River, NJ: Prentice Hall.

Bandura, A. (1986). *Social foundations of thought and action: A social cognitive theory.* Upper Saddle River, NJ: Prentice Hall.

Bandura, A. (1997). *Self-efficacy: The exercise of control.* New York: Freeman.

Bandura, A. (1999). Moral disengagement in the perpetration of inhumanities. *Personality and Social Psychology Review, 3,* 193–209.

Bangerter, A. (2002). Maintaining interpersonal continuity in groups: The role of collective memory processes in redistributing information. *Group Processes & Intergroup Relations, 5,* 203–219.

Bargal, D., Gold, M., & Lewin, M. (Eds.). (1992). The heritage of Kurt Lewin: Theory, research, and practice. *Journal of Social Issues, 48*(2).

Barge, J. K. (2002). Enlarging the meaning of group deliberation: From discussion to dialogue. In L. R. Frey (Ed.), *New directions in group communication* (pp. 159–177). Thousand Oaks, CA: Sage.

Bargh, J. A. (1990). Auto-motives: Preconscious determinants of social interaction. In E. T. Higgins & R. M. Sorrentino (Eds.), *Handbook of motivation and cognition: Foundations of social behavior* (Vol. 2, pp. 93–130). New York: Guilford Press.

Bargh, J. A., & Alvarez, J. (2001). The road to hell: Good intentions in the face of nonconscious tendencies to misuse power. In A. Y. Lee-Chai & J. A. Bargh (Eds.), *The use and abuse of power: Multiple perspectives on the causes of corruption* (pp. 41–55). New York: Psychology Press.

Bargh, J. A., & McKenna, K. Y. A. (2004). The Internet and social life. *Annual Review of Psychology, 55,* 573–590.

Barker, R. G. (1968). *Ecological psychology.* Stanford, CA: Stanford University Press.

Barker, R. G. (1987). Prospecting in ecological psychology: Oskaloosa revisited. In D. Stokols & I. Altman (Eds.), *Handbook of environmental psychology* (Vol. 2, pp. 1413–1432). New York: Wiley.

Barker, R. G. (1990). Recollections of the Midwest Psychological Field Station. *Environment and Behavior, 22,* 503–513.

Barker, R. G., & Associates. (1978). *Habitats, environments, and human behavior: Studies in ecological psychology and eco-behavioral sciences from the Midwest Psychological Field Station, 1947–1972.* San Francisco: Jossey-Bass.

Barlow, S. H., Burlingame, G. M., & Fuhriman, A. (2000). Therapeutic applications of groups: From Pratt's "thought control classes" to modern group psychotherapy. *Group Dynamics, 4,* 115–134.

Barlow, S. H., Burlingame, G. M., Nebeker, R. S., & Anderson, E. (2000). Meta-analysis of medical self-help groups. *International Journal of Group Psychotherapy, 50,* 53–69.

Barnard, C. I. (1938). *The functions of the executive.* Cambridge, MA: Harvard University Press.

Baron, R. A., & Bell, P. A. (1975). Aggression and heat: Mediating effects of prior provocation and exposure to an aggressive model. *Journal of Personality and Social Psychology, 31,* 825–832.

Baron, R. A., & Bell, P. A. (1976). Aggression and heat: The influence of ambient temperature, negative affect, and a cooling drink on physical aggression. *Journal of Personality and Social Psychology, 33,* 245–255.

Baron, R. S. (1986). Distraction–conflict theory: Progress and problems. *Advances in Experimental Social Psychology, 19,* 1–40.

Baron, R. S. (2000). Arousal, capacity, and intense indoctrination. *Personality and Social Psychology Review, 4,* 238–254.

Baron, R. S., Kerr, N. L., & Miller, N. (1992). *Group process, group decision, group action.* Pacific Grove, CA: Brooks/Cole.

Baron, R. S., Vandello, J. A., & Brunsman, B. (1996). The forgotten variable in conformity research: Impact of task importance on social influence. *Journal of Personality and Social Psychology, 71,* 915–927.

Barrera, M., Jr. (1986). Distinctions between social support concepts, measures, and models. *American Journal of Community Psychology, 14,* 413–422.

Barrick, M. R., & Mount, M. K. (1991). The Big Five personality dimensions and job performance: A meta-analysis. *Personnel Psychology, 44,* 1–26.

Barrow, J. C. (1977). The variables of leadership: A review and conceptual framework. *Academy of Management Review, 2,* 231–251.

Bar-Tal, D. (2000). *Shared beliefs in a society: Social psychological analysis.* Thousand Oaks, CA: Sage.

Bartels, L. (May, 2001). No looking back. *Rocky Mountain News.* Retrieved January 3, 2004, from http://www.rockymountainnews.com/drmn/state/article/0,1299,DRMN_21_795883,00.html

Bartholomew, R. E. (1997). Mass hysteria. *British Journal of Psychiatry, 170,* 387–388.

Bartholomew, R. E., & Sirois, F. (1996). Epidemic hysteria in schools: An international and historical overview. *Educational Studies, 22,* 285–311.

Bartis, S., Szymanski, K., & Harkins, S. G. (1988). Evaluation and performance: A two-edged knife. *Personality and Social Psychology Bulletin, 14,* 242–251.

Basden, B. H., Basden, D. R., Bryner, S. & Thomas, R. L., III (1997). A comparison of group and individual remembering: Does collaboration disrupt retrieval strategies? *Journal of Experimental Psychology: Learning, Memory and Cognition, 23,* 1176–1189.

Bass, B. M. (1985a). Good, better, best. *Organizational Dynamics, 13,* 26–40.

Bass, B. M. (1985b). *Leadership and performance beyond expectations.* New York: Free Press.

Bass, B. M. (1990). *Bass and Stogdill's handbook of leadership: Theory, research, and managerial applications* (3rd ed.). New York: Free Press.

Bass, B. M. (1997). Does the transactional–transformational leadership paradigm transcend organizational and national boundaries? *American Psychologist, 52,* 130–139.

Bass, B. M., Avolio, B. J., & Goldheim, L. (1987). Biography and the assessment of transformational leadership at the world-class level. *Journal of Management, 13,* 7–19.

Bass, B. M., & Ryterband, E. C. (1979). *Organizational psychology* (2nd ed.). Boston: Allyn & Bacon.

Batchelor, J. P., & Goethals, G. R. (1972). Spatial arrangements in freely formed groups. *Sociometry, 35,* 270–279.

Bates, B., & Goodman, A. (1986). The effectiveness of encounter groups: Implications of research for counselling practice. *British Journal of Guidance and Counselling, 14,* 240–251.

Batson, C. D. (1975). Rational processing or rationalization? The effect of disconfirming information on a state religious belief. *Journal of Personality and Social Psychology, 32,* 176–184.

Baum, A., Calesnick, L. E., Davis, G. E., & Gatchel, R. J. (1982). Individual differences in coping with crowding: Stimulus screening and social overload. *Journal of Personality and Social Psychology, 43,* 821–830.

Baum, A., & Davis, G. E. (1980). Reducing the stress of high-density living: An architectural intervention. *Journal of Personality and Social Psychology, 38,* 471–481.

Baum, A., Davis, G. E., & Valins, S. (1979). Generating behavioral data for the design process. In J. R. Aiello & A. Baum (Eds.), *Residential crowding and design* (pp. 175–196). New York: Plenum Press.

Baum, A., Harpin, R. E., & Valins, S. (1975). The role of group phenomena in the experience of crowding. *Environment and Behavior, 7,* 185–198.

Baum, A., & Valins, S. (1977). *Architecture and social behavior: Psychological studies of social density.* Mahwah, NJ: Erlbaum.

Baumeister, R. F. (1984). Choking under pressure: Self-consciousness and paradoxical effects of incentives on skillful performance. *Journal of Personality and Social Psychology, 46,* 610–620.

Baumeister, R. F. (1985). The championship choke. *Psychology Today, 19*(4), 48–52.

Baumeister, R. F. (1995). Disputing the effects of championship pressures and home audiences. *Journal of Personality and Social Psychology, 68,* 644–648.

Baumeister, R. F., & Leary, M. R. (1995). The need to belong: Desire for interpersonal attachments as a fundamental human motivation. *Psychological Bulletin, 117,* 497–529.

Baumeister, R. F., & Showers, C. J. (1986). A review of paradoxical performance effects: Choking under pressure in sports and mental tests. *European Journal of Social Psychology, 16,* 361–383.

Baumeister, R. F., & Sommer, K. L. (1997). What do men want? Gender differences and two spheres of belongingness. *Psychological Bulletin, 122,* 38–44.

Baumeister, R. F., Stillwell, A., & Wotman, S. R. (1990). Victim and perpetrator accounts of interpersonal conflict: Autobiographical narratives about anger. *Journal of Personality and Social Psychology, 59,* 994–1005.

Baumeister, R. F., Twenge, J. M., & Nuss, C. K. (2002). Effects of social exclusion on cognitive processes: Anticipated aloneness reduces intelligent thought. *Journal of Personality and Social Psychology, 83,* 817–827.

Bavelas, A. (1948). A mathematical model for group structures. *Applied Anthropology, 7,* 16–30.

Bavelas, A. (1950). Communication patterns in task-oriented groups. *Journal of the Acoustical Society of America, 22,* 725–730.

Bavelas, A., & Barrett, D. (1951). An experimental approach to organization communication. *Personnel, 27,* 367–371.

Bayazit, M., & Mannix, E. A. (2003). Should I stay or should I go? Predicting team members' intent to remain in the team. *Small Group Research, 34,* 290–321.

Beach, S. R. H., & Tesser, A. (2000). Self-evaluation maintenance and evolution: Some speculative notes. In J. Suls & L. Wheeler (Eds.), *Handbook of social comparison: Theory and research* (pp. 123–140). New York: Kluwer Academic/Plenum.

Beach, S. R. H., Tesser, A., Fincham, F. D., Jones, D. J., Johnson, D., & Whitaker, D. J. (1998). Pleasure and pain in doing well, together: An investigation of performance-related affect in close relationships. *Journal of Personality and Social Psychology, 74,* 923–938.

Beaman, A. L., Cole, C. M., Preston, M., Klentz, B., & Steblay, N. M. (1983). Fifteen years of foot-in-the-door research: A meta-analysis. *Personality and Social Psychology Bulletin, 9,* 181–196.

Beauchamp, M. R., Bray, S. R., Eys, M. A., & Carron, A. V. (2002). Role ambiguity, role efficacy, and role performance: Multidimensional and mediational relationships within interdependent sport teams. *Group Dynamics, 6,* 229–242.

Bechtel, R. B. (2002). On to Mars! In R. B. Bechtel & A. Churchman (Eds.), *Handbook of environmental psychology* (pp. 676–685). New York: Wiley. Retrieved July 29, 2004, from http://www.netlibrary.com

Bechtel, R. B., & Churchman, A. (Eds.). (2002). *Handbook of environmental psychology.* New York: Wiley. Retrieved July 28, 2004, from http://www.netlibrary.com

Beck, A. T. (2002). Cognitive models of depression. In R. L. Leahy & E. T. Dowd (Eds.), *Clinical advances in cognitive psychotherapy: Theory and application* (pp. 29–61). New York: Springer.

Becker, F. (2004). *Offices that work: balancing cost, flexibility, and communication.* San Francisco: Jossey-Bass.

Bedell, J., & Sistrunk, F. (1973). Power, opportunity, costs, and sex in a mixed-motive game. *Journal of Personality and Social Psychology, 25,* 219–226.

Bednar, R. L., & Kaul, T. (1978). Experiential group research: Current perspectives. In S. L. Garfield & A. E. Bergin (Eds.), *Handbook of psychotherapy and behavior change* (2nd ed., pp. 769–815). New York: Wiley.

Bednar, R. L., & Kaul, T. (1979). Experiential group research: What never happened. *Journal of Applied Behavioral Science, 15,* 311–319.

Bednar, R. L., & Kaul, T. (1994). Experiential group research: Can the canon fire? In S. L. Garfield and A. E. Bergin (Eds.), *Handbook of psychotherapy and behavior change* (4th ed., pp. 631–663). New York: Wiley.

Beggan, J. K., & Allison, S. T. (1994). Social values. *Encyclopedia of Human Behavior, 4,* 253–262.

Bell, P. A. (1981). Physiological, comfort, performance, and social effects of heat stress. *Journal of Social Issues, 37*(1), 71–94.

Bell, P. A. (1992). In defense of the negative affect escape model of heat and aggression. *Psychological Bulletin, 111,* 342–346.

Bell, P. A., Fisher, J. D., Baum, A., & Greene, T. E. (2001). *Environmental psychology* (5th ed.). Fort Worth, TX: Harcourt Brace.

Bellah, R. N. (1986, February). *Individualism and commitment in American life.* Retrieved January 17, 2004, from http://www.robertbellah.com/lectures_4.htm

Bellah, R. N., Madsen, R., Sullivan, W. M., Swidler, A., & Tipton, S. M. (1985). *Habits of the heart: Individualism and commitment in American life.* New York: Harper & Row.

Bem, D. J. (1972). Self-perception theory. *Advances in Experimental Social Psychology, 6,* 2–62.

Bem, S. L. (1975). Sex role adaptability: One consequence of psychological androgyny. *Journal of Personality and Social Psychology, 31,* 634–643.

Bem, S. L. (1982). Gender schema theory and self-schema theory compared: A comment on Markus, Crane, Bernstein, and Siladi's "Self-schemas and gender." *Journal of Personality and Social Psychology, 43,* 1192–1194.

Bem, S. L. (1985). Androgyny and gender schema theory: A conceptual and empirical integration. *Nebraska Symposium on Motivation, 32,* 179–226.

Benenson, J. F., Apostoleris, N. H., & Parnass, J. (1997). Age and sex differences in dyadic and group interaction. *Developmental Psychology, 33,* 538–543.

Benford, R. D. (1992). Social movements. In E. F. Borgatta & M. L. Borgatta (Eds.), *Encyclopedia of sociology* (Vol. 4, pp. 1880–1887). New York: MacMillan.

Benjamin, L. T., Jr., & Crouse, E. M. (2002). The American Psychological Association's response to *Brown v. Board of Education:* The case of Kenneth B. Clark. *American Psychologist, 57,* 38–50.

Benne, K. D., & Sheats, P. (1948). Functional roles of group members. *Journal of Social Issues, 4*(2), 41–49.

Bennett, H. S. (1980). *On becoming a rock musician.* Amherst: University of Massachusetts Press.

Bennis, W. (1975). *Where have all the leaders gone?* Washington, DC: Federal Executive Institute.

Bennis, W., & Biederman, P. W. (1997). *Organizing genius: The secrets of creative collaboration.* Reading, MA: Addison-Wesley.

Bennis, W., & Nanus, B. (1997). *Leaders: Strategies for taking charge* (2nd ed.). New York: HarperCollins.

Bennis, W. G., & Shepard, H. A. (1956). A theory of group development. *Human Relations, 9,* 415–437.

Berger, J., Wagner, D. G., & Zelditch, M., Jr. (1992). A working strategy for constructing theories: State organizing processes. In G. Ritzer (Ed.), *Studies in metatheorizing in sociology* (pp. 107–123). Thousand Oaks, CA: Sage.

Berger, J., & Zelditch, M., Jr. (1998). *Status, power, and legitimacy: Strategies and theories.* New Brunswick, NJ: Transaction.

Berger, R. E. (1981). *Heart rate, arousal, and the "mere presence" hypothesis of social facilitation.* Unpublished doctoral dissertation. Richmond: Virginia Commonwealth University.

Berger, S. M., Carli, L. C., Garcia, R., & Brady, J. J., Jr. (1982). Audience effects in anticipatory learning: A comparison of drive and practice-inhibition analyses. *Journal of Personality and Social Psychology, 42,* 478–486.

Berger, S. M., Hampton, K. L., Carli, L. L., Grandmaison, P. S., Sadow, J. S., Donath, C. H., & Herschlag, L. R. (1981). Audience-induced inhibition of overt practice during learning. *Journal of Personality and Social Psychology, 40,* 479–491.

Bergman, T. J., Beehner, J. C., Cheney, D. L., & Sayfarth, R. M. (2003). Hierarchical classification by rank and kinship in baboons. *Science, 302,* 1234–1236.

Berkowitz, L. (1953). Sharing leadership in small, decision-making groups. *Journal of Abnormal and Social Psychology, 48,* 231–238.

Berkowitz, L. (1954). Group standards, cohesiveness, and productivity. *Human Relations, 7,* 509–519.

Berkowitz, L. (1962). *Aggression: A social psychological analysis.* New York: McGraw-Hill.

Berkowitz, L. (1971). Reporting an experiment: A case study in leveling, sharpening, and assimilation. *Journal of Experimental Social Psychology, 7,* 237–243.

Berkowitz, L., & Lundy, R. M. (1957). Personality characteristics related to susceptibility to influence by peers or authority figures. *Journal of Personality, 25,* 306–316.

Berman, J. J., & Zimpfer, D. G. (1980). Growth groups: Do the outcomes really last? *Review of Educational Research, 50,* 505–524.

Berndt, T. J. (1992). Friends and friends' influence in adolescence. *Current Directions in Psychological Science, 1,* 156–159.

Berndt, T. J. (1996). Friendships in adolescence. In N. Vanzetti & S. Duck (Eds.), *A lifetime of relationships* (pp. 182–212). Pacific Grove, CA: Brooks/Cole.

Bernthal, P. R., & Insko, C. A. (1993). Cohesiveness without groupthink: The interactive effects of social and task cohesion. *Group and Organizational Management, 18,* 66–87.

Betancourt, H., & Blair, I. (1992). A cognition (attribution)–emotion model of violence in conflict situations. *Personality and Social Psychology Bulletin, 18,* 343–350.

Bettencourt, B. A., Brewer, M. B., Croak, M. R., & Miller, N. (1992). Cooperation and the reduction of intergroup bias: The role of reward structure and social orientation. *Journal of Experimental Social Psychology, 28,* 301–309.

Bettencourt, B. A., & Sheldon, K. (2001). Social roles as mechanism for psychological need satisfaction within social groups. *Journal of Personality and Social Psychology, 81,* 1131–1143.

Biddle, B. J. (1979). *Role theory: Expectations, identities, and behavior.* New York: Academic Press.

Biernat, M., Crandall, C. S., Young, L. V., Kobrynowicz, D., & Halpin, S. M. (1998). All that you can be: Stereotyping of self and others in a military context. *Journal of Personality and Social Psychology, 75,* 301–317.

Biernat, M., & Kobrynowicz, D. (1997). Gender- and race-based standards of competence: Lower minimum standards but higher ability standards for devalued groups. *Journal of Personality and Social Psychology, 72,* 544–557.

Biernat, M., Vescio, T. K., & Green, M. L. (1996). Selective self-stereotyping. *Journal of Personality and Social Psychology, 71,* 1194–1209.

Birch, L. L. (1987). Children's food preferences: Developmental patterns and environmental influences. *Annals of Child Development, 4,* 171–208.

Black, T. E., & Higbee, K. L. (1973). Effects of power, threat, and sex on exploitation. *Journal of Personality and Social Psychology, 27,* 382–388.

Blader, S. L., & Tyler, T. R. (2003). What constitutes fairness in work settings? A four-component model of procedural justice. *Human Resource Management Review, 13,* 107–126.

Blake, R. R., & McCanse, A. A. (1991). *Leadership dilemmas — Grid solutions.* Houston, TX: Gulf.

Blake, R. R., & Mouton, J. S. (1964). *The managerial grid.* Houston, TX: Gulf.

Blake, R. R., & Mouton, J. S. (1978). *The new managerial grid.* Houston, TX: Gulf.

Blake, R. R., & Mouton, J. S. (1980). *The versatile manager: A Grid profile.* Homewood, IL: Dow Jones/Irwin.

Blake, R. R., & Mouton, J. S. (1982). How to choose a leadership style. *Training and Development Journal, 36,* 39–46.

Blake, R. R., & Mouton, J. S. (1984). *Solving costly organizational conflicts: Achieving intergroup trust, cooperation, and teamwork.* San Francisco: Jossey-Bass.

Blake, R. R., & Mouton, J. S. (1985). Presidential (Grid) styles. *Training and Development Journal, 39,* 30–34.

Blake, R. R., & Mouton, J. S. (1986). From theory to practice in interface problem solving. In S. Worchel & W. G. Austin (Eds.), *Psychology of intergroup relations* (2nd ed., pp. 67–87). Chicago: Nelson-Hall.

Blanchard, F. A., Adelman, L., & Cook, S. W. (1975). Effect of group success and failure upon interpersonal attraction in co-operating interracial groups. *Journal of Personality and Social Psychology, 31,* 1020–1030.

Blanchard, F. A., & Cook, S. W. (1976). Effects of helping a less competent member of a cooperating interracial group on the development of interpersonal attraction. *Journal of Personality and Social Psychology, 34,* 1245–1255.

Blanchard, K., & Johnson, S. (1981). *The one minute manager.* New York: Berkley.

Blanchard, K., Zigarmi, D., & Nelson, R. (1993). Situational leadership after 25 years: A retrospective. *Journal of Leadership Studies, 1,* 22–36.

Blanton, H., Crocker, J., & Miller, D. T. (2000). The effects of ingroup versus out-group social comparison on self-esteem in the context of a negative stereotype. *Journal of Experimental Social Psychology, 36,* 519–530.

Blascovich, J., Ginsburg, G. P., & Howe, R. C. (1975). Blackjack and the risky shift, II: Monetary stakes. *Journal of Experimental Social Psychology, 11,* 224–232.

Blascovich, J., Ginsburg, G. P., & Howe, R. C. (1976). Blackjack, choice shifts in the field. *Sociometry, 39,* 274–276.

Blascovich, J., Loomis, J., Beall, A. C., Swinth, K. R., Hoyt, C. L., & Bailenson, J. N. (2002). Immersive virtual environment technology as a methodological tool for social psychology. *Psychological Inquiry, 13,* 103–124.

Blascovich, J., Mendes, W. B., Hunter, S. B., & Salomon, K. (1999). Social "facilitation" as challenge and threat. *Journal of Personality and Social Psychology, 77,* 68–77.

Blascovich, J., Nash, R. F., & Ginsburg, G. P. (1978). Heart rate and competitive decision making. *Personality and Social Psychology Bulletin, 4,* 115–118.

Blass, T. (1991). Understanding behavior in the Milgram obedience experiment: The role of personality, situations, and their interactions. *Journal of Personality and Social Psychology, 60,* 398–413.

Blass, T. (1992). The social psychology of Stanley Milgram. *Advances in Experimental Social Psychology, 25,* 277–329.

Blass, T. (1995). Right-wing authoritarianism and role as predictors of attributions about obedience to authority. *Personality and Individual Differences, 19,* 99–100.

Blass, T. (1996). Attribution of responsibility and trust in the Milgram obedience experiment. *Journal of Applied Social Psychology, 26,* 1529–1535.

Blass, T. (2000a). The Milgram paradigm after 35 years: Some things we now know about obedience to authority. In T. Blass (Ed.), *Obedience to authority: Current perspectives on the Milgram paradigm* (pp. 35–59). Mahwah, NJ: Erlbaum.

Blass, T. (Ed.). (2000b). *Obedience to authority: Current perspectives on the Milgram paradigm.* Mahwah, NJ: Erlbaum.

Blau, P. M. (1964). *Exchange and power in social life.* New York: Wiley.

Bliese, J. R. (1990). The motives of the First Crusaders: A social psychological analysis. *Journal of Psychohistory, 17,* 393–411.

Bliese, P. D., & Halverson, R. R. (1996). Individual and nomothetic models of job stress: An examination of work hours, cohesion, and well-being. *Journal of Applied Social Psychology, 26,* 1171–1189.

Bloch, S., & Crouch, E. (1985). *Therapeutic factors in group psychotherapy.* New York: Oxford University Press.

Blumer, H. (1946). Collective behavior. In A. M. Lee (Ed.), *New outline of the principles of sociology* (pp. 166–222). New York: Barnes & Noble.

Blumer, H. (1951). Collective behavior. In A. M. Lee (Ed.), *Principles of sociology* (pp. 167–224). New York: Barnes & Noble.

Blumer, H. (1957). Collective behavior. In J. B. Gittler (Ed.), *Review of sociology: Analysis of a decade* (pp. 127–158). New York: Wiley.

Blumer, H. (1964). Collective behavior. In J. Gould & W. L. Kolb (Eds.), *Dictionary of the social sciences* (pp. 100–101). New York: Free Press.

Boardman, S. K., & Horowitz, S. V. (Eds.). (1994). Constructive conflict management: An answer to critical social problems? *Journal of Social Issues, 50*(1), 1–211.

Bogardus, E. S. (1954). Group behavior and groupality. *Sociology and Social Research, 38,* 401–403.

Bohrnstedt, G. W., & Fisher, G. A. (1986). The effects of recalled childhood and adolescent relationships compared to current role performances on young adults' affective functioning. *Social Psychology Quarterly, 49,* 19–32.

Boivin, M., Dodge, K. A., & Coie, J. D. (1995). Individual–group behavioral similarity and peer status in experimental play groups of boys: The social misfit revisited. *Journal of Personality and Social Psychology, 69,* 269–279.

Bollen, K. A., & Hoyle, R. H. (1990). Perceived cohesion: A conceptual and empirical examination. *Social Forces, 69,* 479–504.

Bond, C. F. (1982). Social facilitation: A self-presentational view. *Journal of Personality and Social Psychology, 42,* 1042–1050.

Bond, C. F., Jr., Atoum, A. O., & VanLeeuwen, M. D. (1996). Social impairment of complex learning in the wake of public embarrassment. *Basic and Applied Social Psychology, 18,* 31–44.

Bond, C. F., & Titus, L. J. (1983). Social facilitation: A meta-analysis of 241 studies. *Psychological Bulletin, 94,* 265–292.

Bond, M. H. (2002). Reclaiming the individual from Hofstede's ecological analysis—A 20-year odyssey: Comment on Oyserman et al. (2002). *Psychological Bulletin, 128,* 73–77.

Bond, M. H., & Shiu, W. Y. (1997). The relationship between a group's personality resources and the two dimensions of its group process. *Small Group Research, 28,* 194–217.

Bond, R., & Smith, P. B. (1996). Culture and conformity: A meta-analysis of studies using Asch's (1952b, 1956) line judgment task. *Psychological Bulletin, 119,* 111–137.

Bone, E. (1957). *Seven years solitary.* London: McMillan.

Bonito, J. A., & Hollingshead, A. B. (1997). Participation in small groups. *Communication Yearbook, 20,* 227–261.

Bonney, M. E. (1947). Popular and unpopular children: A sociometric study. *Sociometry Monographs,* No. 99, A80.

Bons, P. M., & Fiedler, F. E. (1976). Changes in organizational leadership and the behavior of relationship- and task-motivated leaders. *Administrative Science Quarterly, 21,* 433–472.

Bonta, B. D. (1997). Cooperation and competition in peaceful societies. *Psychological Bulletin, 121,* 299–320.

Booth, A. (1972). Sex and social participation. *American Sociological Review, 37,* 183–193.

Borah, L. A., Jr. (1963). The effects of threat in bargaining: Critical and experimental analysis. *Journal of Abnormal and Social Psychology, 66,* 37–44.

Borgatta, E. F., & Bales, R. F. (1953). Task and accumulation of experience as factors in the interaction of small groups. *Sociometry, 16,* 239–252.

Borgatta, E. F., Couch, A. S., & Bales, R. F. (1954). Some findings relevant to the great man theory of leadership. *American Sociological Review, 19,* 755–759.

Bormann, E. G. (1975). *Discussion and group methods: Theory and practices* (2nd ed.). New York: Harper & Row.

Bornstein, G. (2003). Intergroup conflict: Individual, group, and collective interests. *Personality and Social Psychology Review, 7,* 129–145.

Bornstein, G., Budescu, D., & Zamir, S. (1997). Cooperation in intergroup, *N*-person, and two-person games of chicken. *Journal of Conflict Resolution, 41,* 384–406.

Bornstein, R. F. (1992). The dependent personality: Developmental, social, and clinical perspectives. *Psychological Bulletin, 112,* 3–23.

Bornstein, R. F., Leone, D. R., & Galley, D. J. (1987). The generalizability of subliminal mere exposure effects: Influence of stimuli perceived without awareness on social behavior. *Journal of Personality and Social Psychology, 53,* 1070–1079.

Bouchard, T. J. (1972a). A comparison of two group brainstorming procedures. *Journal of Applied Psychology, 56,* 418–421.

Bouchard, T. J. (1972b). Training, motivation, and personality as determinants of the effectiveness of brainstorming groups and individuals. *Journal of Applied Psychology, 56,* 324–331.

Bouchard, T. J., Barsaloux, J., & Drauden, G. (1974). Brainstorming procedure, group size, and sex as determinants of the problem-solving effectiveness of groups and individuals. *Journal of Applied Psychology, 59,* 135–138.

Bouchard, T. J., Drauden, G., & Barsaloux, J. (1974). A comparison of individual, subgroup, and total group methods of problem solving. *Journal of Applied Psychology, 59,* 226–227.

Bouchard, T. J., & Hare, M. (1970). Size, performance, and potential in brainstorming groups. *Journal of Applied Psychology, 54,* 51–55.

Bourgeois, K. S., & Leary, M. R. (2001). Coping with rejection: Derogating those who choose us last. *Motivation and Emotion, 25,* 101–111.

Bowers, C. A., Braun, C. C., & Morgan, B. B., Jr. (1997) Team workload: Its meaning and measurement. In M. T. Brannick, E. Salas, & C. Prince (Eds.), *Team performance assessment and measurement: Theory, methods, and applications* (pp. 85–108). Mahwah, NJ: Erlbaum.

Bowers, C. A., Pharmer, J. A., & Salas, E. (2000). When member homogeneity is needed in work teams: A meta-analysis. *Small Group Research, 31,* 305–327.

Bowers, C. A., Weaver, J. L., & Morgan, B. B., Jr. (1996). Moderating the performance effects of stressors. In J. E. Driskell & E. Salas (Eds.), *Stress and human performance* (pp. 163–192). Mahwah, NJ: Erlbaum.

Bowers, D. G., & Seashore, S. E. (1966). Predicting organizational effectiveness with a four-factor theory of leadership. *Administrative Science Quarterly, 11,* 238–263.

Bowlby, J. (1980). *Attachment and loss* (Vol. 1). London: Hogarth.

Bradley, P. H. (1978). Power, status, and upward communication in small decision-making groups. *Communication Monographs, 45,* 33–43.

Brady, F. N. (2002). Lining up for Star-Wars tickets: Some ruminations on ethics and economics based on an Internet study of behavior in queues. *Journal of Business Ethics, 38,* 157–165.

Bramel, D., & Friend, R. (1981). Hawthorne, the myth of the docile worker, and class bias in psychology. *American Psychologist, 36,* 867–878.

Brandes, U., Kenis, P., Raab, J., Schneider, V., & Wagner, D. (1999). Explorations into the visualization of policy networks. *Journal of Theoretical Politics, 11,* 75–106.

Brannick, M. T., Salas, E., & Prince, C. (Eds.). (1997). *Team perfor-mance assessment and measurement: Theory, methods, and applications.* Mahwah, NJ: Erlbaum.

Branscombe, N. R. (1998). Thinking about one's gender group's privileges or disadvantages: Consequences for well-being in women and men. *British Journal of Social Psychology, 37,* 167–184.

Branscombe, N. R., Spears, R., Ellemers, N., & Doosje, B. (2002). Intragroup and intergroup evaluation effects on group behavior. *Personality and Social Psychology Bulletin, 28,* 744–753.

Branscombe, N. R., & Wann, D. L. (1994). Collective self-esteem consequences of outgroup derogation when a valued social identity is on trial. *European Journal of Social Psychology, 24,* 641–657.

Brauer, M., Judd, C. M., & Gliner, M. D. (1995). The effects of repeated expressions on attitude polarization during group discussions. *Journal of Personality and Social Psychology, 68,* 1014–1029.

Bray, R. M., Johnson, D., & Chilstrom, J. T., Jr. (1982). Social influence by group members with minority opinions: A comparison of Hollander & Moscovici. *Journal of Personality and Social Psychology, 43,* 78–88.

Brechner, K. C. (1977). An experimental analysis of social traps. *Journal of Experimental Social Psychology, 13,* 552–564.

Brehm, J. W. (1976). Responses to loss of freedom: A theory of psychological reactance. In J. W. Thibaut, J. T. Spence, & R. C. Carson (Eds.), *Contemporary topics in social psychology* (pp. 51–78). Morristown, NJ: General Learning Press.

Brehm, J. W., & Sensenig, J. (1966). Social influence as a function of attempted and implied usurpation of choice. *Journal of Personality and Social Psychology, 4,* 703–707.

Brehm, S. S., & Brehm, J. W. (1981). *Psychological reactance: A theory of freedom and control.* New York: Academic Press.

Brennan, K. A., Clark, C. L., & Shaver, P. R. (1998). Self-report measurement of adult attachment: An integrative overview. In J. A. Simpson & W. S. Rholes (Eds.), *Attachment theory and close relationships* (pp. 46–76). New York: Guilford Press.

Brenner, O. C., & Vinacke, W. E. (1979). Accommodative and exploitive behavior of males versus females and managers versus nonmanagers as measured by the Test of Strategy. *Social Psychology Quarterly, 42,* 289–293.

Brewer, M. B. (1979). In-group bias in the minimal intergroup situation: A cognitive–motivational analysis. *Psychological Bulletin, 86,* 307–324.

Brewer, M. B. (2000). Reducing prejudice through cross-categorization: Effects of multiple social identities. In S. Oskamp (Ed.), *Reducing prejudice and discrimination* (pp. 165–183). Mahwah, NJ: Erlbaum. Retrieved June 22, 2004, from http://www.netlibrary.com

Brewer, M. B., & Brown, R. J. (1998). Intergroup relations. In D. T. Gilbert, S. T. Fiske, & G. Lindzey (Eds.), *The handbook of social psychology* (4th ed., Vol. 2, pp. 554–594). New York: McGraw-Hill.

Brewer, M. B., & Campbell, D. T. (1976). *Ethnocentrism and intergroup attitudes: East African evidence.* New York: Halsted Press.

Brewer, M. B., & Gardner, W. (1996). Who is this "We"? Levels of collective identity and self representations. *Journal of Personality and Social Psychology, 71,* 83–93.

Brewer, M. B., & Kramer, R. M. (1986). Choice behavior in social dilemmas: Effects of social identity, group size, and decision framing. *Journal of Personality and Social Psychology, 50,* 543–549.

Brewer, M. B., Manzi, J. M., & Shaw, J. S. (1993). In-group identification as a function of depersonalization, distinctiveness, and status. *Psychological Science, 4,* 88–92.

Brewer, M. B., & Miller, N. (1984). Beyond the contact hypothesis: Theoretical perspectives on desegregation. In N. Miller & M. Brewer (Eds.), *Groups in contact: The psychology of desegregation* (pp. 281–302). New York: Academic Press.

Brewer, M. B., & Pickett, C. L. (2002). The social self and group identification: Inclusion and distinctiveness motives in interpersonal and collective identities. In J. P. Forgas & K. D. Williams (Eds.), *The social self: Cognitive, interpersonal, and intergroup perspectives* (pp. 255–272). New York: Psychology Press.

Brickner, M. A., Harkins, S. G., & Ostrom, T. M. (1986). Effects of personal involvement: Thought-provoking implications for social loafing. *Journal of Personality and Social Psychology, 51,* 763–770.

Brief, A. P., Buttram, R. T., Elliott, J. D., Reizenstein, R. M., & McCline, R. L. (1995). Releasing the beast: A study of compliance with orders to use race as a selection criterion. *Journal of Social Issues, 51*(3), 177–193.

Brief, A. P., Schuler, R. S., & Van Sell, M. (1981). *Managing job stress.* Boston: Little, Brown.

Brief, A. P., & Weiss, H. M. (2002). Organizational behavior: Affect in the workplace. *Annual Review of Psychology, 53,* 279–307.

Brinthaupt, T. M., Moreland, R. L., & Levine, J. M. (1991). Sources of optimism among prospective group members. *Personality and Social Psychology Bulletin, 17,* 36–43.

Brockner, J. (1995). How to stop throwing good money after bad: Using theory to guide practice. In D. A. Schroeder (Ed.), *Social dilemmas: Perspectives on individuals and groups* (pp. 163–182). Westport, CT: Praeger.

Brockner, J., & Rubin, J. Z. (1985). *The social psychology of conflict escalation and entrapment.* New York: Springer Verlag.

Brockner, J., & Wiesenfeld, B. M. (1996). An integrative framework for explaining reactions to decisions: Interactive effects of outcomes and procedures. *Psychological Bulletin, 120,* 189–208.

Brodbeck, F. C., Kerschreiter, R., Mojzisch, A., Frey, D., & Schulz-Hardt, S. (2002). The dissemination of critical, unshared information in decision-making groups: The effects of prediscussion dissent. *European Journal of Social Psychology, 32,* 35–56.

Bromley, D. G. (1985). Cult facts and fiction. *VCU Magazine, 14*(2), 10–15.

Bronzaft, A. L. (2002). Noise pollution: A hazard to physical and mental well-being. In R. B. Bechtel & A. Churchman (Eds.), *Handbook of environmental psychology* (pp. 499–510). New York: Wiley. Retrieved July 29, 2004, from http://www.netlibrary.com

Brooks, D. (2004, May 15). Columbine: Parents of a killer. *New York Times.* Retrieved May 16, 2004, from http://www.nytimes.com/

Brooks, G. R. (1996). Treatment for therapy-resistant men. In M. P. Andronico (Ed.), *Men in groups: Insights, interventions, and psychoeducational work* (pp. 7–19). Washington, DC: American Psychological Association.

Brown, B. B. (1987). Territoriality. In D. Stokols & I. Altman (Eds.), *Handbook of environmental psychology* (Vol. 1, pp. 505–531). New York: Wiley.

Brown, B. B., & Lohr, N. (1987). Peer group affiliation and adolescent self-esteem: An integration of ego-identity and symbolic-interaction theories. *Journal of Personality and Social Psychology, 52,* 47–55.

Brown, B. B., Mounts, N., Lamborn, S. D., & Steinberg, L. (1993). Parenting practices and peer group affiliation in adolescence. *Child Development, 64,* 467–482.

Brown, J. D., & Dutton, K. A. (1995). The thrill of victory, the complexity of defeat: Self-esteem and people's emotional reactions to success and failure. *Journal of Personality and Social Psychology, 68,* 712–722.

Brown, R. (1974). Further comment on the risky shift. *American Psychologist, 29,* 468–470.

Brown, R. (2000). *Group processes* (2nd ed.). Malden, MA: Blackwell.

Brown, R., Condor, S., Matthews, A., Wade, G., & Williams, J. A. (1986). Explaining intergroup differentiation in an industrial organization. *Journal of Occupational Psychology, 59,* 273–286.

Brown, R. W. (1954). Mass phenomena. In G. Lindzey (Ed.), *The handbook of social psychology* (Vol. 2, pp. 833–876). Cambridge, MA: Addison-Wesley.

Brown, S. M. (1979). Male versus female leaders: A comparison of empirical studies. *Sex Roles, 5,* 595–611.

Brown, S. P. (1996). A meta-analysis and review of organizational research on job involvement. *Psychological Bulletin, 120,* 235–255.

Brown, T. M., & Miller, C. E. (2000). Communication networks in task-performing groups: Effects of task complexity, time pressure, and interpersonal dominance. *Small Group Research, 31,* 131–157.

Brown, V., & Paulus, P. B. (1996). A simple dynamic model of social factors in group brainstorming. *Small Group Research, 27,* 91–114.

Brown, V. R., & Paulus, P. B. (2002). Making group brainstorming more effective: Recommendations from an associative memory perspective. *Current Directions in Psychological Science, 11,* 208–212.

Browning, L. (1978). A grounded organizational communication theory derived from qualitative data. *Communication Monographs, 45,* 93–109.

Brownstein, A. L. (2003). Biased predecision processing. *Psychological Bulletin, 129,* 545–568.

Buckley, W. (1967). *Sociology and modern systems theory.* Upper Saddle River, NJ: Prentice Hall.

Budman, S. H., Demby, A., Feldstein, M., & Gold, M. (1984). The effects of time-limited group psychotherapy: A controlled study. *International Journal of Group Psychotherapy, 34,* 587–603.

Buehler, R., & Griffin, D. (1994). Change-of-meaning effects in conformity and dissent: Observing construal processes over time. *Journal of Personality and Social Psychology, 67,* 984–996.

Bugental, D. B., & Lewis, J. C. (1999). The paradoxical misuse of power by those who see themselves as powerless: How does it happen? *Journal of Social Issues, 55,* 51–64.

Bukowski, W. M., Newcomb, A. F., & Hartup, W. W. (Eds.). (1996). *The company they keep: Friendships in childhood and adolescence.* New York: Cambridge University Press.

Bulman, R. J., & Wortman, C. B. (1977). Attributions of blame and coping in the "real world": Severe accident victims react to their lot. *Journal of Personality and Social Psychology, 35,* 351–363.

Burgoon, J. K. (1983). Nonverbal violations of expectations. In J. M. Wiemann & R. P. Harrison (Eds.), *Sage annual reviews of communication: Nonverbal interaction* (Vol. 11, pp. 11–77). Thousand Oaks, CA: Sage.

Burke, M. J., & Day, R. R. (1986). A cumulative study of the effectiveness of managerial training. *Journal of Applied Psychology, 71,* 232–245.

Burke, P. J. (1967). The development of task and social–emotional role differentiation. *Sociometry, 30,* 379–392.

Burke, P. J. (1974). Participation and leadership in small groups. *American Sociological Review, 39,* 832–842.

Burlingame, G. M., Fuhriman, A., & Johnson, J. E. (2001). Cohesion in group psychotherapy. *Psychotherapy: Theory, Research, Practice, Training, 38,* 373–379.

Burlingame, G. M., Fuhriman, A., & Mosier, J. (2003). The differential effectiveness of group psychotherapy: A meta-analytic perspective. *Group Dynamics, 7,* 3–12.

Burlingame, G. M., Kircher, J. C., & Taylor, S. (1994). Methodological considerations in group psychotherapy research: Past, present, and future practices. In A. Fuhriman & G. M. Burlingame (Eds.), *Handbook of group psychotherapy* (pp. 41–82). New York: Wiley.

Burlingame, G. M., & Layne, C. M. (Eds.). (2001). Group-based interventions for trauma survivors [Special issue]. *Group Dynamics, 5,* 243–314.

Burney, C. (1961). *Solitary confinement* (2nd ed). New York: St. Martin's Press.

Burns, J. M. (1978). *Leadership.* New York: Harper.

Burnstein, E., & Vinokur, A. (1973). Testing two classes of theories about group-induced shifts in individual choice. *Journal of Experimental Social Psychology, 9,* 123–137.

Burnstein, E., & Vinokur, A. (1977). Persuasive arguments and social comparison as determinants of attitude polarization. *Journal of Experimental Social Psychology, 13,* 315–332.

Burnstein, E., & Worchel, P. (1962). Arbitrariness of frustration and its consequences for aggression in a social situation. *Journal of Personality, 30,* 528–540.

Buss, D. M. (1996). The evolutionary psychology of human social strategies. In E. T. Higgins & A. W. Kruglanski (Eds.), *Social psychology: Handbook of basic principles* (pp. 3–38). New York: Guilford Press.

Buss, D. M., & Kenrick, D. T. (1998). Evolutionary social psychology. In D. T. Gilbert, S. T. Fiske, & G. Lindzey (Eds.), *The handbook of social psychology* (4th ed., Vol. 2, pp. 982–1026). New York: McGraw-Hill.

Butcher, J. N., & Hatcher, C. (1988). The neglected entity in air disaster planning: Psychological services. *American Psychologist, 43,* 724–729.

Butler, D., & Geis, F. L. (1990). Nonverbal affect responses to male and female leaders: Implications for leadership evaluations. *Journal of Personality and Social Psychology, 58,* 48–59.

Butler, T., & Fuhriman, A. (1983a). Curative factors in group therapy: A review of the recent literature. *Small Group Behavior, 14,* 131–142.

Butler, T., & Fuhriman, A. (1983b). Level of functioning and length of time in treatment variables influencing patients' therapeutic experience in group psychotherapy. *International Journal of Group Psychotherapy, 33,* 489–505.

Buunk, B. P., & Hoorens, V. (1992). Social support and stress: The role of social comparison and social exchange processes. *British Journal of Clinical Psychology, 31,* 445–457.

Buunk, B. P., Oldersma, F. L., & De Dreu, C. K. (2001). Enhancing satisfaction through downward comparison: The role of relational discontent and individual differences in social comparison orientation. *Journal of Experimental Social Psychology, 37,* 452–467.

Buys, C. J. (1978a). Humans would do better without groups. *Personality and Social Psychology Bulletin, 4,* 123–125.

Buys, C. J. (1978b). On "Humans would do better without groups": A final note. *Personality and Social Psychology Bulletin, 4,* 568.

Byrne, D. (1961). Anxiety and the experimental arousal of affiliation need. *Journal of Abnormal and Social Psychology, 63,* 660–662.

Byrne, D. (1971). *The attraction paradigm.* New York: Academic Press.

Cacioppo, J. T., Hawkley, L. C., & Berntson, G. G. (2003). The anatomy of loneliness. *Current Directions in Psychological Science, 12,* 71–74.

Cahill, S., Fine, G. A., & Grant, L. (1995). Dimensions of qualitative research. In K. S. Cook, G. A. Fine, & J. S. House (Eds.), *Sociological perspectives on social psychology* (pp. 605–628). Boston: Allyn & Bacon.

Caldwell, D. F., & Burger, J. M. (1997). Personality and social influence strategies in the workplace. *Personality and Social Psychology Bulletin, 23,* 1003–1012.

Callaway, M. R., & Esser, J. K. (1984). Groupthink: Effects of cohesiveness and problem-solving procedures on group decision making. *Social Behavior and Personality, 12,* 157–164.

Callaway, M. R., Marriott, R. G., & Esser, J. K. (1985). Effects of dominance on group decision making: Toward a stress-reduction explanation of groupthink. *Journal of Personality and Social Psychology, 49,* 949–952.

Callero, P. L. (1994). From role-playing to role-using: Understanding role as resource. In Conceptualizing structure in social psychology [Special issue]. *Social Psychology Quarterly, 57,* 228–243.

Camacho, L. M., & Paulus, P. B. (1995). The role of social anxiousness in group brainstorming. *Journal of Personality and Social Psychology, 68,* 1071–1080.

Cameron, J. E. (1999). Social identity and the pursuit of possible selves: Implications for the psychological well-being of university students. *Group Dynamics, 3,* 179–189.

Cameron, W. B. (1966). *Modern social movements: A sociological outline.* New York: Random House.

Campbell, D. T. (1958a). Common fate, similarity, and other indices of the status of aggregates of persons as social entities. *Behavioral Science, 3,* 14–25.

Campbell, D. T. (1958b). Systematic error on the part of human links in communication systems. *Information and Control, 1,* 334–369.

Campbell, D. T. (1965). Ethnocentric and other altruistic motives. *Nebraska Symposium on Motivation, 13,* 283–311.

Campbell, L., Simpson, J. A., Stewart, M., & Manning, J. G. (2002). The formation of status hierarchies in leaderless groups: The role of male waist-to-hip ratio. *Human Nature, 13,* 345–362.

Canetti, E. (1962). *Crowds and power.* London: Gollancz.

Cannavale, F. J., Scarr, H. A., & Pepitone, A. (1970). Deindividuation in the small group: Further evidence. *Journal of Personality and Social Psychology, 16,* 141–147.

Cannella, A. A., & Rowe, W. G. (1995). Leader capabilities, succession, and competitive context: A study of professional baseball teams. *Leadership Quarterly, 6,* 69–88.

Cannon-Bowers, J. A., Tannenbaum, S. I., Salas, E., & Volpe, C. E. (1995). Defining team competencies and establishing team training requirements. In R. Guzzo, E. Salas, & Associates, *Team effectiveness and decision making in organizations* (pp. 333–380). San Francisco: Jossey-Bass.

Cantril, H. (1940). *The invasion from Mars*. Princeton: Princeton University Press.

Caplan, N. (1970). The new ghetto man: A review of recent empirical studies. *Journal of Social Issues 26*(1), 59–73.

Caplan, R. D., Vinokur, A. D., Price, R. H., & Van Ryn, M. (1989). Job seeking, reemployment, and mental health: A randomized field experiment in coping with job loss. *Journal of Applied Psychology, 74,* 759–769.

Caporael, L. R. (2000). Evolutionary psychology: Toward a unifying theory and a hybrid science. *Annual Review of Psychology, 52,* 607–628.

Caporael, L. R. (2001). Parts and wholes: The evolutionary importance of groups. In C. Sedikides & M. B. Brewer (Eds.), *Individual self, relational self, collective self* (pp. 241–258). New York: Psychology Press.

Caporael, L. R., & Brewer, M. B. (1995). Hierarchical evolutionary theory: There is an alternative, and it's not creationism. *Psychological Inquiry, 6,* 31–34.

Cappella, J. N. (1985). Controlling the floor in conversation. In A. W. Siegman & S. Feldstein (Eds.), *Multichannel integrations of nonverbal behavior* (pp. 69–103). Mahwah, NJ: Erlbaum.

Carew, D. K., Parisi-Carew, E., & Blanchard, K. H. (1986). Group development and situational leadership: A model for managing groups. *Training and Development Journal, 40*(6), 46–50.

Carli, L. L. (1989). Gender differences in interaction style and influence. *Journal of Personality and Social Psychology, 56,* 565–576.

Carli, L. L. (1999). Gender, interpersonal power, and social influence. *Journal of Social Issues, 55,* 81–99.

Carli, L. L. (2001). Gender and social influence. *Journal of Social Issues, 57,* 725–741.

Carli, L. L. & Eagly, A. H. (Eds.). (2001). Gender, hierarchy, and leadership. *Journal of Social Issues, 57*(4).

Carli, L. L., LaFleur, S. J., & Loeber, C. C. (1995). Nonverbal behavior, gender, and influence. *Journal of Personality and Social Psychology, 68,* 1030–1041.

Carlopio, J. R. (1996). Construct validity of a physical work environment satisfaction questionnaire. *Journal of Occupational Health Psychology, 1,* 330–344.

Carlyle, T. (1841). *On heroes, hero-worship, and the heroic*. London: Fraser.

Carneiro, R. L. (1970). A theory of the origin of the state. *Science, 169,* 239–249.

Carnevale, P. J. D. (1986a). Mediating disputes and decisions in organizations. *Research on Negotiation in Organizations, 1,* 251–269.

Carnevale, P. J. D. (1986b). Strategic choice in mediation. *Negotiation Journal, 2,* 41–56.

Carnevale, P. J. D., & Pruitt, D. G. (1992). Negotiation and mediation. *Annual Review of Psychology, 43,* 531–582.

Carpenter, C. R. (1958). Territoriality: A review of concepts and problems. In A. Roe & G. G. Simpson (Eds.), *Behavior and evolution* (pp. 224–250). New Haven: Yale University Press.

Carrere, S., & Evans, G. W. (1994). Life in an isolated and confined environment: A qualitative study of the role of the designed environment. *Environment and Behavior, 26,* 707–741.

Carroll, J. W. (1987). Indefinite terminating points and the iterated Prisoner's Dilemma. *Theory and Decision, 22,* 247–256.

Carron, A. V. (1982). Cohesiveness in sports groups: Interpretations and considerations. *Journal of Sport Psychology, 4,* 123–128.

Carron, A. V., Colman, M. M., Wheeler, J., & Stevens, D. (2002). Cohesion and performance in sport: A meta-analysis. *Journal of Sport and Exercise Psychology, 24,* 168–188.

Carron, A. V., Widmeyer, W. N., & Brawley, L. R. (1988). Group cohesion and individual adherence to physical activity. *Journal of Sport and Exercise Psychology, 10,* 127–138.

Carson, R. C. (1969). *Interaction concepts of personality*. Chicago: Aldine.

Cartwright, D. (1959). Power: A neglected variable in social psychology. In D. Cartwright (Ed.), *Studies in social power* (pp. 1–14). Ann Arbor, MI: Institute for Social Research.

Cartwright, D. (1978). Theory and practice. *Journal of Social Issues, 34*(4), 168–175.

Cartwright, D., & Harary, F. (1956). Structural balance: A generalization of Heider's theory. *Psychological Review, 63,* 277–293.

Cartwright, D., & Harary, F. (1970). Ambivalence and indifference in generalizations of structural balance. *Behavioral Science, 14,* 497–513.

Cartwright, D., & Zander, A. (Eds.). (1960). *Group dynamics: Research and theory* (2nd ed.). New York: Harper & Row.

Cartwright, D., & Zander, A. (Eds.). (1968). *Group dynamics: Research and theory* (3rd ed.). New York: Harper & Row.

Carvalho, E. R., & Brito, V. C. A. (1995). Sociometric intervention in family therapy: A case study. *Journal of Group Psychotherapy, Psychodrama, & Sociometry, 47,* 147–164.

Carver, C. S., & Scheier, M. F. (1981). *Attention and self-regulation: A control-theory approach to human behavior*. New York: Springer Verlag.

Cascio, W. F. (1995). Whither industrial and organizational psychology in a changing world of work? *American Psychologist, 50,* 928–939.

Castore, C. H., & Murnighan, J. K. (1978). Determinants of support for group decisions. *Organizational Behavior and Human Performance, 22,* 75–92.

Cattell, R. B. (1948). Concepts and methods in the measurement of group syntality. *Psychological Review, 55,* 48–63.

Cavalli, L. (1986). Charismatic domination, totalitarian dictatorship, and plebiscitary democracy in the twentieth century. In C. F. Graumann & S. Moscovici (Eds.), *Changing conceptions of leadership* (pp. 67–81). New York: Springer Verlag.

Cecil, J. S., Hans, V. P., & Wiggins, E. C. (1991). Citizen comprehension of difficult issues: Lessons from civil jury trials. *American University Law Review, 40,* 727–774.

Chagnon, N. A. (1997). *Yanomamö* (5th ed.). Fort Worth, TX: Harcourt Brace.

Chan, D. (1998). Functional relations among constructs in the same content domain at different levels of analysis: A typology of composition models. *Journal of Applied Psychology, 83,* 234–246.

Chang, A., & Bordia, P. (2001). A multidimensional approach to the group cohesion–group performance relationship. *Small Group Research, 32,* 379–405.

Chang, E. C., & Asakawa, K. (2003). Cultural variations on optimistic and pessimistic bias for self versus a sibling: Is there evidence for self-enhancement in the West and for self-criticism in the East when the referent group is specified? *Journal of Personality and Social Psychology, 84,* 569–581.

Chansler, P. A., Swamidass, P. M., & Cammann, C. (2003). Self-managing work teams: An empirical study of group cohesiveness in "natural work groups" at a Harley-Davidson Motor Company plant. *Small Group Research, 34,* 101–120.

Chapman, A. J. (1973). Funniness of jokes, canned laughter, and recall performance. *Sociometry, 36,* 569–578.

Chartrand, T. L., & Bargh, J. A. (1999). The chameleon effect: The perception–behavior link and social interaction. *Journal of Personality and Social Psychology, 76,* 893–910.

Cheek, J. M. (1989). Identity orientations and self-interpretation. In D. M. Buss & N. Cantor (Eds.), *Personality psychology* (pp. 275–285). New York: Springer Verlag.

Cheek, J. M., & Buss, A. H. (1981). Shyness and sociability. *Journal of Personality and Social Psychology, 41,* 330–339.

Chemers, M. M. (1997). *An integrative theory of leadership.* Mahwah, NJ: Erlbaum.

Chemers, M. M. (2000). Leadership research and theory: A functional integration. *Group Dynamics, 4,* 27–43.

Chen, S., Lee-Chai, A. Y., & Bargh, J. A. (2001). Relationship orientation as a moderator of the effects of social power. *Journal of Personality and Social Psychology, 80,* 173-187.

Chen, S., Shechter, D., & Chaiken, S. (1996). Getting at the truth or getting along: Accuracy- versus impression-motivated heuristic and systematic processing. *Journal of Personality and Social Psychology, 71,* 262–275.

Chen, Z., Lawson, R. B., Gordon, L. R., & McIntosh, B. (1996). Groupthink: Deciding with the leader and the devil. *Psychological Record, 46,* 581–590.

Cheng, S. (1997). Epidemic genital retraction syndrome: Environmental and personal risk factors in southern China. *Journal of Psychology and Human Sexuality, 9,* 57–70.

Chertkoff, J. M., Kushigian, R. H., & McCool, M. A., Jr. (1996). Interdependent exiting: The effects of group size, time limit, and gender on the coordination of exiting. *Journal of Environmental Psychology, 16,* 109–121.

Cherulnik, P., & Wilderman, S. (1986). Symbols of status in urban neighborhoods. *Environment and Behavior, 18,* 604–622.

Cheyne, J. A., & Efran, M. G. (1972). The effect of spatial and interpersonal variables on the invasion of group controlled territories. *Sociometry, 35,* 477–487.

Chiu, C., Hong, Y., & Dweck, C. S. (1997). Lay dispositionism and implicit theories of personality. *Journal of Personality and Social Psychology, 73,* 19–30.

Christensen, A., & Jacobson, N. S. (1994). Who (or what) can do psychotherapy: The status and challenge of nonprofessional therapies. *Psychological Science, 5,* 8–12.

Christensen, P. N., & Kashy, D. A. (1998). Perceptions of and by lonely people in initial social interaction. *Personality and Social Psychology Bulletin, 24,* 322–329.

Cialdini, R. B. (2001). *Influence: Science and practice* (4th ed.). Boston: Allyn & Bacon.

Cialdini, R. B., Borden, R., Thorne, A., Walker, M., Freeman, S., & Sloane, L. R. (1976). Basking in reflected glory: Three (football) field studies. *Journal of Personality and Social Psychology, 34,* 366–375.

Cialdini, R. B., & Goldstein, N. J. (2004). Social influence: Compliance and conformity. *Annual Review of Psychology, 55,* 591–621.

Cialdini, R. B., Kallgren, C. A., & Reno, R. R. (1991). A focus theory of normative conduct: A theoretical refinement and reevaluation of the role of norms in human behavior. *Advances in Experimental Social Psychology, 24,* 201–234.

Cialdini, R. B., Reno, R. R., & Kallgren, C. A. (1990). A focus theory of normative conduct: Recycling the concept of norms to reduce littering in public places. *Journal of Personality and Social Psychology, 58,* 1015–1026.

Cialdini, R. B., Wosinska, W., Barrett, D. W., Butner, J., &

Gornik-Durose, M. (1999). Compliance with a request in two cultures: The differential influence of social proof and commitment/consistency on collectivists and individualists. *Personality and Social Psychology Bulletin, 25,* 1242–1253.

Cianni, M., & Romberger, B. (1995). Interactions with senior managers: Perceived differences by race/ethnicity and by gender. *Sex Roles, 32,* 353–373.

Cini, M. A., Moreland, R. L., & Levine, J. M. (1993). Group staffing levels and responses to prospective and new group members. *Journal of Personality and Social Psychology, 65,* 723–734.

Claiborn, C. D., Goodyear, R. K., & Horner, P. A. (2001). Feedback. *Psychotherapy: Theory, Research, Practice, Training, 38,* 401–405.

Clark, G. (1969, November). What happens when the police strike? *New York Times Magazine,* p. 45.

Clark, K. B. (1971). The pathos of power. *American Psychologist, 26,* 1047–1057.

Clark, M. S., Oullette, R., Powell, M. C., & Milberg, S. (1987). Recipient's mood, relationship type, and helping. *Journal of Personality and Social Psychology, 53,* 94–103.

Clark, N. K., Stephenson, G. M., & Kniveton, B. (1990). Social remembering: Quantitative aspects of individual and collaborative remembering by police officers and students. *British Journal of Psychology, 81,* 73–94.

Clark, R. D., III. (1990). Minority influence: The role of argument refutation on the majority position and social support for the minority position. *European Journal of Social Psychology, 20,* 489–497.

Clark, R. D., III. (1999). Effect of number of majority defectors on minority influence. *Group Dynamics, 3,* 303–312.

Clark, R. D., III. (2001). Effects of majority defection and multiple minority sources on minority influence. *Group Dynamics, 5,* 57–62.

Clark, R. D., III, & Sechrest, L. B. (1976). The mandate phenomenon. *Journal of Personality and Social Psychology, 34,* 1057–1061.

Clark, S. (1998). International competition and the treatment of minorities: Seventeenth-century cases and general propositions. *American Journal of Sociology, 103,* 1267–1308.

Clark, S. E., Hori, A., Putnam, A., & Martin, T. P. (2000). Group collaboration in recognition memory. *Journal of Experimental Psychology: Learning, Memory, & Cognition, 26,* 1578–1588.

Clendenen, V. I., Herman, C. P., & Polivy, J. (1994). Social facilitation of eating among friends and strangers. *Appetite, 23,* 1–13.

Coats, S., Smith, E. R., Claypool, H. M., & Banner, M. J. (2000). Overlapping mental representations of self and in-group: Reaction time evidence and its relationship with explicit measures of group identification. *Journal of Experimental Social Psychology, 36,* 304–315.

Cohen, D., & Nisbett, R. E. (1993). Self-protection and the culture of honor: Explaining southern violence. *Personality and Social Psychology Bulletin, 20,* 551–567.

Cohen, D. J., Whitmyre, J. W., & Funk, W. H. (1960). Effect of group cohesiveness and training upon group thinking. *Journal of Applied Psychology, 44,* 319–322.

Cohen, J. L. (1979). Social facilitation: Increased evaluation apprehension through permanency of record. *Motivation and Emotion, 3,* 19–33.

Cohen, L. L., & Swim, J. K. (1995). The differential impact of gender ratios on women and men: Tokenism, self-confidence, and expectations. *Personality and Social Psychology Bulletin, 21,* 876–884.

Cohen, S., Evans, G. W., Stokols, D., & Krantz, D. (1986). *Behavior, health, and environmental stress.* New York: Plenum Press.

Cohen, S., Glass, D. C., & Singer, J. E. (1973). Apartment noise, auditory discrimination, and reading ability in children. *Journal of Experimental Social Psychology, 9,* 407–422.

Cohen, S., & Weinstein, N. (1981). Nonauditory effects of noise on behavior and health. *Journal of Social Issues, 37*(1), 36–70.

Cohen, S., & Wills, T. A. (1985). Stress, social support, and the buffering hypothesis. *Psychological Bulletin, 98,* 310–357.

Cohen, S. G., & Bailey, D. E. (1997). What makes teams work: Group effectiveness research from the shop floor to the executive suite. *Journal of Management, 23,* 239–290.

Coie, J. D., Dodge, K. A., & Kupersmidt, J. B. (1990). Peer group behavior and social status. In S. R. Asher & J. D. Coie (Eds.), *Peer rejection in childhood* (pp. 17–59). New York: Cambridge University Press.

Coleman, P. T. (2000). Intractable conflict. In M. Deutsch & P. T. Coleman (Eds.), *The handbook of conflict resolution: Theory and practice* (pp. 428–450). San Francisco: Jossey-Bass.

Colligan, M. J., & Murphy, L. R. (1982). A review of mass psychogenic illness in work settings. In M. J. Colligan, J. W. Pennebaker, & L. R. Murphy (Eds.), *Mass psychogenic illness: A social psychological analysis* (pp. 33–52). Mahwah, NJ: Erlbaum.

Colligan, M. J., Pennebaker, J. W., & Murphy, L. R. (Eds.). (1982). *Mass psychogenic illness: A social psychological analysis.* Mahwah, NJ: Erlbaum.

Collins, B. E., & Guetzkow, H. (1964). *A social psychology of group processes for decision-making.* New York: Wiley.

Collins, R. L. (2000). Among the better ones: Upward assimilation in social comparison. In J. Suls & L. Wheeler (Eds.), *Handbook of social comparison: Theory and research* (pp. 159–171). New York: Kluwer Academic/Plenum.

Colman, A. M. (1991). Crowd psychology in South African murder trials. *American Psychologist, 46,* 1071–1079.

Conger, J. A. (1999). Charismatic and transformational leadership in organizations: An insider's perspective on these developing streams of research. *Leadership Quarterly, 10,* 145–179.

Conger, J. A., & Kanungo, R. N. (1987). Toward a behavioral theory of charismatic leadership in organizational settings. *Academy of Management Review, 12,* 637–647.

Conroy, J., & Sundstrom, E. (1977). Territorial dominance in a dyadic conversation as a function of similarity of opinion. *Journal of Personality and Social Psychology, 35,* 570–576.

Cook, S. W. (1978). Interpersonal and attitudinal outcomes in cooperating interracial groups. *Journal of Research and Development in Education, 12,* 97–113.

Cook, S. W. (1984). The 1954 social science statement and school desegregation: A reply to Gerard. *American Psychologist, 39,* 819–832.

Cook, S. W. (1985). Experimenting on social issues: the case of school desegregation. *American Psychologist, 40,* 452–460.

Cooley, C. H. (1902). *Human nature and the social order.* New York: Scribner.

Cooley, C. H. (1909). *Social organization.* New York: Scribner.

Cooper, C. L. (1981). Social support at work and stress management. *Small Group Behavior, 12,* 285–297.

Cooper, H. M. (1979). Statistically combining independent studies: A meta-analysis of sex differences in conformity research. *Journal of Personality and Social Psychology, 37,* 131–146.

Corey, M., & Corey, G. (1992). *Groups: Process and practice* (4th ed.). Pacific Grove, CA: Brooks/Cole.

Corning, A. F., & Myers, D. J. (2002). Individual orientation toward engagement in social action. *Political Psychology, 23,* 703–729.

Corsaro, W. A., & Eder, D. (1995). Development and socialization of children and adolescents. In K. S. Cook, G. A. Fine, & J. S. House (Eds.), *Sociological perspectives on social psychology* (pp. 421–451). Needham Heights, MA: Allyn & Bacon.

Coser, L. A. (1956). *The functions of social conflict.* New York: Free Press.

Costa, P., Jr., Terracciano, A., & McCrae, R. R. (2001). Gender differences in personality traits across cultures: Robust and surprising findings. *Journal of Personality and Social Psychology, 81,* 322–331.

Costanzo, P. R. (1970). Conformity development as a function of self-blame. *Journal of Personality and Social Psychology, 14,* 366–374.

Cota, A. A., Evans, C. R., Dion, K. L., Kilik, L., & Longman, R. S. (1995). The structure of group cohesion. *Personality and Social Psychology Bulletin, 21,* 572–580.

Cotton, J. L. (1993). *Employee involvement.* Thousand Oaks, CA: Sage.

Cotton, J. L., & Cook, M. S. (1982). Meta-analyses and the effects of various reward systems: Some different conclusions from Johnson et al. *Psychological Bulletin, 92,* 176–183.

Cottrell, N. B. (1972). Social facilitation. In C. G. McClintock (Ed.), *Experimental social psychology* (pp. 185–236). New York: Holt, Rinehart & Winston.

Coughlin, B. C., & Venkatesh, S. A. (2003). The urban street gang after 1970 [Electronic version]. *Annual Review of Sociology, 29,* 41–64.

Courneya, K. S., & Carron, A. V. (1991). Effects of travel and length of home stand/road trip on the home advantage. *Journal of Sport and Exercise Psychology, 13,* 42–49.

Courtright, J. A. (1978). A laboratory investigation of groupthink. *Communication Monographs, 43,* 229–246.

Cousins, S. D. (1989). Culture and self-perception in Japan and the United States. *Journal of Personality and Social Psychology, 56,* 124–131.

Crago, M., Yates, A., Beutler, L. E., & Arizmendi, T. G. (1985). Height–weight ratios among female athletes: Are collegiate athletics the precursors to an anorexic syndrome? *International Journal of Eating Disorders, 4,* 79–87.

Crandall, C. S. (1988). Social contagion of binge eating. *Journal of Personality and Social Psychology, 55,* 588–598.

Crano, W. D. (2000). Milestones in the psychological analysis of social influence. *Group Dynamics, 4,* 68–80.

Crocker, J., Blaine, B., & Luhtanen, R. (1993). Self-esteem: Cognitive and motivational consequences for prejudice and intergroup behavior. In M. A. Hogg & D. Abrams (Eds.), *Group motivation: social psychological perspectives* (pp. 52–67). London: Harvester Wheatsheaf.

Crocker, J., & Luhtanen, R. (1990). Collective self-esteem and ingroup bias. *Journal of Personality and Social Psychology, 58,* 60–67.

Crocker, J., Luhtanen, R., Blaine, B., & Broadnax, S. (1994). Collective self-esteem and psychological well-being among White, Black, and Asian college students. *Personality and Social Psychology Bulletin, 20,* 503–513.

Crocker, J., & Major, B. (1989). Social stigma and self-esteem: The self-protective properties of stigma. *Psychological Review, 96,* 608–630.

Crocker, J., & McGraw, K. M. (1984). What's good for the goose is not good for the gander: Solo status as an obstacle to occupational achievement for males and females. *American Behavioral Scientist, 27,* 357–369.

Crocker, O. L., Chiu, J. S. L., & Charney, C. (1984). *Quality circles.* Toronto: Methuen.

Cronshaw, S. F., & Lord, R. G. (1987). Effects of categorization, attribution, and encoding processes on leadership perceptions. *Journal of Applied Psychology, 72,* 97–106.

Crosby, F. (1976). A model of egoistical relative deprivation. *Psychological Review, 83,* 85–113.

Cross, S. E., Bacon, P. L., & Morris, M. L. (2000). The relational–interdependent self-construal and relationships. *Journal of Personality and Social Psychology, 78,* 791–808.

Cross, S. E., & Madson, L. (1997). Models of the self: Self-construals and gender. *Psychological Bulletin, 122,* 5–37.

Cross, S. E., & Morris, M. L. (2003). Getting to know you: The relational self-construal, relational cognition, and well-being. *Personality and Social Psychology Bulletin, 29,* 512–523.

Crouch, E. C., Bloch, S., & Wanlass, J. (1994). Therapeutic factors: Interpersonal and intrapersonal mechanisms. In A. Fuhriman & G. M. Burlingame (Eds.), *Handbook of group psychotherapy* (pp. 269–315). New York: Wiley.

Crow, W. J. (1963). A study of strategic doctrines using the Inter-Nation Simulation. *Journal of Conflict Resolution, 7,* 580–589.

Crutchfield, R. S. (1955). Conformity and character. *American Psychologist, 10,* 191–198.

Csoka, L. S., & Bons, P. M. (1978). Manipulating the situation to fit the leader's style—Two validation studies of Leader Match. *Journal of Applied Psychology, 63,* 295–300.

Cummings, J. N. (2004). Work groups, structural diversity, and knowledge sharing in a global organization. *Management Science, 50,* 352–364.

Cunningham, J. D., Starr, P. A., & Kanouse, D. E. (1979). Self as actor, active observer, and passive observer: Implications for causal attributions. *Journal of Personality and Social Psychology, 37,* 1146–1152.

Curhan, J. R., Neale, M. A., & Ross, L. (2004). Dynamic valuation: Preference changes in the context of face-to-face negotiation. *Journal of Experimental Social Psychology, 40,* 142–151.

Dabbs, J. M., Jr., & Ruback, R. B. (1987). Dimensions of group process: Amount and structure of vocal interaction. *Advances in Experimental Social Psychology, 20,* 123–169.

Dale, R. (1952). *Planning and developing the company organization structure.* New York: American Management Association.

Damhorst, M. L. (1990). In search of a common thread: Classification of information communicated through dress. *Clothing and Textiles Research Journal, 8*(2), 1–12.

Dane, F. C., & Wrightsman, L. S. (1982). Effects of defendants' and victims' characteristics on jurors' verdicts. In N. L. Kerr & R. M. Bray (Eds.), *Psychology of the courtroom* (pp. 83–115). New York: Academic Press.

Dansereau, F., Graen, G. C., & Haga, W. (1975). A vertical dyad linkage approach to leadership in formal organizations. *Organizational Behavior and Human Performance, 13,* 46–78.

Dansereau, F., Yammarino, F. J., & Markham, S. E. (1995). Leadership: The multiple-level approaches. *Leadership Quarterly, 6,* 251–263.

Darley, J. (1992). Social organization for the production of evil. *Psychological Inquires, 3,* 199–218.

Darley, J. M. (1995). Constructive and destructive obedience: A taxonomy of principal–agent relationships. *Journal of Social Issues, 51*(3), 125–154.

Darley, J. (2001). Social comparison motives in ongoing groups. In M. A. Hogg & R. S. Tindale (Eds.), *Blackwell handbook of social psychology: Group processes* (pp. 334–351). Malden, MA: Blackwell.

Darley, J. M., & Latané, B. (1968). Bystander intervention in emergencies: Diffusion of responsibility. *Journal of Personality and Social Psychology, 8,* 377–383.

Davidson-Shivers, G. V., Morris, S. B., & Sriwongkol, T. (2003). Gender differences: Are they diminished in online discussions? *International Journal on E-Learning, 2,* 29–36.

Davis, J. H. (1969). *Group performance.* Reading, MA: Addison-Wesley.

Davis, J. H. (1973). Group decision and social interaction: A theory of social decision schemes. *Psychological Review, 80,* 97–125.

Davis, J. H. (1982). Social interaction as a combinatorial process in group decision. In H. Brandstätter, J. H. Davis, & G. Stocker-Kreichgauer (Eds.), *Group decision making* (pp. 27–58). London: Academic Press.

Davis, J. H. (1996). Group decision making and quantitative judgments: A consensus model. In E. H. Witte & J. H. Davis (Eds.), *Understanding group behavior: Consensual action by small groups* (Vol. 1, pp. 35–60). Mahwah, NJ: Erlbaum.

Davis, J. H., Bray, R. M., & Holt, R. W. (1977). The empirical study of decision processes in juries: A critical review. In J. L. Tapp & F. J. Levine (Eds.), *Law, justice, and the individual in society* (pp. 326–361). New York: Holt, Rinehart & Winston.

Davis, J. H., Kameda, T., Parks, C., Stasson, M., & Zimmerman, S. (1989). Some social mechanics of group decision making: The distribution of opinion, polling sequence, and implications for consensus. *Journal of Personality and Social Psychology, 57,* 1000–1012.

Davis, J. H., Kameda, T., & Stasson, M. (1992). Group risk taking: Selected topics. In J. F. Yates (Ed.), *Risk-taking behavior* (pp. 163–199). Chichester, UK: Wiley.

Davis, J. H., Kerr, N. L., Stasser, G., Meek, D., & Holt, R. (1977). Victim consequences, sentence severity, and decision processes in mock juries. *Organizational Behavior and Human Performance, 18,* 346–365.

Davis, J. H., Stasson, M., Ono, K., & Zimmerman, S. (1988). Effects of straw polls on group decision making: Sequential voting pattern, timing, and local majorities. *Journal of Personality and Social Psychology, 55,* 918–926.

Davis, J. R. (1982). *Street gangs: Youth, biker, and prison groups.* Dubuque, IA: Kendall/Hunt.

Davison, K. P., Pennebaker, J. W., & Dickerson, S. S. (2000). Who talks? The social psychology of illness support groups. *American Psychologist, 55,* 205–217.

Dawes, R. M. (1988). *Rational choice in an uncertain world.* San Diego: Harcourt Brace Jovanovich.

de Castro, J. M., Bellisle, F., Feunekes, G. L. J., Dalix, A. M., & de Graaf, C. (1997). Culture and meal patterns: A comparison of the food intake of free-living Americans, Dutch, and French students. *Nutrition Research, 17,* 807–829.

De Dreu, C. K. W. (1997). Productive conflict: The importance of conflict management and conflict issue. In C. K. W. De

Dreu & E. Van de Vliert (Eds.), *Using conflict in organizations* (pp. 9–22). Thousand Oaks, CA: Sage.

De Dreu, C. K. W. (2003). Time pressure and closing of the mind in negotiation. *Organizational Behavior and Human Decision Processes, 91,* 280–295.

De Dreu, C. K. W., & De Vries, N. K. (1996). Differential processing and attitude change following majority versus minority arguments. *British Journal of Social Psychology, 35,* 77–90.

De Dreu, C. K. W., & De Vries, N. K. (Eds.). (2001). *Group consensus and minority influence: Implications for innovation.* Malden, MA: Blackwell.

De Dreu, C. K. W., Nauta, A., & Van de Vliert, E. (1995). Self-serving evaluations of conflict behavior and escalation of the dispute. *Journal of Applied Social Psychology, 25,* 2049–2066.

De Dreu, C. K. W., & Van Lange, P. A. (1995). The impact of social value orientations on negotiator cognition and behavior. *Personality and Social Psychology Bulletin, 21,* 1178–1188.

De Dreu, C. K. W., & Van Vianen, A. E. M. (2001). Responses to relationship conflict and team effectiveness. *Journal of Organizational Behavior, 22,* 309–328.

De Dreu, C. K. W., & Weingart, L. R. (2003). Task versus relationship conflict, team performance, and team member satisfaction: A meta-analysis. *Journal of Applied Psychology, 88,* 741–749.

De Dreu, C. K. W., Weingart, L. R., & Kwon, S. (2000). Influence of social motives on integrative negotiation: A meta-analytic review and test of two theories. *Journal of Personality and Social Psychology, 78,* 889–905.

De Grada, E., Kruglanski, A. W., Mannetti, L., & Pierro, A. (1999). Motivated cognition and group interaction: Need for closure affects the contents and processes of collective negotiations. *Journal of Experimental Social Psychology, 35,* 346–365.

de la Roche, R. S. (1996). Collective violence as social control. *Sociological Forum, 11,* 97–128.

de la Roche, R. S. (2002). Why is collective violence collective? *Sociological Theory, 19,* 126–144.

de Tocqueville, A. (1969). *Democracy in America* (G. Lawrence, Trans.). New York: Doubleday. (Original work published in 1831)

De Vries, N. K., & De Dreu, C. K. W. (2001). Group consensus and minority influence: Introduction and overview. In C. K. W. De Dreu & N. K. De Vries (Eds.), *Group consensus and minority influence: Implications for innovation* (pp. 1–14). Malden, MA: Blackwell.

Dean, L. M., Willis, F. N., & Hewitt, J. (1975). Initial interaction distance among individuals equal and unequal in military rank. *Journal of Personality and Social Psychology, 32,* 294–299.

Deaux, K. (1996). Social identification. In E. T. Higgins & A. W. Kruglanski (Eds.), *Social psychology: Handbook of basic principles* (pp. 777–798). New York: Guilford Press.

Deci, E. L., Nezlek, J., & Sheinman, L. (1981). Characteristics of the rewarder and intrinsic motivation of the rewardee. *Journal of Personality and Social Psychology, 40,* 1–10.

Decker, S. H., & Van Winkle, B. (1996). *Life in the gang: Family, friends, and violence.* New York: Cambridge University Press.

Defoe, D. (1908). *The life and strange surprising adventures of Robinson Crusoe, of York, mariner, as related by himself.* Philadelphia: Altemus.

Delbecq, A. L., & Van de Ven, A. H. (1971). A group process model for problem identification and program planning. *Journal of Applied Behavioral Science, 7,* 466–492.

Delbecq, A. L., Van de Ven, A. H., & Gustafson, D. H. (1975). *Group techniques for program planning.* Glenview, IL: Scott, Foresman.

DeMatteo, J. S., Eby, L. T., & Sundstrom, E. (1998). Team-based rewards: Current empirical evidence and directions for future research. *Research in Organizational Behavior, 20,* 141–183.

Deming, W. E. (1975). On some statistical aids towards economic production. *Interfaces, 5,* 1–15.

Den Hartog, D. N., House, R. J., Hanges, P. J., Ruiz-Quintanilla, S. A., Dorfman, P. W. & Associates (1999). Culture specific and cross-culturally generalizable implicit leadership theories: Are attributes of charismatic/transformational leadership universally endorsed? [Electronic version]. *Leadership Quarterly, 10,* 219–256.

Dennis, A. R., & Valacich, J. S. (1999). Research note: Electronic brainstorming: Illusions and patterns of productivity. *Information Systems Research, 10,* 375–377.

Denvir, B. (1993). *The chronicle of impressionism.* Boston: Little, Brown.

Derlega, V. J., Cukur, C. S., Kuang, J. C., & Forsyth, D. R. (2002). Interdependent construal of self and the endorsement of conflict resolution strategies in interpersonal, intergroup, and international disputes. *Journal of Cross-Cultural Psychology, 33,* 610–625.

Deutsch, M. (1949a). An experimental study of the effects of cooperation and competition upon group process. *Human Relations, 2,* 199–231.

Deutsch, M. (1949b). A theory of cooperation and competition. *Human Relations, 2,* 129–152.

Deutsch, M. (1969). Socially relevant science: Reflections on some studies of interpersonal conflict. *American Psychologist, 24,* 1076–1092.

Deutsch, M. (1973). *The resolution of conflict: Constructive and destructive processes.* New Haven, CT: Yale University Press.

Deutsch, M. (1975). Equity, equality, and need: What determines which value will be used as the basis of distributive justice? *Journal of Social Issues, 31*(3), 137–149.

Deutsch, M. (1980). Fifty years of conflict. In L. Festinger (Ed.), *Retrospections on social psychology* (pp. 46–77). New York: Oxford University Press.

Deutsch, M. (1985). *Distributive justice: A social psychological perspective.* New Haven, CT: Yale University Press.

Deutsch, M. (1994). Constructive conflict resolution: Principles, training, and research. *Journal of Social Issues, 50*(1), 13–32.

Deutsch, M. (2000). Cooperation and competition. In M. Deutsch & P. T. Coleman (Eds.), *The handbook of conflict resolution: Theory and practice* (pp. 21–40). San Francisco: Jossey-Bass.

Deutsch, M., & Coleman, P. T. (Eds.). (2000). *The handbook of conflict resolution: Theory and practice.* San Francisco: Jossey-Bass.

Deutsch, M., & Gerard, H. B. (1955). A study of normative and informational social influences upon individual judgment. *Journal of Abnormal and Social Psychology, 51,* 629–636.

Deutsch, M., & Krauss, R. M. (1960). The effect of threat upon interpersonal bargaining. *Journal of Abnormal and Social Psychology, 61,* 181–189.

Deutsch, M., & Lewicki, R. J. (1970). "Locking in" effects during a game of Chicken. *Journal of Conflict Resolution, 14,* 367–378.

Devine, D. J. (2002). A review and integration of classification systems relevant to teams in organizations. *Group Dynamics, 6,* 291–310.

Devine, D. J., Clayton, L. D., Dunford, B. B., Seying, R., & Pryce, J. (2001). Jury decision making: 45 years of empirical research on deliberating groups. *Psychology, Public Policy, and Law, 7,* 622–727.

Devine, D. J., Clayton, L. D., Philips, J. L., Dunford, B. B., & Melner, S. B. (1999). Teams in organizations: Prevalence, characteristics, and effectiveness. *Small Group Research, 30,* 678–711.

Devine, P. G. (1989). Stereotypes and prejudice: Their automatic and controlled components. *Journal of Personality and Social Psychology, 56,* 5–18.

Devine, P. G. (1995). Prejudice and out-group perception. In A. Tesser (Ed.), *Advanced social psychology* (pp. 467–524). New York: McGraw-Hill.

Devine, P. G., Monteith, M. J., Zuwerink, J. R., & Elliot, A. J. (1991). Prejudice with and without compunction. *Journal of Personality and Social Psychology, 60,* 817–830.

Devine, P. G., Plant, E. A., Amodio, D. M., Harmon-Jones, E., & Vance, S. L. (2002). The regulation of explicit and implicit race bias: The role of motivations to respond without prejudice. *Journal of Personality and Social Psychology, 82,* 835–848.

Devine, P. G., Plant, E. A., & Buswell, B. N. (2000). Breaking the prejudice habit: Progress and obstacles. In S. Oskamp (Ed.), *Reducing prejudice and discrimination* (pp. 185–208). Mahwah, NJ: Erlbaum. Retrieved June 23, 2004, from http://www.netlibrary.com

DeYoung, C. G., Peterson, J. B., & Higgins, D. M. (2002). Higher-order factors of the Big Five predict conformity: Are there neuroses of health? *Personality and Individual Differences, 33,* 533–552.

Di Salvo, V. S., Nikkel, E., & Monroe, C. (1989). Theory and practice: A field investigation and identification of group members' perceptions of problems facing natural work groups. *Small Group Behavior, 20,* 551–567.

Diehl, M., & Stroebe, W. (1987). Productivity loss in brainstorming groups: Toward the solution of a riddle. *Journal of Personality and Social Psychology, 53,* 497–509.

Diehl, M., & Stroebe, W. (1991). Productivity loss in idea-generating groups: Tracking down the blocking effect. *Journal of Personality and Social Psychology, 61,* 392–403.

Diener, E. (1979). Deindividuation, self-awareness, and disinhibition. *Journal of Personality and Social Psychology, 37,* 1160–1171.

Diener, E. (1980). Deindividuation: The absence of self-awareness and self-regulation in group members. In P. B. Paulus (Ed.), *Psychology of group influence* (pp. 209–242). Mahwah, NJ: Erlbaum.

Diener, E., Fraser, S. C., Beaman, A. L., & Kelem, R. T. (1976). Effects of deindividuating variables on stealing by Halloween trick-or-treaters. *Journal of Personality and Social Psychology, 33,* 178–183.

Dienesch, R. M., & Liden, R. C. (1986). Leader/member exchange model of leadership: A critique and further development. *Academy of Management Review, 11,* 618–634.

Dies, R. R. (1994). Therapist variables in group psychotherapy research. In A. Fuhriman & G. M. Burlingame (Eds.), *Handbook of group psychotherapy* (pp. 114–154). New York: Wiley.

Dietz-Uhler, B., & Murrell, A. (1998). Effects of social identity and threat on self-esteem and group attributions. *Group Dynamics, 2,* 24–35.

Digman, J. M. (1990). Personality structure: Emergence of the five-factor model. *Annual Review of Psychology, 41,* 417–440.

Dijke, M. V., & Poppe, M. (2004). Social comparison of power: Interpersonal versus intergroup effects. *Group Dynamics, 8,* 13–26.

Dillard, J. P. (1991). The current status of research on sequential-request compliance techniques. *Personality and Social Psychology Bulletin, 17,* 283–288.

Dion, K. L. (1973). Cohesiveness as a determinant of ingroup–outgroup bias. *Journal of Personality and Social Psychology, 28,* 163–171.

Dion, K. L. (1979). Intergroup conflict and intragroup cohesiveness. In W. G. Austin & S. Worchel (Eds.), *The social psychology of intergroup relations* (pp. 211–224). Pacific Grove, CA: Brooks/Cole.

Dion, K. L. (1990). Group morale. In R. Brown (Ed.), *The Marshall Cavendish encyclopedia of personal relationships: Human behavior, How groups work* (Vol. 15, pp. 1854–1861). North Bellmore, NY: Marshall Cavendish.

Dion, K. L. (2000). Group cohesion: From "field of forces" to multidimensional construct. *Group Dynamics, 4,* 7–26.

Dionne, S. D., Yammarino, F. J., Atwater, L. E., & James, L. R. (2002). Neutralizing substitutes for leadership theory: Leadership effects and common-source bias [Electronic version]. *Journal of Applied Psychology, 87,* 454–464.

Dipboye, R. L. (1977). Alternative approaches to deindividuation. *Psychological Bulletin, 84,* 1057–1075.

Dittrich, J. E., & Carrell, M. R. (1979). Organization equity perceptions, employee job satisfaction, and departmental absence and turnover rates. *Organizational Behavior and Human Performance, 24,* 29–40.

Dobbins, G. H., & Platz, S. J. (1986). Sex differences in leadership: How real are they? *Academy of Management Review, 11,* 118–127.

Dodd, D. K. (1985). Robbers in the classroom: A deindividuation exercise. *Teaching of Psychology, 12,* 89–91.

Dodge, K. A., Gilroy, F. D., & Fenzel, L. M. (1995). Requisite management characteristics revisited: Two decades later. *Journal of Social Behavior and Personality, 10,* 253–264.

Doherty, W. J., Lester, M. E., & Leigh, G. K. (1986). Marriage encounter weekends: Couples who win and couples who lose. *Journal of Marital and Family Therapy, 12,* 49–61.

Doise, W. (1969). Intergroup relations and polarization of individual and collective judgments. *Journal of Personality and Social Psychology, 12,* 136–143.

Dolinski, D., Nawrat, M., & Rudak, I. (2001). Dialogue involvement as a social influence technique. *Personality and Social Psychology Bulletin, 27,* 1395–1406.

Doll, B., Murphy, P., & Song, S. Y. (2003). The relationship between children's self-reported recess problems, and peer acceptance and friendships [Electronic version]. *Journal of School Psychology, 41,* 113–130.

Dollar, N. J., & Merrigan, G. M. (2002). Ethnographic practices in group communication research. In L. R. Frey (Ed.), *New directions in group communication* (pp. 59–78). Thousand Oaks, CA: Sage.

Dollinger, S. J., Preston, L. A., O'Brien, S. P., & DiLalla, D. L. (1996). Individuality and relatedness of the self: An autophotographic study. *Journal of Personality and Social Psychology, 71,* 1268–1278.

Donnerstein, E., Donnerstein, M., Simon, S., & Ditrichs, R. (1972). Variables in interracial aggression: Anonymity, expected retaliation, and a riot. *Journal of Personality and Social Psychology, 22,* 236–245.

Dooley, D., & Catalano, R. (1984). The epidemiology of economic stress. *American Journal of Community Psychology, 12,* 387–409.

Doosje, B. J., & Branscombe, N. R. (2003). Attributions for the negative historical actions of a group. *European Journal of Social Psychology, 33,* 235–248.

Doosje, B., Ellemers, N., & Spears, R. (1995). Perceived intragroup variability as a function of group status and identification. *Journal of Experimental Social Psychology, 31,* 410–436.

Doosje, B., Ellemers, N., & Spears, R. (1999). Commitment and intergroup behavior. In N. Ellemers, R. Spears, & B. Doosje (Eds.), *Social identity: Context, commitment, content* (pp. 84–106). Oxford, UK: Blackwell Science.

Doreian, P. (1986). Measuring relative standing in small groups and bounded social networks. *Social Psychology Quarterly, 49,* 247–259.

Douthitt, E. A., & Aiello, J. R. (2001). The role of participation and control in the effects of computer monitoring on fairness perceptions, task satisfaction, and performance. *Journal of Applied Psychology, 86,* 867–874.

Dovidio, J. F., Brown, C. E., Heltman, K., Ellyson, S. L., & Keating, C. F. (1988). Power displays between women and men in discussions of gender-linked tasks: A multichannel study. *Journal of Personality and Social Psychology, 55,* 580–587.

Dovidio, J. F., Gaertner, S. L., Esses, V. M., & Brewer, M. B. (2003). Social conflict, harmony, and integration. In T. Millon, M. J. Lerner, & I. B. Weiner (Eds.), *Handbook of psychology: Personality and social psychology* (Vol. 5, pp. 485–506). New York: Wiley. Retrieved July 12, 2004, from http://www.netlibrary.com

Dovidio, J. F., Gaertner, S. L., Isen, A. M., Rust, M., & Guerra, P. (1998). Positive affect, cognition, and the reduction of intergroup bias. In C. Sedikides, J. Schopler, & C. A. Insko (Eds.), *Intergroup cognition and intergroup behavior* (pp. 337–366). Mahwah, NJ: Erlbaum.

Driskell, J. E., & Mullen, B. (1990). Status, expectations, and behavior: A meta-analytic review and test of theory. *Personality and Social Psychology Bulletin, 16,* 541–553.

Driskell, J. E., Radtke, P. H., & Salas, E. (2003). Virtual teams: Effects of technological mediation on team performance. *Group Dynamics, 7,* 297–323.

Driskell, J. E., & Salas, E. (1992). Can you study real teams in contrived settings? The value of small group research to understanding teams. In R. W. Swezey & E. Salas (Eds.), *Teams: Their training and performance* (pp. 101–124). Norwood, NJ: Ablex.

Driskell, J. E., Salas, E., & Johnston, J. (1999). Does stress lead to a loss of team perspective? *Group Dynamics, 3,* 291–302.

Druckman, D. (1994). Determinants of compromising behavior in negotiation: A meta-analysis. *Journal of Conflict Resolution, 38,* 507–556.

Dryer, D. C., & Horowitz, L. M. (1997). When do opposites attract? Interpersonal complementarity versus similarity. *Journal of Personality and Social Psychology, 72,* 592–603.

Dubrovsky, V. J., Kiesler, S., & Sethna, B. N. (1991). The equalization phenomenon: Status effects in computer-mediated and face-to-face decision making groups. *Human–Computer Interaction, 6,* 119–146.

Duchon, D., Green, S. G., & Taber, T. D. (1986). Vertical dyad linkage: A longitudinal assessment of antecedents, measures, and consequences. *Journal of Applied Psychology, 71,* 56–60.

Dudley, B. S., Johnson, D. W., & Johnson, R. T. (1997). Using co-operative learning to enhance the academic and social experiences of freshman student athletes. *Journal of Social Psychology, 137,* 449–459.

Duffy, F. (1997). *The new office.* London: Conran Octopus.

Dugo, J. M., & Beck, A. P. (1997). Significance and complexity of early phases in the development of the co-therapy relationship. *Group Dynamics, 1,* 294–305.

Dugosh, K. L., Paulus, P. B., Roland, E. J., & Yang, H. (2000). Cognitive stimulation in brainstorming. *Journal of Personality and Social Psychology, 79,* 722–735.

Dunegan, K. J., Uhl-Bien, M., & Duchon, D. (2002). LMX and subordinate performance: The moderating effects of task characteristics. *Journal of Business & Psychology, 17,* 275–285.

Dunning, D. (2000). Social judgment as implicit social comparison. In J. Suls & L. Wheeler (Eds.), *Handbook of social comparison: Theory and research* (pp. 353–378). New York: Kluwer Academic/Plenum.

Dunning, E. G., Murphy, P. J., & Williams, J. M. (1986). Spectator violence at football matches: Towards a sociological explanation. *British Journal of Sociology, 37,* 221–244.

Durand, D. E. (1977). Power as a function of office space and physiognomy: Two studies of influence. *Psychological Reports, 40,* 755–760.

Durkheim, É. (1966). *Suicide.* New York: Free Press. (Original work published in 1897)

Duval, S., & Wicklund, R. A. (1972). *A theory of objective self-awareness.* New York: Academic Press.

Dvir, T., Eden, D., Avolio, B. J., & Shamir, B. (2002). Impact of transformational leadership on follower development and performance: A field experiment. *Academy of Management Journal, 45,* 735–744.

Eagly, A. H. (1987). *Sex differences in social behavior: A social-role interpretation.* Mahwah, NJ: Erlbaum.

Eagly, A. H., & Carli, L. L. (1981). Sex of researchers and sex-typed communications as determinants of sex differences in influenceability: A meta-analysis of social influence studies. *Psychological Bulletin, 90,* 1–20.

Eagly A. H., Johannesen-Schmidt, M. C., & van Engen, M. L. (2003). Transformational, transactional, and laissez-faire leadership styles: A meta-analysis comparing women and men. *Psychological Bulletin, 129,* 569–591.

Eagly, A. H., & Johnson, B. T. (1990). Gender and leadership style: A meta-analysis. *Psychological Bulletin, 108,* 233–256.

Eagly, A. H., & Karau, S. J. (1991). Gender and the emergence of leaders: A meta-analysis. *Journal of Personality and Social Psychology, 60,* 685–710.

Eagly, A. H., & Karau, S. J. (2002). Role congruity theory of prejudice toward female leaders. *Psychological Review, 109,* 573–598.

Eagly, A. H., Karau, S., & Makhijani, M. (1995). Gender and the effectiveness of leaders: A meta-analysis. *Journal of Personality and Social Psychology, 117,* 125–145.

Eagly, A. H., Karau, S. J., Miner, J. B., & Johnson, B. T. (1994). Gender and motivation to manage in hierarchic organizations: A meta-analysis. *Leadership Quarterly, 5,* 135–159.

Eagly, A. H., Makhijani, M. G., & Klonsky, B. G. (1992). Gender and the evaluation of leaders: A meta-analysis, *Psychological Bulletin, 111,* 3–22.

Eagly, A. H., & Wood, W. (1991). Explaining sex differences in social behavior: A meta-analytic perspective. *Personality and Social Psychology Bulletin, 17,* 306–315.

Eagly, A. H., & Wood, W. (1999). The origins of sex differences in human behavior: Eved dispositions versus social roles. *American Psychologist, 54,* 408–423.

Eagly, A. H., Wood, W., & Diekman, A. B. (2000). Social role theory of sex differences and similarities: A current appraisal. In T. Eckes & H. T. Trautner (Eds.), *The developmental social psychology of gender* (pp. 123–174). Mahwah, NJ: Erlbaum.

Eagly, A. H., Wood, W., & Fishbaugh, L. (1981). Sex differences in conformity: Surveillance by the group as a determinant of male nonconformity. *Journal of Personality and Social Psychology, 40,* 384–394.

Edelstein, M. R. (2002). Contamination: The invisible built environment. In R. B. Bechtel & A. Churchman (Eds.), *Handbook of environmental psychology* (pp. 559–588). New York: Wiley. Retrieved July 30, 2004, from http://www.netlibrary.com

Edman, I. (1919). *Human traits and their social significance.* New York: Houghton Mifflin.

Edney, J. J. (1975). Territoriality and control: A field experiment. *Journal of Personality and Social Psychology, 31,* 1108–1115.

Edney, J. J. (1976). Human territories: Comment on functional properties. *Environment and Behavior, 8,* 31–48.

Edney, J. J., & Bell, P. A. (1984). Sharing scarce resources: Group-outcome orientation, external disaster, and stealing in a simulated commons. *Small Group Behavior, 15,* 87–108.

Edney, J. J., & Grundmann, M. J. (1979). Friendship, group size, and boundary size: Small group spaces. *Small Group Behavior, 10,* 124–135.

Edney, J. J., & Jordan-Edney, N. L. (1974). Territorial spacing on a beach. *Sociometry, 37,* 92–104.

Edwards, D. J. A. (1972). Approaching the unfamiliar: A study of human interaction distances. *Journal of Behavioral Sciences, 1,* 249–250.

Eldredge, N., & Gould, S. J. (1972). Punctuated equilibria: An alternative to phyletic gradualism. In T. M. Schopf (Ed.), *Models in palaeobiology* (pp. 82–115). New York: Freeman.

Ellemers, N., Spears, R., & Doosje, B. (1997). Sticking together or falling apart: In-group identification as a psychological determinant of group commitment versus individual mobility. *Journal of Personality and Social Psychology, 72,* 617–626.

Ellemers, N., Spears, R., & Doosje, B. (Eds.). (1999). *Social identity: Context, commitment, content.* Oxford, UK: Blackwell Science.

Ellemers, N., Wilke, H., & van Knippenberg, A. (1993). Effects of the legitimacy of low group or individual status on individual and collective status-enhancement strategies. *Journal of Personality and Social Psychology, 64,* 766–778.

Elliott, G. C., & Meeker, B. F. (1984). Modifiers of the equity effect: Group outcome and causes for individual performance. *Journal of Personality and Social Psychology, 46,* 586–597.

Ellis, D. G., & Fisher, M. (1994). *Small group decision making* (4th ed.). New York: McGraw-Hill.

Ellsworth, P. C., & Reifman, A. (2000). Juror comprehension and public policy: Perceived problems and proposed solutions. *Psychology, Public Policy, & Law, 6,* 788–821.

Elms, A. C. (1995). Obedience in retrospect. *Journal of Social Issues, 51*(3), 21–31.

Elsbach, K. D., & Sutton, R. I. (1992). Acquiring organizational legitimacy through illegitimate actions: A marriage of institutional and impression management theories. *Academy of Management Journal, 35,* 699–738.

Emerson, R. M. (1954). Deviation and rejection: An experimental replication. *American Sociological Review, 19,* 688–693.

Emerson, R. M. (1962). Power–dependence relations. *American Sociological Review, 27,* 31–40.

Emerson, R. M. (1981). Social exchange theory. In M. Rosenberg & R. H. Turner (Eds.), *Social psychology: Sociological perspectives* (pp. 30–65). New York: Basic Books.

Emler, N., & Cook, T. (2001). Moral integrity in leadership: Why it matters and why it may be difficult to achieve. In B. W. Roberts & R. Hogan (Eds.), *Personality psychology in the workplace* (pp. 277–298). Washington, DC: American Psychological Association.

Emrich, C. G. (1999). Context effects in leadership perception. *Personality and Social Psychology Bulletin, 25,* 991–1006.

End, C. M., Dietz-Uhler, B., Harrick, E. A., & Jacquemotte, L. (2002). Identifying with winners: A reexamination of sport fans' tendency to BIRG. *Journal of Applied Social Psychology, 32,* 1017–1030.

Epley, N., & Gilovich, T. (1999). Just going along: Nonconscious priming and conformity to social pressure. *Journal of Experimental Social Psychology, 35,* 578–589.

Erez, M., Rim, Y., & Keider, I. (1986). The two sides of the tactics of influence: Agent vs. target. *Journal of Occupational Psychology, 59,* 25–39.

Esser, A. H. (1968). Dominance hierarchy and clinical course of psychiatrically hospitalized boys. *Child Development, 39,* 147–157.

Esser, A. H. (1973). Cottage Fourteen: Dominance and territoriality in a group of institutionalized boys. *Small Group Behavior, 4,* 131–146.

Esser, A. H., Chamberlain, A. S., Chapple, E. D., & Kline, N. S. (1965). Territoriality of patients on a research ward. In J. Wortis (Ed.), *Recent advances in biological psychiatry* (pp. 37–44). New York: Plenum Press.

Esser, J. K. (1998). Alive and well after 25 years: A review of groupthink research. *Organizational Behavior and Human Decision Processes, 73,* 116–141.

Esser, J. K., & Lindoerfer, J. S. (1989). Groupthink and the space shuttle Challenger accident: Toward a quantitative case analysis. *Journal of Behavioral Decision Making, 2,* 167–177.

Etzioni, A. (1967). The Kennedy experiment. *The Western Political Quarterly, 20,* 361–380.

Etzioni, A. (1968). A model of significant research. *International Journal of Psychiatry, 6,* 278–280.

Evans, G. W. (1979). Behavioral and physiological consequences of crowding in humans. *Journal of Applied Social Psychology, 9,* 27–46.

Evans, G. W., & Cohen, S. (1987). Environmental stress. In D. Stokols & I. Altman (Eds.), *Handbook of environmental psychology* (Vol. 1, pp. 571–610). New York: Wiley.

Evans, G. W., & Howard, R. B. (1973). Personal space. *Psychological Bulletin, 80,* 334–344.

Evans, G. W., Hygge, S., & Bullinger, M. (1995). Chronic noise and psychological stress. *Psychological Science, 6,* 333–338.

Evans, G. W., & Lepore, S. J. (1992). Conceptual and analytic issues in crowding research. *Journal of Environmental Psychology, 12,* 163–173.

Evans, G. W., Palsane, M. N., Lepore, S. J., & Martin, J. (1989). Residential density and psychological health: The mediating effects of social support. *Journal of Personality and Social Psychology, 57,* 994–999.

Evans, G. W., & Stecker, R. (2004). Motivational consequences of environmental stress. *Journal of Environmental Psychology, 24,* 143–165.

Evans, N. J., & Jarvis, P. A. (1986). The Group Attitude Scale: A measure of attraction to group. *Small Group Behavior, 17,* 203–216.

Exline, R. V. (1963). Explorations in the process of person perception: Visual interaction in relation to competition, sex, and need for affiliation. *Journal of Personality, 31,* 1–20.

Eysenck, H. (1990). Biological dimensions of personality. In L. A. Pervin (Ed.), *Handbook of personality: Theory and research* (pp. 244–276). New York: Guilford Press.

Fabianic, D. (1994). Managerial change and organizational effectiveness in major league baseball: Findings for the eighties. *Journal of Sport Behavior, 17,* 135–147.

Falbo, T. (1977). The multidimensional scaling of power strategies. *Journal of Personality and Social Psychology, 35,* 537–548.

Falbo, T., & Peplau, L. A. (1980). Power strategies in intimate relationships. *Journal of Personality and Social Psychology, 38,* 618–628.

Falloon, I. R. H., Lindley, P., McDonald, R., & Marks, I. M. (1977). Social skills training of outpatient groups: A controlled study of rehearsal and homework. *British Journal of Psychiatry, 131,* 599–609.

Fanon, F. (1963). *The wretched of the earth.* New York: Grove.

Farbstein, J., & Kantrowitz, M. (1978). *People in places: experiencing, using, and changing the built environment.* Upper Saddle River, NJ: Prentice Hall.

Farrell, M. P. (1982). Artists' circles and the development of artists. *Small Group Behavior, 13,* 451–474.

Feeley, T. H. (2000). Testing a communication network model of employee turnover based on centrality. *Journal of Applied Communication Research, 28,* 262–277.

Feld, S. L. (1982). Social structural determinants of similarity among associates. *American Sociological Review, 47,* 797–801.

Feldman, S. (2003). Enforcing social conformity: A theory of authoritarianism. *Political Psychology, 24,* 41–74.

Ferencik, B. M. (1992). The helping process in group therapy: A review and discussion. *Group, 16,* 113–124.

Ferguson, T. J., & Rule, B. G. (1983). An attributional analysis of anger and aggression. In R. G. Geen & E. I. Donnerstein (Eds.), *Aggression: Theoretical and empirical reviews* (Vol. 1, pp. 41–74). New York: Academic Press.

Ferris, G. R., & Rowland, K. M. (1983). Social facilitation effects on behavioral and perceptual task performance measures: Implications for work behavior. *Group and Organization Studies, 8,* 421–438.

Festinger, L. (1950). Informal social communication. *Psychological Review, 57,* 271–282.

Festinger, L. (1954). A theory of social comparison processes. *Human Relations, 7,* 117–140.

Festinger, L. (1957). *A theory of cognitive dissonance.* Stanford, CA: Stanford University Press.

Festinger, L. (1983). *The human legacy.* New York: Columbia University Press.

Festinger, L., Pepitone, A., & Newcomb, T. (1952). Some consequences of deindividuation in a group. *Journal of Abnormal and Social Psychology, 47,* 382–389.

Festinger, L., Riecken, H. W., & Schachter, S. (1956). *When prophecy fails.* Minneapolis: University of Minnesota Press.

Festinger, L., Schachter, S., & Back, K. (1950). *Social pressures in informal groups.* New York: Harper.

Festinger, L., & Thibaut, J. (1951). Interpersonal communication in small groups. *Journal of Abnormal and Social Psychology, 46,* 92–99.

Fiedler, F. E. (1955). The influence of leader–keyman relations on combat crew effectiveness. *Journal of Abnormal and Social Psychology, 51,* 227–235.

Fiedler, F. E. (1964). A contingency model of leadership effectiveness. *Advances in Experimental Social Psychology, 1,* 150–190.

Fiedler, F. E. (1967). *A theory of leadership effectiveness.* New York: McGraw-Hill.

Fiedler, F. E. (1971a). *Leadership.* Morristown, NJ: General Learning Press.

Fiedler, F. E. (1971b). Note on the methodology of Graen, Orris, and Alvarez studies testing the contingency model. *Journal of Applied Psychology, 55,* 202–204.

Fiedler, F. E. (1978). The contingency model and the dynamics of the leadership process. *Advances in Experimental Social Psychology, 12,* 59–112.

Fiedler, F. E. (1981). Leadership effectiveness. *American Behavioral Scientist, 24,* 619–632.

Fiedler, F. E. (1986). The contribution of cognitive resources to leadership performance. *Journal of Applied Social Psychology, 16,* 532–548.

Fiedler, F. E. (1993). The leadership situation and the black box in contingency theories. In M. M. Chemers & R. Ayman (Eds.), *Leadership theory and research: Perspectives and directions* (pp. 1–28). San Diego: Academic Press.

Fiedler, F. E. (1996). Research on leadership selection and training: One view of the future. *Administrative Science Quarterly, 41,* 241–250.

Fiedler, F. E., & Chemers, M. M. (1974). *Leadership and effective management.* Glenview, IL: Scott, Foresman.

Fiedler, F. E., Chemers, M. M., & Mahar, L. (1976). *Improving leadership effectiveness: The Leader Match concept.* New York: Wiley.

Fiedler, F. E., & Garcia, J. E. (1987). *New approaches to leadership: Cognitive resources and organizational performance.* New York: Wiley.

Field, R. H. G. (1979). A critique of the Vroom-Yetton contingency model of leadership behavior. *Academy of Management Review, 4,* 249–257.

Field, R. H. G., & House, R. J. (1990). A test of the Vroom-Yetton model using manager and subordinate reports. *Journal of Applied Psychology, 75,* 362–366.

Fielding, K. S., & Hogg, M. A. (1997). Social identity, self-categorization, and leadership: A field study of small interactive groups. *Group Dynamics, 1,* 39–51.

Filkins, J. W., Smith, C. M., & Tindale, R. S. (1998). An evaluation of the biasing effects of death qualification: A meta-analytic/computer simulation approach. In R. S. Tindale, L. Heath, J. Edwards, E. J. Posavac, F. B. Bryant, Y. Suarez-Balcazar, E. Henderson-King, & J. Myers (Eds.), *Theory and research on small groups* (pp. 153–175). New York: Plenum Press.

Finch, J. F, Barrera, M., Jr., Okun, M. A., Bryant, W. H., Pool, G. J., & Snow-Turek, A. L. (1997). The factor structure of received social support: Dimensionality and the prediction of depression and life satisfaction. *Journal of Social and Clinical Psychology, 16,* 323–342.

Fine, G. A. (1979). Small groups and culture creation. *American Sociological Review, 44,* 733–745.

Fine, G. A., & Holyfield, L. (1996). Secrecy, trust, and dangerous leisure: Generating group cohesion in voluntary organizations. *Social Psychology Quarterly, 59,* 22–38.

Fink, C. F. (1968). Some conceptual difficulties in the theory of social conflict. *Journal of Conflict Resolution, 12,* 412–460.

Finke, R., & Stark, R. (1992). *The churching of America, 1776–1990: Winners and losers in our religious economy.* New Brunswick, NJ: Rutgers University Press.

Finkelstein, S., & Hambrick, D. (1996). *Strategic leadership: Top executives and their organizations.* Minneapolis, MN: West.

Finlay, F., Hitch, G., & Meudell, P. R. (2000). Mutual inhibition in collaborative recall: Evidence for a retrieval-based account. *Journal of Experimental Psychology: Learning, Memory, & Cognition, 26,* 1556–1567.

Finn, J. D., & Rock, D. A. (1997). Academic success among students at risk for school failure. *Journal of Applied Psychology, 82,* 221–234.

Fiorina, C. (2002, October 1). Remarks presented in accepting the Appeal of Conscience Foundation Annual Award, New York [Transcript]. Retrieved June 24, 2004, from http://www.hp.com/hpinfo/execteam/speeches/fiorina/conscience02.html

Fiorina, C. (2003, May 9). Remarks presented at the 8th Annual Coro Northern California leadership luncheon, San Francisco, CA [Transcript]. Retrieved June 24, 2004, from http://www.hp.com/hpinfo/execteam/speeches/fiorina/coro03.html

Fiorina, C. (2004, May 1). Address presented at the Simmons School of Management 25th Annual Conference, Boston [Transcript]. Retrieved June 24, 2004, from http://www.hp.com/hpinfo/execteam/speeches/fiorina/simmons04.html

Fisek, M. H., Berger, J., & Norman, R. Z. (1995). Evaluations and the formation of expectations. *American Journal of Sociology, 101,* 731–746.

Fisher, B. A. (1980). *Small group decision making* (2nd ed.). New York: McGraw-Hill.

Fisher, C. D., & Gitelson, R. (1983). A meta-analysis of the correlates of role conflict and ambiguity. *Journal of Applied Psychology, 68,* 320–333.

Fisher, J. D., & Byrne, D. (1975). Too close for comfort: Sex differences in response to invasions of personal space. *Journal of Personality and Social Psychology, 32,* 15–21.

Fisher, R. (1983). Negotiating power. *American Behavioral Science, 27,* 149–166.

Fisher, R., & Ury, W. (with B. Patton, Ed.). (1981). *Getting to YES: Negotiating agreement without giving in.* Boston: Houghton Mifflin.

Fisher, R., Ury, W., & Patton, B. (1991). *Getting to YES: Negotiating agreement without giving in* (2nd ed.). New York: Penguin.

Fisher, R. J. (1994). Generic principles for resolving intergroup conflict. *Journal of Social Issues, 50*(1), 47–66.

Fisher, W. A., & Fisher, J. D. (1993). A general social psychological model for changing AIDS risk behavior. In J. B. Pryor & G. D. Reeder (Eds.), *The social psychology of HIV infection* (pp. 127–153). Mahwah, NJ: Erlbaum.

Fiske, A. P. (2002). Using individualism and collectivism to compare cultures—A critique of the validity and measurement of the constructs: Comment on Oyserman et al. (2002). *Psychological Bulletin, 128,* 78–88.

Fiske, S. T. (1993a). Controlling other people: The impact of power on stereotyping. *American Psychologist, 48,* 621–628.

Fiske, S. T. (1993b). Social cognition and social perception. *Annual Review of Psychology, 44,* 155–194.

Fiske, S. T., & Goodwin, S. A. (1994). Social cognition research and small group research, a West Side Story or . . . ? In Social cognition in small groups [Special issue]. *Small Group Research, 25,* 147–171.

Fleeson, W., Malanos, A. B., & Achille, N. M. (2002). An intra-individual process approach to the relationship between extraversion and positive affect: Is acting extraverted as "good" as being extraverted? *Journal of Personality and Social Psychology, 83,* 1409–1422.

Fleishman, E. A. (1953). The description of supervisory behavior. *Journal of Applied Psychology, 37,* 1–6.

Fleishman, E. A., & Zaccaro, S. J. (1992). Toward a taxonomy of team performance functions. In R. W. Swezey & E. Salas (Eds.), *Teams: Their training and performance* (pp. 31–56). Norwood, NJ: Ablex.

Flores, P. J. (1997). *Group psychotherapy with addicted populations: An integration of twelve step and psychodynamic theory.* Binghamton, NY: Haworth Press.

Flores, P. J. (2002). The interpersonal approach. In D. W. Brook & H. I. Spitz (Eds.), *The group theory of substance abuse* (pp. 19–36). Binghamton, NY: Haworth Press.

Flowers, M. L. (1977). A laboratory test of some implications of Janis' groupthink hypothesis. *Journal of Personality and Social Psychology, 35,* 888–896.

Flynn, K., & Gerhardt, G. (1989). *The silent brotherhood: Inside America's racist underground.* New York: Penguin.

Foa, U. G., & Foa, E. B. (1971). Resource exchange: Toward a structural theory of interpersonal relations. In A. W. Siegman & B. Pope (Eds.), *Studies in dyadic communication* (pp. 291–325). New York: Pergamon Press.

Foddy, M., & Smithson, M. (1996). Relative ability, paths of relevance, and influence in task-oriented groups. *Social Psychology Quarterly, 59,* 140–153.

Foddy, M., Smithson, M., Schneider, S., & Hogg, M. A. (Eds.). (1999). *Resolving social dilemmas: Dynamic, structural, and intergroup aspects.* New York: Psychology Press.

Fodor, E. M. (1984). The power motive and reactivity to power stresses. *Journal of Personality and Social Psychology, 47,* 853–859.

Fodor, E. M. (1985). The power motive, group conflict, and physiological arousal. *Journal of Personality and Social Psychology, 49,* 1408–1415.

Fodor, E. M., & Riordan, J. M. (1995). Leader power motive and group conflict as influences on leader behavior and group member self-affect. *Journal of Research in Personality, 29,* 418–431.

Fodor, E. M., & Smith, T. (1982). The power motive as an influence on group decision making. *Journal of Personality and Social Psychology, 42,* 178–185.

Folger, R. (1993). Reactions to mistreatment at work. In J. K. Murnighan (Ed.), *Social psychology in organizations: Advances in theory and research* (pp. 161–183). Upper Saddle River, NJ: Prentice Hall.

Folk, G. E., Jr. (1974). *Textbook of environmental physiology.* Philadelphia: Lea & Febiger.

Forgas, J. P. (1998). On feeling good and getting your way: Mood effects on negotiator cognition and bargaining strategies. *Journal of Personality and Social Psychology, 74,* 565–577.

Forgas, J. P., & Williams, K. D. (Eds.). (2001). *Social influence: Direct and indirect processes.* New York: Psychology Press.

Forsyth, D. R. (1980). The functions of attributions. *Social Psychology Quarterly, 43,* 184–189.

Forsyth, D. R. (1990). *Group dynamics* (2nd ed.). Belmont, CA: Brooks/Cole.

Forsyth, D. R. (1994). Norms. In A. S. R. Manstead & M. Hewstone (Eds.), *The Blackwell encyclopedia of social psychology* (pp. 412–417). Malden, MA: Blackwell.

Forsyth, D. R. (Ed.). (1998). Research methods [Special issue]. *Group Dynamics, 2,* 211–320.

Forsyth, D. R. (2000). The social psychology of groups and group psychotherapy: One view of the next century. *Group, 24,* 147–155.

Forsyth, D. R., Berger, R. E., & Mitchell, T. (1981). The effects of self-serving vs. other-serving claims of responsibility on attraction and attribution in groups. *Social Psychology Quarterly, 44,* 59–64.

Forsyth, D. R., & Burnette, J. L. (in press). The history of group research. In S. Wheelan (Ed.), *The handbook of group research and practice.* Thousand Oaks, CA: Sage.

Forsyth, D. R., & Corazzini, J. G. (2000). Groups as change agents. In C. R. Snyder & R. E. Ingram (Eds.), *Handbook of psychological change: Psychotherapy processes and practices for the 21st century* (pp. 309–336). New York: Wiley.

Forsyth, D. R., & Elliott, T. R. (1999). Group dynamics and psychological well-being: The impact of groups on adjustment and dysfunction. In R. Kowalski & M. R. Leary (Eds.), *The social psychology of emotional and behavioral problems: Interfaces of social and clinical psychology* (pp. 339–361). Washington, DC: American Psychological Association.

Forsyth, D. R., Heiney, M. M., & Wright, S. S. (1997). Biases in appraisals of women leaders. *Group Dynamics, 1,* 98–103.

Forsyth, D. R., & Kelley, K. N. (1994). Attribution in groups: Estimations of personal contributions to collective endeavors. *Small Group Research, 25,* 367–383.

Forsyth, D. R., & Kelley, K. N. (1996). Heuristic-based biases in estimations of personal contributions to collective endeavors. In J. L. Nye & A. M. Brower (Eds.), *What's social about social cognition?* (pp. 106–123). Thousand Oaks, CA: Sage.

Forsyth, D. R., Schlenker, B. R., Leary, M. R., & McCown, N. E. (1985). Self-presentational determinants of sex differences in leadership behavior. *Small Group Behavior, 16,* 197–210.

Forsyth, D. R., Zyzniewski, L. E., & Giammanco, C. A. (2002). Responsibility diffusion in cooperative collectives. *Personality and Social Psychology Bulletin, 28,* 54–65.

Foschi, M. (1996). Double standards in the evaluation of men and women. *Social Psychology Quarterly, 59,* 237–254.

Foschi, M., Warriner, G. K., & Hart, S. D. (1985). Standards, expectations, and interpersonal influence. *Social Psychology Quarterly, 48,* 108–117.

Foss, R. D. (1981). Structural effects in simulated jury decision making. *Journal of Personality and Social Psychology, 40,* 1055–1062.

Foti, R. J., Fraser, S. L., & Lord, R. G. (1982). Effects of leadership labels and prototypes on perceptions of political leaders. *Journal of Applied Psychology, 67,* 326–333.

Foti, R. J., & Lord, R. G. (1987). Prototypes and scripts: The effects of alternative methods of processing information on rating accuracy. *Organizational Behavior and Human Decision Processes, 39,* 318–340.

Foushee, H. C. (1984). Dyads and triads at 35,000 feet: Factors affecting group process and aircrew performance. *American Psychologist, 39,* 886–893.

Foy, E., & Harlow, A. F. (1928/1956). *Clowning through life.* New York: Dutton.

Frable, D. E. S., Platt, L., & Hoey, S. (1998). Concealable stigmas and positive self-perceptions: Feeling better around similar others. *Journal of Personality and Social Psychology, 74,* 909–922.

Frager, R. (1970). Conformity and anticonformity in Japan. *Journal of Personality and Social Psychology, 15,* 203–210.

Francis, L. J. (1998). Self-esteem as a function of personality and gender among 8–11 year olds: Is Coopersmith's index fair? *Personality and Individual Differences, 25,* 159–165.

Francis, R. C. (2004). *Why men won't ask for directions: The seduction of sociobiology.* Princeton, NJ: Princeton University Press.

Frank, F., & Anderson, L. R. (1971). Effects of task and group size upon group productivity and member satisfaction. *Sociometry, 34,* 135–149.

Frank, J. D. (1957). Some determinants, manifestations, and effects of cohesiveness in therapy groups. *International Journal of Group Psychotherapy, 7,* 53–63.

Franke, R. H. (1979). The Hawthorne experiments: Review. *American Sociological Review, 44,* 861–867.

Franke, R. H., & Kaul, J. D. (1978). The Hawthorne experiments: First statistical interpretation. *American Sociological Review, 43,* 623–643.

Franken, R. E., & Prpich, W. (1996). Dislike of competition and the need to win: Self-image concerns, performance concerns, and the distraction of attention. *Journal of Social Behavior and Personality, 11,* 695–712.

Franklin, M. E., Jaycox, L. H., & Foa, E. B. (1999). Social skills training. In M. Hersen & A. S. Bellack (Eds.), *Handbook of comparative interventions for adult disorders* (2nd ed., pp. 317–339). New York: Wiley.

Freedman, J. L. (1975). *Crowding and behavior.* San Francisco: Freeman.

Freedman, J. L. (1979). Reconciling apparent differences between responses of humans and other animals to crowding. *Psychological Review, 86,* 80–85.

Freedman, J. L., & Fraser, S. C. (1966). Compliance without pressure: The foot-in-the-door technique. *Journal of Personality and Social Psychology, 4,* 195–202.

Freedman, J. L., & Perlick, D. (1979). Crowding, contagion, and laughter. *Journal of Experimental Social Psychology, 15,* 295–303.

Freeman, K. A. (1996). Attitudes toward work in project groups as predictors of academic performance. *Small Group Research, 27,* 265–282.

Freeman, L. C. (1977). A set of measures of centrality based on betweenness. *Sociometry, 40,* 35–41.

Freeman, L. C. (1979). Centrality in social networks: I. Conceptual clarification. *Social Networks, 1,* 215–239.

French, J. R. P., Jr. (1941). The disruption and cohesion of groups. *Journal of Abnormal and Social Psychology, 36,* 361–377.

French, J. R. P., Jr., Morrison, H., & Levinger, G. (1960). Coercive power and forces affecting conformity. *Journal of Abnormal and Social Psychology, 61,* 93–101.

French, J. R. P., Jr., & Raven, B. (1959). The bases of social power. In D. Cartwright (Ed.), *Studies in social power* (pp. 150–167). Ann Arbor, MI: Institute for Social Research.

Freud, S. (1922). *Group psychology and the analysis of the ego* (J. Strachey, Trans.). London: Hogarth Press and the Institute of Psycho-Analysis.

Frey, L. R. (Ed.). (2002). *Group communication in context: Studies of bona fide groups* (2nd ed). Mahwah, NJ: Erlbaum.

Frey, L. R., Gouran, D. S., & Poole, M. S. (Eds.). (1999). *Handbook of group communication: Theory and research.* Thousand Oaks, CA: Sage.

Friedkin, N. E. (1999). Choice shift and group polarization. *American Sociological Review, 64,* 856–875.

Friedland, N. (1976). Social influence via threats. *Journal of Experimental Social Psychology, 12,* 552–563.

Friedman, S. D., & Saul, K. (1991). A leader's wake: Organization member reactions to CEO succession. *Journal of Management, 17,* 619–642.

Frieze, I. H. (Ed.). (1999). Social influence and social power: Using theory for understanding social issues. *Journal of Social Issues, 55*(1).

Froman, L. A., Jr., & Cohen, M. D. (1969). Threats and bargaining efficiency. *Behavioral Science, 14,* 147–153.

Fromm, E. (1965). *Escape from freedom.* New York: Holt, Rinehart & Winston.

Fry, D. P., & Björkqvist, K. (Eds.). (1997). *Cultural variation in conflict resolution: Alternatives to violence.* Mahwah, NJ: Erlbaum.

Fuegen, K., & Biernat, M. (2002). Reexamining the effects of solo status for women and men. *Personality and Social Psychology Bulletin, 28,* 913–925.

Fuhriman, A., & Burlingame, G. M. (1994a). Group psychotherapy: Research and practice. In A. Fuhriman & G. M. Burlingame (Eds.), *Handbook of group psychotherapy: An empirical and clinical synthesis* (pp. 3–40). New York: Wiley.

Fuhriman, A., & Burlingame, G. M. (Eds.). (1994b). *Handbook of group psychotherapy: An empirical and clinical synthesis.* New York: Wiley.

Fuller, S. R., & Aldag, R. J. (1998). Organizational Tonypandy: Lessons from a quarter century of groupthink phenomenon. *Organizational Behavior and Human Decision Processes, 73,* 163–184.

Gabarro, J. J. (1987). The development of working relationships. In J. W. Lorsch (Ed.), *Handbook of organizational behavior* (pp. 172–189). Upper Saddle River, NJ: Prentice Hall.

Gaertner, L., & Insko, C. A. (2001). On the measurement of social orientations in the minimal group paradigm: Norms as moderators of the expression of intergroup bias. *European Journal of Social Psychology, 31,* 143–154.

Gaertner, L., Sedikides, C., Vevea, J. L., & Iuzzini, J. (2002). The "I," the "we," and the "when": A meta-analysis of motivational primacy in self-definition. *Journal of Personality and Social Psychology, 83,* 574–591.

Gaertner, S. L., & Dovidio, J. F. (2000). *Reducing intergroup bias: The common ingroup identity model.* Philadelphia: Psychology Press.

Gaertner, S. L., Dovidio, J. F., Banker, B. S., Houlette, M., Johnson, K. M., & McGlynn, E. A. (2000). Reducing intergroup conflict: From superordinate goals to decategorization, recategorization, and mutual differentiation. *Group Dynamics, 4,* 98–114.

Gaertner, S. L., Dovidio, J. F., Nier, J. A., Ward, C. M., & Banker, B. S. (1999). Across cultural divides: The value of a superordinate identity. In D. A. Prentice & D. T. Miller (Eds.), *Cultural divides: Understanding and overcoming group conflict* (pp. 173–212). New York: Russell Sage Foundation.

Gaertner, S. L., Dovidio, J. F., Rust, M. C., Nier, J. A., Banker, B. S., Ward, C. M., Mottola, G. R., & Houlette, M. (1999). Reducing intergroup bias: Elements of intergroup cooperation. *Journal of Personality and Social Psychology, 76,* 388–402.

Gaines, S. O., Jr., Marelich, W. D., Bledsoe, K. L., Steers, W. N., Henderson, M. C., Granrose, C. S., Barájas, L., Hicks, D., Lyde, M., Takahashi, Y., Yum, N., Ríos, D. I., García, B. F., Farris, K. R., & Page, M. S. (1997). Links between race/ethnicity and cultural values as mediated by racial/ethnic identity and moderated by gender. *Journal of Personality and Social Psychology, 72,* 1460–1476.

Gaines, S. O., Jr., & Reed, E. S. (1995). Prejudice: From Allport to DuBois. *American Psychologist, 50,* 96–103.

Galinsky, A. D., Gruenfeld, D. H., & Magee, J. C. (2003). From power to action. *Journal of Personality and Social Psychology, 85,* 453–466.

Gallo, P. S., Jr. (1966). Effects of increased incentives upon the use of threat in bargaining. *Journal of Personality and Social Psychology, 4,* 14–20.

Gallupe, R. B., & Cooper, W. H. (1993). Brainstorming electronically. *Sloan Management Review, 35,* 27–36.

Gammage, K. L., Carron, A. V., & Estabrooks, P. A. (2001). Team cohesion and individual productivity: The influence of the norm for productivity and the identifiability of individual effort. *Small Group Research, 32,* 3–18.

Gamson, W. A. (1968). *Power and discontent.* Belmont, CA: Wadsworth.

Gamson, W. A. (1992). The social psychology of collective action. In A. Morris & C. Mueller (Eds.), *Frontiers of social movement theory* (pp. 53–76). New Haven, CT: Yale University Press.

Gamson, W. A., & Scotch, N. (1964). Scapegoating in baseball. *American Journal of Sociology, 70,* 69–70.

Gannon, T. M. (1966). Emergence of the "defensive" group norm. *Federal Probation, 30*(4), 44–47.

Garcia, S. M., Weaver, K., Moskowitz, G. B., & Darley, J. M. (2002). Crowded minds: The implicit bystander effect. *Journal of Personality and Social Psychology, 83,* 843–853.

Gardham, K., & Brown, R. (2001). Two forms of intergroup discrimination with positive and negative outcomes: Explaining the positive–negative asymmetry effect. *British Journal of Social Psychology, 40,* 23–34.

Gardner, J. W. (1965). *The antileadership vaccine.* Annual Report of the Carnegie Corporation. New York: Carnegie Corporation.

Gardner, W. L., Pickett, C. L., & Brewer, M. B. (2000). Social exclusion and selective memory: How the need to belong influences memory for social events. *Personality and Social Psychology Bulletin, 26,* 486–496.

Garner, D. M., & Garfinkel, P. E. (1980). Socio-cultural factors in the development of anorexia nervosa. *Psychological Medicine, 10,* 647–656.

Garner, K., & Deutsch, M. (1974). Cooperative behavior in dyads: Effects of dissimilar goal orientations and differing expectations about the partner. *Journal of Conflict Resolution, 18,* 634–645.

Gastorf, J. W., Suls, J., & Sanders, G. S. (1980). Type A coronary-prone behavior pattern and social facilitation. *Journal of Personality and Social Psychology, 38,* 773–780.

Gaulin, S. J. C., & McBurney, D. H. (2001). *Psychology: An evolutionary approach.* Upper Saddle River, NJ: Prentice Hall.

Gazda, G. M., & Brooks, D. K. (1985). The development of the social/life skills training movement. *Journal of Group Psychotherapy, Psychodrama, and Sociometry, 38,* 1–10.

Gecas, V., & Burke, P. J. (1995). Self and identity. In K. S. Cook, G. A. Fine, & J. S. House (Eds.), *Sociological perspectives on social psychology* (pp. 41–67). Boston: Allyn & Bacon.

Geen, R. G. (1983). Evaluation apprehension and the social facilitation/inhibition of learning. *Motivation and Emotion, 7,* 203–212.

Geen, R. G. (1991). Social motivation. *Annual Review of Psychology, 42,* 377–399.

Geen, R. G. (1995). *Human motivation: A social psychological approach.* Pacific Grove, CA: Brooks/Cole.

Geen, R. G., & Bushman, B. J. (1987). Drive theory: Effects of socially engendered arousal. In B. Mullen & G. R. Goethals

(Eds.), *Theories of group behavior* (pp. 89–109). New York: Springer Verlag.

Geis, R. G., Boston, M. B., & Hoffman, N. (1985). Sex of authority role models and achievement by men and women: Leadership performance and recognition. *Journal of Personality and Social Psychology, 49,* 636–653.

Gemmill, G. (1986). The mythology of the leader role in small groups. *Small Group Behavior, 17,* 41–50.

Genevie, L. E. (Ed.). (1978). *Collective behavior and social movements.* Itasca, IL: Peacock.

George, J. M. (1990). Personality, affect, and behavior in groups. *Journal of Applied Psychology, 75,* 107–116.

George, J. M. (1996). Group affective tone. In M. A. West (Ed.), *Handbook of work group psychology* (pp. 77–93). Chichester, UK: Wiley.

George, J. M., & Brief, A. P. (1992). Feeling good/doing good: A conceptual analysis of the mood at work/organizational spontaneity relationship. *Psychological Bulletin, 112,* 310–329.

George, J. M., & Zhou, J. (2001). When openness to experience and conscientiousness are related to creative behavior: An interactional approach. *Journal of Applied Psychology, 86,* 513–524.

Georgesen, J. C., Harris, M. J. (1998). Why's my boss always holding me down? A meta-analysis of power effects on performance evaluations. *Personality and Social Psychology Review, 2,* 184–195.

Gerard, H. B. (1953). The effect of different dimensions of disagreement on the communication process in small groups. *Human Relations, 6,* 249–271.

Gerard, H. B. (1964). Conformity and commitment to the group. *Journal of Abnormal and Social Psychology, 68,* 209–211.

Gerard, H. B. (1983). School desegregation: The social science role. *American Psychologist, 38,* 869–877.

Gerard, H. B., & Mathewson, G. C. (1966). The effects of severity of initiation on liking for a group: A replication. *Journal of Experimental Social Psychology, 2,* 278–287.

Gerard, H. B., & Orive, R. (1987). The dynamics of opinion formation. *Advances in Experimental Social Psychology, 20,* 171–202.

Gerber, G. L. (1996). Status in same-gender and mixed-gender police dyads: Effects on personality attributions. *Social Psychology Quarterly, 59,* 350–363.

Gergen, K. J., Gergen, M. M., & Barton, W. H. (1973). Deviance in the dark. *Psychology Today, 10,* 129–130.

Gersick, C. J. G. (1989). Marking time: Predictable transitions in task groups. *Academy of Management Journal, 32,* 274–309.

Gerstner, C. R., & Day, D. V. (1997). Meta-analytic review of leader–member exchange theory: Correlates and construct issues. *Journal of Applied Psychology, 82,* 827–844.

Giannetti, C. C., & Sagarese, M. (2001). *Cliques.* New York: Broadway.

Gibb, C. A. (1969). Leadership. In G. Lindzey & E. Aronson (Eds.), *The handbook of social psychology* (Vol. 4, 2nd ed., pp. 205–282). Reading, MA: Addison-Wesley.

Gibb, J. R. (1970). Effects of human relations training. In A. E. Bergin & S. L. Garfield (Eds.), *Handbook of psychotherapy and behavior change.* New York: Wiley.

Gibbons, D., & Olk, P. M. (2003). Individual and structural origins of friendship and social position among professionals. *Journal of Personality and Social Psychology, 84,* 340–351.

Gibson, D. R. (2003). Participation shifts: Order and differentiation in group conversation. *Social Forces, 81,* 1335–1380.

Giesen, M., & McClaren, H. A. (1976). Discussion, distance, and sex: Changes in impressions and attraction during small group interaction. *Sociometry, 39,* 60–70.

Gigone, D., & Hastie, R. (1997). Proper analysis of the accuracy of group judgments. *Psychological Bulletin, 121,* 149–167.

Gilbert, S. J. (1981). Another look at the Milgram obedience studies: The role of the graduated series of shocks. *Personality and Social Psychology Bulletin, 7,* 690–695.

Gilchrist, J. C. (1952). The formation of social groups under conditions of success and failure. *Journal of Abnormal and Social Psychology, 47,* 174–187.

Giles, H. (Ed.). (1977). *Language, ethnicity, and intergroup relations.* London: Academic Press.

Giles, H., & Johnson, P. (1981). The role of language in ethnic group relations. In J. C. Turner & H. Giles (Eds.), *Intergroup behavior* (pp. 199–272). Oxford, UK: Blackwell.

Gill, D. L. (1984). Individual and group performance in sport. In J. M. Silva & R. S. Weinberg (Eds.), *Psychological foundations of sport* (pp. 315–328). Champaign, IL: Human Kinetics.

Gilliland, S. W. (1994). Effects of procedural and distributive justice on reactions to a selection system. *Journal of Applied Psychology, 79,* 691–701.

Ginnett, R. C. (1993). Crews as groups: Their formation and their leadership. In E. L. Wiener, B. G. Kanki, & R. L. Helmreich (Eds.), *Cockpit resource management* (pp. 71–98). San Diego: Academic Press.

Giordano, P. C. (2003). Relationships in adolescence [Electronic version]. *Annual Review of Sociology, 29,* 257–281.

Gire, J. T. (1997). The varying effect of individualism–collectivism on preference for methods of conflict resolution. *Canadian Journal of Behavioral Science, 29,* 38–43.

Gladwell, M. (2000). *The tipping point: How little things can make a big difference.* Boston: Little, Brown.

Glaser, D. (1964). *The effectiveness of a prison and parole system.* Indianapolis: Bobbs-Merrill.

Glass, D. C., & Singer, J. E. (1972). *Urban stress.* New York: Academic Press.

Glass, D. C., Singer, J. E., & Pennebaker, J. W. (1977). Behavioral and physiological effects of uncontrollable environmental events. In D. Stokols (Ed.), *Perspectives on environment and behavior* (pp. 131–151). New York: Plenum Press.

Gleitman, H., Rozin, P., & Sabini, J. (1997). Solomon E. Asch (1907–1996). *American Psychologist, 52,* 984–985.

Godfrey, D. K., Jones, E. E., & Lord, C. G. (1986). Self-promotion is not ingratiating. *Journal of Personality and Social Psychology, 50,* 106–115.

Godwin, R. (Ed.). (2000) *Apollo 13: The NASA mission reports.* Burlington, Ontario, Canada: Apogee.

Goethals, G. R., & Darley, J. M. (1987). Social comparison theory: Self-evaluation and group life. In B. Mullen & G. R. Goethals (Eds.), *Theories of group behavior* (pp. 21–47). New York: Springer Verlag.

Goethals, G. R., & Zanna, M. P. (1979). The role of social comparison in choice shifts. *Journal of Personality and Social Psychology, 37,* 1469–1476.

Goetsch, G. G., & McFarland, D. D. (1980). Models of the distribution of acts in small discussion groups. *Social Psychology Quarterly, 43,* 173–183.

Goffman, E. (1959). *The presentation of self in everyday life.* Garden City, NY: Doubleday.

Goffman, E. (1971). *Relations in public.* Garden City, NY: Doubleday.

Goldberg, L. (1968). Ghetto riots and others: The faces of civil disorder in 1967. *Journal of Peace Research, 2,* 116–132.

Goldberg, L. R. (1993). The structure of phenotypic personality traits. *American Psychologist, 48,* 26–34.

Goldhammer, J. (1996). *Under the influence: The destructive effects of group dynamics.* Amherst, NY: Prometheus.

Golding, W. (1954). *Lord of the flies.* New York: Putnam.

Goldman, F. W., & Goldman, M. (1981). The effects of dyadic group experience in subsequent individual performance. *Journal of Social Psychology, 115,* 83–88.

Goldman, M. (1965). A comparison of individual and group performance for varying combinations of initial ability. *Journal of Personality and Social Psychology, 1,* 210–216.

Goldman, M. (1966). A comparison of group and individual performance where subjects have varying tendencies to solve problems. *Journal of Personality and Social Psychology, 3,* 604–607.

Goldman, M., & Fraas, L. A. (1965). The effects of leader selection on group performance. *Sociometry, 28,* 82–88.

Goldman, M., Stockbauer, J. W., & McAuliffe, T. G. (1977). Intergroup and intragroup competition and cooperation. *Journal of Experimental Social Psychology, 13,* 81–88.

Goldstein, A. P. (2002). *The psychology of group aggression.* New York: Wiley. Retrieved June 12, 2004, from http://www.netlibrary.com

Goldstein, A. P., Heller, K., & Sechrest, L. B. (1966). *Psychotherapy and the psychology of behavior change.* New York: Wiley.

Goleman, D. (1995). *Emotional intelligence.* New York: Bantam.

Goodacre, D. M. (1953). Group characteristics of good and poor performing combat units. *Sociometry, 16,* 168–178.

Goodman, G., & Jacobs, M. K. (1994). The self-help, mutual-support group. In A. Fuhriman & G. M. Burlingame (Eds.), *Handbook of group psychotherapy* (pp. 489–526). New York: Wiley.

Goodman, P. S., & Leyden, D. P. (1991). Familiarity and group productivity. *Journal of Applied Psychology, 76,* 578–586.

Goodstadt, B. E., & Hjelle, L. A. (1973). Power to the powerless: Locus of control and use of power. *Journal of Personality and Social Psychology, 27,* 190–196.

Goodwin, S. A., Gubin, A., Fiske, S. T., & Yzerbyt, V. Y. (2000). Power can bias impression processes: Stereotyping subordinates by default and by design. *Group Processes & Intergroup Relations, 3,* 227–256.

Gordijn, E. H., De Vries, N. K., & De Dreu, C. K. W. (2002). Minority influence on focal and related attitudes: Change in size, attributions, and information processing. *Personality and Social Psychology Bulletin, 28,* 1315–1326.

Gordon, W. (1961). *Synectics: The development of creative capacity.* New York: Harper & Row.

Gorer, G. (1986). *Bali and Angkor: A 1930s pleasure trip looking at life and death.* New York: Oxford University Press.

Gould, S. J. (1991). Exaptation: A crucial tool for an evolutionary psychology. *Journal of Social Issues, 47*(3), 43–65.

Goulding, R. L., & Goulding, M. M. (1979). *Changing lives through redecision therapy.* New York: Brunner/Mazel.

Gouran, D. S. (1999). Communication in groups: The emergence and evolution of a field of study. In L. R. Frey, D. S. Gouran, & M. S. Poole (Eds.), *The handbook of group communication: Theory and research* (pp. 3–36). Thousand Oaks, CA: Sage.

Gouran, D. S., & Hirokawa, R. Y. (1996). Functional theory and communication in decision-making and problem-solving groups: An expanded view. In R.Y. Hirokawa, & M. S. Poole (Eds.), *Communication and group decision making* (2nd ed., pp. 55–80). Thousand Oaks, CA: Sage.

Graeff, C. L. (1983). The situational leadership theory: A critical view. *Academy of Management Review, 8,* 285–291.

Graeff, C. L. (1997). Evolution of situational leadership theory: A critical review. *Leadership Quarterly, 8,* 153–170.

Graen, G. B. (1976). Role-making processes within complex organizations. In M. D. Dunnette (Ed.), *Handbook of industrial organizational psychology* (pp. 1201–1245). Chicago: Rand McNally.

Graen, G. B., & Cashman, J. (1975). A role-making model of leadership in formal organizations: A developmental approach. In J. G. Hunt & L. L. Larson (Eds.), *Leadership frontiers* (pp. 143–166). Kent, OH: Kent State University Press.

Graen, G. B., & Uhl-Bien, M. (1991). The transformation of professionals into self-managing and partially self-designing contributors: Toward a theory of leadership making. *Journal of Management Systems, 3*(3), 33–48.

Graen, G. B., & Uhl-Bien, M. (1995). Relationship-based approach to leadership: Development of leader–member exchange (LMX) theory of leadership over 25 years: Applying a multi-level multi-domain perspective. *Leadership Quarterly, 6,* 219–247.

Granovetter, M. S. (1973). The strength of weak ties. *American Journal of Sociology, 78,* 1360–1380.

Grant, P. R. (1993). Ethnocentrism in response to a threat to social identity. *Journal of Social Behavior and Personality, 8,* 143–154.

Graziano, W. G., Hair, E. C., & Finch, J. F. (1997). Competitiveness mediates the link between personality and group performance. *Journal of Personality and Social Psychology, 73,* 1394–1408.

Graziano, W. G., Jensen-Campbell, L. A., & Hair, E. C. (1996). Perceiving interpersonal conflict and reacting to it: The case for agreeableness. *Journal of Personality and Social Psychology, 70,* 820–835.

Green, L. R., Richardson, D. S., Lago, T., & Schatten-Jones, E. C. (2001). Network correlates of social and emotional loneliness in young and older adults. *Personality and Social Psychology Bulletin, 27,* 281–288.

Green, R. B., & Mack, J. (1978). Would groups do better without social psychologists? *Personality and Social Psychology Bulletin, 4,* 561–563.

Greenberg, C. I., & Firestone, I. J. (1977). Compensatory responses to crowding: Effects of personal space intrusion and privacy reduction. *Journal of Personality and Social Psychology, 35,* 637–644.

Greenberg, J. (1994). Using socially fair treatment to promote acceptance of a work site smoking ban. *Journal of Applied Psychology, 79,* 288–297.

Greenberg, J. (1996). "Forgive me, I'm new": Three experimental demonstrations of the effects of attempts to excuse poor performance. *Organizational Behavior and Human Decision Processes, 66,* 165–178.

Greenhaus, J. H., Parasuraman, S., & Wormley, W. M. (1990). Effects of race on organizational experiences, job performance evaluations, and career outcomes. *Academy of Management Journal, 33,* 64–86.

Greenwald, A. G., Banaji, M. R., Rudman, L. A., Farnham, S. D., Nosek, B. A., & Mellott, D. S. (2002). A unified theory of implicit attitudes, stereotypes, self-esteem, and self-concept. *Psychological Review, 109,* 3–25.

Greenwald, A. G., & Pratkanis, A. R. (1984). The self. In R. S.

Wyer, Jr., & T. K. Srull (Eds.), *Handbook of social cognition* (Vol. 3, pp. 3–26). Mahwah, NJ: Erlbaum.

Greer, D. L. (1983). Spectator booing and the home advantage: A study of social influence in the basketball arena. *Social Psychology Quarterly, 46,* 252–261.

Greitemeyer, T., & Schulz-Hardt, S. (2003). Preference-consistent evaluation of information in the hidden profile paradigm: Beyond group-level explanations for the dominance of shared information in group decisions. *Journal of Personality and Social Psychology, 84,* 322–339.

Greve, D. W. (1993). Gestalt group psychotherapy. In H. I. Kaplan & M. J. Sadock (Eds.), *Comprehensive group psychotherapy* (3rd ed., pp. 228–235). Baltimore: Williams & Wilkins.

Griffin, M. (2001). The phenomenology of the alone condition: More evidence for the role of aloneness in social facilitation. *Journal of Psychology: Interdisciplinary & Applied, 135,* 125–127.

Griffitt, W. (1970). Environmental effects on interpersonal affective behavior: Ambient effective temperature and attraction. *Journal of Personality and Social Psychology, 15,* 240–244.

Griffitt, W., & Veitch, R. (1971). Hot and crowded: Influence of population density and temperature on interpersonal affective behavior. *Journal of Personality and Social Psychology, 17,* 92–98.

Grimes, A. J. (1978). Authority, power, influence and social control: A theoretical synthesis. *Academy of Management Review, 3,* 724–737.

Groff, B. D., Baron, R. S., & Moore, D. L. (1983). Distraction, attentional conflict, and drivelike behavior. *Journal of Experimental Social Psychology, 19,* 359–380.

Grofman, B., & Owen, G. (1982). A game theoretic approach to measuring degree of centrality in social networks. *Social Networks, 4,* 213–224.

Gross, E., & Stone, G. P. (1964). Embarrassment and the analysis of role requirements. *American Journal of Sociology, 70,* 1–15.

Gross, S. R., & Miller, N. (1997). The "golden section" and bias in perceptions of social consensus. *Personality and Social Psychology Review, 1,* 241–271.

Guadagno, R. E., & Cialdini, R. B. (2002). Online persuasion: An examination of gender differences in computer-mediated interpersonal influence. *Group Dynamics, 6,* 38–51.

Guerin, B. (1983). Social facilitation and social monitoring: A test of three models. *British Journal of Social Psychology, 22,* 203–214.

Guerin, B. (1986). Mere presence effects in humans: A review. *Journal of Experimental Social Psychology, 22,* 38–77.

Guerin, B. (1993). *Social facilitation.* New York: Cambridge University Press.

Guerin, B. (1999). Social behaviors as determined by different arrangements of social consequences: Social loafing, social facilitation, deindividuation, and a modified social loafing. *Psychological Record, 49,* 565–578.

Guerin, B., & Innes, J. M. (1982). Social facilitation and social monitoring: A new look at Zajonc's mere presence hypothesis. *British Journal of Social Psychology, 21,* 7–18.

Guetzkow, H., & Gyr, J. (1954). An analysis of conflict in decision-making groups. *Human Relations, 7,* 367–382.

Guimond, A., & Dubé-Simard, L. (1983). Relative deprivation theory and the Quebec nationalist movement: The cognitive–emotion distinction and the personal–group deprivation issue. *Journal of Personality and Social Psychology, 44,* 526–535.

Guinote, A., Judd, C. M., & Brauer, M. (2002). Effects of power on perceived and objective group variability: Evidence that more powerful groups are more variable. *Journal of Personality and Social Psychology, 82,* 708–721.

Gulley, H. E., & Leathers, D. G. (1977). *Communication and group process.* New York: Holt, Rinehart & Winston.

Gully, S. M., Devine, D. J., & Whitney, D. J. (1995). A meta-analysis of cohesion and performance: Effects of level of analysis and task interdependence. *Small Group Research, 26,* 497–520.

Gump, P. V. (1990). A short history of the Midwest Psychological Field Station. *Environment and Behavior, 22,* 436–457.

Gunderson, E. K. E. (1973). Individual behavior in confined or isolated groups. In J. E. Rasmussen (Ed.), *Man in isolation and confinement* (pp. 145–164). Chicago: Aldine.

Gurr, T. R. (1970). *Why men rebel.* Princeton, NJ: Princeton University Press.

Gustafson, D. H., Shukla, R. M., Delbecq, A. L., & Walster, G. W. (1973). A comparative study of differences in subjective likelihood estimates made by individuals, interacting groups, Delphi groups, and nominal groups. *Organizational Behavior and Human Performance, 9,* 280–291.

Guthman, E. (1971). *We band of brothers.* New York: Harper & Row.

Guzzo, R. A. (1995). Introduction: At the intersection of team effectiveness and decision making. In R. A. Guzzo, E. Salas, & Associates, *Team effectiveness and decision making in organizations* (pp. 1–8). San Francisco: Jossey-Bass.

Guzzo, R. A., & Dickson, M. W. (1996). Teams in organizations: Recent research on performance and effectiveness. *Annual Review of Psychology, 47,* 307–338.

Guzzo, R. A., & Shea, G. P. (1992). Group performance and intergroup relations in organizations. In M. D. Dunnette & L. M. Hough (Eds.), *Handbook of industrial and organizational psychology* (2nd ed., Vol. 3, pp. 269–313). Palo Alto, CA: Consulting Psychologists Press.

Guzzo, R. A., Yost, P. R., Campbell, R. J., & Shea, G. P. (1993). Potency in groups: Articulating a construct. *British Journal of Social Psychology, 32,* 87–106.

Haas, D. F., & Deseran, F. A. (1981). Trust and symbolic exchange. *Social Psychology Quarterly, 44,* 3–13.

Haber, G. M. (1980). Territorial invasion in the classroom: Invadee response. *Environment and Behavior, 12,* 17–31.

Haber, G. M. (1982). Spatial relations between dominants and marginals. *Social Psychology Quarterly, 45,* 219–228.

Hackman, J. R. (1987). The design of work teams. In J. W. Lorsch (Ed.), *Handbook of organizational behavior* (pp. 315–342). Upper Saddle River, NJ: Prentice Hall.

Hackman, J. R. (Ed.). (1990). *Groups that work (and those that don't).* San Francisco: Jossey-Bass.

Hackman, J. R. (1992). Group influences on individuals in organizations. In M. D. Dunnette & L. M. Hough (Eds.), *Handbook of industrial and organizational psychology* (2nd ed., Vol. 3, pp. 199–267). Palo Alto, CA: Consulting Psychologists Press.

Hackman, J. R. (2003). Learning more by crossing levels: Evidence from airplanes, hospitals, and orchestras. *Journal of Organizational Behavior, 24,* 905–922.

Hackman, J. R., Brousseau, K. R., & Weiss, J. A. (1976). The interaction of task design and group performance strategies in determining group effectiveness. *Organizational Behavior and Human Performance, 16,* 350–365.

Hackman, J. R., & Morris, C. G. (1975). Group tasks, group interaction process, and group performance effectiveness: A review and proposed integration. *Advances in Experimental Social Psychology, 8,* 47–99.

Hall, E. T. (1966). *The hidden dimension*. New York: Doubleday.

Hall, R. J., & Lord, R. G. (1995). Multi-level information-processing explanations of followers' leadership perceptions. *Leadership Quarterly, 6,* 265–287.

Hallinan, M. T. (1981). Recent advances in sociometry. In S. R. Asher & J. M. Gottman (Eds.), *The development of children's friendships* (pp. 91–115). New York: Cambridge University Press.

Halpern, D. (1995). *Mental health and the built environment: More than bricks and mortar?* London: Taylor & Francis.

Halpin, A. W., & Winer, B. J. (1952). *The leadership behavior of the airplane commander*. Columbus: Ohio State University Research Foundation.

Ham v. S. Carolina, 409 U.S. 524 (1973).

Hamaguchi, E. (1985). A contextual model of the Japanese: Toward a methodological innovation in Japanese studies. *Journal of Japanese Studies, 11,* 289–321.

Hamblin, R. L. (1958). Leadership and crises. *Sociometry, 21,* 322–335.

Hamilton, D. L., & Sherman, S. J. (1989). Illusory correlations: Implications for stereotype theory and research. In D. Bar-Tal, C. F. Graumann, A. W. Kruglanski, & W. Stroebe (Eds.), *Stereotyping and prejudice: Changing conceptions* (pp. 59–82). New York: Springer Verlag.

Hamilton, D. L., & Sherman, S. J. (1996). Perceiving persons and groups. *Psychological Review, 103,* 336–355.

Hamilton, D. L., Sherman, S. J., & Lickel, B. (1998). Perceiving social groups: The importance of the entitativity continuum. In C. Sedikides, J. Schopler, & C. A. Insko (Eds.), *Intergroup cognition and intergroup behavior* (pp. 47–74). Mahwah, NJ: Erlbaum.

Hamilton, V. L., & Sanders, J. (1995). Crimes of obedience and conformity in the workplace: Surveys of Americans, Russians, and Japanese. *Journal of Social Issues, 51*(3), 67–88.

Hamilton, V. L., & Sanders, J. (1999). The second face of evil: Wrongdoing in and by the corporation. *Personality and Social Psychology Review, 3,* 222–233.

Hamilton, W. D. (1964). The genetic evolution of social behavior: I and II. *Journal of Theoretical Biology, 7,* 1–52.

Haney, C., Banks, C., & Zimbardo, P. (1973). Interpersonal dynamics in a simulated prison. *International Journal of Criminology and Psychology, 1,* 69–97.

Hans, V. P., Hannaford-Agor, P. L., Mott, N. L., & Munsterman, G. T. (2003). The hung jury: The American jury's insights and contemporary understanding. *Criminal Law Bulletin, 39,* 33–50.

Hans, V. P., & Vidmar, N. (1982). Jury selection. In N. L. Kerr & R. M. Bray (Eds.), *Psychology of the courtroom* (pp. 39–82). New York: Academic Press.

Hansen, W. B., & Altman, I. (1976). Decorating personal places: A descriptive analysis. *Environment and Behavior, 8,* 491–504.

Hardin, G. (1968). The tragedy of the commons. *Science, 162,* 1243–1248.

Harding, J., Proshansky, H., Kutner, B., & Chein, I. (1969). Prejudice and ethnic relations. In G. Lindzey & E. Aronson (Eds.), *The handbook of social psychology* (2nd ed., Vol. 5, pp. 1–76). Reading, MA: Addison-Wesley.

Hardy, C., & Latané, B. (1986). Social loafing on a cheering task. *Social Science, 71*(2–3), 165–172.

Hardyck, J. A., & Braden, M. (1962). Prophecy fails again: A report of a failure to replicate. *Journal of Abnormal and Social Psychology, 65,* 136–141.

Hare, A. P. (1967). Small group development in the relay assembly testroom. *Sociological Inquiry, 37,* 169–182.

Hare, A. P. (1976). *Handbook of small group research* (2nd ed.). New York: Free Press.

Hare, A. P. (1982). *Creativity in small groups*. Thousand Oaks, CA: Sage.

Hare, A. P. (1985). The significance of SYMLOG in the study of group dynamics. *International Journal of Small Group Research, 1,* 38–50.

Hare, A. P. (1994). Types of roles in small groups: A bit of history and a current perspective. *Small Group Research, 25,* 433–448.

Hare, A. P., & Bales, R. F. (1963). Seating position and small group interaction. *Sociometry, 26,* 480–486.

Hare, A. P., Blumberg, H. H., Davies, M. F., & Kent, M. V. (1994). *Small group research: A handbook*. Norwood, NJ: Ablex.

Hare, A. P., Borgatta, E. F., & Bales, R. F. (1955). *Small groups: Studies in social interaction*. New York: Knopf.

Hare, A. P., Hare, S. E., & Blumberg, H. H. (1998). Wishful thinking: Who has the least preferred coworker? *Small Group Research, 29,* 419–435.

Hare, A. P., & Naveh, D. (1986). Conformity and creativity: Camp David, 1978. *Small Group Behavior, 17,* 243–268.

Harinck, F. (2004). Persuasive arguments and beating around the bush in negotiations. *Group Processes & Intergroup Relations, 7,* 5–18.

Harkins, S. G., & Jackson, J. M. (1985). The role of evaluation in eliminating social loafing. *Personality and Social Psychology Bulletin, 11,* 457–465.

Harkins, S. G., Latané, B., & Williams, K. (1980). Social loafing: Allocating effort or taking it easy. *Journal of Experimental Social Psychology, 16,* 457–465.

Harkins, S. G., & Szymanski, K. (1987). Social loafing and social facilitation: New wine in old bottles. *Review of Personality and Social Psychology, 9,* 167–188.

Harkins, S. G., & Szymanski, K. (1988). Social loafing and self-evaluation with an objective standard. *Journal of Experimental Social Psychology, 24,* 354–365.

Harkins, S. G., & Szymanski, K. (1989). Social loafing and group evaluation. *Journal of Personality and Social Psychology, 56,* 934–941.

Harlow, H. F. (1932). Social facilitation of feeding in the albino rat. *Journal of Genetic Psychology, 41,* 211–221.

Harlow, H. F., & Harlow, M. K. (1966). Learning to love. *American Scientist, 54,* 244–272.

Harlow, R. E., & Cantor, N. (1995). To whom do people turn when things go poorly? Task orientation and functional social contacts. *Journal of Personality and Social Psychology, 69,* 329–340.

Harlow, R. E., & Cantor, N. (1996). Still participating after all these years: A study of life task participation in later life. *Journal of Personality and Social Psychology, 71,* 1235–1249.

Harper, N. L., & Askling, L. R. (1980). Group communication and quality of task solution in a media production organization. *Communication Monographs, 47,* 77–100.

Harrington, B., & Fine, G. A. (2000). Opening the "black box": Small groups and twenty-first-century sociology. *Social Psychology Quarterly, 63,* 312–323.

Harris, J. R. (1995). Where is the child's environment? A group socialization theory of development. *Psychological Review, 102,* 458–489.

Harrison, A. A., Clearwater, Y. A., & McKay, C. P. (Eds.). (1991).

From Antarctica to outer space: Life in isolation and confinement. New York: Springer Verlag.

Harrison, A. A., & Connors, M. M. (1984). Groups in exotic environments. *Advances in Experimental Social Psychology, 18,* 50–87.

Harrod, W. J. (1980). Expectations from unequal rewards. *Social Psychology Quarterly, 43,* 126–130.

Hart, J. W., Bridgett, D. J., & Karau, S. J. (2001). Coworker ability and effort as determinants of individual effort on a collective task. *Group Dynamics, 5,* 181–190.

Härtel, C. E. J., & Härtel, G. F. (1997). SHAPE-assisted intuitive decision making and problem solving: Information-processing–based training for conditions of cognitive busyness. *Group Dynamics, 1,* 187–199.

Hartig, T., Mang, M., & Evans, G. W. (1991). Restorative effects of natural environment experience. *Environment and Behavior, 23,* 3–26.

Harton, H. C., Green, L. R., Jackson, C., & Latané, B. (1998). Demonstrating dynamic social impact: Consolidation, clustering, correlation, and (sometimes) the correct answer. *Teaching of Psychology, 25,* 31–35.

Harvey, J. B. (1988) *The Abilene paradox and other meditations on management.* New York: Wiley.

Haslam, S. A. (2001). *Psychology in organizations: The social identity approach.* Thousand Oaks, CA: Sage.

Haslam, S. A., & Oakes, P. J. (1995). How context-independent is the outgroup homogeneity effect? A response to Bartsch and Judd. *European Journal of Social Psychology, 12,* 469–475.

Hastie, R., Penrod, S. D., & Pennington, N. (1983). *Inside the jury.* Cambridge, MA: Harvard University Press.

Hastorf, A. H., & Cantril, H. (1954). They saw a game. *Journal of Abnormal and Social Psychology, 49,* 129–134.

Hatcher, C., McCarthy, P. (2003, July). From garage to global empire: Carly Fiorina and leadership communication. In *Proceedings of the Australian and New Zealand Communication Association Conference.* Brisbane, Australia: Brisbane Graduate School of Business, Queensland University of Technology. Retrieved June 23, 2004, from http://www.anzca.net/

Hayduk, L. A. (1978). Personal space: An evaluative and orienting overview. *Psychological Bulletin, 85,* 117–134.

Hayduk, L. A. (1983). Personal space: Where we now stand. *Psychological Bulletin, 94,* 293–335.

Hays, R. B., & Oxley, D. (1986). Social network development and functioning during a life transition. *Journal of Personality and Social Psychology, 50,* 304–313.

Haythorn, W., Couch, A. S., Haefner, D., Langham, P., & Carter, L. F. (1956). The effects of varying combinations of authoritarian and equalitarian leaders and followers. *Journal of Abnormal and Social Psychology, 53,* 210–219.

Hazan, C., & Shaver, P. (1987). Romantic love conceptualized as an attachment process. *Journal of Personality and Social Psychology, 52,* 511–524.

Hearne, G. (1957). Leadership and the spatial factor in small groups. *Journal of Abnormal and Social Psychology, 54,* 269–272.

Hechter, M., & Op, K. (Eds.). (2001). *Social norms.* New York: Russell Sage Foundation.

Heffron, M. H. (1972). The naval ship as an urban design problem. *Naval Engineers Journal, 12,* 49–64.

Heider, F. (1958). *The psychology of interpersonal relations.* New York: Wiley.

Heifetz, R. A. (1994). Some strategic implications of William Clinton's strengths and weaknesses. *Political Psychology, 15,* 763–768.

Heilman, M. E. (2001). Description and prescription: How gender stereotypes prevent women's ascent up the organizational ladder. *Journal of Social Issues, 57,* 657–674.

Heilman, M. E., Block, C. J., & Martell, R. F. (1995). Sex stereotypes: Do they influence perceptions of managers? *Journal of Social Behavior and Personality, 10,* 237–252.

Heine, S. J., Kitayama, S., & Lehman, D. R. (2001). Cultural differences in self-evaluation: Japanese readily accept negative self-relevant information. *Journal of Cross-Cultural Psychology, 32,* 434–443.

Heinicke, C. M., & Bales, R. F. (1953). Developmental trends in the structure of small groups. *Sociometry, 16,* 7–38.

Heller, J. F., Groff, B. D., & Solomon, S. H. (1977). Toward an understanding of crowding: The role of physical interaction. *Journal of Personality and Social Psychology, 35,* 183–190.

Helmreich, R. L. (1974). Evaluation of environments: Behavioral observations in an undersea habitat. In J. Lang, C. Burnette, W. Moleski, & D. Vachon (Eds.), *Designing for human behavior.* Stroudsburg, PA: Dowden, Hutchinson, & Ross.

Helmreich, R. L., & Collins, B. E. (1967). Situational determinants of affiliative preference under stress. *Journal of Personality and Social Psychology, 6,* 79–85.

Helmreich, R. L., & Foushee, H. C. (1993). Why crew resource management? Empirical and theoretical bases of human factors training in aviation. In E. L. Wiener, B. G. Kanki, & R. L. Helmreich (Eds.), *Cockpit resource management* (pp. 3–45). San Diego: Academic Press.

Hembroff, L. A. (1982). Resolving status inconsistency: An expectation states theory and test. *Social Forces, 61,* 183–205.

Hembroff, L. A., & Myers, D. E. (1984). Status characteristics: Degrees of task relevance and decision process. *Social Psychology Quarterly, 47,* 337–346.

Hemphill, J. K. (1950). Relations between the size of the group and the behavior of "superior" leaders. *Journal of Social Psychology, 32,* 11–22.

Hemphill, J. K. (1961). Why people attempt to lead. In L. Petrullo & B. M. Bass (Eds.), *Leadership and interpersonal behavior.* New York: Holt, Rinehart & Winston.

Henchy, T., & Glass, D. C. (1968). Evaluation apprehension and the social facilitation of dominant and subordinate responses. *Journal of Personality and Social Psychology, 10,* 446–454.

Henry, K. B., Arrow, H., & Carini, B. (1999). A tripartite model of group identification: Theory and measurement. *Small Group Research, 30,* 558–581.

Hensley, T. R., & Griffin, G. W. (1986). Victims of groupthink: The Kent State University Board of Trustees and the 1977 gymnasium controversy. *Journal of Conflict Resolution, 30,* 497–531.

Heppner, P. P., Kivlighan, D. M., Burnett, J. W., Berry, T. R., Goedinghaus, M., Doxsee, D. J., Hendricks, F. M., Krull, L. A., Wright, G. E., Bellatin, A. M., Durham, R. J., Tharp, A., Kim, H., Brossart, D. F., Wang, L., Witty, T. E., Kinder, M. H., Hertel, J. B., & Wallace, D. L. (1994). Dimensions that characterize supervisor interventions delivered in the context of live supervision of practicum counselors. *Journal of Counseling Psychology, 41,* 227–235.

Hepworth, J. T., & West, S. G. (1988). Lynchings and the economy: A time-series reanalysis of Hovland and Sears (1940). *Journal of Personality and Social Psychology, 55,* 239–247.

Herbert, T. B., & Cohen, S. (1993). Stress and immunity in humans: A meta-analytic review. *Psychosomatic Medicine, 55,* 364–379.

Herek, G. M., Janis, I. L., & Huth, P. (1989). Quality of U.S. decision making during the Cuban missile crisis: Major errors in Welch's reassessment. *Journal of Conflict Resolution, 33,* 446–459.

Herek, G., Janis, I. L., & Huth, P. (1987). Decision-making during international crises: Is quality of process related to outcome? *Journal of Conflict Resolution, 31,* 203–226.

Herman, C. P., Roth, D. A., & Polivy, J. (2003). Effects of the presence of others on food intake: A normative interpretation. *Psychological Bulletin, 129,* 873–886.

Hersey, P. (1985). A letter to the author of "Don't be misled by LEAD." *Journal of Applied Behavioral Sciences, 21,* 152–153.

Hersey, P., & Blanchard, K. H. (1976). Leader effectiveness and adaptability description (LEAD). In J. W. Pfeiffer & J. E. Jones (Eds.), *The 1976 annual handbook for group facilitators* (Vol. 5). La Jolla, CA: University Associates.

Hersey, P., & Blanchard, K. H. (1977). *Management of organizational behavior* (3rd ed.). Upper Saddle River, NJ: Prentice Hall.

Hersey, P., & Blanchard, K. H. (1982). *Management of organizational behavior* (4th ed.). Upper Saddle River, NJ: Prentice Hall.

Hersey, P., Blanchard, K. H., & Johnson, D. E. (2001). *Management of organizational behavior: Leading human resources* (8th ed.). Upper Saddle River, NJ: Prentice Hall.

Heshka, S., & Nelson, Y. (1972). Interpersonal speaking distance as a function of age, sex, and relationship. *Sociometry, 25,* 491–498.

Hewstone, M. (1990). The "ultimate attribution error"? A review of the literature on intergroup causal attribution. *European Journal of Social Psychology, 20,* 311–335.

Hewstone, M., Rubin, M., & Willis, H. (2002). Intergroup bias. *Annual Review of Psychology, 53*(2), 575–604.

Higginbotham, H. N., West, S. G., & Forsyth, D. R. (1988). *Psychotherapy and behavior change: Social, cultural, and methodological perspectives.* New York: Pergamon Press.

Highhouse, S. (2002). A history of the T-group and its early applications in management development. *Group Dynamics, 6,* 277–290.

Hill, C. A. (1991). Seeking emotional support: The influence of affiliative need and partner warmth. *Journal of Personality and Social Psychology, 60,* 112–121.

Hill, C. E., Helms, J. E., Tichenor, V., Spiegel, S. B., O'Grady, K. E., & Perry, E. S. (1988). Effects of therapist response modes in brief psychotherapy. *Journal of Counseling Psychology, 35,* 222–233.

Hill, C. T., & Stull, D. E. (1981). Sex differences in effects of social and value similarity in same-sex friendship. *Journal of Personality and Social Psychology, 41,* 488–502.

Hill, T. E., & Schmitt, N. (1977). Individual differences in leadership decision making. *Organizational Behavior and Human Performance, 19,* 353–367.

Hill, W. F., & Gruner, L. (1973). A study of development in open and closed groups. *Small Group Behavior, 4,* 355–381.

Hilmert, C. J., Kulik, J. A., & Christenfeld, N. (2002). The varied impact of social support on cardiovascular reactivity. *Basic and Applied Social Psychology, 24,* 229–240.

Hinkle, S., & Schopler, J. (1986). Bias in the evaluation of in-group and out-group performance. In S. Worchel & W. G. Austin (Eds.), *Psychology of intergroup relations* (2nd ed., pp. 196–212). Chicago: Nelson-Hall.

Hinsz, V. B. (1995). Goal setting by groups performing an additive task: A comparison with individual goal setting. *Journal of Applied Social Psychology, 25,* 965–990.

Hinsz, V. B., Tindale, R. S., & Vollrath, D. A. (1997). The emerging conceptualization of groups as information processors. *Psychological Bulletin, 121,* 43–64.

Hirokawa, R. Y. (1980). A comparative analysis of communication patterns within effective and ineffective decision-making groups. *Communication Monographs, 47,* 312–321.

Hirokawa, R. Y., & Salazar, A. B. (1999). Task-group communication and decision-making performance. In L. R. Frey, D. S. Gouran, & M. S. Poole (Eds.), *The handbook of group communication: Theory and research* (pp. 167–191). Thousand Oaks, CA: Sage.

Hirt, E. R., Zillmann, D., Erickson, G. A., & Kennedy, C. (1992). Costs and benefits of allegiance: Changes in fans' self-ascribed competencies after team victory versus defeat. *Journal of Personality and Social Psychology, 63,* 724–738.

Hoag, M. J., & Burlingame, G. M. (1997). Evaluating the effectiveness of child and adolescent group treatment: A meta-analytic review. *Journal of Clinical Child Psychology, 26,* 234–246.

Hodson, G., & Sorrentino, R. M. (1997). Groupthink and uncertainty orientation: Personality differences in reactivity to the group situation. *Group Dynamics, 1,* 144–155.

Hoffer, E. (1951). *The true believer.* New York: Harper & Row.

Hoffman, J. R., & Rogelberg, S. G. (2001). All together now? College students' preferred project group grading procedures. *Group Dynamics, 5,* 33–40.

Hofmann, D. A., Morgeson, F. P., & Gerras, S. J. (2003). Climate as a moderator of the relationship between leader–member exchange and content specific citizenship: Safety climate as an exemplar. *Journal of Applied Psychology, 88,* 170–178.

Hofstede, G. (1980). *Culture's consequences: International differences in work-related values.* Thousand Oaks, CA: Sage.

Hogan, R., Curphy, G. J., and Hogan, J. (1994). What we know about leadership: Effectiveness and personality. *American Psychologist, 49,* 493–504.

Hogg, M. A. (1992). *The social psychology of group cohesiveness: From attraction to social identity.* New York: New York University Press.

Hogg, M. A. (1996). Intragroup processes, group structure and social identity. In W. P. Robinson (Ed.), *Social groups and identities: Developing the legacy of Henri Tajfel* (pp. 65–93). Oxford, UK: Butterworth-Heinemann.

Hogg, M. A. (2001). Social categorization, depersonalization, and group behavior. In M. A. Hogg & R. S. Tindale (Eds.), *Blackwell handbook of social psychology: Group processes* (pp. 56–85). Malden, MA: Blackwell.

Hogg, M. A., & Abrams, D. (1999). Social identity and social cognition: Historical background and current trends. In D. Abrams & M. A. Hogg (Eds.), *Social identity and social cognition* (pp. 1–25). Malden, MA: Blackwell.

Hogg, M. A., & Tindale, S. (Eds.). (2001). *Blackwell handbook of social psychology: Group processes.* Malden, MA: Blackwell.

Hogg, M. A., & Turner, J. C. (1987). Intergroup behaviour, self-stereotyping and the salience of social categories. *British Journal of Social Psychology, 26,* 325–340.

Hogg, M. A., & Williams, K. D. (2000). From I to we: Social identity and the collective self. *Group Dynamics, 4,* 81–97.

Hogh, A., & Dofradottir, A. (2001). Coping with bullying in the workplace. *European Journal of Work and Organizational Psychology, 10,* 485–495.

Hollander, E. P. (1958). Conformity, status, and idiosyncrasy credit. *Psychological Review, 65,* 117–127.

Hollander, E. P. (1960). Competence and conformity in the acceptance of influence. *Journal of Abnormal and Social Psychology, 61,* 365–369.

Hollander, E. P. (1961). Some effects of perceived status on responses to innovative behavior. *Journal of Abnormal and Social Psychology, 63,* 247–250.

Hollander, E. P. (1965). Validity of peer nominations in predicting a distance performance criterion. *Journal of Applied Psychology, 49,* 434–438.

Hollander, E. P. (1971). *Principles and methods of social psychology* (2nd ed.). New York: Oxford University Press.

Hollander, E. P. (1981). *Principles and methods of social psychology* (3rd ed.). New York: Oxford University Press.

Hollander, E. P. (1985). Leadership and power. In G. Lindzey & E. Aronson (Eds.), *Handbook of social psychology* (Vol. 2, 3rd ed., pp. 485–537). New York: Random House.

Hollander, E. P. (1993). Legitimacy, power, and influence: A perspective on relational features of leadership. In M. M. Chemers & R. Ayman (Eds.), *Leadership theory and research: Perspectives and directions* (pp. 29–47). San Diego: Academic Press.

Hollander, E. P., & Julian, J. W. (1969). Contemporary trends in the analysis of leadership processes. *Psychological Bulletin, 71,* 387–397.

Hollander, E. P., & Offermann, L. R. (1990). Power and leadership in organizations: Relationships in transition. *American Psychologist, 45,* 179–189.

Hollingshead, A. B. (2001a). Cognitive interdependence and convergent expectations in transactive memory. *Journal of Personality and Social Psychology, 81,* 1080–1089.

Hollingshead, A. B. (2001b). Communication technologies, the Internet, and group research. In M. A. Hogg & R. S. Tindale (Eds.), *Blackwell handbook of social psychology: Group processes* (pp. 557–573). Malden, MA: Blackwell.

Hollingshead, A. B., & McGrath, J. E. (1995). Computer-assisted groups: A critical review of the empirical research. In R. A. Guzzo, E. Salas & Associates, *Team effectiveness and decision making in organizations* (pp. 46–78). San Francisco: Jossey-Bass.

Hollingworth, H. L. (1935). *The psychology of the audience.* New York: American Books.

Holmes, P. (1983). "Dropping out" from an adolescent therapeutic group: A study of factors in the patients and their parents which may influence this process. *Journal of Adolescence, 6,* 333–346.

Holsti, O. R., & North, R. (1965). The history of human conflict. In E. B. McNeil (Ed.), *The nature of human conflict* (pp. 155–172). Upper Saddle River, NJ: Prentice Hall.

Homans, G. C. (1950). *The human group.* New York: Harcourt, Brace & World.

Homans, G. C. (1967). *The nature of social science.* New York: Harcourt, Brace & World.

Homans, G. C. (1974). *Social behavior: Its elementary forms.* San Diego: Harcourt Brace Jovanovich.

Homma, M., Tajima, K., & Hayashi, M. (1995). The effects of misperception of performance in brainstorming groups. *Japanese Journal of Experimental Social Psychology, 34,* 221–231.

Honeywell-Johnson, J. A., & Dickinson, A. M. (1999). Small group incentives: A review of the literature. *Journal of Organizational Behavior Management, 19,* 89–120.

Hooijberg, R., & DiTomaso, N. (1996). Leadership in and of demographically diverse organizations. *Leadership Quarterly, 7,* 1–19.

Horne, A. M., Jolliff, D. L., & Roth, E. W. (1996). Men mentoring men in groups. In M. P. Andronico (Ed.), *Men in groups: Insights, interventions, and psychoeducational work* (pp. 97–112). Washington, DC: American Psychological Association.

Horowitz, I. A., & Kirkpatrick, L. C. (1996). A concept in search of a definition: The effects of reasonable doubt instructions on certainty of guilt standards and jury verdicts. *Law and Human Behavior, 20,* 655–670.

Horwitz, M., & Rabbie, J. M. (1982). Individuality and membership in the intergroup system. In H. Tajfel (Ed.), *Social identity and intergroup relations* (pp. 241–274). New York: Cambridge University Press.

Houle, C. O. (1989). *Governing boards: Their nature and nurture.* San Francisco: Jossey-Bass.

House, R. J. (1971). A path goal theory of leader effectiveness. *Administrative Science Quarterly, 16,* 321–338.

House, R. J., & Aditya, R. N. (1997). The social scientific study of leadership: Quo vadis? *Journal of Management, 23,* 409–473.

House, R. L., & Baetz, M. L. (1979). Leadership: Some empirical generalizations and new research directions. *Research in Organizational Behavior, 1,* 341–423.

House, R. J., Schuler, R. S., & Levanoni, E. (1983). Role conflict and ambiguous scales: Realities or artifacts? *Journal of Applied Psychology, 68,* 334–337.

Houston, T. K., Cooper, L. A., & Ford, D. E. (2002). Internet support groups for depression: A 1-year prospective cohort study. *American Journal of Psychiatry, 159,* 2062–2068.

Hovland, C., & Sears, R. (1940). Minor studies of aggression: VI. Correlation of lynchings with economic indices. *Journal of Psychology, 9,* 301–310.

Howard, J. A. (2000). Social psychology of identities [Electronic version]. *Annual Review of Sociology, 26,* 367–393.

Howard, J. W., & Rothbart, M. (1980). Social categorization and memory for in-group and out-group behavior. *Journal of Personality and Social Psychology, 38,* 301–310.

Howells, L. T., & Becker, S. W. (1962). Seating arrangement and leadership emergence. *Journal of Abnormal and Social Psychology, 64,* 148–150.

Hoyle, R. H., & Crawford, A. M. (1994). Use of individual-level data to investigate group phenomena: Issues and strategies. *Small Group Research, 25,* 464–485.

Hoyle, R. H., Pinkley, R. L., & Insko, C. A. (1989). Perceptions of behavior: Evidence of differing expectations for interpersonal and intergroup interactions. *Personality and Social Psychology Bulletin, 15,* 365–376.

Hoyt, C. L. & Blascovich, J. (2003). Transformational and transactional leadership in virtual and physical environments. *Small Group Research, 6,* 678–715.

Hubbard, J. A., Dodge, K. A., Cillessen, A. H. N., Coie, J. D., & Schwartz, D. (2001). The dyadic nature of social information processing in boys' reactive and proactive aggression. *Journal of Personality and Social Psychology, 80,* 268–280.

Hughes, R. L. (2003). The flow of human crowds [Electronic version]. *Annual Review of Fluid Mechanics, 35,* 169–182.

Huguet, P., Galvaing, M. P., Monteil, J. M., & Dumas, F. (1999). Social presence effects in the Stroop task: Further evidence for an attentional view of social facilitation. *Journal of Personality and Social Psychology, 77,* 1011–1025.

Humphreys, L. (1975). *Tearoom trade* (enlarged ed.). New York: Aldine.

Hunt, J. G., & Peterson, M. F. (1997). International perspectives on international leadership. *Leadership Quarterly, 8,* 203–231.

Hunter, J. A., Platow, M. J., Bell, L. M., Kypri, K., & Lewis, C. A. (1997). Intergroup bias and self-evaluation: Domain-specific self-esteem, threats to identity and dimensional importance. *British Journal of Social Psychology, 36,* 405–426.

Hurley, J. R. (1997). Interpersonal theory and measures of outcome and emotional climate in 111 personal development groups. *Group Dynamics, 1,* 86–97.

Hyman, H. (1942). The psychology of status. *Archives of Psychology, 38*(269).

Hyman, H. M., & Tarrant, C. M. (1975). Aspects of American trial jury history. In R. J. Simon (Ed.), *The jury system in America.* Thousand Oaks, CA: Sage.

Iannaccone, L. R. (1994). Why strict churches are strong. *American Journal of Sociology, 99,* 1180–1211.

Ickes, W., & Barnes, R. D. (1977). The role of sex and self-monitoring in unstructured dyadic interactions. *Journal of Personality and Social Psychology, 35,* 315–330.

Ickes, W., & Turner, M. (1983). On the social advantages of having an older, opposite-sex sibling: Birth order influence in mixed-sex dyads. *Journal of Personality and Social Psychology, 45,* 210–222.

Ilgen, D. R. (1999). Teams embedded in organizations: Some implications. *American Psychologist, 54,* 129–139.

Ilgen, D. R., & Fujii, D. S. (1976). An investigation of the validity of leader behavior descriptions obtained from subordinates. *Journal of Applied Psychology, 61,* 642–651.

Ilgen, D. R., Mitchell, T. R., & Fredrickson, J. W. (1981). Poor performances: Supervisors' and subordinates' responses. *Organizational Behavior and Human Performance, 27,* 386–410.

Immelman, A. (2003). Personality in political psychology. In T. Millon, M. J. Lerner, & I. B. Weiner (Eds.), *Handbook of psychology: Personality and social psychology* (Vol. 5, pp. 599–625). New York: Wiley. Retrieved July 23, 2004, from http://www.netlibrary.com

Indik, B. P. (1965). Organization size and member participation: Some empirical tests of alternate explanations. *Human Relations, 15,* 339–350.

Ingham, A. G., Levinger, G., Graves, J., & Peckham, V. (1974). The Ringelmann effect: Studies of group size and group performance. *Journal of Personality and Social Psychology, 10,* 371–384.

Ingram, R. E., Hayes, A., & Scott, W. (2000). Empirically supported treatments: A critical analysis. In C. R. Snyder & R. E. Ingram (Eds.). *Handbook of psychological change: Psychotherapy processes & practices for the 21st century* (pp. 40–60). New York: Wiley.

Insko, C. A., Gilmore, R., Drenan, S., Lipsitz, A., Moehle, D., & Thibaut, J. (1983). Trade versus expropriation in open groups: A comparison of two types of social power. *Journal of Personality and Social Psychology, 44,* 977–999.

Insko, C. A., Hoyle, R. H., Pinkley, R. L., Hong, G., Slim, R., Dalton, G., Lin, Y., Ruffin, P. P., Dardis, G. J., Bernthal, P. R., & Schopler, J. (1988). Individual–group discontinuity: The role of a consensus rule. *Journal of Experimental Social Psychology, 24,* 505–519.

Insko, C. A., Pinkley, R. L., Hoyle, R. H., Dalton, B., Hong, G., Slim, R., Landry, P., Holton, B., Ruffin, P. F., & Thibaut, J. (1987). Individual–group discontinuity: The role of intergroup contact. *Journal of Experimental Social Psychology, 23,* 250–267.

Insko, C. A., & Schopler, J. (1972). *Experimental social psychology.* New York: Academic Press.

Insko, C. A., & Schopler, J. (1998). Differential distrust of groups and individuals. In C. Sedikides, J. Schopler, & C. A. Insko (Eds.), *Intergroup cognition and intergroup behavior* (pp. 75–107). Mahwah, NJ: Erlbaum.

Insko, C. A., Schopler, J., Drigotas, S. M., Graetz, K., Kennedy, J., Cox, C., & Bornstein, G., (1993). The role of communication in interindividual–intergroup discontinuity. *Journal of Conflict Resolution, 37,* 108–138.

Insko, C. A., Schopler, J., Gaertner, L., Wildschut, T., Kozar, R., Pinter, B., Finkel, E. J., Brazil, D. M., Cecil, C. L., & Montoya, M. R. (2001). Interindividual–intergroup discontinuity reduction through the anticipation of future interaction. *Journal of Personality and Social Psychology, 80,* 95–111.

Insko, C. A., Schopler, J., Graetz, K. A., Drigotas, S. M., Currey, K. P., Smith, S. L., Brazil, D., & Bornstein, G. (1994). Interindividual–intergroup discontinuity in the Prisoner's Dilemma Game. *Journal of Conflict Resolution, 38,* 87–116.

Insko, C. A., Schopler, J., Hoyle, R. H., Dardis, G. J., & Graetz, K. A. (1990). Individual–group discontinuity as a function of fear and greed. *Journal of Personality and Social Psychology, 58,* 68–79.

Insko, C. A., Schopler, J., Kennedy, J. F., Dahl, K. R., Graetz, K. A., & Drigotas, S. M. (1992). Individual–group discontinuity from the differing perspectives of Campbell's realistic group conflict theory and Tajfel and Turner's social identity theory. *Social Psychology Quarterly, 55,* 272–291.

Insko, C. A., Schopler, J., & Sedikides, C. (1998). Personal control, entitativity, and evolution. In C. Sedikides, J. Schopler, & C. A. Insko (Eds.), *Intergroup cognition and intergroup behavior* (pp. 109–120). Mahwah, NJ: Erlbaum.

Insko, C. A., Thibaut, J. W., Moehle, D., Wilson, M., Diamond, W. D., Gilmore, R., Solomon, M. R., & Lipsitz, A. (1980). Social evolution and the emergence of leadership. *Journal of Personality and Social Psychology, 39,* 431–448.

Isenberg, D. J. (1986). Group polarization: A critical review and meta-analysis. *Journal of Personality and Social Psychology, 50,* 1141–1151.

Iverson, M. A. (1964). Personality impressions of punitive stimulus persons of differential status. *Journal of Abnormal and Social Psychology, 68,* 617–626.

Jablin, F. M. (1979). Superior–subordinate communication: The state of the art. *Psychological Bulletin, 86,* 1201–1222.

Jablin, F. M. (1982). Formal structural characteristics of organizations and superior–subordinate communication. *Human Communication Research, 8,* 338–347.

Jackson, J. M. (1987). Social impact theory: A social forces model of influence. In B. Mullen & G. R. Goethals (Eds.), *Theories of group behavior* (pp. 112–124). New York: Springer Verlag.

Jackson, J. M., & Latané, B. (1981). All alone in front of all those people: Stage fright as a function of number and type of co-performances and audience. *Journal of Personality and Social Psychology, 40,* 73–85.

Jackson, J. W., & Smith, E. R. (1999). Conceptualizing social identity: A new framework and evidence for the impact of different dimensions. *Personality and Social Psychology Bulletin, 25,* 120–135.

Jackson, S. E. (1992). Team composition in organizational settings: Issues in managing an increasingly diverse workforce. In S. Worchel, S. Wood, & J. A. Simpson (Eds.), *Group process and productivity* (pp. 138–172). Thousand Oaks, CA: Sage.

Jackson, S. E., May, K. E., & Whitney, K. (1995). Understanding the dynamics of diversity in decision-making teams. In R. A. Guzzo, E. Salas, & Associates (Eds.), *Team effectiveness and decision making in organizations* (pp. 204–261). San Francisco: Jossey-Bass.

Jackson, S. E., & Schuler, R. S. (1995). Understanding human resource management in the context of organizations and their environments. *Annual Review of Psychology, 46,* 237–264.

Jacobs, A. (1974). The use of feedback in groups. In A. Jacobs & W. W. Spradlin (Eds.), *Group as an agent of change.* New York: Behavioral Publications.

Jacobs, D., & O'Brien, R. M. (1998). The determinants of deadly force: A structural analysis of police violence. *American Journal of Sociology, 103,* 837–862.

Jacobs, G. A., Quevillon, R. P., & Stricherz, M. (1990). Lessons from the aftermath of Flight 232: Practical considerations for the mental health profession's response to air disasters. *American Psychologist, 45,* 1329–1335.

Jacobs, M. K., & Goodman, G. (1989). Psychology and self-help groups: Predictions on a partnership. *American Psychologist, 44,* 536–545.

Jacobs, R. C., & Campbell, D. T. (1961). The perpetuation of an arbitrary tradition through several generations of a laboratory microculture. *Journal of Abnormal and Social Psychology, 62,* 649–658.

Jago, A. G. (1978). Configural cue utilization in implicit models of leader behavior. *Organizational Behavior and Human Performance, 22,* 474–496.

James, J. (1951). A preliminary study of the size determinant in small group interaction. *American Sociological Review, 16,* 474–477.

James, J. (1953). The distribution of free-forming small group size. *American Sociological Review, 18,* 569–570.

James, R. (1959). Status and competency of jurors. *American Journal of Sociology, 64,* 563–570.

Janis, I. L. (1972). *Victims of groupthink.* Boston: Houghton Mifflin.

Janis, I. L. (1982). *Groupthink: Psychological studies of policy decisions and fiascos* (2nd ed.). Boston: Houghton Mifflin.

Janis, I. L. (1983). Groupthink. In H. H. Blumberg, A. P. Hare, V. Kent, & M. F. Davis (Eds.), *Small groups and social interaction* (Vol. 2, pp. 39–46). New York: Wiley.

Janis, I. L. (1985). International crisis management in the nuclear age. *Applied Social Psychology Annual, 6,* 63–86.

Janis, I. L. (1989). *Crucial decisions: Leadership in policy making and crisis management.* New York: Free Press.

Janis, I. L., & Mann, L. (1977). *Decision making: A psychological analysis of conflict, choice, and commitment.* New York: Free Press.

Jankowski, M. S. (1991). *Islands in the street: Gangs and American urban society.* Berkeley: University of California Press.

Jarboe, S. C., & Witteman, H. R. (1996). Intragroup conflict management in task-oriented groups: The influence of problem sources and problem analyses. *Small Group Research, 27,* 316–338.

Jehn, K. A. (1994). Enhancing effectiveness: An investigation of advantages and disadvantages of value-based intragroup conflict. *International Journal of Conflict Management, 5,* 223–238.

Jehn, K. A. (1995). A multimethod examination of the benefits and detriments of intragroup conflict. *Administrative Science Quarterly, 40,* 256–282.

Jehn, K. A., & Mannix, E. A. (2001). The dynamic nature of conflict: A longitudinal study of intragroup conflict and group performance. *Academy of Management Journal, 44,* 238–251.

Jehn, K. A., & Shaw, P. P. (1997). Interpersonal relationships and task performance: An examination of mediating processes in friendship and acquaintance groups. *Journal of Personality and Social Psychology, 72,* 775–790.

Jetten, J., Branscombe, N. R., Spears, R., & McKimmie, B. (2003). Predicting the paths of peripherals: The interaction of identification and future possibilities. *Personality and Social Psychology Bulletin, 29,* 130–140.

Jetten, J., & Spears, R. (2004). The divisive potential of differences and similarities: The role of intergroup distinctiveness in intergroup differentiation. *European Review of Social Psychology, 14,* 203–241.

Jetten, J., Spears, R., & Manstead, A. S. R. (1996). Intergroup norms and intergroup discrimination: Distinctive self-categorization and social identity effects. *Journal of Personality and Social Psychology, 71,* 1222–1233.

Jetten, J., Spears, R., & Manstead, A. S. R. (1997). Strength of identification and intergroup differentiation: The influence of group norms. *European Journal of Social Psychology, 27,* 603–609.

Jetten, J., Spears, R., & Postmes, T. (2004). Intergroup distinctiveness and differentiation: A meta-analytic integration. *Journal of Personality and Social Psychology, 86,* 862–879.

Jimerson, J. B. (1999). "Who has next?" The symbolic, rational, and methodical use of norms in pickup basketball. *Social Psychology Quarterly, 62,* 136–156.

Johnson, A. G. (1995). *The Blackwell dictionary of sociology: A user's guide to sociological language.* Malden, MA: Blackwell.

Johnson, C. (1974). Planning for termination of the group. In P. Glasser, R. Sarri, & R. Vinter (Eds.), *Individual change through small groups* (pp. 258–265). New York: Free Press.

Johnson, D. W., & Johnson, R. T. (1989). *Cooperation and competition: Theory and research.* Edina, MN: Interaction.

Johnson, D. W., & Johnson, R. T. (1999). Promoting safe educational and community environments. In A. J. Reynolds, H. J.Walberg, & R. P. Weissberg (Eds.), *Promoting positive outcomes* (pp. 161–196). Washington, DC: Child Welfare League of America.

Johnson, D. W., & Johnson, R. T. (2003). Field testing integrative negotiations. *Peace & Conflict: Journal of Peace Psychology, 9,* 39–68.

Johnson, D. W., Johnson, R. T., & Maruyama, G. (1984). Goal interdependence and interpersonal attraction in heterogeneous classrooms: A meta-analysis. In N. Miller & M. Brewer (Eds.), *Groups in contact: The psychology of desegregation* (pp. 187–212). New York: Academic Press.

Johnson, D. W., Johnson, R. T., & Tjosvold, D. (2000). Constructive controversy: The value of intellectual opposition. In M. Deutsch & P. T. Coleman (Eds.), *The handbook of conflict resolution: Theory and practice* (pp. 65–85). San Francisco: Jossey-Bass.

Johnson, D. W., Maruyama, G., Johnson, R., Nelson, D., & Skon, L. (1981). Effects of cooperative, competitive, and individualistic goal structures on achievement: A meta-analysis. *Psychological Bulletin, 89,* 47–62.

Johnson, F. (1988). Encounter group therapy. In S. Long (Ed.), *Six group therapies* (pp. 115–158). New York: Plenum Press.

Johnson, N. R. (1987). Panic at "The Who concert stampede": An empirical assessment. *Social Problems, 34,* 362–373.

Johnson, R. D., & Downing, L. L. (1979). Deindividuation and valence of cues: Effects on prosocial and antisocial behavior. *Journal of Personality and Social Psychology, 37,* 1532–1538.

Jones, D. (2003, January 27). Few women hold top executive jobs, even when CEOs are female. *USA Today.* Retrieved February 3, 2004, from http://www.usatoday.com/money/jobcenter/2003-01-26-womenceos_x.htm

Jones, E. S., Gallois, C., Callan, V. J., & Barker, M. (1995). Language and power in an academic context: The effects of status, ethnicity, and sex. *Journal of Language & Social Psychology, 14,* 434–461.

Jones, M. B. (1974). Regressing group on individual effectiveness. *Organizational Behavior and Human Decision Processes, 11,* 426–451.

Jones, S. C. (1973). Self- and interpersonal evaluations: Esteem theories versus consistency theories. *Psychological Bulletin, 79,* 185–199.

Jones, W. H., & Carver, M. D. (1991). Adjustment and coping implications of loneliness. In C. R. Snyder & D. R. Forsyth (Eds.), *Handbook of social and clinical psychology: The health perspective* (pp. 395–415). New York: Pergamon Press.

Josephs, R. A., Markus, H. R., & Tafarodi, R. W. (1992). Gender and self-esteem. *Journal of Personality and Social Psychology, 63,* 391–402.

Jourard, S. (1971). *Self-disclosure: An experimental analysis of the transparent self.* New York: Wiley.

Judd, C. M., & McClelland, G. H. (1998). Measurement. In D. T. Gilbert, S. T. Fiske, & G. Lindzey (Eds.), *The handbook of social psychology* (4th ed., Vol. 1, pp. 180–232). New York: McGraw-Hill.

Judge, T. A., Bono, J. E., Ilies, R., & Gerhardt, M. W. (2002). Personality and leadership: A qualitative and quantitative review. *Journal of Applied Psychology, 87,* 765–780.

Jung, C. G. (1924). *Psychological types, or the psychology of individuation* (H. G. Baynes, Trans.). New York: Harcourt, Brace & World.

Jung, D. I., & Sosik, J. J. (2002). Transformational leadership in work groups: The role of empowerment, cohesiveness, and collective efficacy on perceived group performance. *Small Group Research, 33,* 313–336.

Kacmar, K. M., Witt, L. A., Zivnuska, S., & Gully, S. M. (2003). The interactive effect of leader–member exchange and communication frequency on performance ratings. *Journal of Applied Psychology, 88,* 764–772.

Kagan, J., Snidman, N., & Arcus, D. M. (1992). Initial reactions to unfamiliarity. *Current Directions in Psychological Science, 1,* 171–174.

Kagitcibasi, C. (1997). Individualism and collectivism. In J. W. Berry, M. H. Segall, & C. Kagitcibasi (Eds.), *Handbook of cross-cultural psychology: Social behavior and applications* (Vol. 3, pp. 1–49). Boston: Allyn & Bacon.

Kahn, A., Hottes, J., & Davis, W. L. (1971). Cooperation and optimal responding in the Prisoner's Dilemma Game: Effects of sex and physical attractiveness. *Journal of Personality and Social Psychology, 17,* 267–279.

Kahn, R. (1973). *The boys of summer.* New York: HarperCollins.

Kahn, R. L., Wolfe, D. M., Quinn, R. P., Snoek, J. D., & Rosenthal, R. A. (1964). *Organizational stress: Studies in role conflict and ambiguity.* New York: Wiley.

Kalven, H., Jr., & Zeisel, H. (1966). *The American jury.* Boston: Little, Brown.

Kamarck, T. W., Manuck, S. B., & Jennings, J. R. (1990). Social support reduces cardiovascular reactivity to psychological challenge: A laboratory model. *Psychosomatic Medicine, 52,* 42–58.

Kameda, T. (1994). Group decision making and social sharedness. *Japanese Psychological Review, 37,* 367–385.

Kameda, T. (1996). Procedural influence in consensus formation: Evaluating group decision making from a social choice perspective. In E. Witte & J. Davis (Eds.), *Understanding group behavior: Consensual action by small groups* (Vol. 1, pp. 137–161). Mahwah, NJ: Erlbaum.

Kameda, T., Stasson, M. F., Davis, J. H., Parks, C. D., & Zimmerman, S. K. (1992). Social dilemmas, subgroups, and motivation loss in task-oriented groups: In search of an "optimal" team size in division of work. *Social Psychology Quarterly, 55,* 47–56.

Kameda, T., & Sugimori, S. (1993). Psychological entrapment in group decision making: An assigned decision rule and a groupthink phenomenon. *Journal of Personality and Social Psychology, 65,* 282–292.

Kameda, T., & Sugimori, S. (1995). Procedural influence in two-step group decision making: Power of local majorities in consensus formation. *Journal of Personality and Social Psychology, 69,* 865–876.

Kameda, T., Takezawa, M., Tindale, R. S., & Smith, C. M. (2002). Social sharing and risk reduction: Exploring a computational algorithm for the psychology of windfall gains. *Evolution and Human Behavior, 23,* 11–33.

Kampmeier, C., & Simon, B. (2001). Individuality and group formation: The role of independence and differentiation. *Journal of Personality and Social Psychology, 81,* 448–462.

Kanagawa, C., Cross, S. E., & Markus, H. R. (2001). "Who am I?" The cultural psychology of the conceptual self. *Personality and Social Psychology Bulletin, 27,* 90–103.

Kanas, N. (1999). Group therapy with schizophrenic and bipolar patients. In V. L. Schermer & M. Pines (Eds.), *Group psychotherapy of the psychoses: Concepts, interventions and contexts* (pp. 129–147). London: Jessica Kingsley.

Kandel, D. B. (1978). Similarity in real-life adolescent friendship pairs. *Journal of Personality and Social Psychology, 36,* 306–312.

Kanter, R. M. (1977). Some effects of proportions on group life: Skewed sex ratios and responses to token women. *American Journal of Sociology, 82,* 465–490.

Kanzer, M. (1983). Freud: The first psychoanalytic group leader. In H. I. Kaplan & B. J. Sadock (Eds.), *Comprehensive group psychotherapy* (2nd ed., pp. 8–14). Baltimore: Williams & Wilkins.

Kaplan, K. J., Firestone, I. J., Klein, K. W., & Sodikoff, C. (1983). Distancing in dyads: A comparison of four models. *Social Psychology Quarterly, 46,* 108–115.

Kaplan, M. F. (1982). Cognitive processes in the individual juror. In N. L. Kerr & R. M. Bray (Eds.), *Psychology of the courtroom* (pp. 197–220). New York: Academic Press.

Kaplan, M. F., & Miller, C. E. (1983). Group discussion and judgment. In P. B. Paulus (Ed.), *Basic group processes* (pp. 65–94). New York: Springer Verlag.

Kaplan, M. F., & Miller, C. E. (1987). Group decision making and normative versus informational influence: Effects of type of issue and assigned decision rule. *Journal of Personality and Social Psychology, 53,* 306–313.

Kaplan, R. E. (1979). The conspicuous absence of evidence that process consultation enhances task performance. *Journal of Applied Behavioral Science, 15,* 346–360.

Kaplan, R., & Kaplan, S. (1989). *The experience of nature: A psychological perspective.* New York: Cambridge University Press.

Kaplowitz, S. A. (1978). Towards a systematic theory of power attribution. *Social Psychology, 41,* 131–148.

Kapos, M. (1995). *The impressionists and their legacy.* New York: Barnes & Noble.

Karau, S. J., & Kelly, J. R. (1992). The effects of time scarcity and time abundance on group performance quality and interaction process. *Journal of Experimental Social Psychology, 28,* 542–571.

Karau, S. J., & Williams, K. D. (1993). Social loafing: A meta-analytic review and theoretical integration. *Journal of Personality and Social Psychology, 65,* 681–706.

Kashima, Y., Yamaguchi, S., Kim, U., Choi, S., Gelfand, M. J., & Yuki, M. (1995). Culture, gender, and self: A perspective from individualism–collectivism research. *Journal of Personality and Social Psychology, 69,* 925–937.

Katz, A. H. (1993). *Self-help in America: A social movement perspective.* New York: Twayne.

Katz, D., & Kahn, R. L. (1978). *The social psychology of organizations* (2nd ed.). New York: Wiley.

Katz, R. (1977). The influence of group conflict on leadership effectiveness. *Organizational Behavior and Human Performance, 20,* 265–286.

Katz, R., & Tushman, M. (1979). Communication patterns, project performance, and task characteristics: An empirical evaluation and integration in an R & D setting. *Organization Behavior and Group Performance, 23,* 139–162.

Kaul, T. J., & Bednar, R. L. (1986). Experiential group research: Results, questions, and suggestions. In S. L. Garfield & A. E. Bergin (Eds.), *Handbook of psychotherapy and behavior change* (3rd ed., pp. 671–714). New York: Wiley.

Keller, E., & Berry, J. (2003). *The influentials: One American in ten tells the other nine how to vote, where to eat, and what to buy.* New York: Free Press.

Kelley, H. H. (1952). Two functions of reference groups. In G. E. Swanson, T. M. Newcomb, & E. L. Hartley (Eds.), *Readings in social psychology* (2nd ed., pp. 410–414). New York: Holt.

Kelley, H. H. (1979). *Personal relationships: Their structures and processes.* Mahwah, NJ: Erlbaum.

Kelley, H. H., Contry, J. C., Dahlke, A. E., & Hill, A. H. (1965). Collective behavior in a simulated panic situation. *Journal of Experimental Social Psychology, 1,* 20–54.

Kelley, H. H., & Stahelski, A. J. (1970a). Errors in perceptions of intentions in a mixed-motive game. *Journal of Experimental Social Psychology, 6,* 379–400.

Kelley, H. H., & Stahelski, A. J. (1970b). Social interaction basis of cooperators' and competitors' beliefs about others. *Journal of Personality and Social Psychology, 16,* 66–91.

Kelley, H. H., & Stahelski, A. J. (1970c). The inference of intentions from moves in the Prisoner's Dilemma Game. *Journal of Experimental Social Psychology, 6,* 401–419.

Kelley, H. H., & Thibaut, J. W. (1978). *Interpersonal relations: A theory of interdependence.* New York: Wiley.

Kelly, J. R. (2001). Mood and emotion in groups. In M. A. Hogg & R. S. Tindale (Eds.), *Blackwell handbook of social psychology: Group processes* (pp. 164–181). Malden, MA: Blackwell.

Kelly, J. R., Futoran, G. C., & McGrath, J. E. (1990). Capacity and capability: Seven studies of entrainment of task performance rates. *Small Group Research, 21,* 283–314.

Kelly, J. R., & Karau, S. J. (1993). Entrainment of creativity in small groups. *Small Group Research, 24,* 179–198.

Kelly, J. R., & Karau, S. J. (1999). Group decision making: The effects of initial preferences and time pressure. *Personality and Social Psychology Bulletin, 25,* 1342–1354.

Kelman, H. C. (1958). Compliance, identification, and internalization: Three processes of attitude change. *Journal of Conflict Resolution, 2,* 51–60.

Kelman, H. C. (1961). Processes of opinion change. *Public Opinion Quarterly, 25,* 57–78.

Kelman, H. C. (1992). Informal mediation by the scholar/practitioner. In J. Bercovitch & J. Rubin (Eds.), *Mediation in international relations: Multiple approaches to conflict management* (pp. 64–96). New York: St. Martin's Press.

Kelman, H. C., & Hamilton, V. L. (1989). *Crimes of obedience: Toward a social psychology of authority and responsibility.* New Haven, CT: Yale University Press.

Keltner, D., Gruenfeld, D. H., & Anderson, C. (2003). Power, approach, and inhibition. *Psychological Review, 110,* 265–284.

Keltner, D., Young, R. C., Heerey, E. A., Oemig, C., & Monarch, N. D. (1998). Teasing in hierarchical and intimate relations. *Journal of Personality and Social Psychology, 75,* 1231–1247.

Kemery, E. R., Bedeian, A. G., Mossholder, K. W., & Touliatos, J. (1985). Outcomes of role stress: A multisample constructive replication. *Academy of Management Review, 28,* 363–375.

Kennedy, R. F. (1969). *Thirteen days.* New York: Norton.

Kenney, R. A., Schwartz-Kenney, B. M., & Blascovich, J. (1996). Implicit leadership theories: Defining leaders described as worthy of influence. *Personality and Social Psychology Bulletin, 22,* 1128–1143.

Kenny, D. A., Horner, C., Kashy, D. A., & Chu, L. (1992). Consensus at zero acquaintance: Replication, behavioral cues, and stability. *Journal of Personality and Social Psychology, 62,* 88–97.

Kenny, D. A., Kashy, D. A., & Bolger, N. (1998). Data analysis in social psychology. In D. T. Gilbert, S. T. Fiske, & G. Lindzey (Eds.), *The handbook of social psychology* (4th ed., Vol. 1, pp. 233–265). New York: McGraw-Hill.

Kenny, D. A., Kieffer, S. C., Smith, J. A., Ceplenski, P., & Kulo, J. (1996). Circumscribed accuracy among well-acquainted individuals. *Journal of Experimental Social Psychology, 32,* 1–12.

Kenny, D. A., & Zaccaro, S. J. (1983). An estimate of variance due to traits in leadership. *Journal of Applied Psychology, 68,* 678–685.

Kent, S. (1991). Partitioning space: Cross-cultural factors influencing domestic spatial segmentation. *Environment and Behavior, 23,* 438–473.

Kerckhoff, A. C., & Back, K. W. (1968). *The June Bug: A study of hysterical contagion.* New York: Appleton-Century-Crofts.

Kerckhoff, A. C., Back, K. W., & Miller, N. (1965). Sociometric patterns in hysterical contagion. *Sociometry, 28,* 2–15.

Kerckhoff, A. C., & Davis, K. E. (1962). Value consensus and need complementarity in mate selection. *American Sociological Review, 27,* 295–303.

Kerr, N. L. (1983). Motivation losses in small groups: A social dilemma analysis. *Journal of Personality and Social Psychology, 45,* 819–828.

Kerr, N. L. (1995). Norms in social dilemmas. In D. A. Schroeder

(Ed.), *Social dilemmas: Perspectives on individuals and groups* (pp. 31–48). Westport, CT: Praeger.

Kerr, N. L. (2001). Is it what one says or how one says it? Style vs. substance from an SDS perspective. In C. K. W. De Dreu & N. K. De Vries (Eds.), *Group consensus and minority influence: Implications for innovation* (pp. 201–228). Malden, MA: Blackwell.

Kerr, N. L., Aronoff, J., & Messé, L. A. (2000). Methods of small group research. In H. T. Reis & C. M. Judd (Eds.), *Handbook of research methods in social and personality psychology* (pp. 160–189). New York: Cambridge University Press.

Kerr, N. L., Atkin, R. S., Stasser, G., Meek, D., Holt, R. W., & Davis, J. H. (1976). Guilt beyond a reasonable doubt: Effect of concept definition and assigned decision rule on the judgments of mock jurors. *Journal of Personality and Social Psychology, 34,* 282–294.

Kerr, N. L., & Bruun, S. E. (1981). Ringelmann revisited: Alternative explanations for the social loafing effect. *Personality and Social Psychology Bulletin, 7,* 224–231.

Kerr, N. L., & Bruun, S. E. (1983). Dispensability of member effort and group motivation losses: Free-rider effects. *Journal of Personality and Social Psychology, 44,* 78–94.

Kerr, N. L., & Huang, J. Y. (1986). Jury verdicts: How much difference does one juror make? *Personality and Social Psychology Bulletin, 12,* 325–343.

Kerr, N. L., & Kaufman-Gilliland, C. M. (1994). Communication, commitment, and cooperation in social dilemmas. *Journal of Personality and Social Psychology, 66,* 513–529.

Kerr, N. L., & MacCoun, R. J. (1985). The effects of jury size and polling method on the process and product of jury deliberation. *Journal of Personality and Social Psychology, 48,* 349–363.

Kerr, N. L., MacCoun, R. J., & Kramer, G. P. (1996a). Bias in judgment: Comparing individuals and groups. *Psychological Review, 103,* 687–719.

Kerr, N. L., MacCoun, R. J., & Kramer, G. P. (1996b). "When are *N* heads better (or worse) than one?": Biased judgment in individuals and groups. In E. H. Witte & J. H. Davis (Eds.), *Understanding group behavior: Consensual action by small groups* (Vol. 1, pp.105–136). Mahwah, NJ: Erlbaum.

Kerr, N. L., & Tindale, R. S. (2004). Group performance and decision making. *Annual Review of Psychology, 55,* 623–655.

Kerr, S., & Jermier, J. M. (1978). Substitutes for leadership: Their meaning and measurement. *Organizational Behavior and Human Performance, 22,* 375–403.

Kerr, S., Schriesheim, C. A., Murphy, C. J., & Stogdill, R. M. (1974). Toward a contingency theory of leadership based upon the consideration and initiating structure literature. *Organizational Behavior and Human Performance, 12,* 62–82.

Kessler, T., & Mummendey, A. (2001). Is there any scapegoat around? Determinants of intergroup conflicts at different categorization levels. *Journal of Personality and Social Psychology, 81,* 1090–1102.

Keyton, J. (2002). *Communicating in groups: Building relationships for effective decision making.* New York: McGraw-Hill.

Kiesler, C. A., & Corbin, L. H. (1965). Commitment, attraction, and conformity. *Journal of Personality and Social Psychology, 2,* 890–895.

Kiesler, C. A., & Kiesler, S. B. (1976). *Conformity* (2nd ed.). Reading, MA: Addison-Wesley.

Kiesler, C. A., Zanna, M., & Desalvo, J. (1966). Deviation and conformity: Opinion change as a function of commitment, attraction, and presence of a deviate. *Journal of Personality and Social Psychology, 3,* 458–467.

Kiesler, D. J. (1991). Interpersonal methods of assessment and diagnosis. In C. R. Snyder & D. R. Forsyth (Eds.), *Handbook of social and clinical psychology: The health perspective* (pp. 438–468). New York: Pergamon Press.

Kiesler, S., Siegel, J., & McGuire, T. W. (1984). Social psychological aspects of computer-mediated communication. *American Psychologist, 39,* 1123–1134.

Kiesler, S., Sproull, L., & Waters, K. (1996). A prisoner's dilemma experiment on cooperation with people and human-like computers. *Journal of Personality and Social Psychology, 70,* 47–65.

Kilham, W., & Mann, L. (1974). Level of destructive obedience as a function of transmitter and executant roles in the Milgram obedience paradigm. *Journal of Personality and Social Psychology, 29,* 696–702.

Kilmartin, C. T. (1994). *The masculine self.* New York: Macmillan.

Kim, H., & Markus, H. R. (1999). Deviance or uniqueness, harmony or conformity? A cultural analysis. *Journal of Personality and Social Psychology, 77,* 785–800.

Kim, K., & Bonk, C. J. (2002). Cross-cultural comparisons of online collaboration. *Journal of Computer-Mediated Communication, 8.* Retrieved August 28, 2004, from http://www.ascusc.org/jcmc/vol8/issue1/kimandbonk.html

King, G. A., & Sorrentino, R. M. (1983). Psychological dimensions of goal-oriented interpersonal situations. *Journal of Personality and Social Psychology, 44,* 140–162.

King, L. A. (2004). Measures and meaning: The use of qualitative data in social and personality psychology. In C. Sansone, C. C. Morf, & A. T. Panter (Eds.), *The Sage handbook of methods in social psychology* (pp. 173–194). Thousand Oaks, CA: Sage.

King, L. A., & King, D. W. (1990). Role conflict and role ambiguity: A critical assessment of construct validity. *Psychological Bulletin, 107,* 48–64.

Kipnis, D. (1974). *The powerholders.* Chicago: University of Chicago Press.

Kipnis, D. (1984). The use of power in organizations and in interpersonal settings. *Applied Social Psychology Annual, 5,* 179–210.

Kipnis, D., Castell, P. J., Gergen, M., & Mauch, D. (1976). Metamorphic effects of power. *Journal of Applied Psychology, 61,* 127–135.

Kipnis, D., & Consentino, J. (1969). Use of leadership powers in industry. *Journal of Applied Psychology, 53,* 460–466.

Kipper, D. A., & Ritchie, T. D. (2003). The effectiveness of psychodramatic techniques: A meta-analysis. *Group Dynamics, 7,* 13–25.

Kirkpatrick, L. A., & Shaver, P. (1988). Fear and affiliation reconsidered from a stress and coping perspective: The importance of cognitive clarity and fear reduction. *Journal of Social and Clinical Psychology, 7,* 214–233.

Kirkpatrick, S. A., & Locke, E. A. (1991). Leadership: Do traits matter? *Academy of Management Executive, 5*(2), 48–60.

Kirshner, B. J., Dies, R. R., & Brown, R. A. (1978). Effects of experimental manipulation of self-disclosure on group cohesiveness. *Journal of Consulting and Clinical Psychology, 46,* 1171–1177.

Kitayama, S. (2002). Culture and basic psychological theory—Toward a system view of culture: Comment on Oyserman et al. (2002). *Psychological Bulletin, 128,* 89–96.

Kivlighan, D. M., Jr. (1985). Feedback in group psychotherapy: Review and implications. *Small Group Behavior, 16,* 373–386.

Kivlighan, D. M., Jr. (1997). Leader behavior and therapeutic gain: An application of situational leadership theory. *Group Dynamics, 1,* 32–38.

Kivlighan, D. M., Jr., & Goldfine, D. C. (1991). Endorsement of therapeutic factors as a function of stage of group development and participant interpersonal attitudes. *Journal of Counseling Psychology, 38,* 150–158.

Kivlighan, D. M., Jr., McGovern, T.V., & Corazzini, J. G. (1984). Effects of content and timing of structuring interventions on group therapy process and outcome. *Journal of Counseling Psychology, 31,* 363–370.

Kivlighan, D. M., Jr., & Mullison, D. (1988). Participants' perception of therapeutic factors in group counseling: The role of interpersonal style and stage of group development. *Small Group Behavior, 19,* 452–468.

Kivlighan, D. M., Jr., Multon, K. D., & Brossart, D. F. (1996). Helpful impacts in group counseling: Development of a multidimensional rating system. *Journal of Counseling Psychology, 43,* 347–355.

Kivlighan, D. M., Jr., & Tarrant, J. M. (2001). Does group climate mediate the group leadership–group member outcome relationship? A test of Yalom's hypotheses about leadership priorities. *Group Dynamics, 5,* 220–234.

Klausner, E. J., Snyder, C. R., & Cheavens, J. (2000). A hope-based group treatment for depressed older adult outpatients. In G. M. Williamson, D. R. Shaffer, & P. A. Parmelee (Eds.), *Physical illness and depression in older adults: A handbook of theory, research, and practice* (pp. 295–310). Dordrecht, Netherlands: Kluwer Academic.

Klein, K. J., Conn, A. B., Smith, D. B., & Sorra, J. S. (2001). Is everyone in agreement? An exploration of within-group agreement in employee perceptions of the work environment. *Journal of Applied Psychology, 86,* 3–16.

Kleinpenning, G., & Hagendoorn, L. (1993). Forms of racism and the cumulative dimension of ethnic attitudes. *Social Psychology Quarterly, 56,* 21–36.

Klenke, K. (1996). *Women and leadership: A contextual perspective.* New York: Springer Verlag.

Klimoski, R., & Mohammed, S. (1994). Team mental model: Construct or metaphor? *Journal of Management, 20,* 403–437.

Knight, G. P., & Dubro, A. F. (1984). Cooperative, competitive, and individualistic social values: An individualized regression and clustering approach. *Journal of Personality and Social Psychology, 46,* 98–105.

Knight, H. C. (1921). *A comparison of the reliability of group and individual judgment.* Unpublished master's thesis. New York: Columbia University.

Knowles, E. S. (1973). Boundaries around group interaction: The effect of group size and member status on boundary permeability. *Journal of Personality and Social Psychology, 26,* 327–331.

Knowles, E. S. (1980). An affiliative conflict theory of personal and group spatial behavior. In P. B. Paulus (Ed.), *Psychology of group influence* (pp. 133–188). Mahwah, NJ: Erlbaum.

Knowles, E. S., & Bassett, R. L. (1976). Groups and crowds as social entities: The effects of activity, size, and member similarity on nonmembers. *Journal of Personality and Social Psychology, 34,* 837–845.

Knowles, E. S., & Brickner, M. A. (1981). Social cohesion effects on spatial cohesion. *Personality and Social Psychology Bulletin, 7,* 309–313.

Knowles, E. S., & Condon, C. A. (1999). Why people say "yes":

A dual-process theory of acquiescence. *Journal of Personality and Social Psychology, 77,* 379–386.

Knowles, E. S., Kreuser, B., Haas, S., Hyde, M., & Schuchart, G. E. (1976). Group size and the extension of social space boundaries. *Journal of Personality and Social Psychology, 33,* 647–654.

Kochan, T. A., Schmidt, S. M., & DeCotiis, T. A. (1975). Superior–subordinate relations: Leadership and headship. *Human Relations, 28,* 279–294.

Köhler, O. (1926). Kraftleistungen bei Einzel- und Gruppenarbeit [Effort in individual and group work]. *Industrielle Psychotechnik, 3,* 274–282.

Kolb, D. M., & Williams, J. (2003). *Everyday negotiation: Navigating the hidden agendas in bargaining.* San Francisco: Jossey-Bass.

Komorita, S. S., Hilty, J. A., & Parks, C. D. (1991). Reciprocity and cooperation in social dilemmas. *Journal of Conflict Resolution, 35,* 494–518.

Komorita, S. S., & Parks, C. D. (1994). *Social dilemmas.* Dubuque, IA: Brown & Benchmark.

Komorita, S. S., Parks, C. D., & Hulbert, L. G. (1992). Reciprocity and the induction of cooperation in social dilemmas. *Journal of Personality and Social Psychology, 62,* 607–617.

Korda, M. (1975). *Power! How to get it, how to use it.* New York: Ballantine.

Kounin, J. S. (1970). *Discipline and group management in classrooms.* New York: Holt, Rinehart & Winston.

Kounin, J. S., & Gump, P. V. (1958). The ripple effect in discipline. *Elementary School Journal, 59,* 158–162.

Kowalski, R. M. (1996). Complaints and complaining: Functions, antecedents, and consequences. *Psychological Bulletin, 119,* 179–196.

Kowalski, R. M., & Wolfe, R. (1994). Collective identity orientation, patriotism, and reactions to national outcomes. *Personality and Social Psychology Bulletin, 20,* 533–540.

Kowert, P. A. (2002). *Groupthink or deadlock: When do leaders learn from their advisors?* Albany: State University of New York Press.

Kozlowski, S. W. J., & Bell, B. S. (2003). Work groups and teams in organizations. In W. C. Borman, D. R. Ilgen, R. J. Klimoski, & I. B. Weiner (Eds.), *Handbook of psychology: Industrial and organizational psychology* (Vol. 12, pp. 333–376). New York: Wiley.

Krackhardt, D. (2003). *KrackPlot: A social network visualization program.* Retrieved August 23, 2004, from http://www.andrew.cmu.edu/user/krack/krackplot/krackindex.html

Krackhardt, D., & Kilduff, M. (1999). Whether close or far: Social distance effects on perceived balance in friendship networks. *Journal of Personality and Social Psychology, 76,* 770–782.

Krackhardt, D., & Porter, L. W. (1986). The snowball effect: Turnover embedded in communication networks. *Journal of Applied Psychology, 71,* 50–55.

Krakauer, J. (1997). *Into thin air.* New York: Random House.

Kramer, M. W., Kuo, C. L., & Dailey, J. C. (1997). The impact of brainstorming techniques on subsequent group processes: Beyond generating ideas. *Small Group Research, 28,* 218–242.

Kramer, R. M. (1998). Paranoid cognition in social systems: Thinking and acting in the shadow of doubt. *Personality and Social Psychology Review, 2,* 251–275.

Kraus, L. A., Davis, M. H., Bazzini, D. G., Church, M., & Kirchman, C. M. (1993). Personal and social influences on loneliness: The mediating effect of social provisions. *Social Psychology Quarterly, 56,* 37–53.

Krause, C. A. (1978). *Guyana massacre: The eyewitness account.* New York: Berkley.

Krauss, R. M., & Chiu, C. (1998). Language and social behavior. In D. T. Gilbert, S. T. Fiske, & G. Lindzey (Eds.), *The handbook of social psychology* (4th ed., Vol. 2, pp. 41–88). New York: McGraw-Hill.

Krauss, R. M., & Morsella, E. (2000). Communication and conflict. In M. Deutsch & P. T. Coleman (Eds.), *The handbook of conflict resolution: Theory and practice* (pp. 131–143). San Francisco: Jossey-Bass.

Kraut, R. E., Egido, C., & Galegher, J. (1990). Patterns of contact and communication in scientific research collaboration. In J. Galegher, R. E. Kraut, & C. Egido (Eds.), *Intellectual teamwork: Social and technological foundations of cooperative work* (pp. 149–171). Mahwah, NJ: Erlbaum.

Kravitz, D. A., Cohen, J. L., Martin, B., Sweeney, J., McCarty, J., Elliott, E., & Goldstein, P. (1978). Humans would do better without other humans. *Personality and Social Psychology Bulletin, 4,* 559–560.

Kravitz, D. A., & Martin, B. (1986). Ringelmann rediscovered: The original article. *Journal of Personality and Social Psychology, 50,* 936–941.

Kressel, K. (2000). Mediation. In M. Deutsch & P. T. Coleman (Eds.), *The handbook of conflict resolution: Theory and practice* (pp. 522–545). San Francisco: Jossey-Bass.

Krueger, J. (2000). The projective perception of the social world: A building block of social comparison processes. In J. Suls & L. Wheeler (Eds.), *Handbook of social comparison: Theory and research* (pp. 323–351). New York: Kluwer Academic/Plenum.

Krueger, J., & Clement, R. W. (1997). Estimates of social consensus by majorities and minorities: The case for social projection. *Personality and Social Psychology Review, 1,* 299–312.

Kruglanski, A. W., Shah, J. Y., Pierro, A., & Mannetti, L. (2002). When similarity breeds content: Need for closure and the allure of homogeneous and self-resembling groups. *Journal of Personality and Social Psychology, 83,* 648–662.

Kruglanski, A. W., & Webster, D. M. (1991). Group members' reactions to opinion deviates and conformists at varying degrees of proximity to decision deadline and of environmental noise. *Journal of Personality and Social Psychology, 61,* 212–225.

Kuhn, T. S. (1970). *The structure of scientific revolutions* (2nd ed.). Chicago: University of Chicago Press.

Kulic, K. R., Horne, A. M., & Dagley, J. C. (2004). A comprehensive review of prevention groups for children and adolescents. *Group Dynamics, 8,* 139–151.

Kulik, J. A., & Mahler, H. I. M. (1989). Stress and affiliation in a hospital setting: Preoperative roommate preference. *Personality and Social Psychology Bulletin, 15,* 183–193.

Kulik, J. A., & Mahler, H. I. M. (2000). Social comparison, affiliation, and emotional contagion under threat. In J. Suls & L. Wheeler (Eds.), *Handbook of social comparison: Theory and research* (pp. 295–320). New York: Kluwer Academic/Plenum.

Kulik, J. A., Mahler, H. I. M., & Moore, P. J. (1996). Social comparison and affiliation under threat: Effects on recovery from major surgery. *Journal of Personality and Social Psychology, 71,* 967–979.

Kurland, N. B., & Pelled, L. H. (2000). Passing the word: Toward a model of gossip and power in the workplace. *Academy of Management Review, 25,* 428–438.

Kushnir, T. (1984). Social psychological factors associated with the dissolution of dyadic business partnerships. *Journal of Social Psychology, 122,* 181–188.

Kuypers, B. C., Davies, D., & Glaser, K. H. (1986). Developmental arrestations in self-analytic groups. *Small Group Behavior, 17,* 269–302.

Kuypers, B. C., Davies, D., & Hazewinkel, A. (1986). Developmental patterns in self-analytic groups. *Human Relations, 39,* 793–815.

Kwan, V. S. Y., Bond, M. H., Boucher, H. C., Maslach, C., & Gan, Y. (2002). The construct of individuation: More complex in collectivist than in individualist cultures. *Personality and Social Psychology Bulletin, 28,* 300–310.

La Gaipa, J. J. (1977). Interpersonal attraction and social exchange. In S. Duck (Ed.), *Theory and practice in interpersonal attraction* (pp. 129–164). New York: Academic Press.

LaBarge, E., Von Dras, D., & Wingbermuehle, C. (1998). An analysis of themes and feelings from a support group for people with Alzheimer's disease. *Psychotherapy: Theory, Research, Practice, Training, 35,* 537–544.

Lacoursiere, R. B. (1980). *The life cycle of groups.* New York: Human Sciences Press.

LaFrance, M. (1985). Postural mirroring and intergroup relations. *Personality and Social Psychology Bulletin, 11,* 207–217.

Laing, R. D. (1960). *The divided self.* London: Tavistock.

Lakin, M. (1972). *Experiential groups: The uses of interpersonal encounter, psychotherapy groups, and sensitivity training.* Morristown, N.J.: General Learning Press.

Lal Goel, M. (1980). Conventional political participation. In D. H. Smith, J. Macaulay, & Associates (Eds.), *Participation in social and political activities: A comprehensive analysis of political involvement, expressive leisure time, and helping behavior* (pp. 108–132). San Francisco: Jossey-Bass.

Lalonde, R. N. (1992). The dynamics of group differentiation in the face of defeat. *Personality and Social Psychology Bulletin, 18,* 336–342.

Lam, S. K., & Schaubroeck, J. (2000). Improving group decisions by better pooling information: A comparative advantage of group decision support systems. *Journal of Applied Psychology, 85,* 565–573.

Lambert, A. J., Cronen, S., Chasteen, A. L., & Lickel, B. (1996). Private vs. public expressions of racial prejudice. *Journal of Experimental Social Psychology, 32,* 437–459.

Lambert, A. J., Payne, B. K., Jacoby, L. L., Shaffer, L. M., Chasteen, A. L., & Khan, S. R. (2003). Stereotypes as dominant responses: On the "social facilitation" of prejudice in anticipated public contexts. *Journal of Personality and Social Psychology, 84,* 277–295.

Lamm, H., & Myers, D. G. (1978). Group-induced polarization of attitudes and behavior. *Advances in Experimental Social Psychology, 11,* 145–195.

Landau, J. (1995). The relationship of race and gender to managers' ratings of promotion potential. *Journal of Organizational Behavior, 16,* 391–401.

Landsberger, H. A. (1958). *Hawthorne revisited.* Ithaca, NY: Cornell University Press.

Langfred, C. W. (1998). Is group cohesiveness a double-edged sword? An investigation of the effects of cohesiveness on performance. *Small Group Research, 29,* 124–143.

Lanzetta, J. T., & Roby, T. B. (1960). The relationship between certain group process variables and group problem-solving efficiency. *Journal of Social Psychology, 52,* 135–148.

LaPiere, R. (1938). *Collective behavior.* New York: McGraw-Hill.

Larsen, K. S. (1982). Cultural conditions and conformity: The Asch effect. *Bulletin of the British Psychological Society, 35,* 347.

Larson, C. E., & Lafasto, F. M. J. (2001). *Teamwork: What must go right/what can go wrong* (2nd ed.). Thousand Oaks, CA: Sage.

Larson, J. R., & Christensen, C. (1993). Groups as problem solving units: Toward a new meaning of social cognition. *British Journal of Social Psychology, 32,* 5–30.

Larson, J. R., Jr., Christensen, C., & Abbott, A. S., & Franz, T. M. (1996). Diagnosing groups: Charting the flow of information in medical decision-making teams. *Journal of Personality and Social Psychology, 71,* 315–330.

Larson, J. R., Jr., Foster-Fishman, P. G., & Keys, C. B. (1994). The discussion of shared and unshared information in decision-making groups. *Journal of Personality and Social Psychology, 67,* 446–461.

Larson, L. L., Hunt, J. G., & Osborn, R. N. (1976). The great Hi-Hi leader behavior myth: A lesson from Occam's Razor. *Academy of Management Journal, 19,* 628.

Latané, B. (1981). The psychology of social impact. *American Psychologist, 36,* 343–356.

Latané, B. (1996). Strength from weakness: The fate of opinion minorities in spatially distributed groups. In E. Witte & J. Davis (Eds.), *Understanding group behavior: Consensual action by small groups* (Vol. 1, pp. 193–219). Mahwah, NJ: Erlbaum.

Latané, B. (1997). Dynamic social impact: The societal consequences of human interaction. In C. McGarty & S. A. Haslam (Eds.), *The message of social psychology: Perspectives on mind and society* (pp. 200–220). Malden, MA: Blackwell.

Latané, B., & Bourgeois, M. J. (1996). Experimental evidence for dynamic social impact: The emergence of subcultures in electronic groups. *Journal of Communication, 46*(4), 35–47.

Latané, B., & Bourgeois, M. J. (2001). Dynamic social impact and the consolidation, clustering, correlation, and continuing diversity of culture. In M. A. Hogg & R. S. Tindale (Eds.), *Blackwell handbook of social psychology: Group processes* (pp. 235–258). Malden, MA: Blackwell.

Latané, B., & Darley, J. M. (1970). *The unresponsive bystander: Why doesn't he help?* New York: Appleton-Century-Crofts.

Latané, B., & Nida, S. A. (1981). Ten years of research on group size and helping. *Psychological Bulletin, 89,* 308–324.

Latané, B., Williams, K., & Harkins, S. (1979). Many hands make light the work: The causes and consequences of social loafing. *Journal of Personality and Social Psychology, 37,* 822–832.

Latané, B., & Wolf, S. (1981). The social impact of majorities and minorities. *Psychological Review, 88,* 438–453.

Latham, G. P., & Baldes, J. J. (1975). The "practical significance" of Locke's theory of goal settings. *Journal of Applied Psychology, 60,* 122–124.

LaTour, S. (1978). Determinants of participant and observer satisfaction with adversary and inquisitorial modes of adjudication. *Journal of Personality and Social Psychology, 36,* 1531–1545.

LaTour, S., Houlden, P., Walker, L., & Thibaut, J. (1976). Some determinants of preference for modes of conflict resolution. *Journal of Conflict Resolution, 20,* 319–356.

Laughlin, P. R. (1980). Social combination processes of cooperative problem solving groups on verbal intellective tasks. In M. Fishbein (Ed.), *Progress in social psychology* (pp. 127–155). Mahwah, NJ: Erlbaum.

Laughlin, P. R. (1996). Group decision making and collective induction. In E. Witte & J. Davis (Eds.), *Understanding group behavior: Consensual action by small groups* (Vol. 1, pp. 61–103). Mahwah, NJ: Erlbaum.

Laughlin, P. R. (1999). Collective induction: Twelve postulates. *Organizational Behavior and Human Decision Processes, 80,* 50–69.

Laughlin, P. R., Bonner, B. L., & Miner, A. G. (2002). Groups perform better than the best individuals on letters-to-numbers problems. *Organizational Behavior and Human Decision Processes, 88,* 605–620.

Laughlin, P. R., & Hollingshead, A. B. (1995). A theory of collective induction. *Organizational Behavior and Human Decision Processes, 61,* 94–107.

Laughlin, P. R., Zander, M. L., Knievel, E. M., & Tan, T. K. (2003). Groups perform better than the best individuals on letters-to-numbers problems: Informative equations and effective strategies. *Journal of Personality and Social Psychology, 85,* 684–694.

Lawler, E. J. (1975). An experimental study of factors affecting the mobilization of revolutionary coalitions. *Sociometry, 38,* 163–179.

Lawler, E. J., Ford, R. S., & Blegen, M. A. (1988). Coercive capability in conflict: A test of bilateral deterrence versus conflict spiral theory. *Social Psychology Quarterly, 51,* 93–107.

Lawler, E. J., & Thompson, M. E. (1978). Impact of a leader's responsibility for inequity on subordinate revolts. *Social Psychology Quarterly, 41,* 264–268.

Lawler, E. J., & Thompson, M. E. (1979). Subordinate response to a leader's cooptation strategy as a function of type of coalition power. *Representative Research in Social Psychology, 9,* 69–80.

Lawler, E. J., & Yoon, J. (1996). Commitment in exchange relations: Test of a theory of relational cohesion. *American Sociological Review, 61,* 89–108.

Lawrence, B. S. (1996). Organizational age norms: Why is it so hard to know one when you see one? *Gerontologist, 36,* 209–220.

Lawrence, R. J. (2002). Healthy residential environments. In R. B. Bechtel & A. Churchman (Eds.), *Handbook of environmental psychology* (pp. 394–412). New York: Wiley. Retrieved July 29, 2004, from http://www.netlibrary.com

Layne, C. M., Pynoos, R. S., Saltzman, W. R., Arslanagic, B., Black, M., Savjak, N., Popovic, T., Durakovic, E., Mušic, M., Campara, N., Djapo, N., & Houston, R. (2001). Trauma/grief-focused group psychotherapy: School-based postwar intervention with traumatized Bosnian adolescents. *Group Dynamics, 5,* 277–290.

Lazarsfeld, P. F., & Merton, R. K. (1954). Friendship as a social process: A substantive and methodological analysis. In M. Berger, T. Abel, & C. H. Page (Eds.), *Freedom and control in modern society* (pp. 18–66). New York: Van Nostrand.

Le Bon, G. (1960). *The crowd: A study of the popular mind [La psychologie des foules].* New York: Viking Press. (Original work published in 1895)

Lea, M., & Spears, R. (1991). Computer-mediated communication, de-individuation, and group decision-making. In S. Greenberg (Ed.), *Computer-supported cooperative work and groupware* (pp. 155–174). New York: Harcourt Brace Jovanovich.

Leach, C. W., Spears, R., Branscombe, N. R., & Doosje, B. (2003). Malicious pleasure: Schadenfreude at the suffering of another group. *Journal of Personality and Social Psychology, 84,* 932–943.

Leary, M. R. (1983). *Understanding social anxiety.* Thousand Oaks, CA: Sage.

Leary, M. R. (1990). Responses to social exclusion: Social anxiety, jealousy, loneliness, depression, and low self-esteem. *Journal of Social and Clinical Psychology, 9,* 221–229.

Leary, M. R. (2001). Shyness and the self: Attentional, motivational, and cognitive self-processes in social anxiety and inhibition. In W. R. Crozier & L. E. Alden (Eds.), *International handbook of social anxiety: Concepts, research, and interventions relating to the self and shyness* (pp. 217–234). New York: Wiley.

Leary, M. R., & Baumeister, R. F. (2000). The nature and function of self-esteem: Sociometer theory. *Advances in Experimental Social Psychology, 32,* 1–62.

Leary, M. R., & Forsyth, D. R. (1987). Attributions of responsibility for collective endeavors. *Review of Personality and Social Psychology, 8,* 167–188.

Leary, M. R., & Kowalski, R. M. (1995). *Social anxiety.* New York: Guilford Press.

Leary, M. R., Rogers, P. A., Canfield, R. W., & Coe, C. (1986). Boredom in interpersonal encounters: Antecedents and social implications. *Journal of Personality and Social Psychology, 51,* 968–975.

Leary, M. R., Tambor, E. S., Terdal, S. K., & Downs, D. L. (1995). Self-esteem as an interpersonal monitor: The sociometer hypothesis. *Journal of Personality and Social Psychology, 68,* 518–530.

Leary, M. R., Wheeler, D. S., & Jenkins, T. B. (1986). Aspects of identity and behavioral preferences: Studies of occupational and recreational choice. *Social Psychology Quarterly, 49,* 11–18.

Leavitt, H. J. (1951). Some effects of certain communication patterns on group performance. *Journal of Abnormal and Social Psychology, 46,* 38–50.

Lee, E., & Nass, C. (2002). Experimental tests of normative group influence and representation effects in computer-mediated communication: When interacting via computers differs from interacting with computers. *Human Communication Research, 28,* 349–381.

Lee, M. T., & Ofshe, R. (1981). The impact of behavioral style and status characteristics on social influence: A test of two competing theories. *Social Psychology Quarterly, 44,* 73–82.

Lee, P. W. H., Leung, P. W. L., Fung, A. S. M., & Low, L. C. K. (1996). An episode of syncope attacks in adolescent schoolgirls: Investigations, intervention and outcome. *British Journal of Medical Psychology, 69,* 247–257.

Lee-Chai, A. Y., & Bargh, J. A. (Eds.). (2001). *The use and abuse of power: Multiple perspectives on the causes of corruption.* New York: Psychology Press.

Leffler, A., Gillespie, D. L., & Conaty, J. C. (1982). The effects of status differentiation on nonverbal behavior. *Social Psychology Quarterly, 45,* 153–161.

Leichtentritt, J., & Shechtman, Z. (1998). Therapist, trainee, and child verbal response modes in child group therapy. *Group Dynamics, 2,* 36–47.

Leon, G. R. (1991). Individual and group process characteristics of polar expedition teams. *Environment and Behavior, 23,* 723–748.

Leonard, W. M., II. (1980). *A sociological perspective on sport.* Minneapolis: Burgess.

Lepore, S. J., Evans, G. W., & Schneider, M. L. (1991). Dynamic role of social support in the link between chronic stress and psychological distress. *Journal of Personality and Social Psychology, 61,* 899–909.

Lepsius, M. R. (1986). Charismatic leadership: Max Weber's model and its applicability to the rule of Hitler. In C. F. Graumann & S. Moscovici (Eds.), *Changing conceptions of leadership* (pp. 53–66). New York: Springer Verlag.

Leung, K. (1988). Some determinants of conflict avoidance. *Journal of Cross-Cultural Psychology, 19,* 125–136.

Leung, K. (1997). Negotiation and reward allocations across cultures. In P. C. Earley & M. Erez (Eds.), *New perspectives on international industrial/organizational psychology* (pp. 640–675). San Francisco: New Lexington Press/Jossey-Bass.

Leventhal, G. S., Karuza, J., & Fry, W. R. (1980). Beyond fairness: A theory of allocation preferences. In G. Mikula (Ed.), *Justice and social interaction* (pp. 167–218). New York: Springer Verlag.

Leventhal, G. S., & Lane, D. W. (1970). Sex, age, and equity behavior. *Journal of Personality and Social Psychology, 15,* 312–316.

Levesque, M. J. (1997). Meta-accuracy among acquainted individuals: A social relations analysis of interpersonal perception and metaperception. *Journal of Personality and Social Psychology, 72,* 66–74.

Levine, D. I., & D'Andrea Tyson, L. (1990). Participation, productivity, and the firm's environment. In A. S. Blinder (Ed.), *Paying for productivity* (pp. 183–237). Washington, DC: Brookings Institute.

Levine, J. M. (1980). Reaction to opinion deviance in small groups. In P. B. Paulus (Ed.), *Psychology of group influence* (pp. 375–429). Mahwah, NJ: Erlbaum.

Levine, J. M., & Moreland, R. L. (1990). Progress in small group research. *Annual Review of Psychology, 41,* 585–634.

Levine, J. M., & Moreland, R. L. (1995). Group processes. In A. Tesser (Ed.), *Advanced social psychology* (pp. 419–465). New York: McGraw-Hill.

Levine, J. M., & Moreland, R. L. (1998). Small groups. In D. T. Gilbert, S. T. Fiske, & G. Lindzey (Eds.), *The handbook of social psychology* (4th ed., Vol. 2, pp. 415–469). New York: McGraw-Hill.

Levine, J. M., Moreland, R. L., & Choi, H. (2001). Group socialization and newcomer innovation. In M. A. Hogg & R. S. Tindale (Eds.), *Blackwell handbook of social psychology: Group processes* (pp. 86–106). Malden, MA: Blackwell.

Levine, J. M., & Russo, E. M. (1987). Majority and minority influence. *Review of Personality and Social Psychology, 8,* 13–54.

Levine, J. M., & Thompson, L. (1996). Conflict in groups. In E. T. Higgins & A. W. Kruglanski (Eds.), *Social psychology: Handbook of basic principles* (pp. 745–776). New York: Guilford Press.

LeVine, R. A., & Campbell, D. T. (1972). *Ethnocentrism: Theories of conflict, ethnic attitudes, and group behavior.* New York: Wiley.

Levine, S. (1996, March). *The psychobiological consequences of social behavior.* Paper presented at the New York Academy of Sciences Conference on the Integrative Neurobiology of Affiliation, Washington, DC.

Levine, S. V. (1984). Radical departures. *Psychology Today, 18*(8), 21–27.

Levinger, G., Senn, D. J., & Jorgensen, B. W. (1970). Progress toward permanence in courtship: A test of the Kerckhoff-Davis hypothesis. *Sociometry, 33,* 427–433.

Levy, B. (1996). Improving memory in old age through implicit self-stereotyping. *Journal of Personality and Social Psychology, 71,* 1092–1107.

Levy, L. H. (2000). Self-help groups. In J. Rappaport & E. Seidman (Eds.), *Handbook of community psychology* (pp. 591–613). Dordrecht, Netherlands: Kluwer Academic.

Lewin, K. (1936). *Principles of topological psychology.* New York: McGraw-Hill.

Lewin, K. (1943). Forces behind food habits and methods of change. *Bulletin of the National Research Council, 108,* 35–65.

Lewin, K. (1946). Action research and minority problems. *Journal of Social Issues, 2*(4), 34–46.

Lewin, K. (1947). Frontiers in group dynamics. *Human Relations, 1,* 143–153.

Lewin, K. (1948). *Resolving social conflicts: Selected papers on group dynamics.* New York: Harper.

Lewin, K. (1951). *Field theory in social science.* New York: Harper.

Lewin, K., Dembo, T., Festinger, L., & Sears, P. S. (1944). Level of aspiration. In J. M. Hunt (Ed.), *Personality and the behavior disorders* (pp. 333–378). New York: Ronald Press.

Lewin, K., Lippitt, R., & White, R. (1939). Patterns of aggressive behavior in experimentally created "social climates." *Journal of Social Psychology, 10,* 271–299.

Lewis, H. S. (1974). *Leaders and followers: Some anthropological perspectives.* Reading, MA: Addison-Wesley.

Ley, D., & Cybriwsky, R. (1974a). The spatial ecology of stripped cars. *Environment and Behavior, 6,* 53–68.

Ley, D., & Cybriwsky, R. (1974b). Urban graffiti as territorial markers. *Annals of the Association of American Geographers, 64,* 491–505.

Leyens, J., & Corneille, O. (1999). Asch's social psychology: Not as social as you may think. *Personality and Social Psychology Review, 3,* 345–357.

Leyens, J., Cortes, B., Demoulin, S., Dovidio, J. F., Fiske, S. T., Gaunt, R., Paladino, M., Rodriguez-Perez, A., Rodriguez-Torres, R., & Vaes, J. (2003). Emotional prejudice, essentialism, and nationalism: The 2002 Tajfel Lecture. *European Journal of Social Psychology, 33,* 703–717.

Lickel, B., Hamilton, D. L., Wieczorkowska, G., Lewis, A., Sherman, S. J., & Uhles, A. N. (2000). Varieties of groups and the perception of group entitativity. *Journal of Personality and Social Psychology, 78,* 223–246.

Lieberman, M. A. (1993). Self-help groups. In H. I. Kaplan & M. J. Sadock (Eds.), *Comprehensive group psychotherapy* (3rd ed., pp. 292–304). Baltimore: Williams & Wilkins.

Lieberman, M. A. (1994). Growth groups in the 1980s: Mental health implications. In A. Fuhriman & G. M. Burlingame (Eds.), *Handbook of group psychotherapy* (pp. 527–558). New York: Wiley.

Lieberman, M. A., & Golant, M. (2002). Leader behaviors as perceived by cancer patients in professionally directed support groups and outcomes. *Group Dynamics, 6,* 267–276.

Lieberman, M. A., Yalom, I., & Miles, M. (1973). *Encounter groups: First facts.* New York: Basic Books.

Liefooghe, A. P. D., & Davey, K. M. (2001). Accounts of workplace bullying: The role of the organization. *European Journal of Work and Organizational Psychology, 10,* 375–392.

Liese, B. S., Beck, A. T., & Seaton, K. (2002). The cognitive therapy addictions group. In D. Brook & H. Spitz (Eds.), *The group therapy of substance abuse* (pp. 37–57). New York: Haworth Press.

Likert, R. (1967). *The human organization.* New York: McGraw-Hill.

Lind, E. A., Kanfer, R., & Earley, P. C. (1990). Voice, control, and procedural justice: Instrumental and noninstrumental concerns in fairness judgments. *Journal of Personality and Social Psychology, 59,* 952–959.

Lindblom, C. E. (1965). *The intelligence of democracy.* New York: Free Press.

Lindeman, M. (1997). Ingroup bias, self-enhancement and group identification. *European Journal of Social Psychology, 27,* 337–355.

Lindholm, C. (1990). *Charisma.* Malden, MA: Blackwell.

Lindskold, S. (1978). Trust development, the GRIT proposal, and the effects of conciliatory acts on conflict and cooperation. *Psychological Bulletin, 85,* 772–793.

Lindskold, S. (1979). Conciliation with simultaneous or sequential interaction. *Journal of Conflict Resolution, 23,* 704–714.

Lindskold, S. (1986). GRIT: Reducing distrust through carefully introduced conciliation. In S. Worchel & W. G. Austin (Eds.), *Psychology of intergroup relations* (2nd ed., pp. 305–322). Chicago: Nelson-Hall.

Lindskold, S., Albert, K. P., Baer, R., & Moore, W. C. (1976). Territorial boundaries of interacting groups and passive audiences. *Sociometry, 39,* 71–76.

Lindskold, S., & Aronoff, J. R. (1980). Conciliatory strategies and relative power. *Journal of Experimental Social Psychology, 16,* 187–198.

Lindskold, S., & Finch, M. L. (1982). Anonymity and the resolution of conflicting pressures from the experimenter and from peers. *Journal of Psychology, 112,* 79–86.

Linville, P. W., & Fischer, G. W. (1998). Group variability and covariation: Effects on intergroup judgment and behavior. In C. Sedikides, J. Schopler, & C. A. Insko (Eds.), *Intergroup cognition and intergroup behavior* (pp. 123–150). Mahwah, NJ: Erlbaum.

Linville, P. W., Fischer, G. W., & Salovey, P. (1989). Perceived distributions of the characteristics of in-group and out-group members: Empirical evidence and a computer simulation. *Journal of Personality and Social Psychology, 57,* 165–188.

Lippmann, W. (1922). *Public opinion.* New York: Harcourt & Brace.

Lipset, S. M., & Wolin, S. S. (1965). *The Berkeley student revolt.* Garden City, NY: Anchor.

Litman-Adizes, T., Fontaine, G., & Raven, B. (1978). Consequences of social power and causal attribution for compliance as seen by powerholder and target. *Personality and Social Psychology Bulletin, 4,* 260–264.

Little, B. L., & Madigan, R. M. (1997). The relationship between collective efficacy and performance in manufacturing work teams. *Small Group Research, 28,* 517–534.

Littlepage, G. E. (1991). Effects of group size and task characteristics on group performance: A test of Steiner's model. *Personality and Social Psychology Bulletin, 17,* 449–456.

Littlepage, G. E., & Karau, S. J. (1997). Utility and limitations of the SHAPE-assisted intuitive decision-making procedure. *Group Dynamics, 1,* 200–207.

Littlepage, G. E., & Mueller, A. L. (1997). Recognition and utilization of expertise in problem-solving groups: Expert characteristics and behavior. *Group Dynamics, 1,* 324–328.

Littlepage, G. E., Robison, W., & Reddington, K. (1997). Effects of task experience and group experience on group performance, member ability, and recognition of expertise. *Organizational Behavior and Human Decision Processes, 69,* 133–147.

Littlepage, G. E., Schmidt, G. W., Whisler, E. W., & Frost, A. G. (1995). An input–process–output analysis of influence and performance in problem-solving groups. *Journal of Personality and Social Psychology, 69,* 877–889.

Littlepage, G. E., & Silbiger, H. (1992). Recognition of expertise in decision-making groups: Effects of group size and participation patterns. *Small Group Research, 23,* 344–355.

Liu, J. H., & Latané, B. (1998). Extremitization of attitudes: Does thought- and discussion-induced polarization cumulate? *Basic and Applied Social Psychology, 20,* 103–110.

Lloyd, C., Creson, D. L., & D'Antonio, M. S. (1993). A petrochemical plant disaster: Lessons for the future. *Journal of Social Behavior and Personality, 8,* 281–298.

Locke, E. A., Alavi, M., & Wagner, J. A., III (1997). Participation in decision making: An information exchange perspective. *Research in Personnel and Human Resources Management, 15,* 293–331.

Locke, E. A., & Latham, G. P. (1990). *A theory of goal-setting and task performance.* Upper Saddle River, NJ: Prentice Hall.

Locke, E. A., & Latham, G. P. (2002). Building a practically useful theory of goal setting and task motivation: A 35-year odyssey. *American Psychologist, 57,* 705–717.

Lockwood, P., & Kunda, Z. (1997). Superstars and me: Predicting the impact of role models on the self. *Journal of Personality and Social Psychology, 73,* 91–103.

Lodewijkx, H. F. M., & Syroit, J. E. M. M. (1997). Severity of initiation revisited: Does severity of initiation increase attractiveness in real groups? *European Journal of Social Psychology, 27,* 275–300.

Loehlin, J. C. (1997). A test of J. R. Harris's theory of peer influences on personality. *Journal of Personality and Social Psychology, 72,* 1197–1201.

Loewen, L. J., & Suedfeld, P. (1992). Cognitive and arousal effects of masking office noise. *Environment and Behavior, 24,* 381–395.

Lofland, J. (1981). Collective behavior: The elementary forms. In M. Rosenberg & R. H. Turner (Eds.), *Social psychology* (pp. 411–446). New York: Basic Books.

Lofland, L. H. (1995). Social interaction: Continuities and complexities in the study of nonintimate sociality. In K. S. Cook, G. A. Fine, & J. S. House (Eds.), *Sociological perspectives on social psychology* (pp. 176–202). Boston: Allyn & Bacon.

Lois, J. (1999). Socialization to heroism: Individualism and collectivism in a voluntary search and rescue group. *Social Psychology Quarterly, 62,* 117–135.

Long, C. R., Seburn, M., Averill, J. R., & More, T. A. (2003). Solitude experiences: Varieties, settings, and individual differences. *Personality and Social Psychology Bulletin, 29,* 578–583.

Long, S. (Ed.). (1988). *Six group therapies.* New York: Plenum Press.

Longley, J., & Pruitt, D. G. (1980). Groupthink: A critique of Janis's theory. *Review of Personality and Social Psychology, 1,* 74–93.

Lord, R. G. (1977). Functional leadership behavior: Measurement and relation to social power and leadership perceptions. *Administrative Science Quarterly, 22,* 114–133.

Lord, R. G. (1985). An information processing approach to social perceptions, leadership, and behavioral measurement in organizations. *Research in Organizational Behavior, 7,* 87–128.

Lord, R. G., & Alliger, G. M. (1985). A comparison of four information processing models of leadership and social perception. *Human Relations, 38,* 47–65.

Lord, R. G., Binning, J. F., Rush, M. C., & Thomas, J. C. (1978). The effect of performance cues and leader behavior on questionnaire ratings of leadership behavior. *Organizational Behavior and Human Performance, 21,* 27–39.

Lord, R. G., De Vader, C. L., & Alliger, G. M. (1986). A meta-analysis of the relation between personality traits and leadership perceptions: An application of validity generalization procedures. *Journal of Applied Psychology, 71,* 402–410.

Lord, R. G., Foti, R. J., & De Vader, C. L. (1984). A test of leadership categorization theory: Internal structure, information processing, and leadership perceptions. *Organization Behavior and Human Performance, 34,* 343–378.

Lord, R. G., & Maher, K. J. (1991). *Leadership and information processing: Linking perceptions and performance.* Boston: Unwin Hyman.

Lorge, I., Fox, D., Davitz, J., & Brenner, M. (1958). A survey of studies contrasting quality of group performance and individual performance, 1920–1957. *Psychological Bulletin, 55,* 337–372.

Lorge, I., & Solomon, H. (1955). Two models of group behavior in the solution of Eureka-type problems. *Psychometrika, 20,* 139–148.

Lott, A. J., & Lott, B. E. (1965). Group cohesiveness as interpersonal attraction: A review of relationships with antecedent and consequent variables. *Psychological Bulletin, 64,* 259–309.

Lott, B. (2002). Cognitive and behavioral distancing from the poor. *American Psychologist, 57*(2), 100–110.

Lovaglia, M. J., & Houser, J. A. (1996). Emotional reactions and status in groups. *American Sociological Review, 61,* 867–883.

Lovell, J., & Kluger, J. (1994). *Lost moon: The perilous journey of Apollo 13.* New York: Houghton Mifflin.

Lowe, K. B., Kroeck, K. G., & Sivasubramaniam, N. (1996). Effectiveness correlates of transformation and transactional leadership: A meta-analytic review of the MLQ literature. *Leadership Quarterly, 7,* 385–425.

Lucas, R. E., & Diener, E. (2001). Understanding extraverts' enjoyment of social situations: The importance of pleasantness. *Journal of Personality and Social Psychology, 81,* 343–356.

Lucas, R. E., Diener, E., Grob, A., Suh, E. M., & Shao, L. (2000). Cross-cultural evidence for the fundamental features of extraversion. *Journal of Personality and Social Psychology, 79,* 452–468.

Lucas, R. E., & Fujita, F. (2000). Factors influencing the relation between extraversion and pleasant affect. *Journal of Personality and Social Psychology, 79,* 1039–1056.

Luce, R. D., & Raiffa, H. (1957). *Games and decisions.* New York: Wiley.

Lueder, D. C. (1985a). Don't be misled by LEAD. *Journal of Applied Behavioral Science, 21,* 143–151.

Lueder, D. C. (1985b). A rejoinder to Dr. Hersey. *Journal of Applied Behavioral Science, 21,* 154.

Luft, J. (1984). *Groups process: An introduction to group dynamics* (3rd ed.). Palo Alto, CA: Mayfield.

Luhtanen, R., & Crocker, J. (1992). A collective self-esteem scale: Self-evaluation of one's social identity. *Personality and Social Psychology Bulletin, 18,* 302–318.

Luria, S. M. (1990). More about psychology and the military. *American Psychologist, 45,* 296–297.

Lutsky, N. (1995). When is "obedience" obedience? Conceptual and historical commentary. *Journal of Social Issues, 51*(3), 55–65.

Lyman, S. M., & Scott, M. B. (1967). Territoriality: A neglected sociological dimension. *Social Problems, 15,* 236–249.

Maass, A., Ceccarelli, R., & Rudin, S. (1996). Linguistic intergroup bias: Evidence for in-group–protective motivation. *Journal of Personality and Social Psychology, 71,* 512–526.

Maass, A., Milesi, A., Zabbini, S., & Stahlberg, D. (1995). Linguistic intergroup bias: Differential expectancies or in-group protection? *Journal of Personality and Social Psychology, 68,* 116–126.

Maass, A., West, S. G., & Cialdini, R. B. (1987). Minority influence and conversion. *Review of Personality and Social Psychology, 8,* 55–79.

Maassen, G. H., Akkermans, W., & van der Linden, J. L. (1996). Two-dimensional sociometric status determination with rating scales. *Small Group Research, 27,* 56–78.

Maccoby, E. E. (2002). Gender and group process: A developmental perspective. *Current Directions in Psychological Science, 11,* 54–58.

MacCracken, M. J., & Stadulis, R. E. (1985). Social facilitation of young children's dynamic balance performance. *Journal of Sport Psychology, 7,* 150–165.

MacKenzie, K. R. (1994). Group development. In A. Fuhriman & G. M. Burlingame (Eds.), *Handbook of group psychotherapy* (pp. 223–268). New York: Wiley.

MacKenzie, K. R. (1997). Clinical application of group development ideas. *Group Dynamics, 1,* 275–287.

Mackie, D. M. (1987). Systematic and nonsystematic processing of majority and minority persuasive communications. *Journal of Personality and Social Psychology, 53,* 41–52.

Mackie, D. M., Devos, T., & Smith, E. R. (2000). Intergroup emotions: Explaining offensive action tendencies in an intergroup context. *Journal of Personality and Social Psychology, 79,* 602–616.

MacKinnon, C. A. (2003). The social origin of sexual harassment. In M. Silberman (Ed.), *Violence and society: A reader* (pp. 251–258). Upper Saddle River, NJ: Prentice Hall.

MacNair-Semands, R. R. (2002). Predicting attendance and expectations for group therapy. *Group Dynamics, 6,* 219–228.

MacNair-Semands, R. R., & Lese, K. P. (2000). Interpersonal problems and the perception of therapeutic factors in group therapy. *Small Group Research, 31,* 158–174.

MacNeil, M. K., & Sherif, M. (1976). Norm change over subject generations as a function of arbitrariness of prescribed norm. *Journal of Personality and Social Psychology, 34,* 762–773.

Macy, B. A., & Izumi, H. (1993). Organizational change, design, and work innovation: A meta-analysis of 131 North American field studies—1961–1991. *Research in Organizational Change and Development, 7,* 235–313.

Maddux, J. E. (1999). The collective construction of collective efficacy: Comment on Paskevich, Brawley, Dorsch, and Widmeyer (1999). *Group Dynamics, 3,* 223–226.

Magaro, P. A., & Ashbrook, R. M. (1985). The personality of societal groups. *Journal of Personality and Social Psychology, 48,* 1479–1489.

Mai-Dalton, R. R. (1993). Managing cultural diversity on the individual, group, and organizational levels. In M. M. Chemers & R. Ayman (Eds.), *Leadership theory and research: Perspectives and directions* (pp. 189–215). San Diego: Academic Press.

Maier, N. R. F., & Solem, A. R. (1952). The contribution of a discussion leader to the quality of group thinking: The effective use of minority opinions. *Human Relations, 5,* 277–288.

Major, D. A., Kozlowski, S. W. J., Chao, G. T., & Gardner, P. D. (1995). A longitudinal investigation of newcomer expectations, early socialization outcomes, and the moderating effects of role development factors. *Journal of Applied Psychology, 80,* 418–431.

Maki, J. E., Thorngate, W. B., & McClintock, C. G. (1979). Prediction and perception of social motives. *Journal of Personality and Social Psychology, 37,* 203–220.

Malloy, T. E., & Janowski, C. L. (1992). Perceptions and metaperceptions of leadership: Components, accuracy, and dispositional correlates. *Personality and Social Psychology Bulletin, 18,* 700–708.

Manis, M., Cornell, S. D., & Moore, J. C. (1974). Transmission of attitude-relevant information through a communication chain. *Journal of Personality and Social Psychology, 30,* 81–94.

Mann, F. C. (1965). Toward an understanding of the leadership role in formal organizations. In R. Dubin, G. C. Homans, F. C. Mann, & D. C. Miller (Eds.), *Leadership and productivity* (pp. 44–78). San Francisco: Chandler.

Mann, J. H. (1959). A review of the relationships between personality and performance in small groups. *Psychological Bulletin, 56,* 241–270.

Mann, L. (1969). Queue culture. The waiting line as a social system. *American Journal of Sociology, 75,* 340–354.

Mann, L. (1970). The psychology of waiting lines. *American Scientist, 58,* 390–398.

Mann, L. (1980). Cross-cultural studies of small groups. In H. C. Triandis & R. W. Brislin (Eds.), *Handbook of cross-cultural psychology: Social psychology* (Vol. 5, pp. 155–209). Boston: Allyn & Bacon.

Mann, L. (1981). The baiting crowd in episodes of threatened suicide. *Journal of Personality and Social Psychology, 41,* 703–709.

Mann, L. (1988). Cultural influence on group processes. In M. H. Bond (Ed.), *The cross-cultural challenge to social psychology* (pp. 182–195). Thousand Oaks, CA: Sage.

Mann, L., Newton, J. W., & Innes, J. M. (1982). A test between deindividuation and emergent norm theories of crowd aggression. *Journal of Personality and Social Psychology, 42,* 260–272.

Mannix, E. A. (1993). Organizations as resource dilemmas: The effects of power balance on coalition formation in small groups. *Organizational Behavior and Human Decision Processes, 55,* 1–22.

Mantell, D. M., & Panzarella, R. (1976). Obedience and responsibility. *British Journal of Social and Clinical Psychology, 15,* 239–245.

Manz, C. C., & Sims, H. P., Jr. (1982). The potential for "groupthink" in autonomous work groups. *Human Relations, 35,* 773–784.

Manz, C. C., & Sims, H. P., Jr. (2001). *The new superleadership: Leading others to lead themselves.* San Francisco: Berrett-Koehler.

Marcus, D. K. (1998). Studying group dynamics with the social relations model. *Group Dynamics, 2,* 230–240.

Marcus, D. K., & Wilson, J. R. (1996). Interpersonal perception of social anxiety: A social relations analysis. *Journal of Social and Clinical Psychology, 15,* 471–487.

Marcus-Newhall, A., Miller, N., Holtz, R., & Brewer, M. B. (1993). Cross-cutting category membership with role assignment: A means of reducing intergroup bias. *British Journal of Social Psychology, 32,* 125–146.

Markovitz, R. J., & Smith, J. E. (1983). Patients' perceptions of curative factors in short term group psychotherapy. *International Journal of Group Psychotherapy, 33,* 21–39.

Markovsky, B., Smith, L. F., & Berger, J. (1984). Do status interventions persist? *American Sociological Review, 49,* 373–382.

Markus, H. (1978). The effect of mere presence on social facilitation: An unobtrusive test. *Journal of Experimental Social Psychology, 14,* 389–397.

Markus, H. (1980). The self in thought and memory. In D. M. Wegner & R. R. Valacher (Eds.), *The self in social psychology* (pp. 102–130). New York: Oxford University Press.

Markus, H. R., Kitayama, S., & Heiman, R. J. (1996). Culture and "basic" psychological principles. In E. T. Higgins & A. W. Kruglanski (Eds.), *Social psychology: Handbook of basic principles* (pp. 857–913). New York: Guilford Press.

Marmarosh, C. L., & Corazzini, J. G. (1997). Putting the group in your pocket: Using collective identity to enhance personal and collective self-esteem. *Group Dynamics, 1,* 65–74.

Marques, J. M. (1990). The black sheep effect: Out-group homogeneity in social comparison settings. In D. Abrams & M. A. Hogg (Eds.), *Social identity theory: Constructive and critical advances* (pp. 131–151). New York: Springer Verlag.

Marques, J., Abrams, D., & Serôdio, R. G. (2001). Being better by being right: Subjective group dynamics and derogation of ingroup deviants when generic norms are undermined. *Journal of Personality and Social Psychology, 81,* 436–447.

Marrow, A. J. (1969). *The practical theorist: The life and work of Kurt Lewin.* New York: Basic Books.

Marsh, C. (2000). A science museum exhibit on Milgram's obedience research: History, description, and visitors' reactions. In T. Blass (Ed.). *Obedience to authority: Current perspectives on the Milgram paradigm* (pp. 145–159). Mahwah, NJ: Erlbaum.

Marsh, P., & Morris, D. (1988). *Tribes.* Layton, UT: Gibbs Smith.

Martens, R., & Landers, D. M. (1972). Evaluation potential as a determinant of coaction effects. *Journal of Experimental Social Psychology, 8,* 347–359.

Martens, R., Landers, D. M., & Loy, J. (1972). *Sports cohesiveness questionnaire.* Reston, VA: American Association of Health, Physical Education, and Recreation.

Martin, E. D. (1920). *The behavior of crowds.* New York: Harper.

Martin, R., & Hewstone, M. (2001). Conformity and independence in groups: Majorities and minorities. In M. A. Hogg & R. S. Tindale (Eds.), *Blackwell handbook of social psychology: Group processes* (pp. 209–234). Malden, MA: Blackwell.

Marx, K., & Engels, F. (1947). *The German ideology.* New York: International Publishers.

Maslach, C. (1972). Social and personal bases of individuation. *Proceedings of the 80th Annual Convention of the American Psychological Association, 7,* 213–214.

Maslach, C., Santee, R. T., & Wade, C. (1987). Individuation, gender role, and dissent: Personality mediators of situational forces. *Journal of Personality and Social Psychology, 53,* 1088–1093.

Maslach, C., Stapp, J., & Santee, R. T. (1985). Individuation: Conceptual analysis and assessment. *Journal of Personality and Social Psychology, 49,* 729–738.

Maslow, A. H. (1968). *Toward a psychology of being.* New York: Van Nostrand Reinhold.

Mason, C. M., & Griffin, M. A. (2002). Group task satisfaction: Applying the construct of job satisfaction to groups. *Small Group Research, 33,* 271–312.

Mast, M. S. (2002). Female dominance hierarchies: Are they any different from males'? *Personality and Social Psychology Bulletin, 28,* 29–39.

Mathes, E. W., & Guest, T. A. (1976). Anonymity and group antisocial behavior. *Journal of Social Psychology, 100,* 257–262.

Mathes, E. W., & Kahn, A. (1975). Diffusion of responsibility and extreme behavior. *Journal of Personality and Social Psychology, 5,* 881–886.

Mathews, E., Canon, L. K., & Alexander, K. R. (1974). The influence of level of empathy and ambient noise on body buffer zone. *Personality and Social Psychology Bulletin, 1,* 367–369.

Mausner, B. (1954). The effect of one partner's success in a relevant task on the interaction of observer pairs. *Journal of Abnormal and Social Psychology, 49,* 557–560.

Maxmen, J. (1973). Group therapy as viewed by hospitalized patients. *Archives of General Psychiatry, 28,* 404–408.

Maxmen, J. (1978). An educative model for inpatient group therapy. *International Journal of Group Psychotherapy, 28,* 321–338.

Mayadas, N., & Glasser, P. (1985). Termination: A neglected aspect of social group work. In M. Sundel, P. Glasser, R. Sarri, & R. Vinter (Eds.), *Individual change through small groups* (2nd ed., pp. 251–261). New York: Free Press.

Mayer, J. D., & Salovey, P. (1993). The intelligence of emotional intelligence. *Intelligence, 17,* 433–442.

Mayer, T. (1975). *Mathematical models of group structure.* New York: Bobbs-Merrill.

Mayo, E. (1933). *The human problems of an industrial civilization.* Cambridge, MA: Harvard University Press.

Mayo, E. (1945). *The social problems of an industrial civilization.* Cambridge, MA: Harvard University Press.

Mazur, A. (1973). Cross-species comparison of status in established small groups. *American Sociological Review, 38,* 513–529.

Mazur, A., Rosa, E., Faupel, M., Heller, J., Leen, R., & Thurman, B. (1980). Physiological aspects of communication via mutual gaze. *American Journal of Sociology, 86,* 50–74.

McAdam, D., McCarthy, J. D., & Zald, M. N. (1988). Social movements. In N. J. Smelser (Ed.), *The handbook of sociology* (pp. 695–737). Thousand Oaks, CA: Sage.

McAdams, D. P. (1982). Experiences of intimacy and power: Relationships between social motives and autobiographical memory. *Journal of Personality and Social Psychology, 42,* 292–301.

McAdams, D. P. (1995). What do we know when we know a person? *Journal of Personality, 63,* 365–396.

McAdams, D. P., & Constantian, C. A. (1983). Intimacy and affiliation motives in daily living: An experience sampling analysis. *Journal of Personality and Social Psychology, 45,* 851–861.

McAdams, D. P., Healy, S., & Krause, S. (1984). Social motives and patterns of friendship. *Journal of Personality and Social Psychology, 47,* 828–838.

McBurney, D. H., Levine, J. M., & Cavanaugh, P. H. (1977). Psychophysical and social ratings of human body odor. *Personality and Social Psychology Bulletin, 3,* 135–138.

McCallum, D. M., Harring, K., Gilmore, R., Drenan, S., Chase, J., Insko, C. A., & Thibaut, J. (1985). Competition between groups and between individuals. *Journal of Experimental Social Psychology, 21,* 301–320.

McCallum, R., Rusbult, C. E., Hong, G. K., Walden, T., & Schopler, J. (1979). Effects of resource availability and importance of behavior on the experience of crowding. *Journal of Personality and Social Psychology, 37,* 1304–1313.

McCammon, S. L., & Long, T. E. (1993). A post-tornado support group: Survivors and professionals in concert. *Journal of Social Behavior and Personality, 8,* 131–148.

McCauley, C. (1989). The nature of social influence in groupthink: Compliance and internalization. *Journal of Personality and Social Psychology, 57,* 250–260.

McCauley, C. (1998). Groupthink dynamics in Janis's theory of groupthink: Backward and forward. *Organizational Behavior and Human Decision Processes, 73,* 142–162.

McClelland, D. C. (1975). *Power: The inner experience.* New York: Irvington.

McClelland, D. C. (1985). How motives, skills, and values determine what people do. *American Psychologist, 40,* 812–825.

McClelland, D. C., & Boyatzis, R. E. (1982). Leadership motive pattern and long-term success in management. *Journal of Applied Psychology, 67,* 737–743.

McClintock, C. G., Stech, F. J., & Keil, L. J. (1983). The influence of communication on bargaining. In P. B. Paulus (Ed.), *Basic group processes* (pp. 205–233). New York: Springer Verlag.

McClure, B. A. (1998). *Putting a new spin on groups: The science of chaos.* Mahwah, NJ: Erlbaum.

McCoy, J. M. (2002). Work environments. In R. B. Bechtel & A. Churchman (Eds.), *Handbook of environmental psychology* (pp. 443–460). New York: Wiley. Retrieved July 29, 2004, from http://www.netlibrary.com

McDougall, W. (1908). *An introduction to social psychology.* London: Methuen.

McGillicuddy, N. B., Pruitt, D. G., & Syna, H. (1984). Perceptions of firmness and strength in negotiation. *Personality and Social Psychology Bulletin, 10,* 402–409.

McGrath, J. E. (1964). *Social psychology: A brief introduction.* New York: Holt.

McGrath, J. E. (1984). *Groups: Interaction and performance.* Upper Saddle River, NJ: Prentice Hall.

McGrath, J. E. (1997). Small group research, that once and future field: An interpretation of the past with an eye to the future. *Group Dynamics, 1,* 7–27.

McGrath, J. E., & Altermatt, T. W. (2001). Observation and analysis of group interaction over time: Some methodological and strategic choices. In M. A. Hogg & R. S. Tindale (Eds.), *Blackwell handbook of social psychology: Group processes* (pp. 525–556). Malden, MA: Blackwell.

McGrath, J. E., Arrow, H., & Berdahl, J. L. (2000). The study of groups: Past, present, and future. *Personality & Social Psychology Review, 4,* 95–105.

McGraw, K. M., & Bloomfield, J. (1987). Social influence on group moral decisions: The interactive effects of moral reasoning and sex role orientation. *Journal of Personality and Social Psychology, 53,* 1080–1087.

McGrew, J. F., Bilotta, J. G., & Deeney, J. M. (1999). Software team formation and decay: Extending the standard model for small groups. *Small Group Research, 30,* 209–234.

McGuire, J. P., & Leak, G. K. (1980). Prediction of self-disclosure from objective personality assessment techniques. *Journal of Clinical Psychology, 36,* 201–204.

McGuire, T. W., Kiesler, S., & Siegel, J. (1987). Group and computer-mediated discussion effects in risk decision making. *Journal of Personality and Social Psychology, 52,* 917–930.

McGuire, W. J., & McGuire, C. V. (1988). Content and process in the experience of self. *Advances in Experimental Social Psychology, 21,* 97–144.

McKenna, K. Y. A., & Green, A. S. (2002). Virtual group dynamics. *Group Dynamics, 6,* 116–127.

McKersie, R. B., & Walton, R. E. (1992). A retrospective on the behavioral theory of labor negotiations. In Conflict and negotiation in organizations: Historical and contemporary perspectives [Special issue]. *Journal of Organizational Behavior, 13,* 277–285.

McLeod, P. L., Lobel, S. A., & Cox, T. H. (1996). Ethnic diversity and creativity in small groups. *Small Group Research, 27,* 248–264.

McPhail, C. (1991). *The myth of the madding crowd.* Hawthorne, NY: Aldine de Gruyter.

McPhail, C., & Wohlstein, R. R. (1983). Individual and collective behaviors within gatherings, demonstrations, and riots. *Annual Review of Sociology, 9,* 579–600.

McPherson, M., Smith-Lovin, L., & Cook, J. M. (2001). Birds of a feather: Homophily in social networks [Electronic version]. *Annual Review of Sociology, 27,* 415–444.

McRoberts, C., Burlingame, G. M., & Hoag, M. J. (1998). Comparative efficacy of individual and group psychotherapy: A meta-analytic perspective. *Group Dynamics, 2,* 101–117.

Mead, M. (1935). *Sex and temperament.* Oxford, UK: Morrow.

Meadow, A., Parnes, S. J., & Reese, H. (1959). Influence of brainstorming instructions and problem sequence on a creative problem solving test. *Journal of Applied Psychology, 43,* 413–416.

Medalia, N. Z., & Larsen, O. N. (1958). Diffusion and belief in a collective delusion: The Seattle windshield pitting epidemic. *American Sociological Review, 23,* 180–186.

Meerloo, J. A. (1950). *Patterns of panic.* New York: International Universities Press.

Meeus, W. H. J., & Raaijmakers, Q. A. W. (1995). Obedience in modern society: The Utrecht studies. *Journal of Social Issues, 51*(3), 155–175.

Megargee, E. I. (1969). Influence of sex roles on the manifestation of leadership. *Journal of Applied Psychology, 53,* 377–382.

Mehrabian, A. (1972). *Nonverbal communication.* Chicago: Aldine-Atherton.

Mehrabian, A., & Diamond, S. G. (1971). Effects of furniture arrangement, props, and personality on social interaction. *Journal of Personality and Social Psychology, 20,* 18–30.

Mehrabian, A., & Russell, J. A. (1974). A verbal measure of information rate for studies in environmental psychology. *Environment and Behavior, 6,* 233–252.

Mehrabian, A., & Russell, J. A. (1975). The basic emotional impact of environments. *Perceptual and Motor Skills, 38,* 283–301.

Meindl, J. R. (1995). The romance of leadership as a follower-centric theory: A social constructionist approach. *Leadership Quarterly, 6,* 329–341.

Meindl, J. R., Ehrlich, S. B., & Dukerich, J. M. (1985). The romance of leadership and the evaluation of organizational performance. *Academy of Management Journal, 30,* 90–109.

Melamed, B. G., & Wills, T. A. (2000). Comment on Turner (2000). *Group Dynamics, 4,* 150–156.

Melucci, A. (1989). *Nomads of the present: Social movements and individual needs in contemporary society* (J. Keanne & P. Mier, Eds.). Philadelphia: Temple University Press.

Mennecke, B. E., Hoffer, J. A., & Wynne, B. E. (1992). The implications of group development and history for group support system theory and practice. *Small Group Research, 23,* 524–572.

Merei, F. (1958). Group leadership and institutionalization. In E. E. Maccoby, T. M. Newcomb, & E. L. Hartley (Eds.), *Readings in social psychology* (3rd ed., pp. 522–532). New York: Holt, Rinehart & Winston.

Merritt, A. C., & Helmreich, R. L. (1996). Human factors on the flight deck: The influence of national culture. *Journal of Cross-Cultural Psychology, 27,* 5–24.

Messé, L. A., Hertel, G., Kerr, N. L., Lount, R. B., Jr., & Park, E. S. (2002). Knowledge of partner's ability as a moderator of group motivation gains: An exploration of the Koehler discrepancy effect. *Journal of Personality and Social Psychology, 82,* 935–946.

Messé, L., & Sivacek, J. M. (1979). Predictions of others' responses in a mixed-motive game: Self-justification or false consensus? *Journal of Personality and Social Psychology, 37,* 602–607.

Messé, L. A., Stollak, G. E., Larson, R. W., & Michaels, G. Y. (1979). Interpersonal consequences of person perception in two social contexts. *Journal of Personality and Social Psychology, 37,* 369–379.

Messick, D. M. (1999). Dirty secrets: Strategic uses of ignorance and uncertainty. In L. L. Thompson, J. M. Levine, & D. M. Messick (Eds.), *Shared cognition in organizations: The management of knowledge* (pp. 71–87). Mahwah, NJ: Erlbaum.

Messick, D. M., & Brewer, M. B. (1983). Solving social dilemmas: A review. *Review of Personality and Social Psychology, 4,* 11–44.

Meudell, P. R., Hitch, G. J., & Boyle, M. M. (1995). Collaboration in recall: Do pairs of people cross-cue each other to produce new memories? *Quarterly Journal of Experimental Psychology: Human Experimental Psychology, 48*(A), 141–152.

Meudell, P. R., Hitch, G. J., & Kirby, P. (1992). Are two heads better than one? Experimental investigations of the social facilitation of memory. *Applied Cognitive Psychology, 6,* 525–543.

Meumann, E. (1904). Haus- und Schularbeit: Experimente an Kindern der Volksschule [Homework and school work: Experiments with public school children]. *Die Deutsche Schule, 8,* 278–303, 337–359, 416–431.

Meyer, J. P., & Pepper, S. (1977). Need compatibility and marital adjustment in young married couples. *Journal of Personality and Social Psychology, 35,* 331–342.

Michaels, J. W., Blommel, J. M., Brocato, R. M., Linkous, R. A., & Rowe, J. S. (1982). Social facilitation and inhibition in a natural setting. *Replications in Social Psychology, 2,* 21–24.

Michaelsen, L. K., Watson, W. E., & Black, R. H. (1989). A realistic test of individual versus group consensus decision making. *Journal of Applied Psychology, 74,* 834–839.

Michels, R. (1959). *Political parties: A sociological study of the oligarchical tendencies of modern democracy.* New York: Dover. (Original work published in 1915)

Michener, H. A., & Burt, M. R. (1975a). Components of "authority" as determinants of compliance. *Journal of Personality and Social Psychology, 31,* 606–614.

Michener, H. A., & Burt, M. R. (1975b). Use of social influence under varying conditions of legitimacy. *Journal of Personality and Social Psychology, 32,* 398–407.

Michener, H. A., & Lawler, E. J. (1975). The endorsement of formal leaders: An integrative model. *Journal of Personality and Social Psychology, 31,* 216–223.

Middlemist, R. D., Knowles, E. S., & Matter, C. F. (1976). Personal space invasions in the lavatory: Suggestive evidence for arousal. *Journal of Personality and Social Psychology, 33,* 541–546.

Mikolic, J. M., Parker, J. C., & Pruitt, D. G. (1997). Escalation in response to persistent annoyance: Groups versus individuals and gender effects. *Journal of Personality and Social Psychology, 72,* 151–163.

Milanovich, D. M., Driskell, J. E., Stout, R. J., & Salas, E. (1998). Status and cockpit dynamics: A review and empirical study. *Group Dynamics, 2,* 155–167.

Miles, R. H. (1976). A comparison of the relative impacts of role perceptions of ambiguity and conflict by role. *Academy of Management Journal, 19,* 25–35.

Milgram, S. (1963). Behavioral study of obedience. *Journal of Abnormal and Social Psychology, 67,* 371–378.

Milgram, S. (1974). *Obedience to authority.* New York: Harper & Row.

Milgram, S. (1992). *The individual in a social world: Essays and experiments* (2nd ed.). New York: McGraw-Hill.

Milgram, S., Bickman, L., & Berkowitz, L. (1969). Note on the drawing power of crowds of different size. *Journal of Personality and Social Psychology, 13,* 79–82.

Milgram, S., Liberty, H. J., Toledo, R., & Wackenhut, J. (1986). Response to intrusion into waiting lines. *Journal of Personality and Social Psychology, 51,* 683–689.

Milgram, S., & Toch, H. (1969). Collective behavior: Crowds and social movements. In G. Lindzey & E. Aronson (Eds.), *The handbook of social psychology* (Vol. 4, 2nd ed., pp. 507–610). Reading, MA: Addison-Wesley.

Miller, A. G. (1995). Constructions of the obedience experiments: A focus upon domains of relevance. *Journal of Social Issues, 51*(3), 33–53.

Miller, A. G., Collins, B. E., & Brief, D. E. (1995a). Perspectives on obedience to authority: The legacy of the Milgram experiments. *Journal of Social Issues, 51*(3), 1–19.

Miller, A. G., Collins, B. E., & Brief, D. E. (Eds.). (1995b). *Journal of Social Issues, 51*(3).

Miller, C. E., Jackson, P., Mueller, J., & Schersching, C. (1987). Some social psychological effects of group decision rules. *Journal of Personality and Social Psychology, 52,* 325–332.

Miller, C. E., & Komorita, S. S. (1995). Reward allocation in task-performing groups. *Journal of Personality and Social Psychology, 69,* 80–90.

Miller, D. L. (1985). *Introduction to collective behavior.* Belmont, CA: Wadsworth.

Miller, D. T. (2001). Disrespect and the experience of injustice. *Annual Review of Psychology, 52,* 527–553.

Miller, D. T., & Holmes, J. G. (1975). The role of situational restrictiveness on self-fulfilling prophecies: A theoretical and empirical extension of Kelley and Stahelski's triangle hypothesis. *Journal of Personality and Social Psychology, 31,* 661–673.

Miller, D. T., & McFarland, C. (1991). When social comparison goes awry: The case of pluralistic ignorance. In J. Suls and T. A. Wills (Eds.), *Social comparison: Contemporary theory and research* (pp. 287–313). Mahwah, NJ: Erlbaum.

Miller, D. T., & Prentice, D. A. (1996). The construction of social norms and standards. In E. T. Higgins & A. W. Kruglanski (Eds.), *Social psychology: Handbook of basic principles* (pp. 799–829). New York: Guilford Press.

Miller, G. A., Galanter, E., & Pribram, K. H. (1960). *Plans and the structure of behavior.* New York: Holt.

Miller, James G. (1978). *Living systems.* New York: McGraw-Hill.

Miller, Joan G. (2002). Bringing culture to basic psychological theory—Beyond individualism and collectivism: Comment on Oyserman et al. (2002). *Psychological Bulletin, 128,* 97–109.

Miller, J. K., & Gergen, K. J. (1998). Life on the line: The therapeutic potentials of computer-mediated conversation. *Journal of Marital and Family Therapy, 24,* 189–202.

Miller, K. I., & Monge, P. R. (1986). Participation, satisfaction, and productivity: A meta-analytic review. *Academy of Management Journal, 29,* 727–753.

Miller, N., & Brewer, M. B. (1986a). Categorization effects on ingroup and outgroup perception. In J. Dovidio & S. Gaertner (Eds.), *Prejudice, discrimination, and racism: Theory and research* (pp. 209–230). New York: Academic Press.

Miller, N., & Brewer, M. B. (1986b). Social categorization theory and team learning procedures. In R. S. Feldman (Ed.), *The social psychology of education* (pp. 172–198). New York: Cambridge University Press.

Miller, N., & Davidson-Podgorny, G. (1987). Theoretical models of intergroup relations and the use of cooperative teams as an intervention for desegregated settings. *Review of Personality and Social Psychology, 9,* 41–67.

Miller, N., Urban, L. M., & Vanman, E. J. (1998). A theoretical analysis of crossed social categorization effects. In C. Sedikides, J. Schopler, & C. A. Insko (Eds.), *Intergroup cognition and intergroup behavior* (pp. 393–422). Mahwah, NJ: Erlbaum.

Mills, J., Clark, M. S., Ford, T. E., & Johnson, M. (2004). Measurement of communal strength. *Personal Relationships, 11,* 213–230.

Mills, T. M. (1962). A sleeper variable in small groups research: The experimenter. *Pacific Sociological Review, 5,* 21–28.

Mills, T. M. (1979). Changing paradigms for studying human groups. *Journal of Applied Behavioral Science, 15,* 407–423.

Minami, H., & Tanaka, K. (1995). Social and environmental psychology: Transaction between physical space and group-dynamic processes. *Environment and Behavior, 27,* 43–55.

Mintz, A. (1951). Non-adaptive group behavior. *Journal of Abnormal and Social Psychology, 46,* 150–159.

Mischel, W., & DeSmet, A. L. (2000). Self-regulation in the service of conflict resolution. In M. Deutsch & P. T. Coleman (Eds.), *The handbook of conflict resolution: Theory and practice* (pp. 256–275). San Francisco: Jossey-Bass.

Misumi, J. (1985). *The behavioral science of leadership.* Ann Arbor: University of Michigan Press.

Misumi, J. (1995). The development in Japan of the performance–maintenance (PM) theory of leadership. *Journal of Social Issues, 51*(1), 213–228.

Mitchell, R. C., & Mitchell, R. R. (1984). Constructive management of conflict in groups. *Journal for Specialists in Group Work, 9,* 137–144.

Mixon, D. (1977). Why pretend to deceive? *Personality and Social Psychology Bulletin, 3,* 647–653.

Mobley, W. H., Griffeth, R. W., Hand, H. H., & Meglino, B. M. (1979). Review and conceptual analysis of employee turnover process. *Psychological Bulletin, 86,* 493–522.

Modigliani, A., & Rochat, F. (1995). The role of interaction sequences and the timing of resistance in shaping obedience and defiance to authority. *Journal of Social Issues, 51*(3), 107–123.

Moede, W. (1927). Die Richtlinien der Leistungs-Psychologie [Guidelines for the psychology of achievement]. *Industrielle Psychotechnik, 4,* 193–207.

Moemeka, A. A. (1998). Communalism as a fundamental dimension of culture. *Journal of Communication, 48,* 118–141.

Molm, L. D. (1986). Gender, power, and legitimation: A test of three theories. *American Journal of Sociology, 91,* 1156–1186.

Molm, L. D. (1988). The structure and use of power: A comparison of reward and punishment power. *Social Psychology Quarterly, 51,* 108–122.

Molm, L. D. (1994). Is punishment effective? Coercive strategies in social exchange. *Social Psychology Quarterly, 57,* 75–94.

Moore, J. (1991). *Going down in the barrio: Homeboys and homegirls in change.* Philadelphia: Temple University Press.

Moore, L. E. (1973). *The jury.* Cincinnati, OH: Anderson.

Moorhead, G., Ference, R., & Neck, C. P. (1991). Group decision fiascoes continue: Space shuttle Challenger and a revised groupthink framework. *Human Relations, 44,* 539–550.

Moorhead, G., & Montanari, J. R. (1986). An empirical investigation of the groupthink phenomenon. *Human Relations, 39,* 399–410.

Moorhead, G., Neck, C. P., & West, M.S. (1998). The tendency toward defective decision making within self-managing teams:

The relevance of groupthink for the 21st century. *Organizational Behavior and Human Decision Processes, 73,* 327–351.

Moos, R. H., Insel, P. M., & Humphrey, B. (1974). *Preliminary manual for Family Environment Scale, Work Environment Scale, and Group Environment Scale.* Palo Alto, CA: Consulting Psychologists Press.

Morasch, B., Groner, N., & Keating, J. (1979). Type of activity and failure as mediators of perceived crowding. *Personality and Social Psychology Bulletin, 5,* 223–226.

Moreland, R. L. (1985). Social categorization and the assimilation of "new" group members. *Journal of Personality and Social Psychology, 48,* 1173–1190.

Moreland, R. L. (1987). The formation of small groups. *Review of Personality and Social Psychology, 8,* 80–110.

Moreland, R. L. (1997). *Leadership in small groups: Expanding our analytical horizons.* Paper presented at the Interface of Leadership and Team Processes in Organizations: Implications for Understanding Work Effectiveness, George Mason University, Washington, DC.

Moreland, R. L., Argote, L., & Krishnan, R. (1996). Socially shared cognition at work: Transactive memory and group performance. In J. L. Nye & A. M. Brower (Eds.), *What's social about social cognition? Research on socially shared cognitions in small groups* (pp. 57–84). Thousand Oaks, CA: Sage.

Moreland, R. L., & Levine, J. M. (1982). Socialization in small groups: Temporal changes in individual–group relations. *Advances in Experimental Social Psychology, 15,* 137–192.

Moreland, R. L., & Levine, J. M. (2002). Socialization and trust in work groups. *Group Processes & Intergroup Relations, 5,* 185–201.

Moreland, R. L., Levine, J. M., & Cini, M. A. (1993). Group socialization: The role of commitment. In M. Hogg & D. Abrams (Eds.), *Group motivation: Social psychological perspectives* (pp. 105–129). London: Harvester Wheatsheaf.

Moreland, R. L., Levine, J. M., & Wingert, M. L. (1996). Creating the ideal group: Composition effects at work. In E. H. Witte & J. H. Davis (Eds.), *Understanding group behavior: Small group processes and interpersonal relations* (Vol. 2, pp. 11–35). Mahwah, NJ: Erlbaum.

Moreno, J. L. (1934). *Who shall survive? A new approach to the problem of human interrelations.* Washington, DC: Nervous and Mental Disease Publishing Co.

Moreno, J. L. (Ed.). (1960). *The sociometry reader.* New York: Free Press.

Morgan, R. D., & Flora, D. B. (2002). Group psychotherapy with incarcerated offenders: A research synthesis. *Group Dynamics, 6,* 203–218.

Mori, K. (1996). Effects of trust and communication on cooperative choice in a two-person prisoner's dilemma game. *Japanese Journal of Experimental Social Psychology, 35,* 324–336.

Morran, K. D., Stockton, R., Cline, R. J., & Teed, C. (1998). Facilitating feedback exchange in groups: Leader interventions. *Journal for Specialists in Group Work, 23,* 257–268.

Morrill, C. (1995). *The executive way.* Chicago: University of Chicago Press.

Morris, W. N., & Miller, R. S. (1975). Impressions of dissenters and conformers: An attributional analysis. *Sociometry, 38,* 327–339.

Morris, W. N., Worchel, S., Bois, J. L., Pearson, J. A., Rountree, C. A., Samaha, G. M., Wachtler, J., & Wright, S. L. (1976). Collective coping with stress: Group reactions to fear, anxiety, and ambiguity. *Journal of Personality and Social Psychology, 33,* 674–679.

Moscovici, S. (1994). Three concepts: Minority, conflict, and be-havioral styles. In S. Moscovici, A. Mucchi-Faina, & A. Maass (Eds.), *Minority influence* (pp. 233–251). Chicago: Nelson-Hall.

Moscovici, S., Lage, E., & Naffrechoux, M. (1969). Influence of a consistent minority on the responses of a majority in a color perception task. *Sociometry, 12,* 365–380.

Moscovici, S., & Personnaz, B. (1980). Studies in social influence. V. Minority influence and conversion behavior in a perceptual task. *Journal of Experimental Social Psychology, 16,* 270–282.

Moscovici, S., & Zavalloni, M. (1969). The group as a polarizer of attitudes. *Journal of Personality and Social Psychology, 12,* 125–135.

Moser, G., & Uzzell, D. L. (2003). Environmental psychology. In T. Millon, M. J. Lerner, & I. B. Weiner (Eds.), *Handbook of psychology: Personality and social psychology* (Vol. 5, pp. 419–445). New York: Wiley. Retrieved July 15, 2004, from http://www.netlibrary.com

Moskowitz, G. B., & Chaiken, S. (2001). Mediators of minority social influence: Cognitive processing mechanisms revealed through a persuasion paradigm. In C. K. W. De Dreu & N. K. De Vries (Eds.), *Group consensus and minority influence: Implications for innovation* (pp. 60–90). Malden, MA: Blackwell.

Mowat, F. (1977). *Ordeal by ice: The search for the Northwest Passage.* Toronto: McClelland & Steward.

Mowday, R. T., & Sutton, R. I. (1993). Organizational behavior: Linking individuals and groups to organizational contexts. *Annual Review of Psychology, 44,* 195–229.

Moxley, R. L., & Moxley, N. F. (1974). Determining point central-ity in uncontrived social networks. *Sociometry, 37,* 122–130.

Mucchi-Faina, A. (1994). Theoretical perspectives on minority in-fluence: Conversion versus divergence? In S. Moscovici, A. Mucchi-Faina, & A. Maass (Eds.), *Minority influence* (pp. 115–133). Chicago: Nelson-Hall.

Mudrack, P. E. (1989). Defining group cohesiveness: A legacy of confusion? *Small Group Behavior, 20,* 37–49.

Mudrack, P. E., & Farrell, G. M. (1995). An examination of func-tional role behavior and its consequences for individuals in group settings. *Small Group Behavior, 26,* 542–571.

Mulder, M., & Stemerding, A. (1963). Threat, attraction to group, and need for strong leadership. *Human Relations, 16,* 317–334.

Mullen, B. (1986). Atrocity as a function of lynch mob composi-tion: A self-attention perspective. *Personality and Social Psychology Bulletin, 12,* 187–197.

Mullen, B. (1987). Self-attention theory: The effects of group com-position on the individual. In B. Mullen & G. R. Goethals (Eds.), *Theories of group behavior* (pp. 125–146). New York: Springer Verlag.

Mullen, B., Anthony, T., Salas, E., & Driskell, J. E. (1994). Group cohesiveness and quality of decision making: An integration of tests of the groupthink hypothesis. *Small Group Research, 25,* 189–204.

Mullen, B., & Baumeister, R. F. (1987). Group effects on self-attention and performance: social loafing, social facilitation, and social impairment. *Review of Personality and Social Psychology, 9,* 189–206.

Mullen, B., Brown, R., & Smith, C. (1992). Ingroup bias as a func-tion of salience, relevance, and status: An integration. *European Journal of Social Psychology, 22,* 103–122.

Mullen, B., Bryant, B., & Driskell, J. E. (1997). Presence of others and arousal: An integration. *Group Dynamics, 1,* 52–64.

Mullen, B., & Copper, C. (1994). The relation between group co-hesiveness and performance: An integration. *Psychological Bulletin, 115,* 210–227.

Mullen, B., Driskell, J. E., & Salas, E. (1998). Meta-analysis and the study of group dynamics. *Group Dynamics, 2,* 213–229.

Mullen, B., & Hu, L. (1988). Social projection as a function of cognitive mechanisms: Two meta-analytic integrations. *British Journal of Social Psychology, 27,* 333–356.

Mullen, B., Johnson, C., & Salas, E. (1991). Productivity loss in brainstorming groups: A meta-analytic review. *Basic and Applied Social Psychology, 12,* 3–23.

Mullen, B., Rozell, D., & Johnson, C. (1996). The phenomenology of being in a group: Complexity approaches to operationalizing cognitive representation. In J. L. Nye & A. M. Brower (Eds.), *What's social about social cognition?* (pp. 205–229). Thousand Oaks, CA: Sage.

Mullen, B., Salas, E., & Driskell, J. (1989). Salience, motivation, and artifacts as contributors to the relationship between partici-pation rate and leadership. *Journal of Experimental Social Psychology, 25,* 545–559.

Mummendey, A. (1995). Positive distinctiveness and social discrim-ination: An old couple living in divorce. *European Journal of Social Psychology, 25,* 657–670.

Murata, K. (1982). Attribution processes in a mixed-motive inter-action: The role of active observer's behavior. *Behaviormetrika, 12,* 47–61.

Murnighan, J. K. (1986). Organizational coalitions: Structural con-tingencies and the formation process. *Research on Negotiation in Organizations, 1,* 155–174.

Murnighan, J. K., & Conlon, D. E. (1991). The dynamics of in-tense work groups: A study of British string quartets. *Administrative Science Quarterly, 36,* 165–186.

Murphy, S. A., & Keating, J. P. (1995). Psychological assessment of postdisaster class action and personal injury litigants: A case study. *Journal of Traumatic Stress, 8,* 473–482.

Murphy-Berman, V., & Berman, J. (1978). Importance of choice and sex invasions of personal space. *Personality and Social Psychology Bulletin, 4,* 424–428.

Murray, H. A. (1938). *Explorations in personality.* New York: Oxford University Press.

Myers, A. E. (1962). Team competition, success, and the adjust-ment of group members. *Journal of Abnormal and Social Psychology, 65,* 325–332.

Myers, D. G. (1978). The polarizing effects of social comparison. *Journal of Experimental Social Psychology, 14,* 554–563.

Myers, D. G. (1982). Polarizing effects of social interaction. In H. Brandstätter, J. H. Davis, & G. Stocker-Kreichgauer (Eds.), *Group decision making* (pp. 125–161). New York: Academic Press.

Myers, D. G. (2002). *Social psychology.* New York: McGraw-Hill.

Myers, D. G., & Bishop, G. D. (1970). Discussion effects on racial attitudes. *Science, 169,* 778–789.

Myers, D. G., & Lamm, H. (1976). The group polarization phe-nomenon. *Psychological Bulletin, 83,* 602–627.

Myers, D. J. (1997). Racial rioting in the 1960s: An event history analysis of local conditions. *American Sociological Review, 62,* 94–112.

Nagasundaram, M., & Dennis, A. R. (1993). When a group is not a group: The cognitive foundation of group idea generation. *Small Group Research, 24,* 463–489.

Nahavandi, A. (2003). *The art and science of leadership* (3rd ed.). Upper Saddle River, NJ: Prentice Hall.

Nail, P. R., MacDonald, G., & Levy, D. A. (2000). Proposal of a four-dimensional model of social response. *Psychological Bulletin, 126,* 454–470.

National Center for State Courts. (1976). *Facets of the jury system: A survey.* Denver, CO: Research and Information Service.

National Transportation Safety Board. (1994). *A review of flightcrew-involved, major accidents of U.S. air carriers, 1978 through 1990* (Safety Study NTSB/SS-94/01). Washington, DC: Author.

Neck, C. P., & Moorhead, G. (1995). Groupthink remodeled: The importance of leadership, time pressure, and methodical decision-making procedures. *Human Relations, 48,* 537–557.

Nemeth, C. J. (1986). Differential contributions of majority and minority influence. *Psychological Review, 93,* 23–32.

Nemeth, C. J. (1994). The value of minority dissent. In S. Moscovici, A. Mucchi-Faina, & A. Maass (Eds.), *Minority influence* (pp. 3–15). Chicago: Nelson-Hall.

Nemeth, C. J., Endicott, J., & Wachtler, J. (1976). From the '50s to the '70s: Women in jury deliberations. *Sociometry, 39,* 293–304.

Nemeth, C. J., & Kwan, J. L. (1985). Originality of word associations as a function of majority vs. minority influence. *Social Psychology Quarterly, 48,* 277–282.

Nemeth, C. J., & Kwan, J. L. (1987). Minority influence, divergent thinking, and detection of correct solutions. *Journal of Applied Social Psychology, 17,* 788–799.

Nemeth, C., Mayseless, O., Sherman, J., & Brown, Y. (1990). Exposure to dissent and recall of information. *Journal of Personality and Social Psychology, 58,* 429–437.

Nemeth, C., Mosier, K., & Chiles, C. (1992). When convergent thought improves performance: Majority versus minority influence. *Personality and Social Psychology Bulletin, 18,* 139–144.

Nemeth, C. J., & Wachtler, J. (1974). Creating the perceptions of consistency and confidence: A necessary condition for minority influence. *Sociometry, 37,* 529–540.

Nemeth, C. J., & Wachtler, J. (1983). Creative problem solving as a result of majority vs. minority influence. *European Journal of Social Psychology, 13,* 45–55.

Newcomb, A. F., Bukowski, W. M., & Pattee, L. (1993). Children's peer relations: A meta-analytic review of popular, rejected, neglected, controversial, and average sociometric status. *Psychological Bulletin, 113,* 99–128.

Newcomb, T. M. (1943). *Personality and social change.* New York: Dryden.

Newcomb, T. M. (1960). Varieties of interpersonal attraction. In D. Cartwright & A. Zander (Eds.), *Group dynamics: Research and theory* (2nd ed., pp. 104–119). Evanston, IL: Row, Peterson.

Newcomb, T. M. (1961). *The acquaintance process.* New York: Holt, Rinehart & Winston.

Newcomb, T. M. (1963). Stabilities underlying changes in interpersonal attraction. *Journal of Abnormal and Social Psychology, 66,* 376–386.

Newcomb, T. M. (1979). Reciprocity of interpersonal attraction: A nonconfirmation of a plausible hypothesis. *Social Psychology Quarterly, 42,* 299–306.

Newcomb, T. M. (1981). Heiderean balance as a group phenomenon. *Journal of Personality and Social Psychology, 40,* 862–867.

Newcomb, T. M., Koenig, K., Flacks, R., & Warwick, D. (1967). *Persistence and change: Bennington College and its students after 25 years.* New York: Wiley.

Newman, O. (1972). *Defensible space.* New York: Macmillan.

Newton, J. W., & Mann, L. (1980). Crowd size as a factor in the persuasion process: A study of religious crusade meetings. *Journal of Personality and Social Psychology, 39,* 874–883.

Nicholls, J. R. (1985). A new approach to situational leadership. *Leadership and Organization Development Journal, 6*(4), 2–7.

Nielsen, J. M. (1990). *Sex and gender in society: Perspectives on stratification.* Prospect Heights, IL: Waveland Press.

Nielsen, M. E., & Miller, C. E. (1997). The transmission of norms regarding group decision rules. *Personality and Social Psychology Bulletin, 23,* 516–525.

Nier, J. A., Gaertner, S. L., Dovidio, J. F., Banker, B. S., Ward, C. M., & Rust, M. C. (2001). Changing interracial evaluations and behavior: The effects of a common group identity. *Group Processes & Intergroup Relations, 4,* 299–316.

Nisbett, R. E. (1993). Violence and U.S. regional culture. *American Psychologist, 48,* 441–449.

Nisbett, R. E., & Storms, M. D. (1974). Cognitive and social determinants of food intake. H. London & R. E. Nisbett (Eds.), *Thought and feeling: Cognitive alteration of feeling states.* Oxford, UK: Aldine.

Noel, J. G., Wann, D. L., & Branscombe, N. R. (1995). Peripheral ingroup membership status and public negativity toward outgroups. *Journal of Personality and Social Psychology, 68,* 127–137.

Nord, W. R. (1969). Social exchange theory: An integrative approach to social conformity. *Psychological Bulletin, 71,* 174–208.

Norris, F. H., & Murrell, S. A. (1990). Social support, life events, and stress as modifiers of adjustment to bereavement by older adults. *Psychology and Aging, 5,* 429–436.

Nosanchuk, T. A., & Lightstone, J. (1974). Canned laughter and public and private conformity. *Journal of Personality and Social Psychology, 29,* 153–156.

Nowak, A., Szamrej, J., & Latané, B. (1990). From private attitude to public opinion: A dynamic theory of social impact. *Psychological Review, 97,* 362–376.

Nowak, A., Vallacher, R. R., & Miller, M. E. (2003). Social influence and group dynamics. In T. Millon, M. J. Lerner, & I. B. Weiner (Eds.), *Handbook of psychology: Social psychology* (Vol. 5, pp. 383–418). New York: Wiley.

Nutt, P. C. (2002). *Why decisions fail: Avoiding the blunders and traps that lead to debacles.* San Francisco: Berrett-Koehler.

Nye, J. L. (1994). Discussion: The social perceiver as a social being. In Social cognition in small groups [Special issue]. *Small Group Research, 25,* 316–322.

Nye, J. L. (2002). The eye of the follower: Information processing effects on attributions regarding leaders of small groups. *Small Group Research, 33,* 337–360.

Nye, J. L., & Forsyth, D. R. (1991). The effects of prototype-based biases on leadership appraisals: A test of leadership categorization theory. *Small Group Research, 22,* 360–379.

Nyquist, L. V., & Spence, J. T. (1986). Effects of dispositional dominance and sex role expectations on leadership behaviors. *Journal of Personality and Social Psychology, 50,* 87–93.

Nystrom, P. C. (1978). Managers and the Hi-Hi leader myth. *Academy of Management Journal, 21,* 325–331.

O'Connell, P., Pepler, D., & Craig, W. (1999). Peer involvement in bullying: Insights and challenges for intervention. *Journal of Adolescence, 22,* 437–452.

O'Connor, B. P., & Dyce, J. (1997). Interpersonal rigidity, hostility, and complementarity in musical bands. *Journal of Personality and Social Psychology, 72,* 362–372.

Offner, A. K., Kramer, T. J., & Winter, J. P. (1996). The effects of facilitation, recording, and pauses on group brainstorming. *Small Group Research, 27,* 283–298.

Ogrodniczuk, J. S., & Piper, W. E. (2003). The effect of group climate on outcome in two forms of short-term group therapy. *Group Dynamics, 7,* 64–76.

Ohbuchi, K., Chiba, S., & Fukushima, O. (1996). Mitigation of interpersonal conflicts: Politeness and time pressure. *Personality and Social Psychology Bulletin, 22,* 1035–1042.

Ohtsubo, Y., Masuchi, A., & Nakanishi, D. (2002). Majority influence process in group judgment: Test of the social judgment scheme model in a group polarization context. *Group Processes & Intergroup Relations, 5,* 249–261.

Olweus, D. (1997). Tackling peer victimization with a school-based intervention program. In D. P. Fry & K. Björkqvist (Eds.), *Cultural variation in conflict resolution: Alternatives to violence* (pp. 215–231). Mahwah, NJ: Erlbaum.

Olweus, D. (2000). Bullying. In A. E. Kazdin (Ed.), *Encyclopedia of psychology* (Vol. 1, pp. 487–489). Washington, DC: American Psychological Association. Retrieved September 1, 2004, from http://online.psycinfo.com/psycbooks

Ones, D. S., Mount, M. K., Barrick, M. R., & Hunter, J. E. (1994). Personality and job performance: A critique of the Tett, Jackson, and Rothstein (1991) meta-analysis. *Personnel Psychology, 47,* 147–156.

Opotow, S. (2000). Aggression and violence. M. Deutsch & P. T. Coleman (Eds.), *The handbook of conflict resolution: Theory and practice* (pp. 403–427). San Francisco: Jossey-Bass.

Orbell, J., Dawes, R., & van de Kragt, A. (1995). Cooperation under laissez faire and majority decision rules in group-level social dilemmas. In D. A. Schroeder (Ed.), *Social dilemmas: Perspectives on individuals and groups* (pp. 105–116). Westport, CT: Praeger.

Orcutt, J. D. (1973). Societal reaction and the response to deviation in small groups. *Social Forces, 52,* 261–267.

Ormont, L. R. (1984). The leader's role in dealing with aggression in groups. *International Journal of Group Psychotherapy, 34,* 553–572.

Orne, M. T., & Holland, C. H. (1968). On the ecological validity of laboratory deceptions. *International Journal of Psychiatry, 6,* 282–293.

Osborn, A. F. (1957). *Applied imagination.* New York: Scribner.

Osgood, D. W., Wilson, J. K., O'Malley, P. M., Bachman, J. G., & Johnston, L. D. (1996). Routine activities and individual deviant behavior. *American Sociological Review, 61,* 635–655.

Oskamp, S., & Hartry, A. (1968). A factor-analytic study of the double standard in attitudes toward U.S. and Russian actions. *Behavioral Science, 13,* 178–188.

Ostrom, T. M., & Sedikides, C. (1992). Out-group homogeneity effects in natural and minimal groups. *Psychological Bulletin, 112,* 536–552.

Overbeck, J. R., & Park, B. (2001). When power does not corrupt: Superior individuation processes among powerful perceivers. *Journal of Personality and Social Psychology, 81,* 549–565.

Oyserman, D., Coon, H. M., & Kemmelmeier, M. (2002). Rethinking individualism and collectivism: Evaluation of theoretical assumptions and meta-analyses. *Psychological Bulletin, 128,* 3–72.

Oyserman, D., & Saltz, E. (1993). Competence, delinquency, and attempts to attain possible selves. *Journal of Personality and Social Psychology, 65,* 360–374.

Packard, D. (1995). *The HP Way: How Bill Hewlett and I built our company.* New York: HarperCollins.

Page, R. A., & Moss, M. K. (1976). Environmental influences on aggression: The effects of darkness and proximity of victim. *Journal of Applied Social Psychology, 6,* 126–133.

Page, R. C., Weiss, J. F., & Lietaer, G. (2002). Humanistic group psychotherapy. In J. D. Cain (Ed.), *Humanistic psychotherapies: Handbook of research and practice* (pp. 339–368). Washington, DC: American Psychological Association.

Palinkas, L. A. (1991). Effects of physical and social environments on the health and well-being of Antarctic winter-over personnel. *Environment and Behavior, 23,* 782–799.

Palmer, G. J. (1962). Task ability and effective leadership. *Psychological Reports, 10,* 863–866.

Pandey, J., & Singh, P. (1987). Effects of machiavellianism, other-enhancement, and power-position on affect, power feeling, and evaluation of the ingratiator. *Journal of Psychology, 121,* 287–300.

Paris, C. R., Salas, E., & Cannon-Bowers, J. A. (1999). Human performance in multi-operator systems. In P. A. Hancock (Ed.), *Human performance and ergonomics* (2nd ed., pp. 329–386). San Diego: Academic Press.

Park, B., & Rothbart, M. (1982). Perception of out-group homogeneity and levels of social categorization: Memory for the subordinate attributes of in-group and out-group members. *Journal of Personality and Social Psychology, 42,* 1051–1068.

Parker, K. C. (1988). Speaking turns in small group interaction: A context-sensitive event sequence model. *Journal of Personality and Social Psychology, 54,* 965–971.

Parkinson, C. N. (1957). *Parkinson's law and other studies in administration.* Boston: Houghton Mifflin.

Parks, C. D., Henager, R. F., & Scamahorn, S. D. (1996). Trust and reactions to messages of intent in social dilemmas. *Journal of Conflict Resolution, 40,* 134–151.

Parks, C. D., & Komorita, S. S. (1997). Reciprocal strategies for large groups. *Personality and Social Psychology Review, 1,* 314–322.

Parks, C. D., Sanna, L. J., & Posey, D. C. (2003). Retrospection in social dilemmas: How thinking about the past affects future cooperation. *Journal of Personality and Social Psychology, 84,* 988–996.

Parkum, K. H., & Parkum, V. C. (1980). Citizen participation in community planning and decision making. In D. H. Smith, J. Macaulay, & Associates (Eds.), *Participation in social and political activities: A comprehensive analysis of political involvement, expressive leisure time, and helping behavior* (pp. 153–167). San Francisco: Jossey-Bass.

Parsons, H. M. (1976). Work environments. In I. Altman & J. Wohlwill (Eds.), *Human behavior and environment* (Vol. 1, pp. 163–209). New York: Plenum Press.

Parsons, T., Bales, R. F., & Shils, E. (Eds.). (1953). *Working papers in the theory of action.* New York: Free Press.

Paskevich, D. M., Brawley, L. R., Dorsch, K. D., & Widmeyer, W. N. (1999). Relationship between collective efficacy and team cohesion: Conceptual and measurement issues. *Group Dynamics, 3,* 210–222.

Patel, K. A., & Schlundt, D. G. (2001). Impact of moods and social context on eating behavior. *Appetite, 36,* 111–118.

Patterson, M. L. (1975). Personal space—Time to burst the bubble? *Man–Environment Systems, 5,* 67.

Patterson, M. L. (1991). A functional approach to nonverbal exchange. In R. S. Feldman & B. Rimé (Eds.), *Fundamentals of nonverbal behavior* (pp. 458–495). New York: Cambridge University Press.

Patterson, M. L. (1996). Social behavior and social cognition: A parallel process approach. In J. L. Nye & A. M. Brower (Eds.), *What's social about social cognition? Research on socially shared cognitions in small groups* (pp. 87–105). Thousand Oaks, CA: Sage.

Patterson, M. L., Kelley, C. E., Kondracki, B. A., & Wulf, L. J. (1979). Effects of seating arrangement on small group behavior. *Social Psychology Quarterly, 42,* 180–185.

Patterson, M. L., Roth, C. P., & Schenk, C. (1979). Seating arrangement, activity, and sex differences in small group crowding. *Personality and Social Psychology Bulletin, 5,* 100–103.

Patterson, M. L., & Sechrest, L. B. (1970). Interpersonal distance and impression formation. *Journal of Personality, 38,* 161–166.

Paul, G. L. (1967). Strategy of outcome research in psychotherapy. *Journal of Consulting Psychology, 31,* 109–118.

Paulus, P. B. (2000). Groups, teams, and creativity: The creative potential of idea-generating groups. *Applied Psychology: An International Review, 49,* 237–262.

Paulus, P. B., Annis, A. B., Seta, J. J., Schkade, J. K., & Matthews, R. W. (1976). Density does affect task performance. *Journal of Personality and Social Psychology, 34,* 248–353.

Paulus, P. B., & Dzindolet, M. T. (1993). Social influence processes in group brainstorm. *Journal of Personality and Social Psychology, 64,* 575–586.

Paulus, P. B., Dzindolet, M. T., Poletes, G., & Camacho, L. M. (1993). Perception of performance in group brainstorming: The illusion of group productivity. *Personality and Social Psychology Bulletin, 19,* 78–89.

Paulus, P., & Putman, V. (1996, November). *Demonstrating group brainstorming effects.* Paper presented at the Annual Conference of the Society of Southeastern Social Psychologists, Virginia Beach, VA.

Paulus, P. B., & Yang, H. (2000). Idea generation in groups: A basis for creativity in organizations. *Organizational Behavior and Human Decision Processes, 82,* 76–87.

Pavelchak, M. A., Moreland, R. L., & Levine, J. M. (1986). Effects of prior group memberships on subsequent reconnaissance activities. *Journal of Personality and Social Psychology, 50,* 56–66.

Paxton, P., & Moody, J. (2003). Structure and sentiment: Explaining emotional attachment to group. *Social Psychology Quarterly, 66,* 34–47.

Pearce, C. L., & Conger, J. A. (Eds.). (2003). Shared leadership: Reframing the hows and whys of leadership. Thousand Oaks, CA: Sage.

Pearce, C. L., & Sims, H. P., Jr. (2002). Vertical versus shared leadership as predictors of the effectiveness of change management teams: An examination of aversive, directive, transactional, transformational, and empowering leader behaviors. *Group Dynamics, 6,* 172–197.

Pedersen, D. M. (1999). Model for types of privacy by privacy functions. *Journal of Environmental Psychology, 19,* 397–405.

Pelled, L. H., Eisenhardt, K. M., & Xin, K. R. (1999). Exploring the black box: An analysis of work group diversity, conflict, and performance. *Administrative Science Quarterly, 44,* 1–28.

Pelletier, L. G., & Vallerand, R. J. (1996). Supervisors' beliefs and subordinates' intrinsic motivation: A behavioral confirmation analysis. *Journal of Personality and Social Psychology, 71,* 331–340.

Pelz, D. C. (1956). Some social factors related to performance in a research organization. *Administrative Science Quarterly, 1,* 310–325.

Pelz, D. C. (1967). Creative tensions in the research and development climate. *Science, 157,* 160–165.

Pemberton, M. B., Insko, C. A., & Schopler, J. (1996). Memory for and experience of differential competitive behavior of individuals and groups. *Journal of Personality and Social Psychology, 71,* 953–966.

Pemberton, M. B., & Sedikides, C. (2001). When do individuals help close others improve? The role of information diagnosticity. *Journal of Personality and Social Psychology, 81,* 234–246.

Pennebaker, J. W. (1982). Social and perceptual factors affecting symptom reporting and mass psychogenic illness. In M. J. Colligan, J. W. Pennebaker, & L. R. Murphy (Eds.), *Mass psychogenic illness: A social psychological analysis* (pp. 139–153). Mahwah, NJ: Erlbaum.

Pennebaker, J. W. (1997). *Opening up: The healing power of expressing emotions* (rev. ed.). New York: Guilford Press.

Pennington, D. C. (2002). *The social psychology of behavior in small groups.* New York: Psychology Press.

Pennington, N., & Hastie, R. (1986). Evidence evaluation in complex decision-making. *Journal of Personality and Social Psychology, 51,* 242–258.

Pennington, N., & Hastie, R. (1992). Explaining the evidence: Tests of the Story Model for juror decision making. *Journal of Personality and Social Psychology, 62,* 189–206.

Penrod, S., & Hastie, R. (1980). A computer simulation of jury decision making. *Psychological Review, 87,* 133–159.

Penrod, S., & Heuer, L. (1998). Improving group performance: The case of the jury. In R. S. Tindale, L. Heath, J. Edwards, E. J. Posavac, F. B. Bryant, Y. Suarez-Balcazar, E. Henderson-King, & J. Myers (Eds.), *Theory and research on small groups* (pp. 127–152). New York: Plenum Press.

Pepitone, A. (1981). Lessons from the history of social psychology. *American Psychologist, 36,* 972–985.

Pepitone, A., & Reichling, G. (1955). Group cohesiveness and the expression of hostility. *Human Relations, 8,* 327–337.

Pepitone, A., & Wilpinski, C. (1960). Some consequences of experimental rejection. *Journal of Abnormal and Social Psychology, 60,* 359–364.

Pérez, J. A., & Mungy, G. (1996). The conflict elaboration theory of social influence. In E. Witte & J. Davis (Eds.), *Understanding group behavior: Consensual action by small groups* (Vol. 2, pp. 191–210). Mahwah, NJ: Erlbaum.

Perls, F. (1969). *Gestalt therapy verbatim.* Lafayette, CA: Real People Press.

Perls, F., Hefferline, R., & Goodman, P. (1951). *Gestalt therapy: Excitement and growth in the human personality.* New York: Julian Press.

Perrin, S., & Spencer, C. P. (1980). The Asch effect—A child of its time? *Bulletin of the British Psychological Society, 32,* 405–406.

Perrin, S., & Spencer, C. P. (1981). Independence or conformity in the Asch experiment as a reflection of cultural and situational factors. *British Journal of Social Psychology, 20,* 205–210.

Pescosolido, A. T. (2001). Informal leaders and the development of group efficacy. *Small Group Research, 32,* 74–93.

Pescosolido, A. T. (2003). Group efficacy and group effectiveness: The effects of group efficacy over time on group performance and development. *Small Group Research, 34,* 20–42.

Peterson, M. F., Smith, P. B., Akande, A., & Ayestaran, S. (1995). Role conflict, ambiguity, and overload: A 21-nation study. *Academy of Management Journal, 38,* 429–452.

Peterson, R. S. (1997). A directive leadership style in group decision making can be both virtue and vice: Evidence from elite and experimental groups. *Journal of Personality and Social Psychology 72,* 1107–1121.

Peterson, R. S., & Nemeth, C. J. (1996). Focus versus flexibility:

Majority and minority influence can both improve performance. *Personality and Social Psychology Bulletin, 22,* 14–23.

Peterson, R. S., Owens, P. D., Tetlock, P. E., Fan, E. T., & Martorana, P. (1998). Group dynamics in top management teams: Groupthink, vigilance, and alternative models of organizational failure and success. *Organizational Behavior and Human Decision Processes, 73,* 272–305.

Pettigrew, T. F. (1997). Generalized intergroup contact effects on prejudice. *Personality and Social Psychology Bulletin, 23,* 173–185.

Pettigrew, T. F. (2001). The ultimate attribution error: Extending Allport's cognitive analysis of prejudice. In M. A. Hogg & D. Abrams (Eds.), *Intergroup relations: Essential readings* (pp. 162–173). Philadelphia: Psychology Press.

Pettigrew, T. F, & & Tropp, L. R. (2000). Does intergroup contact reduce prejudice: Recent meta-analytic findings. S. Oskamp (Ed.), *Reducing prejudice and discrimination* (pp. 93–114). Mahwah, NJ: Erlbaum. Retrieved June 22, 2004, from http://www.netlibrary.com

Petty, R. E., & Cacioppo, J. T. (1986). The elaboration likelihood model of persuasion. *Advances in Experimental Social Psychology, 19,* 124–205.

Pfeffer, J., & Salancik, G. (1978) *The external control of organizations.* New York: Harper & Row.

Phillips, J. S., & Lord, R. G. (1986). Notes on the practical and theoretical consequences of implicit leadership theories for the future of leadership measurement. *Journal of Management, 12,* 31–41.

Phillips, K. W. (2003). The effects of categorically based expectations on minority influence: The importance of congruence. *Personality and Social Psychology Bulletin, 29,* 3–13.

Phinney, J. S. (1989). Stages of ethnic identity development in minority group adolescents. *Journal of Early Adolescence, 9,* 34–49.

Phinney, J. S. (1996). When we talk about American ethnic groups, what do we mean? *American Psychologist, 51,* 918–927.

Phoon, W. H. (1982). Outbreaks of mass hysteria at workplaces in Singapore: Some patterns and modes of presentation. In M. J. Colligan, J. W. Pennebaker, & L. R. Murphy (Eds.), *Mass psychogenic illness: A social psychological analysis* (pp. 21–31). Mahwah, NJ: Erlbaum.

Pierro, A., Mannetti, L., De Grada, E., Livi, S., & Kruglanski, A. W. (2003). Autocracy bias in informal groups under need for closure. *Personality and Social Psychology Bulletin, 29,* 405–417.

Pigors, P. (1935). *Leadership or domination.* Boston: Houghton Mifflin.

Pilisuk, M., Brandes, B., & van den Hove, D. (1976). Deceptive sounds: Illicit communication in the laboratory. *Behavioral Science, 21,* 515–523.

Pillai, R. (1996). Crisis and the emergence of charismatic leadership in groups: An experimental investigation. *Journal of Applied Social Psychology, 26,* 543–562.

Pillutla, M. M., & Murnighan, J. K. (1996). Unfairness, anger, and spite: Emotional rejections of ultimatum offers. *Organizational Behavior and Human Decision Processes, 68,* 208–224.

Pinsonneault, A., Barki, H., Gallupe, R. B., & Hoppen, N. (1999). Electronic brainstorming: The illusion of productivity. *Information Systems Research, 10,* 110–133.

Pisano, G. P., Bohmer, R. M. J., & Edmondson, A. C. (2001). Organizational differences in rates of learning: Evidence from the adoption of minimally invasive cardiac surgery. *Management Science, 47,* 752–768.

Pittard-Payne, B. (1980). Nonassociational religious participation.

In D. H. Smith, J. Macaulay, & Associates (Eds.), *Participation in social and political activities: A comprehensive analysis of political involvement, expressive leisure time, and helping behavior* (pp. 214–243). San Francisco: Jossey-Bass.

Platania, J., & Moran, G. P. (2001). Social facilitation as a function of mere presence of others. *Journal of Social Psychology, 141,* 190–197.

Platow, M. J., Durante, M., Williams, N., Garrett, M., Walshe, J., Cincotta, S., Lianos, G., & Barutchu, A. (1999). The contribution of sport fan social identity to the production of prosocial behavior. *Group Dynamics, 3,* 161–169.

Plous, S. (1993). *The psychology of judgment and decision making.* New York: McGraw-Hill.

Podsakoff, P. M., & MacKenzie, S. B. (1997). Kerr and Jermier's substitutes for leadership model: Background, empirical assessment, and suggestions for future research. *Leadership Quarterly, 8,* 117–132.

Podsakoff, P. M., MacKenzie, S. B., & Bommer, W. H. (1996). Meta-analysis of the relationships between Kerr and Jermier's substitutes for leadership and employee job attitudes, role perceptions, and performance. *Journal of Applied Psychology, 81,* 380–399.

Polletta, F., & Jasper, J. M. (2001). Collective identity and social movements [Electronic version]. *Annual Review of Sociology, 27,* 283–305.

Polley, R. B. (1989). On the dimensionality of interpersonal behavior: A reply to Lustig. *Small Group Behavior, 20,* 270–278.

Polley, R. B., Hare, A. P., & Stone, P. J. (Eds.). (1988). *The SYMLOG practitioner: Applications of small group research.* New York: Praeger.

Pollis, N. P., Montgomery, R. L., & Smith, T. G. (1975). Autokinetic paradigms: A reply to Alexander, Zucker, and Brody. *Sociometry, 38,* 358–373.

Polzer, J. T. (1996). Intergroup negotiations: The effects of negotiating teams. *Journal of Conflict Resolution, 40,* 678–698.

Polzer, J. T., Kramer, R. M., & Neale, M. A. (1997). Positive illusions about oneself and one's group. *Small Group Research, 28,* 243–266.

Poppe, E. (2001). Effects of changes in GNP and perceived group characteristics on national and ethnic stereotypes in central and eastern Europe. *Journal of Applied Social Psychology, 31,* 1689–1708.

Porter, N., Geis, F. L., Cooper, E., & Newman, E. (1985). Androgyny and leadership in mixed-sex groups. *Journal of Personality and Social Psychology, 49,* 808–823.

Postmes, T., & Spears, R. (1998). Deindividuation and antinormative behavior: A meta-analysis. *Psychological Bulletin, 123,* 238–259.

Postmes, T., & Spears, R. (2002). Behavior online: Does anonymous computer communication reduce gender inequality? *Personality and Social Psychology Bulletin, 28,* 1073–1083.

Postmes, T., Spears, R., & Cihangir, S. (2001). Quality of decision making and group norms. *Journal of Personality and Social Psychology, 80,* 918–930.

Postmes, T., Spears, R., & Lea, M. (2000). The formation of group norms in computer-mediated communication. *Human Communication Research, 26,* 341–371.

Poundstone, W. (1992). *Prisoner's dilemma.* New York: Doubleday.

Prapavessis, H., & Carron, A. V. (1997). Sacrifice, cohesion, and conformity to norms in sport teams. *Group Dynamics, 1,* 231–240.

Prapavessis, H., & Carron, A. V. (1997). Sacrifice, cohesion, and conformity to norms in sport teams. *Group Dynamics, 1,* 231–240.

Pratt, J. H. (1922). The principle of class treatment and their application to various chronic diseases. *Hospital Social Services, 6,* 401–417.

Preiss, J. J. (1968). Self and role in medical education. In C. Gordon & K. J. Gergen (Eds.), *The self in social interaction* (pp. 207–218). New York: Wiley.

Prentice, D. A., & Miller, D. T. (1993). Pluralistic ignorance and alcohol use on campus: Some consequences of misperceiving the social norm. *Journal of Personality and Social Psychology, 64,* 243–254.

Prentice-Dunn, S., & Rogers, R. W. (1980). Effects of deindividuating situation cues and aggressive models on subjective deindividuation and aggression. *Journal of Personality and Social Psychology, 39,* 104–113.

Prentice-Dunn, S., & Rogers, R. W. (1982). Effects of public and private self-awareness on deindividuation and aggression. *Journal of Personality and Social Psychology, 43,* 503–513.

Prentice-Dunn, S., & Rogers, R. W. (1983). Deindividuation and aggression. In R. G. Geen & E. I. Donnerstein (Eds.), *Aggression: Theoretical and empirical reviews* (Vol. 1, pp. 155–171). New York: Academic Press.

Prentice-Dunn, S., & Spivey, C. B. (1986). Extreme deindividuation in the laboratory: Its magnitude and subjective components. *Personality and Social Psychology Bulletin, 12,* 206–215.

Prislin, R., Brewer, M., & Wilson, D. J. (2002). Changing majority and minority positions within a group versus an aggregate. *Personality and Social Psychology Bulletin, 28,* 640–647.

Prislin, R., & Christensen, P. N. (2002). Group conversion versus group expansion as modes of change in majority and minority positions: All losses hurt but only some gains gratify. *Journal of Personality and Social Psychology, 83,* 1095–1102.

Prislin, R., Limbert, W. M., & Bauer, E. (2000). From majority to minority and vice versa: The asymmetrical effects of losing and gaining majority position within a group. *Journal of Personality and Social Psychology, 79,* 385–397.

Probst, T., Carnevale, P. J., & Triandis, H. C. (1999). Cultural values in intergroup and single-group social dilemmas. *Organizational Behavior and Human Decision Processes, 77,* 171–191.

Propp, K. M. (1999). Collective information processing in groups. In L. Frey, D. S. Gouran, & M. S. Poole (Eds.), *The handbook of group communication: Theory and research* (pp. 225–250). Thousand Oaks, CA: Sage.

Pruitt, D. G. (1971). Choice shifts in group discussion: An introductory review. *Journal of Personality and Social Psychology, 20,* 339–360.

Pruitt, D. G. (1983). Strategic choice in negotiation. *American Behavioral Science, 27,* 167–194.

Pruitt, D. G. (1998). Social conflict. In D. T. Gilbert, S. T. Fiske, & G. Lindzey (Eds.), *The handbook of social psychology* (4th ed., Vol. 2, 470–503). New York: McGraw-Hill.

Pruitt, D. G., & Carnevale, P. J. (1993). *Negotiation in social conflict.* Buckingham, UK: Open University Press.

Pruitt, D. G., & Rubin, J. Z. (1986). *Social conflict: Escalation, stalemate, and settlement.* New York: Random House.

Quattrone, G. A. (1986). On the perception of a group's variability. In S. Worchel & W. G. Austin (Eds.), *Psychology of intergroup relations* (2nd ed., pp. 25–48). Chicago: Nelson-Hall.

Quattrone, G. A., & Jones, E. E. (1980). The perception of variability within in-groups and out-groups: Implications for the law of small numbers. *Journal of Personality and Social Psychology, 38,* 141–152.

Quinn, A., & Schlenker, B. R. (2002). Can accountability produce independence? Goals as determinants of the impact of accountability on conformity. *Personality and Social Psychology Bulletin, 28,* 472–483.

Quinn, R. E., & McGrath, M. R. (1982). Moving beyond the single solution perspective. *Journal of Applied Behavioral Science, 18,* 463–472.

Rabbie, J. (1963). Differential preference for companionship under stress. *Journal of Abnormal and Social Psychology, 67,* 643–648.

Radloff, R., & Helmreich, R. (1968). *Groups under stress: Psychological research in SEALAB II.* New York: Irvington.

Ragone, G. (1981). Fashion, "crazes," and collective behavior. *Communications, 7,* 249–268.

Raiffa, H. (1983). Mediation of conflicts. *American Behavioral Science, 27,* 195–210.

Raiffa, H., Richardson, J., & Metcalfe, D. (2003). *Negotiation analysis: The science and art of collaborative decision making.* Cambridge, MA: Harvard Books.

Rail, G. (1987). Perceived role characteristics and executive satisfaction in voluntary sport associations. *Journal of Sport Psychology, 9,* 376–384.

Ranie, L., & Kalsnes, B. (2001, October 10). *The commons of the tragedy: How the internet was used by millions after the terror attacks to grieve, console, share news, and debate the country's response.* Retrieved July 17, 2004, from http://www.pewtrusts.com/pdf/vf_pew_internet_attack_aftermath.pdf

Rantilla, A. K. (2000). Collective task responsibility allocation: Revisiting the group-serving bias. *Small Group Research, 31,* 739–766.

Rapoport, A. (1985). Provision of public goods and the MCS experimental paradigm. *American Political Science Review, 79,* 148–155.

Rapoport, A. (1988). Provision of step-level public goods: Effects of inequality in resources. *Journal of Personality and Social Psychology, 54,* 432–440.

Ratner, R. K., & Miller, D. T. (2001). The norm of self-interest and its effects on social action. *Journal of Personality and Social Psychology, 81,* 5–16.

Raven, B. H. (1965). Social influence and power. In I. D. Steiner & M. Fishbein (Eds.), *Current studies in social psychology* (pp. 371–382). New York: Holt, Rinehart & Winston.

Raven, B. H. (1992). A power/interaction model of interpersonal influence: French and Raven thirty years later. *Journal of Social Behavior and Personality, 7,* 217–244.

Raven, B. H. (1998). Groupthink, Bay of Pigs, and Watergate reconsidered. *Organizational Behavior and Human Decision Processes, 73,* 352–361.

Raven, B. H. (1999). Influence, power, religion, and the mechanisms of social control. *Journal of Social Issues, 55,* 161–186.

Raven, B. H., & Kruglanski, A. W. (1970). Conflict and power. In P. Swingle (Ed.), *The structure of conflict* (pp. 69–110). New York: Academic Press.

Rawlinson, J. W. (2000). Does psychodrama work? A review of the literature. *British Journal of Psychodrama and Sociometry, 15,* 67–101.

Rayner, S. R. (1996). *Team traps.* New York: Wiley.

Read, K. E. (1986). *Return to the high valley: Coming full circle.* Berkeley: University of California Press.

Read, P. P. (1974). *Alive.* New York: Avon.

Reddin, W. J. (1970). *Managerial effectiveness*. New York: McGraw-Hill.

Redl, F. (1942). Group emotion and leaders. *Psychiatry, 5*, 573–596.

Reeder, K., MacFadyen, L. P., Roche, J., & Chase, M. (2004). Negotiating cultures in cyberspace: Participation patterns and problematics. *Language Learning and Technology, 8*, 88–105.

Rees, C. R., & Segal, M. W. (1984). Role differentiation in groups: The relationship between instrumental and expressive leadership. *Small Group Behavior, 15*, 109–123.

Reicher, S. D. (1984). The St. Pauls riot: An explanation of the limits of crowd action in terms of a social identity model. *European Journal of Social Psychology, 14*, 1–21.

Reicher, S. D. (1987). Crowd behavior as social action. In J. C. Turner, M. A. Hogg, P. J. Oakes, S. D. Reicher, & M. S. Wetherell (Eds.), *Rediscovering the social group: A self-categorization theory* (pp. 171–202). Oxford, UK: Blackwell.

Reicher, S. D. (1996). "The Battle of Westminster": Developing the social identity model of crowd behavior in order to explain the initiation and development of collective conflict. *European Journal of Social Psychology, 26*, 115–134.

Reicher, S. D. (2001). The psychology of crowd dynamics. In M. A. Hogg & R. S. Tindale (Eds.), *Blackwell handbook of social psychology: Group processes* (pp. 182–208). Malden, MA: Blackwell.

Reicher, S. D., & Levine, M. (1994). Deindividuation, power relations between groups and the expression of social identity: The effects of visibility to the out-group. *British Journal of Social Psychology, 33*, 145–163.

Reicher, S. D., Spears, R., & Postmes, T. (1995). A social identity model of deindividuated phenomena. In W. Stroebe & M. Hewstone (Eds.), *European review of social psychology* (Vol. 6, pp. 161–198). Chichester, UK: Wiley.

Reichl, A. J. (1997). Ingroup favoritism and outgroup favoritism in low status minimal groups: Differential responses to status-related and status-unrelated measures. *European Journal of Social Psychology, 27*, 617–633.

Reid, A., & Deaux, K. (1996). Relationship between social and personal identities: Segregation or integration. *Journal of Personality and Social Psychology, 71*, 1084–1091.

Reifman, A., Lee, L., & Apparala, M. (2004). *Spreading popularity of two musical artists: A "tipping point" study.* Poster presented at the 5th Annual Meeting of the Society for Personality and Social Psychology, Austin, TX.

Remland, M. S., Jones, T. S., & Brinkman, H. (1995). Interpersonal distance, body orientation, and touch: Effects of culture, gender, and age. *Journal of Social Psychology, 135*, 281–297.

Rempel, J. K., Holmes, J. G., & Zanna, M. P. (1985). Trust in close relationships. *Journal of Personality and Social Psychology, 49*, 95–112.

Reno, R. R., Cialdini, R. B., & Kallgren, C. A. (1993). The transsituational influence of social norms. *Journal of Personality and Social Psychology, 64*, 104–112.

Rentsch, J. R., & Steel, R. P. (1998). Testing the durability of job characteristics as predictors of absenteeism over a six-year period. *Personnel Psychology, 51*, 165–190.

Rhee, E., Uleman, J. S., Lee, H. K., & Roman, R. J. (1995). Spontaneous self-descriptions and ethnic identities in individualistic and collectivistic cultures. *Journal of Personality and Social Psychology, 69*, 142–152.

Rheingold, H. (2002). *Smart mobs: The next social revolution.* Cambridge, MA: Perseus.

Rice, O. K. (1978). *The Hatfields and the McCoys.* Lexington: University Press of Kentucky.

Rice, R. W. (1979). Reliability and validity of the LPC Scale: A reply. *Academy of Management Review, 4*, 291–294.

Rice, R. W., Instone, D., & Adams, J. (1984). Leader sex, leader success, and leadership process: Two field studies. *Journal of Applied Psychology, 69*, 12–31.

Ridgeway, C. L. (1982). Status in groups: The importance of motivation. *American Sociological Review, 47*, 76–88.

Ridgeway, C. L. (1983). *The dynamics of small groups.* New York: St. Martin's Press.

Ridgeway, C. L. (1989). Understanding legitima-tion in informal status orders. In J. Berger, M. Zelditch, Jr., & B. Anderson (Eds.), *Sociological theories in progress: New formulations* (pp. 131–159). Thousand Oaks, CA: Sage.

Ridgeway, C. L. (2001). Social status and group structure. In M. A. Hogg & R. S. Tindale (Eds.), *Blackwell handbook of social psychology: Group processes* (pp. 352–375). Malden, MA: Blackwell.

Ridgeway, C. L., & Balkwell, J. W. (1997). Group processes and the diffusion of status beliefs. *Social Psychology Quarterly, 60*, 14–31.

Ridgeway, C. L., & Walker, H. A. (1995). Status structures. In K. S. Cook, G. A. Fine, & J. S. House (Eds.), *Sociological perspectives on social psychology* (pp. 281–310). Boston: Allyn & Bacon.

Riess, M. (1982). Seating preferences as impression management: A literature review and theoretical integration. *Communication, 11*, 85–113.

Riess, M., & Rosenfeld, P. (1980). Seating preferences as nonverbal communication: A self-presentational analysis. *Journal of Applied Communications Research, 8*, 22–30.

Rimé, B., Philippot, P., Boca, S., & Mesquita, B. (1992). Long-lasting cognitive and social consequences of emotion: Social sharing and rumination. *European Review of Social Psychology, 3*, 225–258.

Ringelmann, M. (1913). Research on animate sources of power: The work of man. *Annales de l'Institut National Agronomique, 2e. série—tome XII*, 1–40.

Riordan, C., & Riggiero, J. (1980). Producing equal-status interracial interaction: A replication. *Social Psychology Quarterly, 43*, 131–136.

Rivera, A. N., & Tedeschi, J. T. (1976). Public versus private reactions to positive inequity. *Journal of Personality and Social Psychology, 34*, 895–900.

Robak, R. W. (2001). Self-definition in psychotherapy: Is it time to revisit self-perception theory? *North American Journal of Psychology, 3*, 529–534.

Robert, H. M. (1971). *Robert's rules of order* (rev. ed.). New York: Morrow. (Originally published in 1915)

Rodin, J. (1976). Crowding, perceived choice, and response to controllable and uncontrollable outcomes. *Journal of Experimental Social Psychology, 12*, 564–578.

Rodin, J., & Baum, A. (1978). Crowding and helplessness: Potential consequences of density and loss of control. In A. Baum & Y. Epstein (Eds.), *Human responses to crowding.* Mahwah, NJ: Erlbaum.

Rodin, J., Solomon, S. K., & Metcalf, J. (1978). Role of control in mediating perceptions of density. *Journal of Personality and Social Psychology, 36*, 988–999.

Roethlisberger, F. J., & Dickson, W. J. (1939). *Management and the worker.* Cambridge, MA: Harvard University Press.

Rofé, Y. (1984). Stress and affiliation: A utility theory. *Psychological Review, 91,* 235–250.

Rogelberg, S. G., & O'Connor, M. S. (1998). Extending the stepladder technique: An examination of self-paced stepladder groups. *Group Dynamics, 2,* 82–91.

Rogelberg, S. G., & Rumery, S. M. (1996). Gender diversity, team decision quality, time on task, and interpersonal cohesion. *Small Group Research, 27,* 79–90.

Rogers, C. (1970). *Encounter groups.* New York: Harper & Row.

Rogers, R. W., & Prentice-Dunn, S. (1981). Deindividuation and anger-mediated interracial aggression: Unmasking regressive racism. *Journal of Personality and Social Psychology, 41,* 63–73.

Rohrbaugh, M., & Bartels, B. D. (1975). Participants' perceptions of curative factors in therapy and growth groups. *Small Group Behavior, 6,* 430–456.

Roll, S., McClelland, G., & Abel, T. (1996). Differences in susceptibility to influence in Mexican American and Anglo females. *Hispanic Journal of Behavioral Sciences, 18,* 13–20.

Rom, E., & Mikulincer, M. (2003). Attachment theory and group processes: The association between attachment style and group-related representations, goals, memories, and functioning. *Journal of Personality and Social Psychology, 84,* 1220–1235.

Rook, K. S. (1984). Promoting social bonding: Strategies for helping the lonely and socially isolated. *American Psychologist, 39,* 1389–1407.

Roos, P. D. (1968). Jurisdiction: An ecological concept. *Human Relations, 21,* 75–84.

Rose, R. (1954). *Twelve angry men.* Chicago: Dramatic Publishing.

Rosenbaum, M. E. (1986). The repulsion hypothesis: On the non-development of relationships. *Journal of Personality and Social Psychology, 51,* 1156–1166.

Rosnow, R. L. (1980). Psychology of rumor reconsidered. *Psychological Bulletin, 87,* 578–591.

Rosnow, R. L., & Kimmel, A. J. (1979). Lives of a rumor. *Psychology Today, 13*(6), 88–92.

Rosnow, R. L., & Rosenthal, R. (1997). *People studying people: Artifacts and ethics in behavioral research.* New York: Freeman.

Rosnow, R. L., Yost, J. H., & Esposito, J. L. (1986). Belief in rumor and likelihood of rumor transmission. *Language and Communication, 6,* 189–194.

Ross, L. (1977). The intuitive psychologist and his shortcomings: Distortions in the attribution process. *Advances in Experimental Social Psychology, 10,* 173–220.

Ross, L., Bierbrauer, G., & Hoffman, S. (1976). The role of attribution processes in conformity and dissent: Revisiting the Asch situation. *American Psychologist, 31,* 148–157.

Ross, L., & Ward, A. (1995). Psychological barriers to dispute resolution. *Advances in Experimental Social Psychology, 27,* 255–304.

Ross, M., & Holmberg, D. (1992). Are wives' memories for events in relationships more vivid than their husbands' memories? *Journal of Social & Personal Relationships, 9,* 585–604.

Ross, W. H., Brantmeier, C., & Ciriacks, T. (2002). The impact of hybrid dispute-resolution procedures on constituent fairness judgments. *Journal of Applied Social Psychology, 32,* 1151–1188.

Ross, W. H., & Conlon, D. E. (2000). Hybrid forms of dispute resolution: Theoretical implications of combining mediation and arbitration. *Academy of Management Review, 25,* 416–427.

Roth, B. E. (1993). Freud: The group psychologist and group leader. In H. I. Kaplan & M. J. Sadock (Eds.), *Comprehensive group psychotherapy* (3rd. ed., pp. 10–21). Baltimore: Williams & Wilkins.

Rothbart, M., Sriram, N., & Davis-Stitt, C. (1996). The retrieval of typical and atypical category members. *Journal of Experimental Social Psychology, 32,* 309–336.

Rothgerber, H. (1997). External intergroup threat as an antecedent to perceptions in in-group and out-group homogeneity. *Journal of Personality and Social Psychology, 73,* 1206–1212.

Rothgerber, H., & Worchel, S. (1997). The view from below: Intergroup relations from the perspective of the disadvantaged group. *Journal of Personality and Social Psychology, 73,* 1191–1205.

Rothman, A. L., & Weintraub, M. I. (1995). The sick building syndrome and mass hysteria. *Neurologic Clinics, 13,* 405–412.

Rotton, J., & Cohn, E. G. (2002). Climate, weather, and crime. In R. B. Bechtel & A. Churchman (Eds.), *Handbook of environmental psychology* (pp. 481–498). New York: Wiley. Retrieved July 30, 2004, from http://www.netlibrary.com

Rouhana, N. N., & Bar-Tal, D. (1998). Psychological dynamics of intractable ethnonational conflicts: The Israeli–Palestinian case. *American Psychologist, 53,* 761–770.

Rouhana, N. N., & Kelman, H. C. (1994). Promoting joint thinking in international conflicts: An Israeli–Palestinian continuing workshop. *Journal of Social Issues, 50*(1), 157–178.

Roy, D. F. (1973). "Banana time"—Job satisfaction and informal interaction. In W. G. Bennis, D. E. Berlew, E. H. Schein, & F. I. Steele (Eds.), *Interpersonal dynamics* (pp. 403–417). Homewood, IL: Dorsey.

Roy, M. C., Gauvin, S., & Limayem, M. (1996). Electronic group brainstorming: The role of feedback and productivity. *Small Group Research, 27,* 214–247.

Rozin, P., Lowery, L., Imada, S., & Haidt, J. (1999). The CAD triad hypothesis: A mapping between three moral emotions (contempt, anger, disgust) and three moral codes (community, autonomy, divinity). *Journal of Personality and Social Psychology, 76,* 574–586.

Ruback, R. B., Dabbs, J. M., Jr., & Hopper, C. H. (1984). The process of brainstorming: An analysis with individual and group vocal parameters. *Journal of Personality and Social Psychology, 47,* 558–567.

Rubin, J. Z. (1980). Experimental research on third-party intervention in conflict: Toward some generalizations. *Psychological Bulletin, 87,* 379–391.

Rubin, J. Z. (1986). Third parties within organizations: A responsive commentary. *Research on Negotiation in Organizations, 1,* 271–283.

Rubin, J. Z. (1994). Models of conflict management. *Journal of Social Issues, 50*(1), 33–46.

Rubin, J. Z., & Brown, B. R. (1975). *The social psychology of bargaining and negotiation.* New York: Academic Press.

Rubin, J. Z., Pruitt, D. G., & Kim, S. H. (1994). *Social conflict: Escalation, stalemate, and settlement* (2nd ed.). New York: McGraw-Hill.

Rubin, M., & Hewstone, M. (1998). Social identity theory's self-esteem hypothesis: A review and some suggestions for clarification. *Personality and Social Psychology Review, 2,* 40–62.

Rubonis, A. V., & Bickman, L. (1991). Psychological impairment in the wake of disaster: The disaster–psychopathology relationship. *Psychological Bulletin, 109,* 384–399.

Rudman, L. A., & Glick, P. (2001). Prescriptive gender stereotypes and backlash toward agentic women. *Journal of Social Issues, 57,* 743–762.

Rugel, R. P., & Meyer, D. J. (1984). The Tavistock group: Empirical findings and implications for group therapy. *Small Group Behavior, 15,* 361–374.

Runcimann, W. G. (1966). *Relative deprivation and social justice.* London: Routledge & Kegan Paul.

Rusbult, C. E. (1983). A longitudinal test of the investment model: The development (and deterioration) of satisfaction and commitment in heterosexual involvements. *Journal of Personality and Social Psychology, 45,* 101–117.

Rusbult, C. E. (1987). Responses to dissatisfaction in close relationships: The exit–voice–loyalty–neglect model. In D. Perman & S. Duck (Eds.), *Intimate relationships: Development, dynamics, and deterioration* (pp. 209–237). Thousand Oaks, CA: Sage.

Rusbult, C. E., & Martz, J. M. (1995). Remaining in an abusive relationship: An investment model analysis of nonvoluntary dependence. *Personality and Social Psychology Bulletin, 21,* 558–571.

Rusbult, C. E., Zembrodt, I. M., & Gunn, L. K. (1982). Exit, voice, loyalty, and neglect: Responses to dissatisfaction in romantic involvements. *Journal of Personality and Social Psychology, 43,* 1230–1242.

Ruscher, J. B., & Duval, L. L. (1998). Multiple communicators with unique target information transmit less stereotypical impressions. *Journal of Personality and Social Psychology, 74,* 329–344.

Rush, M. C., Thomas, J. C., & Lord, R. G. (1977). Implicit leadership theory: A potential threat to the internal validity of the leader behavior questionnaires. *Organizational Behavior and Human Performance, 20,* 93–110.

Rushton, J. P. (1989). Genetic similarity, human altruism, and group selection. *Behavioral and Brain Sciences, 12,* 503–559.

Russell, B. (1938). *Power.* London: Allen & Unwin.

Russell, G. W., & Arms, R. L. (1998). Toward a social psychological profile of would-be rioters. *Aggressive Behavior, 24,* 219–226.

Russell, J. A., & Lanius, U. F. (1984). Adaptation levels and the affective appraisal of environments. *Journal of Environmental Psychology, 4,* 119–135.

Russell, J. A., & Mehrabian, A. (1975). Task, setting, and personality variables affecting the desire to work. *Journal of Applied Psychology, 60,* 518–520.

Ryen, A. H., & Kahn, A. (1975). The effects of intergroup orientation on group attitudes and proxemic behavior: A test of two models. *Journal of Personality and Social Psychology, 31,* 302–310.

Sadler, M. S., & Judd, C. M. (2001). Overcoming dependent data: A guide to the analysis of group data. In M. A. Hogg & R. S. Tindale (Eds.), *Blackwell handbook of social psychology: Group processes* (pp. 497–524). Malden, MA: Blackwell.

Sadler, P., & Woody, E. (2003). Is who you are who you're talking to? Interpersonal style and complementarity in mixed-sex interactions. *Journal of Personality and Social Psychology, 84,* 80–95.

Saegert, S. (1978). High-density environments: Their personal and social consequences. In A. Baum & Y. M. Epstein (Eds.), *Human response to crowding* (pp. 257–281). Mahwah, NJ: Erlbaum.

Sagar, H. A., & Schofield, J. W. (1980). Racial and behavioral cues in Black and White children's perceptions of ambiguously aggressive acts. *Journal of Personality and Social Psychology, 39,* 590–598.

Saks, M. J. (1977). *Jury verdicts.* Lexington, MA: Heath.

Saks, M. J., & Hastie, R. (1978). *Social psychology in court.* New York: Van Nostrand Reinhold.

Saks, M. J., & Marti, M. W. (1997). A meta-analysis of the effects of jury size. *Law and Human Behavior, 21,* 451–467.

Salas, E., & Cannon-Bowers, J. A. (2000). The science of training: A decade of progress. *Annual Review of Psychology, 52,* 471–499.

Sampson, E. E. (1971). *Social psychology and contemporary society.* New York: Wiley.

Sampson, E. E., & Brandon, A. C. (1964). The effects of role and opinion deviation on small group behavior. *Sociometry, 27,* 261–281.

Sampson, R. V. (1965). *Equality and power.* London: Heinemann.

Samuelson, C. D., & Allison, S. T. (1994). Cognitive factors affecting the use of social decision heuristics in resource-sharing tasks. *Organizational Behavior and Human Decision Processes, 58,* 1–27.

Samuelson, C. D., & Messick, D. M. (1995). When do people want to change the rules for allocating shared resources? In D. A. Schroeder (Ed.), *Social dilemmas: Perspectives on individuals and groups* (pp. 144–162). Westport, CT: Praeger.

Sandal, G. M., Vaernes, R., Bergan, T., Warncke, M., & Ursin, H. (1996). Psychological reactions during polar expeditions and isolation in hyperbaric chambers. *Aviation, Space, and Environmental Medicine, 67,* 227–234.

Sandelands, L., & St. Clair, L. (1993). Toward an empirical concept of group. *Journal for the Theory of Social Behavior, 23,* 423–458.

Sanders, G. S. (1981). Driven by distraction: An integrative review of social facilitation theory and research. *Journal of Experimental Social Psychology, 17,* 227–251.

Sanders, G. S., & Baron, R. S. (1977). Is social comparison irrelevant for producing choice shifts? *Journal of Experimental Social Psychology, 13,* 303–314.

Sanders, G. S., Baron, R. S., & Moore, D. L. (1978). Distraction and social comparison as mediators of social facilitation effects. *Journal of Experimental Social Psychology, 14,* 291–303.

Sanders, W. B. (1994). *Gangbangs and drive-bys: Grounded culture and juvenile gang violence.* New York: Aldine de Gruyter.

Sankowsky, D. (1995). Charismatic leader as narcissist: Understanding the abuse of power. *Organizational Dynamics, 23*(4), 57–71.

Sanna, L. J. (1992). Self-efficacy theory: Implications for social facilitation and social loafing. *Journal of Personality and Social Psychology, 62,* 774–786.

Sanna, L. J., & Parks, C. D. (1997). Group research trends in social and organizational psychology: Whatever happened to intragroup research? *Psychological Science, 8,* 261–267.

Sanna, L. J., & Shotland, R. L. (1990). Valence of anticipated evaluation and social facilitation. *Journal of Experimental Social Psychology, 26,* 82–92.

Santee, R. T., & Jackson, S. E. (1982). Sex differences in evaluative implications of conformity and dissent. *Social Psychology Quarterly, 45,* 121–125.

Santee, R. T., & Maslach, C. (1982). To agree or not to agree: Personal dissent amid social pressure to conform. *Journal of Personality and Social Psychology, 42,* 690–700.

Sapp, S. G., Harrod, W. J., & Zhao, L. (1996). Leadership emergence in task groups with egalitarian gender-role expectations. *Sex Roles, 34,* 65–83.

Sarbin, T. R., & Allen, V. L. (1968). Increasing participation in a natural group setting: A preliminary report. *Psychological Record, 18,* 1–7.

Sarri, R. C., & Galinsky, M. J. (1985). In M. Sundel, P. Glasser, R. Sarri, & R. Vinter (Eds.), *Individual change through small groups* (2nd ed., pp. 70–86). New York: Free Press.

Sasfy, J., & Okun, M. (1974). Form of evaluation and audience expertness as joint determinants of audience effects. *Journal of Experimental Social Psychology, 10,* 461–467.

Sattler, D. N., & Kerr, N. L. (1991). Might versus morality explored: Motivational and cognitive bases for social motives. *Journal of Personality and Social Psychology, 60,* 756–765.

Scandura, T. A., & Lankau, M. J. (1996). Developing diverse leaders: A leader–member exchange approach. *Leadership Quarterly, 7,* 243–263.

Schachter, S. (1951). Deviation, rejection, and communication. *Journal of Abnormal and Social Psychology, 46,* 190–207.

Schachter, S. (1959). *The psychology of affiliation.* Stanford, CA: Stanford University Press.

Schachter, S., Ellertson, N., McBride, D., & Gregory, D. (1951). An experimental study of cohesiveness and productivity. *Human Relations, 4,* 229–238.

Schafer, M., & Crichlow, S. (1996). Antecedents of groupthink: A quantitative study. *Journal of Conflict Resolution, 40,* 415–435.

Schauer, A. H., Seymour, W. R., & Geen, R. G. (1985). Effects of observation and evaluation on anxiety in beginning counselors: A social facilitation analysis. *Journal of Counseling and Development, 63,* 279–285.

Schein, E. H. (1961). *Coercive persuasion.* New York: Norton.

Schein, E. H. (1971). *Process consultation: Its role in organization development.* Reading, MA: Addison-Wesley.

Schein, E. H. (1990). Organizational culture. *American Psychologist, 45,* 109–119.

Schein, V. E. (2001). A global look at psychological barriers to women's progress in management. *Journal of Social Issues, 57,* 675–688.

Scheuble, K. J., Dixon, K. N., Levy, A. B., & Kagan-Moore, L. (1987). Premature termination: A risk in eating disorder groups. *Group, 11,* 85–93.

Schlenker, B. R. (1975). Liking for a group following an initiation: Impression management or dissonance reduction? *Sociometry, 38,* 99–118.

Schlenker, B. R., & Bonoma, T. V. (1978). Fun and games: The validity of games for the study of conflict. *Journal of Conflict Resolution, 22,* 7–37.

Schlenker, B. R., & Goldman, H. J. (1978). Cooperators and competitors in conflict: A test of the "triangle model." *Journal of Conflict Resolution, 22,* 393–410.

Schlenker, B. R., Nacci, P., Helm, B., & Tedeschi, J. T. (1976). Reactions to coercive and reward power: The effects of switching influence modes on target compliance. *Sociometry, 39,* 316–323.

Schlenker, B. R., Phillips, S. T., Boniecki, K. A., & Schlenker, D. R. (1995a). Championship pressures: Choking or triumphing in one's own territory. *Journal of Personality and Social Psychology, 68,* 632–643.

Schlenker, B. R., Phillips, S. T., Boniecki, K. A., & Schlenker, D. R. (1995b). Where is the home choke? *Journal of Personality and Social Psychology, 68,* 649–652.

Schlenker, B. R., Pontari, B. A., & Christopher, A. N. (2001). Excuses and character: Personal and social implications of excuses. *Personality and Social Psychology Review, 5,* 15–32.

Schlesinger, A. M., Jr. (1965). *A thousand days.* Boston: Houghton Mifflin.

Schmidt, D. E., & Keating, J. P. (1979). Human crowding and personal control: An integration of the research. *Psychological Bulletin, 86,* 680–700.

Schmidt, N., & Sermat, V. (1983). Measuring loneliness in different relationships. *Journal of Personality and Social Psychology, 44,* 1038–1047.

Schmitt, B. H., Dubé, L., & Leclerc, F. (1992). Intrusions into waiting lines: Does the queue constitute a social system? *Journal of Personality and Social Psychology, 63,* 806–815.

Schmitt, B. H., Gilovich, T., Goore, N., & Joseph, L. (1986). Mere presence and social facilitation: One more time. *Journal of Experimental Social Psychology, 22,* 242–248.

Schmitt, D. R. (1981). Performance under cooperation or competition. *American Behavioral Scientist, 24,* 649–679.

Schmitt, M. T., Silvia, P. J., & Branscombe, N. R. (2000). The intersection of self-evaluation maintenance and social identity theories: Intragroup judgment in interpersonal and intergroup contexts. *Personality and Social Psychology Bulletin, 26,* 1598–1606.

Schneebaum, T. (1969). *Keep the river on your right.* New York: Grove Press.

Schneider, D. J. (2004) *The psychology of stereotyping.* New York: Guilford Press.

Schneider, J., & Cook, K. (1995). Status inconsistency and gender: Combining revisited. In Extending interaction theory [Special issue]. *Small Group Research, 26,* 372–399.

Schofield, J. W. (1978). School desegregation and intergroup relations. In D. Bar-Tal & L. Saxe (Eds.), *The social psychology of education.* Washington, DC: Halstead.

Schofield, J. W., & Sagar, H. A. (1977). Peer interaction patterns in an integrated middle school. *Sociometry, 40,* 130–138.

Schofield, J. W., & Whitley, B. E., Jr. (1983). Peer nomination vs. rating scale measurement of children's peer preferences. *Social Psychology Quarterly, 46,* 242–251.

Schopler, J., & Insko, C. A. (1992). The discontinuity effect in interpersonal and intergroup relations: Generality and mediation. *European Review of Social Psychology, 3,* 121–151.

Schopler, J., Insko, C. A., Currey, D., Smith, S., Brazil, D., Riggins, T., Gaertner, L., & Kilpatrick, S. (1994). The survival of a cooperative tradition in the intergroup discontinuity context. *Motivation and Emotion, 18,* 301–315.

Schopler, J., Insko, C. A., Drigotas, S. M., Wieselquist, J., Pemberton, M., & Cox, C. (1995). The role of identifiability in the reduction of interindividual–intergroup discontinuity. *Journal of Experimental Social Psychology, 31,* 553–574.

Schopler, J., Insko, C. A., Graetz, K. A., Drigotas, S. M., & Smith, V. A. (1991). The generality of the individual–group discontinuity effect: Variations in positivity–negativity of outcomes, players' relative power, and magnitude of outcomes. *Personality and Social Psychology Bulletin, 17,* 612–624.

Schopler, J., Insko, C. A., Graetz, K. A., Drigotas, S., Smith, V. A., & Dahl, K. (1993). Individual–group discontinuity: Further evidence for mediation by fear and greed. *Personality and Social Psychology Bulletin, 19,* 419–431.

Schopler, J., & Layton, B. D. (1972a). *Attributions of interpersonal influence and power.* Morristown, NJ: General Learning Press.

Schopler, J., & Layton, B. D. (1972b). Determinants of the self-attribution of having influenced another person. *Journal of Personality and Social Psychology, 22,* 326–332.

Schriesheim, C. A., Cogliser, C. C., & Neider, L. L. (1995). Is it "trustworthy"? A multiple-levels-of-analysis re-examination of an Ohio State leadership study, with implications for future research. *Leadership Quarterly, 6,* 111–145.

Schriesheim, C. A., & Eisenbach, R. J. (1995). An exploratory and confirmatory factor-analytic investigation of item wording effects on the obtained factor structures of survey questionnaire measures. *Journal of Management, 21,* 1177–1193.

Schubert, M. A., & Borkman, T. J. (1991). An organizational typology for self-help groups. *American Journal of Community Psychology, 19,* 769–787.

Schultz, P. W., Shriver, C., Tabanico, J. J., & Khazian, A. M. (2004). Implicit connections with nature. *Journal of Environmental Psychology, 24,* 31–42.

Schulz-Hardt, S., Frey, D., Luethgens, C., & Moscovici, S. (2000). Biased information search in group decision making. *Journal of Personality and Social Psychology, 78,* 655–669.

Schulz-Hardt, S., Jochims, M., & Frey, D. (2002). Productive conflict in group decision making: Genuine and contrived dissent as strategies to counteract biased information seeking. *Organizational Behavior and Human Decision Processes, 88,* 563–586.

Schuster, B. (1996). Mobbing, bullying, and peer rejection. *Psychological Science Agenda, 9*(4), 12–13.

Schuster, M. A., Stein, B. D., Jaycox, L. H., Collins, R. L., Marshall, G. N., Elliott, M. N., Zhou, A. J., Kanouse, D. E., Morrison, J. L., & Berry, S. H. (2001). A national survey of stress reactions after the September 11, 2001, terrorist attacks. *The New England Journal of Medicine, 345,* 1507–1512.

Schutte, N. S., Malouff, J. M., Bobik, C., Coston, T. D., Greeson, C., Jedlicka, C., Rhodes, E., & Wendorf, G. (2001). Emotional intelligence and interpersonal relations. *Journal of Social Psychology, 141,* 523–536.

Schutz, W. C. (1958). *FIRO: A three-dimensional theory of interpersonal behavior.* New York: Rinehart.

Schutz, W. C. (1992). Beyond FIRO-B. Three new theory-driven measures—Element B: behavior, Element F: feelings, Element S: self. *Psychological Reports, 70,* 915–937.

Schwartz, B., & Barsky, S. F. (1977). The home advantage. *Social Forces, 55,* 641–661.

Schwartz, H., & Jacobs, J. (1979). *Qualitative sociology: A method to the madness.* New York: Free Press.

Schwartz, M. S., & Schwartz, C. G. (1955). Problems in participant observation. *American Journal of Sociology, 60,* 343–354.

Schwartz, S. H. (1994). Are there universal aspects in the structure and contents of human values? *Journal of Social Issues, 50*(4), 19–45.

Schwartz, S. H., & Gottlieb, A. (1976). Bystander reactions to a violent theft: Crime in Jerusalem. *Journal of Personality and Social Psychology, 34,* 1188–1199.

Schwarz, E. D., & Kowalski, J. M. (1992). Malignant memories: Reluctance to utilize mental health services after a disaster. *Journal of Nervous and Mental Disease, 180,* 767–772.

Schwarz, N., Groves, R. M., & Schuman, H. (1998). Survey methods. In D. T. Gilbert, S. T. Fiske, & G. Lindzey (Eds.), *The handbook of social psychology* (4th ed., Vol. 1, pp. 143–179). New York: McGraw-Hill.

Schwarzwald, J., Amir, Y., & Crain, R. L. (1992). Long-term effects of school desegregation experiences on interpersonal relations in the Israeli Defense Forces. *Personality and Social Psychology Bulletin, 18,* 357–368.

Scott, W. A., & Scott, R. (1981). Intercorrelations among structural properties of primary groups. *Journal of Personality and Social Psychology, 41,* 279–292.

Sculley, J. (with J. A. Byrne). (1987). *Odyssey: Pepsi to Apple . . . A journey of adventure, ideas, and the future.* New York: Harper & Row.

Seal, D. W., Bogart, L. M., & Ehrhardt, A. A. (1998). Small group dynamics: The utility of focus group discussion as a research method. *Group Dynamics, 2,* 253–267.

Seashore, S. E. (1954). *Group cohesiveness in the industrial work group.* Ann Arbor, MI: Institute for Social Research.

Seashore, S. E., & Bowers, D. G. (1970). Durability of organizational change. *American Psychologist, 25,* 227–233.

Sedikides, C., Gaertner, L., & Toguchi, Y. (2003). Pancultural self-enhancement. *Journal of Personality and Social Psychology, 84,* 60–79.

Sedikides, C., Schopler, J., & Insko, C. A. (Eds.). (1998). *Intergroup cognition and intergroup behavior.* Mahwah, NJ: Erlbaum.

Seeger, J. A. (1983). No innate phases in group problem solving. *Academy of Management Review, 8,* 683–689.

Seeman, A. A., & Hellman, P. (1975). *Chief!* New York: Avon.

Seeman, M., Seeman, T., & Sayles, M. (1985). Social networks and health status: A longitudinal analysis. *Social Psychology Quarterly, 48,* 237–248.

Seers, A., & Woodruff, S. (1997). Temporal pacing in task forces: Group development or deadline pressure? *Journal of Management, 23,* 169–187.

Seers, A., Keller, T., & Wilkerson, J. M. (2003). Can team members share leadership? Foundations in research and theory. In C. L. Pearce & J. A. Conger (Eds.), *Shared leadership: Reframing the hows and whys of leadership* (pp. 77–102). Thousand Oaks, CA: Sage.

Segal, H. A. (1954). Initial psychiatric findings of recently repatriated prisoners of war. *American Journal of Psychiatry, 111,* 358–363.

Segal, M. W. (1974). Alphabet and attraction: An unobtrusive measure of the effect of propinquity in a field setting. *Journal of Personality and Social Psychology, 30,* 654–657.

Segal, M. W. (1979). Varieties of interpersonal attraction and their interrelationships in natural groups. *Social Psychology Quarterly, 42,* 253–261.

Sekaquaptewa, D., & Thompson, M. (2002). The differential effects of solo status on members of high- and low-status groups. *Personality and Social Psychology Bulletin, 28,* 694–707.

Sekaquaptewa, D., & Thompson, M. (2003). Solo status, stereotype threat, and performance expectancies: Their effects on women's performance. *Journal of Experimental Social Psychology, 39,* 68–74.

Seligman, M. E. P. (1995). The effectiveness of psychotherapy: The Consumer Reports study. *American Psychologist, 50,* 965–974.

Seligman, M. E. P. (1996). Science as an ally of practice. *American Psychologist, 51,* 1072–1079.

Sell, J. (1997). Gender, strategies, and contributions to public goods. *Social Psychology Quarterly, 60,* 252–265.

Sell, J., Griffith, W. I., & Wilson, R. K. (1993). Are women more cooperative than men in social dilemmas? *Social Psychology Quarterly, 56,* 211–222.

Sell, J., Lovaglia, M. J., Mannix, E. A., Samuelson, C. D., & Wilson, R. K. (2004). Investigating conflict, power, and status within and among groups. *Small Group Research, 35,* 44–72.

Sellers, R. M., Rowley, S. A. J., Chavous, T. M., Shelton, J. N., & Smith, M. A. (1997). Multidimensional Inventory of Black Identity: A preliminary investigation of reliability and construct validity. *Journal of Personality and Social Psychology, 73,* 805–815.

Semin, G. R., Gil de Montes, L., & Vlencia, J. F. (2003). Communication constraints on the linguistic intergroup bias. *Journal of Experimental Social Psychology, 39,* 142–148.

Semin, G. R., & Rubini, M. (1990). Unfolding the concept of person by verbal abuse. *European Journal of Social Psychology, 20,* 463–474.

Service, E. R. (1975). *Origins of the state and civilization.* New York: Norton.

Seta, C. E., & Seta, J. J. (1995). When audience presence is enjoyable: The influences of audience awareness of prior success on performance and task interest. *Basic and Applied Social Psychology, 16,* 95–108.

Seta, J. J., Crisson, J. E., Seta, C. E., & Wang, M. A. (1989). Task performance and perceptions of anxiety: Averaging and summation in an evaluative setting. *Journal of Personality and Social Psychology, 56,* 387–396.

Seta, J. J., Seta, C. E., & Donaldson, S. (1991). The impact of comparison processes on coactors' frustration and willingness to expend effort. *Personality and Social Psychology Bulletin, 17,* 560–568.

Shackelford, S., Wood, W., & Worchel, S. (1996). Behavioral styles and the influence of women in mixed-sex groups. *Social Psychology Quarterly, 59,* 284–293.

Shah, J. Y., Kruglanski, A. W., & Thompson, E. P. (1998). Membership has its (epistemic) rewards: Need for closure effects on in-group bias. *Journal of Personality and Social Psychology, 75,* 383–393.

Shambaugh, P. W. (1978). The development of the small group. *Human Relations, 31,* 283–295.

Shamir, B. (1992). Attribution of influence and charisma to the leader: The romance of leadership revisited. *Journal of Applied Social Psychology, 22,* 386–407.

Shaver, P., & Buhrmester, D. (1983). Loneliness, sex-role orientation, and group life: A social needs perspective. In P. B. Paulus (Ed.), *Basic group processes* (pp. 259–288). New York: Springer Verlag.

Shaver, P., Schwartz, J., Kirson, D., & O'Connor, C. (1987). Emotion knowledge: Further exploration of a prototype approach. *Journal of Personality and Social Psychology, 52,* 1061–1086.

Shaw, J. I., & Condelli, L. (1986). Effects of compliance outcome and basis of power on the powerholder–target relationship. *Personality and Social Psychology Bulletin, 12,* 236–246.

Shaw, M. E. (1964). Communication networks. *Advances in Experimental Social Psychology, 1,* 111–147.

Shaw, M. E. (1978). Communication networks fourteen years later. In L. Berkowitz (Ed.), *Group processes.* New York: Academic Press.

Shaw, M. E. (1981). *Group dynamics: The psychology of small group behavior* (3rd ed.). New York: McGraw-Hill.

Shaw, M. E., & Breed, G. R. (1970). Effects of attribution of responsibility for negative events on behavior in small groups. *Sociometry, 33,* 382–393.

Shaw, M. E., & Shaw, L. M. (1962). Some effects of sociometric grouping upon learning in a second grade classroom. *Journal of Social Psychology, 57,* 453–458.

Shaw, Marjorie E. (1932). A comparison of individuals and small groups in the rational solution of complex problems. *American Journal of Psychology, 44,* 491–504.

Sheatsley, P. B., & Feldman, J. J. (1964). The assassination of President Kennedy: A preliminary report on public attitudes and behavior. *Public Opinion Quarterly, 28,* 189–215.

Shebilske, W. L., Jordon, J. A., Goettl, B. P., & Paulus, L. E. (1998). Observation versus hands-on practice of complex skills in dyadic, triadic, and tetradic training-teams. *Human Factors, 40,* 525–540.

Shechtman, Z. (1994). The effect of group psychotherapy on close same-gender friendships among boys and girls. *Sex Roles, 30,* 829–834.

Sheldon, K. M., Elliot, A. J., Kim, Y., & Kasser, T. (2001). What is satisfying about satisfying events? Testing 10 candidate psychological needs. *Journal of Personality and Social Psychology, 80,* 325–339.

Shelly, R. K., Troyer, L., Munroe, P. T., & Burger, T. (1999). Social structure and the duration of social acts. *Social Psychology Quarterly, 62,* 83–95.

Sheppard, B. H. (1983). Managers as inquisitors: Some lessons from the law. In H. Bazerman & R. J. Lewicki (Eds.), *Negotiating in organizations* (pp. 193–213). Beverly Hills, CA: Sage.

Shepperd, J. A. (1993). Productivity loss in performance groups: A motivation analysis. *Psychological Bulletin, 113,* 67–81.

Shepperd, J. A. (1995). Remedying motivation and productivity loss in collective settings. *Current Directions in Psychological Science, 5,* 131–133.

Shepperd, J. A., & Wright, R. A. (1989). Individual contributions to a collective effort: An incentive analysis. *Personality and Social Psychology Bulletin, 15,* 141–149.

Sheridan, C. L., & King, R. G., Jr. (1972). Obedience to authority with an authentic victim. *Proceedings of the 80th Annual Convention of the American Psychological Association, 7,* 165–166.

Sherif, M. (1936). *The psychology of social norms.* New York: Harper & Row.

Sherif, M. (1966). *In common predicament: Social psychology of intergroup conflict and cooperation.* Boston: Houghton Mifflin.

Sherif, M., Harvey, O. J., White, B. J., Hood, W. R., & Sherif, C. W. (1961). *Intergroup conflict and cooperation. The Robbers Cave Experiment.* Norman, OK: Institute of Group Relations.

Sherif, M., & Sherif, C. W. (1953). *Groups in harmony and tension.* New York: Harper & Row.

Sherif, M., & Sherif, C. W. (1956). *An outline of social psychology* (rev. ed.). New York: Harper & Row.

Sherif, M., White, B. J., & Harvey, O. J. (1955). Status in experimentally produced groups. *American Journal of Sociology, 60,* 370–379.

Sherman, J. D. (2002). Leader role inversion as a corollary to leader–member exchange. *Group and Organization Management, 27,* 245–271.

Sherrod, D. R., & Cohen, S. (1979). Density, personal control, and design. In J. R. Aiello & A. Baum (Eds.), *Residential crowding and design* (pp. 217–227). New York: Plenum.

Shiflett, S. (1979). Toward a general model of small group productivity. *Psychological Bulletin, 86,* 67–79.

Shotola, R. W. (1992). Small groups. In E. F. Borgatta & M. L. Borgatta (Eds.), *Encyclopedia of sociology* (Vol. 4, pp. 1796–1806). New York: Macmillan.

Shrauger, J. S. (1975). Responses to evaluation as a function of initial self-perceptions. *Psychological Bulletin, 82,* 581–596.

Shure, G. H., & Meeker, J. R. (1967). A personality/attitude scale for use in experimental bargaining studies. *Journal of Psychology, 65,* 233–252.

Shure, G. H., Rogers, M. S., Larsen, I. M., & Tassone, J. (1962). Group planning and task effectiveness. *Sociometry, 25,* 263–282.

Sias, P. M., & Jablin, F. M. (1995). Differential superior–subordinate relations, perceptions of fairness, and coworker communication. *Human Communication Research, 22,* 5–38.

Sidanius, J., & Pratto, F. (1999). *Social dominance: An intergroup theory of social hierarchy and oppression.* New York: Cambridge University Press.

Silver, W. S., & Bufanio, K. A. (1996). The impact of group efficacy and group goals on group task performance. *Small Group Research, 27,* 347–349.

Silver, W. S., & Bufanio, K. A. (1997). Reciprocal relationships, causal influences, and group efficacy: A reply to Kaplan. *Small Group Research, 28,* 559–562.

Simmel, G. (1902). The number of members as determining the sociological form of the group. *American Journal of Sociology, 8,* 1–46, 158–196.

Simmel, G. (1955). *Conflict.* New York: Free Press.

Simmons, W. W. (2001, January). *When it comes to choosing a boss, Americans still prefer men: Even women prefer a male boss by a two-to-one margin.* Retrieved July 24, 2004 from http://www.gallup.com/poll/content/login.aspx?ci=2128

Simon, B., Glässner-Bayerl, B., & Stratenwerth, I. (1991). Stereotyping and self-stereotyping in a natural intergroup context: The case of heterosexual and homosexual men. *Social Psychology Quarterly, 54,* 252–266.

Simon, B., & Hamilton, D. L. (1994). Self-stereotyping and social context: The effects of relative ingroup size and ingroup status. *Journal of Personality and Social Psychology, 66,* 699–711.

Simon, B., Pantaleo, G., & Mummendey, A. (1995). Unique individual or interchangeable group member? The accentuation of intragroup differences versus similarities as an indicator of the individual self versus the collective self. *Journal of Personality and Social Psychology, 69,* 106–119.

Simon, R. J. (1980). *The jury: Its role in American society.* Lexington, MA: Heath.

Simonson, I., & Nowlis, S. M. (2000). The role of explanations and need for uniqueness in consumer decision making: Unconventional choices based on reasons. *Journal of Consumer Research, 27,* 49–68.

Simonton, D. K. (1980). Land battles, generals, and armies: Individual and social determinants of victory and casualties. *Journal of Personality and Social Psychology, 38,* 110–119.

Simonton, D. K. (1985). Intelligence and personal influence in groups: Four nonlinear models. *Psychological Review, 92,* 532–547.

Simonton, D. K. (1987). *Why presidents succeed.* New Haven, CT: Yale University Press.

Singer, E. (1990). Reference groups and social evaluations. In M. Rosenberg & R. H. Turner (Eds.), *Social psychology: Sociological perspectives* (pp. 66–93). New Brunswick, NJ: Transaction.

Singer, J. E., Baum, C. S. Baum, A., & Thew, B. D. (1982). Mass psychogenic illness: The case for social comparison. In M. J. Colligan, J. W. Pennebaker, & L. R. Murphy (Eds.), *Mass psychogenic illness: A social psychological analysis* (pp. 155–169). Mahwah, NJ: Erlbaum.

Singer, J. E., Brush, C. A., & Lublin, S. C. (1965). Some aspects of deindividuation: Identification and conformity. *Journal of Experimental Social Psychology, 1,* 356–378.

Skinner, B. F. (1953). *Science and human behavior.* New York: Macmillan.

Skinner, B. F. (1971). *Beyond freedom and dignity.* New York: Knopf.

Skinner, E. A., Edge, K., Altman, J., & Sherwood, H. (2003). Searching for the structure of coping: A review and critique of category systems for classifying ways of coping. *Psychological Bulletin, 129,* 216–269.

Slater, P. E. (1955). Role differentiation in small groups. *American Sociological Review, 20,* 300–310.

Slavson, S. R. (1950). Group psychotherapy. *Scientific American, 183*(6), 42–45.

Smart, R. (1965). Social-group membership, leadership, and birth order. *Journal of Social Psychology, 67,* 221–225.

Smeesters, D., Warlop, L., Van Avermaet, E., Corneille, O., & Yzerbyt, V. (2003). Do not prime hawks with doves: The interplay of construct activation and consistency of social value orientation on cooperative behavior. *Journal of Personality and Social Psychology, 84,* 972–987.

Smelser, N. J. (1962). *Theory of collective behavior.* New York: Free Press.

Smith, D. H. (1980). Participation in outdoor recreation and sports. In D. H. Smith, J. Macaulay, & Associates (Eds.), *Participation in social and political activities: A comprehensive analysis of political involvement, expressive leisure time, and helping behavior* (pp. 177–201). San Francisco: Jossey-Bass.

Smith, E. R., Murphy, J., & Coats, S. (1999). Attachment to groups: Theory and management. *Journal of Personality and Social Psychology, 77,* 94–110.

Smith, M. B. (1972). Is experimental social psychology advancing? *Journal of Experimental Social Psychology, 8,* 86–96.

Smith, P. B. (1975). Controlled studies of the outcome of sensitivity training. *Psychological Bulletin, 82,* 597–622.

Smith, P. B. (1980). The outcome of sensitivity training and encounter. In P. B. Smith (Ed.), *Small groups and personal change* (pp. 25–55). New York: Methuen.

Smith, P. B., & Bond, M. H. (1993). *Social psychology across cultures: Analysis and perspectives.* Boston: Allyn & Bacon.

Smith, P. B., Dugan, S., Peterson, M. F., & Leung, K. (1998). Individualism/collectivism and the handling of disagreement. A 23 country study. *International Journal of Intercultural Relations, 22,* 351–367.

Smith, R. H. (2000). Assimilative and contrastive emotional reactions to upward and downward social comparisons. In J. Suls & L. Wheeler (Eds.), *Handbook of social comparison: Theory and research* (pp. 173–200). New York: Kluwer Academic/Plenum.

Smoke, W. H., & Zajonc, R. B. (1962). On the reliability of group judgments and decisions. In J. H. Crisswell, H. Solomon, & P. Suppes (Eds.), *Mathematical methods in small group processes* (pp. 322–333). Stanford, CA: Stanford University Press.

Sniezek, J. A., & Buckley, T. (1993). Becoming more or less uncertain. In N. J. Castellan (Ed.), *Individual and group decision making: Current issues* (pp. 87–108). Mahwah, NJ: Erlbaum.

Snow, D. A., & Oliver, P. E. (1995). Social movements and collective behavior: Social psychological dimensions and considerations. In K. S. Cook, G. A. Fine, & J. S. House (Eds.), *Sociological perspectives on social psychology* (pp. 571–599). Needham Heights, MA: Allyn & Bacon.

Snyder, C. R., & Fromkin, H. L. (1980). *Uniqueness: The human pursuit of difference.* New York: Plenum Press.

Snyder, C. R., Higgins, R. L., & Stucky, R. J. (1983). *Excuses: Masquerades in search of grace.* New York: Wiley.

Snyder, C. R., Ilardi, S., Michael, S. T., & Cheavens, J. (2000). Hope theory: Updating a common process for psychological change. In C. R. Snyder & R. E. Ingram (Eds.), *Handbook of psychological change: Psychotherapy processes and practices for the 21st century* (pp. 128–153). New York: Wiley.

Somech, A. (2003). Relationships of participative leadership with relational demography variables: A multi-level perspective. *Journal of Organizational Behavior, 24,* 1003–1018.

Sommer, R. (1959). Studies in personal space. *Sociometry, 22,* 247–260.

Sommer, R. (1967). Small group ecology. *Psychological Bulletin, 67,* 145–152.

Sommer, R. (1969). *Personal space.* Upper Saddle River, NJ: Prentice Hall.

Sommer, R. (2002). Personal space in a digital age. In R. B. Bechtel & A. Churchman (Eds.), *Handbook of environmental psychology* (pp. 647–660). New York: Wiley. Retrieved July 29, 2004, from http://www.netlibrary.com

Sorokin, P. A., & Lundin, W. A. (1959). *Power and morality: Who shall guard the guardians?* Boston: Sargent.

Sorrels, J. P., & Kelley, J. (1984). Conformity by omission. *Personality and Social Psychology Bulletin, 10,* 302–305.

Sorrentino, R. M., & Boutillier, R. G. (1975). The effect of quantity and quality of verbal interaction on ratings of leadership ability. *Journal of Experimental Social Psychology, 11,* 403–411.

Sorrentino, R. M., & Field, N. (1986). Emergent leadership over time: The functional value of positive motivation. *Journal of Personality and Social Psychology, 50,* 1091–1099.

Spears, R., Doosje, B., & Ellemers, N. (1997). Self-stereotyping in the face of threats to group status and distinctiveness: The role of group identification. *Personality and Social Psychology Bulletin, 23,* 538–553.

Spears, R., Lea, M., & Lee, S. (1990). Deindividuation and group polarization in computer-mediated communication. *British Journal of Social Psychology, 29,* 121–134.

Spears, R., Postmes, T., Lea, M., & Wolbert, A. (2002). When are net effects gross products? The power of influence and the influence of power in computer-mediated communication. *Journal of Social Issues, 58,* 91–107.

Spencer Stuart. (2004). *The 2004 Spencer Stuart route to the top: Our survey of Fortune 700 CEOs provides a snapshot of today's CEOs and the major trends emerging.* Retrieved June 29, 2004, from http://www.spencerstuart.com/

Spencer, H. (1897). *The principles of sociology.* New York: Appleton.

Spencer, R. W., & Huston, J. H. (1993). Rational forecasts: On confirming ambiguity as the mother of conformity. *Journal of Economic Psychology, 14,* 697–709.

Spira, J. L. (1997). Understanding and developing psychotherapy groups for medically ill patients. In J. L. Spira (Ed.), *Group therapy for medically ill patients* (pp. 3–52). New York: Guilford Press.

Squire, S. (1983). *The slender balance.* New York: Pinnacle.

Staats, H., & Hartig, T. (2004). Alone or with a friend: A social context for psychological restoration and environmental preferences. *Journal of Environmental Psychology, 24,* 199–211.

Stafford, L., Dainton, M., & Haas, S. (2000). Measuring routine and strategic relational maintenance: Scale revision, sex versus gender roles, and the prediction of relational characteristics. *Communication Monographs, 67,* 306–323.

Stager, S. F., Chassin, L., & Young, R. D. (1983). Determinants of self-esteem among labeled adolescents. *Social Psychology Quarterly, 46,* 3–10.

Stangor, C., Jonas, K., Stroebe, W., & Hewstone, M. (1996). Influ-

ence of student exchange on national stereotypes, attitudes, and perceived group variability. *European Journal of Social Psychology, 26,* 663–675.

Stasser, G. (1992a). Information salience and the discovery of hidden profiles by decision-making groups: A "thought experiment." *Organizational Behavior and Human Decision Processes, 52,* 156–181.

Stasser, G. (1992b). Pooling of unshared information during group discussions. In S. Worchel, W. Wood, & J. A. Simpson (Eds.), *Group process and productivity* (pp. 48–67). Thousand Oaks, CA: Sage.

Stasser, G., & Dietz-Uhler, B. (2001). Collective choice, judgment, and problem solving. In M. A. Hogg & R. S. Tindale (Eds.), *Blackwell handbook of social psychology: Group processes* (pp. 31–55). Malden, MA: Blackwell.

Stasser, G., Kerr, N. L., & Bray, R. M. (1982). The social psychology of jury deliberations: Structure, process, and product. In N. L. Kerr & R. M. Bray (Eds.), *Psychology of the courtroom* (pp. 221–256). New York: Academic Press.

Stasser, G., & Stewart, D. (1992). Discovery of hidden profiles by decision-making groups: Solving a problem versus making a judgment. *Journal of Personality and Social Psychology, 63,* 426–434.

Stasser, G., Taylor, L. A., & Hanna, C. (1989). Information sampling in structured and unstructured discussions of three- and six-person groups. *Journal of Personality and Social Psychology, 57,* 67–78.

Stasser, G., & Titus, W. (1985). Pooling of unshared information in group decision making: Biased information sampling during discussion. *Journal of Personality and Social Psychology, 48,* 1467–1478.

Stasser, G., & Titus, W. (1987). Effects of information load and percentage of shared information on the dissemination of unshared information during group discussion. *Journal of Personality and Social Psychology, 53,* 81–93.

Stasson, M. F., & Bradshaw, S. D. (1995). Explanations of individual–group performance differences: What sort of "bonus" can be gained through group interaction? *Small Group Research, 26,* 296–308.

Stasson, M. F., Kameda, T., & Davis, J. H. (1997). A model of agenda influences on group decisions. *Group Dynamics, 1,* 316–323.

Staub, E. (1989). *The roots of evil: The origins of genocide and other group violence.* New York: Cambridge University Press.

Staub, E. (1990). Moral exclusion, personal goal theory, and extreme destructiveness. *Journal of Social Issues, 46*(1), 47–64.

Staub, E. (1996). Cultural–societal roots of violence: The examples of genocidal violence and of contemporary youth violence in the United States. *American Psychologist, 51,* 117–132.

Staudacher, C. (1994). *Time to grieve.* San Francisco: HarperCollins.

Staw, B. M., & Ross, J. (1987). Behavior in escalation situations: Antecedents, prototypes, and solutions. *Research in Organizational Behavior, 9,* 39–78.

Steers, R. M., & Porter, L. W. (1991). *Motivation and work behavior* (4th ed.). New York: McGraw-Hill.

Stein, R. T., & Heller, T. (1979). An empirical analysis of the correlations between leadership status and participation rates reported in the literature. *Journal of Personality and Social Psychology, 37,* 1993–2002.

Stein, R. T., & Heller, T. (1983). The relationship of participation rates to leadership status: A meta-analysis. In H. H. Blumberg,

A. P. Hare, V. Kent, & M. Davies (Eds.), *Small groups and social interaction* (Vol. 1, pp. 401–406). New York: Wiley.

Steinel, W., & De Dreu, C. K. (2004). Social motives and strategic misrepresentation in social decision making. *Journal of Personality and Social Psychology, 86,* 419–434.

Steiner, I. D. (1972). *Group process and productivity.* New York: Academic Press.

Steiner, I. D. (1974). Whatever happened to the group in social psychology? *Journal of Experimental Social Psychology, 10,* 94–108.

Steiner, I. D. (1976). Task-performing groups. In J. W. Thibaut, J. T. Spence, & R. C. Carson (Eds.), *Contemporary topics in social psychology* (pp. 393–422). Morristown, NJ: General Learning Press.

Steiner, I. D. (1983). What ever happened to the touted revival of the group? In H. Blumberg, A. Hare, V. Kent, & M. Davies (Eds.), *Small groups and social interaction* (Vol. 2, pp. 539–547). New York: Wiley.

Steiner, I. D. (1986). Paradigms and groups. *Advances in Experimental Social Psychology, 19,* 251–289.

Steinzor, B. (1950). The spatial factor in face to face discussion groups. *Journal of Abnormal and Social Psychology, 45,* 552–555.

Stempfle, J., Hübner, O., & Badke-Schaub, P. (2001). A functional theory of task role distribution in work groups. *Group Processes & Intergroup Relations, 4,* 138–159.

Stephan, F. F., & Mischler, E. G. (1952). The distribution of participation in small groups: An exponential approximation. *American Sociological Review, 17,* 598–608.

Stephan, W. G. (1987). The contact hypothesis in intergroup relations. *Review of Personality and Social Psychology, 9,* 13–40.

Stephan, W. G., & Rosenfield, D. (1982). Racial and ethnic stereotypes. In A. G. Miller (Ed.), *In the eye of the beholder: Contemporary issues in stereotyping.* New York: Praeger.

Stephan, W. G., & Stephan, C. W. (2000). An integrated threat theory of prejudice. In Oskamp, S. (Ed.), *Reducing prejudice and discrimination* (pp. 23–45). Mahwah, NJ: Erlbaum. Retrieved June 24, 2004, from http://www.netlibrary.com

Stern, E. K. (1997). Probing the plausibility of newgroup syndrome: Kennedy and the Bay of Pigs. In P. 't Hart, E. K. Stern, & B. Sundelius (Eds.), *Beyond groupthink: Political group dynamics and foreign policy-making* (pp. 153–189). Ann Arbor: University of Michigan Press.

Sternberg, R. J. (2003). A duplex theory of hate: Development and application to terrorism, massacres, and genocide. *Review of General Psychology, 7,* 299–328.

Sternberg, R. J., & Dobson, D. M. (1987). Resolving interpersonal conflicts: An analysis of stylistic consistency. *Journal of Personality and Social Psychology, 52,* 794–812.

Stevenson, R. J., & Repacholi, B. M. (2003). Age-related changes in children's hedonic response to male body odor. *Developmental Psychology, 39,* 670–679.

Stevenson, W. B., Pearce, J. L., & Porter, L. W. (1985). The concept of "coalition" in organizational theory and research. *Academy of Management Review, 10,* 256–267.

Stewart, A. E., Stewart, E. A., & Gazda, G. M. (1997). Assessing the need for a new group journal. *Group Dynamics, 1,* 75–85.

Stewart, D. D., & Stasser, G. (1998). The sampling of critical, unshared information in decision-making groups: The role of an informed minority. *European Journal of Social Psychology, 28,* 95–113.

Stewart, G. L., & Manz, C. C. (1995). Leadership for self-managing

work teams: A typology and integrative model. *Human Relations, 48,* 747–770.

Stewart, P. A., & Moore, J. C. (1992). Wage disparities and performance expectations. *Social Psychology Quarterly, 55,* 78–85.

Stiles, W. B., Lyall, L. M., Knight, D. P., Ickes, W., Waung, M., Hall, C. L., & Primeau, B. E. (1997). Gender differences in verbal presumptuousness and attentiveness. *Personality and Social Psychology Bulletin, 23,* 759–772.

Stiles, W. B., Shapiro, D. A., & Elliott, R. (1986). "Are all psychotherapies equivalent?" *American Psychologist, 41,* 165–180.

Stogdill, R. M. (1948). Personal factors associated with leadership. *Journal of Psychology, 23,* 35–71.

Stogdill, R. M. (1974). *Handbook of leadership.* New York: Free Press.

Stokes, J. P. (1983). Components of group cohesion: Intermember attraction, instrumental value, and risk taking. *Small Group Behavior, 14,* 163–173.

Stokes, J. P. (1985). The relation of social network and individual difference variables to loneliness. *Journal of Personality and Social Psychology, 48,* 981–990.

Stokols, D. (1972). On the distinction between density and crowding: Some implications for future research. *Psychological Review, 79,* 275–278.

Stokols, D. (1978). In defense of the crowding construct. In A. Baum, J. E. Singer, & S. Valins (Eds.), *Advances in environmental psychology* (Vol. 1, pp. 111–130). Mahwah, NJ: Erlbaum.

Stokols, D., & Altman, I. (Eds.). (1987). *Handbook of environmental psychology* (Vols. 1 & 2). New York: Wiley.

Stolte, J. F., Fine, G. A., & Cook, K. S. (2001). Sociological miniaturism: Seeing the big through the small in social psychology [Electronic version]. *Annual Review of Sociology, 27,* 387–413.

Stoner, J. A. (1968). Risky and cautious shifts in group decisions: The influence of widely held values. *Journal of Experimental Social Psychology, 4,* 442–459.

Stoner, J. A. F. (1961). *A comparison of individual and group decisions involving risk.* Unpublished master's thesis. Cambridge, MA: Massachusetts Institute of Technology.

Stones, C. R. (1982). A community of Jesus people in South Africa. *Small Group Behavior, 13,* 264–272.

Stoop, J. R. (1932). Is the judgment of the group better than that of the average member of the group? *Journal of Experimental Psychology, 15,* 550–562.

Storms, M. D., & Thomas, G. C. (1977). Reactions to physical closeness. *Journal of Personality and Social Psychology, 35,* 319–328.

Storr, A. (1988). *Solitude: A return to the self.* New York: Free Press.

Stout, R. J., Salas, E., & Fowlkes, J. E. (1997). Enhancing teamwork in complex environments through team training. *Group Dynamics: Theory, Research, and Practice, 1,* 169–182.

Stratham, A. (1987). The gender model revisited: Differences in the management styles of men and women. *Sex Roles, 16,* 409–429.

Straus, S. G. (1997). Technology, group process, and group outcomes: Testing the connections in computer-mediated and face-to-face groups. *Human–Computer Interaction, 12,* 227–266.

Strauss, A., & Corbin, J. (1998). *Basics of qualitative research: Techniques and procedures for developing grounded theory* (2nd ed.). Thousand Oaks, CA: Sage.

Strauss, A. L. (1944). The literature on panic. *Journal of Abnormal and Social Psychology, 39,* 317–328.

Strauss, B. (2002). Social facilitation in motor tasks: A review of research and theory. *Psychology of Sport & Exercise, 3,* 237–256.

Street, M. D. (1997). Groupthink: An examination of theoretical issues, implications, and future research suggestions. *Small Group Research, 28,* 72–93.

Streufert, S., & Streufert, S. C. (1986). The development of international conflict. In S. Worchel & W. G. Austin (Eds.), *Psychology of intergroup relations* (2nd ed., pp. 134–152). Chicago: Nelson-Hall.

Strickland, L. H. (1958). Surveillance and trust. *Journal of Personality, 26,* 206–215.

Strickland, L. H., Barefoot, J. C., & Hockenstein, P. (1976). Monitoring behavior in the surveillance and trust paradigm. *Representative Research in Social Psychology, 7,* 51–57.

Strodtbeck, F. L., & Hook, L. H. (1961). The social dimensions of a twelve-man jury table. *Sociometry, 24,* 397–415.

Strodtbeck, F. L., James, R. M., & Hawkins, C. (1957). Social status in jury deliberations. *American Sociological Review, 22,* 713–719.

Strodtbeck, F. L., & Lipinski, R. M. (1985). Becoming first among equals: Moral considerations in jury foreman selection. *Journal of Personality and Social Psychology, 49,* 927–936.

Strodtbeck, F. L., & Mann, R. D. (1956). Sex role differentiation in jury deliberations. *Sociometry, 19,* 3–11.

Stroebe, M. S. (1994). The broken heart phenomenon: An examination of the mortality of bereavement. *Journal of Community and Applied Social Psychology, 4,* 47–61.

Stroebe, W., Diehl, M., & Abakoumkin, G. (1992). The illusion of group effectivity. *Personality and Social Psychology Bulletin, 18,* 643–650.

Stroebe, W., Diehl, M., & Abakoumkin, G. (1996). Social compensation and the Köhler effect: Toward a theoretical explanation of motivation gains in group productivity. In E. Witte & J. Davis (Eds.), *Understanding group behavior: Consensual action by small groups* (Vol. 2., pp. 37–65). Mahwah, NJ: Erlbaum.

Stroebe, W., Stroebe, M. S., Abakoumkin, G., & Schut, H. (1996). The role of loneliness and social support in adjustment to loss: A test of attachment versus stress theory. *Journal of Personality and Social Psychology, 70,* 1241–1249.

Strong, S. R., Hills, H. I., Kilmartin, C. T., DeVries, H., Lanier, K., Nelson, B. N., Strickland, D., & Meyer, C. W., III. (1988). The dynamic relations among interpersonal behaviors: A test of complementarity and anticomplementarity. *Journal of Personality and Social Psychology, 54,* 798–810.

Stryker, S., & Burke, P. J. (2000). The past, present, and future of an identity theory. *Social Psychology Quarterly, 63,* 284–297.

Stryker, S., & Statham, A. (1985). Symbolic interaction and role theory. In G. Lindzey & E. Aronson (Eds.), *The handbook of social psychology* (3rd ed., Vol. 1, pp. 311–378). New York: Random House.

Stuster, J. (1996). *Bold endeavors: Lessons from polar and space exploration.* Annapolis, MD: Naval Institute Press.

Suedfeld, P. (1987). Extreme and unusual environments. In D. Stokols & I. Altman (Eds.), *Handbook of environmental psychology* (Vol. 1, pp. 863–887). New York: Wiley.

Suedfeld, P. (1997). The social psychology of "invictus": Conceptual and methodological approaches to indomitability. In C. McGarty & S. A. Haslam (Eds.), *The message of social psychology: Perspectives on mind in society* (pp. 329–341). Malden, MA: Blackwell.

Suedfeld, P., & Steel, G. D. (2000). The environmental psychology of capsule habitats. *Annual Review of Psychology, 51,* 227–253.

Sugisawa, H., Liang, J., & Liu, X. (1994). Social networks, social support, and mortality among older people in Japan. *Journals of Gerontology, 49,* S3–S13.

Suh, E. J., Moskowitz, D. S., Fournier, M. A., & Zuroff, D. C. (2004). Gender and relationships: Influences on agentic and communal behaviors. *Personal Relationships, 11,* 41–59.

Sulloway, F. J. (1996). *Born to rebel: Birth order, family dynamics, and creative lives.* New York: Pantheon.

Suls, J., Martin, R., & David, J. P. (1998). Person–environment fit and its limits: Agreeableness, neuroticism, and emotional reactivity to interpersonal conflict. *Personality and Social Psychology Bulletin, 24,* 88–98.

Suls, J., & Wheeler, L. (Eds.). (2000). *Handbook of social comparison: Theory and research.* New York: Kluwer Academic/Plenum.

Sumner, W. G. (1906). *Folkways.* New York: Ginn.

Sundstrom, E. (1975). An experimental study of crowding: Effects of room size, intrusion, and goal-blocking on nonverbal behavior, self-disclosure, and self-reported stress. *Journal of Personality and Social Psychology, 32,* 645–654.

Sundstrom, E. (1987). Work environments: Offices and factories. In D. Stokols & I. Altman (Eds.), *Handbook of environmental psychology* (Vol. 1, pp. 733–782). New York: Wiley.

Sundstrom, E. & Altman, I. (1974). Field study of dominance and territorial behavior. *Journal of Personality and Social Psychology, 30,* 115–125.

Sundstrom, E., Bell, P. A., Busby, P. L., & Asmus, C. (1996). Environmental psychology: 1989–1994. *Annual Review of Psychology, 47,* 485–512.

Sundstrom, E., De Meuse, K. P., & Futrell, D. (1990). Work teams: Applications and effectiveness. *American Psychologist, 45,* 120–133.

Sundstrom, E., McIntyre, M., Halfhill, T., & Richards, H. (2000). Work groups: From the Hawthorne studies to work teams of the 1990s and beyond. *Group Dynamics, 4,* 44–67.

Sunwolf. (2002). Getting to "GroupAha!": Provoking creative processes in task groups. In L. R. Frey (Ed.), *New directions in group communication* (pp. 203–217). Thousand Oaks, CA: Sage.

Swap, W. C., & Rubin, J. Z. (1983). Measurement of interpersonal orientation. *Journal of Personality and Social Psychology, 44,* 208–219.

't Hart, P. (1991). Irving L. Janis' Victims of Groupthink. *Political Psychology, 12,* 247–278.

't Hart, P. (1998). Preventing groupthink revisited: Evaluating and reforming groups in government. *Organizational Behavior and Human Decision Processes, 73,* 306–326.

Tajfel, H. (1981). *Human groups and social categories: Studies in social psychology.* Cambridge, UK: Cambridge University Press.

Tajfel, H., & Turner, J. C. (1979). An integrative theory of intergroup conflict. In W. G. Austin & S. Worchel (Eds.), *The social psychology of intergroup relations* (pp. 33–47). Monterey, CA: Brooks/Cole.

Tajfel, H., & Turner, J. C. (1986). The social identity theory of intergroup behavior. In S. Worchel & W. G. Austin (Eds.), *Psychology of intergroup relations* (2nd ed., pp. 7–24). Chicago: Nelson-Hall.

Tanford, S., & Penrod, S. (1983). Computer modeling of influence in the jury: The role of the consistent juror. *Social Psychology Quarterly, 46,* 200–212.

Tanford, S., & Penrod, S. (1984). Social influence model: A formal integration of research on majority and minority influence processes. *Psychological Bulletin, 95,* 189–225.

Tang, J. (1997). The Model Minority thesis revisited: (Counter) evidence from the science and engineering fields. *Journal of Applied Behavioral Science, 33,* 291–314.

Tarde, G. (1903). *The laws of imitation.* New York: Holt.

Tarnow, E. (2000). Self-destructive obedience in the airplane cockpit and the concept of obedience optimization. In T. Blass (Ed.). *Obedience to authority: Current perspectives on the Milgram paradigm* (pp. 111–123). Mahwah, NJ: Erlbaum.

Tata, J., Anthony, T., Hung-Yu, L., Newman, B., Tang, S., Millson, M., & Sivakumar, K. (1996). Proportionate group size and rejection of the deviate: A meta-analytic integration. *Journal of Social Behavior and Personality, 11,* 739–752.

Tate, D. F., & Zabinski, M. F. (2004). Computer and Internet applications for psychological treatment: Update for clinicians. *Journal of Clinical Psychology, 60,* 209–220.

Taub, S. (2001, December 5). *Enron blame game: Accountants take the offensive.* Retrieved March, 3, 2002, from http://www.cfo.com/

Tauer, J. M., & Harackiewicz, J. M. (2004). The effects of cooperation and competition on intrinsic motivation and performance. *Journal of Personality and Social Psychology, 86,* 849–861.

Taylor, D. M., & Moghaddam, F. M. (1994). *Theories of intergroup relations* (2nd ed.). Westport, CT: Praeger.

Taylor, F. W. (1923). *The principles of scientific management.* New York: Harper.

Taylor, H. F. (1970). *Balance in small groups.* New York: Van Nostrand Reinhold.

Taylor, R. B., & Lanni, J. C. (1981). Territorial dominance: The influence of the resident advantage in triadic decision making. *Journal of Personality and Social Psychology, 41,* 909–915.

Taylor, S. E., Klein, L. C., Lewis, B. P., Gruenewald, T. L., Gurung, R. A. R., & Updegraff, J. A. (2000). Biobehavioral responses to stress in females: Tend-and-befriend, not fight-or-flight. *Psychological Review, 107,* 411–429.

Taylor, S. E., & Lobel, M. (1989). Social comparison activity under threat: Downward evaluation and upward contacts. *Psychological Review, 96,* 569–575.

Tedeschi, J. T., Gaes, G. G., & Rivera, A. N. (1977). Aggression and the use of coercive power. *Journal of Social Issues, 33*(1), 101–125.

Tedeschi, J. T., Smith, R. B., III, & Brown, R. C. (1974). A reinterpretation of research on aggression. *Psychological Bulletin, 81,* 540–563.

Teger, A. (1980). *Too much invested to quit.* New York: Pergamon Press.

Tennen, H., McKee, T. E., & Affleck, G. (2000). Social comparison processes in health and illness. In J. Suls & L. Wheeler (Eds.), *Handbook of social comparison: Theory and research* (pp. 443–483). New York: Kluwer Academic/Plenum.

Terkel, S. (1980). *American dreams, lost and found.* New York: Ballantine.

Terry, D. J., & Hogg, M. A. (1996). Group norms and the attitude–behavior relationship: A role for group identification. *Personality and Social Psychology Bulletin, 22,* 776–793.

Tesser, A. (1988). Toward a self-evaluation maintenance model of social behavior. *Advances in Experimental Social Psychology, 21,* 181–227.

Tesser, A. (1991). Emotion in social comparison and reflection processes. In J. Suls & T. A. Wills (Eds.), *Social comparison: Contemporary theory and research* (pp. 117–148). Mahwah, NJ: Erlbaum.

Tesser, A., Campbell, J., & Smith, M. (1984). Friendship choice and performance: Self-evaluation maintenance in children. *Journal of Personality and Social Psychology, 46,* 561–574.

Tetlock, P. E. (1979). Identifying victims of groupthink from public statements of decision makers. *Journal of Personality and Social Psychology, 37,* 1314–1324.

Tetlock, P. E., Peterson, R. S., McGuire, C., Chang, S., & Feld, P. (1992). Assessing political group dynamics: A test of the groupthink model. *Journal of Personality and Social Psychology, 63,* 403–425.

"The Who," the what, but why? (1979, December 5). *Richmond News Leader,* p. A19.

Thibaut, J. W., & Coules, J. (1952). The role of communication in the reduction of interpersonal hostility. *Journal of Abnormal and Social Psychology, 47,* 770–777.

Thibaut, J. W., & Kelley, H. H. (1959). *The social psychology of groups.* New York: Wiley.

Thoits, P. A. (1992). Identity structures and psychological well-being: Gender and marital status comparisons. *Social Psychology Quarterly, 55,* 236–256.

Thomas, E. J., & Fink, C. F. (1961). Models of group problem solving. *Journal of Abnormal and Social Psychology, 63,* 53–63.

Thomas, K. W. (1992). Conflict and negotiation processes in organizations. In M. D. Dunnette & L. M. Hough (Eds.), *Handbook of industrial and organizational psychology* (2nd ed., Vol. 3, pp. 651–717). Palo Alto, CA: Consulting Psychologists Press.

Thomas, W. I. (1928). *The child in America.* New York: Knopf.

Thompson, L. (1990). Negotiation behavior and outcomes: Empirical evidence and theoretical issues. *Psychological Bulletin, 108,* 515–532.

Thompson, L. (1991). Information exchange in negotiation. *Journal of Experimental Social Psychology, 27,* 161–179.

Thompson, L. (2004). *Making the team: A guide for managers* (2nd ed.). Upper Saddle River, NJ: Prentice Hall.

Thompson, L., & Hrebec, D. (1996). Lose–lose agreements in interdependent decision making. *Psychological Bulletin, 120,* 396–409.

Thompson, L., & Nadler, J. (2000). Judgmental biases in conflict resolution and how to overcome them. In M. Deutsch & P. T. Coleman (Eds.), *The handbook of conflict resolution: Theory and practice* (pp. 213–235). San Francisco. Jossey-Bass.

Thoreau, H. D. (1962). *Walden and other writings.* New York: Bantam.

Thorndike, E. L. (1920). Intelligence and its uses. *Harper's Magazine, 140,* 227–235.

Thorne, B. (1993) *Gender play.* New Brunswick, NJ: Rutgers University Press.

Thrasher, F. M. (1927). *The gang.* Chicago: University of Chicago Press.

Thye, S. R. (2000). A status value theory of power in exchange relations. *American Sociological Review, 65,* 407–432.

Tiedens, L. Z. (2001). Anger and advancement versus sadness and subjugation: The effect of negative emotion expressions on social status conferral. *Journal of Personality and Social Psychology, 80,* 86–94.

Tiedens, L. Z., Ellsworth, P. C., & Mesquita, B. (2000). Stereotypes about sentiments and status: Emotional expectations for high- and low-status group members. *Personality and Social Psychology Bulletin, 26,* 560–574.

Tiedens, L. Z., & Fragale, A. R. (2003). Power moves: Complementarity in dominant and submissive nonverbal behavior. *Journal of Personality and Social Psychology, 84,* 558–568.

Tindale, R. S. (1993). Decision errors made by individuals and groups. In N. J. Castellan (Ed.), *Individual and group decision making* (pp. 109–124). Mahwah, NJ: Erlbaum.

Tindale, R. S., Meisenhelder, H. M., Dykema-Engblade, A. A., & Hogg, M. A. (2001). Shared cognitions in small groups. In M. A. Hogg & R. S. Tindale (Eds.), *Blackwell handbook in social psychology: Group processes* (pp. 1–30). Oxford, UK: Blackwell.

Tindale, R. S., Smith, C. M., Thomas, L. S., Filkins, J., & Sheffey, S. (1996). Shared representations and asymmetric social influence processes in small groups. In E. Witte & J. Davis (Eds.), *Understanding group behavior: Consensual action by small groups* (Vol. 1, pp. 81–103). Mahwah, NJ: Erlbaum.

Tjosvold, D. (1986). *Working together to get things done.* Lexington, MA: Lexington Books.

Tjosvold, D. (1995). Cooperation theory, constructive controversy, and effectiveness: Learning from crisis. In R. A. Guzzo, E. Salas, & Associates, *Team effectiveness and decision making in organizations* (pp. 79–112). San Francisco: Jossey-Bass.

Toch, H. (1969). *Violent men.* Chicago: Aldine.

Toennies, F. (1963). *Community and society [Gemeinschaft und Gesellschaft].* New York: Harper & Row. (Original work published in 1887)

Tolnay, S. E., & Beck, E. M. (1996). Vicarious violence: Spatial effects on southern lynchings, 1890–1919. *American Journal of Sociology, 102,* 788–815.

Tolstoy, L. (1952). *War and peace.* Chicago: Encyclopedia Britannica. (Original work published in 1869)

Torrance, E. P. (1954). The behavior of small groups under the stress conditions of "survival." *American Sociological Review, 19,* 751–755.

Torrance, E. P. (1957). Group decision-making and disagreement. *Social Forces, 35,* 314–318.

Tracey, T. J., Ryan, J. M., & Jaschik-Herman, B. (2001). Complementarity of interpersonal circumplex traits. *Personality and Social Psychology Bulletin, 27,* 786–797.

Trafimow, D., Triandis, H. C., & Goto, S. G. (1991). Some tests of the distinction between the private self and the collective self. *Journal of Personality and Social Psychology, 60,* 649–655.

Travis, L. E. (1928). The influence of the group upon the stutterer's speed in free association. *Journal of Abnormal and Social Psychology, 23,* 45–51.

Triandis, H. C. (1995). *Individualism and collectivism.* Boulder, CO: Westview Press.

Triandis, H. C. (1996). The psychological measurement of cultural syndromes. *American Psychologist, 51,* 407–415.

Triandis, H. C., Carnevale, P. J., Gelfand, M., Robert, C., Wasti, A., Probst, T. M., Kashima, E. S., Dragonas, T., Chan, D., Chen, X. P., Kim, U., Kim, K., De Dreu, C., Van de Vliert, E., Iwao, S., Ohbuchi, K., & Schmitz, P. (2001). Culture, personality, and deception in intercultural management negotiations. *International Journal of Cross-Cultural Management, 1,* 73–90.

Triandis, H. C., McCusker, C., & Hui, C. H. (1990). Multimethod probes of individualism and collectivism. *Journal of Personality and Social Psychology, 59,* 1006–1013.

Triandis, H. C., & Suh, E. M. (2002). Cultural influences on personality. *Annual Review of Psychology, 53,* 133–160.

Triplett, N. (1898). The dynamogenic factors in pacemaking and competition. *American Journal of Psychology, 9,* 507–533.

Tropp, L. R., & Wright, S. C. (2001). Ingroup identification as the inclusion of ingroup in the self. *Personality and Social Psychology Bulletin, 27,* 585–600.

Trost, M. R., Maass, A., & Kenrick, D. T. (1992). Minority influence: Personal relevance biases cognitive processes and reverses private acceptance. *Journal of Experimental Social Psychology, 28,* 234–254.

Trujillo, N. (1986). Toward a taxonomy of small group interaction coding systems. *Small Group Behavior, 17,* 371–394.

Tsui, A. S. (1984). A role-set analysis of managerial reputation. *Organizational Behavior and Human Performance, 34,* 64–96.

Tubbs, S. L. (2001). *A systems approach to small group interaction* (7th ed.). New York: McGraw-Hill.

Tubre, T. C., & Collins, J. M. (2000). Jackson and Schuler (1985) revisited: A meta-analysis of the relationships between role ambiguity, role conflict, and job performance. *Journal of Management, 26,* 155–169.

Tucker, C. W., Schweingruber, D., & McPhail, C. (1999). Simulating arcs and rings in gatherings [Electronic version]. *International Journal of Human–Computer Studies, 50,* 581–588.

Tuckman, B. W. (1965). Developmental sequences in small groups. *Psychological Bulletin, 63,* 384–399.

Tuckman, B. W., & Jensen, M. A. C. (1977). Stages of small group development revisited. *Group and Organizational Studies, 2,* 419–427.

Turner, A. L. (2000). Group treatment of trauma survivors following a fatal bus accident: Integrating theory and practice. *Group Dynamics, 4,* 139–149.

Turner, J. C. (1982). Towards a cognitive redefinition of the social group. In H. Tajfel (Ed.), *Social identity and intergroup relations* (pp. 15–40). Cambridge, UK: Cambridge University Press.

Turner, J. C., Hogg, M. A., Oakes, P. J., Reicher, S. D., & Wetherell, M. S. (1987). *Rediscovering the social group: A self-categorization theory.* Malden, MA: Blackwell.

Turner, J. C., & Onorato, R. S. (1999). Social identity, personality, and the self-concept: A self-categorization perspective. In T. R. Tyler, R. M. Kramer, & O. P. John (Eds.), *The psychology of the social self* (pp. 11–46). Mahwah, NJ: Erlbaum.

Turner, M. E., & Pratkanis, A. R. (Eds.). (1998). Theoretical perspectives on groupthink: A twenty-fifth anniversary appraisal. *Organizational Behavior and Human Decision Processes, 73*(2–3).

Turner, M. E., Pratkanis, A. R., Probasco, P., & Leve, C. (1992). Threat, cohesion, and group effectiveness: Testing a social identity maintenance perspective on groupthink. *Journal of Personality and Social Psychology, 63,* 781–796.

Turner, R. H. (1964). Collective behavior. In R. E. L. Faris (Ed.), *Handbook of modern sociology.* Chicago: Rand McNally.

Turner, R. H., & Colomy, P. (1988). Role differentiation: Orienting principles. *Advances in Group Processes, 5,* 1–27.

Turner, R. H., & Killian, L. M. (1972). *Collective behavior* (2nd ed.). Upper Saddle River, NJ: Prentice Hall.

Turner, R. H., & Killian, L. M. (1987). *Collective behavior* (3rd. ed.). Upper Saddle River, NJ: Prentice Hall.

Twenge, J. M. (2001). Changes in women's assertiveness in response to status and roles: A cross-temporal meta-analysis, 1931–1993. *Journal of Personality and Social Psychology, 81,* 133–145.

Twenge, J. M., Baumeister, R. F., Tice, D. M., & Stucke, T. S. (2001). If you can't join them, beat them: Effects of social exclusion on aggressive behavior. *Journal of Personality and Social Psychology, 81,* 1058–1069.

Twenge, J. M., Catanese, K. R., & Baumeister, R. F. (2002). Social exclusion causes self-defeating behavior. *Journal of Personality and Social Psychology, 83,* 606–615.

Twenge, J. M., & Crocker, J. (2002). Race and self-esteem: Meta-analyses comparing Whites, Blacks, Hispanics, Asians, and American Indians and comment on Gray-Little and Hafdahl (2000). *Psychological Bulletin, 128,* 371–408.

Tyerman, A., & Spencer, C. (1983). A critical test of the Sherifs' Robber's Cave Experiments: Intergroup competition and cooperation between groups of well-acquainted individuals. *Small Group Behavior, 14,* 515–531.

U.S. Senate Select Committee on Intelligence (2004). *Report on the U.S. intelligence community's prewar intelligence assessments on Iraq: Conclusions.* Retrieved July 13, 2004, from http://intelligence .senate.gov/

Uchino, B. N., Cacioppo, J. T., & Kiecolt-Glaser, J. K. (1996). The relationship between social support and physiological processes: A review with emphasis on underlying mechanisms and implications for health. *Psychological Bulletin, 119,* 488–531.

Ulbig, S. G., & Funk, C. L. (1999). Conflict avoidance and political participation. *Political Behavior, 21,* 265–282.

Umberson, D., Chen, M. D., House, J. S., Hopkins, K., & Slaten, E. (1996). The effect of social relationships on psychological well-being: Are men and women really so different? *American Sociological Review, 61,* 837–857.

Uris, A. (1978). *Executive dissent: How to say no and win.* New York: AMACOM.

Utman, C. H. (1997). Performance effects of motivational state: A meta-analysis. *Personality and Social Psychology Review, 1,* 170–182.

Utz, S., & Sassenberg, K. (2002). Distributive justice in common-bond and common-identity groups. *Group Processes & Intergroup Relations, 5,* 151–162.

Van de Ven, A. H. (1974). *Group decision-making effectiveness.* Kent, OH: Kent State University Center for Business and Economic Research Press.

Van de Ven, A. H., & Delbecq, A. L. (1971). Nominal versus interacting group process for committee decision making effectiveness. *Academy of Management Journal, 14,* 203–212.

Van de Vliert, E., & Euwema, M. C. (1994). Agreeableness and activeness as components of conflict behaviors. *Journal of Personality and Social Psychology, 66,* 674–687.

Van de Vliert, E., & Janssen, O. (2001). Description, explanation, and prescription of intragroup conflict behaviors. In M. E. Turner (Ed.), *Groups at work: Theory and research* (pp. 267–297). Mahwah, NJ: Erlbaum. Retrieved May 18, 2004, from http:// www.netlibrary.com

van den Bos, K., Wilke, H., & Lind, E. A. (1998). When do we need procedural fairness? The role of trust in authority. *Journal of Personality and Social Psychology, 75,* 1449–1458.

van Engen, M. L. (2001). *Gender and leadership: A contextual perspective.* Unpublished doctoral dissertation. Tilburg, Netherlands: Tilburg University.

Van Hiel, A., & Franssen, V. (2003). Information acquisition bias during the preparation of group discussion: A comparison of prospective minority and majority members. *Small Group Research, 34,* 557–574.

Van Kleef, G. A., & De Dreu, C. K. (2002). Social value orientation and impression formation: A test of two competing hy-

potheses about information search in negotiation. *International Journal of Conflict Management, 13,* 59–77.

Van Kleef, G. A., De Dreu, C. K., & Manstead, A. S. (2004). The interpersonal effects of anger and happiness in negotiations. *Journal of Personality and Social Psychology, 86,* 57–76.

Van Lange, P. A. M. (1999). The pursuit of joint outcomes and equality in outcomes: An integrative model of social value orientation. *Journal of Personality and Social Psychology, 77,* 337–349.

Van Lange, P. A. M. (2000). Cooperation and competition. In A. E. Kazdin (Ed.), *Encyclopedia of psychology* (Vol. 2, pp. 296–300). Washington, DC: American Psychological Association. Retrieved September 19, 2004, from http://online.psycinfo .com/psycbooks

Van Lange, P. A. M., De Bruin, E. M. N., Otten, W., & Joireman, J. A. (1997). Development of prosocial, individualistic, and competitive orientations: Theory and preliminary evidence. *Journal of Personality and Social Psychology, 73,* 733–746.

Van Lange, P. A. M., Ouwerkerk, J. W., & Tazelaar, M. J. (2002). How to overcome the detrimental effects of noise in social interaction: The benefits of generosity. *Journal of Personality and Social Psychology, 82,* 768–780.

van Oostrum, J., & Rabbie, J. M. (1995). Intergroup competition and cooperation within autocratic and democratic management regimes. *Small Group Research, 26,* 269–295.

Van Sell, M., Brief, A. P., & Schuler, R. S. (1981). Role conflict and role ambiguity: Integration of the literature and directions for future research. *Human Relations, 34,* 43–71.

Van Vugt, M., & Hart, C. M. (2004). Social identity as social glue: The origins of group loyalty. *Journal of Personality and Social Psychology, 86,* 585–598.

Van Zelst, R. H. (1952). Sociometrically selected work teams increase production. *Personnel Psychology, 5,* 175–185.

Vandello, J. A., & Cohen, D. (1999). Patterns of individualism and collectivism across the United States. *Journal of Personality and Social Psychology, 77,* 279–292.

Vandello, J. A., & Cohen, D. (2003). Male honor and female fidelity: Implicit cultural scripts that perpetuate domestic violence. *Journal of Personality and Social Psychology, 84,* 997–1010.

Vandello, J. A., & Cohen, D. (2004). When believing is seeing: Sustaining norms of violence in cultures of honor. In M. Schaller & C. S. Crandall (Eds.), *The psychological foundations of culture* (pp. 281–304). Mahwah, NJ: Erlbaum.

Varela, J. A. (1971). *Psychological solutions to social problems.* New York: Academic Press.

Varma, A., & Stroh, L. K. (2001). Different perspectives on selection for international assignments: The impact of LMX and gender. *Cross Cultural Management, 8,* 85–97.

Vecchio, R. P. (1987). Situational leadership theory: An examination of a prescriptive theory. *Journal of Applied Psychology, 72,* 444–451.

Vecchio, R. P., & Boatwright, K. J. (2002). Preferences for idealized styles of supervision [Electronic version]. *Leadership Quarterly, 13,* 327–342.

Veitch, J. A. (1990). Office noise and illumination effects on reading comprehension. *Journal of Environmental Psychology, 10,* 209–217.

Vertue, F. M. (2003). From adaptive emotion to dysfunction: An attachment perspective on social anxiety disorder. *Personality and Social Psychology Review, 7,* 170–191.

Vider, S. (2004). Rethinking crowd violence: Self-categorization theory and the Woodstock 1999 riot. *Journal for the Theory of Social Behaviour, 34,* 141–166.

Villaseñor, V. (1977). *Jury: The people vs. Juan Corona.* Boston: Little, Brown.

Vinacke, W. E. (1971). Negotiations and decisions in a politics game. In B. Lieberman (Ed.), *Social choice.* New York: Gordon & Breach.

Vinokur, A., & Burnstein, E. (1974). The effects of partially shared persuasive arguments on group-induced shifts: A group-problem-solving approach. *Journal of Personality and Social Psychology, 29,* 305–315.

Vinokur, A., & Burnstein, E. (1978). Depolarization of attitudes in groups. *Journal of Personality and Social Psychology, 36,* 872–885.

Vinokur, A., Burnstein, E., Sechrest, L., & Wortman, P. M. (1985). Group decision making by experts: Field study of panels evaluating medical technologies. *Journal of Personality and Social Psychology, 49,* 70–84.

Vinsel, A., Brown, B. B., Altman, I., & Foss, C. (1980). Privacy regulation, territorial displays, and effectiveness of individual functioning. *Journal of Personality and Social Psychology, 39,* 1104–1115.

Vorauer, J. D., & Miller, D. T. (1997). Failure to recognize the effect of implicit social influence on the presentation of self. *Journal of Personality and Social Psychology, 73,* 281–295.

Vroom, V. H. (1973). A new look at managerial decision making. *Organizational Dynamics, 1,* 66–80.

Vroom, V. H. (1974). Decision making and the leadership process. *Journal of Contemporary Business, 3,* 47–64.

Vroom, V. H. (1976). Leadership. In M. D. Dunnette (Ed.), *Handbook of industrial and organizational psychology* (pp. 1527–1551). Chicago: Rand McNally.

Vroom, V. H., & Jago, A. G. (1978). On the validity of the Vroom/Yetton model. *Journal of Applied Psychology, 63,* 151–162.

Vroom, V. H., & Jago, A. G. (1988). *The new leadership: Managing participation in organizations.* Upper Saddle River, NJ: Prentice Hall.

Vroom, V. H., & Mann, F. C. (1960). Leader authoritarianism and employee attitudes. *Personnel Psychology, 13,* 125–140.

Vroom, V. H., & Yetton, P. W. (1973). *Leadership and decision making.* Pittsburgh, PA: University of Pittsburgh Press.

Wageman, R. (1999). Task design, outcome interdependence, and individual differences: Their joint effects on effort in task-performing teams. *Group Dynamics, 3,* 132–137.

Wageman, R. (2001). The meaning of interdependence. In M. E. Turner (Ed.), *Groups at work: Theory and research* (pp. 197–217). Mahwah, NJ: Erlbaum. Retrieved May 18, 2004, from http://www.netlibrary.com

Wagner, D. G., & Berger, J. (1993). Status characteristics theory: The growth of a program. In J. Berger & M. Zelditch, Jr. (Eds.), *Theoretical research programs: Studies in the growth of theory* (pp. 24–63). Stanford, CA: Stanford University Press.

Wagner, J. A. (1994). Participation effects on performance and satisfaction: A reconsideration of research evidence. *Academy of Management Review, 19,* 312–330.

Waldman, D. A., Bass, B. M., & Yammarino, F. J. (1990). Adding to contingent-reward behavior: The augmenting effect of charismatic leadership. *Group and Organization Studies, 15,* 381–394.

Walker, C. J., & Berkerle, C. A. (1987). The effect of state anxiety

on rumor transmission. *Journal of Social Behavior and Personality, 2,* 353–360.

Walker, H. A., Ilardi, B. C., McMahon, A. M., & Fennell, M. L. (1996). Gender, interaction, and leadership. *Social Psychology Quarterly, 59,* 255–272.

Walker, M. B., & Andrade, M. G. (1996). Conformity in the Asch task as a function of age. *Journal of Social Psychology, 136,* 367–372.

Wall, J. A., & Callister, R. R. (1995). Conflict and its management. *Journal of Management, 21,* 515–558.

Wall, V. D., Jr., & Nolan, L. L. (1987). Small group conflict: A look at equity, satisfaction, and styles of conflict management. *Small Group Behavior, 18,* 188–211.

Wallach, M. A., Kogan, N., & Bem, D. J. (1962). Group influence on individual risk taking. *Journal of Abnormal and Social Psychology, 65,* 75–86.

Walsh, D. (2003). *Classroom sociometrics.* Retrieved August 23, 2004, from http://www.classroomsociometrics.com/

Walsh, Y., Russell, R. J. H., & Wells, P. A. (1995). The personality of ex-cult members. *Personality and Individual Differences, 19,* 339–344.

Walther, E., Bless, H., Strack, F., Rackstraw, P., Wagner, D., & Werth, L. (2002). Conformity effects in memory as a function of group size, dissenters and uncertainty. *Applied Cognitive Psychology, 16,* 793–810.

Wang, A. Y., Newlin, M. H., & Tucker, T. L. (2001). A discourse analysis of online classroom chats: Predictors of cyber-student performance. *Teaching of Psychology, 28,* 222–226.

Wann, D. L., Dolan, T. J., McGeorge, K. K., & Allison, J. A. (1994). Relationships between spectator identification and spectators' perceptions of influence, spectators' emotions, and competition outcome. *Journal of Sport and Exercise Psychology, 16,* 347–364.

Ward, R. E., Jr. (2002). Fan violence: Social problem or moral panic? *Aggression and Violent Behavior, 7,* 453–475.

Ware, R., Barr, J. E., & Boone, M. (1982). Subjective changes in small group processes: An experimental investigation. *Small Group Behavior, 13,* 395–401.

Warfield-Coppock, N. (1995). Toward a theory of Afrocentric organizations. *Journal of Black Psychology, 21,* 30–48.

Warner HBO (Production company). (2001). *Do you believe in miracles? The story of the 1980 U.S. Hockey Team* [Videotape]. New York: HBO Studios.

Warr, M. (2002). *Companions in crime: The social aspects of criminal conduct.* New York: Cambridge University Press.

Wasserman, S., & Faust, K. (1994). *Social network analysis: Methods and applications.* New York: Cambridge University Press.

Watson, C., & Hoffman, L. R. (1996). Managers as negotiators: A test of power versus gender as predictors of feelings, behavior, and outcomes. *Leadership Quarterly, 7,* 63–85.

Watson, C. B., Chemers, M. M., & Preiser, N. (2001). Collective efficacy: A multilevel analysis. *Personality and Social Psychology Bulletin, 27,* 1057–1068.

Watson, D., & Clark, L. A. (1997). Extraversion and its positive emotional core. In R. Hogan & J. A. Johnson (Eds.), *Handbook of personality psychology* (pp. 767–793). San Diego: Academic Press.

Watson, R. I., Jr. (1973). Investigation into deindividuation using a cross-cultural survey technique. *Journal of Personality and Social Psychology, 25,* 342–345.

Watson, W. E., Kumar, K., & Michaelsen, L. K. (1993). Cultural diversity's impact on interaction process and performance: Comparing homogeneous and diverse task groups. *Academy of Management Journal, 36,* 590–602.

Webb, N. M., Troper, J. D., & Fall, R. (1995). Constructive activity and learning in collaborative small groups. *Journal of Educational Psychology, 87,* 406–423.

Weber, M. (1946). The sociology of charismatic authority. In H. H. Gert & C. W. Mills (Trans. & Eds.), *From Max Weber: Essay in sociology* (pp. 245–252). New York: Oxford University Press. (Originally published in 1921)

Webster, D. M., & Kruglanski, A.W. (1998). Cognitive and social consequences of the need for cognitive closure. *European Review of Social Psychology, 8,* 133–173.

Webster, M., Jr., & Driskell, J. E., Jr. (1983). Processes of status generalization. In H. H. Blumberg, A. P. Hare, V. Kent, & M. F. Davies (Eds.), *Small groups and social interaction* (Vol. 1, pp. 57–67). New York: Wiley.

Webster, M., Jr., & Hysom, S. J. (1998). Creating status characteristics. *American Sociological Review, 63,* 351–378.

Wech, B. A., Mossholder, K. W., Steel, R. P., & Bennett, N. (1998). Does work group cohesiveness affect individuals' performance and organizational commitment? A cross-level examination. *Small Group Research, 29,* 472–494.

Wegner, D. M. (1987). Transactive memory: A contemporary analysis of the group mind. In B. Mullen & G. R. Goethals (Eds.), *Theories of group behavior* (pp. 185–208). New York: Springer Verlag.

Wegner, D. M., Giuliano, T., & Hertel, P. T. (1985). Cognitive interdependence in close relationships. In W. Ickes (Ed.), *Compatible and incompatible relationships* (pp. 253–276). New York: Springer Verlag.

Weick, K. E. (1985). Systematic observational methods. In G. Lindzey & E. Aronson (Eds.), *The handbook of social psychology* (Vol. 1, 3rd ed., pp. 567–634). New York: Random House.

Weick, K. E. (1990). The vulnerable system: An analysis of the Tenerife air disaster. *Journal of Management, 16,* 571–593.

Weigold, M. F., & Schlenker, B. R. (1991). Accountability and risk taking. *Personality and Social Psychology Bulletin, 17,* 25–29.

Weiner, N., & Mahoney, T. (1981). A model of corporate performance as a function of environmental, organizational and leadership influences. *Academy of Management Journal, 24,* 453–470.

Weingart. L. R. (1997). How did they do that? The ways and means of studying group process. *Research in Organizational Behavior, 19,* 189–239.

Weingart, L. R., Thompson, L. L., Bazerman, M. H., & Carroll, J. S. (1990). Tactical behavior and negotiation outcomes. *The International Journal of Conflict Management, 1,* 7–31.

Weingart, L. R., & Weldon, E. (1991). Processes that mediate the relationship between a group goal and group member performance. *Human Performance, 4,* 33–54.

Weiss, R. F., & Miller, F. G. (1971). The drive theory of social facilitation. *Psychological Review, 78,* 44–57.

Wekselberg, V., Goggin, W. C., & Collings, T. J. (1997). A multifaceted concept of group maturity and its measurement and relationship to group performance. *Small Group Research, 28,* 3–28.

Weldon, E., Jehn, K. A., & Pradhan, P. (1991). Processes that mediate the relationship between a group goal and improved group performance. *Journal of Personality and Social Psychology, 61,* 555–569.

Weldon, E., & Weingart, L. R. (1993). Group goals and group performance. *British Journal of Social Psychology, 32,* 307–334.

Weldon, M. S., & Bellinger, K. D. (1997). Collective memory: Collaborative and individual processes in remembering. *Journal of Experimental Psychology: Learning, Memory, and Cognition, 23,* 1160–1175.

Weldon, M. S., Blair, C., & Huebsch, D. (2000). Group remembering: Does social loafing underlie collaborative inhibition? *Journal of Experimental Psychology: Learning, Memory, & Cognition, 26,* 1568–1577.

Welsh, D. A. (1989). Crisis decision making reconsidered. *Journal of Conflict Resolution, 33,* 430–445.

Werner, C. M., Brown, B. B., & Altman, I. (2002). Transactionally oriented research: Examples and strategies. In R. Bechtel & A. Churchman (Eds.), *Handbook of environmental psychology* (pp. 203–221). New York: Wiley. Retrieved July 30, 2004, from http://www.netlibrary.com

Werner, P. (1978). Personality and attitude–activism correspondence. *Journal of Personality and Social Psychology, 36,* 1375–1390.

West, S. G., Gunn, S. P., & Chernicky, P. (1975). Ubiquitous Watergate: An attributional analysis. *Journal of Personality and Social Psychology, 23,* 55–65.

Weybrew, B. B. (1963). Psychological problems of prolonged marine submergence. In J. N. Burns, R. Chambers, & E. Hendler (Eds.), *Unusual environments and human behavior.* New York: Macmillan.

Wheelan, S. A. (1994). *Group process: A developmental perspective.* Boston: Allyn & Bacon.

Wheelan, S. A., Davidson, B., & Tilin, F. (2003). Group development across time: Reality or illusion? *Small Group Research, 34,* 223–245.

Wheelan, S. A., & Hochberger, J. M. (1996). Validation studies of the group development questionnaire. *Small Group Research, 27,* 143–170.

Wheelan, S. A., & McKeage, R. L. (1993). Developmental patterns in small and large groups. *Small Group Research, 24,* 60–83.

Wheeler, D. D., & Janis, I. L. (1980). *A practical guide for making decisions.* New York: Free Press.

Wheeler, L. (1966). Toward a theory of behavioral contagion. *Psychological Review, 73,* 179–192.

Wheeler, L., & Miyake, K. (1992). Social comparison in everyday life. *Journal of Personality and Social Psychology, 62,* 760–773.

White, H. C., & White, C. A. (1993). *Canvases and careers: Institutional change in the French painting world.* Chicago: University of Chicago Press.

White, R. K. (1965). Images in the context of international conflict. In H. Kelman (Ed.), *International behavior: A social–psychological analysis.* New York: Holt, Rinehart & Winston.

White, R. K. (1966). Misperception and the Vietnam war. *Journal of Social Issues, 22*(3), 1–156.

White, R. K. (1969). Three not-so-obvious contributions of psychology to peace. *Journal of Social Issues, 25*(4), 23–29.

White, R. K. (1977). Misperception in the Arab–Israeli conflict. *Journal of Social Issues, 33*(1), 190–221.

White, R. K. (1990). Democracy in the research team. In S. A. Wheelan, E. A. Pepiton, & V. Abt (Eds.), *Advances in field theory* (pp. 19–22). Thousand Oaks, CA: Sage.

White, R. K. (1992). A personal assessment of Lewin's major contributions. *Journal of Social Issues, 48*(2), 45–50.

White, R. K. (1998). American acts of force: Results and misperceptions. *Peace & Conflict: Journal of Peace Psychology, 4,* 93–128.

White, R. K., & Lippitt, R. (1960). *Autocracy and democracy.* New York: Harper & Row.

White, R. K., & Lippitt, R. (1968). Leader behavior and member reaction in three "social climates." In D. Cartwright and A. Zander (Eds.), *Group dynamics: Research and theory* (3rd ed., pp. 318–335). New York: Harper & Row.

Whitehead, T. N. (1938). *The industrial worker.* Cambridge, MA: Harvard University Press.

Whitley, B. E., Jr. (1999). Right-wing authoritarianism, social dominance orientation, and prejudice. *Journal of Personality and Social Psychology, 77,* 126–134.

Whitley, B. E., Jr. (2002). *Principles of research in behavioral science* (2nd ed.). New York: McGraw-Hill.

Whitney, I., & Smith, P. K. (1993). A survey of the nature and extent of bullying in junior/middle and secondary schools. *Educational Research, 35,* 3–25.

Whitney, K., & Sagrestano, L. M., & Maslach, C. (1994). Establishing the social impact of individuation. *Journal of Personality and Social Psychology, 66,* 1140–1153.

Whittal, M. L., & McLean, P. D. (2002). Group cognitive behavioral therapy for obsessive compulsive disorder. In R. O. Frost & G. Steketee (Eds.), *Cognitive approaches to obsessions and compulsions: Theory, assessment, and treatment* (pp. 417–433). Amsterdam: Pergamon/Elsevier Science.

Whyte, G. (1993). Escalating commitment in individual and group decision making: A prospect theory approach. *Organizational Behavior and Human Decision Processes, 54,* 430–455.

Whyte, G. (1998). Recasting Janis's groupthink model: The key role of collective efficacy in decision fiascoes. *Organizational Behavior and Human Decision Processes, 73,* 185–209.

Whyte, W. F. (1943). *Street corner society.* Chicago: University of Chicago Press.

Whyte, W. F. (1991). *Participatory action research.* Thousand Oaks, CA: Sage.

Wicker, A. W. (1979). *An introduction to ecological psychology.* Pacific Grove, CA: Brooks/Cole.

Wicker, A. W. (1987). Behavior settings reconsidered: Temporal stages, resources, internal dynamics, context. In D. Stokols & I. Altman (Eds.), *Handbook of environmental psychology* (Vol. 1, pp. 613–653). New York: Wiley.

Wicker, A. W. (2002). Ecological psychology: Historical contexts, current conception, prospective directions. In R. Bechtel & A. Churchman (Eds.), *Handbook of environmental psychology* (pp. 114–126). New York: Wiley. Retrieved July 30, 2004, from http://www.netlibrary.com

Wicker, A. W., & August, R. A. (1995). How far should we generalize? The case of a workload model. *Psychological Science, 6,* 39–44.

Wicker, A. W., Kirmeyer, S. L., Hanson, L., & Alexander, D. (1976). Effects of manning levels on subjective experiences, performance, and verbal interaction in groups. *Organizational Behavior and Human Performance, 17,* 251–274.

Widmeyer, W. N. (1990). Group composition in sport. In The group in sport and physical activity [Special issue]. *International Journal of Sport Psychology, 21,* 264–285.

Widmeyer, W. N., Brawley, L. R., & Carron, A. V. (1992). Group dynamics in sports. In T. S. Horn (Ed.), *Advances in sport psychology* (pp. 163–180). Champaign, IL: Human Kinetics.

Wilder, D. A. (1977). Perception of groups, size of opposition, and social influence. *Journal of Experimental Social Psychology, 13,* 253–268.

Wilder, D. A. (1986a). Cognitive factors affecting the success of intergroup contact. In S. Worchel & W. G. Austin (Eds.), *Psychology of intergroup relations* (2nd ed., pp. 49–66). Chicago: Nelson-Hall.

Wilder, D. A. (1986b). Social categorization: Implications for creation and reduction of intergroup bias. *Advances in Experimental Social Psychology, 19,* 293–355.

Wilder, D., & Simon, A. F. (1998). Categorical and dynamic groups: Implications for social perception and interpersonal behavior. In C. Sedikides, J. Schopler, & C. A. Insko (Eds.), *Intergroup cognition and intergroup behavior* (pp. 27–44). Mahwah, NJ: Erlbaum.

Wilder, D. A., Simon, A. F., & Faith, M. (1996). Enhancing the impact of counterstereotypic information: Dispositional attributions for deviance. *Journal of Personality and Social Psychology, 71,* 276–287.

Wilder, D. A., & Thompson, J. E. (1980). Intergroup contact with independent manipulations of in-group and out-group interaction. *Journal of Personality and Social Psychology, 38,* 589–603.

Wildschut, T., Lodewijkx, H. F., Hein, F. M., & Insko, C. A. (2001). Toward a reconciliation of diverging perspectives on interindividual–group discontinuity: The role of procedural interdependence. *Journal of Experimental Social Psychology, 37,* 273–285.

Wildschut, T., Pinter, B., Vevea, J. L., Insko, C. A., & Schopler, J. (2003). Beyond the group mind: A quantitative review of the interindividual–intergroup discontinuity effect. *Psychological Bulletin, 129,* 698–722.

Wilke, H. A. M. (1996). Status congruence in small groups. In E. Witte & J. H. Davis (Eds.), *Understanding group behavior: Small group processes and interpersonal relations* (Vol. 2, pp. 67–91). Mahwah, NJ: Erlbaum.

Williams v. Florida, 399 U.S. 78 (1970).

Williams, J. E., & Best, D. L. (1990). *Measuring sex stereotypes: A multination study.* Thousand Oaks, CA: Sage.

Williams, K. D. (2001). *Ostracism: The power of silence.* New York: Guilford Press.

Williams, K. D., Cheung, C. K. T., & Choi, W. (2000). Cyberostracism: Effects of being ignored over the Internet. *Journal of Personality and Social Psychology, 79,* 748–762.

Williams, K. D., Govan, C. L., Croker, V., Tynan, D., Cruickshank, M., & Lam, A. (2002). Investigations into differences between social- and cyber-ostracism. *Group Dynamics, 6,* 65–77.

Williams, K. D., Harkins, S., & Latané, B. (1981). Identifiability as a deterrent to social loafing: Two cheering experiments. *Journal of Personality and Social Psychology, 40,* 303–311.

Williams, K. D., Jackson, J. M., & Karau, S. J. (1995). Collective hedonism: A social loafing analysis of social dilemmas. In D. A. Schroeder (Ed.), *Social dilemmas: Perspectives on individuals and groups* (pp. 117–141). Westport, CT: Praeger.

Williams, K. D., & Karau, S. J. (1991). Social loafing and social compensation: The effects of expectations of co-worker performance. *Journal of Personality and Social Psychology, 61,* 570–581.

Williams, K. D., Shore, W. J., & Grahe, J. E. (1998). The silent treatment: Perceptions of its behaviors and associated feelings. *Group Processes & Intergroup Relations, 1,* 117–141.

Williams, K. D., & Sommer, K. L. (1997). Social ostracism by coworkers: Does rejection lead to loafing or compensation? *Personality and Social Psychology Bulletin, 23,* 693–706.

Williams, K. Y., & O'Reilly, C. A. (1998). Demography and diversity in organizations: A review of 40 years of research. *Research in Organizational Behavior, 20,* 77–140.

Willis, F. N. (1966). Initial speaking distance as a function of the speakers' relationship. *Psychonomic Science, 5,* 221–222.

Wills, T. A., & Cleary, S. D. (1996). How are social support effects mediated? A test with parental support and adolescent substance use. *Journal of Personality and Social Psychology, 71,* 937–952.

Wills, T. A., & DePaulo, B. M. (1991). Interpersonal analysis of the help-seeking process. In C. R. Snyder & D. R. Forsyth (Eds.), *Handbook of social and clinical psychology: The health perspective* (pp. 350–375). New York: Pergamon Press.

Wills, T. A., & Filer, M. (2000). Social networks and social support. In A. Baum & T. Revenson (Eds.), *Handbook of health psychology* (pp. 209–232). Mahwah, NJ: Erlbaum.

Willsie, D. A., & Riemer, J. W. (1980). The campus bar as a "bastard" institution. *Mid-American Review of Sociology, 5,* 61–79.

Wilson, E. O. (1975). *Sociobiology: The new synthesis.* Cambridge, MA: Belknap Press.

Wilson, M. S. (2003). Social dominance and ethical ideology: The end justifies the means? *Journal of Social Psychology, 143,* 549–558.

Wilson, M. S., & Liu, J. H. (2003). Social dominance orientation and gender: The moderating role of gender identity. *British Journal of Social Psychology, 42,* 187–198.

Wilson, R. K., & Sell, J. (1997). "Liar, Liar . . . ": Cheap talk and reputation in repeated public goods settings. *Journal of Conflict Resolution, 41,* 695–717.

Wilson, S. R. (1992). Face and facework in negotiation. In L. L. Putnam & M. E. Roloff (Eds.), *Communication and negotiation* (pp. 176–205). Thousand Oaks, CA: Sage.

Winquist, J. R., & Larson, J. R., Jr. (1998). Information pooling: When it impacts group decision making. *Journal of Personality and Social Psychology, 74,* 371–377.

Winstead, B. (1986). Sex differences in same sex friendships. In V. J. Derlaga & B. Winstead (Eds.), *Friendship and social interaction.* New York: Springer Verlag.

Winter, D. G. (1973). *The power motive.* New York: Free Press.

Wisman, A., & Koole, S. L. (2003). Hiding in the crowd: Can mortality salience promote affiliation with others who oppose one's worldviews? *Journal of Personality and Social Psychology, 84,* 511–526.

Witteman, H. (1991). Group member satisfaction: A conflict-related account. *Small Group Research, 22,* 24–58.

Wittenbaum, G. M. (1998). Information sampling in decision-making groups: The impact of members' task-relevant status. *Small Group Research, 29,* 57–84.

Wittenbaum, G. M., Hollingshead, A. B., Paulus, P. B., Hirokawa, R. Y., Ancona, D. G., Peterson, R. S., Jehn, K. A., & Yoon, K. (2004). The functional perspective as a lens for understanding groups. *Small Group Research, 35,* 17–43.

Wittenbaum, G. M., Hubbell, A. P., & Zuckerman, C. (1999). Mutual enhancement: Toward an understanding of the collective preference for shared information. *Journal of Personality and Social Psychology, 77,* 967–978.

Wittenbaum, G. M., & Stasser, G. (1996). Management of information in small groups. In J. L. Nye & A. M. Brower (Eds.),

What's social about social cognition? Research on socially shared cognitions in small groups (pp. 3–28). Thousand Oaks, CA: Sage.

Wittenbaum, G. M., Stasser, G., & Merry, C. J. (1996). Tacit coordination in anticipation of small group task completion. *Journal of Experimental Social Psychology, 32,* 129–152.

Wolf, S. (1987). Majority and minority influence: A social impact analysis. In M. P. Zanna, J. M. Olson, & C. P. Herman (Eds.), *Social influences: The Ontario Symposium* (Vol. 5, pp. 207–235). Mahwah, NJ: Erlbaum.

Wolff, S. B., Pescosolido, A. T., & Druskat, V. U. (2002). Emotional intelligence as the basis of leadership emergence in self-managing teams [Electronic version]. *Leadership Quarterly, 13,* 505–522.

Wood, J. V. (1989). Theory and research concerning social comparisons of personal attributes. *Psychological Bulletin, 106,* 231–248.

Wood, J. V. (1996). What is social comparison and how should we study it? *Personality and Social Psychology Bulletin, 22,* 520–537.

Wood, W. (1987). A meta-analytic review of sex differences in group performance. *Psychological Bulletin, 102,* 53–71.

Wood, W., & Eagly, A. H. (2002). A cross-cultural analysis of the behavior of women and men: Implications for the origins of sex differences. *Psychological Bulletin, 128,* 699–727.

Wood, W., Lundgren, S., Ouellette, J. A., Busceme, S., & Blackstone, T. (1994). Minority influence: A meta-analytic review of social influence processes. *Psychological Bulletin, 115,* 323–345.

Wood, W., Polek, D., & Aiken, C. (1985). Sex differences in group task performance. *Journal of Personality and Social Psychology, 48,* 63–71.

Wood, W., Pool, G. J., Leck, K., & Purvis, D. (1996). Self-definition, defensive processing, and influence: The normative impact of majority and minority groups. *Journal of Personality and Social Psychology, 71,* 1181–1193.

Woodman, R. W., & Sherwood, J. J. (1980). The role of team development in organizational effectiveness: A critical review. *Psychological Bulletin, 88,* 166–186.

Worchel, S. (1986). The role of cooperation in reducing intergroup conflict. In S. Worchel & W. G. Austin (Eds.), *Psychology of intergroup relations* (2nd ed., pp. 288–304). Chicago: Nelson-Hall.

Worchel, S., & Brehm, J. W. (1971). Direct and implied social restoration of freedom. *Journal of Personality and Social Psychology, 18,* 294–304.

Worchel, S., Lind, E., & Kaufman, K. (1975). Evaluations of group products as a function of expectations of group longevity, outcome of competition, and publicity of evaluations. *Journal of Personality and Social Psychology, 31,* 1089–1097.

Worchel, S., Rothgerber, H., Day, E. A., Hart, D., & Butemeyer, J. (1998). Social identity and individual productivity within groups. *British Journal of Social Psychology, 37,* 389–413.

Worchel, S., & Teddlie, C. (1976). The experience of crowding: A two-factor theory. *Journal of Personality and Social Psychology, 34,* 30–40.

Worchel, S., & Yohai, S. (1979). The role of attribution in the experience of crowding. *Journal of Experimental Social Psychology, 15,* 91–104.

Word of the Day. (2000, May 10). *Schadenfreude.* Retrieved May 10, 2000, from http://dictionary.reference.com/wordoftheday/archive/2000/05/10.htm

Worringham, C. J., & Messick, D. M. (1983). Social facilitation of running: An unobtrusive study. *Journal of Social Psychology, 121,* 23–29.

Worthington, E. L., Jr., Hight, T. L., Ripley, J. S., Perrone, K. M., Kurusu, T. A., & Jones, D. R. (1997). Strategic hope-focused relationship-enrichment counseling with individual couples. *Journal of Counseling Psychology, 44,* 381–389.

Wright, J. C., Giammarino, M., & Parad, H. W. (1986). Social status in small groups: Individual–group similarity and the social "misfit." *Journal of Personality and Social Psychology, 50,* 523–536.

Wright, S. C., Aron, A., McLaughlin-Volpe, T., & Ropp, S. A. (1997). The extended contact effect: Knowledge of cross-group friendships and prejudice. *Journal of Personality and Social Psychology, 73,* 73–90.

Wright, S. S., & Forsyth, D. R. (1997). Group membership and collective identity: Consequences for self-esteem. *Journal of Social and Clinical Psychology, 16,* 43–56.

Wright, T. L., Ingraham, L. J., & Blackmer, D. R. (1984). Simultaneous study of individual differences and relationship effects in attraction. *Journal of Personality and Social Psychology, 47,* 1059–1062.

Wrightsman, L. S., Nietzel, M. T., & Fortune, W. H. (1998). *Psychology and the legal system* (4th ed.). Pacific Grove, CA: Brooks/Cole.

Wrightsman, L. S., O'Connor, J., & Baker, N. J. (Eds.). (1972). *Cooperation and competition: Readings on mixed-motive games.* Belmont, CA: Wadsworth.

Wrong, D. (1979). *Power: Its forms, bases, and uses.* Chicago: University of Chicago Press.

Wu, J. Z., & Axelrod, R. (1995). How to cope with noise in the iterated prisoner's dilemma. *Journal of Conflict Resolution, 39,* 183–189.

Wyden, P. H. (1979). *Bay of Pigs: The untold story.* New York: Simon & Schuster.

Yablonsky, L. (1959). The delinquent gang as a near group. *Social Problems, 7,* 108–117.

Yablonsky, L. (1962). *The violent gang.* New York: Macmillan.

Yalom, I. D. (1995). *The theory and practice of group psychotherapy* (4th ed). New York: Basic Books.

Yalom, V. J., & Vinogradov, S. (1993). Interpersonal group psychotherapy. In H. I. Kaplan & M. J. Sadock (Eds.), *Comprehensive group psychotherapy* (3rd. ed., pp. 185–195). Baltimore: Williams & Wilkins.

Yamagishi, K. (1994). Social dilemmas. In K. S. Cook, G. A. Fine, & J. S. House (Eds.), *Sociological perspectives on social psychology* (pp. 311–334). Boston: Allyn & Bacon.

Yamagishi, T. (1986). The provision of a sanctioning system as a public good. *Journal of Personality and Social Psychology, 51,* 110–116.

Yammarino, F. J., & Bass, B. M. (1990). Long-term forecasting of transformational leadership and its effects among naval officers: Some preliminary findings. In K. E. Clark & M. B. Clark (Eds.), *Measure of leadership* (pp. 151–169). West Orange, NJ: Leadership Library of America.

Yammarino, F. J., & Bass, B. M. (1991). Personal and situation views of leadership: A multiple levels of analysis approach. *Leadership Quarterly, 2,* 121–139.

Yang, J., & Mossholder, K. W. (2004). Decoupling task and relationship conflict: The role of intragroup emotional processing. *Journal of Organizational Behavior, 25,* 589–605.

Yang, K., & Bond, M. H. (1990). Exploring implicit personality theories with indigenous or imported constructs: The Chinese case. *Journal of Personality and Social Psychology, 58,* 1087–1095.

Yao, R. (1987). *An introduction to fundamentalists anonymous.* New York: Fundamentalists Anonymous.

Yin, R. K. (1993). *Applications of case study research.* Thousand Oaks, CA: Sage.

Yin, R. K. (1994). *Case study research: Design and methods* (2nd ed.). Thousand Oaks, CA: Sage.

Youngs, G. A., Jr. (1986). Patterns of threat and punishment reciprocity in a conflict setting. *Journal of Personality and Social Psychology, 51,* 541–546.

Yrle, A. C., Hartman, S., & Galle, W. P. (2002). An investigation of relationships between communication style and leader–member exchange. *Journal of Communication Management, 6,* 257–268.

Yukelson, D., Weinberg, R., & Jackson, A. (1984). A multidimensional group cohesion instrument for intercollegiate basketball teams. *Journal of Sport Psychology, 6,* 103–117.

Yukl, G. (2002). *Leadership in organizations.* Upper Saddle River, NJ: Prentice-Hall.

Yukl, G., Kim, H., & Falbe, C. (1996). Antecedents of influence outcomes. *Journal of Applied Psychology, 81,* 309–317.

Zaccaro, S. J. (1984). Social loafing: The role of task attractiveness. *Personality and Social Psychology Bulletin, 10,* 99–106.

Zaccaro, S. J. (1995). Leader resources and the nature of organizational problems. *Applied Psychology: An International Review, 44,* 32–36.

Zaccaro, S. J., & Banks, D. J. (2001). Leadership, vision, and organizational effectiveness. In S. J. Zaccaro & R. J. Klimoski (Eds.), *The nature of organizational leadership: Understanding the performance imperatives confronting today's leaders* (pp. 181–218). San Francisco: Jossey-Bass.

Zaccaro, S. J., Blair, V., Peterson, C., & Zazanis, M. (1995). Collective efficacy. In J. E. Maddux (Ed.), *Self-efficacy, adaptation, and adjustment: Theory, research, and application* (pp. 305–328). New York: Plenum Press.

Zaccaro, S. J., Foti, R. J., & Kenny, D. A. (1991). Self-monitoring and trait-based variance in leadership: An investigation of leader flexibility across multiple group situations. *Journal of Applied Psychology, 76,* 308–315.

Zaccaro, S. J., Gilbert, J. A., Thor, K. K., & Mumford, M. D. (1991). Leadership and social intelligence: Linking social perspectives and behavioral flexibility to leader effectiveness. *Leadership Quarterly, 2,* 317–342.

Zaccaro, S. J., Gualtieri, J., & Minionis, D. (1995). Task cohesion as a facilitator of team decision making under temporal urgency. *Military Psychology, 7,* 77–93.

Zajac, E. J., & Westphal, J. D. (1996). Who shall succeed? How CEO/board preferences and power affect the choice of new CEOs. *Academy of Management Journal, 39,* 64–90.

Zajonc, R. B. (1965). Social facilitation. *Science, 149,* 269–274.

Zajonc, R. B. (1980). Compresence. In P. B. Paulus (Ed.), *Psychology of group influence* (pp. 35–60). Mahwah, NJ: Erlbaum.

Zajonc, R. B., Heingartner, A., & Herman, E. M. (1969). Social enhancement and impairment of performance in the cockroach. *Journal of Personality and Social Psychology, 13,* 83–92.

Zald, M., & Ash, R. (1966). Social movement organizations: Growth, decay, and change. *Social Forces, 44,* 327–341.

Zamarripa, P. O., & Krueger, D. L. (1983). Implicit contracts regulating small group leadership. *Small Group Behavior, 14,* 187–210.

Zander, A. (1977). *Groups at work.* San Francisco: Jossey-Bass.

Zander, A. (1979). The psychology of group processes. *Annual Review of Psychology, 30,* 417–451.

Zander, A. (1982). *Making groups effective.* San Francisco: Jossey-Bass.

Zander, A. (1985). *The purposes of groups and organizations.* San Francisco: Jossey-Bass.

Zander, A. (1996). *Motives and goals in groups.* New Brunswick, NJ: Transaction. (originally published in 1971)

Zander, A., Cohen, A. R., & Stotland, E. (1959). Power and relations among the professions. In D. Cartwright (Ed.), *Studies in social power.* Ann Arbor, MI: Institute for Social Research.

Zander, A., Stotland, E., & Wolfe, D. (1960). Unity of group, identification with group, and self-esteem of members. *Journal of Personality, 28,* 463–478.

Zartman, I. W., & Rubin, J. Z. (Eds.). (2000). *Power and negotiation.* Ann Arbor: University of Michigan Press.

Zelditch, M., Jr., & Walker, H. A. (1984). Legitimacy and the stability of authority. *Advances in Group Processes, 1,* 1–25.

Zimbardo, P. G. (1969). The human choice: Individuation, reason, and order versus deindividuation, impulse, and chaos. *Nebraska Symposium on Motivation, 17,* 237–307.

Zimbardo, P. G. (1975). Transforming experimental research into advocacy for social change. In M. Deutsch & H. A. Hornstein (Eds.), *Applying social psychology* (pp. 33–66). Mahwah, NJ: Erlbaum.

Zimbardo, P. G. (1977a). *Psychology and life.* Glenview, IL: Scott, Foresman.

Zimbardo, P. G. (1977b). *Shyness: What it is and what to do about it.* New York: Jones.

Zimbardo, P. G., Butler, L. D., & Wolfe, V. A. (2003). Cooperative college examinations: More gain, less pain when students share information and grades. *Journal of Experimental Education, 71,* 101–125.

Zimbardo, P. G., Maslach, C., & Haney, C. (2000). Reflections on the Stanford Prison Experiment: Genesis, transformations, consequences. In T. Blass (Ed.). *Obedience to authority: Current perspectives on the Milgram paradigm.* Mahwah, NJ: Erlbaum.

Zubek, J. P. (1973). Behavioral and physiological effects of prolonged sensory and perceptual deprivation: A review. In J. E. Rasmussen (Ed.), *Man in isolation and confinement.* Chicago: Aldine.

Zuber, J. A., Crott, H. W., & Werner, J. (1992). Choice shift and group polarization: An analysis of the status of arguments and social decision schemes. *Journal of Personality and Social Psychology, 62,* 50–61.

Zurcher, L. A., Jr. (1969). Stages of development in poverty program neighborhood action committees. *Journal of Applied Behavioral Science, 15,* 223–258.

Zyzniewski, L. E. (2002). *Strategic linguistic bias in intergroup processes.* Unpublished doctoral dissertation. Richmond: Virginia Commonwealth University.

NAME INDEX

Subject Index

Page numbers for definitions are in boldface.